CONTEMPORARY AUTHORS.
c1981-
V.124 2004
37565001442176
CENT

Contemporary Authors®
NEW REVISION SERIES

ISSN 0275-7176

Contemporary Authors®

A Bio-Bibliographical Guide to
Current Writers in Fiction, General Nonfiction,
Poetry, Journalism, Drama, Motion Pictures,
Television, and Other Fields

NEW REVISION SERIES
volume 124

Detroit • New York • San Diego • San Francisco • Cleveland • New Haven, Conn. • Waterville, Maine • London • Munich

Contemporary Authors, New Revision Series, Vol. 124

Project Editor
Scot Peacock

Editorial
Katy Balcer, Shavon Burden, Sara Constantakis, Anna Marie Dahn, Alana Joli Foster, Natalie Fulkerson, Arlene M. Johnson, Michelle Kazensky, Julie Keppen, Joshua Kondek, Thomas McMahon, Jenai A. Mynatt, Judith L. Pyko, Mary Ruby, Lemma Shomali, Susan Strickland, Maikue Vang, Tracey Watson, Thomas Wiloch, Emiene Shija Wright

Research
Michelle Campbell, Tracie A. Richardson, Robert Whaley

Permissions
Margaret Chamberlain, Sue Rudolph

Imaging and Multimedia
Randy Bassett, Dean Dauphinais, Leitha Etheridge-Sims, Lezlie Light, Michael Logusz, Dan Newell, Christine O'Bryan, Kelly A. Quin

Composition and Electronic Capture
Kathy Sauer

Manufacturing
Lori Kessler

© 2004 Thomson Gale, a part of the Thomson Corporation.

Gale and Design™ and Thomson Learning™ are trademarks used herein under license.

For more information, contact
The Gale Group, Inc.
27500 Drake Rd.
Farmington Hills, MI 48331-3535
Or you can visit our internet site at
http://www.gale.com

ALL RIGHTS RESERVED
No part of this work covered by the copyright herein may be reproduced or used in any form or by any means—graphic, electronic, or mechanical, including photocopying, recording, taping, Web distribution, or information storage retrieval systems—without the written permission of the publisher.

This publication is a creative work fully protected by all applicable copyright laws, as well as by misappropriation, trade secret, unfair competition, and other applicable laws. The authors and editors of this work have added value to the underlying factual material herein through one or more of the following: unique and original selection, coordination, expression, arrangement, and classification of the information.

For permission to use material from the product, submit your request via the Web at http://www.gale-edit.com/permissions, or you may download our Permissions Request form and submit your request by fax or mail to:

Permissions Department
The Gale Group, Inc.
27500 Drake Rd.
Farmington Hills, MI 48331-3535
Permissions Hotline:
248-699-8006 or 800-877-4253, ext. 8006
Fax 248-699-8074 or 800-762-4058

Since this page cannot legibly accommodate all copyright notices, the acknowledgments constitute an extension of the copyright notice.

While every effort has been made to secure permission to reprint material and to ensure the reliability of the information presented in this publication, the Gale Group neither guarantees the accuracy of the data contained herein nor assumes any responsibility for errors, omissions or discrepancies. Gale accepts no payment for listing; and inclusion in the publication of any organization, agency, institution, publication, service, or individual does not imply endorsement of the editors or publisher. Errors brought to the attention of the publisher and verified to the satisfaction of the publisher will be corrected in future editions.

LIBRARY OF CONGRESS CATALOG CARD NUMBER 81-640179

ISBN 0-7876-6716-1
ISSN 0275-7176

Printed in the United States of America
10 9 8 7 6 5 4 3 2 1

Contents

Preface vii

Product Advisory Board xi

International Advisory Board xii

CA Numbering System and
Volume Update Chart xiii

Authors and Media People
Featured in This Volume xv

Acknowledgments xvii

Author Listings 1

> **Indexing note:** All *Contemporary Authors* entries are indexed in the *Contemporary Authors* cumulative index, which is published separately and distributed twice a year.
>
> **As always, the most recent Contemporary Authors cumulative index continues to be the user's guide to the location of an individual author's listing.**

Preface

Contemporary Authors (*CA*) provides information on approximately 115,000 writers in a wide range of media, including:

- Current writers of fiction, nonfiction, poetry, and drama whose works have been issued by commercial publishers, risk publishers, or university presses (authors whose books have been published only by known vanity or author-subsidized firms are ordinarily not included)

- Prominent print and broadcast journalists, editors, photojournalists, syndicated cartoonists, graphic novelists, screenwriters, television scriptwriters, and other media people

- Notable international authors

- Literary greats of the early twentieth century whose works are popular in today's high school and college curriculums and continue to elicit critical attention

A *CA* listing entails no charge or obligation. Authors are included on the basis of the above criteria and their interest to *CA* users. Sources of potential listees include trade periodicals, publishers' catalogs, librarians, and other users.

How to Get the Most out of *CA*: Use the Index

The key to locating an author's most recent entry is the *CA* cumulative index, which is published separately and distributed twice a year. It provides access to *all* entries in *CA* and *Contemporary Authors New Revision Series* (*CANR*). Always consult the latest index to find an author's most recent entry.

For the convenience of users, the *CA* cumulative index also includes references to all entries in these Gale literary series: *Authors and Artists for Young Adults, Authors in the News, Bestsellers, Black Literature Criticism, Black Literature Criticism Supplement, Black Writers, Children's Literature Review, Concise Dictionary of American Literary Biography, Concise Dictionary of British Literary Biography, Contemporary Authors Autobiography Series, Contemporary Authors Bibliographical Series, Contemporary Dramatists, Contemporary Literary Criticism, Contemporary Novelists, Contemporary Poets, Contemporary Popular Writers, Contemporary Southern Writers, Contemporary Women Poets, Dictionary of Literary Biography, Dictionary of Literary Biography Documentary Series, Dictionary of Literary Biography Yearbook, DISCovering Authors, DISCovering Authors: British, DISCovering Authors: Canadian, DISCovering Authors: Modules* (including modules for Dramatists, Most-Studied Authors, Multicultural Authors, Novelists, Poets, and Popular/Genre Authors), *DISCovering Authors 3.0, Drama Criticism, Drama for Students, Feminist Writers, Hispanic Literature Criticism, Hispanic Writers, Junior DISCovering Authors, Major Authors and Illustrators for Children and Young Adults, Major 20th-Century Writers, Native North American Literature, Novels for Students, Poetry Criticism, Poetry for Students, Short Stories for Students, Short Story Criticism, Something about the Author, Something about the Author Autobiography Series, St. James Guide to Children's Writers, St. James Guide to Crime & Mystery Writers, St. James Guide to Fantasy Writers, St. James Guide to Horror, Ghost & Gothic Writers, St. James Guide to Science Fiction Writers, St. James Guide to Young Adult Writers, Twentieth-Century Literary Criticism, 20th Century Romance and Historical Writers, World Literature Criticism,* and *Yesterday's Authors of Books for Children.*

A Sample Index Entry:

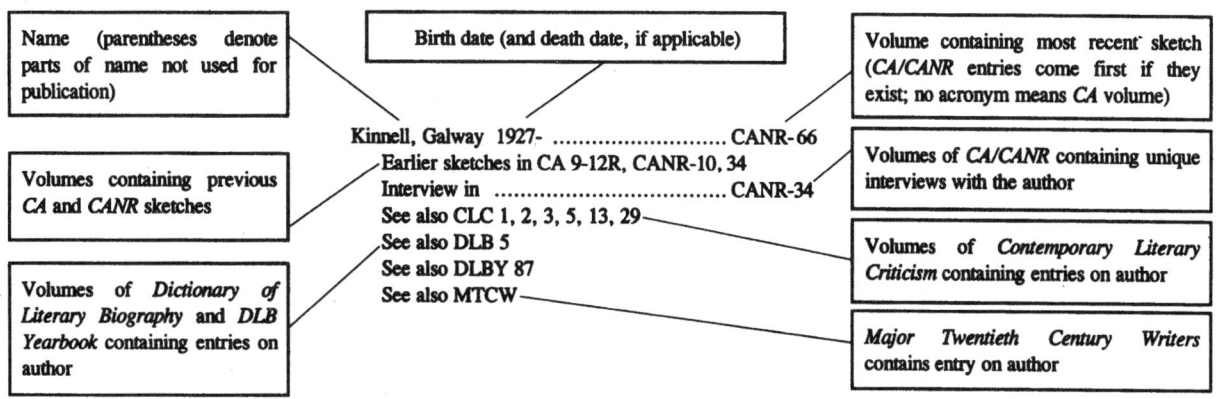

How Are Entries Compiled?

The editors make every effort to secure new information directly from the authors; listees' responses to our questionnaires and query letters provide most of the information featured in *CA*. For deceased writers, or those who fail to reply to requests for data, we consult other reliable biographical sources, such as those indexed in Gale's *Biography and Genealogy Master Index,* and bibliographical sources, including *National Union Catalog, LC MARC,* and *British National Bibliography*. Further details come from published interviews, feature stories, and book reviews, as well as information supplied by the authors' publishers and agents.

An asterisk (*) at the end of a sketch indicates that the listing has been compiled from secondary sources believed to be reliable but has not been personally verified for this edition by the author sketched.

What Kinds of Information Does An Entry Provide?

Sketches in *CA* contain the following biographical and bibliographical information:

- **Entry heading:** the most complete form of author's name, plus any pseudonyms or name variations used for writing

- **Personal information:** author's date and place of birth, family data, ethnicity, educational background, political and religious affiliations, and hobbies and leisure interests

- **Addresses:** author's home, office, or agent's addresses, plus e-mail and fax numbers, as available

- **Career summary:** name of employer, position, and dates held for each career post; resume of other vocational achievements; military service

- **Membership information:** professional, civic, and other association memberships and any official posts held

- **Awards and honors:** military and civic citations, major prizes and nominations, fellowships, grants, and honorary degrees

- **Writings:** a comprehensive, chronological list of titles, publishers, dates of original publication and revised editions, and production information for plays, television scripts, and screenplays

- **Adaptations:** a list of films, plays, and other media which have been adapted from the author's work

- **Work in progress:** current or planned projects, with dates of completion and/or publication, and expected publisher, when known

- **Sidelights:** a biographical portrait of the author's development; information about the critical reception of the author's works; revealing comments, often by the author, on personal interests, aspirations, motivations, and thoughts on writing

- **Interview:** a one-on-one discussion with authors conducted especially for *CA*, offering insight into authors' thoughts about their craft

- **Autobiographical essay:** an original essay written by noted authors for *CA*, a forum in which writers may present themselves, on their own terms, to their audience

- **Photographs:** portraits and personal photographs of notable authors

- **Biographical and critical sources:** a list of books and periodicals in which additional information on an author's life and/or writings appears

- **Obituary Notices** in *CA* provide date and place of birth as well as death information about authors whose full-length sketches appeared in the series before their deaths. The entries also summarize the authors' careers and writings and list other sources of biographical and death information.

Related Titles in the *CA* Series

Contemporary Authors Autobiography Series complements *CA* original and revised volumes with specially commissioned autobiographical essays by important current authors, illustrated with personal photographs they provide. Common topics include their motivations for writing, the people and experiences that shaped their careers, the rewards they derive from their work, and their impressions of the current literary scene.

Contemporary Authors Bibliographical Series surveys writings by and about important American authors since World War II. Each volume concentrates on a specific genre and features approximately ten writers; entries list works written by and about the author and contain a bibliographical essay discussing the merits and deficiencies of major critical and scholarly studies in detail.

Available in Electronic Formats

GaleNet. *CA* is available on a subscription basis through GaleNet, an online information resource that features an easy-to-use end-user interface, powerful search capabilities, and ease of access through the World-Wide Web. For more information, call 1-800-877-GALE.

Licensing. *CA* is available for licensing. The complete database is provided in a fielded format and is deliverable on such media as disk, CD-ROM, or tape. For more information, contact Gale's Business Development Group at 1-800-877-GALE, or visit us on our website at www.galegroup.com/bizdev.

Suggestions Are Welcome

The editors welcome comments and suggestions from users on any aspect of the *CA* series. If readers would like to recommend authors for inclusion in future volumes of the series, they are cordially invited to write the Editors at *Contemporary Authors*, Gale Group, 27500 Drake Rd., Farmington Hills, MI 48331-3535; or call at 1-248-699-4253; or fax at 1-248-699-8054.

Contemporary Authors Product Advisory Board

The editors of *Contemporary Authors* are dedicated to maintaining a high standard of excellence by publishing comprehensive, accurate, and highly readable entries on a wide array of writers. In addition to the quality of the content, the editors take pride in the graphic design of the series, which is intended to be orderly yet inviting, allowing readers to utilize the pages of *CA* easily and with efficiency. Despite the longevity of the *CA* print series, and the success of its format, we are mindful that the vitality of a literary reference product is dependent on its ability to serve its users over time. As literature, and attitudes about literature, constantly evolve, so do the reference needs of students, teachers, scholars, journalists, researchers, and book club members. To be certain that we continue to keep pace with the expectations of our customers, the editors of *CA* listen carefully to their comments regarding the value, utility, and quality of the series. Librarians, who have firsthand knowledge of the needs of library users, are a valuable resource for us. The *Contemporary Authors* Product Advisory Board, made up of school, public, and academic librarians, is a forum to promote focused feedback about *CA* on a regular basis. The six-member advisory board includes the following individuals, whom the editors wish to thank for sharing their expertise:

- **Anne M. Christensen,** Librarian II, Phoenix Public Library, Phoenix, Arizona.

- **Barbara C. Chumard,** Reference/Adult Services Librarian, Middletown Thrall Library, Middletown, New York.

- **Eva M. Davis,** Youth Department Manager, Ann Arbor District Library, Ann Arbor, Michigan.

- **Adam Janowski, Jr.,** Library Media Specialist, Naples High School Library Media Center, Naples, Florida.

- **Robert Reginald,** Head of Technical Services and Collection Development, California State University, San Bernadino, California.

- **Stephen Weiner,** Director, Maynard Public Library, Maynard, Massachusetts.

International Advisory Board

Well-represented among the 115,000 author entries published in *Contemporary Authors* are sketches on notable writers from many non-English-speaking countries. The primary criteria for inclusion of such authors has traditionally been the publication of at least one title in English, either as an original work or as a translation. However, the editors of *Contemporary Authors* came to observe that many important international writers were being overlooked due to a strict adherence to our inclusion criteria. In addition, writers who were publishing in languages other than English were not being covered in the traditional sources we used for identifying new listees. Intent on increasing our coverage of international authors, including those who write only in their native language and have not been translated into English, the editors enlisted the aid of a board of advisors, each of whom is an expert on the literature of a particular country or region. Among the countries we focused attention on are Mexico, Puerto Rico, Spain, Italy, France, Germany, Luxembourg, Belgium, the Netherlands, Norway, Sweden, Denmark, Finland, Taiwan, Singapore, Malaysia, Thailand, South Africa, Israel, and Japan, as well as England, Scotland, Wales, Ireland, Australia, and New Zealand. The sixteen-member advisory board includes the following individuals, whom the editors wish to thank for sharing their expertise:

- **Lowell A. Bangerter,** Professor of German, University of Wyoming, Laramie, Wyoming.

- **Nancy E. Berg,** Associate Professor of Hebrew and Comparative Literature, Washington University, St. Louis, Missouri.

- **Frances Devlin-Glass,** Associate Professor, School of Literary and Communication Studies, Deakin University, Burwood, Victoria, Australia.

- **David William Foster,** Regent's Professor of Spanish, Interdisciplinary Humanities, and Women's Studies, Arizona State University, Tempe, Arizona.

- **Hosea Hirata,** Director of the Japanese Program, Associate Professor of Japanese, Tufts University, Medford, Massachusetts.

- **Jack Kolbert,** Professor Emeritus of French Literature, Susquehanna University, Selinsgrove, Pennsylvania.

- **Mark Libin,** Professor, University of Manitoba, Winnipeg, Manitoba, Canada.

- **C. S. Lim,** Professor, University of Malaya, Kuala Lumpur, Malaysia.

- **Eloy E. Merino,** Assistant Professor of Spanish, Northern Illinois University, DeKalb, Illinois.

- **Linda M. Rodríguez Guglielmoni,** Associate Professor, University of Puerto Rico—Mayagüez, Puerto Rico.

- **Sven Hakon Rossel,** Professor and Chair of Scandinavian Studies, University of Vienna, Vienna, Austria.

- **Steven R. Serafin,** Director, Writing Center, Hunter College of the City University of New York, New York City.

- **David Smyth,** Lecturer in Thai, School of Oriental and African Studies, University of London, England.

- **Ismail S. Talib,** Senior Lecturer, Department of English Language and Literature, National University of Singapore, Singapore.

- **Dionisio Viscarri,** Assistant Professor, Ohio State University, Columbus, Ohio.

- **Mark Williams,** Associate Professor, English Department, University of Canterbury, Christchurch, New Zealand.

CA Numbering System and Volume Update Chart

Occasionally questions arise about the *CA* numbering system and which volumes, if any, can be discarded. Despite numbers like "29-32R," "97-100" and "216," the entire *CA* print series consists of only 268 physical volumes with the publication of *CA* Volume 217. The following charts note changes in the numbering system and cover design, and indicate which volumes are essential for the most complete, up-to-date coverage.

CA First Revision
- 1-4R through 41-44R (11 books)
  Cover: Brown with black and gold trim.
  There will be no further First Revision volumes because revised entries are now being handled exclusively through the more efficient *New Revision Series* mentioned below.

CA Original Volumes
- 45-48 through 97-100 (14 books)
  Cover: Brown with black and gold trim.
  101 through 217 (117 books)
  Cover: Blue and black with orange bands.
  The same as previous *CA* original volumes but with a new, simplified numbering system and new cover design.

CA Permanent Series
- *CAP*-1 and *CAP*-2 (2 books)
  Cover: Brown with red and gold trim.
  There will be no further Permanent Series volumes because revised entries are now being handled exclusively through the more efficient *New Revision Series* mentioned below.

CA New Revision Series
- CANR-1 through CANR-124 (124 books)
  Cover: Blue and black with green bands.
  Includes only sketches requiring significant changes; **sketches are taken from any previously published CA, CAP, or CANR volume.**

If You Have:	You May Discard:
CA First Revision Volumes 1-4R through 41-44R and *CA Permanent Series* Volumes 1 and 2	*CA* Original Volumes 1, 2, 3, 4 and Volumes 5-6 through 41-44
CA Original Volumes 45-48 through 97-100 and 101 through 217	**NONE:** These volumes will not be superseded by corresponding revised volumes. Individual entries from these and all other volumes appearing in the left column of this chart may be revised and included in the various volumes of the *New Revision Series*.
CA New Revision Series Volumes *CANR*-1 through *CANR*-124	**NONE:** The *New Revision Series* does not replace any single volume of *CA*. Instead, volumes of *CANR* include entries from many previous *CA* series volumes. All *New Revision Series* volumes must be retained for full coverage.

A Sampling of Authors and Media People Featured in This Volume

Edward Albee
Albee, a prolific and critically acclaimed playwright, is one of few dramatists to receive three Pulitzer Prize awards. Widely noted by critics for his thematically connected works, which depict a link between human feelings of loss and isolation with an overall collapse of societal values, Albee is the author of many award-winning plays, including *A Delicate Balance, Seascape, Three Tall Women* (Pulitzer Prize winners), and the 1963 Tony Award-winning *Who's Afraid of Virginia Woolf?*, which was adapted to film in 1966. His most recent offering *The Goat, or Who Is Sylvia?*, received the 2002 Tony Award for best new play of the year.

Rick Atkinson
Atkinson is a Pulitzer Prize-winning journalist whose first book, *The Long Gray Line*, received widespread critical attention. Subtitled *The American Journey of West Point's Class of 1966*, the work focuses on one generation of army officers and the tremendous impact the Vietnam War had on their lives. In 2002 Atkinson published *An Army at Dawn: The War in North Africa, 1942-1943*, the first volume of a planned trilogy about the liberation of Europe during World War II.

Derrick A. Bell, Jr.
Bell, a professor of law at New York University School of Law, is considered a pioneer of critical race theory and an important figure in the movement against racial discrimination. Though he had established himself as a talented editor and essayist more than ten years earlier, Bell redefined his place in the literary world with his 1987 book *And We Are Not Saved: The Elusive Quest for Racial Justice*, which addresses racial issues through an intertwining of fictional parables and academic argumentation. In 2004 he published the study *Silent Covenants: Brown v. Board of Education and the Elusive Quest for Racial Justice*.

Helen Caldicott
Caldicott, an Australian-born physician, is an activist whose speeches on the health dangers posed by nuclear fallout helped convince many Australians to protest the testing of nuclear weapons. Since moving to the U.S. in 1977, she has worked to expand the debate over nuclear technology, pushing for a freeze on such weapons. Among her titles are *Missile Envy: The Arms Race and Nuclear War, If You Love This Planet: A Plan to Heal the Earth*, and 2002's *The New Nuclear Danger: George W. Bush's Military-Industrial Complex*.

David Gerrold
Gerrold is the author or editor of over forty books and numerous television scripts. His award-winning novels include *Yesterday's Children* and *Moonstar Odyssey*, as well as the books that comprise his enterprising and entertaining "War against the Chtorr" series. For a young-adult audience, he has also written the science fiction trilogy, known as the "Dingilliad" series. Additionally, Gerrold has written of his experiences as the single father of an adopted son in the popular 2002 novel *The Martian Child: A Novel about a Single Father Adopting a Son*.

Callie Khouri
Khouri is a screenplay writer best known for the 1991 Academy Award-winning film *Thelma and Louise*, about two women from Arkansas whose weekend road trip spins out of control. She marked her directorial debut in 2002 with the Warner Bros. film *Divine Secrets of the Ya-Ya Sisterhood*, based on her adaptation of Rebecca Well's best-selling novel. Khouri also wrote the screenplay for *Something to Talk About*, released in 1995.

Toni Morrison
Nobel laureate Morrison has a central role in the American literary canon, according to many critics, award committees, and readers. Through works such as *The Bluest Eye, Song of Solomon,* and *Beloved,* she proves herself to be a gifted teller of stories in which troubled characters seek to find themselves and their cultural riches in a society that warps or impedes such essential growth. Morrison, who released the novel *Love* in 2003, has also authored such children's books as *The Book of Mean People* with her son Slade Morrison.

Art Spiegelman
Spiegelman's Pulitzer-winning graphic-novel *Maus: A Survivors Tale* is an epic parable of the Holocaust that substitutes mice and cats for human Jews and Nazis. An author and illustrator, Spiegelman has roots that reach into the underground comics scene; in the early 1980s he and his wife, Françoise Mouly, introduced the first issue of the influential comics magazine *Raw*. The duo have also collaborated as editors on the "Little Lit" series of graphic novels for children. In 2001 Spiegelman produced the book *Jack Cole and Plastic Man: Forms Stretched to Their Limits* with graphic designer Chip Kidd.

Acknowledgments

Grateful acknowledgment is made to those publishers, photographers, and artists whose work appear with these authors' essays. Following is a list of the copyright holders who have granted us permission to reproduce material in this volume of *CA*. Every effort has been made to trace copyright, but if omissions have been made, please let us know.

Photographs/Art

Dannie Abse: Abse, photograph by Mark Gerson. © Mark Gerson Photography. Reproduced by permission.

Chinua Achebe: Achebe, photograph by Jerry Bauer. © Jerry Bauer. Reproduced by permission.

Douglas Adams: Adams, photograph by Jerry Bauer. © Jerry Bauer. Reproduced by permission.

Edward Albee: Albee, photograph by Marc Geller. Reproduced by permission of Marc Geller.

Jane Alexander: Alexander, photograph. AP/Wide World Photos. Reproduced by permission.

Rudolfo A. Anaya: Anaya, photograph. AP/Wide World Photos. Reproduced by permission.

John Arden: Arden, photograph by Jerry Bauer. © Jerry Bauer. Reproduced by permission.

Rick Atkinson: Atkinson, photograph. AP/Wide World Photos. Reproduced by permission.

Paul Bailey: Bailey, photograph by Mark Gerson. © Mark Gerson Photography. Reproduced by permission.

Derrick A. Bell, Jr.: Bell, photograph by Mark Bolster. Reproduced by permission of Derrick A. Bell, Jr. and Mark Bolster.

William Peter Blatty: Blatty, photograph. Archive Photos, Inc. Reproduced by permission.

Judy Blume: Blume, photograph by Sigrid Estrada. Reproduced by permission of Judy Blume.

Robert Boswell: Boswell, photograph. AP/Wide World Photos. Reproduced by permission.

James L. Brooks: Brooks, photograph. AP/Wide World Photos. Reproduced by permission.

Helen Caldicott: Caldicott, photograph. AP/Wide World Photos. Reproduced by permission.

Nancy Carlson: Carlson, photograph from *Smile a Lot!* Copyright © 2002 by Nancy Carlson. Reproduced by permission of Carolrhoda Books, a division of Lerner Publishing Group. All rights reserved.

Floyd Cooper: Cooper, photograph by C. J. Soos. Copyright © C. J. Soos. Reproduced by permission of Floyd Cooper.

Joy Cowley: Cowley, photograph. Reproduced by permission.

Jamie Lee Curtis: Curtis, photograph. © Mitchell Gerber/Corbis. Reproduced by permission.

Pamela Ditchoff: Ditchoff, photograph. Reproduced by permission of Pamela Ditchoff.

Sharon M. Draper: Draper, photograph. AP/Wide World Photos. Reproduced by permission.

Rosalyn Drexler: Drexler, photograph. AP/Wide World Photos. Reproduced by permission.

Patricia Duncker: Duncker, photograph by Jerry Bauer. © Jerry Bauer. Reproduced by permission.

Deanne Durrett: Durrett, photograph. Reproduced by permission of Deanne Durrett.

John L. Esposito: Esposito, photograph. AP/Wide World Photos. Reproduced by permission.

Pauline Fisk: Fisk, photograph by Jerry Bauer. © Jerry Bauer. Reproduced by permission.

Ruth Bader Ginsburg: Ginsburg, photograph by Najlah Feanny/Corbis Saba. Reproduced by permission.

Ted Robert Gurr: Gurr, photograph. Reproduced by permission of Ted Robert Gurr.

John E. Hallwas: Hallwas, photograph by Hartmann Photography. Reproduced by permission of John E. Hallwas.

Robert Harris: Harris, photograph by Jerry Bauer. © Jerry Bauer. Reproduced by permission.

Vaclav Havel: Havel, photograph. Getty Images. Reproduced by permission.

Mark Helprin: Helprin, photograph by Jerry Bauer. © Jerry Bauer. Reproduced by permission.

Will Hobbs: Hobbs, photograph by Jean Hobbs. Reproduced by permission of Will Hobbs.

Mary Ann Hoberman: Hoberman, photograph by Helen Neafsey. Reproduced by permission of Mary Ann Hoberman.

Stacy Horn: Horn, photograph. AP/Wide World Photos. Reproduced by permission.

Thomas Hoving: Hoving, photograph. Bettman/Corbis. Reproduced by permission.

David Henry Hwang: Hwang, photograph by Rick Maiman. AP/Wide World Photos. Reproduced by permission.

Alex S. Jones: Jones, photograph. AP/Wide World Photos. Reproduced by permission.

Cynthia Lynn Kadohata: Kadohata, photograph. AP/Wide World Photos. Reproduced by permission.

Garrison Keillor: Keillor, photograph by Ralph Nelson. Prairie Home Productions. Reproduced by permission.

Ken Kesey: Kesey, photograph. AP/Wide World Photos. Reproduced by permission.

Callie Khouri: Khouri, photograph by Julie Markes. AP/Wide World Photos. Reproduced by permission.

Jay Leno: Leno, photograph Archive Photos/Hammond. Reproduced by permission.

Joan Lunden: Lunden, photograph. AP/Wide World Photos. Reproduced by permission.

Mary E. Lyons: Lyons, photograph. © 2003 Mary E. Lyons. Reproduced by permission of Mary E. Lyons.

Louis A. Meyer, Jr.: Meyer, photograph by Annetje Meyer. Reproduced by permission of Louis A. Meyer, Jr.

Toni Morrison: Morrison, photograph. AP/Wide World Photos. Reproduced by permission.

Mary Pope Osborne: Osborne, photograph. Reproduced by permission pf Mary Pope Osborne.

Kevin Philips: Philips, photograph. Diana Walker/Time Life Pictures/Getty Images. Reproduced by permission.

Barbara Ann Porte: Porte, photograph by Venetia Thomas Carigo. Reproduced by permission of Barbara Ann Porte.

Art Spiegelman: Spiegelman, photograph by Jerry Bauer. © Jerry Bauer. Reproduced by permission.

Carlton Stowers: Stowers, photograph by Pat Stowers. Reproduced by permission of Carlton Stowers.

Marlo Thomas: Thomas, photograph by Victor Malafronte. Archive Photos, Inc. Reproduced by permission.

Teresa Toten: Toten, photograph by Matthew Wiley. Red Deer College Press. Reproduced by permission.

Frank E. Vandiver: Vandiver, photograph. Reproduced by permission of Frank E. Vandiver.

Steven Zaillian: Zaillian, photograph. AP/Wide World Photos. Reproduced by permission.

A

* Indicates that a listing has been compiled from secondary sources believed to be reliable, but has not been personally verified for this edition by the author sketched.

AARON, Shale
    See BOSWELL, Robert

*   *   *

ABSE, Dannie 1923-

PERSONAL: Born September 22, 1923, in Cardiff, Wales; son of Rudy (a cinema owner) and Kate (Shepherd) Abse; married Joan Mercer (an art historian), August 4, 1951; children: Keren, Susanna, David. *Ethnicity:* "Welsh." *Education:* Studied at University of Wales, 1941-42, King's College, London, and Westminster Hospital; Royal College of Surgeons, M.R.C.S., 1949; Royal College of Physicians, L.R.C.P., 1950. *Religion:* "Secular-Jewish." *Hobbies and other interests:* Chess.

ADDRESSES: Home—85 Hodford Rd., London NW11 8NH, England; and Green Hollows, Craig-yr-Eos Rd., Ogmore-by-Sea, Glamorgan, Wales. *Agent*—Drury House, 34-43 Russell St., London WC2B 5HA, England.

CAREER: Physician, playwright, novelist, and poet. *Poetry and Poverty* magazine, London, England, editor, 1949-54; Central Medical Establishment (chest clinic), London, part-time physician, 1955-89; freelance writer. Writer-in-residence, Princeton University, 1973-74. *Military service:* Royal Air Force, 1951-55; became squadron leader.

MEMBER: Poetry Society (president, 1978-92), Welsh Academy (president), Royal Society of Literature.

Dannie Abse

AWARDS, HONORS: Charles Henry Foyle award, 1960, for *House of Cowards;* Welsh Arts Council Literature Award, 1970, for *Selected Poems,* and 1979, for *Pythagoras; Jewish Chronicle* Book Award, 1970, for *Selected Poems;* Royal Society of Literature fellow, 1983; Cholmondeley Award, 1985, for distinction in poetry; D.Litt., University of Wales, 1989, and University of Glamorgan, 1993; honorary fellow, Cardiff University, College of Medicine, 1997.

WRITINGS:

PLAYS

Fire in Heaven (three-act in verse; also known as *In the Cage;* first produced in London, England, 1948; also see below), Hutchinson (London, England), 1956, prose version produced as *Is the House Shut?,* in West End, 1964.

Hands around the Wall (three-act), first produced in London, England, 1950.

House of Cowards (three-act; also see below), first produced in London's West End, 1960.

The Eccentric (one-act; first produced in London, England, 1961), Evans Brothers (London, England), 1961.

The Joker (one-act), first produced in London's West End, 1962.

Gone (one-act; also see below), first produced in London's West End, 1962.

Three Questor Plays (contains *In the Cage, House of Cowards,* and *Gone*), Scorpion Press, 1967.

The Dogs of Pavlov (three-act; first produced in London, England, 1969; produced in New York, 1974; also below), Vallentine, Mitchell (London, England), 1973.

Gone in January, first produced in London, England, 1978.

Pythagoras (first produced in Birmingham, England, 1976; also see below), Hutchinson (London, England), 1979.

The View from Row G: Three Plays (contains *House of Cowards, The Dogs of Pavlov* and *Pythagoras*), edited and introduced by Gary A. Davis, Seren Books (Bridgend, Wales), 1990.

Plays anthologized in *Best One-Act Plays, 1960-61,* edited by Hugh Miller, Harrap (London, England), 1963, and *Twelve Great Plays,* edited by L. F. Dean, Harcourt (New York, NY), 1970.

POETRY

After Every Green Thing, Hutchinson (London, England), 1948.
Walking under Water, Hutchinson (London, England), 1952.
Tenants of the House, Hutchinson (London, England), 1957, Criterion (New York, NY), 1959.
Poems, Golders Green, Hutchinson (London, England), 1962.
Dannie Abse: A Selection, Studio Vista (London, England), 1963.
A Small Desperation, Hutchinson (London, England), 1968.
Selected Poems, Oxford University Press (New York, NY), 1970.
Funland: A Poem in Nine Parts, Portland University Library (Portland, OR), 1971.
Funland, and Other Poems, Oxford University Press (New York, NY), 1973.
(With others) *More Words,* British Broadcasting Corp. (London, England), 1977.
Collected Poems, 1948-1976, University of Pittsburgh Press (Pittsburgh, PA), 1977.
Way out in the Centre, Hutchinson (London, England), 1981, published as *One-legged on Ice,* University of Georgia Press (Athens, GA), 1983.
Ask the Bloody Horse, Hutchinson (London, England), 1986.
White Coat, Purple Coat: Collected Poems, 1948-1988, Hutchinson (London, England), 1989.
Remembrance of Crimes Past: Poems, 1986-1989, Hutchinson (London, England), 1990.
Selected Poems, Penguin (Harmondsworth, England), 1994.
On the Evening Road, Hutchinson (London, England), 1994.
Welsh Retrospective, Seren Books (Bridgend, Wales), 1997.
Arcadia, One Mile, Hutchinson (London, England), 1998.
Be Seated, Thou: Poems, 1989-1998, Sheep Meadow Press (Riverdale-on-Hudson, NY), 2000.
Encounters, Hearing Eye (London, England), 2001.
New and Collected Poems, Hutchinson Radius (London, England), 2003.

Poems represented in anthologies, including *Faber Book of Twentieth-Century Verse,* edited by J. F. A. Heath-Stubbs and D. H. Wright, Faber (London, England), 1953; *Presenting Welsh Poetry,* edited by Gwyn Williams, Dufour, 1959; *An Anthology of Modern Verse,* edited by Elizabeth Jennings, Methuen (London, England), 1961; *Mid-Century: English Poetry, 1940-60,* edited by John S. Williams and Meic Stephens, J. M. Dent (London, England), 1969; *Norton Anthology of Modern Poetry,* edited by Richard Ellmann and R. M. O'Clair, Norton (New York, NY), 1973; and *The Oxford Book of Contemporary Verse,* edited by D. J. Enright, Oxford University Press, 1980.

NOVELS

Ash on a Young Man's Sleeve, Hutchinson (London, England), 1954.
Some Corner of an English Field, Hutchinson (London, England), 1956.
O. Jones, O. Jones, Hutchinson (London, England), 1970.
There Was a Young Man from Cardiff, Hutchinson (London, England), 1991.
The Strange Case of Dr. Simmonds and Dr. Glas, Robeson (London, England), 2002, Carroll & Graf (New York, NY), 2003.

EDITOR

(With Stephen Spender and Elizabeth Joan Jennings) *New Poems, 1956,* M. Joseph (London, England), 1956.
(With Howard Sergeant) *Mavericks,* Editions Poetry and Poverty, 1957.
Modern Poets in Focus, Corgi (London, England), Volume 1, 1971, Volumes 3, 5, 1973.
European Verse, Studio Vista (London, England), 1964.
Thirteen Poets, Poetry Book Society, 1972.
Poetry Dimension 2: The Best of the Poetry Year, St. Martin's Press (New York, NY), 1974.
Poetry Dimension: The Best of the Poetry Year (annual), Volumes 3-7, Robson (London, England), 1975-1980.
My Medical School, Robson (London, England), 1978.
Poems for Shakespeare 9, Globe Playhouse (London, England), 1981.
(And author of introduction) *Wales in Verse,* Secker & Warburg (London, England), 1983.
Doctors and Patients, Oxford University Press (Oxford, England), 1984.
(With wife, Joan Abse) *Voices in the Gallery: Poems and Pictures Chosen by Dannie and Joan Abse,* Tate Gallery Publications (London, England), 1986.
(With Joan Abse) *The Music Lover's Literary Companion,* Robson (London, England), 1989.
The Hutchinson Book of Post-War British Poets, Hutchinson (London, England), 1989.
(With Anne Stevenson) *The Gregory Anthology, 1991-1993,* Sinclair-Stevenson (London, England), 1994.
Twentieth-Century Anglo-Welsh Poetry, Seren Books (Bridgend, Wales), 1998.

RADIO AND TELEVISION SCRIPTS

Conform or Die, British Broadcasting Corp. (BBC) Radio, 1956.
No Telegrams, No Thunder, BBC Radio, 1962.
You Can't Say Hello to Anybody, BBC Radio, 1964.
A Small Explosion, BBC Radio, 1964.
Dylan Thomas Lived Here (teleplay), BBC-1, 1975.
Like Poetry (teleplay), BBC 2, 1977.
Pythagoras, BBC Radio 3, 1978.
Return to Cardiff, BBC Wales Television, 1985.
Bookmarks (teleplay), BBC 2, 1986.
A Welsh Life, HTV, 1990.
Case History, BBC Wales Television, 1999.

OTHER

Medicine on Trial, Aldus Books, 1967, Crown (New York, NY), 1969.
A Poet in the Family (autobiography), Hutchinson (London, England), 1974, updated edition published as *Goodbye, Twentieth Century,* Pimlico (London, England), 2001.
(Contributor) *Three Poets, Two Children: Leonard Clark, Vernon Scannell, Dannie Abse, Answer Questions by Two Children,* Thornhill, 1975.
Miscellany One, Poetry Wales Press (Bridgend, Wales), 1981.
A Strong Dose of Myself (essays and stories), Hutchinson (London, England), 1983.
Journals from the Ant Heap, Hutchinson (London, England), 1986.
Intermittent Journals, Seren Books (Bridgend, Wales), 1994.
The Two Roads Taken, (essays, broadcasts, lectures), Enitharmon (London, England), 2003.

Contributor to books, including *How Poets Work,* edited by Tony Curtis, Seren Books (Bridgend, Wales), 1996. Contributor to periodicals, including *New Yorker, Encounter,* and *Times Literary Supplement.*

SIDELIGHTS: Welsh-born Dannie Abse has successfully combined the practice of medicine with the art of writing poetry all of his working life. He was influenced toward a career in medicine by the example of several family members—including his brother Wilfred, who became a psychoanalyst—yet was also charmed in his teens by the rich language he heard in the political speeches of his brother Leo, who was then a vocal supporter of the Republican forces during the Spanish Civil War and later became a member of Parliament. In the *Dictionary of Literary Biography,* Daniel Hoffman explained that "Abse is a poet whose range of experience is wide, whose tone—at once intimate and unselfconscious—is inimitably his own. . . . His poems do not shrink from grappling with the most pressing questions of identity and existence."

At times a reluctant medical student, Abse entertained the notion of giving up medicine altogether, especially after his first book of poems, *After Every Green Thing,* was accepted for publication in 1946. An opportunity to work in the Royal Air Force's Mass Radiography section in London during World War II not only placed Abse closer to his future wife, art historian Joan Mercer, but also laid the groundwork for a clinical career that would give him enough leisure time to write.

For many years Abse's dual careers were discrete in his mind and practice. As he once explained in an essay for *Contemporary Authors Autobiography Series,* "Until the mid-sixties I somehow had not been able to call upon my confrontations with patients, their triumphs and defeats." People would approach him after poetry readings to express their surprise at learning he was a doctor. Despite the poet-physician examples of Keats and Robert Bridges, Abse said, "I felt uneasy about not being able to call upon that dramatic area of my life experience—was it so disturbing? Did I not believe that poetry should be an immersion into reality not an escape from it? . . . Gradually my mind, as it were, became prepared to write poems with medical themes."

This growth was first apparent in *A Small Desperation,* published in 1968. *Books and Bookmen* critic Howard Sergeant remarked that "although Dannie Abse has produced outstanding poems at various stages of his poetic career, there can be little doubt that since he has been writing 'as a whole man' and accepting his medical profession within the total complexity of his experience, his poetry has gained in scope, imaginative depth and psychological insight."

Abse's early work was heavily influenced by Rainer Maria Rilke. "The Uninvited," the only poem from *After Every Green Thing* that Abse remained pleased with through the years, had its genesis in his reading of Rilke's *Letters to a Young Poet.* The early poems are characterized by an extensive use of symbolism, a practice Abse later rejected. His collection of poetry, *Walking under Water,* demonstrates a decline in his former emphasis on the metaphysical and a shift toward the creation of poems drawn from personal experience—a trend that continues in the more conversational poems of *Tenants of the House* and *Poems, Golders Green.*

Abse's Jewish heritage and his family life are among the subjects of his poems in 1981's *Way out in the Centre,* a book in which he continues to explore his dual careers and their relationship to each other. He examines this issue on a deeper personal level in the poem "Lunch and Afterwards," which Douglas Dunn of the *Times Literary Supplement* found insufficient as an explanation of the tension between Abse's "physician's reliance on practical, scientific procedures and his poet's respect for the apparently unreal and irrational, the imagined and mysteriously human factors of life." In the *Dictionary of Literary Biography,* Hoffman observed this and other apparent contradictions in the poet's life, "Abse is 'way out' among English poets as a Welshman, a Jew, a Dionysian, a physician. These sides of his identity isolate him so that he feels he 'travelled without ticket.' Yet he is at the same time 'here . . . in England . . . in the centre,' because his work is rooted in the central English tradition of intimate address to a reader, more concerned to communicate through shared conventions of rhetoric and syntax than to substitute idiosyncratic inventions."

Several critics have commented on Abse's approach to depicting everyday life in his writing. Nathan Zach of the *Jewish Quarterly* wrote, "His poems are in part episodic and in their subject matter remain faithful to reality; a kind of diary-like impressionism." According to *New Statesman*'s Alan Brownjohn, Abse goes further than simply recording reality: "He writes in a restrainedly observant way about urban living, yet he is rarely mundane or patronising." Abse is uncomfortably aware of the difficulties encountered by those living a less privileged existence than himself. Michael Mott of *Poetry* praised Abse for being "willing toughly to accept the chasm between the comfort of his life and the discomfort of his thoughts. The questions he is brave enough to ponder at that chasm's edge, in however quiet a voice, are terrible."

Although Abse often concerns himself with serious issues in his verse, he "shows a clever wit in locating the fun in circumstances both grave and trivial," *Poetry*'s Leroy Searle observed. Some critics have characterized not only Abse's humor but also his poetic voice as particularly Welsh. As William H. Pritchard said in the *Hudson Review,* "Abse, like all good Welshmen, cares about, because he is so endowed with, the singing voice and the sense of humor." Samuel Hazo in *Commonweal* added: "I have a suspicion that Dr. Abse, being a singer in the Welsh sense, . . . is best in those poems of his that are essentially lyrical." Michael O'Neill, writing in the *Times Literary Supplement,* saw in "A Scream," from the 1986 book *Ask the Bloody Horse,* "fluent rhythms, diffusedly musical internal rhymes and casual run-ons" and found "much wit and exuberance" in "Hotel Nights," in the same collection.

Although Abse is best known for his poetry, he has also written several plays. In *The Poetry of Dannie Abse* John Cassidy described the plays as being "concerned with the making of choices and with the recognition of moral imperatives" and "aloof from the main currents moving through English theatre in the sixties and seventies. . . . If they have an affinity to anything outside themselves it is perhaps to the radio play, that underestimated form in which reliance upon language is often virtually complete. . . . The people who inhabit these dramas, whatever their status, are people whose lines are eminently speakable."

"Although he was long well known as a poet," Linden Peach wrote in the *Dictionary of Literary Biography,* ". . . Abse only belatedly came to be seen as a major theatrical voice. Despite generally favorable reviews, his plays were regarded as aloof from the main trends in English theater in the 1960s and 1970s; as ignoring the influences of Eugene O'Neill, Samuel Beckett, and Eugene Ionesco; and as having most affinity with radio plays, a genre in which Abse also worked. His career as a dramatist reflects his concern with complex philosophical issues, and his Jewish background has exerted an increasingly powerful influence on his work."

Peach pointed out that Abse's play *The Dogs of Pavlov* focuses on the readiness of two average people—lovers Kurt and Sally—to inflict pain on others when they are ordered to do so. As Peach described the play, the couple "volunteer to take part in a psychological experiment. They are separated, and Sally is strapped to an electrically wired chair and asked to perform a series of arithmetical calculations. If she gets an answer wrong, a volunteer in another room, who can hear but not see her, is instructed to give her a shock. . . . The experiment is supposedly designed to test the effect of negative reinforcement on learning; in fact, the ostensible subject, Sally, is a confederate of the experimenter and is not being shocked at all but is screaming in simulated pain. The real purpose of the experiment is to see the degree to which the actual subject—the person administering the 'shock'—will ignore his own moral code and carry out the instructions of the experimenter. . . . The play developed out of Abse's thinking in the 1960s—reflected in poems such as 'Postmark,' 'Not Beautiful,' and 'No More Mozart'—about how ordinary Germans during the Holocaust could obey orders to commit atrocities."

Among Abse's other writings are several novels, the first of which, *Ash on a Young Man's Sleeve,* has also been categorized as an autobiography. Despite James D. Finn's complaint in *Commonweal* that Abse's first novel has "a story but no plot," it was this book rather than his poetry that originally won Abse recognition as a promising writer. Speaking with Carolina Moorehead of the London *Times* about his more recent autobiographical work *A Strong Dose of Myself,* Abse referred to himself as "a dilettante doctor" and a professional poet, "because while I do feel that many doctors could do what I do, and probably do it better, no one else can write my verse, however defective it is."

In his novel *The Strange Case of Dr. Simmonds and Dr. Glas,* Abse draws on his medical experiences to fashion a fictional story revolving around Dr. Simmonds, who is practicing medicine in postwar London and despising it. With the end of the war, many refugees are moving into Simmonds's community, particularly Jewish refugees. Simmonds's inherent anti-Semitism is only stirred by this development. But when he comes to know the wife of the Jewish patient he despises most, Simmonds becomes infatuated and is soon plotting to murder her husband and win her for himself. Told through a series of journal entries which chart the doctor's decline into madness, the novel moved a *Kirkus* reviewer to maintain that "Abse works a fascinating riff on the Dr. Jekyll theme without adhering to it slavishly." Claire McKenna, writing in the *British Medical Journal,* noted that the novel "explores the themes of unrequited love, loneliness, unfulfilled potential, and the central tenets of the Hippocratic Oath," while John Quin in the *Lancet* concluded that "Abse has written a splendid and timely meditation on a doctor who chooses evil intent over good."

Asked by Nicholas Wroe in the *Guardian* about whether he had ever considered giving up medicine for a writing career, Abse explained: "I did once consider giving up medicine just after I'd failed a pathology exam. . . . By this time I'd already had a play produced and a book of poems accepted for publication. But I was under great pressure to carry on, both from my brothers and my father, who basically lived vicariously through his sons. I remember him saying, 'I don't care if he's Homer. He's got to earn a living.' And looking back, I'm glad I did stick with it."

BIOGRAPHICAL AND CRITICAL SOURCES:

BOOKS

Cohen, Joseph, editor, *The Poetry of Dannie Abse,* Robson Books (London, England), 1983.
Contemporary Authors Autobiography Series, Volume 1, Gale (Detroit, MI), 1986.
Contemporary Literary Criticism, Gale (Detroit, MI), Volume 7, 1977, Volume 29, 1984.
Contemporary Poets, 6th edition, St. James Press (Detroit, MI), 1996.
Curtis, Tony, *Dannie Abse,* University of Wales (Swansea, Wales), 1985.
Dictionary of Literary Biography, Gale (Detroit, MI), Volume 27: *Poets of Great Britain and Ireland, 1945-1960,* 1984, Volume 245: *British and Irish Dramatists since World War II, Third Series,* 2001.
Robson, Jeremy, editor, *Modern Poets in Focus,* Volume 4, Corgi (London, England), 1972.

PERIODICALS

Anglo-Welsh Review, winter, 1967; spring, 1973.
Booklist, June 1, 2000, Ray Olson, review of *Be Seated, Thou,* p. 1839.
Books and Bookmen, October, 1968, Howard Sergeant, review of *A Small Desperation;* July, 1977.
British Medical Journal, August 31, 2002, Claire McKenna, review of *The Strange Case of Dr. Simmonds and Dr. Glas,* p. 499.
Commonweal, March 18, 1955; October 19, 1973.
Encounter, June, 1973.
Guardian, January 31, 1978; September 29, 2001, Nicholas Wroe, "Is There a Poet in the House?"
Hudson Review, autumn, 1973.
Jewish Quarterly, winter, 1968-69.
Kirkus Reviews, March 1, 2003, review of *The Strange Case of Dr. Simmonds and Dr. Glas,* p. 324.
Lancet, April 11, 1998, Joseph Cady, review of *Welsh Retrospective,* p. 1141; October 24, 1998, Daniel Davies, review of *Arcadia, One Mile,* p. 1397; August 24, 2002, John Quin, review of *The Strange Case of Dr. Simmonds and Dr. Glas,* p. 651.
Listener, October 8, 1970.
Los Angeles Times Book Review, January 29, 1984.
Nassau Literary Review, spring, 1974.
New Statesman, March 6, 1970; May 11, 1973.
New York Times, April 12, 1969.
New York Times Book Review, December 6, 1970.
Poetry, May, 1971; March, 1974.
Spectator, November 24, 2001, P. J. Kavanagh, review of *Goodbye, Twentieth Century,* p. 56.
Times (London, England), February 28, 1983; November 13, 1986.
Times Literary Supplement, August 15, 1968; April 27, 1973; October 11, 1974; November 18, 1977; August 21, 1981, Douglas Dunn, review of *Way out in the Centre;* December 30, 1983; January 23, 1987, Michael O'Neill, review of *Ask the Bloody Horse;* November 2, 1990; August 9, 2002, Paddy Bullard, "Love in Swiss Cottage," p. 20.
World Literature Today, summer, 1998, Daniel T. Lloyd, review of *Twentieth Century Anglo-Welsh Poetry,* p. 625.

ONLINE

Desperado Literature, http://lidiavianu.scriptmania.com/ (July 1, 2002), Lidia Vianu, "Interview with Dannie Abse."

* * *

ACHEBE, (Albert) Chinua(lumogu) 1930-

PERSONAL: Name is pronounced "CHIN-yoo-uh ah-CHAY-bee"; born November 16, 1930, in Ogidi, Nigeria; son of Isaiah Okafo (an Anglican churchman and teacher) and Janet N. Iloegbunam Achebe; married Christiana Chinwe Okoli, September 10, 1961; chil-

Chinua Achebe

dren: Chinelo (daughter), Ikechukwu (son), Chidi (son), Nwando (daughter). *Education:* Church Mission Society School; a colonial government secondary school in which English was enforced; Government College, Umuahia, 1944-47; and University College, Ibadan, 1948-53, B.A. (under London University) 1953; studied broadcasting at the British Broadcasting Corporation, London, 1956. *Hobbies and other interests:* Music.

ADDRESSES: *Home*—P.O. Box 53 Nsukka, Anambra State, Nigeria. *Office*—Institute of African Studies, University of Nigeria, Nsukka, Anambra State, Nigeria; and c/o Bard College, P.O. Box 41, Annandale-on-Hudson, NY 12504. *E-mail*—achebe@bard.edu.

CAREER: Writer. Nigerian Broadcasting Company (NBC), Lagos, Nigeria, talk show producer, 1954-57, controller of Eastern Region in Enugu, Nigeria, 1958-61, founder and director of Voice of Nigeria, 1961-66; University of Nigeria, Nsukka, senior research fellow, 1967-72, professor of English, 1976-81, professor emeritus, 1985—; Anambra State University of Technology, Enugu, pro-chancellor and chair of council, 1986-88; University of Massachusetts—Amherst, professor, 1987-88. Served on diplomatic missions for Biafra during the Nigerian Civil War, 1967-69. Visiting professor of English at University of Massachusetts—Amherst, 1972-75, and University of Connecticut, Afro-American Studies department, 1975-76. University of California, Los Angeles, Regents' lecturer, 1984; Cambridge University, Clare Hall, visiting fellow and Ashby lecturer, 1993; Charles P. Stevenson Professor of Languages and Literatures at Bard College, Annandale-on-Hudson, NY, 1993—; lecturer at universities in Nigeria and the United States; speaker at events in numerous countries throughout the world. Chair, Citadel Books Ltd., Enugu, Nigeria, 1967; founding editor, Heinemann African Writers series, 1962-72, director, Heinemann Educational Books Ltd., Ibadan, Nigeria, 1970—; director, Nwamife Publishers Ltd., Enugu, Nigeria, 1970—. Founder and publisher, *Uwa Ndi Igbo: A Bilingual Journal of Igbo Life and Arts,* 1984—. Governor, Newsconcern International Foundation, 1983. Member, University of Lagos Council, 1966, East Central State Library Board, 1971-72, Anambra State Arts Council, 1977-79, and National Festival Committee, 1983; director, Okike Arts Centre, Nsukka, 1984—. Deputy national president of People's Redemption Party, 1983; president of town union, Ogidi, Nigeria, beginning 1986; goodwill ambassador for U.N. Population Fund, 1999.

MEMBER: International Social Prospects Academy (Geneva), Writers and Scholars International (London), Writers and Scholars Educational Trust (London), Commonwealth Arts Organization (member of executive committee, 1981—), Association of Nigerian Authors (founder; president, 1981-86), Ghana Association of Writers (fellow), Royal Society of Literature (London), Modern Language Association of America (honorary fellow), American Academy and Institute of Arts and Letters (honorary member).

AWARDS, HONORS: Margaret Wrong Memorial Prize, 1959, for *Things Fall Apart;* Rockefeller travel fellowship to East and Central Africa, 1960-1961; Nigerian National Trophy, 1961, for *No Longer at Ease;* UNESCO fellowship for creative artists for travel to United States and Brazil, 1963; Jock Campbell/*New Statesman* Award, 1965, for *Arrow of God;* Commonwealth Poetry Prize, 1972, for *Beware, Soul-Brother, and Other Poems;* Neil Gunn international fellow,

Scottish Arts Council, 1975; Lotus Award for Afro-Asian Writers, 1975; Nigerian National Merit Award, 1979; named to the Order of the Federal Republic of Nigeria, 1979; Commonwealth Foundation senior visiting practitioner award, 1984; *A Man of the People* was cited in Anthony Burgess's 1984 book *Ninety-nine Novels: The Best in England since 1939;* Booker Prize nomination, 1987, for *Anthills of the Savannah;* Champion Award, 1996. D.Litt., Dartmouth College, 1972, University of Southampton, 1975, University of Ife, 1978, University of Nigeria, Nsukka, 1981, University of Kent, 1982, Mount Allison University, 1984, University of Guelph, 1984, and Franklin Pierce College, 1985, Ibadan University, 1989, Skidmore College, 1991, City College of New York, 1992, Fitchburg State College, 1994, Harvard University, 1996, Binghamton University, 1996, Bates College, 1996, Trinity College, Connecticut, 1999; D.Univ., University of Stirling, 1975, Open University, 1989; LL.D., University of Prince Edward Island, 1976, Georgetown University, 1990, Port Harcourt University, 1991; D.H.L., University of Massachusetts—Amherst, 1977, Westfield College, 1989, New School for Social Research, 1991, Hobart and William Smith College, 1991, Marymount Manhattan College, 1991, Colgate University, 1993; nominated for Nobel prize in literature, 2000; German Booksellers Peace Prize for promoting human understanding through literature, 2002.

WRITINGS:

NOVELS

Things Fall Apart, Heinemann (London, England), 1958, Obolensky (New York, NY), 1959, abridged and annotated edition published as *Things Fall Apart: An Adapted Classic,* adapted by Sandra Widner, Globe Fearon (Lebanon, IN), 2000, also published as *Things Fall Apart: With Related Readings,* Paradigm (St. Paul, MN), 2002.

No Longer at Ease, Heinemann (London, England), 1960, Obolensky (New ork, NY), 1961, 2nd edition, Fawcett (Uncasville, CT), 1988.

Arrow of God, Heinemann (London, England), 1964, John Day (New York, NY), 1967.

A Man of the People, John Day (New York, NY), 1966, published with an introduction by K. W. J. Post, Doubleday (New York, NY), 1967.

Anthills of the Savannah, Anchor Books (New York, NY), 1988.

The Voter, Viva Books (Johannesburg, South Africa), 1994.

Home and Exile, Oxford University Press (New York, NY), 2000.

JUVENILE

Chike and the River, Cambridge University Press (Cambridge, England), 1966.

(With John Iroaganachi) *How the Leopard Got His Claws,* Nwankwo-Ifejika (Enugu, Nigeria), 1972, bound with *Lament of the Deer,* by Christopher Okigbo, Third Press (New York, NY), 1973.

The Flute, Fourth Dimension Publishers (Enugu, Nigeria), 1978.

The Drum, Fourth Dimension Publishers (Enugu, Nigeria), 1978.

POETRY

Beware, Soul-Brother, and Other Poems, Nwankwo-Ifejika (Enugu, Nigeria), 1971, Doubleday (New York, NY), 1972, revised edition, Heinemann (London, England), 1972.

Christmas in Biafra, and Other Poems, Doubleday (New York, NY), 1973.

(Editor, with Dubem Okafor) *Don't Let Him Die: An Anthology of Memorial Poems for Christopher Okigbo,* Fourth Dimension Publishers (Enugu, Nigeria), 1978.

(Coeditor) *Aka Weta: An Anthology of Igbo Poetry,* Okike (Nsukka, Nigeria), 1982.

Another Africa, poems and essays, Anchor Books (New York, NY), 1997.

OTHER

The Sacrificial Egg, and Other Stories, Etudo (Onitsha, Nigeria), 1962.

(Contributor) *The Insider: Stories of War and Peace from Nigeria,* Nwankwo-Ifejika (Enugu, Nigeria), 1971.

Morning Yet on Creation Day (essays), Doubleday (New York, NY), 1975.

(Contributor) *In Person—Achebe, Awoonor, and Soyinka at the University of Washington,* University of Washington (Seattle, WA), 1975.

(Editor, with Jomo Kenyatta and Amos Tutuola) *Winds of Change: Modern Stories from Black Africa*, Longman (London, England)), 1977.

The Trouble with Nigeria (essays), Fourth Dimension Publishers (Enugu, Nigeria), 1983, Heinemann (London, England), 1984.

(Editor, with C. L. Innes) *African Short Stories*, Heinemann (London, England), 1984.

The World of the Ogbanje, Fourth Dimension (Enugu, Nigeria), 1986.

Girls at War (short stories), Heinemann (London, England), 1972, Fawcett (Uncasville, CT), 1988.

Hopes and Impediments: Selected Essays 1965-1987, Heinemann (London, England), 1988.

The University and the Leadership Factor in Nigerian Politics, Abic Books (Enugu, Nigeria), 1988.

The African Trilogy, (fiction), Picador (London, England), 1988.

A Tribute to James Baldwin: Black Writers Redefine the Struggle: Proceedings of a Conference at the University of Massachusetts at Amherst, April 22-23, 1988, Featuring Chinua Achebe, University of Massachusetts Press (Amherst, MA), 1989.

(Coeditor) *Beyond Hunger in Africa: Conventional Wisdom and an African Vision*, Currey (London, England), 1990.

(Editor, with C. L. Innes, and contributor) *The Heinemann Book of Contemporary African Short Stories*, Heinemann (London, England), 1992.

(With others) *The South Wind and the Sun*, edited by Kate Turkington, Thorold's Africana Books (Johannesburg, South Africa), 1996.

Another Africa (poems and essay), photographs by Robert Lyons, Anchor Books (New York, NY), 1997.

(With others) *Order and Chaos*, Great Books Foundation (Chicago, IL), 1997.

Conversations with Chinua Achebe, University Press of Mississippi (Jackson, MS), 1997.

Also author of essay collection *Nigerian Topics*, 1988. Contributor to anthologies, including *Modern African Stories*, edited by Ellis Ayitey Komey and Ezekiel Mphahlele, Faber (London), 1964; *Africa Speaks: A Prose Anthology with Comprehension and Summary Passages*, Evans, 1970; and *The Short Century: Independence and Liberation Movements in Africa, 1945-1994*, edited by Okwui Enwezor, Prestel, 2001. Author of foreword, *African Rhapsody: Short Stories of the Contemporary African Experience*, 1994. Founding editor, "African Writers Series," Heinemann, 1962-72; editor, *Okike: A Nigerian Journal of New Writing*, 1971—; editor, *Nsukkascope*, a campus magazine.

Things Fall Apart has been translated into forty-five languages.

ADAPTATIONS: *Things Fall Apart* was adapted for the stage and produced by Eldred Fiberesima in Lagos, Nigeria; it was also adapted for radio and produced by the British Broadcasting Corporation in 1983, and for television in English and Igbo and produced by the Nigerian Television Authority in 1985.

WORK IN PROGRESS: *Our Shared Future*, a series of books focused on the issues affecting children around the world, for UNICEF, edited with Toni Morrison.

SIDELIGHTS: Since the 1950s, Nigeria has witnessed "the flourishing of a new literature which has drawn sustenance both from traditional oral literature and from the present and rapidly changing society," wrote Margaret Laurence in her book *Long Drums and Cannons: Nigerian Dramatists and Novelists*. Thirty years ago, Chinua Achebe, who rejected the British name "Albert" and took his indigenous name "Chinua" in college in 1948, was among the founders of this new literature and over the years many critics have come to consider him the finest of the Nigerian novelists. His achievement has not been limited to his native country or continent (his work has been published in some fifty languages). As Laurence maintained, "Chinua Achebe's careful and confident craftsmanship, his firm grasp of his material and his ability to create memorable and living characters place him among the best novelists now writing in any country in the English language."

On the level of ideas, Achebe's "prose writing reflects three essential and related concerns," observed G. D. Killam in his book *The Novels of Chinua Achebe*, "first, with the legacy of colonialism at both the individual and societal level; secondly, with the *fact* of English as a language of national and international exchange; thirdly, with the obligations and responsibilities of the writer both to the society in which he lives and to his art." Over the past century, African nations have been caught in struggles for identity between tradition, colonialism, and independence. These conflicts, deepened by the continuing presence of economic colonialism and neocolonialism among European educated rulers, has prevented many nations from raising themselves above political and social chaos to achieve true independence. "Most of the problems we see in our politics derive from the moment when we lost our initiative to other people, to colonizers," Achebe noted in a book of essays. He went on to explain: "What I think is the basic problem of a new African country like Nigeria is really what you might call a 'crisis in the soul.' We have been subjected—we have subjected ourselves too—to this period during which we have accepted everything alien as good and practically everything local or native as inferior." "We had all been duped," he wrote. "No independence was given . . . Europe had only made a tactical withdrawal on the political front and while we sang our anthem . . . she was securing her grip behind us in the economic field. And our leaders in whose faces we hurled our disenchantment neither saw nor heard because they were not leaders at all but marionettes."

In order to recognize the virtues of precolonial Nigeria, chronicle the ongoing impact of colonialism on native cultures, and expose present-day corruption, Achebe desired to clearly communicate these concerns first to his fellow countrymen but also to those outside his country. Unlike Kenyan writer Ngugi wa Thiongo and others, who chose to return to writing in their native languages, Achebe judged the best channel for these messages to be English, the language of colonialism. He did so because he wished to repossess the power of description from those, like Conrad, Joyce Cary, and H. Rider Haggard, who had, as he said, secured "an absolute power over narrative" that cast Africans as beasts, savages, and idiots. He explained that language need not to be viewed as an enemy, "but as a tool." Through repossession, he could "help [his] society regain belief in itself and put away the complexes of the years of denigration and self-abasement." He was taking up a long fight against European writers who were "bloody racists" in their descriptions of Africans and Africa.

Achebe's transformation of language to achieve his particular ends distinguishes his writing from that of other English-language novelists. To repossess description of Nigeria in English, he translates Ibo proverbs and weaves them into his stories with Ibo vocabulary, images, and speech patterns. "Among the Ibo the art of conversation is regarded very highly," he wrote in his novel *Things Fall Apart,* "and proverbs are the palm-oil with which words are eaten." "Proverbs are cherished by Achebe's people as . . . the treasure boxes of their cultural heritage," explained Adrian A. Roscoe in *Mother Is Gold: A Study of West African Literature.* "When they disappear or fall into disuse . . . it is a sign that a particular tradition, or indeed a whole way of life, is passing away." Achebe's use of proverbs also has an artistic aim, as Bernth Lindfors suggested in *Folklore in Nigerian Literature.* "Proverbs can serve as keys to an understanding of his novels," commented the critic, "because he uses them not merely to add touches of local color but to sound and reiterate themes, to sharpen characterization, to clarify conflict, and to focus on the values of the society."

Although he has also written poetry, short stories, and essays—both literary and political—Achebe is best known for his novels: *Things Fall Apart, No Longer at Ease, Arrow of God, A Man of the People,* and *Anthills of the Savannah.* Anthony Daniels wrote of Achebe's novels in the *Spectator,* "In spare prose of great elegance, without any technical distraction, he has been able to illuminate two emotionally irreconcilable facets of modern African life: the humiliations visited on Africans by colonialism, and the . . . worthlessness of what replaced colonial rule." Set in this historical context, the novels develop the theme of what happens to a society when change outside distorts and blocks the natural change from within and offer, as Eustace Palmer observed, "a powerful presentation of the beauty, strength and validity of traditional life and values and the disruptiveness of change." Even as he resists the rootless visions of postmodernist globalization, Achebe does not appeal for a return to the ways of the past.

Things Fall Apart and *Arrow of God*—Achebe's first novels—focus on Nigeria's early experience with colonialism, from first contact with the British to widespread British administration. "With remarkable unity of the word with the deed, the character, the time and the place, Chinua Achebe creates in these two novels a coherent picture of coherence being lost, of the tragic consequences" of European colonialism, suggested Robert McDowell in a special issue of *Studies in Black Literature* dedicated to Achebe's work. "There is an artistic unity of all things in these books, which is rare anywhere in modern English fiction."

Things Fall Apart was published in 1958, early in the Nigerian renaissance. Achebe explained why he began writing at this time in an interview with Lewis Nkosi in *African Writers Talking: A Collection of Radio Interviews:* "One of the things that set me thinking was Joyce Cary's novel set in Nigeria, *Mr. Johnson,* which was praised so much, and it was clear to me that this was a most superficial picture . . . not only of the country, but even of the Nigerian character. . . . I thought if this was famous, then perhaps someone ought to try and look . . . from the inside." Charles R. Larson, in *The Emergence of African Fiction,* said of Achebe's success, both in investing his novel of Africa with an African sensibility and in making this view available to African readers: "In 1964 . . . *Things Fall Apart* became the first novel by an African writer to be included in the required syllabus for African secondary school students throughout the English-speaking portions of the continent." As Simon Gikandi recalled in a special issue of *Research in African Literatures,* "Once I had started reading *Things Fall Apart* . . . I could not cope with the chapter-a-day policy. I read the whole novel over one afternoon and it is not an exaggeration to say that my life was never to be the same again. . . . In reading *Things Fall Apart,* everything became clear: the yam was important to Ibo culture, not because of what we were later to learn to call use-value . . . but because of its location at the nexus of a symbolic economy in which material wealth was connected to spirituality and ideology and desire." Later in the 1960s, the novel "became recognized by African and non-African literary critics as the first 'classic' in English from tropical Africa," added Larson.

The novel tells the story of an Ibo village of the late 1800s and one of its great men, Okonkwo. Although the son of a ne'er-do-well, Okonkwo has achieved much in his life. He is a champion wrestler, a wealthy farmer, a husband to three wives, a title-holder among his people, and a member of the select *egwugwu* who represent ancestral spirits at tribal rituals. "The most impressive achievement of *Things Fall Apart,*" maintained David Carroll in his book *Chinua Achebe,* "is the vivid picture it provides of Ibo society at the end of the nineteenth century." He explained: "Here is a clan in the full vigor of its traditional way of life, unperplexed by the present and without nostalgia for the past. Through its rituals the life of the community and the life of the individual are merged into significance and order."

In *Things Fall Apart,* the order of the village is disrupted with the appearance of the white man in Africa and with the introduction of his religion. "The conflict in the novel, vested in Okonkwo, derives from the series of crushing blows which are levelled at traditional values by an alien and more powerful culture causing, in the end, the traditional society to fall apart," observed Killam. Okonkwo is unable to counter the changes that accompany colonialism. In the end, in frustration, he kills an African employed by the British, and then commits suicide, a sin against the tradition to which he had long remained true. The novel thus presents "two main, closely intertwined tragedies," wrote Arthur Ravenscroft in his study *Chinua Achebe,* "the personal tragedy of Okonkwo . . . and the public tragedy of the eclipse of one culture by another." Achebe reclaims the power of description from the colonial writer by depicting both tragedies from within Ibo culture.

Although the author emphasizes the message in his novels, he also received praise for his artistic achievement. As Palmer commented, the work "demonstrates a mastery of plot and structure, strength of characterization, competence in the manipulation of language and consistency and depth of thematic exploration which is rarely found in a first novel." Achebe also achieves balance in recreating the tragic consequences of colonial damage to his culture. Killam noted that "in showing Ibo society before and after the coming of the white man he avoids the temptation to present the past as idealized and the present as ugly and unsatisfactory." And, Killam concluded, Achebe's "success proceeds from his ability to create a sense of real life and real issues in the book and to see his subject from the point of view which is neither idealistic nor dishonest."

Arrow of God, the second novel, takes place in the 1920s after the British have established a presence in Nigeria. The "arrow of god" in the title is Ezeulu, the chief priest of the god Ulu, a deity created to unite Umuaro, a federation of six Ibo villages. As chief priest, Ezeulu is responsible for initiating rituals that structure village life and maintain the unity of the federation, a position with a great deal of political as well as spiritual power. In fact, the central theme of this novel, as Laurence pointed out, is power: "Ezeulu's testing of his own power and the power of his god, and his effort to maintain his own and his god's authority in the face of village factions and of the [Christian] mission and the British administration." "This, then, is a political novel in which different systems of power are examined and their dependence upon myth and ritual compared," wrote Carroll.

In Ezeulu, Achebe presents a study of loss of power in the face of colonial manipulation whose depth he does not understand. After the village council rejects his advice to avoid conflict with a neighboring village, Ezeulu finds himself at odds with his own people and praised by British administrators. The British, seeking a candidate to install as village chieftain, make him an offer, which he refuses and is therefore imprisoned. Caught in the middle with no allies, Ezeulu becomes more and more uncompromising and finally dooms the villages in his rigid opposition to the council. "As in Achebe's other novels," observed Gerald Moore in *Seven African Writers,* "it is the strong-willed man of tradition who cannot adapt, and who is crushed by his virtues in the war between the new, more worldly order, and the old, conservative values of an isolated society." The artistry displayed in *Arrow of God,* Achebe's second portrait of cultures in collision, has drawn a great deal of attention, adding to the esteem in which the writer is held. Charles Miller commented in a *Saturday Review* article that Achebe's "approach to the written word is completely unencumbered with verbiage. He never strives for the exalted phrase, he never once raises his voice; even in the most emotion-charged passages the tone is absolutely unruffled, the control impeccable." Concluded Miller, "It is a measure of Achebe's creative gift that he has no need whatever for prose fireworks to light the flame of his intense drama."

Achebe's three other novels—*No Longer at Ease, A Man of the People,* and *Anthills of the Savannah*—examine Africa in the era of independence. This is an Africa less and less under obvious European administration, but still deeply controlled by it, an Africa struggling to regain its footing in order to stand on its own two feet. Standing in the way of realizing its goal of true independence is the persistence of European values pervasive in modern Africa, an obstacle Achebe continues to scrutinize in each of these novels. Olaniyan commented, "The postcolonial state was determined by, and is an expression of, the political superstructure elaborated by colonial power, and not an outgrowth of the autonomous evolution of the people. . . . The postcolonial state has been unable to escape the logic of its origin in the colonial state: absence of legitimacy with the governed, dependence on coercion, lack of political accountability, a bureaucracy with an extraverted mentality, disregard for the cultivation of a responsive civic community, uneven horizontal integration into the political community such that the government is most felt in the cities, extraction of surplus from the interior to overfeed the capital, and many more!"

In *No Longer at Ease,* set in Nigeria just prior to independence, Achebe extends his history of the Okonkwo family. The central character is Obi Okonkwo, grandson of the tragic hero of *Things Fall Apart.* Obi Okonkwo has been raised a Christian and educated in England. Like many of his peers, he has left the bush behind for a position as a civil servant in Lagos, Nigeria's largest city. "*No Longer at Ease* deals with the plight of [this] new generation of Nigerians," observed Palmer, "who, having been exposed to education in the western world and therefore largely cut off from their roots in traditional society, discover, on their return, that the demands of tradition are still strong, and are hopelessly caught in the clash between the old and the new," the demands the logic of colonialism continues to make on the ruling class.

Many faced with this internal conflict between individualistic and communal values succumb to corruption. Obi is no exception. "The novel opens with Obi on trial for accepting bribes," noted Killam, "and the book takes the form of a long flashback." "In a world which is the result of the intermingling of Europe and Africa . . . Achebe traces the decline of his hero from brilliant student to civil servant convicted of bribery and corruption," wrote Carroll. "It reads like a postscript to the earlier novel [*Things Fall Apart*] because the same forces are at work but in a confused, diluted, and blurred form." In *This Africa: Novels by West Africans in English and French,* Judith Illsley Gleason pointed out how the imagery of each book depicts the changes in the Okonkwo family and the Nigeria they represent. She wrote, "The career of the grandson Okonkwo ends not with a machete's swing but with a gavel's tap," but the legacy that destroys him is the same.

A Man of the People is satire, and in this "novel of disenchantment," Achebe further casts his eye on African politics, taking on, as Moore noted, "the corruption of Nigerians in high places in the central government." The author's eyepiece is the book's narrator Odili, a schoolteacher; the object of his scrutiny is the Honorable M. A. Nanga, Member of Parliament,

Odili's former teacher and a popular bush politician who has risen to the post of Minister of Culture in his West African homeland.

At first, Odili is charmed by the politician but eventually he recognizes the extent of Nanga's abuses and decides to oppose the minister in an election. Odili is beaten, both physically and politically, his appeal to the people heard but ignored because he too has left his roots behind for abstract intellect. The novel demonstrates, according to Shatto Arthur Gakwandi in *The Novel and Contemporary Experience in Africa,* that "the society has been invaded by a wide range of values which have destroyed the traditional balance between the material and the spiritual spheres of life, which has led inevitably to the hypocrisy of double standards." Odili is both victim and perpetrator of these double standards.

Despite his political victory, Nanga, along with the rest of the government, is ousted by a coup. "The novel is a carefully plotted and unified piece of writing," wrote Killam. "Achebe achieves balance and proportion in the treatment of his theme of political corruption by evoking both the absurdity of the behavior of the principal characters while at the same time suggesting the serious and destructive consequences of their behavior to the commonwealth." The seriousness of the fictional situation portrayed in *A Man of the People* became real very soon after the novel was first published in 1966 when Nigeria itself was wracked by a coup.

Two decades passed between the publication of *A Man of the People* and Achebe's 1988 novel, *Anthills of the Savannah.* During this time, rather than flee abroad as he might have done, Achebe became involved in the political struggle between Nigeria and the seceding nation of Biafra, a struggle marked by five coups, a civil war, elections marred by violence, and a number of attempts to return to civilian rule. He worked throughout the war as Biafran Minister of Information. Judging that novels could not express the horrors of the struggle, he wrote poetry, short stories, and essays that mourned and celebrated the attempted revolution.

Anthills of the Savannah is Achebe's return to the novel, and as Nadine Gordimer commented in the *New York Times Book Review,* "It is a work in which twenty-two years of harsh experience, intellectual growth, self-criticism, deepening understanding and mustered discipline of skill open wide a subject to which Mr. Achebe is now magnificently equal." It is a return to the themes of independent Africa informing Achebe's earlier novels but it gives the most significant role to women, who invent a new kind of storytelling, offering a glimmer of hope at the end of the novel. "This is a study of how power corrupts itself and by doing so begins to die," wrote *Observer* contributor and fellow Nigerian Ben Okri. "It is also about dissent, and love."

Three former schoolmates have risen to positions of power in an imaginary West African nation, Kangan. Ikem is editor of the state-owned newspaper; Chris is the country's minister of information; Sam is a military man who has become head of state. Sam's quest to have himself voted president for life sends the lives of these three and the lives of all Kangan citizens into turmoil. Neal Ascherson in the *New York Review of Books,* commented that the novel becomes "a tale about responsibility, and the ways in which men who should know better betray and evade that responsibility."

The turmoil comes to a head in the novel's final pages. All three of the central characters are dead. Ikem, who spoke out against the abuses of the government, is murdered by Sam's secret police. Chris, who flees into the bush to begin a journey of transformation among the people, is shot attempting to stop a rape. Sam is kidnapped and murdered in a coup. "The three murders, senseless as they are, represent the departure of a generation that compromised its own enlightenment for the sake of power," wrote Ascherson. At Achebe's 70th birthday celebration at Bard College, Wole Soyinka commented that "Achebe never hesitates to lay blame for the woes of the African continent squarely where it belongs." And, as Okri observed, "The novel closes with the suggestion that power should reside not within an elite but within the awakened spirit of the people."

Anthills of the Savannah was well-received and earned Achebe a nomination for the Booker Prize. Larson, in *Tribune Books,* estimated that "No other novel in many years has bitten to the core, swallowed and regurgitated contemporary Africa's miseries and expectations as profoundly as *Anthills of the Savannah.*"

Achebe's next book, *Hopes and Impediments: Selected Essays 1965-1987,* essays and speeches written over a period of twenty-three years, is perceived in many ways to be a logical extension of ideas in *Anthills of the Savannah*. In this collection, however, he is not addressing the way Africans view themselves but rather how Africa is viewed by the outside world. The central theme is the corrosive impact of the racism that pervades Western traditional appraisal of Africa. The collection opens with an examination of Joseph Conrad's 1902 novella *Heart of Darkness;* Achebe criticizes Conrad for projecting an image of Africa as "the other world"—meaning non-European and, therefore, uncivilized. Achebe argues that to this day, the Conradian myth persists that Africa is a dark and bestial land. The time has come, Achebe states, to sweep away this racism in favor of new myths and socially "beneficent fiction" which will enable Africans and non-Africans alike to redefine the way they look at the continent. "I am a political writer," he said, and "My politics is concerned with universal communication across racial and cultural boundaries as a means of fostering respect for all people. . . . As long as one people sits on another and are deaf to their cry, so long will understanding and peace elude us."

Achebe continues this critique, after a long silence while he recovered from a serious car crash that left him paralyzed from the waist down, in *Home and Exile,* a memoir in the form of three essays, where he extends his attack on linguistic colonialism in its many forms: "The subject of naming, especially naming to put down, appears in a variety of forms in the course of his deliberations." For instance, he repossesses for the Ibo the word "nation" rather than "tribe." Adebayo, in an article in *Research in African Literatures,* contended that Achebe "resents the colonial categorization of non-Western nationalities as tribes distinguished by primordial affiliations and primitive customs. By sheer force of logic and weight of evidence, Achebe demonstrates that his own people . . . do not share most of the notorious attributes of tribal groups, particularly blood ties and a centralized authority." As Richard Feldstein wrote in a *Literature and Psychology* review, "*Home and Exile* calls for overwriting colonial narratives by painstakingly reviewing their articulation as well as their accumulated details while instituting a counter-discourse of repossession. Repossession . . . calls for the process of re-storying marginalized indigenes who have been silenced by the trauma of dispossession. Repossession presents counter-discursive 'stories,' along with new ways of telling them."

In his writings, Achebe has created a significant body of work in which he offers a close and balanced examination of contemporary Africa and the historical forces that have shaped it. "His distinction is to have [looked back] without any trace either of chauvinistic idealism or of neurotic rejection," maintained Moore. And Busby commended the author's achievement in "charting the socio-political development of contemporary Nigeria." However, Achebe's writing reverberates beyond the borders of Nigeria and beyond the arenas of anthropology, sociology, and political science. As literature, it deals with universal qualities. And, as Killam wrote in his study: "Achebe's novels offer a vision of life which is essentially tragic, compounded of success and failure, informed by knowledge and understanding, relieved by humour and tempered by sympathy, embued with an awareness of human suffering and the human capacity to endure." Concluded the critic, "Sometimes his characters meet with success, more often with defeat and despair. Through it all the spirit of man and the belief in the possibility of triumph endures." In 1990, only weeks after attending a celebration for his 60th birthday, Achebe was paralyzed in an accident in Nigeria, but has continued to publish, teach, and appear in public. He moved to the United States for therapy, and has lived there, "a reluctant refugee," according to Oluwole Adujare in an *African News Service* review, during a dark time of Nigerian dictatorship.

BIOGRAPHICAL AND CRITICAL SOURCES:

BOOKS

Awoonor, Kofi, *The Breast of the Earth,* Doubleday (New York, NY), 1975.
Awosika, Olawale, *Form and Technique in the African Novel,* Sam Bookman (Ibadan, Nigeria), 1997.
Baldwin, Claudia, *Nigerian Literature: A Bibliography of Criticism,* G. K. Hall (Boston, MA), 1980.
Carroll, David, *Chinua Achebe,* Macmillan (New York, NY), 1990.
Champion, Ernest A., *Mr. Baldwin, I Presume: James Baldwin—Chinua Achebe: A Meeting of the Minds,* University Press of America (Lanham, MD), 1995.
Contemporary Literary Criticism, Gale (Detroit, MI), Volume 1, 1973, Volume 3, 1975, Volume 5, 1976, Volume 7, 1977, Volume 11, 1979, Volume 26, 1983, Volume 51, 1988, Volume 75, 1993.
Contemporary Novelists, 7th edition, St. James Press (Detroit, MI), 2001.

Ezenwa-Ohaeto, *Chinua Achebe: A Biography,* Indiana University Press, 1997.

Gakwandi, Shatto Arthur, *The Novel and Contemporary Experience in Africa,* Africana Publishing, 1977.

Gikandi, Simon, *Reading Chinua Achebe: Language and Ideology in Fiction,* Heinemann, 1991.

Gleason, Judith Illsley, *This Africa: Novels by West Africans in English and French,* Northwestern University Press, 1965.

Gurnah, Abdulrazak, editor, *Essays on African Writing: A Re-evaluation,* Heinemann, 1993.

Ihekweazu, Edith, editor, *Eagle on Iroko: Selected Papers from the Chinua Achebe International Symposium, 1990,* Heinemann Education Books (Ibadan, Nigeria), 1996.

Indrasena Reddy, K., *The Novels of Achebe and Ngugi: A Study in the Dialectics of Commitment,* Prestige Books (New Delhi, India), 1994.

International Symposium for Chinua Achebe's 60th Birthday, Heinemann Educational Books (Ibadan, Nigeria), 1996.

Kambaji, Christopher Tshikala, *Chinua Achebe: A Novelist and a Portraitist of His Society,* Vantage Press (New York, NY), 1994.

Killam, G. D., *The Novels of Chinua Achebe,* Africana Publishing, 1969.

Kim, Soonsik, *Colonial and Post-Colonial Discourse in the Novels of Yaeom Sang-Saeop, Chinua Achebe, and Salman Rushdie,* P. Lang (New York City), 1996.

King, Bruce, *Introduction to Nigerian Literature,* Africana Publishing, 1972.

King, Bruce *The New English Literatures: Cultural Nationalism in a Changing World,* Macmillan, 1980.

Laurence, Margaret, *Long Drums and Cannons: Nigerian Dramatists and Novelists,* Praeger (New York, NY), 1968.

Lindfors, Bernth, *Folklore in Nigerian Literature,* Africana Publishing, 1973.

Lindfors, Bernth, *Conversations with Chinua Achebe,* University Press of Mississippi (Jackson, MS), 1997.

McEwan, Neil, *Africa and the Novel,* Humanities Press (Atlantic Highlands, NJ), 1983.

Moore, Gerald, *Seven African Writers,* Oxford University Press (New York, NY), 1962.

Moses, Michael Valdez, *The Novel and the Globalization of Culture,* Oxford University Press (New York, NY), 1995.

Muoneke, Romanus Okey, *Art, Rebellion and Redemption: A Reading of the Novels of Chinua Achebe,* Peter Lang (New York, NY), 1994.

Njoku, Benedict Chiaka, *The Four Novels of Chinua Achebe: A Critical Study,* Peter Lang (New York, NY), 1984.

Ogbaa, Kalu, *Gods, Oracles and Divination,* Africa World Press (Trenton, NJ), 1992.

Ojinma, Umelo, *Chinua Achebe: New Perspectives,* Spectrum Books Ltd. (Ibadan, Nigeria), 1991.

Okoye, E.M., *The Traditional Religion and Its Encounter with Christianity in Achebe's Novels,* 1987.

Okpu, B.M., *Chinua Achebe: A Bibliography,* Libriservice, 1984.

Omotoso, Kole, *Achebe or Soyinka?: A Reinterpretation and a Study in Contrasts,* Hans Zell Publishers, 1992.

Palmer, Eustace, *The Growth of the African Novel,* Heinemann, 1979.

Parker, Michael, *Postcolonial Literatures: Achebe, Ngugi, Desai, Wolcott,* St. Martin's Press (New York, NY), 1995.

Petersen, K. H., *Chinua Achebe: A Celebration,* Heinemann, Dangeroo Press, 1991.

Podis, Leonard A., and Yakubu Saaka, editors, *Challenging Hierarchies: Issues and Themes in Colonial and Postcolonial African Literature,* Peter Lang (New York, NY), 1998.

Simola, Raisa, *World Views in Chinua Achebe's Works,* P. Lang (New York, NY), 1995.

Wren, Robert M., *Achebe's World: The Historical and Cultural Context of the Novels,* Three Continents (Washington, DC), 1980.

PERIODICALS

Africa News Service, May 24, 1999; October 16, 2000; November 27, 2000; September 13, 2002; February 14, 2003.

Africa Today, March, 1995, p. 93.

America, June 22-29, 1991; July 20, 1996; October 14, 2000, p. 24.

Ariel, April, 1992, p. 7.

Black Issues Book Review, September, 2000, p. 54.

Bloomsbury Review, January, 1996, p. 21.

Bookbird, spring, 1998, p. 6.

Booklist, March 1, 1997, p. 1168; August, 1997, p. 1842; January 1, 1998, p. 835; May 15, 2000, p. 1721.

Boston Globe, March 9, 1988.

Callaloo, fall, 1999, p. 1054.
Children's Literature Association Quarterly, winter, 1997, p. 160.
Choice, March, 1995, p. 1059.
Christian Century, April 18, 2001, p. 26.
Christian Science Monitor, November 16, 2000, p. 16.
CLA Journal, March, 1992, p. 303.
College Literature, October, 1992, special issue; winter, 1999, p. 69.
Commonweal, December 1, 1967.
Commonwealth Essays and Studies, fall, 1990.
Ebony, February, 1999, p. 96.
Economist, October 24, 1987.
Emerge, June, 2000, p. 68.
English Journal, March, 1995, p. 49.
Entertainment Weekly, September 26, 1997, p. 74.
Explicator, summer, 2002, p. 229.
Guardian, April 4, 1998, p. TW5; November 18, 2000, p. 6.
Harper's Bazaar, January, 1999, p. 66.
Journal of Commonwealth Literature, spring, 2001, p. 75.
Library Journal, September 15, 1997, p. 74; February 15, 1998, p. 184; May 15, 1998, p. 135; April 15, 2000, p. 87.
Listener, October 15, 1987.
Literature and Psychology, spring-summer, 2002, p. 131.
London Review of Books, October 15, 1981; August 7, 1986; June 22, 1989, p. 16-17.
Los Angeles Times Book Review, February 28, 1988.
Modern Fiction Studies, fall, 1991.
Nation, October 11, 1965; April 16, 1988.
National Post, July 8, 2000, p. B11.
New Statesman, January 4, 1985; September 25, 1987.
New Statesman and Society, July 22, 1988, pp. 41-42; February 9, 1990, p. 30; November 17, 1995, p. 40.
New York Review of Books, March 3, 1988.
New York Times, August 10, 1966; February 16, 1988; August 29, 1999, p. WK2; November 6, 2000, p. B1 and E1.
New York Times Book Review, December 17, 1967; May 13, 1973; August 11, 1985; February 21, 1988; November 12, 1989, p. 55; August 13, 2000, p. 15.
Observer (London), September 20, 1987.
People, January 11, 1999, p. 35; January 25, 1999, p. 33.
Philadelphia Enquirer, August 16, 2000.
Publications of the Modern Language Association of America, January, 1995, p. 30.
Publishers Weekly, February 21, 1994, p. 249; August 4, 1997, p. 54; May 8, 2000, p. 211.
Research in African Literatures 30 (2), 1999; fall, 2001, special issue.
Saturday Review, January 6, 1968.
School Library Journal, December, 1992, p. 146.
Social Education, November-December, 1997, p. 380.
Spectator, October 21, 1960; September 26, 1987; February 24, 2001, p. 39.
Studies in Black Literature, spring, 1971, special issue on Achebe.
Times Educational Supplement, January 25, 1985.
Times Higher Education Supplement, July 16, 1999, p. 22.
Times Literary Supplement, February 3, 1966; March 3, 1972; May 4, 1973; February 26, 1982; October 12, 1984; October 9, 1987.
Tribune Books (Chicago), February 21, 1988.
UNESCO Courier, June, 2001, Amy Otchet "Chinua Achebe: No Longer at Ease in Exile," interview with Achebe, p. 47.
Variety, September 21, 1998, p. 110.
Village Voice, March 15, 1988.
Wall Street Journal, February 23, 1988.
Washington Post, February 16, 1988.
Washington Post Book World, February 7, 1988.
World Literature Today, summer, 1985.
World Literature Written in English, November, 1978.

ONLINE

Pegasos, http://www.kirjasto.sci.fi/ (December 4, 2003), "Author's Calendar."
University Scholars Programme, National University of Singapore, http://www.scholars.nus.edu./ (December 4, 2003).*

* * *

ADAMS, Douglas (Noel) 1952-2001

PERSONAL: Born March 11, 1952, in Cambridge, England; died of an apparent heart attack, May 11, 2001, in Santa Barbara, CA; son of Christopher Douglas (a management consultant) and Janet (a nurse; maiden name, Donovan, present surname, Thrift) Adams; married Jane Elizabeth Belson, 1991; children: Polly Jane Rocket. *Education:* St. John's College, Cambridge, B.A. (with honors), 1974, M.A. *Hobbies*

Douglas Adams

and other interests: Purchasing equipment for recreations he would like to take up, playing acoustic guitar, scuba diving, fiddling with computers.

CAREER: British Broadcasting Corporation (BBC), London, producer and scriptwriter for "Hitchhiker's Guide to the Galaxy" radio and television series, beginning 1978, script editor for television series "Doctor Who," 1978-80; writer, 1978-2001.

MEMBER: Cambridge Footlights Club, which also produced *Monthy Python's* John Cleese, Eric Idle, and Graham Chapman.

AWARDS, HONORS: Best Books for Young Adults List, American Library Association (ALA), 1980, for *The Hitchhiker's Guide to the Galaxy.*

WRITINGS:

"THE HITCHHIKER'S GUIDE TO THE GALAXY" SERIES

The Hitchhiker's Guide to the Galaxy, Pan Books (London, England), 1979, Harmony (New York, NY), 1980.
The Restaurant at the End of the Universe, Pan Books (London, England), 1980, Harmony (New York, NY), 1982.
Life, the Universe and Everything, Harmony (New York, NY), 1982.
So Long, and Thanks for All the Fish, Pan Books (London, England), 1984, Harmony (New York, NY), 1985.
The Hitchhiker's Trilogy (omnibus volume), Harmony (New York, NY), 1984.
The Original Hitchhiker's Radio Scripts, edited with an introduction by Geoffrey Perkins, Harmony (New York, NY), 1985.
The Hitchhiker's Quartet (omnibus volume), Harmony (New York, NY), 1986.
More Than Complete Hitchhiker's Guide, Longmeadow Press (New York, NY), 1987, revised edition published as the *More Than Complete Hitchhiker's Guide Fifty-one Point Eighty,* 1989, unabridged edition, 1994.
Mostly Harmless, Crown (New York, NY), 1992.
The Illustrated Hitchhiker's Guide to the Galaxy, Crown (New York, NY), 1994.
The Ultimate Hitchhiker's Guide, unabridged and complete version, Wings Books (New York, NY), 1996.
(Creator and author of introduction) Terry Jones, *Douglas Adams's Starship Titanic: A Novel,* Harmony Books (New York, NY), 1997.
The Hitchhiker's Guide to the Galaxy: The Authorized Collection, adapted by John Carnell, illustrated by Steve Leialoha, DC Comics, 1997.
Neil Richards, *Douglas Adams's Starship Titanic: The Official Strategy Game,* Three Rivers Press, 1998.
The Salmon of Doubt: Hitchiking the Galaxy One Last Time, Harmony Books (New York, NY), 2002.

Also author of scripts for the "Hitchhiker's Guide to the Galaxy" radio and television programs, BBC-TV, and "Dr. Who" episodes (1978-1980); author, with Steve Meretzky, of interactive computer program.

OTHER

(With others) *Not 1982: Not the Nine o'Clock News Rip-Off Annual,* Faber (London, England), 1981.
(With John Lloyd) *The Meaning of Liff,* Pan Books (London, England), 1983, Harmony (New York, NY), 1984.

(Editor, with Peter Fincham) *The Utterly Utterly Merry Comic Relief Christmas Book,* Fontana (London, England), 1986.

Dirk Gently's Holistic Detective Agency (novel), Simon & Schuster (New York, NY), 1987.

The Long Dark Tea-Time of the Soul (novel), Heinemann, 1988, Simon & Schuster (New York, NY), 1989.

(With Mark Carwardine) *Last Chance to See* (nonfiction), Crown (New York, NY), 1990.

(With Lloyd) *The Deeper Meaning of Liff: A Dictionary of Things There Aren't Words for Yet—but There Ought to Be,* Crown (New York, NY), 1990.

Two Complete Novels (*Dirk Gently's Holistic Detective Agency* and *The Long Dark Tea-Time of the Soul*), Wings Books, 1994.

Dirk Gently's Holistic Detective Agency: Two Complete Novels (contains *Dirk Gently's Holistic Detective Agency* and *The Long Dark Tea-Time of the Soul*), Random House (New York, NY), 1995.

Contributor to *The Great Ape Project: Equality Beyond Humanity,* edited by Peter Singer, St. Martin's, 1993, and *Tales from the Jungle: A Rainforest Reader,* edited by Daniel R. Katz and Miles Chapin, Crown (New York, NY), 1995. Also author of episodes of "Doctor Who" for BBC-TV; coauthor of interactive computer program, "Bureaucracy" and CD-Rom game, "Starship Titanic."

ADAPTATIONS: *Hitchhiker's Guide* has been produced as a stage play, Liverpool (1979); producer Ivan Reitman holds the movie rights to the *Hitchhiker* trilogy; a film version of *The Hitchhiker's Guide to the Galaxy* is to be written by Karey Kirkpatrick and directed by Jay Roach. The screenplay will be based on a draft by Douglas, who was working on it at the time of his death and will be credited as an executive producer.

SIDELIGHTS: When Douglas Adams first dreamed up the cosmic satire *The Hitchhiker's Guide to the Galaxy,* he had no idea his radio series would become so popular as to inspire several novels, a television series, and even an interactive computer game. As the author once commented: "I never set out to be a novelist, because I thought I was just a scriptwriter. When I was asked by Pan Books to turn my radio scripts of *The Hitchhiker's Guide to the Galaxy* into a book, I thought that there were two ways of doing it. I could either do the normal script-novelization hack job, which involves going through the script putting 'he said' or 'she said' (and in the case of my books, 'it said' as well) at the end of each line, or I could have a go at doing it properly. I decided to see if I could do it properly." Adams's first attempt at a novel proved immensely successful, garnering favorable reviews and selling 100,000 copies in its first month alone.

The Hitchhiker's Guide to the Galaxy, as well as its sequels, *The Restaurant at the End of the Universe; Life, the Universe and Everything; So Long, and Thanks for All the Fish;* and *Mostly Harmless,* is "inspired lunacy that leaves hardly a science fictional cliché alive," as *Washington Post Book World* contributor Lisa Tuttle described it. The novels chronicle in stream-of-consciousness style the adventures of Arthur Dent, a hapless and continually bewildered Englishman, wearing his dressing gown throughout the adventures, and his friend Ford Prefect, an alien who has been posing as an unemployed actor for fifteen years. When Ford warns Arthur that Earth is minutes away from demolition to make room for an interstellar bypass, the two hitch a ride on a space vehicle, narrowly escaping the calamity. Traveling through the galaxy with the aid of a computer travel guide, Prefect and Dent encounter a motley array of characters, including Marvin, a terminally depressed robot; Zaphod Beeblebrox, the three-armed, two-headed president of the galaxy; and Slartibartfast, a planet designer whose specialty is fjords.

Many reviewers praised the *Hitchhiker* series for a sense of humor uncommon to most science fiction, and some have likened it to Alice's bewildering travels through Wonderland. Noting that "humorous science fiction novels have notoriously limited audiences," Gerald Jonas of the *New York Times Book Review* declared that *Hitchhiker's Guide* "is a delightful exception." The second *Hitchhiker* volume similarly impressed *Washington Post Book World's* Ron Goulart: "Adams has a gift for sending up the sacred precepts of sf and those who took his vastly successful *The Hitchhiker's Guide to the Galaxy* to their hearts will want to perform similar acts with this sequel." As Richard Brown explained in the London *Times,* "much of the comedy arises from a variety of pseudo-high-tech mis-information"; countering the traditional idea of science as benefactor, Adams portrays science as the embodiment of Murphy's Law—anything that can malfunction, will. Thus while he faults *Hitchhiker* for a "sometimes damagingly sophomoric" tone, John Clute of the *Magazine of Fantasy and Science Fiction* nevertheless remarked that "there is enough joy throughout, enough tooth to the zaniness, and enough rude knowingness about media-hype versions of science fiction, to make *Hitchhiker* one of the genre's rare genuinely funny books." Richard Dawkins commented in his "Lament," that he had been surprised to learn how deeply read in science Adams was: "You can't understand many of the jokes in Hitchhiker if you don't know a lot of advanced science."

Although the plots of the *Hitchhiker* novels are science fictional, Adams asserted, "I'm not a science fiction writer, but a comedy writer who happens to be using the conventions of science fiction for this particular thing." Critics have likewise observed a wider scope in the author's satire. As London *Times* reviewer Philip Howard stated, "Adams has fun with the trendy manners of our time, from worship of the motor car to jogging, and from the pedantry of committee meetings, Point of Order Madam Chairperson, to religious enthusiasm and, engagingly, Sci-Fi itself." Citing Adams's "surreal, comic creativity,"*Listener* contributor Peter Kemp saw "hints from Lewis Carroll and Edward Lear" in the *Hitchhiker* books: "There are logical extensions of mad premises, grotesque creatures with crazily evocative names, chattering objects, moments of satiric farce, and picturesquely absurd landscapes." Others have compared him to Jonathan Swift and Kurt Vonnegut. "Adams tries to make fun of almost every possible concern of humans from their quest for knowledge and power to their obsession with prolonging life," *Dictionary of Literary Biography Yearbook* contributor Michael Adams observed. As a result, his humor targets not only science fiction clichés, but "bureaucracies, bad poets, literary critics, scientific theories, nightclub entertainers, religion, philosophy, labor unions, economists, tax laws, clichés . . . structural linguists, rock 'n' roll, sentimentality, cricket commentators, and Paul McCartney's wealth."

While they are noted for their humor and satire, "it is not just the comic techniques that make Adams's novels worth reading," Robert Reilly asserted in *Twentieth-Century Science Fiction Writers*. "The characters, who may at first appear as mere parodies of science-fiction stereotypes, grow throughout the series into fairly well-rounded comic persons." Michael Adams concurred with this assessment, noting that "one of Adams's main virtues is his gift for characterization. The adventures of Arthur and his friends are entertaining not only for all the last-second escapes from disaster but for how the characters respond to the whims of fate." The author explained to James Brown of the *Los Angeles Times* that many of *Hitchhiker's* characters, including the protagonist, are based on people Adams knows. "Arthur Dent is to a certain extent autobiographical," the novelist said. "He moves from one astonishing event to another without fully comprehending what's going on. He's the Everyman character—an ordinary person caught up in some extraordinary events."

While critics and the author alike found the fourth novel of the Hitchhiker "trilogy" an overextension of the series—the humorist told the *Bloomsbury Review* that "that book was a mistake"—critics praised the fifth novel, *Mostly Harmless*. Carolyn Cushman said in *Locus*, "This time, Adams sinks his teeth into a basic human problem looking for a purpose in life and uses it as a theme, giving *Mostly Harmless* a coherence lacking in the other novels in the series. And it's funny to boot." A reviewer for *Analog Science Fiction and Fact* called it "a hit of bubbly seltzer in a dour, dour world. . . . Adams's cockeyed logic is bound to make you smile."

After the fourth Hitchhiker novel, Adams discovered another venue for his satire. *Dirk Gently's Holistic Detective Agency* introduces a time-machine, a spaceship, an Electric Monk, and Samuel Taylor Coleridge's ghost in solving the murder of a computer executive. Featuring Dirk Gently, a detective who unravels mysteries (usually missing cat cases) by examining the "interconnectedness of all things," the novel is full of coincidence and humor. While "the plot is inventive and often surprising," *Chicago Tribune* writer Christopher Farley found that "at points there is just too much of it." Douglas E. Winter similarly faulted the novel, commenting in the *Washington Post* that the excess of events overshadows the characters: "Missing are the outrageous characterizations that charmed the 'Hitchhiker' books; indeed, save for the quirky Dirk himself, Adams's cast is a wan and almost antiseptic assortment sent over by Central Casting."

In contrast, Toronto *Globe and Mail* reviewer H. J. Kirchhoff maintained that *Dirk Gently's Holistic Detective Agency* "is Adams's best novel. That is, his characters are more fully delineated than in the *Hitch-*

hiker books, the settings more credible and the plot more . . . well, linear." And Farley admitted that "in the end, Adams succeeds because he is flat-out funny. It will make you laugh, and that's the bottom line, even if his line isn't necessarily the shortest distance between two points." "Following a tradition which stretches from Laurence Sterne to P. G. Wodehouse," John Nicholson similarly concluded in the London *Times,* "what signifies most here is the quality of the writing, the asides and allusions, and—above all—the jokes. Mr. Adams scores very high on all counts."

Dirk Gently returns in *The Long Dark Tea-Time of the Soul,* "a clever and funny novel about an English detective, an American girl in a bad mood and a Norse god who sells his soul to an advertising executive," as Cathleen Schine summarized in the *New York Times Book Review.* After failing to prevent the murder of his only client, Dirk turns his attention to a mysterious explosion at an airport check-in counter; the two seemingly unrelated events, as the "holistic" detective knows, have some connection. Along the way, "with a skewed imagination and ironic wit, Douglas Adams romps through modern life's paranoias and absurdities," Jess Bravin remarked in the *Chicago Tribune.* The author's "humor, crisp and intelligent, and his prose—elegant, absurdly literal-minded understatements or elegant, absurdly literal-minded overstatements—are a pleasure to read," Schine claimed.

Nevertheless, the critic believed that "in spite of all the nimble plots, the skillful writing and the underlying wit of his work, Mr. Adams is a bit banal." Marc Conly, however, found that the author's "social awareness and the accuracy of his barbs keep the narrative of *The Long Dark Tea-Time of the Soul* from becoming too frothy," as he wrote in the *Bloomsbury Review.* "Douglas Adams is a dismayed idealist in jester's clothing. His portrayal of modern society, and his unrelenting dissection of the modern style of self-centeredness, make us think, make us laugh, and make us look forward to his next book." "Adams is concerned less with the intricacies of detective novels than with the promulgation of ideas," Bravin similarly contended. With *Tea-Time,* the critic concluded, "Adams affirms his standing as one of England's top exporters of irreverence."

The Deeper Meaning of Liff: A Dictionary of Things There Aren't Words for Yet—but There Ought to Be takes "geographical names with no current meaning and matches them with objects, feelings, actions for which no word exists," wrote a reviewer for the London *Observer,* explaining the content of the "funny, highly perceptive book." However, in his review for *The Spectator,* Richard Ingrams said, "The book might have passed muster as a cheap paperback, but as a hardback, it seems unduly pretentious."

With zoologist Mark Carwardine, Adams traveled to Indonesia, Zaire, New Zealand, China, and Mauritius to research *Last Chance to See.* The book covers people, places, and animals the pair saw on their journeys. All the animals are endangered in some way. *Atlantic* reviewer Jack Beatty asserted that "*Last Chance* makes us care about some hard-pressed animals. . . . It renders this service to nature not through the instrumentalities of science but through those of humanism—rhetoric, irony, cadence, and wit." Commented Beth Levine in the *New York Times Book Review,* "Don't expect any great insights here, but *Last Chance to See* is enjoyable and accessible, and its details on the heroic efforts being made to save these animals are inspirational."

Adams found it very difficult to write and had once to be confined to a hotel room by his publisher to make him finish a novel. "I would never sit down and write for pleasure because it's too much like hard work," he told the *Times* of London, so the pleasure his work continues to give thousands of readers is the more admirable. He had moved to Santa Barbara, California, and was working on the script for a movie, when he died unexpectedly. Unfinished written work and other papers, essays, and speeches have been collected in *The Salmon of Doubt.*

BIOGRAPHICAL AND CRITICAL SOURCES:

BOOKS

Bestsellers 89, Issue 3, Gale (Detroit, MI), 1989.
Contemporary Literary Criticism, Volume 27, Gale (Detroit, MI), 1984.
Dictionary of Literary Biography Yearbook: 1983, Gale (Detroit, MI), 1984.
Gaiman, Neil, *Don't Panic: The Official Hitchhiker's Guide to the Universe Companion,* Pocket Books (New York, NY), 1988.

Richards, Neil, *Douglas Adams Starship Titanic: The Official Strategy Guide,* Three Rivers Press (New York, NY), 1998.

Twentieth-Century Science Fiction Writers, St. James Press (Detroit, MI), 1986.

PERIODICALS

Analog Science Fiction and Fact, September, 1993, p. 164.
Atlantic, March, 1991, p. 131.
Bangkok Post, May 23, 2001.
Bloomsbury Review, December, 1982; May-June, 1989, Marc Conly, interview with Adams.
Booklist, April 15, 2002, p. 1386.
Chicago Tribune, October 28, 1982; March 13, 1985; March 17, 1985; August 25, 1987; March 31, 1989.
Chicago Tribune Book World, October 12, 1980.
Fantasy Review, April, 1985.
Globe and Mail (Toronto), April 4, 1987; June 27, 1987.
GQ 61, December, 1991, Carolina Upcher, interview with Adams.
Greenman Review, August 2, 2002.
Guardian, July 23, 1992, p. 33.
Illustrated London News, September, 1982.
Interzone 66, December, 1992, Stan Nicholls, interview with Adams.
Kirkus Reviews, April 15, 2002, p. 508.
Kliatt Young Adult Paperback Book Guide, July, 1999, p. 5.
Listener, December 18-25, 1980, June 25, 1987.
Locus, October, 1992, p. 37.
London Times, June 18, 1987.
London Times Literary Supplement, September 24, 1982.
Los Angeles Times, April 19, 1985; June 13, 1987; March 17, 1989, May 13, 2001, p. B12.
Los Angeles Times Book Review, December 7, 1980; February 3, 1985; February 3, 1991, p. 4.
Magazine of Fantasy and Science Fiction, February, 1982.
New Scientist, August 18, 2001, p. 47.
Newsweek, November 15, 1982; April 13, 1998.
New York Times, April 9, 1998; May 15, 2001.
New York Times Book Review, January 25, 1981; March 12, 1989; March 17, 1991, p. 22; November 1, 1992.
Observer, December 2, 1990, p. 64; August 12, 2001, p. 15; May 12, 2002.
People, January 10, 1983; May 20, 1991, p. 79.
Publishers Weekly, January 14, 1983, Jennifer Crichton, interview with Adams, p. 47; February 1, 1991, Michele Field, interview with Adams, p. 62; April 15, 2002, p. 43.
Quadrant, September, 2002, p. 84.
Religious Studies Review, January, 1999, p. 99.
Science Fiction Studies, March, 1988, p. 61.
Spectator, December 15, 1990, p. 35.
Times (London), February 7, 1981; September 9, 1982; December 13, 1984; June 18, 1987; November 5, 1988.
Times Literary Supplement, September 24, 1982; May 24, 2002, p. 23.
VOYA, April, 1993, p. 33.
Washington Post, July 23, 1987; March 16, 1989.
Washington Post Book World, November 23, 1980; December 27, 1981; March 24, 1991, p. 4.

ONLINE

BBC-H2G2-Hitchhiker's Guide to the Galaxy, http://www.bbc.co.uk/h2g2/ (December 2, 2003).
Douglas Adams Home Page, http://www.douglasadams.com/ (December 2, 2003).
Floor 42 (fansite), http://www.floor42.com/ (December 2, 2003).
Guardian, http://books.guardian.co.uk/ (December 2, 2003), review of *The Salmon of Doubt.*

OBITUARIES:

PERIODICALS

Los Angeles Times, May 13, 2001, p. B12.
New York Times, May 15, 2001, pp. A21, A23, and E-1.
Times (London, England), May 14, 2001.
Washington Post, May 13, 2001, p. C8.

ONLINE

Guardian, http://booksguardian.co.uk.*

ALBEE, Edward (Franklin III) 1928-

PERSONAL: Surname pronounced *All*-bee; born March 12, 1928, probably in VA; adopted son of Reed A. (part-owner of Keith-Albee theater circuit) and Frances (Cotter) Albee; partner and lifelong friend of composer and music critic William Flanagan (1951-59), playwright Terence McNally (1959-63), decorator William Pennington (1963-71), and artist, Jonathon Thomas (1971—). *Education:* Rye Country Day School, Lawrence, New Jersey, 1940-43, Valley Forge Military Academy, Pennsylvania, 1946-47 (expelled from all three), Choate School, Connecticut, 1944-46 (where he first wrote—a play, a novel, poems, and short stories), Trinity College, Hartford, CT, 1946-47, Columbia University, 1949. *Religion:* None. *Hobbies and other interests:* Travel, playing the harpsichord.

ADDRESSES: Office—14 Harrison St., New York, NY 10013.

CAREER: Writer, producer, and director of plays. Served in the U.S. Army. Worked as continuity writer for WNYC-radio, office boy for Warwick & Legler (advertising agency), record salesman for G. Schirmer, Inc. (music publishers), and counterman in luncheonette of Manhattan Towers Hotel; messenger for Western Union, 1955-58. Producer, with Richard Barr and Clinton Wilder, New Playwrights Unit Workshop, 1963—; director of touring retrospective of his one-act plays including, *The Zoo Story, The American Dream, Fam and Yam, The Sandbox, Box, Quotations from Chairman Mao Tse-Tung, Counting the Ways,* and *Listening,* produced as *Albee Directs Albee,* 1978-79; co-director of Vivian Beaumont Theatre at Lincoln Center for the Performing Arts, New York, NY, 1979-81. Founder of William Flanagan Center for Creative Persons in Montauk, NY, 1971. Lecturer at colleges, including Brandeis University, Johns Hopkins University, and Webster University. Cultural exchange visitor to Latin American countries and the U.S.S.R. for U.S. State Department, 1961, 1963. President of Edward F. Albee Foundation. Resident playwright, Atlantic Center for the Arts, New Smyrna Beach, Florida, 1982. Regents Professor of Drama, University of California at Irvine, 1983-85. Instructor/Artist-in-Residence, University of Houston, 1988—.

MEMBER: PEN American Center, National Academy of Arts and Letters, Dramatists Guild, National Endowment grant-giving council Dramatists Guild Council, governing commission of New York State Council for the Arts, Theater Hall of Fame.

Edward Albee

AWARDS, HONORS: Berlin Festival Award, 1959, for *The Zoo Story,* and 1961, for *The Death of Bessie Smith*; Vernon Rice Memorial Award, and Obie Award, 1960, and Argentine Critics Circle Award, 1961, all for *The Zoo Story*; *The Death of Bessie Smith* and *The American Dream* were chosen as best plays of the 1960-61 season by Foreign Press Association, 1961; Lola D'Annunzio Award, 1961, for *The American Dream*; selected as most promising playwright of 1962-63 season by New York Drama Critics, 1963; New York Drama Critics Circle Award, Foreign Press Association Award, Antoinette Perry Award (Tony), Outer Circle Award, *Saturday Review* Drama Critics Award, and *Variety* Drama Critics' Poll Award, 1963, and *Evening Standard* Award, 1964, all for *Who's Afraid of Virginia Woolf?;* Tony Award nominee for best play, 1964, for *The Ballad of the Sad Café*; with Richard Barr and Clinton Wilder, recipient of Margo Jones Award, 1965, for encouraging new playwrights; Tony Award nominee both for author, and best play, 1965, for *Tiny Alice;* Pulitzer Prize and Tony Award nominee for best play, 1967, for *A Delicate Balance;* Pulitzer Prize and Tony Award nominee for best play, 1975, for *Seascape;* D.Litt., Emerson College, 1967, and Trinity College, 1974; American Academy and

Institute of Arts and Letters Gold Medal, 1980; inducted into Theater Hall of Fame, 1985; Pulitzer Prize and New York Drama Critics Circle Award for *Three Tall Women,* 1994; Obie Award for Sustained Achievement in the American Theater, 1994; Kennedy Center Honoree, 1996; National Medal of Arts, 1996; Tony Award for best play, 2002, for *The Goat, or Who Is Sylvia?*

WRITINGS:

PLAYS, EXCEPT AS NOTED

The Zoo Story, The Death of Bessie Smith, The Sandbox: Three Plays (*The Zoo Story,* first produced [in German] in Berlin at Schiller Theater Werkstatt, September 28, 1959, produced off-Broadway at Provincetown Playhouse, January 14, 1960; *The Death of Bessie Smith,* first produced in Berlin at Schlosspark Theater, April 21, 1960, produced off-Broadway at York Playhouse, February 28, 1961; *The Sandbox,* first produced in New York City at Jazz Gallery, May 15, 1960, produced off-Broadway at Cherry Lane Theatre, February, 1962, directed by author), Coward McCann (New York, NY), 1960, published with *The American Dream* (also see below) as *The Zoo Story and Other Plays,* J. Cape, 1962, and as *The American Dream; and Zoo Story: Two Plays,* Plume (New York, NY), 1997.

(Author of libretto with James Hinton, Jr.) *Bartleby* (opera; adaptation of story by Herman Melville; music by William Flanagan), produced off-Broadway at York Playhouse, January 24, 1961.

The American Dream, with introduction by the author (produced off-Broadway at York Playhouse, January 24, 1961), Coward McCann (New York, NY), 1961.

Fam and Yam (produced in Westport, CT, at White Barn Theatre, August 27, 1960), Dramatists Play Service (New York, NY), 1961.

Who's Afraid of Virginia Woolf? (produced on Broadway at Billy Rose Theatre, October 13, 1962), Atheneum (New York, NY), 1962.

The Ballad of the Sad Café (adaptation of novella of same title by Carson McCullers; produced on Broadway at Martin Beck Theatre, October 30, 1963), Houghton Mifflin (Boston, MA), 1963, Scribner Classics (New York, NY), 2001.

Tiny Alice (produced on Broadway at Billy Rose Theatre, December 29, 1964), Atheneum (New York, NY), 1965.

Malcolm (adaptation of novel of same title by James Purdy; produced on Broadway at Sam S. Shubert Theatre, January 11, 1966), Atheneum, 1966.

A Delicate Balance (produced on Broadway at Martin Beck Theatre, September 22, 1966), Atheneum (New York, NY), 1966, Plume (New York, NY), 1997.

Breakfast at Tiffany's (musical; adaptation of story of same title by Truman Capote; music by Bob Merrill), produced in Philadelphia, PA, 1966, produced on Broadway at Majestic Theatre, December, 1966.

Everything in the Garden (based on play by Giles Cooper; produced on Broadway at Plymouth Theatre, November 29, 1967), Atheneum (New York, NY), 1968.

Box [and] *Quotations from Chairman Mao Tse-Tung* (two interrelated plays; first produced at Studio Arena Theatre, Buffalo, NY; produced on Broadway at Billy Rose Theatre, September 30, 1968), Atheneum (New York, NY), 1969.

All Over (produced on Broadway at Martin Beck Theatre, January 26, 1971; produced in London by Royal Shakespeare Company at Aldwych Theatre, January 31, 1972), Atheneum (New York, NY), 1971.

Seascape (produced on Broadway at Sam S. Shubert Theatre, January 26, 1975, directed by author), Atheneum (New York, NY), 1975.

Counting the Ways [and] *Listening: Two Plays* (*Counting the Ways,* first produced in London by National Theatre Company, 1976, produced by Hartford Stage Company, Hartford, CT, January 28, 1977; *Listening: A Chamber Play* [produced as radio play by British Broadcasting Corp. (BBC), 1976], first produced on stage by Hartford Stage Company, Hartford, January 28, 1977), Atheneum (New York, NY), 1977.

The Lady from Dubuque (produced on Broadway at Morosco Theatre, January 31, 1980), Atheneum (New York, NY), 1980.

Lolita (adaptation of novel of same title by Vladimir Nabokov), first produced in Boston at Wilbur Theatre, January 15, 1981, produced on Broadway at Brooks Atkinson Theatre, March 19, 1981, published as *Lolita: A Play,* Dramatists Play Service (New York, NY), 1984.

The Plays (four volumes), Atheneum (New York, NY), 1981-82.

Alice, A Delicate Balance, Box and Quotations from Chairman Mao Tse-tung, Atheneum (New York, NY), 1982.

Counting the Ways, Listening, All Over, Atheneum (New York, NY), 1982.

Everything in the Garden, Malcolm, The Ballad of the Sad Café, Atheneum (New York, NY), 1982.

The Man Who Had Three Arms, first produced in Miami, FL, at New World Festival, June 10, 1982, directed by the author; produced in Chicago, IL at Goodman Theater, October 4, 1982, directed by the author.

Edward Albee: An Interview and Essays, edited by Julian N. Wasserman, University of St. Thomas, 1983.

Finding the Sun (first produced in 1983, New York premiere at the Signature Theatre Company, February, 1994), Dramatists Play Service (New York, NY), 1994.

Envy in *Faustus in Hell,* (produced Princeton, NJ, 1985).

Marriage Play, first produced at the English Theatre in Vienna, 1987, American premiere at the McCarter Theater in Princeton, NJ, February 22, 1992; *Edward Albee's Marriage Play,* Dramatists Play Service (New York, NY), 1995.

Selected Plays of Edward Albee, Doubleday (Garden City, NY), 1987.

Conversations with Edward Albee, edited by Philip C. Kolin, University Press of Mississippi (Jackson, MS), 1988.

Straight through the Night (novel), Soho (New York, NY), 1989.

Three Tall Women (two-act play; first produced at the English Theatre in Vienna, June, 1991, New York City premiere at the Vineyard Theatre, February 13, 1994), Dutton (New York, NY), 1995.

The Lorca Play, (produced at the Alley Theatre, Houston, TX, April 24, 1992).

Fragments: A Sit Around (premiered at Ensemble Theater of Cincinnati, Cincinnati, OH, November, 1993, New York opening at Signature Theatre Company, 1994), published as *Edward Albee's Fragments: A Sit-Around,* Dramatists Play Service (New York, NY), 1995.

The Play about the Baby, (first produced at Almeida Theatre, London, September 1, 1998; Houston, TX, Alley Theatre, April 11, 2000; New York, February 1, 2001), Dramatists Play Service (New York, NY), 2002, Overlook Press (Woodstock, NY), 2003.

From Idea to Matter: Nine Sculptors . . . , Anderson Gallery (Richmond, VA), 2000.

(With Sam Hunter) *Tony Rosenthal* (literary criticism), Rizzoli (New York, NY), 2000.

(With Carson McCullers) *The Ballad of the Sad Café: Carson McCullers's Novella Adapted to the Stage,* Scribner Classics (New York, NY), 2001.

Occupant, (produced at the John Golden Theatre, New York, 2002).

The Goat, or Who Is Sylvia? (first produced at the John Golden Theatre in New York, March 10, 2002), Overlook Press (Woodstock, NY), 2003.

AUTHOR OF INTRODUCTION

Noel Coward, *Three Plays by Noel Coward: Blithe Spirit, Hay Fever,* [and] *Private Lives,* Delta (New York, NY), 1965.

Phyllis Johnson Kaye, editor, *National Playwrights Directory,* 2nd edition, Eugene O'Neill Theater Center (Waterford, CT), 1981.

(With Sabina Lietzmann) *New York,* Vendome Press (New York, NY), 1981.

Louise Nevelson: Atmospheres and Environments, Clarkson N. Potter (New York, NY), 1981.

Three Tall Women: A Play in Two Acts, Dutton (New York, NY), 1994.

Also author of screenplays, including an adaptation of *Le Locataire* (title means "The Tenant"), a novel by Roland Topor, an adaptation of his *The Death of Bessie Smith,* one about the life of Nijinsky, one about Stanford White and Evelyn Nesbitt, and *A Delicate Balance,* American Film Theater, 1973. Contributor to anthologies, including *American Playwrights on Drama,* edited by Horst Frenz, Hill & Wang, 1965; *The Off-Broadway Experience,* edited by Howard Greenberger, Prentice-Hall, 1971. Also contributor to periodicals, including *Harper's Bazaar, Saturday Review,* and *Dramatists Guild Quarterly.*

ADAPTATIONS: *Who's Afraid of Virginia Woolf?* was adapted and filmed by Warner Bros. in 1966.

SIDELIGHTS: Reviewing the numerous commentaries written about Edward Albee's plays, C. W. E. Bigsby noted in *Edward Albee: A Collection of Critical Essays* that in comparison to Albee "few playwrights . . . have been so frequently and mischievously misunderstood, misrepresented, overpraised, denigrated, and precipitately dismissed." Capsulizing the changing tone of Albee criticism since the early-1960s (when his first play appeared), Bigsby offered this overview:

"Canonized after . . . *The Zoo Story*, [Albee] found himself in swift succession billed as America's most promising playwright, leading dramatist, and then, with astonishing suddenness, a 'one-hit' writer. . . . The progression was essentially that suggested by George in [Albee's] *Who's Afraid of Virginia Woolf?*, 'better, best, bested.'"

To symbolize the curve of Albee's reputation as a dramatist, Bigsby chose a phrase from a play designated by many critics as a dividing line in the playwright's career. T. E. Kalem, for example, in *Time* remarked: "Albee almost seems to have lived through two careers, one very exciting, the other increasingly depressing. From *The Zoo Story* through *The American Dream* to *Who's Afraid of Virginia Woolf?*, he displayed great gusto, waspish humor and feral power. In the succeeding . . . years, he has foundered in murky metaphysics, . . . dabbled in adaptations, . . . and gone down experimental blind alleys." Confusing him with more nihilist European absurdist playwrights, many critics have failed to understand the autobiographical sources of his writing and the more hopeful nature of his message, as Lincoln Konkle pointed out in the *Dictionary of Literary Biography* entry on Albee. Matthew C. Roudané has declared, "Albee's is an affirmative vision of human experience. . . . In the midst of a dehumanizing society, Albee's heroes, perhaps irrationally, affirm living."

However, many critics have praised these same plays. Albee continues to win awards; he has received three Pulitzer Prizes since *Virginia Woolf*, one in 1967 for *A Delicate Balance*, one in 1975, for *Seascape*, and, in 1994, a third for his autobiographical drama *Three Tall Women*. His three Pulitzer Prizes place him in the ranks of such notable dramatists as Tennessee Williams, holder of two Pulitzers, Robert E. Sherwood, a three-time winner, and four-time honoree Eugene O'Neill.

Although stylistically varied, Albee's plays are thematically connected. Gerald Weales in *The Jumping Off Place: American Drama in the 1960s* noted: "Each new Albee play seems to be an experiment in form, in style, . . . and yet there is unity to his work as a whole. This is apparent in the devices and the characters that recur, modified according to context, but it is most obvious in the repetition of theme, in the basic assumptions about the human condition that underlie all his work."

Reviewing Albee's touring retrospective of eight of his one-act plays, "Albee Directs Albee," Sylvie Drake of the *Los Angeles Times* observed: "This condensation of work reveals Albee's consistent and enduring concern with loss. . . . 'Pain is understanding,' says someone in [Albee's play] 'Counting the Ways.' 'It's really loss.' Yes. These plays are *all* about loss." In her analysis of Albee's plays Drake also discovered the following themes: "the chasm between people, [and] their inability to connect except through pain."

John MacNicholas, writing in the *Dictionary of Literary Biography*, said the development of these themes in Albee's plays started with his first play, *The Zoo Story*. According to Brian Way in *American Theatre*, this play, a tale of a fairly prosperous married man and his confrontation on a Central Park bench with a totally alienated young drifter, "is an exploration of the farce and agony of human isolation." George Wellwarth, in *The Theater of Protest and Paradox: Development in the Avant-Garde Drama*, explained the play's thematic content in more detail: "[Albee] is exemplifying or demonstrating a theme. That theme is the enormous and usually insuperable difficulty that human beings find in communicating with each other. More precisely, it is about the maddening effect that the enforced loneliness of the human condition has on the person who is cursed (for in our society it undoubtedly is a curse) with an infinite capacity for love."

Albee's thematic preoccupation with loss of contact between individuals is tied to the playwright's desire to make a statement about American values, as Weales pointed out. "In much of his work," according to the critic, "there is a suggestion . . . that the emptiness and loneliness of the characters are somehow the result of a collapse of values in the Western world, in general, in the United States, in particular." Albee finds the feelings of loss and emptiness prevalent in the society that surrounds him.

Following *The Zoo Story*, three Albee plays opened in New York during 1960-61. All of these—*The Sandbox, The American Dream,* and *The Death of Bessie Smith*—"attack certain features in American society," according to MacNicholas. *The Death of Bessie Smith*, for example, deals with the death of the black singer who bled to death after an automobile accident, apparently because she was denied care at a nearby all-white hospital. *The American Dream* and *The Sandbox* share the same characters—Mommy, Daddy, and

Grandma. MacNicholas feels that these two plays "form a continuum in subject matter and technique; both attack indifference to love, pity, and compassion. In both, . . . the characters . . . live in a kind of moral narcosis."

Allen Lewis, in *American Plays and Playwrights of the Contemporary Theatre,* commented: "*The American Dream* is a wildly imaginative caricature of the American family. . . . [In this play] Albee is the angry young man, tearing apart the antiseptic mirage of American middle-class happiness." The American family of the play is comprised of characters known only as "Mommy" (a domineering shrew), "Daddy" (a weak, hen-pecked husband), and "Grandma" (an older version of "Mommy"). Set in the family's stuffy apartment, the play includes the story of the couple's adoption of a "bumble of joy" whom they destroy after discovering his various defects. (For example, they cut out his tongue when he says a dirty word.) As he grows up, Mommy and Daddy complain that the baby has no head on his shoulders, is spineless, and has feet of clay. They complain again when he dies after having already been paid for. Near the end of the play, the baby's twin appears. He is a handsome young man who describes himself as a "clean-cut midwest farm boy type, almost insultingly good-looking in a typically American way." "The young man," as Frederick Lumley noted in *New Trends in Twentieth Century Drama,* "feels that he is incomplete, he doesn't know what has happened to something within him, but he has no touch, he is unable to make love, to see anything with pity; in fact he has no feeling." Continuing his interpretation of the play, Lewis stated: "The American Dream [of the title] is the young man who is all appearance and no feelings. . . . He says: 'I cannot touch another person and feel love. . . . I have no emotions. . . . I have now only my person . . . my body, my face. . . . I let people love me. . . . I feel nothing.'"

In his preface to *The American Dream,* Albee explains the play's content: "The play is an examination of the American Scene, an attack on the substitution of artificial for real values in our society, a condemnation of complacency, cruelty, emasculation and vacuity; it is a stand against the fiction that everything in this slipping land of ours is peachy-keen." According to MacNicholas, Albee continues his critique of American society in his first three-act play, *Who's Afraid of Virginia Woolf?* Many critics note a relationship between this play and *The American Dream.* Martin Esslin, writing in *The Theatre of the Absurd,* commented: "A closer inspection reveals elements which clearly . . . relate [*Virginia Woolf*] to Albee's earlier work. . . . George and Martha [a couple in the play] (there are echoes here of George and Martha Washington) have an imaginary child which they treat as real, until in the cold dawn of that wild night [in which the action of the play takes place] they decide to 'kill' it by abandoning their joint fantasy. Here the connection to *The American Dream* with its horrid dream-child of the ideal all-American boy becomes clear. . . . Is the dream-child which cannot become real among people torn by ambition and lust something like the American ideal itself?"

Drake found George and Martha of *Virginia Woolf* directly related to Mommy and Daddy of *The American Dream.* Lumley described this evolution: "The Mommy and Daddy of . . . *Virginia Woolf* are this time given names, Martha and George, thus becoming individuals instead of abstract characters. . . . They have been unable to have children; so that their love is mixed-up sexual humiliation, a strong love-hate relationship which makes them want to hurt and claw and wound each other because they know each other and cannot do without one another." In the *Arizona Quarterly,* James P. Quinn described the combination of social criticism and the theme of human isolation in *Virginia Woolf:* "In [the play] the author parodies the ideals of western civilization. . . . Thus, romantic love, marriage, sex, the family, status, competition, power all the 'illusions' man has erected to eliminate the differences between self and others and to escape the . . . burden of his freedom and loneliness come under attack."

Critics noted the continuation of theme and social awareness throughout Albee's work. For example, Harold Clurman, in his *Nation* review of *All Over,* wrote: "Albee is saying [in this play] that despite all the hasty bickering, the fierce hostility and the mutual misunderstandings which separate us, we need one another. We cry out in agony when we are cut off." Bigsby, commenting on the same play, concluded: "Albee's concern in *All Over* is essentially that of his earlier work. He remains intent on penetrating the bland urbanities of social life in an attempt to identify the crucial failure of nerve which has brought individual men and whole societies to the point of not merely soulless anomie but even of apocalypse."

Bigsby also found similar characteristics in Albee's play *Box,* calling it "a protest against the dangerously declining quality of life—a decline marked . . . by the growth of an amoral technology with a momentum and direction of its own." MacNicholas noted Albee's preoccupation with loss in *A Delicate Balance:* "[The play] concerns itself with loss: not loss which occurs in one swift traumatic stroke, but that which evolves slowly in increments of gentle and lethal acquiescence."

Then, in what several critics have referred to as phoenix-like fashion, Albee was seemingly reborn as a popular and critically successful artist during the 1993-94 New York theater season in off- and off-off-Broadway houses similar in spirit to the fringe theaters Albee and his contemporaries helped nourish in the 1960s, during the early days of avant-garde American playwriting. One such artistic enclave, the Signature Theatre, a non-profit company in lower Manhattan, brought Albee aboard as its playwright-in-residence and dedicated an entire season to his works, proving that at least some producers remembered his allegedly forgotten plays. The lineup included a variety of full-length dramas and one-acts, old and new. Among them were *Finding the Sun,* a long 1983 one-act in twenty-two vignettes, involving the interaction of eight characters on a New England beach; *Marriage Play,* Albee's 1987 sparring match between a long-wed husband and wife that elicited several comparisons to *Virginia Woolf;* and *Fragments: A Sit Around.*

Rounding off the list were two one-act collections. The first, *Listening: A Chamber Play,* and *Counting the Ways* were originally presented in London at the National Theatre in 1976, then in America at the Hartford Stage Company in Connecticut. These plays represent Albee's experimental writing in the middle part of his career. In a *New York Times* review, Ben Brantley suggested that both "are essentially linguistic chamber works. . . . Though they are radically different in tone, their preoccupation with the slipperiness of language and perception and with the opacity of what truly lies behind it is much the same. The questions posed reverberate without answers and are often as unapologetically naked as 'Who am I?' 'Who are you?' and 'Do you love me?'"

The next short play bill, collectively entitled *Sand,* was directed by Albee himself and included three representative pieces, *Box* (1968), *The Sandbox* (1960), and *Finding the Sun* (1983). While the Signature season provided him a rare opportunity to revisit several old works and try out new ideas, it was the 1994 New York premiere of his 1991 play *Three Tall Women* a few blocks north at the Vineyard Theater that earned Albee his greatest accolades since *Virginia Woolf,* including a third Pulitzer Prize and the New York Drama Critics Circle Award.

Autobiographical in content, *Three Tall Women* is an examination of the life of a wealthy, boisterous, strong-minded woman nearly a century old. The first act consists of a conversation between this often cantankerous dowager, known only as A; her sympathetic, middle-aged caretaker, B; and C, her twenty-six-year-old lawyer. These are Albee's "three tall women" in their first incarnation. A's physical condition is deteriorating rapidly—she is frequently incontinent and has recently broken an arm that will not heal—and her mental state is precarious. As she attempts to put her affairs in order with C and reminisces about her experiences, she alternates between an amazing perceptiveness and scandalous wit, and amnesic episodes accompanied by childlike tantrums. She can't remember if she is ninety-one or ninety-two, or whether close friends are alive or dead, but can relate tales from her courtship and early years of marriage in great detail.

The fifty-two-year-old B has become inured to the abuse A frequently heaps upon her, and to the personal tasks she must help the older woman perform. In her own climbing years B waxes philosophically about the natural aging process. C is both attracted to and repulsed by the behavior of her elders. She giggles at A's anecdotes of her early sexual escapades (though A claims to have been the "wild one" her behavior was prudish by C's youthful standards), then she is shocked at A's casual, overt racism, bigotry, and insensitivity. The first act ends with A lying in bed lamenting the breakdown in her relationships with her own mother, whom she cared for in her old age, and her homosexual son, who couldn't stand her intolerance and left her when he was still a teenager. Her rambling diatribe ends suddenly, and upon examining her, B announces A has suffered a stroke.

A transformation occurs between acts, and when the curtain rises on the second half of *Three Tall Women,* a mannequin representation of A occupies the bed while the actresses playing A, B, and C are revealed as the same woman at three different stages of life, all attending what will soon be her own deathbed. This partition of the elderly A's life allows the playwright the opportunity to examine his character from three distinct, yet similar points of view.

C remembers her glory days, when she and her sister worked as department store models and cavorted innocently, and not so innocently, with boys, all the while waiting for "the man of my dreams." Hers is the voice of youth and naivete, silly yet romantically appealing. B, the realist, has fresher adult memories of the man of her dreams, including both her and her husband's extramarital affairs. She also recalls, quite vividly, opening her son's mail and finding admiring notes from older men, then arguing with him, and watching him exit her life for the next twenty years. A remembers the six agonizing years it took for her husband to die of cancer, and how she sold her jewelry a little at a time to meet expenses, replacing it with replicas to maintain appearances. In the final moments of the play, the three tall women, multiple facets of the same spirit, share what they feel has been their happiest moment. For the youthful C it is uncertain. It may have been her confirmation or, better yet, perhaps they are still to come. B's happiest moment is the here and now, "half of being adult done," she says, "the rest ahead of me. Old enough to be a *little* wise, past being *really* dumb." As they all join hands A reveals her happiest moment will be "coming to the end of it; yes. . . . That's the happiest moment. When it's all done. When we stop. When we can stop."

Following the success of *Three Tall Women* in New York, Albee admitted in interviews that the play's main character was directly inspired by his own adoptive mother, Frances Cotter Albee, who expelled the eighteen-year-old Albee from his family's home for his homosexuality, and later removed him from her will. As Albee told David Richards of the *New York Times*, "The play is a kind of exorcism. . . . I didn't end up any more fond of the woman after I finished it than when I started. But it allowed me to come to terms with the long unpleasant life she led and develop a little respect for her independence. She was destructive, but she had lots of reasons to be. It's there on the stage, all the good stuff and the bad stuff." Though elements of his own life and family had crept into his plays before, notably in *The American Dream* and *Finding the Sun,* Albee did not feel free enough to write particularly about his mother until after her death at the age of ninety-two in 1990. In the *New Yorker,* John Lahr suggested that the "last great gift a parent gives to a child is his or her own death, and the energy underneath *Three Tall Women* is the exhilaration of a writer calling it quits with the past." Robert Brustein asserted in the *New Republic* that "*Three Tall Women* is a mature piece of writing . . . in which Albee seems to be coming to terms not only with a socialite foster parent, . . . but with his own advancing age."

The rest of the 1990s and the early 2000s continued with further productions but many mixed reviews. *A Delicate Balance* was revived in 1996 to win Tonys for best revival, direction and actor. It also ran successfully in London. *The Play about the Baby,* appearing 1998 through 2001, brought such mixed reactions that it appeared both on best-of-the-year-in-theater and worst-of-the-year-in-theater lists. *The Goat or Who Is Sylvia?* (2002) was Albee's first play on Broadway after the disastrous 1983 production of *The Man Who Had Three Arms,* and Albee warned that it would be his most controversial play because it dealt with bestiality. According to Konkle, its real theme is the mercurial nature of love. *The Goat,* despite divided responses, received the 2002 Tony and Drama Desk Awards for best new play of the year.

As Konkle concluded, Albee, with a career spanning six decades, has influenced some of the most important twentieth-century playwrights, such as Tom Stoppard and David Mamet. More directly, he has supported young artists through the Playwrights Unit and the Flanagan Center. He has received many honorary doctorates, and his plays have been produced all over the world. Many drama critics and scholars credit him with "practically inventing Off-Broadway singlehandedly. . . . He has enjoyed success but not made that his priority, so that he could expand the possibilities of theater and drama and continue to post tough moral and philosophical questions to his audiences."

BIOGRAPHICAL AND CRITICAL SOURCES:

BOOKS

Amacher, Richard E., *Edward Albee,* Twayne (New York, NY), 1969.
Amacher, Richard E., and Margaret Rule, *Edward Albee at Home and Abroad: A Bibliography 1958-June 1968,* AMS Press (New York, NY), 1970.

Bigsby, C. W. E., *Albee,* Oliver & Boyd, 1969.

Bigsby, C. W. E., editor, *Edward Albee: A Collection of Critical Essays,* Prentice-Hall, 1975.

Bloom, Harold, editor, *Edward Albee,* Chelsea House, 1987.

Brown, John Russell, and Bernard Harris, editors, *American Theatre,* Edward Arnold, 1967.

Bryer, Jackson R., editor, *The Playwright's Art: Conversations with Contemporary American Dramatists,* Rutgers University Press (New Brunswick, NJ), 1995.

Cohn, Ruby, *Edward Albee,* University of Minnesota Press (Minneapolis, MN), 1969.

Contemporary Literary Criticism, Gale (Detroit, MI), Volume 1, 1973, Volume 2, 1974, Volume 3, 1975, Volume 5, 1976, Volume 9, 1978, Volume 11, 1979, Volume 13, 1980, Volume 25, 1983, Volume 53, 1989, Volume 86, 1995.

Debusscher, Gilbert, *Edward Albee: Tradition and Renewal,* American Studies Center (Brussels, Belgium), 1967.

De La Fuente, Patricia, editor, *Edward Albee, Planned Wilderness: Interviews, Essays, and Bibliography,* Living Author Series, Number 3, Pan American University (Edinburgh, TX), 1980.

Dictionary of Literary Biography, Volume 7: *Twentieth-Century American Dramatists,* Part I, Gale (Detroit, MI), 1981.

Downer, Alan S., editor, *American Drama and Its Critics: A Collection of Critical Essays,* University of Chicago Press (Chicago, IL), 1965.

Esslin, Martin, *The Theatre of the Absurd,* Doubleday (New York, NY), 1969.

Giantvalley, Scott, *Edward Albee: A Reference Guide,* G. K. Hall, 1987.

Green, Charles Lee, *Edward Albee: An Annotated Bibliography 1968-1977,* AMS Press (New York, NY), 1980.

Gussow, Mel, *Edward Albee: A Singular Journey,* Simon & Schuster, 1999.

Hayman, Ronald, *Edward Albee,* Heinemann (London, England), 1971, Ungar (New ork, NY), 1973.

Hirsch, Foster, *Who's Afraid of Edward Albee,* Creative Arts (Berkeley, CA), 1978.

Kolin, Philip C., and J. Madison Davis, editors, *Critical Essays on Edward Albee,* G.K. Hall (Boston, MA), 1986.

Kolin, Philip C., editor, *Conversations with Edward Albee,* University Press of Mississippi (Jackson, MS), 1988.

Konkle, Lincoln, *Dictionary of Literary Biography, Vol.266: Twentieth-Century American Dramatists, Fourth Series,* Gale (Detroit, MI), 2002.

Lewis, Allan, *American Plays and Playwrights of the Contemporary Theatre,* Crown (New York, NY), 1965.

Lumley, Frederick, *New Trends in Twentieth Century Drama,* 4th edition, Oxford University Press, 1972.

Mayberry, Bob, *Theatre of Discord: Dissonance in Beckett, Albee, and Pinter,* Fairleigh Dickinson University Press, 1989.

McCarthy, Gerald, *Edward Albee,* Macmillan (London, England), 1987.

Paolucci, Anne, *From Tension to Tonic: The Plays of Edward Albee,* Southern Illinois University Press (Carbondale, IL), 1972.

Roudané, Matthew Charles, *Understanding Edward Albee,* University of South Carolina Press (Columbia, SC), 1987.

Roudané, Matthew Charles, *Who's Afraid of Virginia Woolf?: Necessary Fictions, Terrifying Realities,* Twayne Publishers, 1990.

Rutenberg, Michael E., *Edward Albee: Playwright in Protest,* Avon, 1969.

Singh, C.P., *Edward Albee: The Playwright of Quest,* Mittal Publications (Delhi, India), 1987.

Stenz, Anita M., *The Poet of Loss,* Mouton (The Hague, Netherlands), 1978.

Tyce, Richard, *Edward Albee: A Bibliography,* Scarecrow (Metuchen, NY), 1986.

Vos, Nelvin, *Eugene Ionesco and Edward Albee: A Critical Essay,* Eerdmans (Grand Rapids, MI), 1968.

Wagner, Walter, editor, *The Playwrights Speak,* Delacorte (New York, NY), 1967.

Weales, Gerald, *The Jumping Off Place: American Drama in the 1960's,* Macmillan (New York, NY), 1969.

Wellwarth, George, *The Theater of Protest and Paradox: Development in the Avant-Garde Drama,* New York University Press (New York, NY), 1964.

PERIODICALS

Advocate, March 13, 2001, p. 56; April 16, 2002, p. 58.

America, April 2, 1994, p. 18.

American Book Collector, March-April, 1983, p. 37.

American Drama, spring, 1993, special issue; fall 1995, p. 51.

American Theater, September, 1994, p. 38; September 1996, p. 24.

Arizona Quarterly, autumn, 1974.

Asia Africa Intelligence Wire, November 30, 2002.

Atlantic Monthly, April, 1965.

Back Stage, December 8, 2000, p. 56.

Back Stage West, January 18, 2001, p. 10.

Booklist, June 1, 2000, p. 1808.

Books, July, 1966.

Chicago Tribune, March 26, 1979; September 26, 1982; April 9, 1995, sec. 13, p. 2.

Chicago Tribune Book World, September 26, 1982.

Christian Science Monitor, November 10, 1993, p. 12; April 13, 2001, p. 18; April 26, 2002, p. 18.

CLA Journal, 1984, p. 210.

Commonweal, January 22, 1965; April 10, 1992, p. 18; December 3, 1993, p. 17.

Contemporary Drama, spring, 1970, p. 151.

Daily Variety, May 8, 2002, p. 1; August 13, 2002, p. 1; September 10, 2002, p. 15.

Dance Magazine, October, 2002, p. 56.

Detroit News, June 27, 1982.

Educational Theatre Journal, March, 1973, pp. 71 and 80.

Explicator, 1988, p. 46.

Gay and Lesbian Review Worldwide, July-August, 2002, p. 50.

Hollywood Reporter, February 27, 2002, p. 44; March 11, 2002, p. 30.

Houston Chronicle, March 17, 2002, p. 12.

Hudson Review, spring, 1965; winter, 1966-67.

Journal of Evolutionary Psychology, August, 1985, p. 302.

Life, October 28, 1966; May 26, 1967; February 2, 1968.

London Magazine, March, 1969.

Los Angeles Times, October 18, 1978; April 21, 1994, pp. F1, F6; January 8, 2001, p. B6; January 15, 2001, p. F1; August 18, 2002, p. F44.

Modern Drama, December, 1967, p. 274.

Nation, December 18, 1967; March 25, 1968; April 12, 1971; February 23, 1980; April 18, 1981; March 14, 1994, p. 355.

National Observer, December 4, 1967.

New Criterion, June, 2002, p. 54.

New Leader, December 18, 1967; April 19, 1971.

New Republic, January 23, 1965; April 17, 1971; February 2, 1975; April 11, 1981; April 4, 1994, pp. 26, 28; June 17, 1996; April 15, 2002, p. 24.

Newsday, March 26, 1971.

New Statesman, January 23, 1970.

Newsweek, January 4, 1965; March 18, 1968; April 5, 1971; February 10, 1975; March 30, 1981.

New York, May 6, 1996, p. 86; March 25, 2002, p. 133; July 8, 2002, p. 47.

New Yorker, January 22, 1966; April 3, 1971; March 3, 1980; May 30, 1981; May 16, 1994, pp. 102-05; May 27, 1996, p. 138; February 19, 2001, p. 228.

New York Magazine, November, 1993, p. 70.

New York Times, December 27, 1964; January 21, 1965; January 13, 1966; August 16, 1966; September 18, 1966; September 24, 1966; October 2, 1966; August 20, 1967; November 26, 1967; April 4, 1971; April 18, 1971; January 27, 1975; February 4, 1977; May 23, 1978; January 27, 1980; March 1, 1981; March 20, 1981; March 29, 1981; February 23, 1992; November 20, 1993, p. A11; December 1, 1993, p. C17; February 14, 1994, pp. C13, C16; February 20, 1994, p. 5; April 13, 1994, p. C15; August 28, 1994, p. WC1; May 5, 1996, p. H4; June 16, 1996, p. H33; July 25, 1999; April 12, 2000, p. B2, E2; December 6, 2000, p. B1, E1; September 24, 2000; January 28, 2001; February 2, 2001, p. B1, E1; April 8, 2001; February 25, 2002, p. B1, E1; March 11, 2002, p. B1, E1; June 30, 2002, p. 5.

New York Times Magazine, February 25, 1962. p. 30, 64, 66.

New York World Journal Tribune, September 22, 1966; October 2, 1966.

Observer Review, January 19, 1969.

Paris Review, fall, 1966.

People Weekly, February 25, 1980; April 6, 1981.

Pittsburgh Press, February 3, 1974.

Prairie Schooner, fall, 1965; spring, 1966, p.139.

Progressive, August, 1996, Richard Farr, interview with Albee, pp. 60-67.

Recherches Anglaises et Américaine, number 5, summer, 1972, p. 85.

Reporter, December 28, 1967.

San Francisco Chronicle, March 20, 2002, p. D2; November 27, 2002, p. D1.

Saturday Review, June 4, 1966; April 17, 1971; March 8, 1975; May, 1981.

South Central Review, spring, 1990, p. 50.

Studies in Contemporary Satire, 1987, p. 30.

Theatre Arts, March, 1961.

Theatre Survey, November 1993, Rakesh Solomon, interview with Albee on directing *Who's Afraid of Virginia Woolf?*, p. 95.

Time, April 5, 1971; February 10, 1975; May 20, 1996, p. 77.

Transatlantic Review, summer, 1963.

Tri-Quarterly, 1966, p. 182.
Tulane Drama Review, spring, 1963; summer, 1965.
Twentieth-Century Literature: A Scholarly and Critical Journal, spring, 1982, p. 14.
Variety, March 4, 1991, p. 66; January 20, 1992, p. 147; November 8, 1993, p. 30; February 14, 1994, p. 61; November 6, 1995, p. 80; October 27, 1997; April 17, 2000, p. 36; March 13, 2001, p. 47; March 18, 2002, p. 32; May 13, 2002, p. 35; October 14, 2002, p. 38; February 3, 2003, p. 42 and 71.
Village Voice, December 7, 1967; March 21, 1968; October 31, 1968.
Wall Street Journal, December 20, 2000, p. A20; March 13, 2002, p. A16.
Washington Post, February 18, 1979; August 14, 1994.
World Literature Today, autumn, 1995, pp. 799-800.
Writer's Digest, October, 1980.

ONLINE

John F. Kennedy Center for the Performing Arts, http://www.kennedy-center.org/ (December 1, 2003).
University of Houston Web site, http://www.uh.edu/ (December 1, 2003).

OTHER

Edward Albee (video), edited and presented by Melvyn Bragg, London Weekend Television in association with RM Arts, Films for the Humanities, 1996.*

* * *

ALEXANDER, Jane 1939-

PERSONAL: Born October 28, 1939, in Boston, MA; daughter of Thomas Bartlett (a doctor) and Ruth Elizabeth (Pearson) Quigley; married Robert Alexander (an actor and director), July 23, 1962 (divorced, 1969); married Edwin Sherin (a director), March 29, 1975; children: (first marriage) Jason, Jane. *Ethnicity:* "Caucasian; Irish-German-American." *Education:* Attended Sarah Lawrence College, 1957-58; attended University of Edinburgh, 1959-60. *Politics:* Democrat. *Hobbies and other interests:* Birding.

Jane Alexander

ADDRESSES: *Agent*—William Morris Agency, 1325 Avenue of the Americas, New York, NY 10019.

CAREER: Actress, producer, and writer. Member, Charles Playhouse, Boston, MA, 1964-65, and Arena Stage acting company, Washington, DC, 1965-68; associated with American Shakespeare Festival. Chair, National Endowment of the Arts, 1993-97. Has recorded audio books, including *Wuthering Heights,* Random House, and *Rebecca,* Warner. Stage appearances include: Eleanor Bachman, *The Great White Hope,* 1968; Katrina, *Mother Courage and Her Children,* 1970; Mistress Page, *The Merry Wives of Windsor,* 1970; Lavinia, *Mourning Becomes Electra,* 1970; title role, *Major Barbara,* 1971; Kitty Duval, *The Time of Your Life,* 1972; Anne Miller, *Six Rms Riv Vu,* 1972; Jacqueline Harrison, *Find Your Way Home,* 1974; Liz Essendine, *Present Laughter,* 1974; Gertrude, *Hamlet,* 1975; Catherine Sloper, *The Heiress,* 1976; Hilda, *The Master Builder,* 1977; Judge Ruth Loomis, *First Monday in October,* 1978; Joanne, *Losing Time,* 1979; Natalia, *Goodbye Fidel,* 1980; Cleopatra, *Antony and Cleopatra,* 1981; title role, *Hedda Gabler,* 1981; Annie, *Monday after the Miracle,* 1982; Anna, *Old Times,* 1983; Maxine Faulk, *Night of the Iguana,* 1988; Charlotte Blossom, *Approaching Zanzibar,* 1989; Nurse, *Mystery of the Rose Bouquet,* 1989; Joy Davidman,

Shadowlands, 1990; Claire Zachanassian, *The Visit,* 1992; Sara Goode, *The Sisters Rosensweig,* 1993; *Honour,* 1998; *Mourning Becomes Electra,* 2002; *Ghosts,* 2003.

Film appearances include: Eleanor Bachman, *The Great White Hope,* Twentieth Century-Fox, 1970; Nora Tenneray, *A Gunfight,* Paramount, 1971; Dorothy Fehler, *The New Centurions,* Columbia, 1972; Bookkeeper, *All the President's Men,* Warner Bros., 1976; Alicia Hardeman, *The Betsy,* Allied Artists, 1978; Margaret Phelps, *Kramer vs. Kramer,* Columbia, 1979; Lillian Gray, *Brubaker,* Twentieth Century-Fox, 1980; Doris Strelyzk, *Night Crossing,* Buena Vista, 1982; Carol Wetherly, *Testament,* Paramount, 1983; Addy, *City Heat,* Warner Bros., 1984; (and executive producer) Juanelle, *Square Dance* (also known as *Home Is Where the Heart Is*), Island Pictures, 1987; Anna Willing, *Sweet Country,* Cinema Group, 1987; Mrs. Shaw, *Glory,* TriStar, 1989; narrator, *Building Bombs* (documentary), Tara Releasing, 1991; Nurse Edna, *The Cider House Rules,* Miramax, 1999; *The Ring,* 2002.

Television appearances in miniseries include: Eleanor Roosevelt, *Eleanor and Franklin,* American Broadcasting Companies, Inc. (ABC), 1976, and *Eleanor and Franklin: The White House Years,* ABC, 1977; Doris Ashley, *Blood and Orchids,* Columbia Broadcasting System (CBS), 1986; and Blanche Kettman, *Stay the Night,* ABC, 1992. Television appearances in movies include: Anne Palmer, *Welcome Home Johnny Bristol,* CBS, 1971; Karen Walker, *Miracle on 34th Street,* CBS, 1973; Sarah Shaw, *This Is the West That Was,* National Broadcasting Company, Inc. (NBC), 1974; Frances Gunther, *Death Be Not Proud,* ABC, 1975; Mary MacCracken, *A Circle of Children,* CBS, 1977; Mary MacCracken, *Lovey: A Circle of Children, Part II,* CBS, 1978; *Dear Liar,* Public Broadcasting Service (PBS), 1978; Barbara Moreland, *A Question of Love* (also known as *A Purely Legal Matter*), NBC, 1978; Alma Rose, *Playing for Time,* CBS, 1980; Sandy Caldwell, *In the Custody of Strangers,* ABC, 1983; title role, *Calamity Jane,* CBS, 1984; Nora Strangis, *When She Says No,* ABC, 1984; Hedda Hopper, *Malice in Wonderland,* CBS, 1985; Sybil Stockdale, *In Love and War,* NBC, 1987; Ginny Charlson, *Open Admissions,* CBS, 1987; Hanna Dournevald, *A Friendship in Vienna* (also known as *The Devil in Vienna*), Disney Channel, 1988; and Peggy Ryan, *Daughter of the Streets,* ABC, 1990. Episodic television appearances include: host, *Generations,* 1987; *Drug Free Kids: A Parent's Guide,* PBS, 1988; narrator, *Sea Turtles' Last Dance,* PBS, 1988; voice of Emily Dickinson, "Emily Dickinson," *Voices and Visions,* PBS, 1988; narrator, *Sea Turtles: Ancient Nomads,* PBS, 1989; narrator, *They're Doing My Time,* PBS, 1989; *Night of One Hundred Stars III,* NBC, 1990; (and executive producer) Georgia O'Keeffe, "A Marriage: Georgia O'Keeffe and Alfred Stieglitz," *American Playhouse,* PBS, 1991; *The Forty-seventh Annual Tony Awards,* 1993; *The Kennedy Center Honors: A Celebration of the Performing Arts,* CBS, 1993; *New Year* (pilot), 1993; *The Forty-eighth Annual Tony Awards,* 1994; narration, "Dr. Spock the Baby Doc," *Nova,* PBS, 1995; interviewee, "James Earl Jones," *Biography,* Arts and Entertainment, 1995; *Small Steps, Big Strides: The Black Experience in Hollywood,* AMC, 1998; narrator, *Intimate Portrait: Eleanor Roosevelt,* Lifetime, 1999; *Intimate Portrait: Jane Alexander,* Lifetime, 1999; and Regina Mulroney, "Entitled, Part 2," *Law and Order,* NBC, 2000. Co-producer, *Calamity Jane* (movie), CBS, 1984; segment producer, *Dancing* (series), PBS, 1992-93.

MEMBER: Actors' Equity Association, Screen Actors Guild, American Federation of Television and Radio Artists, Women's Action for Nuclear Disarmament (member, board of directors, 1981-88), Wildlife Conservation International (member, board of directors, 1984—), Film Forum (member, board of directors, 1985-90), National Stroke Association (member, board of directors, 1985—), New York Zoological Society (member, advisory board, 1991—, board of directors, 1991), MacDowell Colony (board member), Hornecker Wildlife Institute (board member), American Bird Conservancy (board member).

AWARDS, HONORS: Antoinette Perry Award, Drama Desk Award, and *Theatre World* Award for Best Supporting Actress, all 1969, and Academy Award nomination, Academy of Motion Picture Arts and Sciences, 1970, all for *The Great White Hope;* Golden Globe Award for most promising newcomer—female, Hollywood Foreign Press Association, 1971; Antoinette Perry Award nomination for Best Actress (Dramatic), 1973, for *Six Rms Riv Vu,* 1974, for *Find Your Way Home,* and 1979, for *First Monday in October;* Emmy Award nomination for Best Actress in a Drama or Comedy Special, 1976, for *Eleanor and Franklin;* Academy Award nomination for Best Supporting Actress, 1976, for *All the President's Men;* Television

Critics Circle Award and Emmy Award nomination for Best Actress in a Drama or Comedy Apecial, both 1977, both for *Eleanor and Franklin: The White House Years;* St. Botolph Club Achievement in Dramatic Arts, 1979; Academy Award nomination and Golden Globe Award nomination for Best Supporting Actress, both 1979, both for *Kramer vs. Kramer;* Emmy Award for Outstanding Supporting Actress in a Limited Series or Special, 1981, for *Playing for Time,* and nominations, 1984, for *Calamity Jane,* and 1985, for *Malice in Wonderland;* Israel Cultural Award, 1982; Academy Award nomination and Golden Globe Award nominations for Best Actress, both 1983, both for *Testament;* Helen Caldicott Leadership Award, 1984; Western Heritage Wrangler Award, 1984; Living Legacy Award, Women's International Center, 1988; Obie Award for Best Performance, 1993, for *The Sisters Rosensweig;* Environmental Leadership Award, Eco-Expo; inducted into Theater Hall of Fame, 1993; Muse Award, New York Women in Film, 1993; Lectureship Award, NIH, 1994; Houseman Award, The Acting Company, 1994; University of California at Los Angeles Medal, 1994; Outer Critics Circle Award for Distinguished Voice in Theater, 1994; Helen Hayes Award, American Express Tribute, 1994; Women of Achievement Award, Anti-Defamation League, 1994; D.F.A., Juilliard School, 1994, North Carolina School of the Arts, 1994, University of Pennsylvania, 1995, New School for Social Research, 1996, and Smith College, 1999; Margo Jones Award, 1995; Massachusetts Society Award, 1995; North American Mont Blanc de la Culture Award, 1995; Commonwealth Award, 1995; honorary Ph.D., Duke University, 1996, and Sarah Lawrence College, 1998; L.H.D., College of Santa Fe, 1997; Christopher Reeve Award, Creative Coalition, 1998; Outstanding Leadership for Achievement in Arts, People for the American Way, 1998; Lifetime Achievement Award, Americans for Arts and United States Conference of Mayors, 1999; Harry S Truman Award for Public Service, 1999.

WRITINGS:

(With Greta Jacobs) *The Bluefish Cookbook,* Globe Pequot (Old Saybrook, CT), 1980, 5th revised edition published as *The Bluefish Cookbook: 101 Ways to Get Rid of the Blues,* illustrated by Wezi Swift, 1995.
Command Performance: An Actress in the Theater of Politics (memoir), PublicAffairs (New York, NY), 2000.

Also author, with Sam Engelstad, of *The Master Builder* (adaptation of the play by Henrich Ibsen).

SIDELIGHTS: Acclaimed for her extraordinary versatility, actress Jane Alexander has built a successful career on the stage, in film, and in television. She has also worked as a film and television producer, recorded audiobooks, and coauthored a popular cookbook. From 1993 to 1997 Alexander also headed the National Endowment for the Arts. Her book *Command Performance: An Actress in the Theater of Politics* recounts her time with the U.S. arts agency.

Alexander is the oldest of three children born to orthopedic surgeon Thomas Bartlett Quigley, a pioneer in sports medicine, and former nurse Ruth Elizabeth (Pearson) Quigley. Her paternal grandfather, Daniel Quigley, had been the personal physician to Buffalo Bill in North Platte, Nebraska. Alexander grew up in Brookline, a middle-class suburb of Boston, and in 1957 entered Sarah Lawrence College in Bronxville, New York. She left after two years to study at the University of Edinburgh in Scotland, where she was active in the dramatic club.

After leaving Edinburgh in 1960, Alexander audited a few courses at Harvard University and appeared in a student production of William Shakespeare's *As You Like It* before moving to New York City in 1961 to try her luck on the stage. While looking for work as an actor, she got a secretarial job and studied acting with Mira Rostova. Her first break came when she replaced Sandy Dennis's stand-in in *A Thousand Clowns* at the Eugene O'Neill Theatre. She went on to appear in *Twice over Nightly,* a satirical revue, at the Upstairs at the Downstairs cabaret. By 1964, however, Alexander decided to leave New York to try to find more challenging dramatic parts in regional theater. She joined the repertory cast of the Charles Playhouse in Boston and then joined the Arena Stage in Washington, D.C.

At the Arena Stage, Alexander created the role that launched her career, that of Eleanor Bachman in the world premiere of Howard Sackler's *The Great White Hope* in 1967. The three-act drama focused on the career of Jack Jefferson—the first major role for James Earl Jones—a black prizefighter who becomes world heavyweight champion. The complex and troubled Jefferson emotionally abuses his white mistress, Eleanor, and drives her to suicide before finally losing his title to a white fighter. The following year the play went to Broadway, where it was showered with critical accolades. For her performance in that production, Alexander was awarded Antoinette Perry, Drama Desk, and Theatre World awards. When Alexander starred in the movie version of *The Great White Hope* two years later, she received an Oscar nomination.

Her stage career firmly established, Alexander went on to play major roles in a wide variety of plays on Broadway and elsewhere, such as *Six Rms Riv Vu, Mourning Becomes Electra,* and *The Merry Wives of Windsor,* as well as the title role in the American Shakespeare Festival production of *Major Barbara.* She also appeared in several film and television roles. Among her most admired performances was her Television Critics' Circle Award-winning portrayal of Eleanor Roosevelt in the 1976 television miniseries *Eleanor and Franklin* and its 1977 sequel, *Eleanor and Franklin: The White House Years.* Her role as Alma Rose in the 1980 television movie *Playing for Time,* about a troupe of women musicians at Auschwitz, was also widely respected and won her an Emmy award. Alexander has also narrated several television specials, produced television programming, and recorded audiobook versions of the novels *Wuthering Heights* and *Rebecca.*

In addition to her performing career, Alexander has coauthored an adaptation of Heinrich Ibsen's play *The Master Builder.* With Greta Jacobs, Alexander wrote *The Bluefish Cookbook,* a collection of easy recipes the pair developed in response to the plentiful bluefish that family and friends brought them during summers on Nantucket. The book covers everything from basic filleting and smoking methods to tips on steaming fish in a home dishwasher. Both New England-based reviewers and national critics appreciated the book's range, clarity, and charm. An appraisal by a *Boston Globe* reviewer declared: "Of all the things ever written about bluefish, this . . . is my favorite because, in its breezy elegant way, it approaches the level of wackiness found in the very personality of the bluefish." Popular with readers, *The Bluefish Cookbook* went into five editions in its first fifteen years of publication.

In 1993 President Bill Clinton named Alexander chair of the National Endowment for the Arts. The embattled federal agency had been mired in controversy since the late 1980s over government funding of the arts. Much of the controversy centered on art deemed by some observers to be obscene or sacrilegious—particularly photographs by the late Robert Mapplethorpe, whose work included homoerotic scenes and sexually provocative poses, as well as works by Andres Serrano, best known for "Piss Christ," a photo of a plastic crucifix immersed in a glass of urine. While many had been grumbling for years over whether the U.S. government should be involved at all in financing the arts, such exhibits ignited a once low-key debate, turning it into a bitter war that threatened the NEA's very existence.

Alexander accepted the challenge, and after being confirmed by the U.S. Senate, she was sworn into office by Associate Supreme Court Justice Sandra Day O'Connor on October 8, 1993. According to a writer in *Time,* Alexander, who is described as liberal in her beliefs on artistic freedom, told the subcommittee overseeing the NEA in 1990: "I find it astonishing that after twenty-five years we are not celebrating the enormous success of the NEA. Rather, we're put in a position of defending it. The family of art produces ugly babies as well as beautiful ones, but we have to embrace all of that family." A few years later, she told the *Detroit Free Press* she was "sick of the polemics" that threaten the existence of the NEA. "I see the arts as the solution to our problems and not, in any way, part of the problem. The arts are life-enhancing, and they bring joy. The arts are a community issue. They bring us together, they do not rend us asunder."

During her four-year tenure, Alexander strengthened that organization's partnerships with other federal agencies and convened the first national arts conference, "Art 21: Art Reaches into the 21st Century." She traveled to more than two hundred communities throughout the United States and Puerto Rico and gave speeches emphasizing how arts can improve schools, boost local economies, and build stronger communities. Alexander created the Arts Endowment's World Wide Web Site and initiated measures to improve communications and opportunities for artists and small arts organizations through the Internet.

During her term, the agency's funding was cut by some forty percent. Despite these cuts, Alexander saved the organization from being disbanded entirely. The NEA, which had also received criticism for its tendency to give the majority of its funding to artists in two states, California and New York, while ignoring the rest of the nation, agreed to distribute the money more fairly. In 1997, frustrated over congressional funding, a lack of attention from the Clinton administration, and her desire to return to acting, Alexander resigned her NEA post, but recounts her career as an arts administrator in the book *Command Performance*. Robert Brustein in the *New Republic* described the memoir as "at its best, an honest effort to explore the unholy marriage between politics and art, a relationship that, in this author's case, ended in a rather unhappy divorce." Tom O'Brien, writing in *America*, found *Command Performance* "a graciously written, even funny book." Hap Erstein in the *Washington Times* commented on Alexander's account of her tenure as arts administrator: "Other performances of hers have been more successful, and certainly more widely acclaimed, but this behind-the-scenes look at her days at the helm of the NEA shows it to be unparalleled for gratification and frustration."

BIOGRAPHICAL AND CRITICAL SOURCES:

BOOKS

Newsmakers 1994, Gale (Detroit, MI), 1994.

PERIODICALS

America, July 29, 2000, Tom O'Brien, "Hollywood Meets D.C.," p. 24.
American Theatre, November, 1997, Ron Jenkins, "NEA Wins Vote, Loses Alexander," p. 70; September, 1998, Marilyn Stasio, "Jane Alexander: She Stoops to Conquer," p. 59.
Arts Education Policy Review, September, 2000, Margaret Dee Merrion, review of *Command Performance: An Actress in the Theater of Politics,* p. 38.
Atlanta Journal and Constitution, October 15, 1993.
Back Stage, May 28, 1999, p. 7.
Booklist, June 1, 2000, Mary Carroll, review of *Command Performance,* p. 1829.
Boston Globe, August 17, 1990.
Chicago Tribune, November 14, 1993.
Dance, December, 1997, "Trouble at NEA: Exit Alexander," p. 38.
Detroit Free Press, January 11, 1994.
Library Journal, June 1, 2000, Barbara Hutcheson, review of *Command Performance,* p. 164.
New Republic, August 21, 2000, Robert Brustein, review of *Command Performance,* p. 34.
New York Times, March 30, 1993; July 31, 1993; October 16, 1993.
Publishers Weekly, May 15, 2000, review of *Command Performance,* p. 97.
Time, August 16, 1993.
Washington Times, November 12, 1993; October 9, 1997, Julia Duin, "Alexander's Departure Called 'Huge Loss' to Arts Agency," p. 3; May 28, 2000, Hap Erstein, "Report from the Actress Who Did Time at NEA," p. 8.

* * *

ANAYA, Rudolfo A(lfonso) 1937-

PERSONAL: Born October 30, 1937, in Pastura, New Mexico; son of Martin (a laborer) and Rafaelita (Mares) Anaya; married Patricia Lawless (a counselor), July 21, 1966. *Ethnicity:* "Mexican American/Chicano." *Education:* Attended Browning Business School, 1956-58; University of New Mexico, B.A. (Education), 1963, M.A. (English), 1969, M.A. (guidance and counseling), 1972. *Hobbies and other interests:* Reading, travel, apple orchards.

ADDRESSES: Home—5324 Canada Vista N.W., Albuquerque, NM, 87120. *Office*—Department of English, University of New Mexico, Albuquerque, NM 87131.

CAREER: Public school teacher in Albuquerque, NM, 1963-70; University of Albuquerque, Albuquerque, NM, director of counseling, 1971-73, associate professor, 1974-88, professor of English, 1988-93 (retired), professor emeritus, 1993—. Teacher, New Mexico Writers Workshop, summers, 1977-79. Lecturer, Universidad Anahuac, Mexico City, Mexico, summer, 1974; lecturer at other universities, including University of Haifa, Israel, Yale University, University of Michigan, Michigan State University, University of California—Los Angeles, University of Indiana, and University of Texas at Houston. Quebec Writers Exchange, Trois Rivières, 1982; Brazil International Seminar, 1984. Board member, El Norte Publications/Academia; consultant. Founder and first President, Rio Grande Writers Association. Professor emeritus, University of New Mexico, 1993—.

MEMBER: Modern Language Association of America, American Association of University Professors, Na-

Rudolfo A. Anaya

tional Council of Teachers of English, Trinity Forum, Coordinating Council of Literary Magazines (vice president, 1974-80), Rio Grande Writers Association (founder and first president), La Academia Society, La Compania de Teatro de Albuquerque, Multi-Ethnic Literary Association (New York, NY), Before Columbus Foundation (Berkeley, CA.), Santa Fe Writers Co-op, Sigma Delta Pi (honorary member).

AWARDS, HONORS: Premio Quinto Sol literary award, 1971, for *Bless Me, Ultima;* University of New Mexico Mesa Chicana literary award, 1977; City of Los Angeles award, 1977; New Mexico Governor's Public Service Award, 1978 and 1980; National Chicano Council on Higher Education fellowship, 1978-79; National Endowment for the Arts fellowships, 1979, 1980; Before Columbus American Book Award, Before Columbus Foundation, 1980, for *Tortuga;* New Mexico Governor's Award for Excellence and Achievement in Literature, 1980; literature award, Delta Kappa Gamma (New Mexico chapter), 1981; honorary doctorates from universities including University of New Mexico, 1981, and 1996, Marycrest College, 1984, College of Santa Fe, 1991, University of New England, 1992, California Lutheran University, 1994, and University of New Hampshire, 1997; Corporation for Public Broadcasting script development award, 1982, for "Rosa Linda"; Award for Achievement in Chicano Literature, Hispanic Caucus of Teachers of English, 1983; Kellogg Foundation fellowship, 1983-85; ; Mexican Medal of Friendship, Mexican Consulate of Albuquerque, NM, 1986; PEN Center West Award for *Albuquerque,* 1992; Erna S. Fergusson award for exceptional accomplishment, University of New Mexico Alumni Association, 1994; Art Achievement award, Hispanic Heritage Celebration, 1995; El Fuego Nuevo Award, 1995; Tomas Rivera Mexican American Children's Book Award, 1995, for *The Farlitos of Christmas* and 2000, for *My Land Sings;* Distinguished Achievement Award, Western Literature Association, and Premio Fronterizo, Border Book Festival, both 1997; Arizona Adult Author Award, Arizona Library Association, and De Coleres Hispanic Literature Award, both 2000; National Medal of Arts in literature, Wallace Stegner Award, Center for the American West, National Hispanic Cultural Center Literary Award, and Bravos Award, Albuquerque Arts Alliance, all 2001; National Association of Chicano scholar, and Champion of Change Award, both 2002.

WRITINGS:

Bless Me, Ultima (novel; also see below), Tonatiuh International, 1972.

Heart of Aztlan (novel), Editorial Justa (Berkeley, CA), 1976.

Bilingualism: Promise for Tomorrow (screenplay), Bilingual Educational Services, 1976.

(Editor, with Jim Fisher, and contributor) *Voices from the Rio Grande,* Rio Grande Writers Association Press (Albuquerque, NM), 1976.

(Contributor) Charlotte I. Lee and Frank Galati, editors, *Oral Interpretations,* 5th edition, Houghton (Boston, MA), 1977.

(Contributor) *New Voices 4 in Literature, Language and Composition,* Ginn (Oxford, England), 1978.

(Author of introduction) Sabine Ulibarri, *Mi abuela fumaba puros,* Tonatiuh International, 1978.

(Contributor) *Anuario de letras chicanas,* Editorial Justa (Berkeley. CA), 1979.

(Contributor) *Grito del sol,* Quinto Sol Publications, 1979.

Tortuga (novel), Editorial Justa (Berkely, CA), 1979.

The Season of La Llorona (one-act play), first produced in Albuquerque, NM, at El Teatro de la Compania de Albuquerque, October 14, 1979.

(Translator) *Cuentos: Tales from the Hispanic Southwest, Based on Stories Originally Collected by Juan B. Rael,* edited by Jose Griego y Maestas, Museum of New Mexico Press (Santa Fe, NM), 1980.

(Editor, with Antonio Marquez) *Cuentos Chicanos: A Short Story Anthology,* University of New Mexico Press (Albuquerque, NM), 1980.

(Editor, with Simon J. Ortiz) *A Ceremony of Brotherhood, 1680-1980,* Academia Press, 1981.

The Silence of the Llano (short stories), Tonatiuh/Quinto Sol International, 1982.

The Legend of La Llorona (novel), Tonatiuh/Quinto Sol International, 1984.

The Adventures of Juan Chicaspatas (epic poem), Arte Publico, 1985.

A Chicano in China (nonfiction, travel), University of New Mexico Press (Albuquerque, NM), 1986.

The Farolitos of Christmas: A New Mexican Christmas Story (juvenile), New Mexico Magazine, 1987.

Lord of the Dawn: The Legend of Quetzalcóatl, University of New Mexico Press ((Albuquerque, NM), 1987.

(Editor) *Voces: An Anthology of Nuevo Mexicano Writers,* University of New Mexico Press (Albuquerque, NM), 1987.

Who Killed Don Jose (play), first produced in Albuquerque, NM, at La Compania Menval High School Theatre, July, 1987.

The Farolitos of Christmas (play), first produced in Albuquerque, NM, at La Compania Menval High School Theatre, December, 1987.

(Contributor) *Flow of the River,* or *Corre el Rio,* Hispanic Culture Foundation, 1988.

Selected from "Bless Me, Ultima," Literary Volumes of New York City, 1989.

(Editor, with Francisco Lomeli) *Aztlan: Essays on the Chicano Homeland,* El Norte, 1989.

(Editor) *Tierra: Contemporary Fiction of New Mexico* (short story collection), Cinco Puntos, 1989.

Alburquerque (novel), University of New Mexico Press (Albuquerque, NM), 1992.

Los Matachines (play), produced at La Casa Teatro, Albuquerque, December 10, 1992.

(Author of introduction) Howard Bryan, *Incredible Elfego Baca,* Clear Light (Santa Fe, NM), 1993.

(Author of introduction) *Growing Up Chicana/o,* (anthology), Morrow (New York, NY), 1993.

(Contributor) *Man on Fire: Luis Jimenez = El Hombre en Llamas,* translated by Margarita B. Montalvo, Albuquerque Museum, 1994.

The Anaya Reader, Warner Books, 1995.

(Author of foreword) *Writing the Southwest,* edited by David K. Dunaway, NAL/Dutton, 1995.

Zia Summer (novel), Warner Books, 1995.

(Editor) *Blue Mesa Review, Volume 8: Approaching the Millenium,* Blue Mesa Review/Creative Writing Center, University of New Mexico (Albuquerque, NM), 1996.

(Author of foreword) *Dictionary of Hispanic Biography,* Gale (Detroit, MI), 1996.

(Author of introduction) David L. Witt, *Spirit Ascendant: The Art and Life of Patrocino Barela,* Red Crane Books (Santa Fe, NM), 1996.

Jalamanta: A Message from the Desert (novel), Warner Books, 1996.

(With others) *Muy Macho: Latin Men Confront Their Manhood,* edited by Ray Gonzales, Anchor (New York, NY), 1996.

Rio Grande Fall (novel), Warner Books, 1996.

Abelardo Baeza, *Keep Blessing Us, Ultima: A Teaching Guide for "Bless Me, Ultima" by Rudolfo Anaya,* Easkin Press (Austin, TX), 1997.

Billy the Kid (play), produced at La Casa Teatro, July 11, 1997.

Angie (play), produced at La Casa Teatro, July 10, 1998.

Conversations with Rudolfo Anaya, edited by Bruce Dick and Silvio Sirias, University Press of Mississippi (Jackson, MS), 1998.

(With others) *The Floating Borderlands: Twenty-five Years of U.S. Hispanic Literature,* edited by Lauro Flores, University of Washington Press (Seattle, WA), 1999.

(With others) *Saints and Sinners: The American Catholic Experience through Stories, Memoirs, Essays, and Commentary,* edited by Greg Tobin, Doubleday (New York, NY), 1999.

Shaman Winter, Warner Books, 1999.

An Elegy on the Death of Cesar Chavez, illustrations by Gaspar Enriquez, Cinco Puntos Press, 2000.

FOR CHILDREN

The Farlitos of Christmas, illustrated by Edward Gonzalez, Hyperion (New York, NY), 1995.

Maya's Children, illustrated by Maria Baca, Hyperion (New York, NY), 1996.

Farolitos for Abuelo, illustrated by Edward Gonzales, Hyperion (New York, NY), 1998.

My Land Sings: Stories from the Rio Grande, illustrated by Amy Cordova, Morrow (New York, NY), 1999.

Roadrunner's Dance, illustrated by David Diaz, Hyperion (New York, NY), 2000.

Author of unproduced play "Rosa Linda," for the Corporation for Public Broadcasting; author of unpublished and unproduced dramas for the Visions Project, KCET-TV (Los Angeles). Contributor of short stories, articles, essays, and reviews to periodicals in the United States and abroad, including *La Luz, Bilingual Review-Revista Bilingue, New Mexico Magazine, La Confluencia, Contact II, Before Columbus Review, L'Umano Avventura, 2 Plus 2,* and *Literatura Uchioba;* contributor to *Albuquerque News.* Editor, *Blue Mesa Review;* associate editor, *American Book Review,* 1980-85, and *Escolios;* regional editor, *Viaztlan* and *International Chicano Journal of Arts and Letters;* member of advisory board, *Puerto Del Sol Literary Magazine.* Anaya's manuscript collection is available at the Zimmerman Museum, University of New Mexico, Albuquerque.

WORK IN PROGRESS: *Jamez Spring* (novel), *The Santero's Miracle* (children's book), and *Serafina's Stories* (young adult book), all expected 2004.

SIDELIGHTS: Best known for his first novel, *Bless Me, Ultima,* Rudolfo A. Anaya's writing stems from his New Mexican background and his fascination with the oral tradition of Chicano stories in Spanish *cuentos.* He grew up listening to *cuentistas,* oral storytellers, and wanted to bring their magic into his writing. The mystical nature of these folk tales, together with events from his own life, have had a significant influence on his novels, which portray the experiences of Chicanos in the American Southwest. But the novelist's books are also about faith and the loss of faith. As Anaya explained in *Contemporary Authors Autobiography Series,* his education at the University of New Mexico intensified his questions about his religious beliefs, and this, in turn, led him to write poetry and prose in order to "fill the void." "I lost faith in my God," Anaya wrote, "and if there was no God there was no meaning, no secure road to salvation. . . . The depth of loss one feels is linked to one's salvation. That may be why I write. It is easier to ascribe those times and their bittersweet emotions to my characters."

Bless Me, Ultima, "a unique American novel that deserves to be better known," in *Revista Chicano-Riquena* contributor Vernon Lattin's words, leans heavily on Anaya's background in folklore in its depiction of the war between the evil Tenorio Trementina and the benevolent *curandera* (healer) Ultima. Several critics, such as *Latin American Literary Review*'s Daniel Testa, have praised Anaya's use of old Spanish-American, specifically Chicano, tales in his book. "What seems to be quite extraordinary," averred Testa, ". . . is the variety of materials in Anaya's work. He intersperses the legendary, folkloric, stylized, or allegorized material with the detailed descriptions that help to create a density of realistic portrayal."

The novel is also a *bildungsroman* about a young boy, named Antonio, who grows up, as Anaya did, in a small village in New Mexico around the time of World War II. Most of Antonio's maturation is linked with a struggle with his religious faith and his trouble in choosing between the nomadic way of life of his father's family, and the agricultural lifestyle of his mother's. Reviewers of *Bless Me, Ultima* have lauded Anaya for his depiction of these dilemmas in the life of a young Mexican-American. For example, in *Chicano Perspectives in Literature: A Critical and Annotated Bibliography,* authors Francisco A. Lomeli and Donaldo W. Urioste called this work "an unforgettable novel . . . already becoming a classic for its uniqueness in story, narrative technique and structure." And *America* contributor Scott Wood remarked: "Anaya offers a valuable gift to the American scene, a scene which often seems as spiritually barren as some parched plateau in New Mexico."

Anaya's next novel, *Heart of Aztlan,* influenced by Anaya's involvement in the Chicano movement of the 1960s, is a more political work about a family that moves from a rural community to the city; but as with its predecessor, Anaya mixes in some mystical elements along with the book's social concern for the Chicano worker in capitalist America. Reception of this second book was somewhat less enthusiastic than it was for *Bless Me, Ultima.* Marvin A. Lewis observed in *Revista Chicano-Requena* that "on the surface, the outcome [of *Heart of Aztlan*] is a shallow, romantic, adolescent novel which nearly overshadows the treatment of adult problems. The novel [has] redeeming qualities, however, in its treatment of the urban experience and the problems with racism inherent therein, as well as in its attempt to define the mythic dimension of the Chicano experience." Similarly, *World Literature Today* critic Charles R. Larson felt that *Heart of Aztlan*, along with *Bless Me, Ultima*, "provide[s] us with a vivid sense of Chicano Life since World War II."

Anaya himself says that he was working, in cathartic writings before *Bless Me, Ultima*, without models or mentors for delineating Chicano experiences: "I was still imitating a style and mode not indigenous to the people and setting I knew best. I was desperately seeking my natural voice, but the process by which I formed it was long and arduous." At university, he, along with other Mexican-American students, had been "unprepared by high school to compete. . . . The thought was still prevalent in the world of academia that we were better suited as janitors than scholars." He had to learn English which "was still a foreign language to us," and with the attitudes of teachers who believed learning meant changing to be like them. His life of writing has been a journey of discovery: how to present the reality of Chicano people in the United States from within that experience.

Tortuga, Anaya's third novel, continues in the mythical vein of the author's other works and has been called "Anaya's most accomplished novel" by Antonio Marquez in *The Magic of Words*. The novel concerns a young boy who must undergo therapy for his paralysis and wear a body cast, hence his nickname "Tortuga," which means turtle. "Tortuga," however, also "refers . . . to the 'magic mountain' (with a nod here to Thomas Mann) that towers over the hospital for paralytic children," according to Angelo Restivo in *Fiction International*. While staying at the Crippled Children and Orphans Hospital, Tortuga becomes more spiritually and psychologically mature, and the novel ends when he returns home after his year-long ordeal. As with the novelist's other books, *Tortuga* is a story about growing up; indeed, *Bless Me, Ultima*, *Heart of Aztlan*, and *Tortuga* form a loosely-tied trilogy that depicts the Chicano experience in the southwestern United States over a period of several decades. As the author once told *CA*, these novels "are a definite trilogy in my mind. They are not only about growing up in New Mexico, they are about life."

All of Anaya's novels, including the award-winning quartet *Alburquerque* (the original spelling of the city's name), *Zia Summer, Rio Grande Fall*, and *Shaman Winter*, attempt to find the answers to life's questions, doing so from the perspective of his own personal cultural background and thus offering an opportunity to Mexican-American students of all ages to educate themselves about their culture, heritage and history. "If we as Chicanos do have a distinctive perspective on life," he told John David Bruce-Novoa in *Chicano Authors: Inquiry by Interview*, "I believe that perspective will be defined when we challenge the very basic questions which mankind has always asked itself: What is my relationship to the universe, the cosmos? Who am I and why am I here? If there is a Godhead, what is its nature and function? What is the nature of mankind?" These questions echo the doubts, realizations, and experiences the author has had in his life, and that he links closely to mythology alive in the land and peoples of the Americas, especially in the Mexican/Spanish and Native American cultures which flow together in Anaya. He explained to Bruce-Novoa, "All literature, and certainly Chicano literature, reflects, in its more formal aspects, the mythos of the people, and the writings speak to the underlying philosophical assumptions which form the particular world view of culture. . . . In a real sense, the mythologies of the Americas are the only mythologies of all of us, whether we are newly arrived or whether we have been here for centuries. The land and the people force this mythology on us. I gladly accept it; many or most of the American newcomers have resisted it."

As well as novels, Anaya has written plays and screenplays, two epic poems and other poems, short stories, essays, documentaries, and children's stories. His first epic poem, a mock-heroic piece written in the language of "vatos locos," or crazy barrio Chicanos who jest at almost everything, continues the search for self-definition. In 2000 Anaya published *Elegy on the Death of Cesar Chavez*, another epic poem which celebrates the life and struggles of the famed Chicano labor leader.

Anaya told *CA:* "With fear throbbing in my heart I said goodbye to my mother and father and went off to my first day at school. First grade in Santa Rosa, New Mexico. I didn't know a word of English. But, as time progressed, I learned to read. I wrote great book reviews and illustrated them. I read the Nancy Drew and Hardy Boys mysteries. I read cowboy stories. I read comic books. I had a comic book collection three feet high. I loved stories. Stories are what the old people told. I was raised on the folk tales of the Hispanic New Mexicans.

"I really fell in love with reading when I was a student at the University of Mexico. I read everything in those days when a liberal education meant preparing the student in world literature—multicultural literature.

"I began to write poetry. The Beatnik era was full of poetry and rebellion, and some of that energy became mine. I began to write what I knew best, my childhood, my family, community, place. More like Thomas Wolfe than Hemingway.

"I discovered in the arduous, creative process that the story must be personal. My place. The history, language, and culture of my community.

" I wrote every night, descending into the world of my dreams, the mythos, the images of the unconscious, the world of symbols. My history was tied to the history of my community.

"In the 1970s, the Chicago Movement was born—we gave it birth. We began to write *us*. Identity. The movement spread across the country and continues to this day.

"I don't have a favorite novel. They are all children born of blood, pain, joy, and revelation—the dark world coming into light. Some are fuller of soul, some are weaker in style, but they are all children to be loved.

"We write for ourselves and for others. Messages. A sharing. We write to say we exist. The reader reads and also shouts I too exist! We are all together in the structure, which we call creativity. The structure is a house. We all live there. Some write, some do carpentry, plumbing or doctoring. We all live and share what we do. If it wasn't for those guys, I wouldn't have a house to live in. If it weren't for me, they wouldn't have a book of revelation to read. It all works out in the end.

BIOGRAPHICAL AND CRITICAL SOURCES:

BOOKS

Baeza, Abelardo, *Keep Blessing Us, Ultima: A Teaching Guide for Bless Me, Ultima by Rudolfo Anaya,* Easkin Press (Austin, TX), 1997.

Bruce-Novoa, Juan D., *Chicano Authors: Inquiry by Interview,* University of Texas Press (Austin, TX), 1980, pp. 183-202.

Chavez, John R., *The Lost Land, The Chicano Image of the Southwest,* University of New Mexico Press (Albuquerque, NM), 1984.

Chicano Literature: A Reference Guide, Greenwood Press (Westport, CT), 1985.

Contemporary Authors Autobiography Series, Volume 4, Gale (Detroit, MI), 1986.

Contemporary Literary Criticism, Volume 23, Gale (Detroit, MI), 1983.

Dennis, Philip A., and Wendell Aycock, *Literature and Anthropology,* Texas Tech University Press (Lubbock, TX), 1989, pp. 193-208.

Dick, Bruce, and Silvio Sirias, *Conversations with Rudolfo Anaya,* University Press of Mississippi (Jackson, MS), 1998.

Dictionary of Literary Biography, Volume 82: *Chicano Writers, First Series,* Gale (Detroit, MI), 1989, pp. 24-35.

Fabre, Genvieve, *European Perspectives on Hispanic Literature of the United States,* Arte Publico Press, 1988, pp. 55-65.

Gonzales-Berry, Erlinda, *Paso por Aqui: Critical Essays on the New Mexican Literary Tradition, 1542-1988,* University of New Mexico Press (Albuquerque, NM), 1989, pp. 243-54.

Gonzales, Cesar A., *Rudolfo Anaya: Focus on Criticism* (includes bibliography by Teresa Marquez), Lalo Press (Tempe, AZ), 1990.

Gonzales, Cesar A., *A Sense of Place: Rudolfo A. Anaya: An Annotated Bio-Bibliography,* University of California Press (Berkeley, CA), 1999.

Hispanic Literature Criticism, Gale (Detroit, MI), 1994.

Jimenez, Francisco, editor, *The Identification and Analysis of Chicano Literature,* Bilingual Press (New York, NY), 1979.

Kanellos, Nicolas, editor, *Understanding the Chicano Experience through Literature,* Mexican American Studies, University of Houston Press (Houston, TX), 1981.

Lattin, Vernon E., editor, *Contemporary Chicano Fiction: A Critical Survey,* Bilingual Press/Editorial Bilinguumlal (Binghamton, NY), 1986.

Lomeli, Francisco A., and Donaldo W. Urioste, *Chicano Perspectives in Literature: A Critical and Annotated Bibliography,* Apparition, 1976.

Olmos, Margarite Fernandez, *Rudolfo A. Anaya: A Critical Companion,* Greenwood Press (Westport, CT), 1999.

Reference Guide to American Literature, 3rd edition, St. James Press (Detroit, MI), 1994, p. 57.

Robinson, Cecil, *Mexico and the Hispanic Southwest in American Literature,* University of Arizona Press (Tucson, AZ), 1977.

Ryan, Bryan, *Hispanic Writers,* Gale (Detroit, MI), 1991.

Vassallo, Paul, *Magic of Words: Rudolfo A. Anaya and His Writings,* University of New Mexico Press (Albuquerque, NM), 1982.

PERIODICALS

Agenda: A Journal of Hispanic Issues, July, 1977, p. 46; November, 1979, p. 4 and 33.

Albuquerque Monthly, November, 1981, pp. 26-28.

America, January 27, 1973, p. 72.

American Book Review, March-April, 1979.

American Literature, January, 1979, p. 625.

Americas Review: A Review of Hispanic Literature and Art of the USA, fall-winter, 1996, p. 201.

Aztlan, spring, 1987, pp. 59-68.

Bilingual Review, January-April, 1982, pp. 82-87.

Bloomsbury Review, September-October, 1993, pp. 3, 18.

Booklist, February 1, 1996, p. 915; September 1, 1996, p. 66; May 1, 1997, p. 1500; October 1, 1997, p. 94; April 15, 1998, p. 1389; August 1999, p. 2043; May 1, 2000, p. 1594; December 15, 2000, p. 811 and 823.

Caribe, spring, 1976, p. 113.

Center for Children's Books Bulletin, August, 1997, p. 387.

Children's Book & Play Review, January, 2001, p. 13.

Children's Book Review Service, August, 1997, p. 164; October, 1999, p. 188.

Children's Bookwatch, June, 1997, p. 6; February, 2001, p. 3.

Commonweal, November 5, 1999, p. 24.

Critica, fall, 1986, p. 21.

Critique, 1980, pp. 55-64.

De Colores, 1975, p. 22; fall, 1977, p. 30; spring, 1980, p. 111.

Emergency Librarian, May, 1996, p. 56.

Empire, March, 1980, p. 24.

Environment, March, 1999, p. 8.

Fiction International, number 12, 1980, p. 283.

Hispanic, September, 1994, p. 90; January, 1999, p. 106.

Horn Book Guide, November-December, 1995, p. 727; spring, 1996, p. 53; fall, 1997, p. 257; spring, 2001, p. 27 and 139.

Hungry Mind Review, fall, 1999, p. 34.

Journal for Youth Services in Libraries, summer 1996, p. 414.

Kirkus Reviews, July 15, 1996, p. 1004; December 1, 1998, p. 1696; July 1, 1999, p. 1050; September 15, 1999, p. 1496.

La Confluenzia, July, 1977, p. 61.

La Luz, May, 1973.

Latin American Literary Review, spring-summer, 1977, p. 64 and 70; spring-summer, 1978, p.70.

Library Journal, February 1, 1996, p. 64; September 1, 1996, p. 213; January 1997, p. 51.

Los Angeles Times Book Review, August 30, 1992, p. 8.

MELUS, spring, 1978, p. 71; spring, 1984, pp. 27-32, winter, 1984, pp. 47-57.

Mester, November, 1974, p. 27.

Nation, July 18, 1994, p. 98.

New Mexico Humanities Review, summer, 1979, pp. 5-12.

New York Times Book Review, October 11, 1981, pp. 15; November 29, 1992, p. 22; 36-37; July 2, 1995, p. 15; December 17, 1995, p. 28.

Ploughshares, June 1978, p. 190.

PMLA, January, 1987, pp. 10, 15-17.

Publishers Weekly, May 25, 1992; March 21, 1994, p. 24; April 10, 1994, p. 56; June 5, 1995, p. 41; January 1, 1996, p. 58; July 29, 1996, p. 73; October 6, 1997, p. 58; September 27, 1999, p. 60; October 11, 1999, p. 77; November 20, 2000, p. 68.

Reading Teacher, October, 2001, p. 208.

Revista Chicano-Riquena, spring, 1978, p. 50; summer, 1981, p. 74.

San Francisco Review of Books, June, 1978, pp. 9-12, 34.

School Library Journal, June, 1997, p. 78; September, 1999, p. 218; October, 1999, p. 64; September, 2000, p. 184; January 1, 2001, p. 136.

Skipping Stones, May-August 2001, p. 9.

Sojourners, May, 2001, p. 51.

Southwestern American Literature, 1974, p. 74.

Stone Soup, July-August, 2002, p. 8.

University of Albuquerque Alumni Magazine, January, 1973.

University of New Mexico Alumni Magazine, January, 1973.

Western American Literature, summer, 1997, p. 179.

World Literature Today, spring, 1979, p. 245; spring, 1996, p. 403; autumn 1996, p. 957.

* * *

ARDEN, John 1930-

PERSONAL: Born October 26, 1930, in Barnsley, Yorkshire, England; son of Charles Alwyn (a manager of a glass works) and Annie Elizabeth (a school teacher; maiden name, Layland) Arden; married Margaretta Ruth D'Arcy (a playwright), 1957; children: Francis Gwalchmei (deceased), Finn, Adam, Jacob, Neuss. *Education:* King's College, Cambridge, B.A., 1953; Edinburgh College of Art, diploma, 1955. *Hobbies and other interests:* Antiquarianism, mythology.

ADDRESSES: Agent—c/o Casarotto Ramsay & Associates, National House, 4th Fl., 60-66 Wardour St., London W1V 3HP, England.

CAREER: Architectural assistant in London, England, 1955-57; playwright, 1957—. Fellow in playwriting, University of Bristol, Bristol, England, 1959-60; visiting lecturer in politics and drama, New York University, 1967; Regents' lecturer, University of California, Davis, 1973; writer in residence and playwright in residence, University of New England, Australia, 1975. Cofounder of Corrandulla Arts and Entertainment Club, Corrandulla, Ireland, 1971, and Galway Theatre Workshop, 1975. *Military service:* British Army, Intelligence Corps, 1949-50.

AWARDS, HONORS: British Broadcasting Corp. Northern Region prize for *The Life of Man;* Encyclopaedia Britannica prize, 1959, and Vernon Rice award, 1966, both for *Serjeant Musgrave's Dance: An Unhistorical Parable;* Bristol University fellowship in playwriting, 1959-60; *Evening Standard* (London) "most promising playwright" award, 1960; Trieste Festival prize, 1961, for *Soldier, Soldier;* Arts Council Award, 1973; recipient, with Margaretta D'Arcy, award from Arts Council, 1974, for *The Ballygombeen Bequest* and *The Island of the Mighty: A Play on a Traditional British Theme in Three Parts;The Old Man Sleeps Alone* included in *Best Radio Plays of 1982; Silence among the Weapons: Some Events at the Time of the Failure of a Republic* short-listed for Booker McConnell prize for fiction, 1982; PEN Macmillan Silver Pen award, 1992, for *Cogs Tyrranic;* V. S. Pritchett Award, 1999.

John Arden

WRITINGS:

PLAYS

All Fall Down, produced in Edinburgh, Scotland, 1955.
The Waters of Babylon (also see below), first produced in London at Royal Court Theatre, October 20, 1957; produced in New York City, 1958, and in Washington, DC, at Washington Theatre Club, 1967.
When Is a Door Not a Door? (also see below), first produced in London at Central School of Speech and Drama, 1958.
Live Like Pigs (also see below), first produced in London at Royal Court Theatre, September 30, 1958; produced Off-Broadway at Actor's Playhouse, June 7, 1965.
Serjeant Musgrave's Dance: An Unhistorical Parable (also see below; first produced in London at Royal Court Theatre, October 22, 1959; produced Off-Broadway at Theatre de Lys, March 8, 1966; revised version with John McGrath produced on tour as *Serjeant Musgrave Dances On,* 1972), Methuen (London, England), 1960, Grove (New York, NY), 1962, with notes and commentary by

R. W. Ewart, Longman, 1982, with notes and commentary by Glenda Leeming, Methuen (London, England), 1982, revised 1966 script, Studio Duplicating Service, 1986.

The Workhouse Donkey: A Vulgar Melodrama (also see below; first produced in Sussex, England, at Chichester Festival Theatre, July 8, 1963), Methuen (London, England), 1964, Grove (New York, NY), 1967.

Ironhand (adaptation of Goethe's *Goetz von Berlichingen;* first produced in Bristol, England, at Bristol Old Vic Theatre, November 12, 1963), Methuen (London, England), 1965, Grove (New York, NY), 1967.

Armstrong's Last Goodnight: An Exercise in Diplomacy (also see below; first produced in Glasgow, Scotland, at Glasgow Citizens' Theatre, May 5, 1964; produced in Boston, 1966), Methuen (London, England), 1965, Grove (New York, NY), 1976.

Fidelio (adaptation of libretto by Joseph Sonnleithner and Friedrich Treitschke of opera by Beethoven), first produced in London, 1965.

Left-Handed Liberty: A Play about Magna Carta (commissioned by the City of London to celebrate the 750th anniversary of the sealing of the Magna Carta; first produced in London at Mermaid Theatre, June 14, 1965), Methuen (London, England), 1965, Grove (NewYork, NY), 1966.

The Soldier's Tale (adaptation of libretto by Charles Ramuz of opera by Igor Stravinsky), first produced in Bath, England, 1968.

The True History of Squire Jonathan and His Unfortunate Treasure (also see below), first produced in London at Ambiance Lunch Hour Theatre, June 17, 1968.

The Hero Rises Up: A Romantic Melodrama, Methuen (London, England), 1969.

Two Autobiographical Plays, Methuen (London, England), 1971.

PLAYS; WITH MARGARETTA D'ARCY

The Happy Haven (two-act; also see below), first produced in Bristol at Bristol University, 1960; produced in London at Royal Court Theatre, September 14, 1960; produced in New York City, 1967.

The Business of Good Government: A Christmas Play (one-act; first produced as *A Christmas Play,* in Somerset, England, at Brent Knoll Church of St. Michael, December, 1960; produced in New York City, 1970), Methuen (London, England), 1963, reprinted, 1983, Grove (NewYork, NY), 1967.

Ars Longa, Vita Brevis (one-act; first produced on the West End at Aldwych Theatre by the Royal Shakespeare Co., 1964), Cassell (London, England), 1965.

Friday's Hiding (one-act; also see below), first produced in London, 1965; produced in Edinburgh at the Lyceum Theatre, 1966.

The Royal Pardon; or, The Soldier Who Became an Actor (first produced in Devon, England, at Beaford Arts Centre, September 1, 1966; produced in London at Arts Theatre, 1967), Methuen (London, England), 1967.

(And with Cartoon Archetypical Slogan Theatre) *Harold Muggins Is a Martyr,* first produced in London at Unity Theatre Club, June, 1968.

The Hero Rises Up: A Romantic Melodrama (two-act; first produced in London at Round House Theatre, November 6, 1968), Methuen (London, England), 1969.

(And with Muswell Hill Street Theatre) *Granny Welfare and the Wolf,* first produced in London at Ducketts Common, Turnpike Lane, March, 1971.

(And with Muswell Hill Street Theatre) *My Old Man's a Tory* (one-act), first produced in London at Wood Green, March, 1971.

(And with Socialist Labour League) *Two Hundred Years of Labour History* (two-act), first produced in London at Alexandra Palace, April, 1971.

(And with Writers against Repression) *Rudi Dutschke Must Stay,* first produced in London at British Museum, spring, 1971.

The Ballygombeen Bequest (first produced in Belfast, Northern Ireland, at St. Mary and St. Joseph's College Drama Society, May, 1972; produced in London at Bush Theatre, September 11, 1972), Scripts, 1972.

The Island of the Mighty: A Play on a Traditional British Theme in Three Parts (first produced on the West End at Aldwych Theatre, December 5, 1972), with illustrations by authors, Eyre Methuen (Oxford, England), 1974.

(And with Corrandulla Arts Entertainment Club) *The Devil and the Parish Pump* (one-act), first produced in county Galway, Ireland, at Gort Roe, Corrandulla Arts Centre, April, 1974.

The Non-Stop Connolly Show: A Dramatic Cycle of Continuous Struggle in Six Parts (first produced in Dublin at Liberty Hall, March 29, 1975, produced in London at Ambiance Lunch Hour Theatre, May 17, 1976), Pluto, Parts 1 and 2: *Boyhood 1868-1889* [and] *Apprenticeship, 1889-1896,* 1977, Part 3: *Professional, 1896-1903,* Part 4: *The New World, 1903-1910,* Part 5: *The Great Lockout, 1910-1914,* and Part 6: *World War and the Rising, 1914-1916,* 1978.

(And with Galway Theatre Workshop) *The Crown Strike Play* (one-act), first produced in Galway at Eyre Square, December, 1975.

(And with Galway Theatre Workshop) *Sean O'Scrudu,* first produced in Galway at Coachman Hotel, February, 1976.

(And with Galway Theatre Workshop) *The Mongrel Fox* (one-act), first produced in Galway at Regional Technical College, October, 1976.

(And with Galway Theatre Workshop) *No Room at the Inn* (one-act), first produced in Galway at Coachman Hotel, December, 1976.

(And with Galway Theatre Workshop) *Silence,* first produced in Galway at Eyre Square, April, 1977.

(And with Galway Theatre Workshop) *Mary's Name* (one-act), first produced in Galway at University College, May, 1977.

(And with Galway Theatre Workshop) *Blow-In Chorus for Liam Cosgrave,* first produced in Galway at Eyre Square, June, 1977.

Vandaleur's Folly: An Anglo-Irish Melodrama; The Hazard of Experiment in an Irish Co-operative, Ralahine, 1831 (two-act; first produced at Lancaster University, 1978) Methuen (Oxford, England), 1981.

The Little Gray Home in the West: An Anglo-Irish Melodrama, Pluto, 1982.

RADIO / TELEVISION PRODUCTIONS

The Life of Man (radio play), BBC Radio, 1956.

Soldier, Soldier: A Comic Song for Television (also see below), BBC, 1960.

Wet Fish: A Professional Reminiscence for Television (also see below), BBC, 1961.

The Bagman; or, The Impromptu of Muswell Hill (radio play; also see below), BBC-Radio, 1970.

(With Margaretta D'Arcy) *Keep These People Moving* (radio play; for children), British Broadcasting Corp. (BBC-Radio), 1972.

(With Margaretta D'Arcy) *Portrait of a Rebel* (television documentary about Sean O'Casey), Radio-Telefis Eireann (Dublin), 1973.

To Put It Frankly (radio play), BBC-Radio, 1979.

Pearl: A Play about a Play within a Play (radio play), Eyre Methuen (Oxford, England), 1979.

The Adventures of the Ingenious Gentlemen (two-part adaptation of Cervantes' *Don Quixote*), BBC-Radio, 1980.

Garland for a Hoar Head (radio play), BBC-Radio, 1982.

The Old Man Sleeps Alone (radio play), BBC-Radio, 1982.

(With Margaretta D'Arcy) *The Manchester Enthusiasts* (radio play broadcast in three parts), BBC-Radio, 1984, broadcast on RTE Radio, Dublin, as *The Ralahine Experiment,* 1985.

(With Margaretta D'Arcy) *Whose Is the Kingdom?* (radio play broadcast in nine parts by BBC-Radio, 1988), Methuen (London, England), 1988.

(With Margaretta D'Arcy) *A Suburban Suicide* (radio play), BBC-Radio, 1994.

Little Novels of Wilkie Collins (radio play), 1998.

Woe Alas, the Fatal Cash-Box! (radio plays), Radio 4, 1999.

Wild Ride to Dublin (radio play), BBC-Radio 4, 2003.

Poor Tom Thy Horn is Dry (radio play), BBC-Radio 3, 2003.

COLLECTIONS

Three Plays (contains *The Waters of Babylon, Live Like Pigs,* and *The Happy Haven*), introduction by John Russell Taylor, Penguin (New York, NY), 1964, reprinted, 1984, Penguin (Baltimore, MD), 1965.

Soldier, Soldier, and Other Plays (contains *Soldier, Soldier: A Comic Song for Television, Wet Fish: A Professional Reminiscence for Television, When Is a Door Not a Door?* and *Friday's Hiding*), Methuen (London, England), 1967.

Two Autobiographical Plays (contains *The True History of Squire Jonathan and His Unfortunate Treasure* and *The Bagman; or, The Impromptu of Muswell Hill*), Methuen (London, England), 1971.

Plays (includes *Serjeant Musgrave's Dance: An Unhistorical Parable, The Workhouse Donkey: A Vulgar Melodrama,* and *Armstrong's Last Goodnight: An Exercise in Diplomacy*), Methuen (London, England), 1977, Grove (New York, NY), 1978.

Arden/D'Arcy, Plays One, Methuen (London, England), 1991.

Arden, Plays One and Two, Methuen (London, England), 1994, reprinted, 2002.

OTHER

(With Margaretta D'Arcy) *To Present the Pretence: Essays on the Theatre and Its Public,* Eyre Methuen (Oxford, England), 1977, Holmes & Meier, 1979.

Vox Pop: The Last Days of the Roman Republic (novel), Harcourt (New York, NY), 1982, published as *Silence among the Weapons: Some Events at the Time of the Failure of a Republic,* Methuen (London, England), 1982.

Books of Bale: A Fiction of History (novel), Methuen (London, England), 1988.

(With Margaretta D'Arcy) *Awkward Corners: Essays, Papers, Fragments* (essays), Methuen (London, England), 1988.

Cogs Tyrannic (four stories), Methuen (London, England), 1991.

Jack Juggler and the Emperor's Whore: Seven Tall Tales Linked Together for an Indecorous Toy Theatre (novel), Methuen (London, England), 1995.

Stealing Steps (short stories), Methuen (London, England), 2003.

Contributor to anthologies, including *New English Dramatists,* Penguin, Volume 3, 1961, Volume 4, 1962, and *Scripts 9,* 1972.

SIDELIGHTS: British playwright John Arden may not be as well known outside of his native land as are some of his contemporaries of the radical writers school that emerged during the 1950s and 1960s. But like John Osborne, author of *Look Back in Anger,* and David Edgar, whose many agitprop dramas rocked the stage, Arden takes a hard look at English life, examining the conflicts behind the traditions. As Stanley Lourdeaux described it in a *Dictionary of Literary Biography* article, when the fledgling playwright Arden began his professional career in 1957, "critics hastily placed him with other 'angry young men' of the period. Recent critics have labeled Arden the British [Bertolt] Brecht because of his generally Marxist politics in his recent social drama. But neither his present politics nor the 'angry' nonconformity of his protagonists tells the story of why he gradually rejected the appearance of 1950s social realism for that of improvisation." Writing in *Contemporary Dramatists,* Elaine Turner found that "Arden's plays break through the confinements of realism by using open staging; broad, poetic language; characters bordering on caricature; complex visual imagery; active social settings; and an appropriation of traditional 'popular' forms, like music-hall and medieval theatre, to dramatise the inter-active effects of concepts, ideas, and social organisation on social, personal, and political life."

Arden's early theatrical efforts "scrutinized the basic social tension between aggressive survivors and the institutions meant to pacify them," continued Lourdeaux, who pointed to *The Waters of Babylon,* a 1957 production, as an illustration. It is the story of Sigismanfred Krankiewicz—Krank for short—a Pole who emigrates to London as an architectural assistant (the playwright's original career). When Krank runs up against local authorities for harboring too many boarders, many of them prostitutes, at his private boardinghouse, the immigrant rebels by becoming involved in a corrupt local lottery. Krank's schemes are contrasted against his friend Paul's, who is an amateur anarchist given to building bombs in the name of Polish patriotism. But Polish patriotism "makes little sense to Krank in a world gone mad, as he explains when Paul almost shoots him after learning that he was a soldier in the German army at Buchenwald," noted Lourdeaux. Eventually, Paul does shoot Krank and kill him, though accidentally, and "the random results of the entire scene undermines Krank's clever individualism as well as social justice," as Lourdeaux explained.

In his book *Anger and After: A Guide to the New British Drama,* John Russell Taylor remarked that "behind Arden's work there seems to be brooding one basic principle: not exactly the obvious one that today there are no causes—that would be altogether too facile, and in any case just not true—but that there are too many." In the opinion of Simon Trussler, in his published study *John Arden, The Waters of Babylon* is "extravagantly plotted, generously peopled—a scenically shuttling kaleidoscope of down-at-heel London life in the early 1950s. Coincidence functions here not with the shyly intruding excuses of the well-made play but as a fine art in itself, a satisfaction of improbable expectations. And the characters, a racial mixture of Poles, English, Irish, and West Indians, embody in this comedy of contemporary humours many of the mythic archetypes of urban life, caught from an unexpected angle."

Another Arden work to satirically examine the conflict between the classes is *Live Like Pigs.* Like *The Waters of Babylon,* this play "contains earthy and zestful language and depends greatly on performance," according to Lourdeaux. "Arden presents the chaos of the gypsylike Sawney family who are forced out of their broken run-down tramcar and made to live in the local housing project. The Sawneys quickly manage to insult their new neighbors, the Jacksons, who eventually incite a vigilante group to run the unappreciative vulgar family out of the project."

Live Like Pigs looks "superficially naturalistic, but one has only to consider the sturdy-beggarly tongue in which the Sawneys speak to realize that Arden is here employing a device which was to become more familiar in his historical plays for distinguishing a way of life through its language," said Trussler. "The ballads which introduce the scenes, and the occasional snatches of song within them, underline the danger of approaching the play naturalistically." The purpose of song in this work, the critic continued, "is in marked contrast to the deliberately interruptive purpose it usually serves in Brecht's: balladry is best regarded as another of Arden's invented languages, the problems it poses dramatic rather than musical."

Called by the Irish dramatist Sean O'Casey "far and away the finest play of the present day," *Serjeant Musgrave's Dance: An Unhistorical Parable,* a 1958 Arden drama, centers on a fanatical sergeant of the nineteenth-century British army who exacts a bizarre revenge for the life of a soldier killed by a sniper. He in fact wants no fewer than five men to die to avenge the young private; then he calls for more murders to mark another soldier's death, although that one was accidental. *Serjeant Musgrave's Dance,* in M. W. Steinberg's view, "is largely an exploration of the place of violence in society and our varying responses to it." *Dalhousie Review* writer M. W. Steinberg added that "the moral-political question is given sharpest focus and most acute and challenging dramatic expression through Serjeant Musgrave, a zealot so convinced of the absolute rightness of his cause that he is willing to adopt horrifying means to achieve his goal, and so unswerving and single-minded in his devotion to his avowed purpose that he refuses to be distracted by any consideration not immediately relevant."

"[It] would make for easier acceptance of *Serjeant Musgrave's Dance* if the fanatical sergeant were to be either wholly condemned or wholly approved of," stated G. W. Brandt, the author of *Contemporary Theatre*. "But is it not disturbing to see a morally sensitive man trying to start a public massacre? It is. Does his fanaticism invalidate his moral protest as such? It does not. The contradiction between laudable indignation and reprehensible conclusions drawn from it may either alienate the spectators out of all sympathy with the play (as happened to some critics), or else it may jolt them into stirring moral speculation (as was the experience of some other critics)."

That *Serjeant Musgrave's Dance* evoked a divided, if emotional, reaction in critics proved a point of discussion to Malcolm Page: "Clearly there are grounds for uncertainty about the import of the play; difficulties in comprehension arose mainly because neither method nor subject was what the critics expected," he wrote in *Drama Survey*. The play "suggests that pacifists are not sure enough about what they are trying to do, and have not understood the complexities of the world," Page said. And "there are several other ideas in the play, perhaps too many. Musgrave and his followers are obsessed with guilt at the evil in which they joined, raising the issue of how to expiate it. . . . Musgrave touches, too, on the question of what principle is: where and how can one begin to apply principles in an imperfect world; does the quest of absolute principle lead to madness?"

In another *Drama Survey* article, John Mills reacted both to *Serjeant Musgrave's Dance* and to Page's assessment of it. To Page's opinion that the work asks "why pacifist ideas have not had more influence," Mills responded that "though I agree with much of [Page's] commentary, I think that the play is a little more hopeful than he indicates. For one thing, it seems to me that *Musgrave* is less about pacifism than it is about anarchism, a doctrine [with] which the play tentatively (as Arden himself might put it) agrees."

The playwright does not lack for personal anger, "but he is the dramatist par excellence who translates that anger into situations of a strictly impersonal nature," to quote Arnold P. Hinchcliffe from his book *British Theatre 1950-1970*. "Arden's characters are primarily used as representatives, and his plots bring about conflicts between social groups. His characters, of course, exist as very colourful individuals, but their personality is shaped at all times to suggest what they stand for . . . and add to the picture of the community as a whole. Thus, isolated town or national politics reflected in local government is observed with an accurate social eye and a strong historical sense which combine to 'translate the concrete life of today into terms of poetry that shall at the one time illustrate that life and set it within the historical and legendary tradition of our culture,'" he said, quoting Arden.

To Lourdeaux, Arden "began his career in theater as a trained architect who was guided by the basic foundation of social drama only to turn to more and more explicitly political material. Though at first interested in epic figures like Hitler and King Arthur, Arden tempered his taste to the smaller stature of men like Sigismanfred Krankiewicz and Serjeant Musgrave, whose vivid speech and improvised actions supplanted the significance of seemingly realistic plots. With other fierce survivors like the Sawneys in *Live Like Pigs*, [the playwright] seemed to have settled on contemporary social realism."

Arden's career presented another aspect—collaborating on plays with his wife, Irish actress and playwright Margaretta D'Arcy. The professional partnership was a natural move, as Arden explained in a *Contemporary Authors Autobiography Series* article. "She was closely involved with the most progressive aspects of the theatre of that time, aspects of which I knew nothing, with my limited Shakespearean provincial orientation and my academic (and indeed pompous) attitude towards the stage. She gave me a copy of Brecht—a writer I had only heard of: she introduced me to the works of Beckett, Strindberg, Toller, Behan," he wrote. "Her name now appears, sometimes first, sometimes second, together with mine, upon a great deal of published work which nonetheless the male critics, managements, publishers, and broadcasters, will insist upon referring to as 'Arden's.' Or, worse, 'the Ardens.'" Her name also appears on work of her own, but this did not appear until after the collaborative pieces.

The Non-Stop Connolly Show: A Dramatic Cycle of Continuous Struggle in Six Parts is a marathon collaboration between Arden and D'Arcy; a six-part cycle lasting nearly twenty-four hours, with a huge cast of historical characters, the production traces the life of Irish socialist leader James Connolly from boyhood through the Easter Uprising in 1916, an important and inspiring event in the history of Irish nationalism. Writing of the two traditions in Ireland, "vicious, merciless violence" and pacifism, Desmond Hogan pointed out in *New Statesmen* that Connolly exemplified neither, but "ultimately opted for a bloody revolution on a minor scale not so much to break from Britain but to let out his own protest against Britain's centuries of manhandling Ireland." Although Lourdeaux considers the play "too long and the characters too numerous for viewers to focus exclusively on any one character or action in this complex political tapestry," Hogan suggested that "one feels one is in the presence of great drama and that the drama was made from a cold eye, an eye which like Yeats's, penetrated lies, phobias, images which dressed other images, and came up with—even if only for moments at a stretch—a mind-boggling authenticity."

Concluding an essay on Arden in *Modern Drama*, Joan Tindale Blindheim declared the playwright "a conscious and imaginative explorer of visual effects and stage resources. His knowledge of stage history and his trained eye add dimensions to his work that are often absent from that of more 'literary' writers. There are aspects that must not be ignored when [Arden's] contribution to the drama is considered, and it is through them that he is likely to make a lasting contribution to the theatre too, in helping to break down theatre conventions and in striving towards a richer and more active relationship between actors and audience."

In 1995, Arden produced a sprawling 582-page novel, *Jack Juggler and the Emperor's Whore: Seven Tall Tales Linked Together for an Indecorous Toy Theatre*. The novel follows the life of Jack "Juggler" Pogmoor, a slightly amoral and unscrupulous theater director who is the anti-hero of these tales. Pogmoor's successes in the theater are offset by accusations of sexual delinquency. David Caute, writing in the *Times Literary Supplement*, claimed that "Arden . . . strongly implies that a theatre director cannot be falsely charged with anything." The book's great mystery centers on brother and sister pair Fidelio and Leonora Carver, writer and stage designer for the theater, who are chillingly murdered. Fidelio by an Irish paramilitary leader, Lenora by a British military policeman.

Arden's book received mixed critical reviews. Caute remarked that the novel "is a grim tale in which the make-believe radicalism of the fringe theatre encounters the distinctly untheatrical blood-letting of an Irish nationalism bitterly at war with the British state." However, Caute satirically faulted Arden for his portrayal of some of the female characters: "His portrait of the hysterical radical Carmilla Costello alone is worth a boycott." *Observer* reviewer Michael Coveney found the novel "ramshackle and unruly to the point of indecent excess," yet declared that it "never flags or fails to engage."

Writing in the *International Dictionary of Theatre,* Laurel Brake summarized Arden's career: "A consciousness of society and politics as well as the individual informs John Arden's work as a playwright, critic, and actor. In almost any context one attempts to place him he appears, to his credit, abrasive and anomalous. Loosely implicated in the 'angry young men' group of the 1950s, he countered the commitment of their work with a resolute disengagement; as the universities have expanded to include modern drama in the syllabus of the academy, he observes the tyranny of the 'literary' text of the play and the mistaken valuation of the 'objective'; and as state subsidies have created a secure and, some might say, 'entrenched' British theatre, Arden criticizes a system where selection and production of plays are determined by a director-administrator whose policies are administrative rather than artistic."

In 1997, Arden told *CA* that "since 1978 all my dramatic writing has been for radio. The theatre, whether in Britain or Ireland, has seemed neither able nor willing to provide decent working conditions for playwrights to develop new work in a way which I could cope with. In Britain, this has been largely due to economic reasons: scarcity of resources has led to smaller casts, a terror of taking risks (particularly in the area of political comment), and a significant growth of *bureaucratic* rather than *artistic* control of the business. Public funding for the arts has become subject to the interference of reactionary political policies, while private investment gives priority to creative work suitable for Corporate Image-enhancement. Between the two, the dramatist with something to say is intolerably squeezed. Radio, alas, is now succumbing to these pressures.

"In Ireland there are similar restrictions, with a slightly different colour: a recently developed, officially stimulated (but tacit) *cultural consensus* demands that artists and writers should be part of what might be called 'the authentic national and/or community voice,' as interpreted and reinterpreted in the shifting light of current political developments. This is a category into which it appears I fail to fit, even when I collaborate with the authentically Irish Margaretta D'Arcy, and even though we have lived and worked in the country for over thirty years.

"I have therefore spent most of my time over the last decade-and-a-half writing stories of various sizes, some of them quite short (as in *Cogs Tyrannic*), others extremely long (*Books of Bale* and *Jack Juggler*); up to now I have been lucky enough to have had them accepted for publication. Nearly all of them have dealt in some way with the theatre and its social/political background in various periods of history—ancient Rome in *Silence among the Weapons* (*Vox Pop* for U.S. readers); 16th-century England and Ireland in *Books of Bale;* early 19th-century England in *Cogs Tyrannic;* my own lifetime in another of the *Cogs Tyrannic* tales and in most of *Jack Juggler. Jack Juggler* also includes a theatrical episode of the mid-18th century. I suppose all these stories are concerned with the ability—or inability—of drama and its practitioners to cope with the world beyond the stage, with political lies and suppressions, with overt wars and covert treacheries, with the vagaries of patronage, with the harsh demands of sexual desire and the exigencies of sexual custom at any given time.

"I feel that I have more or less worked these themes out of my system: I really don't know where I'm going to go from here."

Where Arden returned was to the world of radio, a fertile arena with the British Broadcasting Corporation commissioning several hundred plays each year. During the 1990s, he created such plays as *Little Novels of Wilkie Collins,* and *Woe Alas, the Fatal Cash-Box!* The later deals with a frequently used setting, the British public school (equivalent to a private school in the United States), and focuses on the public school experiences of Julius Applewick. A heart-attack victim, Applewick, languishing in a hospital, experiences a series of flashbacks, including being falsely accused of embezzlement. London *Guardian* reviewer Anne Karpf recalled Arden's award-winning 1978 drama *Pearl* and compared *Woe Alas* favorably with it: "Here again he writes with brio and comic indignation, treating the central incidents as melodrama." She concluded that while there are many works based on public school experiences, Arden's is "rich in sap."

BIOGRAPHICAL AND CRITICAL SOURCES:

BOOKS

Anderson, Michael, *Anger and Detachment: A Study of Arden, Osborne and Pinter,* Pitman (London, England), 1976.

Armstrong, William A., general editor, *Experimental Drama*, G. Bell & Sons (London, England), 1963.

Brandt, G. W., *Contemporary Theatre*, Stratford-upon-Avon Studies 4, Edward Arnold (London, England), 1962.

Brown, John Russell, *Theatre Language: A Study of Arden, Osborne, Pinter, and Wesker*, Allen Lane (London, England), 1972.

Contemporary Authors Autobiography Series, Volume 4, Gale (Detroit, MI), 1986.

Contemporary Dramatists, 5th edition, St. James Press (Detroit, MI), 1993.

Contemporary Literary Criticism, Gale (Detroit, MI), Volume 6, 1976, Volume 13, 1980, Volume 15, 1980.

Dictionary of Literary Biography, Volume 13: *British Dramatists since World War II*, Gale (Detroit, MI), 1982.

Gilman, Richard, *Common and Uncommon Masks: Writings on Theatre, 1961-1970*, Random House (New York, NY), 1971.

Gray, Frances, *John Arden*, Grove Press (New York, NY), 1982.

Hayman, Ronald, *John Arden*, Heinemann Educational Books (London, England), 1968.

Hinchcliffe, Arnold P., *British Theatre 1950-1970*, Rowman & Littlefield (London, England), 1974.

Hunt, Albert, *Arden: A Study of His Plays*, Eyre Methuen (Oxford, England), 1974.

International Dictionary of Theatre, Volume 2: *Playwrights*, St. James Press (Detroit, MI), 1994.

Kennedy, Andrew K., *Six Dramatists in Search of a Language: Studies in Dramatic Language*, Cambridge University Press (Cambridge, England), 1975.

Leeming, Glenda, *John Arden*, edited by Ian Scott-Kilvert, Longman (Harlow, England), 1974.

Lowenfels, Walter, editor, *The Playwrights Speak*, Delacorte (New York, NY), 1967.

Lumley, Frederick, *New Trends in 20th Century Drama: A Survey since Ibsen and Shaw*, Oxford University Press (Oxford, England), 1967.

Malick, Javed, *Toward a Theatre of the Oppressed: The Dramaturgy of John Arden*, University of Michigan Press (Ann Arbor, MI), 1995.

Marowitz, Charles *The Encore Reader: A Chronicle of New Drama*, Methuen & Co. (London, England), 1965.

Page, Malcolm, *John Arden*, Twayne (Boston, MA), 1984.

Page, Malcolm, editor, *Arden on File*, Methuen (New York, NY), 1985.

Roy, Emil, *British Drama since Shaw*, Southern Illinois University Press (Carbondale, IL), 1972.

Schvey, Henry I., *From Paradox to Propaganda: The Plays of John Arden*, Hueber (Munich, Germany), 1981.

Taylor, John Russell, *Anger and After: A Guide to the New British Drama*, Methuen (London, England), 1962.

Thomson, Peter, *Plays in Production*, Cambridge University Press (Cambridge, England), 1997, pp. 159-162.

Trussler, Simon, *John Arden*, Columbia University Press (New York, NY), 1973.

Tschudin, Marcus, *A Writer's Theatre: George Devine and the English Stage Company at the Royal Court, 1956-1965*, Lang (London, England), 1972.

Wellworth, George, *The Theatre of Protest and Paradox*, New York University Press (New York, NY), 1964.

Wike, Jonathan, *John Arden and Margaretta D'Arcy: A Casebook*, Garland (New York, NY), 1995.

Williams, Raymond, *Drama from Ibsen to Brecht*, Oxford University Press (Oxford, England), 1969.

Winkler, Elizabeth Hale, "Modern Melodrama: The Living Heritage in the Theatre of John Arden and Margaretta D'Arcy," in *Melodrama*, edited by James Redmond, Cambridge University Press (Cambridge, England), 1992, pp. 255-267.

Worth, Katherine, editor, *Revolutions in Modern English Drama*, Bell (London, England), 1972, pp. 126-135.

PERIODICALS

Contemporary Literature, summer, 1991, Georg Gaston, "An Interview with John Arden," pp. 147-170.

Cross Currents, summer, 1991, Diana Culbertson, "Sacred Victims: Catharsis in the Modern Theatre," pp. 179-194.

Dalhousie Review, fall, 1977, M. W. Steinberg, review of *The Hero Rises Up*, pp. 437-438.

Drama Survey, summer, 1967; winter, 1968.

Guardian (London, England), July 24, 1999, Anne Karpf, "One Small Theft for a Boy," review of *Woe Alas, the Fatal Cash-Box!*, p. 4.

Hibbert Journal, fall, 1966.

Modern Drama, December, 1968, Joan Tindale Blindheim, p. 316; March, 1978, Craig Clinton, review of *The Hero Rise Up*, pp. 55-56; June, 1985,

Michael Cohen, "The Politics of the Earlier Arden," pp. 198-210; March, 1983, Helena Forsas Scott, "Life and Love and Sergeant Musgrave: An Approach to Arden's Play," pp. 1-11.

New Statesman, December 17, 1965, Ronald Bryden, review of *Serjeant Musgrave's Dance,* p. 979; April 11, 1980.

Observer (London), July 11, 1965, Penelope Gilliatt, review of *Serjeant Musgrave's Dance,* p. 21; September 24, 1995, p. 16.

Panjab University Research Bulletin (Arts), October, 1983, Ishwar Dutt, "The Rebel and the Tyrant: An Analysis of Violence in *Serjeant Musgrave's Dance,*" pp. 143-155; April 17, 1986, P. C. David, "Poetry in the Drama of John Arden," pp. 41-50.

Review of English Literature, October, 1966, J. D. Hainsworth, pp. 47-48.

Theatre Research International, fall, 1980, Redmond O'Hanlon, "The Theatrical Values of John Arden," pp. 218-236; spring, 1990, Michael Cohen, "A Defense of D'Arcy and Arden's *Non-Stop Connolly Show,*" pp. 78-88.

Times Literary Supplement, January 7, 1965; March 3, 1978; August 27, 1982; September 29, 1995, p. 24.

Tulane Drama Review, winter, 1966, Richard Gilman, pp. 55-56.

* * *

ASHTON, Dianne 1949-

PERSONAL: Born June 21, 1949, in Buffalo, NY; daughter of Irving (in business) and Miriam (a bookkeeper; maiden name, Keller) Ashton; married Richard M. Drucker (a teacher), October 23, 1988. *Ethnicity:* "Jewish." *Education:* Adelphi University, B.A., 1971; studied at Kibbutz Palmach Tsuba, Israel, 1971; University of Massachusetts—Amherst, graduate study, 1975; Temple University, M.A., 1982, Ph.D. (with distinction), 1986. *Politics:* Democrat. *Religion:* Jewish. *Hobbies and other interests:* Travel, music, art, reading.

ADDRESSES: *Home*—Cherry Hill, NJ. *Office*—Department of Philosophy and Religion, Bunce Hall, Rowan University, 201 Mullica Hill Rd., Glassboro, NJ 08028-1701. E-mail—ashtond@rowan.edu.

CAREER: La Salle University, Philadelphia, PA, lecturer in religion, 1986-88; University of Pennsylvania, Philadelphia, PA, teacher of general studies, 1987; Rowan University, Glassboro, NJ, professor of religion, 1987—, director of American studies, and past chair of Department of Philosophy and Religion. Lecturer at Gratz College and Netzky Institute, 1986-88; Rutgers University, lecturer, 1988; guest lecturer at colleges and universities, including University of Utah, 1989, Temple University, 1992, Ocean County College, Bergen County College, and University of Maryland—College Park, all 1993, and University of Minnesota—Twin Cities, 1996.

AWARDS, HONORS: American Jewish Archives, Franklin fellowship, 1984, Rapoport fellowship, 1988, Marguerite R. Jacobs fellowship, 1999; *Rebecca Gratz: Women and Judaism in Antebellum America* was selected as recommended reading by New Jersey Council for the Humanities, 1998; grant from International Research Institute on Jewish Women.

WRITINGS:

(Editor, with Ellen M. Umansky, and coauthor of introductions) *Four Centuries of Jewish Women's Spirituality: A Sourcebook,* Beacon Press (Boston, MA), 1992.

The Philadelphia Group: A Guide to Archival and Bibliographic Collections, Center for American Jewish History, Temple University (Philadelphia, PA), 1993.

Rebecca Gratz: Women and Judaism in Antebellum America, Wayne State University Press (Detroit, MI), 1997.

Jewish Life in Pennsylvania, Pennsylvania Historical Association, (University Park, PA) 1998.

Contributor to books, including *Communication Theory and Interpersonal Interaction,* edited by Sari Thomas, Ablex Publishing (Norwood, NJ), 1984; *When Philadelphia Was the Capital of Jewish America,* edited by Murray Friedman, Associated University Presses (Philadelphia, PA), 1993; *Active Voices: Women in Jewish Culture,* edited by Maurie Sacks, University of Illinois Press (Urbana, IL), 1995; *Religions of the United States in Practice,* edited by Colleen McDannell, Princeton University Press (Princeton, NJ), 2001; and *Women and American Judaism: Historical Perspectives,* edited by Pamela S. Nadell and Jonathan D. Sarna, Brandeis University Press (Hanover, NJ), 2001. Contributor to periodicals, including *Religious Studies Review, American Jewish History, Jewish Folklore and Ethnology Review, Liturgy,* and *Transformations.*

WORK IN PROGRESS: Research on holidays and rituals in American Jewish life.

SIDELIGHTS: Dianne Ashton once told *CA:* "I have loved the process of writing since childhood. I became an academic because I could always find something to write about by researching other people's lives, even if I could not come up with a story of my own.

"I find the conditions of human life fascinating and religion in all its permutations—belief, material artifacts, culture—probably the most curious thing about being human. I am grateful that so many people appreciate my written work, which emerges almost completely out of my own interests. I pay close attention to the work of scholars I admire in the fields of American studies, Jewish studies, and women's studies, but my research projects appeal primarily to me. I hope they will please others when they are completed. I enjoy the process.

"When I write, I sit down at the computer and just pour words onto the screen as fast as I think of them. I organize, edit, substantiate, cite, and generally improve the flow as I go along. I do countless revisions, but I like revising. I like figuring out better ways to shape a sentence, paragraph, chapter, or phrase.

"I prefer to write about topics that allow me to explore issues and subtleties in American religious life. I think scholarship is more interesting when it is exploring nuances and seeming contradictions than when it is telling a single narrative that overarches a historical era. Nonetheless, I think narrative structure is crucial in a volume. The reader has to like the book! My challenge is to construct an enjoyable, readable, credible, and intellectually challenging book out of the complexities in the material that I have researched. I find it fun."

* * *

ATKINSON, Rick 1952-

PERSONAL: Born Lawrence Rush Atkinson, IV, November 16, 1952, in Munich, West Germany (now Germany); U.S. citizen; son of Larry (a lieutenant colonel in the U.S. Army) and Margaret Jean (a

Rick Atkinson

teacher; maiden name, Howe) Atkinson; married Jane Ann Chestnut (a dentist), May 12, 1979; children: Rush, Sarah. *Education:* East Carolina State University, B.A., 1974; University of Chicago, M.A., 1975.

ADDRESSES: Home—6646 Barnaby St. NW, Washington, DC 20015. *Office*—1150 15th St. NW, Washington, DC 20071. *Agent*—Raphael Sagalyn, The Sagalyn Literary Agency, 4825 Bethesda Ave., Ste. 302, Bethesda, MD 20814.

CAREER: Pittsburg Morning Sun, Pittsburg, KS, reporter, 1976-77; *Kansas City Times,* Kansas City, MO, reporter, 1977-83; *Washington Post,* Washington, DC, investigative reporter, 1983—, deputy national editor, 1985-87, Berlin (Germany) bureau chief, 1993-96, assistant managing editor for projects, 1996—. Guest on television programs, including *Good Morning America.*

AWARDS, HONORS: Pulitzer Prize for National Reporting from Columbia Graduate School of Journalism, 1982; Livingston Award for international reporting from University of Michigan; George Polk Award from Long Island University; John Hancock Award for excellence in business and financial journalism from John Hancock Mutual Life Insurance Co.; other awards in journalism.

WRITINGS:

The Long Gray Line: The American Journey of West Point's Class of 1966, Houghton Mifflin (Boston, MA), 1989.
Crusade: The Untold Story of the Persian Gulf War, Houghton Mifflin (Boston, MA), 1993.
An Army at Dawn: The War in North Africa, 1942-1943, Henry Holt (New York, NY), 2002.

SIDELIGHTS: Rick Atkinson is a Pulitzer Prize-winning journalist whose first book, *The Long Gray Line,* received widespread critical attention. Subtitled *The American Journey of West Point's Class of 1966,* the book focuses on one generation of army officers and the tremendous impact the Vietnam War had on their lives. For the book Atkinson conducted dozens of interviews with class members and their families, and the result is both a historical study and a group biography that *Business Week* reviewer Dave Griffiths called, "the best book out of Vietnam to-date."

When the book's subjects entered the United States Military Academy at West Point as cadets in 1962, they were naive and idealistic, inspired by the academy's motto—Duty, Honor, Country—and by President John F. Kennedy's challenge to "pay any price, bear any burden" for their country. Four difficult years at West Point did little to dampen their patriotic enthusiasm, but by the time they graduated in 1966, the U.S. Government had started sending soldiers to Vietnam to battle the communist North Vietnamese Army for control of the country. The conflict was not yet a divisive issue among the American public, and the cadets expected to "storm across the Pacific, win the war, and return to ticker tape parades, as their fathers had," noted Griffiths. In the next several years, though, the U.S. government's war strategy proved insufficient for gaining control of the country; the heavy American firepower had little effect on the mobile, flexible enemy army, and large numbers of U.S. troops died for minute territorial gains. As casualties mounted and the war effort stalled, many Americans turned against the war, blaming not only the government that directed the war but also the soldiers who fought in it. The United States conceded the country to the North Vietnamese and pulled out of Vietnam in 1973, but the war remained a contentious public issue for many more years.

Vietnam had a tremendous impact on West Point. Faced with widespread resignations after the war ended, the academy was further weakened by a massive cadet cheating scandal that surfaced in 1976. And the admission of women into West Point that same year caused significant turmoil. Not until the 1980s—with the onset of President Ronald Reagan's pro-military rhetoric and the successful 1983 invasion of Grenada, a tiny country in the West Indies that had been led by a Marxist government—did West Point begin to regain its stellar reputation among the American public.

Of the West Point classes that fought in Vietnam, the class of 1966 was hardest hit: thirty out of the class total of 579 died in the war, and more than one hundred were wounded. Among those who died were Buck Thompson, a popular cadet who was mortally wounded when American bombs were dropped in the wrong area, and Frank Rybicki, Jr., who was accidentally killed by his own rifle. Others survived but were badly injured, such as Bill Haneke, who lost a leg, an eye, and part of a foot in Vietnam. Three of the main characters in *The Long Gray Line,* John Wheeler, Tom Carhart, and George Crocker, survived the war but took widely varying paths after it ended. Wheeler and Carhart both resigned their commissions—as did many of their classmates—and became lawyers. Later, they were passionately involved in the efforts to build a memorial to veterans of the war but became enemies in the process: while Wheeler favored the final design—a long, stark stretch of black marble with engraved names of those who died in the war—Carhart was bitterly opposed to it. Unlike Wheeler and Carhart, Crocker's faith in the sanctity of the Army never wavered. He retained his commission after Vietnam ended and eventually became a full colonel.

Atkinson's ability to portray the complexities and scope of these characters' lives drew praise from critics, who noted that this feature gives his book an intimacy and drama normally found in fiction. *Boston Sunday Globe* contributor Cullen Murphy, for instance, commented that "although it is a work of nonfiction, *The Long Gray Line* shares the force and sweep of a *Ben Hur* or *Gone with the Wind.* The cast of characters is vast, and we see them grow and change and interact over a period of two full decades. . . .The result is an awesome feat of biographical reconstruction." Likewise, in his *Philadelphia Inquirer* review Nicholas Proffitt characterized the book as "a compelling collection of personal stories—stories that inspire even as they break your heart. . . .Through Atkinson's meticulous research, we are there during each phase of the cadets' epic journey, there to savor their successes and wince at their failures. We live with them and, in some cases, we die with them." Other critics had particular praise for the author's depiction of the subjects' early years at the academy. Atkinson "provides a remarkable picture of cadet life and of West Point itself," noted James Salter in the *Washington Post Book World.* He added: "The four years at West Point have a powerful romantic aura. . . .You come to have enormous sympathy for the main characters and the classmates who surround them."

Some reviewers felt that *The Long Gray Line*—at almost six hundred pages—is overlong and that the author attempts to tell too many stories. Writing in the Chicago *Tribune Books,* John Eisenhower commented that "in this otherwise brilliant book, [Atkinson] is guilty of overkill. He tries to characterize too many young men, as well as their wives and sweethearts, and as a result all but a few are two-dimensional." *New York Times Book Review* contributor Tom Buckley was more harsh, stating that *The Long Gray Line* "is not so much expanded as bloated—a shapeless grab bag, lacking selectivity, synthesis, a theme or, aside from an uncritical sympathy for one and all, a point of view." And Brian Mitchell of the *National Review* pointed out Atkinson's emphasis on description rather than critical commentary, stating: "The author should make some sense of things."

Still, Mitchell concluded that the book's myriad scenes "are often poignant and compelling, and Atkinson's stars are the kind of characters a novelist would invent if they had not been born." Proffitt praised the author's ability to tell his story through "brief and poetic narratives." "Enormously rich in detail and written with a novelist's brilliance," stated Proffitt, "the pages literally hurry before one." Members of West Point's class of 1966 praised Atkinson's objectivity and accuracy. Reviewing the book in the *Washington Times,* John Wheeler commented: "Why did the class of 1966 bare its soul to a Pulitzer Prize-winning investigative reporter? Because we trust him." The class's regard for the author was evident in October, 1989, when about one hundred former classmates held a ceremony in honor of Atkinson and his book and presented him with a saber. As quoted by *People* magazine correspondent Linda Kramer, the inscription on the saber read: "With Deep Appreciation for What You Have Given to Our Class and The Long Gray Line."

Atkinson once told *CA:* "My interest in the West Point class of 1966 was piqued in 1981 when a graduate from the class, Michael B. Fuller, mentioned that his fifteenth reunion was coming up. I attended the reunion and began what was to be an eight-year effort to reconstruct the tale of this remarkable group of young men."

Atkinson's 1993 work, *Crusade: The Untold Story of the Persian Gulf War,* is a detailed study of the war, events leading up to it, its progression, and its aftermath. Atkinson drew on his own experiences as a journalist in Saudi Arabia during the war; copious military after-action reports; and more than 500 interviews with participants in the war to create this narrative account of the conflict. In *Technology Review,* Jonathan B. Tucker wrote, "Unlike other recent histories, *Crusade* resists the temptation to romanticize its subject and instead provides a clear-eyed, skeptical assessment of the war, the soldiers who fought it, and the weapons they used." Atkinson explores the Pentagon's assertions about the accuracy of its "precision-guided" weapons—proven in combat to be much less accurate than the military claimed, hitting only 25 percent of their targets—and notes that like all wars, the Persian Gulf War was "unpredictable, cruel, and violent, damning the innocent and the guilty alike." In *National Interest,* Paul Wolfowitz wrote that the book "provides a valuable perspective on the conflict," and in the *Economist,* a reviewer noted, "This is among the best books yet written about the Gulf War."

In 2002 Atkinson published *An Army at Dawn: The War in North Africa, 1942-1943,* the first volume of a planned trilogy about the liberation of Europe during World War II. This volume examines the invasion of North Africa by the Allies, which influenced many of the subsequent events of the war. Atkinson relies on battlefield reports and archival material to tell the story of the North African campaign. A *Kirkus Reviews* writer called this "the most thorough and satisfying" history of the North African campaign.

BIOGRAPHICAL AND CRITICAL SOURCES:

BOOKS

Bestsellers 90, Issue 2, Gale (Detroit, MI), 1990.

PERIODICALS

Booklist, August 16, 1993, p. 91; September 1, 1993, John Mort, review of *Crusade: The Untold Story of the Persian Gulf War,* p. 2; November 1, 1996, Karen Harris, review of *Crusade,* p. 522; August, 2002, Gilbert Taylor, review of *An Army at Dawn: The War in North Africa, 1942-1943,* p. 1882.
Boston Sunday Globe, October 1, 1989.
Business Week, October 23, 1989; December 27, 1993, Russell Mitchell, review of *Crusade,* p. 20.
Choice, February, 1994, R. Higham, review of *Crusade,* p. 985.
Contemporary Review, May, 2003, review of *An Army at Dawn,* p. 317.
Economist, January 15, 1994, review of *Crusade,* p. 93.
Foreign Affairs, May-June, 1994, Eliot A. Cohen, review of *Crusade,* p. 141.
Journal of Military History, January, 1994, Steve E. Dietrich, review of *Crusade,* p. 174.
Kirkus Reviews, July 15, 2002, review of *An Army at Dawn,* p.1001.
Library Journal, October 15, 1993, Nader Entessar, review of *Crusade,* p. 78; May 15, 1996, Michael T. Fein, review of *Crusade,* p. 101; August, 2002, Mark Ellis, review of *An Army at Dawn,* p. 114.
National Interest, spring, 1994, Paul Wolfowitz, review of *Crusade,* p. 87.
National Review, November 24, 1989.
New Republic, October 11, 1993, Edward Luttwak, review of *Crusade,* p. 47.
New York Times Book Review, October 22, 1989; November 28, 1993, Mark Laity, review of *Crusade,* p. 16.
People, October 30, 1989.
Philadelphia Inquirer, October 15, 1989.
Publishers Weekly, August 16, 1993, review of *Crusade,* p. 91; July 8, 2002, review of *An Army at Dawn,* p. 38.
Survival, summer, 1995, Jeffrey D. McCausland, review of *Crusade,* p. 163.
Technology Review, May-June, 1994, Jonathan B. Tucker, review of *Crusade,* p. 67.
Time, October 30, 1989.
Tribune Books (Chicago, IL), October 1, 1989.
USA Today, October 13, 1989.
U.S. News and World Report, October 9, 1989.
Wall Street Journal, October 12, 1993, John Lehman, review of *Crusade,* p. A18.
Washington Post Book World, October 8, 1989.
Washington Times, October 9, 1989.*

* * *

AZOULAY, Dan 1960-

PERSONAL: Born June 17, 1960, in Toronto, Ontario, Canada; married Raya Neumann, 1984; children: Alyssa, Adam. *Education:* University of Toronto, B.A., 1983; York University, M.A., Ph.D., 1991.

ADDRESSES: Home—1005 Lemar Rd., Newmarket, Ontario L3Y 1S2, Canada. *Office*—Department of History, McMaster University, 1280 Main St. W, Hamilton, Ontario L8S 4L8, Canada. *E-mail*—dazoulay@yorku.ca.

CAREER: Trent University, Peterborough, Ontario, Canada, sessional instructor, 1989-2002; McMaster University, Hamilton, Ontario, Canada, sessional instructor, 1992—; York University, North York, Ontario, Canada, sessional instructor in history, 1995—; University of Toronto, Toronto, Ontario, Canada, sessional instructor, 2002—.

WRITINGS:

Keeping the Dream Alive: The Survival of the Ontario CCF/NDP, 1950-1963, McGill-Queen's University Press (Montreal, Quebec, Canada), 1997.
(Editor) *Canadian Political Parties: Historical Readings,* Irwin (Toronto, Ontario, Canada), 1999.
Only the Lonely: Finding Romance in the Personal Columns of Canada's Western Home Monthly, 1905-1924, Fifth House Publishers (Calgary, Alberta, Canada), 2000.

Contributor to books, including *Papers in Post-Confederation Ontario History*, edited by E. A. Montigny and L. Chambers, University of Toronto Press (Toronto, Ontario, Canada), 2000. Contributor of articles and reviews to periodicals, including *Journal of Women's History, Ontario History, Labour/Le Travail, Journal of Commonwealth and Comparative Politics*, and *Canadian Historical Review.*

WORK IN PROGRESS: A history of romance in Canada, 1900-1930.

SIDELIGHTS: Dan Azoulay told *CA:* "I am motivated to make Canadian history more accessible to the average person, and I want to contribute to the body of knowledge in my field. I really enjoy wading through historical documents and then piecing bits of evidence together to recreate an era long past. It's a bit like traveling in time and being an investigator all at once. I am influenced by popular historians and journalists who seem to bring history to life better than professional historians do."

B

BAHR, Mary (Madelyn) 1946-

PERSONAL: Born May 20, 1946, in Bemidji, MN; daughter of Frederick J. (a commercial printer) and Frances Mary (a homemaker; maiden name, Larson) Bahr; married Bill James Fritts (a banker), December 27, 1969; children: Jason Erik, Joshua Adam, Jordan Patrick, Jeremy Zachariah. *Education:* College of St. Catherine, B.S., 1968. *Hobbies and other interests:* Reading, writing, visiting zoos, volunteering with son at the humane society, comedy, music, cats.

ADDRESSES: Home and office—807 Hercules Place, Colorado Springs, CO 80906-1130.

CAREER: Minnesota Department of Corrections, library trainee, 1968-69; Presbyterian Medical Center, Denver, CO, medical librarian, 1969-70, registrar of Nursing School, 1971-74; church librarian, 1978-80; Cobb County Public Library, library assistant, 1981-84; Pikes Peak Library District, information and reference technician at Penrose Library, 1990—. Church librarian in Marietta, GA, 1981-84; Cheyenne Mountain School District, member of special education advisory committee, 1991—; volunteer at libraries in Kansas, Georgia, and Colorado. Speaker and leader of workshops.

MEMBER: International Reading Association, Society of Children's Book Writers and Illustrators, Rocky Mountain Society of Children's Book Writers (member of the board, 1990-92; retreat director, 1990-91), Colorado Authors League (member of the board, 1996-97).

AWARDS, HONORS: Writing grant, Highlights Foundation, 1988; Notable Trade Book in Social Studies, National Council for the Social Studies and Children's Book Council, 1992, for *The Memory Box;* Magazine Merit Honor, Society of Children's Book Writers and Illustrators, 1992, for "Letter to a President"; Top Hand Awards, Colorado Author's League, 1993, for *The Memory Box,* "Two Fishermen," and "Letter to a President," and 1994, for "A Little Life Music"; Conference Grant, Colorado Author's League, 1994 and 1996.

WRITINGS:

The Memory Box, illustrated by David Cunningham, Albert Whitman (Morton Grove, IL), 1992.
Jordi's Run, Royal Fireworks, 1997.
If Nathan Were Here, illustrated by Karen A. Jerome, Eerdmans (Grand Rapids, MI), 2000.
My Brother Loved Snowflakes: The Story of Wilson A. Bentley, the Snowflake Man, Boyds Mills Press (Honesdale, PA), 2002.

Contributor to books, including *Guiltless Catholic Parenting from A to Y,* Charis (Ann Arbor, MI), 1995; *God's Abundance: 365 Days to a Simple Life,* Starburst (Lancaster, PA), 1997; *God's Vitamin C for the Hurting Spirit,* Starburst (Lancaster, PA), 1997. Columnist for *New Writer's Magazine,* 1991-93; reviewer for *Five Owls,* 1993—. Contributor of stories, articles, and poems to magazines, including *Living with Children, Liguorian, Writer's Digest, Woman's Touch,* and *Our Little Friend.*

ADAPTATIONS: The Memory Box has been recorded on audio cassette and released by Harcourt Brace (New York, NY), 1996.

SIDELIGHTS: Mary Bahr's books for children have taken on difficult subjects, including Alzheimer's disease and the death of a child. Her first novel, *The Memory Box*, is a story of a young boy who is unexpectedly presented with his grandfather's memory loss due to Alzheimer's disease. Zach, the protagonist, is enthralled by his grandfather's stories every summer, but one summer there is a difference. He finds that his grandfather is not as apt to tell stories as he is to start filling a box with memories of the past. Zach's grandmother encourages him to help with the box, but he does not truly understand why until his grandfather wanders off one day, returning confused and in tears. The elderly man is slowly losing his memory to Alzheimer's. *School Library Journal* reviewer Judy Constantinides called *The Memory Box* "a moving, sympathetic, and ultimately comforting book." And a *Publishers Weekly* contributor added that "love and reassurance fill these pages—along with the sadness of loss and knowledge that there is more to come."

The subject of *If Nathan Were Here* is equally poignant. The story begins with a boy thinking of all the things he would be enjoying if only his best friend, Nathan, were with him. Midway through the book, it is revealed that Nathan has died. The children in his class at school are encouraged to cope with their feelings of loss by creating a memory box, in which they can place tokens of remembrance. The grieving child has no idea what to put in the box, and spends some time in a tree fort he shared with Nathan, thinking it over. His feelings of loss are "simply expressed" and "sympathetic," according to Patricia Pearl Dole in *School Library Journal*. While the story has a "hopeful message," it is all the more worthwhile because it does not offer easy answers, stated Connie Fletcher in *Booklist*. The depiction of grief "feels very real," commented a *Publishers Weekly* reviewer.

Bahr turned to biography with *My Brother Loved Snowflakes: The Story of Wilson A. Bentley, the Snowflake Man*. Wilson Bentley became famous for his pioneering work in photography, using snowflakes as his subjects. Bahr chose to relate Bentley's life from the perspective of the photographer's older brother, Charlie. Her book, which is intended for an elementary-school audience, offers the "emotional heart of the story" rather than cold facts, related Kathleen Kelly MacMillan in *School Library Journal*. MacMillan noted that the book is unclear as to the source of the information presented, but concluded that using Charlie's voice proves an effective way to create "an affectionate and moving portrait" of this unique photographer.

Bahr once told *CA:* "When asked how I became a writer, I answer 'accidentally.' I then go on to explain how my journey really did begin with an accident; how I didn't choose writing so much as writing chose me.

"When I graduated from high school in northern Minnesota, I headed for college in southern Minnesota to become a nurse. I had wanted to be a nurse ever since first grade. But during my third year, while training on a geriatric floor, I came to work one morning to discover that a favorite patient had died during the night. I was upset for a very long time and realized that nursing was not for me. Since the only things I loved as much as the thought of being a nurse were reading, books, and libraries, I decided to become a librarian.

"Oddly enough, my first job after graduation was as a librarian in a hospital library. During this time I met and married Bill Fritts and we became the parents of four sons—Jason, Joshua, Jordan, and Jeremy—the four reasons I eventually began writing for children. They reminded me of growing up and all the powerful feelings that went along with it—the thrill of skating on the lake as the ice cracked, the excitement of riding atop a float in the fourth of July parade, the pride of building a tree fort in the woods, the sadness of walking alone to school while a best friend walked with someone else, the terror of being bullied by a girl on the playground, the panic of a piano recital, the nervousness of being a radio show hostess, the joy of climbing out of a canoe in the middle of the lake, and the ecstasy of falling in love for the first time.

"For the next few years I worked as a church librarian, in a school library, accounting firm library, public library and a library for parole officers of juvenile offenders. But an accident—a horrible accident—changed all of that. One sunshiny Saturday morning, our three-year-old fell under the wheel of a car. I had to pull him out from underneath the wheels and try to stop the bleeding as his brothers screamed in the back seat and Bill barreled through traffic to the hospital. While the small hand was operated on three times, something moved me to write about the incredible people who helped our family survive this nightmare.

The editor for whom I was writing book reviews for the library suggested I send the piece to *Parish Family Digest.* I sent it. They published it, and I've been writing ever since. That's how writing chose me, and that's how I finally discovered what I wanted to be when I grew up.

"I write for children and adults—fiction and nonfiction—books and magazine articles—serious and not so serious—on lots of things that only have one thing in common—they're subjects or ideas or people that I care about—that I'm passionate about—that I must write about.

"For those who ask 'how' to begin the writing journey, the simplest advice I give is 'read what you want to write, and write what you want to read.' But you'd better write it with a passion because if you don't, nobody will want to read your words. . . . If we have a dream, and if we work hard to make that dream come true, I truly believe it will. The trick?. . . . Never, never, never give up."

BIOGRAPHICAL AND CRITICAL SOURCES:

PERIODICALS

Booklist, February 15, 1992, Ilene Cooper, review of *The Memory Box,* p. 1106; April 15, 2000, Connie Fletcher, review of *If Nathan Were Here,* p. 1550.
Bulletin of the Center for Children's Books, February, 1992, p. 148.
Gazette (Colorado Springs, CO), May 21, 2000, review of *If Nathan Were Here,* p. T&B5.
Horn Book Guide, fall, 1992, p. 222.
Magpies, November, 1993, p. 31.
Publishers Weekly, March 30, 1992, review of *The Memory Box,* p. 105; September 25, 1995, p. 58; April 3, 2000, review of *If Nathan Were Here,* p. 80.
School Library Journal, September, 1992, Judy Constantinides, review of *The Memory Box,* p. 196; August, 2000, Patricia Pearl Dole, review of *If Nathan Were Here,* p. 144; September, 2000, review of *My Brother Loved Snowflakes: The Story of Wilson A. Bentley, the Snowflake Man,* p. 209; September, 2002, Kathleen Kelly MacMillan, review of *My Brother Loved Snowflakes,* p. 209.*

BAILEY, Paul 1937-

PERSONAL: Born Peter Harry Bailey, February 16, 1937, in Battersea, London, England; son of Arthur Oswald and Helen (Burgess) Bailey. *Education:* Attended London Central School of Speech and Drama, 1953-56. *Politics:* "Socialist." *Religion:* "Agnostic." *Hobbies and other interests:* Music, literature, tennis.

ADDRESSES: Home—79 Davisville Rd., London W12 9SH, England.

CAREER: Actor, educator, novelist, and playwright. Actor, 1956-63, on television and with the Stratford and Royal Court theatres in London, England; full-time writer. University of Newcastle upon Tyne and University of Durham, literary fellow, 1972-74; North Dakota State University, Fargo, visiting lecturer, 1977-79. Formerly worked in retail.

AWARDS, HONORS: Arts Council of Great Britain Award and Somerset Maugham Travel Award, both 1968, both for *At the Jerusalem;* Authors' Club Award, 1970; E. M. Forster Award, National Institute of Arts and Letters, 1974; Bicentennial Arts fellow, 1976; George Orwell Memorial Prize, 1976; shortlisted for Booker Prize for Fiction, 1977, for *Peter Smart's Confessions,* and 1986, for *Gabriel's Lament;* Royal Society of Literature fellow, 1982.

WRITINGS:

NOVELS

At the Jerusalem, Atheneum (New York, NY), 1967.
Trespasses, J. Cape (London, England), 1970, Harper (New York, NY), 1971.
A Distant Likeness, J. Cape (London, England), 1973.
Peter Smart's Confessions, J. Cape (London, England), 1977.
Old Soldiers, J. Cape (London, England), 1980.
Gabriel's Lament, J. Cape (London, England), 1986, Viking (New York, NY), 1987.
Sugar Cane, Bloomsbury (London, England), 1993.
(Editor) *First Love,* Dent (London, England), 1997.
Kitty and Virgil, Fourth Estate (London, England), 1998, Overlook Press (New York, NY), 2000.

Paul Bailey

Uncle Rudolf, Fourth Estate (London, England), 2002.

PLAYS

At Cousin Henry's (radio play), 1964.
A Worthy Guest, produced in Newcastle upon Tyne, England, 1973, and London, 1974.
Alice, produced in Newcastle upon Tyne, England, 1975.
Crime and Punishment (based on the novel by Feodor Dostoevsky), produced in Manchester, England, 1978.
(With Tristram Powell) *We Think the World of You* (television play), 1980.

OTHER

(With others) *Living in London,* London Magazine Editions (London, England), 1974.

An English Madam: The Life and Work of Cynthia Payne (biography), J. Cape (London, England), 1982.
An Immaculate Mistake: Scenes from Childhood and Beyond (autobiography), Bloomsbury (London, England), 1990, Dutton (New York, NY), 1992.
(Editor) *The Oxford Book of London* (anthology), Oxford University Press (New York, NY), 1995.
(Editor) *The Stately Homo: A Celebration of the Life of Quentin Crisp,* Bantam (New York, NY), 2000.
Three Queer Lives: An Alternative Biography of Naomi Jacob, Fred Barnes, and Arthur Marshall, Hamish Hamilton (London, England), 2001.

Contributor to periodicals, including *New Statesman, Listener, Observer, London Magazine, Sunday Times,* and *Daily Telegraph.*

SIDELIGHTS: Paul Bailey's novels are "characterized by extreme compression," Peter Lewis wrote in the *Times Literary Supplement,* "in an attempt to produce great poetic intensity." Usually concerned with elderly or isolated characters who are suffering from a personal catastrophe in their lives, Bailey's work is often pessimistic. Yet, Thomas J. Cousineau stated in the *Dictionary of Literary Biography,* "Bailey is a writer who possesses a remarkable sensitivity to human relations and an exceptional gift for rendering the inner lives of his characters."

At the Jerusalem, Bailey's first novel, was described as "probably the most original, and certainly the most accomplished, first novel" of 1967 by Alan Ross in *London* magazine. It is set at the Jerusalem retirement home, where Mrs. Gadny has been forced to live. Her struggle against—and eventual failure to adjust to—the loneliness of institutional life is the subject of the novel. "Bailey's social comment," Miles Burrows observed in his *New Statesman* review, "is precise and made with an enviably light touch while never failing to be serious." This blending of the comic and compassionate results, Ross commented, in "a series of portraits remarkable for their insight and tenderness." Because of her inability to adjust to life in the retirement home, and her disturbing memories of past failures to achieve intimacy with others, Mrs. Gadny eventually "breaks and goes from poorhouse to mental institution," J. M. Carroll explained in *Library Journal.* Carroll found *At the Jerusalem* a "sad, almost clinical account of unhappiness in growing old," while a *Times*

Literary Supplement critic praised Bailey for combining "mature understanding with immense control and accomplishment."

Ralph Hicks, the narrator and protagonist of Bailey's second novel, *Trespasses,* is also committed to a mental institution. Following the suicide of his wife, who blames him for her action, Hicks has suffered a breakdown and committed himself. In a series of short narrative fragments, Hicks examines the details of his life as a way to find some sort of sense in it. "He hopes," Cousineau wrote, "that the exploration of his past will awaken in him that sense of a strong personal identity which has until now eluded him." As in *Jerusalem,* the principal theme of *Trespasses* is "estrangement: the subtly inevitable process by which parents and children, men and women, draw tragically and uncomprehendingly apart from one another," a Times Literary Supplement reviewer maintained. The critic went on to conclude that with *Trespasses,* Bailey "establishes a firm place among the best of the younger novelists." Cousineau believed *Trespasses* "may well be Bailey's finest novel."

Estrangement is also an important theme in *A Distant Likeness,* the story of police inspector Frank White, recently deserted by his wife for another man. White's efforts to reconcile himself to this loss are interwoven with his daily police work and his memories and presented in a stream-of-consciousness narration. It is written, noted a Times Literary Supplement critic, "almost entirely in tiny, cryptic paragraphs collected in short batches separated by blank pages." This method is "probably less effective," Cousineau admitted, "than the more explicitly controlled technique of *Trespasses.*" Lewis believed that in this novel Bailey is "aiming at a hyper-concentration of linguistic effect."

The "likeness" of the title refers to the similarity between White and a wife murderer named Belsey who sits silently in his cell and refuses to talk to police. Both men have failed in life and this common failure eventually moves White to give Belsey a knife, hinting to the man that he may want to kill himself with it. Instead, Belsey attacks a guard and White is arrested as his accomplice. Some critics saw the novel's short length and minimal plot as its major flaws. "No amount of ingenuity," a Times Literary Supplement critic concluded, "in the deployment of symbols, the details which echo meaningfully across the pages, the nice attention to minuscule portrayals of settings, can compensate for the final absence of the full-blooded novel which Mr. Bailey's skills might have provided. *A Distant Likeness* is thin stuff."

As in previous Bailey novels, the protagonist of *Peter Smart's Confessions* is caught in a catastrophic situation. The novel begins with Smart waking up in a hospital intensive care ward after a failed suicide attempt. Like Ralph Hicks of *Trespasses,* Smart then decides to write his autobiography as a means of sorting out his life. The result is an often-humorous book filled with the constant chatter of a host of eccentric characters. In fact, as Paddy Kitchen explained in *Listener,* the text of this autobiography consists primarily of "the dialogue of [Smart's] motley and intermittently splendid cast of relations, friends, and employers." "*Peter Smart's Confessions,*" Peter Ackroyd observed in the *Spectator,* "is a sport, a game constantly threatening to get out of hand as Bailey swoops with horrid glee upon each of his characters as they alternately fumble, strut and moan through their lives." The characters, Ackroyd continued, "address the world about themselves, ferocious and furious, helpless and merciless in turn, lying and hesitating." "Irony and humour are not unwelcome in tragedy," Kitchen stated, "but too often here they deteriorate into long-drawn-out badinage. However, there are some brilliant passages." Similarly, Cousineau believed the book's humor "seems to reside more in isolated set pieces . . . than in any underlying novelistic conception."

In *Old Soldiers,* Bailey again deals with elderly characters who are experiencing a painful loss. The novel begins as Victor Harker returns to London for the first time in fifty years. He has come to get away from his hometown for a few days following the recent death of his wife. While visiting St. Paul's Cathedral, Harker meets Harold Standish, another elderly man. Both men served in World War I; they dine together and share their memories of that time. Harker soon realizes that Standish is not what he first seemed to be; he maintains three separate identities—a tramp, an unknown poet, and a retired army officer—and dons each disguise for a few days at a time. Standish's intention is "to escape from himself," Cousineau explained, "and the inevitability of his own death." This need to escape was triggered by an act of cowardice during the war. "I was not entirely persuaded by Paul Bailey's literal explanation of how Standish's protean obsession began," Nicholas Shrimpton of the *New Statesman* allowed. "But in other respects this is a marvelously skillful book, deftly constructed and full of incidental delights." Writing in the *Listener,* John Naughton focused his attention on the book's length, calling it "an exercise in compression, a stylistic experiment conducted to see how far a scenario can be cut to the descriptive bone while still remaining credible." Elaine Feinstien noted in her review for the London *Times* that "to bring us into the presence of the dead and dying and then, without the slightest precautionary numbing of ordinary emotions, bewilder us into laughter is a remarkably difficult manoeuvre. . . . [*Old Soldiers*], however, does just this, and gently, without a taint of black farce." Lewis dubbed *Old Soldiers* the "most completely satisfying" Bailey novel since *At the Jerusalem.*

Gabriel's Lament "is by far [Bailey's] longest work of fiction and encompasses over forty years of English life, from the early years of World War II on," stated Lewis in *Contemporary Novelists.* The novel tells the story of Gabriel, a writer whose life "has been profoundly affected by [his mother's] mysterious absence as well as by the overbearing presence of his outrageously eccentric father, Oswald, one of Bailey's most brilliant creations and a comic character of Dickensian stature," noted Lewis, continuing, "Oswald may make Gabriel suffer, but he simultaneously makes the reader laugh. Bailey achieves a delicate synthesis of the tragic and the comic." Identifying similar characteristics, Boyd Tonkin summarized in the *Listener:* "Bailey's rich comedy and wily narration suggest a link between creation and delusion that places *Gabriel's Lament* squarely inside a Romantic tradition." Jill Johnson commented in the *New York Times Book Review* that "The oppression of Gabriel is so pervasive, so persistent, that his ultimate triumph as a writer, let alone his survival, may be hard to believe," stating also that, "All Mr. Bailey's characters tend to talk like [Oswald], whose speech is mannered and inflated. This blurs the distinctness of the characters and often makes the reading hard going." Neil Philip viewed the novel more positively. He stated in his *British Book News* review that "Bailey maintains Gabriel's rather fussy narrative voice with great skill, and within that constraint unerringly manages a cast of almost Dickensian eccentrics."

Kitty and Virgil is a love story concerning Londoner Kitty Crozier and Virgil Florescu, a Romanian poet who has been forced to flee the dictatorship of Ceausescu because of his anti-government writings. Virgil is a born storyteller who enjoys recounting traditional folktales to the attentive Kitty. She, in turn, is an indexer for a publishing house who is trying to deal with an unpredictable family. "Kitty and Virgil are appealingly unpretentious, sincere, and witty," Ben Donnelly stated in the *Review of Contemporary Fiction.* Judith Kicinski in *Library Journal* called *Kitty and Virgil* "very funny yet deeply tragic," while Paul Whitaker, in his review for the *New Statesman,* described it as "a study of late 1980s England and Romania seen through the distorting lens of a love affair." The critic for *Publishers Weekly* found *Kitty and Virgil* to be "at once a wistful and tender love story and a harrowing account of how people from two utterly different cultures and ways of looking at the world can find, then lose, each other."

Bailey's novel *Uncle Rudolf* again features a Romanian character, this time telling the story of young Andrei, who is brought from Romania to London in 1937 to live with his Uncle Rudolf. Andrei has never before met his relative, and he is unsure why he has been spirited out of his homeland at all. Uncle Rudolf works as a tenor in light opera, and he enjoys some fame, but he is unhappy with performing in what he considers to be an inferior form of entertainment. Behind the scenes, Rudolf also works against the fascist regime which has taken over Romania. Told in retrospect by an elderly Andrei who is seeking to make sense of the events of his life, *Uncle Rudolf* is, according to Paul Binding in the *Spectator,* "a beautifully worked cultural fable, elliptically presented after the manner Bailey has made uniquely his own." Stevie Davies in the *Guardian* found *Uncle Rudolf* "an exquisitely composed novel," while *Observer* contributor Amelia Hill called the novel "a desperately sad tale; a haunting narrative by a haunted man whose inability to fuse the fragments of his childhood condemns him to an unanchored existence, floating between the old world—and words—and the new."

There are recurring themes in all of Bailey's novels, Cousineau noted. "In each novel," he explained, "the stability of the main character's life is undermined by some painful circumstance. . . . It frequently happens as well that the catastrophe is provoked at least in part by the main character's personal inadequacies . . . [and, in addition,] Bailey's characters are generally isolated from normal human relationships." Bailey's great strength, Lewis observed, is his ability to depict the isolation of his characters. "He exposes the vulnerable core at the heart of all individuals," Lewis wrote, "the strategies by which people try to disguise their vulnerability and to protect themselves from the daily assault of reality, including the inevitability of death."

In addition to fiction, Bailey has produced several nonfiction publications, including *An Immaculate Mistake: Scenes from Childhood and Beyond* and *The Oxford Book of London*. *An Immaculate Mistake* is a "slim, unpretentious memoir" of Bailey's life, according to Nisid Hajari in *Entertainment Weekly*. A reviewer in *Publishers Weekly* stated of the biography that it is "varying in intensity, the episodes shine with good humor." *The Oxford Book of London* contains various fiction and nonfiction works, ordered chronologically from 1180 to 1994, which detail life in London. In his *Observer* review, Anthony Quinn described the book as "a fine anthology, that should leave minds as madly divided on the place as they ever were . . . it might be said to unfold a tale of two cities within a single metropolis, one of them home to privilege, the other to privation. Bailey's artful juxtapositions keep this grim divide always before us." Oliver Reynolds faulted the book in the *Times Literary Supplement* for failing to include material describing key aspects of London life, such as "sport," "the Long Room," and the "twin towers." Reynolds stated that, "considering its subject matter, [it] is relatively slim; rather narrow in its choice of materials, it is one of those rare books that a reviewer might wish were longer." Praising *The Oxford Book of London*, Reynolds continued: "The book reads very easily, and is constantly diverting through its juxtaposition of poetry and prose, factual account and gilded memory . . . [it] is cogently ordered and consistently enjoyable."

Bailey has also published two nonfiction books on gay topics. In the first, *The Stately Homo: A Celebration of the Life of Quentin Crisp*, the author collects writings by an openly homosexual English author. Known for his biting humor and flaunting of conventional values, Crisp is best remembered for the autobiographical *The Naked Civil Servant*. Richard Canning in the *Independent* noted that the collection contains "well-chosen excerpts from Crisp's works and pithy recollections" by other writers. Bailey's *Three Queer Lives* presents biographies of writers Naomi Jacob and Fred Barnes and of entertainer Arthur Marshall. According to Cora Lindsay, on *Contemporary Writers*, these three people "succeeded against the odds at a time when being gay was more difficult than it generally is today." Francis King in the *Spectator* found that the book offers "an engaging combination of seriousness and frivolity."

Bailey commented in an interview for *Contemporary Novelists*: "I write novels for many reasons, some of which I have probably never consciously thought of. I don't like absolute moral judgments, the 'placing' of people into types—I'm both delighted and appalled by the mysteriousness of my fellow creatures. I enjoy 'being' other people when I write, and the novels I admire most respect the uniqueness of other human beings. I like to think I show my characters respect and that I don't sit in judgment on them. This is what, in my small way, I am striving for—to capture, in a shaped and controlled form, something of the mystery of life."

BIOGRAPHICAL AND CRITICAL SOURCES:

BOOKS

Contemporary Novelists, 7th edition, St. James Press (Detroit, MI), 2001.
Dictionary of Literary Biography, Volume 14: *British Novelists since 1960,* Gale (Detroit, MI), 1983.

PERIODICALS

Antioch Review, spring, 1971.
Booklist, May 1, 1987, p. 1332.
Books and Bookmen, August, 1967.
British Book News, January 19, 1987, p. 43.
Daily Telegraph (London, England), November 23, 2002, "Books of the Year."
Encounter, September, 1973.
Entertainment Weekly, August 14, 1992, p. 56.
Guardian, September 28, 2002, Stevie Davies, review of *Uncle Rudolf,* p. 27.
Independent (London, England), December 18, 2000, Richard Canning, "The True Importance of Being Quentin," p. 5.
Kirkus Reviews, April 1, 1987, p. 486.
Library Journal, April 15, 1967; January, 2000, Judith Kicinski, review of *Kitty and Virgil,* p. 154.
Listener, July 6, 1967; April 30, 1970; June 14, 1973; June 2, 1977; March 6, 1980; October 2, 1986, pp. 23-24.
London, October, 1976.
London Review of Books, October 23, 1986, p. 16.
New Statesman, June 2, 1967; April 17, 1970; June 15, 1973; June 10, 1977; February 29, 1980; May 28, 1993, p. 38.; September 18, 1998, Paul Whitaker, review of *Kitty and Virgil,* p. 53.

New York Times Book Review, May 21, 1967; October 18, 1987, p. 34.
Observer (London, England), May 28, 1967; June 17, 1973; May 29, 1977; March 2, 1980; October 22, 1995, p. 14; December 15, 2002, Amelia Hill, review of *Uncle Rudolf,* p. 17.
Publishers Weekly, January, 13, 1992, review of *An Immaculate Mistake: Scenes from Childhood and Beyond,* p. 39; January 24, 2000, review of *Kitty and Virgil,* p. 289.
Punch, July 5, 1967; October 1, 1986, p. 59.
Review of Contemporary Fiction, summer, 2000, Ben Donnelly, review of *Kitty and Virgil,* p. 175.
Spectator, April 18, 1970; June 16, 1973; June 4, 1977; June 14, 1980; September 26, 1998, Anita Brookner, review of *Kitty and Virgil,* p. 44; October 20, 2001, Francis King, review of *Three Queer Lives,* p. 47; September 21, 2002, Paul Binding, review of *Uncle Rudolf,* p. 45.
Times (London, England), February 28, 1980.
Times Literary Supplement, June 8, 1967; April 16, 1970; June 29, 1973; May 27, 1977; November 6, 1982; June 21, 1996, p. 32.
USA Today, August 6, 1987, p. 5D.

ONLINE

Contemporary Writers, http://www.contemporarywriters.com/ (November 6, 2003).*

* * *

BALDRIGE, Letitia (Katherine) 1927(?)-

PERSONAL: Born c. 1927, in Miami Beach, FL; (some sources say Omaha, NE); daughter of H. Malcolm and Regina (Connell) Baldrige; married Robert Hollensteiner (a real estate executive), December 27, 1963; children: Clare Louise, Malcolm Baldrige. *Education:* Vassar College, B.A.; University of Geneva, graduate study. *Politics:* Republican. *Religion:* Catholic.

ADDRESSES: Office—151 East 80th St., New York, NY. 10021.

CAREER: Social secretary to Ambassador and Mrs. David Bruce, American Embassy, Paris, France, 1948-51; intelligence officer in Washington, DC, 1951-53; social secretary to Ambassador Clare Boothe Luce, American Embassy, Rome, Italy, 1953-56; Tiffany & Co., New York, NY, public relations director, 1956-60; social secretary to Mrs. John F. Kennedy, the White House, Washington, DC, 1961-63; Letitia Baldrige Enterprises (public relations), Chicago, IL, president, 1964-69; director of consumer affairs, Burlington Industries, 1969-71; Letitia Baldrige Enterprises, Inc., New York, NY, president, 1971—. Lecturer and television hostess.

MEMBER: American Institute of Interior Designers (public relations associate member), Institute of International Education (director), National Home Fashions League of New York, Fashion Group of New York, Women's Forum, Woodrow Wilson National Foundation (director), Committee of Two Hundred.

WRITINGS:

Roman Candle, Houghton Mifflin (Boston, MA), 1956.
Tiffany Table Settings, Crowell (New York, NY), 1959.
Of Diamonds and Diplomats: An Autobiography of a Happy Life, Houghton Mifflin (Boston, MA), 1968.
Home, Viking (New York, NY), 1970.
Juggling: The Art of Balancing Marriage, Motherhood, and Career, Viking (New York, NY), 1976.
(Reviser) *Amy Vanderbilt's Book of Etiquette,* Doubleday (New York, NY), 1978, published as *Amy Vanderbilt's Everyday Etiquette,* Bantam (New York, NY), 1981.
The Entertainers, Bantam (New York, NY), 1981.
Letitia Baldrige's Complete Guide to Executive Manners, edited by Sandi Gelles-Cole, Rawson Associates (New York, NY), 1985, revised edition published as *Letitia Baldrige's New Complete Guide to Executive Manners,* Scribner (New York, NY), 1993.
Letitia Baldrige's Complete Guide to a Great Social Life, illustrations by Raquel Jaramillo, Rawson Associates (New York, NY), 1987.
Letitia Baldrige's Complete Guide to the New Manners for the '90s, illustrations by Denise Cavalieri Fike, Rawson Associates (New York, NY), 1990.
Public Affairs, Private Relations (novel), Doubleday (New York, NY), 1990.
Letitia Baldrige's More Than Manners! Raising Today's Kids to Have Kind Manners and Good Hearts, Rawson Associates (New York, NY), 1997.

(With Rene Verdon) *In the Kennedy Style: Magical Evenings in the Kennedy White House,* Doubleday (New York, NY), 1998.

Legendary Brides: From the Most Romantic Weddings Ever, Inspired Ideas for Today's Brides, HarperCollins (New York, NY), 2000.

A Lady, First: My Life in the Kennedy White House and the American Embassies of Paris and Rome, Viking (New York, NY), 2001.

Class Acts: How Good Manners Create Good Relationships and Good Relationships Create Good Manners, Evans (New York, NY), 2003.

Letitia Baldrige's New Manners for New Times, Scribner (New York, NY), 2001.

Author of syndicated column in the *Los Angeles Times.* Contributor to magazines and newspapers.

SIDELIGHTS: Letitia Baldrige, who was the White House social secretary during the Kennedy administration, writes in her book *Amy Vanderbilt's Everyday Etiquette* that good manners are "nothing more than a combination of kindness and efficiency." In revising Vanderbilt's classic work on the social graces, Baldrige, according to Clarence Petersen in the *Chicago Tribune Book World,* addresses many forms of modern behavior, including "how to fight teen drug problems (talk openly and honestly) and . . . 16 ways to combat loneliness if you're suddenly single."

Since revising *Amy Vanderbilt's Everyday Etiquette,* Baldrige has penned several more books of her own. These titles include volumes about manners, such as *Letitia Baldrige's New Complete Guide to Executive Manners* and *Letitia Baldrige's More Than Manners! Raising Today's Kids to Have Kind Manners and Good Hearts.* Jo Lynn Jennings, reviewing an early edition of the former in the *Journal of Small Business Management,* praised it as "the most comprehensive book yet written on social behavior in American business." Of the latter, a *Booklist* critic concluded that "Baldrige has covered every conceivable social situation" involving children.

Baldrige collaborated with Rene Verdon, the chef who served with her at the Kennedy White House, to produce the 1998 volume *In the Kennedy Style: Magical Evenings in the Kennedy White House.* Verdon provided the recipes and Baldrige provided the reminiscences about the fabulous nights of entertainment at the presidential residence during the Kennedy administration. Raul Nino, discussing *In the Kennedy Style* in *Booklist,* reported that it is "engaging" and "written in an informal style." Baldrige reveals more about her White House service, as well as her employment by U.S. ambassadors to France and Italy, in her second volume of autobiography, *A Lady, First: My Life in the Kennedy White House and the American Embassies of Paris and Rome.* She also recounts how, as a well-qualified graduate of Vassar, she faced a great deal of sexual discrimination while seeking a career during the late 1940s. As Jill Ortner noted in a *Library Journal* review, Baldrige "is detailed but not bitter when describing the real lack of opportunity for women with her credentials." Similarly, a *Publishers Weekly* critic concluded that "Baldrige is an exemplary role model for women because she opened doors by refusing to accept that they were closed."

Not surprisingly, when Baldrige turned to writing about weddings in 2000's *Legendary Brides,* she included the First Lady she had served among the subjects she chose. She also provides details about the weddings of Princess Grace of Monaco, and of Great Britain's nineteenth-century ruler Queen Victoria. In addition to her many works of nonfiction about manners, Baldrige is also the author of a novel, *Public Affairs, Private Relations.* The book centers on a widowed heroine, described as a "Boston blueblood" by Sybil Steinberg of *Publishers Weekly,* who falls in love with a wealthy Jewish entrepreneur. Steinberg remarked that Baldrige's "prose is literate and her story timely."

BIOGRAPHICAL AND CRITICAL SOURCES:

BOOKS

Baldrige, Letitia, *Amy Vanderbilt's Everyday Etiquette,* Bantam (New York, NY), 1981.

PERIODICALS

Booklist, March 1, 1997, Patricia Hassler, review of *Letitia Baldrige's More Than Manners! Raising Today's Kids to Have Kind Manners and Good Hearts,* p. 1100; May 15, 1998, Raul Nino, review of *In the Kennedy Style: Magical Evenings in the Kennedy White House,* p. 1579.

Chicago Tribune Book World, April 26, 1981.
Journal of Small Business Management, April, 1986, Jo Lynn Jennings, review of *Letitia Baldrige's Complete Guide to Executive Manners,* p. 69.
Library Journal, September 15, 2001, Jill Ortner, review of *A Lady First: My Life in the Kennedy White House and the American Embassies of Paris and Rome,* p. 87.
Management Review, April, 1992, Barbara Ettorre, "Letitia Baldrige: Arbiter of Business Manners and Mores," pp. 50-54.
New York Times Book Review, March 24, 2002, Margaret Van Dagens, review of *A Lady, First,* p. 21.
People, May 18, 1998, Sandra McElwaine and Alec Foege, "The Age of Jackie," p. 163.
Publishers Weekly, September 7, 1990, Sybil Steinberg, review of *Public Affairs, Private Relations,* pp. 76-77; August 27, 2001, review of *A Lady, First,* p. 64.

ONLINE

Letitia Baldrige Home Page, http://www.letitia.com/ (July 28, 2002).*

* * *

BALIT, Christina 1961-

PERSONAL: Surname is pronounced Ba-leet; born August 5, 1961, in Manchester, England; daughter of Georges Michelle (an architect) and Patricia (a teacher, cook, actress, and homemaker; maiden name, Rothwell) Balit; married Brian Croucher (an actor), May 8, 1992; children: Sean Georges, Billie Georges (daughter). *Education:* Chelsea School of Art, B.A.; Royal College of Art, M.A.; also attended Morley Theatre School and Questors Theatre School.

ADDRESSES: Home—Pym Lodge, Soles Hill Rd., Shottenden, Kent CT4 8JU, England. *Agent*—Lisa Eveliegh, 26-A Rochester Sq., London NW1 9SA, England.

CAREER: Illustrator and playwright. Tutor at City and Guilds School of Art, London.

AWARDS, HONORS: Travel grant from Thames Television, 1982; award for Outstanding Children's Book of 1995, *Primary English;* Best Books selection, *Junior Education,* 1996.

WRITINGS:

(And illustrator) *My Arabian Home: Leila and Mustapha's Story,* Hampstead Press (New York, NY), 1988.
(Reteller and illustrator) *Atlantis: The Legend of a Lost City,* Holt (New York, NY), 2000.
(And illustrator) *Escape from Pompeii,* Holt (New York, NY), 2003.

ILLUSTRATOR

Michael Morpurgo, *Blodin the Beast,* Fulcrum Publishing (Golden, CO), 1995.
Christopher J. Moore, *Ishtar and Tammuz: A Babylonian Myth of the Seasons,* Kingfisher (New York, NY), 1996.
James Riordan, *The Twelve Labours of Hercules,* Millbrook Press (Brookfield, CT), 1997.
Jacqueline Mitton, *Zoo in the Sky,* Frances Lincoln (London, England), 1998.
Mary Hoffman, *Women of Camelot: Queens and Enchantresses at the Court of King Arthur,* Abbeville Press (New York, NY), 2000.
Jacqueline Mitton, *Kingdom of the Sun: A Book of the Planets,* National Geographic Society (Washington, DC), 2001.
Lois Rock, *Everlasting Stories: A Family Bible Treasury,* Chronicle Books (San Francisco, CA), 2001.
Jacqueline Mitton, *Once upon a Starry Night: A Book of Constellation Stories,* National Geographic Society (Washington, DC), 2003.

PLAYS

Agony for Beginners, produced in Edinburgh, Scotland, and London, 1989.
Woman with Upturned Skirt, produced in London at Grace Theatre, 1992.
The Sentence, produced in London at Old Red Lion Theatre, 1996.

WORK IN PROGRESS: With or without a Horse, a play.

SIDELIGHTS: Christina Balit is primarily an illustrator of children's literature, but she has also written and illustrated her own books, including *Atlantis: The Leg-

end of a Lost City. In this volume, she relates the tale of Atlantis, said to be a great civilization that was eventually submerged deep under the sea. Her version is "gracefully" told, according to a reviewer for *Publishers Weekly.* It begins with Poseidon, the god of the sea. Poseidon falls in love with Cleito, an island girl. They marry, but he hides the fact that he is a god. His power cannot be truly contained, however, and his presence on the island transforms it into a paradise, filled with temples, fountains, and other things of beauty. The inhabitants as well as the land are affected by his presence. They become nobler than ordinary mortals, loving peace and wisdom. Poseidon and Cleito have five sets of twin children; they and their descendants rule the kingdom with wisdom and goodness. In time, however, Poseidon must take his leave. Once he is gone, the Atlanteans slowly revert to normal human behavior. Greed, lust, and ambition lead to strife. Seeing this, Poseidon angrily sends a ferocious storm to drive the once-great island kingdom to the bottom of the sea.

The "luminous illustrations and simple prose" will "captivate a new generation of children intrigued with the mysteries of this timeless legend," stated Laura Scott in *School Library Journal.* Balit's artwork was praised by Scott and other reviewers, including Ilene Cooper, who termed it "quite sophisticated" in her *Booklist* evaluation. Cooper added: "She magnificently portrays Atlantis, with architectural shapes and intricate patterns, all burnished with gold." Stylized designs, reminiscent of Greek figure painting, are used along with a "sumptuous palette" to create "busy, almost psychedelically patterned compositions," with "seemingly endless detail," wrote a *Publishers Weekly* reviewer.

Balit remarked to *CA* on the process of painting her illustrations: "The practical doing of it is benign and gentle, but often very difficult, and I dread distraction. My desk is up a ladder in a loft. There is no window. I rarely speak except to the radio. My days have a rigid pattern, and I get the twitch if I've failed to put in eight hours. I'm desperately unfit, of course—thin and lanky and pinned to a chair, but the production of work is regular and steady. I've learned to estimate how long I need to complete each painting.

"I remember the books I kept as a child, and it was always perfectly clear that I was going to make my own. The Middle East left its mark. The work is littered with it. It made sense to surround myself with reference to history and proto-history of the ancient Near East. I had wandered around those ruins often. They were regular weekend picnics, thanks to my parents. When a book is in print, I pick it up and read it to my children. That's when I notice the pictures I worry about, that I wish I had more time to make, that I imagine re-doing. But it's over. The deadline rules us all, as do book fairs and sales trips and proofs by October. Finally the art work goes back in a drawer, rarely on a wall, because it doesn't belong on one. It belongs in hardback next to the text, in my children's toy box covered in biro and milk.

"So I move on to the next book, trying always to remember that, like an actor, it is my job to honor the text, and not the other way around. I live with an actor, and I feel for him desperately. He can only work when asked, and he shoulders all responsibility for our well-being and upkeep. I can do what I do whether I'm asked or not. I climb that ladder to the loft and just keep doing it. I yearn to write a beautiful play, to paint the perfect book. I blame my parents, of course. They encouraged me not to limit myself to anything, to be confident and go do—go work. If I told them tomorrow that I wanted to drive a train, they'd say 'Great! Why not? Fax us from Mexico.'

"My need to make something from nothing is the reason my blood runs, and I need to keep it thick. I read somewhere that Jacques-Yves Cousteau said 'If we didn't die, we would not appreciate life as we do.' I don't fear dying, but I can't imagine how people live if they don't 'make' things.

BIOGRAPHICAL AND CRITICAL SOURCES:

PERIODICALS

Booklist, September 1, 1996, p. 123; May 15, 2000, Ilene Cooper, review of *Atlantis: The Legend of a Lost City,* p. 1754; January 1, 2002, Todd Morning, review of *Everlasting Stories: A Family Bible Treasury,* p. 854.
Publishers Weekly, July 22, 1996, p. 242; June 19, 2000, review of *Atlantis,* p. 78.
School Library Journal, March, 1989, p. 176; December, 1996, p. 132; May, 2000, Laura Scott, review of *Atlantis,* p. 160; April, 2002, Linda Beck, review of *Everlasting Stories,* p. 140.*

BARTOV, Hanoch 1926-

PERSONAL: Given name is also transliterated as "Hanokh"; born August 13, 1926, in Petach Tikva, Palestine (now Israel); son of Simkha and Miriam Bartov; married Yehudith Shimmer, February 10, 1946 (died April 20, 1998); children: Gillat Bartov Eitam, Omer. *Ethnicity:* "Jewish." *Education:* Attended Hebrew University of Jerusalem, 1946-51.

ADDRESSES: Home—91 Levanon St., Ramat Aviv, Tel Aviv, Israel 69345. *E-mail*—hanochbr@netvision.net.il.

CAREER: Israeli Institute for Applied Social Research, researcher, 1949-51; Kibbutz Ein Ha'Koresh, high school teacher and farmer, 1951-54; Tikhon Khadash, Tel Aviv, Israel, high school teacher, 1955; *Lamerkhav* (Israeli daily newspaper), news editor, 1956-58, U.S. correspondent, 1958-60, columnist, 1960-66; Israeli Embassy, London, England, counselor and cultural officer, 1966-68; *Lamerkhav,* columnist, 1968-71; *Ma'ariv,* Tel Aviv, Israel, newspaper columnist, 1971-90; retired, 1991. Israel Broadcasting Authority, member of board of directors, 1965-66, 1969-72; Omanut La'am (public agency for the arts), member of board of directors, 1986-90, chair, 1990-92. *Military service:* British Army, Jewish Brigade, 1943-46; Israel Defense Forces, Jerusalem Brigade, 1947-49.

MEMBER: International PEN (member of board of directors, Israel Center, 1968-72; president of board of directors, 1990-95), International Theater Institute (president of Israel Center, 1975-79), Hebrew Writers Association (member of executive board, 1968-72), Israel Journalists Association.

AWARDS, HONORS: Ussishkin Prize, 1955, for *Shesh kenafay'im la'ekhad;* Shlonsky Prize, 1965, for *Pitsey bagrut;* Hebrew Writers Association, Valenrod Prize, best short story of the year, 1969, Israel Efrat Prize for essays, 1995, for *Ani Lo Ha'zabar Ha'mithologi;* Prime Minister's Prize, 1974; Yitskhak Sadeh Prize for military history, 1978, for *Daddo;* Bialik Prize for Literature from Tel Aviv Municipality, 1985, for *Be'emtsa Ha'roman;* Shalom Aleykhem House Award, 1995, for *Regel Akhat bakhuts;* President of Israel Prize for body of writings, 1998.

WRITINGS:

NOVELS

Ha'Kheshbon ve'ha'nefesh (title means "The Reckoning and the Soul"), Sifriat Poalim (Tel Aviv, Israel), 1953, revised edition, Ma'ariv (Tel Aviv, Israel), 1988.

Shesh knafayim la'ekhad (stage adaptation by the author first produced in Tel Aviv, Israel, at Habima National Theater, 1958, and on U.S. tour, 1964), Sifriat Poalim (Tel Aviv, Israel), 1954, revised edition, Am Oved (Tel Aviv, Israel), 1973; translation of the stage version published as *Every One Had Six Wings,* World Zionist Organization (Jerusalem, Israel), 1973.

Pitsey bagrut (title means "Growing Pains"), Am Oved (Tel Aviv, Israel), 1965, translation by David S. Segal published as *The Brigade,* Holt (New York, NY), 1968.

Shel mi ata yeled, Am Oved (Tel Aviv, Israel), 1970, translation by Hillel Halkin published as *Whose Little Boy Are You?,* Jewish Publication Society (Philadelphia, PA), 1978.

Habadai (title means "The Lying Man"), Am Oved (Tel Aviv, Israel), 1975.

Be'emtsa Ha'roman (title means "In the Middle of the Novel"), Am Oved (Tel Aviv, Israel), 1984.

Zeh ishl medaber (title means "It's Ishl Speaking"), Ma'ariv (Tel Aviv, Israel), 1990.

Regel Akhat bakhuts (title means "Halfway Out"), Am Oved (Tel Aviv, Israel), 1994.

Lev Shafoukh (title means "A Heart Poured Out"), Zmora-Bitan (Tel Aviv, Israel), 2001.

Mi'tom ad tom (title means "From Innocence to the Very End"), Kineret-Zmora (Tel Aviv, Israel), 2003.

SHORT FICTION COLLECTIONS

Ha'Shuk ha'katan (title means "Little Market"), Sifriat Poalim (Tel Aviv, Israel), 1957.

Lev khakhamim (title means "Heart of the Wise"), Sifriat Poalim (Tel Aviv, Israel), 1962.

Akhot rekhoka (title means "Distant Sister"), Hakibbutz Hameukhad (Tel Aviv, Israel), 1973.

Yehudi Katan (title means "A Little Jew"), Am Oved (Tel Aviv, Israel), 1981.

Mazal Ayala (title means "Ayala's Star"), Ma'ariv (Tel Aviv, Israel), 1988.

Maveth be'Purim (title means "Death on Purim"), Ma'ariv (Tel Aviv, Israel), 1992.

NONFICTION

Arba'ah Isre'elim ve-khol America (travel; title means "Four Israelis All Over America"), Sifriat Poalim (Tel Aviv, Israel), 1961, revised editon, Massada (Tel Aviv, Israel), 1963.

Isre'elim ba'khatsar St. James', Hakibbutz Hameukhad (Tel Aviv, Israel), 1969, translation by Ruth Aronson published as *Israelis at the Court of St. James's,* Vallentine, Mitchell (London, England), 1973.

Zalman Shazar: Deyokno shel nasi (title means "Zalman Shazar: Portrait of a President"), 1973.

Yarid be'Moskva (travel; title means "A Fair in Moscow"), Ma'ariv (Tel Aviv, Israel), 1988.

Daddo: 48 shanim ve'od 20 yom, two volumes, Ma'ariv (Tel Aviv, Israel), 1978, expanded and annotated edition, Zmora-Bitan (Tel Aviv, Israel), 2002, translation by Ina Friedman published as *Dado: 48 Years and 20 More Days,* Ma'ariv (Tel Aviv, Israel), 1981.

Ani Lo Ha'zabar Ha'mithologi (essays; title means "I Am Not the Mythological Sabra"), Am Oved (Tel Aviv, Israel), 1995.

Author of columns "Le'Ruakh Ha'Yom," *Lamerhav,* 1956-70, and "Ha'Prat Ha'Katan," *Ma'ariv,* 1972-90. Contributor to periodicals.

PLAYS

Chatunat haKesef (radio play), first broadcast by Israeli Radio, 1958.

Sa habayta, Yonathan (two-act; title means "Jonathan, Go Home"), first produced in Tel Aviv, Israel, at Zuta Theater, 1962.

Agada Khaya (radio play; title means "Living Legend"), first broadcast by Israeli Radio, 1989.

Author of other radio plays; adaptor of novels and stories for radio.

TRANSLATIONS

Graham Greene, *Maseotai im Dodati* (translation of *Travels with My Aunt*), Am Oved (Tel Aviv, Israel), 1971.

Zhang Xian Liang, *Etz Hameshi* (translation of *Mimosa*), Am Oved (Tel Aviv, Israel), 1985.

Translator of nonfiction works and children's books.

BIOGRAPHICAL AND CRITICAL SOURCES:

BOOKS

Gilboa, Menuha, *Pitsei Zahut* (title means "Identity Pains"), [Tel Aviv, Israel] 1987.

PERIODICALS

Best Sellers, January 15, 1968.
Jewish Quarterly, summer, 1969.
Times Literary Supplement, June 26, 1979, September 3, 1971.
World Literature Today, winter, 1986.

* * *

BAUMEL, Judith 1956-

PERSONAL: Born October 9, 1956, in New York, NY; daughter of Abraham (an educator) and Betty (an educator; maiden name, Fogel) Baumel; married David Ghitelman (a journalist), July 4, 1985; children: Samuel, Aaron. *Education:* Harvard University, B.A. (creative writing; magna cum laude), 1977; Johns Hopkins University, M.A., 1978. *Hobbies and other interests:* Baseball.

ADDRESSES: Home—3530 Henry Hudson Pkwy, No. 12, Bronx, NY 10463. *E-mail*—baumel@adelphi.edu.

CAREER: Educator and poet. Poetry Society of America, New York, NY, director, 1985-88; Adelphi University, Garden City, NY, associate professor of English, 1988—, and director of creative writing program; City College of the City University of New York, instructor in graduate writing program, 1995—. Poet-in-the-schools volunteer.

AWARDS, HONORS: Lloyd McKim Garrison Medal, Harvard University, 1977; Walt Whitman Award, Academy of American Poets, 1987, for *The Weight of Numbers;* New York Foundation for the Arts fellowship for poetry, 1987.

WRITINGS:

POETRY

The Weight of Numbers, Wesleyan University Press (Middletown, CT), 1988.
Now, Miami University Press (Oxford, OH), 1996.

(Translator, with others) Patrizia Cavalli, *My Poems Will Not Change the World: Selected Poems, 1974-1992,* Exile Editions (Toronto, Ontario, Canada), 1998.

Monument, in press.

Contributor of poems and articles to periodicals, including *New Yorker, New Republic, Threepenny Review, New York Times Book Review, Ploughshares, Poetry, Paris Review,* and *American Poetry Review.* Contributor to anthologies, including *Telling and Remembering: A Century of American Jewish Poetry, A Year in Poetry, A Walk on the Wild Side,* and *Sports Poems.*

WORK IN PROGRESS: Dashed Hopes, a book about American women poets.

SIDELIGHTS: Judith Baumel is an English professor at Adelphi University in New York. She has published two books of poetry. Her first collection, *The Weight of Numbers,* won the Walt Whitman Award from the Academy of American Poets in 1987. Baumel's second book of poems is titled *Now.* The title refers to the exact moment that one is living in and the fact that that experience may be what generates future memories. In other words, every "now" has a "then." Elizabeth Millard of *Booklist* called Baumel a "gifted" poet and noted that the author's "language is both simple and rich."

BIOGRAPHICAL AND CRITICAL SOURCES:

PERIODICALS

Booklist, February 1, 1996, Elizabeth Millard, p. 913.

ONLINE

Adelphi University, http://home.adelphi.edu/ (July 10, 2002), "Judith Baumel."

Judith Baumel Home Page, http://members.aol.com/ (January, 1999).*

* * *

BEEVOR, Antony 1946-

PERSONAL: Born December 14, 1946, in London, England; son of John G. and Kinta J. Beevor; married Artemis Cooper, 1988; children: one daughter, one son. *Education:* Attended secondary school at Winchester College, 1960-64; attended University of Grenoble, 1964-65, and Royal Military Academy, Sandhurst, 1965-67.

ADDRESSES: Agent—Andrew Nurnberg Associates, Clerkenwell House, 45-47 Clerkenwell Green, London EC1R 0HT, England.

CAREER: Freelance journalist in the Middle East, 1970; worked in London, England, in marketing and advertising, 1971-72, and in marketing and publishing, 1974-75; writer, 1975—; visiting professor at Birkbeck College, University of London, 2002—. *Military service:* British Army, Royal Hussars, 1965-70; served in Germany; became lieutenant.

MEMBER: Society of Authors (member of management committee), Council of the London Library, Royal Geographical Society (fellow).

AWARDS, HONORS: Runciman Prize, 1992, for *Crete: The Battle and the Resistance;* Chevalier de l'Ordre des Arts et Lettres, 1997; Samuel Johnson Prize, Wolfson Prize for History, and Hawthornden Prize for Literature, 1999, for *Stalingrad: The Fateful Siege, 1942-1943;* fellow, Royal Society of Literature, 1999; Lees-Knowles lecturer at Cambridge, 2002-2003; Longman-History Today Trustees' Award, 2003.

WRITINGS:

The Violent Brink (novel), J. Murray (London, England), 1975.
For Reasons of State (novel), J. Cape (London, England), 1981.
The Spanish Civil War (nonfiction), Orbis, 1982, reprinted, Penguin (New York, NY), 2001.
The Faustian Pact (novel), J. Cape (London, England), 1983.
The Enchantment of Christina von Retzen (novel), Weidenfeld & Nicolson (London, England), 1989.
Inside the British Army, Chatto & Windus (London, England), 1990.
Crete: The Battle and the Resistance, J. Murray (London, England), 1991, Westview (Boulder, CO), 1994.
(With wife, Artemis Cooper) *Paris after the Liberation, 1946-1949,* Doubleday (New York, NY), 1994.

Stalingrad: The Fateful Siege, 1942-1943, Viking (New York, NY), 1998.
The Fall of Berlin, 1945, Viking (New York, NY), 2002, published as *Berlin: The Downfall, 1945,* Viking (London, England), 2002.

Contributor to *No End Save Victory: Perspectives on World War II,* edited by Robert Cowley, Putnam (New York, NY), 2001. Contributor to periodicals.

SIDELIGHTS: Former British Army officer Antony Beevor brings to vivid life the horrors of combat and persecution in books like *Stalingrad: The Fateful Siege, 1942-1943* and *The Fall of Berlin, 1945.* In the first work, Beevor examines "the bitterest and most cruel of all twentieth-century battles," according to *New Statesman* critic Alan Clark. "We all know, or think we know, what happened at Stalingrad," Clark noted. The target was Russia's Caucasian oil field, which Germany's Field Marshal von Paulus was intent on capturing. But the siege came a cropper when von Paulus bungled the first assault. With soldiers on both ends of the conflict at risk, the battle for Stalingrad became more of a tactical exercise waged between the two countries' dictatorial leaders, Adolf Hitler and Josef Stalin. Thus "the graveyards of this century are packed with the bodies of men who died to save the 'face' of their commanders," as Clark remarked.

Stalingrad earned critical praise from journalists ranging from Eliot Cohen of *Foreign Affairs,* who deemed the book "masterly," to *Library Journal*'s Robert Johnson, who called Beevor's work "thoroughly mesmerizing." Gilbert Taylor of *Booklist* said that by focusing on the doomed soldiers' morale, the author "has composed a history of Stalingrad unlikely to be bettered." The British reading public responded to *Stalingrad* as well, hoisting the book to the bestseller lists with 60,000 copies sold in hardcover and another 250,000 in paperback.

Beevor followed *Stalingrad* with *The Fall of Berlin, 1945,* another account of wartime brutality. Reading this book, stated *Boston Herald* writer Roger Miller, "is like viewing some enormous, latter-day Heironymous Bosch painting of the human race in total meltdown." The Russian forces, determined to overtake Germany, laid siege to Berlin in a display of brutality matched only by Stalin, who turned a blind eye to the suffering his soldiers inflicted upon the German civilians. (According to Robert Winder, Stalin shared with Hitler "a belief that wanton disdain for other people's lives was a mark of true greatness.") As Winder wrote in *New Statesman,* "The Red Army went about things in its own unbelievably depraved way: raping the women of Poland and Germany (young, old, nuns, orphans—none was safe), tearing watches, jewels and anything else of value from the land they overran, destroying and burning everything they could not pocket. Rarely has a defeated people been so epically abused."

A *Publishers Weekly* contributor said that Beevor supplies "overheard quotes from the main players" in *The Fall of Berlin,* "making the reader an eavesdropper to Hitler and Stalin's orbiter dicta." "But it isn't Beevor's meticulous exposition of military carnage that will startle readers," commented *Times* critic Richard Morrison. "It's his portrayal of a much more sordid aspect of the Red Army's 'heroic' advance: the ferocious mass rape of two million women." Winder noted Beevor's "coolness and . . . sober lack of sentiment" in recording the atrocities, saying that such emotional distance served the book well. "He wisely does not attempt to compete with his dreadful raw material," concluded Winder, "so his book is a powerful anthology of anguished utterances." What accounted for the Russian troops' apparent ease with which they abused civilians? "There are, as Beevor points out, any number of half-explanations," said Morrison. "The most plausible is that brutality begets brutality. Red Army soldiers were treated deplorably by their own commanders."

The Fall of Berlin was assessed by *Newsweek International* reporter William Underhill (who used the book's U.K. title, *Berlin: The Downfall 1945*) as "a dismal view of humanity that could be numbing over 490 pages. But Beevor gives plenty of all-too-human detail to enliven the narrative."

BIOGRAPHICAL AND CRITICAL SOURCES:

PERIODICALS

Booklist, June 1, 1998, Gilbert Taylor, review of *Stalingrad: The Fateful Siege, 1942-1943,* p. 1712.
Boston Herald, May 26, 2002, Roger Miller, "Author Rises to Task with 'Fall of Berlin,'" p. 058.

Contemporary Review, June, 1999, review of *Stalingrad,* p. 331.

Economist, April 13, 2002, "Burdens of Victory."

Foreign Affairs, November, 1998, Eliot Cohen, review of *Stalingrad,* p. 148.

Guardian (London, England), January 8, 2000, Nicholas Wroe, "Mini-cab to Stalingrad: My Life in Writing" (author interview), p. 11; April 20, 2002, Michael Burleigh, review of *Berlin: The Downfall, 1945,* p. 10.

Houston Chronicle, July 19, 1998, Fritz Lanham, "Suffering in Stalingrad," p. 21.

Journal of Military History, January, 1999, review of *Stalingrad,* p. 213.

Kirkus Reviews, May 15, 1999, review of *Stalingrad,* p. 704; April 1, 2002, review of *The Fall of Berlin, 1945,* p. 464.

Library Journal, May 15 1998, Robert Johnston, review of *Stalingrad,* p. 95.

London Review of Books, July 15, 1999, review of *Stalingrad,* p. 18.

Marine Corps Gazette, March, 2001, Gordon Keiser, "The Whermacht Slaughtered," p. 76.

New Statesman, May 8, 1998, Alan Clark, review of *Stalingrad,* p. 47; April 15, 2002, Robert Winder, "Landscape of Despair," p. 49.

Newsweek International, May 20, 2002, William Underhill, "An Act of Blasphemy," p. 41.

New York Review of Books, November 4, 1999, review of *Stalingrad,* p. 57.

New York Times, August 26, 1998, Richard Bernstein, review of *Stalingrad,* p. B7.

Publishers Weekly, June 9, 1998, review of *Stalingrad,* p. 55; March 11, 2002, review of *The Fall of Berlin, 1945,* p. 59.

Reference and Research Book News, May, 1999, review of *Stalingrad,* p. 23.

Spectator, April 6, 1991; May 2, 1998, review of *Stalingrad,* p. 34.

Sunday Times, June 20, 1999, Cosmo Landesman, "The Ex-Soldier Leading History from the Front," p. N5.

Times (London, England), May 9, 2002, Richard Morrison, "Why Did So Many Russian Soldiers, Having Fought Their Way across Half of Europe, Turn into Violent Gang-Rapists?," p. 7.

Times Literary Supplement, February 4, 1983; April 22, 1983; August 18, 1989; October 23, 1998, Omer Bartov, review of *Stalingrad,* p. 12.

Wall Street Journal, July 8, 1998, Stuart Ferguson, review of *Stalingrad,* p. A13.

ONLINE

Antony Beevor Home Page, http://www.antonybeevor.com/ (June 9, 2002).

* * *

BEHRMAN, Carol H(elen) 1925-

PERSONAL: Born August 24, 1925, in Brooklyn, NY; daughter of Louis (a postal worker) and Sylvia (Leventhal) Bostwick; married Edward Behrman (an accountant), January 22, 1949; children: Bonnie, Joseph, Linda. *Education:* City College (now City College of the City University of New York), B.S.Ed. (cum laude), 1947; graduate study at Columbia University.

ADDRESSES: Agent—c/o Author Mail, Lerner Publishing, 1251 Washington Ave. N., Minneapolis, MN 55401.

CAREER: Writer. Teacher of business education in New York, NY, public schools, 1949-54; freelance writer, 1954-70; teacher of adult secretarial studies in public schools in Fair Lawn, NJ, and River Edge, NJ, 1970-73; Glen Ridge Middle School, Glen Ridge, NJ, teacher of typing and language arts, 1973-87. Conducted writing workshops at New York University, Seton Hall University, and at writers' conferences, including Cape Cod Writers Conference, New Jersey Writers Conference, and Chautauqua Writers Center.

MEMBER: Society of Children's Book Writers and Illustrators, New Jersey Education Association.

AWARDS, HONORS: New Jersey Institute of Technology award, 1988, for *Wanted: One New Dad.*

WRITINGS:

FOR CHILDREN

There's Only One You, Southern Publishing (Nashville, TN), 1973.

Catch a Dancing Star, Dillon (Minneapolis, MN), 1975.

Become Your Own Ideal, Southern Publishing (Nashville, TN), 1980.

The Remarkable Writing Machine, Messner (New York, NY), 1981.

California Summer, Weekly Reader (Columbus, OH), 1982.

Stranger in My Heart, Weekly Reader (Middletown, CT), 1982.

The Wrong Kind, Weekly Reader (Middletown, CT), 1983.

Old Enough to Dream, Weekly Reader (Middletown, CT), 1984.

Miss Dr. Lucy, Review & Herald (Washington, DC), 1984.

Ghost in the Garden, Weekly Reader (Middletown, CT), 1984.

The Christmas Orphan, Weekly Reader (Middletown, CT), 1984.

Friendship Blues, Weekly Reader (Middletown, CT), 1985.

Erica for President, Weekly Reader (Middletown, CT), 1986.

Wendy's Choice, Weekly Reader (Middletown, CT), 1986.

Wanted: One New Dad, Weekly Reader (Middletown, CT), 1988.

Roberto Clemente, Quercus (Englewood Cliffs, NJ), 1990.

Hooked on Writing: Writing Process Activities Grades 4-8, Center for Applied Research in Education (West Nyack, NY), 1990.

Fiddler to the World: The Inspiring Life of Itzhak Perlman, Shoe Tree Press (White Hall, VA), 1992.

The Lancaster Witch, Willowisp (St. Petersburg, FL), 1993.

The Ghost in the Computer, Willowisp (St. Petersburg, FL), 1994.

Programmed for Terror, Willowisp (St. Petersburg, FL), 1994.

Write! Write! Write! Ready-to-Use Writing Process Activities for Grades 4-8, Center for Applied Research in Education (West Nyack, NY), 1995.

Writing Activities for Every Month of the School Year: Ready-to-Use Writing Process Activities for Grades 4-8, Jossey-Bass (San Francisco, CA), 1997.

The Ding Dong Clock, illustrated by Hideko Takahashi, Holt (New York, NY), 1999.

Writing Skills Problem Solver: 101 Ready-to-Use Writing Process Activities for Correcting the Most Common Errors, Center for Applied Research in Education (West Nyack, NY), 2000.

Ready-to-Use Writing Proficiency Lessons and Activities: Fourth Grade Level, Center for Applied Research in Education (Paramus, NJ), 2002.

Ready-to-Use Writing Proficiency Lessons and Activities: Eighth-Grade Level, Jossey-Bass (San Francisco, CA), 2003.

The Indian Wars, Lerner Publishing (Minneapolis, MN), 2004.

"PRESIDENTIAL LEADERS" SERIES

Andrew Jackson, Lerner Publishing (Minneapolis, MN), 2003.

John Adams, Lerner Publishing (Minneapolis, MN), 2004.

Thomas Jefferson, Lerner Publishing (Minneapolis, MN), 2004.

Dwight D. Eisenhower, Lerner Publishing (Minneapolis, MN), 2004.

Herbert C. Hoover, Lerner Publishing (Minneapolis, MN), 2004.

James Madison, Lerner Publishing (Minneapolis, MN), 2004.

John F. Kennedy, Lerner Publishing (Minneapolis, MN), 2004.

Ulysses S. Grant, Lerner Publishing (Minneapolis, MN), 2004.

Contributor to professional, poetry, and children's magazines.

SIDELIGHTS: Children's author Carol H. Behrman has created a wide variety of books, from rhyming picture books to biographies and resource books for elementary-school writing teachers. Her nonfiction works include *The Remarkable Writing Machine,* a history of the typewriter from its invention in the early eighteenth century to its introduction into wide usage in business settings by the early twentieth century. Behrman describes the varieties of the modern machine, its increased sophistication, and the role it played in introducing many women into the business world. For its "terse" writing and "fascinating" topic, Connie Tyrrell recommended the book "for history buffs as well as budding inventors," in her review in *School Library Journal.*

Behrman has written several biographies for young adults, including *Fiddler to the World: The Inspiring Life of Itzhak Perlman.* Perlman's family were early settlers to the newly formed Israel after World War II, and at the age of four, young Itzhak fell ill with polio, which left him permanently paralyzed below the waist. The young boy, who first asked for a violin at the age of three, was playing on the *Ed Sullivan Show* by the age of twelve, and has been considered a world-class classical violinist throughout his adult life. Behrman's biography stresses the obstacles Perlman overcame in order to achieve the level of success he has, but the narrative is also "peppered with quotes that reveal Perlman's wit and good humor," according to Ellen Mandel who reviewed *Fiddler to the World* in *Booklist*. The author places Perlman's life in historical context by providing background information on the settling of Israel after World War II and the 1949 polio epidemic there, the history of violin-making, and the role of the *Ed Sullivan Show* in early television.

Behrman is also the author of a rhyming picture book that teaches young children how to tell time. In *The Ding Dong Clock,* a grandfather clock tolls the hours between twelve in the morning and twelve noon, revealing the activity in the house during each hour. With the family asleep for much of these hours, the author focuses on the moonrise, a cat waking and stretching, a couple of mice cavorting, then finally the milkman delivering milk at five in the morning, followed shortly by the family waking up and beginning their day. A clock on the cover may be used by young listeners for practicing the skill of telling time.

In 2003, Behrman began contributing to the "Presidential Leaders" series. Written by Behrman and other biographers for young readers, the series will eventually include biographies on all forty-three presidents, giving readers a context for understanding the life of the president by also explaining what was going on in the world when that president was alive.

Behrman once told *CA:* "I seem to be able, when writing, to reach into my subconscious, make contact with the eleven- or twelve-year-old me and look out at the world through her mind and her soul. It's a mysterious process that I don't understand, but it works."

BIOGRAPHICAL AND CRITICAL SOURCES:

PERIODICALS

Booklist, May 15, 1992, Ellen Mandel, review of *Fiddler to the World: The Inspiring Life of Itzhak Perlman,* p. 1674.

Bulletin of the Center for Children's Books, October, 1981, review of *The Remarkable Writing Machine,* p. 22.
Kirkus Reviews, January 15, 1999, review of *The Ding Dong Clock,* p. 143.
Kliatt, September, 1992, Elaine R. Goldberg, review of *Fiddler to the World,* p. 27.
School Library Journal, December, 1981, Connie Tyrrell, review of *The Remarkable Writing Machine,* p. 60; June, 1999, Patricia Pearl Dole, review of *The Ding Dong Clock,* p. 91; January, 2003, Kristen Oravec, review of *Andrew Jackson,* p. 147.*

* * *

BELL, Derrick
See BELL, Derrick A(lbert), Jr.

* * *

BELL, Derrick A(lbert), Jr. 1930-
(Derrick Bell)

PERSONAL: Born November 6, 1930, in Pittsburgh, PA; son of Derrick Albert and Ada Elizabeth (Childress) Bell; married Jewel Allison Hairston, June 26, 1960 (died, August, 1990); married Janet Dewart, June 28, 1992; children: (first marriage) Derrick Albert, III, Douglass Dubois, Carter Robeson. *Ethnicity:* "African American." *Education:* Duquesne University, A.B., 1952; University of Pittsburgh, LL.B., 1957.

ADDRESSES: Home—444 Central Park W, Apt. 14B, New York, NY 10025-4358. *Office*—New York University School of Law, Vanderbilt Hall, Room 308, 40 Washington Square St., New York, NY 10012-1099. *E-mail*—derrick.bell@nyu.edu.

CAREER: Law education, author, and lecturer. U.S. Department of Justice, Washington, DC, member of staff of conscientious objector section and civil rights division, 1957-59; National Association for the Advancement of Colored People (NAACP), New York, NY, staff attorney for Legal Defense and Education Fund, Inc., 1960-66; U.S. Department of Health, Education and Welfare, Washington, DC, deputy director of Office of Civil Rights, 1966-68; U.S. Office of Economic Opportunity, Western Center of Law and Pov-

Derrick A. Bell, Jr.

erty at University of Southern California, Los Angeles, director, 1968-69; Harvard University, Cambridge, MA, lecturer, 1969-71, professor of law, 1971-80, 1986-90; University of Oregon, Eugene, professor of law and dean of law school, 1981-85. Visiting professor, New York University, New York, NY, 1991-92. *Military service:* U.S. Air Force, 1952-54; became first lieutenant.

MEMBER: National Conference of Black Lawyers, Society of American Law Schools.

AWARDS, HONORS: Ford Foundation grants, 1972, 1975, 1991, and 1993; National Endowment for the Humanities grant, 1980-81; honorary law degrees, Toogaloo College, 1983, Northeastern University, 1985, Mercy College, 1988, Allegheny College, 1989, and Pace Law School, 1996; Teacher of the Year Award, Society of American Law Schools, 1985; American Book Award, Before Columbus Foundation, 1997, for *Gospel Choirs: Psalms of Survival in an Alien Land Called Home.*

WRITINGS:

UNDER NAME DERRICK BELL (EXCEPT AS NOTED)

(As Derrick A. Bell, Jr.) *Race, Racism, and American Law,* Little, Brown (Boston, MA), 1973, 4th edition, Aspen Law & Business (Gaithersburg, MD), 2000.

(Contributor) Robert J. Haws, editor, *The Age of Segregation: Race Relations in the South, 1890-1945* (essays), University Press of Mississippi (Jackson, MS), 1978.

(Editor, as Derrick A. Bell, Jr.) *Shades of Brown: New Perspectives on School Desegregation,* Teachers College Press, 1980.

(Editor) *Civil Rights: Leading Cases,* Little, Brown (Boston, MA), 1980.

And We Are Not Saved: The Elusive Quest for Racial Justice, Basic Books (New York, NY), 1987.

Faces at the Bottom of the Well: The Permanence of Racism, Basic Books (Boston, MA), 1992.

Confronting Authority: Reflections of an Ardent Protester, Beacon Press (Boston, MA), 1994.

Gospel Choirs: Psalms of Survival in an Alien Land Called Home, Basic Books (New York, NY), 1996.

Afrolantica Legacies, Third World Press (Chicago, IL), 1998.

Ethical Ambition: Living a Life of Meaning and Worth, Bloomsbury (New York, NY), 2002.

(Editor, with Bernestine Singley) *When Race Becomes Real: Black and White Writers Confront Their Personal Histories,* Lawrence Hill Books (Chicago, IL), 2002.

Silent Covenants: Brown v. Board of Education and the Elusive Quest for Racial Justice, Oxford University Press (New York, NY), 2004.

Contributor to law journals.

SIDELIGHTS: Derrick A. Bell, Jr. is a professor of law at New York University School of Law. According to Raoul Dennis in *Black Issues in Higher Education,* he is known variously as "The Race Man, The Steward, The Scold, The Pessimist, and The Realist, among others." He is considered a pioneer of critical race theory and an important figure in the movement against racial discrimination.

Born in Pittsburgh, Pennsylvania, in 1930, Bell is the son of Derrick Bell, Sr., and Ada Elizabeth Childress Bell. His father operated a small rubbish company.

Both Bell's parents taught him the value of activism when he was a boy, and they encouraged him to become educated. He was the first person in his family to go to college. He earned an A.B. degree from Duquesne University, and after graduating in 1952, joined the U.S. Air Force as a lieutenant. While he was stationed in Louisiana, he decided he would integrate a local all-white church. The church allowed him to attend, but told him to sit alone in a pew in the balcony. Bell told the pastor that he wanted to sing in the choir, which forced the church to allow him to mingle with the white members.

After leaving military service in 1954, Bell earned a law degree at the University of Pittsburgh, graduating fourth in his otherwise all-white class. Bell began teaching at Harvard University Law School in 1969 after working for several years as a civil rights lawyer. Although he had been led to believe that he would be the first of several minority faculty members that the university would hire, two years later he was still the only non-white faculty member there; this situation continued for many years, despite his protests.

From 1981 to 1985, Bell was dean of the law school at the University of Oregon, but found the same problem there. He left the deanship when the school refused to give tenure to an Asian woman whom he thought should receive it. He then returned to Harvard, but left in 1990 because of the school's refusal to hire an African-American woman.

Though he had established himself as a talented editor and essayist more than ten years earlier, Bell redefined his place in the literary world with his 1987 book, *And We Are Not Saved: The Elusive Quest for Racial Justice*. It addresses racial issues through an intertwining of fictional parables, which the author calls "chronicles," and academic argumentation. This combination allows Bell to go "beyond the well-worn arguments, answers and accommodations about race that Americans are accustomed to reading," noted Juan Williams in the *Washington Post Book World*.

Between the often-humorous parables are dialogues between two fictional narrators: a fiery 1960s civil rights lawyer named Geneva Crenshaw and a nameless male speaker who, according to *New York Times Book Review* critic Vincent Harding, "reminds us a lot of Mr. Bell." With these two narrators acting as adversaries, moderators, and chorus, *And We Are Not Saved* allows readers to examine racial issues from a unique perspective. "Novels . . . are more illuminating on racial themes [than essays] because they can convey the reality of racial discrimination," wrote Williams, "the cultural biases, legal inequities, sexual rules and the struggle of children to understand so massive a sin, as well as the occasional triumph against all odds." At one point, Geneva Crenshaw is transported back in time to the Constitutional Convention, where she debates with the founding fathers as to the ramifications of drafting legal slavery into the Constitution. In the end, says Harding, Bell asks readers both black and white to "rethink our past in order to re-envision and re-create our common future." Williams observed: "The road to this conclusion is a long one. . . . Bell could have written a much shorter essay and made his point. But the human dimension added by his stories about the pain and psychic costs of flawed modern race relations make the trip worthwhile."

When *And We Are Not Saved* was published, it elicited in readers a kind of determined optimism; Harding placed it "near the center of our continuing discussions of the past, present and future of this nation," while Williams went so far as to say: "It has the potential to shift the national mindset as America continues to climb the mountain of racial problems." Bell himself grudgingly admitted to *New York Times Book Review* interviewer Rosemary L. Bray: "At some point America may actually be a land with opportunity and justice for all." During the following years, however, the face of American racial issues became even more grim, and that optimism turned slowly into indignation. Disgusted with the lack of progress, Bell once again addressed black America with his 1992 novel, *Faces at the Bottom of the Well: The Permanence of Racism*.

Where *And We Are Not Saved* was considered by critics to be melancholy, *Faces at the Bottom of the Well* was seen as scathing and provocative; it was described by Alex Raksin of the *Los Angeles Times Book Review* as "virtually a declaration of war. Declaring that 'black people will never gain full equality in this country,' it is . . . a manifesto of secession." As with his first novel, Bell combines essay with parable to illuminate the plight of the African American: that equality is, ultimately, unattainable. Notable among the stories in *Faces* is a chronicle entitled "Space Traders," in which the entire population of black Americans is sold to extraterrestrials, for an unspecified purpose, in exchange for gold and other resources. "Bell spins this grim and stingingly effective tale around the thesis that 'sanctuary' is a more apt description of black citizenship in America than 'equality,'" wrote Lynne Duke in the *Washington Post Book World.* As with the first book, the parables are interspersed with dialogue, and Geneva Crenshaw even makes a brief return. Raksin called Bell's chronicles "powerful in their eloquence," and while Duke wrote that they can be "overly contrived and laborious to get through, this does not detract from Bell's profoundly engaging theme: Equality, for African-Americans, is a seductive, tranquilizing notion, but nothing more."

In *Confronting Authority,* Bell describes his efforts to convince Harvard University and the University of Oregon to hire minority faculty. Dennis quoted Columbia professor Manning Marable, who said of Bell, "His efforts are flash-points in a larger, longer struggle for racial equality. They are symbolic in meaning, but you have to remember that symbols are very powerful."

In *Ethical Ambition: Living a Life of Meaning and Ambition,* Bell presents his views on how one can maintain integrity while pursuing one's dreams. Bell believes that maintaining integrity is more important than financial security or public acclaim, but he notes that making the correct decision is not always easy.

Bell once commented: "In my writing, there is little of craft and certainly nothing of art, but it serves as a medium of expression which, while only infrequently effectual, remains a soul-satisfying means of speaking out against racism, poverty, and this society's self-deluding conviction that happiness can be purchased, integrity feigned, and the Lord's judgment forever postponed."

BIOGRAPHICAL AND CRITICAL SOURCES:

PERIODICALS

African American Review, summer, 1996, Raymond M. Brown, review of *Confronting Authority: Reflections of an Ardent Protester,* p. 290.
American History Review, December, 1988, p. 1386.
Black Issues in Higher Education, November 27, 1997, p. 48; August 6, 1998, p. 44; December 24, 1998, Michele Collison and Cheryl Fields, review of *Afrolantica Legacies* p. 29.
Booklist, September 15, 1994, Roland Wulbert, review of *Confronting Authority,* p. 87; June 1, 1996, Mary Carroll, review of *Gospel Choirs: Psalms of Survival for an Alien Land Called Home,* p. 1646; January 1, 1998, Bonnie Smothers, review of *Afrolantica Legacies,* p. 750; February 15, 1998, Derrick Bell author interview, p. 952; July-August, 1998, p. 71.
Chicago Daily Law Bulletin, October 4, 1994, p. 2
Choice, January, 1995, L. Bowen, review of *Confronting Authority,* p. 872.
Christian Century, August 11, 1993, Peter T. Nash, review of *Faces at the Bottom of the Well,* p. 789.
Emerge, July-August, 1996, Robert Joiner, review of *Gospel Choirs,* p. 79; July-August, 1998, Katheryn Russell, review of *Afrolantica Legacies,* p. 71.
Freedomways, 1981, p. 123.
Georgia Review, fall, 1995, Sanford Pinsker, review of *Faces at the Bottom of the Well* and *Confronting Authority,* p. 732.
Harvard Blackletter Law Journal, spring, 1995, Adrien Katherine Wing, review of *Confronting Authority,* pp. 161-175.
John Marshall Law Review, summer, 1997, Kevin L. Hopkins, review of *Gospel Choirs,* pp. 1039-1061.
Journal of American History, September, 1988, p. 675.
Journal of Black Studies, January, 1997, Darnell Anderson, review of *Confronting Authority,* p. 421.
Kirkus Reviews, August 1, 2002, review of *Ethical Ambition: Living a Life of Meaning and Worth,* p. 1085.
Law and Social Inquiry, winter, 1998, James Hackney, Jr., review of *Gospel Choirs, Faces at the Bottom of the Well,* and *And We Are Not Saved: The Elusive Quest for Racial Justice,* pp. 141-164.
Library Journal, September 15, 1994, Katherine Dahl, review of *Confronting Authority,* p. 84; May 1, 1996, review of *Gospel Choirs,* p. 116; January, 1998, Ann Burns, review of *Afrolantica Legacies,* p.122.
Los Angeles Daily Journal, October 8, 1992, p. 7.
Los Angeles Times Book Review, August 23, 1992, p. 6.
Michigan Law Review, May, 1993, p. 1175.
Nation, March 19, 1988, p. 382.
New Republic, November 16, 1987, p. 36.
New York Law Journal, June 14, 1996, p. 2.
New York Law School Law Review, winter, 1996, Helen Leskovac, review of *Confronting Authority,* pp. 537-564.
New York Times Book Review, October 11, 1987 p. 7; September 20, 1002, p. 7; July 21, 1996, p. 22; April 5, 1998, p. 30; October 2, 1994, p. 15.

NWSA Journal, fall, 1998, Diane Raymond, p. 216.

Publishers Weekly, August 8, 1994, review of *Confronting Authority,* p. 410; May 6, 1996, review of *Gospel Choirs,* p. 65; December 22, 1997, review of *Afrolantica Legacies,* p. 41; July 22, 2002, review of *Ethical Ambition: Living a Life of Meaning and Worth,* p. 164.

Wall Street Journal, December 4, 1992, p. A7; September 26, p. A12.

Washington Post Book World, November 1, 1987, p. 10; August 23, 1992, p. 1.

* * *

BELUE, Ted Franklin 1954-

PERSONAL: Born January 12, 1954, in Orlando, FL; son of Frank Owens and Myra (Janell) Belue; married July 4, 1977; wife's name Lavina (a computer programmer). *Ethnicity:* "White." *Education:* Florida College, A.A., 1976; Murray State University, B.S., 1982, M.A., 1985. *Politics:* Independent. *Religion:* Christian. *Hobbies and other interests:* Hunting, fishing, primitive camping, eighteenth-century style, eighteenth-century living-history events, acoustic music, "searching for the world's best barbecue."

ADDRESSES: Home—Murray, KY. *Office*—Department of History, Murray State University, P.O. Box 9, Murray, KY 42071-0009; fax: 502-762-6587. *E-mail*—ted.belue@murraystate.edu.

CAREER: Murray State University, Murray, KY, began as lecturer, became senior lecturer in history, 1991—. *Muzzleloader,* staff writer, 1993—; Kentucky Humanities Council, member of speakers' bureau, 1998-99; History Channel (cable television network), technical and script consultant and commentator; performed as "extra" for the film *The Last of the Mohicans,* released by Twentieth Century-Fox in 1991, and for the television broadcasts *River Pirates* and *Frontier Medicine,* both for History Channel, between 1998 and 2000; public lecturer and historical consultant.

MEMBER: Filson Club Historical Society (member of editorial advisory board, 1997-99).

WRITINGS:

The Long Hunt: Death of the Buffalo East of the Mississippi, Stackpole Books (Harrisburg, PA), 1996.

(Editor) Peter Houston, *A Sketch of the Life and Character of Daniel Boone,* Stackpole Books (Harrisburg, PA), 1997.

(Editor) Lyman C. Draper, *The Life of Daniel Boone,* Stackpole Books (Harrisburg, PA), 1998.

The Hunters of Kentucky: A Narrative History of America's First Far West, 1750-1792, Stackpole Books (Harrisburg, PA), 2003.

Contributor to books, including encyclopedias, and to *The Book of Buckskinning VII,* Scurlock Publishing (Texarkana, TX), 1995; and *The Book of Buckskinning VIII,* Scurlock Publishing (Texarkana, TX), 1999. Contributor of about eighty articles to periodicals, including *Filson Club History Quarterly, Blackpowder Annual, Muzzle Blasts, Kentucky Explorer,* and *Bluegrass Unlimited.*

SIDELIGHTS: Ted Franklin Belue once told *CA:* "Early in my life, at least by third grade, I became infatuated with the romance of America's first 'far west,' that being frontier Kentucky, and woodland Indians, especially the Shawnee. In school I realized I had a knack for being able to express myself with a pen. After attending college, I found myself out of work. To make money in 1989, I turned to writing historical nonfiction, marketing my work to magazines. While honing my skills in the trade press, to gain greater credibility I submitted essays to historical quarterlies and encyclopedias. In 1991 Murray State University hired me as an adjunct to teach general history courses, a position I still hold today, and with the same level of insecurity. By September of 1998 I had published three books which continue to sell well.

"I have no idea why I have an interest in frontier history. Nor do I know why I write, other than because I find it intriguing and, at times, profitable. Mark Twain and Jules Verne are my primary nineteenth-century influences; Peter Matthiessen, Ernest Hemingway, and Edward Abbey are my primary twentieth-century influences. Jack London taught me discipline. Typically, when not researching, I write in the mornings beginning about four o'clock, and I pick it up later in the afternoon and night after I come home from work. Often I put in twenty-five to forty hours a week on top of a full-time job. It is a lonely way to make a living, but it satisfies me."

BIOGRAPHICAL AND CRITICAL SOURCES:

PERIODICALS

Humanities: Magazine of the National Endowment for the Humanities, January-February, 1999.

BILLOUT, Guy (René) 1941-

PERSONAL: Surname pronounced "be-you"; born July 7, 1941, in Decize, France; immigrated to United States in 1969; son of René George (a journalist) and Christiane (a bookseller; maiden name, Vichard) Billout. *Education:* Attended Ecole des Arts Appliques de Beaune (France), 1956-60.

ADDRESSES: *Home and office*—380 Rector Pl., 4M, New York, NY 10280. *E-mail*—guy@guybillout.com.

CAREER: Freelance illustrator and writer. Publicis (advertising agency), Paris, France, designer, 1962-66; Thibaud-Lintas (advertising agency), Paris, France, designer, 1966-68.

AWARDS, HONORS: *New York Times* Ten Best Illustrated Books selection, 1973, for *Number Twenty-four,* 1979, for *By Camel or by Car: A Look at Transportation,* 1980, for *Stone and Steel: A Look at Engineering,* and 1982, for *Squid and Spider: A Look at the Animal Kingdom;* Society of Illustrators gold medal, 1974 and 1988, and silver medal, 1984 and 1985; books selected by American Institute of Graphic Arts include *Stone and Steel,* 1980, *Thunderbolt and Rainbow: A Look at Greek Mythology,* 1981, and *Squid and Spider,* 1982.

WRITINGS:

SELF-ILLUSTRATED

Number Twenty-four, Harlin Quist Books (New York, NY), 1973.
By Camel or by Car: A Look at Transportation, Prentice-Hall (Englewood Cliffs, NJ), 1979.
Stone and Steel: A Look at Engineering, Prentice-Hall (Englewood Cliffs, NJ), 1980.
Thunderbolt and Rainbow: A Look at Greek Mythology, Prentice-Hall (Englewood Cliffs, NJ), 1981.
Squid and Spider: A Look at the Animal Kingdom, Prentice-Hall (Englewood Cliffs, NJ), 1982.
The Journey: Travel Diary of a Daydreamer, Creative Education (Mankato, MN), 1993.
Question of Detail, Harlin Quist Books (Paris, France), 1998.
Il y a quelque chose qui cloche, Harlin Quist Books (Paris, France), 1998, published as *Something's Not Quite Right,* David R. Godine (Boston, MA), 2002.

Contributor of illustrations and columns to *Atlantic Monthly,* and of illustrations to *Le Monde, New Republic, Rolling Stone,* and the *New York Times.*

SIDELIGHTS: Guy Billout's illustrated books are indeed reviewed for children, but it is often noted that the highly-stylized artwork and cryptic or sophisticated texts will require adult interpretation for younger audiences. However, the artist's fanciful renderings of everything from wildlife to modern architecture is often considered inspiring for creatively-minded older audiences. While his books cover a variety of subjects, Billout's approach is generally consistent. Although critics have sometimes questioned whether Billout's texts are too difficult or dry for young readers, his illustrations are praised for their exceptional execution and unique, inspiring vision. His stark, poster-like watercolor paintings, with large expanses of space, bold color, and precise linear perspective, are distinguished by whimsical or surreal touches.

Billout's first book, *Number Twenty-four,* is a series of wordless images of a man waiting for bus number twenty-four while before him parade conveyances of all kinds, including a rowboat, a tank, a train, and an airplane, each of which crashes in front of him. Writing in the *New York Times Book Review,* Selma G. Lanes called this "a surreal work, as mysterious as a roomful of René Magritte paintings." Billout added words to his modus operandi in his second book, *By Camel or by Car: A Look at Transportation.* Here, his paintings are "simple nearly to the point of austere yet meticulous in detail, with a bold use of color," according to Connie Tyrrell in *School Library Journal.* Each painting depicts a mode of transportation, accompanied by two paragraphs of text, the first describing the mode in somewhat objective terms, such as speed, life span, and so forth, and the second paragraph adding the personal element, as the author muses on his own experiences with that form of transportation.

Stone and Steel: A Look at Engineering quickly followed *By Camel or by Car.* In it, Billout presents his own special look at a number of architectural marvels, blending fine detail with whimsical additions "that will delight children of all ages," according to S. W. Dobyns in *Science Books & Films*. While Paul Goldberger, writing in the *New York Times Book Review*, felt that Billout's failure to incorporate much factual information in his brief text would frustrate young readers, Leonard S. Marcus, who made a similar judgement in the *Washington Post Book World*, nevertheless noted that "daydreamers will be well in their element" in examining the illustrations in *Stone and Steel*.

For his next book, *Thunderbolt and Rainbow: A Look at Greek Mythology*, Billout envisions a modern-day Manhattan inhabited by the gods of the ancient Greeks. Steam rising from a grate offers proof of the presence of Hephaestus, the god of fire, while Zeus perches atop the Empire State Building, poised to throw his thunderbolt. "The writing is swift and unfailingly interesting," wrote a critic for *Publishers Weekly*. And though not all critics concurred with this assessment, most felt that Billout's visual rendering of ancient Greece in New York City was the true focus of the book. "The illustrations are stunning, striking, original," announced Peter Neumeyer in *School Library Journal*.

For *Squid and Spider: A Look at the Animal Kingdom*, Billout chooses thirteen animals and poses each "in unusual situations or habitats that will get observant readers giggling, thinking, or both," in Ilene Cooper's estimation in *Booklist*. "With their sly wit and eye-catching brilliance, the illustrations are striking and memorable," asserted Ethel R. Twichell in *Horn Book*, while noting that Billout's brief text debunks some popular myths about each creature.

This work was followed more than ten years later by *The Journey: Travel Diary of a Daydreamer*, a return to the cryptic, textual style of his earlier books, accompanied by an equally ambiguous series of visual images. On the left-hand page of each two-page spread, a boy sits at the window of a train looking out on a view that is only partially available. On the right hand side of the spread, the view from the window is expanded and alone, revealing details that completely alter the significance of the partial view. For Susan Scheps, writing in *School Library Journal*, the book works best as "a collection of unusual illustrations that could provide inspiration for creative writers or daydreamers of all ages."

Originally published in French as *Il y a quelque chose qui cloche*, Billout's *Something's Not Quite Right* challenges readers to find the out-of-place element in each seemingly ordinary illustration, with the unusual thing sometimes being the picture's own, single-word caption. For instance, Billout creates a seemingly-normal map of the ancient center of Paris, with one small modification. In this illustration titled "Secession," he slices through the bridges connecting Paris's Ile de la Cite to the Left and Right Banks, allowing the island to drift down the Seine. While many reviewers noted that younger children, and even some older ones, would not understand the irony, humor, and contradiction behind some of the work, *Booklist*'s Gillian Engberg suggested that teens who enjoy the surrealism of Salvador Dali and optical illusions of M. C. Escher would be attracted to *Something's Not Quite Right*. She also added that the illustrations would "make excellent exercises for creative-writing students," an aspect also noted by *Horn Book* reviewer Lolly Robinson, who predicted, "It's easy to see this book as a starting point for creative writing assignments."

Billout once told *CA*: "By education and practice, I am used to solving problems for editorial and advertising. [Upon] becoming an author/illustrator, I discovered my best capacities because I was working with a story of my own. For me, so far, the only field allowing such freedom is illustrated books, and illustrated books are mostly made for children. I would like to create picture books for adults."

BIOGRAPHICAL AND CRITICAL SOURCES:

PERIODICALS

Appraisal, spring, 1980, Douglas B. Sands, review of *By Camel or by Car: A Look at Transportation*, p. 15.

Booklist, March 15, 1982, Ilene Cooper, review of *Thunderbolt and Rainbow: A Look at Greek Mythology*, p. 955; March 1, 1983, Ilene Cooper, review of *Squid and Spider: A Look at the Animal Kingdom*, p. 902; February 15, 2003, Gillian Engberg, review of *Something's Not Quite Right*, p. 1062.

Boston, December, 1983, Charles Matthews, review of *Squid and Spider*, p. 100.

Children's Literature: Annual of the Modern Language Association Seminar on Children's Literature and the Children's Literature Association, 1974, William Anderson, review of *Number Twenty-four*, p. 217.

Design, January-February, 1982, Kenneth Marantz, review of *Thunderbolt and Rainbow,* p. 46.

Esquire, November 11, 1987.

Graphis, November-December, 1998, Veronique Vienne, "Guy Billout's Parallel Universe," p. 50.

Horn Book, April, 1983, Ethel R. Twichell, review of *Squid and Spider,* p. 181; January-February, 2003, Lolly Robinson, review of *Something's Not Quite Right,* p. 52.

New York, December 17, 1973.

New York Times Book Review, November 4, 1973, Selma Lanes, review of *Number Twenty-four,* p. 30; October 14, 1979, George A. Woods, review of *By Camel or by Car,* p. 40; November 9, 1980, Paul Goldberger, review of *Stone and Steel: A Look at Engineering,* p. 67; November 29, 1981, John Russell, review of *Thunderbolt and Rainbow,* p. 42; December 19, 1982, Selma G. Lanes, review of *Squid and Spider,* p. 26.

Publishers Weekly, July 4, 1980, review of *Stone and Steel,* p. 90; December 4, 1981, review of *Thunderbolt and Rainbow,* p. 50; November 12, 1982, review of *Squid and Spider,* p. 67; May 20, 1983, review of *By Camel or by Car,* p. 237; November 15, 1993, review of *The Journey: Travel Diary of a Daydreamer,* p. 78; November 18, 2002, review of *Something's Not Quite Right,* p. 58.

School Library Journal, February 15, 1974, Judith Shor Kronick, review of *Number Twenty-four,* p. 59; December, 1979, Connie Tyrrell, review of *By Camel or by Car,* pp. 71-72; December, 1980, Ruby G. Campbell, review of *Stone and Steel,* p. 58; February, 1982, Peter Neumeyer, review of *Thunderbolt and Rainbow,* p. 64; April, 1983, Margaret Bush, review of *Squid and Spider,* p. 120; February, 1994, Susan Scheps, review of *The Journey,* p. 100; January, 2003, Marianne Saccardi, review of *Something's Not Quite Right,* p. 150.

Science Books & Films, September-October, 1981, S. W. Dobyns, review of *Stone and Steel,* p. 34.

Time, December 20, 1982, Stefan Kanfer, review of *Squid and Spider,* p. 80.

Washington Post Book World, November 9, 1980, Leonard S. Marcus, review of *Stone and Steel,* p. 12; January 10, 1982, Brigitte Weeks and Robert Wilson, review of *Thunderbolt and Rainbow,* p. 10.

Zoom (France), March-April, 1975.

ONLINE

Guy Billout Home Page, http://www.guybillout.com/ (August 2, 2003).*

BILLSON, Janet Mancini 1941-

PERSONAL: Born December 15, 1941, in Hamilton, Ontario, Canada; daughter of Clifford E. (retired from Canadian armed forces) and Kathleen M. (a homemaker; maiden name, Billson) Ramey; married Francis S. Mancini, June, 1968 (divorced, 1978); married Norman T. London (an academic consultant), August 21, 1990; children: Mark F., Kyra M. *Ethnicity:* "White." *Education:* Baldwin-Wallace College, B.A., 1965; Brandeis University, M.A., 1972, Ph.D., 1976. *Politics:* "Democratic." *Religion:* Unitarian. *Hobbies and other interests:* Photography, hiking, gardening, kayaking.

ADDRESSES: Office—Group Dimensions Research, 300 Narragansett Ave., Barrington, RI 02806. *E-mail*—jbillson@aol.com.

CAREER: Rhode Island College, Providence, RI, professor of sociology and women's studies, 1973-91, acting associate dean of students and director of student life, 1984, assistant dean of faculty of arts and sciences, 1984-86; American Sociological Association, Washington, DC, assistant executive officer and director of the academic and professional affairs program, 1991-95; George Washington University, Washington, DC, adjunct professor of sociology and women's studies, 1993-95, professor of sociology, 1995—. Group Dimensions Research, Barrington, RI, director.

MEMBER: American Sociological Association, Sociologists for Women in Society, Society for Applied Sociology, Association for Canadian Studies in the United States, Sociological Practice Association, District of Columbia Sociological Society.

AWARDS, HONORS: Woodrow Wilson fellow, 1965-66; field work fellowship, National Institute of Mental Health, 1966-68; Danforth associate, 1979—; honorary research fellow, University of Exeter, 1981; Pulitzer Prize nomination, 1992, for *Cool Pose: Dilemmas of Black Manhood in America;* award for sociological practice, Sociological Practice Association, 2000; Stuart A. Rice Career Achievement Award, District of Columbia Sociological Society, 2001.

WRITINGS:

Strategic Styles: Coping in the Inner City, University Press of New England (Hanover, NH), 1980.

(With Richard Majors) *Cool Pose: Dilemmas of Black Manhood in America,* Lexington Books (New York, NY), 1992.

Keepers of the Culture: The Power of Tradition in Women's Lives, Lexington Books (New York, NY), 1995.

Pathways to Manhood: Young Black Males Struggle for Identity, Transaction Books (New Brunswick, NJ), 1996.

The Power of Focus Groups for Social and Policy Research, Skywood Press (Barrington, RI), 2002.

(With Kyra Mancini Reis) *Their Powerful Spirit: Inuit Women in a Century of Change,* in press.

Work represented in anthologies, including *Teaching Sociological Practice: A Resource Book,* edited by Carla B. Howery, Novella Perrin, and John Seem, American Sociological Association (Washington, DC), 1993; *Marginality and Society: Issues in Class, Race, and Gender,* edited by Rutledge Dennis, Sage Publications (Newbury Park, CA), 1996; and *Perspectives on Current Social Problems,* edited by Gregg Carter, Allyn & Bacon (New York, NY), 1996.

WORK IN PROGRESS: Women 2000: A Century of Social Change around the World, with Carolyn Fleuhr-Lobban.

SIDELIGHTS: Sociologist Janet Mancini Billson once told *CA:* "I write because I am committed to conducting research with people whose voices are seldom heard—immigrant, Native, and minority women and men. As a sociologist, I find myself driven to understand the impacts of rapid social change on identity (both individual and community). I am especially intrigued by the interlocking identities created by the intersection of race, class, and gender. Writing becomes a natural extension of the research process and a key way to share my insights."

Billson's commitment to sharing her insights concerning minority men and women is evident in her books, among them her 1992 publication *Cool Pose: Dilemmas of Black Manhood in America,* which she wrote with Richard Majors. In this volume Billson and Majors explore the experience of black men in a world that has traditionally offered them few social, political, and economic opportunities. The "cool pose" black men have assumed, according to the authors, is a physical and mental stance that projects braveness, toughness, and detachment, while camouflaging their inner feelings. The pose also may be an outward rebellion toward an insensitive society, while subsequently providing a measure of distance from the black man's oppressor, as a tough, "cool" posture proves threatening, and even frightening, to many other Americans. Writing in the *New York Review of Books,* Andrew Hacker said that "Richard Majors and Janet Billson do much to demystify what they call 'the dilemmas of black manhood.'" Hacker added: "Majors and Billson do not romanticize the young men. They note that if one aspect of 'coolness means poise under pressure,' it can also 'express bitterness, anger, and distrust toward the dominant society.'"

Billson's 1995 book, *Keepers of the Culture: The Power of Tradition in Women's Lives,* features the women of seven cultures in Canada: the Chinese in Vancouver; Iroquois, Jamaicans, and Mennonites in Ontario; the Blood in Alberta; Ukrainian in Saskatchewan; and the Inuit on Baffin Island. Billson studied each of these peoples, interviewing them, in particular, about the role feminism plays in their lives. The author found that cultures in which women are valued are far less likely to embrace feminist ideology than are women in cultures that place less importance on women's roles. She found, too, that women without financial freedom often submit to their culture's traditions because they see no other choice. Billson's book was well-received as an important study of women and culture by reviewers such as Ann Grimes, writing in the *Washington Post Book World. Keepers of the Culture,* Grimes reported, "reads very much like the academic study it is. Nevertheless, it makes a good argument that feminist theories and women's-studies courses should do better at recognizing and incorporating the experiences of women from different cultures."

Commenting on what influences her work, Billson also told *CA:* "The most critical influences have been the spectacular feminist research literature that has emerged in the social sciences since the early 1970s. This perspective forces me to look behind everyday power relations between men and women and to question the 'taken for granted' arrangements between oppressed and oppressors. My Canadian heritage, which includes English, Scottish, and French streams of tradition, has led me to write extensively about women in Canada, and to think cross-culturally.

"My favorite approach involves conducting intensive focus group interviews with women in distinct communities (for example, the Mennonites of Ontario or the Inuit of Baffin Island) and to write as closely to their words as possible. Interviewees (whom I consider 'consultants' rather than 'respondents') have a chance to react to interpretations and hypotheses as they emerge 'in the field,' and always have the opportunity to respond to drafts. Careful reviews of the scholarly literature always precede and find their way into my work, even though my writing style bridges academic and trade audiences. Generally, I write between two and twelve hours a day, depending on the stage of the manuscript and time pressures. I write virtually every day, all year long, because I enjoy the absorption of the writing process.

"The people I meet on my journeys inspire me, as do my colleagues, family, and friends. I like ideas that sit on the edge of two or more disciplines. For example, identity and marginality, two themes that dominate my work, derive their intellectual force from both sociology and psychology. I find myself challenged by trying to figure out why and how people become powerful or powerless, and how they cope with the changing world around them. The more immediate inspiration for my writing comes from kayaking in Narragansett Bay in Rhode Island, or watching the light play on the water and the wind move through the trees. The birds at the feeder outside my study window provide regular companionship and relief from the hard work of writing."

BIOGRAPHICAL AND CRITICAL SOURCES:

PERIODICALS

New York Review of Books, January 28, 1993, pp. 12-15.
Washington Post, June 2, 1992, p. D2.
Washington Post Book World, August 13, 1995, p. 6.

* * *

BLATTY, William Peter 1928-

PERSONAL: Born January 7, 1928, in New York, NY; son of Peter (a carpenter) and Mary (Mouakad) Blatty; married Mary Margaret Rigard, February 18, 1950 (marriage annulled); married Elizabeth Gilman, 1950; married Linda Tuero (a professional tennis player),

William Peter Blatty

July 20, 1975; children: seven. *Education:* Georgetown University, A.B., 1950; George Washington University, M.A., 1954; graduate study overseas. *Religion:* Roman Catholic.

ADDRESSES: *Home*—Montecito, CA. *Agent*—William Morris Agency, 151 El Camino Dr., Beverly Hills, CA 90212.

CAREER: Door-to-door Electrolux vacuum cleaner salesman, 1950; beer truck driver for Gunther Brewing Co., 1950; United States Information Agency, Beirut, Lebanon, editor of *News Review* (weekly magazine), 1955-57; University of Southern California, Los Angeles, CA, publicity director, 1957-58; Loyola University of Los Angeles, Los Angeles, CA, public relations director, 1959-60; full-time novelist and screenwriter, 1960—. Has produced and directed films, all based on his novels of the same titles, *The Exorcist, The Ninth Configuration,* and *Twinkle, Twinkle, "Killer" Kane.* Regular guest on *Tonight Show* television program. *Military service:* U.S. Air Force, Psychological Warfare Division, 1951-54; attained the rank of first lieutenant.

MEMBER: Writers Guild of America.

AWARDS, HONORS: Gabriel Award and Blue Ribbon, American Film Festival, 1969, for *Insight* television series script; Silver Medal, California Literature Medal Award, 1972, for *The Exorcist*; Academy Award for best screenplay based on a work in another medium, Academy of Motion Picture Arts and Sciences, 1973, and August Derleth Award for best film, and Golden Globe Award for best screenplay, both 1974, all for *The Exorcist*; Golden Globe Award for best screenplay, 1981, for *The Ninth Configuration*; L.H.D., Seattle University, 1974.

WRITINGS:

NOVELS

Which Way to Mecca, Jack?, Bernard Geis Associates, 1960.
John Goldfarb, Please Come Home!, Doubleday (New York, NY), 1963.
I, Billy Shakespeare!, Doubleday (New York, NY), 1965.
Twinkle, Twinkle, "Killer" Kane (also see below), Doubleday (New York, NY), 1967, Futura (London, England), 1975, revised as *The Ninth Configuration*, Harper & Row (New York, NY), 1978.
The Exorcist (also see below), Harper (New York, NY), 1971.
Legion (also see below), Simon & Schuster (New York, NY), 1983, also published as *Exorcist III: Legion*, Pocket Books (New York, NY), 1990.
Demons Five, Exorcists Nothing: A Fable, Donald I. Fine Books (New York, NY), 1996.

SCREENPLAYS

The Man from the Diner's Club, Columbia, 1963.
John Goldfarb, Please Come Home! (based on his novel of the same title), Twentieth Century-Fox, 1965.
A Shot in the Dark, United Artists, 1966.
What Did You Do in the War, Daddy?, United Artists, 1966.
Gunn, Paramount, 1967.
The Great Bank Robbery, Warner Bros., 1969.
Darling Lili, Paramount, 1970.

(And producer) *The Exorcist* (based on his novel of the same title), Warner Bros., 1973.
(And director and producer) *Twinkle, Twinkle, "Killer" Kane* (based on his novel of the same title), United Film, 1980.
The Ninth Configuration (based on his novel of the same title), 1980.
(And director) *The Exorcist III* (based on his novel *Legion*), Twentieth Century-Fox, 1990.

OTHER

I'll Tell Them I Remember You (informal biography of his mother, Mary Mouakad Blatty), Norton (New York, NY), 1973.
William Peter Blatty on "The Exorcist": From Novel to Film (nonfiction), Bantam (New York, NY), 1974.
If There Were Demons, Then Perhaps There Were Angels: William Peter Blatty's Own Story of the Exorcist (memoir), illustrated by Rae Smith, ScreenPress Books (Southwold, England), 1999.

Author of *Elsewhere* (novella), included in *999: Twenty-nine Original Tales of Horror and Suspense*, edited by Al Sarrantonio, Perennial Press, 2001. Also author of *Promise Her Anything*, 1962, (and director and producer) *The Baby Sitter*, and *"Insight"* television series script. Contributor of articles to periodicals, including *Saturday Evening Post*, *Coronet*, and *This Week*.

WORK IN PROGRESS: A humorous novel and a psychological/theological thriller.

SIDELIGHTS: Although William Peter Blatty began his career as a writer of comedic screenplays, he achieved greater fame and commercial success in horror films. With his best-selling novel *The Exorcist*, about the expulsion of a demon from a young girl by a Roman Catholic priest, and the major motion picture it engendered, he helped initiate the modern horror film movement. The novel sold thirteen million copies in the United States alone, and the 1973 motion picture based on it broke box-office records, earning $165 million, the first time around. When a remastered version of the motion picture, which included never-before-seen footage, was released in 2000, it garnered another $140 million worldwide. Yet according to the

St. James Guide to Horror, Ghost & Gothic Writers, Blatty had a more earnest desire than to purely entertain. He has used this novel and later *Legion* as works to debate the "existence of God, the soul, and the afterlife, and the nature of good and evil." Despite such high aims, Blatty knew he had a blockbuster on his hands with *The Exorcist,* predicting the book's achievements even before penning the final chapters. "I knew it was going to be a success," he told Garry Clifford of *People.* "I couldn't wait to finish it and become famous."

The youngest son of Lebanese immigrants, Blatty vividly remembers his childhood. Raised primarily by his mother after his parents separated when he was six years old, Blatty recalled her determination to succeed. She strived to support the family by selling her homemade quince jelly along Park Avenue and in front of the Plaza Hotel in New York City. Blatty told Martha MacGregor of the *New York Post,* "My feeling was that if she couldn't come through with some kind of evidence of survival, it couldn't be done." Despite his mother's efforts, however, Blatty still remembers their poverty and numerous evictions, explaining to Clifford: "I'd come home from school, . . . and all the furniture would be piled up in the street. It was pretty savage the way they did it—humiliating for a kid." As a boy he read ghost stories and works by P. G. Wodehouse, but horror did not, and still "does not interest me, so I know little of its practitioners, old or current," he told Lucy A. Snyder in *Dark Planet: Nonfiction.* Among his other favorite authors are such diverse writers as Graham Greene, Dostoyevsky, Robert Nathan, and Ray Bradbury.

A college scholarship to Georgetown University provided Blatty's first real step away from New York City and gave him the inspiration for his first blockbuster. While a student there, he read stories in the *Washington Post* about the exorcism practices used on a fourteen-year-old boy in nearby Mount Rainier, Maryland. Blatty would use the idea of demonic possession, but not retell this particular incident, in *The Exorcist.*

While it was not until the publication of *The Exorcist* that Blatty became well known, his second novel was the subject of a minor controversy. *John Goldfarb, Please Come Home!* chronicles the efforts of a captured American pilot to coach a team of Arabs to victory over the Notre Dame football team; the novel drew loud criticism from Notre Dame officials. University trustees protested that both book and film damaged the school's reputation, and they received an injunction blocking both from distribution. Upheld in the New York State Supreme Court in 1964, the ruling was later overturned in 1965, after Blatty appealed the decision, explaining that he had meant no disrespect to Notre Dame. Once released, however, the movie failed to achieve major success.

After *John Goldfarb, Please Come Home!* Blatty experienced a disappointing period in his career. Both *I, Billy Shakespeare!* and *Twinkle, Twinkle, "Killer" Kane* failed to impress critics. Numerous production changes in his screenplays combined with the sudden death of his mother in 1967 left Blatty emotionally drained. Reaction to these personal problems forced Blatty to retreat to a Lake Tahoe cabin for privacy and reevaluation of his beliefs. Once there, he drafted his first version of *The Exorcist,* a novel that would attain the number two position on the 1971 *Publishers Weekly* best-seller list, and that would remain on the *New York Times*'s best-seller list for fifty-five weeks. *The Exorcist* inspired varied reactions. Many critics acknowledged the sheer readability and mounting suspense of the novel, yet some questioned its validity, both in terms of literary value and intellectual appeal. Webster Schott of *Life* commented: "It's a page-turner *par excellence.* . . . Blatty writes and thinks sophisticated. . . . Faulkner, Blatty is not. But Poe and Mary Shelley would recognize him as working in their ambiguous limbo between the natural and the supernatural." *New York Times Book Review* critic Newgate Callendar shared Schott's observations of the book, noting, "Well researched, written in a literate style, it comes to grips with the forces of evil incarnate, and there are not many readers who will be unmoved."

Newsweek's Peter S. Prescott admitted the novel's wide attraction but denied higher merits, claiming, "I suspect [Blatty] wants his book to be interesting in an intellectual way, but it is not; nevertheless, it is wonderfully exciting." R. Z. Sheppard of *Time,* while decrying any literary and religious aspirations, nonetheless accurately predicted favorable public reaction to the work: "[*The Exorcist*] is a pretentious, tasteless, abominably written, redundant pastiche of superficial theology, comic-book psychology, Grade C movie dialogue and Grade Z scatology. In short [it] will be a bestseller and almost certainly a drive-in movie."

In 1971 Warner Brothers paid over $400,000 for the film rights to the novel allowing Blatty to retain complete control on the set. (He later demanded and was granted similar arrangements on the films *The Ninth Configuration* and *Twinkle, Twinkle, "Killer" Kane,* both based respectively on his novels of the same titles.) Blatty also wrote the film script and produced the movie himself. *The Exorcist*'s ten million budget proved worth the investment in terms of revenues as the film grossed an average of two million per month during its original release. *The Exorcist* effectively became the bar by which later movies about demonic possessions were measured.

Although *The Exorcist* was his first published novel dealing with demonic possession, Blatty had long been interested in the occult and the supernatural. His own informal research into case histories of "possessed" individuals revealed that, although most of the "victims" were probably mentally unbalanced, a small number of cases defied usual psychological and scientific explanations. Fascinated by these apparent anomalies, Blatty fashioned *Exorcist* character "Regan MacNeil" after one such case. He loosely based Regan on a Maryland patient, upon whom, owing to the failure of conventional medical and psychiatric therapies, Catholic priests resorted to the holy rite of exorcism. Blatty's interest in the supernatural continued in personal matters as well as in his writing. After his mother's death, he ultimately convinced himself that her spirit had transcended mortal boundaries, as detailed in the final chapters of *I'll Tell Them I Remember You.*

Although Blatty attempted to make a movie sequel to *The Exorcist* in the late 1970s, he and filmmakers were unable to agree on a plot, and Warner Brothers paid for the rights to make a sequel without Blatty's input. Thus, the resulting *Exorcist 2: The Heretic* was not his work, although some might have thought it so; the same situation came about with the fourth *Exorcist* film, the prequel. For his part, Blatty finds it ironic that he was first known as a comedy writer and not taken seriously when he wanted to do non-comedic work. At the turn of the millennium, the opposite held true. With his work on *The Exorcist* eclipsing all of his earlier work, no one remembers his comedic work or looks for him to again create comedy. And even as the author of *The Exorcist,* Blatty does not consider himself a creator of horror, because, as he explained at the *Well Rounded Web* site, "I don't classify *The Exorcist* as a horror film—it is a psychological thriller."

Blatty's screenplay version of *Legion* was to be his sequel to *The Exorcist.* When he was unable to peddle it to a studio, Blatty rewrote the screenplay as a novel, working intensely over a four-month period. The action of the novel *Legion* takes place fifteen years after *The Exorcist* and involves some of the same characters, including the demon-possessed Father Karras (who did not really die at the end of *The Exorcist*) and Lt. Kinderman, a Jewish detective and philosopher who ruminates on theological questions as he attempts to solve a series of murders. After the success of the novel *Legion* in 1983, Blatty was able to find filmmakers interested in bringing the novel to the big screen, though much of Blatty's theological discussions could not be translated to the screen. So a pared-down version of what *Library Journal*'s James B. Hemesath called a "needlessly complicated plot and overwritten style" premiered in 1990 under the title *Exorcist III: Legion.* At the same time, the novel was re-released under the same title as the movie. Writing in *People,* Ralph Novak lavished praise on the film, calling it "one of the shrewdest, wittiest, most intense and most satisfying horror movies ever made."

Blatty considers the novels *The Exorcist, The Ninth Configuration,* and *Legion* to be a trilogy. As the author explained to Snyder: "Taken together, they are all about the eternal questions that nag at Woody Allen: why are we here? what are we supposed to be doing? why do we die? is there a God?" For example, *The Exorcist* deals with the question of God's existence by treating the topic of demons and the ability of religious faith to combat them. His 1980 film *The Ninth Configuration,* based on the 1978 book of the same title, treats the theme of unselfish love, the "love as a God might love—and that a man will give his life for another," Blatty continued. In the second novel, Hudson Kane, a guerilla war specialist who must come to terms with the moral issues surrounding his career and the Vietnam War, aids fellow officers suddenly suffering from strange obsessions. In addition to describing this plot as "clever" and "gripping," and Blatty's characterizations as "excellent," *Library Journal* reviewer Marilyn Lutz recommended the work. Finally, in *Legion,* Lt. Kinderman ponders the eternal question of suffering by innocents.

In the mid-1990s Blatty returned to his roots, publishing a satiric fable about a movie mogul attempting to make a film called *The Satanist.* Likely based on some of Blatty's own experiences in Hollywood, the "madcap narrative" relies on "heavily caricatured types" for which the reader may have little empathy, noted a *Publishers Weekly* reviewer. It is "silly without being funny," concluded *Library Journal*'s David Bartholomew. In addition to this fictional treatment of movie-making, Blatty has written several nonfiction works about his career: *"The Exorcist": From Novel to Film*, now out of print, and the 1999 memoir *If There Were Demons, Then Perhaps There Were Angels: William Peter Blatty's Own Story of the Exorcist*.

BIOGRAPHICAL AND CRITICAL SOURCES:

BOOKS

Newquist, Roy, *Counterpoint*, Simon & Schuster (New York, NY) 1964.
St. James Guide to Horror, Ghost & Gothic Writers, St. James Press (Detroit, MI), 1998.
Short, R. L., *Something to Believe In*, Harper (New York, NY), 1978.

PERIODICALS

Best Sellers, August, 1983, review of *Legion*, p. 159.
Booklist, April 15, 1983, review of *Legion*, p. 1057.
Books and Bookmen, April, 1972.
Fear, June, 1990, Steve Biodrowski, "Self Possessed: An Interview with William Peter Blatty."
Harper's Bazaar, August, 1972.
Kirkus Reviews, April 1, 1983, review of *Legion*, p. 387; July 15, 1996, review of *Demons Five, Exorcists Nothing*, p. 986.
Kliatt Young Adult Paperback Book Guide, review of *The Exorcist* (audio version), p. 46.
Library Journal, September 1, 1978, Marilyn Lutz, review of *The Ninth Configuration*, p. 1658; May 15, 1983, James B. Hemesath, review of *Legion*, p. 1015; September 1, 1996, David Bartholomew, review of *Demons Five, Exorcists Nothing*, p. 208.
Life, May 7, 1971; December 31, 1971.
Locus, April, 1990, review of *The Exorcist*, p. 35; October, 1990, review of *Legion*, p. 50; March, 1994, review of *The Exorcist*, p. 53.
London Review of Books (London, England), November 17, 1983, review of *Legion*, p. 12.
Los Angeles Times, July 17, 1983, Grover Sales, review of *Legion*, p. 4; September 8, 1985, Pat H. Broeske, review of *Ninth Configuration*, p. 15.

Necrofile, winter, 1997, review of *Demons Five, Exorcists Nothing*, pp. 18+.
Newsweek, May 10, 1971.
New York Post, October 12, 1971; September 1, 1973.
New York Times, October 6, 1973; August 8, 1980; June 27, 1983, Christopher Lehman-Haupt, review of *Legion*, p. C12(L); August 18, 1990, Vincent Canby, review of *The Exorcist III*, p. 13(L).
New York Times Book Review, June 6, 1971; February 11, 1973; November 18, 1973; July 3, 1983, review of *Legion*, p. 9; January 19, 1997, Karen Ray, review of *Demons Five, Exorcists Nothing*, p. 18.
People, March 4, 1974; October 9, 1978; August 14, 1989; September 3, 1990, Ralph Novak, review of *The Exorcist III*, p. 12.
Premiere, March, 2001, Marion Hart, review of *The Exorcist: The Version You've Never Seen*, p. 114.
Publishers Weekly, May 6, 1983, review of *Legion*, p. 88; March 16, 1984, review of *Legion*, p. 85; July 29, 1999, review of *Demons Five, Exorcists Nothing*, pp. 69-70.
Saturday Review, June 5, 1971.
Science Fiction Review, February, 1984, review of *Legion*, p. 38.
Sight and Sound, July, 1999, Mark Kermode, review of *The Ninth Configuration*, p. 50.
Time, June 7, 1971.
Times Literary Supplement, April 19, 1974.
Variety, August 22, 1990, p. 76; September 25, 2000, Robert Koehler, review of *The Exorcist*, p. 60.
Video Review, April, 1991, Ed Hulse, review of *The Exorcist III*, p. 79.
Washington Post, April 4, 1974.
Washington Times, September 23, 2000, Gary Arnold, "Revised *Exorcist* Tormented by Gratuitous Scene," p. 2.
West Coast Review of Books, November, 1978; September, 1983, review of *Legion*, p. 34.*

* * *

BLUME, Judy (Sussman) 1938-

PERSONAL: Born February 12, 1938, in Elizabeth, NJ; daughter of Rudolph (a dentist) and Esther (Rosenfeld) Sussman; married John M. Blume (an attorney), August 15, 1959 (divorced, 1975); married third husband, George Cooper (a writer), June 6, 1987; chil-

Judy Blume

dren: (first marriage) Randy Lee (daughter), Lawrence Andrew; (third marriage) Amanda (stepdaughter). *Education:* New York University, B.S., 1961. *Religion:* Jewish.

ADDRESSES: *Home*—New York, NY. *Agent*—c/o Author Mail, Atheneum, 1230 Avenue of the Americas, New York, NY 10020. *E-mail*—judyb@judyblume.com.

CAREER: Writer of juvenile and adult fiction. Founder and trustee of KIDS Fund, 1981.

MEMBER: Society of Children's Book Writers and Illustrators (member of board), PEN, Authors Guild (member of council; vice president, 2002—), National Coalition Against Censorship (member of board).

AWARDS, HONORS: *New York Times* best books for children list, 1970, Nene Award, 1975, Young Hoosier Book Award, 1976, and North Dakota Children's Choice Award, 1979, all for *Are You There God? It's Me, Margaret;* Charlie May Swann Children's Book Award, 1972, Young Readers Choice Award, Pacific Northwest Library Association, and Sequoyah Children's Book Award of Oklahoma, both 1975, Massachusetts Children's Book Award, Georgia Children's Book Award, and South Carolina Children's Book Award, all 1977, Rhode Island Library Association Award, 1978, North Dakota Children's Choice Award, and West Australian Young Readers' Book Award, both 1980, United States Army in Europe Kinderbuch Award, and Great Stone Face Award, New Hampshire Library Council, both 1981, all for *Tales of a Fourth Grade Nothing;* Golden Archer Award, 1974; Arizona Young Readers Award, and Young Readers Choice Award, Pacific Northwest Library Association, both 1977, and North Dakota Children's Choice Award, 1983, all for *Blubber;* South Carolina Children's Book Award, 1978, for *Otherwise Known As Sheila the Great;* Texas Bluebonnet List, 1980, Michigan Young Readers' Award, and International Reading Association Children's Choice Award, both 1981, First Buckeye Children's Book Award, Nene Award, Sue Hefley Book Award, Louisiana Association of School Libraries, United States Army in Europe Kinderbuch Award, West Australian Young Readers' Book Award, North Dakota Children's Choice Award, Colorado Children's Book Award, Georgia Children's Book Award, Tennessee Children's Choice Book Award, and Utah Children's Book Award, all 1982, Northern Territory Young Readers' Book Award, Young Readers Choice Award, Pacific Northwest Library Association, Garden State Children's Book Award, Iowa Children's Choice Award, Arizona Young Readers' Award, California Young Readers' Medal, and Young Hoosier Book Award, all 1983, all for *Superfudge;* American Book Award nomination, Dorothy Canfield Fisher Children's Book Award, Buckeye Children's Book Award, and California Young Readers Medal, all 1983, all for *Tiger Eyes;* Today's Woman Award, 1981; Eleanor Roosevelt Humanitarian Award, Favorite Author—Children's Choice Award, Milner Award, and Jeremiah Ludington Memorial Award, all 1983; Carl Sandburg Freedom to Read Award, Chicago Public Library, 1984; Civil Liberties Award, Atlanta American Civil Liberties Union, and John Rock Award, Center for Population Options, Los Angeles, both 1986; D.H.L., Kean College, 1987; South Australian Youth Media Award for Best Author, South Australian Association for Media Education, 1988; Most Admired Author, Heroes of Young America Poll, 1989; National Hero Award, Big Brothers/Big Sisters, 1992; Dean's Award, Columbia University College of Physicians and Surgeons, 1993; Margaret

A. Edwards Award for Outstanding Literature for Young Adults, American Library Association, 1996, for lifetime achievement writing for teens; honorary degree from Holyoke College, 2003; Writers for Writers Award, Poets and Writers, 2004.

WRITINGS:

JUVENILE FICTION

The One in the Middle Is the Green Kangaroo, Reilly & Lee, 1969, revised edition, Bradbury (New York, NY), 1981, second revised edition, with new illustrations, 1991.
Iggie's House, Bradbury (New York, NY), 1970.
Are You There God? It's Me, Margaret, Bradbury (New York, NY), 1970.
Then Again, Maybe I Won't (also see below), Bradbury (New York, NY), 1971.
Freckle Juice, Four Winds (New York, NY), 1971.
Tales of a Fourth Grade Nothing, Dutton (New York, NY), 1972.
Otherwise Known As Sheila the Great (also see below), Dutton (New York, NY), 1972.
It's Not the End of the World (also see below), Bradbury (New York, NY), 1972.
Deenie (also see below), Bradbury (New York, NY), 1973.
Blubber, Bradbury (New York, NY), 1974.
Starring Sally J. Freedman As Herself, Bradbury (New York, NY), 1977.
Superfudge, Dutton (New York, NY), 1980.
Tiger Eyes, Bradbury (New York, NY), 1981.
The Pain and the Great One, Bradbury (New York, NY), 1984.
Just As Long As We're Together, Orchard (New York, NY), 1987.
Fudge-a-Mania, Dutton (New York, NY), 1990.
Here's to You, Rachel Robinson, Orchard (New York, NY), 1993.
Double Fudge, Dutton (New York, NY), 2002.
A Judy Blume Collection: Three Novels by Best-selling Author Judy Blume: Deenie; It's Not the End of the World; Then Again, Maybe I Won't, Atheneum (New York, NY), 2003.

OTHER

Forever . . . (young-adult novel), Bradbury (New York, NY), 1975.
Wifey (adult novel), Putnam (New York, NY), 1977.
The Judy Blume Diary, Dell (New York, NY), 1981.
Smart Women (adult novel), Putnam (New York, NY), 1984.
Letters to Judy: What Your Kids Wish They Could Tell You (nonfiction), Putnam (New York, NY), 1986.
The Judy Blume Memory Book, Dell (New York, NY), 1988.
(And producer with son, Lawrence Blume) *Otherwise Known As Sheila the Great* (screenplay; adapted from her novel), Barr Films, 1988.
Summer Sisters (adult novel) Delacorte (New York, NY), 1998.
(Editor) *Places I Never Meant to Be: Original Stories by Censored Writers,* Simon & Schuster (New York, NY), 1999.
(With others) *Author Talk: Conversations with Judy Blume (and Others),* Simon & Schuster (New York, NY), 2000.

Some of Blume's papers are housed in the Kerlan Collection, University of Minnesota.

ADAPTATIONS: *Forever . . .* was adapted as a television film, CBS-TV, 1978; *Freckle Juice* was adapted as an animated film by Barr Films, 1987.

SIDELIGHTS: In the nearly thirty years since she published her first book, Judy Blume has become one of the most popular and controversial authors writing for children. Her accessible, humorous style and direct, sometimes explicit treatment of youthful concerns have won her many fans—as well as critics who sometimes seek to censor her work. Nevertheless, Blume has continued to produce works that are both entertaining and thought-provoking. "Blume has a knack for knowing what children think about and an honest, highly amusing way of writing about it," Jean Van Leeuwen stated in the *New York Times Book Review.*

Many critics attribute Blume's popularity to her ability to discuss openly, realistically, and compassionately the subjects that concern her readers. Her books for younger children, such as *Tales of a Fourth Grade Nothing, Blubber,* and *Otherwise Known As Sheila the Great,* deal with problems of sibling rivalry, establishing self-confidence, and social ostracism. *Tales of a Fourth Grade Nothing* introduces Manhattanite Peter Warren Hatcher and his little brother Fudge. In the book's most memorable scene, Peter learns that his brother Fudge has swallowed his pet turtle. This book won numerous awards from organizations throughout the United States and continues to be a favorite with children. As Mark Oppenheimer noted in the *New York Times Book Review,* by 1996, the title "had sold over six million copies." Blume continued the story begun in *Tales of a Fourth Grade Nothing* with *Superfudge.* In this book, the Hatcher family has moved to Princeton, New Jersey, and Fudge is ready to enter kindergarten. Fudge is still a problem for Peter: he keeps Peter out of the bathroom, sticks stamps all over the baby, and kicks his kindergarten teacher. "No one knows the byways of the under-twelves better than Blume," commented Pamela D. Pollack in *School Library Journal.* Brigitte Weeks of the *Washington Post Book World* remarked that the book demonstrates Blume's ability to create "good clean fun," adding, "Blume's books for younger readers are funny . . . important to children is the clear knowledge that Blume is on their team." In *Double Fudge,* Fudge develops such an obsession with money that his family decides to take him to the mint in Washington, DC, to show him how it is made. There, they run into relatives from Hawaii who end up barging in to stay with them. While the twins Fauna and Flora insist on singing at Fudge's school, their brother enjoys acting like a dog. Peter narrates the humorous events with an appropriate tone of frustration. Terrie Dorio in the *School Library Journal* believed that "Peter is a real twelve-year-old with all the insecurities and concerns of that age." The critic for *Publishers Weekly* praised "the sprightly clip of this cheerful read." Gillian Engberg in *Booklist* found that "Blume's humor and pitch-perfect ear for sibling rivalry and family dynamics will have readers giggling with recognition."

Blume's books for young adults, such as *Are You There God? It's Me, Margaret, Deenie,* and *Just As Long As We're Together* consider matters of divorce, friendship, family breakups, and sexual development, while *Forever . . .* specifically deals with a young woman's first love and first sexual experience. But whatever the situation, Blume's characters confront their feelings of confusion as a start to resolving their problems. In *Are You There God? It's Me, Margaret,* for example, the young protagonist examines her thoughts about religion and speculates about becoming a woman. The result is a book that uses "sensitivity and humor" in capturing "the joys, fears and uncertainty that surround a young girl approaching adolescence," Lavinia Russ wrote in *Publishers Weekly.*

"Blume's books reflect a general cultural concern with feelings about self and body, interpersonal relationships, and family problems," Alice Phoebe Naylor and Carol Wintercorn remarked in the *Dictionary of Literary Biography.* Blume has taken this general concern further, the critics continued, for "her portrayal of feelings of sexuality as normal, and not rightfully subject to punishment, [has] revolutionized realistic fiction for children." Blume's highlighting of sexuality reflects her ability to target the issues that most interest young people; when she first began writing, she "knew intuitively what kids wanted to know because I remembered what I wanted to know," she explained to John Neary of *People Weekly.* "I think I write about sexuality because it was uppermost in my mind when I was a kid: the need to know, and not knowing how to find out. My father delivered these little lectures to me, the last one when I was ten, on how babies are made. But questions about what I was feeling, and how my body could feel, I *never* asked my parents."

Nowhere is Blume's insight into character more apparent than in her fiction for adolescents, who are undeniably her most loyal and attentive audience. As Naomi Decter observed in *Commentary,* "There is, indeed, scarcely a literate girl of novel-reading age who has not read one or more Blume books." Not only does Blume address sensitive themes, she "is a careful observer of the everyday details of children's lives and she has a feel for the little power struggles and shifting alliances of their social relationships," R. A. Siegal commented in *The Lion and the Unicorn.* This realism enhances the appeal of her books, as Walter Clemons noted in a *Newsweek* review of *Tiger Eyes:* "No wonder teen-agers love Judy Blume's novels: She's very good. . . . Blume's delicate sense of character, eye for social detail and clear access to feelings touches even a hardened older reader. Her intended younger audience gets a first-rate novel written directly to them."

Blume reflected on her ability to communicate with her readers in a *Publishers Weekly* interview with Sybil Steinberg: "I have a capacity for total recall. That's my talent, if there's a talent involved. I have this gift, this memory, so it's easy to project myself back to certain stages in my life. And I write about what I know is true of kids going through those same stages." In addition, Blume enjoys writing for and about this age group. "When you're twelve, you're on the brink of adulthood," the author told Joyce Maynard in the *New York Times Magazine,* "but everything is still in front of you, and you still have the chance to be almost anyone you want. That seemed so appealing to me. I wasn't even thirty when I started writing, but already I didn't feel I had much chance myself." As a result, "whether she is writing about female or male sexual awakening, and whatever other adolescent problems, Judy Blume is on target," Dorothy M. Broderick asserted in the *New York Times Book Review.* "Her understanding of young people is sympathetic and psychologically sound; her skill engages the reader in human drama without melodrama."

Blume's style also plays a major role in her popularity; as Adele Geras remarked in *New Statesman,* Blume's books "are liked because they are accessible, warm hearted, often funny, and because in them her readers can identify with children like themselves in difficult situations, which may seem silly to the world at large but which are nevertheless very real to the sufferer." "It's hard not to like Judy Blume," Carolyn Banks elaborated in the *Washington Post Book World.* "Her style is so open, so honest, so direct. Each of her books reads as though she's not so much writing as kaffeeklatsching with you." In addition, Siegal observed that Blume's works are structured simply, making them easy to follow. "Her plots are loose and episodic: they accumulate rather than develop," the critic states. "They are not complicated or demanding."

Another way in which Blume achieves such a close affinity with her readers is through her consistent use of first-person narratives. As Siegal explained: "Through this technique she succeeds in establishing intimacy and identification between character and audience. All her books read like diaries or journals and the reader is drawn in by the narrator's self-revelations." "Given the sophistication of Miss Blume's material, her style is surprisingly simple," Decter similarly commented. "She writes for the most part in the first person: her vocabulary, grammar, and syntax are colloquial; her tone, consciously or perhaps not, evokes the awkwardness of a fifth grader's diary." In *Just As Long As We're Together,* for instance, the twelve-year-old heroine "tells her story in simple, real kid language," noted Mitzi Myers in the *Los Angeles Times,* "inviting readers to identify with her dilemmas over girlfriends and boyfriends and that most basic of all teen problems: 'Sometimes I feel grown up and other times I feel like a little kid.'"

Although Blume's work is consistently in favor with readers, it has frequently been the target of criticism. Some commentators have charged that the author's readable style, with its focus on mundane detail, lacks the depth to deal with the complex issues that she raises. In a *Times Literary Supplement* review of *Just As Long As We're Together,* for example, Jan Dalley claimed that Blume's work "is all very professionally achieved, as one would expect from this highly successful author, but Blume's concoctions are unvaryingly smooth, bland and glutinous." Critical reaction to Blume's young-adult novel *Here's to You, Rachel Robinson* follows a similar theme. The novel's plot concerns the conflicts and eventual reconciliation experienced by thirteen-year-old Rachel and her troubled and self-destructive older brother Charles. Critics noted that while this book maintains the author's tradition of treating the problems of adolescence with empathy and humor, the novel as a whole suffers from a slight superficiality. Wendy E. Betts maintained, for example, that the title character's narrative voice "fails to ring true"; and a reviewer in the *New Yorker* stated that the plot "all begins to look a little like wallpaper as it unrolls before us."

Beryl Lieff Benderly believed that the author's readability sometimes masks what some critics call her "enormous skill as a novelist," as she wrote in a *Washington Post Book World* review of *Here's to You, Rachel Robinson.* "While apparently presenting the bright, slangy, surface details of life in an upper-middle class suburban junior high school, she's really plumbing the meaning of honesty, friendship, loyalty, secrecy, individuality, and the painful, puzzling question of what we owe those we love."

Other reviewers have taken exception to Blume's tendency to avoid resolving her fictional dilemmas in a straightforward fashion, for her protagonists rarely finish dealing with all their difficulties by the end of the book. Many critics, however, think that it is to Blume's credit that she does not settle every problem for her readers. One such critic, Robert Lipsyte, in a *Nation* review maintained that "Blume explores the feelings of children in a nonjudgmental way. The immediate resolution of a problem is never as important as what the protagonist . . . will learn about herself by confronting her life." Lipsyte explained that "the young reader gains from the emotional adventure story both by observing another youngster in a realistic situation and by finding a reference from which to start a discussion with a friend or parent or teacher. For many children, talking about a Blume story is a way to expose their own fears about menstruation or masturbation or death." Countering other criticisms that by not answering the questions they raise Blume's books fail to educate their readers, Siegal likewise suggested: "It does not seem that Blume's books . . . ought to be discussed and evaluated on the basis of what they teach children about handling specific social or personal problems. Though books of this type may sometimes be useful in giving children a vehicle for recognizing and ventilating their feelings, they are, after all, works of fiction and not self-help manuals."

Even more disturbing to some adults is Blume's treatment of mature issues and her use of frank language. "Menstruation, wet dreams, masturbation, all the things that are whispered about in real school halls" are the subjects of Blume's books, related interviewer Sandy Rovner in the *Washington Post.* As a result, Blume's works have frequently been the targets of censorship, and Blume herself has become an active crusader for freedom of expression. She has answers to those who would censor her work for its explicitness. "The way to instill values in children is to talk about difficult issues and bring them out in the open, not to restrict their access to books that may help them deal with their problems and concerns," she said in a Toronto *Globe and Mail* interview with Isabel Vincent. And, as she revealed to Peter Gorner in the *Chicago Tribune,* she never intended her work to inspire protest in the first place: "I wrote these books a long time ago when there wasn't anything near the censorship that there is now," she told Gorner. "I wasn't aware at the time that I was writing anything controversial. I just know what these books would have meant to me when I was a kid."

Others similarly defend Blume's choice of subject matter. For example, Natalie Babbitt asserted in the *New York Times Book Review:* "Some parents and librarians have come down hard on Judy Blume for the occasional vulgarities in her stories. Blume's vulgarities, however, exist in real life and are presented in her books with honesty and full acceptance." And those who focus only on the explicit aspects of Blume's books are missing their essence, Judith M. Goldberger proposed in the *Newsletter on Intellectual Freedom.* "Ironically, concerned parents and critics read Judy Blume out of context, and label the books while children and young adults read the whole books to find out what they are really about and to hear another voice talking about a host of matters with which they are concerned in their daily lives. The grownups, it seems, are the ones who read for the 'good' parts, more so than the children."

Blume, too, realizes that the controversial nature of her work receives the most attention. That causes concern for her beyond any censorship attempts. As the author explained to Maynard: "What I worry about is that an awful lot of people, looking at my example, have gotten the idea that what sells is teenage sex, and they'll exploit it. I don't believe that sex is why kids like my books. The impression I get, from letter after letter, is that a great many kids don't communicate with their parents. They feel alone in the world. Sometimes, reading books that deal with other kids who feel the same things they do, it makes them feel less alone." The volume of Blume's fan mail seems to reinforce the fact that her readers are looking for contact with an understanding adult. Hundreds of letters arrive each week not only praising her books but also asking her for advice or information. As Blume remarked in *Publishers Weekly,* "I have a wonderful, intimate relationship with kids. It's rare and lovely. They feel that they know me and that I know them."

In 1986 Blume collected a number of letters from her readers and published them, along with some of her own comments, as *Letters to Judy: What Your Kids Wish They Could Tell You.* The resulting book, aimed at both children and adults, "is an effort to break the silence, to show parents that they can talk without looking foolish, to show children that parents are human and remember what things were like when they were young, and to show everyone that however trivial the problem may seem it's worth trying to sort it out," wrote Geras. "If parents and children alike read *Letters to Judy,*" advice columnist Elizabeth Winship likewise observed in the *New York Times Book Review,* "it might well help them to ease into genuine conversation. The book is not a how-to manual, but one compassionate and popular author's way to help parents see life through their children's eyes, and feel it through their hearts and souls." Blume feels so strongly about the lack of communication between children and their parents that she used the royalties from *Letters to Judy,* among other projects, to help finance the KIDS Fund, which she established in 1981. Each year, the fund contributes approximately $45,000 to various nonprofit organizations set up to help young people communicate with their parents.

Over the years, Blume's writing has matured and her audience has expanded with each new book. Her first adult novel, *Wifey,* deals with a woman's search for more out of life and marriage; the second, *Smart Women,* finds a divorced woman trying to deal with single motherhood and new relationships. Although these books are directed at a different audience, they share with her juvenile fiction two characteristics: an empathy for the plights and feelings of her characters and a writing style that is humorous and easy to read. Interestingly enough, even in Blume's adult fiction "the voices of the children ring loudest and clearest," Linda Bird Francke declared in a *New York Times Book Review,* praising Blume's *Smart Women* in particular for its portrayal of "the anger, sadness, confusion and disgust children of divorce can feel."

One reason children play such a role in Blume's "adult" fiction may be due to the author's reluctance to direct her works solely toward a narrow audience, as she disclosed in her interview with Steinberg: "I hate to categorize books. . . . I wish that older readers would read my books about young people, and I hope that younger readers will grow up to read what I have to say about adult life. I'd like to feel that I write for everybody. I think that my appeal has to do with feelings and with character identification. Things like that don't change from generation to generation. That's what I really know." "I love family life," the author added in her interview with Gorner. "I love kids. I think divorce is a tragedy, traumatic and horribly painful for everybody. That's why I wrote *Smart Women.* I want kids to read that and to think what life might be like for their parents. And I want parents to think about what life is like for their kids."

Banks commended Blume not only for her honest approach to issues, but for her "artistic integrity": "She's never content to rest on her laurels, writing the same book over and over as so many successful writers do." For instance, *Tiger Eyes,* the story of Davey, a girl whose father is killed in a robbery, is "a lesson on how the conventions of a genre can best be put to use," Lipsyte claimed. While the author uses familiar situations and characters, showing Davey dealing with an annoying younger sibling, a move far from home, and a new family situation, "the story deepens, takes turns," the critic continued, particularly when Davey's family moves in with an uncle who works for a nuclear weapons plant. The result, Lipsyte stated, is Blume's "finest book—ambitious, absorbing, smoothly written, emotionally engaging and subtly political." And even when Blume returns to familiar characters, as she does in the series starting with *Tales of a Fourth Grade Nothing* and *Superfudge,* her sequels "expand on the original and enrich it, so that [the] stories . . . add up to one long and much more wonderful story," Jean Van Leeuwen remarked in a *New York Times Book Review* article about *Fudge-a-Mania.*

"Blume is concerned to describe characters surviving, finding themselves, growing in understanding, coming to terms with life," John Gough noted in *School Librarian.* While the solutions her characters find and the conclusions they make "may not be original or profound," the critic continued, ". . . neither are they trivial. The high sales of Blume's books are testimony to the fact that what she has to say is said well and is well worth saying." While her "willingness to recognize children's serious thoughts about sex, religion and class made her a figure of controversy twenty-five years ago," as Mark Oppenheimer commented in the *New York Times Book Review,* "Blume has become an icon, as famous for those who tried to cleanse libraries of her books as for the books themselves." Faith McNulty concluded in the *New Yorker:* "I find much in Blume to be thankful for. She writes clean, swift, unadorned prose. She has convinced millions of young people that truth can be found in a book and that reading is fun. At a time that many believe may be the twilight of the written word, those are things to be grateful for."

BIOGRAPHICAL AND CRITICAL SOURCES:

BOOKS

Children's Literature Review, Gale (Detroit, MI), Volume 2, 1976, Volume 15, 1988.
Contemporary Literary Criticism, Gale (Detroit, MI), Volume 12, 1980, Volume 30, 1984.
Dictionary of Literary Biography, Volume 52: *American Writers for Children since 1960: Fiction,* Gale (Detroit, MI), 1986.
Fisher, Emma, and Justin Wintle, *The Pied Pipers,* Paddington Press, 1975.
Gleasner, Diana, *Breakthrough: Women in Writing,* Walker, 1980.
Lee, Betsey, *Judy Blume's Story,* Dillon Press, 1981.
Rees, David, *The Marble in the Water: Essays on Contemporary Writers of Fiction for Children and Young Adults,* Horn Book (Boston, MA), 1980, pp. 173-184.

Weidt, Maryann, *Presenting Judy Blume,* Twayne (New York, NY), 1989.

Wheeler, Jill C., *Judy Blume,* Abdo and Daughters (Edina, MN), 1996.

PERIODICALS

Booklist, September 15, 2002, Gillian Engberg, "Fudge Is Back!," p. 235.

Boston Globe, January 30, 1971.

Bulletin of the Center for Children's Books, April, 1970, Zena Sutherland, review of *The One in the Middle Is the Green Kangaroo,* p. 125; May, 1975, Zena Sutherland, review of *Blubber,* p. 142; October, 1993, review of *Here's To You, Rachel Robinson,* p. 39.

Chicago Tribune, September 24, 1978; March 15, 1985.

Christian Science Monitor, May 14, 1979; March 14, 1984.

Commentary, March, 1980.

Commonweal, July 4, 1980.

Detroit Free Press, February 26, 1984.

Detroit News, February 15, 1985.

Detroit News Magazine, February 4, 1979.

English Journal, September, 1972; March, 1976.

Entertainment Weekly, October 11, 2002, Rebecca Ascher Walsh, "The 'Fudge' Report: Are You There, Readers? It's Me, Judy Blume, with a New Children's Book . . . Finally," p. 77.

Five Owls, November-December, 1993, pp 37-38.

Globe and Mail (Toronto, Ontario, Canada), November 17, 1990.

Horn Book, November-December, 2002, Jennifer M. Brabander, review of *Double Fudge,* p. 748.

Kirkus Reviews, September 1, 1973, p. 965; March 15, 1998; September 1, 2002, review of *Double Fudge,* p. 1304.

Lion and the Unicorn, fall, 1978, R. A. Siegal, "Are You There, God? It's Me, Me, Me!: Judy Blume's Self-Absorbed Narrators," pp. 72-77.

Los Angeles Times, December 26, 1987.

Los Angeles Times Book Review, October 5, 1980; August 31, 1986.

Nation, November 21, 1981.

NEA Today, October, 1984, p. 10.

Newsletter on Intellectual Freedom, May, 1981.

New Statesman, November 5, 1976; November 14, 1980; October 24, 1986.

Newsweek, October 9, 1978; December 7, 1981; August 23, 1982.

New Yorker, December 5, 1983; December 13, 1993, p. 116-7.

New York Times, October 3, 1982; February 21, 1984.

New York Times Book Review, May 24, 1970; November 8, 1970; December 9, 1970; January 16, 1972; September 3, 1972; November 3, 1974; December 28, 1975; May 25, 1976; May 1, 1977; November 23, 1980; November 15, 1981; February 19, 1984; June 8, 1986; November 8, 1987, p. 33; November 11, 1990; December 19, 1993, p. 16; November 16, 1997, Mark Oppenheimer, "Why Judy Blume Endures," pp. 44-45; July 19, 1998, p. 18.

New York Times Magazine, December 3, 1978; August 23, 1982.

People Weekly, October 16, 1978; August 16, 1982; March 19, 1984; March 7, 1994, p. 38.

Publishers Weekly, January 11, 1971; October 8, 1973; April 17, 1978; June 24, 2002, review of *Double Fudge,* p. 57; August 12, 2002, Sally Lodge, "The Return of Fudge: Thirty Years On, Judy Blume's Popular Character Is Forever Feisty, Forever Five," p. 150.

Saturday Review, September 18, 1971.

School Librarian, May, 1987.

School Library Journal, August, 1980, Pamela D. Pollack, review of *Superfudge,* pp. 60-61; September, 2002, Terrie Dorio, review of *Double Fudge,* p. 181.

Time, August 23, 1982.

Times Literary Supplement, October 1, 1976; April 7, 1978; January 29-February 4, 1988.

U.S. News and World Report, October 14, 2002, Vicky Hallett, "She Can't Say Farewell to Fudge," p. 12.

Voice of Youth Advocates, December, 1993, p. 287.

Washington Post, November 3, 1981.

Washington Post Book World, August 14, 1977; October 8, 1978; November 9, 1980, Brigitte Weeks, review of *Superfudge,* p. 12; September 13, 1981; February 12, 1984; November 8, 1987.

Wilson Library Bulletin, January, 1994, p. 119.

ONLINE

Judy Blume Web site, http://www.judyblume.com/ (November 6, 2003).

BOSWELL, Robert 1953-
(Shale Aaron)

PERSONAL: Born December 8, 1953, in Sikeston, MO; son of Albert Russell (a teacher) and Annelle (a realtor; maiden name, Eley) Boswell; married Antonya Nelson (a writer), July 28, 1984; children: Jade Nelson, Noah Nelson. *Education:* University of Arizona, Tucson, B.S. (English and psychology), M.A. (rehabilitation counseling), M.F.A, 1984.

ADDRESSES: Office—Department of English, Box 3E, New Mexico State University, Las Cruces, NM 88005. *Agent*—Jane Cushman, 435 East 79th St., Apt. 4M, New York, NY 10021. *E-mail*—rboswell@nmsu.edu.

CAREER: Educator and fiction writer. University of Arizona, Tucson, graduate assistant, 1981-84; instructor in English, 1984-86; Northwestern University, Evanston, IL, assistant professor of English, 1986-89; Warren Wilson College, instructor in M.F.A. program, 1986—; New Mexico State University, Las Cruces, professor of English, 1989—.

MEMBER: Modern Languages Association, Writers Guild, Associated Writing Programs, American Civil Liberties Union.

AWARDS, HONORS: Iowa School of Letters Award for short fiction, 1985, for *Dancing in the Movies;* fellowships from Arizona Commission on the Arts, 1986, National Endowment for the Arts, 1987 and 1993, Guggenheim Foundation, 1989, Illinois Arts Council, 1989, and Lila Wallace/Woodrow Wilson, 1994; John Gassner Playwrighting Award, 1994, for *Tongues;* PEN West Award for best fiction, 1995, for *Living to Be a Hundred;* Philip K. Dick Award finalist, 1996, for *Virtual Death;* Evil Companions Award, 1996;

WRITINGS:

Dancing in the Movies (short stories), University of Iowa Press, 1986.
Crooked Hearts (novel), Knopf (New York, NY), 1987.

Robert Boswell

The Geography of Desire (novel), Knopf (New York, NY), 1989.
Mystery Ride, Knopf (New York, NY), 1993.
Living to Be a Hundred (stories), Knopf (New York, NY), 1994.
(As Shale Aaron) *Virtual Death* (novel), Harper Collins (New York, NY), 1995.
American Owned Love, Knopf (New York, NY), 1997.
Tongues (play), produced by American Southwest Theatre Company (Las Cruces, NM), 1999.
Century's Son, Knopf (New York, NY), 2002.

Work represented in anthologies, including *Best American Short Stories, O. Henry Prize Stories, New Stories from the South, Passages North Anthology, The Pushcart Anthology 2000, Still Wild: An Anthology of Western Stories,* and *Voice Louder Than Words.* Contributor to periodicals, including *New Yorker, Esquire, Harvard Review, TriQuarterly, Colorado Review, Georgia Review, Ploughshares, North American Review, Antioch Review, New Times,* and *Iowa Review.*

SIDELIGHTS: Robert Boswell is an author of both short stories and novels. His first book, *Dancing in the*

Movies, is comprised of six realistic tales about the grimmer aspects of life. The protagonists in these stories are often haunted by guilt or fear. In "The Darkness of Love," for instance, a black police officer realizes that he harbors suspicions against his own race; and in "The Right Thing" a Vietnam War veteran returns home only to suffer jolting recollections of jungle life. Still other tales concentrate on similarly unnerving situations. In "Little Bear" an American soldier in the Korean War experiences mutilation, while in the title tale a college student returns home and finds that his girlfriend is a heroin addict. Ellen Lesser, writing in the *Village Voice,* declared that the tales in *Dancing in the Movies* "add up to stunning performance."

In his first novel, *Crooked Hearts,* Boswell writes of an American family plagued by failure and internal strife. The members of this family, the Warrens, were described by *New York Times* reviewer Michiko Kakutani as "sensitive, eccentric and chronically adolescent." Among the memorable members of the Warren clan are Edward, the father, who longs for the matrimonial harmony that preceded his infidelities; Jill, the mother, who sees moving into a new house as an opportunity for another start in life; son Edward, who also longs for a fresh start, but one away from the other family members; and son Charley, who likewise fantasizes a break from the clan's uncomfortably close—and, thus, often unhealthy—ties. Kakutani called *Crooked Hearts* "a dazzling debut" novel.

Boswell followed *Crooked Hearts* with *The Geography of Desire,* in which Leon Green contrives to overcome unhappiness, including guilt over a past crime, by fleeing the United States for Central America, where he lives seaside as a self-consciously mysterious hotel operator. Unfortunately for Leon, even with a fresh start he finds himself once again in uncomfortable circumstances, this time as part of a love triangle with far-reaching implications. Matters become further complicated when Green, who is already conducting love affairs with both a bookstore manager and a local teenager, becomes romantically obsessed with an American tourist whose past is similarly murky. Boswell, Kakutani noted in the *New York Times,* "expertly delineates the complicated geometry of emotions that develop among these characters." And Paul Skenazy, in his review for Chicago *Tribune Books,* commended Boswell for his "evocative prose and immense lyrical talents." Skenazy deemed *The Geography of Desire* an "often stunning blend of eroticism and intrigue, tall tales and seedy politics."

In 1993 Boswell published *Mystery Ride,* which is, like much of his work, about dysfunctional families and the way in which their lives unfold. It is the story of a couple who moved to a remote farm in Iowa to begin their family. Years later, the wife begins to suffocate in the small town community and leaves with her daughter, only to bring her back to her father as a rebellious teenager. As William Clark of *Publishers Weekly* commented, "*Mystery Ride* is . . . about love and loss, about the ways in which ordinary people endure their lives." Clark also noted that Boswell has "the ability to orchestrate time and point of view, to create characters with unforgettable voices." Another *Publishers Weekly* critic found the book to be "charged with insight, resonating with questions about how one leads a moral, fulfilling life and accepts the mysteries of love."

Boswell's second collection of short stories is titled *Living to Be a Hundred.* Many of the protagonists in these eleven stories are miserable, middle-aged men, looking back on their glory days and trying to pinpoint one specific moment when their lives took a turn for the worst. In "Salt Commons" a man is kidnaped by a crazy woman and mourns all the experiences he never had. In "The Products of Love" a man is in love with his married neighbor, but is too guarded to act on his feelings. And in "The Earth's Crown" a small town grocery store owner's wife is about to leave him when he goes back to a former lover, only to find that she is a surrogate mother. Donna Seaman of *Booklist* reported that *Living to Be a Hundred* was "suffused with beauty and the thrill of surrender," while a *Publishers Weekly* critic felt that "though the collection suffers somewhat from a certain sameness of theme, Boswell's tales are gracefully written and often haunting." *Living to Be a Hundred* received the PEN West Award for fiction in 1995.

American Owned Love, Boswell's fourth novel, uses the Rio Grande River in New Mexico as a major theme for the separation of race and class in America. On one side of the river is Persimmon, a middle-class, white community where promiscuous Gay Schaefer lives with her teenager, Rita. Across the river is Apuro, a virtual shantytown of illegal immigrants. Rudy Salazar lives in Apuro and his crazed distaste for Mexicans that have made it over the river to live in Persimmon brings him into Rita's life. "Boswell has demonstrated a compassionate understanding of dysfunctional families and misfits, and his insights about the self-destructive behavior of most of his characters are both bitingly sharp and tender," commented a *Publishers Weekly* writer. Mary Frances Wilkens of *Booklist* called this novel "beautiful" as it uncovers "happiness and despair on both sides of the river."

Boswell creates another fascinating and unusual family in *Century's Son*. Zhenya is a college professor who is married to Morgan, a successful union activist turned garbage man after the suicide of their twelve-year-old son. Her father, an eccentric Russian writer, suddenly comes to live with them and is the subject of the title, as he falsely claims to be a hundred years old. Along with their daughter Emma and the son she bore at age fourteen, this family has been living in a sort of trance since the death of Philip. The arrival of Zhenya's father shakes their world and forces them to look more closely at their lives. Lawrence Lundgren of *Library Journal* called *Century's Son* a tale of "love and loss, anger and forgiveness, and the truth that offers the possibility of a redeeming life."

BIOGRAPHICAL AND CRITICAL SOURCES:

PERIODICALS

Booklist, March 1, 1994, Donna Seaman, review of *Living to Be a Hundred,* p. 1180; June 1, 1997, Mary Frances Wilkens, review of *American Owned Love,* p. 1654; March 15, 2002, Joanne Wilkinson, review of *Century's Son,* p. 1210.

Kirkus Reviews, February 15, 2002, review of *Century's Son,* p. 203.

Library Journal, January 24, 1994, review of *Living to Be a Hundred,* p. 40; February 24, 1997, p. 63; April 1, 1997, Nancy Pearl, review of *American Owned Love,* p. 122; March 15, 2002, Lawrence Lundgren, review of *Century's Son,* p. 106.

Los Angeles Times Book Review, October 8, 1989, p. 8.

New Yorker, March 1, 1993, review of *Mystery Ride,* p. 115.

New York Times, May 27, 1987; July 2, 1987; September 12, 1989; January 22, 1993, Michiko Kakutani, review of *Mystery Ride,* p. C25.

New York Times Book Review, October 1, 1989, p. 25; May 4, 1997, David Gates, review of *American Owned Love,* p. 24; April 21, 2002, Jonathan Dee, review of *Century's Son,* p. 22.

Ploughshares, winter, 1996-97, Don Lee, "About Robert Boswell: A Profile."

Publishers Weekly, November 16, 1992, review of *Mystery Ride,* p. 44; January 25, 1993, William Clark, interview with Boswell, p. 65; January 24, 1994, p. 40; February 24, 1997, review of *American Owned Love,* p. 63; May 17, 1999, p. 56; March 18, 2002, review of *Century's Son,* p. 79.

Times (London, England), December 27, 1997, Jane Shilling, review of *American Owned Love,* p. 21; July 26, 1997, Sean Coughlan, review of *The Geography of Desire,* p. 13.

Tribune Books (Chicago, IL), October 1, 1989, Section 14, p. 7.

Village Voice, March 18, 1986, p. 48.

Washington Post, October 5, 1989.

ONLINE

New Mexico State University Web site, http://www.nmsu.edu/ (July 21, 2003).

Writers Register, http://www.writersregister.com/ (November 14, 2003).*

* * *

BOULLATA, Issa J. 1929-

PERSONAL: Born February 25, 1929, in Jerusalem, Palestine; son of Joseph (a postmaster) and Barbara (a homemaker; maiden name, Atalla) Boullata; married Marita Seward, August 12, 1960; children: Joseph, Barbara, David, Peter. *Ethnicity:* "Palestinian Arab." *Education:* University of London, B.A. (with first class honors), 1964, Ph.D., 1969. *Politics:* Independent. *Religion:* Christian Orthodox. *Hobbies and other interests:* Chess, travel, music, community service.

ADDRESSES: Home—4070 Madison Ave., Montreal, Quebec H4B 2T7, Canada. *Office*—Institute of Islamic Studies, McGill University, 3485 McTavish St., Montreal, Quebec H3A 1Y1, Canada; fax 514-398-6731. *E-mail*—issa.boullata@mcgill.ca.

CAREER: De La Salle College, Jerusalem, Jordan (now Israel), senior teacher of Arabic literature, 1949-52; Ahliyyah College, Ramallah, Jordan (now Israel), senior teacher of Arabic literature, 1952-53; St.

George's School, Jerusalem, Israel, senior teacher of Arabic literature and deputy headmaster, 1953-68; Hartford Theological Seminary, Hartford, CT, professor of Arabic literature and language, 1968-75; McGill University, Montreal, Quebec, Canada, professor of Arabic literature and language, 1975-99, part-time teacher of Qur'anic studies, Arabic literature, and modern Arab thought, 1999—.

MEMBER: International Comparative Literature Association, Middle East Studies Association of North America, American Association of Teachers of Arabic (president, 1983), Radius of Arab American Writers, Canadian-Arab Organization for Human Rights (president, 1997-98).

AWARDS, HONORS: Arberry Memorial Prize, Pembroke Arabic Research Group, Cambridge, England, 1972; University of Arkansas Press Awards for translations from Arabic, 1993, for *The First Well: A Bethlehem Boyhood,* and 1997, for *The Square Moon.*

WRITINGS:

Outlines of Romanticism in Modern Arabic Poetry (in Arabic), [Beirut, Lebanon], 1960.
Badr Shakir al-Sayyab: His Life and Poetry (in Arabic), [Beirut, Lebanon], 1971.
(Editor and translator) *Modern Arab Poets, 1950-1975,* [Washington, DC], 1976.
(Editor) *Critical Perspectives on Modern Arabic Literature,* [Washington, DC], 1980.
Trends and Issues in Contemporary Arab Thought, [Albany, NY], 1990.
(With Terry DeYoung) *Tradition and Modernity in Arabic Literature,* [Fayetteville, AR], 1997.
A`id ila al Quds (novel in Arabic; title means "Return to Jerusalem"), [Beirut, Lebanon], 1998.
Literary Structures of Religious Meaning in the Qur'an, Curzon Press (London, England), 2000.
Al-Tajriba al-jam̄ilah (correspondence from Jabra I. Jabra; title means "The Beautiful Experience"), [Beirut, Lebanon], 2001.
N̄afidhah àlá al-had̄athah (title means "Modernism in Arabic"), [Beirut, Lebanon], 2002.

Contributor to encyclopedias. Contributor of numerous articles and reviews and some short stories to scholarly journals. Coeditor, *Muslim World,* 1970-80; editor of the annual, *Al-`Arabiyya,* 1978-82; editor of special issues, *Oral Tradition,* 1989, and *Mundus Arabicus,* 1992.

TRANSLATOR

Ahmad Amin, *My Life,* [Leiden, Netherlands], 1978.
Emily Nasrallah, *Flight against Time,* [Charlottetown, Prince Edward Island, Canada], 1987.
Jabra Ibrahim Jabra, *The First Well: A Bethlehem Boyhood,* University of Arkansas Press (Fayetteville, AR), 1995.
Mohamed Berrada, *The Game of Forgetting,* University of Texas Press (Austin, TX), 1996.
Ghada Samman, *The Square Moon,* University of Arkansas Press (Fayetteville, AR), 1998.
Mohamed Berrada, *Fugitive Light,* Syracuse University Press (Syracuse, NY), 2002.

Translator from English into Arabic, including the books *Wallace Stevens* by William York Tindall, [Beirut, Lebanon], 1962; and *Edith Wharton* by Louis Auchincloss, [Beirut, Lebanon], 1962.

WORK IN PROGRESS: Translating into English the tenth-century Arabic classic by Ibn 'Abd Rabbih, *Al-'Iqd al-Farid* (title means "The Unique Necklace"), with Roger Allen, ten volumes; research on the contemporary Arabic novel.

SIDELIGHTS: Issa J. Boullata once told *CA:* "I write in order to express myself and make known my thoughts and feelings. This is best done in my creative Arabic fiction writing. But as a scholar and literary critic, I write mostly in English to present modern Arabic literature and thought and to make Arab culture known in the West. I also translate from Arabic into English for the same purpose. My translations include English renderings of many Arabic poems and of a number of Arabic novels, short stories, and autobiographies. I translate from English to Arabic in order to introduce English or American literature to Arab readers.

"My creative Arabic writing has been influenced by modern fiction writers in the Arab world, as well as in Europe and America. I am fascinated by the way in which words written on paper can be made to create in the mind of the reader a whole universe teeming with characters, events, and images of life and society. Through words I can influence the thoughts and feelings of others with regard to issues I like, causes I defend, and ethical behavior I advocate. But all this has to be done in an artistic manner, aesthetically acceptable and illusively possible.

"As a scholar and literary critic, my purpose in writing is different and so is my method. Here I objectively propose an understanding of a literary work and point out its strengths and/or weaknesses by thorough analysis. I situate it in the context of its social and cultural background, and in the light of its author's life, and I evaluate it on its literary merits of creativity and performance.

"The writing process begins with an idea that I keep mulling over for some time. It perfects itself consciously and unconsciously in my mind before I begin writing. Changes happen during the writing, and new directions for the idea are often opened in the process, but the basic idea remains the mainstay of the written product in the end. Some ideas are deeper than others, stronger in their drive to be expressed, and they eventually result in a better product. I cannot explain this, save by saying that human creativity has its ups and downs. Lucky is the writer who can capture it on the upturn as often as possible—although there is always need for inspiration and exertion of effort."

BIOGRAPHICAL AND CRITICAL SOURCES:

BOOKS

Abdel-Malek, Kamal, and Wael Hellaq, editors, *Tradition, Modernity, and Postmodernity in Arabic Literature,* E. J. Brill (Leiden, Netherlands), 2000.

* * *

BROADWIN, John A. 1944-

PERSONAL: Born April 17, 1944, in Palo Alto, CA; son of Henry (in business) and Bertyl Muller (Berlin) Broadwin. *Ethnicity:* "Caucasian." *Education:* Stanford University, B.A., 1966; University of California—Los Angeles, M.A., 1971. *Hobbies and other interests:* Reading, crossword puzzles, swimming, walking.

ADDRESSES: Home—706 Regal Court, Menlo Park, CA 94025. *Office*—Hubert H. Semans Library, Foothill College, 12345 El Monte Rd., Los Altos Hills, CA 94022. *E-mail*—broadwinjohn@fhda.edu.

CAREER: California State University, Sacramento, CA, assistant catalog librarian, 1972-74; Felix Dietrich Verlag (publisher), Osnabruck, West Germany (now Germany), indexer and translator, 1974-75; National Library of Medicine, Bethesda, MD, selector of medical literature, 1975-79; Letterman Army Institute of Research, San Francisco, CA, administrative librarian, 1979-83; Stanford University, Stanford, CA, head of reference and bibliographic instruction at Engineering Library, 1983-88; Veterans Administration Medical Center, Palo Alto, CA, medical librarian at Health Services Library, 1988-90; Foothill College, Los Altos Hills, CA, collection development librarian at Hubert H. Semans Library, 1990—.

MEMBER: Phi Beta Kappa.

AWARDS, HONORS: Alumni Association Award for Academic Distinction, University of California—Los Angeles, 1971; library associate, National Library of Medicine, 1974-75; Outstanding Achievement Award, U.S. Department of the Army, 1980.

WRITINGS:

(Translator) Timothy W. Mason, *Social Policy in the Third Reich: The Working Class and the 'National Community',* edited by Jane Caplan, Berg Publishers (New York, NY), 1993.
(Translator) Hilmar Hoffmann, *The Triumph of Propaganda: Film and National Socialism, 1933-1945,* Berghahn Books (New York, NY), 1996.
(Translator) Ruth Liepman, *Maybe Luck Isn't Just Chance* (nonfiction), Northwestern University Press (Evanston, IL), 1997.
(Translator) Heinrich Schipperges, *Hildegard of Bingen: Healing and the Nature of the Cosmos,* Markus Wiener Publishers (Princeton, NJ), 1997.
(With Ingeborg Hecht and others) *Invisible Walls: A German Family under the Nuremberg Laws; and To Remember Is to Heal: Encounters between Victims of the Nuremberg Laws,* Northwestern University Press (Evanston, IL), 1999.
(Translator) Piotr O. Scholz, *Eunuchs and Castrati,* Markus Wiener Publishers (Princeton, NJ), 2001.
(Translator) Angelika Konigseder and others, *Waiting for Hope: Jewish Displaced Persons in Post World War II Germany,* Northwestern University Press (Evanston, IL), 2001.

(Translator) Hans Frankenthal, *The Unwelcome One,* Northwestern University Press (Evanston, IL), in press.

WORK IN PROGRESS: Translating the preface to *Les Vrais riches,* for Northwestern University Press (Evanston, IL).

SIDELIGHTS: John A. Broadwin once told *CA:* "While working for a publishing house in Germany in 1974, I happened to see a note posted on a bulletin board at the local university—a professor was looking for someone to translate his article into English for publication in a scientific journal. The subject matter—neuronal responses to peripheral temperature changes in the rat thalamus—wasn't exactly electrifying. But, before I knew it, I was hooked.

"I enjoy the intellectual stimulation of putting someone else's ideas into my native language, trying to give non-English-speaking writers a voice in idiomatic English, especially if the original is worth the effort. Tim Mason's *Social Policy in the Third Reich: The Working Class and the 'National Community'* was just such a work. It also turned out to be quite a chastening experience. Mason was a British historian who wrote in both English and German. Unlike many in the social sciences, he had a flair for writing. So it was a real challenge to translate him back into a language in which he had already established a reputation as a gifted stylist.

"I have always thought it better to make available a good book by someone else than inflict a poorer book of one's own. The only sad thing is that translation is still the Cinderella of scholarship. I only hope that, like the heroine of the fairy tale, translation and translators will receive the honor and respect they deserve."

* * *

BROOKS, James L. 1940-

PERSONAL: Born May 9, 1940, in Brooklyn, NY; son of Edward M. and Dorothy Helen (Sheinheit) Brooks; married Marianne Catherine Morrissey, July 7, 1964 (divorced, 1971); married Holly Beth Holmberg, July 23, 1978; children: (first marriage) Amy Lorraine; (second marriage) Chloe, Cooper, Joseph. *Education:* Attended New York University, 1958-60.

James L. Brooks

ADDRESSES: Office—Gracie Films/Columbia Pictures, Poitier Building, 10202 Washington Blvd., Culver City, CA 90232-3119.

CAREER: Writer, producer, and director. Columbia Broadcasting System (CBS) News, New York, NY, reporter and writer, 1964-66; Wolper Productions, Los Angeles, CA, writer and producer of documentaries, 1966-67; American Broadcasting Co. (ABC), Los Angeles, executive story editor and creator of television series *Room 222,* 1968-69; CBS, Studio City, CA, executive producer and creator of television series *The Mary Tyler Moore Show,* 1970-77; founder of Gracie Films, 1984. Producer, co-creator, and writer for numerous television series and films, 1968—, including *Thursday's Game, Cindy* (musical), *Rhoda, The New Lorenzo Music Show, Friends and Lovers, Lou Grant, Taxi, The Associates, Broadcast News, The Tracey Ullman Show, Sibs, The Simpsons, I'll Do Anything,* and *The Critic;* also producer of films *Big,* 1988, *War of the Roses,* 1989, and executive producer of *Say Anything,* 1989, *Jerry Maguire,* 1996, *As Good As It Gets,* 1997. Appeared as an actor in the film *Modern Romance,* 1981. Guest lecturer, Stanford Graduate School of Communications.

MEMBER: Television Academy of Arts and Sciences, Writers Guild of America, Directors Guild of America, Screen Actors Guild, Academy of Motion Picture Arts and Sciences.

AWARDS, HONORS: Emmy Awards, National Academy of Television Arts and Sciences, for best new series, 1969, for *Room 222,* for outstanding comedy writing, 1971, and 1974-77, and for outstanding comedy series, 1975-77; Peabody Award, Writers Guild of America Award nomination, best teleplay, TV Critics Achievement in Comedy Award, TV Critics Achievement in Series Award, and Humanitas Prize, all 1977, all for *The Mary Tyler Moore Show;* Humanitas Prize, 1977 and 1982, both for *Rhoda;* Peabody Award, 1977 and 1978, Emmy Award for outstanding writing in a drama, 1978-82, and Emmy Award nomination for outstanding drama series, 1978, all for *Lou Grant;* TV Film Critics Circle Award for achievement in comedy and in a series, 1977, Golden Globe Award for best comedy, 1978-80, Humanitas Prize, 1979, and Emmy Award for outstanding comedy series, 1979-81, all for *Taxi;* Academy Award for best film and best adapted screenplay from American Academy of Motion Picture Arts and Sciences, Golden Globe Award, and New York Film Critics Circle Award, all 1984, all for *Terms of Endearment;* Academy Award nomination for best picture and winner of best original screenplay from American Academy of Motion Picture Arts and Sciences, and best picture, best original screenplay, and best director from New York Film Critics Circle, both 1987, for *Broadcast News;* Emmy Awards for outstanding variety or comedy Series, and two Emmy Awards for outstanding writing of a variety or music show, for *The Tracey Ullman Show,* 1986-90; Emmy Award for outstanding animated special and outstanding animated program, 1990, for *The Simpsons*; Academy Awards, best picture, 1996, for *Jerry Maguire,* and best picture and best original screenplay, both 1997, for *As Good As It Gets*; inducted into Hall of Fame, Academy of Television Arts and Sciences, 1998; TV Paddy Chayefsky Laurel award, Writers Guild of America, 1998, for screenplay *As Good As It Gets.*

WRITINGS:

SCREENPLAYS

(Cowriter and coproducer) *Thursday Game* (television film), 1971.

(And coproducer) *Starting Over,* Paramount, 1979.
(And coproducer and director) *Terms of Endearment* (based on the novel by Larry McMurtry), Paramount, 1983.
(And producer and director) *Perfect,* 1985.
(And producer and director) *Broadcast News,* Twentieth Century-Fox, 1987.
(And coproducer and director) *I'll Do Anything,* Columbia Pictures, 1994.
(Cowriter, producer, and director) *As Good As It Gets,* TriStar, 1997.

TELEVISION SERIES

(And creator) *Room 222,* ABC, 1968-69.
(With Ernie Frankel and Robert Hamner) *My Friend Tony,* NBC, 1969.
(And cocreator, with Allan Burnsand executive producer) *The Mary Tyler Moore Show,* CBS, 1970-77.
(With Allan Burns) *Paul Sands in Friends and Lovers,* CBS, 1974.
(With others) *Rhoda,* CBS, 1974-78.
(With Allan Burns) *Lou Grant,* CBS, 1977-82.
(With Allan Burns) *The Associates,* ABC, 1979-80, syndicated, 1982.
(With Allan Burns) *Duck Factory,* NBC, 1984.
(With Allan Burns) *The Tracey Ullman Show,* Fox 1986-90.
(Executive producer, with Matt Groening and Sam Simon) *The Simpsons,* Fox, 1990—.
(With Allan Burns) *The Days and Nights of Molly Dodd,* NBC, 1987-88, Lifetime, 1989.
(With Allan Burns) *Eisenhower and Lutz,* CBS, 1988.

TELEVISION MOVIES

Thursday's Game, ABC, 1974.
(With Stan Daniels and David Davis) *Cindy,* ABC, 1978.
(With others) *The Munsters' Revenge,* NBC, 1981.

SIDELIGHTS: With everything from tear-jerking dramas to irreverent comedies to his credit, screenwriter/producer/director James L. Brooks has established himself as a Hollywood mainstay. *New York Times* correspondent Aljean Harmetz noted that with his "long jaw, black mustache and heavy beard," Brooks "might be Mephistopheles as a stand-up comic. The comedy that gushes out like water from a lawn sprinkler has no edge of nastiness. It is sweet and cheerful and aimed at no one but himself." Brooks made a name for himself in the 1970s as a television writer, and in the ensuing years has performed a myriad of tasks for both television series and feature films, winning both accolades and important awards. Among his notable works for television are the series *Room 222, The Mary Tyler Moore Show, Rhoda, Lou Grant,* and *The Tracey Ullman Show* and for the big screen *Terms of Endearment, Broadcast News,* and *As Good As It Gets.* Brooks served in other capacities such as co-producer—for such other well-known films as *Big, The War of the Roses,* and *Jerry Maguire.* Brooks has been variously described as a mercurial man who can bubble effusively one minute and turn apprehensive the next, and an engaging eccentric who has made a career of mining his own inner turmoil for laughs, and later, for tears.

A self-described "early latchkey" kid who grew up in the New Jersey suburbs of New York City, Brooks dropped out of New York University in the late 1950s to take a job as a copy boy for CBS News. After four years of toil in the newsroom (later the source for his television news-based *Mary Tyler Moore Show* and *Broadcast News*), he managed to work his way up to newswriter and reporter. He left New York City in 1966 to work as a television writer in Los Angeles.

In Hollywood, Brooks began writing and selling scripts for various situation comedies, including *The Andy Griffith Show* and *That Girl.* He landed a full-time job with ABC in 1968 as executive story editor and went on to create the award-winning television series *Room 222.* He returned to CBS in 1970 and scored an immediate hit as creator, writer, and producer of *The Mary Tyler Moore Show.* The series was the first in a string of television hits that eventually included the comedies *Rhoda* and *Taxi* and the drama *Lou Grant.* As the 1970s drew to a close, Brooks had three series running simultaneously (*Taxi, Rhoda,* and *Lou Grant*), all of which reflected the troubled spirit of the decade. Having received numerous Emmy Awards and other citations from the television industry, Brooks decided to move into feature films.

As a would-be movie producer and director, Brooks found himself, in the early 1980s, with an adaptation of a Larry McMurtry novel, an idea for directing it, and no encouragement from the studio brass. "Not commercial," "too downbeat," and "Who would be interested in the problems of this mother and daughter?" were, according to Harmetz's article, just some of the rejection remarks Brooks got when he was trying to pitch *Terms of Endearment.* Finally Brooks got a deal from Paramount, and *Terms of Endearment,* starring Shirley MacLaine, Jack Nicholson, and Debra Winger, was released in 1983. The reaction seemed instantaneous, with critics and public alike responding to the bittersweet comedy of family loyalty and romantic infidelity. Among the many gifted artists involved in the movie, Brooks was singled out for particular praise—even in his handling of the touchy subject of death in what ostensibly appears to be a comedy.

"In adapting [McMurtry's] entertaining and affecting but dramatically diffuse novel, Brooks has contrived to finesse most of the structural defects built into its rambling, episodic nature," noted *Washington Post* critic Gary Arnold. "His touch is so pleasant and the cast so skillful and enjoyable that it may seem immaterial to ask yourself if this narrative is really getting someplace, rather than passing the time agreeably." Arnold continued: "When a decisive crisis [in the film] occurs, Brooks takes even more impressive advantage of the novel's belated, arguably underhanded resort to incurable illness as a cure-all for plot drift. Spectators who feel resentful about the way the movie activates and exploits its concluding, heartbreaking twist of fate will probably be in a clear minority, but it will be difficult for the rest of us to deny that they have a legitimate esthetic complaint."

In a *New York Times* review of *Terms of Endearment,* Vincent Canby admitted that the film "is not a perfect movie," with its scenes of fatal illness and family breakdown. The critic went on to conclude, however, that the work "must be one of the most engaging films of the year, to be cherished as much for the low-pressure way in which it operates . . . as for the fact that it contains what are possibly the best performances ever given by Shirley MacLaine and Jack Nicholson." *Terms of Endearment* went on to capture three major Academy Awards, including best picture and best adapted screenplay for Brooks.

After what is commonly acknowledged as a false start, the 1985 aerobics-love story *Perfect,* Brooks came back with an original screenplay culled from his own past as a writer in a television newsroom. *Broadcast News,* released in 1987, presents the traditional love triangle—between Jane, a savvy network-news producer, Aaron, a brilliant but uncharismatic reporter, and Tom, an attractive if less-than-gifted news anchorman—that evolves into a love quadrangle, as careerism becomes a consuming part of each character. "The story unfolds as a series of 'days in the life of a network news bureau,' and a cautionary tale it is," remarked Sheila Benson in the *Los Angeles Times.* "Brooks is understandably distressed at the state of the news we're getting, in bright, flashy, easily digested 'bites,' a *USA Today,* 'Entertainment Tonight' version of the news."

Broadcast News is "funny, it's intelligent, and it's aimed at the upscale, but what will sell it . . . is that it's all about Washington Media Folk, the people America loves to hate and who, it might be speculated, love to hate themselves," according to *Washington Post* reviewer Tom Shales. *Chicago Tribune* correspondent Dave Kehr observed: "Though Brooks begins with a slightly sitcom-like sense of narrowly defined, single-trait characters—there's the dumb one, the smart one and the compulsive one—he builds on the archetypes to create remarkably full, complex figures, in whom strengths and weaknesses, generous impulses and selfish interests exist side by side." Benson feels that Brooks's "talent for observation and for truthful, careful writing borders on the eerie. He's captured these young people and their pressure-cooker jobs exactly—their banter, their rationalizations, the balance of their lives between work and whatever comes a close second. . . . [Brooks] has seen that a playful sort of ego-speak guards their vulnerability, and he understands that there is a distinct pragmatism to his whiz kids. But he likes them. And there's no way in the world that we won't either."

In *Washington Post* critic Hal Hinson's opinion, *Broadcast News* "never comes close to being a great, penetrating work about television news. It's not a scathing satire like *Network,* nor is it to broadcast journalism what *All the President's Men* was to print. But Brooks's ambitions for [this movie] appear to have been far less exalted. [He instead has crafted] a teasing, affectionately critical satire of his former profession. In the process, he's created a spunky romantic comedy with some of the snappiest lines heard on screen in a long while." Members of the Motion Picture Academy agreed with these assessments, awarding Brooks a best original screenplay Oscar, along with a nomination for best picture.

Broadcast News was the first motion picture released by Brooks's own production company, Gracie Films, named after the famous comedienne Gracie Allen. Brooks created Gracie Films as a refuge for the writer, as he explained in an *American Film* profile. "The justification for Gracie was to try this idea out," he stated, "that we'd consider it a personal failure if more than the original writer's name appeared on the [film] credits. . . . We wanted authorship of movies, not the latest draft from the latest person hired." In addition to its screen-writing and film-producing mission, Gracie Films has provided a launching point for several television series, including the highly irreverent animated comedy *The Simpsons.* In a *Rolling Stone* piece on *The Simpsons,* Bill Zehme stated: "Without Brooks, of course, it is doubtful Simpsonia would have gripped the land. He sponsored the Simpsons' rise by hiring [creator Matt] Groening." Zehme concluded that *The Simpsons* had become "the soul of Fox Broadcasting, dependably notching Top Twenty Nielsen ratings."

The renewed television success brought to Brooks by *The Simpsons* did not interfere with his movie projects. In 1994 he released *I'll Do Anything,* a satire of Hollywood that was originally conceived as a musical but ended up being reshaped into a comedy-romance with one song. Featuring a score largely written by Prince and choreography by the eminent modern dancer Twyla Tharp, *I'll Do Anything* exhibited "the kind of crackling comedic dialogue that is a hallmark of all of Jim Brooks's work," to quote Nancy Griffin in *Premiere.* Griffin added that even after the musical numbers had been excised, "what remains is, incredibly enough, a dazzling, urbane comedy of which Brooks can be justly proud, rich in its navigation through the ethical flytraps and seductions of the entertainment industry." The film failed to draw at the box office, however, a consequence—so Brooks thought—of its inherent complexity. "There is something about me that's at war with simplicity," he told *Premiere.* "And if it is true that the form requires some simplicity, maybe that is it."

In 1996 Brooks added to his list of movie credits with *Jerry Maguire*; and in 1997 *As Good As It Gets,* co-authored with Mark Andrus. *As Good As It Gets* is a romantic comedy about an obsessive-compulsive romance writer, who is anything but nice, and a struggling single-mother waitress, who is the only person at the restaurant who can stand the novelist. As Brooks told Alan Waldman during an interview in *Writers*

Guild of America online, he and Andrus spent over a year polishing the script, which they felt was very risky because the main character is so unlikeable at first. "This was a romantic comedy that didn't insist you root for the couple to make it. I think that's what set it apart," Brooks continued. While this unique aspect worked for some viewers, for others it proved to be too original. Stanley Kauffmann, writing in *New Republic* found the romantic tangle "unbelievable, partly because of the soppiness that eventually comes Nicholson's [romance writer's] way." *Entertainment Weekly*'s Lisa Schwarzbaum shared a similar view, noting that as hard as the stars try, "upon closer inspection [the cute premise], rings falser rather than truer. It's pretty good, but not nearly as good as Brooks gets." Other reviewers begged to differ, however. *National Review* movie critic John Simon praised Brooks for his ability to manipulate viewers' emotions to make them laugh and cry, sometimes simultaneously. In appreciating the comedic aspects of *As Good As It Gets,* Simon pointed to Brooks's dialogue, which he deemed "lively, often bitingly funny," and the screenplay, which "jolts as well as it tickles." Another reviewer found much to like in Brooks's dialogue. "What's perhaps most enjoyable about the movie is its intelligent writing," commented George Meyer of the *Sarasota Herald Tribune*. "The shrewd script sparks even the spikiest insult with originality and turns the wordplay into lines so elegant you'll wish you'd said it." Many viewers appreciated the film's merits, as shown when *As Good As It Gets* was nominated for seven Academy Awards and won two of them. Brooks acted as co-producer of the 2001 movie *Riding in Cars with Boys*, starring Drew Barrymore.

Throughout his career Brooks has remained a writer with an ear for snappy dialogue that lashes out at the listener, that has the ring of authenticity but at the same time tells the viewer: here is something you have never heard before. And he has remained, too, an iconoclastic, almost capricious teller of darker truths. "I'm telling you," Brooks explained in *Premiere,* "I'm a guy trying to get the people right." He does so by showing the weakness and strengths, obsessions and compulsions of his characters. In *Interview* magazine he concluded: "The truth about making movies is—is God help us if it's all that important."

BIOGRAPHICAL AND CRITICAL SOURCES:

PERIODICALS

American Film, May, 1989, p. 44.

Chicago Tribune, April 8, 1984; December 16, 1987; January 3, 1988.

Commonweal, January 29, 1988, p. 49.

Cosmopolitan, February, 1988, p. 40.

Entertainment, January 9, 1998, Liza Schwarzbaum, review of *As Good As It Gets,* p. 42; January 30, 1998, Lisa Schwarzbaum, review of *As Good As It Gets,* p. 46.

Films in Review, January-February, 1997, Rocco Simonelli, review of *Jerry Maguire,* p. 87.

Forbes, November 12, 1990, p. 188.

Interview, April, 1988, p. 92.

Los Angeles Times, November 23, 1983; December 16, 1987; December 20, 1987; January 11, 1988; March 27, 2001, Howard Rosenberg, "There's Not Much to Laugh about in 'Joan', " p. F-10 .

Movieline, April, 1994, p. 36.

Ms., March, 1988, p. 26.

Nation, January 23, 1988, p. 94.

National Review, February 5, 1988, p. 56; February 23, 1998, John Simon, review of *As Good As It Gets,* pp. 57-58.

New Republic, February 1, 1988, p. 26; February 2, 1998, Stanley Kauffmann, review of *As Good As It Gets,* p. 25.

Newsweek, April 17, 1989, p. 72; December 22, 1997, David Ansen, review of *As Good As It Gets,* pp. 85-87.

New York, February 1, 1988, p. 54; December 22, 1997, David Denby, review of *As Good As It Gets,* p. 134.

New Yorker, January 11, 1988, p. 76; April 2, 2001, Nancy Franklin, review of *What about Joan,* pp. 88-89.

New York Times, November 20, 1983; November 23, 1983; December 4, 1983; April 8, 1984; January 7, 1988, p. C19; December 23, 1997, Janet Maslin, review of *As Good As It Gets,* p. B1 (N), p. E1 (L); March 25, 2001, Hilary De Vries, "Joan Cusak Goes for Calm in Sit-com," p. 40 (N).

New York Times Magazine, April 8, 1984; November 4, 2001, A. O. Scott, "Homer's Odyssey: After 12 Years, How Does *The Simpsons* Remain the Best Show on Television?," p. 42.

People, December 21, 1987, p. 10; January 12, 1998, Leah Rozen, review of *As Good As It Gets,* p. 21.

Premiere, February 8, 1988, pp. 84, 86; September, 1989, p. 105; March, 1994, p. 49.

Rolling Stone, June 28, 1990, p. 41.

Sarasota Herald Tribune (Sarasota, FL), December 26, 1997, George Meyer, "*As Good As It Gets* Lives Up to Its Name," p. 9.

Sight and Sound, March, 1998, Xan Brooks, review of *As Good As It Gets,* pp. 38-39.

Vogue, February, 1988, p. 86; April, 1988, p. 198.
Washington Post, October 5, 1979; November 23, 1983; December 13, 1987; December 25, 1987; December 26, 1997, Desson Howe, review of *As Good As It Gets,* p. N34.

ONLINE

Writers Guild of America Web site, http://www.wga.org/ (April 17, 2003), Alan Waldman, interview with James L. Brooks.*

C

CALDICOTT, Helen (Mary) 1938-

PERSONAL: Born August 8, 1938, in Melbourne, Victoria, Australia; daughter of Philip (a factory manager) and Mary Mona Enyd (an interior designer; maiden name, Coffey) Broinowski; married William Caldicott (a physician), December 8, 1962; children: Philip, Penny, William, Jr. *Education:* University of Adelaide, received B.S. (surgery), M.B. (medicine), 1961.

ADDRESSES: Home—245 Highland Ave. W, Newton, MA 02165. *Office*—P.O. Box 348, Arlington, MA 02174. *E-mail*—info@nuclearpolicy.org.

CAREER: Physician, activist, and author. Royal Adelaide Hospital, Adelaide, South Australia, Australia, intern, 1961; general practice of medicine in South Australia, 1963-65; Harvard University Medical School, Cambridge, MA, fellow in nutrition, 1966-68, instructor in pediatrics, 1977-80; Children's Hospital Medical Center, Boston, MA, fellow in nutrition, 1967-68, fellow in cystic fibrosis, 1975-76, associate, 1977-80; Adelaide Children's Hospital, Adelaide, intern, 1972, resident, 1973-74, founder and head of cystic fibrosis clinic, 1975-76. Appeared in documentary films, including *If You Love This Planet,* National Film Board of Canada, 1982, and *In Our Hands,* Action for Nuclear Disarmament, 1982; guest on radio and television programs, including *Merv Griffin Show, Donahue, Today Show, Good Morning, America, 60 Minutes,* and *Nightline.* Ran unsuccessfully for seat in Australian Parliament, 1990.

MEMBER: American Thoracic Society, Royal Australian College of Physicians, Physicians for Social Responsibility (president, 1978-83; president emeritus,

Helen Caldicott

1983—), Medical Campaign against Nuclear War (founder), Women's Action for Nuclear Disarmament (founder), Women's Party for Survival (founder).

AWARDS, HONORS: Prize for clinical medicine from British Medical Association, 1960; Consumer Action Now award, Margaret Mead Award from Environmental Defense Center, Thomas Merton Prize for Peace from Thomas Merton Society, and Humanist of the Year Award from Ethical Society of Boston, all 1980; Gandhi Peace Prize from Promoting Enduring Peace, and SANE Peace Award from SANE Education Fund, both 1981; Humanist of the Year Award from American Association of Humanistic Psychology, and Audubon "A" Award from Massachusetts Audubon Society, both 1982; Woman of the Year Award from Boston College, Peace Award from American Association of University Women, Humanitarian Award from Massachusetts Psychological Association, Elizabeth Blackwell Award from American Medical Women's Association, Abraham L. Sacher Award from Brandeis University, Ansel Adams Award from Second Biennial Fate of the Earth Conference, and Outstanding Writer Award from Massachusetts Bay Association of Writing Programs, all 1984; President's Award from Hofstra University, Integrity Award from John-Roger Foundation, Peace Medal Award from United Nations Association of Australia, and Nobel Peace Prize nomination, all 1985; International Year of Peace Award from Australian Government, 1986; numerous honorary degrees from institutions, including Antioch University, Emmanuel College, Russell Sage College, State University of New York at Binghamton, University of Linkoeping (Linkoeping, Sweden), and University of Notre Dame.

WRITINGS:

(With Nancy Herrington and Nahum Stiskin) *Nuclear Madness: What You Can Do!,* Autumn Press, 1978, new edition published as *Nuclear Madness: What You Can Do; With a New Chapter on Three Mile Island,* Bantam (New York, NY), 1980, revised edition, Norton (New York, NY), 1994.

Missile Envy: The Arms Race and Nuclear War, Morrow (New York, NY), 1984.

If You Love This Planet: A Plan to Heal the Earth, Norton (New York, NY), 1992.

A Passionate Life, Random House Australia (Milsons Point, New South Wales, Australia), 1996, published as *A Desperate Passion: An Autobiography,* Norton (New York, NY), 1996.

(Author of foreword) Gayle Greene, *The Woman Who Knew Too Much: Alice Stewart and the Secrets of Radiation,* University of Michigan Press (Ann Arbor, MI), 1999.

The New Nuclear Danger: George W. Bush's Military-Industrial Complex, New Press (New York, NY), 2002.

SIDELIGHTS: Since her 1971 fight to stop France from testing nuclear weapons over the southern Pacific Ocean, Australian-born physician Helen Caldicott has become "probably the most effective antinuclear speaker" in America, averred Nobel Prize-winning biologist George Wald in a 1979 *Ms.* article. Caldicott's speeches on the health dangers posed by nuclear fallout helped convince many Australians to protest and end the testing; she later led the successful effort to halt uranium mining and exporting in that country also. Since moving to the United States in 1977, Caldicott has focused much of her energy on protesting against nuclear weapons, pushing for a freeze on the building of such weapons, and urging all Americans to become involved in the debate over nuclear technology. In *Nuclear Madness: What You Can Do!,* written with Nancy Herrington and Nahum Stiskin, Caldicott states: "I believe it imperative that the American public understand that nuclear power generation is neither safe, nor clean, nor cheap; that new initiatives are urgently required if we are to avoid nuclear catastrophe in a world armed to the teeth with atomic weapons; and that these initiatives must begin with awareness, concern, and action on the part of the individual citizen. . . . We must educate ourselves . . . then move powerfully as individuals accepting full responsibility for preserving our planet for our descendants."

Caldicott's own awareness of nuclear hazards stemmed in part from her experiences as a pediatrician. In treating patients stricken with cystic fibrosis and leukemia, she realized that even one radioactive particle could damage a cell or a gene, thus making such genetic diseases and cancers more likely. "I decided that promoting the elimination of nuclear weapons and power was part of practicing . . . real preventive medicine," she told an interviewer in *Ms.* The results of her decision included reviving the antinuclear organization Physicians for Social Responsibility and leaving her medical practice to devote more time to educating the public.

Concern for her children also motivated Caldicott to activism. "When my husband and I decided to have our first child, I had nightmares thinking that the baby would live to see the horrors that I'd read about as a girl," she once told a *CA* interviewer. Reading scientific studies of nuclear issues helped solidify her opposition to the technology, showing how weapons tests and routine reactor operation produce substances that affect the entire food chain. Caldicott was particularly troubled to discover that children face the greatest dangers from radiation. Because children are still growing, their cells reproduce quickly; a radiation-damaged cell only reproduces more damaged—cancerous—cells.

From the beginning of her campaign for a nuclear-free world, Caldicott has focused on a personal approach to sharing what she has learned. As a physician and as a parent she addresses church groups, college students, hospital staffs, and labor unions. She reaches many through magazine and newspaper articles, and she speaks on radio and television news programs. Commented Wald in *Ms.,* "She has a gift for making the hard scientific facts meaningful to the public." Using blackboard drawings, Caldicott explains the technological and medical realities, and data collected from government reports and scientific studies fuel her arguments. Yet even while she conveys hard facts, Wald observed, "she doesn't hesitate to raise moral questions or display intense emotions about these matters that are life-threatening in the extreme." To those who criticize her emotional appeal, Caldicott offered her defense in a *Los Angeles Times* article: "This is a very emotional issue. . . . To be unemotional about the end of the world is sick."

Caldicott also spreads her message with her books, which have been deemed useful educational tools. In the *New York Times Book Review* Philip M. Boffey described *Nuclear Madness* as "a primer on the medical hazards of nuclear fission." The critic questioned some of Caldicott's assertions, but he also acknowledged the book's "undeniable strengths," among them clarity, simplicity, a dispassionate tone, and attention to neglected issues. For example, among the issues she discusses is the disposal of radioactive waste; she notes that "even if unbreakable, corrosion-resistant containers could be designed, any storage site on earth would have to be kept under constant surveillance by incorruptible guards, administered by moral politicians living in a stable, warless society, and left undisturbed by earthquakes, natural disasters, or other acts of God for no less than half a million years." *Nuclear Madness* was revised and updated in 1994.

In *Missile Envy: The Arms Race and Nuclear War* Caldicott analyzes the intricacies of defense strategy and the capabilities of nuclear arsenals worldwide. She offers several explanations for the U.S.-USSR arms race and suggests that human nature must change to prevent the annihilation of mankind. Taylor Branch, writing in the *New York Times Book Review,* faulted the author's diagnosis as superficial and criticized her emotional leaps between denunciations and religious appeals, but nonetheless judged Caldicott's arguments regarding specific arms issues convincing. "Caldicott is at her best," Branch reflected, "when she goes into the maw of the doomsday machine itself to describe the missile systems, nuclear warheads and military theories in their deadliest applications." Branch also hailed the author's contention that "the logical consequence of the preparation for nuclear war is nuclear war." In 1995, shortly after the publication of this book, Caldicott was nominated for a Nobel Peace Prize.

If You Love This Planet: A Plan to Heal the Earth is Caldicott's guide to saving the planet from nuclear war and environmental disaster. Drawing on her background as a medical doctor, she first diagnoses the ills of the planet and then outlines a comprehensive plan to save Earth from ourselves. In the final chapter of the book, she recommends that the planet's human residents take up the four "L's" to heal the planet: love, learn, live, and legislate.

A Desperate Passion: An Autobiography chronicles Caldicott's personal and professional trials and triumphs—from a strict childhood where her mother beat her for small infractions to her success in negotiating arms treaties with heads of state. Caldicott writes about how, at the age of nineteen, she read Nevil Shute's novel *On the Beach,* a haunting tale of five people who are waiting to die following a nuclear attack. The horror of the novel stuck with her, and she decided that she would become a medical doctor in order to help as many people as possible. Her grandmother had been the first woman to graduate from medical college in Melbourne, and Caldicott herself was one of the first female physicians to practice in her native Australia. She soon began her second career as a crusader, talking to women's groups about health issues and the dangers of venereal disease, and she was seen by many as strident. As she gradually became more concerned with the potential effects of a nuclear war, she became a crusader on this front, too, founding anti-nuclear groups and eventually winning audiences with leaders like Leonid Brezhnev, Jimmy Carter, and Ronald Reagan. At the same time that she was becoming more renowned professionally, however, Caldicott's personal life fell apart, and she and her husband of twenty-five years divorced. *A Desperate Passion* ends with its author's reflections on becoming a single person. Patricia D'Alessandro wrote in the *Bloomsbury Review* that "Caldicott is an iconoclast who has struggled to rise above the patriarchy in medicine, politics, the peace movement, and her private life. . . . She is endowed with a passion that goes beyond the call of duty, one that could very well be the most important call to arms that we face."

In 2002 Caldicott published *The New Nuclear Danger: George W. Bush's Miltary-Industrial Complex,* which not only provides the general reader with a solid grounding in the Republican Bush administration's defense programs and various weapons projects but also alerts the public to the dire consequences of allowing the U.S. government to continue producing massive amounts of nuclear weapons. The book focuses on the connection between the American weapons arsenal and large corporations, as well as the millions of tax dollars spent on nuclear-weapons projects. Caldicott also clearly explains the medical implications Americans potentially face from carcinogenic nuclear waste. Donna Seaman, a critic for *Booklist,* called *The New Nuclear Danger* a "meticulous, urgent, and shocking report" about nuclear arms in the United States.

Through her writings and lectures Caldicott "has captured the hearts and minds of people around the world," stated scientist Freeman Dyson in the *New Yorker.* "You cannot brush aside her message as the emotional outpouring of a fanatic. She speaks from a solid basis of medical experience." In December of 1982 Caldicott won a lengthy private meeting with U.S. President Ronald Reagan, but she left frustrated because Reagan was "not receptive at all to what I had to say," she recalled in *Missile Envy.* Explained Dyson: "There is prejudice and antipathy on both sides. The military establishment looks on the peace movement as a collection of ignorant people meddling in a business they do not understand, while the peace movement looks on the military establishment as a collection of misguided people protected by bureaucratic formality from all contact with human realities. Both these preconceptions create barriers to understanding." Reflecting on what she has achieved and what remains to be done, Caldicott urges in *Missile Envy:* "It is time for people to rise to their full moral and spiritual height, to take the world on their shoulder like Atlas. . . . Think how much Americans could achieve by using . . . the democracy they have inherited from their forebears. All it takes is willpower and determination. . . . Think of what we are about to destroy."

For an interview with Caldicott, please see *Contemporary Authors,* Volume 124.

BIOGRAPHICAL AND CRITICAL SOURCES:

BOOKS

American Women in Science, 1950 to the Present, Gale (Detroit, MI), 1998.
Caldicott, Helen, *Missile Envy: The Arms Race and Nuclear War,* Morrow (New York, NY), 1984.
Caldicott, Helen, Nancy Herrington, and Nahum Stiskin, *Nuclear Madness: What You Can Do!,* Autumn Press, 1978, new edition published as *Nuclear Madness: What You Can Do; With a New Chapter on Three Mile Island,* Bantam (New York, NY), 1980, revised edition, Norton (New York, NY), 1994.
Contemporary Issues Criticism, Volume 2, Gale (Detroit, MI), 1984.

PERIODICALS

Bloomsbury Review, November-December, 1996, pp. 17, 21.
Booklist, March 1, 1992, p. 1183; March 15, 2002, Donna Seaman, review of *The New Nuclear Danger,* p. 1186.
Business Wire, September 17, 2001, p. 198.
Choice, October, 1992, p. 320.
Family Circle, May 18, 1982.
Harper's, March, 1985.
Kirkus Reviews, July 15, 1996, p. 1017.
Library Journal, April 1, 1992, p. 142; April 15, 2002, Daniel K. Blewett, review of *The New Nuclear Danger,* p. 110.
Los Angeles Times, June 27, 1984.
Ms., July, 1979; July, 1984.
New Yorker, February 6, 1984.
New York Times, May 25, 1979; August 18, 1985; June 2, 1986.
New York Times Book Review, August 26, 1979; July 29, 1984.

People, November 30, 1981.
Publishers Weekly, January 20, 1992, p. 59; March 25, 2002, review of *The New Nuclear Danger,* p. 53.
Sierra, July-August, 1992, p. 91.

ONLINE

No Radiation Web site, http://www.noradioation.org/ (July 12, 2002), "Helen Caldicott."
Radio 4 All, http://www.radio4all.org/ (July 12, 2002), interview with Helen Caldicott.
Women's International Center Web site, http://www.wic.org/ (July 21, 2003), "Helen Caldicott: Peace Is Her Passion."

OTHER

Eight Minutes to Midnight: A Portrait of Dr. Helen Caldicott (film), Physicians for Social Responsibility, 1981. *

* * *

**CARLSON, Nancy L.
See CARLSON, Nancy (Lee)**

* * *

**CARLSON, Nancy (Lee) 1953-
(Nancy L. Carlson)**

PERSONAL: Born October 10, 1953, in Minneapolis, MN; daughter of Walter J. (a contractor) and Louise (a homemaker; maiden name, Carlson) Carlson; married John Barry McCool (a graphic designer), June 30, 1979; children: Kelly Louise, John Patrick, Michael Barry. *Ethnicity:* "Swedish." *Education:* Attended University of Minnesota—Duluth, 1972-73, and Santa Fe Workshop of Contemporary Art, 1975; Minneapolis College of Art and Design, B.F.A. (printmaking), 1976. *Religion:* Christian. *Hobbies and other interests:* "Physical fitness, running, biking, watching my children do sports, skiing. I am also a big figure skating fan."

ADDRESSES: Home—Bloomington, MN. *Agent*—c/o Author Mail, Viking, 375 Hudson St., New York, NY 10014. *E-mail*—nancy@nancycarlson.com.

Nancy Carlson

CAREER: Artist, author, and illustrator, 1975—. Visiting artist at schools, including Bemidji State University, 1983, Minnetonka Schools, MN, 1985, and Minneapolis School of Art and Design, 1986. Lecturer and public speaker. Card buyer for Center Book Shop, Walter Art Center, 1977-80; arts and craft specialist for city of South St. Paul, MN, 1978; illustrator of greeting cards for Recycled Paper Products, 1982. Creator of CD-ROM products. Illustrator of calendars, mugs, T-shirts, posters, hats, and gift wrap. *Exhibitions:* "Commencement Exhibition," Minneapolis College of Art and Design, Minneapolis, MN, 1976; "New Works by Three Artists," Honeywell Plaza, Minneapolis, MN, 1980; "Drawings: Scandinavian Reflections," Dolly Fiterman Gallery, 1980; "Minnesota Women," WARM Gallery, Minneapolis, MN, 1981, 1982; Minnesota State Fair Art Exhibition, 1981; "American Art: The Challenge of the Land," Pillsbury World Headquarters, 1981; "Illustrator's Art," Inland Gallery, Minneapolis, MN, 1982; "Young Minnesota Artists," University Gallery, University of Minnesota, 1982; "Hausman Years: 1975-1982," Minneapolis College of Art and Design, Minneapolis, MN, 1982; "Original Art," Master Eagle Gallery, New York, NY, 1983, 1985; "Alumni Show," Minneapolis College of Art and Design, Minneapolis, MN, 1986; "The Art of Author Illustrator Nancy Carlson," American Swedish Institute, Minneapolis, MN, 1989; "Metaphorical Fish," University Art Museum, 1990; "Children's Book Illustration," Minneapolis College of Art and Design, Minneapolis, MN, 1993; "Children's Book Illustration," Plymouth Church, Minneapolis, MN, 1994; "Whimsical World of Josie Winship and Nancy Carlson," Bloomington Art Center, Bloomington, MN, 1996.

AWARDS, HONORS: Drawing awards from Northshore Arts Festival, 1975, Minnesota State Fair Art Exhibition, 1981, Young Minnesota Artists, University of Minnesota, 1982, Women in International Design, 1983, and Minneapolis Graphic Design Association, 1985; Parents' Choice Award, Parents' Choice Foundation, 1985, for *Louanne Pig in the Talent Show;* Children's Choice Award, 1996, for *Sit Still!*

WRITINGS:

SELF-ILLUSTRATED

Harriet's Recital, Carolrhoda (Minneapolis, MN), 1982.
Harriet and Walt, Carolrhoda (Minneapolis, MN), 1982.
Harriet and the Roller Coaster, Carolrhoda (Minneapolis, MN), 1982.
Harriet and the Garden, Carolrhoda (Minneapolis, MN), 1982.
Harriet's Halloween Candy, Carolrhoda (Minneapolis, MN), 1982.
Loudmouth George and the Cornet, Carolrhoda (Minneapolis, MN), 1983.
Loudmouth George and the New Neighbors, Carolrhoda (Minneapolis, MN), 1983.
Loudmouth George and the Fishing Trip, Carolrhoda (Minneapolis, MN), 1983.
Loudmouth George and the Sixth-Grade Bully, Carolrhoda (Minneapolis, MN), 1983.
Loudmouth George and the Big Race, Carolrhoda (Minneapolis, MN), 1983.
Bunnies and Their Hobbies, Carolrhoda (Minneapolis, MN), 1984.
Louanne Pig in Making the Team, Carolrhoda (Minneapolis, MN), 1985.
Louanne Pig in the Mysterious Valentine, Carolrhoda (Minneapolis, MN), 1985.
Louanne Pig in the Perfect Family, Carolrhoda (Minneapolis, MN), 1985.
Louanne Pig in the Talent Show, Carolrhoda (Minneapolis, MN), 1985.
Louanne Pig in Witch Lady, Carolrhoda (Minneapolis, MN), 1985.
Bunnies and Their Sports, Viking (New York, NY), 1987.
Arnie and the Stolen Markers, Viking (New York, NY), 1987.
Arnie Goes to Camp, Viking (New York, NY), 1988.
I Like Me!, Viking (New York, NY), 1988.
Poor Carl, Viking (New York, NY), 1989.
Arnie and the New Kid, Viking (New York, NY), 1990.
A Visit to Grandma's, Viking (New York, NY), 1991.
Take Time to Relax, Viking (New York, NY), 1991.
What If It Never Stops Raining?, Viking (New York, NY), 1992.
Life Is Fun!, Viking (New York, NY), 1993.
How to Lose All Your Friends, Viking (New York, NY), 1994.
Arnie and the Skateboard Gang, Viking (New York, NY), 1995.
Sit Still!, Viking (New York, NY), 1996.
ABC, I Like Me!, Viking (New York, NY), 1997.
Snowden, Viking (New York, NY), 1997.
It's Going to Be Perfect!, Viking (New York, NY), 1998.
Look Out Kindergarten, Here I Come!, Viking (New York, NY), 1999.
Hooray for Grandparents' Day, Viking (New York, NY), 2000.
Harriet and George's Christmas Treat, Carolrhoda (Minneapolis, MN), 2001.
How About a Hug?, Viking (New York, NY), 2001.
My Best Friend Moved Away, Viking (New York, NY), 2001.
Smile a Lot!, Carolrhoda (Minneapolis, MN), 2002.
There's a Big, Beautiful World Out There!, Penguin Putnam (New York, NY), 2002.
It's Not My Fault, Carolrhoda (Minneapolis, MN), 2003.
My Family Is Forever, Viking (New York, NY), 2004.

ILLUSTRATOR

(As Nancy L. Carlson) Joyce Kessel, *Halloween,* Carolrhoda (Minneapolis, MN), 1980.
(As Nancy L. Carlson) Geoffrey Scott, *Egyptian Boats,* Carolrhoda (Minneapolis, MN), 1981.

(With Trina Schart Hyman, Hilary Knight, and Peter E. Hanson) Pamela Espeland and Marilyn Waniek, *The Cat Walked through the Casserole and Other Poems for Children,* Carolrhoda (Minneapolis, MN), 1984.

Susan Pearson, *The Baby and the Bear,* Viking (New York, NY), 1987.

Susan Pearson, *When the Baby Went to Bed,* Viking (New York, NY), 1987.

Rufus Klein, *Watch Out for These Weirdos,* Viking (New York, NY), 1990.

Susan Pearson, *Lenore's Big Break,* Viking (New York, NY), 1992.

Jacqueline K. Ogburg, *The Masked Maverick,* Lothrop (New York, NY), 1994.

Rick Walton, *What to Do When a Bug Climbs in Your Mouth and Other Poems to Drive You Buggy,* Lothrop (New York, NY), 1995.

Also author of a play, *Ted Just Ted,* for Stages Theatre Company, and an adaptation of *Hooray for Grandparents' Day.*

ADAPTATIONS: The following books have been adapted for audiocassette: *Harriet and Walt,* Live Oak Media, 1984; *Harriet's Recital* (with filmstrip), Random House, 1984, Live Oak Media, 1985; *Harriet and the Roller Coaster,* Live Oak Media, 1985; *Harriet and the Garden,* Live Oak Media, 1985; *Harriet's Halloween Candy,* Live Oak Media, 1985; *Loudmouth George and the Cornet,* Live Oak Media, 1986; *Loudmouth George and the Fishing Trip,* Live Oak Media, 1986; *Loudmouth George and the Sixth-Grade Bully,* Live Oak Media, 1986; *Loudmouth George and the Big Race,* Live Oak Media, 1986; *Loudmouth George and the New Neighbors,* Live Oak Media, 1987; *Louanne Pig in the Talent Show,* Live Oak Media, 1987; *Louanne Pig in Witch Lady,* Live Oak Media, 1987; *Louanne Pig in the Perfect Family,* Live Oak Media, 1987; *Louanne Pig in Making the Team,* Live Oak Media, 1987; *I Like Me!* ("Read Along" cassette series), Weston Woods, 1988, (with filmstrip), Weston Woods, 1988, and Puffin Books, 1997.

WORK IN PROGRESS: Henry's Show and Tell, for Viking.

SIDELIGHTS: Nancy Carlson is "the prolific author/illustrator of some of the most beloved characters in picture books," declared a critic for *Kirkus Reviews.*

With over forty books published, Carlson has charmed young readers for more than two decades with a cast of warm and fuzzy animal characters and small humans who have big hopes and overcome a variety of fears. Critics claim her cartoon-like style is well suited to her gently humorous tales in which dogs, cats, pigs, frogs, and children all undergo typical childhood adventures and sometimes traumas, from learning to be optimistic to realizing the mistake of stealing. Throughout her work, Carlson's characters learn how to cope with a variety of challenging situations in stories that illustrate for young readers how to make the right decision. Reviewers often dub Carlson's books optimistic and upbeat; the author believes, as she noted on her Web site, *Nancy's Neighborhood,* "that life should be fun for everyone, but especially for children." In addition to her busy writing schedule—producing on average two books per year—Carlson also visits over 150 classrooms annually as a guest author and illustrator.

From the age of five, Carlson knew that she wanted to be an artist when she grew up. A lifelong resident of Minnesota, she was raised in Edina, and had, as she noted on her author Web site, "a happy and fulfilling childhood surrounded by an outgoing family." Carlson attended the Minneapolis College of Art and Design, majoring in printmaking, and shortly after graduation, she began illustrating children's books.

Quickly realizing she would rather illustrate books that she had written herself, Carlson began combining her own pictures with stories and produced her first book, *Harriet's Recital,* in 1982. The book features a lovable canine that generally takes on more than she can handle. In the debut title, Harriet becomes a nervous wreck when her ballet teacher, Miss Betty, announces an upcoming recital. Though fearing she will forget every step of her dance routine, Harriet nonetheless builds up her courage for the big day. Carlson wrote four more books about Harriet, including *Harriet's Halloween Candy,* a tale about the negative effects of greed, in which the dog forgets all rules about the art of sharing. She hides all her treats so that not even her brother Walt can find them. Walt also makes an appearance in *Harriet and Walt,* a tale of winter fun. After the first big snowfall, Harriet is anxious to go outside and play, and even ends up having fun despite her mother's demand that she entertain her younger brother as well.

Another favorite of younger readers, Loudmouth George is featured in a quintet of his own books. In

Loudmouth George and the Sixth-Grade Bully, the obstreperous rabbit is tormented by a bully until Harriet helps him find a way to stand up for himself and discourage the troublemaker from any future incidents. In *Loudmouth George and the Big Race,* George figures that, with a bit of practice, a two-mile race will be a cinch for him. However, after repeatedly delaying his training, George finds he is not as prepared for the race as he would like to be. When a family of pigs moves in next door in *Loudmouth George and the New Neighbors,* George intentionally ignores them, thinking that smelly pigs are beneath him. His other neighbors do not feel the same way, however, and enjoy the newly-arrived porcine family. Finally, after listening to the fun the others are having while playing outside, the bigoted bunny gives up and joins in, too, in this "gentle look at prejudice," according to Lee Bock in *School Library Journal.*

Louanne Pig, in turn, stars in her own series of five books. With *Louanne Pig in the Talent Show,* excitement is in the air with the advent of the school talent show. Louanne, however, feels that she has no talents to share, unlike all her friends who plan to show off their unique abilities. After deciding to stay home on the big night, she begins to wonder about all of the fun she will miss. In *Louanne Pig and the Mysterious Valentine,* the little porker becomes excited when a lovely valentine arrives, but she cannot figure out who sent it. With only a bit of green ink to guide her, Louanne must sort through all of her friends to find her secret admirer. Her friend Arnie the cat makes an appearance in *Louanne Pig in Making the Team.* With tryouts for the school's cheerleading team arriving fast, Louanne seeks out the help of Arnie, who in turn asks for her help with his football skills.

A cat who loves mice, Arnie eventually received a book of his own, *Arnie and the Stolen Markers,* in 1987. One day Arnie sees a set of markers for sale at Harvey's Candy and Toy Shop and decides that he must have them. However, since he has wasted all his allowance on candy and his spendthrift friend Louanne refuses to lend him any money, Arnie slips the markers under his shirt and out of the store. Once he returns home, Arnie's mother discovers his thievery and returns him to the store, where the owner makes Arnie work for the stolen marker set. "Brightly spirited characters" help Carlson convey the message to children that stealing is wrong without the author "didactically haranguing the impropriety of stealing" according to Cathy Woodward in *School Library Journal.*

In *Arnie and the New Kid,* Carlson's 1990 picture book, a boy named Philip, who is in a wheelchair, enters Arnie's school. Arnie leads the other children in teasing Philip about his physical disability, but when Arnie injures his leg and finds out how difficult maneuvering on crutches is, he begins to sympathize with Philip. Philip and Arnie begin a friendship that continues long after Arnie's cast is removed. Writing in *School Library Journal,* Ellen Fader praised the happy ending, as well as Carlson's "lighthearted treatment of a common situation." *Bulletin of the Center for Children's Books* critic Deborah Stevenson applauded Carlson's illustrations, saying the characters complemented the text by "convey[ing] emotions that the text left unspoken."

While producing the "Arnie" series, Carlson also worked on other books to help youngsters calm their childhood fears and develop a healthy outlook on life. *Take Time to Relax,* the author's 1991 book, features a family of busy beavers who fill their every waking hour with activities from ballet classes and soccer games to tennis lessons and volleyball matches. When a terrible snowstorm prevents the beaver family from leaving their home, the ambitious family discovers that spending time alone with each other is more important than any other activity. A critic in *Publishers Weekly* liked the "hyperbole and humor" Carlson included in her text and noted that *Take Time to Relax* reinforces "an important message to today's over-programmed families."

Carlson followed *Take Time to Relax* with *What If It Never Stops Raining?,* another book that concentrates on children coping with their anxieties. Young Tim constantly worries about everything, even about a never-ending rain flooding his house. However, with his mother's support, Tim learns how to distinguish between worrying about real dangers, like falling off of the playground equipment, and needless anxiety about unfamiliar situations, like his new school bus driver getting lost. While admitting the ending is "a bit too tidy," a reviewer in *Publishers Weekly* said Carlson "proficiently handled" the delicate subject of how to quiet a child's irrational fears.

More gentle advice for kids comes in *How to Lose All Your Friends,* a tongue-in-cheek self-help book that tells kids how to push in line, tattle on others, and whine, complemented by "zippy" artwork that clearly distinguishes between "having fun and being mean," according to *Booklist*'s Mary Harris Veeder. *A Visit to Grandma's* provides another lesson, this time about the positive effects of change. A rodent family visits grandmother, who has moved to Florida, and little Tina is disappointed at first because her pumpkin-pie-baking grandma has been transformed into a sunglasses-wearing, aerobic-exercising lady. But soon Tina learns to appreciate this new and improved Grandma, even though the apron has been replaced with a jogging suit. "This subtle but important message is served up with jazzy trimmings," commented a contributor for *Publishers Weekly*, "and makes its point deftly."

Patrick is a hyperactive kid, featured in *Sit Still!*, whose mother decides to keep him busy with activities rather than treating his rambunctiousness with medicine. Reviewing the title in *Booklist*, Ilene Cooper thought the book would "cause some controversy." While noting that medication for children similar to Patrick is sometimes helpful, Cooper also predicted that "kids who are hyperactive will appreciate one of their own portrayed in a positive light." Less controversial is the self-confident pig in *I Like Me!* who makes a second appearance in *ABC, I Like Me!*, "a cheery companion book that celebrates the self," according to a critic for *Kirkus Reviews*. Each letter of the alphabet is used to affirm a positive quality about herself. "This concept book vibrates with bright colors, happy thoughts, and joie de vivre," announced Virginia Opocensky in *School Library Journal*. *Booklist*'s Cooper had similar praise for the affirming alphabet book, concluding, "It's hard to be down around a book this up."

A little mouse is ready to begin school in *Look Out Kindergarten, Here I Come!*, in which "Carlson brings her vibrant brand of encouragement to bear," according to a contributor for *Kirkus Reviews*. Reviewing the same title in *School Library Journal*, Marianne Saccardi commented that "the classroom is a cheery, welcoming place, and the story will reassure youngsters who are both eager for and apprehensive about their first school experience."

Carlson did not forget her dog, bunny, and cat friends from the outset of her career. With *Hooray for Grandparents' Day*, Arnie makes a reappearance, though a sad one initially because he does not have anyone to bring to school on Grandparents' Day. When a librarian suggests that he just bring some adult he knows, Arnie discovers that the ones he chooses are all out of town. But when the day comes, other adults in Arnie's life make an appearance, lifting his spirits. *Booklist*'s Cooper lauded "Carlson's goofy-looking animals-as-people," whom she felt were "quite appealing and lighten the story's mood." Harriet the dog and George the bunny are likewise reprised in *Harriet and George's Christmas Treat*. When the two see Mrs. Hoozit leaving the grocery shop at the outset of the holiday season, they figure they will need to avoid her in the future, for it is time for her awful fruitcakes. They manage to stay out of her path all week, but on Christmas Eve brother Walt is cajoled in for a visit, only to run outside praising Mrs. Hoozit's fudge. By the time Harriet and George arrive, however, the fudge is all gone, but still Mrs. Hoozit has a treat for them: she saved a fruitcake from last year. A reviewer for *School Library Journal* commended Carlson for the expressions on her characters, which "are great fun." A *Publishers Weekly* contributor similarly called the book "a holiday joke that feasters young and old can appreciate." *Booklist*'s Denise Wilms also found the book pleasing, describing it as "a light, amusing Christmas treat."

More positive, upbeat messages are offered in *Smile a Lot!* and *There's a Big, Beautiful World Out There!* In the first book, a frog narrator demonstrates that when you are feeling down, the best thing you can do is put a smile on your face. Smiles can work on bullies and moms, the frog advises. "Carlson knows how to make dry humor work for three-year-olds," wrote a contributor for *Kirkus Reviews*, while a writer for *Publishers Weekly* also praised the title, noting that "Carlson goes beyond 'grin and bear it' to give readers a glimpse of karmic justice; in exchange for his upbeat attitude, the frog is justly rewarded." And Shelle Rosenfeld, writing in *Booklist*, similarly commented, "Employing a characteristically charming animal cast, Carlson touts the best way to get through life's ups and downs."

With her 2002 *There's a Big, Beautiful World Out There!*, Carlson provides a subtle response to the terrorist attacks of September 11, 2001. This "reassuring picture book," as Kathy Broderick described it in *Booklist*, features a young girl who looks out her window at the world to discover that it is not as scary as it seems. There may be big, frightening dogs and thunderstorms, but there are also just as many compensating joyous things in the world. Shelley B. Sutherland, writing in *School Library Journal*, felt that Carlson "hits just the right note" in sharing with children their power "to choose between facing frightening things or hiding from them."

Hitting the right note is what Carlson has consistently done in her picture books, according to reviewers. From tales of talkative rabbits and outgoing cats and dogs, to stories of little boys and girls facing their worst fears, Carlson's tales present valuable life lessons without resorting to didacticism. Humor and colorful illustrations are considered the trademarks of her work.

BIOGRAPHICAL AND CRITICAL SOURCES:

PERIODICALS

Booklist, May 15, 1990, p. 1797; October 15, 1992, p. 438; January 1, 1993, p. 810; February 1, 1994, p. 1010; September, 1, 1994, Mary Harris Veeder, review of *How to Lose All Your Friends,* p. 49; June 1, 1995, p. 1782; April 15, 1996, Ilene Cooper, review of *Sit Still!,* p. 1445; April 1, 1997, Ilene Cooper, review of *ABC, I Like Me!,* p. 1337; June 1, 1998, Helen Rosenberg, review of *Look Out Kindergarten, Here I Come!,* p. 1838; July, 1998, Susan Dove Lempke, review of *It's Going to Be Perfect!,* p. 1885; June 1, 2000, Ilene Cooper, review of *Hooray for Grandparents' Day,* p. 1904; April 1, 2001, Carolyn Phelan, review of *My Best Friend Moved Away,* p. 1477; July, 2001, Ilene Cooper, *How About a Hug?,* p. 2017; October 1, 2001, Denise Wilms, review of *Harriet and George's Christmas Treat,* p. 323; September 15, 2002, Shelle Rosenfeld, review of *Smile a Lot!,* p. 238; October 1, 2002, Kathy Broderick, review of *There's a Big, Beautiful World Out There,* p. 332.

Bulletin of the Center for Children's Books, February, 1989, p. 143; May, 1990, Deborah Stevenson, review of *Arnie and the New Kid,* p. 209-210.

Five Owls, September, 1988, p. 8; May, 1990, p. 93; May, 1993, pp. 104, 122.

Horn Book Guide, spring, 1993, p. 23; spring, 1994, p. 28; spring, 1995, p. 28; fall, 1998, Christie Heppermann, review of *It's Going to Be Perfect!,* p. 286; spring, 1999, Peter D. Sieruta, review of *Snowden,* p. 25; spring, 2001, Frieda F. Bastian, review of *Hooray for Grandparents' Day,* p. 31.

Junior Bookshelf, April, 1993, p. 57.

Kirkus Reviews, March 15, 1989, p. 460; May 15, 1990, p. 726; August 15, 1991, p. 1086; August 15, 1994, p. 1122; May 1, 1997, review of *ABC, I Like Me!,* pp. 717-718; May 15, 1998, review of *It's Going to Be Perfect!,* p. 735; May 15, 1999, review of *Look Out Kindergarten, Here I Come!,* p. 797; April 1, 2001, review of *My Best Friend Moved Away,* pp. 495-496; June 15, 2002, review of *Smile a Lot!,* p. 877; August 1, 2002, review of *There's a Big, Beautiful World Out There!,* pp. 123-124.

Magpies, March, 1992, p. 27.

Publishers Weekly, October 9, 1987, p. 84; April 29, 1988, p. 74; September 9, 1988, p. 130; December 9, 1988, p. 61; December, 7, 1990, review of *Take Time to Relax,* p. 81; August 30, 1991, review of *A Visit to Grandma's,* p. 81; November 9, 1992, review of *What If It Never Stops Raining?,* p. 82; March 1, 1993, p. 58; July 26, 1993, review of *Life Is Fun!,* p. 70; October 8, 2001, review of *Harriet and George's Christmas Treat,* p. 63, review of *How About a Hug?,* p. 67; August 26, 2002, review of *Smile a Lot!,* p. 66.

School Library Journal, February, 1988, Cathy Woodward, review of *Arnie and the Stolen Markers,* p. 58; September, 1988, p. 154; June, 1990, Ellen Fader, review of *Arnie and the New Kid,* p. 97; August, 1991, p. 143; November, 1991, p. 90; February, 1993, p. 70; November, 1993, p. 76; August, 1995, p. 121; May, 1997, Elizabeth C. Fiene, review of *I Like Me!,* p. 87; June, 1997, Virginia Opocensky, review of *ABC, I Like Me!,* p. 85; August, 1998, Susan Knell, review of *It's Going to Be Perfect!,* p. 133; January, 1999, Sue Sherif, review of *Snowden,* pp. 79-80; July, 1999, Marianne Saccardi, review of *Look Out Kindergarten, Here I Come!,* p. 67; August, 2000, Sally R. Dow, review of *Hooray for Grandparents' Day!,* p. 144; June, 2001, Gay Lynn van Vleck, review of *My Best Friend Moved Away,* p. 105; October, 2001, review of *Harriet and George's Christmas Treat,* p. 63; December, 2001, Melinda Piehler, review of *How About a Hug?,* p. 97; October, 2002, Kathleen Simonetta, review of *Smile a Lot!,* p. 99; November, 2002, Shelley B. Sutherland, review of *There's a Big, Beautiful World Out There!,* p. 112; February, 2003, Lee Bock, review of *Loudmouth George and the New Neighbors,* p. 96.

Times Educational Supplement, February 19, 1993, p. R2.

ONLINE

Nancy's Neighborhood, http://www.nancycarlson.com/ (May 19, 2003).

* * *

CARRASCO, David 1944-

PERSONAL: Given name is accented on second syllable; born November 23, 1944, in Bainbridge, MD; son of David L. (a coach) and Marjorie (a painter; maiden name, Partin) Carrasco; divorced; children: La Anna Ruth, Octavio Pascal. *Education:* Western Maryland College, B.A., 1967; University of Chicago, M.A., 1972, Ph.D., 1977.

ADDRESSES: Office—Mesoamerican Archive, Princeton University, 1879 Hall, Princeton, NJ 08540.

CAREER: University of Colorado, Boulder, assistant professor, 1976-82, associate professor of religious studies, beginning 1982; Princeton University, Princeton, NJ, visiting professor, 1991-92, professor of history of religions, 1993—, director of the Mesoamerican Archive.

AWARDS, HONORS: Ford Foundation Fellowship for Mexican Americans, 1975-76; Chancellor's Essay Prize from University of Colorado, 1982, for article "Aztec Vision of Place: The Templo Mayor," and Chancellor's Book Prize, 1983, for *Quetzalcoatl and the Irony of Empire;* National Research Council fellow; West Maryland College, honorary doctorate, 1984; University of Colorado, Teaching Excellence Award, 1988; University of Colorado, Faculty Fellowship, 1989.

WRITINGS:

(Editor, with Jane Marie Swanburg) *Waiting for the Dawn: Mircea Eliade in Perspective,* Westview Press (Boulder, CO), 1985.
(With Johanna Broda and Eduardo Matos Moctezuma) *The Great Temple of Tenochtitlan: Center and Periphery in the Aztec World,* University of California Press (Berkeley, CA), 1987.
(Editor) *The Imagination of Matter: Religion and Ecology in Mesoamerican Traditions,* B.A.R. (Oxford, England), 1989.
Religions of Mesoamerica: Cosmovision and Ceremonial Centers, Harper & Row (New York, NY), 1990.
To Change Place: Aztec Ceremonial Landscapes, University Press of Colorado (Niwot, CO), 1991.
(Editor, with Jane Marie Law) *Waiting for the Dawn: Mircea Eliade in Perspective,* foreword by Joseph Mitsuo Kitagawa, photographs by Lawrence G. Desmond, University Press of Colorado (Niwot, CO), 1991.
(With Eduardo Matos Moctezuma) *Moctezuma's Mexico: Visions of the Aztec World,* University Press of Colorado (Niwot, CO), 1992.
(With Scott Sessions) *Daily Life of the Aztecs: People of the Sun and Earth,* Greenwood Press (Westport, CT), 1998.
City of Sacrifice: The Aztec Empire and the Role of Violence in Civilization, Beacon Press (Boston, MA), 1999.
(Editor) *Aztec Ceremonial Landscapes,* University Press of Colorado (Niwot, CO), 1999.
(Editor, with Lindsay Jones and Scott Sessions) *Mesoamerica's Classic Heritage: From Teotihuacan to the Aztecs,* University Press of Colorado (Boulder, CO), 2000.
Quetzalcoatl and the Irony of Empire: Myths and Prophecies in the Aztec Tradition, University of Chicago Press (Chicago, IL), 1982, revised edition, University Press of Colorado (Boulder, CO), 2000.
(Editor) *The Oxford Encyclopedia of Mesoamerican Cultures: The Civilizations of Mexico and Central America,* Oxford University Press (New York, NY), 2001.

Contributor to journals.

SIDELIGHTS: David Carrasco is a professor of historic religions and also director of the Mesoamerican Archive at Princeton University. He specializes in ancient Latin American cultures and has written and/or edited numerous books on the topic.

David Carrasco told *CA* that his primary motivation resulted from his work at the University of Chicago with Mircea Eliade, "the finest historian of religions of this century," and Paul Wheatley, "a leading urban geographer whose work on cities and symbols provides a context for my own work."

He continued: "My close connection to the Templo Mayor project in Mexico City has also led to a number of important collaborations and meetings with internationally known scholars. In 1979 I organized a major seminar, 'Center and Periphery: The Templo Mayor and the Aztec Empire,' which involved thirty major scholars from ten institutions in the United States and Mexico.

"The Templo Mayor is a paradigm of Mesoamerican culture and religion. I have established, with the help of colleagues at the University of Colorado, a five-year interdisciplinary study of the Templo Mayor and the seven thousand objects uncovered in the excavation. An archive of primary and secondary written sources plus photographs of the major treasures from the Templo Mayor is being set up at the University of Colorado to be used for teaching and research."

BIOGRAPHICAL AND CRITICAL SOURCES:

PERIODICALS

Antiquity, June, 2000, N. James, review of *Mesoamerica'a Classic Heritage from Teotihuacan to the Aztecs,* p. 433.
Booklist, September 1, 2001, review of *The Oxford Encyclopedia of Mesoamerican Cultures: The Civilizations of Mexico and Central America,* p. 155.
Choice, November, 2001, review of *The Oxford Encyclopedia of Mesoamerican Cultures,* p. 491.
Times Literary Supplement, February 15, 2001, review of *The Oxford Encyclopedia of Mesoamerican Cultures,* p.11.*

* * *

CHRISTIANSEN, Keith 1947-

PERSONAL: Born January 6, 1947, in Seattle, WA; son of Robert M. (a minister) and Constance (Ahnlund) Christiansen; married Mary Kunzel (an instructor in art), June, 1972; children: Teresa, Regina. *Education:* University of California—Santa Cruz, B.A. (history and French literature), 1969; University of California—Los Angeles, M.A., 1971; Harvard University, Ph.D., 1976. *Religion:* Episcopalian.

ADDRESSES: *Home*—320 Riverside Dr., New York, NY 10025. *Office*—Metropolitan Museum of Art, Fifth Ave. & 82nd St., New York, NY 10028.

CAREER: Metropolitan Museum of Art, New York, NY, assistant curator, 1976-81, associate curator of European paintings, beginning 1981, currently curator of Italian paintings.

AWARDS, HONORS: Fulbright grant, 1975; Mitchell Prize from Jan Mitchell Foundation, 1983, for *Gentile da Fabriano;* Arthur Kingsley Award, 1989, for *Painting in Renaissance Siena, 1420-1500.*

WRITINGS:

Gentile da Fabriano, Cornell University Press (Ithaca, NY), 1982.
(With Mina Gregori) *Caravaggio: The Age of Caravaggio,* Rizzoli International Publication (New York, NY), 1985.
(With Laurence B. Kanter and Carl Brandon Strehlke) *Painting in Renaissance Siena, 1420-1500,* Metropolitan Museum of Art (New York, NY), 1988.
A Caravaggio Rediscovered: "The Lute Player," Metropolitan Museum of Art (New York, NY), 1990.
Italian Painting, Macmillan (New York, NY), 1992.
Andrea Mantegna: Padua and Mantua, G. Braziller (New York, NY), 1994.
(Editor) *Giambattista Tiepolo, 1696-1770,* Metropolitan Museum of Art (New York, NY), 1996.
(Editor, with Maryan W. Ainsworth) *From Van Eyck to Bruegel: Early Netherlandish Painting in the Metropolitan Museum of Art,* Metropolitan Museum of Art (New York, NY), 1998.
(Author of introduction) *Piero della Francesca,* Stanley Moss Books-Sheep Meadow Press (Riverdale-on-Hudson, NY), 2000.
(With Judith W. Mann) *Orazio and Artemisia Gentileschi,* Yale University Press (New Haven, CT), 2001.
(Editor, with Gabriele Finaldi and Xavier Bray), David Davies and John Elliot, *El Greco,* Yale University Press (New Haven, Connecticut), 2003.

Contributor to art and museum journals.

SIDELIGHTS: Keith Christiansen is a curator at the Metropolitan Museum of Art who has written extensively about European paintings and their artists. His illustrated catalogs have garnered wide praise for informative texts offering insights into the artworks illustrated in these books. For example, *Publishers Weekly* reviewer Hugh Lauter Levin applauded *Italian Painting* for "text and illustrations [that] marvelously complement each other in this glorious album." And in a review of *From Van Eyck to Bruegel: Early Netherlandish Painting in the Metropolitan Museum of Art* for *Library Journal,* Kathryn Wekselman called the book a "well-produced volume" that is an "essential acquisition for specialized and academic collections."

Christiansen's books do not simply provide background to the artists and history behind the paintings they discuss, they also illuminate facts that many readers—even those well-versed in art—may not know or fully appreciate. For example, in *Italian Painting* Christiansen points out that Correggio was a master artist whose contributions should be weighed to be on a par of those by Leonardo da Vinci and Michelangelo. Similarly, in his *Orazio and Artemisia Gentileschi* Christiansen is the first writer to discuss the father and daughter artists together in one volume. The result is a book in which the influence these two artists had on each other can be clearly seen. Christiansen writes about how Orazio taught his daughter to be a skilled painter—in fact, one of the most famous female painters of her day—and how she eventually set out on her own to establish her unique style. The book also talks about how Artemisia was raped by Orazio's colleague Tassi, and how the crime and subsequent trial affected them both. "Both artists emerge from these meticulously argued pages as complex and unconventional human beings as well as consummate artists," concluded Donna Seaman in *Booklist.*

BIOGRAPHICAL AND CRITICAL SOURCES:

PERIODICALS

Apollo, January, 1983.
Booklist, March 1, 2002, Donna Seaman, review of *Orazio and Artemisia Gentileschi,* p. 1082.
Library Journal, October 15, 1989, Kathryn W. Finkelstein, review of *Painting in Renaissance Siena, 1420-1500,* p. 79; January, 1993, Douglas F. Smith, review of *Italian Painting,* p. 108; February 1, 1999, Kathryn Wekselman, review of *From Van Eyck to Bruegel: Early Netherlandish Painting in the Metropolitan Museum of Art,* p. 84; March 15, 2002, Sandra Rothenberg, review of *Orazio and Artemisia Gentileschi,* p. 75.
Listener, December 23, 1982.
London Review of Books, March 17, 1983.
New York Times Book Review, December 4, 1994, Michael Kimmelman, review of *Andrea Mantegna: Padua and Mantua,* p. 36.
Publishers Weekly, May 10, 1985, Genevieve Stuttaford, review of *The Age of Caravaggio,* p. 219; September 28, 1992, review of *Italian Painting,* p. 58.
Times Literary Supplement, April 5, 2002, Theodore K. Rabb, "Orazio, Artemisia—and Rome Revived," p. 15.
University of California—Santa Cruz Review, winter, 2001.

* * *

COOK, Harold John 1952-

PERSONAL: Born May 7, 1952, in Evanston, IL; son of John D. and Sybilla (a librarian; maiden name, Avery) Cook; married Faye Marie Getz (an historian), November 30, 1985. *Education:* Cornell College, B.A., 1974; University of Michigan, M.A., 1975, Ph.D., 1981.

ADDRESSES: Office—Wellcome Trust Centre for the History of Medicine, University College, London, 24 Eversholt St., London NW1 1AD, England. *E-mail*—h.cook@ucl.ac.uk.

CAREER: Educator, administrator, and author. Harvard University, Boston, MA, assistant professor and head tutor, 1982-85; University of Wisconsin—Madison, assistant professor, 1985-88, associate professor, 1988-93, professor of history of medicine, 1993-200, chair of department, 1993-98-; Wellcome Trust Center for the History of Medicine, University College, London, London, England, director, 2000—. Visiting assistant professor of history of science, University of Oklahoma, 1981-82; part-time lecturer at Humanities, Sozial- und Kulturgeschichte, Berlin, Germany.

MEMBER: American Historical Association, American Association for the History of Medicine, History of Science Society, Society for the Social History of Medicine, Society for the History of Natural History, North American Conference on British Studies.

WRITINGS:

The Decline of the Old Medical Regime in Stuart London, Cornell University Press (Ithaca, NY), 1986.
Trials of an Ordinary Doctor: Joannes Groenevelt in Seventeenth-Century London, Johns Hopkins University Press (Baltimore, MD), 1994.

Contributor to periodicals, including *Social History of Medicine, American Journal of Legal History, Medical History, Osiris, Bulletin of the History of Medicine, Journal of the History of Ideas, History of Science, Journal of British Studies,* and *Annals of Science.* Work has been collected in anthologies, including *The Scientific Revolution in National Context,* Cambridge University Press, 1992.

WORK IN PROGRESS: Research on early modern English medicine; research on medicine and natural history during the Dutch Golden Age and the rise of the Dutch East India Company.

SIDELIGHTS: Educator Harold J. Cook's works focus on the history of medicine during the seventeenth and early eighteenth centuries. His first book, *The Decline of the Old Medical Regime in Stuart London,* reflects the author's interest in the conservative medical establishment at the time, a subject Cook examines even more acutely in *Trials of an Ordinary Doctor: Joannes Groenevelt in Seventeenth-Century London.* In this second work, Cook reveals "the complexities of professionalism, medical practice, and British society around 1700," according to Gert H. Brieger in the *Journal of the American Medical Association.* Groenevelt was a Dutch physician who moved to London to establish a medical practice. He quickly found himself at odds with the medical community there with his desire to focus on the practice of internal medicine, which inspired jealousy among his peers. Groenevelt was sued by a patient on whom he had operated for gall stones, and his subsequent trial was used as a forum by his enemies to attack him professionally. Although he was eventually exonerated, the trial ruined his reputation and he died penniless. "Though new ideas were flourishing and London and the rest of England were seeing demographic and economic growth," commented Brieger, "the fundamentally conservative nature of British institutions, especially medicine, is readily evident in this gripping story of a man of talent and energy outside the traditional field." *English Historical Review* contributor Paul Slack praised Cook for his research into both Dutch and English primary source material and his ability to bring this research together into "a readable and engrossing narrative work and a work with wider implications."

Cook once told *CA:* "I am deeply interested in the ways in which social experience affects our cultural notions and ideas. In my historical work, therefore, I have tried to integrate social and intellectual history, especially in the areas of the history of medicine and the history of science. Since all people face illness and death, the ways in which they meet them tell much about their culture. My continuing interest, therefore, is to uncover the ways in which social, economic, and political changes in early modern Europe affected medical and scientific ideas, practices, and professions."

BIOGRAPHICAL AND CRITICAL SOURCES:

PERIODICALS

American Historical Review, December, 1995, Anita Guerrini, review of *Trials of an Ordinary Doctor: Joannes Groenevelt in Seventeenth-Century London,* p. 1565.
Choice, January, 1995, G. Eknoyan, review of *Trials of an Ordinary Doctor,* p. 822.
English Historical Review, February, 1997, Paul Slack, review of *Trials of an Ordinary Doctor,* p. 204.
Journal of British Studies, October, 1997, Margaret C. Jacob, review of *Trials of an Ordinary Doctor,* p. 459.
Journal of the American Medical Association, December 13, 1995, Gert H. Brieger, review of *Trials of an Ordinary Doctor,* p. 181.
Times Higher Education Supplement, October 28, 1994, Alice Stewart, review of *Trials of an Ordinary Doctor,* p. 20.
Times Literary Supplement, July 11, 1986.*

ONLINE

Wellcome Trust Centre for the History of Medicine Web site, http://www.ucl.ac.uk/ (July 24, 2003), "Professor Harold Cook."*

COOPER, Floyd 1956-

PERSONAL: Born January 8, 1956, in Tulsa, OK; married; wife's name, Velma; children: Dayton, Kai Noah. *Education:* University of Oklahoma, B.F.A. *Hobbies and other interests:* Basketball, tennis, bicycling, nature walks, movies, all types of music, books.

ADDRESSES: Home—West Orange, NJ. *Agent*—c/o Author Mail, HarperCollins, 1350 Avenue of the Americas, New York, NY 10019.

CAREER: Author and illustrator. Worked in advertising and for Hallmark, Kansas City, MO; freelance illustrator, 1984—.

AWARDS, HONORS: Notable Book selection, American Library Association (ALA), for *Grandpa's Face,* written by Eloise Greenfield; Parents' Choice Award, Parents' Choice Foundation, 1990, for *Laura Charlotte,* written by Kathryn Osebold Galbraith; Coretta Scott King Honor Book for Illustration, ALA, 1994, for *Brown Honey in Broomwheat Tea: Poems,* 1995, for *Meet Danitra Brown,* and 1999, for *I Have Heard of a Land.*

WRITINGS:

SELF-ILLUSTRATED

Coming Home: From the Life of Langston Hughes, Philomel (New York, NY), 1994.
Mandela: From the Life of the South African Statesman, Philomel (New York, NY), 1996.
Cumbayah, Morrow (New York, NY), 1998.

ILLUSTRATOR

Margaret Davidson, *The Story of Jackie Robinson, Bravest Man in Baseball,* Dell (New York, NY), 1988.
Eloise Greenfield, *Grandpa's Face,* Philomel (New York, NY), 1988.
Elizabeth Fitzgerald Howard, *Chita's Christmas Tree,* Bradbury Press (New York, NY), 1989.
Kathryn Osebold Galbraith, *Laura Charlotte,* Philomel (New York, NY), 1990.

Floyd Cooper

Jacqueline Woodson, *Martin Luther King, Jr. and His Birthday,* Silver-Burdett (Parsippany, NJ), 1990.
Karen Lynn Williams, *When Africa Was Home,* Orchard Books (New York, NY), 1991.
Deborah Eaton, *Petey,* Silver Burdett (Parsippany, NJ), 1992.
Denise Burden-Patmon, *Imani's Gift at Kwanzaa,* Modern Curriculum Press (Cleveland, OH), 1992.
Jean Merrill, *The Girl Who Loved Caterpillars: A Twelfth-Century Tale from Japan,* Philomel (New York, NY), 1992.
Virginia M. Fleming, *Be Good to Eddie Lee,* Philomel (New York, NY), 1993.
Joyce Carol Thomas, *Brown Honey in Broomwheat Tea: Poems,* HarperCollins (New York, NY), 1993.
Wade Hudson, selector, *Pass It On: African-American Poetry for Children,* Scholastic (New York, NY), 1993.
Sandra Belton, *From Miss Ida's Porch,* Four Winds Press (New York, NY), 1993.
Gerald Hausman, reteller, *Coyote Walks on Two Legs: A Book of Navajo Myths and Legends,* Philomel (New York, NY), 1993.
Nikki Grimes, *Meet Danitra Brown,* Lothrop (New York, NY), 1994.
Kathryn D. Jones, *Happy Birthday, Dr. King,* Modern Curriculum Press (Cleveland, OH), 1994.

Candy Dawson Boyd, *Daddy, Daddy, Be There,* Philomel (New York, NY), 1995.

Joyce Carol Thomas, *Gingerbread Days: Poems,* HarperCollins (New York, NY), 1995.

Elizabeth Fitzgerald Howard, *Papa Tells Chita a Story,* Simon & Schuster (New York, NY), 1995.

Wade and Cheryl Hudson, selectors, *How Sweet the Sound: African-American Songs for Children,* Scholastic (New York, NY), 1995.

Carol J. Farley, *King Sejong's Secret,* Lothrop (New York, NY), 1995.

Virginia Hamilton, *Jaguarundi,* Blue Sky Press (New York, NY), 1995.

Jane Kurtz, *Pulling the Lion's Tale,* Simon & Schuster (New York, NY), 1995.

Alan Schroeder, *Satchmo's Blues,* Doubleday (New York, NY), 1996.

Nancy Lamb, *One April Morning: Children Remember the Oklahoma City Bombing,* Lothrop (New York, NY), 1996.

Bill Martin and Michael Sampson, *Si Won's Victory,* Celebration Press (Parsippany, NJ), 1996.

Patricia C. McKissack, *Ma Dear's Aprons,* Atheneum (New York, NY), 1997.

Jane Yolen, *Miz Berlin Walks,* Philomel (New York, NY), 1997.

Virginia L. Kroll, *Faraway Drums,* Little, Brown (Boston, MA), 1998.

Joyce Carol Thomas, *I Have Heard of a Land,* HarperCollins (New York, NY), 1998.

Ziporah Hildebrandt, reteller, *Sea Girl and the Dragon King: A Chinese Folktale,* Atheneum (New York, NY), 1998.

James Haskins and Kathleen Benson, *African Beginnings,* Lothrop (New York, NY), 1998.

Amy Littlesugar, *Shake Rag: From the Life of Elvis Presley,* Philomel (New York, NY), 1998.

Amy Littlesugar, *Tree of Hope,* Philomel (New York, NY), 1999.

Robert H. Miller, *Reflections of a Black Cowboy,* 2nd edition, Volume 1: *Cowboys,* 1999, Volume 2: *The Buffalo Soldiers,* 1999, Volume 3: *Pioneers,* 1999, Volume 4: *Mountain Men,* Silver Burdett (Parsippany, NJ), 1999.

Michael Sampson, *Caddie, the Golf Dog,* Tommy Nelson (Nashville, TN), 1999.

Fatima Shaik, *On Mardi Gras Day,* Dial (New York, NY), 1999.

Monalisa DeGross, *Granddaddy's Street Songs,* Jump at the Sun/Hyperion (New York, NY), 1999.

James Haskins and Kathleen Benson, *Bound for America: The Forced Migration of Africans to the New World,* Lothrop (New York, NY), 1999.

Margaret Wise Brown, *A Child Is Born,* Jump at the Sun/Hyperion (New York, NY), 2000.

Jacqueline Woodson, *Sweet, Sweet Memory,* Jump at the Sun/Hyperion (New York, NY), 2000.

Bill Martin, Jr. and Michael Sampson, *City Scenes,* Learning Matters Africa (Durban, South Africa), 2000.

Amy Littlesugar, *Freedom School, Yes!,* Philomel (New York, NY), 2001.

Joyce Carol Thomas, *The Blacker the Berry: Poems,* HarperCollins (New York, NY), 2002.

Nikki Grimes, *Danitra Brown Leaves Town,* HarperCollins (New York, NY), 2002.

Ruth Vander Zee, *Mississippi Morning,* Eerdmans Books (Grand Rapids, MI), 2003.

SIDELIGHTS: Winner of three Coretta Scott King Honor Awards for illustration, author and illustrator Floyd Cooper has brought to life many stories, poems, songs, and works of nonfiction detailing centuries of African-American experience. "Luminous" is perhaps the single most often used word by critics to describe the work of Cooper, who began his career as a children's book illustrator with his work on the 1988 picture book *Grandpa's Face.* Cooper has since been hailed by critics for what a *Publishers Weekly* reviewer called his "painterly, sun-drenched portraits" and Lois F. Anderson lauded as "reveal[ing] keen observations of people and neighborhood" in a *Horn Book* review. He has illustrated nearly fifty picture books by writers from Nikki Grimes to Amy Littlesugar to Jane Yolen to Margaret Wise Brown; additionally, Cooper has also penned several of his own picture books with strong African-American themes.

Born in Tulsa, Oklahoma, in 1956, Cooper first tried his hand at illustration as a three-year-old. As he noted on the *Teachers at Random* Web site, "My earliest recollection of actually doing drawing is on the side of my father's house." While Cooper's father busied himself building, his young son found a stray piece of drywall and began drawing the picture of a "duck of some sort," as Cooper recalled. Though he had to ultimately erase this piece of artwork, he has been drawing ever since. "The biggest influence on me as a child was my mother," Cooper further noted. "She played a major role in my direction. Everything. I lived in the projects as a child. We were from very modest means, but she was always able to instill in me a sense of value that I carry with me today." Cooper's mother also had a wealth of stories which she shared with her imaginative young son.

Cooper attended the University of Oklahoma, where he studied fine art. After graduating, he spent several years in the advertising field and working for Hallmark greeting cards. Moving to New York, he "stumbled into an agent's office" one afternoon after searching for work for several months, and was offered a chance at illustrating his first picture book, *Grandpa's Face,* written by Eloise Greenfield.

The book is a sensitive portrait of a young girl named Tamika who sees her grandfather's expression become scary; unaware that he is practicing for the part of an angry character in a play, she purposely misbehaves to see if he could get angry enough at her to wear such a mean expression. Illustrated in muted pastel tones of gold and rich warm brown, Cooper's work was praised by a *Publishers Weekly* critic for "reinforc[ing] in the pictures the feelings of warmth and affection that exists between generations." Such feelings were also kindled by his artwork for Kathryn Galbraith's *Laura Charlotte,* as a young girl's fear of the dark at bedtime is diminished with the story of how her favorite stuffed animal—an elephant who once belonged to her mother—came to be. Cooper's grainy, "somber-toned illustrations envelop the reader in their warmth as they capture the mood of summer nights and cozy bedrooms," noted a *Publishers Weekly* commentator.

Sandra Belton's *From Miss Ida's Porch* evokes an earlier age as elderly residents of a city's African-American neighborhood gather in the early evening hours and recall musical idols Duke Ellington and Marian Anderson. As a counterpoint to Belton's lyrical prose, Cooper's oil-wash illustrations "add to the warmth and sense of community," according to *School Library Journal* reviewer Elizabeth Hanson. A *Publishers Weekly* commentator noted that Cooper's pictures "affectingly capture the fading light on the young and old faces and complement the nostalgic quality of the story." Cooper opens a similar window to the past in Patricia C. McKissack's *Ma Dear's Aprons,* as young David tells the story of how he can always tell what day of the week it is by the apron his widowed mother, a domestic servant, wears to work. "The love between the mother and son is palpable," noted Maeve Visser Knoth in a *Horn Book* review, "and the composition and colors of the illustration emphasize the strength of the relationship." Also praising Cooper's oil-wash artwork, Hazel Rochman commented in *Booklist* that his illustrations "show the exhausting work, as well as the proud and loving bonds of family."

In addition to stories—both of the African-American experience and of other cultures, such as twelfth-century Japan in his highly praised work for Jean Merrill's *The Girl Who Loved Caterpillars: A Twelfth-Century Tale from Japan*—Cooper has illustrated several collections of verse for younger children, including four volumes by poet Joyce Carol Thomas. Thomas's first collection, *Brown Honey in Broomwheat Tea: Poems,* features watercolor illustrations that a *Publishers Weekly* reviewer characterized as "essentially realistic but enveloped in a haze of light," and that *Booklist* contributor Janice Del Negro noted "invite the viewer to participate in the family gatherings and ritual tea brewing that take place." In Thomas's *Gingerbread Days: Poems,* the twelve poems featured—one for each month of the calendar year—are "made even stronger by Floyd Cooper's glowing golden illustrations," in the opinion of *Horn Book* critic Martha V. Parravano. And praising the illustrator's work for Wade Hudson's compilation *Pass It On: African-American Poetry for Children,* Jane Marino remarked upon Cooper's characteristic "glowing colors and skillfully drawn faces" in her *School Library Journal* review.

In addition to picture books and poetry for young readers, nonfiction works have also benefited from Cooper's artistic talents. In response to the tragedy that occurred in Oklahoma City in 1995, during which nineteen young people were among the many victims that day, Nancy Lamb and Cooper produced *One April Morning: Children Remember the Oklahoma City Bombing*. According to a *Publishers Weekly* reviewer, Cooper's "softly focused renderings of children . . . effectively serve as all-purpose, emotion-laden backdrops to the disquieting but ultimately life-affirming text." *Booklist* critic Kay Weisman asserted that Cooper's "muted pastel illustrations convey the intense emotion of the survivors from a discrete distance."

In 1994, Cooper published his first work as both author and illustrator with *Coming Home: From the Life of Langston Hughes.* Focusing on the poet's lonely childhood and his search for a stable home despite his parents' extended absences, Cooper tells of the writer's early years "in a warm and intimate tone that conveys both the deprivations and sources of strength" in Hughes's youth, according to *Bulletin of the Center for Children's Books* critic Roger Sutton. And Cooper's "writing proves equal to his artwork in highlighting elements that convey the emotion and important events" from Hughes's boyhood, Louise L. Sherman maintained in *School Library Journal.*

Continuing to pursue an interest in biography, Cooper has also written of another black leader in 1996's *Mandela: From the Life of the South African Statesman.* Retaining a focus on his subject's youth, Cooper illuminates the South African leader's philosophical origins as a child growing up in a Transkai village, and outlines the basis of the character that enabled Mandela to withstand personal difficulties—including an almost thirty-year prison term—during decades of fighting to end apartheid in his homeland. Praising Cooper's artwork, a *Publishers Weekly* critic deemed the volume "a forceful, credible picture of a strong and deeply devoted statesman."

In 1996's *Satchmo's Blues,* the early life of trumpeter Louis Armstrong is fictionalized through Alan Schroeder's text and what *Booklist* contributor Bill Ott called "some of [Cooper's] best work." Ott continued: "His soft-focus, two-page spreads . . . use hazy browns and golds to capture the shimmering heat and pulsing rhythm of New Orleans' streets."

Cumbayah is a further solo effort, a book that blends the well-known verses of the spiritual with "glowing illustrations," according to Jane Marino in *School Library Journal,* "to tell a global tale far beyond the words." Each stanza of the song is illustrated with a different group of children and adults from around the world taking part in the singing. Cooper also adds original verses to the song to create a book that "will be welcomed by religious instructors, music teachers and families," thought a contributor for *Publishers Weekly.* And *Booklist*'s Susan Dove Lempke had similar praise, calling *Cumbayah* a "warm, inviting book."

Cooper has explored the African-American experience—both on the individual level and on the larger historical scene—in numerous books in collaboration with other writers. Working with the poet Nikki Grimes, he has provided illustrations for both *Meet Danitra Brown* and the 2002 *Danitra Brown Leaves Town.* Both books relate the tale of a simple friendship through letters between the friends Danitra and Zuri Jackson. Reviewing the first title, a contributor for *Publishers Weekly* commented on "Cooper's misty oil paints [that] depict two proud, happy kids in an often grim urban landscape." *Booklist*'s Hazel Rochman also lauded Cooper's artwork for *Meet Danitra Brown,* remarking favorably upon the "rich shades of brown and purple," while Betsy Hearne, writing in *Bulletin of the Center for Children's Books,* found the pictures "as upbeat as the poetry." In *Danitra Brown Leaves Town,* the two friends must learn to do without each other one summer while Danitra visits relatives. *School Library Journal*'s Catherine Threadgill felt that "Cooper's photo-realist artwork in soft hues . . . is a lovely complement to the girls' many moods." Similar praise came from a critic for *Kirkus Reviews,* who noted that "Cooper's paintings simply burst with energy and expressiveness."

Cooper has also teamed up with James Haskins and Kathleen Benson on titles exploring African as well as African-American history. Their 1998 *African Beginnings* looks at eleven different African cultures, beginning with the Nubian in 3800 B.C., and also including the Egyptian civilization. Various aspects are covered, such as music, dance, Islam, contact with Europe, and eventual slavery. *Booklist*'s Susan Dove Lempke felt that the artwork "reflect[s] Cooper's exceptional ability to capture people's faces [and] portray the varied cultures with dignity and spirit." Eunice Weech, writing in *School Library Journal,* found the same book "a handsomely illustrated overview of Africa's ancient empires." Weech also lauded Cooper's "beautiful double-page spreads" in this "stunning introduction to African history." The same authors worked with Cooper on *Bound for America: The Forced Migration of Africans to the New World,* which provides an overview of the slave trade from Africa to Europe, with its subsequent high loss of life in transport across the Atlantic. "Cooper's strong oil-wash paintings, with their focus on individual faces, make intensely personal these statistics," wrote Hazel Rochman in a *Booklist* review.

Working again with Joyce Carol Thomas, Cooper provided illustrations to a "lyrical tribute to the pioneer spirit," according to *Booklist*'s Ilene Cooper, in a review of the 1998 *I Have Heard of a Land.* This third collaborative effort with Thomas proved equally as successful as the earlier ones. Documenting the black pioneers in the Oklahoma land runs of 1889 and 1893, the book is a poem of praise to one woman who has heard of a land where she can start a new life. Jody McCoy, writing in *School Library Journal,* noted that "the poem is exalted by Cooper's warm, joyous, and majestic paintings." Similarly, Ilene Cooper felt that the author's poetry was "matched by Cooper's always evocative artwork." A contributor for *Publishers Weekly* likewise lauded Cooper's "signature grainy, dreamy oil-wash portraits." Cooper won a Coretta Scott King Honor Award for the illustrations to *I Have Heard of a Land.*

Granddaddy's Street Songs, by Monalisa DeGross, *Faraway Drums,* by Virginia Kroll, and *Sweet, Sweet Memory,* by Jacqueline Woodson all present more personal tales: a grandfather's stories about the good old days; a girl frightened by night sounds of her new neighborhood; or a young girl's preparations for her beloved grandfather's funeral. Alicia Eames praised Cooper's "brightly colored yet softly muted pastels" for *Granddaddy's Street Songs* in a *School Library Journal* review, while *Booklist*'s Stephanie Zvirin found "Cooper's hazy yet saturated oil paintings . . . just right" for *Faraway Drums.* Marianne Saccardi, in a *School Library Journal* review of *Sweet, Sweet Memory,* had similar praise for Cooper's artwork, calling it "the perfect complement for Woodson's gentle text." Saccardi further noted that the artist's faces are "filled with a range of emotions, from sorrow to joy to determination to continue with the business of living."

Working with author Amy Littlesugar, Cooper has created the artwork for three further books. *Shake Rag: From the Life of Elvis Presley* documents the youth of the future rock and roll king in the largely black community of Shake Rag, Tennessee. Here the youthful Presley gained inspiration from the radio and from visits to a predominantly black church and its gospel music. A *Publishers Weekly* reviewer wrote that Cooper's paintings, "luminous as ever and glowing in tones of browns, yellows and earthy greens—draw readers into a fascinating era." In *Tree of Hope,* Littlesugar and Cooper once again "join forces to vividly evoke the past," according to another critic for *Publishers Weekly.* Set during the Great Depression, *Tree of Hope* features a young girl and her adventures with her father, an actor trying to revive Harlem's once popular theaters. The same reviewer further noted that the artist's illustrations "breathe life into both the gritty period cityscapes and the memorable characters." Miriam Lang Budin, writing in *School Library Journal,* also thought Cooper's artwork "capture[s] the emotions that make Littlesugar's characters vivid." Reviewing *Tree of Hope* in *Booklist,* Hazel Rochman noted that the illustrations display "the harsh poverty, the warmth of family bonds, and also the excitement and magic of being part of a show." A further collaborative effort with Littlesugar is the 2001 title *Freedom School, Yes!,* a fictionalized account of the 1964 Mississippi Summer Project and the Freedom Schools opened in the South by volunteers from the North. Barbara Buckley, reviewing the book in *School Library Journal,* called Cooper's artwork "masterful and lush," and further commended his representation of faces which exhibit "exquisite strength and real pain." For Buckley, *Freedom School, Yes!* was a "unique and poignant look at a moment in history." Similar praise came from a reviewer for *Publishers Weekly* who felt Cooper's illustrations were "as radiant as ever, depict[ing] the strength shining in the faces of people newly enlightened."

Cooper additionally provided artwork for an unpublished manuscript from the well-known children's writer Margaret Wise Brown. A nativity tale, *A Child Is Born* is told in verse, and according to a *Publishers Weekly* critic, Cooper's "radiant . . . paintings serve as elegant accompaniment" to Wise's "celebratory" text. A reviewer for *School Library Journal* felt while the text was "spare," Cooper's artwork "will bring forth a thousand words for a parent and child to share."

"My inspiration for illustrating picture books primarily comes from the text," Cooper explained on the *Teachers at Random* Web site. "Someone writes a story, and I'll read it and become totally affected by it. . . . I'll get inspired by what's going on and actually be transported to that place. I want to do that with my art—bring the viewer along with me and tell the story in the same way that I feel it when I read the story. And so that's what I attempt to do with my paintings: to sort of take you into the place that's happening in the story."

BIOGRAPHICAL AND CRITICAL SOURCES:

BOOKS

Children's Literature Review, Volume 60, Gale (Detroit, MI), 2000, pp. 14-28.
Continuum Encyclopedia of Children's Literature, edited by Bernice E. Cullinan and Diane G. Person, Continuum International (New York, NY), 2001, pp. 195-196.

PERIODICALS

Black Issues Book Review, November, 2000, review of *A Child Is Born,* p. 78.

Booklist, September 1, 1992, p. 54; September 15, 1993, Janice Del Negro, review of *Brown Honey in Broomwheat Tea: Poems,* p. 115; February 15, 1994, Hazel Rochman, review of *Meet Danitra Brown,* p. 1085; December 15, 1994, p. 753; May 15, 1996, Kay Weisman, review of *One April Morning: Children Remember the Oklahoma City Bombing,* p. 1583; September 15, 1996, Bill Ott, review of *Satchmo's Blues,* p. 251; February 15, 1997, Hazel Rochman, review of *Ma Dear's Aprons,* p. 1027; February 15, 1998, Susan Dove Lempke, review of *African Beginnings,* pp. 1002-1003; February 15, 1998, Stephanie Zvirin, review of *Faraway Drums,* p. 1008; February 15, 1998, Ilene Cooper, review of *I Have Heard of a Land,* p. 1009; February 15, 1998, Susan Dove Lempke, review of *Cumbayah,* p. 1014; December 15, 1998, Hazel Rochman, review of *Bound for America: The Forced Migration of Africans to the New World,* p. 746; February 15, 1999, Hazel Rochman, review of *Bound for America,* p. 1068; March 1, 1999, Julie Corsaro, review of *Mardi Gras Day,* p. 1223; June 1, 1999, Michael Cart, review of *Granddaddy's Street Songs,* p. 1838; December 15, 1999, Hazel Rochman, review of *Tree of Hope,* p. 790; February 15, 2001, Hazel Rochman, review of *Freedom School, Yes!,* p. 1155, Henrietta M. Smith, review of *Cumbayah,* p. 1160.

Bulletin of the Center for Children's Books, July-August, 1994, Betsy Hearne, review of *Meet Danitra Brown,* p. 357; January, 1995, Roger Sutton, review of *Coming Home: From the Life of Langston Hughes,* p. 162.

Childhood Education, fall, 2001, review of *Freedom School, Yes!,* p. 50.

Horn Book, March-April, 1989, p. 197; November-December, 1993, pp. 743-744; September-October, 1994, Lois F. Anderson, review of *Coming Home,* pp. 604-605; September-October, 1995, pp. 626-627; March-April, 1996, Martha V. Parravano, review of *Gingerbread Days: Poems,* p. 219; May-June, 1997, Maeve Visser Knoth, review of *Ma Dear's Aprons,* p. 310.

Kirkus Reviews, April 15, 1994, review of *Meet Danitra Brown,* p. 557; September 15, 1994, p. 1269; August 1, 1996, pp. 1148-1149; December 15, 2001, review of *Danitra Brown Leaves Town,* p. 1758.

New York Times Book Review, February 12, 1995, p. 13; June 18, 1995, p. 25; February 14, 1999, Peter Keepnews, review of *Shake Rag: From the Life of Elvis Presley,* p. 27.

Publishers Weekly, October 28, 1988, review of *Grandpa's Face,* p. 78; February 9, 1990, review of *Laura Charlotte,* p. 60; October 12, 1992, p. 78; January 18, 1993, review of *Pass It On: African-American Poetry for Children,* p. 471; July 26, 1993, review of *From Miss Ida's Porch,* p. 73; October 11, 1993, review of *Brown Honey in Broomwheat Tea,* p. 87; April 11, 1994, review of *Meet Danitra Brown,* p. 65; October 10, 1994, p. 70; August 26, 1996, review of *Mandela: From the Life of the South African Statesman,* p. 98; January 20, 1997, p. 401; March 23, 1998, review of *Cumbayah,* p. 94; March 30, 1998, review of *Faraway Drums,* p. 81; April 6, 1998, review of *I Have Heard of a Land,* pp. 77-79; November 2, 1998, review of *Shake Rag,* p. 82; January 25, 1999, review of *Satchmo's Blues,* p. 98; February 8, 1999, review of *On Mardi Gras Day,* p. 214; November 29, 1999, review of *Tree of Hope,* p. 70; December 13, 1999, review of *Mandela,* p. 85; December 20, 1999, review of *Ma Dear's Aprons,* p. 82; September 25, 2000, review of *A Child Is Born,* p. 67; November 20, 2000, review of *Miz Berlin Walks,* p. 70; January 8, 2001, review of *Freedom School, Yes!,* p. 65; July 30, 2001, review of *Shake Rag,* p. 87.

School Library Journal, April, 1990, p. 90; December, 1990, p. 22; September, 1992, p. 269; May, 1993, Jane Marino, review of *Pass It On,* pp. 99-100; November, 1993, Elizabeth Hanson, review of *From Miss Ida's Porch,* p. 76; November, 1994, Louise L. Sherman, review of *Coming Home,* pp. 95-96; December, 1994, p. 75; June, 1995, p. 87; January, 1996, p. 107; April 15, 1996, review of *One April Morning,* p. 69; September, 1996, p. 191; May, 1998, Dawn Amsberry, review of *Faraway Drums,* p. 119, Jane Marino, review of *Cumbayah,* pp. 130-131; June, 1998, Eunice Weech, review of *African Beginnings,* p. 130; July, 1998, Jody McCoy, review of *I Have Heard of a Land,* p. 84; July, 1999, Alicia Eames, review of *Granddaddy's Street Songs,* p. 68; November, 1999, Miriam Lang Budin, review of *Tree of Hope,* p. 123; October, 2000, review of *A Child Is Born,* p. 56; January, 2001, Barbara Buckley, review of *Freedom School, Yes!,* p. 104; April, 2001, Marianne Saccardi, review of *Sweet, Sweet Memory,* p. 126; February, 2002, Catherine Threadgill, review of *Danitra Brown Leaves Town,* p. 101; Linda Ludke, December, 2002, review of *Caddie, the Golf Dog,* p. 108.

Teacher Librarian, September, 1998, Shirley Lewis, review of *Cumbaya,* p. 47.

ONLINE

Teachers at Random, http://www.randomhouse.com/teachers/ (May 22, 2003), "Floyd Cooper."*

* * *

COWLEY, (Cassia) Joy 1936-

PERSONAL: Born August 7, 1936, in Levin, New Zealand; daughter of Peter (a builder) and Cassia (Gedge) Summers; married Ted Cowley, 1956 (divorced); married Malcolm Mason (an accountant and writer), 1970 (died, 1985); married Terry Coles, 1989; children: (from first marriage) Sharon, Edward, Judith, James. *Education:* Attended Girls' High School, Palmerston North, Wellington, New Zealand. *Religion:* Roman Catholic. *Hobbies and other interests:* Spinning, fishing, cooking, gardening, fishing, playing with grandchildren, "other soothing pastimes."

ADDRESSES: Home—Te Mangawa, Fish Bay, Kenepuru, R.D. 2, Picton 7372, New Zealand.

CAREER: Writer, 1967—. Pharmacist's apprentice in New Zealand, 1953-56.

AWARDS, HONORS: New Zealand Buckland Literary Award, 1970, for *Man of Straw;* New Zealand Literary Achievement Award, 1980; New Zealand AIM Children's Book Awards, 1982, for *The Silent One,* 1992, for *Bow down Shadrach,* and 1996, for *The Cheese Trap;* Children's Book of the Year awards, 1983, for *The Silent One,* and 1993, for *Bow down Shadrach;* Russell Clark Award, 1985, for *The Duck in the Gun;* New Zealand Commemoration Medal, 1990; Order of the British Empire, 1992, for services to children's literature; Margaret Mahy Lecture Award, 1993; Women's Suffrage Centennial Medal, 1993; Honorary Doctorate of Literature, Massey University, 1994; New Zealand Film and Television Awards, best

Joy Cowley

script television drama for "Mother Tongue," 1994; named patron of the Children's Literature Foundation of New Zealand, 1995; *Boston Globe-Horn Book* Award for Nonfiction, 1999, for *Red-Eyed Tree Frog;* New Zealand Post Children's Junior Fiction Award, 2001, for *Shadrach Girl;* New Zealand Post Children's Picture Book Award for *Brodie,* 2002; Roberta Long Medal, 2002; Children's Literature Foundation of New Zealand "Joy Cowley Picture Book Award" launched, 2003.

WRITINGS:

CHILDREN'S BOOKS

The Duck in the Gun, illustrated by Edward Sorel, Doubleday (New York, NY), 1969, illustrated by Robyn Belton, Shortland (Auckland, New Zealand), 1984.

The Silent One (for teens), illustrated by Hermann Greissle, Knopf (New York, NY), 1981.

The Terrible Taniwha of Timberditch, Oxford University Press (Auckland, New Zealand), 1982.

Old Tuatara, illustrated by Clare Bowes, Department of Education School Publications Branch (Wellington, New Zealand), 1983, published as *Old Lizard*, Nelson (London, England), 1985.

(With Mona Williams) *Two of a Kind* (stories), illustrated by Jane Amos, Blackberry Press (Upper Hutt, New Zealand), 1984.

The Fierce Little Woman and the Wicked Pirate, illustrated by Jo Davies, Shortland (Auckland, New Zealand), 1984.

Salmagundi, illustrated by Philip Webb, Oxford University Press (Auckland, New Zealand), 1985.

Brith the Terrible, Shortland (Auckland, New Zealand), 1986.

Captain Felonius, illustrated by Elizabeth Fuller, Shortland (Auckland, New Zealand), 1986.

The Lucky Feather, illustrated by Philip Webb, Shortland (Auckland, New Zealand), 1986.

My Tiger (stories), illustrated by Jan van der Voo, Shortland (Auckland, New Zealand), 1986.

The King's Pudding, illustrated by Martin Bailey, Shortland (Auckland, New Zealand), 1986.

Mrs. Grindy's Shoes, illustrated by Val Biro, Shortland (Auckland, New Zealand), 1986.

Turnips for Dinner, illustrated by Jan van der Voo, Shortland (Auckland, New Zealand), 1986.

The Train Ride Story, illustrated by Val Biro, Shortland (Auckland, New Zealand), 1987.

Giant on the Bus, illustrated by Ian McNee, Shortland (Auckland, New Zealand), 1987.

Seventy Kilometers from Ice Cream, photographs by Winto Cleal, Department of Education School Publications Branch (Wellington, New Zealand), 1987.

Far Out, Shortland (Auckland, New Zealand), 1988.

The White Horse, Shortland (Auckland, New Zealand), 1988.

Kangaroo from Wooloomooloo, Allan Publishers, 1988.

My Bad Mood, Highgate/Price Milburn (Wellington, New Zealand), 1989.

Pawprints in the Butter: A Collection of Cats, Mallinson Rendel (Wellington, New Zealand), 1991.

Bow down, Shadrach (for teens; book 1 of "Shadrach Trilogy"), illustrated by Robyn Belton, Hodder & Stoughton (Auckland, New Zealand), 1991, Wright Group (Bothell, WA), 1996.

Happy Birthday, Mrs. Felonius, Omnibus (Norwood, Australia), 1992.

Stolen Food: A Maori Legend, Learning Media (Wellington, New Zealand), 1993.

The Day of the Rain, Mallinson Rendel (Wellington, New Zealand), 1993.

Little Unicorn Library: The Park Street Playground, Robotwalk, Custom Book Company (Beecroft, New South Wales), 1993.

Annabel, Wright Group (Bothell, WA) 1993.

The Screaming Mean Machine, Scholastic (New York, NY), 1993.

Gladly Here I Come (for teens; book 2 of Shadrach Trilogy), Penguin (Harmondsworth, England), 1994, Wright Group (Bothell, WA), 1996.

Beyond the Rivers, Scholastic New Zealand (Auckland, New Zealand), 1994.

Song of the River, Wright Group (Bothell, WA), 1994.

Beep and the Telephone, Telecom New Zealand (Wellington, New Zealand), 1994.

Write On! Joy Cowley's Guide for Young Authors, Scholastic New Zealand (Auckland, New Zealand), 1994, published as *A Guide for Young Authors*, Wright Group (Bothell, WA), 1995.

The Day of the Snow, illustrated by Bob Kerr, Mallinson Rendel (Wellington, New Zealand), 1994.

Ten Happy Elephants, Wendy Pye (British Virgin Islands), 1995.

Tulevai and the Sea, Scholastic New Zealand (Auckland, New Zealand), 1995.

The Happy Hens Series (includes *Babysitter Bother, Chicken Dinners,* and *Croack-a-roo-roo-roo*), Scholastic New Zealand (Auckland, New Zealand), 1995.

The Day of the Wind, Mallinson Rendel (Wellington, New Zealand), 1995.

Sea Daughter, Scholastic New Zealand (Auckland, New Zealand), 1995.

The Mouse Bride, paintings by David Christiana, Scholastic (New York, NY), 1995.

The Cheese Trap, Scholastic New Zealand (Auckland, New Zealand), 1995.

Nicketty-Nacketty-Noo-Noo-Noo, Scholastic New Zealand (Auckland, New Zealand), 1995.

Joy Cowley Answers Kids' Questions, Scholastic New Zealand (Auckland, New Zealand), 1995.

Brave Mama Puss, Reed (Auckland, New Zealand), 1995.

Papa Puss to the Rescue, Reed (Auckland, New Zealand), 1995.

Mabel and the Marvelous Meow, Reed (Auckland, New Zealand), 1995.

Oscar in Danger, Reed (Auckland, New Zealand), 1995.

Gracias, the Thanksgiving Turkey, illustrated by Joe Cepeda, Scholastic (New York, NY), 1996.

Snake and Lizard, Wright Group (Bothell, WA), 1996.

Elephant Rhymes, Scholastic (Auckland, New Zealand), 1997.

The Great Bamboozle, Scholastic (Auckland, New Zealand), 1997.

A Haunting Tale, Scholastic (Auckland, New Zealand), 1997.

The Hitchhikers: Stories from Joy Cowley, Scholastic (New York, NY), 1997.

Singing down the Rain, HarperCollins (New York, NY), 1997.

The Bump, Scholastic (Auckland, New Zealand), 1997.

Ticket to the Sky Dance, Viking (Auckland, New Zealand), 1997.

Time for Bed, Little Bear, Wright Group (Bothell, WA), 1997.

Splishy-Sploshy, Wright Group (Bothell, WA), 1997.

Big Moon Tortilla, Boyd's Mill Press (Honesdale, PA), 1998.

Starbright and the Dream-Eater, Penguin New Zealand (Auckland, New Zealand), 1998, HarperCollins (New York, NY), 2000.

The Wild West Gang, HarperCollins (Auckland, New Zealand), 1998.

Big Moon Tortilla, Boyds Mills Press (Honesdale, PA), 1998.

The Rusty, Trusty Tractor, Boyds Mills Press (Honesdale, PA), 1999.

Red-Eyed Tree Frog, Scholastic (New York, NY), 1999.

The Video Shop Sparrow, Millinson Rendel (Wellington, New Zealand), 1999.

Agapanthus Hum and the Eyeglasses, Philomel (New York, NY), 1999.

Shadrach Girl (for teens; book 3 of "Shadrach trilogy"), Penguin, 2000.

Apple Banana Cherry, 2000.

Cricket's Storm, 2000.

Tabby Tiger, Taxi Driver, Wright Group (Bothell, WA), 2001.

Brodie, 2001.

Eating Plums in Bed, 2001.

Pudding, 2001.

Agapanthus Hum and Major Bark, Philomel Books (New York, NY), 2001.

Mrs. Goodstory, Boyd's Mills Press (Honesdale, PA), 2001.

Agapanthus Hum and the Angel Hoot, Philomel Books (New York, NY), 2002.

Pigeon Princess: A Modern Fantasy, 2002.

Duck Walk, 2002.

Weta, 2002.

The Sea Daughter, 2002.

Wishy-Washy Farm, Philomel Books (New York, NY), 2003.

JUVENILE READERS

Author of more than five hundred early reading books, including *Fish in the Trough, A New Friend, Johnny's Guitar, The Fire-Fighters, The Meeting House,* and *Wendy Makes a Poi,* all illustrated by Nancy Parker, Kea Press (Wellington, New Zealand), 1968, published as *The Tui and Sis Books,* Price Milburn (Wellington, New Zealand), 1977.

Author, with June Melser, of "Story Chest Read-Together/Story Box Reading Programme" series, including *Mrs. Wishy-Washy, Smarty Pants, The Big Toe, Boo-Hoo, Grandpa Grandpa, Hairy Bear, The Hungry Giant, In a Dark Dark Wood, Lazy Mary, Obadiah!, One Cold Wet Night, Poor Old Polly, Sing a Song, Three Little Ducks, Woosh!, Yes Ma'am, The Red Rose, To Town, Dan the Flying Man, The Farm Concert, The Jigaree, Meanies, The Monster's Party,* and *Who Will Be My Mother?,* Shortland (Auckland, New Zealand), 1980-83, Wright Group (Bothell, WA), 1988-90.

Author, with June Melser, of "Story Chest Books" series, including *The Birthday Cake, The Dragon, A Terrible Fright, A Barrel of Gold, Clever Mr. Brown, Hungry Monster, Jack-in-the-Box, The Kick-a-Lot Shoes, The Pirates, Wet Grass, Where Is My Spider?, Yum and Yuk, Captain Bumble, Countdown, A Day in Town, The Big Tease, Cat on the Roof, The Ghost and the Sausage, Grandma's Stick, Hatupatu and the Birdwoman, Little Brother's Haircut, The Sunflower That Went FLOP, Tell-Tale,* and *Sun Smile,* Shortland (Auckland, New Zealand), 1981-82, Wright Group (Bothell, WA), 1989-94.

Author, with June Melser, of "Story Chest Ready-Set-Go" series, including *The Bee, The Chocolate Cake, Come with Me, Copy-Cat, Flying, I Want an Ice Cream, Little Pig, Lost, My Home, Plop!, Round and Round, Splosh, To New York, Who Lives Here?, Where Are They Going?, Who's Going to Lick the Bowl?, Horace, The Night Train, The Pumpkin, Rum-Tum Tumm, Sleeping Out, Too Big for Me, What a Mess!,* and *Look for Me,* Shortland (Auckland, New Zealand), 1981-82, Wright Group (Bothell, WA), 1990.

Author, with June Melser and Margaret Mahy, of *Cooking Pot, Fast and Funny, Roly Poly, Sing to the Moon,* and *Tiddalik,* Shortland (Auckland, New Zealand), 1982.

Author of "Story Box Books" series, including *The Pie Thief, The Tale of the Cook, The Trader from Currumbin, The War of the Winds,* and *Poor Old Robot,* Shortland (Auckland, New Zealand), 1982-85.

Author of "Story Chest Ready-to-Read" series, including *Number One, The Biggest Cake in the World, Fasi Sings, Fasi's Fish, Greedy Cat, Our Teacher Miss Pool, Rain Rain, Words, I'm the King of the Mountain, Rosie at the Zoo, The Wild Wet Wellington Wind, Did You Say Five?, The Smile,* and *Where Is Miss Pool?,* Department of Education School Publications Branch (Wellington, New Zealand), 1982-87.

Author, with June Melser, of "Story Chest Get Ready Books," including *The Bicycle, The Big Hill, Feet, The Ghost, Go Go Go, Houses, If You Meet a Dragon, In the Mirror, A Monster Sandwich, Mouse, Night-Time, On a Chair, Painting, The Party, The Storm,* and *The Tree-House,* Arnold Wheaton (Leeds, England), 1983, Wright Group (Bothell, WA), 1990.

Author of "Sunshine Books" series, including *Yuk Soup, Baby Gets Dressed, Big and Little, Buzzing Flies, Dinner! Down to Town, A Hug Is Warm, Huggles' Breakfast, Huggles Can Juggle, Huggles Goes Away, I Am a Bookworm, I Can Fly, I Can Jump, I Love My Family, Ice Cream, Little Brother, The Long Long Tail, Major Jump, My Home, My Puppy, Our Granny, Our Street, The Race, Scat! Said the Cat, Shark in a Sack, Shoo! Snap!, Uncle Buncle's House, Up in a Tree, What Is a Huggles? When Itchy Witchy Sneezes, Along Comes Jake, Bread, Come for a Swim, The Cooking Pot, Dad's Headache, Don't You Laugh at Me! The Giant's Boy, Good for You, Goodbye Lucy, I'm Bigger Than You!, Let's Have a Swim!, Little Car, The Monkey Bridge, Mr. Grump, Mr. Whisper, My Boat, My Sloppy Tiger, Noise, Nowhere and Nothing, Old Grizzly, One Thousand Currant Buns, The Poor Sore Paw, Ratty-Tatty, Red Socks and Yellow Socks, The Seed, Spider Spider, The Terrible Tiger, The Tiny Woman's Coat, Wake Up, Mum!, What Would You Like?, Where Are You Going Aja Rose?,* and *The Wind Blows Strong,* Heinemann (London, England), 1986-87, Wright Group (Bothell, WA), 1986-90.

Author of "Windmill" series, including *Growing, The Little Red Hen, My Little Brother, Splish Splash!, Where Can We Put an Elephant?, Where's the Egg Cup, Lucy's Sore Knee,* and *My Wonderful Chair,* Heinemann (Auckland, New Zealand), 1986-88.

Author of "Jellybeans" series, including *Don't Wake the Baby, The Kangaroo from Wooloomooloo, Lavender the Library Cat, Let's Get a Pet, The Little Brown House, The Magician's Lunch, Morning Dance, The Most Scary Ghost, Mouse Monster, The Plants of My Aunt, Ten Loopy Caterpillars, The Terrible Armadillo, The Train That Ran Away, The Yukadoos, Monster, The Amazing Popple Seed, The Bull and the Matador, Cow Up a Tree, The Difficult Day, The Gumby Shop, A Handy Dragon, The Horrible Thing with Hairy Feet, Mr. Beep, Boggity-Bog, Do-Whacky-Do, The Shoe Grabber, A Silly Old Story, A Walk with Grandpa, The Wonder-Whizz,* and *The Wild Woolly Child,* Shortland (Auckland, New Zealand), 1988-89.

Author of "Cocky's Circle Little Books" series, including *Timothy Flynn, Tom's Trousers,* and *When the Moon Was Blue,* Advertiser Magazines (Artarmon, New South Wales), 1988-89; second series, including *The Things I Like, Cow up a Tree, Do-Whacky-Do, Monster, Across the Nullarbor, The Gonna Bird, The Yellow Tractor,* and *The Wild Woolly Child,* Murdoch Books (North Sydney, New South Wales, Australia), 1990-95.

Author of "Literacy Links," including *The Cabbage Princess, Yellow Overalls, Baba Yaga: A Traditional Russian Tale,* and *A Froggy Tale,* Shortland (Auckland, New Zealand), 1990, 1996.

Author of "Ready to Read Books," including *Hoiho's Chicks, Pukelo Morning, The Shag Goes Fishing, The Water Boatman, The New Cat,* and *Off Goes the Hose!,* Learning Media (Wellington, New Zealand), 1991-97.

Author of "The Story Basket" series, including *Who Spilled the Beans?, Wishy-Washy Day, Ballyhoo!, Cats, Cats, Cats, The Pirate Feast,* and *Water! Water!,* Wright Group (Bothell, WA), 1993-95.

Author of "The Country Kids" series, including *The Boomy Buzzer, Crabs, Egg Stuff, The Island, Leaves, Playhouse, Rabbit Hunt,* and *Running Away,* Heinemann Primary (Auckland, New Zealand), 1996.

Author of "Get-Ready Books," including *The Boogie-Woogie Man: A Play, Brenda's Birthday, The Bridge, Chick's Walk, Dan Gets Dressed, The Escalator, Fishing, The Gifts,* and *What Can Jigarees Do?*, Shortland Publications (Auckland, New Zealand), 1997.

Author of "Ready-Set-Go Books," including *Barn Dance, A Two-Part Chant, Chicken for Dinner, The Clown in the Well, I Love Chickens: A Play, My Brown Cow, My Mum and Dad, Skating, Teeth, Where Is Skunk?* and *Who Can See the Camel?*, Shortland (Auckland, New Zealand), 1997.

Author of "The Wild Wests," including *The Wild West Gang, More of the Wild Wests, The Wild Wests and Pong Castle, The Wild Wests and Haunted Fridge,* HarperCollins (Auckland, New Zealand).

ADULT

Nest in a Falling Tree (novel), Doubleday (New York, NY), 1967.
Man of Straw (novel), Doubleday (New York, NY), 1970.
Of Men and Angels (novel), Doubleday (New York, NY), 1973.
The Mandrake Root (novel), Doubleday (New York, NY), 1976.
The Growing Season (novel), Doubleday (New York, NY), 1979.
(Editor, with Thelma France) *Women Writers of New Zealand 1932-1982,* Colonial (Wellington, New Zealand), 1982.
Heart Attack and Other Stories, Hodder & Stoughton (London, England), 1985.
Aotearoa Psalms: Prayers of a New People (reflections), Catholic Supplies NZ (Wellington, New Zealand), 1989.
Whole Learning: Whole Child, Wright Group (Bothell, WA), 1994.
Joy Cowley Short Stories, HarperCollins (Auckland, New Zealand), 1996.
Psalms Down Under (reflections), Catholic Supplies NZ (Wellington, New Zealand), 1996.
The Complete Short Stories, HarperCollins (Auckland, New Zealand), 1997.
Everything 'round Us Is Praise: Extraordinary Prayers for Ordinary Days, Ave Maria Press (Notre Dame, IN), 1997.

Classical Music (novel), Penguin (Auckland, New Zealand), 1999.
Holy Days (novel), Penguin (Auckland, New Zealand), 2001.

Contributor, *New Zealand Short Stories,* Volume 3, Oxford University Press, 1975. Stories have appeared in New Zealand literary periodicals and school readers; writer of radio scripts for New Zealand Broadcasting Corporation. Several of Cowley's books have been translated into Spanish.

ADAPTATIONS: Carry Me Back, a film produced by Kiwi Film Production/New Zealand Film Commission, and shown at the 1982 Cannes Film Festival, was based on a story by Cowley. *Nest in a Falling Tree* was adapted by Roald Dahl as the film *The Night Digger,* starring Patricia Neal. *The Silent One* has been adapted for film and aired on The Disney Channel. Many of Cowley's books have been recorded as audiotapes. *Fish Bay* a children's video based on Cowley's stories, directed and animated by Bob Stenhouse, 2003.

SIDELIGHTS: Joy Cowley is a prolific, award-winning writer of children's picture books and early reading texts. Cowley was born into a family that did not value books, and her early experience with reading was far from pleasant. Decoding words was difficult for her, and a cruel teacher physically punished her for her slowness. And yet, when another teacher presented her with interesting reading and a positive attitude, Cowley suddenly became an avid and highly competent reader. Before long, Cowley was regularly contributing prose, verse, and drawings to the *Wellington Southern Cross* newspaper. Her parents were in difficult financial circumstances, and when their daughter was sixteen, they told her she would have to quit school to work full-time. The young girl's teachers responded by setting up an arrangement for her to work after school as the editor of the children's page of the local newspaper. The following year, she was offered a full-time position with the paper, but her parents refused to grant permission, feeling that journalists were not a good moral influence. Instead, Cowley was apprenticed to a pharmacist to learn a trade.

Cowley did little in the way of writing for some time after that. She married and had four children, and her writing began again only when her son Edward began having difficulties with reading, similar to those she had experienced as a child. Her first published children's book was *The Duck in the Gun*, about a mother duck who puts off a war by building her nest inside the General's cannon. Cowley established her reputation with her next book, *The Silent One,* which was aimed at an audience of older children. This story, set in the South Pacific, tells how a deaf, mute boy named Jonasi is dreaded and ostracized by superstitious islanders, because of his silence and his friendship with a rare albino turtle. Jonasi and the turtle are perceived as demons, and blamed for both a hurricane and a fatal shark attack. When Jonasi gets his chance to leave the island for a new life and an education at a school for the deaf, the life of his turtle is threatened. Jonasi jumps into the ocean to save it, and disappears forever. *The Silent One* was favorably received by many critics, and it earned Cowley her first AIM Children's Book Award. Virginia Haviland, writing in *Horn Book,* found the prose in *The Silent One* to be "brilliantly evocative of the physical background as well as of the emotional atmosphere." The book "has a haunting quality," asserted a critic for *Bulletin of the Center for Children's Books. Times Educational Supplement* critic Fred Urquhart declared that *The Silent One* "will not be forgotten easily."

As her career progressed, Cowley continued to garner praise for her books for older children and teens, as well as for the scores of picture books and readers she began producing. Reviewers frequently pointed out that her stories could draw in readers of all ages. Reviewing *Salmagundi,* the story of rival factory owners who turn from manufacturing weapons of war to making products for peacetime use, Marcus Crouch commented in *Junior Bookshelf:* "Joy Cowley's story is rich in irony as well as good jokes. . . . Don't be misled by the picture-book format. There is no upper age-limit for its appeal." Cowley has also written several adaptations of traditional folktales. *The Mouse Bride* tells a story found in many cultures, in which a small mouse laments her weakness and desires to marry the strongest husband in the world, thereby seemingly ensuring strong children. Her search takes her to the sun, the cloud, the wind, and finally back again to another mouse before her quest is resolved. *Gracias, the Thanksgiving Turkey* is another retelling of a traditional tale, that of the animal intended for dinner who becomes a pet instead. In Cowley's version, a New York City boy named Miguel receives a gift from his truck-driving father: a crate containing a turkey, to be fattened up for Thanksgiving. Two plot threads create suspense: the question of whether or not Miguel will be able to keep his turkey off the dinner table, and the question of whether his father will really make it home for the holiday. Carolyn Phelan praised Cowley's "distinctive, modern" story, and Selene S. Vasquez called *Gracias* "a heart-warming narrative that captures the boy's close-knit sense of community and family."

Cowley, who has also penned books on the education of children and on children's writing, once explained how she approaches her work for children. "Writing for young people requires a memory; more than that—before starting a book it's necessary to peel away years of adult experience like the layers of an onion, and expose a self that's of an age corresponding with character and reader. Only by being once more ten or fourteen or whatever age I'm writing for, can I evaluate the work. I can 'live' with my characters and understand them as equals."

BIOGRAPHICAL AND CRITICAL SOURCES:

BOOKS

Children's Literature Review, Volume 55, Gale (Detroit, MI), 1999.
St. James Guide to Children's Writers, 5th edition, St. James Press (Detroit, MI), 1999.

PERIODICALS

Best Sellers, August 15, 1967.
Booklist, May 1, 1981, Denise M. Wilms, review of *The Silent One,* p. 102; January 1, 1996, April Judge, review of *The Mouse Bride,* p. 843; September 1, 1996, Carolyn Phelan, review of *Gracias, the Thanksgiving Turkey,* p. 136; November 15, 1997, review of *Singing down the Rain,* p. 565; October 15, 1998, review of *Big Moon Tortilla,* p. 426; March 15, 1999, John Peters, review of *The Rusty, Trusty Tractor,* p. 1332; May 15, 1999, review of *The Rusty, Trusty Tractor,* p. 1332, review of *Red-Eyed Tree Frog,* p. 1696; December 1, 1999, review of *Red-Eyed Tree Frog,* p. 699, review of *The Video Shop Sparrow,* p. 709; April 15, 2000, Sally Estes, review of *Starbright and the Dream Eater,* p. 1543; February 15, 2001, review of *Agapanthus Hum and Major Bark,* p. 1143.

Book Report, November-December, 1986, Mary Lourde, review of *Salmagundi,* p. 54.

Bulletin of the Center for Children's Books, June, 1981, Zena Sutherland, review of *The Silent One,* p. 189; November, 1995, review of *The Mouse Bride,* p. 87; November, 1996, Janice Del Negro, review of *Gracias, the Thanksgiving Turkey,* p. 90; January, 1998, Elizabeth Burns, review of *Singing down the Rain,* p. 157; March, 1999, Janice M. Del Negro, review of *The Red-Eyed Tree Frog,* p. 235, review of *The Rusty, Trusty Tractor,* p. 236; April, 1999, review of *Agapanthus Hum and the Eyeglasses,* p. 275; March, 2001, review of *Agapanthus Hum and Major Bark,* p. 254.

Catholic Library World, March, 1998, review of *Everything 'round Us Is Praise,* p. 45.

Children's Book Review Service, October, 1996, Linda Nelson, review of *Gracias, the Thanksgiving Turkey,* p. 14; December, 1997, review of *Singing down the Rain,* p. 37; October, 1998, review of *Big Moon Tortilla,* p. 20; April, 1999, review of *Agapanthus Hum and the Eyeglasses,* p. 103; June, 1999, review of *Red-Eyed Tree Frog,* p. 121; winter, 1999, review of *Nickety-Nackety Noo-Noo-Noo,* p. 62.

Children's Books, June, 1986, review of *Salmagundi,* p. 12.

Children's Bookwatch, April, 1998, review of *Singing down the Rain,* p. 4; July, 1999, review of *Red-Eyed Tree Frog,* p. 7.

Christian Science Monitor, November 6, 1969, review of *The Duck in the Gun,* p. 8B; August 26, 1999, review of *Red-Eyed Tree Frog,* p. 20.

Five Owls, May, 1999, review of *Red-Eyed Tree Frog,* p. 105.

Horn Book, June, 1981, review of *The Silent One,* pp. 301-302; March, 1999, Lauren Adams, review of *Red-Eyed Tree Frog,* p. 220; January, 2000, review of *Red-Eyed Tree Frog,* p. 45.

Horn Book Guide, spring, 1997, review of *Gracias, the Thanksgiving Turkey,* p. 24; spring, 1998, review of *Singing down the Rain,* p. 27; fall, 1999, reviews of *Big Moon Tortilla* and *The Rusty, Trusty Tractor,* p. 248, review of *Agapanthus Hum and the Eyeglasses,* p. 277, review of *Red-Eyed Tree Frog,* p. 344.

Junior Bookshelf, April, 1986, review of *Salmagundi,* p. 60.

Kirkus Reviews, August 15, 1969, review of *The Duck in the Gun,* p. 853; March 15, 1978, p. 321; October 1, 1981, review of *The Silent One,* p. 1235; October 1, 1995, review of *The Mouse Bride,* pp. 1425-1426; September 15, 1997, review of *Singing down the Rain,* p. 1455; December 1, 1998, review of *Agapanthus Hum and the Eyeglasses,* p. 1732; January 1, 1999, review of *Red-Eyed Tree Frog,* p. 64; October 15, 1999, review of *The Video Shop Sparrow,* p. 1641; August 15, 2001, review of *Mrs. Goodstory,* p. 1209.

Landfall, May, 2000, Marion McLeod, review of *Classical Music,* p. 154.

Library Journal, November, 1969, review of *The Duck in the Gun,* p. 110; February 1, 1975, p. 310.

Magpies, March, 1996, Linnet Hunter, review of *The Mouse Bride,* p. 28; March, 1997, review of *Nicketty-Nackerty, Noo-Noo-Noo,* p. 2; May, 1997, review of *Nicketty-Nackerty, Noo-Noo-Noo,* p. 26; July, 1997, review of *The Great Bamboozle,* p. 7; November, 1997, review of *A Haunting Tale,* p. 5, review of *Ticket to the Sky Dance,* p. 6, review of *Singing down the Rain,* p. 7; March, 1998, Margaret Kedian, review of *The Bump,* pp. 7-8; July, 1998, review of *The Wild West Gang,* p. 8; November, 1998, review of *The Wild West Gang,* p. 2, review of *Starbright and the Dream Eater,* p. 8; March, 1999, Trevor Agnew, interview with Joy Cowley, pp. 1-5; July, 1999, review of *The Video Shop Sparrow* and *Red-Eyed Tree Frog,* p. 7; May, 2001, review of *The Silent One,* p. 7, review of *Apple Banana Cherry,* p. 26.

New York Times Book Review, August 13, 1967, p. 5; December 24, 1972, p. 14.

Observer Review, October 22, 1967.

Publishers Weekly, January 20, 1975, p. 65; April 3, 1978, p. 69; January 16, 1981, review of *The Silent One,* pp. 77, 80; September 30, 1996, p. 86; November 3, 1997, review of *Singing down the Rain,* p. 85; December 21, 1998, review of *Agapanthus Hum and the Eyeglasses,* p. 68; March 1, 1999, review of *The Rusty, Trusty Tractor,* p. 68; November 1, 1999, review of *Agapanthus Hum and the Eyeglasses,* p. 56; January 10, 2000, review of *The Rusty, Trusty Tractor,* p. 70.

Reading Teacher, October, 1999, review of *Red-Eyed Tree Frog,* p. 149; November, 1999, review of *Big Moon Tortilla,* p. 242.

Reading Time, May, 1996, p. 23; August, 1998, John McKenzie, review of *The Wild West Gang,* p. 31; November, 1998, Jilaine Johnson, review of *Starbright and the Dream Eater,* p. 32.

Riverbank Review, winter, 1999, review of *Red-Eyed Tree Frog,* p. 42.

School Librarian, June, 1982, Chris Brown, review of *The Silent One,* p. 128.

School Library Journal, November, 1995, JoAnn Rees, review of *The Mouse Bride,* p. 89; December, 1996, review of *Gracias, the Thanksgiving Turkey,* p. 91; April, 1997, review of *Gracias, the Thanksgiving Turkey,* p. 13; October, 1997, Lisa Falk, review of *Singing down the Rain,* p. 95; November 1, 1998, Roxanne Burg, review of *Big Moon Tortilla,* p. 7; March, 1999, review of *Red-Eyed Tree Frog,* p. 190; April, 1999, review of *Agapanthus Hum and the Eyeglasses,* p. 91; May, 1999, review of *The Rusty, Trusty Tractor,* p. 88; August, 1999, review of *Big Moon Tortilla,* p. 39; December, 1999, review of *The Video Shop Sparrow,* p. 90; June, 2000, Ronni Krasnow, review of *Starbright and the Dream Eater,* p. 142; February, 2001, Laura Scott, review of *Agapanthus Hum and Major Bark,* p. 93; September, 2001, Karen J. Tannenbaum, review of *Mrs. Goodstory,* p. 186.
Times Educational Supplement, August 20, 1982.

ONLINE

Welcome to the World of Joy Cowley, http://www.joycowley.com/ (February, 2002).*

* * *

CRAGGS, Stewart R. 1943-

PERSONAL: Born July 27, 1943, in Ilkley, West Yorkshire, England; married Valerie Gibson (a municipal librarian), 1968; children: Barnaby, Cordelia. *Ethnicity:* "European." *Education:* University of Strathclyde, M.A., 1978, D.Phil., 1982. *Religion:* Church of England.

ADDRESSES: Home—106 Mount Rd., High Barnes, Sunderland SR4 7NN, England; fax: 01-91-525-0258. *E-mail*—stewcraggs@aol.com.

CAREER: University of Sunderland, Sunderland, England, technical services librarian, 1973-81, reader services librarian, 1981-92, development services librarian, 1992-95, professor of music bibliography, 1993; freelance researcher and bibliographer, 1995—. Justice of the peace, 1974-2000.

MEMBER: Chartered Institute of Libraries and Information Professionals (London; fellow).

AWARDS, HONORS: McColvin Gold Medal, best reference book of the year, Library Association, 1990, for *William Walton: A Thematic Catalogue.*

WRITINGS:

William Walton: A Thematic Catalogue, Oxford University Press (Oxford, England), 1977.
William Alwyn: A Catalogue, Bravura, 1985.
Arthur Bliss: A Bio-Bibliography, Greenwood Press (Westport, CT), 1988.
Richard Rodney Bennett: A Bio-Bibliography, Greenwood Press (Westport, CT), 1989.
William Walton: A Catalogue, Oxford University Press (Oxford, England), 1990.
John McCabe: A Bio-Bibliography, Greenwood Press (Westport, CT), 1991.
William Walton: A Source Book, Scolar Press (Brookfield, VT), 1993.
John Ireland: A Catalogue, Discography, and Bibliography, Oxford University Press (Oxford, England), 1993.
Alun Hoddinott: A Bio-Bibliography, Greenwood Press (Westport, CT), 1993.
(Compiler) *Edward Elgar: A Source Book,* Scolar Press (Brookfield, CT), 1995.
William Mathias: A Bio-Bibliography, Greenwood Press (Westport, CT), 1995.
Arthur Bliss: A Source Book, Scolar Press (Brookfield, VT), 1995.
Malcolm Arnold: A Bio-Bibliography, Greenwood Press (Westport, CT), 1998.
Soundtracks: An International Dictionary of Composers for Film, Ashgate Publishing (Burlington, VT), 1998.
(Editor) *William Walton: Music and Literature,* Ashgate Publishing (Burlington, VT), 1999.
Lennox Berkeley: A Source Book, Ashgate Publishing (Burlington, VT), 2000.
Benjamin Britten: A Bio-Bibliography, Greenwood Press (Westport, CT), 2002.
Arthur Bliss: Music and Literature, Ashgate Publishing (Burlington, VT), 2002.
Peter Maxwell Davies: A Source Book, Ashgate Publishing (Burlington, VT), 2003.

WORK IN PROGRESS: A Bibliography of Music Biography, for Ashgate Publishing (Burlington, VT); *Lennox Berkeley: A Bio-Bibliography,* Greenwood Press (Westport, CT); *William Walton: A Catalogue,* 3rd edition, Oxford University Press (Oxford, England); *Alan Bush: A Source Book,* Ashgate Publishing (Burlington, VT); *Alun Hoddinott: A Source Book,* Ashgate Publishing (Burlington, VT); *John Ireland: A Source Book,* Ashgate Publishing (Burlington, VT).

SIDELIGHTS: Stewart R. Craggs told *CA:* "My primary motivation for writing and compiling these kinds of books is a great love of nineteenth- and twentieth-century English music and the work of the particular composers I have chosen over the last twenty years. My work on Sir William Walton, however, extends further back than that to the middle 1950s and onwards. I can, therefore, say that Walton (in particular) and the other composers have greatly influenced and inspired me and my work.

"As you can imagine, it involves a great deal of research, much of it done in London, and working either with people connected with each composer or with the composers themselves; for example: Lady Walton, Lady Bliss, Lady Berkeley, Dr. Rachel O'Higgins (Alan Bush's daughter), Professor Alun Hoddinott, Sir Malcolm Arnold, and Sir Peter Maxwell Davies, together with Mrs. Judy Arnold, Max's manager."

* * *

CURTIS, Jamie Lee 1958-

PERSONAL: Born November 22, 1958; daughter of Tony Curtis (an actor) and Janet Leigh (an actress); married Christopher Guest (an actor, writer, and director), December, 1984; children: Annie, Tom. *Education:* Attended University of the Pacific, 1977. *Hobbies and other interests:* Photography.

ADDRESSES: Home—California. *Agent*—Creative Artists Agency, 9830 Wilshire Blvd., Beverly Hills, CA 90212.

CAREER: Actress, 1977—; author, 1984—. Television appearances include *Death of a Centerfold: The Dorothy Stratten Story,* 1981; *Money on the Side,* 1982;

Jamie Lee Curtis

As Summers Die, 1986; *Anything but Love* (series), 1988-91; *The Heidi Chronicles,* 1995; *Nicholas' Gift,* 1998; *Pigs Next Door* (series), 2000. Film appearances include *Halloween,* 1978; *The Fog,* 1980; *Prom Night,* 1980; *Halloween II,* 1981; *Love Letters,* 1982; *Trading Places,* 1983; *Grandview, U.S.A.,* 1984; *Perfect,* 1984; *A Fish Called Wanda,* 1988; *Blue Steel,* 1989, *Mother's Boys,* 1994; *True Lies,* 1994; *House Arrest,* 1996; *Fierce Creatures,* 1997; *Homegrown,* 1998; *Halloween H2O,* 1998; *Virus,* 1999; *Drowning Mona,* 2000; *The Tailor of Panama,* 2001; *Daddy and Them,* 2001; *Boogeyman,* 2001; *Halloween Resurrection,* 2002; and *Freaky Friday,* 2003.

AWARDS, HONORS: British Academy Award for best supporting actress, 1983, for *Trading Places;* Golden Globe Award for best actress in a television comedy, 1990, for *Anything but Love,* and for best actress in a motion picture, 1995, for *True Lies;* American Comedy Award for funniest actress in a motion picture, and Saturn Award, Academy of Science Fiction, Fantasy, and Horror Films, both 1995, both for *True Lies;*

Emmy nomination, 1998, for *Nicholas' Gift;* awarded star on the Hollywood Walk of Fame, 1998; Woman of the Year, Hasty Pudding Theatricals, 2000.

WRITINGS:

FOR CHILDREN

When I Was Little: A Four-Year-Old's Memoir of Her Youth, illustrated by Laura Cornell, HarperCollins (New York, NY), 1993.
Tell Me Again about the Night I Was Born, illustrated by Laura Cornell, HarperCollins (New York, NY), 1995.
Today I Feel Silly & Other Moods That Make My Day, illustrated by Laura Cornell, HarperCollins (New York, NY), 1998.
Where Do Balloons Go?: An Uplifting Mystery, illustrated by Laura Cornell, HarperCollins (New York, NY), 2000.
I'm Gonna Like Me: Letting Off a Little Self-Esteem, illustrated by Laura Cornell, HarperCollins (New York, NY), 2002.

OTHER

(With mother, Janet Leigh) *There Really Was a Hollywood,* Doubleday (New York, NY), 1984.

WORK IN PROGRESS: My Mommy Hung the Moon, a picture book for HarperCollins.

SIDELIGHTS: Nicknamed the "Scream Queen" for her role as the teenage victim in the 1978 *Halloween,* actor and author Jamie Lee Curtis has come a long way in her career. Enjoying success on both the big and small screens, Curtis made her film debut in a series of low-budget horror films and—by sheer determination—moved from those into comedy and action-adventure hits alongside such big-name stars as Kevin Kline, John Travolta, and Arnold Schwarzenegger. Known by film audiences for her sleek figure and her sly, flirtatious smile, Curtis has overcome both professional and private hurdles as she has forged a successful Hollywood career and started a family with her husband, actor Christopher Guest.

Avoiding stereotypes and pushing the creative envelope is a Curtis trademark, and in 1993 Curtis, the proud parent of an adopted son and daughter, began to forge yet another career as a children's storybook author with *When I Was Little: A Four-Year-Old's Memoir of Her Youth.* That book made it to the *New York Times* best-seller list and has since sold almost a million copies. Curtis has published four more children's books since then, all illustrated by Laura Cornell. And for Curtis, her career as children's author possibly outshines her film career. Speaking with Lisa Birnbach on CBS's *The Early Show* about her 2002 book, *I'm Gonna Like Me: Letting Off a Little Self-Esteem,* Curtis noted, "What I get to do is invite a child on to their parent's lap, and spend fifteen minutes together reading this and then talking about, perhaps, what makes that child like themselves."

The daughter of film stars Tony Curtis and Janet Leigh, Jamie Lee was born on November 22, 1958. Four years later, her parents divorced, and Curtis and her older sister, actress Kelly Curtis, were raised by their mother and stepfather. Try as she might, Curtis could never escape from the shadow of her famous parents. "I've always said I have the longest middle name," she once told an *Esquire* interviewer. "'There goes Jamie Janet-Leigh-and-Tony-Curtis's-Daughter Curtis.' . . . I wanted to be a typical little girl from Smalltown, U.S.A." The desire to escape her celebrity status continued throughout her teen years, which were a difficult time for the soon-to-be actress.

After graduating from high school in 1977, Curtis enrolled at the University of the Pacific, but was unsure what direction she wanted her future life to take. After a semester, she dropped out and, with no formal training as an actress, began auditioning for roles in Hollywood; due to her striking looks, she was quickly signed to Universal Studios, where she worked as an extra and in small roles on television series. "It's just never been hard for me to be someone else," Curtis confided to Neal Karlen in *Rolling Stone* of the ease with which she assumed the occupation of actress. "I think the fact that I had very low self-confidence growing up and in high school made me a good actress. It was easy for me to be a preppie with preppie kids and a hippie with hippie kids. I learned early to be a chameleon, to turn whatever color was needed."

In 1978, Curtis won her first starring role, in the low-budget slasher film *Halloween,* one of the top-grossing B-movies of all time. With this role, nineteen-year-old

Curtis achieved a measure of personal satisfaction in making her own mark on Hollywood. Unfortunately, she soon found herself typecast, with script after script of horror films sent her way. *Prom Night, The Fog,* and *Terror Train* followed in close succession until the young actress turned her back on the horror genre in favor of supporting roles in television films. Her role as a prostitute alongside Dan Ackroyd and Eddie Murphy in 1983's *Trading Places* won her her first major award, the British Academy Award—the United Kingdom's equivalent of an Oscar—for best supporting actress.

Curtis's career flourished in the 1980s with films such as *Perfect,* the comedy hit *A Fish Called Wanda,* and the television series *Anything but Love,* which ran from 1988 to 1991 and netted the actress another prestigious award: the Golden Globe Award for best actress in a television comedy. Marriage, motherhood, and a move to Sun Valley, Idaho, also entered the picture, and after the cancellation of her television series, Curtis retired from television to devote herself to feature film work. In the 1990s, Curtis began acting in a new genre: the action-adventure film. Her role as the mild-mannered wife of an international spy in the 1994 Arnold Schwarzenegger film *True Lies* earned critical praise. Curtis has continued to act in films and in television movies, such as the 1998 *Nicholas' Gift,* for which she received an Emmy nomination. Other notable film appearances include the twentieth anniversary return to her original character in *Halloween H2O,* as well as the 2002 reprisal of the same role in *Halloween: Resurrection.* She has also had leading parts in *Virus, The Tailor of Panama, Daddy and Them,* and the remake of the Disney classic, *Freaky Friday.*

In addition to praise for her acting abilities, reviewers have commended Curtis's picture books for children. *When I Was Little,* published in 1993, describes the growing list of accomplishments made by a proud youngster as she looks back upon infancy: no more "goo and yucky stuff" to eat, no more "floaties" to help her swim, no more being "a handful." Curtis got the idea for the book when her own daughter, Annie, then only four, began telling her about all the wonderful accomplishments she had made, including ceasing to use her pacifier. Curtis simply began taking down a list of such milestones, and the result was her first book, a critical and commercial success. Calling the young girl's perspective on babyhood "truly hilarious," Debra S. Gold wrote in a review for *School Library Journal* that Curtis's "simple text is funny and honest, perfectly capturing that whimsical, innocent way that children view the world."

Inspired by her own experiences of adopting her daughter, Curtis wrote her second book for youngsters, *Tell Me Again about the Night I Was Born.* A *Publishers Weekly* reviewer wrote, "It's hard to imagine a warmer celebration of the special joys of an adopted family." Framed around the retelling of a favorite family story, *Tell Me Again* describes memories of that special moment when they first held their new child. From the ring of the phone in the middle of the night to announce the arrival of their daughter, to the trip to the hospital, the first diaper change, and the first tears of joy, Curtis's book "affirms family love, the pleasure parents feel about new babies, and how pleased children are to hear the story of their birth," according to *School Library Journal* critic Ruth K. MacDonald. Ricki Blackhall, reviewing the picture book in *Magpies,* thought the reader would be in for a "heartwarming surprise." Blackhall went on to note, "This gentle picture book tells of the celebration of the special joys of an adopted family. . . . A wonderful, wonderful book."

With *Today I Feel Silly & Other Moods That Make My Day,* Curtis and Cornell detail thirteen different feelings that a young girl describes having over the course of two weeks. From silly to quiet to cranky to sad, the little redheaded girl presents such moods in rhyming couplets, as in "Moods are just something that happen each day! / Whatever I'm feeling inside is okay." A reviewer for *Publishers Weekly* found such a message "upbeat," and further dubbed the book an "amiable enough outing," despite finding certain "missteps" in the writing. *Booklist*'s Stephanie Zvirin called the same book "colorful [and] energetic," and one that "uses comedy to promote an understanding of common emotions." Similarly, Valerie Caghlan, writing in *Books for Keeps,* lauded the fact that Curtis's book lets children know "that it is normal and acceptable to have mood swings." Caghlan further noted that the book is "engaging and good natured." And Karen MacPherson, writing in the *Pittsburgh Post-Gazette,* felt that Curtis uses "typical good humor" to deal with various emotions, and "amazingly, she does all this in a lilting rhyme that's unforced and witty."

Curtis and Cornell again teamed up for the year 2000 *Where Do Balloons Go?: An Uplifting Mystery.* A little boy lets go of his purple balloon and, watching it float away, wonders what will become of it. Will it catch cold or get married or write postcards back? Curtis found the inspiration for this tale while attending a birthday party with her son, Tom. When rain approached, all the guests took shelter in a gazebo, but one young guest decided to untie all the balloons and as they drifted upward, a little girl asked her mother where all the balloons went. Thus was born a book of questions and exploration rather than of didactic answers.

Curtis employs "snappy rhyme," according to *Horn Book*'s Susan P. Bloom, to ponder these questions. Meanwhile, the artwork shows the balloon out dining or visiting a spa, artistic "nudges adults will enjoy," as Bloom mentioned. The message, Bloom pointed out, is about "holding on and letting go." A reviewer for *Publishers Weekly* felt that the book "may well raise youngsters' spirits," and—like the high-flying balloon did to the young boy in the tale—start imaginations flying "way out there—in a kid-pleasing way." Calling the book a "lighthearted romp," *School Library Journal*'s Marie Orlando commented that "While there are no definite answers to all this speculation, the fun is in the wondering."

Curtis has also celebrated having a positive self-image in her 2002 *I'm Gonna Like Me: Letting Off a Little Self-Esteem*. Again using rhyming text, Curtis describes how a young boy and girl are determined to like themselves even if things are going badly. The little girl says, "I'm gonna like me / when I'm called on to stand. / I know all my letters / like the back of my hand." The little boy in turn says, "I'm gonna like me / when my answer is wrong, / like thinking my ruler / was ten inches long." Once again accompanied by Cornell's artwork, this book is a "pleasant addition" to the genre of self-esteem works, according to Roxanne Burg, writing in *School Library Journal*. *Booklist*'s Karin Snelson noted that author and illustrator team up to "advocate a sort of jubilant self-love," while a contributor for *Publishers Weekly* called the work a "lively, emotionally reassuring picture book." And a critic for *Kirkus Reviews* likewise lauded this celebration "to being individuals," whose "overall message is a good one."

Speaking with Shannon Maughan on *KidsReads.com*, Curtis noted, "It wasn't any grand plan or dream of mine to write a children's book." Yet this "accidental" career has opened up new vistas for Curtis, who continues to write well-received children's books as well as act in movies. As MacPherson commented in her article about the award-winning actress and author, Curtis "is an exception to the rule that most celebrities who want to be writers shouldn't quit their day jobs."

BIOGRAPHICAL AND CRITICAL SOURCES:

BOOKS

Contemporary Theatre, Film, and Television, Volume 32, Gale (Detroit, MI), 2000.
Curtis, Jamie Lee, *When I Was Little: A Four-Year-Old's Memoir of Her Youth,* illustrated by Laura Cornell, HarperCollins (New York, NY), 1993.
Curtis, Jamie Lee, *Today I Feel Silly & Other Moods That Make My Day,* illustrated by Laura Cornell, HarperCollins (New York, NY), 1998.
Curtis, Jamie Lee, *I'm Gonna Like Me: Letting Off a Little Self-Esteem,* illustrated by Laura Cornell, HarperCollins (New York, NY), 2002.
International Dictionary of Films and Filmmakers, Volume 3: *Actors and Actresses,* 4th edition, edited by Tom Pendergast and Sara Pendergast, Gale (Detroit, MI), 2000.

PERIODICALS

Booklist, October 1, 1993, p. 352; October 15, 1996, p. 432; October 15, 1998, Stephanie Zvirin, review of *Today I Feel Silly & Other Moods That Make My Day,* p. 426; October 1, 2002, Karin Snelson, review of *I'm Gonna Like Me: Letting Off a Little Self-Esteem,* p. 334.
Books for Keeps, September, 2001, Valerie Caghlan, review of *Today I Feel Silly & Other Moods That Make My Day,* p. 22.
Children's Book and Play Review, January-February, 2001, Carla Morris, review of *Where Do Balloons Go?: An Uplifting Mystery,* pp. 17-18.
Entertainment Weekly, August 18, 2000, Clarissa Cruz, review of *Where Do Balloons Go?,* p. 120.
Esquire, July, 1985, interview with Jamie Lee Curtis, p. 66.
Horn Book, January-February, 1997, pp. 50-51; November-December, 2000, Susan P. Bloom, review of *Where Do Balloons Go?,* p. 745.

Horn Book Guide, fall, 1999, Jennifer M. Brabander, review of *Tell Me Again about the Night I Was Born,* p. 231.

Kirkus Reviews, August 1, 1996, p. 1149; July 1, 2002, review of *I'm Gonna Like Me,* p. 952.

Magpies, March, 1998, Ricki Blackhall, review of *Tell Me Again about the Night I Was Born,* p. 26.

New York Times, July 17, 1994, Caryn James, review of *True Lies,* p. C13.

Publishers Weekly, July 19, 1993, p. 252; August 5, 1996, review of *Tell Me Again about the Night I Was Born,* p. 441; September 7, 1998, review of *Today I Feel Silly & Other Moods That Make My Day,* p. 94; August 21, 2000, review of *Where Do Balloons Go?,* p. 73; September 30, 2002, review of *I'm Gonna Like Me,* pp. 70-71.

Rolling Stone, July 18-August 1, 1985, Neal Karlen, "Jamie Lee Curtis Gets Serious," p. 35.

School Library Journal, November, 1993, Debra S. Gold, review of *When I Was Little: A Four-Year-Old's Memoir of Her Youth,* p. 78; October, 1996, Ruth K. MacDonald, review of *Tell Me Again about the Night I Was Born,* p. 91; December, 1998, Martha Topol, review of *Today I Feel Silly & Other Moods That Make My Day,* p. 82; December, 2000, Marie Orlando, review of *Where Do Balloons Go?,* p. 106; October, 2002, Roxanne Burg, review of *I'm Gonna Like Me,* p. 100.

ONLINE

BBC News, http://news.bbc.co.uk/ (August 23, 2002), Chris Jones, "Jamie Lee Curtis: The Body Beautiful?"

CBS News, http://www.cbsnews.com/ (October 9, 2002), "*The Early Show* with Lisa Birnbach: Jamie Lee Curtis, Author."

HarperChildrens.com, http://www.harperchildrens.com/ (March 6, 2003), "Jamie Lee Curtis."

KidsReads.com, http://www.kidsreads.com/ (March 6, 2003), Shannon Maughan, "A Talk with Jamie Lee Curtis: Actor, Author, Mom," "Books by Jamie Lee Curtis."

Pittsburgh Post-Gazette Online, http://www.post-gazettte.com/ (November 10, 1998), Karen MacPherson, "Jamie Lee Curtis, One Celebrity Author."

That's a Wrap, http://www.thats-a-wrap.net/ (March 6, 2003), "Total Jamie Lee Curtis."*

CUTLER, Charles L(ocke, Jr.) 1930-1999

PERSONAL: Born September 8, 1930, in Springfield, MA; died, 1999; son of Charles L. (a manufacturer) and Annie (Harris) Cutler; married Katharine Church, July 7, 1962; children: Charles L. III, Pamela. *Education:* Attended Harvard University, 1948-53; University of California—Berkeley, B.A., 1954; University of Edinburgh, graduate study, 1954-55; Springfield College, M.Ed., 1956. *Politics:* Republican. *Religion:* Christian. *Hobbies and other interests:* Writing haiku.

CAREER: Prentice-Hall, Inc., Englewood Cliffs, NJ, production editor, 1956-58; Xerox Education Publications, Middletown, CT, editor, beginning 1959. Member of board of directors of Levi E. Coe Library.

MEMBER: Mensa, Middletown Judo Club.

WRITINGS:

Connecticut's Revolutionary Press, Pequot Press, 1975.

We Made It to 100: Wisdom from the Super Old, Rockfall Press (Rockfall, CT), 1978.

O Brave New Words!: Native American Loanwords in Current English, University of Oklahoma Press (Norman, OK), 1994.

Tracks That Speak: The Legacy of Native American Words in North American Culture, Houghton Mifflin (New York, NY), 2002.

Contributor to *American Heritage* and *American History Illustrated.*

SIDELIGHTS: Charles L. Cutler was the author of two books that explore the legacy of Native American words as they apply to the modern-day English lexicon. *O Brave New Words!: Native American Loanwords in Current English* is a work that "charts new ground," according to *Booklist*'s Kevin Roddy. As the reviewer pointed out, many of the Cutler's "loanwords" from Native tongues relate to "place-names, river names, names of geographical formations, and the like." "Estimating that there are more than one thousand still-current North American Indian loanwords in English," noted Fiona Robertson in *Notes and Queries,* "Cutler reminds us that the AmerIndian languages are 'one of [English's] major vocabulary sources outside the Indo-European family.'"

In a similar vein, the posthumously published *Tracks That Speak: The Legacy of Native American Words in North American Culture* is an "abalone-to-woodchuck tour of the Native American contribution to the American vocabulary," noted a *Kirkus Reviews* contributor. As Cutler related in the book, "You can hardly step outdoors without using words derived from Native American languages." Indeed, such Native words as chipmunk, hickory, and sockeye were "all long at home in the pages of Webster's," wrote the *Kirkus Reviews* critic. A *Publishers Weekly* contributor pointed out that Cutler's work here "leans heavily on an unscholarly bibliography," including articles from popular magazines. The critic added that "the easygoing tone of a magazine article can seem lightweight stretched out over an entire book," but concluded that Cutler was "a much appreciated contributor to magazines."

BIOGRAPHICAL AND CRITICAL SOURCES:

BOOKS

Cutler, Charles L., *Tracks That Speak: The Legacy of Native American Words in North American Culture,* Houghton Mifflin (New York, NY), 2002.

PERIODICALS

American Indian Culture and Research Journal, fall, 1995, Frederick White, review of *O Brave New Words! Native American Loanwords in Current English,* p. 302.

ANQ, spring, 1996, Janine Scancarelli, review of *O Brave New Words!,* p. 56.
Booklist, September 1, 1994, Kevin Roddy, review of *O Brave New Words,* p. 12.
Choice, April, 1995, W. B. McCarthy, review of *O Brave New Words!,* p. 1298.
Ethnohistory, spring, 1996, Donald Lance, review of *O Brave New Words!,* p. 336.
Journal of the West, fall, 2000, Max Oppenheimer, review of *O Brave New Words!,* p. 100.
Kirkus Reviews, March 1, 2002, review of *Tracks That Speak: The Legacy of Native American Words in North American Culture,* p. 303.
Library Journal, October 15, 1994, Amy Boaz Nugent, review of *O Brave New Words!,* p. 72; June 15, 2002, Faye Powell, review of *Tracks That Speak,* p. 74.
Nineteenth-Century Literature, March, 1995, review of *O Brave New Words!,* p. 556.
Notes and Queries, June, 1996, Fiona Robertson, review of *O Brave New Words!,* p. 206.
Plains Anthropologist, May, 1996, Jack Weatherford, review of *O Brave New Words!,* p. 188.
Publishers Weekly, March 11, 2002, review of *Tracks That Speak,* p. 66.
Reference and Research Book News, February, 1995, review of *O Brave New Words!,* p. 42.
Roundup, January, 1995, review of *O Brave New Words!,* p. 23.
Science News, July 6, 2002, review of *Tracks That Speak,* p. 15.*

* * *

**CUTRATE, Joe
See SPIEGELMAN, Art**

D

DANKY, James P. 1947-

PERSONAL: Born October 3, 1947, in Los Angeles, CA; son of Philip H. (a probation officer) and Elizabeth James (an elementary school principal) Danky; married Pamela Johnson (divorced); married Christine Schelshorn (an editor), August 12, 1980; children: Matthew. *Education:* Ripon College, A.B., 1970; University of Wisconsin-Madison, M.A.(library science), 1973. *Hobbies and other interests:* Gardening, raising chickens.

ADDRESSES: Office—State Historical Society of Wisconsin, 816 State St., Madison, WI 53706. *E-mail*—jpdanky@wgs.wisc.edu.

CAREER: State Historical Society of Wisconsin, Madison, newspapers and periodicals librarian, 1973—; University of Wisconsin-Madison, lecturer, 1990—, codirector of Center for the History of Print Culture in Modern America, 1992-2002, director, 2002—. Cooksville Community Center, board of directors and treasurer, 1979-90.

MEMBER: American Historical Association, Organization of American Historians, American Library Association, American Journalism Historians Association.

AWARDS, HONORS: Serials Librarian of the Year, Bowker/American Library Association, 1987; Media Hero, Alternative Media Association, 1993; Alumnus of the Year, University of Wisconsin School of Library and Information Sciences, 1993; Fulbright scholar, British Library, 1991.

WRITINGS:

(Editor) *Undergrounds: A Union List of Alternative Periodicals in Libraries of the United States and Canada,* State Historical Society of Wisconsin (Madison, WI), 1974.

(Editor, with Elliott Shore) *Alternative Materials in Libraries,* Scarecrow Press (Metuchen, NJ), 1982.

(Editor) *Native American Periodicals and Newspapers, 1828-1982,* Greenwood Press (Westport, CT), 1984.

(Editor, with Sanford Berman) *Alternative Library Literature: A Biennial Anthology,* McFarland & Co. (Jefferson, NC), 1984-2001.

(Editor) *Genealogical Research: An Introduction to the Resources of the State Historical Society of Wisconsin,* State Historical Society of Wisconsin (Madison, WI), 1986.

(Editor) *Labor Union Periodicals,* University Publications of America (Bethesda, MD), 1990-99.

(Editor, with Elliott Shore and Ken Fones-Wolf) *The German-American Radical Press: The Shaping of a Left Political Culture, 1850-1940,* University of Illinois Press (Urbana, IL), 1992.

(Editor) *African-American Newspapers and Periodicals: A National Bibliography,* Harvard University Press (Cambridge, MA), 1998.

(Editor, with Wayne A. Wiegand) *Print Culture in A Diverse America,* University of Illinois Press (Urbana, IL), 1998.

Women in Print: Reading, Writing, Publishing in American from the Nineteenth Century to the Present, University of Wisconsin Press (Madision, WI), 2003.

Also contributor to *The History of the Book in America,* Volume 4, for Cambridge University Press; editor of collections on alternative and minority publications held by the State Historical Society of Wisconsin.

WORK IN PROGRESS: Research on newspapers and periodicals of the African Diaspora in Europe, Latin America, and Asia.

SIDELIGHTS: In the strictest definition, James P. Danky is not writer, but the terms editor and compiler do not fully characterize his contributions to literature. Through extensive research, library education, and publishing, Danky has brought to light a body of writing and culture that had previously gone unnoticed. As a librarian at the State Historical Society of Wisconsin and the director of the Center of Print Culture in Modern America at the University of Wisconsin-Madison— where he is also a faculty member in three departments—Danky is committed to increasing public awareness of media sources that are easily overlooked in mainstream library catalogs.

The ten volumes of "Alternative Library Literature" comprise readings from smaller journals and other sources that address topics including human rights, women and children, censorship, multiculturalism and the Third World. Reviewing the 1998-1999 edition of *Alternative Library Literature* for the *Australian Library Journal,* Bob Pymm wrote of Danky and coeditor Sanford Berman, "Their passion has not abated over the years, and their belief in libraries having the potential to make a difference is as strong as ever. Once again this eclectic, irritating, moving, emotional, inconsistent, and enthusing collection sets out to bring to a wider audience [texts] that otherwise would be seen by very few." Danky has also focused his efforts on specific groups, including Native Americans, African Americans, German Americans, and Asian Americans. In a review for *Publishing Research Quarterly,* Albert Henderson called Danky's *African-American Newspapers and Periodicals: A National Bibliography* "an invaluable resource."

In 1999 Danky was honored as the Wisconsin Librarian of the Year for his efforts to make materials on Native Americans, blacks, and women more accessible to a general audience.

BIOGRAPHICAL AND CRITICAL SOURCES:

PERIODICALS

American Libraries, April, 1983, Thomas Nisonger, review of *Alternative Materials in Libraries,* p. 202; January, 2000, "James Danky," p. 94; May, 2001, Cathleen Bourdon, "Airing Alternative Viewpoints," p. 88.

Australian Library Journal, November, 2001, Bob Pymm, review of *Alternative Library Literature, 1998-1999,* pp. 394-395.

Capital Times (Madison, WI), August 9, 1999, "Librarians Honor Danky," p. 1C.

Library Journal, February 1, 1997, Wilda Williams, review of *Alternative Library Literature, 1994-1995,* pp. 114-115; November 15, 1999, Elizabeth Connor, review of *African-American Newspapers and Periodicals,* p. 58; May 1, 2001, Wilda Williams, review of *Alternative Library Literature, 1998-1999,* p. 134.

Publishing Research Quarterly, summer, 2000, Albert Henderson, review of *African-American Newspapers and Periodicals,* p. 94.

Wisconsin State Journal, October 9, 1999, "Historical Society Librarian Honored," p. 2B.

ONLINE

University of Illinois Press Web site, http://www.press.uillinois.edu/ (June 12, 2002).

University of Wisconsin Library Web site, http://www.library.wisc.edu/ (June 12, 2002), "James P. Danky."

University of Wisconsin SLIS Alumni Association Web site, http://www.slis.wisc.edu/ (June 12, 2002).

* * *

D'AVRAY, David L.

PERSONAL: Born in Lusaka, Zambia; son of Hector Anthony (a colonial civil servant) and Audrey Sabina D'Avray; married Julia Caroline Walworth (an art historian), August 14, 1985. *Education:* St. John's College, Cambridge, B.A., 1973; Balliol College, Oxford, D.Phil., 1977. *Religion:* Roman Catholic.

ADDRESSES: *Home*—Flat 16, 1 Hornton St., London W8, England. *Office*—Department of History, University College, University of London, Gower St., London WC1E 6BT, England.

CAREER: Professor of history at University of London, London, England.

WRITINGS:

The Preaching of the Friars: Sermons Diffused from Paris before 1300, Clarendon Press (Oxford, England), 1985.
Death and the Prince: Memorial Preaching before 1350, Oxford University Press (New York, NY), 1994.
(With Nicole Bériou) *Modern Questions about Medieval Sermons: Essays on Marriage, Death, History and Sanctity,* Centro Italiano di studi sull'Alto medioevo (Spoleto, Italy), 1994.
Medieval Marriage Sermons: Mass Communication in a Culture without Print, Oxford University Press (New York, NY), 2001.

Contributor to journals.

SIDELIGHTS: English medieval historian David D'Avray is the author of several books that focus on aspects of life in the Middle Ages. His *Death and the Prince: Memorial Preaching before 1350* "provides readers with a sensitive and supple study" of the subject, according to Alan Fletcher of *Medium Aevum*. D'Avray begins by pointing out that, from the fourth century through the Middle Ages, there was a dearth of archived sermons related to the passing of royalty. By the mid-1300s, "no memorial sermon for a prince [had] survived, except for occasional mentionings," commented *Journal of Religion* writer John Baldwin. That changed at the beginning of the fourteenth century, when memorial texts tied to such influential rulers as Edward I of England began to surface.

D'Avray has taken these unedited manuscripts and, according to Baldwin, "transcribed nearly fifty pages of Latin text, and placed the genre on a solid scholarly basis." The author examines three aspects of memorializing, the reviewer added: first, the "portrayal of individual personality," followed by "representation of political ideology," and finally "attitudes toward death and afterlife." To Jean Dunbabin, writing in *Journal of Ecclesiastical History,* the author "demonstrates that these sermons offer the historian insights into the ways in which political office and its holders were presented by preachers to the wider public." *English Historical Review* contributor R. N. Swanson maintained that individualism is the weaker point of *Death and the Prince*: "To argue that the sermons reveal people as individuals who can be recognized as such if they are sufficiently well known from other sources appears somewhat idiosyncratic," wrote Swanson. Dunbabin had fewer such reservations, stating that D'Avray has produced an "erudite and stimulating work," and adding that the author "has put later medieval historians in his debt by providing them both with material as grist for their mills and with sophisticated interpretative techniques as stimulus to reflection."

In 1997 D'Avray and coauthor Nicole Bériou published *Modern Questions about Medieval Sermons: Essays on Marriage, Death, History and Sanctity,* a collection of historical writings whose "utility and impact," noted R. N. Swanson in *Journal of Ecclesiastical History,* "will vary according to the needs of the reader." Several of the articles "are already in the mainstream; others have hitherto been relatively unknown or inaccessible, but will deservedly soon start to appear in footnotes and bibliographies."

BIOGRAPHICAL AND CRITICAL SOURCES:

PERIODICALS

American Historical Review, October, 1996, Janet Nelson, review of *Death and the Prince: Memorial Preaching before 1350,* p. 1192.
Church History, March, 1997, Daniel Bornstein, review of *Modern Questions about Medieval Sermons: Essays on Marriage, Death, History and Sanctity,* p. 101.
English Historical Review, February, 1997, R. N. Swanson, review of *Death and the Prince,* p. 170.
History, July, 1996, Chistoph Maier, review of *Death and the Prince,* p. 434.
Journal of Ecclesiastical History, April, 1996, Jean Dunbabin, review of *Death and the Prince,* p. 367; January, 1997, R. N. Swanson, review of *Modern Questions about Medieval Sermons,* p. 161.
Journal of Religion, July, 1997, John Baldwin, review of *Death and the Prince,* p. 465.
Medium Aevum, spring, 1996, Alan J. Fletcher, review of *Death and the Prince,* p. 122.
Speculum, April, 1997, Augustine Thompson, review of *Death and the Prince,* p. 461.
Times Literary Supplement, May 31, 1985.*

DESSAIX, Robert 1944-

PERSONAL: Born 1944, in Sidney, New South Wales, Australia. *Education:* Attended Australian National University (studied Russian language and literature); attended Moscow State University, 1966-67 and 1970.

ADDRESSES: Home—Melbourne, Australia. *Agent*—Lyn Tranter, Australian Literary Management, 2 Buckland St., Chippendale, Sydney NSW 2008, Australia.

CAREER: University professor, literary interviewer and commentator, and broadcaster. Australian National University, Canberra, teacher, until 1985; University of New South Wales, Sydney, lecturer in Russian language and literature; ABC Radio National's *Books and Writing* program, producer and presenter, 1985-95; ABC Television, producer and presenter of weekly program *Books and Writing,* 1985—.

AWARDS, HONORS: Shortlisted for Vance Palmer Prize for Fiction, and for Book of the Year award, *The Age,* both 1996, both for *Night Letters.*

WRITINGS:

Turgenev: The Quest for Faith (criticism), Australian National University (Canberra, ACT, Australia), 1980.
(Editor and translator, with Michael Ulman) Grigori Svirski, *A History of Post-War Soviet Writing: The Literature of Moral Opposition* (criticism), Ardis (Ann Arbor, MI), 1981.
(Translator, with Michael Ulman) Boris Vakhtin, *The Sheepskin Coat* [and] *An Absolutely Happy Village* (novellas), Ardis (Ann Arbor, MI), 1990.
(Editor) *Australian Gay and Lesbian Writing: An Anthology,* Oxford University Press (Melbourne, VIC, Australia), 1993.
(Editor, with Helen Daniel) *Picador New Writing* (anthology), Picador Australia (Chippendale, Sydney, NSW, Australia), 1993.
A Mother's Disgrace (autobiography), Angus & Robertson (Pymble, Sydney, NSW, Australia), 1994.
Night Letters (fiction), Macmillan (Sydney, NSW, Australia), 1996, St. Martin's Press (New York, NY), 1997.
and so forth, Pan Macmillan (Sydney, NSW, Australia), 1998.
Corfu: A Novel, Picador (Sydney, NSW, Australia), 2001.

Also editor of *Outrage: Gay and Lesbian Writing,* 1993, and *Oxford Book of Gay and Lesbian Writing,* 1993; author of *A Practical Handbook of Russian Aspect,* 1994; (with Amanda Lohrey and Drusilla Modjeska) *Secrets,* 1997; and *Speaking Their Minds* (a collection of interviews), 1998.

SIDELIGHTS: Robert Dessaix is an Australian educator, critic, and author who has written, translated, and edited works focusing on his main area of academic interest, Russian literature. He has also contributed to the subgenre of Australian homosexual literature with an anthology of gay and lesbian writing, as well his own autobiography, and a work of fiction centering on a gay Australian who travels to Europe after learning he has contracted the AIDS virus.

Dessaix began his literary career with the publication in 1980 of an examination of religious faith in the works of the Russian nineteenth-century author Ivan Turgenev. He later edited and translated, with Michael Ulman, Grigori Svirski's *A History of Post-War Soviet Writing: The Literature of Moral Opposition,* which comprises a consideration of Russian twentieth-century literature, particularly focusing on the literature of dissent within the former Soviet Union. He and Ulman again collaborated in the translation of a pair of comic novellas by Boris Vakhtin, *The Sheepskin Coat* [and] *An Absolutely Happy Village,* which was published in 1990.

Dessaix changed direction with his next work, *Australian Gay and Lesbian Writing: An Anthology,* published in 1994. In this volume, Dessaix has collected literary works featuring gay and lesbian themes by a variety of authors from all periods of Australian literary history and provides supporting material for the texts in the form of biographical notes and a critical introduction. The anthology includes such authors as Dennis Altman, Sumner Locke Elliot, Kate Walker, Henry Handel Richardson, Mary Fallon, Thomas Shapcott, David Herkt, Tim Herbert, Lesbia Harford, Elizabeth Riley, Susan Hampton, Sasha Soldatow, Simon Payne, and Nicholas Jose.

In a review of *Australian Gay and Lesbian Writing* for *Choice,* B. Braendlin noted that having heterosexual writers in addition to homosexual writers forces the reader to examine how homosexual literature is defined, in addition to how sex and gender are related. Tina Muncaster, commenting in the *Australian Book Review,* praised the volume, stating "*Australian Gay and Lesbian Writing* shines through the mass of mediocre publisher's fundraisers as an example of the difference a committed and careful editor can make when assembling source material under a common theme."

A Mother's Disgrace, published in 1994, offers an account of Dessaix's search for identity through a reunion with his biological mother, Yvonne, who had given him up for adoption forty-six years earlier. Elaine Lindsay, writing of *A Mother's Disgrace* in the *Australian Book Review,* commented that his "autobiography may be directed at his mother but it is possible that Dessaix is also readjusting his perceptions of himself." She found, however, that Dessaix's "conversational style . . . does him a disservice for it discourages contemplation and keeps the reader at a passive distance."

Night Letters, Dessaix's 1996 work of fiction, presents a series of letters written by an Australian writer traveling to Venice, Italy, after learning he is HIV positive. Addressed to an unnamed correspondent in Melbourne, the letters are arranged, excerpted, and annotated by the unimaginative fictional editor Igor Miazmov and offer insight into a wide array of topics, including philosophy, religion, literature, cultural history, spiritual quest, and personal awakening. In Venice the narrator meets Professor Eschenbaum. Through the dialog between the two men emerges the story of Donna Scamozzi and her virgin daughter Camilla, the "Disappearing Courtesan," as well as tales of the lives of famous Venetians Casanova and Marco Polo. Throughout the book, the narrator is intensely focused on Dante's *Divine Comedy,* drawing hope and spiritual sustenance from the poet's notion of God as a radiant point of light.

Jeremy Reed of the London *Times* called the book "a poetic masterpiece." Reed wrote, "Not since Edmund White's richly evocative *Nocturnes for the King of Naples* has a gay novelist infused the themes of love and death with so fine a lyric sensibility." The reviewer thought the book was full of hope and a testament to the value of living in the moment. "The outcome is heroic. . . . Illness is viewed as contingent on the will to live, and the future as it is apprehended by the narrator is open-ended and continuous," Reed concluded.

Reviewer Hazel Rowley praised *Night Letters* in the *Australian Book Review.* Noting that "Dessaix excels at second-person narrative," Rowley found the work "intensely pleasurable to read." Dessaix revealed, in an interview with Peter Beilharz, also published in the *Australian Book Review,* that the persona "R," who writes the letters, is "constructed as a fictional voice. It's not my own voice. . . . It's a voice I had to find. It reflects my concerns and, I hope, my enjoyment of play, but it is probably a more self-deprecating voice than my real voice—perhaps more at sea in the world, pretending not to know things that I probably think I do know."

Dessaix's *and so forth* is a collection of some of his short stories and essays from about 1990 to 1998. Several of the essays are from Dessaix's Radio National program. One is about the author's private language, "K," which he invented as a child and still uses when talking to himself. Another deals with other authors who are writing about AIDS and the end of life. Other essays include one about "Anna Karenina," from the novel, and a piece about Aboriginal art and the Australian Outback. *Eclectica* reviewer Ann Skea both liked and disliked the book, saying she preferred Dessaix's essays to his stories. Writing about this mix, she said, "If you want to read Dessaix in his best fictional mode, forget these [short stories] and read *Night Letters* instead." Skea admitted that the reason she disliked some of the author's writings is because she disagrees with him. "As you can tell, Robert Dessaix's writing is not for people who want a quiet uncontroversial read," she concluded. "You don't need to live in Australia to have opinions on gender, sex, colonialism, orientalism, pornography, and art. Dessaix touches on all these topics, and more."

Helen McCullough, in a review for *Screaming Hyena* Web site, wrote: "*and so forth* is not a red hot flash crash change your life sort of book; rather it's a hello Uncle Robert, good to see you again, do come in and have a cup of coffee, and tell us again the one about the stolen picture sort of book. It is recommended for those who already know and like Dessaix. Others should start with *A Mother's Disgrace,* an excellent introduction to the voice and point of view, and a fascinating read."

Dessaix's 2001 novel, *Corfu,* revolves around an unnamed narrator who stops on the Greek island of Corfu on his way home to Australia and stays at the home of writer-actor Kester Berwick while he is away. The narrator comes to know Berwick by reading his letters, diaries, and novels and by meeting Berwick's eccentric friends in the village—expatriates who do not mix with the local people. A series of flashbacks from both the narrator's and Berwick's life make up most of the story. Intertwined throughout the novel are essays on literature befitting the place and circumstance in which the narrator finds himself. For example, when he travels to the island of Lesbos, Dessaix discusses Sappho; Chekhov finds his way into the narrator's reminiscences about the theater; and Homer's Ulysses comes to the fore when he thinks of going home. The narrator also muses on the writings of Cavafy, Emerson, Cicero, Horace, Longus, Tolstoy, and others. Important to the narrator's tale is his failed gay romance and his relationship with the young Australian William, with whom Berwick has also been friendly.

Reviewer Skea wrote, "I was entertained. And surprised, when I had finished, to realize that I had just enjoyed what could well be classified as 'gay fiction.' But to classify it as such would be as limiting as to describe it as 'travel writing,' which is also possible. . . . The narrator's company is entertaining, his travels are exotic, and his adventures, like those of Odysseus, are curiously full of strange encounters."

Times Literary Supplement critic David Horspool viewed the novel less favorably, saying, "Drama . . . happens offstage, while the narrator's thoughts take the spotlight. Dessaix has an eye for comic possibility, but the glimpses he affords . . . are frustratingly brief." Horspool thought Dessaix was too close to his main character, making the book little more than "an elegantly written treatise."

Diana Ward of *Girl Plus Boy* Web site commented that Dessaix's blend of travelogue with fiction and essay does not work as well in *Corfu* as it did in *Night Letters*. Calling *Corfu* "a difficult read," she said she disliked the way literary essay interrupted fiction. Ward also observed that the novel contains "little or no insight" into the lives of the local Greek people and their culture, and she said "the almost exclusive emphasis on male characters . . . makes it seem a little one-dimensional." Although she could not empathize with the narrator, Ward thought "the intricacy of some of the other characters is both wonderful and fantastical."

BIOGRAPHICAL AND CRITICAL SOURCES:

PERIODICALS

Advocate, December 9, 1997, review of *Night Letters,* p. 79.
Australian Book Review, September, 1993, Tina Muncaster, review of *Australian Gay and Lesbian Writing: An Anthology,* pp. 43-44; February, 1994, Elaine Lindsay, review of *A Mother's Disgrace,* pp. 21-22; July, 1994, review of *A Mother's Disgrace,* p. 32; August, 1996, Hazel Rowley, review of *Night Letters,* and Peter Beilharz, interview with Dessaix, pp. 7-8; July, 1998, review of *Speaking Their Minds,* p. 10; November, 1998, review of *and so forth,* p. 19; August, 2001, review of *Corfu: A Novel,* p. 11.
Booklist, November 1, 1997, review of *Night Letters,* p. 454.
Bulletin with Newsweek, December 8, 1998, Diana Simmonds, review of *and so forth,* p. 85; August 14, 2001, Sally Blakeney, review of *Corfu,* p. 71.
Choice, October, 1994, B. Braendlin, review of *Australian Gay and Lesbian Writing,* p. 290.
Kirkus Reviews, September 1, 1997, review of *Night Letters,* p. 1325.
Lambda Book Report, May, 1994, review of *Australian Gay and Lesbian Writing,* p. 34; July, 1995, review of *Australian Gay and Lesbian Writing,* p. 42.
Library Journal, October 1, 1997, review of *Night Letters,* p. 120.
New York Times Book Review, March 18, 1990, p. 12; January 11, 1998, Patrick Farrell, review of *Night Letters,* p. 14; March 7, 1999, review of *Night Letters,* p. 28.
Observer (London, England), December 1, 1996, review of *Night Letters,* p. 16.
Publishers Weekly, October 6, 1997, review of *Night Letters,* p. 75.
Times (London, England), November 26, 1998, Jeremy Reed, "Writing to Survive," review of *Night Letters,* p. 42.
Times Literary Supplement, March 12, 1999, Naomi Price, review of *Night Letters,* p. 23; March 29, 2002, David Horspool, "An Island of Lost Souls," review of *Corfu,* p. 22.

ONLINE

Age Web site, http://www.theage.com.au/ (December 7, 1995), review of *Night Letters.*

Eclectica Online Magazine, http://www.eclectica.org/ (January-February, 1999), Ann Skea, review of *and so forth*; (October-November, 2001), Ann Skea, review of *Corfu*.

Girl Plus Boy Web site, http://www.girlplusboy.com/ (September 23, 2002), Diana Ward, review of *Corfu*.

Premier's Literary Awards Web site, http://www.slv.vic.gov.au/pla/1997/shortlist/ (October 24, 1997).

Screaming Hyena: e-Journal of Queer Writing and Review, http://hares-hyenas.com.au/ (June 30, 1999), Helen McCulloch, review of *and so forth*.*

* * *

DITCHOFF, Pamela (Jane) 1950-

PERSONAL: Born September 21, 1950, in East Lansing, MI; daughter of Ronald Ernest and Beatrice Watson (Porter) Reed; married Paul Alexander Ditchoff, March 28, 1983; children: Dean Reed, Joshua Judson, Deborah Kristine. *Education:* Lansing Community College, A.A. (magna cum laude), 1979; Michigan State University, B.A. (with honors), 1982, M.A. (with honors), 1985.

ADDRESSES: Agent—Jane Dystel, Jane Dystel Literary Agency, Inc., 1 Union Sq. W., New York, NY 10003. *E-mail*—pamela@voyager.net.

CAREER: WFSL-TV, Lansing, MI, copywriter and creative consultant, 1982-84; Quality Dairy, Lansing, MI, advertising agent, 1984-85; Haslett Public Schools, Haslett, MI, instructor in Quest Program for Gifted Children for elementary and middle school students, 1985-89; freelance writer. ASAP Copywriting, owner and sole operator, 1985-87; Lansing Community College, instructor in communication and business, 1986-87; instructor for "Creative Writers in Schools Program" of Michigan, 1989-93; Towar Community Center, volunteer instructor in poetry writing for teenage mothers, 1990-91. Also worked as producer and director, including work on *Artpeace,* c. 1984.

AWARDS, HONORS: Fellowship from Virginia Center for the Creative Arts, 1981; Michigan Addy Certificate of Merit, American Advertising Federation, 1984, for a promotional television campaign, "Come Together in the Heart of Michigan"; Michigan Addy Award for Excellence, 1984, for *Artpeace;* scholar, Southampton Writer's Conference, Long Island University, 1987; named winner of *Amelia* magazine's Bernice Jennings Traditional Poetry Competition, 1988, for "Solution Sestina"; finalist in Eve of St. Agnes Poetry Competition, 1989, for "Negative Capability"; first honorable mention in National Writer's Union Poetry Competition, 1990; *Chicago Review* Award in Fiction, 1991, for "Prodigies"; John Ciardi scholar, Bread Loaf Writer's Conference, 1991; Walter Dakin fellow, Sewanee Writer's Conference, 1998.

Pamela Ditchoff

WRITINGS:

Poetry: One, Two, Three (textbook), Interact Press (El Cajon, CA), 1989.

Lexigram Learns America's Capitals (textbook), Interact Press (El Cajon, CA), 1994.

The Mirror of Monsters and Prodigies (novel), Coffee House Press (Minneapolis, MN), 1995.

Mrs. Beast: A Novel, Bridge Works Publishing (Bridgehampton, NY), 1998.

Seven Days & Seven Sins (fiction), Shaye Areheart Books, (New York, NY), 2003.

Contributor of short stories and poetry to anthologies, including *Vital Signs: Contemporary Fiction about Medicine,* edited by John Mukand, St. Martin's Press (New York, NY), 1990; *Whose Woods These Are,* edited by David Bain, Ecco Press, 1993; and *Home for the Holidays,* Papier-Mache Press, 1997. Contributor of poetry to periodicals, including *River City, Ego, Amelia, Chicago Review, Thema, South Florida Poetry Review, West,* and *Yet Another Small Magazine.*

WORK IN PROGRESS: Two novels.

SIDELIGHTS: Pamela Ditchoff's volume *The Mirror of Monsters and Prodigies* explores the world of the bizarre, specifically the disfigured and otherwise unusual people who for hundreds of years have been not only the object of stares and wonder, but also the entertainment of kings and stars of carnival sideshows. From a set of Siamese twins born in England around 1100 and a museum curator born with a furry tail, to Jo-Jo the Russian Dog-Faced Boy, Ditchoff presents dozens of subjects, each with fascinating and unique features. Although these characters actually existed, Ditchoff has created their voices, developing for each an oral history.

The Mirror of Monsters and Prodigies is an elaboration on Ditchoff's short story "Prodigies," which won a *Chicago Review* award for fiction. While doing research for that story, Ditchoff discovered many references to interesting subjects—people who had been written of because of their physical anomalies—that she was compelled to produce a novel in their honor. But, a deeper, more personal reason also motivated the author to tell of living with an unusual condition; as a child, Ditchoff had a birthmark on her face. The mark has been removed, but the memory of it aids Ditchoff in expressing empathy for others living with unusual physical traits.

Ditchoff, an instructor in creative writing and poetry, has been praised for her novel by critics, among them Melissa Rossi, who wrote in the Seattle weekly newspaper *Eastsideweek:* "This rich and honeyed prose makes this book pop out 3-D in a world of flat, lifeless writing. That her focus is a tour of the oddities of history, that one gains insight into the world of so-called freaks, is merely an added bonus on this voyage of the strange." *Booklist* contributor Kathleen Hughes offered high praise for *The Mirror of Monsters and Prodigies,* declaring, "this engrossing novel is a truly stunning debut work."

Ditchoff once told *CA:* "My primary motivation for writing: I'm miserable if I don't write. I think it's genetic. My paternal grandfather was a newspaper reporter who wrote poetry and fiction for his own enjoyment. I began writing stories and poems when I was around ten years old. As primary is passion; if I don't feel passionately about the subjects and characters, readers won't either."

Ditchoff noted that she is most influenced by "Djuna Barnes, Carson McCullers, Angela Carter, Lewis Nordan, and Harry Crews because their characters are fierce, tender, and three-dimensional." "My love of literature and curiosity for the worlds to be explored between paper pages began with Pearl Buck; I was twelve years old when I read *The Good Earth.*"

"I'm interested in appearances—why and how cultures formulate standards, and how those standards affect individuals. I find great enjoyment in trying to place myself, through extensive research, in history, study the ideas, customs, skills, and art of a particular period, then listen to what my characters have to say. The characters in *The Mirror of Monsters and Prodigies* belong to a culture that appears to be vanishing; a culture whose achievements and contributions have been obscured by myth, legend, and fear. This seems to be due, in part, to a veil of silence drawn over people with abnormalities, who either by choice or by alienation, spoke in whispers. Consequently, they have often been stereotyped in literature as token 'gothics' or as comic figures. I found the history of prodigies to be rich with individuals who distinguished themselves enough to be recorded, who lived at the courts of kings and queens, who acted as spies and couriers, guards and porters, humanitarians, artists, and entertainers.

"Another factor in the disappearance of this culture is that it's become possible to treat or eliminate through medical procedures many conditions that would have been characterized as abnormal: plastic surgery, surgery to separate conjoined and parasitic twins, hormone therapy for hirsutism and select types of growth disorder, and amniocentesis. I expect people will ask if I have an abnormality, and if not, what would I know about being different. In a perfect world, this wouldn't matter; our society has become obsessed with appearances, and advertisers cling to our insecurities like shit on a shovel. I will say that this is a work of fiction drawn from historical record, a record I found fascinating, admirable, and worthy of creative exploration.

"However, having said this, I'll also say that when I was very young, the county fair still included a sideshow. I vividly recall one summer when four performers stood outside as draws: a fat lady, a thin man, a tattooed man, and the Alligator Woman. I got as close as I could. The thin man winked at me, lifted me up onto the platform, and drove a spike into his nose. The tattooed man rippled his muscles. The Alligator Woman offered me her arm and said her skin felt very smooth. It did, like satin. I thought they were marvelous because they didn't look like everyone else. I didn't either; I had a large birthmark on my face. It has never occurred to me that they were kind because of my birthmark; these particular performers were simply kind people. I have one tattoo."

More recently, Ditchoff commented: "The greatest inspiration for the subjects I have chosen [to write about] is a desire to peel back the layers of what may seem strange on the outside and is exquisite on the inside." Ditchoff published a second novel in 2003, *Seven Days & Seven Sins,* which also chronicles the lives of very unique characters, who are each disfigured in a different way. It is described as a modern *Our Town* by the publisher.

BIOGRAPHICAL AND CRITICAL SOURCES:

PERIODICALS

Booklist, September 15, 1995, Kathleen Hughes, review of *The Mirror of Monsters and Prodigies.*
Eastsideweek (Seattle), October 4, 1995, Melissa Rossi, review of *The Mirror of Monsters and Prodigies.*
Lansing State Journal, February 8, 1996.
New York Times Book Review, March 10, 1996, David Guy, review of *The Mirror of Monsters and Prodigies,* p. 17.
Publishers Weekly, July 10, 1995, review of *The Mirror of Monsters and Prodigies,* p. 53.
Town Courier (Mason, MI), October 28, 1995.

* * *

DONLEAVY, J(ames) P(atrick) 1926-

PERSONAL: Born April 23, 1926, in Brooklyn, NY; became Irish citizen, 1967; son of James Patrick and Margaret Donleavy; married Valerie Heron (divorced, 1969); married Mary Wilson Price (an actress), 1970 (divorced); children: (first marriage) Philip, Karen; (second marriage) Rebecca Wallis, Rory. *Education:* Attended Trinity College, Dublin, 1946-49.

ADDRESSES: Home—Levington Park, Mullingar, County Westmeath, Ireland.

CAREER: Writer and playwright. Founder with son Philip Donleavy and producer Robert Mitchell of De Alfonce Tennis Association for the Promotion of the Superlative Game of Eccentric Champions; raises cattle; painter who has exhibited his work in London. *Military service:* U.S. Naval Reserve, served in World War II.

AWARDS, HONORS: Most Promising Playwright Award, London *Evening Standard,* 1961, for *Fairy Tales of New York;* Brandeis University Creative Arts Award, 1961-62, for two plays, *The Ginger Man* and *Fairy Tales of New York;* citation from National Institute and American Academy of Arts and Letters, 1975; American Academy of Arts and Letters grantee, 1975; Worldfest Houston Gold Award, 1992; Cine Golden Eagle Award for writer and narrator, 1993.

WRITINGS:

FICTION

The Ginger Man (novel), Olympia Press (Paris, France), 1955, published with introduction by Arland Ussher, Spearman (London, England), 1956,

McDowell, Obolensky (New York, NY), 1958; complete and unexpurgated edition, Corgi (London, England), 1963, Delacorte (New York, NY), 1965; reprinted with original illustrations by Graham McCallum, Edito-Service (Geneva, Switzerland), 1973; limited edition with illustrations by Skip Liepke, Franklin Library (Franklin Center, PA), 1978.

A Singular Man (novel), Little, Brown (Boston, MA), 1963.

Meet My Maker the Mad Molecule (short stories), Little, Brown (Boston, MA), 1964.

The Saddest Summer of Samuel S (novel), Delacorte/Seymour Lawrence (New York, NY), 1966.

The Beastly Beatitudes of Balthazar B (novel), Delacorte/Seymour Lawrence (New York, NY), 1968.

The Onion Eaters (novel), Delacorte/Seymour Lawrence (New York, NY), 1971.

A Fairy Tale of New York (novel), Delacorte/Seymour Lawrence (New York, NY), 1973.

The Destinies of Darcy Dancer, Gentleman (novel), illustrations by Jim Campbell, Delacorte/Seymour Lawrence (New York, NY), 1977.

Schultz (novel), Delacorte/Seymour Lawrence (New York, NY), 1979.

Meet My Maker the Mad Molecule and *The Saddest Summer of Samuel S,* Dell (New York, NY), 1979.

Leila: Further in the Destinies of Darcy Dancer, Gentleman (novel; sequel to *The Destinies of Darcy Dancer, Gentleman*), Delacorte/Seymour Lawrence (New York, NY), 1983, published as limited edition signed by Donleavy with "A Special Message for the First Edition from J. P. Donleavy," Franklin Library (Franklin Center, PA), 1983, published in England as *Leila: Further in the Life and Destinies of Darcy Dancer, Gentleman,* Allen Lane (London, England), 1983.

Are You Listening, Rabbi Loew? (novel; sequel to *Schultz*), Viking (New York, NY), 1987.

That Darcy, That Dancer, That Gentleman (novel; sequel to *Leila*), Viking (New York, NY), 1990.

The Lady Who Liked Clean Rest Rooms: The Chronicle of One of the Strangest Stories Ever to Be Rumored About Around New York (novella), St. Martin's (New York, NY), 1997.

Wrong Information Is Being Given Out at Princeton, Thomas Dunne Books (New York, NY), 1998.

PLAYS

The Ginger Man (adaptation of his novel of same title; first produced at Fortune Theatre, London, September 15, 1959; produced at Gaiety Theatre, Dublin, October 26, 1959; produced on Broadway at Orpheum Theatre, November 21, 1963; contains introduction "What They Did in Dublin"; also see below), Random House (New York, NY), 1961, published in England as *What They Did in Dublin with The Ginger Man,* MacGibbon and Kee (London), 1962 (also see below).

Fairy Tales of New York (adaptation of his novel *A Fairy Tale of New York;* first produced at Comedy Theatre, London, January 24, 1961; also see below), Random House (New York, NY), 1961.

A Singular Man (first produced at Comedy Theatre, October 21, 1964; produced at Westport County [CT] Playhouse, September 4, 1967; also see below), first published in 1964, Bodley Head (London, England), 1965.

The Plays of J. P. Donleavy (with a preface by the author; contains *What They Did in Dublin with The Ginger Man,The Ginger Man,Fairy Tales of New York,A Singular Man,* and *The Saddest Summer of Samuel S*), photographs of productions by Lewis Morley, Delacorte/Seymour Lawrence (New York, NY), 1972.

The Beastly Beatitudes of Balthazar B (adaptation of his novel of same title), first produced in London, 1981, produced in Norfolk, VA, at Virginia Stage Company, 1986.

Also author of radio play, *Helen,* BBC, 1956.

OTHER

The Unexpurgated Code: A Complete Manual of Survival and Manners, illustrations by the author, Delacorte/Seymour Lawrence (New York, NY), 1975.

De Alfonce Tennis: The Superlative Game of Eccentric Champions, Its History, Accoutrements, Rules, Conduct, and Regimen, Dutton/Seymour Lawrence (New York, NY), 1984.

J. P. Donleavy's Ireland: In All Her Sins and in Some of Her Graces, Viking (New York, NY), 1986.

A Singular Country, Ryan (Peterborough, England), 1989, Norton (New York, NY), 1990.

The History of the Ginger Man, Houghton (Boston, MA), 1994.

An Author and His Image: The Collected Shorter Pieces, Viking (New York, NY), 1997.

Contributor of short fiction and essays to *Atlantic Monthly, Playboy, Queen, Saturday Evening Post,* and *Saturday Review.*

SIDELIGHTS: "If there is an archetypal post-World War II American writer-in-exile it may well be James Patrick Donleavy," writes William E. Grant in a *Dictionary of Literary Biography* essay. The son of Irish immigrant parents, J. P. Donleavy renounced the America of their dreams for an Ireland of his own, and became a citizen when Ireland granted tax-free status to its authors. Although literary success came several years after the publication of his stylistically innovative first novel, *The Ginger Man,* Donleavy is now internationally recognized for having written what many consider to be a modern classic. Referring to the "sense of exile and alienation that seems to haunt his life as well as his work," Grant observes that "even achieving the literary success he thought America would deny him has not lessened his alienation from his country, though it has enhanced the style in which he expresses his exile status." Donleavy now writes at his expansive two-hundred-year-old manor situated on nearly two hundred acres in County Westmeath. "He's a sort of born-again Irishman who enthusiastically embraces the life of a man of letters and leisure, adopting not only an Irish country estate but also the appropriate deportment and brogue," says Peter Ross in the *Detroit News.* "He also happens to be one of the funniest and most audacious writers around."

Donleavy's decision to emigrate, although precipitated by difficulty finding a publisher for his first novel, appears to have been the result of a slowly evolving dissatisfaction with what he refers to in his *Atlantic Monthly* essay, "An Expatriate Looks at America," as "a country corrosive of the spirit." Donleavy explains: "Each time I go to these United States I start anew trying to figure them out. After two weeks I decide that like anywhere, greed, lust and envy make them work. But in America it is big greed, big lust, big envy." Although Donleavy remembers his childhood in the Bronx as peaceful, New York City became an increasingly threatening presence, and the ubiquitous violence made him fearful of death there. He recalls in the *Atlantic Monthly* that "something in one's bowels was saying no to this land. Where my childhood friends were growing up, just as their parents did, to be trapped trembling and terrified in a nightmare." Skeptical of America's treatment of its artists as well, Donleavy felt at the outset of his career that he stood little chance of achieving literary success in a land he describes in the *Atlantic Monthly* as a place "where your media mesmerized brain shuts off when the media does." He adds, "And if I stayed they would, without even trying, or knowing, kill me."

Donleavy was resolved to achieve recognition and relates in a *Paris Review* interview with Molly McKaughan: "I realized that the only way you could ever tackle the world was to write something that no one could hold off, a book that would go everywhere, into everyone's hands. And I decided then to write a novel which would shake the world. I shook my fist and said I would do it." That novel, *The Ginger Man,* is set in post-World War II Dublin and details the hedonistic existence of Sebastian Dangerfield who, according to Alfred Rushton in the Toronto *Globe and Mail,* gave "moral turpitude a new lease on life." While still a student, Donleavy began crafting the novel, but he returned to New York to complete and publish it. He indicates in the *Paris Review* that Scribners, to whom he first took the manuscript, thought it was one of the best ever brought to them; its content, however, prevented them from publishing it. Forty-five publishers rejected the novel because they "thought it was a dirty book—scatological, unreadable, obscene," Donleavy tells David Remnick in the *Washington Post.* "My life literally depended on getting this book into print, and when I couldn't, it just drove me out of America."

In the *Paris Review,* Donleavy recalls his reluctance to edit *The Ginger Man* into acceptability: "I had a sense that the book held itself together on the basis of these scatological parts. That its life was in these parts. And I was quite aware that cutting them would be severely damaging to it." Brendan Behan, the legendary Irish playwright and patriot with whom Donleavy became friends during his Dublin days, suggested sending the manuscript to the Olympia Press in Paris, where it eventually was accepted. Following its publication as part of an overtly pornographic series, however, a lengthy legal battle ensued in which Donleavy emerged as the owner of the publishing house. Despite "the potential for literary damage, publication by Olympia Press had the generally salutary effect of establishing the unexpurgated edition of *The Ginger Man* as an underground classic before complete editions became available," notes Grant. In order to ensure the novel's publication in England, though, and to get it recognized and reviewed, Donleavy agreed to certain cuts, stating in the *Paris Review:* "It was an act of pure practicality. If someone wanted to read the unexpurgated edition, they could buy it in Paris. I had published it as I had written it, so it wasn't wrong, then, to publish it to establish my reputation."

Although Donleavy's reputation had to endure both court battles and censors, his experience as a litigant proved invaluable in negotiating subsequent contracts with publishers. "He's very courtly, but he's a very sharp businessman," comments Donleavy's longtime publisher Seymour Lawrence, according to Samuel Allis in the *Washington Post.* "He does all of his negotiating and, unlike most authors, he understands copyrights. He drives a hard bargain, but he's the most professional author I've ever known." Donleavy's legal and business dealings have also given him a special sense of his profession. Money, says the author in the *Paris Review,* has a dramatic effect upon his writing: "In fact, I would say that money is everything in my profession. One's mind almost becomes a vast cash register. . . . To sit at a desk and think, and write, you must have peace, and to buy peace costs a fortune."

In 1994 Donleavy's *The History of the Ginger Man* was published. In the book Donleavy chronicles his efforts to publish *The Ginger Man* and recounts his struggles to become a writer while supporting his family. The author also reprints his entire correspondence with Olympia Press publisher Maurice Girodias, with whom Donleavy waged a protracted battle for the rights to the novel. Even before the publication of *The History of the Ginger Man,* critics recognized the autobiographical aspects of Donleavy's best-known novel. Sally Eckhoff, writing in the *Voice Literary Supplement,* observes: "In Dangerfield, Donleavy created his prototypical diver into Irish society. Like his hero, the author has a history of Olympic pub-crawling—right down there under the rug with Flann O'Brien." Eckhoff also notes that Donleavy's writing exhibits a strong sense of setting. "Most of *The Ginger Man,*" writes Eckhoff, "takes place in Dublin—the world of dreams, populated by gullible shopkeepers, screaming kids, crooked priests, affectionate laundrywomen with time on their hands, and a pub on every corner with a weird name like 'The Bleeding Horse.'"

Critics were unsure at first how to categorize Donleavy and *The Ginger Man.* Grant observes that the critical establishment "debated whether Donleavy belonged with Britain's Angry Young Men, America's black humorists, or France's existentialists." In his *Doings and Undoings,* Norman Podhoretz calls *The Ginger Man* "fundamentally a book without hope." Similarly, in his *Radical Innocence: Studies in the Contemporary American Novel,* Ihab Hassan considers the novel to be "full of gusto, seething with life, but its energy may be the energy of negation, and its vitality has a nasty edge." The nihilism in *The Ginger Man* "refers us to the postwar, existential era," states Hassan. "Traditional values are not in the process of dying, they have ceased entirely to operate, and their stark absence leaves men to shift for themselves as best they can."

The "freshness" of the characterization of Sebastian Dangerfield was one of the most critically acclaimed aspects of the novel, notes Grant, who adds that some critics recognized that the character "existed almost totally outside any system of ideas." Eckhoff calls *The Ginger Man* "a hilarious, cruel, compassionate book."

Despite the commercial success of Donleavy's subsequent work, the critics generally consider his reputation to rest solely on *The Ginger Man.* "So far as most critics and reviewers are concerned, the later works have been but pale shadows of the first brilliant success, and the publication of each succeeding novel has seen a decline in critical attention," writes Grant. Some critics believe that Donleavy has run out of ideas, that he is refurbishing old material, reworking or resurrecting earlier work. For instance, in a *Harper's* review of *The Destinies of Darcy Dancer, Gentleman,* Michael Malone compares a Donleavy book to Guinness stout: "It's distinctive, it's carbonated, it's brimmed with what Hazlitt called 'gusto,' and those who like it can drink it forever. The ingredients never change." Donleavy pays attention to the critics only in a "fairly superficial way" because, as he says in the *Paris Review,* "A writer must always be aware that he has to be a supreme critic. . . . And only his judgment matters." Allis indicates, however, that Donleavy "displays something close to hostility toward academics and the people who review his books and plays," and that he discourages academic interest in his work because he says, "I never want [to] get that self-conscious of my literary position." Grant suggests that "though none individually rivals the first masterpiece, several of these later works deserve wider attention than they have had from the American reading public and critical establishment alike."

Critics point to several characteristics of *The Ginger Man* that surface in Donleavy's later work. Beneath the bawdy humor lies an inherent despondency, with licentiousness masking the more profound search for love; bizarre, eccentric characters, around whom his books revolve, tend to be alienated, victimized by life, and weakened by impending death. "The novels range from variations of the humorous—slapstick, scatological, sardonic—to the sentimental in an idiosyncratic style that conveys the pressure of time on language," writes Thomas LeClair in *Contemporary Literature.* "But such features of Donleavy's work are finally extensions of and returns to death, the test of man's mettle in landscapes made pale by death's presence."

An awareness of death figures significantly in Donleavy's work, and the question Donleavy's heroes "answer in their own, progressively inefficacious ways," writes LeClair in *Twentieth Century Literature,* is, "How does a man weakened by an awareness of death survive in a world experienced as magical with malevolence?" LeClair observes that "to evade his consciousness of mortality, Sebastian Dangerfield . . . lives a hedonistic life in the present and dreams of relaxed ease for the future"; and the rich and reclusive George Smith of Donleavy's *A Singular Man,* who is absorbed with the idea of death and even builds his own mausoleum, "separates himself from the world in a parody of Howard Hughes' and John Paul Getty's attempts to avoid the disease of life." LeClair notes in *Critique: Studies in Modern Fiction* that "the heroes of *The Saddest Summer of Samuel S, The Beastly Beatitudes of Balthazar B,* and *The Onion Eaters* all attempt to overcome their fear of their own death or their sadness about the death of others through love."

According to Grant, the themes of love and loss are also important in much of Donleavy's work. *The Saddest Summer of Samuel S* is about an eminent literary figure in the United States who undergoes psychoanalysis in Vienna in order to live a more conventional life. Of this novel, Grant writes: "Longing for a love he has never had and cannot find because in spite of his need he cannot give, Samuel S is the victim of a life that cannot be lived over and a destiny that cannot be changed." The character, observes Grant, is withdrawn and "trapped in a life-in-death state of mind with neither belief nor passion to motivate him." Similarly, in *The Beastly Beatitudes of Balthazar B,* a novel that details the lonely life of a wealthy young man whose marriage collapses, the hero is "separated from those he loves . . . and seeks completion by loving others, a simple but impossible quest," says Shaun O'Connell in the *Nation.* Robert Scholes observes in the *Saturday Review* that although this "shy and gentle" character seeks love, "it proves elusive, even harder to keep than to find." And O'Connell sees in Donleavy "the joy of the artist who can embody his vision, however bleak, the self-certainty of the writer who can so eloquently move his hero to name his pain."

However, writing in the *Washington Post Book World* about Donleavy's *The Destinies of Darcy Dancer, Gentleman,* a novel in which a young aristocrat is thwarted in several of his attempts at love, Curt Suplee suggests that "Donleavy does not write novels so much as Oedipal fairy tales: semi-realistic fables in which the same patterns are obsessively reenacted. Invariably, a young man finds himself trapped in a society dominated by hostile father-figures and devoid of the uncritical comfort afforded by mothers. . . . Every time the young man attempts to assert his ego in this world, he fails or is beaten, and flees to succour—either to the manic medium of alcohol or the overt mother-surrogates who provide sex and self-esteem, for a while." O'Connell finds, though, that Donleavy's characters "press the possibilities of life with high style and win many tactical victories of great hilarity . . . before they are defeated," and he believes that "Donleavy's vision of sadness seems earned, won by a search of all the possible routes toward happiness."

Focusing on the bawdy humor in Donleavy's work, critics sometimes fault it for what they consider to be gratuitously lewd language and a reliance upon sexual slapstick. A *Times Literary Supplement* reviewer of *The Onion Eaters,* for instance, states that "the scenes of violence and the sexual encounters suggest an attitude to the human body and its functions, weaknesses and pleasures, which is anything but tender, compassionate, or celebratory." The novel is about a young and handsome character named Clayton Claw Clever Clementine, who in addition to being somewhat freakishly over-endowed sexually, has inherited an Irish manor and must confront what a *New Statesman* contributor refers to as a "bizarre collection of servants and . . . an ever-growing crew of sex-obsessed weirdies." Guy Davenport finds in the *National Review* that "Donleavy is uninterruptedly bawdy, yet his obscenity is so grand and so open, that it rises above giving offense into a realm of its own, unchallenged and wild."

Critics also recognize, however, that Donleavy's humor belies an inherent sadness. "Donleavy writes sad and lonely books," says R. Z. Sheppard in a *Time* review of *The Onion Eaters.* Sheppard finds that Donleavy's fictional worlds are "closed worlds, their boundaries no more distant than the most prominent erectile tissue. Alone, without context or meaning, the flesh is all." Sheppard suggests that the absence of meaning in the novel, as well as its "animal warmth, at once grotesque and touching," is perhaps Donleavy's way of asserting that "this warmth is the only thing about which we can be certain."

Writing in *Newsweek* about Donleavy's nonfiction book *The Unexpurgated Code: A Complete Manual of Survival and Manners,* Arthur Cooper describes Donleavy's humor: "Like Mel Brooks, he knows that bad taste is merely a joke that doesn't get a laugh.

And like Brooks, Donleavy's demonic humor is utterly democratic, thrusting the needle into everyone regardless of race, creed, color, or ability to control one's bowels." Referring to the book as "a collection of bilious and often funny rules for living," Melvin Maddocks observes in *Time* that "between the lines, Donleavy's diatribes manage to say more." Maddocks believes that Donleavy's "visions of grace, chivalry and order" reveal the author as "an inverted romantic, profoundly sad beneath his disguise because he and the world are no better than they happen to be."

Similarly, in a *Midwest Quarterly* assessment of *The Unexpurgated Code,* Charles G. Masinton suggests that "Donleavy normally proceeds by means of instinct, inspiration, and intuition—the tools of a romantic artist. He aims to produce belly laughs and . . . a sympathetic response to his chief characters; he does not set out to impose order and rationality on experience. And instead of elevated language (which he often parodies quite effectively), he records with great skill an earthy vernacular full of both comic and lyric possibilities." While Grant believes that Donleavy's "characteristic tone of pessimism, melancholia, alienation, and human failure . . . suggest Jonathan Swift's misanthropic humor," he also finds it reminiscent of Mark Twain's later work, "which combines pessimism and humor in an elegiac, melancholic, and misanthropic voice."

In the *Los Angeles Times Book Review,* David Hirson laments that while a unique blend of lyricism and farce still characterize Donleavy's later novels, his humor has begun to be derived almost exclusively from overkill. An example is *Are You Listening, Rabbi Loew.* Despite its "dauntingly energetic prose," Hirson believes that the novel ultimately wears out the reader. Writes Hirson, "Funny though boorishness, bodily functions and excessive profanity can be, the effect, finally, is of a joke that takes too long in the telling, a numbingly protracted jape."

The style and language of Donleavy's fiction has attracted a great deal of critical attention over the years. Notes Thomas Lask, "critics keep citing his first book . . . some saying that nothing after it has equaled that first effort, and objecting to his language, which has a syntax of its own, without connectives or prepositions, shifting tense at will." Stylistically innovative, *The Ginger Man* employs not only a shifting point of view (from first to third person) so that Dangerfield becomes both observer and observed but, according to Grant, it "relies on rapidly moving, nearly staccato sentence fragments which capture brilliantly the chaotic and fragmented qualities of Dangerfield's world." In a *Times Literary Supplement* review of *That Darcy, That Dancer, That Gentleman* (the third volume in the trilogy that began with *The Destinies of Darcy Dancer, Gentleman*), Mark Sanderson observes that Donleavy's unusual use of language masks the thinness of the novel's plot. "The stylistic tics remain," writes Sanderson, "a fondness for the present continuous; hyphens reserved for double-barreled surnames; each chapter rounded off by a homespun haiku; semi-colons and question marks entirely absent."

Donleavy explains that his use of language is "designed to reflect the way the mind works," says Lask in a *New York Times* review of *Schultz,* a novel about the exploits of an American producer of vulgar plays in London. In the *Paris Review,* Donleavy offers a more detailed explanation: "You're trying to get what you've written on your page into a reader's mind as quickly as possible, and to keep them seeing it. That is why I use the short, truncated telegraphic sentences. They are the most efficient use of language, and I think the brain puts words together the way I do."

Some critics think Donleavy has become a "prisoner of style," says Paul Abelman in the *Spectator,* that "he has never escaped from the prose techniques which he invented for his fine first novel." Abelman believes that "the style of the later books is not really that of *The Ginger Man* at all but simply one that employs superficial aspects of it and neglects the lyrical essence." Unlike *The Ginger Man,* says Abelman, the other books are "monster prose poems founded on the most plodding, leaden metrical foot known to the English language [the spondee—two stressed syllables regularly repeated]." Abelman, though, considers Donleavy "possibly the greatest lyrical humorist to emerge since the war," and adds that he "has that to his credit which few living writers can claim: a modern classic."

Although Donleavy indicates to Thomas Lask in the *New York Times* that he's as "delighted" with *The Ginger Man* as when he first wrote it, he feels that his subsequent books keep *The Ginger Man* alive. Commenting to Remnick that he does not feel *The Ginger Man* represents his "best work," Donleavy states, "When I pick it up and read it now critically as a piece of writing, in technical terms, it doesn't compare to later books." Acknowledging in the *Paris Review* that his subsequent writing has not provided the pleasure that *The Ginger Man* did, Donleavy says: "I don't think you ever have that again. When an author's recognized, all that leaves him, because that's what he's needed to force himself to go through the terrible agony of being unknown and being able to face the world and the fact that it's a giant, vast place where nearly every man is saying: Dear God, hear my tiny voice."

Another point of interest for critics of Donleavy's writing is the effect that leaving the United States for Ireland has had on the author. Grant believes that "Donleavy remains essentially the exile who once wrote of America, 'there it goes, a runaway horse, with no one in control.'" Donleavy recalls in his *Atlantic Monthly* essay, that "each time you arrive anew in America, you find how small you are and how dismally you impress against the giantness and power of this country where you are so obviously, and with millions like yourself, so totally fatally expendable." Grant notes that this vision is often expressed in Donleavy's portrayal of the United States as a nightmare. In *A Fairy Tale of New York,* for instance, the wife of the Brooklyn-born, Bronx-raised, and European-educated Cornelius Christian dies on their way to New York; and without money or friends, Christian is taken advantage of by everyone. "Affection, loathing, nostalgia and fear are the main components of the attitude he brings to bear upon his native place," writes Julian Moynahan in the *Washington Post Book World,* adding that "hidden away in the book for those who can find it is a good deal of personal revelation, a good deal of alembicated and metamorphosed autobiography." As D. Keith Mano states in the *New York Times Book Review,* the book is "about social impotence and despair. Valleys of humiliation, sloughs of despond." The story focuses on the brutality of New York City; and Christian, who lacks the funds to move, sees emigration as the only answer to his liberation. "Yet Donleavy's thunderous, superb humor has the efficacy of grace," says Mano. "It heals and conquers and ratifies." And a *Times Literary Supplement* contributor, who remarks that "few writers know how to enjoy verbal promiscuity like . . . Donleavy," considers that "it is largely because of the confidence of the style, too, that you come out of the welter of failure and misery feeling good—nastiness is inevitably laced with hilarity and sentiment in his telling it."

Moving to Ireland changed his life "utterly," Donleavy says in the *Paris Review,* adding, "It also romanticized the United States for me so that it became a subject for me as a writer." However, in the *Atlantic Monthly,* Donleavy speaks about the indelibility of his American beginnings: "As far away as you may go, or as foreign as your life can ever become, there is something that always stays stained American in you." About living among the Irish, however, Donleavy remarks in a *Publishers Weekly* interview: "Literally, everywhere you go here, they're half nuts. It's very tough to discover real insanity, because the whole race is like that, and, indeed, this is the place to come if you're not right in the head."

John Kelly writes in the *Times Literary Supplement* that "during a disconsolate return to his native America," Donleavy discovered that "Ireland is a state of mind" and his *J. P. Donleavy's Ireland: In All Her Sins and in Some of Her Graces* "attempts a description of that state of mind." Donleavy recreates his own first exposure to the postwar Dublin that, says Kelly, provided the "raw material" for "Donleavy's myth-making imagination." In a Toronto *Globe and Mail* review of the book, Rushton thinks that "Donleavy belongs to the people he describes, and acknowledges their kinship by giving them their full due." As Kevin E. Gallagher comments in the *Los Angeles Times Book Review,* it is "a love story that, I think never ends for anyone who cares, like this, about a place."

"In [Donleavy's] early seventies, he . . . embarked on what is said to be a series of short novels about New York City," reports Jonathan Yardley in *New York Times Book Review*. Among them are 1997's *The Lady Who Liked Clean Rest Rooms: The Chronicle of One of the Strangest Stories Ever to be Rumored About Around New York* and the following year's *Wrong Information Is Being Given Out at Princeton*. Reviews of these books mimic those of Donleavy's earlier body of work. Critics once again reminded readers that the newer works pale in comparison to the author's hallmark, *The Ginger Man*. Furthermore, as Ellen Beardsley says of *The Lady,* Donleavy's writing contains awkward syntax, elements of "absurdity," and "squalid and lusty moments. . . [that] do not come together with any conviction." In a Publishers Weekly assessment that describes *Wrong Information* as "a muddle that's lewd without purpose and mean-spirited without irony," a critic refers to *The Lady, Wrong Information,* and *The Ginger Man* when declaring: "Donleavy . . . seems fixated on odd or disagreeable people whose bizarre behavior puts them on society's margins." A different *Publishers Weekly* review remarks that the author's characteristic "irreverent but heavy-handed satire" is present in *The Lady,* a "short modern-day fairy tale" in which Donleavy "retains his caustic wit and instinct for outrage." A *Library Journal* review is also reminiscent of past criticisms when it proclaims that *The Lady* has "a sophomoric plot."

A writer for the *Economist* summarized *The Lady:* "Short enough to be a long short story, it is the woebegone tale, Social Education in the suburban climes of Scarsdale, of a lonely, broken, middle-aged woman and her obsessions-poverty, death, hygiene and her own loneliness. With its fractured, semi-incoherent prose it reads like the work of a man who has wrung his best ideas out of himself, and is desperately casting around for fictional straws to cling to." Critics judgments' of Donleavy's characterizations in *The Lady* varied. The protagonist, maintains Susan Salter Reynolds of *Los Angeles Times Book Review,* is "a character of enormous force and dignity." According to the *Publishers Weekly* reviewer, "Donleavy paints a wryly compassionate portrait." Nina Sonenberg's *New York Times Book Review* assessment contends that in a "rich, ribald and touching creation. . . . Donleavy proves himself as much the master of a certain New York social set and train corridor as he is of the psyche of a fresh-mouthed 43-year-old Daughter of the Confederacy." In contrast, Yardley maintains that in "a tale that begs for further elaboration" and "attempts at lighthearted irony bog down in ham-handed sarcasm," the author "displays little real sympathy for [the protagonist and]. . . . since no emotion has been expended on [her] . . . one finds it difficult to summon any." Of Donleavy's *Wrong Information Is Being Given Out at Princeton,* however, Eamon Wall in *The Review of Contemporary Fiction* remarks that the author's "greatest achievement ... is his ability to describe, in such fulsome and elegant detail, post-1945 New York City." Paul Di Filippo, reviewing *Wrong Information* in the *San Francisco Chronicle,* also praises it, maintaining that "happily, the author's patented Amerihibernian roguish spiel-choppy yet fluid, sometimes syntactically jarring, alternately coarse and elegant, shifting whimsically from first person to third-rings as strong as ever."

Donleavy has personally adapted several of his novels as plays, including *The Ginger Man.* Though occasionally the theatrical version has been produced before the novel published, Donleavy tells Sim Horwitz in *Back Stage:* "I've never written an original play, one not based on my novels. I find it almost impossible to write a script without a massive body of material to start with." The writer of Donleavy's entry in *Contemporary Dramatists* finds this problematical: "His novels are usually written from the standpoint of one man, an antihero such as Sebastian Dangerfield or George Smith, but in a play the audience is necessarily aware of other characters simply because they are on the stage. If the central character talks too much," the critic continues, "the audience's sympathy may be drawn toward the reactions of other people to him. A single angle of vision, easy to maintain in a novel, is often hard to achieve in the theater, which is a multi-dimensional medium." Interestingly, the same writer feels that *Fairy Tales of New York,* which was staged before the novel version was published, "is much more successful." With a "changed role for the central character, together with the much greater flexibility of form," this play "allows Donleavy's great gifts for caracature, witty dialogue, and buoyant fun to be more evident."

Although Donleavy's novel *The Ginger Man* remains the standard by which the entirety of his work is measured, his writing has generated the full spectrum of critical response. Ken Lawless in a piece for the *Antioch Review* about *The Destinies of Darcy Dancer, Gentleman,* for example, writes that "no literary artist working in English today is better than J. P. Donleavy, and few merit comparison with him." On the other hand, in the *New York Times Book Review,* Geoffrey Wolff reacts to similar critical assessments of Donleavy's work with: "Nonsense. He is an Irish tenor who sets his blarney to short songs that are sometimes as soft as velvet or good stout, sometimes plangent, elliptical and coarse." However, Grant suggests that "at the very least, he represents the example of a writer who goes very much his own way, eschewing both the popular success of the best-sellers and the literary acclaim of the academic establishment. At best, a case can be made for a few of his novels as primary expressions within the black humorist tradition of modern literature. Certainly he is a foremost American exponent of the Kafkaesque vision of the modern world, and his better works strongly express that sense of universal absurdity at which we can only laugh."

"After all my years of struggle, it makes me realize that in my own way I have conquered America, totally silently, totally from underground and from within and that television or being interviewed doesn't matter," Donleavy relates in the *Paris Review.* In his *Saturday Review* essay, "The Author and His Image," Donleavy ponders the complexities of an author's image in its various aspects from obscurity through success, and concludes: "But you know no matter what you do the world will always finally turn its face away. Back into all its own troubled lives. . . . Forgetting what you wanted them to see. Silent with what you wanted them to say. And empty with what you wanted them to feel. Except somewhere you know there will be a voice. At least once asking. Hey what happened to that guy, did he die, you know the one, who wrote that book, can't remember his name but he was famous as hell. That was the author. And that was his image."

BIOGRAPHICAL AND CRITICAL SOURCES:

BOOKS

Authors in the News, Volume 2, Gale (Detroit, MI), 1976.
Casey, Daniel J., and Robert E. Rhodes, editors, *Irish-American Fiction: Essays in Criticisms,* AMS (New York, NY), 1979.
Contemporary Dramatists, sixth edition, St. James Press (Farmington Hills, MI), 1999.
Contemporary Fiction in America and England, 1950-1970, Gale (Detroit, MI), 1976.
Contemporary Literary Criticism, Gale (Detroit, MI), Volume 1, 1973, Volume 4, 1975, Volume 6, 1976, Volume 10, 1979, Volume 45, 1987.
Contemporary Novelists, St. James Press (Farmington Hills, MI), 2001.
Dictionary of Literary Biography, Gale (Detroit, MI), Volume 6: *American Novelists Since World War II,* 1980, Volume 173: *American Novelists Since World War II, Fifth Series,* 1997.
Dillard, R. H. W., George Garrett, and John R. Moore, editors, *The Sounder Few: Essays from the Hollins Critic,* University of Georgia Press (Athens, GA), 1971.
Donleavy, J. P., *A Singular Country,* Ryan (Peterborough, England), 1989, Norton (New York, NY), 1990.
Donleavy, J. P., *J. P. Donleavy's Ireland: In All Her Sins and in Some of Her Graces,* Viking (New York, NY), 1986.
Donleavy, J. P., *The Ginger Man,* Olympia Press (Paris, France), 1955, published with introduction by Arland Ussher, Spearman, 1956, Obolensky, 1958, complete and unexpurgated edition, Delacorte (New York, NY), 1965.
Donleavy, J. P., *The History of the Ginger Man,* Houghton (Boston, MA), 1994.
Encyclopedia of World Biography Supplement, Volume 19, Gale (Farmington Hills, MI), 1999.
Hassan, Ihab, *Radical Innocence: Studies in the Contemporary American Novel,* Princeton University Press (Princeton, NJ), 1961.
Masinton, Charles G., *J. P. Donleavy: The Style of His Sadness and Humor,* Popular Press (Bowling Green, OH), 1975.
Moore, Harry T, editor, *Contemporary American Novelists,* Southern Illinois University Press (Carbondale, IL), 1964.
Podhoretz, Norman, *Doings and Undoings,* Farrar, Straus (New York, NY), 1964.
Sharma, R. K., *Isolation and Protest: A Case Study of J. P. Donleavy's Fiction,* Humanities Press (Atlantic Highlands, NJ), 1983.
Widmer, Kingsley, *The Literary Rebel,* edited by Moore, Southern Illinois University Press (Carbondale, IL), 1965.

PERIODICALS

America, May 3, 1969; May 10, 1980.
Antioch Review, winter, 1978; winter, 1980, p. 122.
Architectural Digest, November, 1986.
Atlantic Monthly, December, 1968; December, 1976; December, 1977; June, 1979.
Back Stage, June 9, 2000, Sim Horwitz, "The Books Read Easy, The Author Doesn't," p. 7.
Books, November, 1987, p. 29.
Bucknell Review, Volume 22, number 2, 1976.
Chicago Tribune, May 25, 1958; May 19, 1985.
Chicago Tribune Book World, October 28, 1979.
Commonweal, August 15, 1958; December 2, 1966; March 7, 1969; September 14, 1990, p. 518.
Contemporary Literature, summer, 1971.
Critique: Studies in Modern Fiction, Volume 9, number 2, 1967; Volume 12, number 3, 1971; Volume 17, number 1, 1975.
Detroit News, October 2, 1983; June 9, 1985.
Economist, November 10, 1973; April 19, 1997.
Eire-Ireland: A Journal of Irish Studies, fall, 1991.
Gentleman's Quarterly, April, 1994, p. 88.
Globe and Mail (Toronto), October 13, 1984; January 17, 1987; April 18, 1987.

Harper's, December, 1977.

Illinois School Journal, Volume 55, 1975.

Irish Literature Supplement, Volume 3, number 2, 1984.

Journal of Irish Literature, Volume 8, 1979.

Library Journal, June 15, 1997; December, 1998.

Listener, March 13, 1969; May 11, 1978; December 13, 1984, p. 30; October 29, 1987, p. 32; November 2, 1989, p. 35; November 1, 1990, p. 34.

Los Angeles Times, October 28, 1983; June 27, 1997.

Los Angeles Times Book Review, October 7, 1979; May 5, 1985, p. 11; November 16, 1986, p. 11; November 13, 1988, p. 7; May 1, 1994, p. 8.

Meanjin Quarterly, autumn, 1970.

Michigan Academician, winter, 1974; summer, 1976.

Midcontinent American Studies Journal, spring, 1967.

Midwest Quarterly, winter, 1977.

Nation, May 24, 1958; December 14, 1963; January 20, 1969.

National Review, October 18, 1971.

New Campus Review, spring, 1969.

New Leader, December 19, 1977.

New Republic, December 14, 1963; March 1, 1969; July 24, 1971; December 15, 1979.

New Statesman, April 17, 1964; February 7, 1969; July 16, 1971; May 12, 1978; March 28, 1980, p. 483; October 14, 1983.

Newsweek, November 11, 1963; March 21, 1966; November 18, 1968; September 15, 1975.

New Yorker, October 25, 1958; May 16, 1964; October 15, 1966; October 8, 1973; December 19, 1977; July 16, 1990.

New York Herald Tribune Book Review, May 11, 1958.

New York Review of Books, January 2, 1969.

New York Times, May 11, 1958; November 16, 1979; April 17, 1987; October 12, 1988.

New York Times Book Review, November 24, 1963; November 7, 1965; December 5, 1965; March 20, 1966; December 29, 1968; September 5, 1971; September 23, 1973; November 6, 1977; October 7, 1979, p. 14; October 26, 1980; October 11, 1983; October 30, 1983; April 28, 1985, p. 24; November 27, 1988, p. 22; March 4, 1990, p. 38; December 2, 1990, p. 72; July 13, 1997.

Observer (London), October 28, 1984, p. 25; July 6, 1986, p. 24; November 8, 1987, p.28; November 4, 1990, p. 61.

Ohio Review, Volume 14, number 1, 1972.

Paris Review, fall, 1975.

Playboy, May, 1994, p. 34.

Publishers Weekly, April 30, 1979; October 31, 1986; April 7, 1997; October 12, 1998.

Punch, October 21, 1987, p. 64.

Review of Contemporary Fiction, summer, 1999, Eamonn Wall, review of *Wrong Information Is Being Given Out at Princeton,* p. 141.

San Francisco Chronicle, August 8, 1999, Paul Di Filippo, "Grief and Carousing in Donleavy's New York," p. 9.

San Francisco Review of Books, December-January, 1979-1980.

Saturday Review, May 10, 1958; November 23, 1963; November 23, 1968; November 12, 1977; January 20, 1979.

Sean O'Casey Review, Volume 1, number 2, 1975.

Spectator, September 22, 1973; May 13, 1978; April 12, 1980; December 8, 1984, p. 33; July 19, 1986, p. 29; November 28, 1987, p. 36.

Studies in Contemporary Satire, Number 1, 1975.

Time, March 18, 1966; December 6, 1968; July 5, 1971; October 29, 1973; September 22, 1975; November 14, 1977; October 15, 1979.

Times (London), October 13, 1983; July 17, 1986, p. 15; October 29, 1987; March 30, 2002, p. 25.

Times Literary Supplement, April 30, 1964; May 6, 1965; May 5, 1967; March 20, 1969; July 23, 1971; September 7, 1973; May 12, 1978; April 4, 1980, p. 382; October 28, 1983, p. 1185; November 16, 1984, p. 1302; December 19, 1986, p. 1433; February 1, 1991, p. 10; June 24, 1994, p. 36; March 21, 1997, p. 23.

Tribune Books (Chicago), January 25, 1987, p. 6; October 2, 1988, p. 7; June 5, 1994, p. 5.

Twentieth Century Literature, January, 1968; July, 1972.

Village Voice, September 17, 1979.

Virginia Quarterly Review, spring, 1987, p. 56.

Voice Literary Supplement, October, 1988, p. 28.

Washington Post, October 30, 1979; February 24, 1985.

Washington Post Book World, September 30, 1973; November 13, 1977; July 9, 1997.

World Literature Today, summer, 1978; summer, 1980, p. 431; spring, 1984.

Yale Review, October, 1966.

ONLINE

J. P. Donleavy Compendium, unofficial author Web site site, http://www.jpdonleavycompendium.org/ (January 9, 2004).*

* * *

DOZOIS, Gardner R(aymond) 1947-

PERSONAL: Born July 23, 1947, in Salem, MA; son of Raymond (a factory worker) and Dorothy (McSwiggin) Dozois.

ADDRESSES: Home and office—526 Spruce St., Philadelphia, PA 19106. *Agent*—Virginia Kidd, Box 278, Milford, PA 18337.

CAREER: Writer and editor, 1966—. *Isaac Asimov's Science Fiction Magazine,* associate editor, 1976-77, editor, 1985—. Editor of *Isaac Asimov Presents* novel line. *Military service:* U.S. Army, 1966-69; served as military journalist.

MEMBER: Science Fiction Writers of America.

AWARDS, HONORS: Nebula Award for best short story, Science Fiction Writers of America, 1983, for "The Peacemaker," and 1984, for "Morning Child"; several Hugo Awards for his work as an editor.

WRITINGS:

(With George Alec Effinger) *Nightmare Blue,* Berkley Publishing (New York, NY), 1975.
The Fiction of James Tiptree, Jr., Algol Press (New York, NY), 1977.
Visible Man, Berkley Publishing (New York, NY), 1977.
Strangers, Berkley Publishing (New York, NY), 1978.
(With Jack Dann) *Slow Dancing through Time,* Ursus Imprints (Kansas City, MO), 1990.
Geodesic Dreams: The Best Short Fiction of Gardner Dozois, St. Martin's Press (New York, NY), 1992.
Strange Days: Fabulous Journeys with Gardner Dozois, edited by Timothy Szczesuil and Ann A. Broomhead, privately published, 2001.

EDITOR; SCIENCE FICTION SHORT STORY ANTHOLOGIES

A Day in the Life, Harper (New York, NY), 1972.
(Contributor) *Chains of the Sea: Three Original Novellas of Science Fiction,* by Geo. Alec Effinger, Gardner R. Dozois [and] Gordon Eklund, T. Nelson (Nashville, TN), 1973.
(With Jack M. Dann) *Future Power,* Random House (New York, NY), 1976.
Another World, Follett, 1977.
Best Science Fiction Stories of the Year, Dutton (New York, NY), 1977-1981.
(With Jack M. Dann) *Aliens!,* Pocket Books (New York, NY), 1980.
(With Jack M. Dann) *Unicorns!,* Ace Books (New York, NY), 1982.
(With Jack M. Dann) *Magicats!,* Ace Books (New York, NY), 1984.
The Year's Best Science Fiction, Bluejay (New York, NY), 1984-85, St. Martin's Press (New York, NY), 1986-2003.
(With Jack M. Dann) *Beastiary!,* Ace Books (New York, NY), 1985.
(With Jack M. Dann) *Mermaids,* Ace Books (New York, NY), 1986.
(With Jack M. Dann) *Sorcerers!,* Ace Books (New York, NY), 1986.
(With Jack M. Dann) *Demons!,* Ace Books (New York, NY), 1987.
The Best From Isaac Asimov's Science Fiction Magazine, Ace Books (New York, NY), 1988.
(With Jack M. Dann) *Dogtails!,* Ace Books (New York, NY), 1988.
Transcendental Tales from Isaac Asimov's Science Fiction Magazine, foreword by Charles Ardai, Donning (Norfolk, VA), 1989.
(With others) *Writing Science Fiction and Fantasy,* St. Martin's Press (New York, NY), 1991.
(Contributor) *Pulphouse Science-Fiction Short Stories,* Pulphouse (Eugene, OR), 1991.
(With Jack M. Dann) *Unicorns II,* Ace Books (New York, NY), 1992.
Modern Classics of Science Fiction, St. Martin's Press (New York, NY), 1992.
(With Jack M. Dann) *Invaders!,* Ace Books (New York, NY), 1993.
(With Jack M. Dann) *Dragons!,* Ace Books (New York, NY), 1993.
(With Mike Resnick) *Future Earths: Under African Skies,* DAW Books (New York, NY), 1993.
Modern Classic Short Novels of Science Fiction, St. Martin's Press (New York, NY), 1993.
Isaac Asimov's War, Ace Books (New York, NY), 1993.
(With Sheila Williams) *Isaac Asimov's Cyberdreams,* Ace Books (New York, NY), 1994.
Killing Me Softly: Erotic Tales of Unearthly Love, HarperPrism (New York, NY), 1995.
(With Sheila Williams) *Isaac Asimov's Skin Deep,* Ace Books (New York, NY), 1995.
(With Sheila Williams) *Isaac Asimov's Ghosts,* Ace Books (New York, NY), 1995.
(With Jack M. Dann) *Angels!,* Ace Books (New York, NY), 1995.
(With Sheila Williams) *Isaac Asimov's Vampires,* Ace Books (New York, NY), 1996.
Modern Classics of Fantasy, St. Martin's Griffin (New York, NY), 1997.

Dying for It: More Erotic Tales of Unearthly Love, HarperPrism (New York, NY), 1997.
(With Sheila Williams) *Isaac Asimov's Christmas,* Ace Books (New York, NY), 1997.
(With Jack M. Dann) *Timegates,* Ace Books (New York, NY), 1997.
(With Sheila Williams) *Isaac Asimov's Moons,* Ace Books (New York, NY), 1997.
The Good Old Stuff: Adventure SF in the Grand Tradition, St. Martin's Griffin (New York, NY), 1998.
(Coeditor) *Roads Not Taken: Tales of Alternate History,* Del Rey/Ballantine (New York, NY), 1998.
(With Sheila Williams) *Isaac Asimov's Camelot,* Ace Books (New York, NY), 1998.
(With Jack M. Dann) *Nanotech,* Ace Books (New York, NY), 1998.
The Good New Stuff: Adventure SF in the Grand Tradition, St. Martin's Griffin (New York, NY), 1999.
(Coeditor) *Isaac Asimov's Valentines,* Ace Books (New York, NY), 1999.
(With Sheila Williams) *Isaac Asimov's Solar System,* Ace Books (New York, NY), 1999.
(With Sheila Williams) *Isaac Asimov's Utopias,* Ace Books (New York, NY), 2000.
The Mammoth Book of Best New Science Fiction: Thirteenth Anuual Collection, Robinson (London, England), 2000.
Explorers: SF Adventures to Far Horizons, St. Martin's Griffin (New York, NY), 2000.
The Furthest Horizon: SF Adventures to the Far Future, St. Martin's Griffin (New York, NY), 2000.
(With Jack M. Dann) *Aliens among Us,* Ace Books (New York, NY), 2000.
(With Jack M. Dann) *Space Soldiers,* Ace Books (New York, NY), 2000.
(With Sheila Williams) *Isaac Asimov's Mother's Day,* Ace Books (New York, NY), 2000.
(With Jack M. Dann) *Armageddons,* Turtleback Books, 2000.
(With Jack M. Dann) *Genometry,* Ace Books (New York, NY), 2001.
(With Sheila Williams) *Isaac Asimov's Father's Day,* Ace Books (New York, NY), 2001.
(With Sheila Williams) *Isaac Asimov's Halloween,* Ace Books (New York, NY), 2001.
Worldmakers: SF Adventures in Terraforming, St. Martin's Griffin (New York, NY), 2001.
Supermen: Tales of the Posthuman Future, St. Martin's Griffin (New York, NY), 2002.
(With Jack M. Dann) *Beyond Flesh,* Ace Books (New York, NY), 2002.

Contributor of science fiction short stories to periodicals, including *Playboy, Omni, Penthouse, Oui, Analog,* and *Isaac Asimov's Science Fiction Magazine.*

SIDELIGHTS: Gardner R. Dozois is perhaps best known for his several years of service at the helm of *Isaac Asimov's Science Fiction Magazine,* as well as for the many anthologies of short science fiction which he has edited, alone and with others. He is also a writer, however, and has won the prestigious Nebula Award for his own short science fiction stories, "The Peacemaker" and "Morning Child." Dozois wrote a novel, *Strangers,* which appeared in 1978. According to a writer for the fourth edition of the *St. James Guide to Science Fiction Writers,* in *Strangers,* "Dozois presents Joseph Faber, a human from Earth with an alien lover named Liraun." The writer goes on to explain that the couple is "shunned by the non-human Cian and the human trade community," and that "in this tremendously sad story, Dozois develops the theme of alienation, and the impossibility of ever knowing another person—hence the title *Strangers.*" The writer concluded: "This very moving novel is one of the forgotten and ignored classics of the 1970s." Many of Dozois's own short science fiction stories appeared in the 1992 collection *Geodesic Dreams.* This volume prompted a *Publishers Weekly* reviewer to label the author and editor "one of the genre's most exciting writers."

Dozois has also won many awards for his work as an editor. Alone and with others such as Jack Dann, Mike Resnick, and Sheila Williams, he has edited collections of similarly-themed stories culled from various issues of *Isaac Asimov's Science Fiction Magazine.* These titles include *Future Earths: Under South American Skies,* which according to a *Publishers Weekly* critic, "transports readers to South American latitudes that are as exotic and exciting as the farthest stars"; and *Modern Classics of Fantasy,* which prompted Roland Green in *Booklist* to announce that "as an introduction to modern American fantasy, this book could hardly be surpassed." Though Dozois possesses many editorial credits of this type, he is even more strongly associated with his yearly collections, *The Year's Best Science Fiction,* which he began editing in 1984. Reviewers of these volumes frequently use superlatives to describe them, and they typically include tales by such science fiction greats as Nancy

Kress, Ian R. MacLeod, Ursula K. LeGuin, Ben Bova, and Robert Silverberg, as well as others by rising stars in the genre. As J. Stephen Bolhafner concluded in the *St. Louis Post-Dispatch,* "There is no one source that will give you as good a feel for the possibilities of the science fiction genre, and how those possibilities were fulfilled last year, than this annual collection."

BIOGRAPHICAL AND CRITICAL SOURCES:

BOOKS

St. James Guide to Science Fiction Writers, 4th edition, St. James Press (Detroit, MI), 1996.

PERIODICALS

Booklist, December 1, 1996, Roland Green, review of *Modern Classics of Fantasy,* p. 643.
Locus, December, 1997, interview with Gardner Dozois; July, 2002, Gary K. Wolfe, "Locus Looks at Books," pp. 17, 19, 58.
Publishers Weekly, September 14, 1992, review of *Geodesic Dreams,* pp. 114-115; July 5, 1993, review of *Future Earths: Under South American Skies,* p. 68.
St. Louis Post-Dispatch, August 31, 1997, J. Stephen Bolhafner, "As Usual, Dozois' Collection Is Best in Genre," p. 5C.*

* * *

DRAPER, Sharon M(ills) 1950-

PERSONAL: Born 1950, in Cleveland, OH; daughter of Victor D. (a hotel manager) and Catherine (a gardener) Mills; married Larry E. Draper (an educator); children: Wendy, Damon, Crystal, Cory. *Ethnicity:* "African American." *Education:* Pepperdine University, B.A.; Miami University (Oxford, OH), M.A. *Hobbies and other interests:* Reading; "I won't read junk; there's no time to waste on poorly written books."

ADDRESSES: Office—P.O. Box 36551, Cincinnati, OH 45236. *Agent*—Janell Agyeman, Marie Brown Associates Inc., 990 Northeast 82nd Terrace, Miami, FL 33138. *E-mail*—SharonDraper@Mindspring.com.

Sharon M. Draper

CAREER: Public speaker, poet, and author. Walnut Hills High School, Cincinnati, OH, English teacher and head of department, 1970—; Mayerson Academy, associate; Duncanson artist-in-residence at Taft Museum.

MEMBER: International Reading Association, American Federation of Teachers, National Board for Professional Teaching Standards (member of board of directors, 1995—), National Council of Teachers of English, Ohio Council of Teachers of English Language Arts, Conference on English Leadership, Delta Kappa Gamma, Phi Delta Kappa, Women's City Club.

AWARDS, HONORS: First prize, *Ebony* Literary Contest, 1991, for short story "One Small Torch"; Coretta Scott King Genesis Award, American Library Association (ALA), Best Book for Young Adults, ALA, Best Books, Children's Book Council (CBC)/Bank Street College, Books for the Teen Age, New York Public Library, and Notable Trade Book in the Field of Social Studies, National Council for the Social Studies, all 1995, for *Tears of a Tiger,* and all 1998, for *Forged by Fire;* named Outstanding High School English Language Arts Educator, Ohio Council of Teachers of English Language Arts, 1995; Midwest regional winner, National Council of Negro Women Excellence in Teaching Award, 1996; Ohio Governor's Educational Leadership Award, 1996; National Teacher of the Year, 1997; ALA Best Book designation, International Reading Association (IRA) Notable Book designation, and Books for the Teen Age designee, New York Public Library, all 2000, all for *Romiette and Julio;* IRA Children's Choice, 2001, and IRA Young-Adult Choice, 2003, both for *Darkness before Dawn;* CBC Notable Social Studies Trade Book, and ALA among ALA Top Ten Sports Books, both 2003, both for *Double Dutch;* Milken Family Foundation National Educator Award; YWCA Career Woman of Achievement award; Dean's Award, Howard University School of Education; Pepperdine University Distinguished Alumnus Award; Marva Collins Education Excellence Award; named Ohio State Department of Education Pioneer in Education. Honorary degrees include D.H.L, College of Mount Saint Joseph, and D.H., Cincinnati State University.

WRITINGS:

FOR CHILDREN

Ziggy and the Black Dinosaurs, Just Us Books (East Orange, NJ), 1994.

Ziggy and the Black Dinosaurs: Lost in the Tunnel of Time, Just Us Books, (East Orange, NJ), 1996.

Ziggy and the Black Dinosaurs: Shadows of Caesar's Creek, Just Us Books (East Orange, NJ), 1997.

FOR YOUNG ADULTS

Tears of a Tiger, Simon & Schuster (New York, NY), 1994.

Forged by Fire, Simon & Schuster (New York, NY), 1997.

Romiette and Julio, Simon & Schuster (New York, NY), 1999.

Jazzimagination, Scholastic (New York, NY), 1999.

Darkness before Dawn, Simon & Schuster (New York, NY), 2001.

Double Dutch, Simon & Schuster, 2002.

The Battle of Jericho, Simon & Schuster, 2003.

OTHER

Teaching from the Heart: Reflections, Encouragement, and Inspiration, Heinemann (Portsmouth, NH), 2000.

Not Quite Burned Out but Crispy around the Edges: Inspiration, Laughter, and Encouragement for Teachers, Heinemann (Portsmouth, NH), 2001.

Also author of *Let the Circle Be Unbroken* (children's poetry), and *Buttered Bones* (poetry for adults). Contributor of poems and short stories to literary magazines; contributor of essay "The Touch of a Teacher" to *What Governors Need to Know about Education,* Center for Policy Research of the National Governor's Association.

ADAPTATIONS: All of Draper's books have been recorded on audiocassette, Recorded Books.com.

SIDELIGHTS: Sharon M. Draper is a teacher and writer with a philosophy that guides her in how she teaches and what she writes. That philosophy is evident in remarks she made about being honored as the 1997 National Teacher of the Year: "It is a wonderful honor, but also an awesome responsibility—to be the spokesperson and advocate for education in America. I was ready for this challenge, however, because I had been preparing for this work my entire life." Reading, teaching, and writing are all connected for Draper, who wanted to be a teacher since childhood. As she once told an interviewer, "I was an avid reader. I read every single book in the elementary school library, all of them. I did not plan to be a writer until much, much later. I tell students all the time that in order to be a good writer it is necessary first to be a good reader. You need some information in your head. Reading is input. Writing is output. You can't write without input."

Born to Victor and Catherine Mills in Cleveland, Ohio, Draper was the eldest of three children raised in a close-knit neighborhood. Her father worked as a hotel manager and her mother as an administrator at the *Cleveland Plain Dealer.* Theirs was a family where education was a given. The question was not "would you attend college, it was where and to study what," Draper explained in her interview. Draper entered Cleveland Public Schools in the 1950s from a home where she had grown up surrounded by books. Her mother read stories, poems, fairytales, and nursery rhymes to Draper and her siblings from the time they were very young. She recalls a teacher who once "gave me O's for outstanding, saying an A wasn't good enough." A fifth-grade teacher gave Draper and her fellow students poetry by Langston Hughes and Robert Frost. They read and loved Shakespeare. "We didn't know we weren't supposed to be able to do that in fifth grade. She gave it to us and we loved it," Draper said. "It was part of making me the teacher I am today."

Draper attended Pepperdine University as a National Merit Scholar, majoring in English. Upon graduation in 1971, she returned to Ohio where she married and assumed a teaching position in the Cincinnati Public Schools where she still works. Her experience teaching public school since 1972 has given her some definite ideas on the reading habits of teens. "I know what kids like—what they will read, and what they won't. Although I have nothing against Charles Dickens, many teenagers would rather gag than read him. Dickens wrote for his contemporaries—young people of a hundred and fifty years ago. American students might need to know about the world of London in the 1860s, but they would much rather read about their own world first. Not only will they read about recognizable experiences with pleasure, but they will also be encouraged to write as well."

According to an essayist in the *St. James Guide to Young Adult Writers,* "Draper's works address the problems African Americans face in a predominantly white society, specifically stereotyping of black males. They also examine the dynamics of African-American families and communities. Her . . . fiction is energetic and intense, as characters become self aware and attain emotional growth. She often creates mystery plots as a means for characters to be introspective and explore their identities. She sets her books in Cincinnati where she lives and teaches, suggesting a familiarity with her characters and community that enhances their realism."

In 1994 Draper began her "Ziggy" series, writing for a young audience about African-American history and folklore. Ziggy and his friends, who call themselves the Black Dinosaurs, begin their adventures in the first book, *Ziggy and the Black Dinosaurs,* In the second book, *Lost in the Tunnel of Time,* Ziggy and friends, on a field trip to the Ohio River, learn about the Underground Railroad and the tunnels the slaves used to escape the South. In the third volume, *Shadows of Caesar's Creek,* Draper makes connections between African Americans and Native Americans.

In 1994 Draper published the young-adult novel *Tears of a Tiger,* a story about Andy Jackson, a black youth who struggles to make sense of the death of his best friend, Robert, in an automobile accident in which Andy was the driver. Andy must live with his friend's last words: "Oh God, please don't let me die like this! Andy!" The two teenagers had been drinking beer with their friends Tyrone and B. J. in celebration of a victory by their high school basketball team. Tyrone and B. J. are able to move past the awful pain caused by the accident: Tyrone finds support from his girlfriend Rhonda, B. J. through religion. Andy, however, is racked with guilt, grief, and pain that does not subside with time.

According to critics, *Tears of a Tiger* shows the difficulties in healing a damaged teenager. Draper also places in her narrative characters who represent institutional attitudes confronting the young black male: In one episode, teachers discuss how Andy's grief cannot be all that serious since he is black. Andy also internalizes ideas about himself that prevent him from realizing his full capabilities; for example, he thinks he cannot be successful academically because he is a basketball player. Merri Monks, writing in *Booklist,* observed that "Andy's perceptions of the racism directed toward young black males—by teachers, guidance counselors, and clerks in shopping malls—will be recognized by African-American YAs."

Critics of *Tears of a Tiger* found that Draper effectively uses dialog to advance the story. Kathy Fritts, writing in the *School Library Journal,* pointed out that "the characters' voices are strong, vivid, and ring true. This moving novel will leave a deep impression." Furthermore, Draper's use of news stories, journal entries, homework assignments, and letters gives the novel an immediacy that adds to its power. Although some critics faulted Draper for a tendency to be preachy, most commented similarly to Monks, who remarked that the work's "characters and their experiences will captivate teen readers." In *Publishers Weekly,* a reviewer concluded that "the combination of raw energy and intense emotions should stimulate readers." Dorothy M. Broderick, critiquing the work in *Voice of Youth Advocates,* wrote: "Suffice to say, not only is Draper an author to watch for, but that this is as compelling a novel as any published in the last two decades." Roger Sutton, writing in the *Bulletin of the Center for Children's Books,* stated that "rather than a tidy summary of suicide symptoms and 'ways to help,' readers instead get a grave portrait of unceasing despair and a larger picture of how young African-American men like Andy get lost in a system that will not trust or reach out to them." *Tears of a Tiger* received several honors, including the Coretta Scott King Genesis Award.

Forged by Fire, the 1997 sequel to *Tears of a Tiger,* has a similar socially relevant focus. Child sexual abuse and drug addiction replace suicide and racism, yet both books reach a tragic finality. Draper wrote *Forged by Fire*'s first chapter as a short story, "One Small Touch," published in *Ebony*. The novel went on to win Draper her second Coretta Scott King Award.

Gerald Nickelby—a minor character in *Tears of a Tiger*—at age three was burned in a fire when left alone by his mother, Monique. After his hospital stay, Gerald goes to live with his Aunt Queen, a loving and supportive woman. Six years later, Monique reenters Gerald's life after Aunt Queen dies. Monique has married Jordan Sparks, the father of Angel, Gerald's new half-sister. Gerald learns that Sparks has sexually abused Angel and through the testimony of the children, Sparks is sent to prison. When Sparks returns six years later, Monique, who indulges too much in drugs, lets him return to family life where he once again attempts to sexually harm Angel.

Tom S. Hurlburt, reviewing *Forged by Fire* in *School Library Journal,* assessed the book's impact this way: "There's no all's-well ending, but readers will have hope for Gerald and Angel, who have survived a number of gut-wrenching ordeals by relying on their constant love and caring for one another." Candace Smith, writing in *Booklist,* concluded that "Draper faces some big issues (abuse, death, drugs) and provides concrete options and a positive African-American role model in Gerald."

In *Darkness before Dawn* Draper tells the story of high schooler Keisha Montgomery, who has just lost her ex-boyfriend to suicide and now must deal with an overly-aggressive track coach. Debbie Carton in *Booklist* believed that "the graduation scene, in which class president Keisha gives the closing speech, is moving and triumphant, showing Draper and her vibrant characters at their best." While Angela J. Reynolds in *School Library Journal* found that "readers may be overwhelmed by the soap-opera feel of this issue-laden world," Odette Cornwall, writing in the *Journal of Adolescent and Adult Literacy,* concluded that "not only did Draper make Keisha real, but she also wove many prominent social issues faced by young adults today into the story line."

Double Dutch concerns a group of eighth graders with serious problems. Delia cannot read and does not want anyone to find out; her friend Randy fears that his father has deserted the family; and the violent Tolliver twins scare their new classmates. "Draper adeptly paints a convincing portrayal of how young people think, act, feel, and interact with one another," Connie Tyrrell Burns commented in *School Library Journal*. A critic for *Kirkus Reviews* found that "Delia and her friends are delightful, and the reader is rooting for them all the way."

Draper once commented: "I feel very blessed that I have had so much success in such a short time. I hope that my books can continue to make a difference in the lives of young people." In a statement posted on her Web site, Draper proclaimed: "I approach the world with the eyes of an artist, the ears of a musician, and the soul of a writer. I see rainbows where others see only rain, and possibilities when others see only problems."

BIOGRAPHICAL AND CRITICAL SOURCES:

BOOKS

Contemporary Black Biography, Gale (Detroit, MI), Volume 16, 1998.
St. James Guide to Young Adult Writers, 2nd edition, St. James Press (Detroit, MI), 1999.

PERIODICALS

American Libraries, June, 1995, "Two New Awards," p. 487.
American Visions, December-January, 1995, p. 39.
Booklist, November 1, 1994, p. 492; April 1, 1995, p. 1416; March 15, 1996, p. 1278; February 15, 1997, pp. 1016-1017; January 1, 2001, review of *Darkness before Dawn,* p. 939.
Bulletin of the Center for Children's Books, January, 1995, p. 164; June, 1997, p. 355.
Children's Book Review Service, February, 1997, p. 82.

Children's Bookwatch, February, 1995, p. 3.
Christian Science Monitor, May 5, 1997, David Holmstrom, "America's Top Teacher Gives Tough Assignments—and Plenty of Support," p. 12.
Ebony, December, 1990, pp. C18-19.
Emergency Librarian, September, 1996, p. 24.
English Journal, January, 1996, p. 87.
Journal of Adolescent and Adult Literacy, April, 2002, Arina Zonnenberg, review of *Romiette and Julio,* p. 660, and Odette Cornwall, review of *Darkness before Dawn,* p. 661.
Kirkus Reviews, December 1, 1996, p. 1735; June 1, 2002, review of *Double Dutch,* p. 804.
Publishers Weekly, October 31, 1994, p. 64; January 15, 1996, p. 463; March 25, 1996, p. 85; December 16, 1996, p. 61; June 17, 2002, review of *Double Dutch,* p. 66.
School Library Journal, February, 1995, p. 112; March, 1995, p. 202; August, 1996, p. 142; March, 1997, p. 184; September, 1999, Jane Halsall, review of *Romiette and Julio,* p. 222; February, 2001, Angela J. Reynolds, review of *Darkness before Dawn,* p. 117; June, 2002, Connie Tyrrell Burns, review of *Double Dutch,* p. 137.
Social Education, April, 1995, p. 215.
USA Today, April 17, 1997, "An 'A' for Creativity: Variety Is on Teacher of the Year's Lesson Plan," p. D4.
Voice of Youth Advocates, February, 1995, p. 338; June, 1997, p. 108.

ONLINE

Ohio Department of Education Web site, http://schoolimprovement.ode.ohio.gov/ (June 5, 1998), "Sharon Draper."
Sharon Draper Web site, http://sharondraper.com/ (November 4, 2003).

*   *   *

DREXLER, Rosalyn 1926-
(Julia Sorel)

PERSONAL: Born November 25, 1926, in New York, New York; daughter of George and Hilda (maiden name, Sherman) Bronznick; married Sherman Drexler, 1946; children: one daughter, one son.

Rosalyn Drexler

ADDRESSES: *Home*—60 Union St., #1S, Newark, NJ 07105-1430. *Agent*—Georges Borchardt, 136 East 57th St., New York, NY 10022 (literary); Helen Harvey Associates, 410 West 24th St., New York, NY 10011 (drama). *E-mail*—wrestlerarm@msn.com.

CAREER: Playwright, novelist, and painter. Worked briefly as a professional wrestler; taught at Writer's Workshop, University of Iowa, 1976-77; taught art at University of Colorado. Has held one-woman art shows at galleries in New York City, Boston, and Provincetown, RI; her work has been included in group shows at Martha-Jackson, Pace Gallery, Washington Gallery of Modern Art, Guggenheim Museum, and Whitney Museum.

MEMBER: New Dramatists, New York Theatre Strategy, Dramatists Guild, PEN, Actors Studio.

AWARDS, HONORS: Obie Awards from *Village Voice,* 1964, for *Home Movies,* 1979, and 1985; MacDowell fellowship, 1965; Rockefeller grant, 1965, 1968, and 1974; humor prize from *Paris Review,* 1966, for short story, "Dear"; Guggenheim fellowship, 1970-71; Emmy Award for writing excellence from Academy of Television Arts and Sciences, 1974, for *The Lily Show.*

WRITINGS:

NOVELS

I Am the Beautiful Stranger, Grossman (New York, NY), 1965.
One or Another, Dutton (New York, NY), 1970.
To Smithereens, New American Library (New York, NY), 1972, published as *Submissions of a Lady Wrestler,* Mayflower (London, England), 1976.
The Cosmopolitan Girl, M. Evans (New York, NY), 1974.
Starborn: The Story of Jenni Love, Simon & Schuster (New York, NY), 1979.
Tomorrow Is Sometimes Temporary When Tomorrow Rolls Around, Simon & Schuster (New York), 1979.
Bad Guy, Dutton (New York, NY), 1982.
Art Does (Not) Exist, Northwestern University Press (Evanston, IL), 1996.
Dear, Applause (New York, NY), 1997.

UNDER PSEUDONYM JULIA SOREL

Dawn: Portrait of a Teenage Runaway, Ballantine (New York, NY), 1976.
Alex: Portrait of a Teenage Prostitute, Ballantine (New York, NY), 1977.
Rocky, Ballantine (New York, NY), 1977.
See How She Runs, Ballantine (New York, NY), 1978.

PLAYS

The Line of Least Existence and Other Plays, introduction by Richard Gilman, (includes *Home Movies* [produced in New York City at Judson Poet's Theatre, 1964], *Hot Buttered Roll* [produced in New York City at New Dramatists Committee, 1966], *The Investigation* [produced in Boston at Theatre Co. of Boston; first produced in New York City at New Dramatists Committee, 1966], *The Bed Was Full* [produced at New Dramatists Committee, 1967], *The Line of Least Existence* [produced at Judson Poets' Theatre, March 15, 1968], and *Softly, and Consider the Nearness* [produced in New York City at St. Luke's Church, 1969]), Random House (New York, NY), 1967.

(With others) *Collision Course* (twelve plays; includes *Skywriting* by Drexler; produced together in New York City at Cafe au Go Go, May 8, 1968), Random House (New York, NY), 1968.
The Investigation [and] *Hot Buttered Roll,* Methuen (London, England), 1969.
Was I Good?, produced by New Dramatists Committee, 1972.
The Ice Queen, produced in Boston at The Proposition, 1973.
She Who Was He, produced in Richmond, Va., at Virginia Commonwealth University, 1974.
Travesty Parade, produced in Los Angeles at Center Theatre Group, 1974.
Vulgar Lives, produced in New York City at Theatre Strategy, 1979.
The Writer's Opera, produced in New York City at TNC, 1979.
Graven Image, produced in New York City, 1980.
Starburn, produced in New York City, 1983.
Room 17-C, produced in Omaha, 1983.
Delicate Feelings, produced in New York City, 1984.
Transients Welcome, Broadway Play Publishing (New York, NY), 1986.
A Matter of Life and Death, produced in New York City, 1986.
What Do You Call It?, produced in New York City, 1986.
The Heart That Eats Itself, produced in New York City, 1987.
The Flood, produced in 1992.

OTHER

Rosalyn Drexler: Intimate Emotions, Grey Art Gallery, New York University (New York, NY), 1986.

Work represented in anthologies, including *The Bold New Women,* Fawcett, 1966; *New American Review,* New American Library, 1969; and *The Off-Off Broadway Book,* 1972. Author of screenplay *Naked Came the Stranger*; of television script *The Lily Show*; and *Cara Pina,* 1992. Contributor of articles and reviews to periodicals, including *Esquire, Village Voice,* and *Mademoiselle.* Film reviewer for *Vogue.*

SIDELIGHTS: Rosalyn Drexler's dramatic work is based in "a reaction against the intellectualism and pretentiousness which surrounded the theatre of the absurd," as Howard McNaughton wrote in *Contempo-*

rary Dramatists. Her own dramatic works display a verbal dexterity and a delight in lampooning the avant garde art world. "Few contemporary playwrights can equal her verbal playfulness, fearless spontaneity, and boundless irreverence," Michael Smith wrote. "Few in fact, share her devotion to pure writing, preferring their language functional, meaningful, or psychologically 'real.'" Jack Kroll commented: "Drexler presents the spectacle of a playwright with a brilliant gift, not only for language, but for making language work on many levels with the ease and excitement of a Cossack riding his horse everywhere but in the saddle." She has garnered three Obie Awards for her dramatic works. Drexler's novels are humorous slapstick romps that critics have compared to both Kafka and the Marx Brothers. In addition to succeeding as a playwright and novelist, Drexler is also a painter, whose art has been shown in New York City venues.

The play *The Line of Least Existence,* which Kroll found to be "about the total dissonance that occurs whenever living creatures find themselves in any sort of relationship," was deemed by him to be evidence of Drexler's "sweet shrewdness that seems to be talking straight to the most hidden part of you. She has the great and necessary gift of fashioning a new, total innocence out of the total corruption that she clearly sees. With lots of laughs." McNaughton noted in *The Line of Least Existence* "an utterly unpretentious playfulness, in which words are discovered and traded just for their phatic values."

Drexler's play *Hot Buttered Roll* features an aging billionaire, a callgirl hired to entertain him, and a female bodyguard. "The play's central image," McNaughton admitted, "is never clearly stated, but seems to be that of (gendered) man as a sort of transplant patient, his facilities being monitored externally, his needs being canvassed through a huge mail-order system." Benedict Nightingale praised how Drexler uses a preoccupation with "sterile hedonism and dead feelings" to create "arresting dramatic terms." Published in England in the same volume with *Hot Buttered Roll* was Drexler's *The Investigation,* which depicts the police interrogation of a juvenile suspected of murder. According to *Contemporary Dramatists,* the detective conducting the interrogation "is so resourceful that his techniques of sadistic attrition become the main theatrical dynamic."

Skywriting, in the words of the same source, contains "only two characters. . . . The unnamed man and woman . . . who are segregated on either side of the stage, argue about the possession of a huge (projected) picture postcard of clouds." The author of the *Contemporary Dramatists* entry went on to conclude that *Skywriting* "is a very clever and economical play, in which the primordial merges with the futuristic."

Drexler's first novel, 1965's *I Am the Beautiful Stranger,* is the "vital, intense 'diary' of one Selma Silver," as Maggie Rennert in *Book Week* put it. Rennert went on to maintain that Selma's story, as a teenager growing up during the 1930s, "is swift, complete, individual, and universal." Speaking of Drexler's novel *One or Another,* Christopher Lehmann-Haupt in the *New York Times* wrote: "Rosalyn Drexler may very well be the first Marx Sister." Lehmann-Haupt described the novel as being filled with "so many sight, sound and word gags, so many sillinesses and surrealistic—not to mention little grinning obscenities—that the reader soon begins to flinch in anticipation of the next verbal skit and to bark with relieved laughter when it works." Kroll contended that Drexler belongs with Donald Barthelme and Thomas Pynchon as representatives of the "new literary voice." He explained: "The new literary voice comes from some odd and perilous psychic area still being charted, some basic metabolic flashpoint where the self struggles to convert its recurrent breakdowns into new holds on life and reality. . . . Drexler is . . . funny, scary, preternaturally aware she is at the exact center where the new sensibility is being put together cell by cell."

Drexler's exuberant style does not always earn critical acclaim. The novel *To Smithereens* fared less well with critics, though undoubtedly the author drew upon her experience as a women's wrestler to write it. Michael Wood praised the humor and intelligence of the novel and noted that the language "has confidence in its capacity to render precisely the perceptions it is supposed to render." But Anatole Broyard wrote that Drexler "seems almost to strain for irrelevancy, to struggle through a strenuous willed-free association in search of a fashionable zaniness." A critic for the *Times Literary Supplement* found that "the strength of Miss Drexler's writing is in the energy of her prose: every joke is cleancut. And yet she refuses to go inside, to go deeper into her characters' psyches. She has a natural eye and ear but her mistake is in assuming that the number of empty gaps, the things *not* said, will indicate, or evoke, the emptiness of the lives she has created." Another of Drexler's novels is *Bad Guy.* This book, according to Dana Sonnenschein and Juliet Byington in *American Women Writers,* is "about a therapist who uses dream interpretation and psychodrama to treat a teenage rapist/murderer whose role models have all been television characters."

In the author's *The Cosmopolitan Girl,* Sara Sanborn in the *New York Times Book Review* noted that Drexler "weaves a seamy web of parodies that covers the situation perfectly," and stated further that the novel "is a send-up and send-off for the New Woman." Sara Blackburn in *Book World* assessed Drexler's work as a novelist: "She's an absolute original who can take all of the ingredients that usually characterize 'serious' fiction . . . and use them with inventiveness, playfulness, and even hilarity. Wonderfully, it works, and the result is admirable not only for its style and wit, but for its lack of pretense, for the respect it grants its reader in not straining beyond its materials, and for what it achieves; art which is also high entertainment."

BIOGRAPHICAL AND CRITICAL SOURCES:

BOOKS

American Women Writers, 2nd edition, St. James Press (Detroit, MI), 1999.
Contemporary Dramatists, 6th edition, St. James Press (Detroit, MI), 1999.
Contemporary Literary Criticism, Gale (Detroit, MI), Volume 2, 1974, Volume 6, 1976.
Drexler, Rosalyn, *Rosalyn Drexler: Intimate Emotions,* Grey Art Gallery, New York University, 1986.

PERIODICALS

American Theatre, December, 1993, p. 58.
Art in America, September, 2000, Michael Duncan, "Rosalyn Drexler at Mitchell Algus and Nicholas Davies."
Books and Bookmen, June, 1967.
Book Week, June 27, 1965, Maggie Rennert, review of *I Am the Beautiful Stranger,* p. 22.
Book World, March 19, 1972, Sara Blackburn, review of *To Smithereens,* p. 5.
Ms., July, 1975.
Nation, August 31, 1970.
New Statesman, February 27, 1969.
Newsweek, April 1, 1968; February 9, 1970; June 1, 1970, Jack Kroll, review of *One or Another,* p. 87; March 10, 1975.
New York Review of Books, August 10, 1972, Michael Wood, review of *To Smithereens,* p. 14.
New York Times, June 5, 1970; February 21, 1972.
New York Times Book Review, June 28, 1970; March 30, 1975, Sara Sanborn, review of *The Cosmopolitan Girl,* p. 4.
Publishers Weekly, February 12, 1996, p. 59.
Times Literary Supplement, September 14, 1973.
Village Voice, March 28, 1968, Michael Smith, review of *The Line of Least Existence,* p. 50.*

* * *

DUNCKER, Patricia 1951-

PERSONAL: Born June 29, 1951, in Kingston, Jamaica; daughter of Noel Aston and Sheila Joan (maiden name, Beer) Duncker. *Ethnicity:* "White—West Indian origins." *Education:* Studied at Bedales School in mid-1960s; Newnham College, Cambridge, B.A., 1973; St. Hugh's College, Oxford, D. Phil. (English and German Romanticism), 1979. *Politics:* "Extreme." *Religion:* Catholic. *Hobbies and other interests:* Traveling in remote, unpopulated landscapes.

ADDRESSES: Office—Department of English and American Studies, University of East Anglia, Norwich, Norfolk, UK NR4 7TJ. *Agent*—Victoria Hobbs, A. M. Heath and Company, Ltd., 79 St. Martin's Lane, London WC2N 4AA, England.

CAREER: University of Wales, Aberystwyth, teacher of writing, literature, and feminist theory, developer of writing courses, 1991-2002; University of East Anglia, professor of prose fiction, teaching writing at undergraduate and postgraduate levels, 2002—.

MEMBER: Society of Authors (British).

AWARDS, HONORS: Dillon's First Fiction Award, and McKitterick Prize, both 1997, for *Hallucinating Foucault.*

WRITINGS:

Sisters and Strangers: An Introduction to Contemporary Feminist Fiction, Blackwell (Cambridge, MA), 1992.

Patricia Duncker

Hallucinating Foucault, Serpent's Tail (New York, NY), 1996.
Monsieur Shoushana's Lemon Trees, Serpent's Tail (New York, NY), 1997.
(With Susan Dodd and Ruth Moon Kempher) *Insides Out: Stories by Susan Dodd, Patricia Duncker and Ruth Moon Kempher,* Kings Estate Press (Florida), 1997.
The Doctor: A Novel, Ecco Press (New York, NY), 1999, published as *James Miranda Barry,* Serpent's Tail (New York, NY), 1999.
Writing on the Wall: Selected Essays, Pandora/Rivers Oram Publishers, 2002.
The Deadly Space Between, Ecco Press/HarperCollins (New York, NY), 2002.
Seven Tales of Sex and Death, Picador (London, England), 2003.

EDITOR

In and Out of Time: Lesbian Feminist Fiction, Onlywomen Press, 1990.

(With Vicky Wilson, and contributor) *Cancer: Through the Eyes of Ten Women,* drawings by Catherine Arthur, Pandora Press (San Francisco, CA), 1996.
(With Janet Thomas) *The Woman Who Loved Cucumbers: Short Stories by Women from Wales,* Honno (Dinas Powys, South Glamorgan, Wales), 2002.
(With Janet Thomas) *Mirror, Mirror,* Honno (Dinas Powys, South Glamorgan, Wales), 2004.

Author's works have been translated into French, German, Italian, Dutch, Greek, and Lithuanian.

WORK IN PROGRESS: "Fourth novel."

SIDELIGHTS: Patricia Duncker, professor of creative writing (prose fiction) at the University of East Anglia, won wide critical acclaim for her first book of fiction in 1996, *Hallucinating Foucault.* Her debut novel reflects Duncker's worldliness; containing elements of the thriller and the romance, it nonetheless eludes easy classification.

Although it bears a postmodern title, *Hallucinating Foucault* does not explicitly deal with French philosopher Michel Foucault's life and work. Instead it recasts the philosopher's main themes—madness, death, sexuality, and crime—in a love story about the passion between writer and reader. As a nameless twenty-two-year-old graduate student conducts his doctoral research, he becomes increasingly enamored with his subject, French novelist Paul Michel. Although he produces "carefully controlled and austere works," Michel leads a "flamboyant, wild and reckless, homosexual lifestyle," according to Jill Adams in *Barcelona Review.* Obsessed with understanding the hidden meanings in Michel's work, the narrator travels to France to meet him and discovers letters revealing the author's own extraliterary interest in Foucault. Adams deemed the book an "easily accessible, titillating, richly symbolic narrative full of intrigue, suspense, and romance." *Bookweb* reviewer Linda M. Castellitto said that "passion is indeed evident in the pages of this book, in which a graduate student travels quite far—both emotionally and geographically—to find writer Paul Michel . . . in order to consummate their literary love affair."

Duncker's second book is a collection of thirteen stories, *Monsieur Shoushana's Lemon Trees.* The book includes the title story plus "The Crew from M6,"

"Aria Nova," "A Woman Alone," and the novella "The Arrival Matters." This collection has been praised by reviewers, who are especially pleased with "The Arrival Matters," the story of the last days of an elderly woman's life and the passing on of her powerful knowledge to a young apprentice. The woman is a member of a group of magicians linked by love and the supernatural. "The Crew from M6" deals with a film crew's taping of life inside a community of intellectual lesbians and the betrayal of the women by a male member of the crew. Other stories are concerned with women and their abusive husbands, lesbian love, and the aspects of power and freedom in relationships.

Pam Barrett of the London *Sunday Times* called the book a "bewitching collection." Dennis Dodge of *Booklist* found it ambiguous at times but called Duncker's prose "spare and clean" and her stories "powerfully evocative." Graham Fraser of the *Review of Contemporary Fiction* commented that some of Duncker's characters serve only to convey a "heavy-handed 'message,'" but he praised "The Arrival Matters," calling it "by far the most engaging" story in the collection. Fraser thought the collection as a whole was "varied and captivating" and that several of the stories exhibit "a wicked sense of sociosexual satire." Barbara Hoffert praised the collection's originality and said the stories are told in a voice that "glints like metal left out in the sun." She thought "The Crew from M6" was "superb." A *Publishers Weekly* contributor found the collection to be "honed by precise, hard and luminous wordcraft."

Like *Hallucinating Foucault,* Duncker's *Monsieur Shoushana's Lemon Trees* is set in sunny France, where Duncker has lived, in addition to Germany, Wales, England, and her childhood home of Jamaica. "As a writer I have no identity that is rooted in a country, no home, no origins," Duncker said, describing her personal perspective on her work in a Serpent's Tail press release titled "Private/Public." "Most of the exiled writers within my tradition sat in foreign towns dreaming of their particular mass of forest, rocks, stones or bricks. Joyce sat in Trieste . . . imagining Dublin. Lawrence went south, to France, to Italy, then sailed away to New Mexico, never forgetting . . . all the grey landscapes of Northern England. . . . I think about all this and I begin smiling."

Duncker's second novel is based on the life of James Miranda Barry, the nineteenth-century colonial doctor, who after his death was revealed to have been a woman. Duncker once told *CA:* "Barry is, for me, a fascinating subject because he embodies so many of my intellectual interests: the disruption of gender, cross-dressing, identity both as masquerade and as deliberate disguise. But there are personal connections too. Barry worked in Jamaica, which is my country of origin. He knew the landscapes I know. And, by chance, he was important for my mother's research work on the free-coloreds and their resistance to further colonial exploitation in the early days after the abolition in 1838. Barry was present during one of the major slave uprisings, the Trelawny rebellion in 1831. He wrote, 'I served under Sir Willoughby Cotton during the Rebellion and the burning of the plantations by the Negroes.' My mother was not especially interested in Barry's gender, but she was in his medical reforms; I am interested in both.

"Barry was an outsider wherever he went. He had a formidable temper. He was a great favorite with the ladies. He fought many duels. He loved uniforms, dressing up and parades. He was very vain concerning his appearance. I have done a good deal of research on the period of Barry's life, especially on gruesome nineteenth-century tropical diseases and medical theories of the time. Barry was a very successful doctor partly because he was a hygiene fetishist and demanded that everything—bodies, floors, linen, nurses—should be scrubbed clean. He used to mutter 'dirty beasts, dirty beasts' at the soldiers.

"This is a narrative about origins, identity and exile but I am not writing a biography. I am inventing the story of James Barry, his public life, her inner life. About which we know nothing."

Published as *The Doctor* in the United States and *James Miranda Barry* elsewhere, the book was widely reviewed for its intriguing subject matter. In an interview with Nicholas Wroe of the *Guardian,* Duncker said she began writing the novel in 1991 but became stalled when she could not decide whether to refer to the main character as "he" or "she." She had also written a short story, published in 1989, based on Barry's life. By 1997, Duncker was ready to resume work on the novel, settling on first- and third-person narration to work around the gender problem. Said Wroe, "The resulting book is an absorbing literary-historical novel that probes with an exuberant intelligence the complex relationship between what things are and what they seem."

In an interview with the *Guardian* writer Raekha Prasad, Duncker said, "I think there are underworlds of gender. There are a lot of people who feel very unhappy in the roles ascribed to them. Writing can expand your notion of what a man or a woman can be." Prasad called the book a "meaty, compulsive novel." Sarah Chinn of the *Advocate* wrote that the novel "shimmers through Barry's life, trying to get at the heart of what it means to live a pretense—one that awards the pretender a status far above what s/he could otherwise expect."

Guardian writer Alex Clark did not write as favorably about the novel; he said the author "presents a confusing and at times willfully obscure piece of picaresque writing." Commenting on the way Barry came to live as a man—it was the idea of his widowed mother and a group of men surrounding her, concocted to ensure that the eleven-year-old girl could go to medical school and live a successful life—Clark said Barry's life was "created by a powerful cartel of other men." He found the book typical of the modern historical novel and the character of Barry somewhat poorly developed where the inner life is concerned. "Duncker writes expressively and with much passion, but too often she appears to be struggling with the burden of her material, and veering wildly between clumsily handled idiom and register . . . and a more considered treatment of her main themes and concerns," Clark commented, even though he added that handling the material would be "a tall order for any writer."

Aisling Foster of the London *Times* also concluded that the novel does not help the reader to know Barry's character in depth. Foster observed that Duncker's thorough research often left too many gaps needing to be filled by imagination, including the uncertainty over the identity of Barry's father. A little too much historical information about the period, Foster thought, made it appear as if "historic backdrops are wheeled on and off." However, Foster stated, "This is an engrossing story, featuring an authentic hero who is satisfyingly stranger than fiction."

Miranda Seymour of the London *Sunday Times* commented that perhaps the novel offers too much about the kitchen maid-turned-performer Alice Jones's career (Jones is Barry's lifelong lover in Duncker's novel). She found no other flaws, however, and called the book "richly atmospheric," with "the murky excitement of a Victorian thriller." Seymour thought Duncker handled historical gaps brilliantly, filling them "with glorious bravado and an imagination of magnificent, focused intensity."

John Vernon, writing for the *New York Times Book Review,* found the Jones character somewhat out of place. He wrote, "From her first appearance, Alice either stretches our belief or makes us squirm. In a crucial oversight, her language is bleached of any historical markers, of any class or regional dialect." Vernon also pointed out that the novel's ending—in which Jones is interviewed by a journalist seeking the truth about Barry's gender after his death—might be enjoyed by some readers as "immensely playful and entertaining." However, he wrote, "Others will feel robbed, will think that this very talented writer is trying to have it both ways—and will lament so belated a deconstruction of her own fondness for the trappings of romance." All in all, though, Vernon concluded that *The Doctor* "is written with spirit and a good heart. Its historical details are rich and authentic, and its tone combines sensory immediacy and ironic detachment."

Duncker published her third novel, *The Deadly Space Between,* in 2002. She once told *CA*: "*The Deadly Space Between* is a psychological thriller. I love thrillers. I love the plots, the desperate characters, the spies, the cops or the detectives, amateur and professional, the settings, fast-paced psycho-narratives, chases in any form of vehicle, threats, sexual menace, blood everywhere, secrets, twists, revelations. But . . . there is one element in the thriller that has always irritated and disappointed me. The motive. I am always let down by the motive. I can never believe that this huge elaborate artifice was generated by mere jealousy, greed, passion, revenge. So I decided to write a claustrophobic, horrifying tale, with a tight cast of characters, sexual scenes for adults, a thrilling chase, and all the trimmings. But the tale would hinge entirely on the complexity and ambiguity of the motive. For me, the greatest psychological thriller of all time is Sophocles' *Oedipus Rex*. This is the story of a man who murders his father and marries his mother in the fulfillment of a prophecy. But he is unaware of their identities. Oedipus is both the criminal and the detective, and, best of all, There Is No Motive. He didn't even know he'd done it.

"So, my third novel is an Oedipal thriller which attempts to answer the following questions. The first question is raised by Mary Wollstonecraft, who doesn't see the point of the story [*Oedipus Rex*]. 'What moral lesson can be drawn from the story of Oedipus, the favourite subject of such a number of tragedies?' she wrote. 'The gods impel him on, and, led imperiously by blind fate, though perfectly innocent, he is fearfully punished, with all his hapless race, for a crime in which his will had no part.' And the other question is posed by Roland Barthes. Barthes adores the figure of the Father in Freud's theoretical writings. 'Death of the Father,' he pointed out, 'would deprive literature of many of its pleasures. If there is no longer a Father, why tell stories? Doesn't every narrative lead back to Oedipus?'

"Freud's case histories are fascinating because they are psycho-thrillers. Who did what to whom? When? How? Why? In Sophocles' *Oedipus,* the Father gets bumped off early on, offstage. And in Freud's versions of the Oedipus drama, the Father is unchanging, a forbidding monolithic black slab of patriarchy. What about making the Father the centre of the action? And so I created Roehm, who is the stranger in my story, the man with no past, the seductive listener, who leaves no trace.

"My fiction comes out of my reading and my deepest intellectual concerns. But I like books to have a strong sense of place. So I do a lot of traveling research. I drove the route my characters take over the mountain. I spent weeks in the mountains of Chamonix, where key scenes in the novel take place. I interviewed the police, who thought I was barking mad and said so. I wandered the snow peaks, holding my breath in fear on the edge of the ice precipice. You can write convincingly about fear if you too have been afraid, and one comment in the book is absolutely real. The guide ropes up his party, ready to traverse the first razor edge of ice and says, 'If you must fall off, fall to the right. It's only 400 feet. If you fall off to the left it's 7,000 feet down.'"

The Deadly Space Between is the story of a precocious eighteen-year-old boy, Toby Hawk, and his mother, Isobel, a painter who bore her son at age fifteen by a married man no longer in their lives. Mother and son are isolated and close, with a relationship that is sometimes incestuous. Iso's Aunt Luce and her lesbian lover, Liberty, play a somewhat stabilizing role in their lives. When "Iso" starts dating the mysterious hulking Roehm, Toby is at first jealous but later becomes obsessed with the man, who shows sexual favor toward the boy as well as his mother. (The book takes its title from Melville's phrase about transgression of "the deadly space between.") Roehm is powerful and intense, with an icy touch and an elusive existence. His relationship with Iso threatens to break mother and son apart, but near the end of the story they reunite to save themselves from him in a terrifying glacial Alpine setting. In the end, they discover Roehm's incredible secret after Iso confesses to his murder. Throughout the book, Duncker makes reference to Mary Shelley's *Frankenstein,* Freud's theories about sexuality, *Oedipus Rex,* Faust, the composer Weber, and other classics.

Some reviewers enjoyed these parallels; others thought them too obtrusive. William Skidelsky of the *Times Literary Supplement* said they "have a bamboozling, rather than elucidating, effect." He said *The Deadly Space Between* is "never less than engaging to read, but is not entirely convincing as a work of literature." Sinclair McKay of the London *Daily Telegraph* commented that the tale combines all these elements "with the logic of a bad dream." Yet, he also called the story "rich in atmosphere" and concluded, "It's overwrought, but then what good spooky folk tale isn't?"

Phil Baker of the London *Sunday Times* called *The Deadly Space Between* "farcically bad." He pointed out that a boy who had Toby's strange relationship with his mother "would be too disturbed to write the cheerily reasonable narrative" attributed to the teen. Baker said the book suffers from "thematic over-obviousness and . . . bad allegory." A contributor to *Kirkus Reviews* described the book as "overwrought in content, gracefully subdued in tone: an entertainment that falls short of its apparently lofty goals."

Jessica Mann of the London *Sunday Telegraph* had a much more favorable view of the *The Deadly Space Between.* Remarking that Duncker "writes beautifully with a flamboyant immediacy," Mann found Duncker's plot "complex, her characters' motives persuasively ambiguous" and said the relationship between Toby and Roehm has "the requisite appurtenances of a creepy horror story." Even so, Mann said she would not be as haunted by *The Deadly Space Between* as she was by the classic Frankenstein and Count Dracula horror stories. A *Publishers Weekly* contributor found the novel "erotically charged and, finally, enigmatic" and "grotesquely repellant yet sinuously compelling." The reviewer pointed out, however, that one source

Duncker failed to acknowledge was Henry James' *The Turn of the Screw.*

In the interview with Wroe of the *Guardian,* Duncker said her aunt, the poet Patricia Beer, also her namesake, had a tremendous influence on her as a writer, even though the two women had a stormy personal relationship (Beer died in 1999). Duncker said, "If you look, a lot of writers do seem to have another writer somewhere in their lives. She was the writer in mine. . . . She was the first person to take me seriously. She told me, very politely, what was good and what was nonsense. . . . I read everything she wrote and she has shaped my mind. I hugely admire her ruthless imagination." Duncker also said her writing has always been fueled by a voracious appetite for reading. And Beer passed along to her niece the high standards by which a writer should work, revising and perfecting each piece, never succumbing to sloppiness. This perfectionism has resulted in Duncker's having an unpublished novel and many unpublished poems stored away for future work. Yet the joy of publishing, for Duncker, is to please her readers. "I know how thrilling it is for me to read a book that excites me," she said, "so to think I might have given that pleasure to someone else is wonderful."

BIOGRAPHICAL AND CRITICAL SOURCES:

BOOKS

Writers Directory, 16th edition, edited by Miranda H. Ferrara, St. James Press (Detroit, MI), 2001.

PERIODICALS

Advocate, April 25, 2000, Sarah Chinn, review of *The Doctor,* p. 82.
Booklist, February 1, 1997, review of *Hallucinating Foucault,* p. 925; March 15, 1998, Dennis Dodge, review of *Monsieur Shoushana's Lemon Trees,* p. 1200.
Book World, February 9, 1997, review of *Hallucinating Foucault,* p. 8.
Choice, May, 1997, review of *Hallucinating Foucault,* p. 1495.
Daily Telegraph (London, England), March 23, 2002, Sinclair McKay, "Crying Out for Mummy: An Oedipal Ghost Story Satisfies Sinclair McKay," review of *The Deadly Space Between,* p. NA.
Guardian (London, England), May 31, 1999, Raekha Prasad, "Women: Prisoner of Gender," author interview, p. 8; July 10, 1999, Alex Clark, "Is There a Doctor in This Woman?," review of *James Miranda Barry,* p. 10; August 12, 2000, Nicholas Wroe, "A Shadow at My Shoulder," author interview.
Independent, May 29, 1999, Julie Wheelwright, "Transit and Transgression," author interview, p. S12.
Kirkus Reviews, March 15, 1998, review of *Monsieur Shoushana's Lemon Trees,* p. 355; May 15, 2002, review of *The Deadly Space Between,* p. 682.
Library Journal, December, 1996, review of *Hallucinating Foucault,* p. 142; March 15, 1998, Barbara Hoffert, review of *Monsieur Shoushana's Lemon Trees,* p. 98.
London Review of Books, September 18, 1997, review of *Monsieur Shoushana's Lemon Trees,* p. 14.
New Statesman & Society, March 1, 1996, review of *Hallucinating Foucault,* p. 37.
New Yorker, April 14, 1997, review of *Hallucinating Foucault,* p. 85.
New York Times Book Review, February 16, 1997, review of *Hallucinating Foucault,* p. 15; December 13, 1998, review of *Hallucinating Foucault,* p. 36; March 12, 2000, John Vernon, "Adventures in Cross-Dressing: A Fictionalized Life of James Barry: Doctor, Duelist, Woman," review of *The Doctor,* p. 38.
Observer (London, England), July 20, 1997, review of *Hallucinating Foucault,* p. 17; December 30, 2001, review of *The Deadly Space Between,* p. 14.
Publishers Weekly, October 21, 1996, review of *Hallucinating Foucault,* p. 68; February 16, 1998, review of *Monsieur Shoushana's Lemon Trees,* p. 204; May 6, 2002, review of *The Deadly Space Between,* p. 32.
Review of Contemporary Fiction, fall, 1998, Graham Fraser, review of *Monsieur Shoushana's Lemon Trees,* p. 255.
San Francisco Review, January, 1997, review of *Hallucinating Foucault,* p. 31.
Sewanee Review, October, 1998, review of *Hallucinating Foucault,* p. 675.
Signs: Journal of Women in Culture and Society, spring, 1994, review of *Sisters and Strangers: An Introduction to Contemporary Feminist Fiction,* p. 806.
Spectator, November 16, 1996, review of *Hallucinating Foucault,* p. 43; July 17, 1999, Kate Hubbard, review of *James Miranda Barry* (*The Doctor*), p. 31.

Sunday Telegraph (London, England), March 24, 2002, Jessica Mann, "Son, Lover and Cook," review of *The Deadly Space Between*, p. NA.
Sunday Times (London, England), August 16, 1998, Pam Barrett, review of *Monsieur Shoushana's Lemon Trees*, p. 14; June 13, 1999, Miranda Seymour, "Girls Will Be Boys," review of *James Miranda Barry*, p. 13; March 31, 2002, Phil Baker, "Gothic Horrors That Refuse to Die," review of *The Deadly Space Between*, p. 44.
Time, March 3, 1997, review of *Hallucinating Foucault*, p. 76.
Times (London, England), June 17, 1999, Aisling Foster, "Novel Doctoring of the Truth," review of *James Miranda Barry*, p. 43.
Times Literary Supplement, March 22, 1996, review of *Hallucinating Foucault*, p. 22; August 29, 1997, review of *Monsieur Shoushana's Lemon Trees*, p. 24; June 11, 1999, Juliet Fleming, review of *James Miranda Barry* (*The Doctor*), p. 24; March 29, 2002, William Skidelsky, "Sinister Affections," review of *The Deadly Space Between*, p. 23.
Tribune Books (Chicago, IL), March 2, 1997, review of *Hallucinating Foucault*, p. 3.
Village Voice, February 11, 1997, review of *Hallucinating Foucault*, p. 53.

ONLINE

American Booksellers Association Bookweb, http://www.bookweb.org/ (November 18, 1997), Linda M. Castellitto, review of *Hallucinating Foucault*.
Barcelona Review, http://www.barcelonareview.com/ (November 18, 1997), Jill Adams, review of *Hallucinating Foucault*.
Serpent's Tail, http://www.serpentstail.com/ (November 18, 1997), "Private/Public," interview with Patricia Duncker.

* * *

DURHAM, Walter T. 1924-

PERSONAL: Born October 7, 1924, in Nashville, TN; son of George Franklin and Celeste (McAlister) Durham; married Anna Armstrong Coile, April 23, 1949; children: Anna Durham Windrow, Robert Coile, James Franklin, Elizabeth Durham Lindsey. *Ethnicity:* "Caucasian; English, Scottish." *Education:* Attended University of Wisconsin—Madison, 1943-44; Vanderbilt University, B.A., 1948, M.A., 1955. *Politics:* Democrat. *Religion:* United Methodist. *Hobbies and other interests:* Travel, politics, music.

ADDRESSES: Home and office—1010 Durham Dr., Gallatin, TN 37066. *E-mail*—WTDurham@bellsouth.net.

CAREER: Durham Manufacturing Co., Inc., Gallatin, TN, partner, 1948-73, chair, 1973-98. State of Tennessee, appointed state historian, 2002. Gallatin Aluminum Products Co., Inc., cofounder and treasurer, 1958-63, president, 1963-73; First and Peoples National Bank, chair of board of directors, 1964-92; First American National Bank, chair of advisory board, 1992-96. Tennessee State Industrial Development Commission, member, 1963-72. Tennessee Library Advisory Council, chair, 1991-93; White House Conference on Library and Information Services, member of task force, 1991—. Tennessee American Revolution Bicentennial Commission, member, 1973-75; Tennessee Heritage Alliance, founding president, 1982; Tennessee Historical Records Advisory Board, member, 1993-96; Tennessee Historical Commission, past chair; Cumberland Museum and Science Center, member of board of directors; Hermitage, member of board of trustees; APTA Endowment Trust, member of board of trustees. Gallatin Chamber of Commerce, past president. Tennessee Annual Conference of the United Methodist Church, past chair of board of trustees; Tennessee Conference Methodist Youth Fellowship, president, 1939-40. *Military service:* U.S. Army Air Forces, 1943-46; served in Italy and Africa; became sergeant.

MEMBER: Architectural Aluminum Manufacturers Association (past divisional vice president and member of board of directors), Tennessee Building Material Association (vice president, 1967), Tennessee Historical Society (president, 1973-75), Sumner County Historical Society (past president), Phi Beta Kappa, Pi Sigma Alpha, Sigma Nu, Gallatin Lions Club (past president), Vanderbilt Alumni Association (past member of board of directors), Friends of Vanderbilt Library (member of board of directors; past president), Heard Library Society.

AWARDS, HONORS: Distinguished Service Award, Gallatin Jaycees, 1968; Award of Merit, American Association for State and Local History, 1973; Distinguished Public Service Award, Volunteer State Community College, 1974; Tennessee History Book Award, Tennessee Historical Commission and Tennessee Library Association, 1991; Library Leadership Award, Vanderbilt University, 1994; John H. Thweatt Archival Advancement Award, Tennessee Archivists Society, 2002.

WRITINGS:

The Great Leap Westward: A History of Sumner County, Tennessee, from Its Beginnings to 1805, Sumner County Library Board (Gallatin, TN), 1969.

Old Sumner: A History of Sumner County, Tennessee, from 1805 to 1861, Sumner County Library Board (Gallatin, TN), 1972.

A College for This Community, Sumner County Library Board (Gallatin, TN), 1974.

Daniel Smith, Frontier Statesman, Sumner County Library Board (Gallatin, TN), 1976.

The Building Supply Dealer in Tennessee: A History of the Tennessee Building Material Association, 1925-1976, Tennessee Building Material Association (Nashville, TN), 1976.

James Winchester, Tennessee Pioneer, Sumner County Library Board (Gallatin, TN), 1979.

Rebellion Revisited: A History of Sumner County, Tennessee, from 1861 to 1870, Sumner County Museum Association (Gallatin, TN), 1982.

Nashville, the Occupied City: The First Seventeen Months—February 16, 1862 to June 30, 1863, Tennessee Historical Society (Nashville, TN), 1985.

(With James W. Thomas) *A Pictorial History of Sumner County, Tennessee, 1796-1986,* Sumner County Historical Society (Gallatin, TN), 1986.

Reluctant Partners: Nashville and the Union, July 1, 1863 to June 30, 1865, Tennessee Historical Society (Nashville, TN), 1987.

Before Tennessee: The Southwest Territory, 1790-1796, Rocky Mount Historical Association (Piney Flats, TN), 1990.

Wynnewood, Bledsoe's Lick, Castalian Springs, Tennessee, Bledsoe's Lick Historical Association (Castalian Springs, TN), 1994.

(With James W. Thomas and John F. Creasy) *A Celebration of Houses Built before 1900 in Sumner County, Tennessee,* Sumner County Historical Society (Gallatin, TN), 1996.

Volunteer Forty-Niners: Tennessee and the California Gold Rush, Vanderbilt University Press (Nashville, TN), 1997.

The Life of William Trousdale, Soldier, Statesman, Diplomat, 1790-1872, Clark Chapter, United Daughters of the Confederacy (Gallatin, TN), 2001.

(With Glenda Milliken) *Gallatin 200: A Time Line History Celebrating the Bicentennial of Gallatin, Tennessee,* Hillsboro Press (Franklin, TN), 2002.

Josephus Conn Guild and Rose Mont: Politics and Plantation in Nineteenth-Century Tennessee, Hillsboro Press (Franklin, TN), 2003.

Contributor to books, including *Tennessee State of the Nation,* 2nd edition, edited by Larry H. Whiteaker and W. Calvin Dickinson, American Heritage Custom Publishing (New York, NY), 1995. Contributor to history journals, including *Tennessee Historical Quarterly, Journal of Confederate History, Journal of East Tennessee History, Middle Tennessee Genealogy, Confederate Veteran,* and *Cumberland.*

WORK IN PROGRESS: A biography of a colorful early Tennessee member of Congress.

SIDELIGHTS: Walter T. Durham once told *CA:* "I am motivated by a personal interest in bringing relatively obscure historical experiences to a readership who may find them helpful in preparing for the future by better understanding the past. I have been inspired by the glories and the baseness of the westward movement in American history and challenged by the prospect of looking at the people who gave it those characteristics. It may be the old question of reconciling our less than noble human qualities with our propensity to hitch our wagons to a star."

* * *

DURRETT, Deanne 1940-

PERSONAL: Born February 3, 1940, in Oklahoma City, OK; daughter of David M. (a farmer) and June (a homemaker; maiden name, Capps) Grantham; married Franklin Dan Durrett (an engineer), August 28, 1959; children: Timothy Dan, Joy Lynn. *Ethnicity:* "American." *Education:* Attended Southwestern State College, 1958-59. *Politics:* Republican. *Religion:*

Deanne Durrett

Christian. *Hobbies and other interests:* Pets; collecting hats, Beanie and Buddy Bears, and Precious Moments figurines; dancing; playing board games and cards.

ADDRESSES: *Agent*—c/o Author Mail, Kidhaven Press, 10911 Technology Place, San Diego, CA 92127. *E-mail*—deannedurrett@deannedurrett.com.

CAREER: Writer, wife, and mother.

MEMBER: Society of Children's Book Writers and Illustrators (regional advisor, 1989-94).

AWARDS, HONORS: Nonfiction Honor List selection, *Voice of Youth Advocates*, 1999, for *Unsung Heroes of World War II: The Story of the Navajo Code Talkers;* Books for the Teen Age selection, New York Public Library, 1999, for *Healers*.

WRITINGS:

My New Sister, the Bully, Abingdon (Nashville, TN), 1985.
Organ Transplants, Lucent Books (San Diego, CA), 1993.
Jim Henson ("The Importance of" series), Greenhaven Press (San Diego, CA), 1994, revised edition, Kidhaven Press (San Diego, CA), 2002.
Angels ("Opposing Viewpoints" series), Greenhaven Press (San Diego, CA), 1996.
Norman Rockwell ("The Importance of" series), Greenhaven Press (San Diego, CA), 1996.
Healers ("American Indian Lives" series), Facts on File (New York, NY), 1997.
Unsung Heroes of World War II: The Story of the Navajo Code Talkers, Facts on File (New York, NY), 1998.
Dominique Moceanu, Lucent Books (San Diego, CA), 1999.
The Abortion Conflict: A Pro/Con Issue, Enslow Publishers (Berkeley Heights, NJ), 1999.
Teen Privacy Rights: A Hot Issue, Enslow Publishers (Berkeley Heights, NJ), 2001.
Jonas Salk, Kidhaven Press (San Diego, CA), 2002.
Jim Henson, Kidhaven Press (San Diego, CA), 2002.
George W. Bush, Kidhaven Press (San Diego, CA), 2003.
Alexander Graham Bell, Kidhaven Press (San Diego, CA), 2003.
Arizona ("Seeds of a Nation" series), Kidhaven Press (San Diego, CA), 2003.
Oklahoma ("Seeds of a Nation" series), Kidhaven Press (San Diego, CA), 2003.
The 1900s, Kidhaven Press (San Diego, CA), 2004.
The 1910s, Kidhaven Press (San Diego, CA), 2004.
The 1950s, Kidhaven Press (San Diego, CA), 2004.
Rattlesnakes, Kidhaven Press (San Diego, CA), 2004.

Contributor to *Highlights for Children*.

WORK IN PROGRESS: *Right to Vote,* part of Facts on File's "American Rights" series.

SIDELIGHTS: Deanne Durrett fell into writing by accident. When, in 1970, her husband joined a partnership to buy a weekly newspaper, Durrett began writing a humor column for the paper. Though the partnership dissolved, Durrett continued writing her humor column. She recalled on her Web site, "It was love at first sight! I loved seeing myself in print and then I had a dream!" While writing that column, she honed her craft and began writing children's stories, the first of which she sold to *Highlights for Children* in 1972. "When I began following my dream, I was told that I would need to write a million words before I could be published. So, I started on my million words. . . . I wanted to be published and I was willing to do whatever it took," she continued. "Before too many years passed, I was selling almost everything I wrote." Her writings include twenty books, mostly nonfiction titles, including biographies, overviews of states, and books on controversial topics in the news.

After writing the middle-grade novel *My New Sister, the Bully,* Durrett focused her attention on magazines and newspaper articles for awhile. She then turned to nonfiction, making her debut almost ten yeas later with *Organ Transplants.* "I agreed to write the book because I found the subject interesting, but I did not know anything about organ transplants," she recalled on her Web site, and though the research was painstaking, Durrett was propelled forward by her fascination with the subject and the encouragement of her critique group. This 1993 book launched her career as a nonfiction author, and she has produced as steady stream of nonfiction works since that debut. Although she only attended college for one year, she continued her education by taking college-writing courses and participating in a critique group. Every new book leads her to new knowledge about the subject under study and the writing process. As she shared with *CA,* she likes to think of this as a personal university of never-ending learning.

Art had been a favorite subject of Durrett while she was in school, so she took particular pleasure in writing biographies of two creative Americans, artist Norman Rockwell and puppeteer Jim Henson. Using many quotations of Rockwell, Durrett chronicles his life and artwork in *Norman Rockwell.* About the very popular Muppets creator, *Jim Henson* originally was geared for readers aged twelve and older, while the 2002 revised publication was meant for third- and fourth-grade readers. "When I started writing about Jim Henson, I had seen Kermit and Cookie Monster, but I had never seen the man who created them," Durrett recalled on her Web site. "As I worked, I developed a deep admiration for the man Jim Henson was. He had a dream and he followed it. He believed that learning should be fun. He also believed in family entertainment that reached all ages."

Durrett, who has written several books on the Southwest and Native Americans, has a personal connection to the region. Her great-grandfather settled in Indian Territory in the late 1800s and lived with the Comanches for nearly two decades. As she explained on her Web site, "They adopted him into the tribe, and he established a friendship with the Comanches that lasted long after Oklahoma gained statehood." Born and raised in Oklahoma, Durrett hunted arrow heads in the family's cotton fields. In addition to writing overviews about Arizona and Oklahoma for the "Seeds of a Nation" series, Durrett profiles Native Americans in two collective biographies, *Healers* and *Unsung Heroes of World War II: The Story of the Navajo Code Talkers.* In *Healers,* which Carrie Eldridge dubbed "excellent" in *Voice of Youth Advocates,* Durrett introduces readers to a dozen Native-American men and women who are healers. Some of the individuals the author discusses practice traditional Native-American healing while others, including nurses, a medical school professor, and one of the first Native Americans to earn an M.D., practice modern medicine. In the process, she demonstrates that contemporary and native medicine have long grown up side by side, and provides some "gripping examples" of this situation, noted Christine Hepperman in *Horn Book Guide.*

Similarly, in the award-winning title *Unsung Heroes of World War II,* Durrett publicizes the heroic though little-known efforts of a group of Navajos who as U.S. Marines developed an unbreakable combat code that was instrumental in defeating the Japanese forces in the Pacific theater during World War II. Because the information surrounding this program was finally declassified in 1969, Durrett was able to trace the activities of the Code Talkers from the creation of the program to the time of declassification in her "well-written text," to quote Eldon Younce of *School Library Journal. Booklist*'s Roger Leslie also praised the work, judging it "a worthwhile acquisition for both its military and cultural value." This portrayal of an unusual part of American history inspired the creation of the motion picture *Windtalker,* the story of a Marine who is assigned to protect a Code Talker, with orders to shoot him if he should be captured.

Among Durrett's other individual biographies are those of gymnast Dominique Moceanu, polio vaccine creator Jonas Salk, inventor Alexander Graham Bell, and U.S.

President George W. Bush. While the subjects of her collective biographies and these "more famous" people might seem to have little in common, they are all people who have achieved great success in their lives. As she explained on her Web site, it is the personal qualities that allow them to do great things that interest Durrett: "I want to know about people . . . the ones who made great accomplishments and those who did little things that mean a lot."

In addition to biographies, Durrett has penned books about the states of Arizona and her home state of Oklahoma, and overviews of such contentious issues as teen privacy rights and abortion. She approaches each new project with enthusiasm. "I never know what the day will bring or who will enrich my life," she once told *CA*. "Maybe I will unearth a gold nugget of information everyone else overlooked. Perhaps it will add the perfect touch to my chapter or lead to the mother lode of another idea for a book. One thing is for sure, something will excite me. I love discovery and sharing the adventure with my readers." She concluded, "I love to write! Fiction is pure pleasure but nonfiction is discovery!"

BIOGRAPHICAL AND CRITICAL SOURCES:

PERIODICALS

Booklist, November 1, 1998, Roger Leslie, review of *Unsung Heroes of World War II: The Story of the Navajo Code Talkers,* p. 481; January 1, 2001, Gillian Engberg, review of *The Abortion Conflict: A Pro/Con Issue,* p. 934; November 1, 2002, Francisca Goldsmith, review of *Jim Henson* and *Jonas Salk,* pp. 486-487.

Book Report, September-October, 1997, Annette Thibodeaux, review of *Norman Rockwell,* p. 48.

Horn Book Guide, fall, 1993, review of *Organ Transplants,* p. 352; spring, 1995, review of *Jim Henson,* p. 148; spring, 1997, Anne Deifendeifer, review of *Norman Rockwell,* p. 137; fall, 1997, Christine Hepperman, review of *Healers,* pp. 398-399; spring, 2001, Maeve Visser Knoth, review of *The Abortion Conflict,* p. 96; fall, 2001, Mary R. Holt, review of *Teen Privacy Rights: A Hot Issue,* p. 335.

School Library Journal, May, 1996, p. 138; March, 1997, Pat Katka, review of *Norman Rockwell,* p. 199; January, 1999, Eldon Younce, review of *Unsung Heroes of World War II,* p. 138; August, 1999, Laura Glaser, review of *Dominique Moceanu,* p. 168; June, 2001, Lisa Denton, review of *Teen Privacy Rights,* p. 168; October, 2002, Shauna Yusko, review of *Jonas Salk,* p. 182; April, 2003, Kate Kohlbeck, review of *Alexander Graham Bell,* p. 179.

Seventeen, June, 2003, Seth Mnookin, "Somebody's Watching You," p. 152.

Voice of Youth Advocates, August, 1997, Carrie Eldridge, review of *Healers,* pp. 200-201; August, 1999, review of *Unsung Heroes of World War II,* p. 162.

ONLINE

Deanne Durrett Home Page, http://www.deannedurrett.com/ (October 30, 2002).

E

EKMAN, Kerstin (Lillemor) 1933-

PERSONAL: Born August 27, 1933, in Risinge, Sweden; father, a manufacturer. *Education:* Uppsala University, Uppsala, Sweden, M.A., 1957.

ADDRESSES: Home—Sweden. *Agent*—c/o Author Mail, Doubleday, 1540 Broadway, New York, NY 10036.

CAREER: Writer. Worked as high school teacher of Swedish and Swedish literature; literary critic, television writer and producer.

AWARDS, HONORS: Best Swedish Detective Story Prize, 1961, for *Tre sma maestare;* elected to Swedish Academy, 1978 (resigned in protest, 1989, due to Academy's insufficient support to Salman Rushdie); Selma Lagerloef Prize, 1989; Award for Best Crime Novel from the Swedish Crime Academy; August Prize; Literary Prize of the Nordic Council, for *Haendelser vid vatten,* translation published as *Blackwater.*

WRITINGS:

Menedarna, Bonnier (Stockholm, Sweden), 1970.
Moerker och blaebaersris (title means "Darkness and Blueberry Scrub"), [Sweden], 1972, Literaturfraemjandet (Stockholm, Sweden), 1990.
Haexringarna (first novel in tetralogy; title means "The Witches' Rings"), Bonnier (Stockholm, Sweden), 1974, translation by Linda Schenck published as *Witches' Rings,* Norvik Press (Chester Springs, PA), 1997.
Springkaellan (second novel in tetralogy), Bonnier (Stockholm, Sweden), 1976, translation by Linda Schenck published as *The Spring,* Norvik Press (Chester Springs, PA), 2002.
Vykort fraan Katrineholm, Bonnier (Stockholm, Sweden), 1977.
Aenglahuset (third novel in tetralogy; title means "House of Angels"), Bonnier (Stockholm, Sweden), 1979.
Doedsklockan, (detective novel; title means "The Death Knell"), Bonnier (Stockholm, Sweden), 1979.
En stad av ljus (fourth novel in tetralogy; title means "A Town of Light"), Bonnier (Stockholm, Sweden), 1983.
Hunden, Bonnier (Stockholm, Sweden), 1986.
Roevarna i Skuleskogen (novel; title means "The Robbers in Skule Forest"), Bonnier (Stockholm, Sweden), 1988, translation by Anna Paterson published as *The Forest of Hours,* Chatto & Windus (London, England), 1998.
Knivkastarens kvinna (verse epic; title means "The Knife Thrower's Woman"), MaenPocket (Stockholm, Sweden), 1991.
Haendelser vid vatten, Bonnier (Stockholm, Sweden), 1993, translation by Joan Tate published as *Blackwater,* Doubleday (New York, NY), 1996.
Raetten att haeda, Svenska rushdiekommitten (Stockholm, Sweden), 1994.
Goer mig levande igen, Bonnier (Stockholm, Sweden), 1996, translation by Joan Tate published as *Under the Snow,* Doubleday (New York, NY), 1998.
Rovarna i Skuleskogen, translation by Anna Paters published as *The Forest of House,* Chatto & Windus (London, England), 1998.
Guds barmhaertighet, Bonnier (Stockholm, Sweden), 1999.

Urminnes tecken, Bonnier (Stockholm, Sweden), 2000.
Springkallan, translation by Linda Schenck published as *The Spring,* Norvik Press (Norwich, England), 2001.
The Angel House, preface by Sarah Death, Norvik Press (Chester Springs, PA), 2002.

Also author of *30 meter mord,* 1959; *Han roer paa sig,* 1960; *Kalla famnen,* 1960; *Tre sma maestare* (detective novel; title means "Three Little Masters"), 1961; *Den brinnnande ugnen,* 1962; *Pukehornet,* 1967; and *Mine Herrar. . . ,* 1986.

SIDELIGHTS: Before she became a full-time author, Kerstin Ekman was a teacher and literary critic as well as active in the film and television industry as a writer and producer. She began her writing career as an author of popular detective novels. One of them, *Tre sma maestare,* won the prize for Best Swedish Detective fiction in 1961.

With *Doedsklockan,* Ekman began writing a more psychological novel, with only the bare bones of the traditional detective novel still in evidence. In his contribution to the *Encyclopedia of World Literature* Lars G. Warme noted, "[Ekman] now places greater emphasis on psychological complications and on the way characters interact as a group. The author also gives particular attention to the description of milieu: The autumnal landscape and the details surrounding a moose hunt are based on exact observation and evoked with remarkable concreteness."

In *Menedarna,* published in 1970, Ekman examined an actual historical event, the 1915 Utah execution of the Swedish labor agitator and songwriter Joe Hill in the early years of the IWW (Industrial Workers of the World).

Kerstin Ekman's novel, *Haendelser vid vatten,* translated by Joan Tate as *Blackwater,* "is being marketed as a thriller—but of the longer, denser and more erotic variety, the kind that comes along once every few years and usually attracts a big audience," wrote Beverly Lowry in the *New York Times Book Review.* The novel traces how the murders of a man and woman affect the rural Swedish community of Blackwater and specific townspeople eighteen years later. Writing in *Publishers Weekly,* Sybil Steinberg praised the novel as "splendid fiction, dark and compelling . . . told smoothly through multiple points of view." Commenting on Ekman's descriptive prose, *Washington Post Book World* contributor Sven Birkerts observed: "Ekman's somber moods are most effective. Nature here is no picturesque backdrop, but an animated presence, the kind we might ourselves register if we were lost in the deep woods at sunset." Similarly, Lowry remarked: "Throughout the novel, Ms. Ekman's descriptions of the countryside are lush and lovingly rendered. Landscape—what we've come to call the environment—becomes a character here, as fully developed and as important to the plot as human beings."

As investigation of the murders—which had remained unsolved for nearly twenty years—resumes due to new evidence, the village of Blackwater draws tightly in to protect its own. Seemingly shocked by the crime but suspicious of any questions about the past, the residents reject implications that a Blackwater citizen could be the perpetrator. Birkerts praised Ekman's ability to create vivid characters: "It is a thrilling tangle, this cast of characters that seems to generate more and more darkness as we turn the pages." Describing *Blackwater* as a fascinating, gripping, and dutifully crafted narrative, Lowry concluded: "Ms. Ekman provides us with a rich adventure, the kind of long, lush page-turner many of us crave but rarely get our hands on."

Ekman's *Under the Snow* is another psychological thriller set in a small village in northern Sweden. In the dead of winter Police Constable Torsson receives a call from the village of Rakisjokk. Artist and teacher Matti Olsson has been killed, forcing Torsson to get there by the only means possible in winter: a 25-mile trek on skis across a frozen lake. When he arrives, however, the inhabitants don't want to talk and what they do say doesn't seem logical. Unexplainable details appear, and Torsson is unable to blame anything but the terrible cold for Olsson's death.

By accident, the case is reopened when Olsson's friend David Malm makes a summer visit and meets a girl who has hit a reindeer with her car. In the car, Malm discovers a knapsack containing a bloody noose covered with human hair. This revelation forces Torsson to return to the village, now in the midst of Arctic summer. "Slowly and painfully, the two penetrate the peculiar psychology of people who live half their lives in darkness, cut off from the rest of the world. Ekman's brilliant evocation of a place and culture above the Arctic Circle is as compelling and mysterious as the crime itself," wrote Cynthia Johnson in *Library Journal.*

In 1997 the first volume of the tetralogy, *Witches' Rings,* was published in English. The saga spans the last hundred years in a farming town in rural Sweden as industrialization begins to affect the villages. Unlike the tightly plotted *Blackwater, Witches' Rings* revolves around three women, Sara Sabine Lans, her daughter Edla, and Edla's daughter Tora. *New York Times* writer Margaret Livesey noted, "Here [Ekman] is primarily interested in realism, and it is realism with a vengeance. Thus she avoids the choices that have comforted Western readers. Tess of the D'Urbervilles, for example, undergoes many of the same trials as Sara and her descendants, but Thomas Hardy makes Tess a heroine, a woman whose suffering has meaning and whose life is shaped by majestic forces of destiny. In contrast, Ekman's characters can hardly qualify as heroines; they suffer without redemption of any kind."

The tone of the book is set from the opening page: "This was Sara Sabine Lans: gray as a rat, poor as a louse, pouchy and lean as a vixen in summer. No one called her by her given name. . . . She had her children and the croft with its potato patch, a cottage nearly smothered by lilacs as the years passed, but where happiness had no place. . . . She smoked hams for the farmers. That was her cleanest job. Otherwise, there was nothing so coarse, so filthy or so foul that she wouldn't do it. She scrubbed down cowsheds in the spring. She took in laundry and helped with butchering. She laid out the dead. She toiled all her life for leftovers and favors. She was hardy as grass, prickly as nettles."

In the early pages, Edla comes the closest to being the main character. At the age of thirteen, she goes to work at Isaksson's inn. Her life at home has been so poor that neither her endless work nor the table that serves for her bed seem bad at all. She appreciates the abundant food and the glimpse of exotic passengers who stop at the inn. She soon gets pregnant and comes to term without even knowing it. When she gives birth on a lonely country road and falls into a fever and dies without ever knowing she had a daughter, Ekman reveals the unrelenting brutality of poverty that was often the case in the nineteenth-century Swedish countryside.

Livesey concluded, "No reader would want to daydream herself back into this time and place. What the novel accomplishes, however, is something much more important: it reminds us, in the most immediate fashion, just how much our world has changed—even as it forces us to recognize how stubbornly persistent the emotional undercurrents of that world may turn out to be."

The second book in the series, translated as *The Spring,* focuses on the lives of three different women. Bakery owner Torn struggles against a male-dominated culture while Freida, an overworked washerwoman, silently endures her fate. The third, Ingrid, is a passionate rebel determined to get an education and rise above her environment. A *Kirkus Reviews* contributor praised the book, writing, "Ekman's masterly dramatizations of the contrasts between home and hearth and the intimidating wider world beyond them—whose uncertainty is crystallized in the recurring theme of the need for pure drinking water—as well as her precise characterizations and robust humor, make the moving novel (after *Witches' Rings,* 1997), an essential component of what begins to look like an extended work of major importance."

BIOGRAPHICAL AND CRITICAL SOURCES:

BOOKS

Ekman, Kerstin, *Witches' Rings,* Norvik Press (Chester Springs, PA), 1997.
Encyclopedia of World Literature, 3rd edition, St. James Press (Detroit, MI), 1999, p. 19.
Robinson, Lillian S., editor, *Modern Women Writers,* Continuum Press (New York, NY), 1996.
Zuck, Virpi, editor, *Dictionary of Scandinavian Literature,* Greenwood Press (New York, NY), 1990.

PERIODICALS

Booklist, January 1, 1998, Bill Ott, review of *Under the Snow,* p. 782.
Kirkus Reviews, October 15, 1997, review of *Witches' Rings,* p. 1549; November 1, 1997, review of *Under the Snow,* p. 405.
Library Journal, January, 1996, p. 141; December, 1997, Cynthia Johnson, review of *Under the Snow,* p. 150.

New Statesman and Society, April 21, 1995, p. 37.
New Yorker, March 30, 1998, review of *Under the Snow,* p. 123.
New York Times Book Review, March 17, 1996, p. 24; March 9, 1997, review of *Blackwater,* p. 28; February 22, 1998, Margot Livesey, review of *Witches' Rings* and *Under the Snow,* p. 28; February 14, 1999, review of *Under the Snow,* p. 32.
Observer (London, England), October 24, 1999, review of *The Forest of Hours,* p. 15.
Publishers Weekly, December 4, 1995, p. 51; November 10, 1997, review of *Witches' Rings,* p. 57; November 24, 1997, review of *Under the Snow,* p. 53.
St. Louis Post-Dispatch, October 26, 1997, Jan Garden Castro, review of *Under the Snow,* p. 5C.
Scandinavian Studies, winter, 1998, Linda Havery Rugg, review of *Roevarna i Skuleskogen,* p. 425.
Times (London, England), November 8, 1997, Emily Bearn, review of *Under the Snow,* p. 20; November 12, 1998, Ruth Scurr, review of *The Forest of Hours,* p. 42.
Times Literary Supplement, November 20, 1998, Heather O'Donoghue, review of *The Forest of Hours,* p. 21; November 30, 2001, Julia Lovell, review of *The Spring,* p. 24.
Tribune Books (Chicago, IL), February 16, 1997, review of *Blackwater,* p. 8.
Washington Post Book World, March 3, 1996, p. 9.
World Literature Today, spring, 1997, Margaretta Mattsson, review of *Goer mig levande igen,* p. 405; autumn, 1999, review of *Guds barmhaertighet,* p. 764.*

* * *

ERICSON, Richard V(ictor) 1948-

PERSONAL: Born September 20, 1948, in Montreal, Quebec, Canada; son of John William and Elizabeth Mary (Hinkley) Ericson; married Diana Lea McMillan, May 31, 1969; children: Matthew Simon. *Education:* University of Guelph, B.A., 1969; University of Toronto, M.A., 1971; Cambridge University, Ph.D., 1974, Litt.D., 1991.

ADDRESSES: Home and office—Principal's Residence, Green College, University of British Columbia, 6201 Cecil Green Park Rd., Vancouver, British Columbia V6T 1Z1, Canada; fax 604-822-8742. E-mail—ericson@interchange.ubc.ca.

CAREER: Cambridge University, Churchill College, Cambridge, England, instructor in sociology, 1971-73; University of Alberta, Edmonton, Alberta, Canada, assistant professor of sociology, 1973-74; University of Toronto, Toronto, Ontario, Canada, assistant professor, 1974-79, associate professor, 1979-82, professor of criminology and sociology, 1982-93, director of Centre of Criminology, 1992-93; University of British Columbia, Vancouver, British Columbia, Canada, professor of sociology and law and principal of Green College, 1993—. University of Edinburgh, visiting research associate, 1974; Cambridge University, fellow commoner of Churchill College, 1979, visiting fellow at Institute of Criminology, 1979 and 1984-85, overseas fellow, 1984-85; Carleton University, Ottawa, Ontario, Canada, Porter Lecturer, 1983; Arizona State University, visiting research professor, 1991; University of Sydney, Parsons Lecturer, 1992; Oxford University, honorary visiting fellow at Green College, 1993—, visiting fellow of All Souls College, 1998-99; University of Toronto, associate senior fellow of Massey College, 1996—; University of Paris X—Nanterre, visiting professor, 1999; lecturer at many other colleges and universities. University of British Columbia Press, member of publications committee, 1995—.

MEMBER: Royal Society of Canada (fellow).

AWARDS, HONORS: Killam fellow, Canada Council for the Arts, 1998-2000; grants from Social Sciences and Humanities Research Council of Canada, Social Science Federation of Canada, Esso Corp., Royal Society of Canada, Government of Alberta, Office of the Solicitor General of Canada, Ontario Ministry of Corrections, Connaught Fund, Donner Foundation, Canada Council, Canada Ministry of Transport, Law Reform Commission of Canada, Law Commission of Canada, and Laidlaw Foundation.

WRITINGS:

Young Offenders and Their Social Work, Saxon House (Farnborough, England), 1975.
Criminal Reactions: The Labelling Perspective, Saxon House (Farnborough, England), 1975.
(With B. Burtch) *The Silent System: An Inquiry into Prisoners Who Suicide* (monograph), Centre of Criminology, University of Toronto (Toronto, Ontario, Canada), 1979.

Making Crime: A Study of Detective Work, Butterworth (Toronto, Ontario, Canada), 1981, revised edition, University of Toronto Press (Toronto, Ontario, Canada), 1993.

(With J. Chan) *Decarceration and the Economy of Penal Reform* (monograph), Centre of Criminology, University of Toronto (Toronto, Ontario, Canada), 1981.

Reproducing Order: A Study of Police Patrol Work, University of Toronto Press (Toronto, Ontario, Canada), 1982.

(With P. Baranek) *The Ordering of Justice: A Study of Accused Persons As Dependents in the Criminal Process,* University of Toronto Press (Toronto, Ontario, Canada), 1982.

(With M. McMahon) *Policing Reform: A Study of the Reform Process and Police Institution in Toronto* (monograph), Centre of Criminology, University of Toronto (Toronto, Ontario, Canada), 1984.

(With S. Voumvakis) *News Accounts of Attacks on Women: A Comparison of Three Toronto Newspapers* (monograph), Centre of Criminology, University of Toronto (Toronto, Ontario, Canada), 1984.

(With P. Baranek and J. Chan) *Visualizing Deviance: A Study of News Organizations,* University of Toronto Press (Toronto, Ontario, Canada), 1987.

(With P. Baranek and J. Chan) *Negotiating Control: A Study of New Sources,* University of Toronto Press (Toronto, Ontario, Canada), 1989.

(With K. Carriere) *Crime Stoppers: A Study in the Organization of Community Policing,* Centre of Criminology, University of Toronto (Toronto, Ontario, Canada), 1989.

(With P. Baranek and J. Chan) *Representing Order: Crime, Law, and Justice in the News Media,* University of Toronto Press (Toronto, Ontario, Canada), 1991.

(Editor, with J. Gladstone and C. Shearing, and contributor) *Criminology: A Reader's Guide* (monograph), Centre of Criminology, University of Toronto (Toronto, Ontario, Canada), 1991.

(Editor, with N. Stehr, and contributor) *The Culture and Power of Knowledge: Inquiries into Contemporary Societies* (monograph), deGruyter (New York, NY), 1992.

(Editor and contributor) *Crime and the Media* (monograph), Dartmouth (Aldershot, England), 1995.

(With K. Haggerty) *Policing the Risk Society,* University of Toronto Press (Toronto, Ontario, Canada), 1997.

(Editor, with N. Stehr, and contributor) *Governing Modern Societies,* University of Toronto Press (Toronto, Ontario, Canada), 2000.

(Editor, with A. Doyle, and contributor) *Risk and Morality,* University of Toronto Press (Toronto, Ontario, Canada), 2003.

(With A. Doyle and D. Barry) *Insurance As Governance,* University of Toronto Press (Toronto, Ontario, Canada), 2003.

Contributor to books. Contributor to academic journals, including *Canadian Journal of Criminology, British Journal of Criminology, Annals of the American Academy of Political and Social Sciences, Canadian Review of Sociology and Anthropology, Journal of Military and Political Sociology, Economy and Society, British Journal of Sociology,* and *International Journal of Culture, Politics, and Society. Canadian Journal of Sociology,* founding coeditor, 1973—, editor in chief, 1982-86; corresponding editor, *Media, Culture, and Society,* 1990-94.

* * *

ESPOSITO, John L(ouis) 1940-

PERSONAL: Born May 19, 1940, in Brooklyn, NY; son of John and Mary (Marotta) Esposito; married Dr. Jeannette Paisker (a corporate manager), July 31, 1965. *Ethnicity:* "Italian." *Education:* St. Anthony College, B.A., 1963; St. John's University, Jamaica, NY, M.A., 1966; attended University of Pennsylvania, 1969, and Middle East Center for Arab Studies, Shemlan, Lebanon, 1971-72; Temple University, Ph.D., 1974. *Hobbies and other interests:* "Running (8 miles), reading and music, watching reruns of *Law and Order.*"

ADDRESSES: Home—4149 Parkglen St. NW, Washington, DC 20007. *Office*—CMCU/ICC 260, Walsh School of Foreign Services, Georgetown University, Washington, DC 20057-1052. *Agent*—The Lavin Agency, 872 Massachusetts Ave., Cambridge, MA 02139-3073. *E-mail*—jle2@georgetown.edu.

CAREER: Rosemont College, Rosemont, PA, instructor, 1966-69, assistant professor of theology, 1969-72; College of the Holy Cross, Worcester, MA, assistant professor, 1972-75, associate professor, 1975-82, professor of religious studies, 1984-95, chair of department, 1975-84, chair, International Studies Committee, 1984-86, director, Center for International Studies, 1987-91, Loyola professor of Middle East studies,

John L. Esposito

1991-95; Fletcher School of Law and Diplomacy, Tufts University, adjunct professor of diplomacy, 1986-93, professor of Islamic studies, 1987-99; Georgetown University, Washington, DC, School of Foreign Service, founding director of the Center for Muslim-Christian Understanding and professor of religion and international affairs and Islamic studies, 1993—, university professor, 2000—. Oberlin College, visiting professor of Asian studies, 1986; visiting scholar, Center for the Study of World Religions, Harvard University, 1979-80; senior associate of St. Antony's College, Oxford, 1982-83; researcher in the Middle East, South Asia, and Southeast Asia; lecturer at Tel Aviv University, Hebrew University of Jerusalem, Haifa University, Hebron University, Al-Azhar University, American University of Cairo, Kuwait University, and King Abdul Aziz University; lecturer for U.S. Department of State and U.S. Agency for International Development. Member of Committee on Faiths of the World; member of National Council of Churches Task Force on Muslim-Christian Relations; consultant to Independent Broadcasters Associates and National Public Radio.

MEMBER: Middle East Studies Association (member of board of directors, 1983-86; president, 1988-89), American Council for the Study of Islamic Societies (member of board of directors, 1984—; vice president, 1986-89; president, 1989-91), American Academy of Religion, American Society for the Study of Religion, Council on the Study of Religion, College Theology Society (chair of World Religions Section, 1978-80), Society for the Scientific Study of Religion, Middle East Institute, International Studies Association, Association of Pakistan and Indic-Islamic Studies, Council on Foreign Relations, Association of Asian Studies, Maghreb Studies Association, American Oriental Society.

AWARDS, HONORS: Fellowship from St. John's University, 1965; National Defense Foreign Language Fellowship from University of Pennsylvania, 1969, for Arabic; fellowship from Middle East Center for Arab Studies; Faculty Fellowship, College of the Holy Cross, 1977, 1982-83, 1990-91; Visiting Scholar, Center for the Study of World Religions, Harvard University, 1979-80; Elected Senior Associate, St. Antony's College, Oxford University, 1982-83; National Endowment for the Humanities Interpretive Residential Grant, 1990-93; U.S. Institute for Peace, 1992-93.

WRITINGS:

- (Editor and contributor) *Islam and Development: Religion and Sociopolitical Change,* Syracuse University Press (Syracuse, NY), 1980.
- (Editor and translator, with John J. Donohue) *Islam in Transition: Muslim Perspectives,* Oxford University Press (New York, NY), 1982.
- *Women in Muslim Family Law,* Syracuse University Press (Syracuse, NY), 1982.
- (Editor and contributor) *Voices of Resurgent Islam,* Oxford University Press (New York, NY), 1983.
- *Islam and Politics,* Syracuse University Press (Syracuse, NY), 1984, 4th edition, 1998.
- (Editor and contributor) *Islam and Public Life in Asia,* Asia Society (New York, NY), 1985.
- (Editor) *Islam in Asia: Religion, Politics, and Society,* Oxford University Press (New York, NY), 1987.
- *Islam: The Straight Path,* Oxford University Press (New York, NY), 1988, 3rd edition, 1998.
- (Editor) *The Iranian Revolution: Its Global Impact,* Florida International University Press (Miami, FL), 1990.

(With Yvonne Yazbeck Haddad, John O. Voll, Kathleen Moore, and David Sawan) *The Contemporary Islamic Revival: A Critical Survey and Bibliography,* Greenwood Press (New York, NY), 1991.

The Islamic Threat: Myth or Reality?, Oxford University Press (New York, NY), 1992, 3rd edition, 1999.

(Editor in chief) *The Oxford Encyclopedia of the Modern Islamic World,* four volumes, Oxford University Press (New York, NY), 1995.

(With John O. Voll) *Islam and Democracy,* Oxford University Press (New York, NY), 1996.

(Editor) *Political Islam: Revolution: Radicalism, or Reform?,* Lynne Rienner Publishers (Boulder, CO), 1997.

(With Yvonne Yazbeck Haddad, Elizabeth Hiel, and Hibba Abugideiri) *The Islamic Revival since 1988: A Critical Survey and Bibliography,* Greenwood Press (Westport, CT), 1997.

(Editor, with Yvonne Yazbeck Haddad) *Islam, Gender and Social Change,* Oxford University Press (New York, NY), 1998.

(Editor, with Yvonne Yazbeck Haddad) *Muslims on the Americanization Path?,* Scholars Press (Atlanta, GA), 1998.

(Editor) *The Oxford History of Islam,* Oxford University Press (New York, NY), 1999.

(Editor, with Azzam Tamimi) *Islam and Secularism in the Middle East,* C. Hurst (London, England), 2000, New York University Press (New York, NY), 2000.

(Editor, with Michael Watson) *Religion and Global Order,* University of Wales Press (Cardiff, Wales), 2000.

(Editor, with R. K. Ramazani) *Iran at the Crossroads,* Palgrave (New York, NY), 2001.

(Editor, with Yvonne Yazbeck Haddad) *Daughters of Abraham: Feminist Thought in Judaism, Christianity, and Islam,* University Press of Florida (Gainesville, FL), 2001.

(Editor, with Zafar Ishaq Ansari) *Muslims and the West: Encounter and Dialogue,* Center for Muslim-Christian Understanding, Georgetown University (Washington, DC), 2001.

(With John O. Voll) *Makers of Contemporary Islam,* Oxford University Press (New York, NY), 2001.

(Editor, with Yvonne Yazbeck Haddad and Jane I. Smith) *Religion and Immigration: Christian, Jewish, and Muslim Experiences in the United States,* Rowman & Littlefield, (Walnut Creek, CA), 2002.

Unholy War: Terror in the Name of Islam, Oxford University Press (New York, NY), 2002.

What Everyone Needs to Know about Islam, Oxford University Press (New York, NY), 2002.

(With Darrell J. Fasching and Todd Lewis) *World Religions Today,* Oxford University Press (New York, NY), 2002.

(Editor in chief) *The Oxford Dictionary of Islam,* Oxford University Press (New York, NY), 2003.

Contributor to anthologies, including *Teaching about Religion in Public Schools,* edited by Nicholas Piediscalzi, Argus Communications (Niles, IL), 1977; *The Islamic Impact,* edited by Yvonne Y. Haddad, Syracuse University Press (Syracuse, NY), 1983; *Islam: The Political and Religious Life of a Community,* edited by Marjorie Kelly, Praeger (New York, NY), 1984; *Movement and Issues in World Religions: Religious Ideology and Politics,* edited by C. H. Fu, Greenwood Press (Westport, CT), 1985; *Islam, Ethnicity, and the State,* edited by Myron Weiner and Ali Banuazizi, University of California Press (Berkeley, CA), 1986; *Islamic Reassertion in Pakistan: The Application of Islamic Laws in a Modern State,* edited by Anita M. Weiss, Syracuse University Press (Syracuse, NY), 1986.

Contributor to Middle Eastern and Islamic studies journals.

WORK IN PROGRESS: The Islamic World: Past and Present (three volumes), and *The Future of Islam,* both for Oxford University Press.

SIDELIGHTS: John L. Esposito once told *CA*: "Early in my study of Islam I became fascinated by the extent to which religion and politics were intertwined. Contrary to modern Western presuppositions, Islam is a total way of life in which religion is integral to state, law, and society. The Shariah, the sacred law of Islam, epitomizes this historic approach, providing a comprehensive blueprint for individual and public life that encompasses worship as well as family, criminal, and commercial law. In my travels I was struck by the extent to which Islam continued to inform Muslim societies despite Western inspired processes of modernization in politics, law, and education. I became particularly interested in the issue of tradition and change, in the relationship of religion to modernization: (1) Does the emergence of modern Muslim societies necessitate progressive Westernization and secularization? (2) Is there evidence of cultural continuity and modern change? (3) To what extent does Islam inhibit or inform the modern transformation of Muslim countries? These are the questions which have shaped much of my subsequent thinking, research, and writing.

"I began with the study of women in Islam—in particular with the relationship of law to social change, focusing on Muslim family law. The status of women in the family has been of central significance for Islamic society from earliest times. Muslim family law (marriage, divorce, and inheritance) has long been viewed as the heart of Islamic law. Modern reform in family law is an index of social change (both real and ideal) and illustrates Islamic reform, its methodology and problems. I began with a comparative study of women in Egypt and Pakistan and progressively extended my travel and research to include North Africa, the Middle East, and South Asia. As a result, I published a series of articles on various aspects of Muslim women's changing role in society and a book, *Women in Muslim Family Law*.

"Realizing the tension between the Islamic tradition and the modern secular state, with its separation of religion and politics, I broadened my study toward the role of Islam in modern socio-political change from both a theoretical and a practical perspective. The need for such materials had grown out of my experience in trying to teach about Islam in modern Muslim societies at Holy Cross. As a result, a colleague, John J. Donohue, and I translated and edited *Islam in Transition: Muslim Perspectives* which provides direct access to modern Muslim thinkers as they grapple with the problems confronting Islam in a period of rapid change. Complementing this approach, *Islam and Development* provided country case studies, ranging from Nigeria to Malaysia.

"During the 1970s Americans became progressively more aware of and concerned about stability in the Middle East. The Arab oil embargo in 1973, the Iranian Revolution in 1978-79, and the seizure of the grand Mosque in Saudi Arabia in 1979 contributed to an explosion of coverage of events in the Muslim world. Frustrated by our ignorance of Islam and contemporary Muslim societies and convinced of the importance for both the public and policy makers to better understand the nature of Islamic revivalism and its implications, I brought together a number of leading Islamic leaders and intellectuals with Americans from academia, government, and the corporate world. As a result *Voices of Resurgent Islam* was published. It provides a historical and ideological perspective on the revival of Islam. The volume includes studies of major figures such as the Ayotallah Khomeini, Muammar Qaddafi, and leaders of the Muslim Brotherhood. Despite these materials, my experience in teaching and consulting reinforced a desire to provide a general introduction for students, government practitioners, and academics in the West who wished to understand the motivating factors, ideology, and actors in Muslim politics today. *Islam and Politics* and my subsequent work focus on the role of Islam in Muslim politics and the issues which it raises both for Muslims and policy makers.

"As I continue to travel, from the Sudan to Indonesia, I am reinforced in my belief that Islam remains an omnipresent reality and force with which we must come to terms. Yet, this is not a monolithic phenomenon. Differences in Islamic visions are accompanied by profound disagreements regarding the implementation of Islamic rule and law. One need only think of leaders (Anwar Sadat and Ayatollah Khomeini), countries (Egypt, Saudi Arabia, Malaysia), and organizations (from peaceful to terrorist). For the vast majority of Muslims, the resurgence of Islam continues to be a reassertion of cultural identity, formal religious observance, family values, and morality, leading to be a better, more Islamic society through a process of gradual social change. A disaffected, desperate minority believe that violent revolution is the only possibility. I believe that if Muslim governments fail to satisfy the political and economic needs of their societies and fail to pursue a path of modernization which is sensitive to their Islamic heritage, Muslim societies will remain in a precarious position in which stability is based, more often than not, on authoritarian rule and force. Such situations will encourage popular antiestablishment disturbances and, at times, revolt. However, if these governments strive to achieve a new synthesis which provides more continuity between the demands of modernity and their Islamic tradition, then a broad range of possibilities exists. In situations such as Iran and Lebanon, where there is an anti-American reaction, it will be important for us to remember that anti-Americanism does not come from Islam or Muslim belief itself but rather may follow from American presence (government and multinational) as a reaction to U.S. policies in a country or region.

"As events in the Muslim world continue to unfold, we must recall that Muslims stand at a crossroads.

Whereas the process of modernization began in the West and has occurred for several centuries, Muslim countries have endured the centuries-long dominance of European colonialism and enjoyed independence for only several decades. The political and socioeconomic character and institutions of Muslim states are far from established. Alongside the education, power, and wealth of the few still stands the poverty and illiteracy of many, compounded by authoritarian regimes as well as superpower politics. It is within this context that many Muslim societies struggle to harness their resources and determine their futures."

Since the publication of the books mentioned in Esposito's interview with *CA,* he has written and edited many more on the subject of Islam and Islamic nations, making him one of the world's most knowledgeable authorities on Islam. His books have found especially wide readership since the terrorist attacks on the United States in 2001. Esposito has also given talks to universities, government agencies, and the U.S. military and has been an advisor to the U.S. Congress and to the President George W. Bush administration.

Esposito's book *Islam: The Straight Path* is an introduction to the faith, beginning with the prophet Muhammad and the Quran and continuing with basic dogma and the creation of the Muslims as a religious and social community. It covers the Crusades, the Abbasid Caliphate, and the Umayyads during the medieval period and then delves into the Ottoman, Safavid, and Mughal empires before dealing with Islamic divisions into Sunni and Shiite, the Druze, and the Ismailis. Esposito also thoroughly addresses the theology and law of Islam and their practices and discusses the premodern revivalist movements that have attempted to reclaim ancient traditions in the modern world. In addition, he deals with modernist movements that are attempting to do away with some of these ancient teachings and adapt Islam to the changing conditions of present-day society. Esposito also discusses contemporary Islam, whose dominant theme is resurgence. Many Islamist groups believe in a return to original Islamic sources and to Islamic law and are opposed to Western secularism and to corruption and social injustice. The most radical believe it is right to bring about violent revolution to effect these changes. Esposito discusses Islam and its variations in practice and belief in the Muslim countries, in Europe, and in the United States.

Danny Yee, in a review for *Danny Yee's Book Reviews,* was disappointed that Islam in Asia is only lightly covered in the book. However, he said, "As history . . . *The Straight Path* works well, giving a good feel for Islam's historical depth and geographical reach." James F. DeRoche of *Library Journal* praised the third edition of the book for its incorporation of recent developments in Pakistan and the Middle East, as well as the rising number of Muslims in the United States. He complimented Esposito on his unbiased scholarly prose that is "both straightforward and highly readable."

One of Esposito's most reviewed books is *The Islamic Threat: Myth or Reality?,* first published in 1992, with a third edition published in 1999. After the September 11, 2001, attacks on the United States, the book became popular among the general reading public striving to understand why the attacks took place and what the future may hold regarding Islamic terrorists. Esposito points out flaws in the way the United States and other Western countries regard Islamic nations. In a review for *Commonweal,* George Perkovich wrote, "The nations that have led the world through the twentieth century have little idea how to engage with these societies in anything but frightened, befuddled, and adversarial terms." Esposito writes in his book, "It is important that the vacuum created by the end of the cold war not be filled by exaggerated fears of Islam as a resurgent 'evil empire' at war with the new world order and a challenge to global stability." Instead, U.S. leaders should ask how their policy can transform a perceived Islamic threat into an opportunity to work toward a common global future, Esposito said.

Yet, Perkovich found that Esposito "never completely answers this question. Instead . . . he deconstructs the myth and image of raging monolithic 'Islamic fundamentalism.'" Instead of the term "fundamentalism," which he believes conjures too much of a Christian and Western stereotype and suggests a threat that does not exist, Esposito speaks of Islamic "activism" or "revivalism." Esposito also considers the dividedness among Islamic countries and the abuse by many Islamic leaders of religious faith to build political power. He suggests that the revivalists would probably stop short of installing completely democratic governments, ruling out participation by leaders and political parties not in full alignment with their religious beliefs. Esposito also focuses on the many Islamic groups, such as Egypt's Muslim Brotherhood, which fulfill real social and economic needs of the people.

The author also warns the U.S. government against minimizing reasons given by Muslims for their criticism of the United States: its support of Israel, its imperialism, and its support of certain oppressive regimes while ignoring atrocities such as the Serbian slaughter of Bosnian Muslims (against which the U.S. military later intervened). Esposito concludes that the United States must recognize the right of Islamically oriented states to exist in accordance with its policy that all people have a right to determine their future and choose their representatives. However, said Perkovich, U.S. support of human rights and political participation in Muslim countries will fail "if it is heavy-handed and self-righteous. It requires nuance, pragmatism, and an empathetic tolerance of context. These are precisely the attributes vitiated by our current portrayal of the fundamentalist threat."

Harold Vogelaar of the *Christian Century* described *The Islamic Threat* as "one of the finest attempts to explore the reality and the myth behind this renewed fear of Islam. One hopes this book will be read by all who sincerely think of Islam as the 'household of Satan' threatening Christian faith, and also by those who do not fear Islam but consider it a political and social threat." Antony T. Sullivan of the *Arab Studies Quarterly* wrote, "Esposito makes special efforts to demonstrate just how misleading are so many of the stereotypes which continue to impede Western comprehension of Islam and contemporary Islamic revivalism. American media and governmental elites would do well to give his analysis careful attention." Sullivan congratulated Esposito for "this gracefully written contribution to public enlightenment concerning our Muslim neighbors."

Esposito is not without critics, however. Stephen Howe, in a review for *New Statesman & Society,* found little that was new in Esposito's arguments, saying that many Arab writers, notably Edward Said, had made the same points. Howe remarked that Esposito "creates . . . an excessively homogenized image of a western media campaign against Islam. [Yet,] most of those he quotes are drawn from very narrow circles of pundits, far-right politicians and pro-Israel propagandists." Kirin Aziz Chaudhry, writing in the *Political Science Quarterly,* pointed out that *The Islamic Threat* "is vulnerable to a number of criticisms. . . . It makes an argument that is already quite well represented in the Middle East area studies literature. . . . It fails to analyze the empirical material in a way that illuminates the consequences of different policies. . . . Esposito . . . accepts the notion that the Islamic revival is a global phenomenon that, its diversity notwithstanding, can be analyzed as such." An *Economist* contributor thought Esposito covered too much ground to make an effective argument. "In trying so hard to be comprehensive, he blurs the distinction between the important and the less important," the contributor wrote. He gives "too little weight to such crucial influences as Zionism and the kneejerk support of the United States for Israel. And he hardly mentions the economic plight of much of the Muslim world."

A *Middle East* journal contributor praised *The Islamic Threat,* saying, "This lucid, often provocative, study is intended to reach not only students or specialists but a wider general public. It always remains objective and can only help spread mutual understanding instead of the alienation, fear and mutual resentment which are too commonly found."

In another widely reviewed book, *Islam and Democracy,* Esposito and coauthor John O. Voll explore the possibilities of combining Islamic societies and democracy through case studies from six primarily Islamic countries: Iran, Pakistan, Egypt, Algeria, Malaysia and Sudan. The authors examine three operational concepts of Islam which could establish a form of democracy in Islamic nations, although this form might not look like Western democracy. These concepts are *shura* (consultation of the people by the leaders on conduct of the state), *ijma* (consensus or collective judgment of the community), and *ijtihad* (independent interpretive judgment, in which the people apply informed interpretation of divine guidance to the problems and issues of their time).

Esposito and Voll attempt to "refute the common Western view that political Islam and democracy are antithetical," said Joshua Muravchik in a review for *First Things: A Monthly Journal of Religious and Public Life.* Muravchik took issue with the authors on several points. He observed, "Indeed there is something unserious about this whole work, beginning with its failure to take frank account of the current dearth of democracy in the Islamic world. . . . The Islamic world boasts a variety of regimes, but what most of them share is a tendency toward tyranny." Muravchik acknowledged that the authors make a good point in that the Christian world evolved into democracy through basic principles of the religion and that the Islamic world may do so through the principles mentioned above. Still, the reviewer wrote that "much progress needs to be made before Islam makes its peace with democracy. That progress, however, will find no help from the likes of Esposito and Voll, with their relentless apologies for the most retrograde elements in the Islamic world and their insistent obfuscation of the basic principles of democracy as nothing more than a Western 'style'." William B. Quandt of *Foreign Affairs* thought the authors' inclusion of the leadership of Hassan Turabi of Sudan "detracts from an otherwise sensible discussion of reform in failing political systems."

Mahmood Monshipouri, in a review for the *Review of Politics,* found that *Islam and Democracy* "offers no concrete policy guidelines" for implementing democracy in Islamic societies. He wrote, "The broad and abstract nature of the discussions . . . does not allow room for drawing an important distinction between democracies and . . . protective regimes. . . . Elections . . . have plunged some countries . . . into endless trouble." Monshipouri also thought a discussion of why Muslim women play such a minuscule role in their countries' governments should have been included. Even so, Monshipouri concluded that *Islam and Democracy* has a "depth of analysis regarding the complex and dynamic relationships between Islamic resurgence and democratization" and that the authors "make their case very elegantly and cogently, and support their arguments with meticulously investigated case studies."

Political Science Quarterly reviewer Stephen Pelletiere said he believed the authors do not come "to grips with the problem they have set for themselves." His primary question went unanswered: If Islam itself is not causing the violence being carried out in its name, what is causing it? Pelletiere concluded that the book is valuable as a resource about general Islamic religious practice and movements, but he said, "learning about a religious phenomenon specifically tied to present day politics is not on offer here." Similary, Adam Tarock of the *Australian Journal of Political Science* called the book simply "a very valuable addition to the literature on Islam and Islamic societies."

Middle Eastern Studies contributor Gabriel Warburg, in a lengthy review of *Islam and Democracy,* wrote, "The authors seem to glorify political participation and civil society, as opposed to authoritarian oppressive regimes. However, both seem mistaken attempts to transplant Western ideas and institutions into regions which do not seem to be ready or willing to embrace them." Reza Afshari, in a review for *Journal of Church and State,* believed likewise, saying, "In countries under discussion, the sociopolitical and economic realities are too messy to be neatly remade by any single ideological paradigm, religious or secular; and, most likely, peoples will stumble from one painful experimentation to another on the bumpy road to a very uncertain future. No historical judgment is appropriate; no premature scholarly celebration, however subdued, is called for." Afshari also disagreed with the authors' assessment of case studies, concluding, "Islamic revivalism has aggravated the existing national divisions and political conflicts, often exacerbating the tensions associated with economic inequality, factionalism, and religious-ethnic diversities. Only time would tell whether politicization of Islam for these countries was anything more than an addition to the twentieth century's list of self-inflicted wounds."

Charles E. Butterworth, in a review for *Arab Studies Quarterly,* concluded, "John Esposito and John Voll have provided an excellent portrait of the status of democracy in the Islamic world today. Their deep understanding of Islam, familiarity with Islamic culture, and solid knowledge of Islamic history make their exposition highly readable and most persuasive. Scholars, students, and even the generally interested public will learn from it."

Esposito was both editor and contributor to the 1997 volume, *Political Islam: Revolution, Radicalism, or Reform?* The book grew out of a conference at the Center for Muslim-Christian Understanding at Georgetown University, which is directed by Esposito. It is divided into three sections: "Political Islam as Illegal Opposition," "Islam in the Political Process," and "The International Relations of Political Islam." Chapters are written by authoritative voices on the subject of Islam, including Lisa Anderson, Mohsen M. Milani, S. V. R. Nasr, Raymond William Baker, Yvonne Yazbeck Haddad, Barnett R. Rubin, John O. Voll, and Esposito. Containing many of the same arguments presented in Esposito's earlier work, *The Islamic Threat,* this book furthers that discussion, with several of the chapters built around country studies, discussing regional governmental arrangements and economies.

Studies in Comparative International Development reviewer Jillian Schwedler wrote, "Although most comparativists continue to broadly essentialize and exclude Islamic regions from their comparative models, the contributors to this volume have done a tremendous job not only in presenting a valuable set of well-researched and informative case studies, but moving beyond a rearticulation of Esposito's 1992 thesis." Schwedler thought Baker's chapter on the emerging centrist Islamist movement in Egypt is "one of the volume's most engaging contributions," because it shows that a movement can be nonviolent and fruitful and can be carried out from the grassroots level. The reviewer recommended this book for Middle East specialists but especially for those who are not specialists, saying they will find a "wealth of empirical information describing the diversity of Islamist movements, economic and institutional constraints," as well as many possibilities for comparing political styles of the regimes across regions.

Louis J. Cantori, in a review of *Political Islam* for the *American Political Science Review,* remarked that the book "may be one of the single most important scholarly volumes on the controversial subject of political Islam." He praised the book's authors and its organization, which, he said, "separates radical political Islam as a numerically less important phenomenon from reformist Islam and Islam as a worldwide power." Cantori concluded: "This volume is rich in its analysis of the general characteristics of political Islam and also in its important case studies. . . . In the process of telling its complex story so effectively, the volume throws into contrast the conceptual barrenness of a mainstream political science whose intrinsic pluralism fails in application to the non-Western world." Glenn E. Perry, in a review for *Perspectives on Political Science,* praised the volume, stating that it "presents enlightened analyses of matters that are scarcely ever treated in the U.S. mass media or in materials such as general political science textbooks in other than an ill-informed and prejudiced fashion." Perry touted the book as "essential reading for all those who are seriously concerned about Middle Eastern affairs or religion and politics generally." He also concluded, "It should be a high priority for libraries and should be assigned to students in a variety of courses."

Arab Studies Quarterly contributor Antony T. Sullivan also highly recommended *Political Islam.* Referring to the contributions as being "uniformly of excellent quality," Sullivan said the book should be "required reading by those charged with the formulation of American foreign policy" and that it "qualifies as that rare compendium deserving of the most careful attention by scholars and government officials alike." Commenting on Esposito's chapter on the Persian Gulf states, Sullivan wrote that the author "notes that the change of attitude by Islamists in many Arab countries from censure of to support for [Saddam] Hussein after he seized Kuwait was occasioned by America's decision to take the lead in ousting Iraq from that country." Sullivan quotes Esposito as saying, "Saddam Hussein might be wrong, . . . but it is not America who should correct him." Sullivan continued, "Esposito notes the inconsistency of American insistence on rigorous implementation of all U.N. resolutions concerning Iraq and its prevention of similar resolutions from being enforced that have been directed against Israel." In conclusion, Sullivan found that, "On all counts, this book simply represents a five-star performance."

Robert Springborg, in a review of *Political Islam* for the *Australian Journal of Political Science,* observed, "The volume is a very useful antidote to those interpretations that see political Islam as a monolithic, threatening force, invariably opposed to Western interests and even 'Western civilisation' writ large. . . .The collection argues that . . . political Islam can be a force for stabilising and even democratizing political orders, rather than one for *fitna,* the 'chaos' so much decried by Islamic political theory and jurisprudence, to say nothing of being feared by those Washington decision-makers." As'ad AbuKhalil, in a review for the *Journal of Palestine Studies,* commented on Yvonne Haddad's chapter on the Palestinians, saying she "presents a detailed reading of the position of fundamentalists on the peace process, although she can be criticized for cleaning up the language of the fundamentalists. . . . This is not meant to imply that the so-called peace process is just and sound; it needs to be derailed because it merely perpetuates the historical injustices against the Palestinian people. But the fundamentalists, given their rhetoric and actions, are not the logical candidates for the restoration of any kind of justice." AbuKhalil also said John Voll, in his chapter on the relations between Islamist groups, "wisely discredits the international Islamist conspiracy theory, while providing information on some common features shared by world fundamentalist organizations." AbuKhalil concluded by saying, "Those who wish to begin studying the subject of political Islam to escape the misconceptions abundant in Western books and newspapers should read this book."

Middle East Policy reviewer Mahmood Monshipouri, in a review of *Political Islam,* commented on Rubin's chapter, "Arab Islamists in Afghanistan," saying the author "reminds us that Arab Islamists continue to be active in Afghanistan so long as the international community is not providing Afghans with any reliable alternative to the aid they provide. Rubin's reasoning concerning the internal logic of violence in the Arab world is well established: the omnipresent violence . . . is traceable neither to a handful of activists returning from Afghanistan nor to other exogenous sources; rather, its roots are indigenous. In the post-Cold War world, Rubin warns, one needs to be aware of the illusion as well as the danger of replacing the Soviet Communist threat with the 'undifferentiated image of the fundamentalist terrorist.'" Although Monshipouri said he would have liked to see more emphasis on the issue of globalization and that he thought Turkey should have been included among the countries discussed, he closed his review by saying, "In a rigorous account of what continues to be a little-understood subject, Professor Esposito and the other contributors to this volume have sparked a lively discussion in both academic and policy circles about the impacts, both real and potential, of political Islam. This book is a must-read for anybody eager to probe beneath the surface of this challenging subject."

Esposito collaborates with Yvonne Yazbeck Haddad as editor of several books, one of which is *Islam, Gender and Social Change*. A compilation of case studies from a variety of nations and Muslim contexts, the book contains eleven essays and is divided into two sections, one focusing on conceptual issues and the other on the case studies themselves. Gender relations and politics in Islamic nations are discussed in relation to class, politics, personal identity, and religion. In a chapter on state-sponsored feminism in Egypt, Mervat Hatem outlines state programs for the education of women that channel them into traditional feminine roles, such as those of teacher, nurse, and secretary. Rural women's labor in farming has been disregarded, with the ownership of land being designated primarily to men. And while education and professional reforms brought women some gains, personal status laws governing marriage, divorce, and inheritance were left to the strictly conservative religious authorities. In recent years, the government has placed more emphasis on motherhood as the primary role of women, discouraging women from joining the professions and even the workforce, except in dire economic need, and then only when covering themselves to remove all traces of their gender.

Journal of Women's History writer Jasamin Rostam-Kolayi pointed out, "Hatem's conclusions have significant implications for women challenging the state. She alerts us to the limitations of state feminism, the secular state's strategic positioning of family issues in the domain of religion, and the modernizing dynamic within Islamist discourses which replicates unequal gender relations. Studies that feature Islamist women themselves, however, present more nuanced and conflicting findings." May Seikaly's essay on women and work in Bahrain includes interviews with many modern-day women, who insist that it is their right to work to help support their families as long as their jobs include gender-segregated workplaces and they wear *hijab*, or traditional Muslim dress. Another essay, by Afsaneh Najmabadi, includes writings from the Persian-language women's magazine *Zanan*, founded in 1992. Many of the magazine's contributors have written articles that redefine terms reinforcing the subordination of women so that they "envision more cooperative, egalitarian relations between husband and wife and a more equal status for women in society," said Rostam-Kolayi. Yet, she pointed out that the author does not say who *Zanan*'s readers are, and she concludes that progressive strides advocated by the magazine are not being made in many Muslim nations.

With Azzam Tamimi, Esposito edited the collection of essays *Islam and Secularism in the Middle East*, published in 2000. In a review for the *Middle East Journal*, Henry Munson said the book suffers from a "moral myopia" common to Middle Eastern studies. Munson found the book to be mainly a critique of the prevalent secularist tendency to regard Muslims combining religion and politics as dangerous extremists. He found flaws in essayist Peter Berger's work, "Secularism in Retreat," which makes the claim that "the critique of secularity common to all the resurgent movements is that human existence bereft of transcendence is an impoverished . . . condition." Munson asks whether the volume's essayists could not simply accept the fact that life without some form of religion is impoverished for all people, without an effort to create a religious state.

Esposito has edited two books on Iran. The second, *Iran at the Crossroads*, edited with R. K. Ramazani, presents the conflict between a fledgling Iranian democracy headed by President Mohammad Khatami and a parliament and the superior rule of the Islamic component, headed by the Ayatollah Ali Khamenei and his militant conservative forces. While Iran is being introduced to the concepts of democracy and has twice elected its president, the religious leader wields the greater power in the country. Essayist Mohsen Milani predicts that a full transition to democracy in Iran will be slow and violent, and he recommends collaboration between the two leaders as far as possible. Essayist Farideh Farhi writes about the necessary adjustment of the Iranian political system to socioeconomic, political, and cultural changes, including changes in women's rights. Farhi stresses that political discussion about change in Iran is far ahead of actual changes. Essayist Haleh Esfandiari also writes about the gains Iranian women have made and the techniques of organization and lobbying they have learned in pursuit of greater freedoms. In a review for *Middle East Policy,* Mahmood Monshipouri commented that both authors' chapters "could have benefited from a much more in-depth analysis of the legal traditions and paternalistic attitudes still pervasive in all aspects of Iran's society and polity." Monshipouri also thought that greater attention to the study of art and cinema in Iranian culture would have improved these chapters, since it is through these media that many changes are being effected.

Other chapters in the book focus on Iran's economic problems; the religious jurist in Iran; Iranian foreign policy toward Russia, Central Asia, and the Caucasus after the collapse of the Soviet Union; European perspectives on Iran; the alienation between the United States and Iran; and Iran's national interest, including the globalization of its economics and communications. Monshipouri concluded his review with some criticisms, saying, the book "seems to have ignored some new developments, such as the attitude of Iranian policy makers and academia to the processes of globalization and Iran's global interests. One of the areas inadequately explored . . . is that of the decline of Islamic ideology and leadership. Islamic political ideology . . . has been more seriously called into question by a disenchanted public, the youth culture and many other forms of protest. Sorely missing from this volume is a detailed discussion of the state of human rights in Iran in view of the current practice of public flogging, limits to religious freedoms, the closure of reformist newspapers, and cultural and political disputes over what constitutes universal human rights." However, the reviewer said, "Criticisms apart, this book is a valuable contribution to our understanding of the complexities and contradictions inherent in Iranian politics and society." In a review for *Library Journal,* Nader Entessar called *Iran at the Crossroads* "engaging and informative" and "scholarly yet accessible."

Esposito and coauthor John O. Voll published *Makers of Contemporary Islam* in 2001. This book is an overview of the lives and writings of nine Muslim activist intellectuals of the second half of the twentieth century, whose works span three different periods in the development of modern Islamic thought and who represent Islamic societies from North Africa to Southeast Asia. These nine controversial figures have been both accepted and rejected by their people or by political leaders, and many are at cross purposes with other Islamic activists in their regions. The nine figures are: Ismail Ragi al-Faruqi, Khurshid Ahmad, Maryam Jameelah, Hasan Hanafi, Rashid Ghannoushi, Hasan Turabi, Abdolkarim Soroush, Anwar Ibrahim, and Abdurrahman Wahid. A major theme of the book is whether Shari'a, or Islamic law, should be established as the governing law of Muslim nations. In a review for the *Middle East Journal,* Linda S. Walbridge objected to some copyediting errors but said the book nevertheless "makes a valuable contribution to the study of modern Islamic movements. It allows the reader to see how the 'intellectual descendants' of major figures such as Sayyid Qutb and al-Mawdudi have incorporated or rejected their forebears' ideas in shaping the discourse of Islam in the modern world." Michael R. Fischbach, in a review for the *Journal of Palestine Studies,* stated that Esposito and Voll's work fills a "void in the literature on Islamic resurgence" by illuminating the role of intellectuals.

In the aftermath of the September 11, 2001, attacks on the United States by the Islamic extremist organization al-Qaeda and its leader Osama bin Laden, Esposito wrote two books to help the American public and other Westerners understand what might have been the motives behind the attacks. The first of these is *Unholy War: Terror in the Name of Islam.* In this book, Esposito explains in detail the important Muslim concept of *jihad* (religious war) and its many interpretations, from one of personal striving for religious obedience to the most extreme, which calls for open aggression against those thought to be the "infidels." Esposito includes a brief biography of bin Laden and of other Islamic extremists whose teachings have, over time, given rise to the modern-day thinking that is responsible for terrorist acts such as suicide bombings and the destruction of the World Trade Centers and the Pentagon attack in 2001, using American passenger planes. Esposito reiterates some of the points made in earlier books, such as *The Islamic Threat,* that many Muslims object to the U.S. support of Israel and to its aggressive presence in the Middle East. The author also shows how economic conditions and political underdevelopment in Muslim nations have contributed to anger and resentment toward the United States, and he examines the struggle for women's rights in Muslim countries.

According to reviewer Muqtedar Khan, in the *Washington Report on Middle East Affairs,* Esposito "unravels the layered complexity of global politics and explains how the phenomenon of global terrorism articulated in the language of Islam has emerged as a counterforce to Pax Americana." Khan said, "Esposito also addresses the loud claims of American neoconservatives that Islam itself, not just radical Muslims, is inherently incompatible with the cluster of values which some pretentious Westerners call Western and liberals call universal." Esposito, in his book, expresses concern that the so-called war on terrorism, with its military, rather than diplomatic, thrust, will prove counterproductive to peace and instead call forth more terrorist attacks on Western countries.

Khan and other reviewers noted a shift in Esposito's position on Islamic revivalism from his 1992 book *The Islamic Threat* to the present volume. In his earlier work the author seemed not to believe that extremists would carry their *jihad* as far as they have, but in *Unholy War* he notes that a lot has happened regarding the Muslim world since 1992. He advises Western leaders to rethink their policies on Islamic nations and makes it clear that American meddling in Muslim affairs has made the world more dangerous for Islam and for Americans. Khan concluded that Esposito's *Unholy War* "is a masterful rendition by a scholar in his prime. . . . Journalists, academics, students, policymakers and attentive people who care about the ramifications of 9/11 cannot afford not to pick up this book. Once they do, they will put it down only to reflect on the issues it raises."

In an opposite and somewhat angry review, Patrick Clawson of *Commentary* found that, in contrast to Esposito's earlier book, *The Islamic Threat,* "we now learn that when modern extremists call for jihad against Muslims deemed un-Islamic, or for spreading the religion by the sword, they are following well-established tradition. . . . As in his previous book, Esposito searches in *Unholy War* for ways to blame the West for every ill of the Muslim world. . . . Esposito's eagerness to attack the West at every turn stands in sharp contrast to his habit of excusing troubling Islamist practices." Clawson concluded, "It may be tempting to dismiss the intellectual tendency represented by Esposito as inconsequential—after all, U.S. policy toward Islamist radicals and those who harbor them has of late been rather tough. But . . . those who downplayed the dangers posed by the currents of radical Islam had become, by the early 1990s, an entrenched academic elite, while those sounding the alarm were effectively marginalized. The shock delivered to the United States nine months ago has reopened this broad discussion, and in the world of opinion there are encouraging signs of a more realistic appraisal of our adversaries."

In a more favorable review, Nader Entessar of *Library Journal* called *Unholy War* "essential reading for every concerned citizen" who wants to understand Islam and its struggles. A *Publishers Weekly* contributor called the book "a welcome antidote against simplistic attitudes toward Islam." A reviewer for *Kirkus Reviews* described the book as "a primer on modern varieties of terrorism and a well-reasoned plea for tolerance" in these times. A contributor to *About.com* commented, "Anyone interested in learning what sorts of political, religious and social factors have led to the current state of Islam, and perhaps what sorts of changes may be necessary for a long-term improvement . . . would be hard-pressed to find a better starting point than Esposito's book."

What Everyone Needs to Know about Islam is a compilation of the most pressing questions Esposito has been asked in his many talks about Islam. He provides answers to such questions as "What do Muslims believe?, What is the Muslim scripture?, What is meant by Holy War?," and "Why do Muslims hate us?" This is a short and simple book, accessible to the general public, and highly informative on the subject of the world's one billion Muslims.

Esposito has edited three reference works on Islam: *The Oxford Encyclopedia of the Modern Islamic World, The Oxford History of Islam,* and *The Oxford Dictionary of Islam.* Reviewers found the first to be more suited to a general audience and to students than to scholarly researchers but to contain a wide variety of relative subjects, with some 750 entries. The two basic types of articles—with word counts that range from 500 to 10,000—are those covering Islamic religious, legal, and political topics as well as biographies of some 100 contemporary Islamic leaders and scholars.

These articles are listed under their proper names or Arabic-Islamic terms. The second type of article is listed under English terms and covers broad concepts, such as Economics, Literature, Medicine, Cinema, Dress, Human Rights, Women in Islam, and Health Care. *Journal of the American Oriental Society* reviewer Ira M. Lapidus found the first type of article to be the encyclopedia's strongest aspect. Some of the topics of the second type were adequately covered, Lapidus pointed out, but others were too brief to give a full understanding of the issues without using the bibliography to read further. Lapidus found the topic of Muslim minorities in non-Muslim countries to be the most lacking. Although he wrote that the *Oxford Encyclopedia of the Modern Islamic World* "will not work well as a reference work for scholarly research," Lapidus concluded that, "All in all, this work is a useful addition to the repertoire of research and information tools, and is particularly welcome for making Islamic subjects accessible and intelligible to a wider non-scholarly public." Sandy Whiteley of *Booklist* also found the encyclopedia most useful to the general public, but she praised Esposito's efforts, saying he "has recruited more than 450 distinguished contributors from the fields of art history, religion, science, anthropology, political science, and other disciplines. . . . Every attempt has been made to provide a balanced approach, and the inclusion of contributors from many parts of the world has helped to avoid what the editor calls the 'pitfalls of Orientalism.'"

The Oxford History of Islam contains fifteen chapters and more than 300 colorful illustrations. Imad-ad-Dean Ahmad, in a review for *Middle East Policy,* said the book covers "most areas of interest to those who would widen their knowledge of Islamic history from 'Muhammad and the Caliphate' to 'Contemporary Islam.'" Ahmad found the first chapter, written by Fred M. Donner, on early Muslim history to the Mongol conquest to be "marred by oversimplifications and allusions that are impenetrable by the novice." He praised other chapters, however, calling Majid Fakhry's article on the complexities of Islamic philosophy and theology perhaps the best. The reviewer also enjoyed the chapter on art and architecture, by Sheila S. Blair and Jonathan M. Bloom, for its carefully chosen illustrations and for the authors' "appreciation for the theological significance of Islamic art as well as for its artistic merits." Ahmad praised Nehemia Lentzion's chapter "Islam in Africa to 1800" and Jane I. Smith's chapter on Muslim-Christian interactions. He also commented favorably on chapters related to modern Muslim states, the globalization of Islam, and on Esposito's own chapter on contemporary Islam. Harold S. Vogelaar of the *Christian Century* highly recommended the volume "because John Esposito has done so masterful a job of presenting a history of Islam that moves with integrity from its humble origins to its current worldwide significance." Vogelaar said the writers "select out of a vast ocean of material those events, people and ideas that make a particular topic lucid and understandable, especially for readers new to the field." Michael W. Ellis, in a review for *Library Journal,* called the book "meticulous and thorough, readable and comprehensive." Michael R. Fischbach, in a review for the *Journal of Palestine Studies,* said the *Oxford History of Islam* "surely will come to be regarded as a standard work in the field for years to come."

Esposito more recently told *CA:* " In 1978-79, as a result of the impact of the Iranian revolution, I was offered several book contracts. The experience of writing books and realizing their potential audiences and impact, set me on a path, which has been rewarding in every sense of the term. My wife, Jeanette Esposito, has been the most important influence as well as the desire to build bridges of understanding between the Muslim world and the West.

"My writing process has varied a bit, but generally my pattern has been to rise very early, get a good run in, then write and edit for much of the day when my schedule permits. On days when I have other commitments, the ability to write very early in the daya allows me to do a good deal of writing before I leave the house.

"Among my favorite books are my two post 9/11 books, *Unholy War: Terror in the Name of Islam,* and *What Everyone Needs to Know about Islam. Unholy War* enabled me to place 9/11 and global terrorism within a broader context. *What Everyone Needs to Know about Islam* provided an opportunity to address the many questions about Islam and Muslims I received from the media, government officials, and general audiences in a q & a format. *Islam: The Straight Path* and *The Islamic Threat: Myth or Reality?* have had long 'careers,' going through several editions/ revisions and being used by very diverse audiences. *The Oxford History of Islam* has enjoyed great success because of both its text and rich array of illustrations.

"I want people to know about the richness and diversity of Islam (as a religion and civilization), and Muslim cultures and to appreciate that there is a Judeo-Christian-Islamic tradition. I want Muslims to better understand their shared historic past and current relationships and challenges.

BIOGRAPHICAL AND CRITICAL SOURCES:

BOOKS

Directory of American Scholars, 10th edition, Gale (Detroit, MI), 2001.

PERIODICALS

AB Bookman's Weekly, June 21, 1982, review of *Women in Muslim Family Law,* p. 4835.
American-Arab Affairs, summer, 1985, review of *Islam and Politics,* p. 124.
American Historical Review, October, 1981, review of *Islam and Development: Religion and Sociopolitical Change,* p. 894; October, 1986, Charles J. Adams, review of *Islam and Politics,* p. 969.
American Libraries, May, 1996, review of *The Oxford Encyclopedia of the Modern Islamic World,* p. 65.
American Political Science Review, March, 1986, review of *Islam and Politics,* p. 347; March, 1989, Clarke E. Cochran, review of *Islam in Asia: Religion, Politics, and Society,* p. 255; March, 1999, Louis J. Cantori, review of *Political Islam: Revolution: Radicalism, or Reform?,* p. 220.
American Reference Books Annual, 1996, review of *The Oxford Encyclopedia of the Modern Islamic World,* p. 628.
Arab Studies Quarterly, summer, 1993, Antony T. Sullivan, review of *The Islamic Threat: Myth or Reality?,* p. 130; spring, 1999, Charles E. Butterworth, review of *Islam and Democracy,* p. 100; fall, 1999, Antony T. Sullivan, review of *Political Islam,* p. 109.
Asian Affairs, February, 1989, Anthony Hyman, review of *Islam in Asia,* p. 77; October, 1993, Ivor Lucas, review of *The Islamic Threat,* p. 328; February 2001, Peter Clark, review of *The Oxford History of Islam,* p. 70.
Australian Journal of Political Science, July, 1997, Adam Tarock, review of *Islam and Democracy,* p. 314; July, 1998, Robert Springborg, review of *Political Islam,* p. 307.

Best Sellers, February, 1985, review of *Islam and Politics,* p. 426.
Booklist, September 15, 1988, review of *Islam: The Straight Path,* p. 102; May 1, 1995, Sandy Whiteley, review of *The Oxford Encyclopedia of the Modern Islamic World,* p. 1588.
Bookwatch, November, 1991, review of *Islam and Politics,* 3rd edition, p. 7.
Book World, March 24, 1991, review of *Islam: The Straight Path,* p. 13; October 21, 2001, review of *The Islamic Threat,* 3rd edition, and *Islam and Democracy,* p. 15.
Choice, April, 1981, review of *Islam and Development,* p. 1154; June, 1982, review of *Women in Muslim Family Law,* p. 1448; June, 1984, review of *Voices of Resurgent Islam,* p. 1483; March, 1985, review of *Islam and Politics,* p. 1010; September, 1987, review of *Islam in Asia,* p. 150; April, 1989, review of *Islam: The Straight Path,* p. 1349; June, 1991, review of *The Iranian Revolution: Its Global Impact,* p. 1708; February, 1993, review of *The Iranian Revolution,* p. 923; March, 1993, M. Swartz, review of *The Islamic Threat,* p. 1174; December, 1996, review of *Islam and Democracy,* p. 685; June, 1998, L. J. Cantori, review of *Political Islam,* p. 1781; November, 1998, S. Ward, review of *Islam, Gender and Social Change,* p. 536; July-August, 2000, G. R. G. Hambly, review of *The Oxford History of Islam,* p. 2033; June, 2002, M. Swartz, review of *The Islamic Threat,* p. SF-5, S. Ward, review of *Islam, Gender and Social Change,* p. SF-6, G. R. G. Hambly, review of *The Oxford History of Islam,* p. SF-14, L. J. Cantori, review of *Political Islam,* p. SF-23, P. L. Redditt, review of *World Religions Today,* p. 1786.
Christian Century, February 24, 1988, review of *Islam and Politics,* 2nd edition, p. 195; December 1, 1993, Harold Vogelaar, review of *The Islamic Threat,* p. 1214; August 16, 2000, Harold S. Vogelaar, review of *The Oxford History of Islam,* p. 841.
Christianity and Crisis, October 19, 1992, Dale L. Bishop, review of *The Islamic Threat,* p. 361.
Christian Science Monitor, January 5, 1993, George D. Moffett III, review of *The Islamic Threat,* p. 11; July 10, 1996, Judith Caesar, review of *Islam and Democracy,* p. 14.
Commentary, June, 2002, Patrick Clawson, "The Expert," review of *Unholy War: Terror in the Name of Islam,* p. 61.

Commonweal, December 7, 1990, review of *Islam: The Straight Path,* p. 727; February 12, 1993, George Perkovich, review of *The Islamic Threat,* p. 21.

Contemporary Review, March, 1985, review of *Voices of Resurgent Islam,* p. 163.

Contemporary Sociology, September, 1988, Hamid Dabashi, "What Is to Be Done? The Enlightened Thinkers and an Islamic Renaissance," p. 599; March, 1994, Mary-Jane Deeb, review of *The Islamic Threat,* p. 256.

Current History, February, 1994, William F. Finan, review of *The Islamic Threat,* p. 92.

Digest of Middle East Studies, summer, 1993, review of *The Islamic Threat,* p. 15.

Economist, March 13, 1993, review of *The Islamic Threat,* p. 102.

Ethics & International Affairs, annual, 1999, Sohail Hashmi, review of *Political Islam,* p. 272.

First Things: A Monthly Journal of Religion and Public Life, January, 1996, Bernard Lewis, review of *The Oxford Encyclopedia of the Modern Islamic World,* p. 40; January, 1997, Joshua Muravchik, review of *Islam and Democracy,* p. 47.

Foreign Affairs, summer, 1984, review of *Voices of Resurgent Islam,* p. 1263; April, 1985, review of *Islam and Politics,* p. 927; February, 1993, review of *The Islamic Threat,* p. 180; September-October, 1996, William B. Quandt, review of *Islam and Democracy,* p. 154.

Guardian Weekly, March 24, 1991, review of *Islam: The Straight Path,* p. 27; April 25, 1993, review of *The Islamic Threat,* p. 29.

History Today, February, 1991, William Montgomery Watt, review of *Islam: The Straight Path,* p. 59.

International Affairs, July, 1993, Maria Holt, review of *The Islamic Threat,* p. 610; January, 2001, John Anderson, review of *Religion and Global Order,* p. 196.

International Journal of Middle East Studies, May, 1991, Richard C. Martin, review of *Islam: The Straight Path,* p. 238; November, 1993, John P. Entelis, review of *The Islamic Threat,* p. 684; August, 1997, Leonard Binder, review of *Islam and Democracy,* p. 427.

Journal of Asian Studies, May, 1988, Robert L. Winzeler, review of *Islam in Asia,* p. 323.

Journal of Church and State, spring, 1982, review of *Islam and Development,* p. 383; spring, 1987, Juan R. I. Cole, review of *Islam and Politics,* p. 342; autumn, 1988, William R. Roff, review of *Islam in Asia,* p. 597; summer, 1992, Raphael Israeli, review of *The Iranian Revolution,* p. 616; summer, 1994, Barbara R. von Schlegell, review of *The Islamic Threat,* p. 614; spring, 1998, Reza Afshari, review of *Islam and Democracy,* p. 469-470.

Journal of Democracy, October, 1997, Ibrahim A. Karawan, review of *Islam and Democracy,* p. 170.

Journal of Developing Areas, April, 1986, Tareq Y. Ismael, review of *Islam and Politics,* p. 400; spring, 1998, Michael Johnson, review of *Political Islam,* p. 417.

Journal of Interdisciplinary History, winter, 1992, Manochehr Dorraj, review of *The Iranian Revolution,* p. 569.

Journal of Law and Religion, winter-summer, 2000, Jorn Thielmann, review of *Islam and Politics,* p. 615-619, Harold S. Vogelaar, review of *The Islamic Threat,* p. 625-626.

Journal of Marriage and the Family, February, 1983, review of *Women in Muslim Family Law,* p. 237.

Journal of Palestine Studies, summer, 1993, Richard W. Bulliet, review of *The Islamic Threat,* p. 105; autumn, 1997, Lawrence Tal, review of *Islam and Democracy,* p. 106; summer, 1998, As'ad AbuKhalil, review of *Political Islam,* p. 114; summer, 2000, Michael R. Fischbach, review of *The Oxford History of Islam,* p. 116; autumn, 2001, Michael R. Fischbach, review of *Makers of Contemporary Islam,* p. 100.

Journal of Peace Research, August, 1994, Dieter Senghaas, review of *The Islamic Threat,* p. 361.

Journal of Politics, February, 1982, review of *Islam and Development,* p. 297.

Journal of Religion, January, 1984, review of *Islam and Development,* p. 133.

Journal of the American Academy of Religion, summer, 1993, Gisela Webb, review of *Islam: The Straight Path,* p. 359; March, 2000, Nayereh Tohidi, review of *Islam, Gender and Social Change,* p. 178.

Journal of the American Oriental Society, April-June, 1997, Ira M. Lapidus, review of *The Oxford Encyclopedia of the Modern Islamic World,* p. 390.

Journal of Third World Studies, spring, 1996, Rolin G. Mainuddin, review of *The Islamic Threat,* p. 233; spring, 2001, Amalendu Misra, review of *Political Islam,* p. 307.

Journal of Women's History, winter, 1999, Jasamin Rostam-Kolayi, review of *Islam, Gender and Social Change,* p. 205.

Kirkus Reviews, August 1, 1992, review of *The Islamic Threat,* p. 961; April 15, 2002, review of *Unholy War,* p. 542.

Library Journal, December, 1984, review of *Islam and Politics,* p. 2286; September 15, 1988, review of *Islam: The Straight Path,* p. 74; March 15, 1995, James F. DeRoche, review of *The Oxford Encyclopedia of the Modern Islamic World,* p. 62; April 15, 1996, review of *The Oxford Encyclopedia of the Modern Islamic World,* p. 42; May 1, 1998, James F. DeRoche, review of *Islam: The Straight Path,* 3rd edition, p. 103; October 1, 1998, review of *Islam: The Straight Path,* 3rd edition, p. 61; November 15, 1999, Michael W. Ellis, review of *The Oxford History of Islam,* p. 74; February 15, 2001, Nader Entessar, review of *Iran at the Crossroads,* p. 186; November 15, 2001, Martha Cornog, Elizabeth J. Plantz, reviews of *The Oxford History of Islam, The Islamic Threat,* 3rd edition, and *Islam: The Straight Path,* 3rd edition, p. 82; May 1, 2002, Nader Entessar, review of *Unholy War,* p. 119.

London Review of Books, August 1, 1996, review of *The Oxford Encyclopedia of the Modern Islamic World,* p. 26.

Middle East, December, 1992, review of *The Islamic Threat,* p. 41.

Middle Eastern Studies, July, 1999, Gabriel Warburg, review of *Islam and Democracy,* p. 178.

Middle East Journal, summer, 1981, review of *Islam and Development,* p. 417; spring, 1983, review of *Women in Muslim Family Law,* p. 298; summer, 1985, review of *Islam and Politics,* p. 428; summer, 1989, Carolyn Fluehr-Lobban, review of *Islam: The Straight Path,* p. 542; summer, 1991, John C. Campbell, review of *The Iranian Revolution,* p. 504; spring, 1992, review of *Islam and Politics,* p. 341; autumn, 1995, review of *The Oxford Encyclopedia of the Modern Islamic World,* p. 692; summer, 1997, review of *Islam and Democracy,* p. 461; winter, 1998, review of *Political Islam,* p. 141; summer, 2001, Henry Munson, review of *Islam and Secularism in the Middle East,* p. 520, review of *The Oxford History of Islam,* p. 527; winter, 2002, Linda S. Walbridge, review of *Makers of Contemporary Islam,* p. 174.

Middle East Policy, April, 1992, review of *The Islamic Threat,* p. 145; fall, 1992, Grace Halsell, review of *The Islamic Threat,* p. 145; January, 1998, Mahmood Monshipouri, review of *Political Islam,* p. 198; April, 1998, review of *Political Islam: Revolution,* p. 198; October, 2000, Imad-ad-Dean Ahmad, review of *The Oxford History of Islam,* p. 197; December, 2001, Mahmood Monshipouri, review of *Iran at the Crossroads,* p. 154.

Muslim World, January, 1990, Leila Fawaz, review of *Islam: The Straight Path,* p. 53; April, 1993, Ibrahim M. Abu-Rabi, review of *The Islamic Threat,* p. 192; April, 1998, Cari Salisbury, review of *Islam and Democracy,* p. 197.

New Statesman & Society, April 9, 1993, Stephen Howe, review of *The Islamic Threat,* p. 56.

Newsweek, February 18, 1991, review of *Islam: The Straight Path,* expanded edition, p. 62.

New York Law Journal, June 7, 2002, Edward A. Purcell, Jr., review of *Unholy War,* p. 2.

New York Times Book Review, December 13, 1992, Nikki R. Keddie, review of *The Islamic Threat,* p. 7.

Orbis, spring, 1993, Daniel Pipes, review of *The Islamic Threat,* p. 313.

Pacific Affairs, summer, 1988, Judith Nagata, review of *Islam in Asia,* p. 317.

Parameters: U.S. Army War College Quarterly, summer, 1997, review of *Islam and Democracy,* p. 137.

Perspective, November, 1981, review of *Islam and Development,* p. 164; March, 1985, review of *Islam and Politics,* p. 42.

Perspectives on Political Science, summer, 1993, review of *The Iranian Revolution,* p. 138; winter, 1998, Glenn E. Perry, review of *Political Islam: Revolution,* p. 47.

Political Science Quarterly, spring, 1993, Kiren Aziz Chaudhry, review of *The Islamic Threat,* p. 170; fall, 1997, Stephen Pelletiere, review of *Islam and Democracy,* p. 516.

Publishers Weekly, July 22, 1988, Penny Kaganoff, review of *Islam: The Straight Path,* p. 53; November 8, 1999, review of *The Oxford History of Islam,* p. 62; April 29, 2002, review of *Unholy War,* p. 53.

Reference & Research Book News, August, 2001, review of *Iran at the Crossroads,* p. 41.

Religious Studies Review, July, 1981, review of *Islam and Development,* p. 269; April, 1984, review of *Women in Muslim Family Law,* p. 193; July, 1984, review of *Voices of Resurgent Islam,* p. 307; July, 1985, review of *Islam and Politics,* p. 313; October, 1990, review of *Islam: The Straight Path,* p. 363.

Review of Politics, winter, 1997, Mahmood Monshipouri, review of *Islam and Democracy,* p. 197.

Studies in Comparative International Development, summer, 1999, Jillian Schwedler, review of *Political Islam: Revolution,* p. 70.

Times Educational Supplement, July 9, 1993, review of *The Islamic Threat,* p. 24.

Times Higher Education Supplement, September 15, 1995, Shabbir Akhtar, review of *The Oxford Encyclopedia of the Modern Islamic World,* p. 26.

Times Literary Supplement, December 2, 1988, review of *Islam and Politics,* p. 1353.

University Press Book News, December, 1991, review of *Islam and Politics,* 3rd edition, p. 5.

Village Voice Literary Supplement, June, 1991, review of *Islam: The Straight Path,* expanded edition, p. 17.

Wall Street Journal, October 30, 1992, Daniel Pipes, review of *The Islamic Threat,* p. A11; August 14, 2000, Eric Ormsby, "Bookshelf: The Inner and Outer Life of a World Religion," p. A16.

Washington Report on Middle East Affairs, August, 2002, Muqtedar Khan, review of *Unholy War,* p. 104.

ONLINE

About.com: Agnosticism, Atheism, http://atheism.about.com/ (August 7, 2002), review of *Unholy War.*

Danny Yee's Book Reviews Online, http://dannyreviews.com/ (September 2, 2000), Danny Yee, review of *Islam: The Straight Path.*

Islamic Bookstore.com, http://islamicbookstore.com/ (August 7, 2002), review of *The Oxford History of Islam.*

F

FILTZER, Donald (Arthur) 1948-

PERSONAL: Born January 8, 1948, in Baltimore, MD; son of David L. (an orthopedic surgeon) and Frances (Sacks) Filtzer. *Education:* Wesleyan University, B.A. (cum laude), 1969; University of Glasgow, Ph.D., 1976. *Politics:* Marxist.

ADDRESSES: Office—Department of Sociology, University of East London, Longbridge Rd., Dagenham, Essex RM8 2AS, England.

CAREER: University of Birmingham, Birmingham, England, research fellow at Centre for Russian and East European Studies, c. 1978; University of East London, Dagenham, Essex, England, began as reader, became professor of Russian history.

WRITINGS:

(Editor and translator) I. I. Rubin, *A History of Economic Thought,* Ink Links (London, England), 1979.
(Editor and author of introduction) E. A. Preobrazhensky, *The Crisis of Soviet Industrialization,* M. E. Sharpe (Armonk, NY), 1980.
Soviet Workers and Stalinist Industrialization: The Formation of Modern Soviet Production Relations, 1928-1941, Pluto Press (London, England), 1986.
Soviet Workers and De-Stalinization: The Consolidation of the Modern System of Soviet Production Relations, 1953-1964, Cambridge University Press (Cambridge, England), 1992.
The Khrushchev Era: De-Stalinization and the Limits of Reform in the USSR, 1953-1964, [London, England], 1993.
Soviet Workers and the Collapse of Perestroika: The Soviet Labour Process and Gorbachev's Reforms, 1985-1991, [Cambridge, England], 1994.
Soviet Workers and Late Stalinism: Labour and the Restoration of the Stalinist System after World War II, Cambridge University Press (Cambridge, England), 2002.

Contributor to anthologies, including *Labour in Transition: The Labour Process in Eastern Europe and China,* edited by Chris Smith and Paul Thompson, [London, England], 1992. Contributor to periodicals, including *Challenge, Critique, Europe-Asia Studies, Slavonic and East European Review, Social History,* and *Soviet Studies.*

WORK IN PROGRESS: Research on the social history of the U.S.S.R. in the immediate postwar period, 1945-1953.

SIDELIGHTS: In the *Times Literary Supplement,* reviewer Geoffrey Hosking hailed Donald Filtzer's *Soviet Workers and Stalinist Industrialization: The Formation of Modern Soviet Production Relations, 1928-1941* as "one of the most important contributions of recent years to Soviet social history." In the book, Filtzer asserted that Soviet workers of the 1930s assumed enough control over production to undermine all authoritarian attempts to govern them. The production demands of the young Soviet regime required an enormous work force, and this in itself forced planners to make concessions to the working class. Laziness, theft, and slipshod work habits had to be tolerated. Incentive programs to reward good workers were resented by other members of the work force. Treating work infringements as criminal offenses only encouraged middle-level management to cover up for subordinates and peers. Filtzer concluded that the stalemate created by Soviet workers more than fifty years ago has not abated. It contributes to the country's present reputation for waste and corruption in the workplace, poor quality of production, and an ongoing shortage of manual laborers. Hosking told his readers that Filtzer's "account of how the situation has arisen is vivid and instructive." He concluded: "This is a book which should be pondered by anyone who wants to understand the state of the Soviet Union today."

BIOGRAPHICAL AND CRITICAL SOURCES:

PERIODICALS

Slavonic and East European Review, April, 1998, Martin McCauley, review of *Soviet Workers and the Collapse of Perestroika: The Soviet Labour Process and Gorbachev's Reforms, 1985-1991,* p. 308.
Times Literary Supplement, May 27, 1987, Geoffrey Hosking, review of *Soviet Workers and Stalinist Industrialization: The Formation of Modern Soviet Production Relations, 1928-1941.*

* * *

FISK, Pauline 1948-

PERSONAL: Born September 27, 1948, in London, England; daughter of Gordon and Millicent Fisk; married David Davies (an architect), February 12, 1972; children: Nathaniel, Nancy, Beulah, Idris, Grace. *Education:* Attended Wimbledon County School for Girls, 1959-66. *Religion:* "Non-Conformist." *Hobbies and other interests:* Walking, reading, weaving.

ADDRESSES: Agent—Laura Cecil Agency, 17 Alwyne Villas, London N1 2HG, England.

CAREER: Writer.

Pauline Fisk

MEMBER: Society of Authors.

AWARDS, HONORS: Smarties Prize for Children's Books, overall winner and winner of nine-to-eleven-year-old group, Book Trust (England), and Whitbread Award for Children's Books shortlist, Booksellers Association of Great Britain and Ireland, both 1990, both for *Midnight Blue.*

WRITINGS:

The Southern Hill (stories), Lion (Batavia, IL), 1972.
Midnight Blue (novel for young people), Lion (Batavia, IL), 1990.
Telling the Sea (novel for young people), Lion (Batavia, IL), 1992.
Tyger Pool, Bodley Head Children's Books (London, England), 1994.
Sabrina Fludde, [England], 2001, published as *The Secret of Sabrina Fludde,* Bloomsbury Children's Books (New York, NY), 2002.

WORK IN PROGRESS: Lavender Castle, an animated television series, with fantasy artist Rodney Matthews, filmmaker Gerry Anderson, and composer and musician Rick Wakeman. Also working on the next installment of *The Secret of Sabrina Fludde* trilogy.

SIDELIGHTS: In 1990 Pauline Fisk won the most generous prize available to children's authors—the Smarties book award—for her first novel for young people, *Midnight Blue*. Fisk, who had been writing since she was a little girl, stopped writing for a time after the births of her five children. Finally she made time to write *Midnight Blue* by working on the novel in the early hours of the morning.

Midnight Blue was described by the Smarties jury—and book critics as well—as a gripping example of the classic conflict between good and evil. "The story is, in every sense, marvelous," wrote a reviewer for *Junior Bookshelf*. "The magical elements in it are closely integrated. There is no contrivance, and the action evolves naturally out of the characters and their situation. The same might be said of a number of other stories, but what makes this one so very special is the telling." A reviewer for the London *Sunday Times* explained, "*Midnight Blue* is the kind of book that casts a life-long spell over the imagination. It emerges as an original work which is far greater than the sum of its parts."

Fisk grew up in the suburbs of South London, and according to an article published on the BBC Web site, she was a shy young girl, uncomfortable in the world that she found surrounding her, so she began creating a world all of her own. "At the age of nine . . . she decided to become an author [and] began to write her own stories and poems based on characters form her favourite books."

She went on to write several more children's books after her award-winning *Midnight Blue*. *Tyger Pool*, a book tackling the difficult topic of the death of a young girl's mother, won praise from critics for the way Fisk handled the subject matter. At the *Healthy Books* Web site, a critic found *Tyger Pool* to be "full of symbol and can be read on several levels." Fisk wrote it as a story of fantasy in which the battle between good and evil also plays out.

In 2002 Fisk published *The Secret of Sabrina Fludde*, which begins with a young girl floating down a river, the Sabrina Fludde, not knowing from where she has come. All that she remembers is that her name is Abren. As she gathers bits and pieces of her past, she realizes that for some unknown reason, she is living out a legend. However, she knows that in order to survive, she must somehow change the ending of the classic story. A reviewer for *Locus* called this book "an evocative mix of old legend, faerie forces, and contemporary urban survival." *The Secret of Sabrina Fludde* has been planned as the first part of a trilogy.

Fisk once told *CA*: "I began to write fiction and poetry at the age of nine, giving up only after the publication of a book of short stories in 1972, when my first child was born. It seemed to me at that time that the obsessional drives of a writer were incompatible with motherhood. I am now striving, after fifteen years away from it, to prove otherwise! *Midnight Blue* was begun at the worst possible time, after the birth of my fifth child, when I still had a toddler at home as well. But the need to hear what increasingly felt like my 'lost inner voice' was so strong that there was no gainsaying it. Thankfully, now that all my children are at school, I don't have to write at five in the morning anymore!

"Since I decided at the age of nine that I would be a writer, there has never been another career that has attracted me. My only interest when I left school at age eighteen was to 'discover the world' (as I put it then), aware of how limiting my youth and experience were for a potential novelist! 'Discovering the world' found me living in central London, opposite King's Cross Station in the red light district; in Brixton in south London; and out in the wilds of Worcestershire in a laborer's cottage without running water or electricity, two miles away from the nearest road. It found me working for such disparate employers as the Boys' Brigade (an alternative organization to the Boy Scouts) and J. P. Donleavy, the author, in southern Ireland. I worked for the Spastics' Society in London, helping to organize fundraising events, and as an assistant in a social services department, where my discoveries about the nature of the society in which I lived came as something of a shock.

"'Discovering the world' in the heady 1960s and early 1970s also meant making some (limited as I see them now, but major as they seemed at the time) discoveries about myself. Those were exciting times, whatever anybody thinks of them now! Of everything I've done, the career of motherhood has been the one that has been the one that has called from me more wit, intelligence, and stamina than any other. It continually turns my whole life upside down, and in it I've 'discovered more of life' than I did in all the rest put together—and more about myself.

"My method of writing is less one of invention than of discovering the story that's already inside me. I begin by slinging down ideas indiscriminately, and then I work on them to find the story that I know is in there somewhere. I feel like a sculptor, hacking at stone or wood to get at the shape that's hidden in it. Or like a composer writing music (I go over what I'm writing again and again, mostly out loud, to make sure that what I hear is what I'm meant to hear).

"The plot of *Midnight Blue* grew out of the description of a smoke-filled balloon flight in the book *Nazca: The Flight of the Condor I* by Jim Woodman and the Shropshire legend of the Arthurian 'Wild Edric,' who is claimed to slumber beneath a range of hills known as the Stiperstones. The house on Highholly Hill is a (now ruined) farmhouse where my family lived while our own home was being rebuilt. I wrote about Shropshire, blending elements and places together, out of the sheer good sense of writing about what I know.

"I write for children, again, because they're what I know. I'm surrounded by them. They're the ones I want to entertain. I also write for children out of my own vivid memories of childhood, and my own often-painful struggle to reach adulthood—to get out into the world at large. My childhood memories are of great frustration and despair. I sympathize with many of the struggles that children—often lonely, to all intents and purposes trapped by the circumstances of their lives—go through, and with many of their hopes and aspirations and fears, when they contemplate their approaching adult lives.

"I may not always write for children (I hope I'll have a go at all sorts of things) but I suspect that loneliness and weakness will be a recurring theme.

"The success of *Midnight Blue* has been very gratifying after a half-a-lifetime's wait to even begin. But I'm aware, despite everything, that this is still an apprenticeship; I've got so much to learn (in a sense I hope I *always* will have so much to learn). Graham Greene likened a first novel to a short, sharp sprint into which the runner puts all he's got, and everything after to the long-distance race.

"He's a particularly favorite writer, whose skills I admire, not least his ability to 'lift' a story out of the ordinary onto another plane. Bruce Chatwin and Sylvia Plath are favorite writers at the moment. Jack Clemo, George Herbert, and Bob Dylan are favorite poets too. The single book that has influenced me most is the Bible, both in its language and for the content and quality of its epic tale. It never fails to provoke, surprise, and stir me.

"Among children's writers, A. A. Milne has always been a favorite—I wouldn't be writing today without the stimulus of his character Winnie-the-Pooh—and Hans Christian Andersen and (dare I admit it?) *Enid Blyton!* Favorite children's books now are *The Homecoming* by Cynthia Voigt and *Goodnight, Mr. Tom* by Michelle Margorian.

"J. R. R. Tolkein's *Lord of the Rings* influenced me greatly in my younger days. And something he said is never far out of my mind now, as I struggle to write realistically for children—but with hope—about our difficult world: 'That on callow, lumpish, and selfish youth, sorrow and the shadow of death can bestow dignity and sometimes even wisdom.'"

BIOGRAPHICAL AND CRITICAL SOURCES:

PERIODICALS

Books for Keeps, March, 1998, review of *Telling the Sea,* p. 14.
Books for Your Children, spring, 1995, review of *Tyger Pool,* p. 17.
Children's Bookwatch, June, 1992, review of *Telling the Sea,* p. 4.
Fear, April, 1991.
Horn Book Guide, January, 1990.
Junior Bookshelf, December, 1990, p. 292; December, 1994, review of *Tyger Pool,* p. 223.
Locus, June, 2002, review of *The Secret of Sabrina Fludde,* p. 35.
Observer (London, England), October 28, 2001, review of *Sabrina Fludde,* p. 16.

Publishers Weekly, November 30, 1990; May 20, 2002, review of *The Secret of Sabrina Fludde,* pp. 65-66.

School Librarian, August, 1992, review of *Telling the Sea,* p. 113.

School Library Journal, July, 2002, Sharon Grover, review of *The Secret of Sabrina Fludde,* p. 119.

Sunday Times (London, England), November 23, 2001, review of *Sabrina Fludde,* p. 20.

Times Educational Supplement (London, England), April 8, 1990, p. H-8; November 11, 1994, review of *Tyger Pool,* p. R3.

ONLINE

BBC Online, http://www.bbc.co.uk/ (February 24, 2003), "Pauline Fisk—Stories That Teach Children to Love Life."

Healthy Books Web site, http://www.healthybooks.org.uk/ (February 24, 2003), review of *Tyger Pool.**

* * *

FLOOGLEBUCKLE, Al
See SPIEGELMAN, Art

* * *

FORD, Judy 1944-

PERSONAL: Born February 12, 1944, in Glendale, CA. *Education:* Willamette University, B.A., 1966; University of Washington, Seattle, M.S.W., 1976.

ADDRESSES: *Office*—P.O. Box 834, Kirkland, WA 98083.

CAREER: Psychotherapist in private practice, Kirkland, WA.

WRITINGS:

Wonderful Ways to Love a Child, Conari Press (Berkeley, CA), 1995.

Wonderful Ways to Love a Teen—Even When It Seems Impossible, Conari Press (Berkeley, CA), 1996.

Wonderful Ways to Love a Grandchild, Conari Press (Berkeley, CA), 1997.

Blessed Expectations: Nine Months of Wonder, Reflection, and Sweet Anticipation, Conari Press (Berkeley, CA), 1997.

Wonderful Ways to Be a Family, Conari Press (Berkeley, CA), 1998.

Wonderful Ways to Be a Stepparent, Conari Press (Berkeley, CA), 1999.

(With daughter, Amanda Ford), *Between Mother and Daughter: A Teenager and Her Mom Share the Secrets of a Strong Relationship,* Conari Press (Berkeley, CA), 1999.

Getting Over Getting Mad: Positive Ways to Manage Anger in Your Most Important Relationships, Conari Press (Berkeley, CA), 2001.

BIOGRAPHICAL AND CRITICAL SOURCES:

ONLINE

Judy Ford Home Page, http://www.judyford.com/ (June 17, 2003).

* * *

FOTOPOULOS, Takis 1940-

PERSONAL: Born October 14, 1940, in Greece; son of Constantine (a civil servant) and Georgia (Fotaki) Fotopoulos; married Sia Mamareli (a lawyer and claims adjuster), July, 1966; children: Costas. *Education:* University of Athens, LL.B., 1963, degree in economics and politics, 1965; London School of Economics and Political Science, London, M.Sc., 1968.

ADDRESSES: *Home*—20 Woodberry Way, London N12 0HG, England; fax: 02-08-446-1633. *E-mail*—takis@fotopoulos1.fsnet.co.uk.

CAREER: University of North London, London, England, senior lecturer in economics, 1969-89; *Democracy and Nature,* editor, 1992—.

WRITINGS:

Dependent Development: The Case of Greece, Exantas (Athens, Greece), 1985.

The Gulf War: The First Battle in the North-South Conflict, Exantas (Athens, Greece), 1991.
The Neoliberal Consensus and the Crisis of the Growth Economy, Gordios (Athens, Greece), 1993.
The New World Order and Greece, Kastaniotis (Athens, Greece), 1997.
Towards an Inclusive Democracy: The Crisis of the Growth Economy and the Need for a New Liberatory Project, Cassell (New York, NY), 1997.
Drugs: An Alternative Approach, Free Press (Athens, Greece), 1999.
The New Order in the Balkans, Staxy (Athens, Greece), 1999.
Religion, Autonomy, Democracy: The Rise of New Irrationalism, Free Press (Athens, Greece), 2000.
Globalization, the Left, and Inclusive Democracy, Ellinika Grammata (Athens, Greece), 2002.

Columnist for the Athenian daily, *Eleftherotypia,* 1990—. Contributor to periodicals, including *Democracy and Nature.*

Fotopoulos's work has been translated into French, German, Italian, Spanish, and Greek.

SIDELIGHTS: Takis Fotopoulos once told *CA*: "My primary motivation in writing has been to develop a new political project; that is, the project for an inclusive democracy (political, economic, ecological, and democracy in the social realm). The aim of this project is to reintegrate society with economy, polity, and nature. It represents a synthesis of the socialist and democratic traditions, which also encompasses the new social movements (feminist, green, et cetera). I started developing this project in my articles for the journal *Democracy and Nature,* and I further expanded it in my books, *Towards an Inclusive Democracy: The Crisis of the Growth Economy and the Need for a New Liberatory Project* and *Globalization, the Left, and Inclusive Democracy.*"

* * *

FREED, Lynn (Ruth) 1945-

PERSONAL: Born July 18, 1945, in Durban, South Africa; immigrated to the United States in 1967, naturalized citizen, 1977; daughter of Harold Derrick (an actor) and Anne (a theatre director; maiden name, Moshal) Freed; children: Jessica Peta. *Education:* University of the Witwatersrand, B.A., 1966; Columbia University, M.A., 1968, Ph.D., 1972.

ADDRESSES: *Agent*—Jennifer Rudolph Walsh, William Morris Agency, Inc., 1325 Ave. of the Americas, New York, NY 10019. *E-mail*—lrfreed@ucdavis.edu.

CAREER: Writer, 1975—; currently University of California, Davis, professor of English.

MEMBER: PEN America, Authors Guild.

AWARDS, HONORS: Yaddo fellowships, 1985, 1987, 1991, 1994; WIT Fellow, Columbia University, 1969, Bay Area Book Reviewers Association award for fiction, and "Notable Books of the Year" listee, *New York Times,* both 1986, for *Home Ground;* MacDowell fellowships, 1986, 1987; National Endowment for the Arts fellowship, 1987; Rockefeller Foundation fellowship at Bellagio, 1989; Guggenheim Foundation fellowship, 1990; Fellowship grants from the Camargo Foundation, the Lannan Foundation, The John D. and Catherine T. MacArthur Foundation; "Notable Books of the Year" listee, *New York Times,* 1993, for *The Bungalow;* Inaugural Katherine Anne Porter Award from the American Academy of Arts and Letters for *House of Women.*

WRITINGS:

Heart Change, New American Library (New York, NY), 1982.
Home Ground, Summit Books (New York, NY), 1986.
The Bungalow, Poseidon Press (New York, NY), 1993.
The Mirror: A Novel, Crown Publishers (New York, NY), 1997.
Friends of the Family, Story Line Press (Ashland, OR), 2000, originally published as *Heart Change,* New American Library (New York, NY), 1982.
House of Women, Little, Brown (New York, NY), 2002.

Contributor to anthologies, including *Shaking Eve's Tree: Short Stories of Jewish Women,* edited by Sharon Niederman, Jewish Publication Society, 1990; *The Confidence Women: 26 Women Writers at Work,* edited by Eve Shelnutt, Longstreet Press (Atlanta, GA), 1991;

Best Short Stories of 1992, edited by Robert Stone, Houghton (Boston, MA), 1992; *Thoughts of Home: Reflections on Families, Houses, and Homelands,* Hearst Books, 1995; and *Bookworms: Great Writers and Readers Celebrate Reading,* edited by Laura Furman and Elinore Standard, Carroll & Graf, 1996. Also contributor of stories, articles, and reviews for children and adults to periodicals, including *Harper's, House and Garden, House Beautiful, Mirabella, New Yorker, New York Times, Southwest Review, Travel and Leisure, Washington Post Book World,* and *Zyzzyva.*

WORK IN PROGRESS: A collection of short stories.

SIDELIGHTS: Lynn Freed is an expatriate South African whose novels about her home country cast a mordant eye on the liberal, *petit bourgeois* whites among whom she grew up. Freed's novel *Home Ground* created a stir in South Africa. Readers of the work attempted to pry bits of autobiography from the fiction, and her subsequent works have been similarly treated. "Time, memory, identity, continuity, and exile: Freed is caught up in a white South African version of expatriation in which one never finally leaves home, or, if so, then home never finally leaves one," wrote Stephen Clingman in the *Boston Sunday Globe.* "The refreshing aspect of her [work], however, is how these deeper themes are enmeshed with a positively wicked sense of humor.... She makes you laugh, and she tells the dirty domestic secrets white South Africans want to forget."

In *Home Ground,* Freed introduced Ruth Frank, a young Jewish girl coming of age in South Africa during the 1950s and 1960s. The country's social and political situation is filtered through Ruth's experiences as well as those of her family of eccentric stage actors. *Washington Post Book World* commentator Jonathan Yardley called *Home Ground* "a rarity," a novel about childhood and adolescence "that never lapses into self-pity, that rings true in every emotion and incident, that regards adults sympathetically if unsparingly, that deals with serious thematic material, and that is quite deliciously funny." Yardley concluded: "*Home Ground* is all this and more: it is also the flip side of rites-of-passage literary tradition, for its narrator is not a boy but a girl." Some critics, such as *New York Times Book Review* contributor Janette Turner Hospital, suggested that *Home Ground* is not a political novel but rather a metaphor for South Africa. Noted Hospital: "The Franks are South Africa in miniature. They are a theatrical family: second-rate, self-obsessed, histrionic, always requiring an audience.... More than twenty years later the reader feels a shiver of recognition: South African politics as soap opera; P. W. Botha's Government as second-rate stage director, casting itself in the grand melodramas, convinced of its own tragic and misunderstood role."

When *Home Ground* first appeared in South Africa, newspaper headlines hinted that it might be banned. This did not occur, but in an interview with Harriet Stix in the *Los Angeles Times,* Freed recalled how disconcerted some people were after reading the book. People were "just horrified.... I was considered a traitor, and this by people who are highly critical of the government," she said. Even so, *Home Ground* became a critical and commercial success. As Hospital wrote, "Freed's guileless child-narrator takes us *inside* the neurosis of South Africa. We experience it in a way that is qualitatively different from watching the most graphic of news clips.... Freed may not have quite the literary reach of Nadine Gordimer, but her vantage point of privileged outcast gives, I think, a more disturbing inner view of that awful, intricate symbiosis between black and white."

Ruth Frank returns as an adult narrator in Freed's novel *The Bungalow,* first published in 1993. In *The Bungalow,* Ruth returns to South Africa to visit her ailing father and to escape a troubled marriage. She finds solace with a former lover, a liberal white landowner, and stays on in his seaside bungalow after he is murdered. Once again Ruth is confronted by the odd mixture of liberalism and intolerance that informs her social peers in South Africa, and it is their foibles and fears she exposes in her narrative. *St. Louis Dispatch* reviewer Robert DiAntonio wrote that *The Bungalow* "is both a revealing portrait of contemporary South African society and a poignant account of one woman's search for independence and fulfillment.... While *The Bungalow* deals with social attitudes, its strength lies in Freed's extraordinary ear for dialogue and her ability to universalize her characters' plights." As Glenda Adams noted in the *New York Times Book Review,* however, Freed clearly offers warnings to the middle-class South African whites she writes about, both liberal and conservative. "We see in Lynn Freed's fiction what we might fail to recognize from passing news stories about political change," concluded Adams. "The drinks by the pool and the refurbishing have continued. The troubles are still awaited. The cataclysm is yet to come."

The author broke with the contemporary settings and situations of her previous novels in *The Mirror: A Novel.* Alice Joyce wrote in *Booklist,* "Set in the period between the world wars, Freed's latest novel exhibits the splendidly controlled prose of a master at once maintaining a remarkable level of tension in combination with surprising displays of humor."

The novel consists of the fictional memoirs of Agnes La Grange. Agnes, (she gave herself the name La Grange), is a lower-class seventeen-year-old English woman who emigrates to Durban, South Africa, to work as a housekeeper for a wealthy Jewish couple. The "old Jew," as she calls her still-strong, old employer, presents her with a full-length mirror. Completely unsurprised by his sexual advances, she watches their reflections in the mirror as they make love on a regular basis in her little maid's room and eventually conceive a child. After the birth of the child, she takes a cash settlement from the old man and buys the Railway Hotel. From then on she's on her way. She acquires more property, a husband, several lovers, a subsequent divorce, and the trappings of refinement.

Critics have praised Freed's successful realization of Agnes's character, writing that Freed has taken the reader to the larger-than-life territory of Flaubert's Emma Bovary and Defoe's *Moll Flanders.* Agnes keeps her money in a purse around her neck and never dignifies her various lovers by name, referring to them as "the old Jew," "the newspaperman," "the tycoon," "the hunter," "the banker." She takes what she wants, saying, "I'd never been able to stand a good girl, all the dark things buried away."

"The question at the heart of Agnes's story," noted Andy Solomon in the *San Francisco Chronicle,* "is whether fulfillment can even be possible when the choice is between independence and love." Nor is she much touched by the joys of motherhood. "The whole thing felt like a form of service. . . I wondered how women the world over, natives included, went in for this sort of thing time after time." Only when Allega's musical talents bring her to the attention of the child's father and she moves in with them does she have any real feelings for the girl. The *Guardian* reviewer commented, "The qualities with which Freed endows her heroine are fundamentally masculine, and through this comes a subtle but inescapable feminist message which makes *The Mirror* more than a colonial family saga. Moreover, Freed gives Agnes a voice and an indomitable attitude which captivates and mesmerizes the reader."

House of Women explores the depth and intensity of mother-daughter relationship, coming of age, and the awful power of isolation. Written in the style of Greek tragedies, the narrative draws from the myth of the goddess Demeter and her daughter Persephone, who is abducted and taken to the underworld by Hades.

Freed's version begins with Thea, who is brought up in a grand estate in 1960s South Africa with her mother, Nalia, a one-time opera diva and Holocaust survivor who escaped with her family's money to South Africa. As in a fairy tale, no man, not even Thea's wealthy father, whom Nalia has come to hate, is allowed into the house. The gates are chained at night and their native servant Maude sees that Thea never goes out alone. Her father shows up for a visit, bringing with him an older man he calls the Syrian but who really seems to be a relative. Soon it is apparent that her father has somehow promised him Thea as a bride.

Seventeen-year-old Thea is so eager to see the world beyond the walls that when the Syrian literally cuts the chains of the castle, she submits to abduction and boards his boat for his island home. A *Publishers Weekly* reviewer wrote, "Like a Jean Rhys antiheroine, Theadora strikes out fiercely against the world, but is helpless in the face of male desire. And like Rhys, Freed imagines a world in which major events are only ambiguously described, but domestic details are sensuously immediate."

Three years later, after the birth of twin girls, Thea convinces her husband to allow her to return to visit her mother. She learns Nalia is dying, and a discovered journal provides her with answers to many of her mother's secrets.

Lisa Shea, writing in *O, The Oprah Magazine,* called *House of Women* "a quietly suspenseful tale of a marriage that is both an escape from a powerfully sexual mother and manipulative father and an unpredictable journey to the heart of her authentic desires."

BIOGRAPHICAL AND CRITICAL SOURCES:

PERIODICALS

Booklist, September 1, 1997, Alice Joyce, review of *The Mirror: A Novel,* p. 57; January 1, 2002, Eileen Hardy, review of *House of Women,* p. 808.

Book World, October 12, 1997, review of *The Mirror,* p. 4.

Boston Sunday Globe, January 3, 1993.

Entertainment Weekly, September 12, 1997, Margot Mifflin, review of *The Mirror,* p. 133.

Forward, January 29, 1993.

Guardian (London, England), February 12, 2000, Isobel Montgomery, review of *The Mirror,* p. 11.

Illustrated London News, June, 1986.

Library Journal, August, 1997, Ann H. Fisher, review of *The Mirror,* p. 126; April 1, 1998, Katie Arwood, Connie Fillinger, Jon Mihleich, review of *The Mirror,* p. 152; April 1, 1999, Michael Rogers, review of *Home Ground,* p. 134; March 1, 2001, Michael Rogers, review of *Friends of the Family,* p. 135; January, 2002, Cheryl L. Conway, review of *House of Women,* p. 151.

Los Angeles Times, March 20, 1983, Don Strachan, review of *Heart Change,* p. 7; December 14, 1986; February 24, 2002, Susan Salter Reynolds, review of *House of Women,* p. R-11.

New York Times Book Review, August 17, 1986, Ari Goldman, interview with Lynn Freed, p. 7; August 17, 1986, Janette Turner Hospital, review of *Home Ground,* p. 7; March 21, 1993, Brooke Allen, review of *The Bungalow,* p. 17; September 21, 1997, Brooke Allen, review of *The Mirror,* p. 13; February 24, 2002, Kathryn Harrison, review of *House of Women,* p. 10; March 3, 2002, review of *House of Women,* p. 18; June 2, 2002, review of *House of Women,* p. 23.

O, The Oprah Magazine, February 2002, Lisa Shea, review of *House of Women,* p. 115.

Publishers Weekly, November 19, 2001, review of *House of Women,* p. 47; June 23, 1997, review of *The Mirror,* p. 68.

St. Louis Dispatch, January 3, 1993.

San Francisco Chronicle, September 7, 1997, Andy Solomon, review of *The Mirror,* p. 3.

Times Literary Supplement, May 9, 1986; June 12, 2002, Lucy Dallas, review of *House of Women,* p. 25.

Village Voice, October 28, 1986.

Washington Post Book World, August 24, 1986; January 20, 2002, review of *House of Women,* p. T06.

Writer, June 2002, Sarah Anne Johnson, interview with Lynn Freed, p. 29.

ONLINE

Lynn Freed Home Page, http://www.lynnfreed.com/ (May 2, 2002).

G

GAY, Kathlyn 1930-

PERSONAL: Born March 4, 1930, in Zion, IL; daughter of Kenneth Charles (an accountant) and Beatrice (Anderson) McGarrahan; married Arthur L. Gay (an elementary school teacher), August 28, 1948; children: Martin, Douglas, Karen. *Education:* Attended Northern Illinois University, two years. *Politics:* Democrat.

ADDRESSES: Home—11633 Bayonet Ln., New Port Richey, FL 34654. *E-mail*—kgay@microd.com.

CAREER: Church World Service, Christian Rural Overseas Program (CROP), editor and public relations writer in Elkhart, IN, and New York, NY, 1962-66; Juhl Advertising Agency, Elkhart, IN, publicity and public relations writer, 1966; freelance writer, 1966—; partner in rental business, 1971—. Community relations director for Americana Healthcare Center, 1976-79; instructor in creative writing, Elkhart Area Career Center, beginning 1970. Past writer for political campaigns, including Mayor Richard J. Daley's political campaign in Chicago, IL, 1967. Writing consultant to Lyons & Carnahan, 1969-70, Ginn & Co., 1971, and Science Research Associates, 1972-73.

MEMBER: Authors Guild, Society of Children's Book Writers and Illustrators.

AWARDS, HONORS: Honorable mention, *Writer's Digest* short story contest, 1962; first prize in literary section, Northern Indiana Arts Festival, 1965, for one-act play; "Outstanding Book" selection, National Council for the Social Studies and National Science Teachers' Association, 1983, for *Acid Rain,* and 1988, for *Silent Killers: Radon and Other Hazards;* "one of the most important books on education" selection, National Education Association convention, 1987, for *Crisis in Education: Will the United States Be Ready for the Year 2000?;* Notable Books for Young People selection, American Library Association (ALA), 1993, for *Global Garbage: Exporting Trash and Toxic Waste;* Books for the Teen Age list, New York Public Library, 1994, for *Church and State: Government and Religion in the United States* and *Caretakers of the Earth,* 1995, for *Getting Your Message Across* and *Pregnancy: Private Decisions, Public Debates,* and 1996, for *Keep the Buttered Side Up: Food Superstitions from around the World;* ALA recommended list for YA books on terrorism, 2000, for *Silent Death: The Threat of Chemical and Biological Terrorism.*

WRITINGS:

Girl Pilot, Messner (New York, NY), 1966.
Money Isn't Everything: The Story of Economics at Work, Delacorte (New York, NY), 1967.
Meet the Mayor of Your City, Hawthorn (New York, NY), 1967.
Meet Your Governor, Hawthorn (New York, NY), 1968.
Beth Speaks Out, Messner (New York, NY), 1968.
Careers in Social Service, Messner (New York, NY), 1969.
Where the People Are: Cities and Their Future, Delacorte (New York, NY), 1969.
The Germans Helped Build America, Messner (New York, NY), 1971.

Proud Heritage on Parade, Contemporary Drama Service (Colorado Springs, CO), 1972.

Core English: English for Speakers of Other Languages, Ginn (Lexington, MA), 1972.

A Family Is for Living: The Changing Family in a Changing World, Delacorte (New York, NY), 1972.

Our Working World, Science Research Associates (Palo Alto, CA), 1973.

Body Talk, Scribner (New York, NY), 1974.

Be a Smart Shopper, Messner (New York, NY), 1974.

(With Ben E. Barnes) *The River Flows Backward,* Ashley Books (Port Washington, NY), 1975.

What's in a Name?, Elkhart Community Schools (Elkhart, IN), 1975.

Care and Share: Teenagers and Volunteerism, Messner (New York, NY), 1977.

Look Mom! No Words!, Houghton (Boston, MA), 1977.

(With son Martin Gay and Marla Gay) *Get Hooked on Vegetables,* Messner (New York, NY), 1978.

(Coauthor) *English around the World,* Scott, Foresman (Glenview, IL), 1979.

(With Martin Gay) *Eating What Grows Naturally,* illustrated by Brian Byrn, And Books (South Bend, IN), 1980.

(With Ben E. Barnes) *Your Fight Has Just Begun,* Messner (New York, NY), 1980.

(With Ben E. Barnes) *Beginner's Guide to Better Boxing,* McKay (New York, NY), 1980.

(Coauthor) *I Like English,* Scott, Foresman (Glenview, IL), 1981.

English for a Changing World, Scott, Foresman (Glenview, IL), 1981.

Boxes and More Boxes, Houghton (Boston, MA), 1981.

(Coauthor) *Family Living,* Prentice-Hall (Englewood Cliffs, NJ), 1982, 3rd edition, 1988.

Junkyards, Enslow Publishers (Hillside, NJ), 1982.

Acid Rain, F. Watts (New York, NY), 1983.

Cities under Stress, F. Watts (New York, NY), 1985.

The Greenhouse Effect, F. Watts (New York, NY), 1986.

Ergonomics: Making Products and Places Fit People, Enslow Publishers (Hillside, NJ), 1986.

Crisis in Education: Will the United States Be Ready for the Year 2000?, F. Watts (New York, NY), 1986.

The Rainbow Effect: Interracial Families, F. Watts (New York, NY), 1987.

Changing Families: Meeting Today's Challenges, Enslow Publishers (Hillside, NJ), 1988.

Science in Ancient Greece, F. Watts (New York, NY), 1988.

Silent Killers: Radon and Other Hazards, F. Watts (New York, NY), 1988.

Bigotry, Enslow Publishers (Hillside, NJ), 1989.

Ozone, F. Watts (New York, NY), 1989.

Adoption and Foster Care, Enslow Publishers (Hillside, NJ), 1990.

They Don't Wash Their Socks!: Sports Superstitions, Walker (New York, NY), 1990.

Water Pollution, F. Watts (New York, NY), 1990.

Cleaning Nature Naturally, Walker (New York, NY), 1991.

Air Pollution, F. Watts (New York, NY), 1991.

Garbage and Recycling, Enslow Publishers (Hillside, NJ), 1991.

Day Care: Looking for Answers, Enslow Publishers (Hillside, NJ), 1992.

Church and State: Government and Religion in the United States, Millbrook (Brookfield, CT), 1992.

Global Garbage: Exporting Trash and Toxic Waste, F. Watts (New York, NY), 1992.

Caution! This May Be an Advertisement: Teen Guide to Advertising, F. Watts (New York, NY), 1992.

Caretakers of the Earth, Enslow Publishers (Hillside, NJ), 1993.

The Right to Die: Public Controversy, Private Matter, Millbrook (Brookfield, CT), 1993.

Getting Your Message Across, Macmillan (New York, NY), 1993.

Breast Implants: Making Safe Choices, Macmillan (New York, NY), 1993.

Pregnancy: Private Decisions, Public Debates, F. Watts (New York, NY), 1994.

Rainforests of the World, ABC-Clio Press (Santa Barbara, CA), 1994.

The New Power of Women in Politics, Enslow Publishers (Hillside, NJ), 1994.

Pollution and the Powerless: The Environmental Justice Movement, F. Watts (New York, NY), 1994.

I Am Who I Am: Speaking Out about Multiracial Identity, F. Watts (New York, NY), 1995.

Keep the Buttered Side Up: Food Superstitions from around the World, Walker (New York, NY), 1995.

(With Martin Gay) *Encyclopedia of North American Eating and Drinking Traditions, Customs, and Rituals,* ABC-Clio Press (Santa Barbara, CA), 1995.

Rights and Respect: What You Need to Know about Gender Bias and Sexual Harassment, Millbrook (Brookfield, CT), 1995.

(With Martin Gay) *Heroes of Conscience: A Biographical Dictionary,* ABC-CLIO (Santa Barbara, CA) 1996.

Saving the Environment: Debating the Costs, F. Watts (New York, NY), 1996.

(With son Douglas Gay) *The Not-So-Minor Leagues,* Millbrook (Brookfield, CT), 1996.

(With Martin Gay) *The Information Superhighway,* Holt (New York, NY), 1996.

Communes and Cults, Twenty-First Century Books (New York, NY), 1997.

Militias: Armed and Dangerous, Enslow Publishers (Hillside, NJ), 1997.

Neo-Nazis: A Growing Threat, Enslow Publishers (Hillside, NJ), 1997.

(With Martin Gay) *Emma Goldman,* Lucent Books (San Diego, CA), 1997.

(Coauthor) *After the Shooting Stops: The Aftermath of War,* Twenty-First Century Books (New York, NY), 1998.

Who's Running the Nation?: How Corporate Power Threatens Democracy, F. Watts (New York, NY), 1998.

Child Labor: A Global Crisis, Millbrook (Brookfield, CT), 1998.

(With Martin Gay) *Encyclopedia of Political Anarchy,* ABC-CLIO (Santa Barbara, CA), 1999.

Leaving Cuba: From Operation Pedro Pan to Elian, Twenty-First Century Books (New York, NY), 2000.

Silent Death: The Threat of Chemical and Biological Terrorism, Twenty-First Century Books (New York, NY), 2001.

(With Christine Whittington) *Body Marks: Tattooing, Piercing, and Scarification,* Millbrook (Brookfield, CT), 2002.

Epilepsy: The Ultimate Teen Guide, Scarecrow (Lanham, MD), 2002.

The Encyclopedia of Women's Health Issues, Oryx (Phoenix, AZ), 2002.

Eating Disorders: Anorexia, Bulimia, and Binge Eating, Enslow (Hillside, NJ), 2003.

Cultural Diversity: Conflicts and Challenges, Scarecrow (Lanham, MD), 2003.

Abortion: Understanding the Debate, Enslow (Hillside, NJ), 2004.

Death and Dying A-Z, Greenhaven (San Diego, CA), 2004.

Volunteering: The Ultimate Teen Guide, Scarecrow (Lanham, MD), in press.

Also author of teaching manuals, including activities and stories for numerous publishers. Contributor to books, including *Spotlights,* Houghton (Boston, MA), 1986; and *Currents,* Houghton (Boston, MA), 1986. Contributor to *Childcraft Annual,* Field Enterprises (Chicago, IL), 1969, *The New Book of Knowledge,* and *Collier's Encyclopedia.* Contributor to "Young America Basic Reading" series, Lyons & Carnahan (Chicago, IL). Contributor of articles and short stories to periodicals, including *Women in Business, Michiana Magazine, Better Homes and Gardens, Red Cross Journal, Success, Highlights for Children,* and *Popular Medicine.*

"VOICES FROM THE PAST" SERIES; WITH MARTIN GAY

World War I, Twenty-First Century Books (New York, NY), 1995.

World War II, Twenty-First Century Books (New York, NY), 1995.

War of 1812, Twenty-First Century Books (New York, NY), 1995.

Spanish-American War, Twenty-First Century Books (New York, NY), 1995.

Revolutionary War, Twenty-First Century Books (New York, NY), 1995.

Civil War, Twenty-First Century Books (New York, NY), 1995.

Korean War, Twenty-First Century Books (New York, NY), 1996.

Persian Gulf War, Twenty-First Century Books (New York, NY), 1996.

Vietnam War, Twenty-First Century Books (New York, NY), 1996.

WORK IN PROGRESS: *American Radicals, American Landmarks,* and *What Americans Believe.*

SIDELIGHTS: With over a hundred books to her credit, Kathlyn Gay has established herself as a prolific writer of nonfiction information books for teens and juvenile readers. Gay has explored topics including environmental issues, politics, military history, sports, manufacturing, multiculturalism, and pressing social concerns in books that are held up as examples of what a good informational title should be. Gay's works are "insightful, well-researched, and intellectually stimulating," according to *Booklist*'s Stephanie Zvirin. Her books have also been called "relevant [and] engrossing," by *Booklist*'s Roger Leslie, and "factual, well-organized, straightforward, and readable," by Diane P. Tuccillo in *School Library Journal.* Neither does Gay steer away from "thorny contemporary issues," noted Chris Sherman in *Booklist.* "Writing, for me," Gay once told *CA,* "has become a way of life, and I could not imagine trying to function as an individual without exercising this form of communication."

Born in Zion, Illinois, in 1930, Gay was brought up in a community controlled by a church group that originated at the turn of the twentieth century. "'Outsiders' were seldom welcome in this community," Gay once noted in *CA,* "and it was here I learned the real dangers of 'exclusiveness' and isolation. Even at nine and ten years old I felt there was little opportunity for growth in a closed community. What is good and right and productive in life takes many forms, not just one. Each of us may come from a different place and still arrive at the same goal or end." Such an upbringing instilled in Gay a fervent belief in a pluralistic society and a respect for individual difference, concerns reflected in many of her nonfiction titles. Gay started writing when she was ten, publishing articles for her elementary school newspaper. As she grew up, she more and more began to define herself by such writing, dreaming of a career in journalism or perhaps advertising.

Attending Northern Illinois University, she met her future husband, Arthur L. Gay; they married in 1948. Gay's husband was an educator, and the family lived variously in Barrington, Illinois, Ventura, California, and then for thirty-six years in Elkhart, Indiana. Gay did not realize her youthful dreams of becoming a professional writer until her daughter was born in 1957. In fact, the expectant mother penned her first article, which was subsequently published in a travel magazine, in the hospital the very day her daughter was born. The subsequent fifteen dollars she earned for the article convinced Gay that she could build a career in writing. Working part time in a variety of jobs and raising a family, Gay still found time to turn out articles on her portable typewriter. More articles followed, and then some textbooks and teaching materials for the educational market. From there, she branched out to writing books on a wide range of topics of interest for young readers. Soon Gay had built a thriving career as a nonfiction writer for young adults and juvenile readers, collaborating with her husband on some titles, or with her children—as they grew older—on others.

Gay has written numerous books on environmental topics, beginning with the award-winning 1983 *Acid Rain,* a discussion of one of the hottest ecological issues of the 1980s. Gay explicates the impacts of such end results of pollution in a book that has "short chapters with clear explanations," according to Paula J. Lacey in *Voice of Youth Advocates.* She does the same about the build-up of carbon dioxide in the atmosphere in *The Greenhouse Effect,* "a balanced, well-written book on a difficult and important technology-induced problem of our time," as Indira Nair noted in a review for *Appraisal.* Similarly, *School Library Journal* critic Meryl Silverstein found the same book to be "a thorough overview and introduction to a complex and difficult problem." The threat posed by a hole in the ozone layer is examined in *Ozone,* an "outstanding introduction to a complex problem, enhanced by lucid writing," according to a critic for *Kirkus Reviews.* Toxic dangers are explored in *Silent Killers: Radon and Other Hazards.*

Gay also shows how insects and microorganisms can be used in *Cleaning Nature Naturally,* "impressively researched" with a "carefully balanced perspective," as a contributor for *Kirkus Reviews* described the book. "This is a thorough look at an expanding technology with a few sparks of wit here and there," added Paula J. Lacey in *Voice of Youth Advocates.* Various forms of pollution are dealt with in subsequent titles. *Water Pollution* tackles that issue head on, examining both causes and effects. Charles Harmon, writing in *Booklist,* felt that "Gay's discussion of protective and cleanup measures merit special praise." The author also provides a "well-documented, thought-provoking study" in her *Air Pollution,* according to Mary Romano Marks in *Booklist.* A critic for *Kirkus Reviews* had similar praise, calling the book a "comprehensive, up-to-date, well-balanced look at our industrialized society's poisoning of the air we breathe." Addressing the issue of recycling, Gay penned *Garbage and Recycling,* a "short book," according to Herbert J. Mason in *Science Books and Films,* "but the author has made every word count." More environmental solutions are proposed in *Saving the Environment: Debating the Costs,* while in *Rainforests of the World,* Gay presents a reference handbook covering that unique ecosystem.

Gay tackles controversial social issues in numerous other titles. Her 1989 *Bigotry* is "a comprehensive and well-documented account of the complex problems of bigotry and prejudice," according to Sylvia V. Meisner, writing in *School Library Journal.* Not only racial, but also gender, sexual, and economic prejudices are explored in this "worthwhile tool for research papers," as Meisner further noted. One form of such bias is further examined in *Rights and Respect: What You Need to Know about Gender Bias and Sexual Harassment,* a book written in "an anecdotal style that is very readable," according to Chris Sherman in *Booklist.* Gay used her own personal experiences growing up in a closed society in *Communes and Cults,* a discussion of both religious and secular societies. Looking at groups from the Branch Davidians of Waco, Texas, to Jim Jones's People's Temple, she provides "a valuable title, clearly written, and informative," thought Libby K. White in *School Library Journal.* In *Neo-Nazis: A Growing Threat,* she looks at far-right cults in "a scary, informative introduction to the subject," according to *Booklist*'s Jean Franklin.

Turning to social issues with more of a personal concern, Gay authored *Pregnancy: Private Decisions, Public Debates,* examining the controversy around abortion. Lois McCulley, writing in *School Library Journal,* felt that "superior writing and a well-organized, thoughtful presentation mark this volume." Likewise, a contributor for *Kirkus Reviews* found the book to be a "well-informed overview," as well as "lively." For *Booklist*'s Stephanie Zvirin, Gay "does her customarily balanced, well-documented job" in this title. Euthanasia is the subject of *The Right to Die: Pubic Controversy, Private Matter,* a book presented "in lucid, interesting, and easily understood language," as noted by *School Library Journal*'s Kathryn Havris, who also felt that "this book is a great place to start for information" for the continuing debate over the right to die. A writer for *Kirkus Reviews* also praised Gay's "fully-documented, well-integrated" approach to the subject. Education comes under the Gay lens in *Crisis in Education: Will the United States Be Ready for the Year 2000?,* an outline of the basic issues shaping education and educational reform in the mid-1980s. A *Booklist* commentator lauded Gay for approaching the topic "without jargon or preaching" and for discussing "many hotly debated issues with considerable fairness."

Other nonfiction titles from Gay deal with multiculturalism. *I Am Who I Am: Speaking Out about Multiracial Identity* earned a starred *Booklist* review from Stephanie Zvirin, who called it "positive, supporting, and informative," and won similar praise from Brenda Moses in *Voice of Youth Advocates,* as "an excellent source for information." *Changing Families: Meeting Today's Challenges* and *The Rainbow Effect: Interracial Families* are two titles that deal with the ever-developing and altering nature of families in the United States. Rosie Peasley, writing in *School Library Journal,* found *Changing Families* "an excellent presentation," and both "accepting and hopeful" of new family arrangements.

Political issues and government are examined in some of Gay's titles. The separation of government and religion is analyzed in *Church and State: Government and Religion in the United States,* a book that evidences "Gay's even-handedness," according to Dem Polacheck in *Voice of Youth Advocates.* "Gay has performed admirably in presenting the issues," Polacheck further commented. *Cities under Stress* takes a look at the state of the urban centers in America, while *The New Power of Women in Politics* focuses on women in politics from Abigail Adams to today. "Gay treats her subjects as working leaders in public life," declared Mary Harris Veeder in a *Booklist* review, "not as oddities." And in the 1999 *Who's Running the Nation?: How Corporate Power Threatens Democracy,* Gay looks at the corporate threat to democracy in "an insightful analysis of current social trends," according to Jonathan Betz-Zall, writing in *School Library Journal.* From the robber barons of the nineteenth century to today's corporate welfare, the history of such abuses of power is presented in a "well-documented account," as Betz-Zall further described the title.

Lighter in tone are sports books, such as *They Don't Wash Their Socks!: Sports Superstitions,* which *Voice of Youth Advocates* critic Sari Feldman felt was a "fine hilo title" about an "entertaining" topic. Amateur boxing is the subject of *Your Fight Has Just Begun,* "an enthusiastic initiation to a subject about which little has been written specifically for teens," according to a reviewer for *Booklist.* Richard Luzer, writing in *School Library Journal,* also felt that Gay and her coauthor, Ben E. Barnes, "do an excellent job of capturing a very special American subculture." Minor league baseball takes center stage in *The Not-So-Minor Leagues,* written with one of her sons, Douglas Gay. Debbie Carton, reviewing the title in *Booklist,* thought it would make an "excellent addition to basic baseball collections."

Gay displays her wide range of researching and writing abilities in many other titles dealing with military history and wars in which Americans have fought.

Writing in the "Voices from the Past" series in collaboration with her son Martin, the authors offer brief overviews of wars, including causes, battles, outcomes, and ample quotations from people involved in the conflicts, tracing the history of American warfare from the Revolutionary War to the Persian Gulf War over two hundred years later. Reviewing *Civil War, World War I,* and *World War II* in *School Library Journal,* Rosalyn Pierini commented upon the "serviceably written texts . . . interwoven with excerpts from letters, diaries, and newspaper accounts." Hazel Rochman, in a *Booklist* review of *World War I* and *World War II,* similarly praised the personal quoted material that "enlivens the facts." Rochman also predicted that "the military drama will draw readers." Reviewing *Vietnam War* and *Korean War* in *Booklist,* Susan Dove Lempke applauded how Gay "evenhandedly discusses the divisiveness surrounding the conflict" of Vietnam and also how she "shows the atrocities committed by all sides." Roxy Ekstrom, writing in *Voice of Youth Advocates,* felt that *Vietnam War* "presents a concise, comprehensive, clear and unbiased overview." Barbara Jo McKee, reviewing *Persian Gulf War* in *Voice of Youth Advocates,* wrote that Gay "describes in detail" the events of that conflict in an economical manner. For McKee, the volume could be "very useful" not only at the middle school level, but also for "high school students who are reluctant readers or who want a concise version of the war." Judith L. Miller, reviewing the same title in *School Library Journal,* called it "a clearly written, objective overview of the military conflict."

Gay takes a different look at war in her *Silent Death: The Threat of Chemical and Biological Warfare,* an investigation of the use and proliferation of such weaponry. *Booklist*'s Roger Leslie thought the book's "content" was "so staggering that the author need only present information in a straightforward manner to rouse the reader." Similarly, Ann G. Brouse, writing in *School Library Journal,* felt that while "this information is alarming, the presentation is not alarmist." *After the Shooting Stops: The Aftermath of War* is another view on war, or rather on its aftermath in social, political, and technological terms. Allison Trent Bernstein called this book a "solid addition" in a *School Library Journal* review. *Booklist*'s Roger Leslie felt that the book offers "an easy-to-read, information-packed history lesson."

In other titles, Gay continues to demonstrate her versatility. *Science in Ancient Greece* takes a look at scientific achievements in that ancient culture, while *Leaving Cuba: From Operation Pedro Pan to Elian* traces the experiences of children who have fled Castro's Cuba. Reviewing the latter title, Nell Beram, writing in *Horn Book Guide,* commended Gay's "rich narrative." *Voice of Youth Advocates* critic Delia A. Culberson likewise lauded this "well-documented book [that] looks at the various aspects of the Cuban diaspora and its impact on Cubans and their American hosts."

Among the author's popular and well-respected encyclopedias and reference guides are *Encyclopedia of Women's Health Issues,* and *Encyclopedia of Political Anarchy.* Gay offers two hundred alphabetical entries in the first title, including controversies in women's health, concise biographies, and entries on sexual abuse, abortion, dieting, obesity and a wealth of other topics. "The book's approach is evenhanded," noted a *Booklist* reviewer, who also felt that "the reading level should be comfortable for both general adults and teen audiences." Barbara M. Bibel, writing in *Library Journal,* called the same title "a good starting point for research on gender issues in healthcare policy." In her *Encyclopedia of Political Anarchy,* written in collaboration with son Martin, Gay attempts to clear up what she feels is one of the most misunderstood political movements in history. Her one hundred and seventy entries include short biographical profiles on people from Mary Wollstonecraft to Emma Goldman and Noam Chomsky, and on topics from the Haymarket affair to the Black Panthers. The first English-language encyclopedia of anarchism, the work is "well-written," according to Stephen L. Hupp in *Library Journal,* and a "very useful curriculum-support tool," as a *Booklist* contributor noted. Douglas Wooley, reviewing the book in *School Library Journal,* found the articles "cogent [and] concise."

Gay is expanding on this work with another title on radicalism and dissent in the United States. This involves, as Gay told *CA,* "both peaceful and violent protests that have been part of the American scene since colonial times and have had much to do with shaping and changing the nation." Gay further explained, "Unfortunately, I believe that dissent is being stifled today and that those who do not accept the established point of view are being ostracized, harassed, or assaulted. It will be a challenge to present profiles of American radicals who represent various movements and ideologies—individuals who have challenged the state, the church, political parties, the military, and big industry. I hope to cover such historical periods as the American Revolution; the abolitionists and early women's rights and utopianism movements; anarchism, socialism, and labor reform movements; civil rights and peace movements; and social and environmental justice."

"Through the written word," Gay told *CA*, "I feel I have been able to share with young people and adults some of the observations and impressions I have had on what it means to be a person, a productive human being. So many different conditions and factors shape each one of us as individuals that I am often amazed we are able to understand one another at all. Happily, though, there are many experiences in life that are common to all of us and a writer can draw on these in stories and articles to help readers see, hear, feel with real or imaginary people."

BIOGRAPHICAL AND CRITICAL SOURCES:

PERIODICALS

Appraisal, winter, 1987, Indira Nair, review of *The Greenhouse Effect,* pp. 28-29; summer, 1995, Carol Bilge, review of *Pollution and the Powerless: The Environmental Justice Movement,* pp. 23-24.

Booklist, June 1, 1980, review of *Your Fight Has Just Begun,* p. 1418; December 1, 1986, review of *Crisis in Education: Will the United States Be Ready for the Year 2000?,* p. 567; January 1, 1991, Charles Harmon, review of *Water Pollution,* p. 919; December 1, 1991, Mary Romano Marks, review of *Air Pollution,* p. 686; August, 1994, Stephanie Zvirin, review of *Pregnancy: Private Decisions, Public Debates,* p. 2036; February 15, 1995, Mary Harris Veeder, review of *The New Power of Women in Politics,* p. 1068; June 1, 1995, Stephanie Zvirin, review of *I Am Who I Am: Speaking Out about Multiracial Identity,* p. 1756; October 1, 1995, Chris Sherman, review of *Rights and Respect: What You Need to Know about Gender Bias and Sexual Harassment,* p. 300; December 15, 1995, Hazel Rochman, review of *World War I* and *World War II,* p. 700; May 15, 1996, Debbie Carton, review of *The Not-So-Minor Leagues,* p. 1577; July, 1996, Sally Estes, review of *The Information Superhighway,* p. 1816; September 1, 1996, Frances Bradburn, review of *Saving the Environment: Debating the Costs,* p. 71; November 15, 1996, Susan Dove Lempke, review of *Korean War* and *Vietnam War,* p. 582; April 1, 1997, review of *Heroes of Conscience: A Biographical Dictionary,* pp. 1356-1357; September 1, 1997, Jean Franklin, review of *Neo-Nazis: A Growing Threat,* p. 70, Chris Sherman, review of *Communes and Cults,* p. 70; August, 1998, Roger Leslie, review of *After the Shooting Stops: The Aftermath of War,* p. 1982; December 1, 1998, Lauren Peterson, review of *Science in Ancient Greece,* p. 678; July, 1999, review of *Encyclopedia of Political Anarchy,* p. 1973; March 1, 2001, Roger Leslie, review of *Leaving Cuba: From Operation Pedro Pan to Elian,* p. 1270; April 1, 2001, Roger Leslie, review of *Silent Death: The Threat of Chemical and Biological Terrorism,* p. 1458; August, 2002, review of *Encyclopedia of Women's Health Issues,* pp. 2010-2011; December 1, 2002, Roger Leslie, review of *Body Marks: Tattooing, Piercing, and Scarification,* p. 654.

Bulletin of the Center for Children's Books, February, 1992, Deborah Stevenson, review of *Caution! This May Be an Advertisement: Teen Guide to Advertising,* p. 155; June, 1993, Deborah Stevenson, review of *Breast Implants: Making Safe Choices,* pp. 314-315; October, 1996, Susan S. Verner, review of *Saving the Environment,* p. 59.

Choice, April, 1997, W. Arant, review of *Encyclopedia of North American Eating and Drinking Traditions, Customs and Rituals,* pp. 1307-1308; July-August, 2002, J. M. Coggan, review of *Encyclopedia of Women's Health Issues,* p. 1938.

Five Owls, May, 1993, Mary Lou Burket, review of *Caution! This May Be an Advertisement,* p. 108.

Horn Book Guide, fall, 1993, Barbara Barstow, review of *Breast Implants,* p. 352; spring, 1997, Carolyn Shute, review of *Saving the Environment,* p. 97; spring, 1999, Peter D. Sieruta, review of *Who's Running the Nation?: How Corporate Power Threatens Democracy,* p. 89; spring, 2001, Nell Beram, review of *Leaving Cuba,* p. 96; fall, 2001, Peter D. Sieruta, review of *Silent Death,* p. 337.

Kirkus Reviews, June 15, 1978, review of *Get Hooked on Vegetables,* p. 641; August 1, 1986, review of *Ergonomics: Making Products and Places Fit People,* p. 1211; October 1, 1989, review of *Ozone,* p. 1474; November 1, 1991, review of *Air Pollution,* pp. 1401-1402, review of *Cleaning Nature Naturally,* p. 1402; August 1, 1993, review of *The Right to Die: Public Controversy, Private Matter,* p. 1000; June 1, 1994, review of *Pregnancy,* p. 774.

Library Journal, June 1, 1990, review of *Ozone,* p. 88; July, 1999, Stephen L. Hupp, review of *Encyclopedia of Political Anarchy,* pp. 80-81; December, 2002, Barbara M. Bibel, review of *Encyclopedia of Women's Health Issues,* p. 106.

Reference and User Services Quarterly, summer, 2003, Jennifer M. Boudreaux, review of *The Encyclopedia of Women's Health Issues,* p. 364.

School Library Journal, January, 1981, Richard Luzer, review of *Your Fight Has Just Begun,* p. 69; August, 1986, Meryl Silverstein, review of *The Greenhouse Effect,* p. 100; March, 1988, Rosie Peasley, review of *Changing Families: Meeting Today's Challenges,* p. 219; December, 1988, Diane P. Tuccillo, review of *Silent Killers: Radon and Other Hazards,* p. 126; September, 1989, Sylvia V. Meisner, review of *Bigotry,* p. 280; September, 1993, Kathryn Havris, review of *The Right to Die,* pp. 254-255; July, 1994, Lois McCulley, review of *Pregnancy,* p. 123; February, 1996, Rosalyn Pierini, review of *Civil War, World War I,* and *World War II,* p. 106; February, 1997, Judith L. Miller, review of *Persian Gulf War,* p. 115; July, 1997, Libby K. White, review of *Communes and Cults,* pp. 102-103; September, 1998, Allison Trent Bernstein, review of *After the Shooting Stops,* p. 216; March, 1999, Jonathan Betz-Zall, review of *Who's Running the Nation?,* p. 221; November, 1999, Douglas Wooley, review of *Encyclopedia of Political Anarchy,* p. 78; January, 2001, Sylvia V. Meisner, review of *Leaving Cuba,* p. 144; April, 2001, Ann G. Brouse, review of *Silent Death,* p. 158; October, 2002, Elaine Baran Black, review of *Body Marks,* p. 182.

Science Books and Films, January, 1987, Thomas T. Liao, review of *Ergonomics,* p. 172; May, 1989, Wilton T. Adams, review of *Silent Killers,* p. 296; October, 1991, Herbert J. Mason, review of *Garbage and Recycling,* p. 204; September, 2001, David W. Lillie, review of *Silent Death,* pp. 209-210.

Voice of Youth Advocates, April, 1984, Paula J. Lacey, review of *Acid Rain,* p. 46; August, 1990, Sari Feldman, review of *They Don't Wash Their Socks!: Sports Superstitions,* p. 174; February, 1992, Paula Lacey, review of *Cleaning Nature Naturally,* p. 393; February, 1993, Dem Polacheck, review of *Church and State: Government and Religion in the United States,* p. 368; October, 1995, Brenda Moses, review of *I Am Who I Am,* p. 247; February, 1997, Roxy Ekstrom, review of *Vietnam War,* pp. 345-346; June, 1997, Barbara Jo McKee, review of *Persian Gulf War,* p. 130; June, 2001, Delia A. Culberson, review of *Leaving Cuba,* pp. 140, 142.

ONLINE

AuthorsDen.com, http://www.authorsden.com/ (May 25, 2003), "Kathlyn Gay."

Link-On: The Book Web of Kathlyn Gay, http://ourworld.compuserve.com/homepages/kathy/ (May 26, 2003).*

* * *

GERROLD, David 1944-

PERSONAL: Born David Jerrold Friedman, January 24, 1944, in Chicago, IL; son of Lewis (a photographer) and Johanna (Fleischer) Friedman; children: Sean. *Education:* Attended University of Southern California; California State University—Northridge, B.A.

ADDRESSES: Home and office—9420 Reseda Blvd., No. 804, Northridge, CA 91328. *Agent*—Barbara Bova, Barbara Bova Literary Agency, 3951 Gulfshore Blvd., PH 1-B, Naples, FL 34103. *E-mail*—davgerrold@compuserve.com.

CAREER: Science-fiction writer, 1967—. Taught screenwriting at Pepperdine University, Malibu, CA, 1982-99.

AWARDS, HONORS: Hugo Award nomination, World Science Fiction Society, 1968, for *The Trouble with Tribbles;* Nebula Award nomination, Science Fiction and Fantasy Writers of America, 1972, for "In the Deadlands," and 1977, for *Moonstar Odyssey;* Hugo Award nomination, World Science Fiction Society, and Nebula Award nomination, Science Fiction and Fantasy Writers of America, both 1972, for *When Harlie Was One,* and both 1973, for *The Man Who Folded Himself;* Skylark Award, 1979; Nebula Award for Best Novelette, Science Fiction and Fantasy Writers of America, 1994, Hugo Award for Best Novelette, World Science Fiction Society, 1995, Homer Award, Lambda Award nominee, and winner of the *Locus* Readership

Poll, all for *The Martian Child: A Novel about a Single Father Adopting a Son;* Spectrum Award, 2001, Hal Clement Award for Young Adults, Golden Duck Awards, 2002, Lambda Award nominee, and Nebula Award nomination, Science Fiction and Fantasy Writers of America, all for *Jumping off the Planet.*

WRITINGS:

SCIENCE FICTION; EXCEPT AS NOTED

(With Larry Niven) *The Flying Sorcerers* (novel), Ballantine (New York, NY), 1971.

(Editor, with Stephen Goldin) *Protostars*, Ballantine (New York, NY), 1971.

(Editor, with Stephen Goldin) *Generation*, Dell (New York, NY), 1972.

Space Skimmer (novel), Ballantine (New York, NY), 1972.

When Harlie Was One, Doubleday (New York, NY), 1972, revised and expanded as *When Harlie Was One (Release 2.0),* 1988.

With a Finger in My I (short stories; contains "In the Deadlands"), Ballantine (New York, NY), 1972.

Battle for the Planet of the Apes (novelization adapted from the screenplay by John William Corrington and Joyce Hooper Corrington), Universal Publishing & Distributing (New York, NY), 1973.

The Man Who Folded Himself, Random House (New York, NY), 1973.

The World of Star Trek, Ballantine (New York, NY), 1973.

The Trouble with Tribbles, Ballantine (New York, NY), 1973.

(Editor) *Alternities* (anthology), Dell (New York, NY), 1974.

(Editor) *Emphasis* (anthology), Ballantine (New York, NY), 1974.

(Editor) *Ascents of Wonder* (anthology), Popular Library (New York, NY), 1977.

The Galactic Whirlpool (novelization from *Star Trek*), Bantam (New York, NY), 1977.

Moonstar Odyssey (novel), Signet (New York, NY), 1977.

Deathbeast (novel), Popular Library (New York, NY), 1978.

Enemy Mine (novelization of movie), Berkeley (New York, NY), 1985.

Encounter at Farpoint (novelization from *Star Trek*), Pocket Books (New York, NY), 1987.

Chess with a Dragon, illustrated by Daniel Torres, Walker (New York, NY), 1987.

Under the Eye of God, Bantam (New York, NY), 1993.

A Covenant of Justice, Bantam (New York, NY), 1994.

Fatal Distractions!: Eighty-seven of the Very Best Ways to Get Beaten, Eaten, Maimed, and Mauled on Your PC (nonfiction), Waite Group Press (Corte Madera, CA), 1994.

Worlds of Wonder: How to Write Science Fiction and Fantasy (nonfiction), Writer's Digest Books (Cincinnati, OH), 2001.

The Martian Child: A Novel about a Single Father Adopting a Son (adapted from a novelette that first appeared in the September, 1994, issue of *Magazine of Fantasy and Science Fiction*), Tor (New York, NY), 2002.

"WAR AGAINST CHTORR" SERIES

A Matter for Men, Timescape Books (New York, NY), 1983.

A Day for Damnation, Timescape Books (New York, NY), 1984.

A Rage for Revenge, Bantam (New York, NY), 1989.

A Season for Slaughter, Bantam (New York, NY), 1993.

"DINGILLIAD" SERIES

Jumping off the Planet, Tor (New York, NY), 2000.
Bouncing off the Moon, Tor (New York, NY), 2001.
Leaping to the Stars, Tor (New York, NY), 2002.

"TALES OF THE STAR WOLF" SERIES

Yesterday's Children, Dell (New York, NY), 1972, revised as *Starhunt,* Popular Library (New York, NY), 1978.

Voyage of the Star Wolf, Bantam (New York, NY), 1990.

The Middle of Nowhere, Bantam (New York, NY), 1994.

Blood and Fire, BenBella Books (Dallas, TX), 2004.

TELEPLAYS

The Trouble with Tribbles (episode of *Star Trek* television series, NBC-TV, telecast December 29, 1967), Ballantine (New York, NY), 1973.

Also author of a revision of *I, Mudd*, first produced in 1967, and coauthor of *The Cloud Minders*, first produced in 1968, both as episodes for *Star Trek*, and of *More Troubles, More Tribbles* and *Bem*, both for the animated *Star Trek* series. Story editor of *Land of the Lost*, 1974, and for the first season of *Star Trek: The Next Generation*. Also author of scripts for *Logan's Run, Tales from the Darkside, Twilight Zone, The Real Ghost Busters, Superboy*, and *Babylon 5*.

OTHER

Gerrold's columns have appeared in *Starlog, PC-Techniques, Visual Developer, Yahoo, GalaxyOnline*, and *Galileo*. Contributor to *Future Life, InfoWorld, PC Magazine, A+ Magazine, Profiles, Creative Computing*, and *Personal Computing*.

WORK IN PROGRESS: *A Method for Madness, A Time for Treason*, and *A Case for Courage*, further installments in the "War against the Chtorr" series.

SIDELIGHTS: Author or editor of over forty books and numerous television scripts, David Gerrold "is among the best and most inventive SF writers of his generation," according to a contributor for *St. James Guide to Science Fiction Writers*. Gerrold's award-winning novels include *When Harlie Was One, The Man Who Folded Himself, Yesterday's Children*, and *Moonstar Odyssey*, as well as the books that comprise his enterprising and entertaining "War against the Chtorr" series. For a young-adult audience, he has also written a science fiction trilogy, the *Dingilliad* series, including *Jumping off the Planet, Bouncing off the Moon*, and *Leaping to the Stars*. Additionally, Gerrold has written of his experiences as the single father of an adopted son in the popular 2002 novel *The Martian Child: A Novel about a Single Father Adopting a Son*. Indeed, as Colleen Power noted in an essay on the author in *Reader's Guide to Twentieth-Century Science Fiction*, the teaching of important experiences is at the very heart of Gerrold's works: "Gerrold feels that the most meaningful stories are those which provide an experience, or knowledge, that can be adapted into everyday life." Power also noted that, in general, Gerrold's "characterizations are outstanding . . . , giving his readers rich memories of glorious villains and complex heroes." However, for the *St. James* critic, "Gerrold's literary career has never quite jelled as it might have." According to this contributor, Gerrold's "ability to move easily between novels and screenplays . . . has arguably distracted him from focusing on either."

For Gerrold himself, his writing is all about "growth," as he once commented in an interview with *Contemporary Authors* (*CA*). "Everybody has that one thing inside that he doesn't want to look at too closely because it hurts too much—like being picked last to play ball—that gives him a feeling of insecurity. Whatever it is, there's that one thing. My stories are about the person who suddenly finds himself in a situation where, in order to survive, he must get right down in there, find that part of him that hurts, and deal with it. That's called growth. That fascinates me, the idea of how much it is possible for an individual to grow beyond his or her apparent limitations. That is my central theme, and whether I intend it to or not, it shows up in anything I write, even the easy stuff that's meant just for fun."

Born in 1944, in Chicago, Illinois, Gerrold grew up in California's San Fernando Valley. He was an early fan of science fiction, active also in the fan scene. He once commented that what led him to science fiction as a child was the same thing that leads others there: "It's an escape literature," he noted in his interview with *CA*. "Children who have trouble adjusting to their environment for one reason or another seek escape; some go into drugs, some go into some kind of fantasy world, some go into science fiction. I had always been an inveterate reader, and I stumbled into science fiction by a fellow named [Robert A.] Heinlein. There was this book labeled *Rocketship Galileo*, and I said, 'Gee, I like rocketships. That's terrific.' After I'd gone through about six of Heinlein's juveniles, I used the card catalogue to discover that there were about twenty more Heinlein's I hadn't read, and that led me into adult science fiction. I was there for ten years, and then *Star Trek* came on the air."

By this time, Gerrold had passed through two different high schools, a junior college, had participated in cinema classes at the University of Southern California, and was taking theater courses at California State College—Northridge where he eventually earned his B.A. in theater arts. He had dabbled in filmmaking and had taken some writing courses. However, inspired by the new television show *Star Trek* and feeling confident in his knowledge of the science-fiction genre, he decided to send in some story ideas to the producers "to demonstrate what I thought a good science-fiction story for television should be," he explained in his *CA* interview. "Of course it was terribly prideful to think that with no experience at all I could be writing for TV, but it turned out that there were very few television writers who really understood science fiction. Someone who had a grasp of science fiction was more in demand for *Trek* than someone who understood TV writing, because TV writing doesn't require much intelligence, as the current state of television demonstrates."

In 1967, Gerrold wrote "The Trouble with Tribbles," a script dealing with the havoc caused by harmless looking little furry creatures. Nominated for a Hugo, the script was turned into one of the most popular *Star Trek* episodes of all time. The episode was identified by Fox TV in a 1997 special as "the most popular science fiction episode in television history," according to information on Gerrold's Web site. *Star Trek* celebrated its thirtieth anniversary in 1996 with a digitally adapted segment of the "The Trouble with Tribbles" mixed in with an episode featuring the cast of the then current *Star Trek* incarnation, *Deep Space Nine*.

This early success paved the way for Gerrold to continue with a career in writing. More television scripts followed, and in 1971, collaborating with science-fiction novelist Larry Niven, he published his first novel, *The Flying Sorcerers,* a humorous look at how one planet makes the changeover from reliance on magic to science and industry. Edra Bogle, writing in the *Dictionary of Literary Biography,* found this a "hilarious account." Between 1972 and 1973, Gerrold produced nine books, including two nonfiction titles about *Star Trek,* an anthology, a short-story collection, and five novels. Gerrold's first solo novel was *When Harlie Was One,* a work nominated for both a Hugo and a Nebula. This book deals with artificial intelligence in a realistic and meaningful manner, claimed reviewers. The Harlie of the title is a giant computer. "Examining the problematic morality of a sentient computer," wrote Bogle, "Gerrold speculates on the use of knowledge by humans, the purpose of humanity, and the nature of God." Bogle also found the novel "innovative," yet also felt that the "determinedly upbeat ending undercuts any substantive answers to the question raised."

Space Skimmer, also from 1972, deals with the search for a lost galactic empire, while *Yesterday's Children* takes the form of space opera, dealing with the mutinous conflict between a captain and the first officer of a space ship. A reviewer for the *Times Literary Supplement* found *Yesterday's Children* to be "that rare thing in the genre: a study of character." The same reviewer concluded: "*Yesterday's Children* remains a solidly worked-out SF novel with unusually good characterization." Gerrold later revised this novel as *Starhunt,* the first of a series of novels (including *Voyage of the Star Wolf, The Middle of Nowhere,* and *Blood and Fire*) that "has a strong smell of the sea behind it," according to Tom Easton in an *Analog* review of *The Middle of Nowhere.* These novels feature Jon Korie, executive officer of the space ship LS-1187, and his battle against the evil Morthan empire, a race of genetically altered proto-humans. Easton, writing in *Analog,* also had praise for *Voyage of the Star Wolf,* calling it "a tale of intense frustration and terror that delivers a lesson or two in leadership." Combined in these novels, as in several others, is the Harlie artificial intelligence of Gerrold's earlier novel. Writing in *Science Fiction Chronicle,* Don D'Ammassa felt that with *Voyage of the Star Wolf* Gerrold "singlehandedly elevated [the war-in-space novel] to a level no one else has equaled." Reviewing *The Middle of Nowhere* in *Booklist,* Carl Hays lauded this example of "intelligent and entertaining hard sf that remains blessedly free of the militaristic stereotypes rampant in other examples of the subgenre."

Gerrold's *The Man Who Folded Himself,* from 1973, "shows a growing maturity of thought and emphasis," according to Bogle. This book takes a premise straight from the pages of Heinlein—a folding or convolution in time wherein the protagonist continues to meet himself in different periods. A nineteen-year-old student, with the aid of a special belt, time travels and meets with a half-dozen different versions of himself at different ages. A *Publishers Weekly* contributor felt that "Gerrold is such a good writer that he keeps us reading through the most confusing shifts of time, space and character—right into pre-history." A reviewer for the *Times Literary Supplement* had similar praise, calling the book "most impressive," and also noting the "uncanny allegorical force" of the tale.

Following this enormous burst of creativity in the span of only two years, Gerrold slowed down in production for a time, working on screenplays and contributing to anthologies, and living for a time in Ireland and New York. His novel *Moonstar Odyssey* appeared in 1977, and tells of an artificially habitable planet where the inhabitants choose their gender at puberty. This search for "self-fulfillment," as Bogle describes the theme, is also evident in the 1978 novel, *Deathbeast.*

Returning to California, Gerrold created the television show *Land of the Lost,* started teaching creative writing at Malibu's Pepperdine University, and continued working on the first of the novels in his "War against the Chtorr" series. *A Matter for Men,* the initial novel in the series, eventually appeared in 1983, and the second, *A Day for Damnation,* was published the following year. These two books set the stage for the series—Earth faced with an alien invasion of a sort inspired by H. G. Wells's *War of the Worlds.* Indeed, the critic for *St. James Guide to Science Fiction Writers* thought the novels of Gerrold's series present "at least the second-best alien invasion story ever published," next to *War of the Worlds.* A plague has hit the planet, but soon the survivors discover that this sickness is the first stage of an attack by Chtorran invaders, or worms, huge caterpillar-like creatures with fangs. The worms are not alone in the invasion; they carry the entire ecosystem of their world, a system far older and more vicious than anything on Earth. The battle is seen through the eyes of Jim McCarthy, about twenty at the opening of *A Matter for Men.* McCarthy grows into manhood over the course of the novels even as Earth is dying around him. The native plants and animals of Earth have been attacked by the Chtorran ecosystems, and McCarthy has lost friends and loved ones to the invaders.

The action continues in *A Day for Damnation,* and in *A Rage for Revenge* McCarthy is captured by a group of human-Chtorran renegades. The contributor for *St. James Guide to Science Fiction Writers* felt that the strength of this title lay in the fact that its protagonist "has not, yet, turned into the same caliber of monster as his human and Chtorran enemies." The fourth novel in the series, *A Season for Slaughter,* explores the themes of "personal responsibility and alienation," according to the same contributor. In this installment, McCarthy continues to learn more about the nature of the Chtorran threat, though it is still unclear if humanity will be able to counter it. *Booklist*'s Roland Green felt that this fourth volume "continues in the classic mold of intelligent action-sf." Writing in *Analog,* Easton noted that "the series moves from ignorance toward understanding. For McCarthy, this means he's growing up, learning how to be a decent human being." D'Ammassa, writing in *Science Fiction Chronicle,* had further praise, claiming that this fourth volume "continues the narrative with power and effectiveness." D'Ammassa additionally called the novel "gritty, engaging, and unsettling." Fans are still waiting for the series to continue with the next projected volume in the series, *A Method for Madness.*

With *Under the Eye of God* and *A Covenant of Justice,* Gerrold presents another pair of interlinking books. These deal with an immortal race of vampire-like creatures and dragons, the Regency, who rule a forgotten world in a distant corner of the Milky Way. Two bounty hunters are forced by the Regency to hunt down a fugitive, someone who could possibly overthrow their regime. D'Ammassa, writing in *Science Fiction Chronicle,* found the first in the duo, *Under the Eye of God,* "entertaining but maddening" because of Gerrold's use of "farcical humor." A reviewer for *Library Journal,* however, found the same title an "engaging tale of tongue-in-cheek adventure." In a *Booklist* review of the second novel in the series, *A Covenant of Justice,* Denise Winters felt that the author "is able to infuse his electrifying adventures with humor . . . while keeping the action cascading."

Though his books can generally be enjoyed by all ages, Gerrold has also written specifically for the young-adult and juvenile audiences with his "Dingilliad" series, a trilogy that includes *Jumping off the Planet, Bouncing off the Moon,* and *Leaping to the Stars.* The books feature the adventures of Charles Dingillian in "a genuinely powerful coming-of-age story," according to *Booklist*'s Roland Green. In the first novel, young Charles 'Chigger' Dingillian and his two brothers are leaving on a trip to the moon with their father, recently separated from their mother. Set in the twenty-first century, the book posits an Earth that is hugely overcrowded. Such trips to the moon are done via an orbiting magnetic elevator system. But Chigger, the middle sibling, soon begins to see that his dad is in fact kidnapping his children from their mother. Through the character of Chigger, readers experience "the smuggling and big-business intrigue that simmers in a world where international corporatism has made all borders irrelevant," according to a reviewer for *Publishers Weekly.* The same contributor felt that Gerrold writes with "just the right mix of preteen braggadocio and heartbreak." Green, writing in *Booklist,* concluded, "this is sometimes over-the-top but always recognizably the creation of a major talent."

For *Library Journal*'s Jackie Cassada, this novel also showed echoes of Heinlein's juvenile fiction and "should appeal to YA as well as general readers."

Chigger's adventures continue in *Bouncing off the Moon,* in which the three brothers move off the Earth, one step ahead of a deadly plague and financial debacle, bound for the moon. There they undergo a series of adventures and misadventures that make them wonder whether someone is out to murder them. A critic for *Publishers Weekly* had praise for this continuation of the series, calling it an "engaging, believable, and eventually riveting book." Green, however, writing in *Booklist,* felt that this second title lacked "the exuberant creativity and tight narrative of its predecessor." A contributor for *Kirkus Reviews* has similar reservations, finding the plot "claustrophobic but probably okay for the YA audience."

Leaping to the Stars concludes the series, with Chigger signing on as a colonist to the Outbeyond—a distant colony of planet Earth—in a desperate attempt to escape the rival powers pursuing him on the moon. In his possession is Harlie, the artificial intelligence which competing powers on the moon seek. Chigger is also accompanied by his two brothers as well as his divorced parents, but on the way to Outbeyond, they are beset by fellow travelers, the fundamentalist group called the Revelationists, who want to destroy Harlie. A critic for *Publishers Weekly* noted that the book had "obvious" appeal for young adults, "but plenty of adults are also sure to enjoy this thoughtful adventure." *Booklist*'s John Mort also found that Gerrold has a "fresh voice" and that the dialogue between Chigger and his Harlie is "also intriguing—even rather touching." Cassada also commended the novel in a *Library Journal* review, remarking on the "derring-do in the style of early Heinlein."

Gerrold shares some of the lessons he has learned in his more than three decades of writing in the 2001 *Worlds of Wonder: How to Write Science Fiction and Fantasy,* a "fairly standard set of the basics," according to *Booklist*'s Green, who predicted that writers-to-be "will appreciate his clarity and lack of condescension." *Library Journal*'s Denise S. Sticha observed that "Gerrold passionately discusses the challenges and excitement of writing sf" in this "welcome addition."

A further departure for Gerrold is his 2002 *The Martian Child,* adapted from a 1994 novelette of the same title. In this expanded version, Gerrold creates a fictionalized memoir of his own experiences as a gay, single father of an adopted son. The book covers the first two difficult years the father and adopted eight-year-old boy were together. "The heart-searing moments are many but never overwritten, thanks to Gerrold's bright, efficient exposition," noted Ray Olson in a *Booklist* review.

Gerrold has produced an interesting and intriguing body of work since his breakthrough teleplay, "The Trouble with Tribbles." This includes over two dozen novels, and more nonfiction titles and short story collections, along with edited volumes and contributions to anthologies. Praised for his characterizations as well as his unique voice, Gerrold remains humble about the role of a writer. As he concluded in his *CA* interview, "I believe there's nothing inherently special about a writer; he's just a human being who has learned to use the language precisely enough to be coherent in the communication of his ideas. There are lots of people who have the skill to be writers who just never have the determination to sit down at a typewriter, or the feeling that what they have to say is important enough. But what distinguishes the real writer from the guy who's just putting words on paper is that he is reporting back his experiences; that is, he uses his life as a laboratory and reports back on what he has discovered in that laboratory. It is a continual process of discovery of self, and when a writer is able to report something that he has discovered about himself, he is reporting something that he has discovered about the human condition. When he does that, and other people recognize the truth of it, there is one more piece of truth in the world than there was before, and more understanding."

BIOGRAPHICAL AND CRITICAL SOURCES:

BOOKS

Contemporary Authors, Volumes 93-96, interview with David Gerrold, Gale (Detroit, MI), 1980.
Dictionary of Literary Biography, Volume 8: *Twentieth-Century American Science-Fiction Writers,* Gale (Detroit, MI), 1981, pp. 189-192.
Encyclopedia of Science Fiction, edited by John Clute and Peter Nicholls, St. Martin's Press (New York, NY), 1992.
New Encyclopedia of Science Fiction, edited by James Gunn, Viking (New York, NY), 1988.

Reader's Guide to Twentieth-Century Science Fiction, compiled and edited by Marilyn P. Fletcher, American Library Association (Chicago, IL), 1989, pp. 248-251.

St. James Guide to Science Fiction Writers, 4th edition, edited by Jay Pederson, St. James Press (Detroit, MI), 1996.

PERIODICALS

Analog, April, 1991, Tom Easton, review of *Voyage of the Star Wolf,* pp. 181-182; April, 1993, Tom Easton, review of *A Season for Slaughter,* pp. 160-162; September, 1995, Tom Easton, review of *The Middle of Nowhere,* pp. 181-183.

Booklist, November 15, 1992, Roland Green, review of *A Season for Slaughter,* p. 582; April 1, 1994, Dennis Winters, review of *A Covenant of Justice,* p. 1426; March 15, 1995, Carl Hays, review of *The Middle of Nowhere,* p. 1313; March 1, 2000, Roland Green, review of *Jumping off the Planet,* p. 1200; February 1, 2001, Roland Green, review of *Worlds of Wonder: How to Write Science Fiction and Fantasy,* p. 1034; March 1, 2001, Roland Green, review of *Bouncing off the Moon,* p. 1233; March 1, 2002, John Mort, review of *Leaping to the Stars,* pp. 1098-1099; June 1, 2002, review of *The Martian Child: A Novel about a Single Father Adopting a Son,* p. 1675.

Book World, March 30, 1975.

Kirkus Reviews, February 15, 2001, review of *Bouncing off the Moon,* p. 222; April 15, 2002, review of *The Martian Child,* p. 515.

Kliatt, March, 1994, Sister Avila Lamb, review of *Under the Eye of God,* p. 16; May, 1995, Howard G. Zaharoff, review of *The Middle of Nowhere,* p. 14.

Lambda Book Report, September, 2002, Thom Nickels, review of *Leaping to the Stars,* p. 16, Greg Herren, review of *The Martian Child,* pp. 16-17.

Library Journal, December, 1993, review of *Under the Eye of God,* p. 180; March 15, 2000, Jackie Cassada, review of *Jumping off the Planet,* p. 132; March 15, 2001, Denise S. Sticha, review of *Worlds of Wonder,* p. 91; March 15, 2002, Jackie Cassada, review of *Leaping to the Stars,* p. 111.

Locus, February, 1991, review of *Voyage of the Star Wolf,* p. 56; June, 1991, review of *A Rage for Revenge,* p. 48; June, 1994, review of *A Covenant of Justice,* p. 57.

Publishers Weekly, February 4, 1974; May 13, 1974, review of *The Man Who Folded Himself;* January 3, 1977; June 5, 1978; March 6, 2000, review of *Jumping off the Planet,* p. 88; February 19, 2001, review of *Bouncing off the Moon,* p. 73; February 12, 2002, review of *Leaping to the Stars,* p. 166.

Science Fiction Chronicle, March, 1991, Don D'Ammassa, "1990's Novels in Review," review of *Voyage of the Star Wolf,* p. 28; April, 1993, Don D'Ammassa, review of *A Season for Slaughter,* p. 33; February, 1994, Don D'Ammassa, review of *Under the Eye of God,* p. 34; February, 1995, Don D'Ammassa, review of *Fatal Distractions,* p. 35.

Times Literary Supplement, February 15, 1974, review of *Yesterday's Children;* June 14, 1974, review of *The Man Who Folded Himself.*

Village Voice, June 13, 1974.

ONLINE

David Gerrold Home Page, http://www.gerrold.com/ (August 22, 2003).*

* * *

GILDEA, Robert 1952-

PERSONAL: Born September 12, 1952, in Egham, England; son of Denis (a civil servant) and Hazel (a counselor) Gildea; married Lucy-Jean Lloyd, March 21, 1987; children: Rachel, Georgia, William. *Education:* Merton College, Oxford, B.A., M.A., 1974; attended St. Antony's College, Oxford, 1974-76; St. John's College, Oxford, D.Phil., 1978.

ADDRESSES: Office—Merton College, Oxford University, Oxford OX1 4JD, England; fax (0)186-528-6500. *E-mail*—robert.gildea@merton.ox.ac.uk.

CAREER: Educator and historian. Kings College, University of London, London, England, lecturer in history, 1978-79; Oxford University, Oxford, England, fellow and tutor in modern history at Merton College, 1979—, reader in modern history, 1996—.

MEMBER: Royal Historical Society (fellow), Chevalier dans L'Ordre des Palmes Academiques.

WRITINGS:

Education in Provincial France, 1800-1916, Oxford University Press (Oxford, England), 1983.
Barricades and Borders: Europe, 1800-1916, Oxford University Press (Oxford, England), 1987, 2nd edition, 1996.
France, 1870-1914, Longman (London, England), 1988, 2nd edition, 1996.
The Past in French History, Yale University Press (New Haven, CT), 1994.
France since 1945, Oxford University Press (New York, NY), 1996.
Marianne in Chains: In Search of the German Occupation, Pan Macmillan (London, England), 2002.

Contributor to periodicals, including London *Sunday Times.*

SIDELIGHTS: Robert Gildea is a history professor with expertise in French history who has published books on topics ranging from the history of education to French politics. He is especially interested in the "truth" with regard to the historical records of the country, and in his 1994 book, *The Past in French History,* examines how politics and memory combine to create history. Gildea discovered that history is a virtual battlefield to French people, with constant bickering between the political Left and Right about what truly happened.

In his *Marianne in Chains: In Search of the German Occupation,* Gildea seeks to further uncover the myths interwoven in France's history. The book focuses on the period of the German Occupation during World War II and focuses in detail on one small town in the Loire valley, Chinon. The author asserts that there have historically been three major myths about how the French people behaved during the Occupation: they were either resistors, collaborators, or victims. In order to research his subject, Gildea moved to France for a year, studied national and local archives, and conducted many interviews. In addition to creating a vivid day-to-day picture of life in Chinon during this period, Gildea succeeded in a "dismantling of the Resistance legend," according to Frank McLynn in *New Statesman.* Though many who lived through the Occupation claimed to have participated in the Resistance, this book clearly shows that most were simply trying to live their lives and survive on a day-to-day basis. As Gildea concludes in *Marianne in Chains,* no more that two percent of the population resisted, and McLynn cited as one of Gildea's best qualities as author "an acutely developed sense of historical irony." Patrick Marnham, writing for the *Sunday Telegraph,* added that "Gildea has succeeded in giving us a startlingly original view of what we thought was a familiar period." The critic went on to note that "the great strength of *Marianne in Chains* is its narrow focus." Douglas Johnson praised the work in his review for the *Spectator* as "a fine, thought-provoking book," and also called it "excellent and well-documented."

BIOGRAPHICAL AND CRITICAL SOURCES:

PERIODICALS

Daily Telegraph (London, England), April 6, 2002, David Horspool, "Occupational Hazzards."
European History Quarterly, October, 1997, Judith F. Stone, review of *France since 1945,* p. 596.
Historical Journal, March, 1998, D. L. L. Parry, review of *The Past in French History,* p. 311.
History Today, August, 1997, Martin Evans, review of *France since 1945,* p. 54; June, 2002, Martin Evans, review of *Marianne in Chains,* pp. 57-58.
New Statesman, April 1, 2002, Frank McLynn, review of *Marianne in Chains,* p. 54.
Spectator, March 23, 2002, Douglas Johnson, review of *Marianne in Chains,* p. 56.
Sunday Telegraph (London, England), March 17, 2002, Patrick Marnham, "Not As Noir As It Was Painted," p. 5; March 31, 2002, p. 15.
Times (London, England), April 24, 2002, M. R. D. Fox, "Subtle Lack of Resistance in a France Occupied by Appeasement," p. 17.
Times Literary Supplement, May 3, 2002, Richard Vinen, review of *Marianne in Chains,* p. 6.*

* * *

GINSBURG, (Joan) Ruth Bader 1933-

PERSONAL: Born March 15, 1933, in Brooklyn, NY; daughter of Nathan (a furrier) and Celia (Amster) Bader; married Martin David Ginsburg (a professor), June 23, 1954; children: Jane Carol, James Steven.

Ruth Bader Ginsburg

Education: Cornell University, B.A., 1954; Harvard University, graduate study, 1956-58; Columbia University, LL.B., 1959. *Religion:* Jewish.

ADDRESSES: *Office*—c/o Supreme Court of the United States, 1 First St. NE, Washington, DC 20543.

CAREER: Justice, educator, and attorney. Admitted to the Bar of New York State, 1959; New York District Court, law clerk, 1959-61; Rutgers University School of Law, Newark, NJ, assistant professor, 1963-66, associate professor, 1966-69, professor of law, 1969-72; Columbia University, New York, NY, professor of law, 1972-81; admitted to the Bar of the District of Columbia, 1975; U.S. Court of Appeals for the District of Columbia, justice, 1980-93; U.S. Supreme Court, Washington, DC, associate justice, 1993—. American Civil Liberties Union, New York, NY, general counsel, 1973-80, member of national board of directors, 1974-80.

MEMBER: American Bar Association, American Law Institute, Council on Foreign Relations, American Foreign Law Association (member of board of directors, beginning 1970; vice president, beginning 1973), Women's Law Fund (member of board of directors), Association of American Law Schools (member of executive committee, 1972), Association of Bar of the City of New York (member of executive committee, beginning 1974), Phi Beta Kappa, Phi Kappa Phi.

AWARDS, HONORS: Honorary LL.D. from University of Lund, 1969; American Academy of Arts and Sciences fellow, 1982—.

WRITINGS:

(With Anders Bruzelius) *Civil Procedure in Sweden*, M. Nijhoff (the Hague, Netherlands), 1965.

(Translator and author of introduction with Anders Bruzelius) *The Swedish Code of Judicial Procedure*, F. B. Rothman (South Hackensack, NJ), 1968.

(Editor) *Business Regulation in the Common-Market Nations*, Volume I, McGraw-Hill (New York, NY), 1969.

A Selective Survey of English-Language Studies on Scandinavian Law, F. B. Rothman (South Hackensack, NJ), 1970.

(With Herma Hill Kay and Kenneth M. Davidson) *Text, Cases, and Materials on Sex-based Discrimination* ("American Casebook" series), West Publishing (St. Paul, MN), 1974, selections published as *Text, Cases, and Materials on Constitutional Aspects of Sex-based Discrimination*, 1974.

(Author of foreword) Clare Cushman, editor, *Supreme Court Decisions and Women's Rights: Milestones to Equality*, CQ Press (Washington, DC), 2001.

Coauthor of *The Legal Status of Women under Federal Law: Report to the United States Commission on Civil Rights*, 1974. Contributor to books, including *International Cooperation in Litigation*, edited by Hans Smit, M. Nijhoff (The Hague, Netherlands), 1965. Contributor to law journals, including *Journal of Family Law, American Journal of Comparative Law, International and Comparative Law Quarterly, Vital Speeches of the Day, International Lawyer, American Bar Association Journal,* and *Harvard Law Review*. Member of editorial board, *American Journal of Comparative Law,* 1966-72, and *American Bar Association Journal,* 1972-75.

Ginsburg's papers are archived at the Library of Congress, Washington, DC.

SIDELIGHTS: Key events in U.S. Supreme Court Justice Ruth Bader Ginsburg's life helped establish her as a strong advocate for civil liberties and women's rights. President Bill Clinton's first Supreme Court appointee in 1993, Ginsburg was also the second woman to serve on the Supreme Court. Her life and experiences both in and out of her career as an attorney and educator fueled her efforts to help American women gain equal social and legal rights while also shaping her moderate political views.

Born in Brooklyn, New York, on March 15, 1933, Ginsburg is the second daughter of Nathan and Celia Bader. Her older sister, Marilyn, died at the age of eight, before Ruth started school. The Baders lived in the Flatbush section of Brooklyn, a working-class neighborhood of Jewish, Italian, and Irish immigrants. Ginsburg's mother instilled in Ruth the value of education through frequent trips to the library, and stressed the importance of attending college.

After high school, Ginsburg attended Cornell University, where she met her future husband, Martin Ginsburg. An excellent student, she was elected to Phi Beta Kappa and graduated as the top woman in her class. Married the year she graduated, Ginsburg decided to attend law school—Martin Ginsburg had already enrolled at Harvard Law School and Ruth planned to follow suit—but those plans were derailed when Martin was drafted into the U.S. Army. The couple moved to Fort Sill in Lawton, Oklahoma, where they had their first child. Returning to Harvard after two years in Oklahoma, Ruth Ginsburg was admitted to Harvard Law School. In her second year of law school Martin was diagnosed with testicular cancer, and during his radiation therapy and surgery she tended to their daughter as well keeping both her and Martin current in their classwork.

At Harvard Ginsburg first encountered the hostility towards women that she would battle throughout her career, when a professor reportedly asked the nine women in Ginsburg's graduating class how it felt to take the places of more-deserving men. Undaunted by such negativity, Ginsburg excelled at her studies and won a coveted position on the *Harvard Law Review.*

Following his graduation, Martin Ginsburg accepted a position in New York City and Ruth transferred to Columbia Law School, where she earned a position on the *Columbia Law Review* and graduated first in her class in 1959. Despite this Ginsburg once again faced gender-based hostility and found difficulty obtaining a clerkship, but was hired by district court judge Eddie L. Palmieri. In 1961 she joined Columbia's comparative law project, traveling to Sweden to study that country's judicial system. Ginsburg's research resulted in a translation of Swedish judicial proceedings, as well as the book *Civil Procedure in Sweden.* In 1963 she joined the faculty of Rutgers University Law School and also worked as an attorney for the American Civil Liberties Union (ACLU).

At the ACLU Ginsburg became the first director of that organization's Women's Rights project, for which she litigated sex-discrimination cases. In her capacity as director, she argued six cases before the U.S. Supreme Court that involved gender-based discrimination. Recognizing the Court's gradual shift to a moderate stance, Ginsburg selected cases highlighting gender inequality that had male rather than female plaintiffs, and won five of the six cases she argued.

In 1972 Ginsburg became the first woman to receive tenure as a professor at Columbia Law School. Through her accomplishments as a teacher and her success with the ACLU, she came to the attention of President Jimmy Carter, who appointed her to the U.S. Court of Appeals for the District of Columbia Circuit in 1980. As a justice, Ginsburg became known for being conscientious and fair-minded. In 1993, when U.S. Supreme Court Justice Byron R. White resigned, President Bill Clinton became the first Democratic president to nominate a Supreme Court Justice in over a quarter century. He chose Ginsburg, calling her the "Thurgood Marshall of women's rights." She was confirmed to the seat by a Senate vote of 97-3. Although she is considered a liberal, Ginsburg often votes with her conservative bench-mates to promote judicial restraint.

BIOGRAPHICAL AND CRITICAL SOURCES:

BOOKS

Breedson, Carmen, *Ruth Bader Ginsburg: Supreme Court Justice,* Enslow Publishers (Springfield, NJ), 1995.

PERIODICALS

Affilia, spring, 1994, Carol H. Meyer, "The First Feminist Activist I Ever Met," p. 85.

American Bar Association Journal, October, 1993, Stephanie B. Goldberg, "The Second Woman Justice: Ruth Bader Ginsburg Talks Candidly about a Changing Society," p. 40.

Life, May 1, 1999, p. 52.

National Law Journal, August 16, 1993, Thomas E. Baker, "Discomfiting Glimpses of (Hopefully) Old Ways," p. 15; October 11, 1993, David Sive, "Will Justice Ginsburg Color Court Green?," p. 18.

New York University Law Review, April, 2000, Martha Craig Daughtrey, "Women and the Constitution: Where We Are at the End of the Century," pp. 1-25.

ONLINE

Oyez Project, www.oyez.org/ (September 1, 2003), "Ruth Bader Ginsburg."*

* * *

GOODHUE, Thomas W. 1949-

PERSONAL: Born March 5, 1949, in Montebello, CA; son of Wallace T. and Mary Virginia (Gray) Goodhue; married Karen Pohlig (a yarn shop owner), May 13, 1975. *Ethnicity:* "Gringo." *Education:* Stanford University, B.A. (cum laude), 1971; Union Theological Seminary, M.Div., 1975; City College of the City University of New York, M.S., 1982. *Politics:* "Neoliberal/progressive." *Religion:* Christian.

ADDRESSES: Office—Long Island Council of Churches, 1644 Denton Green, Hempstead, NY 11550. *E-mail*—tgoodhue@suffolk.lib.ny.us.

CAREER: Pastor of United Methodist churches in Kailua, HI, 1975-77, and Kahaluu, HI, 1977-78; teacher at church-sponsored school in New York, NY, 1978-85; pastor of United Methodist churches in Island Park, NY, 1985-92, and Bay Shore, NY, 1992-99. Long Island Council of Churches, Hempstead, NY, presenter of weekly radio commentary, 1988-91, vice president, 1991-94, president, 1994-97, executive director, 1999—. United Methodist Center of Far Rockaway, vice president, 1985-92; Long Island Multi-Faith Forum, member; Building Bridges (interfaith education program), creator; Long Island Interfaith Disaster Response, founder, 2001. Windward Coalition of Churches, clergy coordinator, 1975-77; Hawaii Council of Churches, member of executive committee, 1977-78; member of board of directors, Health and Welfare Council of Long Island, 1999—, Fight for Families Coalition, 2000—, and United Way of Long Island, 2002—. Member, board of directors, Long Island Housing Partnership; WLIW-TV, member of community advisory board.

MEMBER: Phi Beta Kappa.

AWARDS, HONORS: Columbia University School of International Affairs, international fellow, 1974-75; Catholic Book Award; Educational Press Association Award.

WRITINGS:

Kaahumanu: Queen of Hawaii, Women of Courage, 1985.

Stories for the Children of Light, Sunday Publications (Lake Worth, FL), 1986.

Sharing the Good News with Children (collected writings), St. Anthony Messenger Press (Cincinnati, OH), 1992.

Curious Bones: Mary Anning and the Birth of Paleontology, Morgan Reynolds (Greensboro, NC), 2002.

Contributor of articles, essays, and reviews to periodicals, including *Anglican and Episcopal History, Northeastern Geological and Environmental Sciences, Journal of Ecumenical Studies, Momentum, Share, Christian Century, Midstream, Newsday, Education Week,* and *New Republic.*

WORK IN PROGRESS: A longer biography of Mary Anning, *Fossil Hunter: The Life and Times of Mary Anning,* for Academic Press; a biography of Hawaiian Queen Kaahumanu.

SIDELIGHTS: Thomas W. Goodhue told *CA:* "I first became fascinated with Mary Anning while teaching kindergartners at the Riverside Church Weekday School in New York. Sharing the enthusiasm of five year olds for prehistoric creatures, I loved reading to them about dinosaurs and fossil hunters. I kept noticing references to the teenage girl who started the first dinosaur craze. Unable to find any factual account of her life—or any other books for children about female paleontologists—I started researching and writing a short summary of her life. This led to an article for the teachers' magazine *Instructor* in 1985, a children's sermon published in my collection *Sharing the Good News,* and a lasting obsession to learn more about this remarkable woman.

"What I find most fascinating about Anning are the paradoxes of her life. She was working class but formed friendships with wealthy fossil collectors and scholars. She had no formal education but helped shape the development of geology, biology, and paleontology. She was deeply pious herself, but her discoveries rattled the beliefs of millions of people. She could not vote herself, but she helped overturn the corrupt, aristocratic political machine that had dominated her town.

* * *

GORAK, Jan 1952-

PERSONAL: Born October 12, 1952, in Blackburn, England; son of Jozef (a road mender) and Mary (a nurse; maiden name, Niland) Gorak; married Irene Elizabeth Mannion, November 17, 1984. *Education:* University of Warwick, B.A., 1975; attended University of Leeds, 1975-77; University of Southern California, M.A., 1981, Ph.D., 1983. *Politics:* "Disillusioned independent." *Hobbies and other interests:* Film, music (especially rock music).

ADDRESSES: *Office*—Department of English, University of Denver, University Park, Denver, CO 80208. *E-mail*—jgorak@du.edu.

CAREER: University of the Witwatersrand, Johannesburg, South Africa, lecturer in English, 1984-87, senior lecturer in English, 1987-88; University of Denver, Denver, CO, visiting associate professor, 1988-89, professor of English, 1991—.

MEMBER: Modern Language Association of America, American Society for Eighteenth-Century Studies, T. S. Eliot Society, Rocky Mountain Modern Language Association.

AWARDS, HONORS: Pringle Prize, English Academy of Southern Africa, 1986, for the article "Deus Artifex: Transformations of a Topos"; Mellon fellow of American Society for Eighteenth-Century Studies at University of Texas—Austin; Humanities fellow, Oregon State University.

WRITINGS:

God the Artist: American Novelists in a Post-Realist Age, University of Illinois Press (Urbana, IL), 1987.
Critic of Crisis: A Study of Frank Kermode, University of Missouri Press (Columbia, MO), 1987.
The Alien Mind of Raymond Williams, University of Missouri Press (Columbia, MO), 1988.
The Making of the Modern Canon: Genesis and Crisis of a Literary Idea, Athlone Press (London, England), 1990.
(Editor) *Canon vs. Culture: Reflections on the Current Debate,* Garland Publishing (New York, NY), 2000.
(Editor) *Northrop Frye on Twentieth-Century Culture,* University of Toronto Press (Toronto, Ontario, Canada), 2003.

Contributor to books, including *The Legacy of Northrop Frye,* edited by Alvin A. Lee and Robert D. Denham, University of Toronto (Toronto, Ontario, Canada), 1994; *Teaching Contemporary Literary Theory to Undergraduates,* edited by Dianne F. Sadoff and William E. Cain, MLA Publications (New York, NY), 1994; *The Cambridge History of Literary Criticism,* Volume 4, edited by Claude Rawson and H. B. Nisbet, Cambridge University Press (New York, NY), 1997; and *Northrop Frye: Eastern and Western Perspectives,* edited by Jean O'Grady, [Toronto, Ontario, Canada], 2002. Contributor to academic journals, including *English Studies in Africa, Denver Quarterly Theater Journal,* and *Rocky Mountain Modern Language Association Journal.*

WORK IN PROGRESS: *Civilization from Outside: Studies in the Emigration of an Idea.*

SIDELIGHTS: Jan Gorak once told *CA:* "I am one of a number of displaced academic personnel trekking the five continents after the breakup of the British university system. Not surprisingly, my books reflect the darker areas of interest of the scholar in exile. In *God the Artist: American Novelists in a Post-Realist Age,* I examined the effect of the destructive creator-god on modern literary culture. In *Critic of Crisis: A Study of Frank Kermode* and *The Alien Mind of Raymond Williams,* I showed how that culture induces a sense of crisis and alienation in its strongest critical exponents. Future projects will no doubt have a similar emphasis on the skeptical, restless, deracinated intelligence induced by an intellectual life of perpetual motion."

Gorak more recently told *CA:* "In *The Making of the Modern Canon: Genesis and Crisis of a Literary Idea,* I set myself the task of understanding whether all the nasty things said about that monolithic entity 'the canon' had any basis in fact or even in fiction. Perhaps to my surprise—for I have never considered myself a particularly conservative person—I found that they did not. Accordingly, I set out to understand what 'canon' did mean in the literary culture from early Elizabethan times to our own. I am now engaged in a similar enterprise for the idea of 'civilization.' Such tasks, perhaps less important than the collective uplift of a generation, are necessary if the past is not to fall into permanent disrepair."

Gorak later added: "My recent work on Northrop Frye has been the byproduct of my interest in the emigrating idea of civilization. But the excellence of Frye's work and the hugeness of his contribution has caused me to reopen my investigation into the question of civilization, to look again at what the future inquiry, so central to enlightened thinking and so increasingly remote to our own, can tell us about that question. I am increasingly drawn to writers like Diderot and Hume, for whom the humanities represent a way of suspending certainty and opening real investigation. I would say that the years since I was last in touch with *Contemporary Authors* have been years in which I have widened my reading considerably and have attempted to tap the positive potential of suspending my own convictions. I hope some of this comes through in what I am writing.

"I have also become more convinced that not much can come of a critical writing not immersed in the detail of the world its subjects inhabit. When I began to edit Frye, it was a source of constant delight to suspend oneself in the everyday life of 1920s and 1930s Toronto, a life that Frye himself thought rather narrow and philistine, but which seems a fertile seedbed for his own 'anti-modernistic' poetics. The possibilities of a criticism informed by milieu and moment seem much broader and deeper to me in 2002 than they did in 1992, and I imagine my work will reflect that conviction."

* * *

GRAHAM, Daniel O., Jr. 1952-

PERSONAL: Born June 3, 1952, in KY; son of Daniel O. (an army officer) and Ruth M. Graham; married Judith Hanson, December 22, 1976; children: Daniel, Rebecca, Rachael, Eve, John, Madeline. *Education:* College of William and Mary, B.A.; University of Alabama, M.B.A. *Politics:* Conservative. *Religion:* Roman Catholic. *Hobbies and other interests:* Sailing, home brewing.

ADDRESSES: Home and office—9117 Saranac Ct., Fairfax, VA 22032. *E-mail*—dograham@erols.com.

CAREER: U.S. Army, career officer, 1974-83, leaving the service as captain; Kentec Corp., Arlington, VA, president, 1983-86; Graham Associates, Fairfax, VA, principal, 1986—. High Frontier, member of board of directors, 1983-85.

MEMBER: National Futures Association.

AWARDS, HONORS: Military: Distinguished Service Medal. *Literary:* Compton Crook Award, best science fiction book by a new author, 1996, for *The Gatekeepers.*

WRITINGS:

(With wife, Judith H. Graham) *The Writing System Workbook,* Preview Press, 1994.
The Gatekeepers (science fiction), Baen Books (Riverdale, NY), 1995.
The Politics of Meaning (humor), Preview Press, 1995.
(Editor) *Confessions of a Cold Warrior* (biography), Preview Press, 1995.
(With Roxann Dawson) *Entering Tenebrea,* Pocket Books (New York, NY), 2001.

(With Roxann Dawson) *Tenebrea's Hope,* Pocket Books (New York, NY), 2001.

(With Roxann Dawson) *Tenebrea Rising,* Pocket Books (New York, NY), 2002.

Business editor, *Journal of Practical Applications in pace,* 1985-86.

WORK IN PROGRESS: The Peacemakers, a sequel to *The Gatekeepers;* research on the northern Renaissance, including the Peasants' War.

SIDELIGHTS: Daniel O. Graham, Jr. once told *CA:* "Since leaving the United States Army in 1983, I have remained self-employed—teaching, consulting, and writing. I pursue my passion for current affairs, enabling technologies, traditional morals, and writing. I study Mark Twain for wit and style, and I use Alfred Hitchcock's method of story-boarding scenes to move the plot."

* * *

GRANT, Anne Underwood 1946-

PERSONAL: Born February 24, 1946, in Savannah, GA; daughter of William Emmett (in insurance business) and Ruth (Pollock) Underwood; married Maxwell Berry Grant, Jr.; children: Elizabeth Keats, Leighton Kyle. *Ethnicity:* "Caucasian." *Education:* University of North Carolina—Chapel Hill, A.B., 1970, graduate study, 1971; attended Warren Wilson College, 1994. *Politics:* "Unaffiliated." *Religion:* "Raised Episcopal." *Hobbies and other interests:* Gardening, reading, tennis.

ADDRESSES: Home—587 George Chastain Rd., Horse Shoe, NC 28742. *E-mail*—annieug@sprynet.com.

CAREER: North Carolina Arts Council, Raleigh, NC, community associate, c. early 1970s; Good Will Publishers, Gastonia, NC, communications director, c. early 1980s; Underwood Grant Advertising, Charlotte, NC, president, c. 1980s-middle 1990s. Tarradiddle Players, president, c. 1990s.

MEMBER: Mystery Writers of America (member of board of directors, 1977-99; president of Southeast chapter, 1997-99), Southern Mystery Gathering (chair, 1998).

WRITINGS:

MYSTERY NOVELS

Multiple Listing, Dell (New York, NY), 1998.
Smoke Screen, Dell (New York, NY), 1998.
Cuttings, Dell (New York, NY), 1999.
Voices in the Sand, Overmountain Press, 2000.

WORK IN PROGRESS: A garden book; a literary novel set in Chapel Hill, NC, in the 1920s; two fantasies.

BIOGRAPHICAL AND CRITICAL SOURCES:

ONLINE

Anne Underwood Grant Home Page, http://www.underwoodgrant.com/ (May 7, 2003).

* * *

GRANT, Skeeter
    See SPIEGELMAN, Art

* * *

GURR, Ted Robert 1936-

PERSONAL: Born February 21, 1936, in Spokane, WA; son of Robert Lucas and Anne (Cook) Gurr; married Erika Brigitte Klie (a research assistant), February 20, 1960 (died, May 6, 1980); married Barbara Harff (a political scientist), January 14, 1981; children: (first marriage) Lisa Anne, Andrea Mariel. *Education:* Reed College, B.A., 1957; Princeton University, additional study, 1958-59; New York University, Ph.D., 1965. *Politics:* Independent. *Hobbies and other interests:* Antiquities, travel, photography.

ADDRESSES: Home—485 College Ave., Boulder, CO 80302. *Office*—Department of Political Science, University of Maryland, 0145 Tydings Hall, College Park, MD 20742. *E-mail*—tgurr@umd.edu.

Ted Robert Gurr

CAREER: Educator and author. *American Behavioral Scientist,* Princeton, NJ, assistant to the editor, 1958-60, assistant editor, 1960-61, associate editor, 1963-64; Princeton University Center of International Studies, Princeton, NJ, research associate, 1965-67, faculty associate and assistant professor of political science, 1967-69; Northwestern University, Evanston, IL, associate professor, 1969-72, professor of political science, 1972-74, Payson S. Wild Professor of Political Science, 1974-84, chairman of department, 1977-80; University of Colorado, Boulder, professor of political science and director of Center for Comparative Politics, 1985-89; University of Maryland, professor of political science, 1989—. Visiting assistant professor of political science, New York University, 1966-67; visiting fellow, Cambridge University Institute of Criminology, 1976; visiting scholar, La Trobe University, Australia, 1981. Codirector of task force on history of violence, National Commission on the Causes and Prevention of Violence, 1968-69; visiting professorship, University of Uppsala, Sweden, 1996-97.

MEMBER: International Peace Science Society, International Studies Association, International Society for the Study of Aggression (fellow), Social Science History Association, American Political Science Association, Phi Beta Kappa.

AWARDS, HONORS: Woodrow Wilson fellowship, 1957; Ford Foundation fellowship, 1970; Woodrow Wilson Foundation Prize from American Political Science Association, 1971, for *Why Men Rebel*; Guggenheim fellowship, 1972-73; German Marshall Fund senior fellowship, 1976; Fulbright senior research fellowship to Australia, 1981; United States Institute of Peace fellowship, 1988-89; University of Leiden research fellow, 1993.

WRITINGS:

(With Alfred de Grazia) *American Welfare,* New York University Press (New York, NY), 1961.
New Error-compensated Measures for Comparing Nations: Some Correlates of Civil Violence (monograph), Center of International Studies, Princeton University (Princeton, NJ), 1966.
(With Charles Ruttenberg) *The Conditions of Civil Violence: First Test of a Causal Model* (monograph), Center of International Studies, Princeton University (Princeton, NJ), 1967.
(With Charles Ruttenberg) *Cross-National Studies of Civil Violence,* Center for Research in Social Systems, American University (Washington, DC), 1968.
(Editor and contributor with Hugh Davis Graham) *Violence in America: Historical and Comparative Perspectives,* National Commission on the Causes and Prevention of Violence, 1969, published as *History of Violence in America,* Praeger (New York, NY), 1969, revised edition, Sage Publications (Beverly Hills, CA), 1979.
Why Men Rebel, Princeton University Press (Princeton, NJ), 1970.
(Editor, with Francisco J. Moreno) *Basic Courses in Comparative Politics: An Anthology of Syllabi,* Sage Publications for the International Studies Association (Beverly Hills, CA), 1970.
(With Muriel McClelland) *Political Performance: A Twelve-Nation Study,* Sage Publications (Beverly Hills, CA), 1971.
Politimetrics: An Introduction to Quantitative Macropolitics, Prentice-Hall (Englewood Cliffs, NJ), 1972.
(Editor, with Ivo K. Feierabend and Rosalind Feierabend) *Anger, Violence, and Politics,* Prentice-Hall (Englewood Cliffs, NJ), 1972.
(With Harry Eckstein) *Patterns of Authority: A Structural Basis for Political Inquiry,* Wiley-Interscience (New York, NY), 1975.

Rogues, Rebels, and Reformers: A Political History of Urban Crime and Conflict, Sage Publications (Beverly Hills, CA), 1976.

(With Peter N. Grabosky and Richard C. Hula) *The Politics of Crime and Conflict: A Comparative History of Four Cities,* Sage Publications (Beverly Hills, CA), 1977.

Comparative Studies of Political Conflict and Change, Inter-University Consortium for Political and Social Research, 1978.

(Editor and contributor) *Handbook of Political Conflict: Theory and Research,* Free Press (New York, NY), 1980.

The Quality of Life and Prospects for Change in Bermuda: A Report to the Government of Bermuda on a Sample Survey, Bermuda Press, 1984.

(Coauthor) *The State and the City,* University of Chicago Press (Chicago, IL), 1987.

(Editor) *Violence in America,* Sage Publications (Newbury Park, CA), 1989.

(Coeditor) *Revolutions of the Late Twentieth Century,* Westview Press (Boulder, CO), 1991.

Minorities at Risk: A Global View of Ethnopolitical Conflicts, United States Institute of Peace Press (Washington, DC), 1993.

(Coauthor) *Ethnic Conflict in World Politics,* Westview Press (Boulder, CO), 1994.

(Coeditor) *Preventive Measures: Building Risk Assessment and Crisis Early Warning Systems,* Rowman & Littlefield (Lanham, MD), 1998.

Peoples versus States: Minorities at Risk in the New Century, United States Institute of Peace Press (Washington, DC), 2000.

(Coeditor) *Journeys through Conflict: Narratives and Lessons,* Rowman & Littlefield (Lanham, MD), 2001.

Contributor to books, including *World Politics and Tension Areas,* edited by Feliks Gross, New York University Press, 1966; *Law and Civil War in the Modern World,* edited by Wolfgang Friedman and John Norton Moore, Johns Hopkins University Press, 1975; *The Uses of Controversy in Sociology,* edited by Lewis A. Coser and Otto N. Larsen, Free Press, 1976; *The Politics of Terror: A Reader in Theory and Practice,* edited by Michael Stohl, Dekker, 1978; *Indicator Systems for Political, Economic, and Social Analysis,* edited by Charles Taylor, Ölgeschlager, 1980; *History and Crime: Implications for Criminal Justice Policy,* edited by James A. Inciardi, Sage Publications, 1980; *World Handbook of Political and Social Indicators,* 3rd edition, edited by Charles Taylor and David Jodice, Yale University Press, 1983; *The Public and the Private,* edited by Jan-Erik Lane, Sage Publications, 1985; *Yearbook of State Violence and State Terrorism,* edited by Michael Stohl and George Lopez, Greenwood Press, 1985; and *Crime and Justice: An Annual Review of Research,* Volume III, 1981.

Coeditor, "Sage Professional Papers in Comparative Politics," Sage Publications, 1969-75. Associate editor of *World Politics,* 1967-68; *Comparative Political Studies,* member of editorial board, 1969—, editor, 1979-80.

SIDELIGHTS: Ted Robert Gurr is a professor of political science and the author of several books focusing on political violence, civil conflict, and ethnopolitics. In addition, Gurr has served as a policy-related consultant in various capacities, including the Lyndon Johnson Administration's National Commission on the Causes and Prevention of Violence and the White House-initiated State Failure Task Force. Gurr was called as an expert witness for the defense in political trials in South Africa and has served as president of the International Studies Association. In the 1970s he began the Policy Project, which coded important information on political bodies throughout the world's independent states between 1800 through the 1970s, creating a databank used by scores of scholars studying democracies and autocracies.

Gurr's early writings center on civil violence and political conflict worldwide. His *Why Men Rebel* won the Woodrow Wilson Prize as the best U.S. book on political science in 1970. In the late 1980s Gurr began work on the Minorities at Risk Project, which he founded at Maryland's Center for International Development and Conflict Management. The project follows and analyzes the status and conflicts of over 300 politically active communal groups worldwide. This work influenced most of his writings in the 1990s, including *Minorities at Risk: A Global View of Ethnopolitical Conflicts.* At the core of this book is a huge classification system, listing by region all 233 ethnocultural groups in the world that have had some kind of political rebellion since 1945. William J. Foltz of the *American Political Science Review* explained that Gurr codes such groups in five categories: "ethnonationalists, large groups with a history and dream of autonomy; indigenous peoples, conquered descendants of original inhabitants; ethnoclasses, low-status minorities descended from slaves or immigrants; militant sects, communities politically defined by religion; and communal contenders, culturally distinct groups seeking to retain or augment their share of the national pie." In addition to placing each group in a category, Gurr gauges how much political and economic difficulty they undergo, as well as determining the degree of cultural uniqueness relative to their country's society as a whole. As Ivan Light explained in his review of *Minorities at Risk,* "Gurr measures cultural difference on the basis of his evaluation of how different minorities are from the dominant culture in respect to ethnicity, language, religion, customs, historical origin, and residence patterns." Mahmood Monshipouri in *Human Rights Quarterly* called *Minorities at Risk* "an impressive and brilliant compilation." He also acknowledged that the book "is by far one of the most seminal and rigorous contributions in the area of ethnicity, politics, and human rights."

In 2000 Gurr published *Peoples versus State: Minorities at Risk in the New Century,* a follow-up to *Minorities at Risk* that includes statistical analyses of the conflicts. In this work Gurr notes that "by the mid 1990s armed conflict within states had abated: there was a pronounced decline in the onset of new ethnic wars and a shift in many ongoing wars from fighting to negotiation." The author then goes on to give his analysis of the reason for the decline, along with interesting empirical data for the ethnic groups he studied. Another feature of the book is the inclusion of several short stories of actual ethnic conflicts, such as the Copts in Egypt, and the Turks of Germany. According to Nikolas K. Gvosdev in the *Journal of Church and State, Peoples versus State* "is an extremely useful piece of scholarship, based on careful analysis." Gvosdev also commended Gurr for compiling a resource that "allows the reader to compare and contrast both the demands articulated by different minority groups as well as the differing responses of different types of regimes around the world."

BIOGRAPHICAL AND CRITICAL SOURCES:

PERIODICALS

American Journal of Sociology, January, 1971; September, 1992, John A. Hall, review of *Revolutions of the Late Twentieth Century,* p. 396.

American Political Science Review, March, 1971; December, 1992, Charles Tilly, review of *Revolutions of the Late Twentieth Century,* p. 1984; June, 1994, William J. Foltz, review of *Minorities at Risk: A Global View of Ethnopolitical Conflicts,* p. 513.

Annals of the American Academy of Political and Social Science, November, 1977; January, 1996, Radha Kumar, review of *Ethnic Conflict in World Politics,* p. 269.

Choice, December, 2000, P. Barton-Kriese, review of *Peoples versus States: Minorities at Risk in the New Century,* p. 777.

Commercial Appeal, August 29, 1999. p. B6.

Contemporary Sociology, September, 1977.

Foreign Affairs, November-December, 2000, p. 170.

Human Rights Quarterly, August, 1994, Mahmood Monshipouri, review of *Minorities at Risk,* pp. 580-584.

International Affairs, January, 2001, Amit Gupta, review of *Peoples versus States,* p. 194.

Journal of Church and State, autumn, 2000, Nikolas K. Gvosdev, review of *Peoples versus State,* p. 848.

Journal of Commonwealth and Comparative Politics, November, 2001, Roland Axtmann, review of *Peoples versus States,* p. 186.

Journal of Politics, August, 1973, November, 1977, February, 1978.

New York Times, July 30, 1969.

New York Times Book Review, April 12, 1970.

Political Science Quarterly, winter, 1988, Martin Shefler, review of *The State and the City,* p. 753.

Public Administration, winter, 1988, p. 471.

Saturday Review, May 22, 1971.

Social Research, spring, 1971.

Social Science Quarterly, December, 1977.

Society, January-February, 1995, Ivan Light, review of *Minorities at Risk,* p. 92.

Virginia Quarterly Review, summer, 1970.

Yale Journal of International Law, winter, 2001, pp. 290-292.

ONLINE

University of Maryland Web site, http://www.bsos.umd.edu/ (March 2, 2001).*

H

HALLWAS, John E(dward) 1945-

PERSONAL: Born May 24, 1945, in Waukegan, IL; son of Emil Ferdinand (a building contractor) and Ruth Edna (Wells) Hallwas; married Garnette Verna Stockstad, January 3, 1966; children: John Darrin, Evan Bradley. *Education:* Western Illinois University, B.S., 1967, M.A., 1968; University of Florida, Ph.D., 1972. *Hobbies and other interests:* Nature study, fitness walking, bicycling.

ADDRESSES: Home—31 Shorewood Dr., Macomb, IL 61455-9746. *Office*—Department of English, Western Illinois University, Macomb, IL 61455; fax: 309-298-2781. *E-mail*—JE-Hallwas@wiu.edu.

CAREER: University of Florida, Gainesville, member of English faculty, summer, 1970; Western Illinois University, Macomb, began as assistant professor, became associate professor, 1970-81, professor of American literature, 1981—, distinguished professor, 1992-93, director of Regional Collections at University Library, 1979—. Spoon River College, Macomb, IL, part-time faculty member, 1987—. Visiting lecturer at Carl Sandburg College, 1976, Monmouth College, 1979, Black Hawk College, 1990, and University of Illinois, Urbana-Champaign, 1995.

MEMBER: Society for the Study of Midwestern Literature, Society of Midland Authors, Association for the Study of Literature and the Environment, Illinois State Historical Society, McDonough County Historical Society (president, 1981-1983), Phi Beta Kappa, Phi Kappa Phi.

John E. Hallwas

AWARDS, HONORS: Grants from Illinois Humanities Council, 1975, 1978, 1979, 1980, 1981, 1982, 1985; Faculty Service Award, National University Continuing Education Association, 1981, for excellence in adult-education programming; Citizen of the Year Award, city of Macomb, IL, 1990, for civic contributions; John Whitmer Historical Association Award, best article category, 1990, for the article "Mormon Nauvoo from a Non-Mormon Perspective"; Superior Achievement Award, Illinois State Historical Society, 1992, for *Macomb: A Pictorial History;* Mid-America Award, Society for the Study of Midwestern Literature, 1994, for distinguished contributions to the study of Midwestern literature; *Spoon River Anthology* was named an "Outstanding Academic Book" of the year, *Choice,* 1995; Mormon History Association Award, best documentary, and John Whitmer Historical Association Award, best book, both 1996, for *Cultures in Conflict;* Nominations for the National Book Award, for Nonfiction and the Pulitzer Prize for Nonfiction, both 1998, for *The Bootlegger.*

WRITINGS:

The Western Illinois Poets (monograph), Western Illinois University (Macomb, IL), 1975.
(Editor, with Dennis J. Reader) *The Vision of This Land: Studies of Vachel Lindsay, Edgar Lee Masters, and Carl Sandburg,* Western Illinois University (Macomb, IL), 1976.
(Editor) *Western Illinois University Libraries: A Handbook,* Western Illinois University (Macomb, IL), 1980.
(Editor, with Jerrilee Cain-Tyson and Victor Hicken) *Tales from Two Rivers,* Western Illinois University (Macomb, IL), Volume 1, 1981, Volume 2, 1982, Volume 3, 1984, Volume 4 (with David R. Pichaske), 1987, and Two Rivers Arts Council (Macomb. IL), Volume 5 (with Alfred J. Lindsey), 1990, Volume 6 (with Lindsey), 1996.
The Poems of H.: The Lost Poet of Lincoln's Springfield, Ellis Press (Peoria, IL), 1982.
The Conflict (play), produced at Argyle Park Theatre, 1982.
Four on the Frontier (one-act plays; includes "Warrior at Sundown," "American Prophet," "Abolitionist in Congress," and "The Backwoods Preacher"), performed on a tour of western Illinois communities, 1982-83.
Western Illinois Heritage, Illinois Heritage Press (Macomb, IL) 1983.
Thomas Gregg: Early Illinois Journalist and Author (monograph), Western Illinois University (Macomb, IL), 1983.
McDonough County Heritage, Illinois Heritage Press (Macomb, IL), 1984.
(Editor, with Robert Graybill, Judy Hample, and others) *Teaching the Middle Ages,* Volume II, Studies in Medieval and Renaissance Teaching (Warrensburg, MO), 1985.
(With Gene Kozlowski) *The Paper Town* (play), produced at Argyle Park Theatre, 1985.
Illinois Literature: The Nineteenth Century, Illinois Heritage Press (Macomb, IL), 1986.
(Author of introduction) Eliza W. Farnham, *Life in Prairie Land,* University of Illinois Press (Urbana, IL), 1988.
(Author of introduction) James Gray, *The Illinois,* University of Illinois Press (Urbana, IL), 1989.
Studies in Illinois Poetry, Stormline Press (Champaign, IL), 1989.
Macomb: A Pictorial History, G. Bradley Publishing (St. Louis, MO), 1990.
(Editor) Edgar Lee Masters, *Spoon River Anthology: An Annotated Edition,* University of Illinois Press (Urbana, IL), 1992.
(Author of introduction) Carl Sandburg, *Chicago Poems: Carl Sandburg,* University of Illinois Press (Urbana, IL), 1992.
The Legacy of the Mines: Memoirs of Coal Mining in Fulton County, Illinois, Spoon River College (Canton, IL), 1993.
(With Roger D. Launius) *Cultures in Conflict: A Documentary History of the Mormon War in Illinois,* Utah State University Press (Logan, UT), 1995.
(Editor, with Roger D. Launius) *Kingdom on the Mississippi Revisited: Nauvoo in Mormon History,* University of Illinois Press (Urbana, IL), 1996.
The Bootlegger: A Story of Small-Town America, University of Illinois Press (Urbana, IL), 1998.
(Author of introduction) Robert J. Burdette, *The Drums of the 47th,* University of Illinois Press (Urbana, IL), 1999.
First Century: A Pictorial History of Western Illinois University, Western Illinois University (Macomb, IL), 1999.
Keokuk and the Great Dam, Arcadia Publishing (Chicago, IL), 2001.
McDonough County Historic Sites, Arcadia Publishing (Chicago, IL), 2002.

Coeditor of the series "Prairie State Books," University of Illinois Press, 1987—. Contributor to books, including *Exploring the Midwestern Literary Imagination:*

Essays in Honor of David D. Anderson, edited by Marcia Noe, Whitston (Troy, NY), 1993. Author of *Prairie State Journal: Inventing Illinois,* a weekly program broadcast by public radio stations in Illinois, 1992-93. Author of "Our Regional Heritage," a weekly column, *Macomb Journal,* 1981-84, "Visions and Values," a weekly self-syndicated column, 1984-85, and "Passages," a weekly column, *Jacksonville Journal Courier,* 1987-88. Contributor of about ninety articles and reviews to periodicals, including *Prairie Journal, Old Northwest, Great Lakes Review, Journal of Mormon History, Illinois Magazine, Illinois Issues, MidAmerica,* and *Journal of the Illinois State Historical Society. Western Illinois Regional Studies,* cofounder, 1978, coeditor, 1978-92, editorial chair, 1980-92; founding editor, *Essays in Literature,* 1973-79, and *Western Illinois Reader,* 1987-89; editor, *McDonough County Historical Society Newsletter,* 1981-90.

Author of introduction for *Life in a Prairie Land,* by Eliza W. Farnham, *The Illinois,* by James Gray, and *The Drums of the 47th,* by Robert J. Burdette, all published by the University of Illinois Press.

WORK IN PROGRESS: *Dime Novel Desperadoes,* an account of Ed and Lon Maxwell (alias Williams), Midwestern outlaws of wide notoriety between 1874 and 1881.

SIDELIGHTS: John E. Hallwas is professor of American literature at Western Illinois University and a noted regional historian who has written numerous books on the history of western Illinois and the surrounding Midwest.

Hallwas brings his scholarship of Edgar Lee Masters and Western Illinois history to bear on a new edition of the classic *Spoon River Anthology.* John Hollander praised Hallwas's edition, noting, "It provides a wealth of information that frames specific historical, biographical, and autobiographical background for names, persons, places, and situations alluded to and invoked by the epitaphs in *Anthology.* Hallwas brings to bear on the text and its history a detailed overview of previous scholarship, and a knowledge of Illinois history in particular, that will be invaluable for anyone not only writing on Masters, but working in American studies generally. He is also authoritatively knowledgeable about the critical reception of the book and its history."

Edited by Hallwas and Roger D. Launius, the 1998 book *Kingdom on the Mississippi Revisited: Nauvoo in Mormon History* comprises a collection of fourteen articles on the history of the Mormon Church. This period of Mormon Church history is referred to as the Nauvoo era. The articles, written by Mormons and non-Mormons alike, give different perspectives of the Mormon experience in the Midwest. *Mississippi Revisited,* wrote Steven Epperson in the *Journal of American Ethnic History,* "aims to provide a rough overview of the main events, personalities, institutions, and issues during the turbulent 'Mormon' era of Nauvoo, Illinois, from 1839 to 1846, when concerted Mormon settlement transformed a malaria-plagued, riverfront village into a metropolis rivaling Chicago in size and intrigue."

In *The Bootlegger: A Story of Small-Town America,* Hallwas examines the Midwest of Bonnie and Clyde. Nominated for both the National Book Award for Nonfiction and the Pulitzer Prize, *The Bootlegger* uses that life story of Kelly Wagle, a bootlegger in Prohibition Colchester, Illinois, to tell the story of the town.

Wagle was seen by most of the town as a sort of Robin Hood figure, and when he was gunned down in front of his house, 1,000 out of the 1,300 citizens of Colchester turned out at his funeral. Most critics wrote, however, that the real protagonist of the book is the failed coal mining town of Colchester itself. A *Publishers Weekly* writer noted, "A coal-mining community in the nineteenth century, Colchester became so imbued by death that inhabitants began to see a mysterious 'Woman in Black,' an embodiment of the town's deepest anxieties."

Throughout the book, Hallwas examines how modernization and industrialization contributed to the disintegration of community in Colchester and other Illinois communities. Dale F. Farris concluded in *Library Journal,* "This deeply interrelated history reveals a rich understanding of rural, Midwestern America in the early twentieth century, the impact of coal mining on a town's economy, the widespread ambivalence toward 1920s Prohibition, and the fascination with the gangster lifestyle of a small-town hood."

Keokuk and the Great Dam, published in 2002, is the story of the first dam built across the Mississippi River in Keokuk, Iowa. Completed between 1910 and 1913, the dam was the first hydroelectric project on the Mississippi river and the world's second largest dam at the time. Hallwas uses extensive archival material to show the entrepreneurial spirit of the town to get the project started and the enormity of the construction effort.

Hallwas once told *CA:* "Most of my writing relates to and interprets the cultural heritage of western Illinois, where I have spent all of my adult life. Although I was raised more than two hundred miles away, in northern Illinois, I have lived here for more than thirty years, and I know more about the landscape, towns, people, and history of western Illinois than I will ever know about any other place. This is my home territory, a corn-and-soybean empire of expanding farms and declining villages, small cities and unsophisticated people, and I am deeply engaged with it.

"Life is enriched if people live in a place where they can feel a part of a meaningful cultural tradition. As a historian, editor, essayist, and literary scholar, I have tried to promote that kind of consciousness—often called a sense of place—and to reflect the culture of my region clearly enough so that readers anywhere might find it compelling.

"In recent years I have been especially interested in community history, with its dramatic interplay of will and circumstance, its portrayal of cultural construction, and its reflection of American myth in local experience. In a nation devoted to self-realization, and now obsessed with individualism and divided into factions, we need to understand our cultural environment far better than we do, and to value the common experience far more than we do. We need to build community. If writing promotes that, it will have cultural significance, whether or not it reaches a national audience.

"Although I do not write poetry, three poets from my region have had a significant influence on my work. Vachel Lindsay, Edgar Lee Masters, and Carl Sandburg were deeply rooted in this part of the country, and they too were engaged with the culture of Illinois and the Midwest and concerned with the renewal of meaning and community in America. Their works were often profoundly influenced by American myth (as I point out with respect to Masters, for example, in my annotated edition of *Spoon River Anthology,* and my historical books, such as *Cultures in Conflict* and *The Bootlegger,* display a considerable awareness of American myth as I examine and portray the roots of social conflict and the significance of cultural change.

"I often teach courses at Western Illinois University that relate closely to my work as a writer—courses such as American Myth, Illinois Literature, and Non-fictional Creative Writing. At Spoon River College, also located in my hometown, I frequently teach courses in Illinois history. Over the years I have also lectured on historical and literary topics in more than one hundred Illinois communities, and I teach workshops in writing nonfiction."

BIOGRAPHICAL AND CRITICAL SOURCES:

PERIODICALS

Bloomsbury Review, March, 1999, review of *The Bootlegger: A Story of Small-Town America,* p. 16.
Booklist, September 15, 1998, Margaret Flanagan, review of *The Bootlegger: A Story of Small-Town America,* p. 176.
Choice, June, 1994, J. J. Patton, review of *Spoon River Anthology: An Annotated Edition,* p. 1580; March 1996, review of *Cultures in Conflict: A Documentary History of the Mormon War in Illinois,* p. 1202; January, 1999, review of *The Bootlegger: A Story of Small-Town America,* p. 953;
Church History, September, 1997, Clyde R. Forsberg, review of *Kingdom on the Mississippi: Nauvoo in Mormon History,* p. 624.
Journal of American Ethnic History, spring, 1999, Steven Epperson, review of *Kingdom on the Mississippi: Nauvoo in Mormon History,* p. 167.
Journal of Religious History, June, 1998, Jennifer Clark, review of *Kingdom on the Mississippi: Nauvoo in Mormon History,* p. 241.
Journal of the Early Republic, winter, 1998, Richard D. Shiels, review of *Kingdom on the Mississippi: Nauvoo in Mormon History,* p. 743.
Library Journal, August, 1998, Dale F. Farris, review of *The Bootlegger: A Story of Small-Town America,* p. 109.
New Republic, July 27, 1992, John Hollander, review of *Spoon River Anthology: An Annotated Edition,* p. 47.
Parnassus: Poetry in Review, fall, 1993, Turner Cassity, review of *Spoon River Anthology: An Annotated Edition,* and *Chicago Poems,* p. 38.

Publishers Weekly, July 20, 1998, review of *The Bootlegger: A Story of Small-Town America,* p. 196.

Utopian Studies, spring, 1999, Louis J. Kern, review of *Kingdom on the Mississippi: Nauvoo in Mormon History,* p. 275.

Western Historical Quarterly, spring, 1997, Thomas G. Alexander, review of *Kingdom on the Mississippi: Nauvoo in Mormon History,* p. 83.

ONLINE

H-Net: Humanities and Social Sciences Online, http://www2.h-net.msu.edu/ (May, 1999), review of *The Bootlegger: A Story of Small-Town America.*

University of Illinois Press, http://www.press.uillinois.edu/ (May 4, 2002), review of *The Bootlegger: A Story of Small-Town America.**

* * *

HARRIS, Robert (Dennis) 1957-

PERSONAL: Born March 7, 1957, in Nottingham, England; son of Dennis Harris (a printer) and Audrey (Hardy) Harris; married Gillian Hornby (a journalist), 1988; children: Holly Miranda, Matilda Felicity, Charlie Robert Nicholas, Samuel Orlando Hornby. *Education:* Selwyn College, Cambridge, B.A. (with honors), 1978. *Politics:* "Supporter of the British Labour Party." *Hobbies and other interests:* Reading history, walking, fishing, listening to music.

ADDRESSES: Home—The Old Vicarage, Kintbury, Berkshire RG17 9TR, England.

CAREER: Writer. British Broadcasting Corporation (BBC-TV), London, England, researcher and film director for *Tonight, Nationwide,* and *Panorama,* 1978-81, reporter for *Newsnight,* 1981-85, and for *Panorama,* 1985-87; *Observer,* London, England, political editor, 1987-89; Thames TV, London, England, political reporter for *This Week,* 1988-89; *Sunday Times,* London, England, political columnist, 1989-92.

WRITINGS:

(With Jeremy Paxman) *A Higher Form of Killing: The Secret Story of Gas and Germ Warfare,* Chatto & Windus (London, England), 1982, published as *A*

Robert Harris

Higher Form of Killing: The Secret Story of Chemical and Biological Warfare, Hill & Wang (New York, NY), 1982, reprinted under original title, Random House (New York, NY), 2002.

Gotcha!: The Media, the Government, and the Falklands Crisis, Faber & Faber (London, England), 1983.

The Making of Neil Kinnock, Faber & Faber (London, England), 1984.

Selling Hitler, Pantheon (New York, NY), 1986.

Good and Faithful Servant: The Unauthorized Biography of Bernard Ingham, Faber & Faber (London, England), 1990.

NOVELS

Fatherland, Random House (New York, NY), 1992.
Enigma, Random House (New York, NY), 1995.
Archangel, Hutchinson (London, England), 1998.
Pompeii, Random House (New York, NY), 2003.

Harris's work has been translated into several languages.

ADAPTATIONS: *Fatherland* was adapted as a TV movie for Home Box Office (HBO). *Archangel* has been adapted for audio cassette. *Enigma* was adapted as a film in 2001.

SIDELIGHTS: Robert Harris had written several books of nonfiction during the 1980s before the publication of his popular 1992 novel *Fatherland.* Constructed around the premise that Adolf Hitler led the Nazis to victory in World War II, with Germany defeating both Great Britain and the Soviet Union and fighting the United States to an uneasy deadlock, *Fatherland* became a bestseller, selling three million copies worldwide. Several of Harris's previous nonfiction works, such as *A Higher Form of Killing: The Secret Story of Chemical and Biological Warfare* and *Gotcha!: The Media, the Government, and the Falklands Crisis,* also deal with war and its repercussions. In *Selling Hitler* Harris details the 1983 hoax in which a counterfeiter claimed to have discovered the diaries of the dead Nazi leader.

A true account of the Hitler diary hoax, *Selling Hitler,* reveals the extent to which greed influenced the publishing industry to overlook the veracity of the (supposedly) newly discovered diaries in favor of their marketability. "One merit of Robert Harris's thorough and mordantly funny account of the diaries scandal in *Selling Hitler* is that he lets no one off the hook," commented *New York Times Book Review* critic James Markham. The diaries were originally obtained by a reporter for the German magazine *Stern;* according to Jonathan Alter in *Newsweek,* "Executives at *Stern*'s parent company, Gruner and Jahr, smelled money. Not wanting to see the bubble burst, *Stern* subjected the papers to only the most cursory handwriting examination." Markham noted in the *New York Times Book Review* that Harris presents "an unsettling portrait of the press baron, Rupert Murdoch, who aggressively bought up rights to the diaries for his corporation . . . and then nonchalantly dismissed their fraudulence with an unhappily memorable one-liner: 'After all, we are in the entertainment business.'" *New Statesman* reviewer Paul Hallam wrote that Harris tells this "sick saga . . . with skill and wit."

The first of Harris's novels, *Fatherland,* unfolds in docudrama style. The setting is 1964, on the eve of an important visit by the president of the United States, Joseph P. Kennedy, to the German Fuhrer, Adolf Hitler, in a Berlin which is now the site of the grandiose Great Hall (built to the specifications of Nazi architect Albert Speer, the building can accommodate 180,000 people). The Allies have lost World War II, the wartime British prime minister, Winston Churchill, is in exile in Canada, and Germany now controls all of Europe and a good part of the Soviet Union. Against this background a German police detective, Xavier March, investigates the murder of a Nazi party official and in the course of his probe unearths a terrible secret with wide-ranging implications. Pursued by the Gestapo, March attempts to publicize a crime of immeasurable dimensions—the systematic murder of millions of European Jews, whom the world believes to have been nonviolently relocated to the East. "March's inquiries jeopardize the crowning achievement of Hitler's three decades in office: world peace," commented Mark Horowitz in the *Los Angeles Times Book Review.* Coming at a time when the American president is making overtures to end the cold war with Germany, "revelations of a Holocaust would make appeasement impossible," Horowitz explained.

New York Times Book Review critic Newgate Callendar wrote that *Fatherland* is an "absorbing, expertly written novel. . . . [It] is a bleak book. But what concerns the author is the indestructibility of the human spirit, as exemplified by Xavier March." In *Time* John Skow stated that Harris's "brooding, brown-and-black setting of a victorious Nazi regime is believable and troubling, the stuff of long nights of little sleep." And in the *Los Angeles Times Book Review* Horowitz remarked that "*Fatherland* works fine as a sly and scary page-turner."

Harris followed *Fatherland* with his second novel, *Enigma.* Like its predecessor, *Enigma* is a World War II thriller, this time set in a secret code-breaking headquarters in England. At the height of the war, brilliant-but-inexperienced researcher Thomas Jericho has managed to crack a Nazi code nicknamed Shark—but the marathon effort has led to his nervous breakdown. Before his recovery is complete, however, Jericho is called back to work on an even tougher Nazi code: Enigma, which is generated on new four-rotor encrypting machines. With a battalion of American warships about to lock horns with German U-boats, it is vital that the code be cracked in time to ensure an Allied victory. Complications further ensue when Jericho suspects his new love, Claire Romilly, of being a spy.

"The second novel is always the most difficult, especially after a big hit," wrote Clive Ponting in *New Statesman & Society.* The critic acknowledged Harris's sophomore effort as an "ultimately . . . formulaic thriller whose location cannot disguise its rather ordinary plot," though Ponting added that the author does provide "a good pace." John Skow in *Time* found more to like in *Enigma,* saying that the results of Harris's efforts to portray genius are "worthy and believable, if not luminous." And to a *Publishers Weekly* contributor, the novel is "a rare mix of cerebral and visceral thrills that features risky exploits complementing the exhilarating challenge [of] solving daunting puzzles within puzzles." Apart from being an international bestseller, *Enigma* was the subject of a BBC documentary on the making of a thriller.

The author is "at his best," wrote Skow, in his third novel, *Archangel.* In the "what-if" tradition of *Fatherland, Archangel* takes on modern Russian history, exploring the implications of a pro-Stalinist cult which discovers the long-lost son of the late dictator and seeks to bring the scion to power. Such a premise powers the novel's theme: "Scratch the surface of post-Soviet Russia," commented *New Statesman* contributor Kate Saunders, "and you will find unreconstructed, bloody-minded old commies." While this over-the-top plot could be the stuff of potboilers, Harris "makes you believe it as it's happening," in the words of *New York Times* writer Christopher Lehmann-Haupt. To Michael Specter of the *New York Times Book Review,* the author "has given those of us who retain some literary nostalgia for the Evil Empire exactly what we have been waiting for." "Building on accurate historical sense," noted *Booklist* contributor Gilbert Taylor, Harris describes would-be historical events compellingly enough to "[reward] readers with a thoroughly thrilling tale."

Harris's 2003 novel, *Pompeii,* spins a new twist on an old tale. According to a reviewer for the *Economist,* "Mr Harris sticks to the *Enigma* formula of placing fictional characters . . . into an authentic setting." The book takes place in A.D. 79 in the Roman Empire two days before the eruption of Mount Vesuvius. The fictional protagonist, civil engineer Marcus Attilus Primus, is elected to investigate the water supply blockage to the aqueduct along the Bay of Naples. His findings lead him to believe bigger problems may be on the horizon and with the approval of his admiral, Attilus sails to Pompeii to get to the root of the problem, which lies at the base of Mount Vesuvius. Although readers are familiar with the tragic ending of this familiar tale, "the events are handled with a skill that kept me turning the pages," Jasper Griffin wrote in the *Spectator.* He concluded that "Harris has done his homework" in depicting the "picture of life" during ancient Rome. The *Economist* reviewer called *Pompeii,* "an engaging thriller with no small lesson for our own times."

BIOGRAPHICAL AND CRITICAL SOURCES:

PERIODICALS

Booklist, September 15, 1995, Gilbert Taylor, review of *Enigma,* p. 142; November 1, 1998, Gilbert Taylor, review of *Archangel,* p. 451; October 15, 2003, Kristine Huntley, review of *Pompeii,* p. 390.

Books, autumn, 1999, review of *Archangel,* p. 20.

Bookseller, May 23, 2003, "Death of a Boom Town: Robert Harris Exlpores the Final Hours of Pompeii," p. 30.

Economist (US), November 28, 1998, review of *Archangel,* p. 89; September 6, 2003, review of *Pompeii,* p. 76.

Entertainment Weekly, October 20, 1995, Michael Giltz, review of *Enigma,* p. 58; February 5, 1999, review of *Archangel,* p. 64; November 21, 2003, Jennifer Reese, "Blast from the Past: Robert Harris's Pompeii Vividly Imagines the Two Days before the Vesuvius Blew Its Top," p. 88.

Europe, March, 2000, Robert Guttman, review of *Archangel,* p. 36.

Guardian, September 5, 1995, Roy Ackerman, "First among Sequels," p. 12.

Kirkus Reviews, August 15, 1995, review of *Enigma,* p. 1130; November 1, 1998, review of *Archangel,* p. 1552; September 15, 2003, review of *Pompeii,* p. 1145.

Library Journal, October 1, 1995, Dawn Anderson, review of *Enigma,* p. 119; January, 1999, Roland Person, review of *Archangel,* p. 150; October 15, 2003, Jane Baird review of *Pompeii,* p. 98.

Los Angeles Times Book Review, July 5, 1992, Mark Horowitz, review of *Fatherland,* pp. 2, 9; February 1, 1999, review of *Archangel,* p. 9.

National Review, February 22, 1999, review of *Archangel,* p. 51.

New Statesman, May 1, 1987, Paul Hallam, review of *Selling Hitler;* October 16, 1998, Kate Saunders, review of *Archangel,* p. 57.

New Statesman & Society, Sept 1, 1995, Clive Ponting, review of *Enigma,* p. 33; September 15, 2003, Philip Kerr, review of *Pompeii,* p. 48.

Newsweek, May 26, 1986, Jonathan Alter, review of *Selling Hitler,* p. 70; February 1, 1999, review of *Archangel,* p. 66.

New York Review of Books, December 17, 1992, pp. 38-44.

New York Times, October 11, 1995, Alan Riding, "An Enigma Wrapped in a Mystery," p. C17; January 21, 1999, Christopher Lehmann-Haupt, review of *Archangel,* p. E9.

New York Times Book Review, April 13, 1986, James Markham, review of *Selling Hitler,* June 28, 1992, Newgate Callendar, review of *Fatherland,* pp. 11-12; p. 28; October 22, 1995, Peter Vansittart, review of *Enigma,* p. 46; February 14, 1999, Michael Specter, review of *Archangel,* p. 10.

Observer (London, England), February 13, 1983; June 9, 1996, review of *Enigma,* p. 16; September 27, 1998, review of *Archangel,* p. 14; October 3, 1999, review of *Archangel,* p. 16.

People, October 30, 1995, J. D. Reed, review of *Enigma,* p. 42.

Publishers Weekly, September 11, 1995, review of *Enigma,* p. 74; November 30, 1998, review of *Archangel,* p. 49; October 27, 2003, review of *Pompeii,* p. 45.

School Library Journal, June, 1996, Carol Beall, review of *Enigma,* p. 168.

Spectator, March 12, 1983, pp. 20-22; August 26, 1995, Kingsley Amis, review of *Enigma,* p. 26; September 26, 1998, Douglas Hurd, review of *Archangel,* p. 45; November 21, 1998, review of *Archangel,* p. 43; November 28, 1999, review of *Archangel,* p. 46; October 4, 2003, Jasper Griffin, "Fire from Heaven," p. 53.

Sunday Times (London, England), September 13, 1998, Norman Stone, "Stalin and Me, a Bit of a Thriller," p. N4.

Time, July 6, 1992, John Skow, review of *Fatherland,* pp. 75-76; October 23, 1995, John Skow, review of *Enigma,* p. 102; February 15, 1999, John Skow, review of *Archangel,* p. 80.

Times Educational Supplement, April 3, 1983, p. 27; July 19, 1996, review of *Enigma,* p. R6.

Times Literary Supplement, September 22, 1995, Keith Jeffrey, review of *Enigma,* p. 22; September 25, 1998, Richard Overy, review of *Archangel,* p. 21.

Tribune Books (Chicago, IL), November 19, 1995, review of *Enigma,* p. 6.

Virginia Quarterly Review, autumn, 1999, review of *Archangel,* p. 131.

Washington Post Book World, July 11, 1982, pp. 1-2; October 15, 1995, review of *Enigma,* p. 4.*

* * *

HARVOR, Beth
See HARVOR, (Erica) Elisabeth (Arendt Deichmann)

* * *

HARVOR, (Erica) Elisabeth (Arendt Deichmann) 1936-
(Beth Harvor)

PERSONAL: Born June 26, 1936, in Saint John, New Brunswick, Canada; daughter of Lauritz Kjeld Deichmann (a potter) and Erica Louise Gregg (a potter; maiden name, Matthiesen); married Stig Harvor (an architect), November 16, 1957 (divorced, 1977); children: Finn, Richard. *Education:* Studied nursing at Saint John General Hospital, 1954-1956; Concordia University, Montreal, Quebec, M.A., 1986.

ADDRESSES: Home—Toronto, Ontario, Canada. *Office*—c/o Writers Union of Canada, 40 Wellington Street East, Third Floor, Toronto, Ontario, Canada M5E 1C7. *Agent*—Hilary McMahon, Westwood Creative Artists, 94 Harbord Street, Toronto, Ontario, Canada M5S 1G6. *E-mail*—eharvor@sympatico.ca.

CAREER: Novelist, poet, and short story writer. Algonquin College, Ottawa, Ontario, Canada, conductor of workshops on women and writing, 1973-76; Concordia University, Montreal, Quebec, Canada, sessional lecturer, 1986-87, 1995-97, writer-in-residence, 1996-1997; York University, Downsview, Ontario, sessional lecturer in writing program, 1987-93; Ottawa Public Library and Carleton University, writer-in-residence, 1993-94. University of New Brunswick, writer-in-residence, 1994-95, instructor, 1995; Humber School for Writers, instructor, 1996-98, 2000-2003; Saskatoon Public Library, writer-in-residence, 1998-99.

AWARDS, HONORS: First prize, Canadian Broadcasting Corporation (CBC) New Canadian Writing Series, 1965, and CBC-Ottawa short story competition, 1970;

fellow, Fonds F.C.A.C. pour l'aide et le soutien a la recherche, 1985-86; League of Canadian Poets' National Poetry Prize, 1989 and 1991; Malahat Long Poem Prize, 1990; National Magazine Award for poetry, 1991; Confederation Poets' Prize for best poem published in *Arc,* 1991 and 1992; Gerald Lampert Memorial Award (co-winner), 1992, for *Fortress of Chairs;* Governor General's Award finalist, 1996, for *Let Me Be the One;* Pat Lowther Award finalist, 1998, for *Long Cold Green Evenings of Spring;* Alden Nowlan Award for Excellence in English-Language Literary Arts, 2000; grants from Canada Council, Ontario Arts Council, Toronto Arts Council, and Woodcock Foundation; fellow, Concordia University.

WRITINGS:

- (Under name Beth Harvor) *Women and Children* (stories), Oberon Press (Ottawa, Ontario, Canada), 1973, revised edition published as *Our Lady of All the Distances,* 1991.
- *If Only We Could Drive Like This Forever* (stories), Penguin Canada (Markham, Ontario, Canada), 1988, revised edition, 2004.
- *Fortress of Chairs* (poems), Signal Editions (Montreal, Quebec, Canada), 1992.
- *Let Me Be the One,* HarperCollins (Toronto, Ontario, Canada), 1996.
- (Editor) *The Long Cold Green Evenings of Spring,* Signal Editions (Montreal, Quebec, Canada), 1997.
- *A Room at the Heart of Things: The Work That Came to Me,* Vehicule Press (Montreal, Quebec, Canada), 1997.
- *The Long Cold Green Evenings of Spring* (poems), Signal Editions (Montreal, Quebec, Canada), 1998.
- *Excessive Joy Injures the Heart* (novel), McClelland & Stewart (Toronto, Ontario, Canada), 2000.
- *All Times Have Been Modern* (novel), Penguin Canada (Markham, Ontario, Canada), 2004.

Work represented in anthologies in Canada, United States and Europe, including *Best American Short Stories,* Houghton Mifflin, 1971; *The Penguin Book of Modern Short Stories,* Penguin, 1982; and *More Stories by Canadian Women,* Oxford University Press, 1987. Contributor of poems, articles, stories, and reviews to magazines and newspapers, including *New Yorker, Hudson Review, Prism International, Event, New Quarterly, Fiddlehead, Our Generation against Nuclear War, American Voice, Saturday Night, Malahat Review, New Quarterly, Globe & Mail, Gazette* (Montreal), *Toronto Star,* and *Ottawa Citizen.*

ADAPTATIONS: One of Harvor's stories, "Summer Mournings," was dramatized on CBC-TV in 1975. Other works have been read on *CBC Anthology,* CBC's *Festival of Fiction,* etc.

SIDELIGHTS: In *Let Me Be the One* Elisabeth Harvor offers eight intimate stories that capture her characters' lives during a rare moment of insight. Many of the characters in the book try to cope with the predicament of being human by entering the territory of the desperate wish. (Let me be the one he loves best. Let me be the one to escape. Let me be the one to make something of my life.) Judith Timson wrote in *Maclean's* that "Harvor is a brave writer" who "depicts women teetering on the brink of failure, women who cannot inspire confidence even in their own divorce lawyers." Megan Harlan, commenting in *New York Times Book Review,* called the contents of the book "eight stunning stories about identity and its discontents . . . [that] are given an engaging structure by the wry, mercurial wanderings of the characters' minds." It was chosen one of the ten best books of 1996 by the *Toronto Star,* the *Saint-John Telegraph Journal* and after its distribution in the United States, one of the best books of 1997 for the Librarians' Choice Awards. *Let Me Be the One* was also a finalist (in fiction) for Canada's prestigious Governor General's Award for Fiction.

When she begins to have trouble sleeping, Claire Vornoff, the protagonist of Harvor's 2000 novel, *Excessive Joy Injures the Heart,* drives out into the country to become a client of Declan Farrell, an acupuncturist and iconoclast in the medical establishment. An education (of sorts) ensues. Calling the book "intricately textured, with surreal juxtapositions," critic Maureen Garvey, writing in *Quill and Quire,* commented that Claire Vornoff's obsessive intensity is "utterly believable and mesmerizing, and that her anxiously heightened awareness animates a world of sensual immediacy. . . . This is really wonderful writing—polished, well plotted, affecting and unsettling." In this novel, Harvor also includes minute details that challenge her readers' preconceived ideas about love and sorrow. According to a contributor for *Publishers Weekly,* "In lucidly charting Claire's emotional and erotic attachment, Harvor is reminiscent of a classic novelist of another generation, Christina Stead and, like Stead, she has a masterly grasp of the psychological states of women on the margins of society."

BIOGRAPHICAL AND CRITICAL SOURCES:

BOOKS

Oxford Companion to Canadian Literature, 2nd edition, Oxford University Press (New York, NY), 1992.

PERIODICALS

Booklist, April 1, 1997, review of *Let Me Be the One,* p. 1281; February 5, 2002, review of *Excessive Joy Injures the Heart,* p. 992.
Books in Canada, March, 1993, review of *Fortress of Chairs,* p. 50.
Canadian Book Review Annual, 1996, review of *Let Me Be the One,* p. 185; 1998, review of *Long Cold Green Evenings of Spring,* p. 227.
Globe & Mail, March 12, 1988; May 8, 1999, review of *A Room at the Heart of Things: The Work That Came to Me,* p. D15.
Kirkus Reviews, February 1, 1997, review of *Let Me Be the One,* p. 160.
Library Journal, March 1, 2002, Karen Munro, review of *Excessive Joy Injures the Heart,* p. 139.
Maclean's, November 18, 1996, review of *Let Me Be the One,* p. 82; December 9, 1996, review of *Let Me Be the One,* p. 64.
New York Times Book Review, July 20, 1997, review of *Let Me Be the One,* p. 20.
Publishers Weekly, February 17, 1997, review of *Let Me Be the One,* p. 209; February 4, 2002, review of *Excessive Joy Injures the Heart,* p. 50.
Quill & Quire, December, 1992, review of *Fortress of Chairs,* p. 16; September, 1996, review of *Let Me Be the One,* p. 65.

ONLINE

Elisabeth Harvor Web site, http://www.elisabethharvor.com/ (March 24, 2003).

HASWELL, Richard H(enry) 1940-

PERSONAL: Born January 30, 1940, in Springfield, MO; son of Richard Ellis (a college teacher) and Alice (a homemaker; maiden name, Sherwood) Haswell; married Judith Baker (marriage ended); married Janis Eileen Tedesco (a university teacher), June, 1994; children: (first marriage) Elizabeth Susan, Christine Baker. *Ethnicity:* "Anglo." *Education:* University of Missouri—Columbia, B.A., 1961, Ph.D., 1967; University of Washington, Seattle, WA, M.A., 1962. *Hobbies and other interests:* Coleoptery.

ADDRESSES: Home—1014 Memphis Dr., Corpus Christi, TX 78412. *Office*—Department of English, Texas A & M University—Corpus Christi, Corpus Christi, TX 78412. *E-mail*—rhaswell@falcon.tamucc.edu.

CAREER: Washington State University, Pullman, WA, professor of English, 1962-96; Texas A & M University—Corpus Christi, Corpus Christi, TX, Haas Professor of English, 1996—.

MEMBER: National Council of Teachers of English, Conference on College Composition and Communication (member of executive committee, 1995-98), Phi Beta Kappa.

AWARDS, HONORS: Woodrow Wilson fellow, 1961-62.

WRITINGS:

(Editor, with John Ehrstine) *A Baker's Dozen,* Star Publishing (Belmont, CA), 1979, 3rd edition, 1992.
(Editor, with John Ehrstine and Robert Wilkinson) *The HBJ Reader,* Harcourt (San Diego, CA), 1987.
Gaining Ground in College Writing: Tales of Development and Interpretation, Southern Methodist University Press (Dallas, TX), 1991.
(Coauthor) *Comp Tales: An Introduction to College Composition through Its Stories,* Longman (New York, NY), 2000.
(Editor) *Beyond Outcomes: Assessment and Instruction within a University Writing Program,* Ablex Publishing (Norwood, NJ), 2001.

Contributor of more than forty scholarly articles to professional journals. Translator from Spanish and French.

WORK IN PROGRESS: Gendership: Strategizing Gender for the Student of English, with wife, Janis Tedesco Haswell; an assessment of writing; research on interpretation theory and writing.

SIDELIGHTS: Richard H. Haswell once told *CA:* "There is the world outside us, which we know we have to share with others. And there is the world inside us, which we do not have to share. I believe that the inner world should be shared, and I praise all the forms of expression that serve—music, painting, sculpture, dance, cinema, photography, hobby, gesture, et cetera. Above all, I believe in language. There is no better road between selves.

"Professionally I am committed to helping people in college learn to build and maintain that road. My research and writing, and my preoccupations with evaluation and development, center on ways teachers can help their students communicate their singular inside worlds to others. It doesn't matter if what's inside is anger over a personal slight, insight into design problems of an exercise treadmill, or understanding derived from twenty years' study of Sufi religion. Whatever is inside does not readily come out; it needs encouragement.

"Of course, language can be used to hide from others and to deceive others about one's inner world. There is no end to the hurt of such language. I do not teach that kind of communication. I unteach it. My writings promote honesty, sincerity, and authenticity in language, whether reading or writing. From such practice I cannot help but believe, though perhaps I am sanguine in doing so, that more good has and always will come than harm."

* * *

HAVEL, Vaclav 1936-

PERSONAL: Born October 5, 1936, in Prague, Czechoslovakia (now Czech Republic); son of Vaclav M. (a building contractor and restaurateur) and Bozena (Vavreckova) Havel; married Olga Splichalova, 1964 (died, January 27, 1996); married Dagmar Havlova, January 4, 1997. *Education:* Attended technical college, 1955-57, and Prague Academy of Art, 1962-67.

Vaclav Havel

ADDRESSES: Agent—Aura Pont Agency, Radilcka 99, 150 00 Prague, Czech Republic.

CAREER: Playwright and politician. ABC Theatre, Prague, Czechoslovakia, stagehand, 1959-60; Theatre on the Balustrade, Prague, stagehand, 1960-61, assistant to artistic director, 1961-63, literary manager, 1963-68, resident playwright, 1968; imprisoned for dissent, 1977, 1979-83, and 1989; president of Czechoslovakia, 1989-92; president of Czech Republic, 1993-2003. *Military service:* Czech Army, 1957-59.

MEMBER: PEN (member of board of directors), Union of Writers (Czechoslovakia), Charter 77 (co-founder), Committee for the Defense of the Unjustly Persecuted (VONS).

AWARDS, HONORS: Austrian State Prize for European Literature, 1969; Obie awards, *Village Voice,* 1970, for *The Increased Difficulty of Concentration,*

1984, for *A Private View,* and, 1985-86, for *Largo Desolato;* Erasmus Prize, 1986; Los Angeles Drama Critics Circle Award, 1988, for *Largo Desolato;* German Booksellers Association prize, 1989; Olof Palme prize, 1989; Simon Bolívar prize, UNESCO, 1990; President's Award, PEN Center USA West, 1990; Charlemagne prize, Sonning prize, Averell Harriman Democracy Award, B'Nai Brith prize, Freedom Award, Raoul Wallenberg Human Rights Award, and International Book Award, all 1991; Onassis Prize Athinai, Order of White Eagle, and Golden Honorary Order of Freedom, all 1993; Indira Gandhi prize, Philadelphia Liberty Medal, and Jackson H. Ralston Prize in International Law, all 1994; Geuzenpenning, Catalonia international prize, and Future of Hope Award, all 1995; Order of the Bath and Virgin Mary's Land Cross, both 1996; Prix Special, International Association of Theatrical Critics (France), Statesman of the Year award (co-recipient with German President Roman Herzog), Institute for East-West Studies, J. William Fulbright prize, and Peace and Democracy award (Burma), all 1997; Compostela Group prize (Spain), 1998; First Decade award, *Gazeta Wyborcza* (Poland), Open Society prize (Hungary), and St. Adalbert Foundation prize (Slovakia), all 1999; Evelyn F. Burkey award, Authors Guild of America, Olympic Gate award, International Olympic Committee, Foundation Stätsbrugerlicher Stiftung, and Wild Geese award (Prague), all 2000. Recipient of honorary degrees from numerous institutions, including Columbia University, Hebrew University—Jerusalem, Lehigh University, University of Brussels, Harvard University, University of New South Wales, Trinity College—Dublin, and various universities in the Czech Republic.

WRITINGS:

PLAYS; IN ENGLISH TRANSLATION

Zahradni slavnost (also see below; first produced in Prague, Czechoslovakia, 1963), [Czechoslovakia], 1964, translation by Vera Blackwell published as *The Garden Party,* J. Cape (London, England), 1969.

Vyrozumeni (also see below; first produced in Prague, Czechoslovakia, 1965; produced Off-Broadway, 1968), Dilia, 1965, translation by Vera Blackwell published as *The Memorandum,* J. Cape (London, England), 1967.

Ztizena moznost soustredeni (first produced in Prague, Czechoslovakia, 1968; produced in New York, NY, 1969), Dilia, 1968, translation by Vera Blackwell published as *The Increased Difficulty of Concentration,* J. Cape (London, England), 1972.

Sorry: Two Plays (contains *Audience* and *Vernisaz;* also see below), translation by Vera Blackwell, Methuen (London, England), 1978.

A Private View (one-act plays; contains *Interview, A Private View,* and *The Protest*; translation by Vera Blackwell, produced in New York, NY, 1983, produced as *The Vanek Plays,* London, England, 1990), portions included in *The Vanek Plays: Four Authors, One Character,* translation by M. Pomichalek and A. Mozga, University of British Columbia Press (Vancouver, British Columbia, Canada), 1987.

Pokouseni (first produced in Vienna, Austria, 1985; produced by the Royal Shakespeare Company; translation by Marie Winn produced in New York, NY, 1989), translation by George Thiener, Faber & Faber (Boston, MA), 1988.

Largo Desolato (produced in Bristol, England; translation by Marie Winn produced in New York, NY, 1986), translation by Tom Stoppard, Faber & Faber (Boston, MA), 1987.

The Garden Party, and Other Plays, Grove Press (New York, NY), 1993.

Selected Plays, 1984-1987 (included *Largo Desolato* and *Temptation*), Faber & Faber (Boston, MA), 1988.

Redevelopment, translation by James Saunders, Faber & Faber (Boston, MA), 1994.

The Beggar's Opera, translation by Paul Wilson, Cornell University Press (Ithaca, NY), 2001.

Also author of *The Conspirators,* 1971, *The Mountain Hotel,* 1974, *Mistake,* and *The Guardian Angel;* author of adaptation of John Gay's 1765 work *The Beggar's Opera,* 1972. Contributor to anthologies, including *Three Eastern European Plays,* 1970.

IN CZECH

(With Ivan Vyskocil) *Autostop* (play; title means "Hitchhike"), first produced in Prague, Czechoslovakia, 1961.

Protokoly (anthology; title means "Protocols"; contains plays *Zahradni slavnost* and *Vyrozumeni,* two essays, and selected poems), introduction by Jan Grossman, Mlanda Fronta, 1966.

Hry 1970-1976 (plays; contains *Spiklenci, Zebracka Opera, Horsky Hotel, Audience,* and *Vernisaz*), Sixty-Eight Publishing House (Toronto, Ontario, Canada), 1977.

Pokouseni: Hra o deseti obrazech, Obrys/Kontur (Munich, Germany), 1986.

Dalkovy Vyslech: Rozhovor s Karlem Hvizdalou, Rozmluvy, 1986.

Asanace: Hra o peti jednanich, Obrys/Kontur, 1988.

Letni premitani, Odeon, 1991.

Sila bessilsnykh, Polifakt, 1991.

Hry: soubor her z let 1963-1988 (plays), Lidove noviny, 1992.

Vazeni obcane: projevy cervenec 1990—ecervenec 1992, Lidove noviny, 1992.

Antikaody: Vaclav Havel, Odeon, 1993.

Deset dopiseu Olze (correspondence), Vybor dobre veule, 1997.

Hovory s Havly: Dalkove rozhovory s Vaclavem Havlem a s Ivanem M. Havlem, Zdenek Susa, 1999.

Havel's speeches were collected and published in annual editions, Paseka, 1992-1998.

OTHER

(With others) *The Power of the Powerless: Citizens against the State in Central Eastern Europe,* edited by John Keane, M. E. Sharpe (Armonk, NJ), 1985.

Vaclav Havel; or, Living in Truth (essay collection), edited by Jan Vladislav, Faber & Faber (Boston, MA), 1987.

Letters to Olga: June 1979 to September 1982 (correspondence), translated by Paul Wilson, Knopf (New York, NY), 1988.

Disturbing the Peace: A Conversation with Karel Hvizdala (interviews), translated by Paul Wilson, Knopf (New York, NY), 1990.

Open Letters: Selected Writings, edited by Paul Wilson, Knopf (New York, NY), 1991.

Summer Meditations (essays), translated by Paul Wilson, Knopf (New York, NY), 1992.

A Word about Words, Cooper Union (New York, NY), 1992.

The Art of the Impossible: Politics As Morality in Practice; Speeches and Writings, 1990-1996, translated by Paul Wilson and others, Knopf (New York, NY), 1997.

Responsibility, Safety, Stability: Vaclav Havel concerning NATO: Selected Speeches, Articles, and Interviews, 1990-1999, North Atlantic Treaty Organization, 1999.

(Author of introduction) Allen Ginsburg, *Spontaneous Mind: Selected Interviews, 1958-1996,* HarperCollins (New York, NY), 2001.

Also author of monograph on writer/painter Joseph Capek, 1963, and of *Slum Clearance,* 1987. Contributor to *New York Review of Books* and other periodicals.

Havel's writings have been translated into numerous languages.

ADAPTATIONS: *Letters to Olga* was set to music and performed by Petr Kotik and the S.E.M. Ensemble, 1989.

SIDELIGHTS: Vaclav Havel's unique career has led him from early praise as a promising dramatic talent to the presidency of a free Czechoslovakia. Havel enjoyed early success as a playwright in his home country, where his first three plays—*The Garden Party, The Memorandum,* and *The Increased Difficulty of Concentration*—were acclaimed for their inventive take on bureaucracy and its effects in creating a dehumanized society. After the Soviet invasion of 1968, however, Havel's works were banned and the dramatist himself became the target of government harassment and imprisonment for his outspokenness. Nevertheless, Havel's works found staging in the Western world, increasing his fame and leading *Tulane Drama Review* critic Henry Popkin to call Havel "the leading Czech dramatist since Karel Capek." In the meantime, Havel gained renown at home for his willingness to suffer government retribution in order to air his views on freedom and human rights. As a result, the sweeping changes that took place in Eastern Europe in late 1989 not only led to the reinstatement of Havel's plays on the Czech stage, but also to his election as president of Czechoslovakia, a position he held until February of 2003.

According to Popkin, Havel's first play, *The Garden Party,* "touches upon the discomforts endured by political bureaucracy as it makes its transition from Stalinism to an awkward and severely limited liberalism." The play concerns the career of Hugo Pludek, who, continually mouthing platitudes and political slogans, rises rapidly to control of the Office of Liquidation and the Office of Inauguration. The play focuses on efforts to dissolve the Office of Liquidation, which, however, can only dissolve itself—an impossibility since, once the process was begun, the office would no longer exist to finish the job. In the *Tulane Drama Review* Jan Grossman described *The Garden Party* as dominated by cliché: "Man does not use cliché, cliché uses man. Cliché is the hero, it causes, advances, and complicates the plot, determining human action, and deviating further and further from our given reality, creates its own." Marketa Goetz-Stankiewicz elaborated, noting in *The Silenced Theatre* that Havel's main concern in the play is "the power of language as a perpetuator of systems, a tool to influence man's mind and therefore one of the strongest (though secret) weapons of any system that wants to mould him."

The Memorandum also concerns the political power of language, in this instance the distortion of language by bureaucracy. Havel's second play revolves around Ptydepe, an artificial and incomprehensible language designed to make all office communication precise and unemotional. The fall and rise of an office manager as a result of his inability to use the new language constitutes the play's main action. A writer for the *Times Literary Supplement* commented: "In *The Garden Party* Havel showed us words dominating human beings: the phrase is the real hero of the piece, creating the situations and complicating them, directing human destinies instead of being their tool. In *Vyrozumeni*—to use the original Czech title of *The Memorandum*—man finds himself enmeshed not merely in a succession of phrases but in a whole language." As Grossman explained, "Man makes an artificial language which is intended to render communication perfect and objective, but which actually leads to constantly deepening alienation and disturbance in human relations."

Despite its treatment of serious issues and themes, *The Memorandum* is an amusing, entertaining play. Clive Barnes of the *New York Times,* for example, called it a "witty, funny and timely" political satire, while *Nation* critic Robert Hatch considered it a "bureaucratic burlesque." Havel's use of his invented language contributes to the comic and absurd aspects of the play. As Paul I. Trensky elaborated in the *Slavic and East European Journal,* "The scenes with the greatest force of absurd comedy are those in which Ptydepe is given voice directly." "The theory of the new languages discussed in the play is brilliantly worked out," Martin Esslin similarly stated in *The Theatre of the Absurd.* In addition, Esslin remarked, "Havel is a master of the ironical, inverted repetition, of almost identical phrases in different contexts."

After Havel was silenced by the Czech authorities, his *The Increased Difficulty of Concentration* was produced in New York City by the Lincoln Center Repertory Theatre. The play depicts the attempts of philosopher Dr. Eduard Huml to deal with a series of challenges: the contrary demands of his wife and mistress; the dictation of a pedantic essay to a beautiful secretary; and his participation in an experiment that requires him to answer the questions of a temperamental computer. The form of the drama is variable; "chronology has been banished from the premises," observed *Washington Post* writer David Richards, so that "Havel's scenes follow one another with a blithe disregard for logic." Thus a character may exit and re-enter on opposite ends of the stage, and scenes fluctuate back and forth in time.

Cue reviewer Marilyn Stasio found the work a "potent satiric drama" that, "for all its ominous undertones, [is] an inescapably funny play." Mel Gussow in the *New York Times* judged the play to be "gentler" than *The Memorandum,* while a *Variety* critic considered it "a better play than Havel's earlier work, . . . with application beyond the border of eastern Europe." In his review for the *Nation,* Harold Clurman noted the play's importance for a Czech audience: "The speech that seems almost embarrassingly out of place with us, a speech in which the central character declares his conviction that the truth of life cannot be measured by computers or bureaucratic dictates but only by the motivations of the human heart, is what Havel meant his play to say. That is what gave it social force in his country. . . . Thus the play, a farce of no great subtlety, becomes something vital to the Czech citizen forever under the vigilant and evil eye—of who can say just what." But Richards suggested that *The Increased Difficulty of Concentration* is entertaining no matter who the audience, calling it "a decidedly unusual comedy, full of the slapstick invention and mishap that Havel obviously sees as a measure of our absurd world."

Although Havel received many invitations to work in the West after 1968, he chose to remain in Czechoslovakia, afraid that if he left he would not be allowed back in the country. Forbidden to work in the theater, he devoted much of his time to speaking out against government oppression. In 1969, for example, he visited steel mills in Ostrava and spoke to union members about workers and intellectuals cooperating to defend the freedoms gained in the spring of 1968. This led to government surveillance of the playwright and his family; and even members of his audience became victims of police reprisals, such as when his adaptation of *The Beggar's Opera* was produced by amateurs in 1975. In 1977 Havel became one of the three principal spokesmen for the Charter 77 manifesto, which charged the Czech government with human- and civil-rights violations and called for compliance with the provisions of the Helsinki Agreement. After joining with the artists, writers, intellectuals, and working people of the Charter 77 movement, Havel was arrested and imprisoned several times.

These experiences are reflected in many of Havel's later works, including the three "Vanek" plays, staged together as *A Private View* and *Largo Desolato*. The three short plays of *A Private View*, consisting of *Interview*, the title piece, and *The Protest*, "are linked both thematically and by the presence in each of a mild-mannered, steel-cored autobiographical character named Ferdinand Vanek, dissident artist and outsider in hopeless conflict with an oppressive social order," as Helen Dudar explained in the *New York Times*. The first play shows Vanek being offered favors by his factory foreman if he will inform on himself; the second brings the artist in contact with a bourgeois couple who refuse to understand his cause; and the third portrays Vanek's encounter with a fellow artist who uses convoluted logic to avoid signing a political protest. "In each of the plays we see how others react to [Vanek] . . . and to his martyrdom," commented Gussow, "how each wears his guilt as a badge of identity: the price of prosperity is the loss of humanity. Vanek has become a public conscience and his very presence is a 'living reproach' to those who are compromisers and cowards."

"All three plays suggest what their author has been publicly saying," stated London *Times* writer Benedict Nightingale: "that lies erode the human spirit, and honesty, once lost, will take time to recover." But while the plays point out this truth, they do so without preaching or being simplistic. As Nightingale observed, the play's "point is the stronger for Havel's unerring refusal to idealize his main character or to damn his less principled acquaintances." *A Private View* "reminds us of the importance of the artist as provocateur," concluded Gussow. "Despite his victimization, Havel has retained his comic equilibrium and his sense of injustice. Confronted by public and private absurdities, the artist clings to first principles: self-respect and an unquenchable morality."

In the award-winning *Largo Desolato*, Havel "has once again attempted to transmute the nightmare of totalitarian repression into bleak comedy of high linguistic absurdity," Frank Rich maintained in the *New York Times*. The protagonist, dissident writer Leopold Kopriva, is tormented both by government thugs who watch over and interrogate him and an assortment of friends, fans, and well-wishers who continually remind him of their expectations for him. But while *Largo Desolato* deals with issues of the artistic conscience, it is also a comedy; Irving Wardle of the London *Times*, in his review of the Tom Stoppard translation, praised the play as "a wonderfully comic and unself-pitying piece of work: a notable instance of how adversity can sharpen the power of irony."

Havel also brings an ironic edge to *Temptation*, which transports the legend of Faust into a modern totalitarian society. Havel's Dr. Foustka is an institute scientist whose forbidden studies conjure the appearance of Fistula, a being who grants the doctor the ability to get ahead with the bureaucracy and with women. When Foustka's study is discovered, however, he begins a chain of deception that leads to a surprising twist. As with Havel's previous work, proposed Rich, in *Temptation* "even simple words (starting with 'morality') are inverted in meaning by a state that demands intellectual conformity and that governs by fear. It's Mr. Havel's incredible gift," Rich continued, that "he spins out the nightmare of repression in intricate verbal comedy to match that of Tom Stoppard." Nightingale likewise praised the playwright's verbal skill: "It says much for Havel's passion and skill that his satiric updating of the Faust legend remains so eloquent," the critic wrote, describing *Temptation* as "a study of the moral convolutions of the dissident in a corrupt society." "As in Havel's early work," concluded Wardle, "the shape is indestructibly elegant, full of ironic echoes and balanced repetitions which become funnier with every recurrence; and in which all the allegorical elements are progressively sharpened to a political cutting edge."

Although Havel's works involve bureaucratic situations and contain a political edge, there is a universality to his plays, according to critics. As Wardle commented, in such works as *Largo Desolato* "the brilliance of the piece is that it extends beyond its own country to the civil rights public at large." And because his plays deal with the dehumanization of man within the increasing mechanization of society, Havel has also been labeled an absurdist and, in fact, credited with bringing the absurdist method to Czechoslovakia. However, Grossman considered Havel's drama not absurd but "appellative": "His plays are inventive, artificial; but this quality has nothing to do with romantic fantasies or . . . unbridled insanity." The critic elaborated: "Havel's artificial structuring of the world is made up of real, even commonplace and banal, components, joined most reasonably into a whole."

Thus grounded in reality, Havel's plays remain decidedly allegorical; the protagonist of a Havel play is political bureaucracy itself, or a mechanism of bureaucracy which controls not only the characters, but also the plot and action of the play. For Havel, Grossman maintained, the mechanization of man is not just a theme, "but the central subject, from which his technique derived and on which it is focused." As a *Times Literary Supplement* reviewer similarly observed: "In his preoccupation with the logical and the illogical Havel is a second Lewis Carroll, except that many people in Prague who saw his plays came out laughing 'with a chill up their spine.' His theatre could be the theatre of the absurd but it is not: his central theme is mechanization and what it makes a man, but mechanization is a gimmick rather than an inescapable factor in progress (as Capek might have seen it). It is clear that Havel's master in ideas was Kafka and in expression Ionesco," the critic concluded. "His is something of a genius whose promise is even greater than his performance."

In 1975 Havel's adaptation of British playwright John Gay's *The Beggar's Opera* eluded censors for one memorable performance. Havel used the play to lambaste the communist regime, and the work brought down the wrath of authorities on the Czech playwright, forcing him out of the theater. In 2003 an English translation of Havel's version of *The Beggar's Opera* saw a stage revival in London and in book form. It differs from Gay's version in that Havel adopts a colloquial style, a comic tone, and includes original subplots that satirize collectivism and the loss of individuality under communism. As Ming-Ming Shen Kuo of *Library Journal* noted, even in the English version, the "political overtones remain sharp." Ian Shuttleworth of the *Financial Times* maintained that the work "brilliantly succeeds in being an indictment of the labyrinthine strategies of deception and the informant networks of the Communist state." Although the Czech people no longer suffer under communist rule, the play can be "read equally in a contemporary context of 'spin,'" Shuttleworth continued, "where everyone is repeatedly trying to justify even to themselves the unjustifiable, and self-interest is served by selling oneself out to the big boys. Goodbye dictatorship of the proletariat, hello global market."

Although he has been acclaimed for his dramatic works, Havel is also known for his development as a political philosopher; Toronto *Globe and Mail* contributor Peter C. Newman, for instance, called the writer "the most influential theorist on the nature of totalitarianism and dissent." During his censorship by the Czech government, Havel's ideas were often spread underground, and while in prison many of them found their way out in the form of Havel's letters to his wife. Published as *Letters to Olga,* these correspondences provide "a rare opportunity for meditation that has been all too rare in the life of a profound philosopher," Roger Scruton remarked in the London *Times.* Similarly, *Disturbing the Peace: A Conversation with Karel Hvizdala* provides Havel with an opportunity to "provoke, enchant and illuminate," as Cameron Smith asserted in the Toronto *Globe and Mail.* This series of tape-recorded interviews from 1985 "is an excursion into humanity's great themes, as Havel himself encountered them—life, death, God, art, freedom, responsibility, courage, fear—by one of the grand figures of our time."

In *Disturbing the Peace* Havel notes the following of his country: "The idea that a writer is the conscience of his nation has its own logic and its own tradition here. For years, writers have stood in for politicians: they were renewers of the national community, maintainers of the national language, interpreters of the national will. This tradition has continued under totalitarian conditions, where it gains its own special coloring: the written word seems to have acquired a kind of heightened radioactivity—otherwise they wouldn't lock us up for it!" This tradition notwithstanding, Havel was frequently quoted as saying that he would rather be a playwright than a statesman.

Just as his plays "don't simply shrug and walk away" and "say that people and societies do have to make choices," as *Los Angeles Times* writer Dan Sullivan observed, throughout his life Havel has complied with what he has seen as his duty. As he was quoted by Henry Kamm in the *New York Times:* "I have repeatedly said my occupation is writer. . . . I have no political ambitions. I don't feel myself to be a professional politician. But I have always placed the public interest above my own. . . . And if, God help us, the situation develops in such a way that the only service that I could render my country would be to [accept public office], then of course I would do it." These circumstances arose during Czechoslovakia's political upheaval in 1989, when Havel emerged as the leader of the opposition to the Communist government. In a unanimous vote by Czechoslovakia's parliament, Havel was chosen to serve as president, and when free elections were held the following year he was reaffirmed as his country's leader.

The volume *Open Letters* collects various writings that showcase Havel's eloquence as a statesman, ranging from his first words of protest in 1965 to what Irving Howe in the *New York Times Book Review* called his "soberly triumphant" inaugural address of 1990. Havel's essays, noted Tony Judt in the *Times Literary Supplement,* "show a complex political and moral sensibility. They are written with wonderful clarity and directness; whatever posterity will say of Havel's plays, there can be no doubt that, as an author, he has a rare gift for metaphor and example." *Summer Meditations,* which includes writings from Havel's early years in public office, focuses mainly on the issue of morality in politics. Havel, commented Steven Lukes in the *Times Literary Supplement,* uses words "for uplift and exhortation: the President as Preacher. They are, needless to say, meditations far more articulate and intelligent than any other current world statesman is likely to produce." As quoted by Lukes, Havel writes that "politics is not essentially a disreputable business; and to the extent that it is, it is only disreputable people who make it so."

In 1997 Havel released *The Art of the Impossible: Politics As Morality in Practice,* a collection of speeches delivered between 1990 and 1996 as president first of Czechoslovakia and then the Czech Republic. George Stephanopoulos in the *Los Angeles Times Book Review* observed that these speeches address all the relevant questions facing modern European politics—NATO's future, European integration, East-West relations, as well as globalization—but "more interesting, and lasting, are Havel's meditations on the timeless questions of politics and philosophy: What is the nature of civic responsibility? When do the ends justify the means in state-craft? Can intellectuals serve with integrity in the political arena? Is it possible for people who hold political power to 'live in truth' and approach the ideal of 'politics as morality in practice?'" Noting the Czech president's silence regarding certain government policies in these speeches, Douglas A. Sylva in the *New York Times Book Review* pointed out that Havel "cares much more about what his people think and feel than how they should resolve specific political questions."

Critical reception to *The Art of the Impossible* called attention to the uniqueness Havel demonstrated in his role as president. Jean Bethke Elshtain, writing in *Commonweal,* saw Havel as struggling with the dichotomy of being both an intellectual and a politician as well as demonstrating a great concern for morality in politics: "Havel's great fear is that relinquishing a politics of high morality often leads to a politics of brute instrumentality; thus, he rejects politics that is simply 'the art of the possible.'" Preston Jones in *First Things* considered Havel's references to a transcendent force distinctive: "Yet that he speaks about such things openly, and not merely for political reasons, sets him apart from the great majority of the industrialized world's public officials." Stephanopoulos found that Havel's "words are a sorely needed antidote to the grandiosity that infects so many who practice politics and the apathy that characterizes so many who live in our society but ignore the duties of citizenship."

After losing in the Czech Republic's parliamentary elections in 2003, Havel and his second wife, Czech actress Dagmar Veskrnova, retired to their home in the seaside town of Algarve, where he planned to write his memoirs.

BIOGRAPHICAL AND CRITICAL SOURCES:

BOOKS

Contemporary Literary Criticism, Gale, (Detroit, MI), Volume 25, 1983, Volume 58, 1990, Volume 65, 1991.
Czech Literature since 1956: A Symposium, edited by William E. Harkins and Paul I. Trensky, Bohemica (New York, NY), 1980, pp. 103-118.

Drama Criticism, Volume 6, Gale, (Detroit, MI) 1996.

Esslin, Martin, *The Theatre of the Absurd,* revised edition, Doubleday (New York, NY), 1969.

Esslin, Martin, *Reflections: Essays on Modern Theatre,* Doubleday (New York, NY), 1969.

Goetz-Stankiewicz, Marketa, *The Silenced Theatre: Czech Playwrights without a Stage,* University of Toronto Press (Toronto, Ontario, Canada), 1979.

Goetz-Stankiewicz, Marketa, and Phyllis Careys, editors, *Critical Essays on Vaclav Havel,* Hall (New York, NY), 1999.

Havel, Vaclav, *Disturbing the Peace: A Conversation with Karel Hvizdala,* translation by Paul Wilson, Knopf (New York, NY), 1990.

Havel, Vaclav, *Summer Meditations,* translation by Paul Wilson, Knopf (New York, NY), 1992.

Keane, John, *Vaclav Havel: A Political Tragedy in Six Acts,* Bloomsbury Press (London, England), 1999.

Kriseova, Eda, *Vaclav Havel: The Authorized Biography,* translation by Caleb Crain, St. Martin's Press (New York, NY), 1993.

The Labyrinth of the Word: Truth and Representation in Czech Literature, Oldenbourg (Munich, Germany), 1995, pp. 144-157.

Matustik, Martin J., *Postnational Identity: Critical Theory and Existential Philosophy in Habemas, Kierkegaard, and Havel,* Guilford (New York, NY), 1993.

Simmons, Michael, *The Reluctant President: The Political Life of Vaclav Havel,* Methuen (London, England), 1991.

Symynkywicz, Jeffrey, *Vaclav Havel and the Velvet Revolution,* Dillon Press (New York, NY), 1995.

Twentieth-Century European Drama, edited by Brian Docherty, St. Martin's Press (New York, NY), 1994, pp. 172-182.

Vladislav, Jan, editor, *Vaclav Havel; or, Living in Truth,* Faber & Faber (London, England), 1987.

PERIODICALS

Back Stage, June 18, 1999, Karl Levett, review of *Largo Desolato,* p. 56.

Booklist, June 1, 2001, Jack Helbig, review of *The Beggar's Opera,* p. 1825.

Chicago Tribune, December 30, 1989; February 22, 1990.

Christianity and Literature, fall, 1994, Phyllis Carey, "Face to Face: Samuel Beckett and Vaclav Havel," pp. 43-57.

Commonweal, October 24, 1997, Jean Bethke Elshtain, "Philosopher President," pp. 23-24.

Cross Currents, Volume 10, 1991, Marketa Goetz-Stankiewicz, "Shall We Dance? Reflections on Vaclav Havel's Plays," pp. 213-222; summer, 1992, Phyllis Carey, "Living the Lies: Vaclav Havel's Drama," pp. 200-211; fall, 1997, Walter H. Capps, "Interpreting Vaclav Havel," pp. 301-316.

Cue, December 13, 1969.

Czechoslovak and Central European Journal, winter, 1991, Paul I. Trensky, "Vaclav Havel's 'Temptation Cycle,'" pp. 84-95.

Essays in Theatre, May, 1992, Michael L. Quinn, "Delirious Subjectivity: Four Scenes from Havel," pp. 117-132.

Financial Times, January 21, 2003, Ian Shuttleworth, "New Spin on Havel's Old Satire Theatre *The Beggar's Opera,*" p. 15.

First Things, December, 1998, p. 61.

Globe and Mail (Toronto, Ontario, Canada), April 30, 1988; October 28, 1989; December 30, 1989; January 6, 1990; June 23, 1990.

Humanist, May-June, 1994, p. 40; November-December, 1994, p. 39.

Insight on the News, August 8, 1994, p. 37.

Kenyon Review, spring, 1993, Robert Skloot, "Vaclav Havel: The Once and Future Playwright," pp. 223-231.

Library Journal, May 15, 2001, Ming-Ming Shen Kuo, review of *The Beggar's Opera,* p. 124.

Los Angeles Times, February 15, 1989; February 22, 1989; December 4, 1989; December 10, 1989; December 17, 1989; January 13, 1990; February 23, 1990.

Los Angeles Times Book Review, April 3, 1988; June 29, 1997, p. 11.

Maclean's, August 17, 1998, p. 52.

Modern Drama, March, 1984, M. C. Bradbrook, "Vaclav Havel's Second Wind," pp. 124-132; winter, 1997, Jude R. Meche, "Female Victims and the Male Protagonist in Vaclav Havel's Drama," pp. 468-476.

Nation, May 27, 1968; December 22, 1969.

New Statesman, July 22, 1994, p. 32.

Newsweek, July 18, 1994, p. 66.

New Yorker, May 18, 1968; February 17, 2003, David Remnick, "Exit Havel," p. 90.

New York Review of Books, August 4, 1977; March 22, 1979; August 15, 1991, Dana Emigerova and Lubos Beniak, "'Uncertain Strength': An Interview with Vaclav Havel," pp. 6, 8; September 24, 1992, George F. Kennan, review of *Summer Mediations,* pp. 3-4.

New York Times, May 6, 1968; October 22, 1969; December 5, 1969; December 14, 1969; November 20, 1983; November 21, 1983; March 23, 1986; March 26, 1986; March 31, 1988; February 5, 1989; April 9, 1989; December 8, 1989; December 17, 1989; December 18, 1989; December 23, 1989; December 30, 1989; January 12, 1990; January 13, 1990; June 27, 1990; May 26, 1991, Irving Howe, review of *Open Letters,* p. 5.

New York Times Book Review, May 8, 1988; May 26, 1991; June 7, 1992; August 3, 1997, p. 17; October 11, 1998, review of *The Art of the Impossible,* p. 32.

New York Times Magazine, October 25, 1987.

Observer Review, December 17, 1967.

Plays and Players, August, 1971.

Progressive, April, 1993, Erwin Knoll, review of *Open Letters, Summer Meditations,* and *Living in Truth,* pp. 40-43.

Prompt, number 12, 1968.

Representations summer, 1993, Martin Prochazka, "Prisoner's Predicament: Public Privacy in Havel's *Letters to Olga,*" pp. 126-154.

Sewanee Review, spring, 1992.

Slavic and East European Journal, spring, 1969, Paul I. Trensky, "Vaclav Havel and the Language of the Absurd," pp. 42-65.

Slavic and East European Performance, spring, 1992, M. Quinn, review of *Largo Desolato,* pp. 8-12; spring, 1996, Jarka Burian, "Vaclav Havel's Notable Encounters in His Early Theatrical Career," pp. 13-29.

Slavic Review, summer, 1992, Alfred Thomas, reviews of *The Vanek Plays* and *Living in Truth,* pp. 348-351.

Style, summer, 1991, Veronika Ambros, "Fictional World and Dramatic Text: Vaclav Havel's Descent and Ascent," pp. 310-319.

Thought, September, 1991, Phyllis Carey, "Contemporary World Drama 101: Vaclav Havel," pp. 317-328.

Time, June 14, 1968; July 25, 1969.

Times (London, England), October 15, 1986; February 12, 1987; May 2, 1987; April 27, 1988; February 29, 1989; March 4, 1989; February 17, 1990; March 7, 1990; June 8, 1990.

Times Literary Supplement, March 7, 1968; March 10, 1972; October 21, 1991; September 25, 1992.

Tulane Drama Review, spring, 1967.

Variety, December 17, 1969.

Washington Post, August 26, 1988; February 22, 1989; May 15, 1989; October 27, 1989; January 7, 1990; January 9, 1990; March 4, 1990.

Washington Post Book World, June 14, 1992.

World and I, August, 2001, Lesley Chamberlain, "Play It Again, Vaclav: The Wisdom of Havel's Plays," p. 76.

World Literature Today, summer, 1981, Marketa Goetz-Stankiewicz, "Vaclav Havel: A Writer for Today's Season," pp. 389-393; spring, 1991, Karen von Kunes, "The National Paradox: Czech Literature and the Gentle Revolution," pp. 327-240.*

* * *

HEILIGMAN, Deborah 1958-

PERSONAL: Born April 24, 1958, in Allentown, PA; daughter of Nathan (a physician) and Helen (Rockmaker) Heiligman; married Jonathan Weiner (an author), May 29, 1982; children: Aaron, Benjamin. *Education:* Brown University, A.B. (religious studies), 1980. *Religion:* Jewish.

ADDRESSES: Home—3040 Yorkshire Rd., Doylestown, PA 18901. *E-mail*—deborah@deborahheiligman.com.

CAREER: Author of children's books. Scholastic Inc., New York, NY, editor, 1981-85.

MEMBER: Authors Guild, Authors League of America, Society of Children's Book Writers and Illustrators.

AWARDS, HONORS: Distinguished alumnus award, Allen High School, 1993; Notable Children's Trade Book in the Field of Social Studies, National Council for the Social Studies/Children's Book Council, 1995, for *Barbara McClintock: Alone in Her Field.*

WRITINGS:

Into the Night, illustrated by Melissa Sweet, Harper & Row (New York, NY), 1990.

Barbara McClintock: Alone in Her Field, illustrated by Janet Hamlin, Scientific American Books for Young Readers (New York, NY), 1994.

Mary Leakey: In Search of Human Beginnings, illustrated by Janet Hamlin, Scientific American Books for Young Readers (New York, NY), 1995.

Pockets, illustrated by Suzanne Duranceau, Hyperion (New York, NY), 1995.

On the Move, illustrated by Lizzy Rockwell, HarperCollins (New York, NY), 1996.

From Caterpillar to Butterfly, illustrated by Bari Weissman, HarperCollins (New York, NY), 1996.

Mike Swan, Sink or Swim, illustrated by Chris L. Demarest, First Choice Chapter Books (New York, NY), 1998.

The Story of the Titanic, illustrated by James Watling, Random House (New York, NY), 1998.

The New York Public Library Kid's Guide to Research, Scholastic (New York, NY), 1998, also published as *The Kid's Guide to Research.*

Too Perfect, illustrated by Deborah Kogan Ray, Grosset & Dunlap (New York, NY), 1999.

The Mysterious Ocean Highway: Benjamin Franklin and the Gulf Stream, Raintree Steck-Vaughn (Austin, TX), 2000.

Honeybees, illustrated by Carla Golembe, National Geographic Society (Washington, DC), 2002.

Babies: All You Need to Know, illustrated by Laura Freeman, National Geographic Society (Washington, DC), 2002.

Earthquakes, Scholastic (New York, NY), 2002.

High Hopes: A Photobiography of John F. Kennedy, National Geographic Society (Washington, DC), 2003.

Contributor to magazines, including *Ladies Home Journal, Sesame Street Parents Guide,* and *Parents.*

SIDELIGHTS: After working as a children's book editor in the mid-1980s, Deborah Heiligman began creating her own children's books. She has penned both fiction and nonfiction titles, including two biographies of female scientists, *Barbara McClintock: Alone in Her Field,* and *Mary Leakey: In Search of Human Beginnings.* Books about insects, titles for emergent readers, and even a research guide for students are all subjects written about by Heiligman. Like many people who eventually become writers, Heiligman appreciated books from an early age, as she once recalled to *CA:* "I remember so clearly the first time I checked a book out of the library. I was in kindergarten. We went to the school library—I can still see the warm wood of the floor, the card catalogue, the heavy doors. I can still smell the books—they smelled warm and musky. I can still feel those first books I pulled off the shelf. They had hard covers, and soft, worn pages. The book I checked out was *What Is a Butterfly?*"

Heiligman continued: "I brought it home; I felt as though I were carrying a real treasure. My mother read it to me, sitting on my bed. I was so small my legs did not reach to the side of the bed. But the world became larger and larger with each word she read. This book told me everything I wanted to know about how a caterpillar becomes a butterfly. I was in a whole new world. I wanted to explore every nook and cranny. I kept reading nonfiction, and then branched out into fiction, longer books, encyclopedias, and magazines. While I was growing up, I had many friends and did all kinds of wonderful things. But the one anchor in my life was always my love of reading. Reading was like magic for me. I found, too, that I loved to write, and that I was pretty good at it."

Thus a career in publishing was a natural fit for Heiligman, who graduated from Brown University in 1980. She married and worked for New York City publisher Scholastic for several years before striking out on her own. As she once recalled to *CA,* "The magic came full circle . . . [in 1995] when an editor asked me to write a picture book on how a caterpillar turns into a butterfly! I had long been searching for my first butterfly book, but it was out of print. So I was able to write my own!" Heiligman had a personal investment in this book, as she told *CA,* "I wrote the book the month after my mother died, and I poured into it memories of her, and all of my books, and the wonders of the world, and of life. From a funny-looking caterpillar comes a beautiful Painted Lady butterfly. And life comes full circle too, as I dedicated *From Caterpillar to Butterfly* to my first son, Aaron, who loves books even more than I do, if that is possible."

As a child, Heiligman was entranced by nonfiction, a love she continues to demonstrate in her writings. And since research is an integral part of nonfiction writing, Heiligman offered her knowledge of research tools to readers in *The New York Public Library Kid's Guide to Research.* Geared to students in grades four through eight, this "short and complete" title, to quote Edith Ching of *School Library Journal,* gives practical advice on note taking, interviewing, evaluating Internet sources, and conducting surveys, as well as using secondary sources. For somewhat older readers, Heiligman also wrote about a historical science mystery—the Gulf Stream. In *The Mysterious Ocean Highway: Benjamin Franklin and the Gulf Stream,* the author traced the history of scientific investigation of this powerful ocean current, beginning with Franklin's discoveries and ending with a description of contemporary scientific investigations. Several reviewers evaluated the book for *Appraisal,* including Linda de Lyon Friel, who praised its "scientifically accurate" and "concise" information, and Robert Newman, who concluded that *The Mysterious Ocean Highway* is "a well written and fascinating tale of discovery and mapping."

Heiligman's ability to tell a story in an easy-to-understand way led her to write a number of books for emergent readers, including *Honeybees* and *Babies: All You Need to Know. Honeybees* is an information-packed book of "fascinating details" about the secret life of bees, noted *Booklist*'s Carolyn Phelan. Although Edith Ching, writing in *School Library Journal,* pointed out several flaws in the work, she also dubbed it overall an "attractive addition." *Babies* is also packed with "interesting information," though it suffers from "an uneven presentation," according to Martha Topol of *School Library Journal.* Yet a *Kirkus Reviews* commentator also found it "a satisfying introduction" to infants and predicted that this "upbeat and fun" title would be useful for families expecting a new member.

BIOGRAPHICAL AND CRITICAL SOURCES:

PERIODICALS

Appraisal, spring-summer-fall, 2000, Linda de Lyon Friel, review of *The Mysterious Ocean Highway: Benjamin Franklin and the Gulf Stream,* p. 39; spring-summer-fall, 2000, Robert Newman, review of *The Mysterious Ocean Highway,* p. 39.

Booklist, November 15, 1994, p. 596; October 1, 1998, Mary Ellen Quinn, review of *The New York Public Library Kid's Guide to Research,* p. 362; October 15, 1999, Hazel Rochman, review of *The Mysterious Ocean Highway,* p. 437; May 1, 2002, Carolyn Phelan, review of *Honeybees,* p. 1529; October 1, 2002, Kathy Broderick, review of *Babies: All You Need to Know,* p. 328.

Horn Book Guide, July, 1990, p. 38; spring, 1999, Peter D. Sieruta, review of *The New York Public Library Kid's Guide to Research,* p. 84.

Kirkus Reviews, August 15, 2002, review of *Babies,* p. 1225.

Publishers Weekly, July 27, 1998, review of *The New York Public Library Kid's Guide to Research,* p. 79.

Reading Teacher, October, 1997, review of *From Caterpillar to Butterfly,* p. 152.

School Library Journal, January, 1991, p. 74; August, 1996, p. 138; February, 1999, Edith Ching, review of *The New York Public Library Kid's Guide to Research,* p. 119; May, 2002, Edith Ching, review of *Honeybees,* p. 138; October, 2002, Martha Topol, review of *Babies,* p. 146.

ONLINE

Deborah Heiligman Home Page, http://www.deborahheiligman.com/ (July 30, 2003).*

* * *

HELPRIN, Mark 1947-

PERSONAL: Born June 28, 1947, in New York, NY; son of Morris (a motion picture executive) and Eleanor (Lynn) Helprin; married Lisa Kennedy (a tax attorney and banker), June 28, 1980; children: Alexandra Morris, Olivia Kennedy. *Education:* Harvard University, A.B., 1969; A.M., 1972; postgraduate study at Magdalen College, Oxford, 1976-77. *Politics:* "Roosevelt Republican." *Religion:* Jewish.

ADDRESSES: *Office*—c/o Author Mail, Harcourt Brace Jovanovich, Inc., 15 East 26th St., New York, NY 10010.

CAREER: Writer. Hudson Institute, senior fellow; Harvard University, Cambridge, MA, former instructor. *Military service:* Israeli Infantry and Air Force, field security, 1972-73; British Merchant Navy.

MEMBER: American Academy in Rome.

AWARDS, HONORS: PEN/Faulkner Award, National Jewish Book Award, and American Book Award nomination, all 1982, all for *Ellis Island and Other Stories;*

Mark Helprin

American Academy and Institute of Arts and Letters Prix de Rome, 1982; Guggenheim fellow, 1984; World Fantasy Award for Best Novella, World Fantasy Convention, 1997, for *A City in Winter: The Queen's Tale;* Mightier Pen Award, Center for Security Policy, 2001.

WRITINGS:

A Dove of the East and Other Stories, Knopf (New York, NY), 1975.
Refiner's Fire: The Life and Adventures of Marshall Pearl, a Foundling (novel), Knopf (New York, NY), 1977.
Ellis Island and Other Stories, Seymour Lawrence/Delacorte (New York, NY), 1981.
Winter's Tale (novel), Harcourt (San Diego, CA), 1983.
Swan Lake (children's book), illustrated by Chris Van Allsburg, Houghton (Boston, MA), 1989.
A Soldier of the Great War (novel), Harcourt (New York, NY), 1991.
Memoir from Antproof Case (novel), Harcourt (New York, NY), 1995.
A City in Winter: The Queen's Tale, illustrated by Chris Van Allsburg, Viking (New York, NY), 1996.
The Veil of Snows, illustrated by Chris Van Allsburg, Viking (New York, NY), 1997.

Editor, with Shannon Ravenel, of *The Best American Short Stories, 1988.* Contributor of numerous short stories and articles to periodicals, including *New Yorker, Esquire, New Criterion, National Review, Commentary, Weekly Standard,* and *New York Times Magazine*; contributing editor, *Wall Street Journal.*

SIDELIGHTS: Mark Helprin is a writer whose fiction is marked by language "more classical than conversational," observed Michiko Kakutani in the *New York Times,* and one who shapes his short stories and novels "less to show my place in the world than to praise the world around me." Explaining his artistic distance from the sparse, clean prose of writers such as American author Ernest Hemingway, Helprin told Jon D. Markman of the *Los Angeles Times,* "My models are the *Divine Comedy,* and the *Bible* and Shakespeare—where they use language to the fullest." Helprin's political concerns—he pursued Middle Eastern studies in graduate school and later served in the Israeli Infantry and Air Force—figure in his newspaper and magazine articles; his books, he has often said with little elaboration, are religious.

Majoring in English as an undergraduate at Harvard, Helprin wrote short stories and sent them to the *New Yorker* with no luck until 1969, when the magazine accepted two at the same time. These became part of his first book, *A Dove of the East and Other Stories,* in which critics have noted the author's grand depictions of nature as a source of strength and healing and his concern with characters who survive loss, particularly that of loved ones.

Some critics were impressed with the wide range of settings and the graceful prose exhibited in *A Dove of the East.* In the *Saturday Review* Dorothy Rabinowitz described Helprin's stories as "immensely readable," some "quite superb," writing that his "old-fashioned regard shines through all his characters' speeches, and his endorsement gives them eloquent tongues. Now and again the stories lapse into archness, and at times, too, their willed drama bears down too heavily. But these are small flaws in works so estimably full of talent and . . . of character." Amanda Heller, however, complained in the *Atlantic Monthly* that, as a result of Helprin's "dreamy, antique style," the stories' "sameness of tone" becomes monotonous. "It appears that Helprin is striving for loveliness above all else," Heller commented, "a tasteful but hardly compelling goal for a teller of tales."

Duncan Fallowell allowed in the *Spectator* that some selections from *A Dove of the East and Other Stories* are "unbeatably vague," but praised Helprin for "recognising the intrinsic majesty" of seemingly meaningless events, because, as Fallowell wrote, "he is also a seeker after truth. Bits of it are squittering out all over the place, sufficiently to fuse into a magnetic centre and make one recognise that the book is not written by a fool." Dan Wakefield, even more appreciative of Helprin's work, observed: "The quality that pervades these stories is love—love of men and women, love of landscapes and physical beauty, love of interior courage as well as the more easily obtainable outward strength. The author never treats his subjects with sentimentality but always with gentleness of a kind that is all too rare in our fiction and our lives."

Helprin's first novel, *Refiner's Fire: The Life and Adventures of Marshall Pearl, a Foundling,* further interested critics. A *New Yorker* reviewer found that Helprin describes the protagonist's boyhood "lyrically and gracefully" and proves himself to be "a writer of great depth and subtle humor." For Joyce Carol Oates the problem is "where to begin" in admiring a novel she described as a "daring, even reckless, sprawling and expansive and endlessly inventive 'picaresque' tale." She added: "At once we know we are in the presence of a storyteller of seemingly effortless and artless charm; and if the exuberant, extravagant plotting of the novel ever becomes tangled in its own fabulous inventions, and its prodigy of a hero ever comes to seem more allegorical than humanly 'real,' that storytelling command, that lovely voice is never lost."

With *Ellis Island and Other Stories* Helprin secured his place among contemporary writers, winning for this work a PEN/Faulkner Award, a National Jewish Book Award, and an American Book Award nomination—a rare feat for a collection of short stories. Though some critics, such as Anne Duchene in the *Times Literary Supplement,* found that Helprin's language sometimes overwhelms his intent, the greater critical response was laudatory. In the *Washington Post Book World,* Allen Wier called the collection "beautifully written and carefully structured. . . . His rich textures alone would be enough to delight a reader, but there is more: wonderful *stories,* richly plotted, inventive, moving without being sentimental, humorous without being cute." Harry Mark Petrakis stated in the *Chicago Tribune* that in *Ellis Island and Other Stories* Helprin "reveals range and insight whether he is writing of children or adults, of scholars, tailors, and lovers. His eye is precise and his spirit is compassionate, and when we finish the stories we have been rewarded, once more, with that astonishing catalyst of art." Reynolds Price, writing for the *New York Times Book Review,* cited as particularly memorable "The Schreuderspitze," in which a photographer who has lost his wife and son in a car accident risks his life to climb a mountain in an effort to regain his spirit; the first half of the title novella, and "North Light," which Price called "a brief and frankly autobiographical recollection of battle nerves among Israeli soldiers, a lean arc of voltage conveyed through tangible human conductors to instant effect."

Winter's Tale, Helprin's second novel, held a place on the *New York Times* bestseller list for four months despite mixed critical opinion. Seymour Krim, writing for *Washington Post Book World,* described the allegorical novel as "the most ambitious work [Helprin] . . . has yet attempted, a huge cyclorama" with a theme "no less than the resurrection of New York from a city of the damned to a place of universal justice and hope." In Krim's view, however, the novel reveals itself to be "a self-willed fairy tale that even on its own terms refuses to convince." In the *Chicago Tribune Book World* Jonathan Brent called the book "a pastiche of cliches thinly disguised as fiction, a maddening welter of earnest platitudes excruciatingly dressed up as a search for the miraculous." In the opinion of *Newsweek*'s Peter S. Prescott, "Helprin fell into the fundamental error of assuming that fantasy can be vaguer than realistic fiction."

In the view of Benjamin de Mott of the *New York Times Book Review,* however, neither through the unique and compelling characters nor "merely by studying the touchstone passages in which description and narrative soar highest" can the reader "possess the work": "No, the heart of this book resides unquestionably in its moral energy, in the thousand original gestures, ruminations, . . . writing feats that summon its audience beyond the narrow limits of conventional vision, commanding us to see our time and place afresh."

Detroit News reviewer Beaufort Cranford found that the book "fairly glows with poetry. Helprin's forte is a deft touch with description, and he has as distinct and spectacular a gift for words an anyone writing today." Further, Cranford noted, "Helprin's fearlessly understated humor shows his comfort with a narrative that in a less adroit grasp might seem too much like a fairy tale."

Openers contributor Ann Cunniff, who also caught the humor in *Winter's Tale,* praised "the beautiful, dreamlike quality" of some passages and Helprin's "frequent references to dreams." "All my life," Helprin explained to Cunniff, "I've allowed what I dream to influence me. My dreams are usually very intense and extremely detailed and always in the most beautiful colors. . . . Frequently, I will dream, and simply retrace that dream the day after when I write. It's just like planning ahead, only I do it when I'm unconscious."

In 1989 Helprin collaborated with illustrator Chris Van Allsburg on *Swan Lake.* Michael Dirda wrote in the *Washington Post Book World,* "The book is so attractive—in its story, illustrations and general design—that by comparison the original ballet almost looks too ethereal." In the *Chicago Tribune,* Michael Dorris raved, "This is one of those rare juvenile classics that will keep you awake to its conclusion . . . [and] will become, I predict, among those precious artifacts your grownup children will someday request for their own children." Helprin and Van Allsburg also combined their talents in 1996's *A City in Winter: The Queen's Tale* and 1997's *The Veil of Snows.*

In *A Soldier of the Great War,* which Shashi Tharoor described in the *Washington Post Book World* as "marvelously old-fashioned" and "a mammoth, elegiac, moving exegesis on love, beauty, the meaning of life and the meaninglessness of war," Helprin seemed to have transcended the criticism leveled at his earlier work. According to John Skow in *Time,* in this tale of the old Italian soldier Alessandro, Helprin has "simplified his language, though he still works up a good head of steam, and he has moderated his enthusiasm for phantasmagoric set pieces. He has also picked themes—war and loss, youth and age—that suit a large, elaborate style." Ted Solotaroff commented in the *Nation* that in *A Soldier of the Great War* Helprin takes "his penchant for life's heightened possibilities and transcendent meanings down into the vile trenches and nightmarish forests and jammed military prisons of the Italian sector of the war." Tharoor concluded: "Clearly a writer of great sensitivity, remarkable skill and capacious intellect, Helprin relishes telling stories in the grand manner, supplying details so complete as to leave the reader in no doubt about the texture of each place and the feelings of each character in it."

Helprin produced yet another expansive, picaresque novel with the mysteriously titled *Memoir from Antproof Case,* which was published in 1995. The story is the memoir of an elderly narrator who relates his fantastic and vivid life in a document he keeps locked inside an ant-proof case. While packing a pistol and hiding from his enemies in Brazil, the narrator describes his early life near New York City, his stay in a Swiss insane asylum, his involvement in World War II, his marriage to a wealthy heiress, and his employment with—and scheme to steal from—a powerful investment brokerage. While telling his life's story, the narrator divulges an odd obsession: the hatred of coffee, including the substance itself as well as the people who drink it. *Los Angeles Times Book Review* contributor Adam Begley described the novel thusly: "More odd mysteries than the anti-coffee mania await unraveling; lyrical passages brim with high-toned literary prose; broad comic riffs announce themselves with take-my-wife subtlety; and tall tales sprout magically at every turn, fed by a steady stream of flamboyant exaggeration."

Critics were positive in their appraisal of *Memoir from Antproof Case,* commending the author's trademark high-wire prose styling and his creation of another unusual, colorful, and rambling narrative. Terry Teachout, riting in the *Washington Post Book World,* called the novel "long, extravagant, daring, occasionally tedious but more often impressively compelling." Similarly, *New York Times Book Review* contributor Sven Birkerts remarked that the story "is rendered with great anecdotal charm and is embroidered throughout with vivid descriptions and delightful reflections." Not all reviewers' comments were positive; Begley, for instance, noted a "lurching Ping-Pong pattern" in the novel in which "suspense alternates with silliness," and Teachout declared that certain elements of *Memoir from Antproof Case* are "exasperating in the extreme." However, Teachout concluded, while "Helprin is a bit of a blowhard, . . . he is also one of the most ambitious novelists of our day."

In addition to his nine fictional works, Helprin wrote articles for the *Wall Street Journal* from 1985 to 2000.

"Many people would probably be surprised to know that the same man who writes political commentary for the *Wall Street Journal* cites as his motto a line from Dante's *Inferno* that translates 'Love moved me, and makes me speak,'" remarked *American Enterprise* reviewer, John Meroney. Helprin also came to the political forefront in 1996, when word leaked out that he was the author of presidential candidate Bob Dole's strong resignation speech from the U.S. Senate. Meroney quoted from the speech: "I will run for President as a private citizen, a Kansan, an American, just a man." Dole's speech was "an unusually lyrical oration by the Kansas solon's dry standards," commented *Salon.com* contributor Mark Schapiro, who continued by noting that "Helprin's soaring words were widely credited with at least temporarily recharging Dole's languishing presidential campaign."

In 2001 Helprin was awarded the Mightier Pen Award by the Century for Security Policy. The Center's president and chief executive officer, Frank Gaffney, Jr., stated that Helprin is "one of the most important writers at work today." "Helprin's creative flair is tempered by intelligence, wisdom, and experience," noted John Elvin in *Insight on the News* in reference to Helprin's receipt of the Mightier Pen award.

BIOGRAPHICAL AND CRITICAL SOURCES:

BOOKS

Concise Dictionary of American Literary Biography Supplement: Modern Writers, 1900-1998, Gale (Detroit, MI), 1998.
Contemporary Literary Criticism, Gale (Detroit, MI), Volume 7, 1977, Volume 10, 1979, Volume 22, 1982, Volume 32, 1985.
Contemporary Novelists, 7th edition, St. James Press (Detroit, MI), 2001.
Dictionary of Literary Biography Yearbook: 1985, Gale (Detroit, MI), 1986.
Encyclopedia of American Literature, Continuum (New York, NY), 1999.
Modern American Literature, Gale (Detroit, MI), 1996.

PERIODICALS

American Enterprise, July, 2001, John Meroney, interview with Helprin, p. 14.
Atlantic Monthly, October, 1975.
Boston Globe, July 12, 1995, Michael Kenney, "Waging a War after All," p. 41.
Chicago Tribune, March 29, 1981; November 12, 1989.
Chicago Tribune Book World, March 29, 1981; October 9, 1983; October 23, 1988; November 12, 1989.
Commentary, June, 1981, pp. 62-66.
Detroit News, February, 23, 1982; March 14, 1982; October 9, 1983.
Globe and Mail (Toronto, Ontario, Canada), January 7, 1984; October 6, 1984.
Harper's, November, 1977.
Insight on the News, May 14, 2001, John Elvin, "A Mightier Pen for a Master Wordsmith," p. 35.
Los Angeles Times, November 8, 1984.
Los Angeles Times Book Review, September 25, 1983; May 5, 1991; May 14, 1995, p. 2.
Nation, June 10, 1991.
New Statesman, February 13, 1976.
Newsweek, September 19, 1983.
New Yorker, October 17, 1977.
New York Review of Books, February 23, 1978; August 15, 1991.
New York Times, January 30, 1981; March 5, 1981, Michiko Kakutani, "The Making of a Writer," p. 17; September 2, 1983.
New York Times Book Review, November 2, 1975; January 1, 1978; March 1, 1981; September 4, 1983; March 25, 1984; May 5, 1991, Thomas Keneally, review of *A Soldier of the Great War,* pp. 1-2; April 9, 1995, p. 3; January 4, 1998, review of *The Veil of Snows,* p. 20.
Openers, fall, 1984.
Publishers Weekly, February 13, 1981.
Saturday Review, September 20, 1975.
School Library Journal, February, 1999, review of *A City in Winter* (audiobook), p. 68; May, 1999, Tricia Finch, review of *Veil of Snows* (audiobook), p. 70.
Spectator, April 24, 1976.
Time, July 6, 1981; October 3, 1983; November 13, 1989; May 20, 1991.
Times Literary Supplement, March 13, 1981; November 25, 1983.
Tribune Books (Chicago, IL), June 9, 1996, p. 10.
Village Voice, May 28, 1991.
Washington Post Book World, February 22, 1981; September 25, 1983; November 5, 1989; May 5, 1991; March 26, 1995, p. 3.

ONLINE

Mark Helprin Bibliography, http://www.lib.ncsu.edu/staff/kamorgan/helprin-bib.html/ (May 11, 2003).
Salon.com, http://www.salon.com/ (August 14, 2003), Mark Schapiro, "Rewriting Bob Dole" (interview).
Wall Street Journal Online, http//www.wsj.com/ (August 9, 2000), "A Chat with Mark Helprin."*

* * *

HOBBS, Will(iam Carl) 1947-

PERSONAL: Born August 22, 1947, in Pittsburgh, PA; son of Gregory J. and Mary (Rhodes) Hobbs; married Jean Loftus (a literary agent, formerly a teacher), December 20, 1972. *Education:* Stanford University, B.A., 1969, M.A., 1971. *Hobbies and other interests:* Hiking in the mountains and canyons, white water rafting, archeology, natural history.

ADDRESSES: Office—c/o Author Mail, HarperCollins Children's Books, 1350 Avenue of the Americas, New York, NY 10019.

CAREER: Educator and children's author. Pagosa Springs, CO, and Durango, CO, public schools, taught junior high and senior high reading and English, 1973-89; writer, 1990—.

MEMBER: Authors Guild, Society of Children's Book Writers and Illustrators, Phi Beta Kappa.

AWARDS, HONORS: Notable Trade Book in the Field of Social Studies, National Council for the Social Studies/Children's Book Council (NCSS/CBC), 1988, and Colorado Blue Spruce Young Adult Book Award, 1992, both for *Changes in Latitudes;* NCSS/CBC Notable Trade Book in the Field of Social Studies, 1989, Best Books for Young Adults, American Library Association (ALA), 1989, and Teachers' Choice citation, International Reading Association (IRA), and Regional Book Award, Mountains and Plains Booksellers Association, both 1990, all for *Bearstone;* Pick of the Lists, American Booksellers Association (ABA), 1991, ALA Best Books for Young Adults and Best Books for Reluctant Young Adult Readers citations, 1992,

Will Hobbs

ALA 100 Best Young Adult Books of the Past Twenty-five Years, 1994, and California Young Readers Medal, 1995, all for *Downriver;* ALA Best Books for Young Adults, 1993, for *The Big Wander;* ABA Pick of the Lists, and ALA Best Books for Young Adults, both 1993, and Spur Award, Western Writers of America, and Colorado Book Award, all for *Beardance;* NCSS/CBC Notable Trade Book in the Field of Social Studies, 1995, for *Kokopelli's Flute;* ALA Top Ten Best Books for Young Adults and Quick Picks for Reluctant Young Adult Readers, and NCSS/CBC Notable Trade Book in the Field of Social Studies, both 1996, Spur Award, and Colorado Book Award, all for *Far North;* ABA Pick of the Lists, 1997, and Edgar Allan Poe Award, Mystery Writers of America, 1998, both for *Ghost Canoe;* ABA Pick of the Lists, 1997, and Colorado Center for the Book Award, 1998, both for *Beardream;* IRA Young Adult Choice selection, 1998, for *River Thunder;* ALA Best Books for Young Adults and Quick Picks for Reluctant Young Adult Readers, ABA Pick of the Lists, and IRA Teachers' Choice, all 1998, all for *The Maze;* Best Books for Young Adults and Quick Picks for Reluctant Young Adult Readers, ALA, Pick of the Lists, ABA, and Notable Children's Trade Book in Social Studies, NCSS/CBC, all 1999, all for *Jason's Gold.* All Hobbs's titles have been nominated for various state readers' choice awards.

WRITINGS:

Changes in Latitudes, Atheneum (New York, NY), 1988.
Bearstone, Atheneum (New York, NY), 1989.
Downriver, Atheneum (New York, NY), 1991.
The Big Wander, Atheneum (New York, NY), 1992.
Beardance, Atheneum (New York, NY), 1993.
Kokopelli's Flute, Simon & Schuster (New York, NY), 1995.
Far North, Morrow (New York, NY), 1996.
Beardream, illustrated by Jill Kastner, Simon & Schuster (New York, NY), 1997.
Ghost Canoe, Morrow (New York, NY), 1997.
River Thunder, Delacorte (New York, NY), 1997.
Howling Hill, illustrated by Jill Kastner, Morrow (New York, NY), 1998.
The Maze, Morrow (New York, NY), 1998.
Jason's Gold, Morrow (New York, NY), 1999.
Down the Yukon, HarperCollins (New York, NY), 2001.
Wild Man Island, HarperCollins (New York, NY), 2002.
Jackie's Wild Seattle, HarperCollins (New York, NY), 2003.
Leaving Protection, HarperCollins (New York, NY), 2004.

Contributor of articles to periodicals, including *Horn Book, ALAN Review, Journal of Youth Services in Libraries, Journal of Adolescent and Adult Literacy, Book Links, Signal, Voices from the Middle, Voice of Youth Advocates,* and numerous state journals.

ADAPTATIONS: Hobbs's novels are available in unabridged audiocassette recordings from Recorded Books, Inc., Bantam Doubleday Dell Audio, and Listening Library. *Bearstone* was adapted as a play by Karen Glenn, published in *Scholastic Scope,* January 14, 1994; *Jason's Gold* and *Down the Yukon* were adapted as plays published in *READ* magazine.

SIDELIGHTS: Author Will Hobbs has a unique way of beginning each day. He winds up a toy pterodactyl and watches it cross his desk. By the time it gets to the other side, he must start writing. That's the deal. For about six hours a day he commits himself to the task of putting something on paper, and, as he explained in an interview for *Authors and Artists for Young Adults* (*AAYA*), "I owe at least three books, especially *Beardance,* to that little guy. I might have given up if it hadn't been for my deal with the pterodactyl." Hobbs's wilderness-based novels, which include *Bearstone, Kokopelli's Flute,* and *Far North,* have been well received by both his young-adult audience and reviewers alike, in part because he knows his audience; Hobbs taught reading and English for seventeen years, mostly in Durango, Colorado. In the *Colorado Reading Council Journal,* Hobbs stated: "I believe that if kids come to care about and identify with the characters in stories, they will also learn more about and ultimately care more about preserving the treasures of our natural world."

Hobbs's father was an engineer in the U.S. Air Force, so the family moved often. Born in Pittsburgh, Pennsylvania, the author was only six months old when the family moved to the Panama Canal Zone. After that, family moves included Virginia, Alaska, California, and Texas. Being close to his three brothers and one sister made the moves easier. They were all involved in scouting, and Hobbs developed a love for nature and the outdoors at an early age. He explained in his interview that his mother "contributed the gusto to my makeup. She feels that life is best lived as an adventure. At the age of seventy-three she rafted the Grand Canyon." His father introduced him to rivers in Alaska. Hobbs recounted, "Years later he joined me for three trips up the Pine River, where *Bearstone* takes place. It's my idea of heaven on earth, and I'll always be able to find him up there."

Although Hobbs has hiked and backpacked in many regions, it was the Southwest that captured his imagination. He spent two summers during high school and two during college in New Mexico as a guide and camp director at Philmont Scout Ranch. In 1973, together with his wife, Jean, he moved to southwestern Colorado, near the San Juan Mountains and the Weminuche Wilderness, the largest wilderness area in Colorado. Hobbs lives at the edge of Durango, in a wooded area adjoining thousands of acres of public land, and from his writing desk he looks out at snow-capped mountain peaks.

Hobbs was thirty-three before he started writing novels, the first being *Bearstone,* which took six different manuscripts and eight years before it was published. In the *California Reader,* Hobbs noted that the writing of *Bearstone* "fulfilled my dream of setting a story for others to enjoy in the upper Pine River country of the Weminuche Wilderness, one of three favorite places in the geography of my heart." It is in wilderness settings such as this that many of Hobbs's characters are tested—to push themselves and to learn their limits. Their journeys are often difficult.

Bearstone tells the story of Cloyd, a Ute Indian boy from Utah who has been sent by his tribe to spend the summer with an old rancher named Walter. Angry and hostile, Cloyd distrusts the old man's affection. While exploring the mountains nearby, Cloyd discovers an Indian burial site and a small bearstone and begins his self-discovery as he renames himself "Lone Bear" and learns how to "live in a good way," as his grandmother has taught him. An incident concerning a hunter who illegally kills a grizzly bear forces Cloyd to face the dilemma of whether to tell and get revenge, or keep silent. *School Library Journal* contributor George Gleason described *Bearstone* as "far above other coming-of-age stories."

Cloyd's story continues in *Beardance,* which Hobbs published in 1993. Cloyd and Walter ride into the mountains together in search of a lost gold mine when they hear about the sighting of a mother grizzly with three cubs. While searching for the cubs Cloyd meets a wildlife biologist on the same trail and ultimately risks his life by staying on alone, with winter approaching, in a heroic attempt to save two orphaned grizzly cubs. "Cloyd's first experiences with spirit dreams are particularly well done," said *Horn Book* writer Elizabeth S. Watson of *Beardance*. Praising Hobbs's "satisfying conclusion," Merlyn Miller observed in *Voice of Youth Advocates* that the book "weaves Native American legends with real adventure. Not only is Cloyd connected with his ancestry, but he's focused with courage, determination, and strength."

The character of Cloyd, the protagonist of both *Bearstone* and *Beardance,* is based on a student from a Durango group home whom Jean Hobbs had taught. The old rancher who teaches Cloyd so much about life and forgiveness is also based on someone Hobbs knows. The author had helped this rancher bring in hay, gaining a feel for the ranching life and listening to his stories about the mine he planned to reopen someday. *Beardream,* Hobbs's first picture book, also focuses on these characters. Illustrated by Jill Kastner, *Beardream* describes how a boy called Short Tail awakens an oversleeping grizzly bear from hibernation, and how, in ancient times, the Ute people learned the beardance from the bears. In an author's note at the end of *Beardream,* Hobbs stated: "It is my belief that future generations of the human family will have greater and greater need for the inspiration of native wisdom, which sees humankind not apart from nature, but as a part of nature." "This tale . . . is respectfully told, but it may be confusing to readers," stated Leda Schubert in a *School Library Journal* review. In a *Journal of Adolescent and Adult Literacy* article, a critic recommended that *Beardream* be read aloud in order that the listener may "experience the beautiful . . . language that is a hallmark of Hobbs's work."

Although *Bearstone* was the first novel Hobbs wrote, it was not the first to be published; *Changes in Latitudes,* written second, was released in 1988. The author explained that this story came much more easily for him, after the many revisions of *Bearstone*. As he explained to *AAYA,* Hobbs starts his stories "usually with a single image that I have a strong feeling about." The image in this case came from a photo from *National Geographic* of a sea turtle swimming underwater. Letting his imagination take over, the author wondered what it would be like to swim with the turtles, and he developed a story in which he could encourage readers to care about endangered species. What he ended up with is a novel about two kinds of endangered species: the turtles and a human family on the verge of breaking up. The novel's title is drawn from Jimmy Buffett's song "Changes in Latitudes, Changes in Attitudes."

In the novel, Travis, the oldest of three kids, is cynical and self-absorbed. At sixteen he attempts to hide himself from his problems by withdrawing into his own "cool" world. On vacation in Mexico with his mother, who has taken the trip without their father, Travis is only close to his little brother, Teddy. It is through Teddy that Travis becomes interested in the plight of the sea turtles. Nancy Vasilakis, writing in *Horn Book,* applauded Hobbs's talents as he "neatly balances the perilous situation of these ancient lumbering sea creatures against the breakdown of his family." She also commended the author for his "sensitive ear for the language of the young." When Teddy dies trying to rescue some of the turtles, Travis discovers that he can't run away from problems and relationships, and that hurt will, indeed, make you stronger.

Hobbs's third novel, *Downriver,* is set in the Grand Canyon, and the idea came from Hobbs's desire to have readers experience one of the great American adventures. Having rowed his raft through the rapids of the Grand Canyon ten times himself, Hobbs knows intimately the dangers and the beauty of the journey. Narrated by Jessie, a fifteen-year-old girl who has been sent away from home, this adventure story takes seven teens down the Grand Canyon where they are tested over and over again. Jessie and the rest of the group, known as "The Hoods in the Woods," leave their leader behind and take off on their own, consequently making their own decisions and living with the consequences. *Downriver* "is exquisitely plotted, with nail-biting suspense and excitement," wrote George Gleason in *School Library Journal. Booklist's* Candace Smith felt that "the ending is too tidy," but commended the novel's rafting scenes. "The scenery description is beautiful and the kids are believable," stated *Voice of Youth Advocates* writer Mary Ojibway.

Jessie and her companions are back together in *River Thunder,* published in 1997. In this story Jessie gets a chance to row the entire Colorado River through the Grand Canyon by herself. Unexpectedly high water on the river forces the entire group to confront their fears and to face the raging rapids of the Colorado together if they are to survive. In *Voice of Youth Advocates,* Cindy Lombardo felt that this sequel is "uninspired," perhaps due to a shortage of character development. Deborah Stevenson in the *Bulletin of the Center for Children's Books* commented that although the interpersonal relationships bog down the beginning of the novel, once the crew is on the river "Hobbs's terrific and involving descriptions" compensate for any shortcomings. "The vivid descriptions deliver high-volume excitement sure to entice many readers," said *School Library Journal's* Joel Shoemaker.

Hobbs was fourteen years old in 1962, the same age as Clay Lancaster in *The Big Wander.* "I recognize a kindred spirit in Clay Lancaster. We both have an adventuring outlook, we're both romantics, and goofy things tend to happen to both of us," Hobbs explained. He placed Clay in Glen Canyon in the last summer before it was flooded by Lake Powell. To write the story, Hobbs kept an image in his mind of a boy, a burro, and a dog adventuring in a "blank spot on the map," the magnificent canyon country of Utah. Clay and his brother head for the southwest to look for a missing uncle, but the brother returns home. On his own, with no one to tell him what to do, Clay begins a journey that leads him to a Navajo family, through remote canyons, and eventually to his uncle. In the process he has adventures escaping quicksand, flash floods, and bad guys, and also finds time for a little romance. Reviewer Kathleen Beck was quick to praise *The Big Wander,* calling it "a rousing adventure with an appealing hero" in her *Voice of Youth Advocates* review. *Booklist* critic Chris Sherman similarly hailed the work, describing it as "an adventure that most teens would love to experience themselves."

When Hobbs writes a story, first he does research about the settings, backgrounds, and historical events that will provide the story's foundation. For *The Big Wander* he hiked into his settings, then studied maps, photos, and writings about the canyons and other places that would make their way into his fiction. In addition to reading, he watched old westerns in the evenings, knowing that he wanted Clay's uncle to be a former rodeo star. He also developed ten plot outlines. Hobbs's protagonists have to learn to survive alone, but ultimately achieve personal goals by establishing a strong relationship with someone else. Even with such planning, according to Hobbs, *The Big Wander* turned out differently than he had anticipated.

In 1995's *Kokopelli's Flute,* fantasy enters Hobbs's western settings. Thirteen-year-old Tepary Jones and his dog, Dusty, journey to the ruins of an ancient Anasazi cliff house overlooking the canyons near Tepary's home on a seed farm in New Mexico. Hoping to see a total eclipse of the full moon from this remote location, Tep soon realizes that he is not alone when he surprises looters searching for Anasazi artifacts. Picking up an old flute made of eagle bone that the looters dropped in their hurry to get away, the teen finds himself in the grip of an ancient magic, which transforms him each night into a bushy-tailed woodrat. With the help of dog, Dusty, Tep is able to track down the looters and also obtain medicinal herbs that save his mother from a deadly sickness. Hobbs "blends fantasy with fact so smoothly that the resulting mix can be consumed without question," wrote Darcy Schild in a *School Library Journal* review, while in *Voice of Youth Advocates* Nancy Zachary called *Kokopelli's Flute* "an engaging and delightful tale."

Published in 1996, *Far North* takes readers into the rugged wilderness of Canada's Northwest Territories. Gabe Rogers, almost sixteen and fresh from Texas, has enrolled in a boarding school in Yellowknife in order to be closer to his father, who works on nearby diamond exploration rigs. His roommate, Raymond Providence, a native boy from a remote Dene village, decides to quit school after only a few months, and on a flight home in a small bush plane both Raymond and Gabe end up stranded on the banks of the Nahanni River. This winter survival story was described by *Horn Book* contributor Mary M. Burns as "a thrill-a-minute account of their struggle, against seemingly impossible odds." The critic added that *Far North* "is not just another page-turner; there are deeper issues addressed," such as the differences between the two boys' cultures. Diane Tuccillo stated in *Voice of Youth Advocates:* "This classic Hobbs adventure takes readers to a rugged, amazing wilderness few know. Characters are well-drawn, and excitement and energy penetrate their entire trek." The American Library Association named *Far North* one of the Top Ten Young Adult Books of 1996.

Also in the outdoor adventures vein, 1997's *Ghost Canoe* is Hobbs's first mystery novel, and the 1998 winner of the Edgar Allan Poe Award for Best Young Adult Mystery. Set in 1874 along the storm-tossed coast of Washington's Olympic Peninsula, this story follows fourteen-year-old Nathan MacAllister, the son of a lighthouse keeper. When a mysterious shipwreck leaves behind a set of unexplained footprints on the shore, Nathan suspects something is amiss. Writing in *School Library Journal*, Gerry Larson called *Ghost Canoe* "a winning tale that artfully combines history, nature, and suspense." In the *Bulletin of the Center for Children's Books,* Elizabeth Bush noted that although the book's mystery is predictable, there is enough action "to keep the pages flipping."

Although he has experienced first-hand many of the adventures he writes about, Hobbs's descriptions of hang gliding in *The Maze* are based on time spent with friends who fly, watching them jump off cliffs and soar. Like Icarus, young protagonist Rick Walker attempts to fly out of his own personal labyrinth, a life of foster homes and dead ends. "Rick is a richly-textured character," noted Sarah K. Herz in her *Voice of Youth Advocates* review. Hobbs set the story in the Maze, a remote region of Canyonlands National Park in Utah, an area noted for its beauty. Todd Morning, in a review for *School Library Journal,* asserted: "What sets this book apart is the inclusion of fascinating details about the condors and hang gliding, especially the action-packed description of Rick's first solo flight above the canyons. . . . Many young readers will find this an adventure story they can't put down." "Hobbs spins an engrossing yarn, blending adventure with a strong theme," said *Horn Book* writer Mary M. Burns.

Set amid the Klondike gold rush of 1897-98, *Jason's Gold* follows young Jason Hawthorn as he races to catch up to his brothers who have taken off for the gold fields in Canada's Yukon. Along the way he meets the not-yet-famous Jack London, but mostly he travels alone, with King, a husky he rescues from a madman. As he did in *Far North,* Hobbs creates an action-packed adventure story filled with vivid descriptions of bone-chilling cold, personal courage, and friendship.

Down the Yukon, the sequel to *Jason's Gold,* features a now sixteen-year-old Jason Hawthorn and Jamie Dunavant, who is still Jason's girlfriend. As the book begins, Jason's brother Ethan loses the family sawmill business in a poker game. In order to recover the property, Jamie and Jason decide to compete in a canoe race to Nome in which the winner receives $20,000 in prize money. Unfortunately, the same characters who swindled the business from Ethan have also entered the race, and they manage to sabotage the brothers' canoe. "The ending, though predictable, features an appropriate twist," remarked *Booklist* critic Catherine Andronik. In her *School Library Journal* review, Vicki Reutter stated that *Down the Yukon* is "more exciting than its predecessor."

A sea-kayaking trip in southeast Alaska with his wife inspired the setting for Hobbs's novel *Wild Man Island.* Fourteen-year-old Andy Galloway, the book's narrator, has enjoyed a guided sea-kayaking vacation. On the last day he decides to leave the other travelers for just a few hours in order to visit the waterfall where his archaeologist father accidentally met his death years before. Then a storm arises, washing Andy's kayak ashore on a remote and wild island. Hunger, cold, and grizzly bears threaten Andy's life until a Newfoundland dog befriends him and leads him to a cave whose only inhabitant is a seemingly wild man. "Hobbs resolves the story's complexities in ways that protect the characters' integrity," commented Joel Shoemaker in *School Library Journal.* In the *Journal of Adolescent and Adult Literacy,* James Blasingame agreed that the novel's "conflicts are resolved in a satisfying conclusion." *Wild Man Island* is "a well-paced novel," added *Horn Book*'s Burns, while a *Kirkus* reviewer commended the novel as "a rugged, satisfying episode for outdoorsy readers."

Jackie's Wild Seattle takes its name from a wildlife rehabilitation center in Seattle, Washington, that is central to this book's plot. Shannon and her brother become involved in their Uncle Neal's work with animals when they spend their summer vacation with him, and help rescue coyotes, bear cubs, raccoons and birds of prey. Mary R. Hoffman wrote in *School Library Journal,* "this exciting, poignant, and beautifully developed story covers a crucial few weeks for several people whose lives intertwine to change and benefit all. . . . This story will reach deep into the hearts of young readers."

In the summer of 2002, Hobbs had the opportunity to work on a salmon troller in southeast Alaska. He'd met a teacher from Craig, on Prince of Wales Island, who had earned her way through college working on her father's fishing boat. She invited him to work on their boat, and write a novel about life on a salmon troller. The result was *Leaving Protection,* a heart-pounding adventure on Alaska's stormy seas.

When sixteen-year-old Robbie Daniels leaves his home in Port Protection for the nearby fishing town of Craig, hoping to find work as a deckhand for king salmon season, he can hardly believe hid good fortune when legendary fisherman Tor Torsen unexpectedly hires him on. Out on the open ocean, alone with Tor, Robbie discovers his mysterious captain is not only fishing, he's searching along the coastline for historic metal plaques buried by early Russian explorers laying claim to Alaska. When Robbie learns how valuable these possession plaques are, he fears for his life, as Tor's wrath and a violent storm at sea put his courage and wit to the ultimate test.

BIOGRAPHICAL AND CRITICAL SOURCES:

BOOKS

Authors and Artists for Young Adults, Volume 39, Gale (Detroit, MI), 2001.
Encyclopedia of Children's Literature, Continuum (New York, NY), 2001.
Gallo, Donald R., editor, *Speaking for Ourselves Too,* National Council of Teachers of English, 1993.
Hobbs, Will, *Beardream,* Simon & Schuster (New York, NY), 1997.
Hobbs, Will, *Ghost Canoe,* Morrow (New York, NY), 1997.
Writers for Young Adults, edited by Ted Hipple, Scribner (New York, NY), 1997, pp. 121-129.

PERIODICALS

ALAN Review, fall, 1994.
Booklist, March 1, 1991, Candace Smith, review of *Downriver,* p. 1377; October 15, 1992, p. 424; May 1, 1997; September 1, 1997, p. 106; September 1, 1998, p. 126; February 15, 2000, Jeanette Larson, review of *Ghost Canoe* (audiobook), p. 1128; March 15, 2000, review of *Jason's Gold,* p. 1340; April 1, 2001, Catherine Andronik, review of *Down the Yukon,* p. 1482; November 15, 2001, Anna Rich, review of *Down the Yukon* (audiobook), p. 589; April 15, 2002, review of *Wild Man Island,* p. 1395.
Bulletin of the Center for Children's Books, April, 1997, Elizabeth Bush, review of *Ghost Canoe,* p. 285; July, 1997, Deborah Stevenson, review of *River Thunder,* pp. 397-398.
California Reader, winter, 1992, pp. 15-16.
Colorado Reading Council Journal, spring, 1993, pp. 7-9.
Five Owls, fall, 2001, review of *Kokopelli's Flute, The Maze, Downriver,* and *Beardance,* p. 2.
Horn Book, May-June, 1988, p. 358; January-February, 1993, p. 91; January-February, 1994, Elizabeth S. Watson, review of *Beardance,* p. 70; March-April, 1996; November-December, 1996, p. 745; September-October, 1998, Mary M. Burns, review of *The Maze,* p. 609; July-August, 2002, Mary M. Burns, review of *Wild Man Island,* p. 462.
Journal of Adolescent and Adult Literacy, September, 1997, review of *Beardream,* p. 83; May, 2000, Joel Taxel, review of *The Maze,* pp. 780-781; February, 2003, James Blasingame, review of *Wild Man Island,* pp. 442-443.
Journal of Youth Services in Libraries, spring, 1995.
Kirkus Reviews, March 15, 1997, p. 462; March 15, 2002, review of *Wild Man Island,* p. 413; March 15, 2003, review of *Jackie's Wild Seattle,* p. 468.
Kliatt, September, 1999, p. 8; March, 2002, review of *Wild Man Island,* p. 11.
Publishers Weekly, February 12, 1988, p. 88; February 1, 1991, pp. 80-81; November 2, 1992, p. 72; October 12, 1998, review of *Howling Hill,* p. 77.

School Library Journal, March, 1988, pp. 212, 214; September, 1989, p. 272; March, 1991, George Gleason, review of *Downriver,* p. 212; November, 1992, p. 92; December, 1993, p. 134; October, 1995, p. 134; April, 1997, Leda Schubert, review of *Beardream,* p. 104; September, 1997, Joel Shoemaker, review of *River Thunder,* p. 217; October 1998, Virginia Golodetz, review of *Howling Hill,* p. 102; May, 2001, Vicki Reutter, review of *Down the Yukon,* p. 150; October, 2001, Sandra L. Doggett, review of *Down the Yukon* (audiobook), p. 89; May, 2002, Joel Shoemaker, review of *Wild Man Island,* p. 154.

Voice of Youth Advocates, August, 1991, Mary Ojibway, review of *Downriver,* pp. 171-172; December, 1992, p. 279; December, 1993, p. 292; February, 1996, p. 372; February, 1997, p. 328; October, 1997, Cindy Lombardo, review of *River Thunder,* p. 244; February, 1999, Sarah K. Herz, review of *The Maze,* p.434; June, 2001, review of *Down the Yukon,* p. 122.

* * *

HOBERMAN, Mary Ann 1930-

PERSONAL: Born August 12, 1930, in Stamford, CT; daughter of Milton and Dorothy (Miller) Freedman; married Norman Hoberman (an architect, artist, and illustrator), February 4, 1951; children: Diane, James, Charles, Margaret. *Education:* Smith College, B.A., 1951; Yale University, M.A. 1985. *Politics:* Liberal Democrat. *Hobbies and other interests:* Gardening, reading, tennis, music.

ADDRESSES: Home—98 Hunting Ridge Rd., Greenwich, CT 06831. *Agent*—Gina Maccoby Literary Agency, P. O. Box 60, Chappaqua, NY 10514-0060.

CAREER: Writer, poet, speaker, consultant, artist-in-the-schools, 1955—. Founder and member of The Pocket People (children's theater group), 1968-75; Fairfield University, Fairfield, CT, adjunct professor, 1980-83.

AWARDS, HONORS: Book Week Poem Award, Children's Book Council, 1976; American Book Award, 1983, for *A House Is a House for Me;* National Council of Teachers of English award, 2003, for poetry for children.

Mary Ann Hoberman

WRITINGS:

CHILDREN'S BOOKS

All My Shoes Come in Two's, illustrated by Norman Hoberman, Little, Brown (Boston, MA), 1957.

How Do I Go?, illustrated by Norman Hoberman, Little, Brown (Boston, MA), 1958.

Hello and Good-by, illustrated by Norman Hoberman, Little, Brown (Boston, MA), 1959.

What Jim Knew, illustrated by Norman Hoberman, Little, Brown (Boston, MA), 1963.

Not Enough Beds for the Babies, illustrated by Helen Spyer, Little, Brown (Boston, MA), 1965.

A Little Book of Little Beasts, illustrated by Peter Parnall, Simon & Schuster (New York, NY), 1973.

The Looking Book, illustrated by Jerry Joyner, Knopf (New York, NY), 1973.

The Raucous Auk, illustrated by Joseph Low, Viking (New York, NY), 1973.

Nuts to You and Nuts to Me, illustrated by Ronni Solbert, Knopf (New York, NY), 1974.

I Like Old Clothes, illustrated by Jacqueline Chwast, Knopf (New York, NY), 1976.

Bugs, illustrated by Victoria Chess, Viking (New York, NY), 1976.

A House Is a House for Me, illustrated by Betty Fraser, Viking (New York, NY), 1978.

Yellow Butter, Purple Jelly, Red Jam, Black Bread: Poems, illustrated by Chaya Burstein, Viking (New York, NY), 1981.

The Cozy Book, illustrated by Tony Chen, Viking (New York, NY), 1982.

Mr. and Mrs. Muddle, illustrated by Catharine O'Neill, Little, Brown (Boston, MA), 1988.

A Fine Fat Pig, and Other Animal Poems, illustrated by Malcah Zeldis, HarperCollins (New York, NY), 1991.

Fathers, Mothers, Sisters, Brothers: A Collection of Family Poems, illustrated by Marilyn Hafner, Little, Brown (Boston, MA), 1991.

(Editor) *My Song Is Beautiful: Poems and Pictures in Many Voices,* Little, Brown (Boston, MA), 1994.

The Cozy Book, illustrated by Betty Frazer, Little, Brown (Boston, MA), 1995.

One of Each, illustrated by Marjorie Priceman, Little, Brown (Boston, MA), 1997.

The Seven Silly Eaters, illustrated by Marla Frazee, Harcourt (San Diego, CA), 1997.

The Llama Who Had No Pajama, illustrated by Betty Fraser, Harcourt (San Diego, CA), 1998.

Miss Mary Mack: A Hand-Clapping Rhyme, illustrated by Nadine Bernard Westcott, Little, Brown (Boston, MA), 1998.

And to Think That We Thought We Would Never Be Friends, illustrated by Kevin Hawkes, Crown (New York, NY), 1999.

The Marvelous Mouse Man, illustrated by Laura Forman, Harcourt (San Diego, CA), 1999.

The Eensy-Weensy Spider, Little, Brown (Boston, MA), 2000.

There Once Was a Man Named Michael Finnegan, Little, Brown (Boston, MA), 2001.

You Read to Me, I'll Read to You: Very Short Stories to Read Together, Little, Brown (Boston, MA), 2001.

It's Simple, Said Simon, illustrated by Meilo So, Knopf (New York, NY), 2001.

Bill Grogan's Goat, Little, Brown (Boston, MA), 2002.

The Marvelous Mouse Man, illustrated by Laura Forman, Harcourt (San Diego, CA), 2002.

The Looking Book, illustrated by Laura Huliska-Beith, Little, Brown (Boston, MA), 2002.

Right Outside My Window, illustrated by Nicholas Wilton, Mondo (New York, NY), 2002.

Whose Garden Is It?, illustrated by Jane Dyer, Harcourt (San Diego, CA), 2004.

Also author of adaptation of *Mary Had a Little Lamb,* Little Brown (New York, NY), 2003, and *Yankee Doodle,* Little, Brown (Boston, MA), 2004.

WORK IN PROGRESS: Third volume of *You Read to Me, I'll Read to You;* other picture books.

SIDELIGHTS: According to an essayist for the *St. James Guide to Children's Writers,* "Mary Ann Hoberman is a poet who likes to write poetry, who can hardly wait to finish one poem so she can start on another. She especially likes to write for children, because she enjoys rhythm and rhyme as they do. For Hoberman, an odd fact or the sound of a name catches her ear, or rhythm catches her feet, and she can't get rid of it. So she writes her poem to be free of it; then she is able to turn her attention to another poem."

Among Hoberman's most popular titles is *You Read to Me, I'll Read to You: Very Short Stories to Read Together,* a collection of thirteen stories-in-rhyme meant to be read aloud by two friends who alternate reading the lines of each poem. Differently-colored texts distinguish between the two parts. *Horn Book Magazine* reviewer Roger Sutton wrote that "each poem bounces back and forth between readers beautifully." Judy Freeman in the *Instructor* noted that the poems "will encourage children to read with each other or with a grown-up." *School Library Journal* contributor Mary Ann Carcich found *You Read to Me, I'll Read to You* to be "a valuable addition to picturebook collections."

In *The Marvelous Mouse Man,* Hoberman retells in verse the traditional story of the Pied Piper. This time, however, the mouse man uses a cheese-scented fan to draw the mice out of town. But then things go wrong: the cats follow the mice, and the dogs follow the cats, and the children follow their pets out of town as well. Wendy Lukehart in the *School Library Journal* believed that "Hoberman's poem is skillfully constructed." A critic for *Publishers Weekly* concluded, "Hoberman's agile and comical verse cleverly contorts a classic and adds a second star: an appealing young heroine."

Hoberman's verses, the essayist for the *St. James Guide to Children's Writers* believed, "will cause giggles as they are read to the preschool child and by the primary grader. Young children will relate to Hoberman's rhythms and to the fine illustrations.... These works may even encourage the reader to try a rhyme, a picture of his own, or to read another book of poetry."

Hoberman told *CA:* "I've been writing forever! Even before I knew how to write, when I was four and five years old, I used to make up stories for myself and to tell to my little brother. We had a game—we called it 'Drawing Pictures and Telling Stories'—where I would draw little stick figures in a comic book sequential format and narrate their adventures. And I was always making up poems and songs for myself while I played in the yard and, especially, while I swung on my swing.

"In a long lifetime the influences on one's work are myriad, most of them by now forgotten, but I must always credit fairy tales read to me when I was very young for awakening my ear and imagination. Walter de la Mare, especially, in his collection *Told Again*, a book I still have, brought me unfathomable joy and made me decide that I too would someday be a writer.

"If I ever had a regular writing process, it is long gone! I get ideas everywhere and at any time—on my morning walks, in my bed at night, driving around town on errands, talking with friends. I write mainly with a fountain pen on a yellow lined pad and I gravitate around my house to wherever the sunshine is. It is only when I have a first or even second draft that I approach the computer.

"Of all my books my favorite is a tiny one, long out of print, called *Hello and Good-by*. It contains many of my early and still favorite poems and is illustrated with simple line drawings by my husband Norman. I specifically asked that it be small enough for a little child's hands, a somewhat unusual format in those days. I only have a few shabby well-read family copies, which makes it even more precious.

"If my books awaken some children to a love of language, to a sense of the magical qualities in individual words and their combinations, to a feeling that they, too, can make up poems and stories, I am grateful. But even more, I want my books to bring joy and delight to their young readers and listeners—simple joy and delight."

BIOGRAPHICAL AND CRITICAL SOURCES:

BOOKS

Children' Literature Review, Volume 22, Gale (Detroit, MI), 1991.
St. James Guide to Children's Writers, 5th edition, St. James Press (Detroit, MI), 1999.
Something about the Author Autobiography Series, Volume 18, Gale (Detroit, MI), 1994.

PERIODICALS

Book, March-April, 2002, "Recommended Children's Reading," p. 81.
Booklist, August, 2001, John Peters, review of *You Read to Me, I'll Read to You,* p. 2124; July, 2002, Hazel Rochman, review of *The Looking Book,* p. 1859; August, 2002, Julie Cummins, review of *Right Outside My Window,* p. 1972.
Horn Book, November-December, 2001, Roger Sutton, review of *You Read to Me, I'll Read to You,* p. 766.
Instructor, April, 2002, Judy Freeman, review of *You Read to Me, I'll Read to You,* p. 14.
New York Times Book Review, April 15, 2001, review of *It's Simple, Said Simon,* p. 24; January 20, 2002, review of *You Read to Me, I'll Read to You,* p. 14.
Publishers Weekly, April 23, 2001, "All A-Board!," p. 80; August 6, 2001, review of *You Read to Me, I'll Read to You,* p. 89; March 18, 2002, review of *The Marvelous Mouse Man,* p. 102; April 15, 2002, review of *The Looking Book,* p. 63; April 29, 2002, review of *Right Outside My Window,* p. 68.
School Library Journal, May, 2001, Piper L. Nyman, review of *There Once Was a Man Named Michael Finnegan,* p. 142; August, 2001, Mary Ann Carcich, review of *You Read to Me, I'll Read to You,* p. 153; April, 2002, Carol Schene, review of *Bill Grogan's Goat,* p. 132; May, 2002, Wendy Lukehart, review of *The Marvelous Mouse Man,* p. 117; June, 2002, Dona Ratterree, review of *The Looking Book,* p. 97.

ONLINE

Mary Ann Hober Home Page, http://www.maryannhoberman.com/ (November 24, 2003).

* * *

HOOD, Roger (Grahame) 1936-

PERSONAL: Born June 12, 1936, in Bristol, England; son of Ronald Hugo Frederick (a stockbroker's dealer) and Phyllis Eileen (a homemaker; maiden name, Murphy) Hood; married Barbara Blaine (a housing adviser), July, 1963 (divorced, July, 1985); married Nancy Colquitt Lynah Stebbing (a director of leisure and arts), October 5, 1985; children: Catharine Rachael. *Ethnicity:* "White European." *Education:* London School of Economics and Political Science, London, B.Sc., 1957; Cambridge University, Ph.D., 1963.

ADDRESSES: Home—63 Iffley Rd., Oxford OX4 1EF, England. *Office*—c/o All Souls College, Oxford University, Oxford OX1 4AL, England; fax: 44-1-86-527-4445. *E-mail*—roger.hood@crim.ox.ac.uk.

CAREER: University of London, London School of Economics and Political Science, London, England, research officer, 1957-58 and 1961-63; University of Durham, Durham, England, lecturer in social administration, 1963-67; Cambridge University, Cambridge, England, fellow of Clare Hall and assistant director of research, director of postgraduate studies, and secretary to Institute of Criminology, 1967-73; Oxford University, Oxford, England, reader, 1973-95, professor of criminology, 1995-2003, fellow of All Souls College, 1973-2003, emeritus fellow, 2003—, sub-warden of the college, 1994-96, director of Centre for Criminological Research, beginning 1973. Columbia University, visiting professor, 1971; University of Virginia, visiting distinguished professor of law, 1980-82 and 1984-90; Florida State University, Ball Lecturer, 1996; University of Hong Kong, visiting distinguished professor, 2003-04; speaker at other institutions, including University of the Saarland, University of Frankfurt, and University of Hull. Parole Board for England and Wales, member, 1972-73; Social Science Research Council, member of Committee for Social Sciences and the Law, 1975-79; Judicial Studies Board, member, 1979-85; British Home Office, member of Departmental Committee to Review the Parole System, 1987-88. Amnesty International, member of international panel of jurists, Commission of Inquiry into the Death Penalty in America, 1993, foreign secretary of Death Penalty Panel, 1998—; also served as expert consultant on the death penalty to United Nations.

MEMBER: British Academy (fellow), British Society of Criminology (president, 1987-89), Academy of Learned Societies for the Social Sciences (academician).

AWARDS, HONORS: Joseph L. Andrews Award, American Association of Law Librarians, 1976, for *Criminology and the Administration of Criminal Justice: A Bibliography;* Sellin-Glück Award, American Society of Criminology, 1986; commander, Order of the British Empire, 1995; honorary D.C.L., Oxford University, 1999; decorated honorary Queen's Counsel, 2000.

WRITINGS:

Sentencing in Magistrates' Courts, Stevens (London, England), 1962.
Borstal Re-Assessed, Heinemann Educational (London, England), 1965.
(With Richard Sparks) *Key Issues in Criminology,* Weidenfeld & Nicolson (London, England), 1970.
Sentencing the Motoring Offender, Heinemann Educational (London, England), 1972.
(Editor and contributor) *Crime, Criminology, and Public Policy: Essays in Honour of Sir Leon Radzinowicz,* Heinemann Educational (London, England), 1974.
Tolerance and the Tariff: Some Reflections on Fixing the Time Prisoners Serve in Custody, National Association for the Care and Resettlement of Offenders (London, England), 1974.
(Editor, with Leon Radzinowicz) *Criminology and the Administration of Criminal Justice: A Bibliography,* Mansell (London, England), 1976.
(With Leon Radzinowicz) *A History of English Criminal Law and Its Administration,* Volume V: *The Emergence of Penal Policy,* Stevens (London,

England), 1986, published as *The Emergence of Penal Policy in Victorian and Edwardian England,* Oxford University Press (Oxford, England), 1990.
- (Editor) *Crime and Criminal Policy in Europe: Proceedings of a European Colloquium,* Centre for Criminological Research, Oxford University (Oxford, England), 1989.
- *The Death Penalty: A World Survey,* United Nations (New York, NY), 1989, 3rd edition, Oxford University Press (Oxford, England), 2002.
- (With Graca Cordovil) *Race and Sentencing: A Study in the Crown Court,* Oxford University Press (Oxford, England), 1992.
- (With Stephen Shute) *The Parole System at Work: A Study of Rick-Based Decision-Making,* Research, Development, and Statistics Directorate, Home Office (London, England), 2000.
- (With Stephen Shute) *Ethnic Minorities in the Criminal Courts: Perceptions of Fairness and Equal Treatment,* Lord Chancellor's Department (London, England), 2003.

Contributor to books, including *Collected Studies in Criminological Research,* Volume I, Council of Europe (Strasbourg, France), 1966; *Parole: Its Implications for the Criminal Justice and Penal Systems,* edited by D. A. Thomas, Institute of Criminology, Cambridge University (Cambridge, England), 1974; *Crime, Proof, and Punishment: Essays in Memory of Sir Rupert Cross,* edited by C. Tapper, Butterworth (London, England), 1981; *The Crime and Justice Handbook,* edited by Michael Tonry, Oxford University Press (New York, NY), 1998; and *The Death Penalty: Abolition in Europe,* Council of Europe Publishing (Strasbourg, France), 1999, 2nd edition, 2003. General editor, "Clarendon Studies in Criminology," Oxford University Press (Oxford, England), 1994-97. Contributor of articles and reviews to law journals and newspapers. *British Journal of Criminology,* member of editorial board, 1973-88, and past coeditor; member of editorial board of *Crime and Justice: Annual Review of Research,* 1988-99, and *European Journal of Crime, Criminal Law, and Criminal Justice,* 1993—.

SIDELIGHTS: Roger Hood once told *CA:* "My prime motivation to work in the field of criminology has been to attempt to bring a greater understanding, rationality, justice, and humanity to the discussion of the problem of crime and the punishment of offenders."

HORN, Stacy 1956-

PERSONAL: Born June 3, 1956, in VA. *Education:* Attended Tufts University; School of the Museum of Fine Arts, Boston, M.A., B.F.A, 1978; New York University, M.A., 1989. *Hobbies and other interests:* Drummer in Manhattan samba group.

ADDRESSES: Office—Echo Communications Group, 97 Perry St., No. 13, New York, NY 10014; fax 212-292-0909. *Agent*—Betsy Lerner, The Gernert Company, 136 East 57th St., Floor 18, New York, NY 10022-2923. *E-mail*—horn@echonyc.com.

CAREER: Founder and director, Echo Communications Group, New York, NY, 1989—.

WRITINGS:

- *Cyberville: Clicks, Culture, and the Creation of an Online Town,* Warner Books (New York, NY), 1998.
- *Waiting for My Cats to Die: A Morbid Memoir,* St. Martin's Press (New York, NY), 2001.

Editor, with Theresa M. Senft, "Sexuality and Cyberspace" issue of *Women & Performance: A Journal of Feminist Theory,* 1997.

WORK IN PROGRESS: The Restless Sleep: Inside New York City's Cold Case Squad, for Viking (New York, NY), winter, 2005.

SIDELIGHTS: Stacy Horn is one of the pioneers in creative uses for the Internet. In 1989, before the growth of such online services as Compuserv and America Online, Horn used severance pay from a previous job to launch the online service Echo Communications from her tiny Greenwich Village apartment. Echo, which stands for East Coast Hang Out, quickly developed a reputation as a particularly imaginative and literate cyberspace community—an online site where members log on to "chat" about diverse subjects. By 1992 Echo had 1,500 members, nearly forty percent of them female. This made Echo's electronic bulletin board the most female-oriented in cy-

Stacy Horn

berspace, and Horn created a mentor program to orient new women members of the service. Horn's experience with Echo gave her the opportunity to study gender differences in online behavior, experience she drew on as coeditor of the 1997 "Sexuality and Cyberspace" issue of *Women & Performance: A Journal of Feminist Theory.*

The story of how Echo developed into such a popular online community became the subject of Horn's first book, *Cyberville: Clicks, Culture, and the Creation of an Online Town.* The book is Horn's analysis of what cyberspace communities are and emphasizes the human nature of this technological world. "I'd say that everybody . . . has a trace of an ache," she writes, "that is satisfied, at least for a minute each day, by a familiar group and by a place that will always be there. This is what online communities offer: a connection to people." Horn comments on the relationships that develop in such communities and emphasizes that conflicts arise in cyberspace just as they do elsewhere, but that this is part of the way a community develops: "This is how communities are formed. Not by creating a place and putting out a welcome sign. They are formed and strengthened through the resolution of conflict."

Horn is also frank about the potential for romance online. "I started Echo to meet guys," she writes, admitting that "Cyberspace is a most erotic medium." Sexuality emerges, Horn explains, despite the fact that members have only words with which to communicate online. "The illusion of free and unbiased communication can only be maintained . . . as long as people hide. . . . In time, if you act yourself, gender is revealed. Because we do take our bodies with us." Several Echo members openly flirt, and some eventually meet. According to Jeff Yang in *Mademoiselle,* Horn says that Echo has introduced many happy couples. "Echo is a regular Peyton Place," quipped Horn.

Reviewers enjoyed the warmth and humor they found in *Cyberville. Publishers Weekly* particularly appreciated the book's accessibility, noting that Horn eschews the jargon and self-importance found in other writing on the subject of cyberspace. Harold Goldberg, in the *New York Times Book Review,* praised *Cyberville* as "a breathless mixture of essays and rants that are rife with sagacity and introspection." Although Goldberg was disappointed that Horn did not provide more details about Echo as a business concern, he admired the book's overall tone and message. "*Cyberville* resonates," he concluded, "because, beyond helping us get inside the technology that separates us as much as it brings us together, the words of the author and of the Echoids are about the souls of people."

The flourishing of other online chat rooms has eroded Echo's fan base, but it is still thriving as a cultural and literate site, with links to book excerpts, music and film reviews, and information on the arts. One of the more recent postings to the site concerns Horn's second book, *Waiting for My Cats to Die: A Morbid Memoir.* In this book Horn examines her eccentricities as she descends into an early mid-life crisis: her obsession with death, her television habits, her slavish devotion to two sick house cats, and her occasional encounters with the ghost in her apartment. The short chapters seek answers to some of life's larger questions and dwell upon the inevitable disappointments. A *Publishers Weekly* reviewer described the work as a "remarkably candid account of one woman's acceptance of aging, piqued with heartening moments of exhilaration." In her *St. Petersburg Times* review of *Waiting for My Cats to Die,* Samantha Puckett wrote: "The conversational tone is engaging. It's as though [Horn is] sitting across the table from you, having a casual chat. . . .

And you like her right away. She's funny and smart and willing to share all her shortcomings with you." *Booklist* contributor Jenny McLarin found the work anything but morbid; rather, McLarin called it "a strong and lovely statement about the joy of life."

Horn told *CA:* "I got interested in writing in the third grade, when a girl in my class wrote a story and stood up and read it to the class. I'd been making up stories in my head for as long as I could think, and it never occurred to me to write them down. 'You can do that?' I was jealous of her. Angry at myself for not thinking of it myself, I immediately got to work."

BIOGRAPHICAL AND CRITICAL SOURCES:

BOOKS

Horn, Stacy, *Cyberville: Clicks, Culture, and the Creation of an Online Town,* Warner Books (New York, NY), 1998.

Horn, Stacy, *Waiting for My Cats to Die: A Morbid Memoir,* St. Martin's Press (New York, NY), 2001.

PERIODICALS

Analog, October, 1997, p. 153.

Atlanta Journal-Constitution (Atlanta, GA), April 14, 1998, Frances Katz, "ECHO Founder Tells of Life in Online Town," p. C5.

Booklist, January 1, 2001, Jenny McLarin, review of *Waiting for My Cats to Die: A Morbid Memoir,* p. 884.

Library Journal, December, 1997, p. 143.

Link-Up, November-December, 1996, Gary M. Stern, "Echo: The Virtual Salon of NYC," p. 12.

Mademoiselle, October, 1993, p. 170.

New York Times Book Review, February 15, 1998.

Publishers Weekly, November 24, 1997, p. 61; January 29, 2001, Lynn Andriani, "PW Talks with Stacy Horn" and review of *Waiting for My Cats to Die,* p. 77.

St. Petersburg Times, February 11, 2001, Samantha Puckett, "Obsessing over Life with Humor," p. 4D.

ONLINE

EchoNYC, http://www.echonyc.com/ (February 20, 2003), author's Web site.

HOVING, Thomas (Pearsall Field) 1931-

PERSONAL: Born January 15, 1931, in New York, NY; son of Walter (in business) and Mary Osgood (Field) Hoving; married Nancy Melissa Bell (a management consultant), October 3, 1953; children: Petrea Bell. *Education:* Princeton University, B.A. (summa cum laude), 1953, M.F.A., 1958, Ph.D., 1959.

ADDRESSES: Home and office—Hoving Associates, 150 East 73rd St., New York, NY 10021. *E-mail*—tomhoving@earthlink.net.

CAREER: Museum and cultural affairs consultant, author. Metropolitan Museum of Art, Department of Medieval Art and the Cloisters, New York, NY, curatorial assistant, 1959-60, assistant curator, 1960-63, associate curator, 1963-65, curator, 1965-66; New York City commissioner of parks, New York, NY, 1966-67, administrator of recreation and cultural affairs, 1967; Metropolitan Museum of Art, director, 1967-77; management consultant, 1977—. Correspondent and interviewer for American Broadcasting Co. (ABC-TV) feature news program *20/20.* Director of International Business Machines (IBM) Americas, H. S. Stuttman Co., and Manhattan Industries. *Military service:* U.S. Marine Corps, 1953-55; became first lieutenant.

MEMBER: American Institute of Architects (honorary member).

AWARDS, HONORS: National Council of the Humanities fellowship, 1955; Kienbusch and Haring fellowship, 1957; distinguished citizen award from Citizens Budget Committee, 1966; award from *Cue* magazine, 1966; LL.D. from Pratt Institute, 1967; distinguished achievement award from Advertising Club of America, 1968; LL.D. from Princeton University, 1968; D.F.A. from New York University, 1968; Litt.D. from Middlebury College, 1968.

WRITINGS:

The Sources of the Ivories of the Ada School (Ph.D. thesis), Princeton University Press (Princeton, NJ), 1960.

(Editor) *The Chase, the Capture: Collecting at the Metropolitan,* Metropolitan Museum of Art (New York, NY), 1975.

Thomas Hoving

Two Worlds of Andrew Wyeth: Kuerners and Olsons, Metropolitan Museum of Art (New York, NY), 1976.

Tutankhamun: The Untold Story, Simon & Schuster (New York, NY), 1978.

King of the Confessors, Simon & Schuster (New York, NY), 1981.

Masterpiece (novel), Simon & Schuster (New York, NY), 1986.

Discovery! (novel), Simon & Schuster (New York, NY), 1989.

Making the Mummies Dance: Inside the Metropolitan Museum of Art, Simon & Schuster (New York, NY), 1993.

(With Andrew Wyeth) *Andrew Wyeth: Autobiography, As Told to Thomas Hoving,* Bulfinch (Boston, MA), 1995.

False Impressions: The Hunt for Big-Time Art Fakes, Simon & Schuster (New York, NY), 1996.

Greatest Works of Art of Western Civilization, Artisan/Workman (New York, NY), 1997.

Art for Dummies, foreword by Andrew Wyeth, IDG Books Worldwide (Foster City, CA), 1999.

The Art of Dan Namingha, Abrams (New York, NY), 2000.

Author of Metropolitan Museum of Art guidebooks and art calendars. Consultant to *Museums, New York* and author of its column "Happenings." Contributor of articles to *Apollo, House Beautiful,* and *Metropolitan Museum of Art Bulletin.* Editor for *Connoisseur.*

SIDELIGHTS: Thomas Hoving joined the curatorial staff of the Metropolitan Museum of Art in New York City in 1959 after James J. Rorimer, the museum director at that time, heard Hoving lecture at New York's Frick Collection on the Annibale Carracci frescoes of the Farnese Gallery in Rome. Hoving started as a curatorial assistant in the Cloisters, the Metropolitan's collection of medieval art, which includes a number of intact medieval cloisters, or enclosed colonnades, brought over from Europe. Hoving quickly moved up to curator of the Met's Cloisters, in part because of his discovery of the twelfth-century medieval ivory, the controversial Bury St. Edmunds Cross. Following that, Hoving took a brief respite from the art world by joining the New York City Parks Department as commissioner under the auspices of 1966 mayor John Lindsay. Building a reputation for himself as a great public relations man for the parks system, Hoving was soon romanced back to the Metropolitan when, in 1967, his former mentor Rorimer died and Hoving was appointed the new director of the largest art museum in the world.

Hoving spent ten years at the Met, striving to change the museum's operations and attempting to make art more accessible to all people, which at times rattled many a cage in the New York art community. As he recalled in a *New York Metro* online interview by Michael Gross, "When I became the director of the Metropolitan Museum of Art, it was stodgy, gray, run by elitists. I said, 'Hey, let's kick the thing around.' I wanted to attract young people to the museum." Hoving's idea of having blockbuster exhibits, advertising in newspapers and magazines, and encouraging loitering on the building's front steps introduced a new generation to the exciting possibilities of visual art. Considered a maverick during his ten-year tenure with the Met, Hoving is today recognized as a significant force in creating and sustaining interest in museums and art collections.

Since his departure from the Met, Hoving has been writing about his many adventures in the art world, particularly about his tenure at the Met. His writing has shattered myths, reputations, and pretenses of the world art community. Though some critics have considered his work controversial, claiming his sense of detail too sketchy or too embellished, or Hoving's truths to be his truths alone, Hoving's books have been very popular with the public. His titles have spent many weeks on *The New York Times* bestseller lists. Answering his critics in his online interview, Hoving stated: "It's virtually impossible to cheapen a great work of art by popularizing it!" What he suggests in his books instead is that one need not have vast education or prior knowledge of art works to enjoy the experience of attending a museum.

In 1977, Hoving's book *Tutankhamun: The Untold Story* was published to coincide with the first American tour of the treasures of the ancient Egyptian pharaoh. Hoving's work joined the "King Tut" craze, but with a twist. In this volume the author discusses the fascinating and controversial tale of Howard Carter's discovery of King Tutankhamun's tomb in 1922 and his celebratory, and clandestine, "pilfering" of the archaeological site. Barbara G. Mertz thought the book somewhat clarified the real picture of archaeology and Egyptology, commenting that *Tutankhamun* "gives considerable insight into the sometimes sordid, sometimes amusing complications that affect all human activities, even archaeology."

Hoving's *King of the Confessors* reveals the history and capture of the Bury St. Edmunds cross, a twelfth-century medieval ivory. Here the reader discovers Hoving's obsessive involvement and pursuit, on an international scale, of the controversial acquisition of this damaged, incomplete, yet highly valuable medieval artifact. The cross cost the Met $600,000, a very large sum by 1960s standards. In a 1980 interview with *Contemporary Authors* Hoving explained, "That twelfth-century cross, which I consider to be one of the greatest works of art ever created . . . changed my life. . . . It is owing to that cross that I became director of the Metropolitan." Accusing Hoving of self-aggrandizement, Walter Goodman, writing for the *New York Times Book Review,* stated, "The promotional pizazz that marked Mr. Hoving's reign at the Met is here devoted to himself. He concedes that ambition generally overcame his scruples." But Goodman also admitted that the work supplies "a remarkable tale of international espionage, art history and museum one-upmanship." Long-time art critic and philosopher Arthur Danto, writing for the *Nation,* described Hoving's tale as though Hoving were a knight, adding, "I liked the cheerful amorality of the quest, and the glimpse into the underside of the museum world, full of monsters."

Hoving's next two works were fiction. In his 1986 novel *Masterpiece,* he introduces a woman and a man bent on professional advancement, creating an acquisition competition between the Metropolitan Museum of Art in New York and the National Gallery in Washington, DC. Their chemistry clashes as well in their rival attempts to attain a rare and valuable Velasquez painting. Finding some of Hoving's text embarrassingly laughable, *New York Times Book Review* contributor Lawrence Weschler asked, "Does anyone really sound like that?" Weschler mused that Hoving may have been "simply lampooning the entire blockbuster genre—but parody has to be at least as well written as the genre it upends, and *Masterpiece* isn't." A *Kirkus Reviews* critic found the work "as styleless as any middlebrow thrill," but conceded that *Masterpiece* "cries out for celluloid."

Hoving's second attempt at fiction, *Discovery!,* is a sequel to *Masterpiece,* revisiting Foster and Cartwright, now married. The couple find themselves on an archaeological dig in Italy and knee-deep in underworld intrigue and corruption. A *Kirkus Reviews* contributor suggested that "the hundred pages or so of connoisseurship (much of it erotic) are worth the novel's failings."

Probably Hoving's most popular work came in 1993 with his best-selling publication *Making the Mummies Dance: Inside the Metropolitan Museum of Art.* Abandoning fiction, Hoving discusses how he achieved greatness by gaining and inventing the avant-garde directorship of the Metropolitan Museum of Art in New York for the ten years between 1967 and 1977. The memoir also recounts Hoving's experiences as director of Manhattan's municipal parks and his decision to return to the Met even though it was known to be a staid—some would say elitist—place. The book's title refers to a comment made by New York Mayor John Lindsay, who told Hoving to "make the mummies dance" in order to wake up the "dead" museum.

In *Making the Mummies Dance* Hoving counts himself a success for his many staff changes and programs designed to broaden the museum's appeal. However, a few critics suggested that his recollection of events was not always accurate. *Art History* contributor Hilton Kramer noted that Hoving's one self-laudatory tale about an alleged investigation into the hiring practices at the Met just prior to his being given the directorship is full of error, miscalculations of dates, details, names, and titles. In his review of *Mummies,* Kramer quoted Michael Kimmelman of the *New York Times,* "'This anecdote . . . is vintage Hoving for its combination of skulduggery, one-upmanship, bravado and unreliability.'" James Gardner in the *National Review* wrote, "If this were a better book, it would probably be far less enjoyable." Gardner called the book "a vulgar crowdpleaser."

Other reviewers were more charitable in their estimations of *Making the Mummies Dance.* Jo Ann Lewis in the *Washington Post* praised Hoving's work as a "riveting, revealing and outrageously nasty social document about the '70s art world that has set phone lines buzzing, faxes humming and—not incidentally—the book climbing up the *New York Times* bestseller list." Hoving's honesty made many people nervous as he discussed such things as his own and his staff administrators' characters, infidelities, and failed exhibits. But he also covers the grand achievements such as developing small installation shows and blockbuster exhibits of dead and living artists, face-lifting the building itself, increasing the permanent collection, and turning the little bookstore into a spacious first-floor adventure-in-shopping for art books, gifts, and even moderate market reproductions. Hoving's thick-skinned, aggressive business-like approach and trail-blazing has been seen as the prototype and catalyst for change in the way museums are managed now and how people in America approach art today. In an interview with Lewis, Hoving explained, "When I went back to the Met, I was no longer a curator: I was a politician who'd learned how the city worked, and how businesses worked, and I wanted to get things done."

Eric Gibson, contributor to *Insight on the News,* offered two reasons for the importance of *Making the Mummies Dance.* The first is that "Hoving's career ushered in the 'modern' museum. . . . His book provides the most detailed chronicle yet of this fateful transformation of our museums." The second reason for the book's significance is that "it provides a sobering glimpse of just what a museum director is prepared to do to secure a treasured acquisition. . . . Whether we like it or not, Hoving is the first of an entirely new breed of museum director." Gibson viewed this story and the attitude of the man who tells it as "the unrepentant, wink-at-the-audience pride of an inveterate seducer." Defending Hoving's controversial tactics, Gibson stated that "Hoving at least possessed a knowledge and a love of art," adding, "This book is necessary reading for anyone who wants to understand how we have gotten where we are today, and what has been lost along the way."

Hoving has also written a catalog meant to accompany a retrospective art exhibit of Andrew Wyeth in 1995 at the Nelson-Atkins Museum of Art in Kansas City. Having interviewed the much-loved and respected American watercolorist Andrew Wyeth in 1976, Hoving gleaned comments made by Wyeth about each of the over four thousand pieces he had painted down to just those that would appear in the 1995 Kansas City exhibit. He titled the show's catalog *Andrew Wyeth: Autobiography.* Though his initial publication of the Wyeth interview did not sell as well as Hoving would have liked, he is proud of it and asserted: "The artist was very cooperative. The book marks the first time an art historian ever interviewed Wyeth."

In the 1996 book *False Impressions: The Hunt for the Big-Time Art Fakes,* Hoving again boldly tells art tales, but this time blasting away at forgers and the dupes who have been taken in by them. After at least three decades in the art-buying and museum business, Hoving shows how some of the world-famous art forgers have wielded their craft. He discusses how colleagues from other major museums have been taken in by these forgers. Though hoodwinked himself on at least three occasions, still Hoving names himself as one "fake-buster" who can sniff out any forgery. Contributing to the *Sewanee Review,* Malcolm Goldstein thought Hoving felt "obvious pleasure" when "recounting the mistakes of his colleagues in the museum world. . . . One would expect greater charity, or at least greater restraint, from so intelligent and learned a man." In *Business Week* Thane Peterson wrote, "Fascinating as it is, *False Impressions* shares many of the weaknesses of *Mummies.* Hoving can't resist the unkind rumor." But in the Lewis interview Hoving's wife, Nancy, defended her husband: "Stepping on toes has never been a problem for him: He doesn't feel it, so he doesn't think anybody else does either."

London *Observer* writer Jay Rayner gave Hoving credit for a story well told: "The book is at its most enjoyable when he is recounting the detective work that led to the uncovering of great fakes." Likewise, *Washington Post* correspondent Philip Kopper described *False Impressions* as fascinating: "Hoving is best when writing about things and people he knows and likes. Consequently there is gold here." Kopper went even further to wryly suggest its validity as an excellent reference book for art collectors and art students but added, "When [*False Impressions*] finds its place on the shelf as the text for Art Fakes 101, let it be without the jacket's clowning pictures that telegraph the author's posturing prose inside. For that is not where this informing book's value lies."

Hoving's *Greatest Works of Art of Western Civilization* was published in 1997. What makes this standard oversized coffee-table book of art different is that the artworks featured are handpicked by Hoving himself, presenting them as "the ones that changed my life. . . . All I cared about were my reactions and whether they mirrored the power, the mystery, and the magnetism of the works themselves." *Library Journal* contributor Eric Bryant wrote that Hoving's annotations accompanying each work of art, outside of a one-page introduction, are "brief, often gossipy commentaries." Bryant also noted that while many of the 111 works have been featured in other books, many are surprises, and further implies that Hoving's name as the former director of the Metropolitan Museum of Art in New York should be ample justification for examining *Greatest Works*.

The personal computer era spawned a number of books "for dummies," and eventually the series spilled into other areas of expertise, from wine and book collecting to art appreciation. Thus it was that Hoving was asked to pen *Art for Dummies: A Reference for the Rest of Us!*, a book that introduces general readers to art history, collecting art, evaluating talent, and visiting museums. As a *Town and Country* reviewer put it, the author "revels in the opportunity to demystify art without denigrating it." *Library Journal* contributor Douglas F. Smith also found the work "delightful," concluding that it that it is a "terrific book for students. . .and old hands alike."

In a *Contemporary Authors* interview, Hoving responded to questions about his career and his work as an author of books. When asked how he writes he answered, "Very fast. . . . I write in longhand—anywhere, on planes, in cars. Then a secretary types it up. *Tutankhamun* took just two drafts, whereas letters can sometimes take up to twelve drafts." *Contemporary Authors* asked Hoving what art writers he admired, and his answer was sure and succinct, "Longhi, Max Friedlaender, Krautheimer, and Panofsky." While he felt Kenneth Clark's *Civilisation* to be admirable in the main, Hoving accused Clark of omitting Germany "almost entirely." Since his departure from the Met, Hoving has enjoyed working as editor of *Connoisseur* magazine, performing management consulting with his business partner/wife Nancy, sitting in as columnist of "Happenings" for *Museums, New York,* and reporting and interviewing on the American Broadcasting Company's (ABC) news program *20/20*. Hoving once told *CA:* "I thoroughly enjoy it. . . . [All] these activities go to support my writing, which I like better than anything."

For a previously published interview, see entry in *Contemporary Authors,* Volume 101.

BIOGRAPHICAL AND CRITICAL SOURCES:

BOOKS

Hess, John L., *The Grand Inquisitors,* Houghton Mifflin (Boston, MA), 1974.

PERIODICALS

America, May 15, 1982, p. 387.
American History Illustrated, November, 1987, p. 10.
Art in America, June, 1986, p. 18; June, 1986, p. 28; January, 1987, p. 19.
ARTnews, March, 1993, p. 60; January, 2000, Milton Esterow, review of *Art for Dummies: A Reference for the Rest of Us!,* p. 124.
Atlantic, January, 1982, p. 88.
Atlantic Monthly, June, 1996, p. 126.
Booklist, November 1, 1992, p. 466; May 1, 1996, p. 1481; December 15, 1997, Donna Seaman, review of *Greatest Works of Art of Western Civilization,* p. 677.
Business Week, February 1, 1993, p. 13; June 3, 1996, p. 15.
Chicago Tribune Book World, October 22, 1978.
Connoisseur, January, 1982, p. 1.
Cosmopolitan, December, 1981, p. 22.

Economist, January 23, 1993, p. 83.
House Beautiful, January, 1982, p. 33.
Insight on the News, February 8, 1993, p. 22.
Library Journal, November 1, 1992, p. 83; May 15, 1996, p. 57; October 15, 1997, Eric Bryant, review of *Greatest Works of Art of Western Civilization,* p. 58; October 15, 1999, Douglas F. Smith, review of *Art for Dummies,* p. 66.
Nation, February 8, 1993, p. 166.
National Review, December 11, 1981, p. 1496; March 1, 1993, p. 65.
New Republic, April 12, 1993, p. 36.
New York, December 7, 1981, p. 61.
New Yorker, February 8, 1993, p. 106.
New York Review of Books, March 4, 1993, p. 8.
New York Times, December 26, 1978.
New York Times Book Review, November 12, 1978; January 3, 1993, p. 1; May 19, 1996, p. 20.
People Weekly, October 26, 1981, p. 32; December 1, 1986, p. 20.
Publishers Weekly, May 8, 1987, p. 60; June 16, 1989, p. 57; June 21, 1989, p. 58; November 23, 1992, p. 45; February 26, 1996, p. 90; June 19, 2000, review of *The Art of Dan Namingha,* p. 74.
Time, November 16, 1981, p. 141; September 1, 1986, p. 85.
Town & Country, September, 1999, "Opening Your Eyes," p. 110.
U.S. News and World Report, August 13, 2001, Andrew Curry, "Medieval Questions," p. 47.
Washington Post Book World, November 26, 1978.
Wilson Library Bulletin, January, 1982, p. 385.

ONLINE

New York Metro Web site, http://www.newyorkmetro.com/ (February 21, 2003), interview with Hoving.*

* * *

HWANG, David Henry 1957-

PERSONAL: Surname pronounced "Wong"; born August 11, 1957, in Los Angeles, CA; son of Henry Yuan (a banker) and Dorothy Yu (a professor of piano; maiden name, Huang) Hwang; married Ophelia Y. M. Chong (an artist), September 21, 1985 (divorced, October, 1989); married Kathryn A. Layng (an actress), December 17, 1993; children: (second marriage) Noah.

David Henry Hwang

Education: Stanford University, B.A., 1979; attended Yale University School of Drama, 1980-81. *Politics:* Democrat. *Hobbies and other interests:* Violin.

ADDRESSES: Home—New York, NY. *Agent*—William Craver, Authors and Artists Agency, 19 West 44th St., Suite 1000, New York, NY 10036; and Tory Metzger, Creative Artists Agency, 9830 Wilshire Blvd., Beverly Hills, CA 90212. *E-mail*—fob@idt.net.

CAREER: Playwright; director of plays, including *A Song for a Nisei Fisherman,* 1980, *The Dream of Kitamura,* 1982, and *F.O.B.,* 1990; Asian American Theatre Center, San Francisco, CA, dramaturg, 1987—. Co-founder, Stanford Asian American Theatre Project; Theatre Communications Group, member of board of directors, 1987—. Menlo-Atherton High School, Menlo Park, CA, teacher of English and writing, 1980. Member of board of directors, President's Committee on the Arts and Humanities, 1994—; China Institute, 1993—; and Center for Arts and Culture, 1998.

MEMBER: Writers Guild of America, Dramatists Guild (member of board of directors, 1988—), Young Playwrights, Inc., American Civil Liberties Union, PEN (member of board of directors, 1990—), Theatre Communications Group (vice president, 1999—), Phi Beta Kappa.

AWARDS, HONORS: Drama-Logue award, 1980, 1986, 1997; Obie Award for best play, *Village Voice*, 1981, for *F.O.B.*, and for best playwriting, 1997, for *Golden Child*; Drama Desk Award nomination, 1982, for *Family Devotions* and *The Dance and the Railroad*; CINE Golden Eagle, 1983, for television production *The Dance and the Railroad*; Rockefeller playwright-in-residence award and National Endowment for the Arts artistic associate fellowship, 1983-84; Guggenheim fellowship, 1984; National Endowment for the Arts, and New York State Council on the Arts fellowships, both 1985; Antoinette Perry "Tony" Award for best play, Outer Critics Circle Award for best Broadway play, John Gassner Award, and Drama Desk Award, all 1988, and Pulitzer Prize nomination, 1989, all for *M. Butterfly*; Los Angeles Drama Critics Award, 1991; Tony Award nomination for best play, and Outer Critics Circle Award nomination for best Broadway play, both 1998, both for *Golden Child*; Obie Award for playwriting, 1997; honorary D.L., Columbia College, 1998.

WRITINGS:

PLAYS

F.O.B. (two-act; title means "Fresh off the Boat"; also see below), produced in Stanford, CA, 1978, produced off-Broadway, 1980.

The Dance and the Railroad (also see below; produced in New York, NY, 1981; produced off-Broadway, 1981), Dramatists Play Service (New York, NY), 1990.

Family Devotions (also see below), produced off-Broadway, 1981.

Sound and Beauty (two one-acts; includes *The House of Sleeping Beauties*, based on a novella by Yasunari Kawabata, and *The Sound of a Voice* [also see below]), produced off-Broadway, 1983.

F.O.B. [and] *The House of Sleeping Beauties*, Dramatists Play Service (New York, NY), 1983.

Broken Promises: Four Plays (contains *F.O.B.*, *The Dance and the Railroad*, *Family Devotions*, and *The House of Sleeping Beauties*), Avon (New York, NY), 1983.

The Sound of a Voice, Dramatists Play Service (New York, NY), 1984.

Rich Relations (also see below), produced off-Broadway, 1986.

As the Crow Flies, produced in Los Angeles, CA, 1986.

Broken Promises (includes *The Dance and the Railroad* and *The House of Sleeping Beauties*), produced in London, England, 1987.

My American Son (television drama), Home Box Office, 1987.

M. Butterfly (produced in Washington, DC, 1988; produced on Broadway, 1988; also see below), Plume (New York, NY), 1989.

One Thousand Airplanes on the Roof (musical; produced in New York, 1988), music by Philip Glass, Gibbs-Smith, 1989.

F.O.B. and Other Plays (includes *Rich Relations*), Plume (New York, NY), 1990.

The Voyage (opera), music by Philip Glass, produced in New York, NY, 1992.

Bondage (one-act; produced at the Humana Theatre Festival, 1992), in *The Best American Short Plays 1992-93*, Applause Theatre Book (New York, NY), 1993.

Face Value, produced in Boston, MA, 1993.

M. Butterfly (screenplay; based on his play), Warner Bros., 1993.

Golden Gate (screenplay), Samuel Goldwyn, 1994.

Golden Child, produced in New York, NY, 1996, produced on Broadway, 1998.

The Silver River (musical), music by Bright Sheng, produced in Santa Fe, NM, 1998.

(Adapter) Henrik Ibsen, *Peer Gynt,* produced in Providence, RI, 1998.

Trying to Find Chinatown: The Selected Plays of David Henry Hwang, Theatre Communications Group, 1999.

(Coauthor of book, with Robert Falls and Linda Woolverton) *Aïda* (rock musical), music by Elton John, lyrics by Tim Rice, produced on Broadway, 1999.

(Contributor) *The Square*, produced in New York, NY, 2001.

(Adaptor) *Flower Drum Song* (based on the musical by Oscar Hammerstein II and Richard Rodgers; produced in Los Angeles, CA, 2001), Theatre Communications Group (New York, NY), 2003.

(Adaptor with Neil LaBute) *Possession* (screenplay; based on the novel by A. S. Byatt), Warner Bros., 2002.

Also author, with Frederic Kimball, of teleplay *Blind Alleys*, 1985. Plays represented in anthologies, including *Between Worlds: Contemporary Asian-American*

Plays, New Plays USA 1, Best Plays of 1981-1982, Best Short Plays of 1982, and Best Plays of 1987-1988.

SIDELIGHTS: Enjoying an unusually swift ascent to prominence on the American stage, David Henry Hwang gained widespread praise for his very first play in 1980 and went on to earn a Antoinette Perry—"Tony"—Award and a Pulitzer Prize nomination. Many of Hwang's plays refer to the experiences of Asian immigrants living in the United States and to East-West relations, leading some reviewers to pigeonhole him as an Asian author. Yet he has also written a science-fiction libretto, a cable television program on Middle East/Central American politics, and several non-Asian-themed plays. Hwang's Chinese-American heritage has been both "a minor detail, like having red hair," as he remarked in a New York Times Magazine interview, and the inspiration for most of his successful plays. Mingling Chinese influences with those of his birth country and in the process addressing wider concerns of race, gender, and culture, Hwang is "the first U.S. playwright to become an international phenomenon in a generation," according to William A. Henry III, writing in Time.

Hwang had just graduated from Stanford University when his first play, F.O.B., was accepted for production at the prestigious National Playwrights Conference at Connecticut's O'Neill Theater Center in 1979; the following year producer Joseph Papp brought the play to New York's off-Broadway circuit where it won an Obie Award as the best new play of the season. First performed at Stanford, the drama focuses on Steve, a young Chinese immigrant "fresh off the boat," and the two Chinese-American students he meets in Los Angeles. The male student scorns Steve, preferring to renounce Steve's Chinese heritage; the woman tries to accommodate both traditions and becomes a pivot between the two men. Wrote Frank Rich in the New York Times, "The subject of the evening is a very old one: the price that minorities pay to assimilate in mainstream America. But David Henry Hwang . . . is too rambunctious to tell a familiar story in a tired way." One unusual aspect of F.O.B., Rich noted, is a technical innovation: in the second act Hwang employs Chinese theatrical techniques to present his characters as figures from Chinese mythology. Rich also enjoyed the "comic verve" Hwang displays throughout and, while recognizing some flaws of construction and characterization in the work, asserted that the playwright "hits home far more often than he misses. . . . If West and East don't precisely meet in F.O.B., they certainly fight each other to a fascinating standoff."

Hwang's next two plays, The Dance and the Railroad and Family Devotions, also focus on Chinese Americans. The first examines two nineteenth-century Chinese men working on the transcontinental railroad; the second looks at a well-established Chinese-American family of the twentieth century. Rich deemed Railroad "leaner" and "more accomplished" than F.O.B., though similar to the earlier play in its mixture of American comedy and oriental technique and its interest in immigrant concerns. The play explores the confrontation between Ma, a new arrival to the United States, and Lone, who has been in America for two years. Sold into servitude by his parents after studying Chinese opera, Lone is a cynic who distances himself from the other laborers with daily dance sessions away from camp. Ma persuades Lone to teach him to dance, and during their workouts the two men explore their pasts and share their thoughts on the future. Judging the play "witty, poetic and affecting," Rich described Hwang as "a true original" with a "startling and far-ranging theatrical voice." Family Devotions also earned Rich's admiration, though the critic suggested that Hwang loses control of his plot near the play's end. The farcical drama hinges on the conflict between a wealthy, Americanized Chinese family of fanatical born-again Christians and an austere, atheist uncle from Communist China who comes to visit. Rich and New Yorker critic Edith Oliver both judged Family Devotions among Hwang's funniest plays.

Departing from the Chinese-American angle, Hwang followed Family Devotions with a pair of stylized one-act plays set in Japan and jointly titled Sound and Beauty. The House of Sleeping Beauties reinvents a novella by Yasunari Kawabata, making Kawabata a character in a variation of his own story about a brothel of comatose virgins wherein elderly men sleep beside the drugged women as a means of accepting their own mortality. In Hwang's version, Kawabata visits the brothel to research a book, but becomes increasingly involved in the place and thoughts of his own mortality despite himself. The second play, The Sound of a Voice, pits a samurai warrior against a bewitching female hermit. Thinking she has the power to destroy men, the warrior plans to kill the hermit, but several weeks as her guest in the forest change his heart, with unexpected results. Writing in the Los Angeles Times,

Dan Sullivan judged *The Sound of a Voice* "a skillfully ordered and beautifully written play" that combines the simplicity and mystery of folk tales with an insightful look at male and female psychology. Rich, reviewing both one-acts in the *New York Times,* found *The Sound of a Voice* flawed by overemphasized symbolism and both plays hobbled by Hwang's "efforts to duplicate the mood of Japanese literature and theater." Even so, admitted Rich, Hwang "is not standing still." The critic deemed *Sound and Beauty* "an earnest, considered experiment furthering an exceptional young writer's process of growth."

Hwang suffered his first critical failure with the 1986 play *Rich Relations,* characterized by Rich as "tired." Although not about Asian Americans, the play includes several elements characteristic of Hwang's earlier works: materialism and wealth, evangelical Christianity, and a family at odds. Noted Jeremy Gerard in the *New York Times Magazine,* "The playwright didn't disagree with the charge" that he was treading familiar ground."*Rich Relations* was another attempt to write a spiritual farce," Hwang told Gerard."It's about my family—except that they're not Asians." Ultimately the playwright found the flop liberating. As he related in a *Los Angeles Times* article, "I felt I'd done something I was pleased with and proud of—and everybody spat on it and I was still happy I did it. That gives you tremendous exhilaration, because the next time you want to pursue whatever it is you really want, it's not going to hurt that much if people don't like it."

Hwang bounced back from failure in 1988 with the popular *M. Butterfly,* based on a true story of a French diplomat and his Chinese lover, who turned out to be not only a spy but a man. Debuting in Washington, D.C., and quickly moving on to Broadway, the play pleased audiences and many critics, earning a Pulitzer Prize nomination and a Tony Award. Surprised by such success, Hwang told *Los Angeles Times* interviewer Sylvie Drake that some of his play's appeal may derive from its use of Italian and Chinese opera music. Also, he said, "People associate a certain level of exoticism with the East; therefore they'll come to the theater to see this." Hwang decided to give audiences what they expected, "in spades, and at the same time try to subvert it by talking about exactly why it is that audiences are attracted to this material *at the time* that they are being attracted to it."

Hwang's strategy was to exploit parallels between the espionage incident and the Giacomo Puccini opera *Madama Butterfly,* which tells of a Japanese woman who falls in love with an European, is spurned, and commits suicide. In Hwang's play, the diplomat, Gallimard, represents Puccini's Westerner, Pinkerton; Gallimard's Butterfly is Song Liling, a Chinese opera diva/spy in drag who appears to fall in love with Gallimard. To Hwang, explained Rich, "a cultural icon like *Madama Butterfly* bequeaths the sexist and racist roles that burden Western men: Gallimard believes he can become 'a real man' only if he can exercise power over a beautiful and submissive woman, which is why he's so ripe to be duped by Song Liling's impersonation of a shrinking butterfly." Hwang's parallel includes a crucial twist: "At the beginning of the play," he asserted in a *Washington Post* interview, "the Frenchman sees himself as Pinkerton—he's found this beautiful Madame Butterfly in China. And by the end of the play he kind of realizes that it is he, the Frenchman, that has been sacrificed for love, that the spy was actually the Pinkerton who preyed on his love."

M. Butterfly drew both acclaim and criticism. Several reviewers applauded its ambition, richness, and drama, while others found its characterizations and plot twists unbelievable. Contrasting the work with other American plays, Rich observed that "instead of reducing the world to an easily digested cluster of sexual or familial relationships, Mr. Hwang cracks open a liaison to reveal a sweeping, universal meditation on two of the most heated conflicts—men versus women, East versus West—of this or any other time." In another *New York Times* review, however, John Gross judged *M. Butterfly* better as a personal tragedy than a wide-ranging play of ideas: calling it "a mess, intellectually speaking," Gross nonetheless admitted that "at its best it sweeps one up in a tense emotional drama." In the *New Yorker,* Edith Oliver described the play as "funny, mysterious, and often beautiful" and labeled Hwang the most "audacious, imaginative, [and] gifted" young playwright in America.

Hwang's *Golden Child,* produced at the Joseph Papp Public Theater in 1996 and directed by James Lapine, begins in the back seat of a taxi when Andrew Kwong, a young Chinese American about to become a father, receives a visit from the ghost of his grandmother, Eng Ahn, who urges him to honor his ancestors and his origins. In a clever bit of theatrical sleight-of-hand, Kwong transforms into his grandfather, Eng Tieng-Bin, as Eng Ahn simultaneously becomes the child she once was. Most of the play takes place in a small

Chinese village at the turn of the twentieth century. Within this milieu Hwang explores the disruption of feudal traditions as Tieng-Bin returns from abroad to his three wives with new ideas about marriage, education, and religion. Tieng-Bin sees Christianity as a route to a more modern world. His religious conversion has startling effects on the members of his household as each of his three wives struggles to come to terms with his spiritual and social reawakening. Ben Brantley, writing in the *New York Times,* found *Golden Child* less caustic than earlier plays like *Family Devotions,* writing that it "has the evenhandedness of a debate moderator who wants, above all, to be fair." Calling the play "likable, educational and, at times, very poignant," Brantley also added that "it's never able to generate much urgency." On the other hand, David Sterritt noted in the *Christian Science Monitor* that "while *Golden Child* is not likely to cause as much stir as Hwang's controversial *M. Butterfly* did . . . he [still] thoughtfully probes the topics he raises, weaving them into a domestic story that is increasingly melodramatic until enough destructive and self-destructive acts have occurred to match the music from *La Traviata* that provides the play's motifs." Sterritt also noted that the "play's most involving material clusters around issues of what it means to be born again in a spiritual sense . . . and a historical sense, as forward-thinking Chinese people look for ways of entering a new era dominated by Western values."

Hwang captivated stage audiences in 2001 with his updated adaptation of the 1958 Oscar Hammerstein II and Joseph Fields text of *Flower Drum Song.* C. Y. Lee, author of the novel, and the Rodgers and Hammerstein Organization gave Hwang permission to use his full artistic creativity in the reworking of this musical. "My original idea was to show both the cultural conflict and the closeness of the Chinese family. [That's hard to do] on stage, but David managed to simplify it. You really see the relationships and the love between these characters," praised Lee in a *USAToday.com* interview with Elysa Gardner. In the same interview, Hwang remembered how some Asian Americans—himself included—were offended by certain stereotypes that appeared in the original libretto. He began to rethink his negative opinion after seeing a revival of *The King and I* on Broadway when he realized that "Rodgers and Hammerstein musicals are . . . more complex" than they might seem on first viewing.

In Hwang's adaptation he strengthens the female protagonist, Mei-Li, from a shy, mail-order bride to a feisty young woman fleeing China due to her father's problems with the Maoist regime. He changes the musical's setting to an old-style Chinese opera house in 1960's San Francisco that is run by a man whose son, Ta, transforms it into a Western-style nightclub when no opera is playing. Another alteration by Hwang is that some of the musical pieces appear at different points in the action than they did in the original musical.

The modernization of a classic musical earned a somewhat mixed response from theatre critics. "Hwang has made the show a richer, more nuanced exploration of the immigrant experience," asserted *Time* critic Richard Zoglin of *Flower Drum Song,* adding that "the show works because it doesn't condescend." "While it contains a workable premise and more assertive characters, the new book's themes are both clichéd and not terribly compelling," remarked *Hollywood Reporter* writer Frank Scheck. In a contrasting *Hollywood Reporter* review, Jay Reiner praised Hwang for his ability to revive "a flawed musical" from its "near-dead" status. Reiner admitted, however, that "there is a price to be paid for telling the story in this new way" with the consequence that Mei-Li and Ta's love story "sometimes gets lost in the shuffle and it's not always convincing." Judith Newmark noted in a review for *Knight Ridder/Tribune News Service:* "Hwang emphasizes respect for Chinese artistic tradition while [taking] a lighthearted, romantic look at assimilationist issues." In his *Variety* piece, Steven Oxman noted that Gordon Davidson, artistic director of the Center Theater Group in Los Angeles, felt that "the tension between the old and new is better realized . . . and therefore more affecting and more universal."

Hwang took the mixed critical response in stride. In a *Knight Ridder/Tribune News Service* article by Karen D'Souza he was quoted as saying: "I'm sure there will be extremists on both ends who will never like this project. There will be the Asian Americans who say that *Flower Drum* shouldn't be revived under any circumstances, and there will be the musical theater lovers who will dismiss this as a politically correct exercise. But you can't worry about expectations. You have to just do your work and roll the dice."

In a reflection of his versatility and willingness to overstep traditional boundaries, Hwang exercised his imagination in a different genre with his 1988 science-fiction collaboration with composer Philip Glass and scene designer Jerome Sirlin. Conceived and directed by Glass, *One Thousand Airplanes on the Roof* is a multimedia project in which Hwang's text served as a narrative framework for Glass's music and Sirlin's set and projection images. The play concerns a character who may have been kidnaped by visiting aliens. "She longs to discuss her experience, but knows her tale will be dismissed," explained Allan Kozinn in a *New York Times* review. "To appear sane, she has to deny it happened; but she fears that repressing this momentous experience will drive her crazy." The character's confusion and distress are illumined by ever-changing images of cities, grids, and stars projected on the set by Sirlin, whose work, according to *Washington Post* contributor Pamela Sommers, "steals the show." Sommers criticized Hwang's narrative as uneven, summarizing the evening as "intermittently compelling and disappointing . . . intriguing if perplexing." Kozinn, however, praised Hwang for his "rich, gripping monologue."

In another break from traditional theatre, in 1999 Hwang turned his considerable talents toward writing the book for the Disney-produced rock musical *Aïda*, in collaboration with Robert Falls and Linda Woolverton. With new music by Elton John and Tim Rice, the multi-award-winning musical retells the love story of Radames and Aïda. "Falls and Hwang have accented some universal resonance in the tale which gives the show necessary weight," wrote *Variety* reviewer Chris Jones of the 2000 Broadway production.

Moving from stage to screen, Hwang joined forces with Neil LaBute and Laura Jones to adapt *Possession,* a novel by A. S. Byatt that was awarded the Booker Prize, into a film. The storyline focuses upon romances occurring in parallel times and worlds: the Victorian Era and the present day. Two modern academics (portrayed by Aaron Eckhart and Gwyneth Paltrow) strive together to find a connection between the romantic lives of two Victorian poets, as unlikely as that connection might seem at first glance. *Possession* is a "witty, literate . . . mesmerizing . . . [and] devilishly clever screenplay," said Kirk Honeycutt in a *Hollywood Reporter* review.

"Hwang is a very clever and gifted playwright," acknowledged Jack Kroll of the playwright's career in *Newsweek.* Successful and praised at age twenty-three and the recipient of a coveted Tony award by age thirty, through his work for both stage and screen he continues to address universal issues through his imagination and vision, and has justifiably won a wide audience. "The main weakness of his writing," assessed Henry in *Time,*"is that its purpose often seems more political than literary, more attuned to social issues than to the private struggles of the human heart. The final scene of *M. Butterfly,* when the agony of one soul finally takes precedence over broad-ranging commentary, is among the most forceful in the history of the American theater. . . . If Hwang can again fuse politics and humanity, he has the potential to become the first important dramatist of American public life since Arthur Miller, and maybe the best of them all."

BIOGRAPHICAL AND CRITICAL SOURCES:

BOOKS

Asian-American Literature, Gale (Detroit, MI), 1999.
Contemporary Dramatists, 6th edition, St. James Press (Detroit, MI), 1999.
Contemporary Literary Criticism, Volume 55, Gale (Detroit, MI), 1989.
Contemporary Theatre, Film, and Television, Volume 5, Gale (Detroit, MI), 1988.
Dictionary of Literary Biography, Gale (Detroit, MI), 2000.
Encyclopedia of American Literature, Continuum (New York, NY), 1999.
Street, Douglas, *David Henry Hwang,* Boise State University Press, 1989.

PERIODICALS

Amerasia Journal, winter, 1994, p. 93.
Back Stage West, January 25, 2001, Charlene Baldridge, review of *F.O.B.*, p. 19.
Christian Science Monitor, November 29, 1996, p. 15.
Daily Variety, October 21, 2002, Robert Hofler, review of *Flower Drum Song,* pp. 1-2.
Hollywood Reporter, October 15, 2001, Jay Reiner, review of *Flower Drum Song,* pp. 6-7; August 9, 2002, Kirk Honeycutt, review of *Possession,* pp. 11-12; October 18, 2002, Frank Scheck, review of *Flower Drum Song,* pp. 15-16.
House and Garden, September, 1991, p. 72.
Journal of Dramatic Theory and Criticism, spring, 1991; fall, 1992.

Knight Ridder/Tribune News Service, October 12, 2001, Karen D'Souza, interview with Hwang, p. K7128; October 16, 2002, Judith Newmark, review of *Flower Drum Song,* p. K5257.

Literary Review, winter, 1999, Bonnie Lyons, interview with David Hwang, p. 230.

Los Angeles Times, February 19, 1986; March 26, 1988; June 7, 1988; October 30, 1988.

Modern Drama, March, 1990, pp. 59-66.

Nation, April 23, 1988, pp. 577-578.

New Republic, April 25, 1988, pp. 28-29; November 1, 1993, p. 72.

Newsweek, April 4, 1988, p. 75; October 26, 1992, p. 62.

New York, April 11, 1988, pp. 117-19; October 24, 1988, p. 145; October 26, 1992, p. 91; December 9, 1996, p. 76.

New Yorker, November 2, 1981; April 4, 1988, p. 72; October 11, 1993, p. 123; December 2, 1996, p. 121.

New York Times, June 10, 1980; March 31, 1981; July 12, 1981; October 19, 1981; November 7, 1983; April 22, 1986; February 25, 1988; March 21, 1988; March 25, 1988; April 10, 1988; May 22, 1988; June 5, 1988; September 24, 1988; November 23, 1988; December 11, 1988; December 16, 1988; May 20, 1990; November 10, 1996, p. H5; November 20, 1996, p. C20; November 21, 1996, p. B2; December 5, 1997, p. E2; March 24, 2000, Ben Brantley, review of *Aïda,* p. B26; October 14, 2001, Bernard Weinraub, review of *Flower Drum Song,* p. AR7.

New York Times Magazine, March 13, 1988.

People, January 9, 1984.

Rolling Stone, February 10, 1994, p. 52.

Theater, spring-summer, 1989, pp. 24-27.

Theatre Journal, March, 1990; December, 2002, Sun Hee Teresa Lee, review of *Flower Drum Song,* pp. 640-642.

Time, April 4, 1988, p. 74; August 14, 1989; October 26, 1992, p. 80; October 4, 1993, p. 85; October 28, 2002, Richard Zoglin, review of *Flower Drum Song,* p. 63.

Times (London, England), March 17, 1989; April 22, 1989.

Variety, December 13, 1999, Chris Jones, review of *Aïda,* p. 117; October 8, 2001, Steven Oxman, review of *Flower Drum Song,* p. 27; June 3, 2002, Robert Hofler, review of *Flower Drum Song,* p. A8.

Washington Post, February 10, 1988; December 10, 1988.

ONLINE

USAToday, http://www.usatoday.com/ (May 12, 2003), Elysa Gardner, interview with Hwang and C. Y. Lee.*

J

JEFFARES, A(lexander) Norman 1920-

PERSONAL: Born August 11, 1920, in Dublin, Ireland; son of Cecil Norman (a university accountant) and Agnes (a civil servant; maiden name, Fraser) Jeffares; married Jeanne Agnes Calembert (a potter, and homeopath), July 29, 1947; children: Felicity Anne Sekine. *Education:* University of Dublin, B.A., 1943, Ph.D., 1946; Oriel College, Oxford, M.A., 1946, D.Phil., 1948. *Religion:* Church of Ireland. *Hobbies and other interests:* Traveling, rebuilding old houses, drawing, motoring.

ADDRESSES: Office—Craighead Cottage, Fife Ness, Crail, Fife KY10 3XN, Scotland.

CAREER: University of Dublin, Trinity College, Dublin, Ireland, lecturer in classics, 1943-45; University of Gröningen, Gröningen, Holland, lecturer in English, 1946-49; University of Edinburgh, Edinburgh, Scotland, lecturer in English, 1949-51; University of Adelaide, Adelaide, Australia, Jury Professor of English Language and Literature, 1951-56; University of Leeds, Leeds, England, professor of English literature, 1957-74, head of English department, 1957-74, chairman of School of English, 1961-64; University of Stirling, Stirling, Scotland, professor of English studies, 1974-86, professor emeritus, 1986—. Has lectured in the United States, Canada, India, Australia, the Middle East, France, Germany, Belgium, Italy, the USSR, and elsewhere. Vice president, Film and Television Council of South Australia, 1951-56; Australian Humanities Research Council, secretary, 1954-57, corresponding member for Great Britain and Ireland, 1958-70; Scottish Arts Council, chairman of literature committee, 1977-80, vice chairman, 1980-84; Muckhart Community Council, vice chairman, 1979—. Member, Arts Council of Great Britain, 1980-84; director, Yeats International Summer School, 1969-71, and Colin Smythe (publisher), 1979—; Academic Advisory Services, Crail, Scotland, managing director, 1970—.

MEMBER: International Association for the Study of Anglo-Irish Literature (founding chairman, 1967-68; honorary cochairman, 1970-73; honorary life president, 1973—), PEN Scotland (president, 1986-89), Scottish Book Trust (chariman, 1985-88), Australian Academy of Humanities (fellow), Association for Commonwealth Literature and Language Studies (chairman, 1966-69; honorary fellow, 1970—), Royal Society of Edinburgh, (fellow; vice president, 1989-90), Royal Society of Arts (fellow), Royal Society of Literature (fellow), Royal Commonwealth Society (fellow), National Book League Scotland (chairman, 1985-86), Athenaeum Club.

AWARDS, HONORS: Honorary doctorates from University of Lille, 1977, University of Ulster, 1990, and University of Sterling, 2001; honorary fellow of Trinity College, 1978.

WRITINGS:

W. B. Yeats: Man and Poet, Yale University Press (New Haven, CT), 1949, reprinted, 1962, revised edition published as *W. B. Yeats: A New Biography,* Hutchinson (London, England), 1988.

The Poetry of W. B. Yeats, Barron's, 1961.

George Moore, Longman (London, England), 1965.

(With Walter Fitzwilliam Starkie) *Homage to Yeats, 1865-1965,* University of California, William Andrews Clark Memorial Library, 1966.

A Commentary on the Collected Poems of W. B. Yeats, Stanford University Press (Stanford, CA), 1968, revised edition published as *A New Commentary on the Poems of W. B. Yeats,* 1984.

George Moore's Mind and Art, edited by Graham Owens, Oliver & Boyd (London, England), 1968, Barnes & Noble (Totowa, NJ), 1970.

The Circus Animals: Essays on W. B. Yeats, Stanford University Press (Stanford, CA), 1970.

W. B. Yeats, Humanities Press, 1971.

(With A. S. Knowland) *A Commentary on the Collected Plays of W. B. Yeats,* Stanford University Press (Stanford, CA), 1975.

Jonathan Swift, Longman (London, England), 1976.

Brought Up in Dublin (poems), Colin Smythe (Gerrards Cross, England), 1987.

Brought Up to Leave (poems), Colin Smythe (Gerrards Cross, England), 1987.

Parameters of Irish Literature in English, Colin Smythe (Gerrards Cross, England), 1987.

(Co-selector) *Ireland's Women: Writings Past and Present,* Gill & Macmillan, (Dublin, Ireland), 1994.

Images of Invention: Essays on Irish Writing, Colin Smythe (Gerrards Cross, England), 1996.

The Irish Literary Movement, Gill & Macmillan (Dublin, Ireland), 1998.

Contributor to journals.

EDITOR

Maria Edgeworth, *Castle Rackrent and Other Stories,* Thomas Nelson (London, England), 1953.

Seven Centuries of Poetry: Chaucer to Dylan Thomas, Longmans, Green (London, England), 1955, revised edition, 1960.

Benjamin Disraeli, *Sybil,* Thomas Nelson (London, England), 1957.

(With M. Bryn Davies) *The Scientific Background,* Pitman, 1958.

Poems of W. B. Yeats, Macmillan (London, England), 1962.

William Cowper, *Selected Poems and Letters,* Oxford University Press (Oxford, England), 1963.

Oliver Goldsmith, *A Goldsmith Selection,* Macmillan (London, England), 1963.

Selected Plays of W. B. Yeats, Macmillan (London, England), 1964.

William Butler Yeats, *Selected Prose,* Macmillan (London, England), 1964.

William Butler Yeats, *Selected Criticism,* Macmillan (London, England), 1964.

(With K. G. W. Cross) *In Excited Reverie: A Centenary Tribute to William Butler Yeats, 1865-1939,* Macmillan (London, England), 1965.

Walt Whitman, *Selected Poems and Prose,* Oxford University Press (New York, NY), 1966.

William Congreve, *Incognita* [and] *The Way of the World,* Edward Arnold (London, England), 1966, University of South Carolina Press (Columbia, SC), 1970.

Eleven Plays of William Butler Yeats, Macmillan (New York, NY), 1967.

Oliver Goldsmith, *She Stoops to Conquer,* St. Martin's Press (New York, NY), 1967.

William Congreve, *Love for Love,* St. Martin's Press (New York, NY), 1967.

Fair Liberty Was All His Cry: A Tercentenary Tribute to Jonathan Swift, 1667-1745, St. Martin's Press (New York, NY), 1967.

Richard Sheridan, *The School for Scandal,* St. Martin's Press (New York, NY), 1967.

Richard Sheridan, *The Rivals,* Macmillan (London, England), 1967.

Jonathan Swift, *Swift,* Macmillan (New York, NY), 1968.

Thomas Crawford, *Scott's Mind and Art,* Oliver & Boyd (Edinburgh, Scotland), 1969, Barnes & Noble (Totowa, NJ), 1970.

George Farquhar, *The Beaux Stratagem,* Oliver & Boyd (Edinburgh, Scotland), 1972.

George Farquhar, *The Recruiting Officer,* Oliver & Boyd (Edinburgh, Scotland), 1973.

Restoration Comedy, four volumes, Rowman & Littlefield (London, England), 1974.

Jonathan Swift, Longman (London, England), 1976.

W. B. Yeats: The Critical Heritage, Routledge & Kegan Paul (London, England), 1977.

Yeats, Sligo, and Ireland, Colin Smythe (Gerrards Cross, England), 1980.

A History of Anglo-Irish Literature, Schocken (New York, NY), 1982.

A New Commentary on the Poems of W. B. Yeats, Stanford University Press (Stanford, CA), 1984.

W. B. Yeats, *The Poems of William Butler Yeats: A New Selection,* Macmillan (London, England), 1984.

W. B. Yeats: A New Biography, Hutchinson (London, England), 1988, Farrar, Straus & Giroux (New York, NY), 1989, revised edition, Continuum (New York), 2001.

Yeats the European, Colin Smythe (Gerrards Cross, England), 1989.

Yeats's Poems, Macmillan (London, England), 1989.

W. B. Yeats, *The Love Poems,* Kyle Cathie (London, England), 1990.

Yeats's Vision, Arrow Books, 1990.

Yeats: Poems of Place, Tern Press, 1991.

(With Anna White) *Always Your Friend: Letters between Maud Gonne and W. B. Yeats,* Hutchinson (London, Enagland), 1992.

(Coeditor) *Joycechoyce: The Poems in Verse and Prose of James Joyce,* Kyle Cathie (London, England), 1992.

(And author of introduction and notes) Jonathan Swift, *The Selected Poems,* Kyle Cathie (London, England), 1992.

(With Antony Kamm) *Irish Childhoods,* Gill & Macmillan (Dublin, Ireland), 1992.

(Coeditor) *The Gonne-Yeats Letters, 1893-1938,* W. W. Norton (New York, NY), 1993.

(Coeditor) Maud Gonne, *The Autobiography of Maud Gonne: A Servant of the Queen,* University of Chicago Press (Chicago, IL), 1995.

(And author of introduction and notes) W. B. Yeats, *The Secret Rose: Love Poems of W. B. Yeats,* Roberts Rinehart (New York, NY), 1998.

(And author of introduction) *Ireland's Love Poems: Wonder and a Wild Desire,* Kyle Cathie (London, England), 2000.

(And author of introduction and notes) Oliver St. John Gogarty, *Poems and Plays of Oliver St. John Gogarty,* Colin Smythe (Gerrards Cross, England), 2001.

(With Anna MacBride White and Christina Bridgewater) Iseult Gonne, *Letters to W. B. Yeats and Ezra Pound from Iseult Gonne, a Girl That Knew All Dante Once,* Palgrave Macmillan (New York, NY), 2003.

General editor of book series, including "Writers and Critics," 1960-73; "New Oxford English," 1963—; "Macmillan Histories of Literature," 1978—; and "York Classics," 1985—. Editor of magazines, including *Review of English Literature,* 1960-67, *Ariel,* 1970-72, and *York Handbooks,* 1984—; joint editor, *Biography and Criticism,* 1963-73. Literary editor, "Fountainwell Drama Texts," 1968-75; coeditor, "York Notes," 1980—.

WORK IN PROGRESS: A volume of poems; *Images of Imagination,* a collection of essays.

SIDELIGHTS: Although A. Norman Jeffares's scholarship ranges in interest from the works of fourteenth-century poet Geoffrey Chaucer to twentieth-century literature, his principal concern is with the life and writings of Irish writer William Butler Yeats. *Washington Post Book World* reviewer George O'Brien called Jeffares "the dean of Anglo-Irish Yeats scholars."

Jeffares's book *W. B. Yeats: Man and Poet,* first published in 1949, is an introductory study that chronologically examines Yeats's life and poetry. Bernard O'Donoghue in the *Times Literary Supplement* called it "an important part of Yeats studies over the past forty years." Drawing upon more recent scholarship and previously unpublished notebooks and letters, Jeffares rewrote his original biography in 1989. Retitled *W. B. Yeats: A New Biography,* the book is "neither a biography nor a critical study," explained Joseph Coates in the Chicago *Tribune Books,* ". . . but a chronological narrative of the continuous link between the life and the work at the point where one became the other—a biography of Yeats' creative sensibility." *New York Times* critic Michiko Kakutani noted that "the volume's main usefulness is as a kind of reference book [especially for] the reader interested in the genesis of individual poems."

Coates complimented Jeffares on his approach to examining the poetry. Jeffares, Coates believed, "avoids the curse of explication by converting it into an entertaining kind of name- and image-dropping that smells more of the pub than of the classroom." Other critics have found Jeffares's method less satisfying. "While such a well-dressed and urbane biography of Yeats is certainly welcome," wrote O'Brien, "this work also inevitably brings to mind a line the poet himself addressed to his verse: 'There's more enterprise / In walking naked.'" Despite his own reservations, O'Donoghue found that "the new book, like the old, is a good introduction to the life and works, to be used with Jeffares's invaluable *Commentary* on the poems."

In *A Commentary on the Collected Poems of W. B. Yeats,* Jeffares presents a closer, disciplined reading of the poetry. Again including significant biographical data, Jeffares elaborates on the poems' literary allusions and parallels as well as the poet's use of mythology and symbolism. "This work of quiet and very great scholarship," a *Virginia Quarterly Review* critic stated, "collects between two covers in the most matter of fact way all that the Yeats poems are about." According to a reviewer for the *Times Literary Supplement*, lecturers, undergraduates and research students "will find this a useful and labour-saving book. Professor Jeffares's almost complete effacement of his own personality is typical of the objective devotion and the patient industry which his great countryman has always exacted from him."

Turning to the plays of Yeats, Jeffares provides an annotated guide to the poet's theatrical work in a companion volume to the *Collected Poems* titled *A Commentary on the Collected Plays of W. B. Yeats*. He addresses the problems of the plays' obscurity and provides interpretation with glosses on difficult terms and names, summaries of various critical responses, and histories of production and publication. "It is a testimony to the success of the *Commentary*," Edward Engelberg concluded in his review for the *Sewanee Review*, "that it leaves us with a very good idea of how much remains to be done with the plays."

During Ireland's civil war, soldiers from the Irish Free State burned many of the letters between Maud Gonne, an Irish Catholic radical, and Yeats when they invaded Gonne's home. Jeffares offers a collection of the letters that survived in *The Gonne-Yeats Letters, 1893-1938*. The lengthy friendship between Yeats and Gonne inspired some of the poet's best verse, and this fact is documented in this volume. Although only twenty-nine letters in the collection were actually written by Yeats, enough information can be derived from them to help understand Yeats's life-long obsession for Gonne. With the addition of significant editorial notes, Daniel Patrick King of *World Literature Today* noted, "The result is a valuable picture of two uncommon people."

The success of *Images of Invention: Essays on Irish Writing* comes from Jeffares's profound knowledge of Irish authors and their writings. With essays on writers from the seventeenth to the twentieth century, he provides a major introduction to students of Irish literature. According to Geoffrey Heptonstall of *Contemporary Review*, Jeffares "has a scholar's eye for detail, a critic's perception of the subtle connection, the underlying theme."

Ireland's Love Poems: Wonder and a Wild Desire is a collection that includes writers from Jonathan Swift to Seamus Heaney. The central theme in this volume of poems selected by Jeffares is love, an expression in Irish literary tradition that there is no shortage of. According to Patricia Monaghan of *Booklist*, "Collections of Irish poetry don't get any better than this." Whether the poem is traditional or modern, or the writer male or female, these poems offer the reader an authoritative insight into the essence of Irish literature.

BIOGRAPHICAL AND CRITICAL SOURCES:

BOOKS

Dictionary of Irish Literature, Greenwood Press (Westport, CT), 1996.

PERIODICALS

America, October 20, 1990, Elizabeth Bergmann Loizeaux, review of *W. B. Yeats: A New Biography*, p. 277.
American Scholar, autumn, 1993, John P. Sisk, review of *The Gonne-Yeats Letters, 1893-1938*, p. 616.
Antioch Review, spring, 1993, review of *The Gonne-Yeats Letters, 1893-1938*, p. 301.
Atlantic, January, 1993, Conor Cruise O'Brien, review of *The Gonne-Yeats Letters, 1893-1938*, p. 117.
Booklist, February 1, 2002, Patricia Monaghan, review of *Ireland's Love Poems: Wonder and a Wild Desire*, p. 917.
Choice, May, 1993, B. Quinn, review of *The Gonne-Yeats Letters, 1893-1938*, p. 1466; September, 1996, review of *W. B. Yeats: Man and Poet*, p. 126; May, 1997, review of *Images of Invention: Essays of Irish Writing*, p. 1496.
Christian Science Monitor, March 15, 1990, Thomas D. D'Evelyn, review of *W. B. Yeats: A New Biography*, p. 13; January 19, 1993, Merle Rubin, review of *The Gonne-Yeats Letters, 1893-1938*, p. 13.
Commonweal, August 13, 1993, Elizabeth Shannon, review of *The Gonne-Yeats Letters, 1893-1938*, p. 24.
Contemporary Review, October, 1992, Geoffrey Heptonstall, review of *Always Your Friend*, p. 219; March, 1997, Geoffrey Heptonstall, review of *Images of Invention: Essays of Irish Writing*, p. 164.
Criticism, fall, 1969.

Economist, June 5, 1965; April 25, 1992, review of *The Gonne-Yeats Letters, 1893-1938,* pp. 100, 116.

English Literature in Transition 1880-1920, February, 1997, review of *W. B. Yeats: Man and Poet,* p. 252.

Georgia Review, fall, 1994, Patricia Meyer Spacks, review of *The Gonne-Yeats Letters, 1893-1938,* p. 610.

James Joyce Quarterly, spring-summer, 1995, Sebastian D. G. Knowes, review of *Joycechoyce: The Poems in Verse and Prose of James Joyce,* p. 777; summer-fall, 1998, David Holdeman, review of *Images of Invention,* p. 930.

Library Journal, November 1, 1992, Judy Mimken, review of *The Gonne-Yeats Letters, 1893-1938,* p. 85.

Modern Language Review, July, 1977.

New Leader, January 22, 1990, Phoebe Pettingell, review of *W. B. Yeats: A New Biography,* p. 15; January 25, 1993, Phoebe Pettingell, review of *The Gonne-Yeats Letters, 1893-1938,* p. 17.

New Yorker, February 8, 1993, George Steiner, review of *The Gonne-Yeats Letters, 1893-1938,* p. 109.

New York Times, January 2, 1990, Michiko Kakutani, review of *W. B. Yeats: A New Biography,* p. B2.

New York Times Book Review, January 10, 1993, Seamus Deane, review of *The Gonne-Yeats Letters, 1893-1938,* p. 13.

Poetry, April, 1968.

Publishers Weekly, October 1992, review of *The Gonne-Yeats Letters, 1893-1938,* p. 65.

Reference & Research Book News, September, 1996, review of *W. B. Yeats: Man and Poet,* p. 56.

Saturday Review, December 11, 1965.

Sewanee Review, winter, 1976; summer, 1994, Ben Howard, review of *The Gonne-Yeats Letters, 1893-1938,* p. 84.

Southern Review, summer, 1993, Vereen Bell, review of *The Gonne-Yeats Letters, 1893-1938,* p. 629.

Times Educational Supplement, January 27, 1978.

Times Literary Supplement, June 24, 1965; January 2, 1968; January 8, 1971; July 26, 1974; October 10, 1975; June 29, 1984; March 10, 1989, p. 252; May 11, 1990, p. 493; April 24, 1992, Penelope Fitzgerald, review of *The Gonne-Yeats Letters, 1893-1938,* p. 5; September 27, 1996, Norman Vance, review of *Images of Invention,* p. 13; September 27, 1996, review of *Ireland's Women,* p. 32; February 1, 2002, Edna Longley, review of *Poems and Plays of Oliver St. John Gogarty,* p. 25.

Tribune Books (Chicago, IL), November 19, 1989, p. 5.

Virginia Quarterly Review, spring, 1969.

Washington Post Book World, February 25, 1990, p. 6.

World Literature Today, autumn, 1990, William Pratt, review of *W. B. Yeats: A New Biography,* p. 643; spring, 1996, Daniel Patrick King, review of *The Gonne-Yeats Letters, 1893-1938,* p. 411.

ONLINE

Norton Poets Online, http://www.wwnorton.com/ (June 4, 2002), biography of A. Norman Jeffares.

* * *

JILES, Paulette 1943-

PERSONAL: Born April 4, 1943, in Salem, MO; immigrated to Canada, 1969; married. *Education:* University of Missouri, B.A. (Spanish literature), 1969.

ADDRESSES: Home—San Antonio, TX. *Agent*—Liz Darhansoff, Darhansoff & Verrill Literary Agency, 179 Franklin St., 4th Floor, New York, NY 10013.

CAREER: Writer, poet. Canadian Broadcasting Corp. (CBC-Radio), Toronto, Ontario, Canada, freelance reporter, 1968-69; journalism consultant to native Canadian communication groups in Arctic region, 1973-83; David Thompson University, Nelson, British Columbia, Canada, instructor, 1983-84; Phillips Academy, Andover, MA, writer-in-residence, 1987-88; appeared in documentary film *Rose's House,* 1976.

AWARDS, HONORS: President's Gold Medal, 1973; Pat Lowther Memorial award, 1984; Gerald Lampert award, 1974; Governor General's Award, 1984, for *Celestial Navigation;* A.C.T.R.A. award, 1989, for *Money and Blankets;* "Read This!" choice citation from *Good Morning America,* 2002, for *Enemy Women.*

WRITINGS:

Rose's House (screenplay), National Film Board of Canada (Montreal, Quebec, Canada), 1976.

Sitting in the Club Car Drinking Rum and Karma-Kola: A Manual of Etiquette for Ladies Crossing Canada by Train (novella), Polestar Press (Winlaw, British Columbia, Canada), 1986.

The Late Great Human Road Show (novel), Talonbooks (Vancouver, British Columbia, Canada), 1986.

Cousins (novel), Knopf (New York, NY), 1991.

North Spirit: Travels among the Cree and Ojibway Nations and Their Star Maps, Hungry Mind (St. Paul, MN), 1995, published as *North Spirit: Sojourns among the Cree and Ojibway,* Doubleday Canada (Toronto, Ontario, Canada), 1995.

Enemy Women (novel), Morrow (New York, NY), 2002.

POETRY

Waterloo Express, Anansi (Toronto, Ontario, Canada), 1973.

Celestial Navigations, McClelland & Stewart (Toronto, Ontario, Canada), 1984.

The Jesse James Poems, Polestar Press (Winlaw, British Columbia, Canada), 1988.

Blackwater, Knopf (New York, NY), 1988.

Song to the Rising Sun: A Collection, Polestar Press (Winlaw, British Columbia, Canada), 1989.

Flying Lessons: Selected Poems, Oxford University Press (Toronto, Ontario, Canada), 1995.

Also author of radio plays *My Mother's Quilt,* 1987, and *Money and Blankets,* 1988. Work represented in anthologies, including *Canada First,* edited by P. Anson, Anansi, 1970, and *Mindscapes.* Contributor of short stories to *Saturday Night.*

ADAPTATIONS: *Enemy Women* has been optioned for a motion picture.

SIDELIGHTS: Novelist and poet Paulette Jiles became nationally recognized in 2002 with the publication of her historical novel *Enemy Women.* Although many reviewers cited *Enemy Women* as her first novel, Jiles is in fact an accomplished writer with many other books to her credit. Well before *Enemy Women* hit the stands, Jiles had become well known in her adopted country of Canada for what *New York Times Book Review* contributor George Garrett called, "a realized sense of place—places really . . . a real world with sharp corners and edges and with real people with muscles and bones, minds and spirits, hopes and memories, characters who cast shadows." Among her works are the novel *Cousins* and the poetry collections *Blackwater* and *Celestial Navigation,* the latter winning Canada's prestigious Governor General's award in 1985.

Jiles's first volume of poetry, *Waterloo Express,* met with an enthusiastic reception in 1973. Dennis Lee commented in *Saturday Night* that "the author is often presented in folk outline: she laments a string of busted love affairs, hits the road again and again to forget, and can talk as sardonic and lowdown as any blues momma. Yet the TNT and agony she drags around come crackling out in images of manic brilliance, controlled by a frequently superb ear." Linda Rogers of *Canadian Literature* was similarly impressed with Jiles's use of language. Her "images have a life of their own," Rogers explained, and "in visual terms, the poems are like the paintings of Marc Chagall. Gorgeous disconnected figures float by. . . . All the paraphernalia of life's circus is assembled in a giant mobile moving in the wind."

It was over a decade before Jiles's second book, *Celestial Navigation,* was published. Containing twenty-one poems from *Waterloo Express,* the volume also includes many newer poems, comprising a "collection that derives its dynamic energy from Jiles's skill with language," wrote *Books in Canada* reviewer Judith Fitzgerald. "Whether she focuses on interpersonal relationships or interplanetary movements, all things flourish where she turns her eyes." *Celestial Navigation,* which also includes several long, narrative prose poems, uses storytelling to create what *Canadian Poetry* essayist Susan J. Schenk called "a distinctively female, profoundly personal response to experience. . . . [T]he voice talking . . . is for Jiles a means of both displacing personal experience, locating it in the experiences of others, and revealing intensely personal thoughts and emotions."

Jiles's 1988 verse collection, *Blackwater,* was her first volume to be published in the United States, where she was born and raised. The collection incorporates her *Jesse James Poems,* a montage of poetry and contemporary newspaper articles, photographs, and other artifacts related to the outlaw gang that Garrett termed "a major achievement" through Jiles's ability to colorfully recreate, "with an eccentric linking of narrative points of view . . . the rowdy, bloody adventures and misadventures of the James boys." *Blackwater* also contains several short prose works, as well as Jiles's 1986 comic novella, *A Manual of Etiquette for Ladies Crossing Canada by Train,* which was published in Canada under the title *Sitting in the Club Car Drinking Rum and Karma-Kola.* A parody of the 1940s detective novels of Raymond Chandler and Dashiell Hammett, *A Manual of Etiquette* follows its heroine as she avoids the payment of $50,000 in overdue bills by fleeing across country.

Song to the Rising Sun contains both poetry and several of Jiles's radio scripts. The collection focuses on the poet's recollections of her youth, growing up in Missouri's Ozark Mountain region around a number of colorful—and talkative—friends, neighbors, and relatives. "The poet's voice sounds everywhere with a strong incantatory beat and a marked use of repetition," according to *Contemporary Women Poets* contributor Patience Wheatley. Jiles's 1995 collection, *Flying Lessons: Selected Poems,* incorporates some poems from *Song to the Rising Sun* along with new material. Jiles has also published *North Spirit: Sojourns among the Cree and Ojibway,* a 1995 nonfiction work that recounts her experiences while living among Canada's northern tribes in the 1970s and 1980s.

It was the 2002 novel *Enemy Women* that became Jiles's first bestseller. The Civil War-era story is based upon Jiles's own family history and on research she did on women prisoners in Missouri during the Civil War. Set in the Ozark region of Missouri, the novel recounts the wartime experiences of Adair Randolph Colley, an eighteen-year-old thrown into desperate circumstances with little more than her wits to guide her. After Adair's father is beaten and taken away by the Union militia, she follows the troops in hopes of finding out his whereabouts. Instead she is arrested as a Confederate spy and consigned to a women's penitentiary in St. Louis. Amidst the horrifying conditions of the jail, Adair falls in love with the Union officer in charge of the facility, and he helps her to escape even as he leaves the post himself for active duty in the front lines. Christine Wald-Hopkins in the *Denver Post* called *Enemy Women* "a patchwork of varied and disparate pieces—a love story, a grownup girl-and-horse story, a little personal family history, straight historical exposition and a narrative pieced together by period documents."

Enemy Women became a bestseller after it was chosen as the second "Read This!" selection by the television show *Good Morning America.* The book's success was also propelled by reviews and by the popularity of Civil War titles in general. Like *Cold Mountain* before it, *Enemy Women* reveals another side to the famous conflict, that of civilian suffering and the unjust incarceration of innocent people who were merely under suspicion of collaboration with the enemy. According to Linda Brazill in the *Capital Times,* "It's the intimate knowledge of how things worked, smelled and tasted more than a hundred years ago that lend [Jiles's] tale its strength and immediacy. Jiles covers what should be familiar territory by now—the Civil War—but she makes it seem like not only a new story but one that is more related to contemporary history and politics than I would have imagined possible." Brazill further noted that Jiles is "a talented writer whose book is filled with memorable images and passages that beg to be read a second time." A reviewer for the *Tampa Tribune* noted that Jiles's "poetic experience rings through in her prose. The narrative is rich with exquisitely sensual descriptions of the sights, smells, and sounds of a country at war."

According to Michelle Vellucci in *People, Enemy Women* succeeds "because of the vitality of its heroine. Adair is a spitfire with a brash sense of humor and a will of granite. Hers is a love story with grit." In the *Houston Chronicle* Eileen McClelland noted that the "storyteller's skill provides a breezy read through . . . heavy matters that serve as an interesting backdrop to a romantic journey. . . . It's easy to cheer Adair on in her wild journey home."

BIOGRAPHICAL AND CRITICAL SOURCES:

BOOKS

Contemporary Literary Criticism, Volume 13, Gale (Detroit, MI), 1980.

Contemporary Women Poets, St. James Press (Detroit, MI), 1997.

PERIODICALS

Books in Canada, October, 1984, pp. 27-28; January-February, 1987, p. 15.
Canadian Forum, August, 1974; August-September, 1987, pp. 48-49.
Canadian Literature, summer, 1974; spring, 1988, pp. 209-211.
Canadian Poetry, spring/summer, 1987, pp. 67-79.
Capital Times (Madison, WI), May 17, 2002, Linda Brazill, "Civil War Woman's Tale Comes to Life," review of *Enemy Women,* p. A13.
Christian Science Monitor, March 7, 2002, Ray Burson, review of *Enemy Women,* p. 20.
Denver Post, March 24, 2002, review of *Enemy Women,* p. EE-03.
Houston Chronicle, April 14, 2002, Eileen McClelland, "Fighting Woman," review of *Enemy Women,* p. 18.
Knight Ridder/Tribune News Service, February 19, 2003, John Mark Eberhart, review of *Enemy Women,* p. K5766.
Library Journal, February 15, 2002, Ann Fleury, review of *Enemy Women,* p. 178.
New York Times Book Review, October 23, 1988, p. 22; February 24, 2002, John Vernon, "P.O.W.," p. 9.
People, February 11, 2002, Michelle Vellucci, review of *Enemy Women,* p. 41.
Publishers Weekly, December 20, 1991, review of *Cousins,* p. 79; January 7, 2002, review of *Enemy Women,* p. 46; July 15, 2002, Daisy Maryles, "GMA Makes an 'Enemy'," p. 18.
Quill & Quire, December, 1986, p. 38.
St. Louis Post-Dispatch, February 3, 2002, Colleen Kelly Warren, "Novel Set in Missouri Blends Love Story with the Civil War," review of *Enemy Women,* p. G8.
Saturday Night, December, 1973; December, 1977.
Tampa Tribune, March 3, 2002, "Civil War Story Captures Human Spirit," review of *Enemy Women,* p. 4.

ONLINE

Readers Read Web site, http://www.readersread.com/ (February, 2003), interview with Paulette Jiles.*

JONES, Alex S. 1946-

PERSONAL: Born November 19, 1946, in Greeneville, TN; son of John M. (a newspaper publisher) and Arnold (a homemaker; maiden name, Susong) Jones; married Susan E. Tifft (a journalist), September 21, 1985. *Education:* Washington and Lee University, B.A., 1968. *Politics:* Democrat. *Religion:* Episcopalian.

ADDRESSES: Home—Apt. 61, 1 Waterhouse St., Cambridge, MA 02138-3612. *Office*—Joan Shorenstein Center on the Press, Politics and Public Policy, John F. Kennedy School of Government, 79 JFK St., 2nd Floor Taubman, Cambridge, MA 02138. *Agent*—Kathy Robbins, Robbins Office Inc., 405 Park Ave. 9th Floor, New York, NY 10022.

CAREER: Journalist, writer, broadcaster. *Daily Post-Athenian,* Athens, TN, managing editor, 1974-78; *Greeneville Sun,* Greeneville, TN, editor, 1978-83; *New York Times,* New York, NY, business reporter, 1983-92; WNYC-AM Radio, New York, NY, host of *On the Media,* 1993; Public Broadcasting System (PBS-TV), New York, NY, host and executive editor, *Media Matters,* 1996—; Duke University, Durham, NC, coholder of Eugene Patterson Professorship of Journalism, 1998-2000; Harvard University, Joan Shorenstein Center on the Press, Politics, and Public Policy, lecturer, director, 2000—. Appalshop, member of board of directors; International Center for Journalists, member of board of directors. Has appeared on numerous television shows, including *The News Hour, Nightline, McLaughlin Report,* and *The Charlie Rose Show. Military service:* U.S. Naval Reserve, active duty, 1968-71; became lieutenant junior grade.

MEMBER: Committee of Concerned Journalists, New York Media Project, Harvard Club of New York City.

AWARDS, HONORS: Nieman fellowship, 1981-82; Pulitzer Prize, specialized reporting, 1987, for "The Fall of the House of Bingham" in the *New York Times;* "Ten Best Business Books of 1991" citation from *Business Week,* for *The Patriarch: The Rise and Fall of the Bingham Dynasty; New York Times* "notable book" citation, 1991, for *The Patriarch;* "five best nonfiction

Alex S. Jones

books of 1999" citation from *Time* magazine, 2000, for *The Trust: The Private and Powerful Family behind the New York Times.*

WRITINGS:

(With wife, Susan E. Tifft) *The Patriarch: The Rise and Fall of the Bingham Dynasty,* Summit Books (New York, NY), 1991.
(With Susan E. Tifft) *The Trust: The Private and Powerful Family behind the New York Times,* Little, Brown (Boston, MA), 1999.

Contributor to *Brill's Content, Freedom Forum Media Studies Journal, Columbia Journalism Review, Nieman Reports,* and *American Journalism Review.* Member of advisory board, *Columbia Journalism Review.*

SIDELIGHTS: Alex S. Jones is the director of the Joan Shorenstein Center on the Press, Politics, and Public Policy, a division of Harvard University's John F. Kennedy School of Government. A Pulitzer Prize-winning journalist himself, Jones is recognized as an authority on the media in both its print and electronic forms. Through his duties at the Shorenstein Center and his work as executive editor and host of *Media Matters,* a Public Broadcasting System (PBS) television show, Jones seeks to explain "how the press affects politics and public policy," as he told the *Harvard Gazette.*

From 1998 through 2000 Jones shared the Eugene C. Patterson Professorship of the Practice of Journalism with his wife, former *Time* magazine staff member Susan E. Tifft. Together Tifft and Jones have written two books, *The Patriarch: The Rise and Fall of the Bingham Dynasty* and *The Trust: The Private and Powerful Family behind the New York Times. The Patriarch* grew out of Jones's Pulitzer Prize-winning series for the *New York Times* on the Bingham family of Louisville, Kentucky, and their ownership of the highly respected *Louisville Courier-Journal.* The volume documents the intersection between the public business decisions and the private rivalries that ultimately tore the family apart and precipitated the sale of its various newspaper holdings. A *Publishers Weekly* reviewer described the work as an "enthralling, juicy, prodigiously researched saga" that abounds in "withering portrayals" of quarreling family members.

The Trust is a multigenerational history of the family behind the *New York Times.* Since 1896 members of the Ochs-Sulzberger family have owned and published the nation's best-known newspaper, passing the leadership from father to son through four generations. Through all that time, the newspaper has made its name on the quality of its journalism rather than catering to passing whim. While Tifft and Jones see much to admire in the continuing power and prestige of the *New York Times,* their account also details the difficulties besetting a single family dynasty seeking to maintain leadership for the periodical. A *Business Week* reviewer noted that *The Trust* "should stand as the definitive story of the *Times* for years to come." The reviewer added that Tifft and Jones "have produced a remarkable chronicle—a sprawling panorama spanning five generations. It encompasses countless power struggles, broken marriages, embarrassing infidelities, and other assorted dirty laundry. It also tells a story of power and endurance." Christopher B. Daly in *The*

American Prospect likewise felt that the book "is certain to stand as the definitive work on the subject for a good long while," and noted that the authors supply "an air of suspense that lasts right up to the final chapter." And a *Publishers Weekly* contributor concluded that, after reading *The Trust*, "it's hard not to admire the ongoing effectiveness of an epic family institution in a world of new media upstarts and gargantuan corporate mergers."

BIOGRAPHICAL AND CRITICAL SOURCES:

PERIODICALS

American Prospect, January 17, 2000, Christopher B. Daly, review of *The Trust: The Private and Powerful Family behind the New York Times,* p. 58.
Booklist, September 15, 1999, Vanessa Bush, review of *The Trust,* p. 198.
Business Week, October 4, 1999, "The Arthurian Legends: A Tale of the Times," p. 19.
Fortune, October 11, 1999, Andrew Ferguson, "News without Fear or Favor (or the Funnies)," p. 82.
Newsweek, September 27, 1999, Laura Shapiro, "All of the Family's News," p. 48.
New York Times Book Review, April 14, 1991, p. 1; September 26, 1999, Ron Chernow, "Who's In Charge Here," p. 8.
Publishers Weekly, February 8, 1991, Genevieve Stuttaford, review of *The Patriarch: The Rise and Fall of the Bingham Dynasty,* p. 42; August 23, 1999, review of *The Trust,* p. 35.
Time, April 29, 1991, William A. Henry III, review of *The Patriarch,* p. 74.
Washington Monthly, November, 1999, Nelson W. Polsby, review of *The Trust,* p. 52.

ONLINE

Harvard Gazette, http://www.news.harvard.edu/gazette/ (April 20, 2000), article about Jones with biography.*

K

KADOHATA, Cynthia 1956(?)-

PERSONAL: Born 1956 (some sources say 1957), in Chicago, IL. *Education:* Attended Los Angeles City College; received degree from University of Southern California; attended graduate programs at the University of Pittsburgh and Columbia University.

ADDRESSES: Agent—Andrew Wylie, Wylie, Aitken & Stone, Inc., 250 West 57th St., Suite 2106, New York, NY 10107.

CAREER: Writer. Worked variously as a department store clerk and waitress.

AWARDS, HONORS: Whiting Writer's Award from the Mrs. Giles Whiting Foundation; a grant from the National Endowment for the Arts.

WRITINGS:

The Floating World, Viking (New York, NY), 1989.
In the Heart of the Valley of Love, Viking (New York, NY), 1992.
Kira-Kira, Atheneum (New York, NY), 2004.

Contributor of short stories to periodicals, including *New Yorker, Grand Street, Ploughshares,* and *Pennsylvania Review.*

SIDELIGHTS: Cynthia Kadohata's background and experience are mirrored in her novels about young Asian-American women coming of age. Kadohata

Cynthia Kadohata

grew up in a family that moved often—to Illinois, Michigan, Georgia, Arkansas, and California. These experiences of traveling from town to town and state to state are a basic element of her first novel, *The Floating World.* In her second novel, *In the Heart of the Valley of Love,* she uses other autobiographical material. In a *Publishers Weekly* interview with Lisa

See, Kadohata related that she has always had "paranoid dreams" about the future and writing the science fiction novel *In the Heart of the Valley of Love* "may have purged my fears." One episode in this book is based on a serious accident Kadohata experienced; a car jumped a curb and hit her, mangling her right arm. The author told See that writing about the incident was a way of dealing with it: "I thought this was a way for me to come out of the closet, in a sense. I have friends who have never seen my arm." Kadohata added that because she uses her own experiences in her writing, the distinction between reality and fiction is sometimes confusing. She pointed out that "sometimes I can't remember if something has happened to me or to my character. My memories become their memories, and their memories become mine."

Kadohata's debut novel, *The Floating World,* is told through the voice of twelve-year-old Olivia. The story depicts the journey of a Japanese-American family searching for economic and emotional security in post-World War II America. Kadohata uses Olivia's character to portray the family dynamics and interactions that occur as they travel, eat, and even sleep in the same room together. In a passage that reveals the significance of the book's title, Olivia explains this itinerant life: "We were travelling then in what she [Obasan, Olivia's grandmother] called *ukiyo,* the floating world. The floating world was the gas station attendants, restaurants, and jobs we depended on, the motel towns floating in the middle of fields and mountains. In old Japan, *ukiyo* meant the districts full of brothels, tea houses and public baths, but it also referred to change and the pleasures and loneliness change brings. For a long time, I never exactly thought of us as part of any of that, though. *We* were stable, travelling through an unstable world while my father looked for jobs."

In addition to the physical journey, Kadohata illustrates Olivia's internal journey in *The Floating World.* Due to the close quarters of her family's living arrangements, Olivia is exposed to adult issues at an early age. She witnesses the tension that exists between her parents, their quiet arguments, and even their love making. In addition, she is constantly subjected to her eccentric grandmother's frequently abusive behavior. Finally the family finds a stable home in Arkansas where Olivia matures from young teen to young adult. It is during this time that she learns to understand the ways of her parents and grandmother and to develop her own values. *Los Angeles Times Book Review* contributor Grace Edwards-Yearwood commended this portrayal, pointing out that "Kadohata writes compellingly of Olivia's coming of age, her determination to grow beyond her parents' dreams."

The Floating World received many favorable reviews. Diana O'Hehir in the *New York Times Book Review* claimed that Kadohata's "aim and the book's seem to be one: to present the world affectionately and without embroidery. To notice what's there. To see it as clearly as you can." Caroline Ong, a *Times Literary Supplement* contributor, defined the narrative of *The Floating World* as "haunting because of its very simplicity and starkness, its sketchy descriptions fleshing out raw emotions and painful truths." Susanna Moore, writing in the *Washington Post Book World,* judged that *The Floating World* would be a better book if it had been written in the style of a memoir. But, she conceded that "Kadohata has written a book that is a child's view of the floating world, a view that is perceptive, unsentimental and intelligent." *New York Times* critic Michiko Kakutani praised Kadohata's ability to handle painful moments with humor and sensitivity. The reviewer concluded these "moments not only help to capture the emotional reality of these people's lives in a delicate net of images and words, but they also attest to Ms. Kadohata's authority as a writer. *The Floating World* marks the debut of a luminous new voice in fiction."

In the Heart of the Valley of Love is a futuristic novel concerning survival and quality of life in Los Angeles in the year 2052. In this world Kadohata pits the haves and have-nots against one another. Both are gun-toting communities without morals, law, or order. Amidst this chaos, the main character, a nineteen-year-old orphan of Asian and African descent named Francie, relates her story of endurance. Some critics found this second novel relatively disappointing. Barbara Quick in the *New York Times Book Review* criticized the book for lack of conviction and imagination, and further noted that the main character, with only a few alterations, is the same as Kadohata's earlier protagonist. In a similar vein, Michiko Kakutani argued that "unfortunately, Ms. Kadohata's vision of the future is not sufficiently original or compelling. . . . *Heart of the Valley* is an uncomfortable hybrid: a pallid piece of futuristic writing, and an unconvincing tale of coming of age." The reviewer noted, however, that "the writing in this volume is lucid and finely honed, often lyrical and occasionally magical." Other reviewers, however, were thoroughly impressed by Kadohata's work. *Los Angeles Times Book Review* contributor Susan Heeger lauded Kadohata as "masterful in her evocation of physical, spiritual and cultural displacement. . . . The message of this marvelous though often painful book is that our capacity to feel deep emotion—our own and others'—just might bind us together, and save us from ourselves."

Kadohata's status as a new voice for Japanese Americans has brought the author both satisfaction and frustration. Writing in the *Globe and Mail,* Rui Umezawa praised her work: "This is perhaps the greatest joy in reading works of writers from this newly formed tradition. The reader gets a view of another culture from both the inside and the outside. Concepts previously thought foreign suddenly become accessible—at times even moving—making a mockery of pessimistic academics who declare that true understanding of another culture is an impossible dream." In the interview with See, Kadohata summarized her thoughts about the significance of being an Asian-American writer: "For the first time in my life, I saw that there could be expectations of me not only as a writer but as an Asian- American writer. On the one hand, I felt like, 'Leave me alone.' On the other hand, I thought, 'This is a way I can assert my Asianness.' I wrote the book, and I'm Asian, and I'm the only person who could have written it." At the same time, however, Kadohata has weathered criticism that her work is historically inaccurate because it does not conform to the experience of other Japanese Americans, and even that she has been "socially irresponsible" in presenting Obasan as a flawed and difficult character. This type of thinking, the author told See, is misguided. "One Japanese interviewer . . . asked me if in *The Floating World* I was saying that all Japanese grandmothers are abusive and in conflict with themselves. Of course not! Obasan was a character in a novel—not a person representing all Japanese grandmothers. He said that Amy Tan and Maxine Hong Kingston were catering to white people, but I think they and other Asian-American writers are just writing from their hearts. Why should their work or my work stand for all Asians? That's impossible."

BIOGRAPHICAL AND CRITICAL SOURCES:

BOOKS

Kadohata, Cynthia, *The Floating World,* Viking (New York, NY), 1989.

PERIODICALS

Amerasia Journal, winter, 1997, Lynn M. Itagaki, review of *In the Heart of the Valley of Love,* p. 229.
America, November 18, 1989, Eve Shelnutt, review of *The Floating World,* p. 361.
Antioch Review, winter, 1990, review of *The Floating World,* p. 125.
Belles Lettres, spring, 1993, review of *In the Heart of the Valley of Love,* p. 46.
Booklist, June 15, 1992, Gilbert Taylor, review of *In the Heart of the Valley of Love,* p. 1807.
Globe and Mail (Toronto, Ontario, Canada), August 5, 1989.
Library Journal, June 15, 1992, Cherry W. Li, review of *In the Heart of the Valley of Love,* p. 102.
Los Angeles Times Book Review, July 16, 1989, p. 12; August 23, 1992, pp. 1, 8; May 2, 1993, review of *The Floating World,* p. 10.
New York Times, June 30, 1989, Michiko Kakutani, review of *The Floating World,* p. B4; July 28, 1992, Michiko Kakutani, review of *In the Heart of the Valley of Love,* p. C15.
New York Times Book Review, July 23, 1989, Diana O'Hehir, review of *The Floating World,* p. 16; August 30, 1992, Barbara Quick, review of *In the Heart of the Valley of Love,* p. 14.
Publishers Weekly, May 12, 1989, review of *The Floating World,* p. 279; June 1, 1992, review of *In the Heart of the Valley of Love,* p. 51; August 3, 1992, Lisa See, "Cynthia Kadohata," pp. 48-49.
School Library Journal, January, 1990, Anne Paget, review of *The Floating World,* p. 127.
Time, June 19, 1989, review of *The Floating World,* p. 65.
Times Literary Supplement, December 29, 1989, Caroline Ong, review of *The Floating World,* p. 1447.
U.S. News & World Report, December 26, 1988, Miriam Horn and Nancy Linnon, "New Cultural Worlds," p. 101.

Washington Post Book World, June 25, 1989, pp. 5, 7; August 16, 1992, p. 5.*

* * *

**KEILLOR, Gary (Edward)
See KEILLOR, Garrison**

* * *

KEILLOR, Garrison 1942-

PERSONAL: Born Gary Keillor, August 7, 1942, in Anoka, MN; son of John Philip (a railway mail clerk and carpenter) and Grace Ruth (a homemaker; maiden name, Denham) Keillor; married Mary C. Guntzel, September 1, 1965 (divorced, May, 1976); married Ulla Skaerved (a social worker), December 29, 1985 (divorced); married; wife's name Jenny; children: (first marriage) Jason, (third marriage) a daughter. *Education:* University of Minnesota, B.A., 1966, graduate study, 1966-68. *Politics:* Democrat. *Religion:* Plymouth Brethren.

ADDRESSES: Office—c/o *A Prairie Home Companion,* Minnesota Public Radio New Media, 45 East 7th St., Saint Paul, MN 55101 *Agent*—American Humor Institute, 80 Eighth Ave., No. 1216, New York, NY 10011.

CAREER: Writer. KUOM-Radio, Minneapolis, MN, staff announcer, 1963-68; Minnesota Public Radio, St. Paul, MN, producer and announcer, 1971-74, host and principal writer for weekly program *A Prairie Home Companion,* 1974-87 and 1993—; host of *Garrison Keillor's American Radio Company of the Air,* 1989-1993.

AWARDS, HONORS: George Foster Peabody Broadcasting Award, 1980, for *A Prairie Home Companion;* Edward R. Murrow Award from Corporation for Public Broadcasting, 1985, for service to public radio; *Los Angeles Times* Book Award nomination, 1986, for *Lake Wobegon Days;* Grammy Award for best nonmusical recording, 1987, for *Lake Wobegon Days;* Ace Award, 1988; Best Music and Entertainment Host Award, 1988; Gold Medal for spoken English, American Academy of Arts and Letters, 1990; inducted into Museum of Broadcast Communications and Radio Hall of Fame, 1994; National Humanities Medal, National Endowment for the Humanities, 1999.

Garrison Keillor

WRITINGS:

G.K. the DJ, Minnesota Public Radio, 1977.
The Selected Verse of Margaret Haskins Durber, Minnesota Public Radio, 1979.
Happy to Be Here: Stories and Comic Pieces, Atheneum (New York, NY), 1982, expanded edition, Penguin (New York, NY), 1983.
Lake Wobegon Days (novel), Viking (New York, NY), 1985.
Leaving Home: A Collection of Lake Wobegon Stories, Viking (New York, NY), 1987.
We Are Still Married: Stories and Letters, Viking (New York, NY), 1989.
WLT: A Radio Romance, Viking (New York, NY), 1991.

The Book of Guys, Viking (New York, NY), 1993.

Cat, You Better Come Home, illustrated by Steve Johnson, Viking (New York, NY), 1995.

The Old Man Who Loved Cheese, illustrated by Anne Wilsdorf, Little, Brown (Boston, MA), 1996.

Wobegon Boy, Viking (New York, NY), 1997.

(Editor, with Katrina Kenison) *The Best American Short Stories: 1998,* Houghton (Boston, MA), 1998.

Me: By Jimmy (Big Boy) Valente, Governor of Minnesota. As Told to Garrison Keillor, Viking (New York, NY), 1999.

(Coauthor) *Minnesota Days: Our Heritage in Stories, Art, and Photos,* Voyageur (Stillwater, MN), 1999.

In Search of Lake Wobegon, with photographs by Richard Olsenius, Viking (New York, NY), 2001.

Lake Wobegon Summer 1956, Viking (New York, NY), 2001.

(Editor and author of introduction) *Good Poems* (anthology), Viking (New York, NY), 2002.

Love Me, Viking (New York, NY), 2003.

Contributor of articles and stories to periodicals, including *New Yorker, Harper's* and *Atlantic Monthly.*

RECORDINGS

A Prairie Home Companion Anniversary Album, Minnesota Public Radio, 1980.

The Family Radio, Minnesota Public Radio, 1982.

News from Lake Wobegon, Minnesota Public Radio, 1982.

Prairie Home Companion Tourists, Minnesota Public Radio, 1983.

Ten Years on the Prairie: A Prairie Home Companion 10th Anniversary, Minnesota Public Radio, 1984.

Gospel Birds and Other Stories of Lake Wobegon, Minnesota Public Radio, 1985.

A Prairie Home Companion: The Final Performance, Minnesota Public Radio, 1987.

More News from Lake Wobegon, Minnesota Public Radio, 1988.

Lake Wobegon Loyalty Days: A Recital for Mixed Baritone and Orchestra, Minnesota Public Radio, 1989.

Local Man Moves to City, Highbridge, 1991.

(With Frederica von Stade) *Songs of the Cat,* Highbridge, 1991.

Keillor has also recorded his book *Lake Wobegon Days.*

SIDELIGHTS: Born on August 7, 1942, in Anoka, Minnesota, Garrison Keillor was the third of six children born into a conservative religious family. His father, John Philip, worked as a railroad clerk and carpenter to support his family. Gary, however, had his eye on a literary career from a young age. In fact, at the age of thirteen, he started calling himself "Garrison" for professional reasons. His single-minded focus and hard work would pay off in later years as he became a household name.

With the words "It's been a quiet week in Lake Wobegon, my hometown," radio humorist and author Keillor introduced his monologue on his long-running Minnesota Public Radio program, *A Prairie Home Companion.* The stories he told over the air, based partly on his memories of growing up in semi-rural Anoka, Minnesota, were among the highlights of the live-broadcast show—an eclectic mixture of comedy and music (including bluegrass, blues, ethnic folk, choral, gospel, opera, and yodeling)—which reached an audience of about four million listeners per week by the time it went off the air in 1987. It reached a great many more people in its last year when the Disney Channel obtained cable television broadcasting rights.

As principal writer and host of the show, Keillor also revealed his humor in the commercials he wrote for the sponsors of his program, including Ralph's Pretty Good Grocery ("If you can't find it at Ralph's, you can probably get along without it"), Bertha's Kitty Boutique ("For persons who care about cats"), the Chatterbox Cafe ("Where the coffeepot is always on, which is why it always tastes that way"), Bob's Bank ("Neither a borrower nor a lender be; so save at the sign of the sock"), the Sidetrack Tap ("Don't sleep at our bar; we don't drink in your bed"), and especially those Powdermilk Biscuits ("Heavens, they're tasty") that "give shy persons the strength to get up and do what needs to be done."

Many critics place Keillor in the tradition of such American humorists as Ring Lardner, James Thurber, and Mark Twain. Like Twain, who gained a reputation traveling on the American lecture circuit in the last years of the nineteenth and first years of the twentieth century, Keillor's audience originally came from his live performances. Roy Blount, Jr., writing in the *New York Times Book Review* about *A Prairie Home Companion,* stated that it was "impossible to describe. Everyone I have met who has heard it has either been dumbfounded by it, or addicted to it, or both." "The same is true of Keillor's prose," Blount continued, referring to a series of pieces written for the *New Yorker* and collected in *Happy to Be Here: Stories and Comic Pieces.* However, "many of these pieces," wrote Peter A. Scholl in the *Dictionary of Literary Biography Yearbook: 1987,* "show the witty and urbane Keillor rather than the wistful, wandering storyteller in exile from Lake Wobegon, where 'smart doesn't count for very much.'"

In 1985, the publication of *Lake Wobegon Days* brought Keillor's small town to national prominence. Beginning with the first explorations of the French traders in the eighteenth century, Keillor goes on to describe the town's history up to the present day. But Lake Wobegon is, according to Mary T. Schmich in the *Chicago Tribune,* "a town that lies not on any map but somewhere along the border of his imagination and his memory." Keillor described it in *Lake Wobegon Days:* "Bleakly typical of the prairie, Lake Wobegon has its origins in the utopian vision of nineteenth-century New England Transcendentalists, but now is populated mainly by Norwegians and Germans. . . . The lake itself, blue-green and sparkling in the brassy summer sun and neighbored by the warm-colored marsh grasses of a wildlife-teeming slough, is the town's main attraction, though the view is spoiled somewhat by a large grain elevator by the railroad track."

Lake Wobegon, in Keillor's stories, becomes a sort of American Everytown, "the ideal American place to come from," wrote Scholl. "One of the attributes of home in Keillor's work is evanescence. . . . Dozens of his stories concern flight from Lake Wobegon, and the title of his radio show gains ironic force with the realization that it was adapted from the Prairie Home Lutheran cemetery in Moorhead, Minnesota; we are permanently at home only when we are gone." Yet "the wonderful thing about Keillor's tone in detailing life as it is lived in Lake Wobegon is not derived from his pathos knowing he can never go home again," Scholl continued. "He refuses to emphasize his status as exile in the novel [*Lake Wobegon Days*]. The wonder flows from his understanding that the complicated person he has become . . . is truly no step up from the guy down in the Sidetrack Tap he might have been had he never left home in the first place."

Keillor left *A Prairie Home Companion* in June of 1987, deciding that he needed more time to devote to his writing, and, suggested Schmich, to escape the unwanted fame that dogged his heels in Minnesota. His next book, *Leaving Home,* consisted of edited versions of his monologues from the last months of the show, many of them about people leaving Lake Wobegon. "Every once in a while," declared Richard F. Shepard in the *New York Times,* "the author slips into a poetic mood and you know he is saying goodbye to a world that was, a goodbye he makes clear as he goes along." The book, Shepard concluded, "says what it has to say with a rare, dry humor that is in what we like to believe is the very best American tradition." "His humor," Scholl stated, "is sustained by his comic faith, which like Powdermilk Biscuits, helps readers and listeners 'get up and do what needs to be done.'"

Keillor lived briefly in Denmark with his Danish wife Ulla Skaerved, then returned to the United States and set up a residence in New York City. In 1989, he began a new radio program, *Garrison Keillor's American Radio Company of the Air.* Although one of his later books, *We Are Still Married,* mostly reprints pieces that appeared originally in the *New Yorker,* he has not yet exhausted his stories about the denizens of his quiet hometown. "In some hidden chamber of our hearts," wrote David Black in *Rolling Stone,* "most of us, no matter where we live, are citizens of Lake Wobegon," the place where, according to Keillor, "all the women are strong, all the men are good-looking, and all the children are above average."

Keillor made another foray into the world of novel writing with his 1992 release, *WLT: A Radio Romance.* The book is about Ray and Roy Soderbjerg, two brothers who establish a radio station during the glory days of radio in 1926. They bumble through their new enterprise, booking acts small and smaller as they explore the frontier of radio broadcasting. Acts such as the Shepherd Boys (a gospel group), Lily Dale (a wheelchair-bound woman with a seductive voice), and the Shoe Shine Boys (a folk group) compete with radio melodramas like *Adventures in Homemaking* and *Noontime Jubilee*. Brother Ray is a lecherous man who chases after any female who comes within his realm, whereas Roy craves the country life. The station "adopts" boy broadcaster Francis With, whose parents have either died or gone mad, and he is molded into the ubiquitous announcer Frank White, who becomes the station's top draw. The novel chronicles decades of the station's rise until television becomes the draw of the day.

The novel shows the appeal of radio during its golden days, the struggling personalities involved, the backstage hijinks, and the listeners' loyalties. Critical reaction to the book was mixed. Anne Bernays, writing in the *New York Times Book Review*, claimed that the work, unusual for the man so known for his humor, "is a much darker book than one would expect. . . . Mr. Keillor's famous grin now covers a grimace." She related that this undertone is one of her main problems with the work: "Funny and energetic as *WLT* is, the book's subtext of what can only be described as disappointment disappoints. I ended up wishing Mr. Keillor had let me laugh more; he still has the humorist's singular and worthy touch." Elizabeth Beverly of *Commonweal* criticized Keillor's style in writing the book, claiming that the chapters are too short and choppy: "They seriously hinder his ability to tell a story from the inside. There's not enough room to move, not enough time to fill in background information." Beverly concluded that "Keillor the novelist doesn't know what he wants. He cannot hear what he wants. He is learning to work in a medium which, in this case, has resisted him. This novel is a failed venture, but bespeaks a great hope." While Michael Ratcliffe, writing in the London *Observer*, remarked that Keillor's novel is "very funny," he found fault with its structure, claiming that it is "not really a novel at all. Keillor is an intensive miniaturist, but he is driving a stretched limo here. . . . *Radio Romance* is like a brilliant bedding plant: it flowers as floribundantly as promised in the photograph, but puts down no roots to grow."

Keillor's next work was a book of short stories and vignettes called *The Book of Guys*. A comic spinoff of the work of Robert Bly, the Minnesota poet who wrote bestselling works about male bonding in the wilderness, *The Book of Guys* tracks the struggles with manhood experienced by such diverse protagonists as Dionysius and Buddy the Leper. Roy Bradley, Boy Broadcaster, for example, hails from the tongue-twisting village Piscacatawamaquoddymoggin, and his tale is as much one of a broken heart as of his radio vocation. Lonesome Shorty, a cowboy who takes to collecting china, ends up in conflict over how his hobby has created conflict in his previously conventional life. "Keillor puts on the mantle of guyness, with its repeating pattern of male bonding and rugged manly embraces, and camps around in it," commented Susan Jeffreys of *New Statesman & Society*.

Jeffreys claimed that the book "is the best thing he has done since *Lake Wobegon Days;* maybe even better." Lisa Zeidner praised the work in the *New York Times Book Review,* calling it "an endearingly acerbic collection." Zeidner, however, found that Keillor is not necessarily at his peak when he is pointing out the differences between the sexes: "The most substantial tales aren't really about manhood at all, but about the arbitrariness and absurdity of modern success, especially in show business," she commented. "He drags his heroes through the mud of contemporary culture and teaches them the essential tongue-in-cheek Lake Wobegon lesson . . . 'not to imagine we *are* someone but to be content being who we are.'"

The novel *Wobegon Boy* is the third of Keillor's Lake Wobegon books. The story follows John Tollefson as he leaves Lake Wobegon and takes a job at a radio station at a college in upstate New York. John's life is complicated as he enters into a partnership to open a restaurant, falls in love and gets married, experiences the death of his father, and is forced to resign from the station before finally pulling himself together. Julian Ferraro, commenting in the *Times Literary Supplement,* observed that this novel follows its Lake Wobegon predecessors in that "an intelligent, sensitive, liberal-arts-educated son of an insular community in the Midwest breaks free and lives a relatively sophisticated, cosmopolitan life on the East Coast, without ever being able fully to shed the vestiges of the values and attitudes of his home town."

Wobegon Boy's critical reception reflects Keillor's reputation as a storyteller. Ferraro found that "Keillor is . . . at his best as an energetic storyteller, and it is the various comic interludes—the 'dozens of stories of shame and degradation'—that provide the book's most entertaining moments." Reviewing the novel in the *Washington Post Book World,* Michael Kernan revealed: "Though I can't get enough of the Keillor stories on tape, I find his written version of the same material much less effective." Alex Heard in the *New York Times Book Review,* referring to Keillor's earlier book *Lake Wobegon Days* as a "part novel, part super-casual" hybrid, argued that "this time the hybrid, while often sharp and funny, doesn't work as well . . . mainly because Keillor is trying to make Tollefson . . . a three-dimensional character—as opposed to the 2-D vehicles for comic experiences and observations that populate Lake Wobegon. That's admirable, but it creates a slippery situation that sometimes squirts out of Keillor's hands." Kernan concluded with the view that Keillor "appears to ramble on for pages about this and that, entertaining us but not moving us, and then suddenly, at the very end, he pulls everything together and gives meaning and brightness to all that has gone before."

The novel *Lake Wobegon Summer 1956* tells of fourteen-year-old Gary trying to come to terms with his life in rural Minnesota, his sexual yearning, a job as the local newspaper's sportswriter, and his family's religious beliefs. "There is a good deal of *Catcher in the Rye* here: the lonely teenager who sees everything with an x-ray and dyspeptic eye," Jonathan Mirsky noted in the *Spectator.* "But it is less soft-centred and, to use Holden Caulfield's favourite word, less 'phony' than Salinger's too-admired book." Don McLeese in *Book* found that "Keillor's eye for evocative detail and penchant for parody give the novel the breezy charm of a summer reverie." Caroline Hallsworth, reviewing the novel in *Library Journal,* concluded: "Keillor's wry vignettes of Gary's summer of change and turmoil are laced with his trademark self-deprecating humor."

In the 2003 autobiographical novel *Love Me,* Larry Wyler leaves Minnesota and his sweetheart for New York City, hoping to become a famous writer. For a time he seems successful both at writing and womanizing, but his success lasts only a short time, and Wyler is soon brought low. He returns to Minnesota and a job as an advice columnist, giving out words of comfort under the pseudonym Mr. Blue.

Besides his adult fiction, Keillor has also written two books for children, *Cat, You Better Come Home* and *The Old Man Who Loved Cheese,* both of which feature his trademark sense of the absurd. In *Cat, You Better Come Home,* Keillor fictionalizes the life of a feline who wants more than she gets in her own house, so she runs away to a life of show business, only to return broken down to the man who loves her. *The Old Man Who Loved Cheese* features Wallace P. Flynn, a man whose love for the dairy product causes him to lose his wife and his family. However, after he realizes that the joys of human companionship are much more satisfying than his favorite food, he gives it up and his life is restored.

In 1999 Keillor was awarded the National Humanities Medal and was honored at a White House dinner hosted by President Bill Clinton. In July of 2001, Keillor underwent heart surgery at the Mayo Clinic in Rochester, Minnesota. He made a full recovery and continued to broadcast his show and write.

"Keillor's most lasting fame," according to an essayist for *Contemporary Popular Writers,* "will likely center around the *Prairie Home Companion.* With this radio show, Keillor has made a lasting contribution to the literary world, the art of story-telling, public broadcasting, and American culture in general by reviving in the 1980s and 1990s the pre-television tradition of gathering around the radio to listen to variety shows, comedies, and dramas. In this way, Keillor has answered the public's need for old-fashioned, wholesome, family-style entertainment, as well as for nostalgia for a simpler time and a less complicated lifestyle."

BIOGRAPHICAL AND CRITICAL SOURCES:

BOOKS

Contemporary Literary Criticism, Volume 40, Gale (Detroit, MI), 1986.
Contemporary Popular Writers, St. James Press (Detroit, MI), 1997.
Dictionary of Literary Biography Yearbook: 1987, Gale (Detroit, MI), 1988.
Encyclopedia of World Biography Supplement, Volume 22, Gale (Detroit, MI), 2002.
Keillor, Garrison, *Lake Wobegon Days,* Viking (New York, NY), 1985.
Lee, Judith Yaross, *Garrison Keillor: A Voice of America,* University Press of Mississippi (Jackson, MS), 1991.

PERIODICALS

Atlantic, October 8, 1997, Katie Bolick, "It's Just Work."

Book, September, 2001, Don McLeese, reviews of *Lake Wobegon Summer 1956* and *In Search of Lake Wobegon,* p. 80.

Booklist, June 1 and 15, 1996, p. 1732; January 1, 2003, review of *Good Poems,* p. 791.

Chicago Tribune, March 15, 1987.

Chicago Tribune Book World, January 24, 1982.

Children's Book Review Service, June, 1995, p. 124; July, 1996, p. 147.

Christian Century, July 21-28, 1982; November 13, 1985; March 22, 2003, "Wobegon Poets: A Prairie Poem Companion," p. 20.

Commonweal, April 10, 1992, p. 26.

Country Journal, January, 1982.

Detroit Free Press, September 8, 1985.

Detroit News, September 1, 1985.

Esquire, May, 1982.

Irish Times, March 7, 1998.

Kirkus Reviews, April 1, 1996, p. 532.

Library Journal, September 1, 2001, Caroline Hallsworth, review of *Lake Wobegon Summer 1956,* p. 234; March 1, 2003, Rochelle Ratner, review of *Good Poems* (audiobook), p. 136.

National Review, December 8, 1997; April 19, 1999.

New Statesman & Society, January 14, 1994, p. 40.

New York Times, October 31, 1982; August 20, 1985; October 31, 1985; October 21, 1987; August 26, 2001.

New York Times Book Review, February 28, 1982; August 25, 1985; November 10, 1991, p. 24; December 12, 1993, p. 13; May 21, 1995, p. 20; October 26, 1997, p. 14; March 28, 1999, p. 8.

Observer (London, England), January 19, 1992, p. 53; December 3, 1995, p. 16.

Publishers Weekly, September 13, 1985; May 8, 1995, p. 294; April 1, 1996, p. 74.

Rolling Stone, July 23, 1981.

Saturday Review, May-June, 1983.

School Library Journal, July, 1995, p. 78; May, 1996, p. 93; March, 2003, Sheila Shoup, review of *Good Poems,* p. 261.

Seattle Post-Intelligencer, October 7, 1999.

Spectator, November 24, 2001, Jonathan Mirsky, review of *Lake Wobegon Summer 1956,* p. 54.

Time, November 9, 1981; February 1, 1982; September 2, 1985; November 4, 1985; November 22, 1993, p. 82; December 11, 1995, p. 77.

Times Literary Supplement, February 27, 1998, p. 21.

Utne Reader, September-October, 2001, Karen Olson, "The News . . . As Seen from Lake Wobegon," p. 92.

Washington Post, August 23, 1989; July 9, 2001; July 15, 2001.

Washington Post Book World, January 18, 1982; November 28, 1993, p. 1; November 30, 1997, p.1.

Yale Review, January, 1993, p. 148.

ONLINE

Minnesota Author Biographies Project, http://people.mnhs.org/ (June 11, 2003).

Prairie Home Companion Web site, http://phc.mpr.org/ (June 11, 2003).

Prime Time Online, http://www.rny.com/ (November 13, 2001), Jeff Baenen, "Garrison Keillor Spins More Tales from Lake Wobegon."*

* * *

KESEY, Ken (Elton) 1935-2001
(O. U. Levon, a joint pseudonym)

PERSONAL: Born September 17, 1935, in La Junta, CO; died from complications following surgery for liver cancer, November 10, 2001, in Eugene, OR; son of Fred A. and Geneva (Smith) Kesey; married (Norma) Faye Haxby, May 20, 1956; children: Shannon A., Zane C., Jed M. (deceased), Sunshine M. *Education:* University of Oregon, B.A., 1957; Stanford University, graduate study, 1958-61, 1963.

CAREER: Novelist, artist, and farmer. Night attendant in psychiatric ward, Veterans Administration Hospital, Menlo Park, CA, 1961; Intrepid Trips, Inc. (motion picture company), president, 1964; *Spit in the Ocean* (magazine), editor, beginning 1974; University of Oregon, instructor in novel-writing, beginning 1990.

AWARDS, HONORS: Woodrow Wilson fellowship; Saxton Fund fellowship, 1959; Distinguished Service award, State of Oregon, 1978; Robert Kirsh Award, *Los Angeles Times,* 1991, for lifetime of work.

WRITINGS:

One Flew over the Cuckoo's Nest (novel), Viking (New York, NY), 1962, 40th anniversary edition, illustrated and with new introduction by Kesey, 2002.

Ken Kesey

Sometimes a Great Notion (novel), Viking (New York, NY), 1964.
(Contributor) *The Last Whole Earth Catalog: Access to Tools,* Portola Institute, 1971.
(Editor, with Paul Krassner, and contributor) *The Last Supplement to the Whole Earth Catalog,* Portola Institute, 1971.
(Compiler and contributor) *Kesey's Garage Sale* (interviews and articles, including "An Impolite Interview with Ken Kesey," and screenplay "O'Tools from My Chest"), introduction by Arthur Miller, Viking (New York, NY), 1973.
(Author of introduction) Paul Krassner, editor, *Best of "The Realist": The Sixties' Most Outrageously Irreverent Magazine,* Running Press, 1984.
Demon Box (essays, poetry, and stories, including "The Day after Superman Died," "Good Friday," "Finding Doctor Fung," "Run into the Great Wall," and "The Search for the Secret Pyramid"), Viking (New York, NY), 1986.
Little Tricker the Squirrel Meets Big Double the Bear (juvenile), illustrations by Barry Moser, Penguin (New York, NY), 1988.
(Under joint pseudonym O. U. Levon [anagram for "University of Oregon novel"] with others, and author of introduction) *Caverns* (mystery novel), Penguin (New York,NY), 1989.
The Further Inquiry (autobiographical screenplay), photographs by Ron Bevirt, Viking (New York, NY), 1990.
The Sea Lion (juvenile), Viking (New York, NY), 1991.
Sailor Song, Viking (New York, NY), 1992.
Last Go Round, Viking (New York, NY), 1994.
*Kesey's Jail Journal: Cut the M***** Loose,* Viking (New York, NY), 2003.

Also author of unpublished novels, "End of Autumn" and "Zoo," and of "Seven Prayers by Grandma Whittier," an unfinished novel serialized 1974-81 in *Spit in the Ocean.* Work included in anthologies, including *Stanford Short Stories 1962,* edited by Wallace Stegner and Richard Scowcroft, Stanford University Press, 1962. Contributor of articles to periodicals, including *Esquire, Rolling Stone,* and *Oui.*

A collection of Kesey's manuscripts is housed at the University of Oregon.

ADAPTATIONS: One Flew over the Cuckoo's Nest was adapted for the stage by Dale Wasserman and produced on Broadway, 1963, revived in 1971 and 2001, and published as *One Flew over the Cuckoo's Nest: A Play in Three Acts,* S. French (New York, NY), 1970, new edition with criticism, edited by John C. Pratt, 1973, revised edition, 1974; adapted for film by United Artists, 1975; and adapted for audiobook, 1998. *Sometimes a Great Notion* was adapted for film by Universal, 1972.

SIDELIGHTS: Ken Kesey, a writer and cultural hero of the mid-twentieth-century's so-called psychic frontier, is best known for his widely read novel *One Flew over the Cuckoo's Nest* and the insightful contemporary novel *Sometimes a Great Notion.* Kesey's works are set in California and Oregon, two locations representing two facets of Kesey's experience that provided the major tensions in his works. Oregon represents traditional rural family values and self-reliance inherited from Baptist pioneer stock; California is associated with the countercultural revolution in which Kesey played an important role during his lifetime. Therefore Kesey's name is often associated with the American West Coast and the hippie movement that centered itself there during the 1960s. Though he eventually adopted a more critical stance in regard to the alternative lifestyle he once championed, Kesey's later works remain haunted by fond references to the uninhibited life he enjoyed as a member of the Merry Pranksters, a group that traveled America in a bus when experimental drug use was at its peak. His novels, plays, screenplays, and essays express the author's intrepid quest for heightened consciousness in which he explored magic, hypnotism, mind-altering or psychoactive drugs, the occult, Eastern religions, and esoteric philosophies. His works also carry forward the American literary traditions of the Transcendentalists and the Beats as well as the frontier humor and vernacular style established by nineteenth-century humorist and novelist Mark Twain.

Kesey was born and raised "a hard-shell Baptist" in Colorado and Oregon, he once told Linda Gaboriau in a *Crawdaddy* interview. He accompanied his father on many hunting and fishing trips in the Pacific Northwest and developed a deep respect for nature. His love of the outdoors was matched by his fascination with extraordinary experience. He studied theatrical magic and learned to perform illusions. "I . . . did shows all through high school and in college," he once told Gaboriau. "I went from this into ventriloquism (and even had a show on TV), and from ventriloquism into hypnotism. And from hypnotism into dope. But it's always been the same trip, the same kind of search."

After high school Kesey auditioned for film roles in Hollywood before entering the University of Oregon in Eugene, where he majored in speech and communications and gained experience in acting and writing for radio and television. An active athlete during both high school and college, he won a scholarship as an outstanding college wrestler. Each of Kesey's interests figure largely in his works. Hunting and fishing are strategically important events in the two major works that established his literary reputation. His characters are physically strong and ready to compete against overwhelming pressure to conform to standards or submit to authorities that oppose their well-being. His style incorporates techniques borrowed from theatre and film such as flashbacks, fade-outs, and jump cuts, and he evidences a familiarity with the conventions of horror films and popular Westerns.

Kesey married his high school sweetheart, Faye Haxby, while at the University of Oregon, and moved to California where he enrolled in Stanford University's creative writing program. There he met Wallace Stegner, Richard Scowcroft, Malcolm Cowley, and Frank O'Connor—writers who were also literary critics—as well as fellow students Wendell Berry, Larry McMurtry, and Robert Stone. He also encountered the cultural radicalism then developing in Perry Lane, a section of Stanford patterned after the haven of the Beat movement in San Francisco's North Beach. According to *Free You* contributor Vie Lovell, to whom Kesey dedicated *One Flew over the Cuckoo's Nest,* the Perry Lane group "pioneered what have since become the hallmarks of hippie culture: LSD and other psychedelics too numerous to mention, body painting, light shows and mixed media presentations, total aestheticism, be-ins, exotic costumes, strobe lights, sexual mayhem, freakouts and the deification of psychoticism, eastern mysticism, and the rebirth of hair."

When Lovell suggested Kesey take part in the drug experiments being conducted at the Veterans Administration Hospital at Menlo Park, he accepted. There he was paid to ingest various psychoactive drugs and report on their effects. This experience, together with his experiences as an aide at the V.A. Hospital, led Kesey to write *One Flew over the Cuckoo's Nest.*

One Flew over the Cuckoo's Nest is a celebration of the resilience of the human spirit as seen in the characteristically American resistance to corrupt authority. The novel tells how Randle Patrick McMurphy, a cocky, fast-talking inmate of a prison farm who has had himself committed to a mental hospital to avoid work, creates upheaval in the ward that is so efficiently and repressively directed by Nurse Ratched. His self-confidence and irrepressible sense of humor inspire the passive, dehumanized patients to rebel against Ratched and the "Combine" of society she represents. McMurphy ultimately sacrifices himself in the process of teaching his fellow patients the saving lessons of laughter and self-reliance.

Contemporary audiences reacted positively to Kesey's novel. In the early 1960s *One Flew over the Cuckoo's Nest* presented a critique of an American society that had been portrayed in the 1950s as a lonely crowd of organization men who could achieve affluence only through strict conformity. That critique continued to suit the mood of the 1970s and 1980s because larger themes were also involved: the modern technological world as necessarily divorced from nature; contemporary society as repressive; authority as mechanical and destructive; and contemporary man as weak, frightened, and sexless, a victim of rational but loveless forces beyond his control. The novel's message—that people need to get back in touch with their world, to open doors of perception, to enjoy spontaneous sensuous experience, and to resist the manipulative forces of a technological society—was particularly appealing to the young. By the 1970s it was the contemporary novel most frequently used in college courses.

American audiences have appreciated the work in its incarnations as play, novel, and film. The stage version by Dale Wasserman appeared on Broadway with Kirk Douglas starring as McMurphy in 1963 and was revived in 1971, and again in 2001 when it was produced by Chicago's Steppenwolf theater company and starred actor Gary Sinise. The film version, directed by Milos Forman and starring Jack Nicholson, was a box office hit and won six Academy Awards in 1975.

Kesey's novel has been analyzed by critics beyond the literary realm due to the breadth of subjects, issues, and disciplines it includes. In *Lex et Scientia,* the official journal of the International Academy of Law and Science, Ralph Porzio described *One Flew over the Cuckoo's Nest* as "a cornucopia of source material from disciplines so numerous and varied as to challenge the mind and imagination." Porzio observed that it touches upon psychology, psychiatry, medicine, literature, human relations, drama, art, cosmology, law, religion, American culture, and folk culture through a kaleidoscopic blend of tragedy, pathos, and humor. A partial list of topics that show up in various analyses the book include: patterns of romance, patterns of comedy, patterns of tragedy, black humor, the absurd, the hero in modern dress, the comic Christ, folk and western heroes, the fool as mentor, the Grail Knight, attitudes toward sex, abdication of masculinity, the politics of laughter, mechanistic and totemistic symbols, the comic strip, the ritualistic father-figure, and the psychopathic savior.

Ronald Wallace, writing in *The Last Laugh: Form and Affirmation in the Contemporary American Comic Novel,* connected the novel directly to Kesey's early interest in comic books by pointing out that its main characters are drawn from ancient conventions of comedy. Wallace perceived in Nurse Ratched and McMurphy respectively the *aiazon*—the boastful, deluded fool—and the *eiron*—the witty self-deprecator who defeats his opponent by hiding his skill and intelligence. Furthermore, Wallace saw McMurphy as a "Dionysian Lord of Misrule" who "presides over a comic fertility ritual and restores instinctual life to the patients." In a *Critique* review, Terry G. Sherwood noticed the balance between comic strip conventions and those belonging to the serious novel, since the work's major confrontation is between good and evil. *Journal of Narrative Technique* reviewer Michael Boardman pointed out the novel's power as a classic tragedy because it portrays a character opposed by forces from within himself as well as from others. The conflict between Ratched and McMurphy becomes a struggle between McMurphy's need for freedom as an individual and his need to survive in a hostile environment by conforming to oppressive standards. The conventions of the Western novel with its characters, colloquialisms, and frontier values are also present in *One Flew over the Cuckoo's Nest,* observed Richard Blessing in the *Journal of Popular Culture.* Blessing wrote, "Essentially, the McMurphy who enters the ward is a frontier hero, an anachronistic paragon of rugged individualism, relentless energy, capitalistic shrewdness, virile coarseness and productive strength. He is Huck Finn with muscles, Natty Bumppo with pubic hair. He is the descendant of the pioneer who continually fled civilization and its feminizing and gentling influence."

While many reviewers saw much to learn from the book, the brand of individualism and freedom presented in McMurphy's behavior approaches anarchy too closely for others. The mayhem he raises by throwing plates and butter at walls, shouting obscenities, breaking windows, sneaking prostitutes into the ward, and stealing boats, claimed Bruce E. Wallis in *Cithara,* is not a foundation for lasting sanity and self-esteem beyond reproach. The best opposition to society's more repressive forces, Wallis maintained, may not, after all, be man's sexual and nonrational capacities.

Some critics were alarmed by the novel's portrayal of women. Leslie Horst noted in *Lex et Scientia* that Kesey's depiction of Nurse Ratched is demeaning; in fact, "considerable hatred of women is justified in the logic of the novel. The plot demands that the dreadful women who break the rules men have made for them become the targets of the reader's wrath." Viewing the novel primarily from the aspect of gender, Robert Forrey in *Modern Fiction Studies* claimed that "the premise of the novel is that women ensnare, emasculate, and, in some cases, crucify men." On the other hand, Wallace contended that there is no misogyny intended in Kesey's reversal of traditionally assigned gender-appropriate roles, which Wallace related to all comic literature "from Aristophanes to Erica Jong." Boardman suggested that Ratched is not meant to represent womankind, but to be the incarnation of evil required by the novel's dramatic action. In *The Art of Grit: Ken Kesey's Fiction,* M. Gilbert Porter reported Kesey's comment that any good story needs a villain that is truly recognizably evil if the writer is to fulfill his ethical purpose, that of standing "between the public and evil. . . . The good writer in [Kesey's] opinion is a person of 'power' and character who guards faithfully that axis of human choice."

In his book *Ken Kesey,* Barry Leeds commented that Kesey's second novel, *Sometimes a Great Notion,* is superior to *One Flew over the Cuckoo's Nest* because it is "a far more artistically impressive work on several levels. In terms of structure, point of view, theme, it is more ambitious, more experimental, and ultimately more successful." *Sometimes a Great Notion* reflects Kesey's Oregon background and the concerns of the upper Northwest region. The title refers to the folk-song refrain "Sometimes it seems a great notion / to jump in the river and drown," and signals one of the book's themes: the relatively high suicide rate in the Wakonda logging town and others like it. In the novel independent loggers Hank and Leland Stamper are at odds with their union-dominated community and with each other. After Hank involves his Ivy-league-educated half-brother's mother in a sexual relationship, Leland seeks revenge by seducing Hank's wife. The novel approaches these events from a variety of points of view to reveal what the brothers learn from each other.

Like William Faulkner, Kesey comments on the subjectivity of perception by using the cinematic device of multiple perspectives. To make the medium of fiction more fit for his purpose, he liberates himself from the chronological order used in most conventional novels. He also employs conscious authorial intrusion. Innovative use of italics, capital letters, and parentheses help him replicate in print the confusion, moral bankruptcy, and future shock his characters face.

In many ways, the conflict between the Stamper brothers corresponds to Kesey's own inner conflicts. During his college years, the conflict between his down-home athletic nature and his more artistic and intellectual side became more obvious. He could socialize with both intellectuals and more active groups, but they did not usually find each other mutually acceptable. The brothers in *Sometimes a Great Notion* embody these conflicting impulses. As he once explained to Gordon Lish in a *Genesis West* interview: "I want to find out which side of me really is: the woodsy, logger side—complete with homespun homilies and crackerbarrel corniness, a valid side of me that I like—or its opposition. The two Stamper brothers in the novel are each one of the ways I think I am."

In 1963, as Kesey was finishing *Sometimes a Great Notion,* a developer forced the evacuation of Perry Lane, and the Keseys moved to La Honda where he continued as a leader of the psychedelic movement. For the next few years he set aside his writing and sought an alternative with Neal Cassady and other kindred spirits in a group called the Merry Pranksters. His curiosity about altered states of consciousness stimulated by the experiments at the V.A. Hospital, Kesey continued his experimental drug use with the group at La Honda. Evolving from private parties to public parties to large-scale public events, the groups' "acid-tests" introduced light shows, psychedelic art, mixed-media presentations, and acid rock music to the growing hippie culture.

Headed for the New York World's Fair and the events surrounding the publication of *Sometimes a Great Notion,* the Pranksters crossed the country in a 1939 International Harvester bus decorated with bright colors applied at random. Kesey's accounts of those days appear in *Kesey's Garage Sale, Demon Box,* and *The Further Inquiry.*

Critics have referred to *Kesey's Garage Sale* as the book in which the destructive potential of drugs caught up with the author. It contains his screenplay "Over the Border," based on his 1967 flight to Mexico to avoid prosecution for marijuana possession. After witnessing the squalor and anti-American sentiments of small Mexican towns, and after his son survived a close brush with death, Kesey returned to California to serve a short sentence at the San Mateo County Jail and the San Mateo Sheriff's Honor Camp. Afterward, he moved to a farm in Pleasant Hill, Oregon, near Eugene. Many fans sought him out at the farm, looking for drug experiences or a place to live, and numbered in the hundreds each week during the 1970s. *Demon Box,* Kesey's 1986 collection of shorter works written in the '70s and '80s, reflects on both his pleasant and unpleasant experiences in the counterculture.

The Further Inquiry, Kesey's 1990 retrospective on the Merry Prankster years, examines the 1960s and 1970s from a more mature perspective. Structured as a mock trial, the screenplay pits a prosecutor named Chest against the testimony of the various Pranksters. Dierdre English observed in the *New York Times Book Review* that, for the author, "the Pranksters were not pioneers but 'unsettlers,' and their destination was no destination. And one not need blame LSD and marijuana for the sins of heroin and cocaine to admit that the acid revolution did leave some dead Indians behind." In this trial, Kesey "is at once confessing to the damage done and asking for equal consideration of the righteous fun the Pranksters wreaked," English explained. "Uptight America was in desperate need of what they provided: an astoundingly successful communal exorcism of the stifling spirits of the 50s' conformity. In the current cultural atmosphere, a new puritanism about sex, drugs and rebellious play, it would be liberating to quaff a hit of what the Pranksters had—their all-out excitement, spontaneity and spoofing. But some of their ideas of fun no longer amuse." English concluded that the group is only partly acquitted by this defense, especially when compared to other accounts of their activities such as Paul Perry's *On the Bus: The Complete Guide to the Legendary Trip of Ken Kesey and the Merry Pranksters and the Birth of the Counterculture.*

Taking experimental literary risks in the 1980s, Kesey wrote the children's book *Little Trickler the Squirrel Meets Big Double the Bear.* In this story, as in his other books, good conquers evil in the form of a little squirrel who decides to stop the bullying of a local tyrant. He also worked with thirteen creative-writing graduate students to write *Caverns,* a mystery novel, leaving it to the students to see that it was published. The novel begins in 1934 when an itinerant evangelist named Loach discovers a cave decorated with archetypical "drawings that will challenge conventional ideas about American archaeology and Western religion," Alfred Bendixen related in the *New York Times Book Review.* The story follows Loach from his discovery of the cave, to the murder of a photographer and a subsequent prison term, and finally to his quest to rediscover the cave, accompanied by an archaeologist, a reporter, a priest, two mediums, and a large cast of motley characters. Bendixen added, "The book is probably best described as a partly successful attempt to fuse the adventures of Indiana Jones with the cosmic spirit and multiple perspectives of 'The Canterbury Tales.'" However, Madison Smartt Bell commented in the *Voice Literary Supplement* "The result less resembles *The Canterbury Tales* than an uneven day at the Mingus Jazz Workshop. It's fun to isolate the solos; Kesey's seem the strongest, probably because they are the most recognizable. . . . Most scenes and characters are slightly overdrawn, giving the book a cartoon quality which is nonetheless appealing—it has the same amiably sarcastic relation to the junk adventure novels of the '30s and '40s that the Indiana Jones movies have to old serials. At the same time there are some moving and revealing moments." Bendixen observed that the novel is weakened by the lack of a unified authorial voice, its large cast of mostly unsympathetic characters, and its emphasis on plot and comic misadventures, yet it succeeds in being "a revolutionary model for the teaching of creative writing" by "reminding us . . . that the novel requires an individual voice, fully realized characters and a clear sense of time and place."

Working on the *Caverns* group project helped break the writer's block Kesey encountered half-way through his novel *Sailor Song,* a result of the tragic death of his son Jed in 1984. He finished the novel nine years later, making it his first adult novel in two decades. *Sailor Song* features trademark Kesey zaniness, especially in the details surrounding the plot. It takes place a few years in the future, where most of the ecological disasters that were predicted to happen during the 1980s actually do. There is global warming, nuclear pollution in the oceans, high rates of cancer, and drug addiction. The story is set in the run-down Alaskan fishing village of Kuinak, where residents as diverse as refugees, travelers, and DEAPS—Descendants of Early Aboriginal Peoples—try to make a comfortable home in an increasingly uncomfortable world. Ike Sallas, the hero of the novel, is a former crop duster who, when his daughter died of an ecologically based illness, took revenge on the world by dumping fertilizers on state fairs and other places where people congregated. After being caught he became a middle-class hero. Years later, living in Kuinak, he still inspires admiration among the natives. Enter Nicholas Levertov, an albino Hollywood movie producer, who stalks into this relatively untouched paradise scouting for a location to shoot his next movie. However, as Levertov soon makes clear, he intends to change Kuinak forever by turning it into a tourist attraction. The citizenry of the village go berserk, with some residents wanting the money to be gained by complying with Levertov's desires and others wanting the village to remain untouched.

Critical reception to Kesey's novel was mixed. "*Sailor Song* does not make one single particle of sense," complained *New York Times Book Review* critic Donald E. Westlake, who dubbed the book "a long-awaited return, maybe too long," for Kesey. Westlake criticized the structure of the book and concluded that "the novel, having been incoherent from the beginning, turns apocalyptic at the end, which doesn't in any way help." Roger Rosenblatt, writing in the *New Republic,* also had complaints about *Sailor Song.* "Kesey could have been a pretty good writer-writer, but chose instead to be a culture-writer. . . . Style to the culture-writer is not writing, but a kind of animated macho typing." Rosenblatt averred that "the new novel is plotless and idealess and pointless in its overflow of parables, anecdotes and caricatures. . . . His writing screams its own insecurity." Yet critic Joe Chidley in *Maclean's* had a different view of *Sailor Song,* praising Kesey's eccentric world and noting that the author's "patient development of a world about to self-destruct is fascinating. And he successfully weaves a moving and mature love story into the complicated tale." Chidley argued that with *Sailor Song* Kesey "proves that despite the long hiatus, he is still in full control of the narrative form" and shows himself to be a "prodigious talent that has been absent for far too long."

In a departure from much of his work, Kesey explores the world of the dime-novel western with his 1994 book *Last Go Round,* written with friend Ken Babbs and based on a story Kesey's father told about the 1911 Pendleton Round Up, where an African-American bronco rider, an older Native American, and a young boy from Tennessee battled to win the title of World Champion All Round Cowboy of the West. Kesey used this story as inspiration, creating his novel out of an amalgam of facts and his own imagination. Jackson Sundown, the Native American, manages to retain his dignity whether he is drinking or not. Johnathan E. Lee Spain is the naive young Tennessean and the story's narrator, and George Fletcher is the black bronco rider. Kesey throws these characters together into a variety of adventures, all for one less-than-lofty goal: to win the silver saddle, and also manages to inject a 1990s race sensitivity into a novel of an earlier time.

Janet Burroway, writing in the *New York Times Book Review,* claimed that with *Last Go Round* the authors "produced a pulp-thin plot . . . together with an excess of episode, inflated atmosphere and wonders of prowess, just what's demanded in the formula for the original dime westerns." She believed that the novel shows great promise but hoped Kesey's future efforts would be more focused: "we cheer him back on the bronc, hoping this is not the absolute Last Go Round. But neither does this novel win the silver saddle." Dick Roraback summed up the novel in the *Los Angeles Times Book Review* by calling it "Entertaining. Wacky. Sometimes Sappy." Unfortunately for Burroway, *Last Go Round* was true to its title: it was Kesey's last work of fiction.

Though Kesey's works are few in number, they are considered significant additions to that body of writing that seeks to explore and extend the limits of the human spirit. His fiction displays a distinctive blending of a unique American tradition: As an extension of the Beat movement it reflects the concerns and attitudes of American Transcendentalists such as Ralph Waldo Emerson, Henry David Thoreau, and Walt Whitman. Kesey's approach to cherished American traditions and values is original and engaging, and his humor grows naturally out of the situations and idioms of his characters. He displays a skill for creating the revealing anecdote and readily perceives both the rational and more complex sides of human nature, giving his characters the spiritual depth necessary to fully represent themes of freedom and the moral responsibilities of creativity. His innovative fictional technique and self-criticism are notable. Furthermore, in keeping with Kesey's oft-cited declaration that he would "rather live a novel than write one," his personal quests made him an influential leader in culture as well as literature.

Kesey died of complications from surgery for liver cancer on November 10, 2001, shortly before the republication of his classic *One Flew over the Cuckoo's Nest.* For this fortieth anniversary edition, Kesey added a new introduction and twenty-five drawings he made during the period when he worked in a mental institution.

Following Kesey's death, various writers paid homage to him, citing ways in which Kesey had influenced both them and culture as a whole. A *People* writer said that Kesey's mantra that "It is possible to be different without being a threat" was one he followed throughout his life. In *Entertainment Weekly* Chris Nashawaty spoke of how he once sat next to Kesey during a meal at the Sundance Film Festival, and Kesey spoke of his long and interesting life to the young journalist. When Nashawaty entertained Kesey with a description of the beauty of the starry constellations that could be seen in the Sahara Desert, Kesey wished to write down the exact location of the place so that he might include it in "his list of wonders yet to discover."

BIOGRAPHICAL AND CRITICAL SOURCES:

BOOKS

Acton, Jay, Alan Le Mond, and Parker Hodges, *Mug Shots: Who's Who in the New Earth,* World Publishing, 1972.

Allen, Mary, *The Necessary Blankness: Women in Major American Fiction of the Sixties,* University of Illinois Press, 1976.

Billingsley, Ronald G., *The Artistry of Ken Kesey,* University of Oregon, 1971.

Concise Dictionary of American Literary Biography, 1968-1988, Gale (Detroit, MI), 1989.

Contemporary Literary Criticism, Gale (Detroit, MI), Volume 1, 1973, Volume 3, 1975, Volume 6, 1976, Volume 11, 1979, Volume 46, 1987, Volume 64, 1991.

Cook, Bruce, *The Beat Generation,* Scribner (New York, NY), 1971.

Dictionary of Literary Biography, Gale (Detroit, MI), Volume 2: *American Novelists since World War II,* 1978, Volume 16: *The Beats: Literary Bohemians in Postwar America,* 1983.

Harris, Charles B., *Contemporary American Novelists of the Absurd,* College & University Press, 1971.

Kesey, Ken, *Kesey's Garage Sale,* Viking (New York, NY), 1973.

Kesey, Ken, *One Flew over the Cuckoo's Nest,* Viking (New York, NY), 1962, 40th anniversary edition, 2002.

Kesey, Ken, *Sometimes a Great Notion.* Viking (New York, NY), 1964.

Kesey, Ken, *The Further Inquiry,* Viking (New York, NY), 1990.

Krassner, Paul, *How a Satirical Editor Became a Yippie Conspirator in Ten Easy Years,* Putnam (New York, NY), 1971.

Labin, Suzanne, *Hippies, Drugs, and Promiscuity,* Arlington House, 1972.

Leeds, Barry H., *Ken Kesey,* F. Ungar (New York, NY), 1981.

Perry, Paul, *On the Bus: The Complete Guide to the Legendary Trip of Ken Kesey and the Merry Pranksters and the Birth of the Counterculture,* Thunder's Mouth Press, 1990.

Porter, M. Gilbert, *The Art of Grit: Ken Kesey's Fiction,* University of Missouri Press, 1982.

Wallace, Ronald, *The Last Laugh: Form and Affirmation in the Contemporary American Comic Novel,* University of Missouri Press, 1971.

Wolfe, Tom, *The Electric Kool-Aid Acid Test,* Farrar, Straus (New York, NY), 1968.

PERIODICALS

Annals of the American Academy of Political and Social Science, Volume 376, 1968.
CEA Critic, Volume 37, 1975.
Children's Book Review Service, winter, 1992, p. 71.
Cithara, Volume 12, 1972.
Crawdaddy, Volume 29, 1972.
Critique, Volume 5, 1962; Volume 13, 1971.
Free You, Volume 2, 1968.
Genesis West, fall, 1963.
Harper's, August, 1994, p. 22.
Inc., August, 2001, review of *Sometimes a Great Notion,* p. 91.
Journal of American Studies, Volume 5, 1971.
Journal of Narrative Technique, Volume 9, 1979.
Journal of Popular Culture, winter, 1971.
Kirkus Reviews, May 15, 1994, p. 651.
Kliatt, September, 1998, review of *One Flew over the Cuckoo's Nest* (audiobook), p. 62.
Lex et Scientia, Volume 13, issues 1-2, 1977.
Library Journal, April 15, 1998, review of *One Flew over the Cuckoo's Nest* (audiobook), p. 134; February 1, 2002, Michael Rogers, p. 138.
Los Angeles Times Book Review, August 31, 1986; September 18, 1994, p. 6.
Maclean's, September 7, 1992, p. 50.
Modern Fiction Studies, Volume 19, 1973; Volume 21, 1975.
Nation, February 23, 1974.
New Republic, October 26, 1992.
New Statesman, October 10, 1986.
New Yorker, April 21, 1962; December 1, 1975.
New York Herald Tribune, February 25, 1962; July 27, 1964; August 2, 1964.
New York Review of Books, September 10, 1964.

New York Times, July 27, 1964; January 18, 1966; March 12, 1966; October 21, 1966; August 4, 1986; July 7, 1994, p. C18.

New York Times Book Review, February 4, 1962; August 2, 1964; August 18, 1968; October 7, 1973; August 4, 1986; September 14, 1986; December 31, 1989; January 21, 1990; December 9, 1990; August 23, 1992, p. 5; July 10, 1994, p. 11.

Northwest Review, spring, 1963; spring, 1977.

Observer, July 25, 1993, p. 25.

People, March 22, 1976.

Publishers Weekly, April 25, 1994, p. 53; August 1, 1994, p. 28.

Rocky Mountain Review, Volume 43, number 1, 1989.

Rolling Stone, March 7, 1970; September 27, 1973; July 18, 1974; October 5, 1989.

School Library Journal, November, 1991, p. 101.

Time, February 16, 1962; July 24, 1964; February 12, 1965; September 8, 1986.

Times Literary Supplement, February 24, 1966; February 25, 1972.

Voice Literary Supplement, February 2, 1990.

Washington Post, June 9, 1974.

Washington Post Book World, August 10, 1986; July 9, 1995, p. 12.

Western American Literature, Volume 9, 1974; Volume 10, 1975; Volume 22, 1987.

Whole Earth Review, spring, 2002, review of *One Flew over the Cuckoo's Nest,* p. 81.

Wisconsin Studies in Contemporary Literature, Volume 5, 1964; Volume 7, 1966.

ONLINE

Books and Writers, http://www.kirjasto.sci.fi/ (May 12, 2003).

OBITUARIES:

PERIODICALS

Book, March-April, 2002, David Bowman, pp. 34-35.

Entertainment Weekly, November 23, 2001, Chris Nashawaty, p. 16.

Los Angeles Times, November 11, 2001, p. A1.

New York Times, November 11, 2001, p. A34.

People, November 26, 2001, p. 156.

Time, November 19, 2001, p. 27.

Times (London, England), November 12, 2001, p. 19.

Washington Post, November 11, 2001, p. C6.*

* * *

KHOURI, Callie (Ann) 1957-

PERSONAL: Born November 27, 1957, in San Antonio, TX; daughter of Eli, Jr. (a surgeon) and Virginia Mae (a homemaker; maiden name, Uland) Khouri; married David Weaver Warfield (a writer and producer), June 2, 1990. *Education:* Attended Purdue University; studied at Strasburg Institute.

ADDRESSES: *Agent*—c/o International Creative Management, 8942 Wilshire Blvd., Beverly Hills, CA 90211.

CAREER: Screenplay writer, film producer, and author of nonfiction. Producer (with Dean O'Brien) of film *Thelma and Louise,* Metro-Goldwyn-Mayer/Pathe, 1991; director of film *Divine Secrets of the Ya-Ya Sisterhood,* 2002. Formerly worked as an actor, theater apprentice, and waiter in Nashville, TN; produced music videos for performers Robert Cray, Alice Cooper, and the Commodores; worked as a production company receptionist in Los Angeles, CA; also worked as a lecturer.

MEMBER: Hollywood Women's Political Committee, Fairness and Accuracy in Reporting (member of advisory board), Women's Media Watch Project.

AWARDS, HONORS: Academy Award for best original screenplay, Golden Globe Award, and Writers Guild of America West Award, all 1991, all for *Thelma and Louise; Glamour* Woman of the Year award, 1991; Feminist of the Year Award, Feminist Majority Foundation, 1991; U.S. West Literary Award, PEN Center West, and Matrix Award, New York Women in Communication, both 1992.

WRITINGS:

SCREENPLAYS

Thelma and Louise, Metro-Goldwyn-Mayer/Pathe, 1991.

Callie Khouri

Something to Talk About, Warner Bros., 1995.
Thelma and Louise and Something to Talk About: Screenplays, Grove Press (New York, NY), 1996.
Divine Secrets of the Ya-Ya Sisterhood (based on the book by Rebecca Wells), Warner Bros., 2002.

Contributor to books, including *Zen and the Art of Screenwriting,* by William Froug, Silman-James Press (Los Angeles, CA), 1996.

SIDELIGHTS: Callie Khouri has written the screenplays for the controversial 1991 Academy Award winning film *Thelma and Louise* as well as for the 1995 film *Something to Talk About.* She also adapted Rebecca Wells's bestselling novel *Divine Secrets of the Ya-Ya Sisterhood* as a film which appeared in theaters during the summer of 2002.

Khouri's best-known work, *Thelma and Louise,* is the story of two female friends from Arkansas whose weekend road trip in a 1966 Thunderbird convertible spins out of control. Thelma, played by Geena Davis, is a homemaker trapped in an unhappy marriage to an abusive husband. Louise, played by Susan Sarandon, is an emotionally scarred waitress with her own relationship troubles. The trip begins innocently enough, until Louise shoots and kills a thug at a roadside honky-tonk who tries to rape the outgoing Thelma. Running from the incident, the two women suddenly find themselves fugitives from the law, committing more crimes and setting the scene for the film's dramatic finale.

Newsweek contributor Jack Kroll remarked that *Thelma and Louise* initially "seems like an obvious feminizing of male-buddy road movies," but the latter part of the film "churns up terrific momentum, and the writing and direction fuse into a genuine pop myth about two women who discover themselves through the good old American ways of cars and criminality." In an online interview with Khouri on *SydField.com,* Syd Field noted: "*Thelma and Louise* has been one of my favorite teaching films. It has great structure . . . great visuals . . . great direction by Ridley Scott . . . but what really grabbed me was the depth of the two characters." Writing in *Entertainment Weekly,* Ty Burr praised the film's "superior writing, acting, and directing," while in *Commonweal* contributor Richard Alleva called Khouri "talented and usually inventive," and deemed her screenplay for *Thelma and Louise* a "juicy script." Calling the film a "cultural milestone," Alleva concluded that *Thelma and Louise* "is the first feminist film that is also a work of absolute nihilism. Dismayingly, undeniably, it's a lot of fun, too." Responding to the controversy surrounding the female-perpetrated violence in *Thelma and Louise,* Khouri told *Time* contributor Janice C. Simpson: "This is an adventure film. It's a film about women outlaws. People should just relax."

In *Something to Talk About* Khouri introduces Grace King Bichon, a wealthy Southern woman who learns that her husband is having an affair. *New Republic* contributor Stanley Kauffmann called the film "a flossy rich-people romance about a horsey Southern family" that contains "irresolute writing." Reviewing the movie for *New York,* David Denby remarked that "Khouri has a knack for creating pungent women" and deemed *Something to Talk About* "a good movie about the way powerful families give you life and squeeze it out of you at the same time."

Khouri's 2002 film adaptation, *Divine Secrets of the Ya-Ya Sisterhood,* "boasts rock-solid performances, witty writing and Grande dame helpings of Southern comfort," according to Ellen Futterman in her review for the *St. Louis Post-Dispatch.* Mick LaSalle noted in his *San Francisco Chronicle* appraisal that the film exhibits "freshness" in its exploration of the relationship between a mother and her daughter. As the film opens, Sidda Lee Walker has truthfully discussed her unpleasant childhood with a reporter from *Time.* Her mother, Vivi, is deeply insulted by Sidda's comments and refuses to speak with her. In an attempt to reconcile the two parties, Vivi's lifelong friends, the Ya-Yas, kidnap Sidda and reveal the circumstances of Vivi's life to her daughter.

Khouri's directoral debut earned somewhat mixed reviews. *Film Journal International's* Shirley Sealy called *Divine Secrets of the Ya-Ya Sisterhood* "lively, daft, and . . . energized," adding that Khouri's version of the novel by Rebecca Wells "has been considerably restructured from the book, and the changes by writer-director Callie Khouri . . . are all to the good." Sealy felt that the movie would be enjoyed by men and women alike. Richard Schickel of *Time* remarked that the tragic components of the novel are lost in the attempt to produce "an all-forgiving comedy," while *Guardian* contributor Peter Bradshaw described the film as "cloying." "Screenwriter Khouri has clearly worked overtime to try to make the modern story and flashbacks reinforce one another," wrote Todd McCarthy in his *Variety* review. "Khouri's direction, however, is less focused," McCarthy added. In a *Christian Century* review, John Petrakis stated: "*Divine Secrets* is a tale of forgiveness. What is remarkable about the film is the plethora of moral themes and ethical dilemmas that the filmmakers manage to cram into it."

BIOGRAPHICAL AND CRITICAL SOURCES:

PERIODICALS

Christian Century, June 26, 1991, pp. 656-657; July 3, 2002, John Petrakis, review of *Divine Secrets of the Ya-Ya Sisterhood,* p. 43.
Commonweal, September 13, 1991, pp. 513-515.
Daily Variety, June 6, 2002, Shalini Dore and Jill Feiwell, "Secrets Revealed," p. 35.
Entertainment Weekly, January 10, 1992, pp. 73-74; April 10, 1992, p. 8; February 2, 1996, pp. 64-66; June 14, 2002, Rebecca Ascher-Walsh, p. 24.
Film Journal International, June, 2002, Shirley Sealy, review of *Divine Secrets of the Ya-Ya Sisterhood,* p. 35.
Glamour, August, 1991, p. 142; December, 1991, pp. 78-83.
Guardian, September 27, 2002, Peter Bradshaw, review of *Divine Secrets of the Ya-Ya Sisterhood,* p. 19.
Houston Chronicle, June 5, 2002, "Divine Inspiration," p. 2.
Los Angeles Times, June 4, 2002, Patrick Goldstein, review of *Divine Secrets of the Ya-Ya Sisterhood,* p. F1; June 7, 2002, Kenneth Turan, review of *Divine Secrets of the Ya-Ya Sisterhood,* p. F1.
Maclean's, August 14, 1995, p. 55.
New Republic, September 11, 1995, pp. 26-27.
Newsweek, May 27, 1991, pp. 59-60; August 7, 1995, p. 60.
New York, August 14, 1995, pp. 42-43; June 10, 2002, Peter Rainer, review of *Divine Secrets,* pp. 108-109.
People, June 23, 1997, p. 45.
Premiere, December, 1991, p. 133; October, 2001, Laura Morice, review of *Divine Secrets of the Ya-Ya Sisterhood,* p. 67.
Rolling Stone, April 18, 1991, pp. 97-98.
St. Louis Post-Dispatch, June 7, 2002, Ellen Futterman, review of *Divine Secrets of the Ya-Ya Sisterhood,* p. E2.
San Francisco Chronicle, November 8, 2002, Mick LaSalle, review of *Divine Secrets of the Ya-Ya Sisterhood,* p. D8.
Sight and Sound, Gilda Williams, review of *Divine Secrets of the Ya-Ya Sisterhood,* p. 43.
Time, June 24, 1991, pp. 52-56; August 14, 1995, p. 67; June 10, 2002, Richard Schickel, review of *Divine Secrets of the Ya-Ya Sisterhood,* p. 70.
US Weekly, June 17, 2002, Andrew Johnston, review of *Divine Secrets of the Ya-Ya Sisterhood,* p. 62.
Variety, March 30, 1992, p. 17; May 13, 2002, Todd McCarthy, review of *Divine Secrets of the Ya-Ya Sisterhood,* pp. 27-28.

ONLINE

Salon.com, http://www.salon.com/ (June 7, 2002), Stephanie Zacharek, review of *Divine Secrets of the Ya-Ya Sisterhood.*

SydField.com, http://www.sydfield.com/ (May 12, 2003), interview with Khouri.*

* * *

KING, (David) Clive 1924-

PERSONAL: Born April 24, 1924, in Richmond, Surrey, England; married Jane Tuke, 1948 (divorced, 1974); married Penelope Timmins, 1974; children: two daughters (one from each marriage), one son. *Education:* Downing College, Cambridge, B.A., 1948; attended School of Oriental and African Studies (London, England), 1966-67.

ADDRESSES: Home—Norfolk, England. *Agent*—Caroline Walsh, David Highham Associates, 5-8 Lower John St., London W1F 9HA, England.

CAREER: British Council, administrative officer in Amsterdam, Netherlands, 1948-50; student welfare officer in Belfast, Ireland, 1950-51; lecturer in Aleppo, Syria, 1951-54; visiting professor in Damascus, Syria, 1954-55; lecturer and director of studies in Beirut, Lebanon, 1960-66; education advisor for East Pakistan Education Centre in Dacca, East Pakistan (now Bangladesh), 1967-71; and education officer in Madaras, India, 1971-73. East Sussex County Council, Rye, England, warden, 1955-60; author, 1973—. *Military service:* Royal Navy Volunteer Reserve, 1943-46, became sub-lieutenant.

AWARDS, HONORS: Guardian commended notation, 1977, and *Boston Globe-Horn Book* Honor Book for Fiction, 1980, for *Me and My Million.*

WRITINGS:

Hamid of Aleppo, Macmillan (London, England), 1958.
The Town That Went South, illustrated by Maurice Bartlett, Macmillan (London, England, and New York, NY), 1959.
Stig of the Dump, Penguin (Harmondsworth, England), 1963, American edition illustrated by Edward Ardizzone, Penguin (New York, NY), 1993.
The Twenty-two Letters, decorations by Richard Kennedy, Hamilton (London, England), 1966.
The Night the Water Came, Longman Young (Harmondsworth, England), 1973, Crowell (New York, NY), 1982.
Snakes and Snakes, illustrated by Richard Kennedy, Kestrel (Harmondsworth, England), 1975.
Me and My Million, Kestrel Books (Harmondsworth, England), 1976, Crowell (New York, NY), 1979.
The Devil's Cut, illustrated by Val Biro, Hodder & Stoughton (London, England), 1978.
Ninny's Boat, illustrated by Ian Newsham, Kestrel (Harmondsworth, England), 1980, Macmillan (New York, NY), 1981.
The Birds from Africa, illustrated by Diana Groves, Macdonald Educational (London, England), Silver Burdett (Morristown, NJ), 1980.
The Sound of Propellors, illustrated by David Parkins, Viking (London, England), 1986.
The Seashore People, Viking Kestrel (Harmondsworth, England), 1987.
(Compiler) *Adventure Stories,* illustrated by Brian Walker, Kingfisher Books (London, England), 1988, (New York, NY), 1993.
A Touch of Class, Bodley Head (London, England), 1995.

"INNER-RING HIPSTERS" SERIES

Accident, illustrated by Jacqueline Atkinson, Benn (London, England), 1976.
First Day Out, illustrated by Jacqueline Atkinson, Benn (London, England), 1976.
The Secret, illustrated by Jacqueline Atkinson, Benn (London, England), 1976.
Highjacks, Lowjacks, illustrated by Jacqueline Atkinson, Benn (London, England), 1976.

PLAYS

Poles Apart, produced in London, England, 1975.
The World of Light, produced in London, England, 1976.
Get the Message, produced in London, England, 1987.

Also author of *Good Snakes, Bad Snakes,* a television play, 1977.

ADAPTATIONS: Stig of the Dump was adapted for audio in 1988 and reissued in an abridged format in 1999 by Puffin (Harmondsworth, England). It was also dramatized for television by the British Broadcasting Corporation, 2002.

SIDELIGHTS: Clive King has drawn on his experiences in far-flung regions of the world to create what have become classics of children's literature, according to reviewers. In particular, his novel *Stig of the Dump* has continued to attract readers, many years after its original publication in 1963. *Stig of the Dump* follows the story of Barney, an eight-year-old lad, who discovers Stig, a Stone Age man, living in the chalk pit the townspeople have been using as a dump. Stig is very inventive in finding uses for the things townspeople have been throwing away. Marcus Croch reviewed the book's initial publication for *Twentieth-Century Children's Writers,* noting that the "initial concept is brilliant." The book continued to garner praise upon its republication in 1993. *Junior Bookshelf* reviewer Marcus Crouch remarked, "the joy evoked by the story is as great as it was thirty years ago."

Some of King's other books for young readers that explore fantastic situations include *The Town That Went South* and *Me and My Million.* In *The Town That Went South,* King describes the reactions of the people of Ramsly when their town comes adrift from the land and carries them off to various adventures. A *Times Literary Supplement* reviewer called the book "a brilliantly ingenious piece of escapism for intelligent readers between ten and one hundred." *Me and My Million* tells the more realistic story of Ringo, an amoral young thief who cannot read, who helps his brother steal a valuable painting. Ringo's inability to read such things as street signs leads to a series of misadventures over the course of the story. Jane Powell of the *Times Literary Supplement* noted that the book is "written in a very colloquial style with . . . zip and verve."

Critics have noted King's ability to portray interesting historical situations and ideas in his novels. His tales provide readers with a grounding in history, myths and legends, and geography. For example, in *The Twenty-two Letters,* he tells of the invention of the modern alphabet in what Stephanie Nettell described as a "cunningly plotted" and "splendid novel" in her *Times Literary Supplement* review. Similarly, *Ninny's Boat,* "King's most ambitious novel," according to

Twentieth-Century Children's Writers contributor Marcus Crouch, takes place in the Dark Ages. It revolves around the plight of Ninny, a slave of the Angles, a tribe living in what is now Denmark, who plan to take a boat in search of a new land. Through his resourcefulness and his friendship with Offa (who is leading the voyage), Ninny earns a place in the boat. When the Angles invade what was to become Britain, Ninny undertakes many adventures and discovers that he himself is a Briton. "*Ninny's Boat* is a big story about great events and with big ideas behind it," commented Crouch in *Twentieth-Century Children's Writers,* "but it is presented in human terms with life-sized people." *Horn Book*'s Paul Heins also praised the work for its "exciting narrative [that] is full of humorous wordplay, and the clever" use of historical elements.

BIOGRAPHICAL AND CRITICAL SOURCES:

BOOKS

Twentieth-Century Children's Writers, 4th edition, St. James Press (Detroit, MI), 1995.

PERIODICALS

Books for Keeps, March, 2002, Christopher Roberts, review of *Stig of the Dump,* p. 16.
Growing Point, January, 1987, review of *The Sound of Propellors,* pp. 4732-4735.
Horn Book, February, 1980; April, 1982, Paul Heins, review of *Ninny's Boat,* p. 165.
Instructor and Teacher, May, 1982, Allan Yeager, review of *The Night the Water Came,* p. 105.
Junior Bookshelf, December, 1987, review of *The Seashore People,* pp. 275-276; February, 1994, Marcus Crouch, review of *Stig of the Dump,* p. 33.
Kirkus Reviews, April 1, 1982, review of *The Night the Water Came,* pp. 418-419.
New Statesman, May 25, 1973; May 21, 1976; November 21, 1980.
Newsweek, December 17, 1979.
New York Herald Tribune Book Review, June 8, 1958.
New York Times Book Review, March 28, 1982.
Observer (London, England), November 26, 1967; December 12, 1976; November 30, 1986.
School Librarian, August, 1987, Joanna McClatchey, review of *The Sound of Propellors,* p. 254; May, 1988, Chris Stephenson, review of *The Seashore People,* p. 56; May, 1989, J. Lavis, review of *Adventure Stories,* p. 75.

School Library Journal, May, 1982, review of *The Night the Water Came,* p. 64; April, 1993, Kenneth E. Lowen, review of *Adventure Stories,* p. 143.

Times Literary Supplement, May 20, 1960; November 30, 1967; June 15, 1973; April 2, 1976; November 28, 1986, Stephanie Nettell, review of *The Twenty-two Letters,* p. 1347; October 23, 1987.

Young Reader's Review, June, 1967.*

* * *

KOZLOWSKI, Theodore T(homas) 1917-

PERSONAL: Born May 21, 1917, in Buffalo, NY; son of Theodore (in insurance sales) and Helen (Zamiara) Kozlowski; married Maude K. Peters, June 29, 1954. *Education:* Syracuse University, B.S., 1939; Duke University, M.A., 1941, Ph.D., 1947; Massachusetts Institute of Technology, graduate study, 1942-43; University of Buffalo (now State University of New York at Buffalo), postdoctoral study, summers, 1948, 1949.

ADDRESSES: Home—Carlsbad by the Sea, 2855 Carlsbad Blvd., No. S-326, Carlsbad, CA 92008.

CAREER: University of Massachusetts—Amherst, Amherst, MA, assistant professor, 1947-48, associate professor, 1948-50, professor and head of botany department, 1950-58; University of Wisconsin—Madison, Madison, WI, professor of forestry, 1958-72, A. J. Riker Professor of Forestry, 1972-84, Wisconsin Alumni Research Foundation Senior Distinguished Research Professor of Forestry, 1984-87, chair of Department of Forestry, 1961-64, director of Biotron, 1977-87; University of California—Santa Barbara, Santa Barbara, CA, adjunct professor of environmental studies, 1987-93; University of California—Berkeley, Berkeley, CA, visiting scholar in environmental studies, policy, and management, 1993-98; retired, 1998. University of Pennsylvania, visiting professor, 1954-55; Society of American Foresters, visiting scientist, 1963, 1966, 1968, 1969, 1970; Intercounty Fulbright lecturer, 1964-65; American Institute of Biological Sciences, visiting biologist, 1970-71; Purdue University, John S. Wright Visiting Scientist, 1971; University of Nebraska, George Lamb Lecturer, 1974; University of Washington, Seattle, George S. Long Lecturer, 1978. Visiting lecturer at universities and research institutes throughout the world, including Oxford University, University of Lisbon, Warsaw Architectural College, University of Tokyo, Beijing University, Shanghai Research Institute of Plant Physiology, Federal Cacao Research Institute, and Forest Research Institutes in Malaysia and Nigeria. Consultant to many organizations and institutions, including Oak Ridge National Laboratory, National Park Service, U.S.-Australia Cooperative Science Program, Environment Assessment Council, U.S.-Israel Binational Science Foundation, Food and Agriculture Organization of the United Nations, International Council for Research in Agroforestry, Stanford Research Institute, Syracuse Research Co., Natural Environment Research Council (England), and several commercial organizations. *Military service:* U.S. Army Air Forces, 1942-46; became captain.

MEMBER: International Society of Arboriculture, International Union of Forest Research Organizations, Botanical Society of America (chair, Northeastern section, 1958), American Society of Plant Physiologists (chair, Northeastern section, 1958), Ecological Society of America, Society of American Foresters (chapter chair, 1961; chair of committee on tree physiology, 1963), American Institute of Biological Sciences, Phi. Societas Forestalis Fenniae (Finland; honorary member), Societas Botanicorum Poloniae (Poland; honorary member), Scandinavian Society of Plant Physiology, Wisconsin Arborists Association (honorary life member), Phi Beta Kappa, Sigma Xi, Phi Kappa Phi, Alpha Zeta, Phi Sigma.

AWARDS, HONORS: International Society of Arboriculture, Authors' Award, 1963, Arboricultural Research Award, 1976, and merit award, 1987; senior Fulbright research scholar, Oxford University, 1964-65; research fellow, International Shade Tree Conference, 1969-72; Barrington Moore Biological Research Award, Society of American Foresters, 1974; merit award, Botanical Society of America, 1984; distinguished achievement award, College of Environmental Science and Forestry, State University of New York, 1986; merit award, Wisconsin Arborists Association, 1987; C. W. Ralston Distinguished Alumnus Award, School of Forestry and Environmental Studies, Duke University, 1988; honorary degrees include Doctor of Science, Université Catholique de Louvain, 1978, State University of New York, 1988, and Agricultural University of Poznan, Poland, 1992.

WRITINGS:

(With Paul J. Kramer) *Physiology of Trees,* McGraw-Hill (New York, NY), 1960.

(Editor) *Tree Growth,* Ronald Press (New York, NY), 1962.

Water Metabolism in Plants, Harper (New York, NY), 1964.

(Editor) *Water Deficits and Plant Growth,* Academic Press (San Diego, CA), Volume I: *Development, Control, and Measurement,* 1968, Volume II: *Plant Water Consumption and Response,* 1968, Volume III: *Plant Responses and Control of Water Balance,* 1972, Volume IV: *Soil Water Measurement, Plant Responses and Breeding for Drought Resistance,* 1976, Volume V: *Water and Plant Disease,* 1978, Volume VI: *Woody Plant Ecosystems,* 1981, Volume VII: *Additional Woody Crop Plants,* 1983.

Growth and Development of Trees, Academic Press (San Diego, CA), Volume I: *Seed Germination, Ontogeny and Shoot Growth,* 1971, Volume II: *Cambial Growth, Root Growth, and Reproductive Growth,* 1971.

(Editor) *Seed Biology,* Academic Press (San Diego, CA), Volume I: *Importance, Development, and Germination,* 1972, Volume II: *Germination Control, Metabolism, and Pathology,* 1972, Volume III: *Insects and Seed Collection, Storage, Testing, and Certification,* 1972.

(Editor, with G. C. Marks) *Ectomycorrhizae: Their Ecology and Physiology,* Academic Press (San Diego, CA), 1973.

(Editor) *Shedding of Plant Parts,* Academic Press (San Diego, CA), 1973.

(Editor, with C. E. Ahlgren) *Fire and Ecosystems,* Academic Press (San Diego, CA), 1974.

(Editor, with J. B. Mudd) *Responses of Plants to Air Pollution,* Academic Press (San Diego, CA), 1975.

(Editor, with P. de T. Alvim) *Ecophysiology of Tropical Crops,* Academic Press (San Diego, CA), 1977.

Tree Growth and Environmental Stresses, University of Washington Press (Seattle, WA), 1979.

(With Paul J. Kramer) *Physiology of Woody Plants,* Academic Press, (San Diego, CA), 1979, 2nd edition (with Stephen G. Pallardy), 1997.

(Editor, with T. W. Tibbitts) *Controlled Environment Guidelines for Plant Research,* Academic Press (San Diego, CA), 1979.

(Editor) *Flooding and Plant Growth,* Academic Press (San Diego, CA), 1984.

(With Paul J. Kramer and Stephen G. Pallardy) *The Physiological Ecology of Woody Plants,* Academic Press, (San Diego, CA), 1991.

(With Stephen G. Pallardy) *Growth Control in Woody Plants,* Academic Press, (San Diego, CA), 1997.

Consulting editor, "Physiological Ecology," a series of monographs, texts, and treatises, Academic Press (San Diego, CA), 1968-88. Contributor of more than 400 articles on the physiology of woody plants to botanical journals. Member of editorial board, *Forest Science,* 1950-71, *Ecology,* 1968-70, and *Bio-Science,* beginning 1983; associate editor, *American Midland Naturalist,* 1965-71, and *Canadian Journal of Forest Research,* 1970-76; member of editorial advisory board, *Tree Physiology,* beginning 1985.

L

LAW, Jonathan 1961-

PERSONAL: Born April 24, 1961, in Westonzoyland, Somerset, England; son of Stanley James (a headmaster) and Dianne (Croome) Law; married Catherine Hodgson, April 12, 1997; children: one daughter, one son. *Education:* Keble college, Oxford, B.A., 1983. *Religion:* Anglican. *Hobbies and other interests:* Literature and arts, music, walking, the countryside.

ADDRESSES: Office—Market House Books Ltd., Market Sq., Aylesbury, Buckinghamshire, England.

CAREER: Editorial and research assistant to historian and biographer Jeremy Wilson, 1987-89; Market House Books Ltd., Aylesbury, Buckinghamshire, England, editor and writer, 1989—.

WRITINGS:

(Editor) *European Culture: A Contemporary Companion,* Cassell (London, England), 1993.
(Principal editor) *Brewer's Theatre,* Cassell (London, England), 1994.
(Editor) *Brewer's Cinema,* Cassell (London, England), 1995.
(Editor) *One Thousand Great Lives,* Robinson, 1996.
(Editor) *Cassell Companion to Cinema,* Cassell (London, England), 1997.
(Principal editor) *Cassell Companion to Theatre,* (London, England), 1997.
(Joint editor) *Who's Who in the Twentieth Century,* Oxford University Press (Oxford, England), 1999.
(Joint editor) *The Penguin Dictionary of Proverbs,* 2nd edition, Penguin (London, England), 2000.
(Joint editor) *The New Penguin Dictionary of Theatre,* Penguin (London, England), 2001.
(Editor) *Oxford Compendium of English,* Volume I: *Oxford Language Reference.* Oxford University Press (Oxford, England), 2001.
(Principal editor) *The Macmillan Dictionary of Contemporary Phrase and Fable,* Macmillan (London, England), 2002.
(Joint editor) *The Macmillan Encyclopedia 2003,* Macmillan (London, England), 2002.

Contributor to dictionaries, encyclopedias, and other reference books.

* * *

LENO, Jay 1950-

PERSONAL: Born James Douglas Muir Leno, April 28, 1950, in New Rochelle, NY; son of Angelo and Cathryn Leno; married Mavis Nicholson, November 30, 1980. *Education:* Emerson College, graduated, 1973. *Hobbies and other interests:* Antique motorcycles and automobiles.

ADDRESSES: Home—Los Angeles, CA. *Office*—c/o NBC Enterprises, 3500 Olive Dr., 15th Fl., Burbank, CA 91510-7885.

CAREER: Television personality, actor, comedian, writer. Rolls Royce auto mechanic and deliveryman; stand-up comedian at venues, including Carnegie Hall

Jay Leno

and Caesar's Palace; performed as opening act for Henry Mancini, Johnny Mathis, John Denver, James Brown, Tom Jones, and Perry Como; *Good Times,* CBS, writer, 1974; *Jay Leno and the American Dream,* Showtime, host and producer, 1986; *The Tonight Show,* NBC, exclusive guest host, 1987-92, host, 1992—. Appeared on television show episodes, including *Laverne and Shirley,* ABC, 1976; *Alice,* CBS, 1976; *The Marilyn McCoo and Billy Davis, Jr. Show,* CBS, 1977; *Saturday Night Live,* NBC, 1986; *Baywatch,* syndicated, 1989; *Seinfeld,* NBC, 1990; *Fresh Prince of Bel-Air,* NBC, 1990; *Home Improvement,* ABC, 1991; *Mad about You,* NBC, 1992; *The Larry Sanders Show,* 1992; *Homicide: Life on the Street,* NBC, 1993; *The Nanny,* CBS, 1993; *Ellen,* ABC, 1994; *Dennis Miller Live,* 1994; *Friends,* NBC, 1994; *Caroline in the City,* NBC, 1995; *Third Rock from the Sun,* 1996; *Just Shoot Me,* 1997; and *Late Night with David Letterman,* NBC. Other television appearances include *Jay Leno's Family Comedy Hour,* 1987; *The 42nd Annual Primetime Emmy Awards,* 1990; *Happily Ever After: Fairy Tales for Every Child,* 1995; and *Our Planet Tonight.* Appeared in films, including *The Silver Bears,* EMI Films, 1977; *Fun with Dick and Jane,* Columbia, 1977; *American Hot Wax,* Paramount, 1978; *Americathon,* Lorimar/Warner Bros., 1979; *Collision Course,* De Laurentiis Entertainment/Interscope Communications, 1988; *Dave,* Warner Bros., 1993; *Wayne's World 2,* Paramount, 1993; *We're Back! A Dinosaur's Story,* Amblin, 1993; *The Flintstones,* Universal/Hanna-Barbera/Amblin, 1994; *Major League II,* Warner Bros., 1994; *The Birdcage* (also known as *Birds of a Feather*), Metro-Goldwyn-Mayer/United Artists, 1996; *Meet Wally Sparks,* Trimark, 1997; *Contact,* Warner Bros., 1997; *In & Out,* Paramount, 1997; and *Mad City,* Warner Bros., 1997.

AWARDS, HONORS: Writers Guild of America nomination, 1987; Emmy Award for Best Musical or Variety Series, 1995, and Outstanding Technical Direction, 1996, for the *Tonight Show;* Emmy Award for Best Musical or Variety Series nomination, 1996 and 1997, for the *Tonight Show;* Best Political Humorist, *Washingtonian Magazine; Tonight Show* named Favorite Television Show in Europe and TV Guide Favorite Late Night Show.

WRITINGS:

- (Editor) *Headlines: Real but Ridiculous Samplings from America's Newspapers,* photographs by Gary Bernstein, cartoons by Jack Davis, Warner (New York, NY), 1989.
- (Editor) *More Headlines: Real but Ridiculous Samplings from America's Newspapers,* photographs by Joseph Del Valle, cartoons by Jack Davis, Warner (New York, NY), 1991.
- (Editor) *Headlines III: Not the Movie, Still the Book: Real but Ridiculous Samplings from America's Newspapers,* photographs by Joseph Del Valle, cartoons by Jack Davis, Warner (New York, NY), 1991.
- (Editor) *Headlines IV: The Next Generation: More Out-of-This World Headlines from the Bestselling Series,* photographs by Joseph Del Valle, cartoons by Jack Davis, Warner (New York, NY), 1992.
- (Editor) *Jay Leno's Headlines. Books I, II, III,* Wings (New York, NY), 1992.
- (Editor) *Jay Leno's Police Blotter: Real-Life Crime Headlines from "The Tonight Show with Jay Leno,"* Andrews McMeel (Kansas City, MO), 1994.

(With Bill Zehme) *Leading with My Chin,* HarperCollins (New York, NY), 1996.

(Author of introduction) Jon Macks, *Heaven Talks Back: An Uncommon Conversation,* Simon & Schuster (New York, NY), 1998.

(Author of introduction) *Faces of Time: Seventy-five Years of Time Magazine Cover Portraits,* edited by Frederick Voss, Little, Brown (Boston, MA), 1998.

(With Dennis Homstrom and others) *The Complete Idiot's Guide to Motorcycles,* Alpha Books (Indianapolis, IN), 2001.

(Author of introduction) Dennis Adler, *The Art of the Sports Car: The Greatest Designs of the Twentieth Century,* HarperCollins (New York, NY), 2002.

SIDELIGHTS: Born in New Rochelle, New York, and raised in Andover, Massachusetts, late-night television host Jay Leno began his show-business career as a standup comedian. Performing his comedy routines around the country, making as many as three hundred appearances a year, Leno eventually procured a spot as the guest host of the popular late-night program *The Tonight Show,* which starred Johnny Carson. With Carson's retirement from the show, Leno stepped in as his successor, beating out other contenders, including David Letterman. Now dubbed by the media "The King of Late Night," Leno's *Tonight Show* began topping late-night television ratings in 1995 and became completely dominant by the late 1990s.

Leno's 1996 autobiography, *Leading with My Chin,* details his rise to fame from small comedy clubs to his late-night television success. The son of an Italian-American father and a Scottish mother who immigrated to the United States alone at the age of eleven, Leno has apparently always had a heart for comedy. His fifth-grade report card read: "If Jay spent as much time studying as he does trying to be a comedian, he'd be a big star." Leno's autobiography does not break from his comedic tendencies. In the book, he lightheartedly shares anecdotes of his rise to fame, including early gigs in mental institutions and strip clubs. One memorable appearance Leno describes in his book is performing for a group of Orthodox Jews only to find that the audience was really expecting to be entertained by a Yiddish storyteller.

Leading with My Chin is not the first book that Leno wrote. He capitalized on his affiliation with *The Tonight Show* to compile and edit more than four hundred newspaper headlines, material from one of the show's featured routines, to create *Headlines: Real but Ridiculous Samplings from America's Newspapers.* Over the years, five more *Headlines* books have emerged. When the first *Headlines* was published in 1989, *Booklist* reviewer Steve Weingartner, citing the book's entertaining material and the popularity of Leno, stated, "This material should attract an avid audience." Excerpts from the book include, "Researchers call murder a threat to public health" and "Condom week starts with a cautious bang." When *More Headlines* was published in 1991, a *Kliatt* reviewer concluded that Leno's "follow-up is equally humorous." Book five in the *Headlines* series concentrated on crime headlines, but is similar to the first four books.

Critics and fans often point to Leno's record as a fundraiser for charitable causes. The royalties from his second book, *More Headlines,* were donated to a foundation that funds pediatric AIDS programs. The "nice-guy image," as perceived by some reviewers of *Leading with My Chin,* is at odds with the expectations raised by a Hollywood autobiography. Alex Tresniowski in *People,* pointed out that "no one is criticized, no action regretted, no demon wrestled with" in *Leading with My Chin.* Tresniowski described the book as "a homey, joke-filled whitewash of any splotches on Leno's squeaky-clean facade." *Entertainment Weekly* reviewer Bret Watson questioned how Leno survived the battle to inherit Johnny Carson's throne as host of *The Tonight Show* as well as the inside story on Leno's "agonizing decision to fire Helen Kushnick, his manager of seventeen years." Watson was left wishing Leno had offered "insights into his private struggles or intriguing perspectives on the famous people he has known." *New York Times Books Review* contributor Bill Carter felt that such criticism was beside the point. "That's not what Mr. Leno is about; he is about performing," Carter wrote.

Few would quarrel with the assertion that Leno is one of the hardest-working entertainers in Hollywood. His rare absences from *The Tonight Show* have been precipitated by serious illness; otherwise, he is at his interviewer's desk five nights each week. While he has a staff to help him prepare his monologues and other well-known bits, he contributes mightily to the writing of each episode, often completing the next night's monologue after finishing a show. While he makes light of politics, observers have also noted a distinct point of view in his comedy, making him a force to be reckoned with during election years. Not surprisingly, presidential candidates vie for the opportunity to be on *The Tonight Show*. In an essay for the *St. James Encyclopedia of Popular Culture,* a contributor stated: "Leno is perceived as a hard worker and a perfectionist, thus endearing him to other hard-working Americans." According to Peter Bart in *Variety,* "With his relentless twinkle, he works the room, works the press, works the charity circuit. He is the professional good guy who has usurped the place of the naughty neurotics. And he is definitely a winner."

Leno once told *People,* "When I was a kid growing up . . . I had dyslexia. My mother told me that I would always have to work twice as hard as the other kids just to get the same grades. It's the same now. I'm not better than anybody else doing this job; I just think maybe I work harder than some."

BIOGRAPHICAL AND CRITICAL SOURCES:

BOOKS

Adler, Bill, *The World of Jay Leno: His Humor and His Life,* Carol Publishing (New York, NY), 1992.
Carter, Bill, *The Late Shift: Letterman, Leno, and the Network Battle for the Night,* Hyperion (New York, NY), 1994.
Contemporary Newsmakers, Gale (Detroit, MI), 1989.
Leno, Jay, editor, *Headlines: Real but Ridiculous Samplings from America's Newspapers,* Warner (New York, NY), 1989.
Leno, Jay, *Leading with My Chin,* with Bill Zehme, HarperCollins (New York, NY), 1996.
St. James Encyclopedia of Popular Culture, St. James (Detroit, MI), 2000.
Walker, Jay, *The Leno Wit: His Life and Humor,* Morrow (New York, NY), 1997.

PERIODICALS

Advertising Age, May 25, 1992, p. 24; November 30, 1993, pp. 1-3.
Booklist, January 1, 1990, p. 870.
Boston, May, 1992, pp. 16-21.
Chicago Tribune Books, January 14, 1990, p. 4.
Cosmopolitan, December, 1993, pp. 70-72; May, 1996, pp. 180-185.

Entertainment Weekly, August 14, 1992, pp. 20-27; February 11, 1994, p. 63; April 22, 1994, p. 12; November 3, 1995, p. 19; March 15, 1996, p. 52; October 11, 1996, pp. 84-85; November 8, 1996, p. 11.
Esquire, October, 1995, pp. 98-105.
Insight on the News, July 22, 1991, pp. 42-44.
Kliatt, January, 1991, p. 55.
Ladies Home Journal, February, 1997, p. 166.
Life, November, 1993, p. 100.
Newsweek, June 29, 1992, p. 56; January 25, 1993, pp. 60-63.
New Yorker, November 9, 1992, pp. 46-65.
New York Times, January 30, 1994, p. 28; September 24, 2000, Marshall Sella, "The Stiff Guy vs. the Dumb Guy," p. 72.
New York Times Book Review, November 17, 1996, p. 24.
People, December 24, 1990, pp. 56-59; August 23, 1993, pp. 46-49; October 14, 1996, p. 39; May 6, 2002, Michael A. Lipton, "Funny Man at Work," p. 64.
Playboy, December, 1990, pp. 57-69; October, 1996, pp. 51-60.
Publishers Weekly, January 15, 1996, p. 320.
Redbook, July, 1992, pp. 48-51.
Runner's World, November, 1994, pp. 42-45.
Time, March 16, 1992, pp. 58-62.
TV Guide, April 11, 1992, pp. 16-21; August 15, 1992, p. 27; January 30, 1993, pp. 49-51; August 28, 1993, pp. 18-23; October 22, 1994, pp. 28-33; October 5, 1996, pp. 14-22; April 13, 2002, Jason Gay, "The Hardest-Working, Least Talked About, Most Popular Man in Show Business," p. 16.
Vanity Fair, July, 1991, pp. 48-50.
Variety, May 29, 2000, Peter Bart, "Building the Leno Legend," p. 2.
Washingtonian, November, 1993, pp. 76-80.
Woman's Day, March 10, 1992, pp. 36-40.

ONLINE

E! Online, http://www.eonline.com/ (August 25, 1997).
NBC Online, http://www.nbc.com/ (August 19, 1997).*

* * *

LERMAN, Eleanor 1952-

PERSONAL: Born 1952, in New York, NY.

ADDRESSES: *Home*—10460 Queens Blvd., #20H, Flushing, NY 11375-7325.

CAREER: Poet.

AWARDS, HONORS: Juniper Prize from University of Massachusetts, for *Come the Sweet By and By;* recipient of fiction grants from New York Foundation for the Arts.

WRITINGS:

POETRY

Armed Love, Wesleyan University Press (Middletown, CT), 1973.
Come the Sweet By and By, University of Massachusetts Press (Amherst, MA), 1975.
The Mystery of Meteors, Sarabande Books (Louisville, KY), 2001.

Contributor to periodicals.

SIDELIGHTS: Eleanor Lerman has drawn praise for her three books of poetry that depict in graphic terms what one critic described as "glimpses of life in a drug-torn Lesbian ghetto." Lerman's works show an unease with mundane living and a preference for the heightened tension—and occasional horrors—of love. Her poems touch upon suicide threats, Lesbian infidelity, and torture, both physical and mental. *Poetry* contributor Sandra M. Gilbert described Lerman as "a notable scholar of cruelty and despair," noting also that the poetry "is tender, witty, elegant, even beautiful. . . . Here . . . is an intensity of vision that tells us we're in the presence of something wholly authentic—love poems, hate poems, horror poems, written with scalpels on the nerve-endings."

Lerman, who published her first volume of poetry at age twenty-one, is adept at presenting herself in a variety of moods. "Fresh resilience rather than wry weariness is her hallmark," noted Sally M. Gall in *Shenandoah.* "Sometimes she flaunts a heroic Lesbianism in the fatuous face of the establishment. At other times she reveals all the vulnerability and romanticism of a sensitive girl in her very, very early twenties. She can be lighthearted, toughminded, fierce, tender, mystical, and romantic." *Sewanee Review* essayist Paul Ramsey observed of Lerman's work: "The poems are clear in wildness, disturbing, brilliantly lighted, often felt as wholes. . . . [They] are not easy to forget."

Lerman's blatant baring of both emotions and surroundings has disturbed some critics and impressed others. "Such terrifying simplicity, such hunger for love are bound to unnerve us and stir us," wrote X. J. Kennedy in the *New York Times Book Review.* "Much of the time, though, the raw facts just remain on their page like meat left in its butcher's paper, untouched by deep understanding or by art." In a contrasting review in *Parnassus: Poetry in Review,* Mark Halliday expressed favor for that which Kennedy disdained. "There is a raw meat quality to Lerman's work: it shows no signs of academic curing, no workshop seasoning, nor does it smell like any dish cooked in the kitchen of a major American poet past or present," stated Halliday. "But what lies thick and red on the page is not a catalogue of facts—Lerman's poetry is too (literally) fantastic for that—but of emotions, volatile and potentially volatile." Halliday considered Lerman's first volume, *Armed Love,* "a bravely naked book, far more alive than the tidy intellectual constructions of the other young poets I had in hand. . . . After reading *Armed Love* I felt I had been taken somewhere, to a special place with uncommon noises and colors."

While *Armed Love* drew comparisons with Rimbaud, Jerome McGann found parallels with Emily Dickinson evident in Lerman's second collection, *Come the Sweet By and By.* "The traumatized settings are familiar enough," McGann commented in a *Times Literary Supplement* review. "What distinguishes her work in this mode is its humaneness, as if ordinary people in very typical American places, doing commonplace things, had unexpectedly discovered themselves and their environment to be possessed. The poems record how people try to maintain their most basic human feelings—love in particular—despite the fearful sense that the world they live in is out of their control."

Halliday expressed some frustration with *Come the Sweet By and By.* The poems, he wrote, "tend to merge into one endless demented monologue, with pauses only for breath. If you read three or four poems in a row you are lulled (despite the vigor and pain of the voice and the extremeness of the imagery) into a dazed, non-discriminating mood whose dominant thought is merely, What will she think of next?" The critic continued: "[Lerman] fears the reader, she fears her own memories, and she fears poetry—because all of these are forces calling upon her to impose order on her emotions. Lerman thrives on painful passion. She doesn't want anything to be wrapped up neatly and put away; she cherishes the vibrant irresolution that washes over from one fiercely unhappy poem to the next." McGann offered a counter opinion, maintaining that *Come the Sweet By and By* "moves so far beyond the tortured power of her first volume . . . that one hardly believes she has reached this level of rhythmic competence and emotional wisdom so quickly."

It was a quarter century between the publication of *Come the Sweet By and By* and Lerman's next poetry collection, *The Mystery of Meteors*. During the interim, she told Gavin Grant of *Booksense*, "I was doing some writing for a while," such as short stories. "But mostly, no, I was just living my life—the wrong kind of life, as it turns out. I wish I could make my absence from struggling with literature into something romantic . . . but it's much more mundane." Lerman added that during her hiatus from writing "I thought, for years, that I had absolutely nothing to say, but as soon as I decided to try to write poetry again, wham—I couldn't stop. It surprised even me."

The Mystery of Meteors takes on a wide range of subjects: ancient Egypt, physics, memory, the Internet, and love. Sandra Yannone of *Lambda Book Report* wondered if some of Lerman's earlier gifts had grown rusty with disuse: "Lerman's poetry certainly reflects her ability to have adapted her style to the times," noted Yannone. "However most of the poems lack a certain focus as well as a certain precision of language." More impressed was *Library Journal* reviewer Louis McKee, who said that Lerman "has returned, older, wiser, and stronger, with poems of depth and resonance." Indeed, the poet that emerges in this collection confronts "the static but unrelentingly demanding realm of middle age," in the words of *Booklist*'s Donna Seaman.

Comparing the "angry young poet" of the *Armed Love* days to her more mature incarnation, Lerman remarked to Grant that "I'm so much more amused now than I was when I was younger. (It was not politically correct to find anything amusing when I was in my twenties.) But I can go back and read what I wrote and understand how strong my feelings were—they're equally strong now, only not so angry. I've gone through some mighty struggles with myself—I'm sure we all have . . . so I'm trying to enjoy the calm. And be philosophical about whatever comes next."

BIOGRAPHICAL AND CRITICAL SOURCES:

BOOKS

Contemporary Literary Criticism, Volume 9, Gale (Detroit, MI), 1978, pp. 328-332.

PERIODICALS

Booklist, March 15, 2001, Donna Seaman, review of *The Mystery of Meteors,* p. 1347.
Kirkus Reviews, February 1, 2001, review of *The Mystery of Meteors,* p. 152.
Lambda Book Report, April, 2002, Sandra Yannone, review of *The Mystery of Meteors,* p. 24.
Library Journal, February 1, 2001, Louis McKee, review of *The Mystery of Meteors,* p. 100; April 15, 2002, Barbara Hoffert, review of *The Mystery of Meteors,* p. 90.
New York Times Book Review, February 17, 1974, X. J. Kennedy, review of *Armed Love,* p. 6.
Parnassus: Poetry in Review, spring-summer, 1976, Mark Halliday, review of *Armed Love,* pp. 235-242.
Poetry, October, 1975, Sandra Gilbert, review of *Armed Love,* pp. 53-54.
Sewanee Review, spring, 1974, Paul Ramsey, review of *Armed Love,* pp. 404-405.
Shenandoah, fall, 1974, Sally Gall, review of *Armed Love,* pp. 59-61.
Times Literary Supplement, December 10, 1976, Jerome McGann, "The Love That's Left," p. 1563.
Washington Post Book World, May 26, 1974, Norma Procopiow, review of *Armed Love,* p. 3.

ONLINE

Booksense, http://www.booksense.com/ (July 16, 2002), Gavin J. Grant, "Very Interesting People."*

* * *

LEVON, O. U.
See KESEY, Ken (Elton)

LEWIS, Naomi

PERSONAL: Born in Norfolk, England. *Education:* Attended London University.

ADDRESSES: *Home*—13 Red Lion Sq., London WC1R 4QF, England.

CAREER: Author and poet. Worked as a noted critic of adult and children's literature, *New Statesman* and London *Observer;* as a broadcaster, British Broadcasting Corporation (BBC-Radio), England; as a school teacher in England and, briefly, Switzerland; for most of her writing life, worked as tutor of creative writing for adults.

AWARDS, HONORS: Eleanor Farjeon Award, 1974; Travelling Scholarship, Society of Authors; Fellow of the Royal Society of Literature.

WRITINGS:

A Visit to Mrs. Wilcox (for adults; essays), Cresset Press (London, England), 1957.
(Author of verse text) *The Butterfly Collector,* illustrated by Fulvio Testa, Anderson (London, England), 1978, Prentice-Hall (New York, NY), 1979.
(Author of verse text) *Leaves,* illustrated by Fulvio Testa, Andersen (London, England), 1980, Peter Bedrick (New York, NY), 1983.
Once upon a Rainbow, illustrated by Gabriele Eichenauer, Cape (London, England), 1981.
Come with Us (poems), illustrations by Leo Lionni, Andersen (London, England), 1982.
(With Janice Thompson) *Marco Polo and Wellington: Search for Solomon,* Cape (London, England), 1982.
(With Deborah King) *Puffin,* Cape (London, England), Lothrop (New York, NY), 1984.
(With Deborah King) *Swan,* Cape (London, England), Lothrop (New York, NY), 1985.
A School Bewitched (based on Edith Nesbit's *Fortunatus Rex, or The Mystery of the Disappearing Schoolgirls*), illustrated by Errol Le Cain, Blackie (London, England), 1985.
The Stepsister, illustrated by Allison Reed, Hutchinson (London, England), Dial Books (New York, NY), 1987.
(With James Kruess) *Johnny Longnose* (picture book with poetry by Lewis), illustrated by Stasys Eidrigevicius, North-South Books (New York, NY), 1989.
The Mardi Gras Cat (poetry), Heinemann (London, England), 1993.

RETELLER

The Three Golden Hairs: A Story from the Brothers Grimm, illustrated by Francoise Tresy, Hutchinson (London, England), 1983.
Jutta Ash, *Jorinda and Joringel* (based on *Jorinde und Joringel* by the Brothers Grimm), Andersen (London, England), 1984.
(And author of introduction) *Stories from the Arabian Nights,* illustrated by Anton Pieck, Methuen (London, England), Holt (New York, NY), 1987.
Cry Wolf and Other Aesop Fables, illustrated by Barry Castle, Methuen (London, England), Oxford University Press (New York, NY), 1988.

TRANSLATOR

Haroun Tazieff, *South from the Red Sea,* Lutterworth Press (London, England), 1956.
(And author of notes and introduction) Hans Christian Andersen, *Hans Christian Andersen's Fairy Tales,* illustrated by Philip Gough, Puffin (London, England), 1981.
Hans Christian Andersen, *The Wild Swans,* illustrated by Angela Barrett, E. Benn (London, England), Peter Bedrick (New York, NY), 1984.
Hans Christian Andersen, *The Flying Trunk and Other Stories from Hans Andersen,* Andersen (London, England), Prentice-Hall (New York, NY), 1986.
Heide Helene Beisert, *My Magic Cloth: A Story for a Whole Week,* illustrated by Beisert, North-South Books (London, England, and New York, NY), 1986.
Jutta Ash, *Wedding Birds* (adapted from a traditional German song), Andersen (London, England), 1986.
Hans Christian Andersen, *The Swineherd,* illustrated by Dorothee Duntze, North-South Books (New York, NY), 1987.
(And author of introduction) Hans Christian Andersen, *The Snow Queen,* illustrated by Angela Barrett, Holt (New York, NY), 1988.

(And author of introduction) *Proud Knight, Fair Lady: The Twelve Laïs of Marie de France,* illustrated by Angela Barrett, Viking (New York, NY), 1989.

Jacob and Wilhelm Grimm, *The Frog Prince,* illustrated by Binette Schroeder, North-South Books (New York, NY), 1989.

Siegfried P. Rupprecht, *The Tale of the Vanishing Rainbow,* illustrated by Jozef Wilkon, North-South Books (New York, NY), 1989.

(And author of introduction) Hans Christian Andersen, *The Nightingale,* illustrated by Josef Palecek, North-South Books (New York, NY), 1990.

Kurt Baumann, *Three Kings,* illustrated by Ivan Gantschev, North-South Books (New York, NY), 1990.

Hans Christian Andersen, *Thumbelina,* North-South Books (New York, NY), 1990.

Hans Christian Andersen, *The Steadfast Tin Soldier,* illustrated by P. J. Lynch, Andersen (London, England), 1991, Harcourt (San Diego, CA), 1992.

Kurt Baumann, *The Hungry One: A Poem,* illustrated by Stasys Eidrigevicius, North-South Books (New York, NY), 1993.

Charles Perrault, *Puss in Boots,* illustrated by Stasys Eidrigevicius, North-South Books (New York, NY), 1994.

(And author of introduction) Hans Christian Andersen, *The Emperor's New Clothes,* illustrated by Angela Barrett, Walker (London, England), Candlewick Press (Cambridge, MA), 1997.

Hans Christian Andersen, *Elf Hill: Tales from Hans Christian Andersen,* illustrated by Emma Chichester Clark, Frances Lincoln (London, England), 1999.

COMPILER

(And author of introduction) Christina Rossetti, *Christina Rossetti* (poems), E. Hulton (London, England), 1959.

The Best Children's Books of . . . , six annual volumes, Hamish Hamilton (London, England), 1963-69.

(And annotator and author of introduction) Emily Brontë, *A Peculiar Music* (poems), Bodley Head (London, England), Macmillan (New York, NY), 1971.

(And annotator) *Fantasy Books for Children* (short essays on over two hundred books), National Book League (London, England), 1975, new edition, 1977.

(And author of introduction and notes) Edith Nesbit, *Fairy Stories,* illustrated by Brian Robb, E. Benn (London, England), 1977.

(And author of notes and introduction) *The Silent Playmate* (collection of doll stories), illustrated by Harold Jones, Gollancz (London, England), 1979, Macmillan (New York, NY), 1981.

A Footprint on the Air: An Anthology of Nature Verse, illustrated by Liz Graham-Yool, Hutchinson (London, England), 1983.

(Contributor and author of essay) *Messages: A Book of Poems,* Faber & Faber (London, England), 1985.

Jacob and Wilhelm Grimm, *Grimms' Fairy Tales,* illustrated by Lidia Postma, Hutchinson (London, England), 1985, published as *The Twelve Dancing Princesses and Other Tales from Grimm,* Dial Books (New York, NY), 1986.

William Shakespeare, *A Midsummer Night's Dream,* illustrated by Sylvie Monti, Hutchinson (London, England), 1988.

(Author of introductory accounts of each story) *Classic Fairy Tales to Read Aloud,* illustrated by Jo Worth, Kingfisher (New York, NY), 1996.

Rocking Horse Land and Other Classic Tales of Dolls and Toys, illustrated by Angela Barrett, Candlewick Press (Cambridge, MA), 2000.

Also author and compiler of other titles. Author of essays for each of four volumes of *Twentieth-Century Children's Writers,* St. James Press (New York, NY), starting 1978. Author of introductions for *King Arthur* by Henry Gilbert, *Robin Hood,* by Louis Rhead, and eight other books in the "Henry Holt Little Classics" series; *East o' the Sun and West o' the Moon,* translated by George W. Dasent, illustrated by P. J. Lynch, Candlewick Press (Cambridge, MA), 1995; and *The Fairy Tale of My Life* by Hans Christian Andersen, Cooper Square Press, 2000. Contributor to periodicals, including *New York Times, Harper's, New Review, Encounter,* London *Observer, Listener, Times Literary Supplement,* and *Times Educational Supplement.*

SIDELIGHTS: A highly respected writer, critic, and anthologist, Naomi Lewis's particular gift is for writing introductory essays, which, critics have noted, are often as exciting as the main text. Her own works include stories and verse for the young; she considers her two best works (both for all ages) to be *Messages,* her major poetry anthology, and *The Mardi Gras Cat,* a much acclaimed book of original poems. As an editor, reteller, and translator, she is a well-known specialist on the works of Hans Christian Andersen. Of her work as a commentator and editor for occasional anthologies, a reviewer for *Junior Bookshelf* remarked: "What sets Naomi Lewis in a class apart from the general run of critics today is her breadth of sympathies and her ability to see the course of literature whole, so that each new book can be set into its proper slot in the grand structure." Chris Powling, in an interview in *Books for Keeps* commented, "No one is more respected in the world of children's books."

One of four children, Lewis grew up in a house full of books. She became a known professional writer in a quick leap and by a curious route. While still a young teacher, she heard of the prestigious *New Statesman* literary competitions. She sent in three entries under three different names; all three were winners. The next week she won again—and again. Each writing was in a different style, and so the competition was very challenging. One day she took courage and telephoned the *New Statesman* to see if they could use her as a critic. The obvious "no" was quickly reversed when she identified herself by the top name she'd used in the competitions. From that day on, she began writing for the paper. A year and a half later, a critical piece of hers was given the star page (called Books in General). It promptly brought requests for her writings from American periodicals as well as from United Kingdom agents and publishers. She began to write regularly for the London *Observer,* becoming a leading critic as well as the children's book editor. She also became a broadcaster in a range of departments (talks, features, literary discussion programs, etc.) on radio for the BBC. Her first book, *A Visit to Mrs. Wilcox,* a collection of her essays from various publications, is now a collector's piece, and includes her essays "Face at the Window," which discusses the child in adult literature, and "Afternoon at the Grange."

Her work on children's books as a critic, poet, and writer was to come. She began writing occasional reviews and was soon asked to produce *The Best Children's Books* series, an annual British publication providing descriptive classifications of children's books. A *Times Literary Supplement* reviewer of the 1965 edition found that Lewis "applies to children's books the standards of adult criticism that the best of them deserve." She was asked to write introductions for children's collections. Invitations to write original text for children's book illustrators came soon; among these were *Leaves* and *The Butterfly Collector* with illustrator Fulvio Testa. In *Leaves,* Lewis presents "a quiet, contemplative text," according to Kristi Thomas Beavin in *School Library Journal.* The verse presents the question, which has the better life, the evergreens, who always have leaves? Or the trees that lose their leaves, but are renewed fresh and green each spring? A contributor for *Publishers Weekly* noted that the "brilliant paintings" of illustrator Fulvio Testa "glorify Lewis's ballad."

Lewis went on to write the text for artist Deborah King's *Puffin* and *Swan,* books that explain the life cycles of very different birds. *Puffin* follows the experiences of one such seabird, as he first learns to fly, eventually migrating across the Atlantic and evading an oil slick. "The text," wrote Kay O'Connell in *School Library Journal,* "is nicely attuned to the age level, supplying the story elements of the life cycle in an enjoyable style." O'Connell also felt that the book was "as satisfying to read as good fiction." Denise M. Wilms, writing in *Booklist,* likewise thought the tale "reads like a quiet short story rather than a typical fact book." More praise came from a reviewer for *Junior Bookshelf,* who called *Puffin* "a picture book of high quality, unusual appeal and engaging talent." Lewis does much the same in *Swan,* which details the life cycle of that bird using one fictionalized Bewick swan as an example. Here she describes that animal's annual journey to the Arctic, avoiding hunters en route. A contributor for *Publishers Weekly* praised this title, calling it "as accessible and entertaining as fiction." Similar laudatory remarks came from a *Booklist* reviewer, who singled out Lewis's "poetically phrased text," concluding that the book was "an uncommonly effective nonfiction treatment of a sparsely covered topic."

Some critics have thought that poetry is Lewis's preferred form, and she has won much critical acclaim for her books of verse for young readers. A group of mice take the main stage in *Come with Us,* an "enchanting book," according to a reviewer for *Junior Bookshelf,* who also felt that Lewis's "rhymes sparkle." *Once upon a Rainbow* follows the magical partly-rhyming journey of Anna as she climbs the rainbow and travels to the seven Rainbow Lands where, in each, she meets its one-colored creatures. Only by inventing a verse can she escape to the next land. A contributor for *Junior Bookshelf* found this "an engaging fantasy." And in *The Mardi Gras Cat,* Lewis presents a compendium of original poems on felines; a hidden human story is touched upon in each. Her poems are "choice," as Kate Kellaway noted in the *Observer*. Kellaway further called the poetry "off-beat [and] sympathetic to each cat's singularity." More praise came from a reviewer for *Junior Bookshelf*, who called Lewis's poetry "keenly perceptive, . . . witty . . . , passionate." Each poem uses a different style, depending on the type of cat described. The title cat, for example, has a "blues" poem, where the ship's cat has a sea shanty; different again are the convent cat, the Venice cat, and the strange ballad of the Scottish wild cat. A. N. Wilson, writing for the London *Evening Standard*, praised Lewis's writing, saying, "T. S. Eliot, take a back seat. This is a poetic collection of distinctive cats which is absolutely magical." Wilson went on to say that Lewis's poems "will, I predict, soon be a part of every literate-person's nursery-lore."

Reviewers have noted that Lewis's books, such as *A Peculiar Music* and *Proud Knight, Fair Lady: The Twelve Laïs of Marie de France* have made these works available to young readers for the first time. Her collection of poems by Emily Brontë in *A Peculiar Music*, with its long opening introduction, is addressed to all readers, including "intelligent adolescents whose imaginations may be expected to be fired not only by the poems themselves but also" from the additional material the author provides, wrote Roy Fuller in the *Listener*. Another poetry collection, *A Footprint on the Air: An Anthology of Nature Verse*, is a choice of poems and lyrics on animals, plants, insects, and such. Among the gathered poets are Stevie Smith and Emily Dickinson, as well as Lewis herself. The title piece is the most anthologized of Lewis's poems. The editor of *Growing Point* called it a "provocative, discriminating collection for the thoughtful and the word-loving."

Lewis's major poetry collection, *Messages*, is "a sophisticated and eclectic grouping of fine poetry," according to Dawna Lisa Buchanan-Berrigan in *School Library Journal*. Alan Brownjohn, writing in the *Times Literary Supplement*, under the heading "Made to Endure," likewise found this a "rich and substantial volume." Included in this collection are poems by classical poets, contemporary poets, and children themselves. The wide range of the collection includes poems spanning approximately four hundred years. This "enticing introduction to poetry," as *New Statesman*'s Gillian Wilce described *Messages*, presents the classics of English literature as well as examples from haiku, ballads, and lesser-known poets.

Lewis as compiler has also collected classic stories and fairy tales in various volumes. Her *Classic Fairy Tales to Read Aloud* gathers twenty-three tales not only from traditional sources but also from contemporary writers such as Joan Aiken, Susan Price, and William Mayne. Chris Stephenson, writing in *School Librarian*, found this a "book to revel in and cherish." Nikki Gamble of the *Times Educational Supplement* called the book "a delightful collection, an excellent introduction to the fairy tale." Gamble further noted that Lewis's "authoritative and engaging introductions whet the appetite, setting the context of each tale, making connections with similar tales and inviting the reader to explore deeper into the world of the fairy tale." In the London *Daily Telegraph*, Mary Hoffman pointed out that these introductions and annotations by Lewis are "a bonus." And Nina Bawden of the London *Evening Standard*, calling Lewis "incomparable," considered *Classic Fairy Tales to Read Aloud* a "pure delight for all ages."

Stories about dolls and toys are collected in two other books, *The Silent Playmate: A Collection of Doll Stories* and *Rocking Horse Land and Other Classic Tales of Dolls and Toys*. The first title is an anthology of poems and excerpts from novels, with a foreword to each entry. "Those who cherish doll stories will enjoy the variety," wrote *Booklist*'s Ilene Cooper of that volume. A contributor for *Junior Bookshelf* had further positive words for *The Silent Playmate*, noting that "Lewis brings her vast knowledge and her individual flair to this collection." Six tales are gathered in *Rocking Horse Land*, a book filled with "wonderment," according to a reviewer for *Publishers Weekly*. Adèle Geras in the *Times Educational Supplement* considered Lewis to be "the most inspired of compilers," and Anne Knickerbocker, writing in *School Library Journal*, thought the tales in the book "have a timeless quality about them with appealing plots for children."

An acclaimed reteller and translator, Lewis has brought the works of writers from Aesop to Andersen to vivid life for modern readers. A rare and haunting Grimm Brothers tale finds new life in Lewis's *Jorinda and Joringel*, almost a poem in itself, which was also included in *Classic Fairy Tales*. In Lewis's introduction to this piece in its later publication, she wrote, "With its swift pace and clearshot detail, it is like the experience of a dream." Something of a Cinderella story, the tale of *The Stepsister* is "well written for reading aloud," according to a reviewer for *Publishers Weekly*.

The tale tells of a mean stepmother and her awful daughter, Rose, who dislike the kindhearted stepdaughter, also named Rose. After marrying a prince, Rose is tossed into a well by her stepmother, who tries to substitute her daughter for the young bride. Unable to be deceived, the devoted prince embarks on a search for his true love. Lewis's retelling of *Stories from the Arabian Nights* was also praised by critics. Here are not only Ali Baba and Aladdin, but some lesser-known tales. *Booklist*'s Carolyn Phelan found Lewis's versions in this collection "delightful," calling the book "a fine, new English rendition of an old favorite." Similarly, *School Library Journal* critic Ruth M. McConnell called the edition an "enchanting, attractive addition to any folktale collection." Aesop's tales sometimes are given interesting, updated morals by Lewis in *Cry Wolf and Other Aesop Fables*. Twelve stories are gathered in this "sophisticated collection," as a critic for *Kirkus Reviews* described the book.

As a translator, Lewis has also introduced or re-introduced classic tales to a new generation. She presents a Perrault classic, *Puss in Boots*, with an English rendering that "is smooth and accessible," according to a reviewer for *Publishers Weekly*. *Booklist*'s Phelan found that same translation "graceful, readable, and concise." *Proud Knight, Fair Lady* is a gathering that "celebrates the art of courtly love," according to *Horn Book*'s Mary M. Burns. Translated from Anglo-Norman French, Lewis's skill "makes it easy to understand why these stories enthralled late twelfth-century courtiers," Burns further commented. This book is, according to the *Listener*'s Susan Jeffreys, "just right for any brooding bookworms on your Christmas list." Kimi Patton, writing in *Wilson Library Journal,* found these to be "stories from another world." Critics also noted that Lewis's introduction proved as exciting as the tales told in her book.

Lewis's version of *The Snow Queen,* one of her Andersen translations, is, remarked Aidan Warlow in *School Librarian,* a "magnificent edition." A contributor to *Publishers Weekly* found that same tale "faithful to its piercing sweetness." Her translation of *The Wild Swans* is "faithful in romantic spirit to the nineteenth-century Dane, yet congenial to contemporary ears," according to Selma G. Lanes in the *New York Times Book Review*. A critic for *Junior Bookshelf* also had praise for Lewis's translation of *The Wild Swans,* calling it "a most unusual haunting version." Susan H. Patron lauded the book for its "rich literary quality" in a *School Library Journal* review. "The real thing," is how an *Observer* reviewer typified Lewis's translation of the twelve stories in *Hans Andersen's Fairy Tales,* while a contributor for *Publishers Weekly* praised *The Emperor's New Clothes* as a "witty new edition" with a "lively" text. *Horn Book*'s Ann A. Flowers commended *The Emperor's New Clothes,* finding the translation "smooth and contemporary" and further noting that the text "easily transmits the wry humor that distinguishes the story." Jackie Wullschlager of *Financial Times,* also the author of a biography on Andersen, considered *The Emperor's New Clothes* to be "exquisitely witty . . . Naomi Lewis's translation is superb, and this elegant work would be a sophisticated present for anyone." Lewis also translates nine Andersen tales in *Elf Hill: Tales from Hans Christian Andersen*. Adèle Geras, writing in the *Times Educational Supplement,* noted that "Lewis enchants" the reader "with simple, graceful" renditions of classic and less well-known tales. Nicolette Jones of the *Sunday Times* called *Elf Hill* "a must" and praised the "heart-stopping elegance" of the tales.

Lewis told *CA:* "The real fact about me is that I am a writer, possessed by *words* and their sound since the age of four or so when I began to read. At six—I remember the moment—I made a discovery. I was reading a mild poem about fairies, I'm quite sure—but the shape and sound struck a strange chord within me. 'I think *I* can do that,' were my unspoken words. (I had not yet encountered the word 'Eureka.') I promptly wrote surely the worst poem in the world (no doubt on fairies). But it did scan correctly. From that time on, poetry was my passion. When I started writing prose (for the *New Statesman*) I found that writing a critical piece was very much like writing a poem."

BIOGRAPHICAL AND CRITICAL SOURCES:

PERIODICALS

Booklist, January 1, 1982, Ilene Cooper, review of *The Silent Playmate: A Collection of Doll Stories,* p. 599; January 1, 1985, Denise M. Wilms, review of *Puffin,* p. 642; May 1, 1986, review of *Swan,* p. 1314; February 1, 1988, Carolyn Phelan, review of *Stories from the Arabian Nights,* p. 935; April 15, 1994, Carolyn Phelan, review of *Puss in Boots,* p. 1531.

Books for Keeps, November, 1990, Chris Powling, interview with Lewis, pp. 14-15.

Bulletin of the Center for Children's Books, February, 1984.

Daily Telegraph (London), December 7, 1996, Mary Hoffman, review of *Classic Fairy Tales to Read Aloud.*

Evening Standard (London), October, 1993, A. N. Wilson, review of *The Mardi Gras Cat;* December 16, 1996, Nina Bawden, review of *Classic Fairy Tales to Read Aloud.*

Financial Times (London), December 13, 1997, Jackie Wullschlager, review of *The Emperor's New Clothes.*

Growing Point, January, 1980; March, 1984, review of *A Footprint on the Air: An Anthology of Nature Verse,* pp. 4226-4227; November, 1985, p. 4538; January, 1989, pp. 5081-5082.

Horn Book, February, 1982; November-December, 1989, Mary M. Burns, review of *Proud Knight, Fair Lady: The Twelve Laïs of Marie de France,* p. 781; November-December, 1997, Ann A. Flowers, review of *The Emperor's New Clothes,* pp. 688-689.

Junior Bookshelf, June, 1980, review of *The Silent Playmate,* p. 135; October, 1981, review of *Hare and Badger Go to Town, p. 199;* June, 1982, review of *Once upon a Rainbow,* p. 94; August, 1982, review of *Come with Us,* pp. 133-134; February, 1984, review of *A Footprint on the Air,* p. 34; October, 1984, review of *The Wild Swans,* p. 200, review of *Puffin,* p. 203; February, 1986, review of *Messages: A Book of Poems,* pp. 35-36; June, 1989, pp. 132-133; February, 1994, review of *The Mardi Gras Cat,* p. 17.

Kirkus Reviews, June 15, 1986, pp. 937-938; January 15, 1987, review of *Jorinda and Joringel,* p. 136; June 15, 1987, review of *Hare and Badger Go to Town,* p. 926; August 1, 1987, pp. 1159-1160; September 1, 1987, p. 1322; November 1, 1988, review of *Cry Wolf and Other Aesop Fables,* p. 1607.

Listener, December 30, 1971, Roy Fuller, review of *A Peculiar Music: Poems for Young Readers,* p. 911; November 6, 1980; December 7, 1989, Susan Jeffreys, review of *Proud Knight, Fair Lady,* p. 34.

Los Angeles Times Book Review, October 23, 1988.

New Statesman, November 8, 1985, Gillian Wilce, review of *Messages,* p. 28.

New York Times Book Review, November 11, 1979, pp. 58, 64; December 2, 1984, Selma G. Lanes, review of *The Wild Swans,* pp. 52-53; July 9, 1989.

Observer (London, England), December 23, 1979, p. 36; November 28, 1993, Kate Kellaway, review of *The Mardi Gras Cat,* p. 12; July 30, 1995, review of *Hans Andersen's Fairy Tales,* p. 17.

Publishers Weekly, April 10, 1972, p. 58; July 9, 1979, review of *The Snow Queen,* p. 106; August 13, 1979, p. 66; September 16, 1983, review of *Leaves,* p. 125; June 27, 1986, review of *Swan,* p. 86; July 24, 1987, review of *The Stepsister,* p. 185; May 2, 1994, review of *Puss in Boots,* p. 308; July 7, 1997, review of *The Emperor's New Clothes,* pp. 67-68; December 6, 1999, review of *Elf Hill: Tales from Hans Christian Andersen,* p. 77; November 13, 2000, review of *The Emperor's New Clothes,* p. 106; November 20, 2000, review of *Rocking Horse Land and Other Classic Tales of Dolls and Toys,* p. 70.

School Librarian, December, 1979, Aidan Warlow, review of *The Snow Queen,* p. 347; November, 1987, Mary Medlicott, review of *Stories from the Arabian Nights,* p. 334; February, 1997, Chris Stephenson, review of *Classic Fairy Tales to Read Aloud,* p. 33.

School Library Journal, January, 1980, p. 64; October, 1982, p. 142; April, 1984, Kristi Thomas Beavin, review of *Leaves,* p. 105; December, 1984, Susan H. Patron, review of *The Wild Swans,* p. 67; March, 1985, Kay O'Connell, review of *Puffin,* p. 154; August, 1986, Dawna Lisa Buchanan-Berrigan, review of *Messages,* p. 102; May, 1987, Ronald A. Van De Voorde, review of *Jorinda and Joringel,* p. 85; February, 1988, Ruth M. McConnell, review of *Stories from the Arabian Nights,* pp. 80-81; February, 1994, Susan Scheps, review of *The Snow Queen,* p. 76; July, 1994, Linda Boyles, review of *Puss in Boots,* p. 97; November, 1997, Marilyn Iarusso, review of *The Emperor's New Clothes,* p. 76; January, 2000, Miriam Lang Budin, review of *Elf Hill,* p. 107; April, 2001, Anne Knickerbocker, review of *Rocking Horse Land and Other Classic Tales of Dolls and Toys,* p. 115.

Sunday Times (London), December 18, 1999, Nicolette Jones, review of *Elf Hill,* p. 19.

Times Educational Supplement, November 20, 1981, p. 31; November 2, 1984, p. 26; June 7, 1985, p. 55; February 13, 1987, p. 48; February 28, 1997, Nikki Gamble, review of *Classic Fairy Tales to Read Aloud;* December 10, 1999, Adèle Geras, review of *Elf Hill,* p. 33; December 1, 2000, Adèle Geras, review of *Rocking Horse Land,* p. 24.

Times Literary Supplement, June 9, 1966, review of *The Best Children's Books of 1965,* p. 519; July 2,

1970, p. 714; December 14, 1979; July 24, 1981, p. 841; November 9, 1984; November 29, 1985, Alan Brownjohn, review of *Messages,* p. 1361.

Wilson Library Bulletin, November, 1989, Kimi Patton, review of *Proud Knight, Fair Lady,* p. 11; April, 1994, Cathi Dunn MacRae, review of *The Hungry One,* pp. 125-126.

* * *

LINDENBAUM, Pija 1955-

PERSONAL: Born April 27, 1955, in Sundsvall, Sweden; daughter of Gosta Lindenbaum (a director) and Barbro Kalin Olsson (a teacher); married Mikael Nilsson (an artist), May 18, 1989; children: Alva. *Education:* Attended Konstfackskolan, 1975-79.

ADDRESSES: Home—Sulitelmav. 13, 167 35 Bromma, Sweden. *Office*—Bjurholmsg. 3A, 116 38 Stockholm, Sweden.

CAREER: Writer and illustrator.

AWARDS, HONORS: Heffaklumpen Award, 1990, for *Else-Marie and Her Seven Little Daddies;* Best Illustrated Books of 1992 selection, *New York Times,* for *Boodil, My Dog;* Illustrator of the Year Award, Bologna Children's Book Fair, 1993; Elsa Beskow Award, Swedish Library Association, 1993, for *Louie.*

WRITINGS:

SELF-ILLUSTRATED; IN ENGLISH TRANSLATION

Else-Marie and Her Seven Little Daddies (originally published as *Elsi-Marie och småpapporna*), translated by Gabrielle Charbonnet, Holt (New York, NY), 1991.

Boodil, My Dog, translated by Gabrielle Charbonnet, Holt (New York, NY), 1992.

Bridget and the Gray Wolves, translated by Kjersti Board, R & S (New York, NY), 2001.

Bridget and the Muttonheads, translated by Kjersti Board, R & S (New York, NY), 2002.

ILLUSTRATOR; BOOKS IN ENGLISH TRANSLATION

Barbro Lindgren, *Louie,* translated by Steven T. Murray, R & S (New York, NY), 1993.

Astrid Lindgren, *Mirabelle,* translated by Elisabeth Kallick Dyssegaard, Farrar, Straus & Giroux (New York, NY), 2003.

ILLUSTRATOR; BOOKS IN SWEDISH

Moni Nilsson-Brännström, *Tsatsiki och Morsan,* Natur och Kultur (Stockholm, Sweden), 1995.

Annika Holm, *Stick, sa Matilda Markström,* Rabén & Sjögren (Stockholm, Sweden), 1995.

Moni Nilsson-Brännström, *Tsatsiki och Farsan,* Natur och Kultur (Stockholm, Sweden), 1996.

Annika Holm, *Den stora oredan,* Rabén & Sjögren (Stockholm, Sweden), 1997.

Starke Arvid, Alfabeta (Stockholm, Sweden), 1997.

Moni Nilsson-Brännström, *Bara Tsatsiki,* Natur och Kultur (Stockholm, Sweden), 1998.

(Self-illustrated) *Gittan och gråvargarna,* Rabén & Sjögren (Stockholm, Sweden), 2001.

Also published in Swedish, *Britten och Prins Benny,* 1996, and *Glossas Café,* 1998.

ADAPTATIONS: Else-Marie and Her Seven Little Daddies was adapted into a play.

SIDELIGHTS: Swedish author and illustrator Pija Lindenbaum has received international recognition for her small, but well-regarded body of work. Winner of an Illustrator of the Year Award from the Bologna Children's Book Fair and the Elsa Beskow Award for best illustrated children's book published in Sweden, Lindenbaum caught the attention of reviewers with her first book, *Elsi-Marie och småpapporna,* published in English as *Else-Marie and Her Seven Little Daddies.* Here, the author/illustrator uses the story of Snow White and the Seven Dwarfs as a springboard for a tale that some felt was a parable about alternative family structures. Else-Marie has seven tiny little fathers who do all the things that ordinary fathers do, including going to work, reading the paper, and putting Else-Marie to bed at night. Still, Else-Marie dreads the day when her seven little daddies come to pick her up from her play group, because then all her friends with ordinary-sized, singular fathers will find out about her very different situation. Describing the book as an "offbeat treat," a *Kirkus Reviews* critic found *Else-Marie and Her Seven Little Daddies* "a whimsical Swedish import with a unique premise."

Lindenbaum's wry bending of traditional fairy tales is apparent in subsequent picture books, as well, such as *Bridget and the Gray Wolves,* which draws loosely on the story of Little Red Riding Hood. Here, a timid little girl goes on a walk into the forest with her day-care group and gets lost. Suddenly, she is surrounded by a pack of gray wolves, but instead of inspiring terror, the wolves bring out the boss in Bridget, and she soon has the whole pack rounded up to play a game of hospital. She eventually puts them to bed and sings them to sleep, and in the morning, finds her way back to her day-care center. Although the author does not offer insight into how Bridget sheds her timidity, young people "may well enjoy this unexpected turn on the theme of summoning one's courage," contended a reviewer in *Publishers Weekly*. A good deal of the book's humor is found in the illustrations of cowed wolves being bossed around by a preschooler, noted Maryann H. Owen in *School Library Journal*. Readers familiar with Lindenbaum's earlier books, including *Else-Marie and Her Seven Little Daddies* and *Boodil, My Dog,* "will recognize the winning blend of sweetness and weirdness here," remarked Deborah Stevenson in *Bulletin of the Center for Children's Books.*

Bossy Bridget returns in *Bridget and the Muttonheads,* in which the now intrepid youngster wanders off from the hotel pool while on vacation with her parents and befriends some sheep who are stranded on a tiny island. Readers will enjoy another view of "Bridget's steadfast march to the beat of her own odd and quirky drummer," concluded GraceAnne A. DeCandido in *Booklist*.

Lindenbaum once told *CA:* "When my first manuscript with illustrations, *Else-Marie and Her Seven Daddies,* was completed, wrapped in a parcel and on its way to being published, I didn't realize that the book would be given such a reception, or that it would arouse such feeling in readers from different countries. I only thought that I had written a fairy tale, an unbelievable story to laugh at.

"But people wanted to know who the author was, and how I really felt. It was quite amusing to me that people talked more about me than about the book.

During the Book Fair in Bologna that year, a German publisher asked my publisher for a copy of the book to take to her psychiatrist. Some people didn't think it was possible to publish it. But there were many who dared, and that has made me very happy and grateful. In Sweden, *Else-Marie and Her Seven Daddies* was awarded three literary prizes and grants; it was also dramatized for a production.

BIOGRAPHICAL AND CRITICAL SOURCES:

PERIODICALS

Booklist, December 15, 2001, Gillian Engberg, review of *Bridget and the Gray Wolves,* p. 740; August, 2002, GraceAnne A. DeCandido, review of *Bridget and the Muttonheads,* p. 1973; May 15, 2003, Todd Morning, review of *Mirabelle,* p. 1672.

Bulletin of the Center for Children's Books, September, 2001, Deborah Stevenson, review of *Bridget and the Gray Wolves,* pp. 25-26.

Kirkus Reviews, October 15, 1991, review of *Else-Marie and Her Seven Little Daddies.*

Publishers Weekly, November 29, 1991, review of *Else-Marie and Her Seven Little Daddies,* p. 51; November 9, 1992, review of *Boodil, My Dog,* p. 82; September 3, 2001, review of *Bridget and the Gray Wolves,* p. 87.

School Library Journal, March, 1992, Alexandra Marris, review of *Else-Marie and Her Seven Little Daddies,* p. 216; November, 2001, Maryann H. Owen, review of *Bridget and the Gray Wolves,* p. 128; January, 2003, Heather E. Miller, review of *Bridget and the Muttonheads,* p. 105.*

* * *

LUNDEN, Joan 1950-

PERSONAL: Born Joan Elise Blunden, September 9, 1950, in Fair Oaks, CA; daughter of Erle Murray (a physician) and Gladyce Lorraine (Somervill) Blunden; married Michael Krauss (a television producer), September 10, 1978 (divorced, 1992); married Jeff Konigsberg (a summer camp owner), 2000; children: (first marriage) Jamie Beryl, Lindsay Leigh, Sarah Emily; (second marriage) Kate Elizabeth, Max Aaron. *Education:* Attended Universidad de Las Americas, 1968-72; American River Junior College, A.A., 1972.

Joan Lunden

ADDRESSES: *Home*—CT. *Agent*—Debra Goldfarb, Creative Artists Agency, 9830 Wilshire Blvd., Beverly Hills, CA 90212-1825.

CAREER: Motivational speaker, writer, television host and producer. Joni Lisa Charm and Modeling School of Sacramento, Sacramento, CA, owner and manager, 1972-73; KCRA-TV and KCRA-Radio, Sacramento, co-anchor and producer, 1973-75; WABC-TV, New York, NY, reporter for *Eyewitness News*, 1975-80, co-anchor of weekend newscasts, 1976-80; ABC-TV, New York, NY, co-host of *Good Morning America*, 1980-97, host of television specials, *Behind Closed Doors*, 1994-99; Arts & Entertainment Network, New York, NY, host and producer, *Behind Closed Doors*, 2000—. Has also appeared on numerous television programs and in videos, including *Joan Lunden Workout America*.

MEMBER: Mothers Against Drunk Driving (national spokesperson).

AWARDS, HONORS: Outstanding Mother of the Year, National Mother's Day Committee, 1982-83; Spirit of Achievement Award, Albert Einstein College of Yeshiva University; Young Women's Christian Association (YWCA) Outstanding Women's Awards Speaker; National Women's Political Caucus Award; New Jersey Division on Civil Rights Award; Baylor University Outstanding Woman of the Year Award; Matrix Award from New York Women in Communications, 1991.

WRITINGS:

(With Ardy Friedburg) *Good Morning, I'm Joan Lunden,* Putnam (New York, NY), 1986.
(With first husband, Michael Krauss, and Sue Castle) *Joan Lunden's Mothers Minutes,* Warner Books (New York, NY), 1986.
(With Michael Krauss and Sue Castle) *Your Newborn Baby: Everything You Need to Know,* Warner Books (New York, NY), 1988.
(With Laura Morton) *Joan Lunden's Healthy Cooking,* Little, Brown (Boston, MA), 1996.
(With Laura Morton) *Joan Lunden's Healthy Living: A Practical, Inspirational Guide to Creating Balance in Uour Life,* Crown (New York, NY), 1997.
(With Andrea Cagan) *Joan Lunden's A Bend in the Road Is Not the End of the Road: Ten Positive Principles for Dealing with Change,* Morrow (New York, NY), 1998.
Wake-Up Calls: Making the Most out of Every Day, McGraw-Hill (New York, NY), 2001.

Author of syndicated column, *Parent's Notes.*

ADAPTATIONS: *Wake-Up Calls: Making the Most out of Every Day,* was adapted for audio cassette.

SIDELIGHTS: For nearly twenty years Joan Lunden was the co-host of *Good Morning America* for the American Broadcasting Company (ABC-TV). To her legions of fans, Lunden presented the positive image of a working mother who could balance parenting, television duties, and daring physical feats such as bungee jumping and mountain-climbing. As the celebrity host of such a visible network show, Lunden experienced a certain on-air intimacy with her viewers and thus used her own personal experiences at times to illustrate the triumphs and vicissitudes of motherhood, marriage and divorce, weight loss, and physical fitness. This same intimacy is an ingredient in her nonfiction books that deal with such topics as nutrition, self-image, personal philosophy, and child-rearing.

Born and raised in California, Lunden began her broadcasting career as a reporter for KCRA-TV in Sacramento. She signed with ABC-TV in 1975 and began her career there as a newscaster. She joined the staff of *Good Morning America* in 1980 and was the show's indefatigable co-host until 1997, when she left her spot without rancor to host and produce television specials. Since then she has worked in her *Behind Closed Doors* series and has enjoyed a lucrative secondary career as a motivational speaker and author. *People* reviewer Jennifer Wulff noted that a typical Lunden title "offers a helping hand to anyone in need of encouragement."

One of Lunden's earliest books, *Good Morning, I'm Joan Lunden*, is an autobiography which tells of her association with ABC and *Good Morning America*. She describes how she survived the industry at a time when women were given on-air jobs simply for their looks and fired quickly if the ratings dropped; she was able to use her intelligence and quick-thinking to overcome coworkers who thought she was a no-talent "Barbie" and attracted the attention of network executives. Lunden gives a behind-the-scenes look at network television and some of its personalities as well as glimpses into her personal life. David Owen in the *New Republic* commented: "Lunden and her coauthor have a . . . feel for narrative. . . . Lunden's life story is genuinely interesting, even a little inspiring."

When Lunden's children from her first marriage were very young, she authored several titles on motherhood and baby care, including *Your Newborn Baby: Everything You Need to Know*. Later, when she needed to lose weight and increase her physical stamina, she released *Joan Lunden's Healthy Cooking* and *Joan Lunden's Healthy Living: A Practical, Inspirational Guide to Creating Balance in Your Life*. *People* writer Alex Tresniowsky called *Joan Lunden's Healthy Cooking*, "one lively cookbook. . . . [It] amounts to a blueprint for anyone determined to reinvent themselves." *Booklist* contributor Sue-Ellen Beauregard noted that *Joan Lunden's Healthy Living* is "upbeat and chatty" while presenting its suggestions for health and well being "in a most readable fashion."

Since she left *Good Morning America* Lunden has written books that encourage readers to embrace change and to move through transitional periods with strength and calm. *A Bend in the Road Is Not the End of the Road: Ten Positive Principles for Dealing with Change* is based very closely on the insights she gained into herself after being told she was being taken off the morning television show. A similar spirit animates *Wake-Up Calls: Making the Most out of Every Day*, a collection of aphorisms and short passages of inspirational writing that Lunden had collected over many years. In a *Booklist* review of *Wake-Up Calls*, Nancy Spillman concluded that Lunden's "personal touch adds zest to the mix."

In 2003 Lunden and her husband, Jeff Konigsberg, became parents of twins born to a surrogate mother. Lunden continues to produce and host *Behind Closed Doors* specials for the Arts & Entertainment network.

BIOGRAPHICAL AND CRITICAL SOURCES:

PERIODICALS

Booklist, April 1, 1997, Sue-Ellen Beauregard, review of *Joan Lunden's Healthy Living: A Practical Inspirational Guide to Creating Balance in Your Life*, p. 1274; September 1, 1998, Ilene Cooper, review of *Joan Lunden's A Bend in the Road Is Not the End of the Road: Ten Positive Principles for Dealing with Change*, p. 4; September 1, 2000, Ilene Cooper, review of *Wake-Up Calls: Making the Most out of Every Day*, p. 4; June 1, 2001, Nancy Spillman, review of *Wake-Up Calls*, p. 1906.

Good Housekeeping, January, 1998, Joanna Powell, "'I Was Addicted to Security,'" p. 84; November, 1998, Joan Lunden, "Letting Go," p. 114.

Library Journal, April 15, 1997, Lisa S. Wise, review of *Joan Lunden's Healthy Living: A Practical, Inspirational Guide to Creating Balance in Your Life*, p. 102; October 15, 1998, January Adams, review of *Joan Lunden's A Bend in the Road Is Not the End of the Road*, p. 86; June 1, 1999, Nann Blaine Hilyard, review of *Joan Lunden's A Bend in the Road Is Not the End of the Road*, p. 207.

New Republic, March 30, 1987, p. 35.

People, May 6, 1996, Alex Tresniowsky, review of *Joan Lunden's Healthy Cooking*, p. 30; June 9, 1997, "Sunrise, Sunset: After 17 Years as Co-host, Joan Lunden Decides to Leave ABC's Troubled 'Good Morning America'," p. 58; November 13, 2000, Jennifer Wulff, review of *Wake-Up Calls*, p.

53; March 10, 2003, Jill Smolowe, "Teaming with Love: Thanks to Surrogate Deborah Bolig, TV Host Joan Lunden Prepares to Parent Twins at 52," p. 88.

Publishers Weekly, October 5, 1998, review of *Joan Lunden's A Bend in the Road Is Not the End of the Road,* p. 63.*

* * *

LYONS, Mary E(velyn) 1947-

PERSONAL: Born November 28, 1947, in Macon, GA; daughter of Joseph and Evelyn Lyons; married Paul Collinge (owner of a used and rare bookstore). *Education:* Appalachian State University, B.S., 1970, M.S., 1972; University of Virginia, doctoral study. *Hobbies and other interests:* Playing Irish penny whistle and banjo, performing with the group Virgil and the Chicken Heads.

ADDRESSES: Home—Charlottesville, VA. *Agent*—c/o Author Mail, Atheneum, 1230 Avenue of the Americas, New York, NY 10020.

CAREER: Writer. Has worked as a reading teacher at elementary and middle schools in North Carolina and in Charlottesville, VA, and as a school librarian at elementary, middle, and high schools, Charlottesville.

AWARDS, HONORS: Best Books for Young Adults, American Library Association (ALA), and Carter G. Woodson Book Award, National Council for the Social Studies (NCSS), both 1991, both for *Sorrow's Kitchen;* Teacher Scholar Award, National Endowment for the Humanities, 1991-92; Notable Children's Trade Book in the Field of Social Studies, NCSS/Children's Book Council (CBC), 1992, for *Raw Head, Bloody Bones,* 1996, for *Keeping Secrets,* and 1994, for *Stitching Stars;* ALA Best Books for Young Adults, and Golden Kite Award for fiction, Society of Children's Book Writers and Illustrators, both 1992, Jane Addams Children's Book Award Honor, 1993, and Parents' Choice Award, 1996, all for *Letters from a Slave Girl;* ALA Notable Book designation, 1993, and Carter G. Woodson Award, 1994, both for *Starting Home;* Books for the Teen Age, New York Public Library, 1995, for *Deep Blues;* Carter G. Woodson Elementary Merit Book, 1995, for *Master of Mahogany;* Jefferson Cup

Mary E. Lyons

Series Award, Virginia Library Association, 1996, for "African-American Artists and Artisans" series; three Virginia Foundation for the Humanities fellowships.

WRITINGS:

FOR YOUNG PEOPLE

Sorrow's Kitchen: The Life and Folklore of Zora Neale Hurston, Scribner (New York, NY), 1990.

(Editor) *Raw Head, Bloody Bones: African-American Tales of the Supernatural,* Scribner (New York, NY), 1991.

Letters from a Slave Girl: The Story of Harriet Jacobs, Scribner (New York, NY), 1992.

The Butter Tree: Tales of Bruh Rabbit, illustrated by Mireille Vautier, Holt (New York, NY), 1995.

Keeping Secrets: The Girlhood Diaries of Seven Working Writers, Holt (New York, NY), 1995.

The Poison Place (novel), Atheneum (New York, NY), 1997.

(With Muriel M. Branch) *Dear Ellen Bee: A Civil War Scrapbook of Two Union Spies,* Atheneum (New York, NY), 2000.

Knockabeg: A Famine Tale, Houghton (Boston, MA), 2001.

(Editor) *Feed the Children First: Memories of the Great Hunger,* Atheneum (New York, NY), 2002.

"AFRICAN-AMERICAN ARTISTS AND ARTISANS" SERIES

Starting Home: The Story of Horace Pippin, Painter, Scribner (New York, NY), 1993.

Stitching Stars: The Story Quilts of Harriet Powers, Scribner (New York, NY), 1993.

Master of Mahogany: Tom Day, Free Black Cabinet-maker, Scribner (New York, NY), 1994.

Deep Blues: Bill Traylor, Self-Taught Artist, Scribner (New York, NY), 1994.

Painting Dreams: Minnie Evans, Visionary Artist, Houghton (Boston, MA), 1996.

(Editor) *Talking with Tebé: Clementine Hunter, Memory Artist,* Houghton (Boston, MA), 1998.

OTHER

A Story of Her Own: A Resource Guide to Teaching Literature by Women, National Women's History Project, 1985.

SIDELIGHTS: Mary E. Lyons has turned a search for personal roots into a literary exploration of the South. "My way of finding home" is how Lyons explains her work. In award-winning fiction and nonfiction titles for middle-grade readers and young adults, Lyons has explored the lives of historically marginalized members of our society, both African Americans and women. Her nonfiction works for pre-teens include the highly praised "African-American Artists and Artisans" series, and her books for young adults include *Sorrow's Kitchen: The Life and Folklore of Zora Neale Hurston, Letters from a Slave Girl: The Story of Harriet Jacobs,* and *The Poison Place.* Her books celebrate the "triumph of the human spirit," Lyons once explained. "As corny as it might sound, that's what the subjects of my books have accomplished. As women and African Americans, they had to overcome neglect and prejudice to build creative and full lives." Lyons has thus far specialized in telling the stories of creative artists. Most important, however, most of her protagonists and subjects are of the South, and taken collectively, their tales fill in missing pieces of the social history of that part of the United States.

After becoming burned out after several years working as a reading teacher, Lyons returned to college to become credentialed as a school librarian, a position she held for the final six years of her public school career. By 1988 another impulse began guiding her. "Life has a weird way of sending us what we need to complete ourselves," Lyons noted. "When I was a reading teacher, I discovered that my eighth-grade classes enjoyed stories by women writers and African-American writers. They especially loved the humorous folktales collected by Zora Neale Hurston. There was no biography of her in the school library for the students to read, so I wrote my first book, *Sorrow's Kitchen: The Life and Folklore of Zora Neale Hurston.*" There was also a resonance in Hurston's life with her own that piqued Lyons's interest in the black writer. "I found out that Hurston was the only southerner in the Harlem Renaissance, and I identified with that. I knew how it felt to be the only one with a southern accent, that you had to hide it sometimes because of southern stereotypes. Look at television, for example. If they want to depict an ignorant person, they often give him or her a southern accent." Hurston's forthrightness, her sincerity, and her need for honesty also appealed to Lyons.

What resulted is a book that is part biography, part introduction to the works of Hurston. Lyons traces Hurston's life from her childhood in Eatonville, Florida, at the turn of the twentieth century through her fight to become educated, her participation in the Harlem Renaissance, and finally to her collecting and preserving the folklore of both her native South and of the West Indies. Researching and writing the book was a challenge for Lyons, who stated that "history classes have always made me yawn." But now history took on a new meaning; not simply a list of dates and battles, but within the context of a person's life. "I had to relearn everything I had studied years before in high school and college," Lyons noted. "World War I, the Depression, World War II, the civil rights movement. This time I studied with Zora in mind. Now I like learning history, especially when it's told from a woman's point of view."

"I was very fortunate with this first book," Lyons recalled. "Unknown to me, the timing was perfect. Interest in Hurston was growing at the time. There was an Off-Broadway show about her, a PBS production in the works, several adult biographies were underway, and all her books were being reprinted in new editions. I worked with one publisher on my manuscript for nine months, and when they rejected it, I quickly reworked it and sent it off to Scribner. The editor there bought it almost immediately." Critical reception was as positive as that of the publishing community. *Booklist*'s Hazel Rochman observed that the "strength of Lyons's book is that she includes long excerpts from Hurston's works, set off within each chapter by a handsome border design." Elizabeth S. Watson, writing in *Horn Book,* called the book "fascinating, enlightening, stimulating, and satisfying," and also noted Lyons's use of extended quotes from Hurston's writing. The biography was chosen as a Best Book for Young Adults by the American Library Association, one of several awards and honors it garnered. Most important, as far as Lyons is concerned, is the fact that it allowed young readers intrigued by the life of Hurston the means to search out the woman's writings.

Lyons used Hurston's writings as a springboard for her second book, *Raw Head, Bloody Bones: African-American Tales of the Supernatural. Raw Head, Bloody Bones* incorporates some of the stories and tales Hurston collected as well as others compiled by the Federal Writers' Project during the 1930s. Some of the fifteen stories of ghosts and demons that Lyons retells are cast in the Gullah dialect spoken by African-American inhabitants of the South Carolina and Georgia coasts, where Lyons lived as a child. *Booklist*'s Denia Hester warned that the "timid and fainthearted" should beware, as this "collection of African- American tales is a bone chiller . . . a scary good read." A critic in *Publishers Weekly* observed that the tales "derive their bewitching quality from the rhythms of the spoken word and the dancelike quality of early African-American speech" that combine to "provide a quixotic contrast to the often gruesome subject matter."

The success of her books prompted Lyons to leave behind her career as a school librarian for the world of professional writing. "I am fortunate that my husband operates a used and rare bookshop. He has been a great help in researching the books I've written and has been very supportive of my decision to become a full-time writer. It hasn't been easy financially, but I have successful women friends in the corporate world whose jobs are not as satisfying as mine." During her last year of full-time work in the schools, Lyons researched what would become her third title—one of her personal favorites and one of her best-selling books. *Letters from a Slave Girl* is an account of the early life of Harriet Ann Jacobs, a slave who later fled to the North and became, through her writings, an important voice in the abolitionist movement.

Lyons meticulously researched Jacobs's life, relying heavily on the woman's autobiography, and recreated her life from age twelve to twenty-nine in letters Jacobs might have written. A *Kirkus Reviews* critic deemed the book "a moving evocation of the tragedies inflicted by slavery." The fictional letters detail the loss of Jacobs's mother and the forced separation of her family after the death of one owner. There is a letter to her dead father after she is denied permission to attend his funeral; another letter to the man she loves describing how she has decided to accept the attentions of a relatively kind white man in order to escape those of her brutal master. Jacobs ran away from her owners and hid for seven years in a crawl space under the eaves of her grandmother's cabin, eventually escaping to the North in 1842. A *Kirkus Reviews* critic noted that the "style Lyons creates for Harriet—a luminous character, gentle and resolute—is graceful and direct," while a *Horn Book* reviewer declared *Letters from a Slave Girl* to be "historical fiction at its best." A contributor in *Publishers Weekly* also found much to praise in the book, describing it as a "searing epistolary work" that "stirringly celebrates the strength of the human spirit."

In 1993 Lyons initiated an impressive series detailing the lives of African-American artists and artisans, some of whom had been overlooked during their lifetimes. "I've always loved the decorative arts," she explained, "and in 1990, I found several scholarly books describing a group of African-American artists and artisans—from blacksmiths to quilt-makers—whose works were highly respected by folklorists and art historians. But most people, including children, were not familiar with them. . . . I began tracking down articles about the artists. I showed slides of their work to children, who loved the art. Even more, they liked the idea that a person can be artistic in many ways, that you don't have to have a degree from an art school to be creative." Lyons decided to honor the artists with books that, as much as possible, would allow the artists to speak for themselves. She also wanted to show how their art tells the stories of their lives.

The first title in the series, *Starting Home,* features self-taught painter Horace Pippin, whose works include many scenes from World War I, where he fought in the first U.S. all-black regiment to fight overseas. Wounded in the war and left unable to lift his right hand above shoulder level, Pippin went on to become a highly renowned folk artist. Lyons's second subject was Harriet Powers, and in *Stitching the Stars* she profiles this former slave who "wrote" stories in quilts with needle and thread. (Slaves were forbidden to read or write but instead told stories by sewing them.) Powers's two story quilts are now on display at the Museum of American History and are considered priceless examples of folk art. Reviewing both titles for *Booklist,* Rochman noted that "Lyons's sensitive commentary will draw middle-grade readers to look at the paintings and photographs." Reviewing *Stitching Stars* in the *Bulletin of the Center for Children's Books,* Deborah Stevenson remarked that "Lyons's lively writing stitches concepts together with smoothness and clarity. . . . [This] is both an unusual take on history and a reminder of the democratic possibilities of art."

In *Master of Mahogany* and *Catching the Fire* Lyons tells the stories of a cabinetmaker and a blacksmith, respectively. Born of free parents in 1801, Thomas Day became one of the most successful cabinetmakers in pre-Civil War North Carolina, and his works have become collector's items. In *Master of Mahogany* "Lyons does an excellent job of piecing together the sketchy details of Day's life, of which little is known," wrote a reviewer for *Horn Book.* In *Catching the Fire,* Lyons presents the life and work of Philip Simmons, a blacksmith whose gates, fences, and railings decorate the city of Charleston, South Carolina, where Simmons has lived most of his life. Based on personal interviews with Simmons and those who have worked with him, the book was dubbed "an engrossing biography" by a *Kirkus Reviews* critic and "engaging" by a reviewer in *Horn Book.* Stevenson concluded in *Bulletin of the Center for Children's Books* that *Catching the Fire* would be "useful not only as an introduction to a gifted professional craftsman, but also a reminder of how unexpected things can become art when executed with authority."

Other visual artists in the series include Bill Traylor in *Deep Blues,* Minnie Evans in *Painting Dreams,* and Clementine Hunter in *Talking with Tebé.* Lyons's personal favorite in the series is *Deep Blues,* which details the life and works of Traylor, who was born into slavery in Alabama in 1856 and did not begin painting until he was eighty. His works are now acclaimed and exhibited throughout the United States. A critic in *Horn Book* noted that "Lyons's perceptive commentary . . . points out possible connections between Traylor's life as a farmer and the subject matter of his works." Minnie Evans was forty-three before she began to draw pictures that were based on dreams that had haunted her all her life. Born into poverty and untrained as an artist, Evans did not let this stop her, nor would she be stopped by her family and friends who thought she was crazy. "Lyons has brought us the life and work of an African-American folk artist who succeeded despite community prejudice," commented *Booklist*'s Rochman. In the final book in the series, Lyons presents the art of Clementine Hunter, called Tebé, whose work portrays the life of a southern laborer. This story is told through Hunter's own words in magazine and newspaper articles and in tape-recorded interviews.

Other books from Lyons include *Keeping Secrets, The Butter Tree: Tales of Bruh Rabbit,* and *The Poison Place.* In the first of these titles, Lyons blends her own commentary with excerpts from the girlhood diaries of seven nineteenth-century women writers; Louisa May Alcott, Charlotte Forten, Sarah Jane Foster, Kate Chopin, Alice Dunbar-Nelson, Ida B. Wells, and Charlotte Perkins Gilman. Lyons demonstrates how keeping a diary helped each of these young writers eventually develop a public voice. A critic in *Kirkus Reviews* noted that "Lyons writes with style and feeling, creating a strong sense of each individual life story, even as she gives us a social history of what it was like to be a woman at that time." A *Horn Book* reviewer called the work "a fascinating look at the public and private lives" of these writers that explores "issues of femininity, social expectations, family, and racism." In a somewhat lighter vein, Lyons has also retold African-American trickster tales in *The Butter Tree.* The six tales from South Carolina included here involve the usual scenario of a small animal tricking a much larger one, and as a critic in *Publishers Weekly* noted, "undoubtedly helped the enslaved originators of these tales endure their own oppression." "Bruh" as well as "brer" is a variant of "brother," an indication that the slaves held this wily rabbit close to their hearts. *Horn Book*'s Maeve Visser Knoth noted that "Lyons's skilled retellings are brief and uncluttered, recalling the oral tradition. She uses few adjectives, yet her language is colorful and evokes regional flavor."

A novel, *The Poison Place* is by its author's account the most difficult of her books thus far—difficult in terms of researching and writing. Beginning in 1989 with the scrap of an idea, Lyons finally returned to the work years later. The book uses historical fact as its background, detailing the lives of two men. One is Charles Willson Peale, the eighteenth-century portraitist and founder of the first museum of natural history in the United States, the Peale Museum in Philadelphia. The other is Moses Williams, Peale's former slave, who became a silhouette cutter and the first black professional artist in post-revolutionary America. The novel is told through the voice of Williams on a nighttime tour with his young daughter through the museum. Williams's own struggle for survival is contrasted to Peale's story and that of his museum. As Rachelle M. Bilz noted in *Voice of Youth Advocates,* "Moses's lifelong quest for freedom is intertwined with the Peale family's success and failure." Through the narrator's revelations, the reader is led to wonder how much responsibility Peale himself had in the eventual poisoning of his own son, a taxidermist in the museum who died from the arsenic he used in his work. Bilz concluded that the novel was "fast paced and well written . . . sure to appeal to historical fiction fans." A contributor in *Kirkus Reviews* called the novel "a riveting work of historical fiction."

Lyons deals with the Irish Potato Famine of the nineteenth century in two books, the novel *Knockabeg: A Famine Tale* and the nonfiction *Feed the Children First: Memories of the Great Hunger. Knockabeg* mixes creatures and characters from Irish folklore with real-life characters. The fairy folk known as the Nuckelavees have put a curse on Ireland's potatoes, causing a famine and a war between the fairies and the mortals. A critic for *Publishers Weekly* found that "the action shifts between (and often intersects) both worlds, detailing the impact of famine on the human community as well as the wounded faeries' war stories when they return to heal the residents of Knockabeg." Kit Vaughan in *School Library Journal* concluded: "Don't expect an entirely happy ending in this story, which includes some gruesome descriptions of the effects of the potato famine on the mortals of Knockabeg."

Feed the Children First: Memories of the Great Hunger is a collection of comments made by Irish men and women who lived through a devastating potato famine in Ireland. Their accounts include descriptions of the many deaths that occurred—some one quarter of the population perished—as well as remembrances of the voyages many of them made to start new lives in North America. Diane S. Marton in *School Library Journal* found that these firsthand accounts "bear witness not only to unbearable suffering, but also to the humanity, dignity, and endurance of a people." "The personal voices and images in this collection bring the horror of the Irish potato famine very close," added Hazel Rochman in *Booklist.* Margaret A. Bush in *Horn Book* concluded that *Feed the Children First* is "a powerful introduction to Ireland's history and to the human devastation of a country in extreme poverty."

Lyons continues to pen historical fiction and to write for young readers. "I can't imagine writing for anyone besides young people," the author once stated. "They like to be told the truth and can handle complexities that adults can't." She also maintains contact with her audience by frequent visits to schools. "Teachers often expect a black author to show up because so many of my books have dealt with African-American issues. I'm always flattered that people assume I'm black; it means I'm doing my job as a writer. But now I consider myself not only a writer of black history or of women's history, but increasingly as a historian of the South." For Lyons this means giving a voice to those who have not been heard before. "Many people I write about have never had a chance to speak for themselves. In articles already written about them, you don't really hear their voices. I want to let my subjects tell their own stories in a form accessible to young readers."

BIOGRAPHICAL AND CRITICAL SOURCES:

BOOKS

Twentieth-Century Children's Writers, 4th edition, St. James Press (Detroit, MI), 1995.

PERIODICALS

Booklist, December 15, 1990, Hazel Rochman, review of *Sorrow's Kitchen: The Life and Folklore of Zora Neale Hurston,* p. 866; January 1, 1992, Denia Hester, review of *Raw Head, Bloody Bones: African-American Tales of the Supernatural,* pp. 830-831; November 15, 1993, Hazel Rochman, review of *Starting Home: The Story of Horace Pippin, Painter* and *Stitching Stars: The Story Quilts of Harriet Powers,* pp. 618-619; October 1,

1994, Ilene Cooper, review of *Master of Mahogany: Tom Day, Free Black Cabinetmaker*, p. 322; November 15, 1994, Hazel Rochman, review of *Deep Blues: Bill Traylor, Self-Taught Artist*, p. 598; July, 1996, Hazel Rochman, review of *Painting Dreams: Minnie Evans, Visionary Artist*, pp. 1825-1826; September 1, 1997, Carolyn Phelan, review of *Catching the Fire: Philip Simmons, Blacksmith*, p. 117; December 1, 1997, Randy Meyer, review of *The Poison Place*, p. 616; November 1, 2000, Carolyn Phelan, review of *Dear Ellen Bee: A Civil War Scrapbook of Two Union Spies*, p. 540; December 15, 2001, Hazel Rochman, review of *Feed the Children First: Irish Memories of the Great Hunger*, p. 725.

Bulletin of the Center for Children's Books, January, 1991, p. 124; February, 1992, p. 162; November, 1992, p. 79; December, 1993, Deborah Stevenson, review of *Stitching Stars*, p. 128; December, 1994, p. 136; September, 1996, p. 21; October, 1997, Deborah Stevenson, review of *Catching the Fire*, p. 57.

Horn Book, March-April, 1991, Elizabeth S. Watson, review of *Sorrow's Kitchen*, p. 216; November, 1992, review of *Letters from a Slave Girl: The Story of Harriet Jacobs*, p. 729; March-April, 1994, Ellen Fader, review of *Starting Home,* and Ellen Fader, review of *Stitching Stars*, p. 219; November, 1994, review of *Master of Mahogany*, p. 750; March, 1995, review of *Deep Blues*, p. 221; September, 1995, review of *Keeping Secrets: The Girlhood Diaries of Seven Women Writers* and Maeve Visser Knoth, review of *The Butter Tree: Tales of Bruh Rabbit*, p. 614; September-October, 1997, review of *Catching the Fire*, p. 592; September-October, 1998, Susan P. Bloom, review of *Talking with Tebé: Clementine Hunter, Memory Artist*, p. 620; March-April, 2002, Margaret A. Bush, review of *Feed the Children First*, p. 229.

Kirkus Reviews, November 1, 1992, review of *Letters from a Slave Girl*, p. 1380; June 1, 1995, review of *Keeping Secrets;* July 1, 1997, review of *Catching the Fire;* October 1, 1997, review of *The Poison Place;* July 1, 1998, p. 968.

Publishers Weekly, October 25, 1991, review of *Raw Head, Bloody Bones*, p. 69; October 26, 1992, review of *Letters from a Slave Girl*, pp. 72-73; February 20, 1995, review of *The Butter Tree*, p. 206; September 18, 2000, review of *Dear Ellen Bee*, p. 112; July 23, 2001, review of *Knockabeg: A Famine Tale*, p. 78; December 10, 2001, review of *Feed the Children First*, p. 71.

Reading Today, April, 2001, Lynne T. Burke, review of *Dear Ellen Bee*, p. 32.

School Library Journal, January, 1991, p. 119; December, 1992, p. 113; February, 1994, Maria B. Salvadore, reviews of *Starting Home* and *Stitching Stars*, p. 113; October, 1994, Joanne Kelleher, review of *Master of Mahogany*, p. 136; January, 1995, p. 127; July, 1995, p. 100; July, 1996, p. 93; September, 1997, Margaret C. Howell, review of *Catching the Fire*, p. 233; November, 1997, Sally Margolis, review of *The Poison Place*, p. 120; September, 1998, Judith Constantinides, review of *Talking with Tebé*, p. 221; October, 2000, Patricia B. McGee, review of *Dear Ellen Bee*, p. 164; September, 2001, Kit Vaughan, review of *Knockabeg*, p. 226; March, 2002, Diane S. Marton, review of *Feed the Children First*, p. 254.

Voice of Youth Advocates, February, 1991, p. 378; December, 1992, p. 282; October, 1995, p. 252; December, 1997, Rachelle M. Bilz, review of *The Poison Place*, p. 318.

ONLINE

Lyons Den Web site, http://www.lyonsdenbooks.com/ (April 18, 2003).*

M

major, devorah 1952-

PERSONAL: Born 1952, in Berkeley, CA; daughter of Reginald Allman and Helen Gabriel Major; children: Yroko and Iwa. *Ethnicity:* African American. *Education:* San Francisco State University, degrees in health education and African-American studies.

ADDRESSES: Home—P.O. Box 423634, San Francisco, CA 94102. *Agent*—Janell Walden Agyeman, 636 NE 72nd Street, Miami, FL 33138. *E-mail*—dmajor1@ix.netcom.com.

CAREER: Poet, novelist, performer, editor. Former librarian, African-American Historical Society. Koncepts Cultural Gallery, Oakland, CA, editor of community arts magazine and Web site; leader of writing workshops as an artist-in-residence.

MEMBER: Daughters of Yam.

AWARDS, HONORS: First Novelist Award, Black Caucus American Library Association, 1996, for *An Open Weave;* Josephine Mills Award for Literary Excellence, PEN Oakland, 1997, for *Street Smarts;* named poet laureate of San Francisco, CA, 2002.

WRITINGS:

(Editor) *Ascension II,* San Francisco African-American Historical & Cultural Society (San Francisco, CA), 1983.
(With Opal Palmer Adisa) *Traveling Women,* Jukebox Press (Oakland, CA), 1989.
An Open Weave (novel), Seal Press (Seattle, WA), 1995.
Street Smarts (poetry), Curbstone Press (Willimantic, CT), 1996.
Brown Glass Windows (novel), Curbstone Press (Willimantic, CT), 2002.
With More Than Tongue (poetry), Creative Arts (Berkeley, CA), 2002.
Where River Meets Ocean (poetry), City Lights Books (Monroe, OR), 2003.

Contributor of short stories to anthologies, including *Pushcart XII,* 1987; *I Hear a Symphony,* Penguin, 1995; and *Streetlights: Urban Stories of the Black Experience,* Doubleday, 1996. Contributor of essays to anthologies, including *California Childhoods,* Creative Arts Books, 1988; *A Single Mother's Companion,* Seal Press, 1995; *Something to Savor,* Womens Press, 1996; and *Father Songs,* Beacon Press, 1997. Contributor of poetry to anthologies, including *Practicing Angels; Other Side of That Window,* 1992; *Adam of Ife,* 1993; and *Poetry Like Bread,* 1995. Poetry featured in recordings, including *Fierce/Love; America Fears the Drum;* and *Who Sane/Who Sane.* Contributor to periodicals, including *Zyzzyva, Onthebus, Black Scholar, Shooting Star, Caprice,* and *Callaloo.* Producer, with Opal Palmer Adisa, of *The Tongue Is a Drum,* a poetry-and-music sound recording.

SIDELIGHTS: devorah major (whose name is often cited in lower-case) is a poet, essayist, performer, and poetry teacher, whose first novel, *An Open Weave,* has a lyrical style. The story revolves around the female members of an extended African-American family. While waiting to celebrate a birthday party for teenager Imani, the family and their friends reminisce about their pasts. Grandmother Ernestine, though blind, seems to see deep within the family members and is the one who keeps the family from splintering. Her adopted daughter, Iree, sees into the future during epileptic seizures. The story also relates Imani's determination not to desert a pregnant friend, Amanda, who has been abandoned by her family. "If the title [*An Open Weave*] doesn't suggest a symbolic underpinning," commented *Melus* reviewer John Meagher, "then the names and mysterious events lead the reader to believe there is more than meets the eye."

Lisa Nussbaum, in *Library Journal*, observed, "Down-to-earth, gritty, and honest, the story shows how these women weather difficult situations" through love and friendship. A contributor for *Kirkus Reviews* concluded, "Amanda finds at Imani's home a family she has been looking for in all the wrong places—and Imani understands with newfound appreciation the ultimate power of community."

Dulcy Brainard, in *Publishers Weekly*, had this assessment of major's collection of poetry, *Street Smarts*: "Musical and energetic, major's work calls for a live voice to release its emotional power." Brainard wished that the author had delved more deeply into difficult issues, yet called the work "compelling."

Major's second novel is "set in the shadows of redevelopment—really in the '80s before developers finished putting up all the buildings" in the Western Addition area of San Francisco, the author told Wanda Sabir in a *San Francisco Bay View* interview. *Brown Glass Windows* takes place among the "walking wounded," in the words of *Booklist*'s Kier Graff. Like *An Open Weave*, the story centers on a large African-American family in San Francisco. The Everman family has faced its share of demons, from prejudice to postwar trauma to drug addiction; the narration is split between an unnamed third person and the ghost of an African slave of America's past. The presence of otherworldly characters imbues *Brown Glass Windows* with "a heavy dose of magical realism," according to a *Publishers Weekly* contributor. The same reviewer speculated that such a literary tactic might turn away some readers, while "others will be intrigued by the depth and history it lends to . . . the realities of racial prejudice and, above all, the many-layered truths of families."

In spring 2002 Major came home one night to find a message in her fax machine. She had been named San Francisco's poet laureate, chosen over fellow finalists Diane De Prima and Jack Hirschman. Major succeeded Janice Mirikitani, "and I thought that in terms of the politics of the situation it was unlikely that they would give it to me," Major told Sabir. However, she felt it "was, 'like wow'" to realize that two women of color had been chosen sequentially, Sabir's article added. As Sabir related, Major's term as poet laureate was to focus on "living memorials," places where people could gather, reflect on life and death, "and perhaps emerge with a poem."

The poet is particularly interested in showing young people the consequences of violence. "We . . . see the memorials, the balloons, bottles and flowers when the kid is shot on the corner. There are so many, and some people just drive by them." Desensitizing people to killing leads to more killing: "I think there's a big sense of people aren't seeing it—especially people who live in other neighborhoods [who] consistently and conservatively ignore the humanity of the victims with words similar to those used to dehumanize the Palestinians, like 'Palestinian mothers celebrate the deaths of their children, while Jewish women mourn their young,'" Major remarked in Sabir's interview. "That's why people can look at all the youth being killed in the Middle East and not do anything because the people are not people. They are being objectified."

BIOGRAPHICAL AND CRITICAL SOURCES:

PERIODICALS

Black Scholar, winter, 1996, review of *An Open Weave*, p. 66; winter, 1996, review of *Street Smarts*, p. 66.
Bloomsbury Review, July, 1996, review of *An Open Weave*, p. 21.
Booklist, May 1, 2002, Keir Graff, review of *Brown Glass Windows*, p. 1508.
Bookwatch, May, 1996, review of *Street Smarts*, p. 7.
Choice, April 1996, review of *An Open Weave*, p. 1310.
Kirkus Reviews, August 1, 1995, review of *An Open Weave*, pp. 1050-1051; April 15, 2002, review of *Brown Glass Windows*, p. 526.
Kliatt Young Adult Paperback Book Guide, May, 1997, review of *An Open Weave*, p. 8.

Library Journal, September 1, 1995, review of *An Open Weave,* pp. 208-209; November 1, 1995, review of *An Open Weave,* p. 80; March 15, 1996, review of *An Open Weave,* p. 43; May 1, 1996, review of *Street Smarts,* pp. 97-98.

Melus, summer, 1998, John Meagher, review of *An Open Weave,* p. 210.

Publishers Weekly, July 31, 1995, review of *An Open Weave,* p. 71; March 18, 1996, review of *Street Smarts,* p. 67; May 6, 2002, review of *Brown Glass Windows,* p. 38.

ONLINE

San Francisco Bay View, http://www.sfbayview.com/ (July 16, 2002), Wanda Sabir, interview with Devorah Major.*

* * *

McARTHUR, Nancy

PERSONAL: Born in Cleveland, OH; daughter of W. R. (in sales) and Irene (a homemaker) McArthur. *Education:* Baldwin-Wallace College, B.A.

ADDRESSES: Home and office—P.O. Box 296, Berea, OH 44017-0296. *E-mail*—mcarthur@apk.net.

CAREER: Freelance writer. Baldwin-Wallace College, Berea, OH, part-time lecturer in journalism; also worked in public relations connected with the performing arts.

MEMBER: Society of Children's Book Writers and Illustrators, Authors Guild, Authors League of America, Mystery Writers of America, Sisters in Crime.

WRITINGS:

How to Do Theatre Publicity, Good Ideas (Berea, OH), 1978.
Megan Gets a Dollhouse, illustrated by Megan Lloyd, Scholastic (New York, NY), 1988.
Pickled Peppers, illustrated by Denise Brunkus, Scholastic (New York, NY), 1988.
The Plant That Ate Dirty Socks, Avon (New York, NY), 1988.
The Return of the Plant That Ate Dirty Socks, Avon (New York, NY), 1990.
The Adventure of the Buried Treasure, illustrated by Irene Trivas, Scholastic (New York, NY), 1990.
The Adventure of the Backyard Sleepout, illustrated by Irene Trivas, Scholastic (New York, NY), 1992.
The Escape of the Plant That Ate Dirty Socks, Avon (New York, NY), 1992.
The Secret of the Plant That Ate Dirty Socks, Avon (New York, NY), 1993.
More Adventures of the Plant That Ate Dirty Socks, Avon (New York, NY), 1994.
The Plant That Ate Dirty Socks Goes Up in Space, Avon (New York, NY), 1995.
Mystery of the Plant That Ate Dirty Socks, Avon (New York, NY), 1996.
The Plant That Ate Dirty Socks Gets a Girlfriend, Avon (New York, NY), 1997.
The Adventure of the Big Snow, illustrated by Mike Reed, Scholastic (New York, NY), 1998.
The Plant That Ate Dirty Socks Goes Hollywood, Avon (New York, NY), 1999.
The Plant That Ate Dirty Socks (stage play), Dramatic Publishing (Woodstock, IL), 2000.

Contributor to books, including *Stories for Free Children,* McGraw-Hill (New York, NY), 1982. Contributor to periodicals, including *Writer.*

SIDELIGHTS: Nancy McArthur once told *CA:* "I got interested in being a writer when I was about ten or eleven. My first published writing was in my high school newspaper.

"People ask me how I got the idea for my most popular book, *The Plant That Ate Dirty Socks.* One day I thought of the title, jotted it down, and threw it into my idea files. I write down any ideas, even if I don't know what I could possibly do with them. It is amazing how many random ideas turn out to be useful.

"To make up stories, I often ask myself questions. If I have an action in mind, to start developing a character I ask 'What kind of person would do this?' If I start with a character, I wonder 'What would this person do in such-and-such a situation?' So I thought, 'Who would really want a plant that eats dirty socks?' A very messy kid, of course. I remembered that when I was a kid, I was the messy one in the family. My brother and sister were very neat. So I gave my messy-boy character a neatness-nut little brother to drive him crazy. That funny conflict gave me the start for my story.

"In addition to using my imagination and experience, I also do research for realistic details to make my settings and characters lifelike. My books begin with a very messy rough draft, slowly constructed, while I figure out the story. Although I start with some ideas, many more emerge as I write."

BIOGRAPHICAL AND CRITICAL SOURCES:

PERIODICALS

Booklist, September 15, 1988, p. 169.
School Library Journal, December, 1988, p. 89.

* * *

MEDHURST, Martin J. 1952-

PERSONAL: Born October 15, 1952, in Alton, IL; son of Maurice A. (a company president) and Wilma L. Medhurst; married Margaret M. Gentzel, August 11, 1979 (divorced, 1988); married Laurel A. Canglose, October 31, 1989; children: Monica, James Snedden, Julia Marie. *Ethnicity:* "Caucasian." *Education:* Wheaton College, B.A., 1974; Northern Illinois University, M.A., 1975; Pennsylvania State University, Ph.D., 1980. *Politics:* Republican. *Religion:* Roman Catholic.

ADDRESSES: Home—4719 Hunington, Bryan, TX 77802. *Office*—c/o Department of Speech Communication, Texas A&M University, College Station, TX 77843; fax: 979-845-6594. *E-mail*—m-medhurst@tamu.edu.

CAREER: University of California—Davis, Davis, CA, assistant professor, 1979-85, associate professor of rhetoric, 1985-88; Texas A & M University, College Station, TX, associate professor, 1988-91, professor of speech communication, 1991—, coordinator of Program in Presidential Rhetoric at Center for Presidential Studies, George Bush School of Government and Public Service, 1993-2003, associate department head, 1991-98, Naomi Lewis faculty fellow in liberal arts, 1993, 1994. M. J. Medhurst and Associates, president and chief executive officer, 1985-87. Lecturer at colleges and universities, including Indiana University—Bloomington, Purdue University, Kansas State University, Emerson College, Pennsylvania State University, Calvin College, University of Nevada—Las Vegas, and California State University—Chico; guest on television and radio programs.

MEMBER: International Society for the History of Rhetoric, National Communication Association, Religious Communication Association, Rhetoric Society of America, Society for Historians of American Foreign Relations, Center for the Study of the Presidency, Council of Editors of Learned Journals, Western States Communication Association, Southern States Communication Association.

AWARDS, HONORS: National Communication Association, Anniversary Prize Fund Award, 1982, for "Political Cartoons As Rhetorical Form: A Taxonomy of Graphic Discourse," and Marie Hochmuch Nichols Award, 1995 and 1997; publication award, Religious Communication Association, 1983, for "From Duche to Provoost: The Birth of Inaugural Prayer"; Moody grant, Lyndon Baines Johnson Research Foundation, 1984; grants from Texas Committee for the Humanities and National Endowment for the Humanities, 1995, and George Bush Presidential Library Foundation, 1999.

WRITINGS:

(Editor, with Thomas W. Benson, and contributor) *Rhetorical Dimensions in Media: A Critical Casebook,* Kendall/Hunt (Dubuque, IA), 1984, 2nd edition, 1991.
(Editor, with Alberto Gonzalez and Tarla Rai Peterson, and contributor) *Communication and the Culture of Technology,* Washington State University Press (Pullman, WA), 1990.
(With Robert L. Ivie, Philip Wander, and Robert L. Scott) *Cold War Rhetoric: Strategy, Metaphor, and Ideology,* Greenwood Press (Westport, CT), 1990, revised edition, Michigan State University Press (East Lansing, MI), 1997.

(Editor and contributor) *Landmark Essays on American Public Address,* Hermagoras Press (Davis, CA), 1993.

Dwight D. Eisenhower: Strategic Communicator, Greenwood Press (Westport, CT), 1993.

(Editor and contributor) *Eisenhower's War of Words: Rhetoric and Leadership,* Michigan State University Press (East Lansing, MI), 1994.

(Editor and contributor) *Beyond the Rhetorical Presidency,* Texas A & M University Press (College Station, TX), 1996.

(Editor, with H. W. Brands) *Critical Reflections on the Cold War: Linking Rhetoric and History,* Texas A & M University Press (College Station, TX), 2000.

(Editor, with Kurt Ritter) *Presidential Speechwriting: From the New Deal to the Reagan Revolution and Beyond,* Texas A & M University Press (College Station, TX), 2003.

(Editor, with Martin Carcasson, Wynton C. Hall, and B. Wayne Howell) *Presidential Rhetoric: An Annotated Bibliography,* Texas A & M University Press (College Station, TX), in press.

Contributor to books, including *Television Studies: Textual Analysis,* edited by Gary Burns and Robert J. Thompson, Praeger (New York, NY), 1989; *The Modern Presidency and Crisis Rhetoric,* edited by Amos Kiewe, Praeger (New York, NY), 1993; *U.S. Presidents As Orators: A Bio-Critical Sourcebook,* edited by Halford R. Ryan, Greenwood Press (Westport, CT), 1995; and *Rhetoric and Community: Unity and Fragmentation,* edited by J. Michael Hogan, University of South Carolina Press (Columbia, SC), 1998. Founding editor and senior editor of "Rhetoric and Public Affairs Series," Michigan State University Press (East Lansing, MI), 1993—; series editor, "Presidential Rhetoric Series," Texas A & M University Press (College Station, TX), 1996—, and "A Rhetorical History of the United States: Significant Moments in American Public Discourse," Michigan State University Press (East Lansing, MI), 2003—. Contributor of more than forty articles and reviews to academic journals, including *Communication Studies* and *Armed Forces and Society. Quarterly Journal of Speech,* book review editor, 1987-89, associate editor, 1990-92; founding editor, *Rhetoric and Public Affairs,* 1998—; associate editor, *Western Journal of Speech Communication,* 1982-86, and *Communication Monographs,* 1990-92; guest editor, *Communication Education,* 1989; member of editorial board, *Critical Studies in Mass Communication,* 1993-97, and *Presidential Studies Quarterly,* 2002—.

WORK IN PROGRESS: The Eisenhower Persuasions: Rhetoric, Politics, and Leadership; Ghost: A History and Criticism of Presidential Speechwriting, with Thomas W. Benson; *Eisenhower and the Atoms for Peace Campaign, 1953-1961.*

* * *

MEGLIN, Nick 1935-

PERSONAL: Born July 30, 1935, in Brooklyn, NY; married Lucille Guerriero (a medical secretary), December 28, 1956 (divorced, 1980); children: Diane Elizabeth, Christopher Allen. *Education:* Brooklyn Queens College (now Brooklyn College of the City University of New York); School of Visual Arts, B.F.A., 1976. *Hobbies and other interests:* Tennis, camping, theater.

ADDRESSES: Office—Mad, 485 Madison Ave., New York, NY 10022.

CAREER: Mad (magazine), New York, NY, editor, 1956—. Instructor at School of Visual Arts, New York, NY, beginning 1972. *Military service:* U.S. Army, illustrator, 1958-60.

MEMBER: American Society of Composers, Authors and Publishers, Dramatists Guild, Society of Illustrators, Writers Guild, National Eagle Scout Association.

WRITINGS:

On-the-Spot Drawing, Watson-Guptill (New York, NY), 1969.

Fountain Pen Drawing, Grosset (New York, NY), 1973.

Superfan, illustrated by Jack Davis, New American Library (New York, NY), 1973.

The Art of Humorous Illustration, Watson-Guptill (New York, NY), 1973, updated edition published as *Humorous Illustration: The Top Artists of Our Time Talk about Their Work,* foreword by Federico Fellini, 2001.

Superfan . . . Again!, illustrated by Jack Davis, New American Library (New York, NY), 1974.

(Editor) Don Martin and Dick DeBartolo, *"Mad's" Don Martin Steps Further Out,* Warner Books (New York, NY), 1975.
Honor the Godfather, New American Library (New York, NY), 1976.
Mad Stew, illustrated by Anthony D'Adamo, Warner Paperback (New York, NY), 1977.
Rotten Rhymes and Other Crimes, illustrated by Al Jaffee, New American Library (New York, NY), 1978.
(Editor) Barry Siegel, *"Mad" Clobbers the Classics,* Warner Books (New York, NY), 1982.
A "Mad" Look at the Fifties, illustrated by George Woodbridge, Warner Books (New York, NY), 1985.
A "Mad" Look at the Sixties, illustrated by George Woodbridge, Warner Books (New York, NY), 1988.
(Editor, with Don Edwing) Bob Clarke, *Spy vs. Spy: The Updated Files, #2,* Warner Books (New York, NY), 1989.
(Editor) *Mad's Creature Presentation,* Warner (New York, NY), 1993.
(Editor, with John Ficarra) *Mad about the Movies,* Mad Books (New York, NY), 1998.
(Editor, with John Ficarra) *Mad about TV,* Mad Books (New York, NY), 1999.
(With daughter, Diane Meglin) *Drawing from Within: Unleashing Your Creative Potential,* Warner (New York, NY), 1999.
(Editor, with John Ficarra) *The Mad Bathroom Companion,* Mad Books (New York, NY), 2000.
(Editor, with John Ficarra) *The Mad Bathroom Companion, Number Two,* Mad Books (New York, NY), 2001.
(Editor, with John Ficarra) *The Mad Gross Book,* Mad Books (New York, NY), 2001.
(Editor, with John Ficarra) *Mad about Super Heroes,* Mad Books (New York, NY), 2002.

Also editor of *Mad: The Half-Wit and Wisdom of Alfred E. Neuman.*

WORK IN PROGRESS: A Broadway musical, film scripts, two books on drawing and illustration, a *Mad* encyclopedia.

SIDELIGHTS: Although his name is hardly a household word, Nick Meglin has exercised an enormous influence over popular culture over the last half century. Meglin began editing *Mad* magazine in the 1950s and continues to coedit the periodical today, in an era when *Mad*'s antic forms of satire and parody have become pervasive forces in American humor. Meglin, himself an illustrator and writer, did not foresee a lengthy stay at *Mad* when he began editing it in 1956. However, an almost unprecedented degree of editorial freedom and the opportunity to work with several generations of comic illustrators have kept him at the helm for decades.

Poking fun at America—its politics, entertainment, music, morals, and attitudes—has been the hallmark of *Mad* magazine since its inception. In the 1950s its broad satire was a novel, and daring, way to challenge authority. Now that this form of humor has become widely popular, *Mad* has managed to weather competition from television, computers, and stand-up comedy to continue its zany bashing of a nation's sacred cows. In an interview in *Pop Culture* magazine, Meglin said that while "trying to be funny on demand is not an easy thing," he has enjoyed working at *Mad*. "What has kept my interest and my excitement and my exuberance all these years is the people I'm dealing with. The freelancers are among the most talented, brilliant, fun people in the world. That's been my saving grace—I love these people and of course my staff. My partner, John Ficarra, and I really do have a much better time than I think you would find in a room full of accountants arguing about whether you carry the three or debit the five. I think I've been blessed with that kind of situation—that's what keeps it fun." As for the irreverent humor and cartooned sight gags, Meglin says they are devised with no particular eye toward the audience's age, educational level, or gender. He said: "You just hope somebody picks it up and reads it and laughs, then you consider yourself a success."

Although many of the books Meglin has written or edited have to do with *Mad,* some of them also present his more serious views as an illustrator. *Drawing from Within: Unleashing Your Creative Potential,* written with his daughter, Diane, encourages artists of all talent levels to express themselves through the visual arts. *Humorous Illustration: The Top Artists of Our Time Talk about Their Work* offers profiles of fourteen masters of cartoon humor, some of them well known for their regular contributions to *Mad.* Bill Radford in the Colorado Springs *Gazette* praised *Humorous Illustration* for its "insights into the artists' philosophies, styles and work habits."

As it enters the corporate era as part of the Time-Warner conglomerate, *Mad* has incorporated color and advertising to help boost its bottom line. According to its editors, however, the changes have not extended into the humorous intentions of the magazine; if anything, *Mad* has become edgier without resort to the gratuitous vocabulary and subject matter in other media. Meglin told *Pop Culture* magazine: "All magazines and books and newspapers are suffering because reading is getting to be a lost art. . . . So our competition today isn't another humor magazine, it never has been. The only magazine consistently funnier than us is *The Congressional Record*." He added that the market for collectibles, which includes vintage *Mad* issues, art work, and drawings, has enhanced the current viability of the periodical. "We are part of the culture," he concluded, "and that's a phenomenon we ourselves are amazed at."

Meglin once told *CA:* "I have always worked in areas and on subjects I have first had experience in—illustration, sports, humor, opera, and theater. I consider myself a writer who draws rather than an illustrator who writes, since my drawing is of a serious approach and much of my writing is in a lighter vein. I follow the films of [Federico] Fellini, the musicals of Stephen Sondheim, comics Robert Klein, Garry Shandling, and Jerry Seinfeld, composers Nino Rota and John Barry, and the field of American illustration in general."

BIOGRAPHICAL AND CRITICAL SOURCES:

PERIODICALS

Denver Business Journal, November 23, 2001, L. Wayne Hicks, "It's a Mad, Mad, Mad, Mad World," p. 38A.
Gazette (Colorado Springs, CO), July 8, 2001, Bill Radford, "Books Take You Back to the Drawing Board," p. LIFE2.
Library Journal, November 15, 1999, Daniel Lombardo, review of *Drawing from Within: Unleashing Your Creative Potential,* p. 68; September 1, 2002, Steve Raiteri, review of *Mad about Super Heroes,* p. 150.
Publishers Weekly, August 16, 1999, review of *Drawing from Within,* p. 75.

ONLINE

News Observer Online, http://www.newsobserver.com/ (April 3, 2003), author interview.

Pop Culture Web site, http://www.popcultmag.com/ (April 3, 2003), author interview.*

* * *

MEYER, L. A.
See MEYER, Louis A(lbert), Jr.

* * *

MEYER, Louis A(lbert), Jr. 1942-
(L. A. Meyer)

PERSONAL: Born August 22, 1942, in Johnstown, PA; son of Louis, Sr. (an army officer) and Martha (a homemaker; maiden name, Keytack) Meyer; married Annetje Lawrence (a retailer), May 28, 1966; children: Matthew, Nathaniel. *Education:* University of Florida, B.A. (English literature), 1964; graduate study in painting, Columbia University, 1970; Boston University, M.F.A. (painting), 1973. *Politics:* Independent.

ADDRESSES: *Home and office*—P.O. Box 9, Corea, ME 04624. *E-mail*—ameyer@acadia.net.

CAREER: Painter and author. Rockland High School, Rockland, MA, art teacher, 1974-81; cofounder of Sweetback Graphics (textile design and imprinting firm), 1981; cofounder of Clair de Loon Gallery (art gallery), Bar Harbor, ME, 1984—, and co-owner, Blue Loon Studio Gallery, Birch Harbor, ME. *Military service:* U.S. Navy, 1964-68; became lieutenant.

WRITINGS:

The Gypsy Bears, Little, Brown (Boston, MA), 1971.
The Clean Air and Peaceful Contentment Dirigible Airline, Little, Brown (Boston, MA), 1972.
(As L. A. Meyer) *Bloody Jack: Being an Account of the Curious Adventures of Mary "Jacky" Faber, Ship's Boy* (young-adult novel), Harcourt (San Diego, CA), 2002.

WORK IN PROGRESS: A sequel to *Bloody Jack.*

SIDELIGHTS: Louis A. Meyer, Jr. published two children's picture books while attending art school in Boston in the early 1970s before writing his 2002

Louis A. Meyer, Jr.

adventure novel *Bloody Jack: Being an Account of the Curious Adventures of Mary "Jacky" Faber, Ship's Boy*. His first work, *Gypsy Bears*, follows a family of human-like bears who must leave their home in Romania because of a famine in their homeland. But King Zoltan and Maria, the mama and papa bear, along with their two cubs, find it difficult to make a living by entertaining people with their music as everyone seems to be afraid of them wherever they go. After becoming incarcerated in a zoo, they quickly escape and eventually make their way to Yellowstone Park, where they are allowed to continue their happy, gypsy ways without fear. Although Muriel Kolb, who reviewed *Gypsy Bears* for *Library Journal,* complained that Meyer pushes his anthropomorphic story too far, a reviewer for *Publishers Weekly* called this "a refreshing and delightful fantasy." Meyer's second picture book, *The Clean Air and Peaceful Contentment Dirigible Airline*, in which an eccentric inventor builds a flying machine that eventually replaces the airplane and the family car, garnered praise for its "bold and brassy" illustrations from *Library Journal* reviewer Carol Chatfield.

Thirty years later, Meyer published an altogether different sort of book for young people, a historical adventure for young adults. In *Bloody Jack,* Meyer creates an exciting, fast-paced plot, a resourceful heroine, and an intriguing setting, claimed reviewers, when orphaned twelve-year-old Mary decides to disguise herself as a boy and sign onto a British warship in late eighteenth-century London. Mary must learn the arduous job of a ship's boy, and the opportunities for her to show her mettle are frequent in the face of predatory shipmates, a clash with pirates, and a shipwreck. Throughout, she must maintain her disguise as "Jacky" despite the ongoing changes of puberty and her growing feelings for another of the ship's young sailors.

"The action in Jacky's tale will entertain readers with a taste for adventure," contended Carolyn Phelan in *Booklist,* who praised Meyer's effective use of period detail and the strength of Jacky's narrative voice. While not a "rousing, swashbuckling tale of pirates and adventures on the high seas," according to Kit Vaughan in *School Library Journal, Bloody Jack* is "a good story" with a strong, likeable heroine, this critic concluded. Other reviewers were even more enthusiastic in their praise, including a critic for *Publishers Weekly,* who applauded Meyer's "Dickensian flair" in depicting the hardships of an orphaned child living on the streets of London, and extolled "the spirited heroine's wholly engaging voice." Likewise, for a critic in *Kirkus Reviews,* Meyer "has penned a rousing old-time girl's adventure story, with an outsized heroine who is equal parts gutsy and vulnerable." *Bloody Jack* is "a first-rate read," this reviewer concluded.

"I was born in Johnstown, Pennsylvania, in 1942, and spent the next thirteen years as an Army brat, living in Germany and up and down the East Coast of the United States," Meyer told *CA*. "I liked being an Army kid, despite all the constant moving—my mother informs me we moved twenty-six times, and I know I went to twelve different schools before I go out of high school. There was always a lot of great boy stuff to do on Army bases and there was a real camaraderie among the kids—you made friends fast and you saw them go just as quick.

"After my father retired, I went to high school in Conemaugh, Pennsylvania, and Fort Myers, Florida, and college at the University of Florida in Gainesville. While at college, I met my future wife, Annetje Lawrence. Upon graduation with a degree in English literature, I bid the aforementioned Ms. Lawrence goodbye forever and put in a summer as a floor sweeper in Chicago and then hitchhiked around Mexico and the southern United States. Being imminently draftable during the Vietnam-war era and not wanting to have my throat cut in some hot and bug-infested foxhole, I joined the Navy and four months later, I was a spanking new officer in the U.S. Navy, assigned to the Mediterranean Fleet. The closest I got to combat was in various bars in Italy, France, Spain, and Malta. During this time, I also renewed my acquaintance with the inestimable Ms. Annetje Lawrence, and in 1966, during one of my few times in port, we were married.

"After my release from the service, we did our year in New York City, where I worked as a social worker and took graduate art courses at Columbia University. We then relocated to Scituate, Massachusetts, and I enrolled in Boston University's Master of Fine Arts program, receiving my M.F.A. in painting in '73. While at Boston University, I published two children's picture books with Little, Brown, and Company. I taught high school art for seven years at Rockland High School in Rockland, Massachusetts, and we had two sons, Matthew and Nathaniel, who are both now painters and teachers. We left teaching in 1981 to set up a silk screen printing and design shop in Fort Myers Beach, Florida, and soon had retail shops both there and in Bar Harbor, Maine. (We had purchased land on the downeast coast of Maine in 1971 and had built a house, and we have summered there ever since.)

"Several years ago, we closed up the Florida operation and moved to Maine full time, and we now have the Clair de Loon Gallery in Bar Harbor and the Blue Loon Studio Gallery in Birch Harbor, Maine. We live in the small fishing village of Corea.

"About the birth of Jacky Faber, protagonist of *Bloody Jack:* My wife and I have a small art gallery in Bar Harbor, Maine, wherein we sell matted and framed prints of my art work. We sell quite a few of these prints, and they all have to be matted and framed, and I'm the one that gets to do it. While the work is gratifying—people are buying my artwork after all—it is repetitive and the mind is free to wander. So, one day in the summer of 2000, I'm framing away in my workshop and listening to British and Celtic folk music on our local community radio station, when the host of the program plays a long string of early nineteenth-century songs that feature young girls dressing up as boys and following their boyfriends out to sea, the most well known of these being 'Jackaroe' and 'Canadi-i-o.' These generally end up with the girl being found out quickly and happily marrying either the boy or the captain. It occurred to me, however, to wonder what it would be like if the girl, instead of seeking to be with her lover, connives to get on board a British warship in order to just eat regularly and have a place to stay, her being a starving orphan on the streets of late 1700s London. What would she have to do to pull off this deception for a long period of time? How would she handle the 'necessary' things? What if she goes through the changes of adolescence while on board in the company of 408 rather rough men and boys, and her not having much of a clue as to what is happening to her? What if this ship goes into combat and she has to do her dangerous duty? And, finally, what if she falls in love with one of the boys and can never tell him of her female nature?

"I started making notes and seven months later *Bloody Jack* was done."

BIOGRAPHICAL AND CRITICAL SOURCES:

PERIODICALS

Booklist, November 15, 2002, Carolyn Phelan, review of *Bloody Jack: Being an Account of the Curious Adventures of Mary "Jacky" Faber, Ship's Boy,* p. 595.

Kirkus Reviews, March 15, 1972, review of *The Clean Air and Peaceful Contentment Dirigible,* p. 322; August 1, 2002, review of *Bloody Jack,* p. 1137.

Library Journal, May 15, 1971, Muriel Kolb, review of *The Gypsy Bears,* p. 1806; February 15, 1973, Carol Chatfield, review of *The Clean Air and Peaceful Contentment Dirigible,* p. 646.

Publishers Weekly, February 15, 1971, review of *The Gypsy Bears,* p. 79; October 7, 2002, review of *Bloody Jack,* p. 74.

School Library Journal, September, 2002, Kit Vaughan, review of *Bloody Jack,* p. 229.

* * *

MICUCCI, Charles (Patrick, Jr.) 1959-

PERSONAL: Surname is pronounced "Mee-*koo*-chee"; born October 25, 1959, in Camp Lejeune, NC; son of Charles P. (in U.S. Marine Corps) and Jeanne (a secretary; maiden name, Findley) Micucci. *Education:* Attended Northern Illinois University, New York University, and School for the Visual Arts.

ADDRESSES: Agent—c/o Author Mail, Houghton Mifflin, 222 Berkeley, Boston, MA 02116-3764.

CAREER: Writer and illustrator.

WRITINGS:

SELF-ILLUSTRATED

A Little Night Music, Morrow (New York, NY), 1989.
The Life and Times of the Apple, Orchard Books (New York, NY), 1992.
The Cabbie Who Stole New York City, Bantam (New York, NY), 1992.
The Life and Times of the Honeybee, Ticknor & Fields (New York, NY), 1995.
The Life and Times of the Peanut, Houghton Mifflin (Boston, MA), 1997.
The Life and Times of the Ant, Houghton Mifflin (Boston, MA), 2003.

ILLUSTRATOR

Alfred Tennyson, *The Brook,* Orchard Books (New York, NY), 1994.
Fred Arrig, *The Baseball Star,* Whistlestop (Mahwah, NJ), 1995.
Mary Packard, *The Happy Trick-or-Treaters,* Scholastic (New York, NY), 1996.
Jon Chardiet, *Parker Penguin, Big Brother Blues,* Scholastic (New York, NY), 1998.
Bernice Chardiet, *The Easter Ribbit,* Scholastic (New York, NY), 1998.
Jon Chardiet, *Parker Penguin and the Winter Games,* Scholastic (New York, NY), 1999.
Joyce Milton, *Hieroglyphs,* Grosset & Dunlap (New York, NY), 2000.

OTHER

The Life and Times of the Apple was also published in *Scott Foresman Reading, Grade 2,* Scott Foresman (Glenview, IL), 2000; *The Easter Ribbit* was also published in *Hop to It! A Scholastic Easter Treasury,* Scholastic (New York, NY), 2003.

SIDELIGHTS: Charles Micucci's first book for children, *A Little Night Music,* describes the adventures of a musical house cat whose nocturnal violin playing stirs several other animals—a trio of mice, a pair of cardinals, and the family dog—into a joyous frenzy of dancing. Patricia Pearl commented in *School Library Journal,* "The text is simple and poetic as it tells of paws tapping, singing, twirling, whisking, and prancing . . . with grace and energy." A *Publishers Weekly* reviewer described Micucci's watercolor illustrations as "warmly lyrical."

Micucci followed *A Little Night Music* with *The Life and Times of the Apple,* a picture book which examines the growth cycle, uses, varieties, and history of the popular fruit. As part of his research for the book, the author planted twenty-three apple seeds and kept them in his apartment; two were eventually transplanted successfully to New York City's Central Park. Critical response to *The Life and Times of the Apple* was positive. A contributor to *Kirkus Reviews* remarked that "Micucci's lucid text flows logically from one topic to another," and in *Horn Book,* Carolyn K. Jenks asserted that the "watercolor-and-pencil illustrations are simple and clear, providing superb information."

After the success of *The Life and Times of the Apple,* Micucci created several other highly regarded nonfiction titles for children built on the same model, beginning with *The Life and Times of the Honeybee.* "This book reminds us that original artwork can be more precise and just as spectacular as photographs in children's nonfiction," remarked Stephanie Zvirin in *Booklist.* In order to clarify the complexity of bee behavior, Micucci manipulates perspective and scale in his watercolor illustrations of the bees' role in pollination, production of honey, division of labor, and reproduction, according to reviewers. Though the book is packed with information, the text is liberally and judiciously sprinkled with illustrations, and a friendly cartoon bee swoops through the pages as well, adding a lightly humorous touch. "Information about honeybees has never been more interesting," wrote Diane Nunn in *School Library Journal.*

Micucci then brought his winning style to another homely topic in *The Life and Times of the Peanut.* His text tells of the history, cultivation, and uses to which peanuts have been put by people all over the world, and his illustrations, offset by a dancing cartoon peanut, make the facts come alive, claimed reviewers.

"What sets this book apart is Micucci's amusing and creative techniques for bringing statistics to life," asserted Susan Dove Lempke in *Booklist*, singling out the author's visual rendering of the fact that the annual production of peanuts worldwide averages out to nine pounds per person. A reviewer for *Kirkus Reviews* similarly praised Micucci's artful combination of text and illustration, "making this a captivating compendium, as wholesome and substantial as a peanut butter sandwich."

Micucci's next nonfiction title for children, *The Life and Times of the Ant*, has been equally well received, with *Booklist*'s Kay Weisman remarking that the book "offers succinct text and an impressive amount of information presented in an attractive, picture-book format." Combining information on life cycle, behavior, varieties, and role in the ecosystem with illustrations that are alternately realistic and humorous, Micucci brings his characteristic style and approach to this perennially favorite topic in children's nonfiction. Here, a realistic rendering of worker ants, for example, is accompanied by a cartoon rendering of an ant in armor, in order to clarify the idea being presented. As with his earlier nonfiction titles on small, child-friendly topics, *The Life and Times of the Ant* was favorably compared to other works on this popular topic. The book "makes a readable, engaging alternative to the many photographic treatments of the subject," concluded a contributor to *Kirkus Reviews*.

Micucci once remarked, "Writing and illustrating children's books gives me an opportunity to communicate with the future of the world."

BIOGRAPHICAL AND CRITICAL SOURCES:

PERIODICALS

Booklist, February 1, 1995, Stephanie Zvirin, review of *The Life and Times of the Honeybee*, p. 1003; May 1, 1997, Susan Dove Lempke, review of *The Life and Times of the Peanut*, p. 1496; April 15, 2003, Kay Weisman, review of *The Life and Times of the Ant*, p. 1473.

Horn Book, May-June, 1992, Carolyn K. Jenks, review of *The Life and Times of the Apple*, pp. 356-357; fall, 1997, Shela M. Geraty, review of *The Life and Times of the Peanut*, p. 361; May-June, 2003, Betty Carter, review of *The Life and Times of the Ant*, p. 370.

Kirkus Reviews, January 15, 1992, review of *The Life and Times of the Apple*, p. 118; February 15, 1997, review of *The Life and Times of the Peanut*, p. 303; January 1, 2003, review of *The Life and Times of the Ant*, p. 64.

Publishers Weekly, March 10, 1989, review of *A Little Night Music*, p. 88; January 13, 1992, p. 57.

School Library Journal, July, 1989, Patricia Pearl, review of *A Little Night Music*, p. 73; March, 1992, p. 232; April, 1995, Diane Nunn, review of *The Life and Times of the Honeybee*, p. 126; May, 1997, Blair Christolon, review of *The Life and Times of the Peanut*, p. 122; May, 2003, Margaret Bush, review of *The Life and Times of the Ant*, p. 140.*

* * *

MORRISON, Chloe Anthony Wofford
See MORRISON, Toni

* * *

MORRISON, Toni 1931-
(Chloe Anthony Wofford Morrison)

PERSONAL: Born Chloe Anthony Wofford, February 18, 1931, in Lorain, OH; daughter of George and Ramah (Willis) Wofford; married Harold Morrison, 1958 (divorced, 1964); children: Harold Ford, Slade Kevin. *Education:* Howard University, B.A., 1953; Cornell University, M.A., 1955.

ADDRESSES: Office—Department of Creative Writing, Princeton University, 185 Nassau St., Princeton, NJ 08544-0001. *Agent*—International Creative Management, 40 West 57th St., New York, NY 10019.

CAREER: Texas Southern University, Houston, TX, instructor in English, 1955-57; Howard University, Washington, DC, instructor in English, 1957-64; Random House, New York, NY, senior editor, 1965-85; State University of New York—Purchase, associate professor of English, 1971-72; State University of New York—Albany, Schweitzer Professor of the Humanities, 1984-89; Princeton University, Princeton, NJ, Robert F. Goheen Professor of the Humanities, 1989—. Visiting lecturer, Yale University, 1976-77,

Toni Morrison

and Bard College, 1986-88; Clark Lecturer at Trinity College, Cambridge, and Massey Lecturer at Harvard University, both 1990.

MEMBER: American Academy and Institute of Arts and Letters, National Council on the Arts, Authors Guild (council), Authors League of America.

AWARDS, HONORS: National Book Award nomination and Ohioana Book Award, both 1975, both for *Sula;* National Book Critics Circle Award and American Academy and Institute of Arts and Letters Award, both 1977, both for *Song of Solomon;* New York State Governor's Art Award, 1986; National Book Award nomination and National Book Critics Circle Award nomination, both 1987, Pulitzer Prize for Fiction, Robert F. Kennedy Award, and American Book Award, Before Columbus Foundation, 1988, all for *Beloved;* Elizabeth Cady Stanton Award, National Organization of Women; Nobel Prize in Literature, 1993; Pearl Buck Award, Rhegium Julii Prize, Condorcet Medal (Paris, France), and Commander of the Order of Arts and Letters (Paris, France), all 1994; Medal for Distinguished Contribution to American Letters, National Book Foundation, 1996; National Humanities Medal, 2001; subject of Biennial Toni Morrison Society conference in Lorain, Ohio.

WRITINGS:

FICTION

The Bluest Eye, Holt (New York, NY), 1969, reprinted, Plume (New York, NY), 1994.
Sula, Knopf (New York, NY), 1973.
Song of Solomon, Knopf (New York, NY), 1977.
Tar Baby, Knopf (New York, NY), 1981.
Dreaming Emmett (play), first produced in Albany, NY, January 4, 1986.
Beloved, Knopf (New York, NY), 1987.
Jazz, Knopf (New York, NY), 1992.
Playing in the Dark: Whiteness and the Literary Imagination, Harvard University Press (Cambridge, MA), 1992.
The Dancing Mind (text of Nobel Prize acceptance speech), Knopf (New York, NY), 1996.
Paradise, Knopf (New York, NY), 1998.
Love, Knopf (New York, NY), 2003.

FOR CHILDREN; WITH SON SLADE MORRISON

The Big Box, illustrated by Giselle Potter, Hyperion/Jump at the Sun (New York, NY), 1999.
The Book of Mean People, illustrated by Pascal Lemaître, Hyperion (New York, NY), 2002.
The Book of Mean People Journal, illustrated by Pascal Lemaître, Hyperion (New York, NY), 2002.
The Lion or the Mouse? ("Who's Got Game?" series), illustrated by Pascal Lemaître, Scribner (Mew York, NY), 2003.
The Ant or the Grasshopper? ("Who's Got Game?" series), illustrated by Pascal Lemaître, Scribner (New York, NY), 2003.
The Poppy or the Snake? ("Who's Got Game?" series), illustrated by Pascal Lemaître, Scribner (New York, NY), 2004.

MUSIC

(Author of lyrics) André Previn, *Four Songs for Soprano, Cello, and Piano,* Chester Music (London, England), 1995.

(Author of lyrics) Richard Danielpour, *Spirits in the Well: For Voice and Piano,* Associated Music Publishers (New York, NY), 1998.

Also author of lyrics for André Previn's *Honey and Rue,* commissioned by Carnegie Hall, 1992, and Richard Danielpour's *Sweet Talk: Four Songs,* 1996.

EDITOR

The Black Book (anthology), Random House (New York, NY), 1974.
Race-ing Justice, En-Gendering Power: Essays on Anita Hill, Clarence Thomas, and the Construction of Social Reality, Pantheon (New York, NY), 1992.
To Die for the People: The Writings of Huey P. Newton, Writers and Readers (New York, NY), 1995.
Toni Cade Bambara, *Deep Sightings and Rescue Missions: Fiction, Essays, and Conversations,* Pantheon (New York, NY), 1996.
(With Claudia Brodsky Lacour) *Birth of a Nation'Hood: Gaze, Script, and Spectacle in the O. J. Simpson Case,* Pantheon (New York, NY), 1997.

Contributor of essays and reviews to numerous periodicals, including *New York Times Magazine.* Contributor to *Arguing Immigration: The Debate over the Changing Face of America,* edited by Nicolaus Mills, Simon & Schuster (New York, NY), 1994.

ADAPTATIONS: *Beloved* was adapted to a 1998 film of the same title, starring Oprah Winfrey, Danny Glover, Thandie Newton, and Kimberly Elise, and was directed by Jonathan Demme. Morrison books, including *Jazz, Beloved, Tar Baby, Paradise, Song of Solomon* and *The Bluest Eye,* have been adapted to audio cassette.

WORK IN PROGRESS: Lyrics to *Margaret Garner,* an opera composed by Richard Danielpour, expected to premiere at the Michigan Opera Theatre, May, 2005; three more books in the "Who's Got Game" series.

SIDELIGHTS: Nobel laureate Toni Morrison has a central role in the American literary canon, according to many critics, award committees, and readers. Her award-winning novels chronicle small-town African-American life, employing "an artistic vision that encompasses both a private and a national heritage," to quote *Time* magazine contributor Angela Wigan. Through works such as *The Bluest Eye, Song of Solomon,* and *Beloved,* Morrison proves herself to be a gifted storyteller of stories in which troubled characters seek to find themselves and their cultural riches in a society that warps or impedes such essential growth. According to Charles Larson, writing in the *Chicago Tribune Book World,* each of Morrison's novels "is as original as anything that has appeared in our literature in the last twenty years. The contemporaneity that unites them—the troubling persistence of racism in America—is infused with an urgency that only a black writer can have about our society."

Morrison has also proved herself to be an able creator of children's books, working in collaboration with her son Slade Morrison. Together the two writers have produced the rhyming parable *The Big Box* and *The Book of Mean People,* a child's eye view of the world—as seen by a rabbit. They have also collaborated on a series of retellings of the tales from Aesop, titled "Who's Got Game?"

Morrison's artistry has attracted critical acclaim as well as commercial success; *Dictionary of Literary Biography* contributor Susan L. Blake called the author "an anomaly in two respects" because "she is a black writer who has achieved national prominence and popularity, and she is a popular writer who is taken seriously." Indeed, Morrison has won several of modern literature's most prestigious citations, including the 1977 National Book Critics Circle Award for *Song of Solomon,* the 1988 Pulitzer Prize for *Beloved,* and the 1993 Nobel Prize for Literature, the first African American to be named a laureate. *Atlantic* correspondent Wilfrid Sheed noted: "Most black writers are privy, like the rest of us, to bits and pieces of the secret, the dark side of their group experience, but Toni Morrison uniquely seems to have all the keys on her chain, like a house detective. . . . She [uses] the run of the whole place, from ghetto to small town to ramshackle farmhouse, to bring back a panorama of black myth and reality that [dazzles] the senses."

According to Jean Strouse, writing in *Newsweek,* Morrison "comes from a long line of people who did what they had to do to survive. It is their stories she tells in her novels—tales of the suffering and richness, the eloquence and tragedies of the black American experience." Morrison was born Chloe Anthony Wofford in Lorain, Ohio, a small industrial town near the shores of Lake Erie. *New York Review of Books* correspondent Darryl Pinckney described her particular community as "close enough to the Ohio River for the people who lived [there] to feel the torpor of the South, the nostalgia for its folkways, to sense the old Underground Railroad underfoot like a hidden stream."

Two important aspects of Chloe Wofford's childhood—community spirit and the supernatural—inform Toni Morrison's mature writing. In a *Publishers Weekly* interview, Morrison suggested ways in which her community influenced her. "There is this town which is both a support system and a hammer at the same time," she noted. "Approval was not the acquisition of things; approval was given for the maturity and the dignity with which one handled oneself. Most black people in particular were, and still are, very fastidious about manners, very careful about behavior and the rules that operate within the community. The sense of organized activity, what I thought at that time was burdensome, turns out now to have within it a gift—which is, I never had to be taught how to hold a job, how to make it work, how to handle my time."

On several levels the pariah—a unique and sometimes eccentric individual—figures in Morrison's fictional reconstruction of black community life. "There is always an elder there," she noted of her work in *Black Women Writers (1950-1980): A Critical Evaluation.* "And these ancestors are not just parents, they are sort of timeless people whose relationships to the characters are benevolent, instructive, and protective, and they provide a certain kind of wisdom." Sometimes this figure imparts his or her wisdom from beyond the grave; from an early age Morrison absorbed the folklore and beliefs of a culture for which the supernatural holds power and portent. Strouse stated that Morrison's world, both within and outside her fiction, is "filled with signs, visitations, ways of knowing that [reach] beyond the five senses."

As a student, Morrison earned money by cleaning houses; "the normal teenage jobs were not available," she recalled in a *New York Times Magazine* profile by Claudia Dreifus. "Housework always was." Some of her clients were nice; some were "terrible," Morrison added. The work gave her a perspective on black-white relations that touched Morrison's later writing.

As she told Dreifus, "In [*The Bluest Eye*] Pauline lived in this dump and hated everything in it. And then she worked for the Fishers, who had this beautiful house, and she loved it. She got a lot of respect as their maid that she didn't get anywhere else." While never explicitly autobiographical, Morrison's fictions draw upon her youthful experiences in Ohio. In an essay for *Black Women Writers at Work* she claimed: "I am from the Midwest so I have a special affection for it. My beginnings are always there. . . . No matter what I write, I begin there. . . . It's the matrix for me. . . . Ohio also offers an escape from stereotyped black settings. It is neither plantation nor ghetto."

After graduating with honors from high school, Morrison attended Howard University, where she earned a degree in English. During this time, she also decided to change her first name to Toni. Morrison then earned a master's degree in English literature from Cornell. During this period, Morrison met and married her husband, an architect with whom she had two sons. In 1955, Morrison became an English instructor at Texas Southern University. Two years later, she returned to Howard University, teaching English until 1964. It was during her stint at Howard that Morrison first began to write. When her marriage ended in 1964, Morrison moved to New York, where she supported herself and her sons by working as a book editor at Random House. Morrison held this position until 1985, during which time she influenced several prominent black writers.

Morrison's own writing career took off in the late 1960s, and several themes and influences were in early evidence. "It seems somehow both constricting and inadequate to describe Toni Morrison as the country's preeminent black novelist, since in both gifts and accomplishments she transcends categorization," wrote Jonathan Yardley in the *Washington Post Book World,* "yet the characterization is inescapable not merely because it is true but because the very nature of Morrison's work dictates it. Not merely has black American life been the central preoccupation of her . . . novels . . . but as she has matured she has concentrated on distilling all of black experience into her books; quite purposefully, it seems, she is striving not for the particular but for the universal." In her work, critics claim, Morrison strives to lay bare the injustice inherent in the black condition and blacks' efforts, individually and collectively, to transcend society's unjust boundaries. Blake noted that

Morrison's novels explore "the difference between black humanity and white cultural values. This opposition produces the negative theme of the seduction and betrayal of black people by white culture . . . and the positive theme of the quest for cultural identity." *Newsweek* contributor Strouse observed: "Like all the best stories, [Morrison's] are driven by an abiding moral vision. Implicit in all her characters' grapplings with who they are is a large sense of human nature and love—and a reach for understanding of something larger than the moment."

Quest for self is a motivating and organizing device in Morrison's fiction, as is the role of family and community in nurturing or challenging the individual. In the *Times Literary Supplement,* Jennifer Uglow suggested that Morrison's novels "explore in particular the process of growing up black, female and poor. Avoiding generalities, Toni Morrison concentrates on the relation between the pressures of the community, patterns established within families, . . . and the developing sense of self." According to Dorothy H. Lee in *Black Women Writers (1950-1980),* Morrison is preoccupied "with the effect of the community on the individual's achievement and retention of an integrated, acceptable self. In treating this subject, she draws recurrently on myth and legend for story pattern and characters, returning repeatedly to the theory of *quest.* . . . The goals her characters seek to achieve are similar in their deepest implications, and yet the degree to which they attain them varies radically because each novel is cast in unique human terms." In Morrison's books, blacks must confront the notion that all understanding is accompanied by pain, just as all comprehension of national history must include the humiliations of slavery. She tempers this hard lesson by preserving "the richness of communal life against an outer world that denies its value" and by turning to "a heritage of folklore, not only to disclose patterns of living but also to close wounds," in the words of *Nation* contributor Brina Caplan.

Although Morrison herself told the *Chicago Tribune* that there is "epiphany and triumph" in every book she writes, some critics find her work nihilistic and her vision bleak. "The picture given by . . . Morrison of the plight of the decent, aspiring individual in the black family and community is more painful than the gloomiest impressions encouraged by either stereotype or sociology," observed Diane Johnson in the *New York Review of Books.* Johnson continued, "Undoubtedly white society is the ultimate oppressor, and not just of blacks, but, as Morrison [shows], . . . the black person must first deal with the oppressor in the next room, or in the same bed, or no farther away than across the street."

Morrison is a pioneer in the depiction of the hurt inflicted by blacks on blacks; for instance, her characters rarely achieve harmonious relationships but are instead divided by futurelessness and the anguish of stifled existence. Uglow wrote: "We have become attuned to novels . . . which locate oppression in the conflicts of blacks (usually men) trying to make it in a white world. By concentrating on the sense of violation experienced within black neighborhoods, even within families, Toni Morrison deprives us of stock responses and creates a more demanding and uncomfortable literature." *Village Voice* correspondent Vivian Gornick contended that the world Morrison creates "is thick with an atmosphere through which her characters move slowly, in pain, ignorance, and hunger. And to a very large degree Morrison has the compelling ability to make one believe that all of us (Morrison, the characters, the reader) are penetrating that dark and hurtful terrain—the feel of a human life—simultaneously." Uglow concluded that even the laughter of Morrison's characters "disguises pain, deprivation and violation. It is laughter at a series of bad, cruel jokes. . . . Nothing is what it seems; no appearance, no relationship can be trusted to endure."

Other critics detect a deeper undercurrent to Morrison's work that contains just the sort of epiphany for which she strives. "From book to book, Morrison's larger project grows clear," remarked Ann Snitow in the *Voice Literary Supplement.* "First, she insists that every character bear the weight of responsibility for his or her own life. After she's measured out each one's private pain, she adds on to that the shared burden of what the whites did. Then, at last, she tries to find the place where her stories can lighten her readers' load, lift them up from their own and others' guilt, carry them to glory. . . . Her characters suffer—from their own limitations and the world's—but their inner life miraculously expands beyond the narrow law of cause and effect." *Harvard Advocate* essayist Faith Davis wrote that despite the mundane boundaries of Morrison's characters' lives, the author "illuminates the complexity of their attitudes toward life. Having reached a quiet and extensive understanding of their situation, they can endure life's calamities. . . . Morrison never allows us to become indifferent to these people. . . . Her citizens . . . jump up from the pages vital and strong because she has made us care about the pain in their lives." In *Ms.,* Margo Jefferson concluded that Morrison's books "are filled with loss—lost friendship, lost love, lost customs, lost possibilities. And yet there is so much life in the smallest acts and gestures . . . that they are as much celebrations as elegies."

Morrison sees language as an expression of black experience, and her novels are characterized by vivid narration and dialogue. *Village Voice* essayist Susan Lydon observed that the author "works her magic charm above all with a love of language. Her soaring . . . style carries you like a river, sweeping doubt and disbelief away, and it is only gradually that one realizes her deadly serious intent." In the *Spectator,* Caroline Moorehead likewise noted that Morrison "writes energetically and richly, using words in a way very much her own. The effect is one of exoticism, an exciting curiousness in the language, a balanced sense of the possible that stops, always, short of the absurd."

Although Morrison does not like to be called a poetic writer, critics often comment on the lyrical quality of her prose. "Morrison's style has always moved fluidly between tough-minded realism and lyric descriptiveness," said *Newsweek* contributor Margo Jefferson. "Vivid dialogue, capturing the drama and extravagance of black speech, gives way to an impressionistic evocation of physical pain or an ironic, essay-like analysis of the varieties of religious hypocrisy." Uglow wrote: "The word 'elegant' is often applied to Toni Morrison's writing; it employs sophisticated narrative devices, shifting perspectives and resonant images and displays an obvious delight in the potential of language." *Nation* contributor Earl Frederick concluded that Morrison, "with an ear as sharp as glass . . . has listened to the music of black talk and deftly uses it as the palette knife to create black lives and to provide some of the best fictional dialogue around today."

In the mid-1960s, Morrison completed her first novel, *The Bluest Eye.* Although she had trouble getting the book into print—the manuscript was rejected several times—it was finally published in 1969. At age thirty-eight, Morrison was a published author, and her debut, set in Morrison's hometown of Lorain, Ohio, portrays "in poignant terms the tragic condition of blacks in a racist America," to quote Chikwenye Okonjo Ogunyemi in *Critique.* In *The Bluest Eye,* Morrison depicts the onset of black self-hatred as occasioned by white-American ideals such as "Dick and Jane" primers and Shirley Temple movies. The principal character, Pecola Breedlove, is literally maddened by the disparity between her existence and the pictures of beauty and gentility disseminated by the dominant white culture. As Phyllis R. Klotman noted in the *Black American Literature Forum,* Morrison "uses the contrast between Shirley Temple and Pecola . . . to underscore the irony of black experience. Whether one learns acceptability from the formal educational experience or from cultural symbols, the effect is the same: self-hatred." Darwin T. Turner elaborated on the novel's intentions in *Black Women Writers (1950-1980).* Morrison's fictional milieu, wrote Turner, is "a world of grotesques—individuals whose psyches have been deformed by their efforts to assume false identities, their failures to achieve meaningful identities, or simply their inability to retain and communicate love."

Blake characterized *The Bluest Eye* as a novel of initiation, exploring that common theme in American literature from a minority viewpoint. Ogunyemi contended that, in essence, Morrison presents "old problems in a fresh language and with a fresh perspective. A central force of the work derives from her power to draw vignettes and her ability to portray emotions, seeing the world through the eyes of adolescent girls." Klotman, who called the book "a novel of growing up, of growing up young and black and female in America," concluded her review with the comment that the "rite of passage, initiating the young into womanhood at first tenuous and uncertain, is sensitively depicted. . . . *The Bluest Eye* is an extraordinarily passionate yet gentle work, the language lyrical yet precise—it is a novel for all seasons."

The 1994 reissue of *The Bluest Eye* prompted a new set of appraisals. In an *African American Review* piece, Allen Alexander found that religious references—from both Western and African sources—"abound" in the novel's pages. "And of the many fascinating religious references," Alexander continued, "the most complex . . . are her representations of and allusions to God. In Morrison's fictional world, God's characteristics are not limited to those represented by the traditional Western notion of the Trinity: Father, Son and Holy Ghost." Instead, Morrison presents God as having "a fourth face, one that is an explanation for all those things—the existence of evil, the suffering of the innocent and just—that seem so inexplicable in the face of a religious tradition that preaches the omnipotence of a benevolent God." Cat Moses used the forum of *African American Review* to contribute an essay outlining the blues aesthetic in *The Bluest Eye*. The narrative's structure, Moses wrote, "follows a pattern common to traditional blues lyrics: a movement from an initial emphasis on loss to a concluding suggestion of resolution of grief through motion." In depicting the transition from loss to "movin' on," said the essayist, *The Bluest Eye* "contains an abundance of cultural wisdom."

In 1973's *Sula,* Morrison once again presents a pair of black women who must come to terms with their lives. Set in a Midwestern black community called The Bottom, the story follows two friends, Sula and Nel, from childhood to old age and death. Snitow claimed that through *Sula,* Morrison discovered "a way to offer her people an insight and sense of recovered self so dignified and glowing that no worldly pain could dull the final light." Indeed, *Sula* is a tale of rebel and conformist in which the conformity is dictated by the solid inhabitants of The Bottom and even the rebellion gains strength from the community's disapproval. *New York Times Book Review* contributor Sara Blackburn contended, however, that the book is "too vital and rich" to be consigned to the category of allegory. Morrison's "extravagantly beautiful, doomed characters are locked in a world where hope for the future is a foreign commodity, yet they are enormously, achingly alive," wrote Blackburn. "And this book about them—and about how their beauty is drained back and frozen—is a howl of love and rage, playful and funny as well as hard and bitter." In the words of *American Literature* essayist Jane S. Bakerman, Morrison "uses the maturation story of Sula and Nel as the core of a host of other stories, but it is the chief unification device for the novel and achieves its own unity, again, through the clever manipulation of the themes of sex, race, and love. Morrison has undertaken a . . . difficult task in *Sula.* Unquestionably, she has succeeded."

Other critics have echoed Bakerman's sentiments about *Sula*. Yardley stated: "What gives this terse, imaginative novel its genuine distinction is the quality of Toni Morrison's prose. *Sula* is admirable enough as a study of its title character, . . . but its real strength lies in Morrison's writing, which at times has the resonance of poetry and is precise, vivid and controlled throughout." Turner also claimed that in *Sula* "Morrison evokes her verbal magic occasionally by lyric descriptions that carry the reader deep into the soul of the character. . . . Equally effective, however, is her art of narrating action in a lean prose that uses adjectives cautiously while creating memorable vivid images." In her review, Davis concluded that a "beautiful and haunting atmosphere emerges out of the wreck of these folks' lives, a quality that is absolutely convincing and absolutely precise." *Sula* was nominated for a National Book Award in 1974.

From the insular lives she depicted in her first two novels, Morrison moved in *Song of Solomon* to a national and historical perspective on black American life. "Here the depths of the younger work are still evident," said Reynolds Price in the *New York Times Book Review,* "but now they thrust outward, into wider fields, for longer intervals, encompassing many more lives. The result is a long prose tale that surveys nearly a century of American history as it impinges upon a single family." With an intermixture of the fantastic and the realistic, *Song of Solomon* relates the journey of a character named Milkman Dead into an understanding of his family heritage and hence, himself. Lee wrote: "Figuratively, [Milkman] travels from innocence to awareness, i.e., from ignorance of origins, heritage, identity, and communal responsibility to knowledge and acceptance. He moves from selfish and materialistic dilettantism to an understanding of brotherhood. With his release of personal ego, he is able to find a place in the whole. There is, then, a universal—indeed mythic—pattern here. He journeys from spiritual death to rebirth, a direction symbolized by his discovery of the secret power of flight. Mythically, liberation and transcendence follow the discovery of self." Blake suggested that the connection Milkman discovers with his family's past helps him to connect meaningfully with his contemporaries; *Song of Solomon,* Blake noted, "dramatizes dialectical approaches to the challenges of black life." According to Anne Z. Mickelson in *Reaching Out: Sensitivity and Order in Recent American Fiction by Women,* history itself "becomes a choral symphony to Milkman, in which each individual voice has a chance to speak and contribute to his growing sense of well-being."

Mickelson also observed that *Song of Solomon* represents for blacks "a break out of the confining life into the realm of possibility." Charles Larson commented on this theme in a *Washington Post Book World* review. The novel's subject matter, Larson explained, is "the origins of black consciousness in America, and the individual's relationship to that heritage." However, Larson added, "skilled writer that she is, Morrison has transcended this theme so that the reader rarely feels that this is simply another novel about ethnic identity. So marvelously orchestrated is Morrison's narrative that it not only excels on all of its respective levels, not only works for all of its interlocking components, but also—in the end—says something about life (and death) for all of us. Milkman's epic journey . . . is a profound examination of the individual's understanding of, and, perhaps, even transcendence of the inevitable fate of his life." Gornick concluded: "There are so many individual moments of power and beauty in *Song of Solomon* that, ultimately, one closes the book warmed through by the richness of its sympathy, and by its breathtaking feel for the nature of sexual sorrow."

Song of Solomon, which won the National Book Critics Circle Award in 1977, was also the first novel by a black writer to become a Book-of-the-Month Club selection since Richard Wright's *Native Son* was published in 1940. *World Literature Today* reviewer Richard K. Barksdale called the work "a book that will not only withstand the test of time but endure a second and third reading by those conscientious readers who love a well-wrought piece of fiction." Describing the novel as "a stunningly beautiful book" in her *Washington Post Book World* piece, Anne Tyler added: "I would call the book poetry, but that would seem to be denying its considerable power as a story. Whatever name you give it, it's full of magnificent people, each of them complex and multilayered, even the narrowest of them narrow in extravagant ways." Price deemed *Song of Solomon* "a long story, . . . and better than good. Toni Morrison has earned attention and praise. Few Americans know, and can say, more than she has in this wise and spacious novel."

Morrison clearly attained the respect of the literary community, but even in the face of three well-received novels, she did not call herself a writer. "I think, at bottom, I simply was not prepared to do the adult thing, which in those days would be associated with the male thing, which was to say, 'I'm a writer,'" she told Dreifus in 1994. "I said, 'I am a mother who writes,' or 'I am an editor who writes.' The word 'writer' was hard for me to say because that's what you put on your income-tax form. I *do* now say, 'I'm a writer.' But it's the difference between identifying one's work and being the person who does the work. I've always been the latter."

Still, critics and readers had no doubt that Morrison was a writer. Her 1981 book *Tar Baby* remained on bestseller lists for four months. A novel of ideas, the work dramatizes the fact that complexion is a far more subtle issue than the simple polarization of black and white. Set on a lush Caribbean Island, *Tar Baby* explores the passionate love affair of Jadine, a Sorbonne-educated black model, and Son, a handsome knockabout with a strong aversion to white culture. According to Caplan, Morrison's concerns "are race, class, culture and the effects of late capitalism—heavy freight for any narrative. . . . She is attempting to stabilize complex visions of society—that is, to examine competitive ideas. . . . Because the primary function of Morrison's characters is to voice representative opinions, they arrive on stage vocal and highly conscious, their histories symbolically indicated or merely sketched. Her brief sketches, however, are clearly the work of an artist who can, when she chooses, model the mind in depth and detail." In a *Dictionary of Literary Biography Yearbook* essay, Elizabeth B. House outlined *Tar Baby*'s major themes: "the difficulty of settling conflicting claims between one's past and present and the destruction which abuse of power can bring. As Morrison examines these problems in *Tar Baby*, she suggests no easy way to understand what one's link to a heritage should be, nor does she offer infallible methods for dealing with power. Rather, with an astonishing insight and grace, she demonstrates the pervasiveness of such dilemmas and the degree to which they affect human beings, both black and white."

Tar Baby uncovers racial and sexual conflicts without offering solutions, but most critics found that Morrison indicts all of her characters—black and white—for their thoughtless devaluations of others. *New York Times Book Review* correspondent John Irving claimed: "What's so powerful, and subtle, about Miss Morrison's presentation of the tension between blacks and whites is that she conveys it almost entirely through the suspicions and prejudices of her black characters. . . . Miss Morrison uncovers all the stereotypical racial fears felt by whites and blacks alike. Like any ambitious writer, she's unafraid to employ these stereotypes—she embraces the representative qualities of her characters without embarrassment, then proceeds to make them individuals too." *New*

Yorker essayist Susan Lardner praised Morrison for her "power to be absolutely persuasive against her own preferences, suspicions, and convictions, implied or plainly expressed," and Strouse likewise contended that the author "has produced that rare commodity, a truly public novel about the condition of society, examining the relations between blacks and whites, men and women, civilization and nature. . . . It wraps its messages in a highly potent love story." Irving suggested that Morrison's greatest accomplishment "is that she has raised her novel above the social realism that too many black novels and women's novels are trapped in. She has succeeded in writing about race and women symbolically."

Reviewers praised *Tar Baby* for its provocative themes and for its evocative narration. *Los Angeles Times* contributor Elaine Kendall called the book "an intricate and sophisticated novel, moving from a realistic and orderly beginning to a mystical and ambiguous end. Morrison has taken classically simple story elements and realigned them so artfully that we perceive the old pattern in a startlingly different way. Although this territory has been explored by dozens of novelists, Morrison depicts it with such vitality that it seems newly discovered." In the *Washington Post Book World*, Webster Schott claimed: "There is so much that is good, sometimes dazzling, about *Tar Baby*—poetic language, . . . arresting images, fierce intelligence—that . . . one becomes entranced by Toni Morrison's story. The settings are so vivid the characters must be alive. The emotions they feel are so intense they must be real people." Maureen Howard stated in *New Republic* that the work "is as carefully patterned as a well-written poem. . . . *Tar Baby* is a good American novel in which we can discern a new lightness and brilliance in Toni Morrison's enchantment with language and in her curiously polyphonic stories that echo life." Schott concluded: "One of fiction's pleasures is to have your mind scratched and your intellectual habits challenged. While *Tar Baby* has shortcomings, lack of provocation isn't one of them. Morrison owns a powerful intelligence. It's run by courage. She calls to account conventional wisdom and accepted attitude at nearly every turn."

In addition to her own writing, Morrison during this period helped to publish the work of other noted black Americans, including Toni Cade Bambara, Gayle Jones, Angela Davis, and Muhammad Ali. Discussing her aims as an editor in a quotation printed in the *Dictionary of Literary Biography,* Morrison said, "I look very hard for black fiction because I want to participate in developing a canon of black work. We've had the first rush of black entertainment, where blacks were writing for whites, and whites were encouraging this kind of self-flagellation. Now we can get down to the craft of writing, where black people are talking to black people." One of Morrison's important projects for Random House was *The Black Book,* an anthology of items that illustrate the history of black Americans. *Ms.* magazine correspondent Dorothy Eugenia Robinson described the work: "*The Black Book* is the pain and pride of rediscovering the collective black experience. It is finding the essence of ourselves and holding on. *The Black Book* is a kind of scrapbook of patiently assembled samplings of black history and culture. What has evolved is a pictorial folk journey of black people, places, events, handcrafts, inventions, songs, and folklore. . . . *The Black Book* informs, disturbs, maybe even shocks. It unsettles complacency and demands confrontation with raw reality. It is by no means an easy book to experience, but it's a necessary one."

While preparing *The Black Book* for publication, Morrison uncovered the true and shocking story of a runaway slave who, at the point of recapture, murdered her infant child so it would not be doomed to a lifetime of servitude. For Morrison, the story encapsulated the fierce psychic cruelty of an institutionalized system that sought to destroy the basic emotional bonds between men and women, and worse, between parent and child. "I certainly thought I knew as much about slavery as anybody," Morrison told an interview for the *Los Angeles Times.* "But it was the interior life I needed to find out about." It is this "interior life" in the throes of slavery that constitutes the theme of Morrison's novel *Beloved.* Set in Reconstruction-era Cincinnati, the book centers on characters who struggle fruitlessly to keep their painful recollections of the past at bay. They are haunted, both physically and spiritually, by the legacies slavery has bequeathed to them. According to Snitow, *Beloved* "staggers under the terror of its material—as so much holocaust writing does and must."

While the book was not unanimously praised—*New Republic* writer Stanley Crouch cited the author for "almost always [losing] control" and of not resisting "the temptation of the trite or the sentimental"—many critics considered *Beloved* to be Morrison's masterpiece. In *People,* V. R. Peterson described the novel as "a brutally powerful, mesmerizing story about the inescapable, excruciating legacy of slavery. Behind each new event and each new character lies another event and another story until finally the reader meets a community of proud, daring people, inextricably bound by culture and experience." Through the lives of ex-slaves Sethe and her would-be lover Paul D, readers "experience American slavery as it was lived by those who were its objects of exchange, both at its best—which wasn't very good—and at its worst, which was as bad as can be imagined," wrote Margaret Atwood in the *New York Times Book Review.* "Above all, it is seen as one of the most viciously antifamily institutions human beings have ever devised. The slaves are motherless, fatherless, deprived of their mates, their children, their kin. It is a world in which people suddenly vanish and are never seen again, not through accident or covert operation or terrorism, but as a matter of everyday legal policy." *New York Times* columnist Michiko Kakutani contended that *Beloved* "possesses the heightened power and resonance of myth—its characters, like those in opera or Greek drama, seem larger than life and their actions, too, tend to strike us as enactments of ancient rituals and passions. To describe *Beloved* only in these terms, however, is to diminish its immediacy, for the novel also remains precisely grounded in American reality—the reality of Black history as experienced in the wake of the Civil War."

Beloved may be an American novel, but its images and influences come from the British Romantic tradition, theorized Martin Bidney in *Papers on Language and Literature.* "Simply to list a few of [the book's] major episodes—ice skating, boat stealing, gigantic shadow, carnival 'freak' show, water-voices sounding the depths—is almost to create a rapidly scrolled plot synopsis of Wordsworth's *Prelude,*" Bidney wrote. "When Baby Suggs declares that the only grace we will receive is the grace we can 'imagine,' or when Sethe tells how Paul D's visionary capacity makes 'windows' suddenly have 'view,' we hear the voice of William Blake." The critic also saw traces of Keats in the scenes of Paul D's musings "on the superiority of imagined love to mere physical sex." But the achievement of the novel ultimately belongs to Morrison, Bidney added: "These few examples are by no means a complete listing of all the Romantic allusive motifs that combined to help make *Beloved* the visionary masterwork it is."

Acclaim for *Beloved* came from both sides of the Atlantic. In his *Chicago Tribune* piece, Larson claimed that the work "is the context out of which all of Morrison's earlier novels were written. In her darkest and most probing novel, Toni Morrison has demonstrated once again the stunning powers that place her in the first ranks of our living novelists." *Los Angeles Times Book Review* contributor John Leonard likewise expressed the opinion that the novel "belongs on the highest shelf of American literature, even if half a dozen canonized white boys have to be elbowed off. . . . Without *Beloved* our imagination of the nation's self has a hole in it big enough to die from." Atwood stated: "Ms. Morrison's versatility and technical and emotional range appear to know no bounds. If there were any doubts about her stature as a preeminent American novelist, of her own or any other generation, *Beloved* will put them to rest." London *Times* reviewer Nicholas Shakespeare concluded that *Beloved* "is a novel propelled by the cadences of . . . songs—the first singing of a people hardened by their suffering, people who have been hanged and whipped and mortgaged at the hands of white people—the men without skin. From Toni Morrison's pen it is a sound that breaks the back of words, making *Beloved* a great novel."

But for all its acclaim, *Beloved* became the object of controversy when the novel failed to win either the 1987 National Book Award or the National Book Critics Circle Award. In response, forty-eight prominent African-American authors—including Maya Angelou, Alice Walker, and John Wideman—signed a letter to the editor that appeared in the January 24, 1988, edition of the *New York Times.* The letter expressed the signers' dismay at the "oversight and harmful whimsy" that resulted in the lack of recognition for *Beloved.* The "legitimate need for our own critical voice in relation to our own literature can no longer be denied," declared Morrison's peers. The authors concluded their letter with a tribute to Morrison: "For all of America, for all of American letters, you have advanced the moral and artistic standards by which we must measure the daring and the love of our national imagination and our collective intelligence as a people." The letter sparked fierce debate within the New York literary community, "with some critics accusing the authors of the letter of racist manipulation," according to an entry in *Newsmakers 1988. Beloved* ended up winning the Pulitzer Prize for 1988.

Morrison's subsequent novel, *Jazz,* is "a fictive re-creation of two parallel narratives set during major historical events in African-American history—

Reconstruction and the Jazz Age," noted *Dictionary of Literary Biography* writer Denise Heinze. Set primarily in New York City during the 1920s, the novel's main narrative involves a love triangle between Violet, a middle-aged woman; Joe, her husband; and Dorcas, Joe's teenage mistress. When Dorcas snubs Joe for a younger lover, Joe shoots and kills Dorcas. Violet seeks to understand the dead girl by befriending Dorcas's aunt, Alice Manfred. Simultaneously, Morrison relates the story of Joe and Violet's parents and grandparents. In telling these stories, Morrison touches on a number of themes: "male/female passion," as Heinze commented; the movement of blacks into large urban areas after Reconstruction; and, as is usually the case with her novels, the effects of racism and history on the African-American community. Morrison also makes use of an unusual storytelling device: an unnamed, intrusive, and unreliable narrator.

"The standard set by the brilliance and intensity of Morrison's previous novel *Beloved* is so high that *Jazz* does not pretend to come close to attaining it," stated *Kenyon Review* contributor Peter Erickson. Nevertheless, many reviewers responded enthusiastically to the provocative themes Morrison presents in *Jazz*. "The unrelenting, destructive influence of racism and oppression on the black family is manifested in *Jazz* by the almost-total absence of the black family," stated Heinze. Writing in the *New York Review of Books*, Michael Wood remarked that "black women in *Jazz* are arming themselves, physically and mentally, and in this they have caught a current of the times, a not always visible indignation that says enough is enough." Several reviewers felt that Morrison's use of an unreliable narrator impeded the story's effectiveness. Erickson, for instance, averred that the narrator "is not inventive enough. Because the narrator displays a lack of imagination at crucial moments, she seems to get in the way, to block rather than to enable access to deeper levels." But Heinze found that Morrison's unreliable narrator allows the author to engage the reader in a way that she has not done in her previous novels: "in *Jazz* Morrison questions her ability to answer the very issues she raises, extending the responsibility of her own novel writing to her readers." Heinze concluded: "Morrison thereby sends an invitation to her readers to become a part of that struggle to comprehend totality that will continue to spur her genius."

Morrison's "genius" was recognized a year after the publication of *Jazz* with a momentous award: the Nobel Prize for Literature. The first black and only the eighth woman to win the award, Morrison told Dreifus that "it was as if the whole category of 'female writer' and 'black writer' had been redeemed. I felt I represented a whole world of women who either were silenced or who had never received the imprimatur of the established literary world." In describing the author after its selection, the Nobel Committee noted, as quoted by Heinze: "She delves into the language itself, a language she wants to liberate from the fetters of race. And she addresses us with the luster of poetry." In 1996, Morrison received another prestigious award, the National Book Foundation Medal for Distinguished Contribution to American Letters; this was followed by the National Humanities Medal in 2001.

In *Paradise,* Morrison's first novel after winning the Nobel Prize, noted *America* contributor Hermine Pinson, "the writer appears to be reinterpreting some of her most familiar themes: the significance of the 'ancestor' in our lives, the importance of community, the concept of 'home,' and the continuing conundrum of race in the United States. The title and intended subject of the text—Paradise—accommodates all of the foregoing themes." Like *Beloved, Paradise* "centers on a catastrophic act of violence that begs to be understood," *National Catholic Reporter* contributor Judith Bromberg explained. "Morrison meticulously peels away layer upon layer of truth so that what we think we know, we don't until she finally confronts us with raw truth." The conflict, and the violence that results from it, comes out of the dedicated self-righteousness of the leading families of the all-black town of Ruby, Oklahoma. "The story begins in Oklahoma in 1976," Pinson said, "when nine men from the still all-black town of Ruby invade the local convent on a mission to keep the town safe from the outright evil and depravity that they believe is embodied in the disparate assembly of religious women who live there." "In a show of force a posse of nine descend on the crumbling mansion in the predawn of a summer morning, killing all four of the troubled, flawed women who have sought refuge there," Bromberg stated.

Many reviewers recognized Morrison's accomplishment in *Paradise*. John Kennedy of *Antioch Review* called Morrison's opening chapter "Faulknerian"; with its "rich, evocative and descriptive passages, it is a haunting introduction to the repressed individuality that stalks 'so clean and blessed a mission.'" The novel "is full of challenges and surprises," wrote *Christian Century* reviewer Reggie Young. "Though it does not quite come up to the standard of Morrison's masterwork, *Beloved,* this is one of the most important novels of the decade." "This is Morrison's first novel since her 1993 *Jazz,*" summed up Emily J. Jones in *Library Journal,* "and it is well worth the wait."

In addition to her novels, Morrison has also published in other genres. *Playing in the Dark: Whiteness and the Literary Imagination* is a collection of three lectures that Morrison gave at Harvard University in 1990. Focusing on racism as it has manifested itself in American literature, these essays of literary criticism explore the works of authors such as Willa Cather, Mark Twain, and Ernest Hemingway. In 1992, Morrison edited *Race-ing Justice, En-Gendering Power: Essays on Anita Hill, Clarence Thomas, and the Construction of Social Reality,* eighteen essays about Thomas's nomination to the U.S. Supreme Court.

Turning her attention to younger readers, Morrison collaborated with her son Slade on a 1999 picture book called *The Big Box,* based on a story Slade made up when he was nine. Morrison provided the verse for a tale of three children living in "a big brown box [with] three big locks"; the children have been sent there by their parents, who feel the high-spirited and imaginative youngsters "can't handle their freedom." These children have all done something to upset the parents: Patty is too talkative in the library; Liza Sue allows the chickens to keep their eggs; and Mickey plays when he should not. The adults do not like rebellious children and so put them away, not even bothering to listen to their repeated protest: "I know that you think / You're doing what is best for me. / But if freedom is handled just *your* way / Then it's not my freedom or free."

While the tale ends happily, the generally downbeat tone of the story made some critics wary of the children's book. A contributor for *Publishers Weekly* faulted the picture book for having "little of the childlike perspective that so masterfully informs *The Bluest Eye.*" A *Horn Book* contributor likewise complained of the "heavy-handed irony" that informs much of the book. Hazel Rochman of *Booklist* decided that *The Big Box* "will appeal most to adults who cherish images of childhood innocence in a fallen world." Ellen Fader, writing in *School Library Journal,* felt the book "will have a hard time finding its audience," as it appears to be for children, but the message "requires more sophistication." A critic for *Kirkus Reviews,* however, noted that the message of the book is "valid" and "strongly made," calling the work "a promising children's book debut." And a reviewer for *Journal of Adolescent and Adult Literacy* also had praise for the title, remarking favorably upon the "haunting message about children who don't fit the accepted definitions of . . . 'normal.'"

Teaming up again with her son Slade, Morrison published another juvenile title in 2002, *The Book of Mean People,* a "bittersweet volume [that] takes meanness in stride and advocates kindness as the antidote," observed a contributor for *Publishers Weekly.* The narrative is a catalog of the things adults do to kids that kids often interpret as being mean. Grownups shout when something is wrong, make children eat things they do not like, and even dictate the time youngsters are to be in bed. These thoughts seemingly come from a bunny featured in the illustrations by Pascal Lemaître. Overall, this second children's title enjoyed a more positive critical reception than the first. A *Kirkus Reviews* critic thought that young readers "who know just what the young narrator is talking about may take to heart the closing advice to smile in the face of frowns." *School Library Journal*'s Judy Constantinides felt that "the book could be used as a springboard to discuss anger and shouting." Evette Porter, writing in *Black Issues Book Review,* found *The Book of Mean People* "a witty yet candid look at anger from the perspective of a child." The book was published in tandem with an interactive journal so that children can record their responses to situations that make them feel angry and helpless. A reviewer for *Publishers Weekly* thought that the questions supplied as writing prompts in the journal "encourage reflection," while Porter commented that the journal could "serve as a preschool primer in anger-management therapy."

As interesting as such writing projects are, however, it is Morrison's adult fiction that has secured her place among the literary elite. Morrison is an author who labors contentedly under the labels bestowed by pigeonholing critics. She has no objection to being called a black woman writer, because, as she told an interviewer for the *New York Times,* "I really think the range of emotions and perceptions I have had access to as a black person and a female person are greater than those of people who are neither. . . . My world did not shrink because I was a black female writer. It just got bigger." Nor does she strive for that much-vaunted universality that purports to be a hallmark of fine fiction. "I never asked Tolstoy to write for me, a little colored girl in Lorain, Ohio," she told an interviewer for the *New Republic.* "I never asked [James] Joyce not to mention Catholicism or the world of Dublin. Never. And I don't know why I should be asked to explain your life to you. We have splendid writers to do that, but I am not one of them. It is that business of being universal, a word hopelessly stripped of meaning for me. [William] Faulkner wrote what I suppose could be called regional literature and had it published all over the world. That's what I wish to do. If I tried to write a universal novel, it would be water. Behind this question is the suggestion that to write for black people is somehow to diminish the writing. From my perspective there are only black people. When I say 'people,' that's what I mean."

Black woman writer or simply American novelist, Morrison is a prominent and respected figure in modern letters. As testament to her influence, something of a cottage industry has arisen of Morrison assessments. According to a *Time* article, the author "has inspired a generation of black artists, . . . produced seismic effects on publishing . . . [and] affected the course of black-studies programs across the U.S." Several books and dozens of critical essays are devoted to the examination of her fiction. Though popular acceptance of her work has seldom flagged, Morrison found her *Song of Solomon* shooting to the bestseller lists again after being selected by talk-show host Oprah Winfrey as a book-club pick in 1996; in 2002, *Sula* was the novel chosen to close out Winfrey's popular discussion group. The author's hometown of Lorain, Ohio, is the setting for the biennial Toni Morrison Society Conference; a 2000 gathering attracted 130 scholars from around the globe.

In the *Detroit News,* Larson suggested that Morrison's has been "among the most exciting literary careers of the last decade" and that each of her books "has made a quantum jump forward." Ironically, House commended Morrison for the universal nature of her work. "Unquestionably," House wrote, "Toni Morrison is an important novelist who continues to develop her talent. Part of her appeal, of course, lies in her extraordinary ability to create beautiful language and striking characters. However, Morrison's most important gift, the one which gives her a major author's universality, is the insight with which she writes of problems all humans face. . . . At the core of all her novels is a penetrating view of the unyielding, heartbreaking dilemmas which torment people of all races." Snitow noted that the author "wants to tend the imagination, search for an expansion of the possible, nurture a spiritual richness in the black tradition even after 300 years in the white desert." Lee concluded of Morrison's accomplishments: "Though there are unifying aspects in her novels, there is not a dully repetitive sameness. Each casts the problems in specific, imaginative terms, and the exquisite, poetic language awakens our senses as she communicates an often ironic vision with moving imagery. Each novel reveals the acuity of her perception of psychological motivation of the female especially, of the Black particularly, and of the human generally."

"The problem I face as a writer is to make my stories mean something," Morrison stated in an interview in *Black Women Writers at Work.* "You can have wonderful, interesting people, a fascinating story, but it's not about anything. It has no real substance. I want my books to always be about something that is important to me, and the subjects that are important in the world are the same ones that have always been important." In *Black Women Writers (1950-1980),* she elaborated on this idea. Fiction, she wrote, "should be beautiful, and powerful, but it should also work. It should have something in it that enlightens; something in it that opens the door and points the way. Something in it that suggests what the conflicts are, what the problems are. But it need not solve those problems because it is not a case study, it is not a recipe." The author who said that writing to her "is discovery; it's talking deep within myself" told the *New York Times Book Review* that the essential theme in her growing body of fiction is "how and why we learn to live this life intensely and well."

BIOGRAPHICAL AND CRITICAL SOURCES:

BOOKS

American Decades, 1970-1979, edited by Victor Bondi, Gale (Detroit, MI), 1995.
Authors and Artists for Young Adults, Volume 22, Gale (Detroit, MI), 1997.
Awkward, Michael, *Inspiriting Influences: Tradition, Revision, and Afro-American Women's Novels,* Columbia University Press (New York, NY), 1989.

Bell, Roseann P., editor, *Sturdy Black Bridges: Visions of Black Women in Literature,* Doubleday (New York, NY), 1979.

Bjork, Patrick Bryce, *The Novels of Toni Morrison: The Search for Self and Place within the Community,* Peter Lang (New York, NY), 1992.

Black Literature Criticism, Volume 2, Gale (Detroit, MI), 1992.

Bloom, Harold, editor, *Toni Morrison,* Chelsea House (Philadelphia, PA), 1990.

Bruccoli, Matthew J., editor, *Toni Morrison's Fiction,* University of South Carolina Press (Columbia, SC), 1996.

Century, Douglas, *Toni Morrison,* Chelsea House (Philadelphia, PA), 1994.

Christian, Barbara, *Black Women Novelists: The Development of a Tradition, 1892-1976,* Greenwood Press (Westport, CT), 1980.

Contemporary Literary Criticism, Gale (Detroit, MI), Volume 4, 1975, Volume 10, 1979, Volume 22, 1982, Volume 55, 1989, Volume 81, 1994, Volume 87, 1995.

Cooey, Paula M., *Religious Imagination and the Body: A Feminist Analysis,* Oxford University Press (New York, NY), 1994.

Cooper-Clark, Diana, *Interviews with Contemporary Novelists,* St. Martin's Press (New York, NY), 1986.

Coser, Stelamaris, *Bridging the Americas: The Literature of Paule Marshall, Toni Morrison, and Gayl Jones,* Temple University Press (Philadelphia, PA), 1995.

Dictionary of Literary Biography, Gale (Detroit, MI), Volume 6: *American Novelists since World War II,* 1980, Volume 33: *Afro-American Fiction Writers after 1955,* 1984, Volume 143: *American Novelists since World War II, Third Series,* 1994.

Dictionary of Literary Biography Yearbook: 1981, Gale (Detroit, MI), 1982.

Dictionary of Literary Biography Yearbook: 1993, Gale (Detroit, MI), 1994.

Dictionary of Twentieth-Century Culture, Gale (Detroit, MI), Volume 1: *American Culture after World War II,* 1994, Volume 5: *African American Culture,* (Detroit, MI), 1996.

Evans, Mari, editor, *Black Women Writers (1950-1980): A Critical Evaluation,* Doubleday (New York, NY), 1984.

Furman, Jan, *Toni Morrison's Fiction,* University of South Carolina Press (Columbia, SC), 1996.

Gates, Henry Louis, Jr. and K. A. Appiah, editors, *Toni Morrison: Critical Perspectives Past and Present,* Amistad (New York, NY), 1993.

Harding, Wendy, and Jacky Martin, *A World of Difference: An Inter-Cultural Study of Toni Morrison's Novels,* Greenwood Press (Westport, CT), 1994.

Harris, Trudier, *Fiction and Folklore: The Novels of Toni Morrison,* University of Tennessee Press (Knoxville, TN), 1991.

Heinze, Denise, *The Dilemma of "Double-Consciousness": Toni Morrison's Novels,* University of Georgia Press (Athens, GA), 1993.

Holloway, Karla, and Dematrakopoulos, Stephanie, *New Dimensions of Spirituality: A Biracial and Bicultural Reading of the Novels of Toni Morrison,* Greenwood Press (Westport, CT), 1987.

Jones, Bessie W. and Audrey L. Vinson, editors, *The World of Toni Morrison: Explorations in Literary Criticism,* Kendall/Hunt (Dubuque, IA), 1985.

Kramer, Barbara, *Toni Morrison, Nobel Prize-Winning Author,* Enslow (Springfield, NJ), 1996.

Ledbetter, Mark, *Victims and the Postmodern Narrative; or, Doing Violence to the Body: An Ethic of Reading and Writing,* St. Martin's Press (New York, NY), 1996.

McKay, Nellie, editor, *Critical Essays on Toni Morrison,* G. K. Hall (Boston, MA), 1988.

Mekkawi, Mod, *Toni Morrison: A Bibliography,* Howard University Library (Washington, DC), 1986.

Mickelson, Anne Z., *Reaching Out: Sensitivity and Order in Recent American Fiction by Women,* Scarecrow Press (Metuchen, NY), 1979.

Middleton, David L., *Toni Morrison: An Annotated Bibliography,* Garland (New York, NY), 1987.

Modern American Literature, 5th edition, St. James Press (Detroit, MI), 1999.

Morrison, Toni, and Slade Morrison, *The Big Box,* illustrated by Giselle Potter, Hyperion/Jump at the Sun (New York, NY), 1999.

Newsmakers: 1998 Cumulation, Gale (Detroit, MI), 1999.

Notable Black American Women, Book 1, Gale (Detroit, MI), 1992.

Otten, Terry, *The Crime of Innocence in the Fiction of Toni Morrison,* University of Missouri Press (Columbia, MO), 1989.

Page, Philip, *Dangerous Freedom: Fusion and Fragmentation in Toni Morrison's Novels,* University Press of Mississippi (Jackson, MS), 1996.

Peach, Linden, *Toni Morrison,* St. Martin's Press (New York, NY), 1995.

Rainwater, Catherine and William J. Scheick, editors, *Contemporary American Women Writers: Narra-*

tive Strategies, University Press of Kentucky (Lexington, KY), 1985, pp. 205-207.

Rice, Herbert William, *Toni Morrison and the American Tradition: A Rhetorical Reading,* Peter Lang (New York, NY), 1995.

Rigney, Barbara Hill, *The Voices of Toni Morrison,* Ohio State University Press (Columbus, OH), 1991.

Ruas, Charles, *Conversations with American Writers,* Knopf (New York, NY), 1985.

St. James Guide to Young Adult Writers, 2nd edition, St. James Press (Detroit, MI), 1999.

Samuels, Wilfred D. and Clenora Hudson-Weems, *Toni Morrison,* Twayne (Boston, MA), 1990.

Smith, Valerie, editor, *New Essays on Song of Solomon,* Cambridge University Press (New York, NY), 1995.

Tate, Claudia, editor, *Black Women Writers at Work,* Continuum (New York, NY), 1986, pp. 117-31.

Taylor-Guthrie, Danille, editor, *Conversations with Toni Morrison,* University Press of Mississippi (Jackson, MS), 1994.

Weinstein, Philip M., *What Else but Love?: The Ordeal of Race in Faulkner and Morrison,* Columbia University Press (New York, NY), 1996.

Willis, Susan, *Specifying: Black Women Writing the American Experience,* University of Wisconsin Press (Madison, WI), 1987.

PERIODICALS

African American Review, fall, 1993, Jane Kuenz, "'The Bluest Eye': Notes on History, Community, and Black Female Subjectivity," p. 421; summer, 1994, pp. 189, 223; fall, 1994, p. 423; winter, 1994, pp. 571, 659; spring, 1995, p. 55; winter, 1995, pp. 567, 605; spring, 1996, p. 89; summer, 1998, Allen Alexander, "The Fourth Face: The Image of God in Toni Morrison's *The Bluest Eye,*" p. 293; fall, 1998, review of *Beloved,* p. 415; winter, 1998, review of *Beloved,* p. 563; spring, 1999, review of *Beloved,* p. 105; summer, 1999, review of *Beloved,* p. 325; winter, 1999, Cat Moses, "The Blues Aesthetic in Toni Morrison's *The Bluest Eye,*" p. 623; spring, 2000, Martha Cutter, "The Story Must Go On and On," p. 61, and Cynthia Dobbs, "Circles of Sorrow, Lines of Struggle," p. 362; summer, 2000, E. Shelley Reid, "Beyond Morrison and Walker: Looking Good and Looking Forward in Contemporary Black Women's Stories," p. 313; fall, 2000, Katy Ryan, "Revolutionary Suicide in Toni Morrison's Fiction," p. 389; June 22, 2001, "The One All-Black Town Worth the Pain," "Toni Morrison and the Burden of the Passing Narrative," "Toni Morrison's Jazz and the City," and "Toni Morrison, Oprah Winfrey, and Postmodern Popular Audiences"; December 22, 2001, "Furrowing All the Brows: Interpretation and the Transcendent in Toni Morrison's *Paradise*"; March 22, 2002, "Inscriptions in the Dust," and "Reading and Insight in Toni Morrison's *Paradise.*"

America, August 15, 1998, Hermine Pinson, review of *Paradise,* p. 19.

American Historical Review, February, 1994, p. 327.

American Imago, winter, 1994, p. 421.

American Literature, March, 1980, pp. 87-100; January, 1981; May, 1984; May, 1986; March, 1999, review of *Jazz,* p. 151.

Antioch Review, summer, 2000, John Kennedy, review of *Paradise,* p. 377.

Atlantic, April, 1981.

Black American Literature Forum, summer, 1978; winter, 1979; winter, 1987.

Black Issues Book Review, November-December, 2002, Evette Porter, "The Morrison's Meanies," p. 39; May-June, 2003, Suzanne Rust, review of *The Ant or the Grasshopper,* p. 57.

Black Issues in Higher Education, October 26, 2000, Hilary Hurd, "At Home with Toni Morrison," p. 26.

Black Scholar, March, 1978.

Black World, June, 1974.

Bloomsbury Review, September, 1999, review of *The Big Box,* p. 22.

Booklist, February 15, 1998, review of *Jazz* and *Paradise,* p. 979; June 1, 1999, review of *Paradise,* p. 1797; August, 1999, Hazel Rochman, review of *The Big Box,* p. 2067; May 15, 2003, Francisca Goldsmith, review of *The Ant or the Grasshopper,* p. 1660.

Books and Culture, May, 1998, review of *Paradise,* p. 38.

Callaloo, October-February, 1981; winter, 1999, review of *Song of Solomon,* p. 121; fall, 2000, review of *Sula,* p. 1449.

Centennial Review, winter, 1988, pp. 50-64.

Chicago Tribune, October 27, 1987.

Chicago Tribune Books, August 30, 1988.

Chicago Tribune Book World, March 8, 1981.

Children's Bookwatch, November, 1999, review of *The Big Box,* p. 6.

Christian Century, March 18, 1998, Reggie Young, review of *Paradise,* p. 322.

Christian Science Monitor, October 5, 1987, Merle Rubin, review of *Beloved.*

CLA Journal, June, 1979, pp. 402-414; June, 1981, pp. 419-440; September, 1989, pp. 81-93.

Classical and Modern Literature, spring, 1998, review of *Jazz,* p. 219.

Commentary, August, 1981.

Commonweal, October 9, 1998, review of *Paradise,* p. 24.

Contemporary Literature, winter, 1983, pp. 413-429; fall, 1987, pp. 364-377.

Critique, Volume 19, number 1, 1977, Chikwenye Okonjo Ogunyemi, pp. 112-120; spring, 2000, Carl Malmgren, "Texts, Primers, and Voices in Toni Morrison's *The Bluest Eye,*" p. 251.

Detroit News, March 29, 1981.

Economist, June 6, 1998, p. 83.

Entertainment Weekly, January 23, 1998, review of *Paradise,* p. 56.

Essence, July, 1981; June, 1983; October, 1987; May, 1995, p. 222.

Explicator, summer, 1993, John Bishop, review of *The Bluest Eye,* p. 252; fall, 1994, Edmund Napieralski, "Morrison's *The Bluest Eye,*" p. 59.

First World, winter, 1977.

Globe and Mail (Toronto, Ontario, Canada), June 12, 1999, review of *Paradise* and *Song of Solomon,* p. D4.

Harper's Bazaar, March, 1983.

Harvard Advocate, Volume 107, number 4, 1974.

Horn Book, September, 1999, review of *The Big Box,* p. 598.

Hudson Review, spring, 1978; summer, 1998, review of *Paradise,* p. 433.

Hungry Mind Review, spring, 1998, review of *Playing in the Dark: Whiteness and the Literary Imagination,* p. 55; fall, 1999, review of *The Big Box,* p. 33.

Jet, February 12, 1996, p. 4.

Journal of Adolescent and Adult Literacy, review of *The Big Box,* p. 795.

Kenyon Review, summer, 1993, Peter Erickson, review of *Jazz,* p. 197.

Kirkus Reviews, July 15, 1999, review of *The Big Box,* p. 1136; September 1, 2002, review of *The Book of Mean People,* p. 1316.

Knight-Ridder/Tribune News Service, September 19, 2000, Sandy Bauers, "Unabridged Version of Toni Morrison's 'Bluest Eye' Now Available."

Library Journal, February 15, 1998, Emily J. Jones, review of *Paradise,* p. 172; October 15, 1999, review of *Paradise* (audio version), p. 123.

London Review of Books, May 7, 1998, review of *Paradise,* p. 25.

Los Angeles Times, March 31, 1981; October 14, 1987; November 1, 1998, "A Conversation between Michael Silverblatt and Toni Morrison," p. 2.

Los Angeles Times Book Review, August 30, 1987, John Leonard, review of *Beloved;* January 11, 1998, review of *Paradise,* p. 2.

Maclean's, March 30, 1998, review of *Paradise,* p. 65.

Massachusetts Review, autumn, 1977.

MELUS, fall, 1980, pp. 69-82.

Minority Voices, fall, 1980, pp. 51-63; spring-fall, 1981, pp. 59-68.

Modern Fiction Studies, spring, 1988.

Mosaic (Winnipeg, Manitoba, Canada), June, 1996, Laurie Vickroy, "The Politics of Abuse: The Traumatized Child in Toni Morrison and Marguerite Duras," p. 91.

Ms., June, 1974; December, 1974; August, 1987; March, 1998, review of *Paradise,* p. 80.

Nation, July 6, 1974; November 19, 1977; May 2, 1981; January 17, 1994, p. 59; January 26, 1998, review of *Paradise,* p. 25.

National Catholic Reporter, May 22, 1998, Judith Bromberg, review of *Paradise,* p. 35.

New Republic, December 3, 1977; March 21, 1981; October 19, 1987, Stanley Crouch, review of *Beloved;* March 27, 1995, p. 9; March 2, 1998, review of *Paradise,* p. 29.

New Statesman, May 22, 1998, review of *Paradise,* p. 56.

Newsweek, November 30, 1970; January 7, 1974; September 12, 1977; March 30, 1981, "Black Magic" (cover story); September 28, 1987, Walter Clemons, review of *Beloved;* January 12, 1998, review of *Paradise,* p. 62.

New York, April 13, 1981.

New Yorker, November 7, 1977; June 15, 1981; January 12, 1998, review of *Paradise,* p. 78.

New York Post, January 26, 1974.

New York Review of Books, November 10, 1977; April 30, 1981; November 19, 1992, p. 7; February 2, 1995, p. 36; June 11, 1998, review of *Paradise,* p. 64.

New York Times, November 13, 1970; September 6, 1977; March 21, 1981; August 26, 1987; September 2, 1987, Michiko Kakutani, review of *Beloved;* January 24, 1988; January 6, 1998, review of *Paradise,* p. E8.

New York Times Book Review, November 1, 1970; December 30, 1973; June 2, 1974; September 11, 1977; March 29, 1981; September 13, 1987, Margaret Atwood, "Haunted by Their Nightmares," p. 1; October 25, 1992, p. 1; January 11, 1998, review of *Paradise,* p. 6; May 31, 1998, review of *Paradise,* p. 23; May 2, 1999, review of *Paradise,* p. 32.

New York Times Magazine, August 22, 1971; August 11, 1974; July 4, 1976; May 20, 1979; September 11, 1994, Claudia Dreifus, "Chloe Wofford Talks about Toni Morrison," p. 1372.

Observer (London, England), March 29, 1998, review of *Paradise,* p. 15; March 14, 1999, review of *Beloved,* p. 14.

Obsidian, spring/summer, 1979; winter, 1986, pp. 151-161.

Papers on Language and Literature, summer, 2000, Martin Bidney, "Creating a Feminist-Communitarian Romanticism in Beloved," p. 271.

People, July 29, 1974; November 30, 1987; May 18, 1998, p. 45.

Perspectives on Contemporary Literature, 1982, pp. 10-17.

Philadelphia Inquirer, April 1, 1988.

PR Newswire, February 20, 2003, "Michigan Opera Theatre, Cincinnati Opera, and Opera Company of Philadelphia Announce the Co-commission of *Margaret Gardner* by Composer Richard Danielpour and Librettist Toni Morrison."

Publishers Weekly, July 17, 1987, review of *Beloved;* August 21, 1987; March 2, 1998, p. 29; July 12, 1999, review of *The Big Box,* p. 95; May 1, 2000, Daisy Maryles, "Score: Winfrey 33, Morrison 3," p. 20; April 8, 2002, "Oprah: 46 and Out"; September 9, 2002, review of *The Book of Mean People,* p. 68; November 11, 2002, review of *The Book of Mean People Journal,* pp. 66-67; June 2, 2003, review of *The Ant or the Grasshopper,* p. 50.

Quill and Quire, January, 1998, review of *Paradise* (audio version), p. 33.

Saturday Review, September 17, 1977.

School Library Journal, September, 1999, Ellen Fader, review of *The Big Box,* p. 227; November, 2002, Judith Constantinides, review of *The Book of Mean People,* p. 132.

Southern Review, autumn, 1987.

Spectator, December 9, 1978; February 2, 1980; December 19, 1981.

Studies in American Fiction, spring, 1987; autumn, 1989.

Studies in Black Literature, Volume 6, 1976.

Time, September 12, 1977; March 16, 1981; September 21, 1987; April 27, 1992; October 18, 1993; June 17, 1996, p. 73.

Times (London), October 15, 1987, Nicholas Shakespeare, review of *Beloved.*

Times Literary Supplement, October 4, 1974; November 24, 1978; February 8, 1980; December 19, 1980; October 30, 1981; October 16-22, 1987; March 5, 1993; March 27, 1998, review of *Paradise,* p. 22.

U.S. News and World Report, October 19, 1987.

Village Voice, August 29, 1977; July 1-7, 1981.

Vogue, April, 1981; January, 1986.

Voice Literary Supplement, September, 1987; December, 1992, p. 15.

Wall Street Journal, January 20, 1998, review of *Paradise,* p. A16.

Washington Post, February 3, 1974; March 6, 1974; September 30, 1977; April 8, 1981; February 9, 1983; October 5, 1987.

Washington Post Book World, February 3, 1974; September 4, 1977; December 4, 1977; March 22, 1981; September 6, 1987; November 8, 1992, p. 3; January 11, 1998, review of *Paradise,* p. 1.

Women's Journal, April, 1999, review of *Paradise,* p. 20.

Women's Review of Books, December, 1992, p. 1; April, 1998, review of *Paradise,* p. 1.

World Literature Today, summer, 1978; spring, 1993, p. 394.

ONLINE

Biography.com, http://www.biography.com/ (February 12, 2003), "Morrison, Tony."

New York Times, http://www.nytimes.com/ (January 11, 1998) Brooke Allen, "The Promised Land."

Voices from the Gaps, http://voices.cla.umn.edu/ (February 12, 2003), "Toni Morrison."*

* * *

MURPHY, Peter 1956-

PERSONAL: Born January 9, 1956, in Australia; son of Harry (a civil engineer) and Joan (Azar) Murphy; partner of Christine Mintrom (an occupational therapist). *Education:* La Trobe University, B.A. (with first class honors), 1979, Ph.D., 1985.

ADDRESSES: Home—27/183 Kerr St., Fitzroy, Victoria 3065, Australia. *Office*—*Thesis Eleven* Editorial Office, School of Politics, Sociology, and Anthropology, La Trobe University, Bundoora, Victoria 3803, Australia; and School of Information Management, Victoria University of Wellington, P.O. Box 600, Wellington, New Zealand. *E-mail*—peter.murphy@vuw.ac.nz.

CAREER: New School for Social Research, New York, NY, visiting professor and research fellow, 1986; University of Ballarat, Ballarat, Victoria, Australia, lecturer, 1988-93, senior lecturer in politics, 1994-97; Baylor University, Waco, TX, visiting professor of political science, 1996-97; La Trobe University, Bundoora, Victoria, Australia, research fellow at School of Sociology, Politics, and Anthropology, 1997; Looksmart International (database publisher), senior editor, 1998-2001; Victoria University of Wellington, Wellington, New Zealand, senior lecturer in communications, 2001—. Ohio State University, visiting scholar in Hellenic languages and literatures, 1994; Panteion University, visiting scholar in communication and mass media, 1995.

WRITINGS:

(Coeditor) *The Left in Search of a Center,* University of Illinois Press (Urbana, IL), 1996.

The Scales of Justice, Humanities (Atlantic Highlands, NJ), 1997.

(With Sophie Watson) *Surface City: Sydney at the Millennium,* Pluto Press Australia (Annandale, New South Wales, Australia), 1997.

Civic Justice: From Greek Antiquity to the Modern World, Humanity Books (Amherst, NY), 2001.

(Coeditor) *Agon, Logos, Polis,* Franz Steiner Verlag (Stuttgart, Germany), 2001.

(Coauthor) *Dialectic of Romanticism: A Critique of Modernism,* Continuum (New York, NY), in press.

Contributor to books, including *Between Postmodernity and Totalitarianism,* MIT Press (Cambridge, MA), 1992; *Troubled Bodies,* Duke University Press (Durham, NC), 1995; *Building Cities,* Artmedia Press (London, England), 1999; and *What These Ithakas Mean: Readings in Cavafy,* Hellenic Literary and Historical Archive (London, England), 2002. Contributor to journals, including *Diaspora, Journal of Modern Greek Studies, Social Sciences Abroad, Praxis International,* and *Social Research.* Coeditor, *Thesis Eleven: Journal of Critical Theory and Historical Sociology,* 1990—; special issue editor, *South Atlantic Quarterly,* 1998.

WORK IN PROGRESS: Portal: Civic Power, Geopolitics, and the Origins of Intellectual Capital.

N

NIMMO, Jenny 1944-

PERSONAL: Born January 15, 1944, in Windsor, Berkshire, England; daughter of Francis (a physicist) Nimmo and Phyllis Marguerite Johnson; married David Wynn Millward (an artist and illustrator), 1974; children: two daughters, one son. *Education:* Private boarding schools, 1950-60.

ADDRESSES: Home—Henllan Mill, Llangynyw, Welshpool, Powys SY21 9EN, Wales. *Agent*—David Highham Associates, 5-8 Lower John St., Golden Sq., London W1F 9HA, England. *E-mail*—jennynimmo@aol.com.

CAREER: Theatre Southeast, Sussex and Kent, England, actress and assistant stage manager, 1960-63; governess in Amalfi, Italy, 1963; British Broadcasting Corp. Television, London, England, photographic researcher, 1964-66, assistant floor manager, 1966-68, 1971-74, director and writer of children's programs for *Jackanory,* 1970; full-time writer, 1975—.

AWARDS, HONORS: Austrian Ministry of Culture Prize, 1975, for *The Bronze Trumpeter;* Smarties Award, Rowntree Mackintosh Co., 1986, and Tir na n-Og Award, Welsh Books Council, 1987, both for *The Snow Spider;* Smarties Gold Award, six-to-eight-years category, Booktrust, 1997, for *The Owl Tree.*

WRITINGS:

FOR CHILDREN; FICTION

The Bronze Trumpeter, illustrated by Caroline Scrace, Angus & Robertson (London, England), 1975.

Tatty Apple, illustrated by Priscilla Lamont, Methuen (London, England), 1984.

The Snow Spider (first book in the "Snow Spider" trilogy; also see below), illustrated by Joanna Carey, Methuen (London, England), 1986, Dutton (New York, NY), 1987.

Emlyn's Moon (second book in the "Snow Spider" trilogy; also see below), illustrated by Joanna Carey, Methuen (London, England), 1987, published as *Orchard of the Crescent Moon,* Dutton (New York, NY), 1989.

The Red Secret, illustrated by Maureen Bradley, Hamish Hamilton (London, England), 1989.

The Chestnut Soldier (third book in the "Snow Spider" trilogy; also see below), Methuen (London, England), 1989, Dutton (New York, NY), 1991.

The Bears Will Get You!, Methuen (London, England), 1990.

Jupiter Boots, Heinemann (London, England), 1990.

Ultramarine, Methuen (London, England), 1990, Dutton (New York, NY), 1992.

Delilah and the Dogspell, Methuen (London, England), 1991.

Rainbow and Mr. Zed (sequel to *Ultramarine*), Methuen (London, England), 1992, Dutton (New York, NY), 1994.

(Reteller) *The Witches and the Singing Mice,* illustrated by Angela Barrett, Collins (London, England), Dial (New York, NY), 1993.

The Stone Mouse, illustrated by Helen Craig, Walker (London, England), 1993.

(Reteller) *The Starlight Cloak,* illustrated by Justin Todd, Collins (London, England), Dial (New York, NY), 1993.

The Breadwitch, illustrated by Ben Cort, Heinemann (London, England), 1993.

The Snow Spider Trilogy (contains *The Snow Spider, Emlyn's Moon,* and *The Chestnut Soldier*), Mammoth (London, England), 1993.

Delilah and the Dishwasher Dogs, Methuen (London, England), 1993.

Griffin's Castle, Methuen (London, England), 1994, Orchard (New York, NY), 1997.

Wilfred's Wolf, illustrated by husband, David Wynn Millward, Bodley Head (London, England), 1994.

Granny Grimm's Gruesome Glasses, illustrated by David Wynn Millward, A. & C. Black (London, England), 1995.

Ronnie and the Giant Millipede, illustrated by David Parkins, Walker (London, England), 1995.

Alien on the Ninety-ninth Floor, illustrated by Martin Chatterton, Heinemann (London, England), 1996.

The Witch's Tears, illustrated by Paul Howard, Collins (London, England), 1996.

Gwion and the Witch, illustrated by Jac Jones, Pont Books (Llandysul, Wales), 1996.

The Owl Tree, illustrated by Anthony Lewis, Walker (London, England), 1997.

Hot Dog, Cool Cat, illustrated by David Wynn Millward, Mammoth (London, England), 1997.

Seth and the Strangers, Mammoth (London, England), 1997.

The Dragon's Child, illustrated by Alan Marks, Hodder & Stoughton (London, England), 1997.

Delilah Alone, illustrated by Georgien Overwater, Mammoth (London, England), 1997.

(Reteller) *Thumbelina,* illustrated by Phillida Gili, Macdonald Young (Hove, England), 1997.

Branwen, illustrated by Jac Jones, Pont Books (Llandysul, Wales), 1998.

The Rinaldi Ring, Mammoth (London, England), 1999.

Toby in the Dark, illustrated by Helen Craig, Walker (London, England), 1999.

The Box Boys and the Magic Shell, Hodder & Stoughton (London, England), 1999.

The Box Boys and the Fairground Ride, Hodder & Stoughton (London, England), 1999.

Esmeralda and the Children Next Door, illustrated by Paul Howard, Methuen (London, England), 1999, Houghton (Boston, MA), 2000.

Dog Star, Walker (London, England), 1999.

The Box Boys and the Bonfire Cat, Hodder & Stoughton (London, England), 1999.

The Box Boys and the Dog in the Mist, Hodder & Stoughton (London, England), 1999.

Ill Will, Well Nell, Mammoth (London, England), 2000.

The Strongest Girl in the World, illustrated by Paul Howard, Egmont (London, England), 2001.

Milo's Wolves, Mammoth (London, England), 2001.

Tom and the Pterosaur, Walker (London, England), 2001.

Something Wonderful, illustrated by Debbie Boon, Collins (London, England), Harcourt (San Diego, CA), 2001.

The Bodigulpa ("Shock Shop" series), Macmillan (London, England), 2001.

Midnight for Charlie Bone, Egmont (London, England), Orchard (New York, NY), 2002.

Time Twister, Egmont (London, England), 2002, published as *Charlie Bone and the Time Twister,* Orchard (New York, NY), 2003.

Beak and Whisker, illustrated by Ailie Busby, Egmont (London, England), 2002.

Night of the Unicorn, Walker (London, England), 2003.

Pig on a Swing, Hodder (London, England), 2003.

Invisible Vinnie, Corgi (London, England), 2003.

ADAPTATIONS: The three books of the "Snow Spider" trilogy, *The Snow Spider, Emlyn's Moon,* and *The Chestnut Soldier,* have all been adapted as children's programs for British television. Several of Nimmo's works have been recorded.

WORK IN PROGRESS: A third book in the "Children of the Red King" series.

SIDELIGHTS: Author of over fifty books for young readers, including picture books, first readers, and longer novels, Jenny Nimmo began to receive much notice as a children's author in the 1980s. Her first book, *The Bronze Trumpeter,* was published in 1975, and led *Times Literary Supplement* contributor Ann Thwaite to call her "a new writer of considerable imagination and skill." That title, with its Sicilian setting and cascading images and plot that flows like a meandering river, set the tone for much of Nimmo's fantasy fiction to come. Readers are, by the end of the book, "left so dumbstruck that one almost expects to find the book erasing itself as the last page is finished," according to George Hunt, writing in *Books for Keeps.* The novel surely presaged the beginning of a fine writing career, yet the responsibility of raising her three children kept Nimmo from publishing another book until 1984.

Since then, the writer has more than made up for lost time, with her ambitious "Snow Spider" trilogy, and major fantasies such as *Ultramarine, Rainbow and Mr.*

Zed, Griffin's Castle, Milo's Wolves, and the 2002 Midnight for Charlie Bone. Popular shorter books from Nimmo include a trio of tales about a magical cat that casts spells on dogs. These include Delilah and the Dogspell, Delilah and the Dishwasher Dogs, and Delilah Alone. Magic and fantasy also infuse Nimmo's other short novels for beginning readers, such as The Dragon's Child, Witch's Tears, and Toby in the Dark. Additionally, Nimmo has created diverting entertainment for younger readers with picture books such as Esmeralda and the Children Next Door and Something Wonderful.

Nimmo related in Twentieth-Century Children's Writers: "I live and work in a rural community in Wales where my three bilingual children grew up in an old but vigorous culture. Here place names hark back to legend and it seems to me that the past is still part of the rhythm of everyday life. My books are concerned with the very real problem of growing children, and most of them are set in a landscape which is undeniably magical; they are described as fantasies." School Librarian contributor Donna White affirmed that "Wales has a powerful hold on [the] imagination" of this "relative newcomer to children's fantasy."

Born in Windsor, Berkshire, England, in 1944, Nimmo was an only child, and with the death of her father when she was only five, her life became even more circumscribed. She partly grew up on her uncle's free-range chicken farm. At age nine, she changed schools, which she detested. At eleven she began attending a secondary school and earned encouragement to become an actress. She also developed an early and abiding interest in music. Books and writing were also early interests for Nimmo; she read her way through the junior school library and had to be given special permission to use the senior school library. She began to write her own stories—usually on the scary side and with at least one dead body—and entertained her friends with her spooky tales. Leaving school, she went on to work in theater for a time, and then for the BBC in various positions. She married the artist and illustrator David Wynn Millward in 1974, settled in Wales, and had three children. Millward has illustrated several of her titles.

Crediting part of her vivid imagination to the influence of the Welsh countryside, Nimmo has received accolades for her faithful renditions of this history-filled landscape. To win the Tir na n-Og Award, one must present a Welsh language book, or, for an English language book, depict an authentic Welsh setting while raising the standard of writing for children and young people. Nimmo's The Snow Spider earned this honor for doing just that. Ten-year-old Gwyn Griffiths, the protagonist of The Snow Spider, is having a tough time adjusting to his sister's death, his mother's inability to control her grieving, and his father's accusations that Gwyn is to blame for their loss. In an effort to help, Gwyn is given five strange birthday gifts from his mystic grandmother. He must use these oddities to look inside himself to find the magical powers that have long resided in his bloodline. Throughout the journey, Gwyn is taken aback when he sees his dead sister's ghostly image appear in a spider's sorcerous web. As any ten-year-old might, he disobeys his grandmother and reveals his secret while experimenting with powers greater than his ability to control. His newfound magic creates a dichotomy, for now he must choose either to join his sister in a different world or to go back home. According to Horn Book critic Mary M. Burns, "Gwyn is a very real ten-year-old . . . conscious that he is different from his classmates, touchingly anxious to belong and to be loved." Zena Sutherland, writing for the Bulletin of the Center for Children's Books, found The Snow Spider a "cohesive and compelling" story that has "depth and nuance."

The mysterious alternate world of Gwyn's Welsh home returns in Orchard of the Crescent Moon (published in England as Emlyn's Moon); this time Gwyn's neighbor Nia is the person seeking a special talent, which she must then use to rescue her friend Emlyn. Like its predecessor, Emlyn's Moon demonstrates "the 'realness' of the child characters, despite their close access to ancient magical powers," David Bennett noted in Books for Keeps. A Publishers Weekly critic similarly observed, in a review of Orchard of the Crescent Moon, that while the story has fantasy elements, it is "rooted in the miseries of family misunderstandings and sorrows." "Emlyn's Moon confirms all our hopes" about Nimmo's "unusual talents," Marcus Crouch asserted in Junior Bookshelf. "This is a rich, moving and amusing story, one which demands and receives the reader's total capitulation."

The trilogy concludes with The Chestnut Soldier, in which Gwyn is approaching his fourteenth birthday and still exercising his magical powers. This time his irresponsibility causes him to lose control of one of the powers he received on his tenth birthday. His carelessness endangers a weak-spirited, wounded soldier resting at a home in the village. Since the power can thwart Gwyn, he must call on his grandmother and ancestor Gwydion to exorcise the evil force from the soldier's abducted spirit. *The Chestnut Soldier* contains many parallels to the ancient Welsh legends known as the Mabinogion, but was favored least by critic Beth E. Andersen. In *Voice of Youth Advocates,* the reviewer faulted the "relentlessly oppressive moodiness" of the characters and the "disappointingly anti-climactic finish." *School Library Journal* contributor Virginia Golodetz, however, applauded the book and stated that "Nimmo has skillfully woven the ancient story into the modern one, making it accessible to those who do not know the legend." Donna White also praised the concluding volume in *School Librarian,* calling it "Nimmo's best book to date."

"As her major work grows in scale and complexity, Nimmo has turned to the creation of small, simpler worlds," Crouch observed in *Twentieth-Century Children's Writers*. *The Red Secret,* for instance, is a simple tale of Tom, a city boy whose family moves to the country, and how he rescues a wounded fox cub and makes friends in the process. *Growing Point*'s Margery Fisher praised the "concise, pictorial and energetic prose" of Nimmo's book, which she predicted would enliven the easy-to-read format for the reader. Similarly told with "quiet assurance and [Nimmo's] instinct for the right turn of phrase," according to Crouch in *Junior Bookshelf,* is *Jupiter Boots,* the story of young Timothy's encounter with a pair of fancy footwear. *The Stone Mouse* also demonstrates the author's "special kind of mastery in the little book," Crouch stated in another *Junior Bookshelf* review. The relationship between Ted, his sister Elly, and a talking stone mouse makes for "a strangely engaging read" in which "the reader is invited to consider many themes," Sue Smedley concluded in *School Librarian.*

Nimmo has also turned her talents to more comic effect, as in her stories about a cat with magical powers. Readers are first introduced to the gifted feline in *Delilah and the Dogspell,* when Delilah begins to shrink all the dogs who annoy her down to mouse size. After one of the miniaturized dogs befriends a lonely girl and Delilah goes too far by shrinking the Prime Minister's favorite pet, peace and order are finally restored. "The book is a romp, splendidly done," David Churchill wrote in *School Librarian,* recommending the story for both reading aloud or alone, while Fisher noted in *Growing Point* that this "racy bit of nonsense [is] based on a sturdy recognition of the relationship of dogs and cats." The trouble-making witch-cat returns in *Delilah and the Dishwasher Dogs,* in which Delilah is kidnapped by an evil fortune teller and must be rescued by the neighborhood cats. "The story is well delivered, with interesting and stretching vocabulary," stated Janet Sims in *School Librarian,* making for a book that is "exciting, funny, and extremely readable." Delilah is once again reprised in *Delilah Alone.* When her owners go on holiday, the feline is so miffed that she runs away; her only protection as she embarks on the many adventures waiting outside her front door is her ability to shrink other animals. Liz Baynton-Clarke, writing in *School Librarian,* found this "an engaging story with plenty of action throughout and lots of appeal for the seven-to-nine age group."

More humor and fantasy are blended in several other short novels from Nimmo. A feline and canine take center stage in *Hot Dog, Cool Cat,* in which the animals in question are best buddies, yet they belong to owners who do not really understand them. While the dog is large and full of energy, his older owners are quiet; the cat, on the other hand, is reclusive but lives in a family with an active youngster who always wants to play. Finally the two animals decide on a simple solution: they will trade places. *School Librarian*'s Lynne Taylor found this "humorous story . . . just right for young children starting chapter reading." Young Fred helps an alien in a department store in *Alien on the Ninety-ninth Floor,* and in return shares the alien's powers to become invisible. Their subsequent adventures in the store's toy department is "a real hoot," according to A. R. Williams in the *Junior Bookshelf.* In *Ronnie and the Giant Millipede,* a seven year old gets a new pair of boots and cannot stop himself from stomping on everything he comes across. The family ultimately has to move out to the country, to a cottage far away from neighbors so that Ronnie's constant stomping does not bother anybody else. But there, he finally meets his match in a giant millipede who makes him change his ways. Linda Saunders, reviewing the book in *School Librarian,* called it an "enjoyable cautionary tale," and "very amusing. . . . An excellent first novel for eight year olds to read for themselves."

Nimmo also produces scary predicaments for young readers. Toby is a panda who comes to life in *Toby in* the Dark in order to come to the aid of three siblings left in the care of the awful Mrs. Malevant. This lady, hired to watch the children, is so sour that she has taken all happiness from the house. Deepa Earnshaw praised this novel in *School Librarian*, noting that "Nimmo has created a mischievous, endearing character in Toby." Kit Spring, writing in the *Observer*, also found much to like in the book. "There's just enough nastiness in Mrs. Malevant to keep hearts pounding," Spring wrote. Nimmo blends science fiction and terror in *Seth and the Strangers*, in which a young boy learns to deal with his own past and the abuse from his stepfather. *School Librarian* contributor Julia Marriage felt this is "an excellent short novel." A benevolent witch is at the heart of *The Witch's Tears*, in which the mysterious Mrs. Scarum arrives at the home of the Blossom family one stormy night and weeps crystal tears, proving she is, indeed, a witch. The children of the family, Theo and Dodie—waiting for their father— are fearful, but in the end, she helps in the safe return of Mr. Blossom. *The Dragon's Child* features young Dando, a youthful dragon, who is befriended by an orphaned girl, Manon. Together they form a bond and attempt to stay out of the way of an amazing assortment of fantasy creatures, including the evil Doggins who love chasing dragons. Lord Drum, who captures Dando, ultimately learns from these two an important lesson about love and freedom. Roy Blatchford, writing in *Books for Keeps,* lauded Nimmo's ability "to craft fiction that has a genuine sense of wonder for the young reader." Cherrie Warwick, reviewing the novel in *School Librarian,* summarized the theme of the book: "The possession of magic is a responsibility—to recognise it and use it well. Ignorance of this makes us fearful and cruel."

Nimmo also uses playful picture books for her message-driven stories. *Esmeralda and the Children Next Door* features young Esmeralda, "a force to be reckoned with," according to Kate Kellaway in an *Observer* review. The girl, born to circus performers, is the strong woman of the circus, able to carry both parents on her shoulders. Seemingly born for this role, she is not really happy in it, though her parents are oblivious to this. Esmeralda feels out of place, shunned by other kids because of her size. All the while she yearns to be a tightrope walker instead of a weight lifter. But when she catches a falling limb, thus saving a sleeping baby, she begins to see some value in her strength. For a *Horn Book* reviewer, this story is "poignant and interestingly askew rather than humorous." Lisa Dennis, writing in *School Library Journal,* found it a "curious picture book," yet Kellaway was more positive in her evaluation, calling it a "lovely, moving book."

Something Wonderful is a further picture book that looks at serious issues in a playful manner. Little Hen lacks self-esteem; she is indeed small and does not even have a nice name like the other chickens. But she finally discovers her real power when she saves the eggs that other hens have absent-mindedly abandoned. She takes care of them until they hatch with such diligence that she becomes the pride of the barnyard. "Youngsters," wrote Anne Parker in a *School Library Journal* review, "will enjoy and identify with this story about one small animal's special gift." *Booklist*'s Shelle Rosenfeld similarly commended the "soothing and sound" message of Nimmo's picture book, that "determination and perseverance, not preconceptions, make the difference."

Nimmo returned to a supernatural setting for *Ultramarine,* in which she "again combines fantasy elements with the psychological growth of her protagonists to weave solid entertainment," according to a *Publishers Weekly* critic. Ned and Nell are uneasy when they are scheduled to spend a week alone with an aunt and grandmother they've never met; during their unsettling stay, they learn that their real mother actually drowned when they were young and that their father may have been a sea creature known as a kelpie. This discovery leads them to aid a mysterious stranger in rescuing sea creatures, creating a "tantalizing blend" of elements where the children's "realities are every bit as fascinating as their fantasies," as Jody McCoy remarked in *Voice of Youth Advocates.* "The dream-like, secretive quality of the narrative mesmerizes the reader until the children's mystery is fully revealed," Kathryn Jennings wrote in *Bulletin of the Center for Children's Books* in recommending this "haunting story."

Rainbow and Mr. Zed continues the story of Nell, who is adjusting to life without Ned, who has joined their father at sea. Remaining with distant relatives, Nell— whose true name is Rainbow—has been sent to the estate of the mysterious Mr. Zed, who seems to know all about her secret heritage. Nell soon discovers that Mr. Zed is actually her late mother's evil brother, and he wants to use Nell to gain power and revenge against her father. "In a chilling and eerie story that weaves back and forth between fantasy and reality," as *Booklist* writer Kay Weisman described it, "Nell comes to terms with her uniqueness" and thwarts her uncle's sinister plans. *Rainbow and Mr. Zed* "is exciting, moving, and deeply committed to the preservation of the world," Crouch asserted in *Junior Bookshelf,* concluding: "Great stuff this, with much fun to match the terrors, an exciting adventure worked out in terms of vividly realised characters, all confirmation—if such were needed—that here is an important writer at the height of her powers."

Nimmo moves to an urban setting for *Griffin's Castle,* a tale of an eleven-year-old girl who finds magical help in the carved animals on the walls of Cardiff Castle in Wales. The girl, Dinah, needs such help to defeat the intentions of her mother's boyfriend, Gomer, who plans to sell off the old house they have moved into. Once Gomer is defeated, Dinah also discovers that her animal protectors have gone. A critic for *Kirkus Reviews* called this novel a "brooding fantasy," and "a well-told story with unusually strong characters." Elizabeth Bush, writing in the *Bulletin of the Center for Children's Books*, felt that the book "stumbles" at certain plot points, but concluded that "readers charmed by an emotionally vulnerable heroine surrounded by moldy walls and foggy Cardiff streets will be pleased." Crouch, writing in *Junior Bookshelf,* thought *Griffin's Castle* was Nimmo's "most substantial offering since the 'Ultramarine' sequence." Crouch concluded, "Beautifully written, finely imagined to the last detail, this is a fantasy the more powerful because it obeys strict rules and reconciles the differences of magic and reality."

In *The Rinaldi Ring,* twelve-year-old Eliot, an American, is sent to live with English cousins when his mother dies. But once there, he falls captive to the ghost of a girl who once lived in his room. Helena Thompson, reviewing that title in the *Times Educational Supplement,* felt that Nimmo "pacifies the ghosts she raises with assured sensitivity." With *Milo's Wolves,* Nimmo creates a "Frankestein story for the twenty-first century," according to Nikki Gamble in *Books for Keeps.* Milo, father of the family and an actor with a knack for storytelling, tells his three children that they have a long-lost brother, Gwendal, who is coming to live with them. The boy, who has spent most of his life in a clinic, does not resemble either parent, and he seems to be pursued by mysterious figures in gray. Laura, his sister, is shocked and amazed by the arrival of this unknown sibling, and even more so when Gwendal leaves the family to seek protection in the Pyrenees. Gamble lauded Nimmo's ability to "vividly create . . . a haunting setting" for the novel.

In her 2002 novel, *Midnight for Charlie Bone,* Nimmo begins the first of a projected five-part "Children of the Red King" series, about a ten-year-old boy, Charlie, who discovers he has amazing powers and is sent to a special school to develop them. With obvious similarities to the popular "Harry Potter" books, Nimmo's novel features a boy with the power to look at photographs and actually hear the conversations and thoughts that were happening at the time the picture was taken. He is sent by his less than loving grandmother to Bloor's Academy, where gifted children such as Charlie improve their special skills. But once at the school, he falls on hard times, caught up in old intrigues and falling afoul of the evil headmaster. Also, after looking at one picture, he pursues the trail of a missing girl that might lead him to the mystery of his own father. A contributor for *Publishers Weekly* dubbed the work "ersatz Harry Potter," though *Booklist*'s Sally Estes was more laudatory. She found the book an "exciting, fast-paced adventure tale." *School Library Journal*'s Eva Mitnick also praised the novel, noting that "the writing is deft, most of the characters are intriguing, and Charlie Bone is an appealing boy."

In an assessment of the author's career in *Twentieth-Century Children's Writers,* Marcus Crouch further lauded Nimmo, stating that she "is a living example of the basic formula for success in an author: write what you know. She works in big ideas on a small canvas, which she fills with the figures of her own rural community. Magic or no magic, hers is a real world, viewed with a keen and understanding eye and with rich appreciation of its fun and its folly."

BIOGRAPHICAL AND CRITICAL SOURCES:

BOOKS

Children's Literature Review, Volume 44, Gale (Detroit, MI), 1997.

Continuum Encyclopedia of Children's Literature, edited by Bernice E. Cullinan and Diane G. Person, Continuum International (New York, NY), 2001.

Cooling, Wendy, *Interview with Jenny Nimmo,* Egmont (London, England), 2003.

Twentieth-Century Children's Writers, 4th edition, St. James Press (Detroit, MI), 1995, pp. 706-707.

PERIODICALS

Booklist, May 1, 1993, p. 1605; August, 1994, p. 2064; February 15, 1995, Kay Weisman, review of *Rainbow and Mr. Zed;* September 15, 2001, Shelle Rosenfeld, review of *Something Wonderful,* p. 233; January 1, 2002, Sally Estes, review of *Midnight for Charlie Bone,* p. 892.

Bookseller, January 18, 2002, review of *Midnight for Charlie Bone,* p. 48.

Books for Keeps, September, 1986, p. 25; March, 1989, David Bennett, review of *The Snow Spider* and *Emlyn's Moon,* p. 19; January, 1997, George Hunt, review of *The Bronze Trumpeter,* p. 25; November, 1997, Roy Blatchford, review of *The Dragon's Child,* p. 23; July, 2001, Nikki Gamble, review of *Milo's Wolves,* pp. 26-27.

Bulletin of the Center for Children's Books, July-August, 1987, Zena Sutherland, review of *The Snow Spider,* p. 216; July-August, 1992, Kathryn Jennings, review of *Ultramarine,* p. 301; April, 1997, Elizabeth Bush, review of *Griffin's Castle,* pp. 291-292.

Growing Point, May, 1989, Margery Fisher, review of *The Red Secret,* p. 5172; November, 1991, Margery Fisher, review of *Delilah and the Dogspell,* p. 5602.

Horn Book, September-October, 1987, Mary M. Burns, review of *The Snow Spider,* p. 613; September, 1993, p. 611; July-August, 2000, review of *Esmeralda and the Children Next Door,* p. 438.

Junior Bookshelf, February, 1985, p. 28; February, 1988, Marcus Crouch, review of *Emlyn's Moon,* p. 51; April, 1989, pp. 65-66; February, 1991, Marcus Crouch, review of *Jupiter Boots,* p. 26; August, 1992, Marcus Crouch, review of *Rainbow and Mr. Zed,* pp. 158-159; December, 1993, Marcus Crouch, review of *The Stone Mouse,* p. 235; December, 1994, Marcus Crouch, review of *Griffin's Castle,* pp. 229-230; December, 1995, pp. 214-215; August, 1996, A. R. Williams, review of *Alien on the Ninety-ninth Floor,* p. 150, and *Delilah and the Dishwasher Dogs,* pp. 150-151; October, 1996, review of *The Witch's Tears,* p. 194.

Kirkus Reviews, April, 1997, review of *Griffin's Castle,* p. 560; December 15, 2002, review of *Midnight for Charlie Bone,* p. 1854.

Magpies, March, 1996, review of *Ronnie and the Giant Millipede,* p. 22.

Observer (London, England), May 30, 1999, Kit Spring, review of *Toby in the Dark,* p. 13; October 24, 1999, Kate Kellaway, review of *Esmeralda and the Children Next Door,* p. 13.

Publishers Weekly, June 9, 1989, review of *Orchard of the Crescent Moon,* p. 68; March 9, 1992, review of *Ultramarine,* p. 58; August 2, 1993, p. 81; June 18, 2001, review of *Something Wonderful,* pp. 80-81; December 9, 2002, review of *Midnight for Charlie Bone,* p. 85.

School Librarian, February, 1988, p. 21; November, 1991, Donna White, "Welsh Legends through English Eyes: An American Viewpoint," pp. 130-131; February, 1992, David Churchill, review of *Delilah and the Dogspell,* p. 21; November, 1993, Sue Smedley, review of *The Stone Mouse,* p. 157; May, 1994, Janet Sims, review of *Delilah and the Dishwater Dogs,* p. 62; May, 1996, Linda Saunders, review of *Ronnie and the Giant Millipede,* p. 64; August, 1996, Gillian Cross, review of *The Witch's Tears,* p. 108; August, 1997, Liz Baynton-Clarke, review of *Delilah Alone,* p. 147, Linda Saunders, review of *The Owl Tree,* p. 147; November, 1997, Cherrie Warwick, review of *The Dragon's Child,* p. 192, Lynne Taylor, review of *Hot Dog, Cool Cat,* pp. 192-193, Julia Marriage, review of *Seth and the Strangers,* p. 201; summer, 1998, Janet Sims, review of *Branwen,* p. 89; autumn, 1999, Deepa Earnshaw, review of *Toby in the Dark,* p. 132; autumn, 2001, Alison A. Smith, review of *Milo's Wolves,* p. 159; spring, 2002, Vida Conway, review of *Something Wonderful,* p. 20.

School Library Journal, July, 1991, Virginia Golodetz, review of *The Chestnut Soldier,* p. 74; November, 1992, p. 74; February, 1995; June, 1997, Virginia Golodetz, review of *Griffin's Castle,* p. 124; April, 2000, Lisa Dennis, review of *Esmeralda and the Children Next Door,* p. 111; September, 2001, Anne Parker, review of *Something Wonderful,* p. 202; February, 2003, Eva Mitnick, review of *Midnight for Charlie Bone,* p. 146.

Times Educational Supplement, April 9, 1999, Helena Thompson, review of *The Rinaldi Ring,* p. 23.

Times Literary Supplement, April 4, 1975, Ann Thwaite, "Time and Again," review of *The Bronze Trumpeter,* p. 362.

Voice of Youth Advocates, October, 1991, Beth E. Andersen, review of *The Chestnut Soldier,* p. 248; June, 1992, Jody McCoy, review of *Ultramarine,* p. 113.

ONLINE

Channel4.com, http://www.channel4.com/ (February 14, 2003), "Jenny Nimmo."

O

OSBORNE, Mary Pope 1949-

PERSONAL: Born May 20, 1949, in Fort Sill, OK; daughter of William P. (a colonel in the U.S. Army) and Barnette (a homemaker; maiden name, Dickens) Pope; married Will Osborne (an actor, author, playwright, and theater director), May 16, 1976. *Education:* University of North Carolina—Chapel Hill, B.A., 1971. *Hobbies and other interests:* Reading, gardening, traveling, taking long drives, making bread and soup, playing with her Norfolk terrier Bailey.

ADDRESSES: Home and office—Northwest Connecticut. *Agent*—c/o Author Mail, Random House, 1745 Broadway, New York, NY 10019.

CAREER: Author, editor, and lecturer. *Scholastic News Trails* magazine, New York, NY, assistant editor, 1973-79. Worked variously as a medical assistant in Monterey, CA; as a window dresser in Carmel, CA; as a travel agent in Washington, DC, and New York, NY; as an acting teacher in the Bronx, NY; and as a bartender and waitress in New York, NY.

MEMBER: Authors Guild (elected council member; chairman of Children's Book Committee; president, 1993-97 and 1997-2001), Authors Guild Foundation (elected president and vice-president), Authors League Fund (board of directors), Authors Registry (founding director), Authors League of America, PEN International.

AWARDS, HONORS: Annual Award, Woodward Park School (Brooklyn, NY), and Children's Choice selection, International Reading Association/Children's

Mary Pope Osborne

Book Council (IRA/CBC), both 1983, and Most Popular Children's Novel of the Northern Territory of Australia citation, 1986, all for *Run, Run, As Fast As You Can;* Children's Book of the Year list, Child Study Association of America, 1986, for *Last One Home;* Pick of the List, *American Bookseller,* 1986, for *Mo to the Rescue;* "Outstanding and Worthy of Note" citation, Virginia Library Association, 1990, for *The Many*

Lives of Benjamin Franklin;* Pick of the List, *American Bookseller,* and Best Books of the Year, *Parents' Magazine,* both 1991, both for *Moonhorse;* Best Books of the Year list, *School Library Journal,* Blue Ribbon Book, *Bulletin of the Center for Children's Books,* and Notable Children's Trade Book in the Field of Social Studies, National Council for the Social Studies/Children's Book Council (NCSS/CBC), all 1991, and Utah Children's Book Award, 1993, all for *American Tall Tales;* Best Books of the Year list, Bank Street College, 1992, for both *Spider Kane and the Mystery under the May-Apple* and *Dinosaurs before Dark,* which also won the Diamond State (Delaware) Reading Association Award; Edgar Award finalist for Best Juvenile Mystery, Mystery Writers of America, 1993, for *Spider Kane and the Mystery at Jumbo Nightcrawler's;* Notable Children's Trade Book in the Field of Social Studies, NCSS/CBC, 1993, for *Mermaid Tales from around the World;* Distinguished Alumni Award, University of North Carolina—Chapel Hill, 1994; Orbis Pictus Honor Award, National Council of Teachers of English, 1996, for *One World, Many Religions: The Ways We Worship;* Distinguished Contribution to the Arts, New York Carolina Club; named one of Top 100 Authors, Educational Paperback Association; Children's Choice selection, IRA/CBC, for *Standing in the Light: The Captive Diary of Catharine Carey Logan, Delaware Valley, Pennsylvania, 1763;* Children's Choice Award, Association of Booksellers for Children, for *Dolphins at Daybreak* and *Midnight on the Moon.*

WRITINGS:

Mo to the Rescue (also see below), illustrated by DyAnne DiSalvo-Ryan, Dial (New York, NY), 1985.
Moonhorse, illustrated by David McPhail, Knopf (New York, NY), 1988, illustrated by S. M. Saelig, Knopf (New York, NY), 1991.
Mo and His Friends (sequel to *Mo to the Rescue*), illustrated by DyAnne DiSalvo-Ryan, Dial (New York, NY), 1989.
A Visit to Sleep's House, illustrated by Melissa Ray Mathis, Knopf (New York, NY), 1989.
(Editor) *The Calico Book of Bedtime Rhymes from around the World,* illustrated by T. Lewis, Contemporary Books (Chicago, IL), 1990.
(Compiler) *Bears, Bears, and Bears: A Treasury of Stories, Songs, and Poems about Bears,* illustrated by Karen Lee Schmidt, Silver Press (Englewood Cliffs, NJ), 1990, Simon & Schuster (New York, NY), 1992.
Spider Kane and the Mystery under the May-Apple (also see below), illustrated by Victoria Chess, Knopf (New York, NY), 1992.
Spider Kane and the Mystery at Jumbo Nightcrawler's (sequel to *Spider Kane and the Mystery under the May-Apple*), illustrated by Victoria Chess, Knopf (New York, NY), 1993.
Molly and the Prince, illustrated by Elizabeth Sayles, Knopf (New York, NY), 1994.
Rocking Horse Christmas, illustrated by Ned Bittinger, Scholastic (New York, NY), 1997.
Happy Birthday, America, illustrated by Peter Catalanotto, Roaring Brook Press (Brookfield, CT), 2003.

YOUNG-ADULT NOVELS

Run, Run, As Fast As You Can, Dial (New York, NY), 1982.
Love Always, Blue, Dial (New York, NY), 1984.
Best Wishes, Joe Brady, Dial (New York, NY), 1984.
Last One Home, Dial (New York, NY), 1986.

NONFICTION

The Story of Christopher Columbus: Admiral of the Ocean Sea, illustrated by Stephen Marchesi, Dell (New York, NY), 1987, reprinted, Gareth Stevens Publishing (Milwaukee, WI), 1997.
The Many Lives of Benjamin Franklin, Dial (New York, NY), 1990.
George Washington: Leader of a New Nation, Dial (New York, NY), 1991.
The Life of Jesus in Masterpieces of Art, Viking (New York, NY), 1998.
One World, Many Religions: The Ways We Worship, Knopf, 1996, revised and enlarged edition, 2002.

"MAGIC TREE HOUSE" SERIES

Dinosaurs before Dark, illustrated by Sal Murdocca, Random House (New York, NY), 1992.
The Knight at Dawn, illustrated by Sal Murdocca, Random House (New York, NY), 1993.

Mummies in the Morning, illustrated by Sal Murdocca, Random House (New York, NY), 1993.

Pirates Past Noon, illustrated by Sal Murdocca, Random House (New York, NY), 1994.

Night of the Ninjas, illustrated by Sal Murdocca, Random House (New York, NY), 1995.

Afternoon on the Amazon, illustrated by Sal Murdocca, Random House (New York, NY), 1995.

Sunset of the Sabertooth, illustrated by Sal Murdocca, Random House (New York, NY), 1996.

Midnight on the Moon, illustrated by Sal Murdocca, Random House (New York, NY), 1996.

Dolphins at Daybreak, illustrated by Sal Murdocca, Random House (New York, NY), 1997.

Ghost Town at Sundown, illustrated by Sal Murdocca, Random House (New York, NY), 1997.

Lions at Lunchtime, illustrated by Sal Murdocca, Random House (New York, NY), 1998.

Polar Bears past Bedtime, illustrated by Sal Murdocca, Random House (New York, NY), 1998.

Vacation under the Volcano, illustrated by Sal Murdocca, Random House (New York, NY), 1998.

Day of the Dragon King, illustrated by Sal Murdocca, Random House (New York, NY), 1998.

Viking Ships at Sunrise, illustrated by Sal Murdocca, Random House (New York, NY), 1998.

Hour of the Olympics, illustrated by Sal Murdocca, Random House (New York, NY), 1998.

Tigers at Twilight, illustrated by Sal Murdocca, Random House (New York, NY), 1999.

Tonight on the Titanic, illustrated by Sal Murdocca, Random House (New York, NY), 1999.

Buffalo before Breakfast, illustrated by Sal Murdocca, Random House (New York, NY), 1999.

Civil War on Sunday, illustrated by Sal Murdocca, Random House (New York, NY), 2000.

Dingoes at Dinnertime, illustrated by Sal Murdocca, Random House (New York, NY), 2000.

Revolutionary War on Wednesday, illustrated by Sal Murdocca, Random House (New York, NY), 2000.

Earthquake in the Early Morning, illustrated by Sal Murdocca, Random House (New York, NY), 2001.

Twister on Tuesday, illustrated by Sal Murdocca, Random House (New York, NY), 2001.

Good Morning, Gorillas, illustrated by Sal Murdocca, Random House (New York, NY), 2002.

Stage Fright on a Summer Night, illustrated by Sal Murdocca, Random House (New York, NY), 2002.

Thanksgiving on Thursday, illustrated by Sal Murdocca, Random House (New York, NY), 2002.

High Tide in Hawaii, illustrated by Sal Murdocca, Random House (New York, NY), 2003.

"MERLIN MISSIONS" SERIES ("MAGIC TREE HOUSE" BOOKS)

Christmas in Camelot, illustrated by Sal Murdocca, Random House (New York, NY), 2002.

Haunted Castle on Hallow's Eve, illustrated by Sal Murdocca, Random House (New York, NY), 2003.

Summer of the Sea Serpent, illustrated by Sal Murdocca, Random House (New York, NY), 2004.

"MAGIC TREE HOUSE RESEARCH GUIDE" SERIES

(With husband, Will Osborne) *Dinosaurs: A Nonfiction Companion to "Dinosaurs before Dark,"* illustrated by Sal Murdocca, Random House (New York, NY), 2000.

(With Will Osborne) *Knights and Castles: A Nonfiction Companion to "The Knight at Dawn,"* illustrated by Sal Murdocca, Random House (New York, NY), 2000.

(With Will Osborne) *Mummies and Pyramids: A Nonfiction Companion to "Mummies in the Morning,"* illustrated by Sal Murdocca, Random House (New York, NY), 2001.

(With Will Osborne) *Pirates: A Nonfiction Companion to "Pirates Past Noon,"* illustrated by Sal Murdocca, Random House (New York, NY), 2001.

(With Will Osborne) *Rain Forests: A Nonfiction Companion to "Afternoon on the Amazon,"* illustrated by Sal Murdocca, Random House (New York, NY), 2001.

(With Will Osborne) *Titanic: A Nonfiction Companion to "Tonight on the Titanic,"* illustrated by Sal Murdocca, Random House (New York, NY), 2002.

(With Will Osborne) *Space: A Nonfiction Companion to "Midnight on the Moon,"* illustrated by Sal Murdocca, Random House (New York, NY), 2002.

(With Will Osborne) *Dolphins and Sharks: A Nonfiction Companion to "Dolphins at Daybreak,"* illustrated by Sal Murdocca, Random House (New York, NY), 2003.

(With Will Osborne) *Twisters and Other Terrible Storms: A Nonfiction Companion to "Twister on Tuesday,"* illustrated by Sal Murdocca, Random House (New York, NY), 2003.

(With sister, Natalie Pope Boyce) *The Revolutionary War: A Nonfiction Companion to "Revolutionary War on Wednesday,"* illustrated by Sal Murdocca, Random House (New York, NY), 2004.

(With Natalie Pope Boyce) *Ancient Greece and the Olympics: A Nonfiction Companion to "Hour of the Olympics,"* illustrated by Sal Murdocca, Random House (New York, NY), 2004.

HISTORICAL FICTION

Standing in the Light: The Captive Diary of Catherine Carey Logan, Delaware Valley, Pennsylvania, 1763 ("Dear America" series), Scholastic (New York, NY), 1998.

Adaline Falling Star, Scholastic (New York, NY), 2000.

My Secret War: The World War II Diary of Madeline Beck, Long Island, New York, 1941 ("Dear America" series), Scholastic (New York, NY), 2000.

"MY AMERICA" SERIES; HISTORICAL FICTION

My Brother's Keeper: Virginia's Diary, Gettysburg, Pennsylvania, 1863, Scholastic (New York, NY), 2000.

After the Rain, Scholastic (New York, NY), 2002.

(With Will Osborne) *A Time to Dance,* Scholastic (New York, NY), 2003.

RETELLINGS

Beauty and the Beast, illustrated by Winslow Pinney Pels, Scholastic (New York, NY), 1987.

Pandora's Box, illustrated by Lisa Amoroso, Scholastic (New York, NY), 1987.

(With Will Osborne) *Jason and the Argonauts,* illustrated by Steve Sullivan, Scholastic (New York, NY), 1988.

(With Will Osborne) *The Deadly Power of Medusa,* illustrated by Steve Sullivan, Scholastic (New York, NY), 1988.

Favorite Greek Myths, illustrated by Troy Howell, Scholastic, 1989.

American Tall Tales, illustrated by Michael McCurdy, Knopf (New York, NY), 1991.

Mermaid Tales from around the World, illustrated by Troy Howell, Scholastic (New York, NY), 1993.

Haunted Waters (based on the German fairy tale "Undine"), Candlewick Press (Cambridge, MA), 1994.

Favorite Norse Myths, illustrated by Troy Howell, Scholastic (New York, NY), 1996.

Favorite Medieval Tales, illustrated by Troy Howell, Scholastic (New York, NY), 1998.

Kate and the Beanstalk, illustrated by Giselle Potter, Atheneum (New York, NY), 2000.

The Brave Little Seamstress, illustrated by Giselle Potter, Atheneum (New York, NY), 2002.

New York's Bravest, illustrated by Steve Johnson and Lou Fancher, Knopf (New York, NY), 2002.

"TALES FROM 'THE ODYSSEY'" SERIES; RETELLINGS

The One-Eyed Giant, illustrated by Troy Howell, Hyperion Books (New York, NY), 2002.

The Land of the Dead, illustrated by Troy Howell, Hyperion Books (New York, NY), 2002.

Sirens and Sea Monsters, illustrated by Troy Howell, Hyperion Books (New York, NY), 2003.

The Grey-Eyed Goddess, illustrated by Troy Howell, Hyperion Books (New York, NY), 2003.

Return to Ithaca, illustrated by Troy Howell, Hyperion Books (New York, NY), 2004.

Contributor to books, including *When I Was Your Age: Original Stories about Growing Up,* edited by Amy Ehrlich, Candlewick Press (Cambridge, MA), 1996. Contributor of introductions to *Treasure Island,* by Robert Louis Stevenson, Scholastic (New York, NY), 2002, and *Tenggren's Golden Tales from the Arabian Nights,* retold and illustrated by Gustaf Tenggren, Golden Books/Random House (New York, NY), 2003. Osborne's books have been translated into more than fifteen languages.

ADAPTATIONS: The first twenty-three volumes of the "Magic Tree House" series were released individually as book and audio cassette combination packages, read by the author, by Random House and Listening Library, 1999-2003. The series also has been released on audio cassette in collected editions: *Magic Tree House Collection,* Books One through Four, Imagination Studio, 2000; Books Five through Eight, Imagination Studio, 2001; Books Nine through Twelve, Imagination Studio, 2001; Books Thirteen through Sixteen, Listening Library, 2002; Books Seventeen through Twenty, Imagination Studio, 2002; and Books Twenty-one through Twenty-four, Imagination Studio, 2002. The first eight books were released on compact disc as *Magic Tree House Gift Edition,* 2001, which also includes an interview with Osborne. *The Magic Tree House CD Edition* includes the next eight volumes of the series and was released by Random House, 2002. The first eight volumes of the "Magic Tree House" series were released on audio cassette in two-packs by Imagination Studio, 2003. *Adaline Falling Star* was released on audio cassette by Random House, 2001. *American Tall Tales* was released on audio cassette by Audio Bookshelf, 2003. *Tales from "The Odyssey"* was released on two audio cassettes by HarperAudio, 2003. *Standing in the Light: The Captive Diary of Catherine Carey Logan, Delaware Valley, Pennsylvania, 1763* was made into a television movie by Home Box Office.

WORK IN PROGRESS: Winter of the White Wizard, the fourth volume of the "Merlin Missions" series.

SIDELIGHTS: A popular, prolific author for children and young adults, Mary Pope Osborne is considered a versatile writer who has contributed successfully to many of the genres encompassed by juvenile literature. Directing her books to an audience that ranges from preschool through high school, she has written picture books, realistic fiction, historical fiction, young-adult novels, nonfiction, and retellings, and has edited collections of stories, poetry, and songs. Osborne is also the creator of several series and related volumes. She is perhaps best known for writing the "Magic Tree House" books, a best-selling, multi-volume collection of time-travel fantasies for primary graders. In these works, in which brother and sister Jack and Annie enter an enchanted tree house and have adventures in the past, present, and future, Osborne blends exciting plots with historical and scientific facts while emphasizing the power of books and reading. The author also has created two additional series to accompany her "Magic Tree House" volumes. The first of these, the "Merlin Mission" series, features stories about Jack and Annie that are inspired by myths and legends and are twice as long as their counterparts in the original series. With her husband, Will, a writer who also is an actor, playwright, and theater director, Osborne created the "Magic Tree House Research Guide" series, a collection of informational books that serve as companion volumes to several of the fictional titles in the main series. In addition, Osborne is the author of three volumes in the "My America" series, historical fiction in diary form about a young girl who witnesses the Battle of Gettysburg in 1863 and writes about both it and the aftermath of the Civil War; two stories about Sheriff Mo, an amiable beaver who makes friends with the raccoons, frogs, and mice in his pond community; two detective tales for early readers that feature Spider Kane, a brilliant arachnid sleuth who also is a talented jazz clarinetist; picture-book retellings from *The Odyssey* by the ancient Greek writer Homer; collaborations with Will Osborne on two episodes from Ovid's *Metamorphoses,* the adventures of Jason and his Argonauts and the slaying of the monster Medusa by the warrior Perseus; retellings of myths and legends from America, Greece, and Norway, among other international sources; and collections of mermaid tales and stories and poems from the Middle Ages.

In addition to her series books, Osborne has written several distinguished individual volumes in the genres of fiction and nonfiction. As a biographer, she has described the lives of Jesus, Christopher Columbus, George Washington, and Benjamin Franklin; in her fiction, Osborne also includes real-life characters such as Plato, Squanto, William Shakespeare, and Clara Barton, in addition to Columbus and Washington. The author is well known for writing *One World, Many Religions: The Ways We Worship,* an informational book that explains the tenets of seven major religions—Buddhism, Christianity, Confucianism, Hinduism, Islam, Judaism, and Taoism. Osborne brings a feminist perspective to several of her books. Her original works often depict the journeys, both physical and emotional, that are undertaken by female characters. As a reteller, Osborne has retold the familiar tales "Beauty and the Beast" and "Pandora's Box" and the less familiar German fairy tale "Undine." Her retellings of "Jack and the Beanstalk" and "The Brave Little Tailor" feature clever young women as protagonists rather than the males who appear in the traditional versions. For her collection *American Tall Tales,* Osborne created Sally Ann Thunder Ann Whirlwind, a composite of several characters, to supplement male figures like Paul Bunyan, Davy Crockett, and John Henry.

As a literary stylist, Osborne is noted for writing clear, lively, well-paced prose in both her stories and her informational books. She often includes forewords and afterwords in her books that provide historical context and personal information about her research and writing. As a creator of fiction, Osborne is praised for her delineation of and sensitivity to her characters as well as for her sympathetic exploration of the effects of war, racism, divorce, mental illness, and other issues on young people. As a writer of nonfiction, Osborne is commended for her scholarship and for bringing out the humanity of her subjects. Although she has been criticized for creating some books that are trite and predictable, Osborne generally is recognized as a writer of range and ability, one who truly understands children and what appeals to them. A reviewer in *Publishers Weekly* stated that Osborne "has great talent for presenting scientific facts and historic detail in an exciting, fast-paced format for kids," while Deborah Hopkinson of *BookPage* concluded, "There's definitely something magical about Mary Pope Osborne."

Born in Fort Sill, Oklahoma, Osborne is the daughter of William P. Pope, a retired colonel in the United States Army, and Barnette Dickens Pope, a homemaker; the author has used her mother's maiden name as the surname for some of her characters. Osborne has a twin brother, a younger brother, and an older sister, Nancy, who collaborated with her on *The Revolutionary War: A Nonfiction Companion to "Revolutionary War on Wednesday,"* a volume in the "Magic Tree House Research Guide" series. As a young girl, Osborne moved a great deal with her family. She lived in Salzburg, Austria, for three years as well as in Oklahoma, in Florida, and in four different army posts in Virginia and North Carolina.

Although moving was not traumatic for Osborne because of the close relationship that she shared with her family, other things were. She noted in *School Library Journal,* "I was very terrified as a child. I suffered from every possible kind of fear. I would imagine, constantly, terrible things happening to myself or my family. I was always trying to fight against that." In her writings, as she told *School Library Journal,* she hopes to provide young girls with "female heroes," characters she believes would have helped curb her anxieties as a child. Writing on the "Magic Tree House" Web site about her literary influences, Osborne noted, "I read all kinds of books when I was little. But I especially loved the 'Little House on the Prairie' books [by Laura Ingalls Wilder], *The Little Princess* [by Frances Hodgson Burnett], and the 'Uncle Wiggily Stories' [by Howard R. Garis]. I also loved a big thick book of Bible stories that was written in an old-fashioned style and took me a really long time to read." Writing on the Barnes & Noble Web site about the latter title, *Egermeier's Bible Story Book* by Elsie E. Egermeier, Osborne recalled, "By the time I was eleven, I'd read Egermeier's Bible stories three times. My love for old stories and Western history began with this book, as well as a thirst to learn about the different cultures and religions of the period." When asked on the "Magic Tree House" Web site if the characters in her best-known series are based on real people, Osborne replied, "My characters are a combination of real people and my imagination and research. My two brothers and I used to pretend lots of things together—that we were cowboys, soldiers, etc. That's the basis for the whole series."

When she was fifteen, Osborne's father retired from the army and moved their family to a small town in North Carolina. Osborne found that she missed the adventure and changing scenery of her early years. She found these things at the local community theater, which was located a block from her home. Osborne began to spend all of her free time in the theater; she acted in plays and also worked backstage. After graduating from high school, she decided to major in drama at the University of North Carolina—Chapel Hill. However, in her junior year, she discovered the world of mythology and became interested in studying comparative religions. She switched her major to religion and immersed herself in learning about other cultures. After receiving her bachelor's degree in 1971, Osborne traveled abroad for a year. She went back to Europe, lived in a cave in Crete for six weeks, and joined a group of young Europeans who were heading to the East. With this group, Osborne visited sixteen Asian countries, including Iraq, Iran, India, Nepal, Afghanistan, Turkey, Lebanon, Syria, and Pakistan. She encountered several dangerous situations, like an earthquake in northern Afghanistan and a riot in Kabul. Osborne wrote on the Web site for the Children's Book Council that her trip "often was a horrendous journey. Throughout much of the trip, I was terrified. . . . I was constantly ill and constantly frightened." It did not help her situation that the leader of her band of travelers turned out to be, as Osborne said, "insane." When she became infected with blood poisoning in Katmandu, Osborne was forced to end her travels. In a crowded hospital ward of Nepalese women, none of whom spoke English, she discovered J. R. R. Tolkien's fantasy trilogy *The Lord of the Rings,* a book that her traveling companions had kept in their van. Osborne noted, "For two weeks, all I did was read and sleep. . . . By the time I finished the trilogy, . . . I had the emotional strength to start my long journey home." Osborne concluded, "That journey irrevocably changed me. Experience was gathered that serves as a reference point every day of my life. I encountered worlds of light and worlds of darkness—and planted seeds of the imagination that led directly to my being an author of children's books."

After returning to the United States, Osborne recovered from her illness and headed out again. She moved to Monterey, California, and worked as a medical assistant. In 1974, she moved to Washington, DC, and worked as a travel agent, specializing in tours of Russia and Eastern Europe. Osborne moved to New York City in 1975 and began to work with the Russian Travel Bureau. In 1976, she married Will Osborne, with whom she had fallen in love when she saw him in the lead role of a musical about the outlaw Jesse James. The day after their wedding, the couple took off on a theater tour. While on the road, Osborne began to write. She also worked a variety of jobs when not traveling with theatrical productions: for example, Osborne was a drama teacher at a nursing home in the Bronx and also worked with runaway teens, as a bartender, and as an assistant editor of a magazine for children. In 1979, she began the story that would become her first published book, the semi-autobiographical young-adult novel *Run, Run, As Fast As You Can,* which was published in 1982.

In *Run, Run, As Fast As You Can,* eleven-year-old Hallie Pines, a girl from a military family, moves to Virginia when her father retires. Hallie wants to join the three most popular girls at her new school; at first, the girls encourage her, but then they reject her cruelly. For comfort, Hallie turns to her eight-year-old brother Mickey, but soon discovers that he has terminal cancer. By facing the clique's rejection of her as well as her brother's death, Hallie is forced to reexamine her values. Writing in *Horn Book,* Karen M. Klockner commented that Osborne "writes naturally about the interaction among children and of children with adults." Writing in the *Times Literary Supplement,* Judith Elkin said, "The portrait of a girl caught up in the difficult age between childhood and adolescence . . . is well drawn," while Margery Fisher of *Growing Point* concluded that the work "has a candour and directness which are refreshing."

Osborne's second novel for young people, *Love Always, Blue,* is a work that addresses the difficulties that children experience when their parents separate; it also deals with the subject of mental illness. Fourteen-year-old Blue Murray is a girl who lives with her mother, an upwardly mobile socialite, in North Carolina while her father, an aspiring playwright, lives in New York City's Greenwich Village. Blue blames her mom for the separation, discounting her explanation that her husband was extremely hard to live with. After a series of encounters with her mother, Blue is allowed to visit her dad in New York. During their time together, Dad's emotional problems come to the fore, and Blue finds it hard to deal with his depression. Although she meets a nice young man and likes being in the Village, Blue decides to go home early, and her father agrees to get therapy. Writing in *School Library Journal,* Denise L. Moll commented, "This one is much better than many in the plethora of dealing-with-divorce titles." Although she called the structure of Osborne's story weak, Zena Sutherland of *Bulletin of the Center for Children's Books* dubbed *Love Always, Blue* "perceptive in its delineation of the complexity of human relationships." Ilene Cooper of *Booklist* deemed the novel "an engrossing story of family relationships that will give young people a perception about adult depression." Osborne also is the creator of two additional contemporary YA novels, *Best Wishes, Joe Brady,* the story of the romance between eighteen-year-old Sunny Dickens and the title character, a former soap-opera actor who is starring in a dinner theater production in her North Carolina hometown, and *Last One Home,* which describes twelve-year-old Bailey's struggles following her parents' divorce, her father's projected remarriage, and her brother's departure for the service.

In 1992, Osborne produced the first of her "Magic Tree House" books, *Dinosaurs before Dark.* The volume introduces eight-year-old Jack, an inquisitive boy who also is a careful planner and researcher, and seven-year-old Annie, who is intrepid and impetuous. The siblings live in the fictional town of Frog Creek, Pennsylvania. One day, the pair go out into the woods near their home and discover a tree house filled with books. The tree house belongs to Morgan le Fay, a sorceress who is the fairy sister of King Arthur and who, in the "Magic Tree House" series, is the head librarian of Camelot. Jack and Annie find that by reading one of le Fay's books, looking at an illustration, and making a wish, they can be transported to the time and place that the page depicts. The children travel to a wide variety of periods and locations, including prehistory in the initial story. In subsequent volumes, Jack and Annie go to such places as medieval and Elizabethan England; ancient Egypt, Greece, Ireland, and Rome; the Old West; feudal Japan; America during the Revolutionary and Civil Wars; the ocean; and outer space. Accompanied on some of their adventures by Teddy, an enchanted dog who actually is a magician, Jack and Annie are given various assignments to complete by Morgan le Fay; these assignments, often riddles that the children must decipher, include quests to find books from ancient libraries so that they can be preserved in Camelot. Through their adventures, which often involving helping other people or animals, the siblings meet such individuals as knights, ninjas, mummies, pirates, cowboys, Vikings, and cave people; in addition, they interact with well-known historical figures, such as nurse Clara Barton in *Civil War on Sunday* and playwright William Shakespeare in *Stage Fright on a Summer Night*. Characteristically, Jack and Annie find themselves in precarious situations, although some of them have humor or panache. The duo face a saber-toothed tiger, a hungry shark, an African gorilla, an Indian tiger, and vampire bats. In addition, the siblings find themselves in Pompeii before the eruption of Mount Vesuvius, in San Francisco during the Great Earthquake, and on the *Titanic* during its fateful voyage. No matter what they confront, the children, who each grow a year older over the course of the series, conquer their fears, act bravely, learn from their experiences (Jack always takes copious notes), and return home safely in time for dinner.

The "Magic Tree House" series, which has sold more than twelve million copies, is extremely popular with both children and adults. Children enjoy the exciting stories—for example, approximately two thousand young readers are enrolled in the "Magic Tree House" Fan Club—while teachers often use the books as supplementary reading in their classrooms. In assessing the series, critics have commented on the quick pacing, cliffhanger-style chapter endings, and realistic dialogue as well as on Osborne's consistent creativity and integration of knowledge and imagination. Praising the books as successful combinations of fun, learning, and adventure, reviewers have pointed out that the series excels in inspiring children to read by providing early primary graders with high-quality chapter books that they can absorb easily. By joining Jack and Annie in the Magic Tree House, children learn that books can transport them anywhere, from ancient history to the far-flung future. In addition, the series is noted for teaching children about history and geography and for introducing them to new facts and vocabulary words. Young readers also learn about research and note-taking skills, as modeled by Jack; about other cultures; and about the value of literature, community, and the natural world. Although some critics have accused the series of being contrived, most consider it to be both educational and entertaining, a valuable way for children to delight in learning. Writing in *The Continuum Encyclopedia of Children's Literature*, Mary Ariail Broughton stated, "The books in this collection, although fiction, contain a lot of factual information, making them useful and enjoyable supplements for thematic studies." Writing in *Children's Literature*, Lois Rubin Gross explained that the series "provides nicely paced excitement for young readers."

Published in 1996, *One World, Many Religions: The Ways We Worship* is considered one of Osborne's most accomplished nonfiction titles. In this work, the author uses essay-styled chapters to describe the history, beliefs, traditions, and rituals of the faiths that she represents. Calling the work an "excellent source for religious shelves," Ilene Cooper of *Booklist* reported that Osborne "covers the world's major religions, introducing them in a way that will appeal to young readers." Elizabeth Bush of *Bulletin of the Center for Children's Books* reflected, "This exceptionally handsome overview offers middle graders a thoughtful overview of world religions." A critic in *Newsweek* concluded, "Osborne's clear, precise style serves her subject very well. This book has an unforced dignity that's rare in children's literature." Writing in *BookPage*, Alice Cary called *One World, Many Religions* "a superb new book. . . . Osborne's writing is lucid and informative—full of dignity and respect, managing to strike just the right tone without talking down to young readers or going over their heads." Cary concluded, "Whether you're an atheist, Muslim, Baptist, or anything else, my guess is you'll find the volume not only interesting, but fair to all, with neither biases nor judgments." In 2002, *One World, Many Religions* was reissued in a revised edition in which Osborne expands on her discussion of Islam.

Osborne frequently mixes fiction and historical fact in her works. With *Adaline Falling Star*, a novel for middle graders published in 2000, she was praised for doing so in a particularly memorable way. In this work, the author takes little-known figure Adaline Falling Star Carson, the real daughter of famed frontier scout Kit Carson and his Arapaho wife Singing Wind, and creates a story about her early life. After the death of her mother, eleven-year-old Adaline is sent by her father to live with his cousins in St. Louis so that he can join John Fremont's expedition through the Rocky Mountains. In St. Louis, Adaline is viewed as a halfbreed, a savage who is expected to work as a servant. After being mistreated by her cousins, she pretends to be mute. Adaline's only friend in St. Louis is Caddie, an African girl who works in the kitchen and helps her to escape from her cousins. When Adaline learns that the Fremont expedition is over, she heads to Colorado. On her journey, she meets danger and becomes injured but also makes friends with a stray dog that she feels embodies her mother's spirit. Disguised as a boy, Adaline finds work on a steamboat before being reunited with her father. Compared to Mark Twain's novel *The Adventures of Huckleberry Finn, Adaline Falling Star* generally is considered one of Osborne's most effective works. A reviewer in *Horn Book* observed that in *Adaline Falling Star* Osborne "puts memorable faces on the noble, the well intentioned, and the deceived, all of whom shaped our country's history." Marie Orlando of *School Library Journal* noted, "While this touching and exciting novel will absorb readers from beginning to end, it is the unique writing style that makes it truly extraordinary." A writer in *Publishers Weekly* concluded, "Osborne strikes out in a new direction in this assured novel. . . . Adaline possesses a wisdom marked by an often heartbreaking sense of humor."

In her collection *American Tall Tales,* Osborne introduced readers to Mose Humphreys, a fireman who lived in the 1840s and is often considered America's first urban folk hero. In *New York's Bravest,* published in 2002, she revises her initial account of Mose in a picture-book retelling. In the book, dedicated to the New York City firefighters who gave their lives on September 11, 2001, Osborne draws on both legends and published accounts to create her version of the larger-than-life volunteer fireman. Eight-foot-tall Mose is bigger, stronger, and more courageous than any of his counterparts. One day, he disappears in a hotel fire near the Hudson River and is never seen again. Subsequent rumors place Mose in various locations until he becomes mythic—the very spirit of New York. Writing in *Booklist,* Stephanie Zvirin and Beth Leistensnider claimed readers receive a glimpse "of the courage, selflessness, determination, and danger" contained in the life of a firefighter. A critic in *Kirkus Reviews* said that *New York's Bravest* is a "stirring picture-book tribute to the 343 firefighters who died on that terrible day." A commentator in *Publishers Weekly* concluded, "Past and present combine to stirring effect in this tall tale with real-world reverberations."

In assessing her career, Osborne once wrote, "I feel that the years I spent traveling in Asia, the different jobs I've held, the theater career of my husband, our life in New York among a small community of writers, actors, musicians, and artists, my Southern military background, my family, my editor, my work with runaway teenagers, and my interests in philosophy and mythology have all informed and shaped my work." A visiting lecturer at schools and libraries, she often asks children, teachers, and librarians for their input on the "Magic Tree House" series; for example, they have helped her to decide on titles for her books and have made suggestions as to where Jack and Annie should go next. In a brief autobiography posted on the "KidsReads.com" Web site, Osborne talked about the "Magic Tree House" series and its effect on her: "The contact I now have with children has brought overwhelming joy into my life. I love the letters I get from them and I love reading countless 'Magic Tree House' stories that they've written. I feel as if these kids and I are all exploring the creative process together, using our imaginations plus our reading and writing skills to take us wherever we want to go. This, I tell my fellow authors, is true magic." When asked by Deborah Hopkinson of *BookPage* if she thinks that she will ever tire of writing the "Magic Tree House" books, Osborne replied, "How could I? I get to throw myself into every single subject. Besides I have an incredible audience. . . . How could I disappoint them?"

BIOGRAPHICAL AND CRITICAL SOURCES:

BOOKS

Cullinan, Bernice E., and Diane G. Person, editors, *Continuum Encyclopedia of Children's Literature,* Continuum (New York, NY), 2001.

PERIODICALS

Booklist, April 15, 1984, Ilene Cooper, review of *Love Always, Blue,* p. 750; October 1, 1996, Ilene Cooper, review of *One World, Many Religions: The Ways We Worship,* p. 336; September 1, 2002, Stephanie Zvirin and Beth Leistensnider, review of *New York's Bravest,* p. 115.

Bulletin of the Center for Children's Books, January, 1984, Zena Sutherland, review of *Love Always, Blue,* p. 94; January, 1997, Elizabeth Bush, review of *One World, Many Religions,* p. 183; May 1, 2003, Julie Cummins, review of *Happy Birthday, America,* p. 1605.

Growing Point, January, 1984, Margery Fisher, review of *Run, Run, As Fast As You Can,* p. 4187.

Horn Book, June, 1982, Karen M. Klockner, review of *Run, Run, As Fast As You Can,* pp. 291-292; May, 2000, review of *Adaline Falling Star,* p. 318.

Kirkus Reviews, July 1, 2002, review of *New York's Bravest,* p. 96.

Newsweek, December 2, 1996, review of *One World, Many Religions.*

Publishers Weekly, January 31, 2000, review of *Adaline Falling Star,* p. 108; June 24, 2002, review of *New York's Bravest,* p. 56.

School Library Journal, January, 1984, Denise L. Moll, review of *Love Always, Blue,* p. 88; March, 2000, Marie Orlando, review of *Adaline Falling Star,* pp. 240-241; November, 2000, interview with Mary Pope Osborne, p. 19; July, 2003, Angela J. Reynolds, review of *Sirens and Sea Monsters,* p. 148.

Times Literary Supplement, September 30, 1983, Judith Elkin, review of *Run, Run, As Fast As You Can.*

ONLINE

Barnes & Noble, http://www.barnesandnoble.com/ (May 26, 2003), "Meet the Writers: Mary Pope Osborne."

BookPage, http://www.bookpage.com/ (January, 1997), Alice Cary, review of *One World, Many Religions;* (December, 2001), Deborah Hopkinson, "The Magic of Mary Pope Osborne."

Children's Book Council, http://www.cbcbooks.org/ (May 26, 2003), "Mary Pope Osborne."

Children's Literature, http://www.childrenslit.com/ (May 26, 2003), Lois Rubin Gross, review of *Tonight on the Titanic.*

KidsReads.com, http://www.kidsreads.com/ (May 26, 2003), Shannon Maughan, "Mary Pope Osborne Branches Out with the Magic Tree House," and "Mary Pope Osborne: Author Information."

"Magic Tree House" Home Page, http://www.randomhouse.com/ (May 26, 2003).*

P

PETERSON, Cris 1952-

PERSONAL: Born October 25, 1952, in Minneapolis, MN; daughter of Willard C. (an engineer) and Carmen (a political consultant; maiden name, Fossom) Hoeppner; married Gary Peterson (a dairy farmer), February 10, 1973; children: Ben, Matt, Caroline. *Ethnicity:* "Norwegian/German." *Education:* University of Minnesota, B.S., 1972. *Politics:* Republican. *Religion:* Lutheran. *Hobbies and other interests:* Flower gardening, quilting, knitting, collecting antiques, participating in a variety of sports.

ADDRESSES: Home and office—23250 South Williams Rd., Grantsburg, WI 54840. *Agent*—Karen Klockner, Transatlantic Literary Agency, 72 Glengowan Rd., Toronto, Ontario M4N 1G4, Canada. *E-mail*—fourcubs@grantsburgtelcom.net.

CAREER: Dairy farmer and substitute teacher in Grantsburg, WI, 1973—; insurance agent, Grantsburg, 1986—; Universal Press Syndicate, Kansas City, MO, nationally syndicated columnist, 1992-2000. Local historical society, president, 1974-86; 4-H Club, general leader, 1986-94; Sunday school superintendent, 1993—; new children's literature consultant for regional elementary schools.

MEMBER: International Reading Association, Society of Children's Book Writers and Illustrators.

AWARDS, HONORS: Author of the Month citation, *Highlights for Children,* October, 1989; Science Feature of the Year citation, *Highlights for Children,* 1992, for article "New Dining for Dairy Cows;" Woman's Award for Children's Literature, Ohio Farm Bureau, 1995, for *Extra Cheese, Please!: Mozzarella's Journey from Cow to Pizza,* and for *Harvest Year;* Book of the Year Award, Wisconsin Farm Bureau, 2000, and Woman's Award for Children's Literature, Ohio Farm Bureau, both for *Century Farm: One Hundred Years on a Family Farm;* selected as Woman of the Year, American Women in Agriculture, 2002.

WRITINGS:

Extra Cheese, Please!: Mozzarella's Journey from Cow to Pizza, photographs by Alvis Upitis, Boyds Mills Press (Honesdale, PA), 1994.
Harvest Year, photographs by Alvis Upitis, Boyds Mills Press (Honesdale, PA), 1996.
Horsepower: The Wonder of Draft Horses, photographs by Alvis Upitis, Boyds Mills Press (Honesdale, PA), 1997.
Century Farm: One Hundred Years on a Family Farm, photographs by Alvis Upitis, Boyds Mills Press (Honesdale, PA), 1999.
Amazing Grazing, photographs by Alvis Upitis, Boyds Mills Press (Honesdale, PA), 2002.
Wild Horses: Black Hills Sanctuary, photographs by Alvis Upitis, Boyds Mills Press (Honesdale, PA), 2003.

Also authored "Huckleberry Bookshelf," a weekly children's book column appearing in newspapers nationwide, for Universal Press Syndicate. Contributor of stories and articles, including "New Dining for Dairy Cows," to periodicals such as *Highlights for Children, Cricket,* and others.

WORK IN PROGRESS: A hisory of the North American fur trade; a photo essay on big farm machines.

SIDELIGHTS: Cris Peterson has expanded her multiple roles of dairy farmer, mother, 4-H leader, and teacher into another dimension as the author of picture books that both express her love of farm life and explain facets of it to suburban and urban children. After photographer Alvis Upitis visited the Peterson family's dairy farm in Wisconsin to shoot photographs for a magazine article about century farms, he and Peterson have worked together on picture books about farming and ranching. Peterson's longtime interest in children's books also led her to create and successfully sell a children's book review column, *Huckleberry Bookshelf,* to Universal Press Syndicate, which licensed it for use to newspapers across the nation until 1998. Additionally, for over a decade, Peterson has spoken frequently on reading, writing, history, and farming.

"My writing career began when I gave mouth-to-mouth resuscitation to a newborn calf and I knew I had a good story," Peterson recalled at Boyds Mills Press Web site. "The calf lived. The story sold. Both were named 'Breathless.'" Peterson got the idea for *Extra Cheese, Please!: Mozzarella's Journey from Cow to Pizza,* after attending a writers' workshop in 1988. "I knew I wanted to help kids understand where their food comes from," she stated in *The Bridge.* However, self doubts and her busy daily life on the farm prevented her from developing the story for over two years. Finally Alvis Upitis convinced Peterson to move writing a book higher on her list of things to do, and *Extra Cheese, Please!,* a book that provides children with an inside view of every step in the cheese production process, came about. "Already a self-proclaimed dairy cow expert, I spent a day at our local cheese factory learning the cheese-making process," Peterson noted in *The Bridge.* "I formed the resulting information into a tightly written, somewhat boring text." Boyds Mills Press accepted the idea for publication, but it took another two years of working closely with an editor for Peterson to complete the final version.

First, Peterson had to rewrite the story in her own voice, making it "more personalized" so "a kid in the city" could understand it. Following her editor's suggestion, she wrote the next version as a letter to a child "who had never seen a cow," according to *The Bridge. Extra Cheese, Please!* begins on the author's dairy farm—where Annabelle the cow has a calf and produces milk—and follows each step of the process, including milking the cows, pasteurizing the milk, converting milk into curds and whey, processing these byproducts at the cheese factory, packaging the resulting cheese, and selling it at a retail store for its final destination as part of a pizza. The book also includes a glossary and Peterson's own pizza recipe. Then came the time-consuming task of filling in all the necessary photos with Upitis. In order to create the photo of kids eating pizza for the cover of the book, Peterson cooked a total of twelve pizzas and gave her family indigestion. Despite all the hard work, however, she felt the final product was worth it, and so did reviewers. Among its enthusiasts number *School Library Journal*'s Carolyn Jenks, who called the book "attractive and informative," and *Booklist*'s Kay Weisman, who commented that the "clear, simple text" makes it "an appealing addition to primary farm and nutrition units."

In the process of writing *Extra Cheese, Please!,* Peterson had learned important lessons about writing children's books, skills that brought about her second work, again about the origins of food. In *Harvest Year,* a "very nicely executed photographic essay," to quote Paula M. Fleming of *Catholic Library World,* Peterson tells about a wide variety of crops that are harvested annually throughout the United States. Following a calendar format, she explains when, where, and how crops get from the tree or field. According to Lee Bock of *School Library Journal,* Peterson's "spare and clear [text], with well-chosen details" makes this book "engaging."

Peterson took a broader look at farming in her 1999 title, *Century Farm: One Hundred Years on a Family Farm.* Though Peterson was born and raised in Minnesota, when she married Gary Peterson, she became part of a farming family that had worked the same land for five generations—over one hundred years. For her book, Peterson imagined herself telling the farm's story from her husband's point of view, creating "a distinctly personal story," a *Kirkus Reviews* contributor noted. While the technology used on the farm has changed, and these changes are reflected in the photographs that range from sepia tones from the family album to Upitis's full-color images, an appreciation of the family and the hard work of farming has remained the same over the years. *Booklist*'s Susan Dove Lempke praised Peterson's "smooth, personal, descriptive narrative," while a *Publishers Weekly* critic praised the visual presentation, calling it a "warm volume . . . [with] a pleasing mixture of old and new." In a review for the *Bulletin of the Center for Children's Books,* Janice M. DelNegro praised the visual and textual presentation of the book, remarking on Peterson's "friendly and congenial tone" and the "squeaky clean, wholesome farm setting" portrayed in the illustrations. Eldon Younce of *School Library Journal* found the photo captions "interesting," as well, remarking that they "add even more information" to a work that clearly evinces Peterson's knowledge and appreciation of farming.

For many children, the word "farm" conjures images of animals, like horses. Peterson has created two books about horses, one about these animals in the farm setting, another about the wild horses of the West. Although draft horses no longer play the role they once did on many farms, they are raised for pleasure and still used productively among such technology-eschewing populations as the Amish. Peterson celebrates the draft horse in her title *Horsepower: The Wonder of Draft Horses.* Introducing readers to the three main types of draft horses—Belgians, Clydesdales, and Percherons—she uses "appealing details," to quote Deborah Stevenson of the *Bulletin of the Center for Children's Books.* Peterson covers a range of topics, such as the training of a young foal, shows and competitions, and workaday farm life. Reviewers found much to like about the work. Writing in *School Library Journal,* Maura Bresnahan deemed it a "fine effort," noting that the "short, smoothly written text . . . nicely balances the past and present." Likewise, a *Kirkus Reviews* critic found "fascinating nuggets of draft-horse lore . . . embedded in the simple text," which reminds readers of both the beauty and importance to our nation of these gentle giants.

In *Wild Horses: Black Hills Sanctuary,* on the other hand, the author takes a look at the wild mustangs at the Black Hills Sanctuary in western South Dakota. Peterson explains how "cowboy-conservationist" Dayton Hyde purchased 11,000 acres of range in 1980 and created this preserve, where rescued mustangs are free to live out their lives in a natural state. According to *School Library Journal* reviewer Carol Schene, the "sparse, flowing text melds with vivid color photos to capture the beauty of these creatures." Writing in *Publishers Weekly,* a contributor claimed that Peterson and Upitis again had created "another eye-catching story of unusual interest."

Crucial to any ungulate, wild or tame, is fodder, a topic that is the focus of Peterson's *Amazing Grazing.* In this "accessible title," to use *School Library Journal* reviewer Carolyn Janssen's description, Peterson describes the environmentally sound practices of three Montana cattle ranchers. Remarking that little has been written for children on this topic, *Booklist*'s Helen Rosenberg complimented author and illustrator, respectively, on the "cleary written text" and "beautifully formatted color photos" presented in *Amazing Grazing.*

BIOGRAPHICAL AND CRITICAL SOURCES:

PERIODICALS

Booklist, March 15, 1994, Kay Weisman, review of *Extra Cheese, Please!: Mozzarella's Journey from Cow to Pizza,* pp. 1368-1369; September 15, 1996, Susan DeRonne, review of *Harvest Year,* p. 224; March 1, 1999, Susan Dove Lempke, review of *Century Farm: One Hundred Years on a Family Farm,* p. 1210; April 1, 2002, Helen Rosenberg, review of *Amazing Grazing,* pp. 1322-1323.

Bulletin of the Center for Children's Books, April, 1997, Deborah Stevenson, review of *Horsepower: The Wonder of Draft Horses,* p. 292; March, 1999, Janice M. DelNegro, review of *Century Farm,* p. 253.

Catholic Library World, March, 1997, Paula M. Fleming, review of *Harvest Year,* p. 55; December, 2001, Rosanne Steitz, review of *Horsepower,* p. 133.

Farm Journal, December, 2002, Pamela Henderson, "Read'em and Reap," review of *Amazing Grazing,* p. S-1.

Horn Book, 1999, review of *Century Farm.*

Kirkus Reviews, February 1, 1997, review of *Horsepower,* p. 226; February 1, 1999, review of *Century Farm,* p. 227.

Knight Ridder/Tribune News Service, March 9, 1994, Cathy Collison, review of *Extra Cheese Please!*

Plays, May, 2001, review of *Horsepower,* p. 69.

Publishers Weekly, February 1, 1999, review of *Century Farm,* p. 85; December 9, 2002, review of *Wild Horses: Black Hills Sanctuary,* p. 84.

Reading Teacher, November, 1997, review of *Harvest Year,* pp. 256-257; October, 1998, review of *Horsepower,* p. 168.

School Library Journal, April, 1994, Carolyn Jenks, review of *Extra Cheese, Please!,* pp. 121-122; November, 1996, Lee Bock, review of *Harvest*

Year, p. 117; April, 1997, Maura Bresnahan, review of *Horsepower,* p. 130; April, 1999, Eldon Younce, review of *Century Farm,* p. 122; April, 2002, Carolyn Janssen, review of *Amazing Grazing,* p. 180; March, 2003, Carol Schene, review of *Wild Horses,* p. 223.

ONLINE

Boyds Mills Press Web Site, http://www.boydsmillspress.com/ (September 9, 2003), "Cris Peterson."
Transatlantic Literary Agency, http://www.tla1.com (November 3, 2003), "Cris Peterson."

OTHER

Peterson, Cris, *The Bridge* (publicity newsletter), "Kissing Calves and Birthing Elephants: One Writer's Journey to a Book," Boyds Mills Press (Honesdale, PA), March, 1994.

* * *

PFEIFFER, Janet (B.) 1949-

PERSONAL: Born February 23, 1949, in Brooklyn, NY; daughter of Clayton L. (an electrician) and Rae I. (a secretary; maiden name, Sole) Pfeiffer; married Richard Mazzacca (divorced, April, 1984); married Kenneth R. MacDougall, October 13, 1996; children: (first marriage) Richard, Tonia, Christopher, Donna. *Ethnicity:* "Italian/German." *Education:* Englewood Cliffs College (now St. Peter's College), A.A., 1969. *Religion:* Roman Catholic. *Hobbies and other interests:* Race-walking, photography, music, hiking.

ADDRESSES: Home and office—Pfeiffer Power Seminars, 182 Schoolhouse Rd., Oak Ridge, NJ 07438.

CAREER: Home Maintenance Service, past owner; Pfeiffer Power Seminars, president. Anger management consultant, motivational speaker, and writer; teacher at educational institutions, including Learning Annex; guest on television and radio programs. WGHT-Radio, past cohost of the program *Upward Bound;* Reunion of Hearts: Reconciling and Reconnecting Estranged Families, founder; volunteer with Youth Group Ministries, Rainbows for All God's Children, Visions Adult Group, Chilton Hospital, and Habitat for Humanity; counselor at a shelter for battered women; committee member and keynote speaker for the Week without Violence, sponsored by the national YWCA, 1997; National Police Suicide Foundation, member of support staff; consultant to Hoffman-La Roche and U.S. Postal Service.

AWARDS, HONORS: First place awards, Garden State Writer's Challenge, 1994, for *The Angel and the Gift,* and 1995, for *The Orchids of Gateway Lane;* photography awards; athletic awards include gold medal from a New Jersey state race-walking competition, 1994, as well as gold, silver, and bronze medals in national marathons, 1994-95.

WRITINGS:

The Seedling's Journey, Fairway Press (Lima, OH), 1994.
The Angel and the Gift: A Second Chance, Winston-Derek (Nashville, TN), 1996.
The Orchids of Gateway Lane: Galen's Message of Peace, Winston-Derek (Nashville, TN), 1996.
Jordan's Promise, Winston-Derek (Nashville, TN), 1998.
Dying to Be Safe: Ultimate Solutions to Violence, privately printed, 2001.

Contributor to periodicals, including *Living Solo.*

WORK IN PROGRESS: Clayton's Symphony (tentative title).

SIDELIGHTS: Janet Pfeiffer once commented: "When I was thirty-three years old, after thirteen years of marriage, my husband left me with four young children to raise on my own. Needing an income, but also needing to be at home with my children, I began a very successful business that I ran from home.

"During the years that followed my divorce, my life became increasingly difficult. I began a ten-year battle with bulimia, incurred devastating financial loss due to years of legal battles surrounding my divorce, and suffered estrangement from my children for many years. My self esteem plummeted and depression pulled me deeper into despair.

"However, my faith in God and the ever-present goodness that surrounds us got me through all of this. For more than twenty years I have been involved in all aspects of personal growth, attended workshops and lectures on everything from spirituality to holistic healing to physical fitness, psychic development, and anger management. Not sure of my purpose in life, I continually searched for answers. I wrote *The Seedling's Journey* in 1993. It is the story of a little seedling that ends up inside the crevice of a rock. He complains that life is unfair, but soon learns to be thankful for what he has and to 'grow where he is planted.' At this point, my purpose in life became very clear: God was directing me to where he wanted me to be, and that was to help others find inner peace and harmony with one another.

"After *The Seedling's Journey* was released, I began to do a lot of promotional work and talked extensively about how my life paralleled that of the young seedling. I began lecturing on anger management, conflict resolution, forgiveness, goal-setting, and random acts of kindness. I now have a very successful career as a consultant and motivational speaker.

"I believe that there is good in everyone and everything, and that life is a series of lessons to be learned. Our greatest teacher is pain. The more painful the situation, the greater the lesson. When we learn that lesson, we emerge stronger, wiser, more patient, more loving, and much more understanding.

"Through all of the pain, I learned more about myself than I ever imagined possible. I learned that there was an incredible amount of untapped potential within me and that I needed to discover, develop, and share it with the world. I became excited about creating a very new and successful life for myself.

"I continued my writing and am working on a series of inspirational books for young people and adults. All contain valuable lessons and messages of hope in various aspects of life: cherishing relationships, defeating the enemy by making him your friend, being able to feel a sense of peace and hope when death takes a loved one, and *celebrating* (not merely accepting) the uniqueness and differences within each one of us. All of my stories are taken from my own personal experiences in life that have taught me lessons; all are messages from God.

"I have lived life with a new-found sense of enthusiasm and self-power. In addition to my career in lecturing and writing, I also cohosted my own radio talk show on personal growth issues, facilitated couples in divorce negotiations, and I present ongoing workshops on anger management and more. I have won awards in writing and photography, and I am a former state and national medalist on race-walking competitions. I just celebrated my fifteen-year anniversary of walking no less than twelve miles a day every single day of the year.

"Two of the most influential books in my life have been Mandino's *The Greatest Salesman in the World* and Barbara Sher's *I Can Do Anything if Only I Know What That Is*. These books have helped me to gain control over my own life by making conscious choices to be happy, healthy, peaceful, and successful. I believe, as Barbara puts it, that we are all created with certain gifts and talents and that, when we develop and use these talents for the good of all, we find happiness and success. I believe that God allowed me to experience serious pain and loss in my life so that I could learn the lessons that I now share with many others through my writing and lecturing. I would not trade my life for anyone's."

* * *

PHILLIPS, Bob 1940-

PERSONAL: Born December 25, 1940, in Denver, CO; son of Richard Ross (in sales) and Evelyn (a homemaker; maiden name, East; present surname, Fordham) Phillips; married Pamela Joy MacDonald (a gift shop manager), November 28, 1964; children: Lisa Joy Phillips Ortman, Christine Lynne Phillips Anderson. *Education:* Biola College (now Biola University), B.A., 1964; California State University—Fresno, M.A., 1977; Trinity Seminary, Newburg, IN, Ph.D. *Politics:* Republican. *Religion:* Baptist. *Hobbies and other interests:* Karate, motorcycle riding, exploring caves.

ADDRESSES: Office—Hume Lake Christian Camps, 64144 Hume Lake Rd., Hume Lake, CA 93628.

CAREER: Hume Lake Christian Camps, Hume Lake, CA, assistant director, 1964-74; associate pastor of counseling ministries at a church in Fresno, CA, 1974-78; Fresno Counseling Center, Fresno, staff member, 1978-80; Hume Lake Christian Camps, executive director, 1980—. Licensed marriage, family, and child counselor; Pointman Leadership Institute, executive director.

WRITINGS:

The Great Future Escape, Vision House (Ventura, CA), 1973.

The World's Greatest Collection of Clean Jokes, Vision House (Ventura, CA), 1974.

More Good Clean Jokes, Harvest House (Eugene, OR), 1974.

The Last of the Good Clean Jokes, Harvest House (Eugene, OR), 1975.

Redi-Reference, Harvest House (Eugene, OR), 1975.

(With Ken Poure) *Praise Is a Three-Letter Word,* Regal Books (Glendale, CA), 1975.

The All-American Joke Book, Harvest House (Eugene, OR), 1976.

Lots o' Laughs, Fleming Revell (Old Tappan, NJ), 1976.

(Editor, with Tim LaHaye) *The Act of Marriage,* Zondervan (Grand Rapids, MI), 1976.

(Editor, with Judy Messer) *To Know Him Is to Love Him,* Beta Books (San Diego, CA), 1976.

A Time to Laugh, Harvest House (Eugene, OR), 1977.

The Pre-Marital Workbook, Harvest House (Eugene, OR), 1977.

How Can I Be Sure? A Pre-Marriage Inventory, Harvest House (Eugene, OR), 1978.

A Humorous Look at Love and Marriage, Harvest House (Eugene, OR), 1981.

(With Tim LaHaye) *Anger Is a Choice,* Zondervan (Grand Rapids, MI), 1982.

The World's Greatest Collection of Heavenly Humor, Harvest House (Eugene, OR), 1982.

(With Charlie Tremendous Jones) *Wit and Wisdom,* Harvest House (Eugene, OR), 1985.

The Return of the Good Clean Jokes, Harvest House (Eugene, OR), 1986.

(With Charlie Tremendous Jones) *Humor Is Tremendous,* Tyndale (Wheaton, IL), 1988.

The Best of the Good Clean Jokes, Harvest House (Eugene, OR), 1989.

The Delicate Art of Dancing with Porcupines: Learning to Appreciate the Finer Points of Others, Regal Books (Glendale, CA), 1989.

The World's Greatest Collection of Daffy Definitions [and] *The World's Greatest Collection of Riddles,* Harvest House (Eugene, OR), 1989.

The All-New Clean Joke Book, Harvest House (Eugene, OR), 1990.

Good Clean Jokes for Kids, Harvest House (Eugene, OR), 1991.

Powerful Thinking for Powerful Living, Harvest House (Eugene, OR), 1991.

Awesome Good Clean Jokes for Kids, Harvest House (Eugene, OR), 1992.

Bob Phillips' Encyclopedia of Good Clean Jokes, Harvest House (Eugene, OR), 1992.

In Pursuit of Bible Trivia, two volumes, Harvest House (Eugene, OR), 1992, published as *The Ultimate Bible Trivia Challenge,* 1992.

Redi-Reference Daily Bible Reading Plan, Harvest House (Eugene, OR), 1992.

Bible Brainteasers: Heavenly Fun, Harvest House (Eugene, OR), 1993.

Friendship, Love, and Laughter: Inspirational Quotes to Live By, Harvest House (Eugene, OR), 1993.

Loony Good Clean Jokes for Kids, illustrated by Norm Daniels, Harvest House (Eugene, OR), 1993.

Phillips' Book of Great Thoughts and Funny Sayings, Tyndale (Wheaton, IL), 1993.

The Best of the Good Clean Jokes Perpetual Calendar, Harvest House (Eugene, OR), 1993.

Ultimate Good Clean Jokes for Kids, Harvest House (Eugene, OR), 1993.

Wacky Good Clean Jokes for Kids, illustrated by Norm Daniels, Harvest House (Eugene, OR), 1993.

Crazy Good Clean Jokes for Kids, Harvest House (Eugene, OR), 1994.

Goofy Good Clean Jokes for Kids!, Harvest House (Eugene, OR), 1994.

The Awesome Book of Bible Trivia, Harvest House (Eugene, OR), 1994.

The Great Bible Challenge, Harvest House (Eugene, OR), 1994.

The Unofficial Liberal Joke Book: For the Politically Incorrect, illustrated by Nate Owens, Harvest House (Eugene, OR), 1994.

More Awesome Good Clean Jokes for Kids, Harvest House (Eugene, OR), 1995.

Nutty Good Clean Jokes for Kids, Harvest House (Eugene, OR), 1995.

(With Michael Reagan) *The All-American Quote Book,* Harvest House (Eugene, OR), 1995.

The Bible Olympics, Harvest House (Eugene, OR), 1995.

The World's Greatest Collection of Knock-Knock Jokes, Barbour (Uhrichsville, OH), 1995.

What to Do until the Psychiatrist Comes: How to Counsel Yourself and Others, Harvest House (Eugene, OR), 1995.

(With Steve Russo) *Wild and Woolly Clean Jokes for Kids,* Harvest House (Eugene, OR), 1995.

Jest Another Good Clean Joke Book, Harvest House (Eugene, OR), 1996.

The World's All-Time Best Collection of Good Clean Jokes, Galahad Books (New York, NY), 1996.

Tricks, Stunts, and Good Clean Fun, Harvest House (Eugene, OR), 1996.

Sillier Stunts and Terrific Tricks for Kids, Harvest House (Eugene, OR), 1997.

Silly Stunts and Terrific Tricks for Kids, Harvest House (Eugene, OR), 1997.

(With Steve Russo) *Squeaky Clean Jokes for Kids,* Harvest House (Eugene, OR), 1997.

The Star Spangled Quote Book, Harvest House (Eugene, OR), 1997.

Totally Cool Clean Jokes for Kids, Harvest House (Eugene, OR), 1997.

(With Howard Hendricks) *Values, Virtues, and Great Thoughts,* Questar Publishers (Sisters, OR), 1997.

The Best Ever Book of Good Clean Jokes, Galahad Books (New York, NY), 1998.

Over the Hill and On a Roll, Harvest House (Eugene, OR), 1998.

Awesome Animal Jokes for Kids!, Harvest House (Eugene, OR), 1998.

The World's Best Collection of Great Games, Harvest House (Eugene, OR), 1998.

The World's Most Crazy, Wacky, and Goofy Good Clean Jokes for Kids, Galahad Books (New York, NY), 1999.

The World's Greatest Knock-Knock Jokes for Kids, Harvest House (Eugene, OR), 2000.

Phillips' Collection of Awesome Quotations, Harvest House (Eugene, OR), 2001.

What to Do until the Psychiatrist Comes: Controlling Your Emotions, before They Control You, Harvest House (Eugene, OR), 2001.

Contributor to books, including *The Big Book of Questions and Answers: The Bible As Told in the Old Testament,* edited by David M. Howard, Jr., Publications International (Lincolnwood, IL), 1992.

Kevin Phillips

SIDELIGHTS: Author of over sixty books, Bob Phillips once commented: "I am what is called a 'born again Christian.' I feel that as a Christian I have a responsibility to be an influence in my society with regard to the teachings of Jesus Christ. My writing is varied, from clean joke books to religious and family topics, and in all of these I have endeavored to carry forth my moral convictions. Martin Luther said, 'If you want to influence the world—pick up your pen.' I hope that in some small way my writings will influence my world for good."

BIOGRAPHICAL AND CRITICAL SOURCES:

PERIODICALS

Voice of Youth Advocates, April, 1993, p. 57.

* * *

PHILLIPS, Kevin (Price) 1940-

PERSONAL: Born November 30, 1940, in New York, NY; son of William Edward (a state administrator) and Dorothy (Price) Phillips; married Martha Henderson (Republican staff director of the U.S. House of Representatives Budget Committee), September 23, 1968;

children: Andrew, Alexander. *Education:* Colgate University, A.B., 1961; Harvard University, LL.B., 1964; also attended University of Edinburgh, 1959-60. *Politics:* Republican. *Religion:* Protestant.

ADDRESSES: *Home*—5115 Moorland Rd., Bethesda, MD 20014. *Office*—American Political Research Corp., 7316 Wisconsin Ave., Bethesda, MD 20014.

CAREER: Administrative assistant to Congressman Paul Fino, 1964-68; special assistant to campaign manager of "Nixon for President" committee, 1968-69; special assistant to U.S. Attorney General, 1969-70; American Political Research Corp., Bethesda, MD, president, 1971—. Commentator on National Public Radio, CBS Radio Network, and CBS Television.

MEMBER: New York Bar Association, Washington DC Bar Association, Phi Beta Kappa, Pi Sigma Alpha.

AWARDS, HONORS: National Book Critics Circle award nomination, 1991, for *The Politics of Rich and Poor: Wealth and the American Electorate in the Reagan Aftermath.*

WRITINGS:

The Emerging Republican Majority, Arlington House (New Rochelle, NY), 1969.
(With Paul H. Blackman) *Electoral Reform and Voter Participation: Federal Registration, a False Remedy for Voter Apathy,* American Enterprise Institute for Public Policy Research (Washington, DC), 1975.
Mediacracy: American Parties and Politics in the Information Age, Doubleday (New York, NY), 1975.
Post-Conservative America: People, Politics, and Ideology in a Time of Crisis, Random House (New York, NY), 1982.
Staying on Top: The Business Case for a National Industrial Strategy, Random House (New York, NY), 1984, published as *Staying on Top: Winning the Trade War,* Vintage Books (New York, NY), 1986.
The Politics of Rich and Poor: Wealth and the American Electorate in the Reagan Aftermath, Random House (New York, NY), 1990.
Boiling Point: Republicans, Democrats and the Decline of Middle Class Prosperity, Random House (New York, NY), 1993.
Arrogant Capital: Washington, Wall Street, and the Frustration of American Politics, Little, Brown (Boston, MA), 1994.
The Cousins' Wars: Religion, Politics, and the Triumph of Anglo-America, Basic Books (New York, NY), 1999.
Wealth and Democracy: A Political History of the Rich, Broadway Books (New York, NY), 2002.
The Dynastic Presidency: Family, Politics, and Fortune in the Bush Era, Viking (New York, NY), 2004.

Also author of columns for King Features Syndicate, 1970—. Columnist for *Los Angeles Times;* contributor to *New York Times* and *Washington Post.* Editor and publisher of *The American Political Report.*

SIDELIGHTS: Kevin Phillips is considered one of America's premier political analysts. He skyrocketed to public notice with his first book, *The Emerging Republican Majority.* Only twenty-eight years old when the book was published, Phillips already had political experience—he served as a special assistant in voting trends analysis to Richard Nixon's campaign manager, John N. Mitchell, in the successful Republican campaign of 1968. Phillips later followed Mitchell to the Attorney General's office, again working as a special assistant. *The Emerging Republican Majority* correctly predicted the shift from liberalism to conservativism that took place beginning with Nixon's re-election in 1972, as well as coining the term "Sun Belt," and recognizing the political reemergence of the South. In the book, Phillips suggested new ways in which Republicans could gain the political support they needed to dominate American politics.

Political dogma in the late 1960s mandated that Republicans could not come to power without appealing to liberal voters, especially young people and minorities—groups already aligned with the Democratic party, or unaffiliated. Phillips saw Nixon's election in 1968 as the end of a Democratic preeminence in American politics that had begun with Franklin D. Roosevelt's New Deal in the 1930s. He also saw that the Republican party could create an alliance between dissatisfied conservatives in the South, in the Midwest, and on the West Coast, in combination with Roman

Catholics, blue-collar workers, and prosperous suburbanites—a section of the voting public that could give Republicans victory without appealing to liberals. By 1972, a version of Phillips's plan was in effect, and conservatives returned to power in America.

Phillips left the Attorney General's office in 1970, and became president of the American Political Research Corporation in 1971. He continued to state his views through *The American Political Report* and *The Business and Public Affairs Fortnightly,* periodicals he edited and published himself. In addition, he wrote several more examinations of contemporary American politics. *Mediacracy: American Parties and Politics in the Communications Age,* published in 1975, examined the emerging importance of the information industry in American politics. In *Post-Conservative America: People, Politics, and Ideology in a Time of Crisis,* Phillips draws parallels between contemporary America, Weimar Germany, and sixteenth-century Europe, in order to look at two possible political futures for the United States: a shift toward authoritarianism, or disintegration of the two-party political system. *Staying on Top: The Business Case for a National Industrial Strategy,* suggests possible solutions for the trading and industrial problems of the United States, including a more aggressive trade policy and expansion of "economic nationalism."

In *The Politics of Rich and Poor,* Phillips contends that throughout the past twenty years, and especially during Ronald Reagan's presidency—years dominated by conservative Republican politics—the rich have gotten richer and the poor have gotten poorer. Citing data from national magazines and government reports, Phillips shows that during the 1980s average incomes from the poorest 10 percent of the population dropped 10.5 percent. At the same time, the average incomes from the wealthiest 10 percent rose 24.4 percent, and the average incomes of the top 1 percent increased over 74 percent. In addition, the economic policies of the 1980s produced record numbers of millionaires and billionaires, while farmers, middle-income workers, inner-city poor, and the unemployed saw prosperity recede from their grasp.

Phillips sees two historical precedents and a political effect in this accumulation of wealth in the hands of the rich. The precedents lie in the "Gilded Age" (roughly the 1890s) and the "Roaring 20s," both eras of laissez-faire economics marked by government deregulation and low taxes, and directed by conservative Republicans. They were also marked, says Phillips, by hard times for farmers and an increase in indigent poor. Both eras ended in periods of Populist upheaval. The political effect of the Reagan years, Phillips believes, will be similar: a backlash of Populist origins—farmers, middle-income white-collar workers, and the poor—against the politicians in power. These predictions were realized in the presidential elections of 1992, which brought a Democratic president into office for the first time in twelve years.

"The 1980s were a second Gilded Age," writes Phillips in *The Politics of Rich and Poor,* "in which many Americans made and spent money abundantly. Yet as the decade ended, too many stretch limousines, too many enormous incomes and too much high fashion foreshadowed a significant shift of mood. A new plutocracy—some critics were even using the word 'oligarchy'—had created a new target for populist reaction. A small but significant minority of American liberals had begun to agitate the economy's losers—minorities, young men, female heads of households, farmers, steelworkers and others." Phillips continued, "Television audiences were losing their early-eighties fascination with the rich. And many conservatives, including President George Bush himself, were becoming defensive about great wealth, wanton moneymaking and greed. . . . The 1980s boom in the Boston-Washington megalopolis, coupled with hard times on the farm and in the Oil Patch, produced a familiar economic geography—a comparative shift of wealth toward . . . income groups already well off."

In reviewing *The Politics of Rich and Poor,* Priscilla Painton, writing in *Time,* stated that "Phillips brings the authority of statistics and history to his argument: with an elegant weaving of charts and cultural observations, he paints a picture of the Reagan decade as America's third period of 'heyday capitalism,' when the poor got poorer, the middle class has to get rich in order to retain a middle-class life-style, and being rich had to be redefined to account for the tripling in the number of multimillionaires." Ronald Reagan, writes Garry Wills in the *New York Review of Books,* "brought in a new elite of glitterati whom Phillips denounces, here, as betrayers of right-wing populism. The [Republican] party has given itself back to those 'economic royalists' Phillips denounced in 1968. He is admirably consistent. No one else has assembled a more scathing assault on the 1980s as a time of economic exploitation."

Other reviewers were not so enthusiastic. *Fortune* magazine reviewer Walter Olson, and Allen Randolph, writing for the *National Review,* both pointed out that, contrary to Phillips's contention, the tax structure as revised under President Reagan actually resulted in an increase in tax revenues from the taxpayers in the highest brackets. Olson further declared that the dip in unemployment in Reagan's second term helped create higher wages for lower income workers in restaurants—resulting in costs (which Phillips decries) that were in turn passed to consumers. Randolph stated that "the author's curious resentment of the prosperity of the Reagan Era is omnipresent and burdensome—but . . . if there is one thing that we have learned from recent events it is that resentment does not make for sound economics."

Phillips's own political stance in this book has attracted as much attention as his views. "Phillips's biting polemic against the Reagan years is . . . most surprising," wrote Ronald Brownstein in the *Los Angeles Times Book Review.* "As a former aide to Richard Nixon, Phillips usually is described as a Republican analyst. But in recent years he has actually assumed a new role; the conservative who dares to say that liberals are right. This book should confirm him in that improbable position." Olson in particular perceived Phillips as a liberal Democrat in Republican's clothing, stating, "His current book represents a sort of wet-winged emergence from the ideological chrysalis." "It may be that a Democratic comeback will have to wait for a severe economic downturn," stated Michael Waldman in the *Nation.* "Phillips makes a persuasive case that, should this occur, principled progressives will have an opportunity to reshape the political landscape." But Phillips himself stated in *Newsweek,* "I don't see any reason to concede the conservative label to those people who are survival-of-the-fittest disrupters of a lot of ordinary Americans' lives."

One of Phillips's follow-ups to *The Politics of Rich and Poor* is 1994's *Arrogant Capital: Washington, Wall Street, and the Frustration of American Politics.* As Timothy A. Byrnes reported in *Commonweal,* in *Arrogant Capital* "Phillips sets out to explain why gridlock and the stalemates of American government cannot be cured simply by the imposition of party government. The American government, he argues, has been taken over by a new class of parasites," Byrnes continued. "Lawyer-lobbyists and other special-interest pleaders have proliferated wildly and turned Washington, D.C. into a cosmopolitan capital . . . far out of touch with the common citizenry, and far too entrenched to allow for the kind of innovation and new directions the country desperately needs." Though an *Economist* reviewer disagreed with many of Phillips's viewpoints, the critic conceded that the author might well be "accurately reflecting the country's mood." Similarly, while a *Publishers Weekly* critic was not convinced of the efficacy of Phillips's proposed solutions to the problem he describes in *Arrogant Capital,* the critic praised him for setting "an agenda for debate."

The Cousins' Wars: Religion, Politics, and the Triumph of Anglo-America, which saw print in 1999, was something of a change of pace for Phillips. As Cedric B. Cowing pointed out in the *Historian,* "Because it is historical, the book should have a better shelf life than the author's recent tracts and will rank with his classic, *The Emerging Republican Majority.*" *The Cousins' Wars* traces the influence of British and American religious divisions from the British Civil War, to the American Revolution, to the American Civil War, and predicts they will continue to have a strong role in future political conflicts. Jeremy Black concluded in the *English Historical Review* that "the comparisons and links [Phillips] draws between the wars are interesting and he writes in an engaging fashion."

In 2002's *Wealth and Democracy: A Political History of the American Rich,* Phillips "takes a much broader approach" towards the "relationships between politics and wealth" than he did in *The Politics of Rich and Poor,* according to David Siegfried in *Booklist.* Though John B. Judis in the *New York Times Book Review* did not completely agree with Phillips's analysis in *Wealth and Democracy,* he conceded that the volume "has its moments, principally as a jeremiad against the financial excesses of the late 1990s." Thomas Ferguson in the *Washington Post*'s *Book World* was more complimentary, stating that "*Wealth and Democracy* brings the usual mind-numbing litanies of statistics and historical data vividly to life." He went on to conclude that "Phillips's discussion of America now is especially detailed and compelling."

BIOGRAPHICAL AND CRITICAL SOURCES:

PERIODICALS

Booklist, May 1, 2002, David Siegfried, review of *Wealth and Democracy: A Political History of the American Rich,* p. 1490.

Book World, May 19, 2002, Thomas Ferguson, "Following the Money," p. 7.

Business Week, September 17, 1984, pp. 12, 16.

Christian Science Monitor, September 4, 1969.

Commonweal, November 4, 1994, Timothy A. Byrnes, review of *Arrogant Capital: Washington, Wall Street, and the Frustration of American Politics,* pp. 26-27.

Economist, October 8, 1994, review of *Arrogant Capital,* pp. 99-100.

English Historical Review, September, 2000, Jeremy Black, review of *The Cousins' Wars: Religion, Politics, and the Triumph of Anglo-America,* p. 991.

Fortune, July 16, 1990, pp. 113-114.

Historian, fall, 2000, Cedric B. Cowing, review of *The Cousins' Wars,* p. 208.

Los Angeles Times, January 1, 1985.

Los Angeles Times Book Review, June 10, 1990, pp. 1, 8

Nation, July 3, 1982, pp. 20-22; August 13-20, 1990, pp. 175-176.

National Observer, December 22, 1969.

National Review, August 6, 1990. p. 44.

New Republic, September 6, 1982, pp. 28-30.

Newsweek, July 23, 1990, p. 19.

New York Times, June 21, 1990.

New York Times Book Review, May 24, 1975, p. 10; October 21, 1984, pp. 37-38; June 24, 1990, pp. 1, 26-27; May 12, 2002, John B. Judis, "Decline and Fall," p. 12.

Publishers Weekly, July 4, 1994, review of *Arrogant Capital,* p. 48; April 22, 2002, review of *Wealth and Democracy,* p. 61, interview with Kevin Phillips, p. 62.

Saturday Review, September 13, 1969.

Time, August 1, 1969; June 25, 1990, p. 69.

Washington Post Book World, August 15, 1982, p. 7; November 25, 1984, pp. 4, 6; July 8, 1990, pp. 1, 9.*

* * *

PORTE, Barbara Ann 1943-

PERSONAL: Born May 18, 1943, in New York, NY; daughter of a pharmacist and a lawyer. *Education:* Attended Iowa State University; Michigan State University, B.S., 1965; Palmer Graduate School of Library and Information Science, Long Island University, M.S., 1969.

Barbara Ann Porte

ADDRESSES: Home—P.O. Box 16627, Arlington, VA 22215.

CAREER: Writer. Nassau Library System, Uniondale, NY, chief, Children's Services Division, 1974-86.

MEMBER: National Women's Book Association; Author's Guild; Children's Book Guild of Washington, D.C.

AWARDS, HONORS: Notable Book designation, American Library Association (ALA), for *Harry's Visit, Harry's Dog,* and *Harry in Trouble;* "Pick of the List," American Booksellers Association, 1985, for *The Kidnapping of Aunt Elizabeth,* 1995, for *Chickens! Chickens!,* and 1997, for *Tale of a Tadpole* and *Harry's Pony;* Children's Books of the Year, Child Study Association of America, 1986, for *Harry's Mom,* and 1992, for *Harry Gets an Uncle;* Best Books, *Parents' Magazine* and *Learning,* for *Ruthann and Her Pig;*

Best Books for Young Adults, ALA, for *Something Terrible Happened;* Parents' Choice Picture Book Honor, Parents' Choice Foundation, 1995, for *Chickens! Chickens!;* Best Science Books for Children citation, *Scientific American,* 1997, and NTSA Outstanding Science Trade Books for Children, 1998, both for *Tale of a Tadpole;* Anne Izard Storyteller's Choice award, 2000, for *Hearsay: Strange Tales from the Middle Kingdom;* NEST literary classic selection, for *Ma Jiang and the Orange Ants;* Parents Guide to Children's Media award and Capitol Choices Selection, both 2000, for *If You Ever Get Lost: The Adventures of Julia and Evan;* Books for the Teen Age designation, New York Public Library, 2003, for *Beauty and the Serpent: Thirteen Tales of Unnatural Animals.*

WRITINGS:

Harry's Visit, illustrated by Yossi Abolafia, Greenwillow (New York, NY), 1983.

Jesse's Ghost and Other Stories, Greenwillow (New York, NY), 1983.

Harry's Dog, illustrated by Yossi Abolafia, Greenwillow (New York, NY), 1984.

Harry's Mom, illustrated by Yossi Abolafia, Greenwillow (New York, NY), 1985.

The Kidnapping of Aunt Elizabeth, Greenwillow (New York, NY), 1985.

I Only Made Up the Roses, Greenwillow (New York, NY), 1987.

Harry in Trouble, illustrated by Yossi Abolafia, Greenwillow (New York, NY), 1989, reprinted as an "I Can Read Book," HarperCollins (New York, NY), 2002.

The Take-along Dog, illustrated by Emily Arnold McCully, Greenwillow (New York, NY), 1989.

Ruthann and Her Pig, illustrated by Sucie Stevenson, Orchard Books (New York, NY), 1989.

Fat Fanny, Beanpole Bertha, and the Boys, illustrated by Maxie Chambliss, Orchard Books (New York, NY), 1991.

Harry Gets an Uncle, illustrated by Yossi Abolafia, Greenwillow (New York, NY), 1991, reprinted as an "I Can Read Book," HarperCollins (New York, NY), 2002.

Taxicab Tales, illustrated by Yossi Abolafia, Greenwillow (New York, NY), 1992.

A Turkey Drive and Other Tales, illustrated by Yossi Abolafia, Greenwillow (New York, NY), 1993.

Leave That Cricket Be, Alan Lee, illustrated by Donna Ruff, Greenwillow (New York, NY), 1993.

When Grandma Almost Fell off the Mountain and Other Stories, illustrated by Maxie Chambliss, Orchard Books (New York, NY), 1993.

Something Terrible Happened (for young adults), Orchard Books (New York, NY), 1994.

When Aunt Lucy Rode a Mule and Other Stories, illustrated by Maxie Chambliss, Orchard Books (New York, NY), 1994.

Harry's Birthday, illustrated by Yossi Abolafia, Greenwillow (New York, NY), 1994, reprinted as an "I Can Read Book," HarperCollins (New York, NY), 2003.

Chickens! Chickens!, illustrated by Greg Henry, Orchard Books (New York, NY), 1995.

Black Elephant with a Brown Ear (in Alabama), illustrated by Bill Traylor, Greenwillow (New York, NY), 1996.

Surprise! Surprise! It's Grandfather's Birthday (picture book), illustrated by Bo Jia, Greenwillow (New York, NY), 1997.

Harry's Pony, illustrated by Yossi Abolafia, Greenwillow (New York, NY), 1997, reprinted as an "I Can Read Book," HarperCollins (New York, NY), 2004.

Tale of a Tadpole (picture book), illustrated by Annie Cannon, Orchard Books (New York, NY), 1997.

Hearsay: Strange Tales from the Middle Kingdom, illustrated by Rosemary Feit Covey, Greenwillow Books (New York, NY), 1998.

He's Sorry, She's Sorry, They're Sorry Too: Stories (for adults), Hanging Loose Press (Brooklyn, NY), 1998.

If You Ever Get Lost: The Adventures of Julia and Evan, illustrated by Nancy Carpenter, Greenwillow Books (New York, NY), 2000.

Ma Jiang and the Orange Ants, illustrated by Annie Cannon, Orchard Books (New York, NY), 2000.

Beauty and the Serpent: Thirteen Tales of Unnatural Animals, illustrated by Rosemary Feit Covey, Simon & Schuster (New York, NY), 2001.

Contributor to anthologies, including *Funny You Should Ask,* edited by David Gale, Delacorte (New York, NY), 1992; *Don't Give Up the Ghost,* edited by Gale, Delacorte, 1993; *Birthday Surprises,* edited by Johanna Hurwitz, Morrow Junior Books (New York, NY), 1995; and *New Handbook for Storytellers,* edited by Caroline Feller Bauer, ALA, 1993.

Contributor of stories, poems, essays, and reviews to newspapers and literary magazines, including *Advocate, Book Links, Confrontation, Earth's Daughters,*

Green's Magazine, Hanging Loose, Karamu, Newsday, New York Times, Phoebe, 13th Moon, San Jose Studies, School Library Journal, and *Washington Post Book World.*

ADAPTATIONS: *Jesse's Ghost and Other Stories* is available as a talking book from the Library of Congress. *Harry's Dog* is available as a cassette tape, from Random House. *Harry's Pony* was adapted as a play by Metropolitan Teaching and Learning. *Seduction,* a short story, is scheduled to be made into a film.

WORK IN PROGRESS: A young adult novel, *Roxana.*

SIDELIGHTS: Best known for her popular "Harry" books for beginning readers, Barbara Ann Porte has also written a wide variety of books for the middle grader, including a collection of macabre stories and several funny family tales, as well as thought-provoking novels for young adults dealing with biracial families and painful subjects like AIDS, divorce, and death. Critics have praised her for her skillful storytelling, lively dialogue, convincing characterization, and humor.

Born in New York City, the daughter of a lawyer mother and a storytelling pharmacist father, Porte and her two sisters grew up telling stories to one another. Every night their mother read aloud to them, even after they could read on their own. Their father told them: "Read something every day and write something every day, no matter what else you do with your lives."

Despite her love of books, however, Porte majored in the more practical subject of agriculture in college, in both Iowa and Michigan. After she married and had children, however, she returned to school to become a librarian. Porte began her writing career with three stories for the "Read-alone Books" series about the small boy narrator, Harry, who lives with his single-parent dentist dad. *Harry's Visit* describes his reluctance when invited to spend a day with old friends of his father and their children. That is, until one of the children invites him to shoot a few baskets. "Shoot some baskets? He must be joking. I am just a little taller than one of Snow White's dwarfs," is Harry's first reaction. As Zena Sutherland of the *Bulletin of the Center for Children's Books* observed, "The treatment is light but the emotions are deep and universal."

In *Harry's Dog,* Harry makes up some wild tales when his allergic father discovers a dog in the house. However, a home is found for the dog, and Harry finds his father a suitable pet: a goldfish. "As logical and winsome as ever," commented Karen Jameyson of *Horn Book Magazine.* Although the theme of *Harry's Mom* is serious, beginning with the opening "I, Harry, am an orphan," Zena Sutherland of the *Bulletin of the Center for Children's Books* stated, "The author has proved herself adept at investing simply presented situations with emotional substance—here, both humor and sadness." The wise father helps Harry recognize all the loving people in his life, including an aunt and four grandparents, and from them Harry learns about his daredevil, sports-reporter mother. A "quietly satisfying story," commented Denise M. Wilms of *Booklist.* Interspersed with books about other families and books for older readers, several other stories, including *Harry in Trouble, Harry Gets an Uncle, Harry's Birthday,* and *Harry's Pony,* continue the series with the slightly over-anxious lad inevitably discovering his worries were in vain and that lost library cards, wedding responsibilities, and birthday surprises can have happy conclusions.

In another series of books aimed for the preschooler or beginning independent reader, *The Take-along Dog* introduces Sam Rabinowitz, his sister Abigail, and their parents, a taxi driver father and artist mother. Because of their mother's fear of dogs, the children must take their little dog, Benton, with them wherever they go, even to places where dogs are not permitted, until the day Benton protects Mother from a larger dog and wins her appreciation and friendship. *School Library Journal* contributor Pamela Miller noted that *The Take-along Dog,* which among other summer activities depicts Sam taking ballet lessons, "subtly emphasizes important human values [such as] acknowledgment of a parent's fear . . . and the negation of gender stereotypes." In the second of the series, *Taxicab Tales,* Father entertains his family with tales of his day and the unusual passengers he has met. "Porte is an expert at creating unity from bits and pieces, half-truths, absolutes, and maybes—the stuff that real life and great stories are made of," said Heide Piehler in a *School Library Journal* review. *A Turkey Drive and Other Tales,* the third chapter book of the series, is narrated by Abigail and uses Mother's artwork as a springboard. A *Kirkus Reviews* commentator maintained that Porte "keeps the book moving with unexpected plot-twists, comical detail, impeccable timing, and a rare ear for natural, funny dialogue." Quraysh

Ali of *Booklist* found that in *A Turkey Drive* Porte "ties together little pieces of sense, nonsense, and stream-of-consciousness to arrive at the wittiest conclusions." A *Publishers Weekly* reviewer described the book as a collection of "quirky, loosely connected tales," adding: "Porte's energetic imagery and plotting keep the pages turning."

Diverging from her normal population of urban children, Porte turns to a Chinese-American boy in *Leave That Cricket Be, Alan Lee*. Determined to catch a cricket he hears chirping, Alan learns that crickets sing by rubbing their wings, that his great-uncle Clem used to make cricket cages as a boy in China, and that Chinese legend has it that crickets bring good luck. Once caught, however, the cricket no longer sings, so Alan lets it go and is rewarded by its song. A *Kirkus Reviews* critic contended that the narrative is rather long, but added that it is "propelled by plenty of lively realistic dialogue [and] artfully reveals a lot" about the family interrelationships. Jody McCoy in *School Library Journal* likewise felt that the text is a bit long for reading at one sitting, but praised the "deliciously poetic passages [that] beg to be read aloud."

Middle graders are the audience for Porte's *Jesse's Ghost and Other Stories,* a collection of twelve eerie short stories that *Publishers Weekly* advised "be read in daylight, with people around." *Booklist* reviewer Denise M. Wilms described them as "sometimes elegant stories [that] have a haunting quality to them." Zena Sutherland of the *Bulletin of the Center for Children's Books* noted that the writing style "often [captures] the cadence of the oral tradition." This same oral tradition is particularly evident in tales featuring two sisters, Stella and Zelda, who prevail upon their grandmother to tell them a story in *When Grandma Almost Fell off the Mountain and Other Stories,* and hear her account of traveling to Florida by car with the girls' parents in the 1930s. The grandmother's "colorful words, brisk descriptions, and unerring choice of subjects" entertain the sisters (and readers) and add a "rich multigenerational flavor," according to a *Kirkus Reviews* commentator.

In a companion book, *When Aunt Lucy Rode a Mule and Other Stories,* the girls prod their aunt to recount her childhood memories, which include visiting her grandmother in the mountains and getting stung by bees. A *Publishers Weekly* reviewer stated that Porte "liberally sprinkles the text with the kind of rich natural phrasing associated with oral storytelling." *School Library Journal* contributor Nancy Menaldi-Scanlan pointed out that for today's children who equate vacation with "a trip to Disney World or to some other prepackaged funhouse," Porte offers "a sense of old-fashioned good times and down-home humor."

"A fresh and innovative present-tense narrative," as Betsy Hearne described it in the *Bulletin of the Center for Children's Books,* Porte's *Ruthann and Her Pig* tells of Ruthann and her pet pig, Henry Brown. Visitor Cousin Frank, however, also becomes attached to Henry. The ensuing correspondence between cousins, the discovery of a long-lost grandfather, and Henry's fate all add up to reading-aloud fun that Hearne pronounced "distinctively done." Hearne offered a similar estimation of *Fat Fanny, Beanpole Bertha, and the Boys,* noting that "with the same present-tense immediacy that distinguished her narrative in *Ruthann and Her Pig,*" Porte relates the story of two fifth-grade girls, friends since kindergarten, who share a difficult time. Bertha's father has vanished in the Bermuda Triangle, and Fanny's parents are secretly divorced. Sally T. Margolis stated in *School Library Journal* that "Porte approaches the problem novel from left field with zesty humor, unique characters, and unlikely plot developments." Harried Bertha has to look after her eight-year-old younger brothers (triplets) while her mother works two jobs, and overweight Fanny eats excessively while brooding about her folks. "It's the characterizations of this odd lot that make the story a standout," commented Ilene Cooper in *Booklist*. "Fresh and funny, yet it packs a punch."

For older readers, *The Kidnapping of Aunt Elizabeth* features fifteen-year-old Ashley Rush who, for a school project on family history, collects stories from assorted relatives. *School Library Journal* contributor Heide Piehler noted that "Porte establishes herself as a masterful storyteller, [who can create] memorable characters and a seemingly endless supply of engaging tales." A mixture of invention and authenticated folk and fairy tales, the combination makes for "fast moving and captivating reading," according to *Voice of Youth Advocates* contributor Margaret J. Porter.

Another of Porte's well-received books for teens, *I Only Made Up the Roses,* focuses on a seventeen-year-old narrator, Cydra, who lives with her white mother, black stepfather, and younger half-brother Perley. "A wonderful, intelligent book," Myrna Feldman wrote in *Voice of Youth Advocates,* with all the feelings and experiences of a biracial family "explored and handled by contemporary, educated, liberal individuals." Beginning with southern step-grandfather's funeral and concluding with Thanksgiving, the string of short stories revolve around incidents in a family spanning three continents. "Thematic reflections on racial prejudice, family adjustment, and life cycles are delivered by a personable protagonist," wrote Betsy Hearne in the *Bulletin of the Center for Children's Books.*

Selected as one of ALA's Best Books for Young Adults, and a departure from Porte's usual lighthearted fare, *Something Terrible Happened* tells the story of Gillian, whose father died of addictions brought home from Vietnam, and whose mother is stricken with AIDS. Although raised in New York, Gillian identifies with her mother and grandmother, "Island" women of Caribbean heritage. As her mother's condition worsens, Gillian is sent to Tennessee to stay with her white uncle and his family. Her mother's death forces Gillian to grow up, gaining strength from the wealth of folktales she had been brought up on, and learning acceptance and self-reliance. *Horn Book* reviewer Ellen Fader praised this "compelling" story and predicted readers will be captivated by "this gritty, engaging, fast-moving tale of one young girl's fight for emotional survival." A *Kirkus Reviews* critic commented that the author "enlivens a refreshingly cliche-free narrative with the folktales this multiracial family of strong women tell each other." Deborah Stevenson of *Bulletin of the Center for Children's Books* concluded, "The final effect is dreamy and somewhat adult, but there's a verisimilitude in the wandering and an intimacy in the portrayals that keep the book an absorbing read." A reviewer for *Publishers Weekly* observed, "Once in concert with its unique rhythm, the reader will burrow into this story and relish its nuggets of insight."

Porte first met illustrator Greg Henry at a faculty art exhibition at Hampton University, her husband's alma mater. When she discovered that the young painter had grown up on a chicken farm in Guyana, she was ecstatic. "I majored in agriculture in college and received a two-year foundation grant, partially based on my own interest in chickens," she explained. The serendipitous result was the book *Chickens! Chickens!,* of which Betsy Hearne of the *Bulletin of the Center for Children's Books* commented: "This buoyant story will snag listeners with its infectious silliness." Hearne identified the theme as "follow your dream" and summarized the book as "a lot of fun."

In another book inspired by pictures, *Black Elephant with a Brown Ear (in Alabama),* ten stories describe what a survivor of slavery and farmer, almost ninety years old, drew and painted. Deborah Stevenson quoted Porte in *Bulletin of the Center for Children's Books* as saying, "When I look at many of Bill Traylor's pictures, I think of them as stories that he told himself. Seeing them, I tell myself different stories." The stories range from hilarity to heroism, pieces about pigs and dogs, run-away goat carts and circus performers. *School Library Journal* contributor Pam Gosner explained how Porte chose ten out of over twelve hundred paintings the African-American artist had made and how she created imaginative tales about each. "Porte's writings, which are light and folksy in tone, explore a world of possibilities," she declared. Susan Dove Lempke in *Booklist* observed that "while the stories tend to wander and be somewhat insubstantial, they have a certain charm," and Lempke suggested that creative writing and art teachers might find this book useful in encouraging their own students to try out the method.

Porte followed an award-winning science book, *Tale of a Tadpole,* with *Hearsay: Strange Tales from the Middle Kingdom.* The latter work is a compendium of original stories and folktales from China. A *Publishers Weekly* reviewer found the retellings were not "culturally authentic," but added that Porte made up for that drawback with her "contagious passion for the exotic." Nancy Vasilakis of *Horn Book* greeted the work warmly, saying that the author helps "to create a fascination and surprisingly intimate picture of Chinese life over countless generations." A single Chinese tale is the basis for Porte's 2000 book, *Ma Jiang and the Orange Ants.* Set in the past, the story tells of how the young heroine, Ma Jiang, copes when her father goes off to war and leaves in her hands the family business—raising and selling "orange ants" whose hunting skills provide pest control in gardens. Porte adds a note at the end of the story detailing the use of ants in agriculture; Linda Ludke of *School Library Journal* deemed *Ma Jiang* "a captivating tale with a charming heroine who will speak to today's children."

If You Ever Get Lost: The Adventures of Julia and Evan is a collection of "nine sweet stories," as Linda Plevak put it in *School Library Journal,* centering on young siblings whose curious personalities carry them all over town. Definitely less sweet is Porte's 2001 release, *Beauty and the Serpent: Thirteen Tales of Unnatural Animals*. The characters in this teen-reader volume include, as Starr LaTronica noted in a *School Library Journal* review, "puppies from hell, escalator-dwelling cats, murderous crows, and a coma-inducing snake tattoo with a life of its own." A *Kirkus Reviews* contributor thought that Porte "is in top form" with this book.

"What seems of most interest to people these days is that I continue to write with pencil on paper, and to finish up on a manual typewriter," Porte told *CA* in 2002. "My reason: Crossing out by hand doesn't interrupt my train of thoughts; calling up a new screen effectively ends my work for the day. I fear future demands from publishers for 'electronic type.' I breathe easier anytime I hear of improvements in scanning equipment.

"The artist Constantin Brancusi put it so well when he said, 'It is not making things that is difficult, but putting ourselves in the condition to make them.' I keep on trying. I read, I walk, I spend more and more time studying the visual arts.

"Over a decade ago, having seen an exhibition of appliqué work by the Japanese artist Ayako Miyawaki, I wrote an essay titled, 'After Appliqué Contemplating the Art of Writing.' All these years later it still serves as a touchstone for me, containing, as it does, everything I know on the topic. Like Ms. Miyawaki, I, too, use what's around. I select carefully, aware that often what's most important is knowing what to leave out. I arrange and rearrange my pieces, at last 'stitch' them together as seamlessly as I can.

"I'm unable to write—anything—a book, or a story, or a poem, or an essay, until I can see its pattern, how it will look on the page. By this I do not mean an outline. For me, an outline is a structure imposed from without. A pattern is an organic form, internally inevitable; an organizing principle that is different for everything I write, and needs to be discovered every time I start, sometimes rediscovered. I think this concept of pattern is implicit in all of the arts, underlies what makes any work beautiful—beautiful in the truest meaning of the word, a medium for that which is essential, that which is always suggesting something beyond itself. In any event, it's what I'm forever after—seeking to create something beautiful that will last."

BIOGRAPHICAL AND CRITICAL SOURCES:

PERIODICALS

Best Sellers, August, 1985, review of *The Kidnapping of Aunt Elizabeth*, p. 197.
Book Links, March, 1997, p. 21.
Booklist, August, 1983, review of *Harry's Visit*, p. 1470; October 15, 1983, Denise Wilms, review of *Jesse's Ghost and Other Stories*, p. 366; May 15, 1984, October 15, 1985, Denise Wilms, review of *Harry's Mom*, p. 343; May 1, 1987, review of *I Only Made Up the Roses*, p. 1362; March 1, 1989, review of *Harry in Trouble*, p. 1199; June 15, 1989, review of *The Take-along Dog*, p. 1826; October 1, 1989, review of *Ruthann and Her Pig*, p. 354; February 15, 1991, review of *I Only Made Up the Roses*, p. 1217; March 1, 1991, review of *Fat Fanny, Beanpole Bertha, and the Boys*, p. 1388; August, 1991, review of *Harry Gets an Uncle*, p. 2159; April 1, 1992, review of *Taxicab Tales*, p. 1451; April 1, 1993, review of *When Grandma Almost Fell off the Mountain and Other Stories*, p. 1441; April 15, 1993, Quraysh Ali, review of *A Turkey Drive and Other Tales*, p. 1516; September 1, 1993, review of *Leave That Cricket Be, Alan Lee*, p. 70; April 1, 1994, review of *Harry's Birthday*, p. 1466; September 15, 1994, review of *Something Terrible Happened*, p. 125; February 1, 1995, review of *Chickens! Chickens!*, p. 1011; April 1, 1995, review of *Something Terrible Happened*, p. 1403; May 15, 1996, Susan Dove Lempke, review of *Black Elephant with a Brown Ear (in Alabama)*, p. 1584; August, 1997, review of *Tale of a Tadpole*, p. 1907, review of *Harry's Pony*, p. 1910; October 15, 2000, John Peters, review of *Ma Jiang and the Orange Ants*, p. 446.
Book Report, March, 1984, review of *Jesse's Ghost and Other Stories*, p. 35; January, 1995, review of *Something Terrible Happened*, p. 35; March, 1995, review of *Something Terrible Happened*, p. 40.
Bookwatch, June, 1998, review of *He's Sorry, She's Sorry, They're Sorry Too: Stories*, p. 9.
Bulletin of the Center for Children's Books, July-August, 1983, Zena Sutherland, review of *Harry's Visit*, p. 217; March, 1984, Zena Sutherland, review of *Jesse's Ghost and Other Stories*, p. 134; July-August, 1984, review of *Harry's Dog*, p. 211; December, 1985, Zena Sutherland, review of

Harry's Mom, pp. 75-76; June, 1987, Betsy Hearne, review of *I Only Made Up the Roses*, p. 194; February, 1989, review of *Harry in Trouble*, p. 155; January, 1990, Betsy Hearne, review of *Ruthann and Her Pig*, p. 119; April, 1991, Betsy Hearne, review of *Fat Fanny, Beanpole Bertha, and the Boys*, p. 202; June, 1992, review of *Taxicab Tales*, p. 274; July, 1993, review of *A Turkey Drive and Other Tales*, p. 356; May, 1994, review of *Harry's Birthday*, p. 298; December, 1994, Deborah Stevenson, review of *Something Terrible Happened*, p. 143; April, 1995, Betsy Hearne, review of *Chickens! Chickens!*, p. 284; June, 1996, review of *Black Elephant with a Brown Ear (in Alabama)*, p. 350; October, 1997, review of *Harry's Pony*, p. 65; May, 1998, review of *Hearsay: Strange Tales from the Middle Kingdom*, p. 335.

Childhood Education, November, 1983, review of *Harry's Visit*, p. 138; November, 1985, review of *The Kidnapping of Aunt Elizabeth*, p. 138; number 5, 1990, review of *Harry in Trouble*, p. 336; spring, 1992, review of *Harry Gets an Uncle*, p. 176; summer, 1992, review of *Taxicab Tales*, p. 245.

Children's Book Review Service, September, 1983, review of *Jesse's Ghost and Other Stories*, p. 10; April, 1985, review of *The Kidnapping of Aunt Elizabeth*, p. 100; August, 1987, review of *I Only Made Up the Roses*, p. 158; spring, 1989, review of *The Take-along Dog*, p. 133; October, 1989, review of *Ruthann and Her Pig*, p. 20; June, 1991, review of *Fat Fanny, Beanpole Bertha, and the Boys*, p. 128; spring, 1993, review of *When Grandma Almost Fell off the Mountain and Other Stories*, p. 137; September, 1993, review of *Leave That Cricket Be, Alan Lee*, p. 7; February, 1995, review of *Something Terrible Happened*, p. 83; May, 1995, review of *Chickens! Chickens!*, p. 111; April, 1996, review of *Black Elephant with a Brown Ear (in Alabama)*, p. 103; July, 1997, review of *Surprise! Surprise! It's Grandfather's Birthday*, p. 150; July, 1998, review of *Hearsay*, p. 156.

Children's Bookwatch, October, 1993, review of *Leave That Cricket Be, Alan Lee*, p. 4.

Emergency Librarian, November, 1986, review of *Harry's Dog*, p. 47; September, 1989, review of *Harry in Trouble*, p. 49; January, 1990, review of *Ruthann and Her Pig*, p. 50.

English Journal, January, 1996, review of *Something Terrible Happened*, p. 89.

Horn Book, June, 1983, review of *Harry's Visit*, p. 299; August, 1984, Karyn Jameyson, review of *Harry's Dog*, pp. 463-464; May-June, 1985, review of *The Kidnapping of Aunt Elizabeth*, p. 313; November, 1987, review of *I Only Made Up the Roses*, p. 745; May, 1989, review of *The Take-along Dog*, p. 362; review of *Harry in Trouble*, p. 391; July, 1989, review of *Ruthann and Her Pig*, p. 70; January, 1990, review of *Ruthann and Her Pig*, p. 65; July, 1991, review of *Fat Fanny, Beanpole Bertha, and the Boys*, p. 460; January-February, 1992, review of *Harry Gets an Uncle*, pp. 66-67; May, 1992, review of *Taxicab Tales*, p. 338; May-June, 1993, review of *When Grandma Almost Fell off the Mountain and Other Stories*, p. 330, review of *A Turkey Drive and Other Tales*, p. 348; September, 1994, review of *Harry's Birthday*, p. 584; November-December, 1994, Ellen Fader, review of *Something Terrible Happened*, p. 737; March-April, 1995, review of *Chickens! Chickens!*, p. 187; September, 1997, review of *Harry's Pony*, p. 577; July-August, 1998, Nancy Vasilakis, review of *Hearsay*, p. 496.

Horn Book Guide, fall, 1991, review of *Fat Fanny, Beanpole Bertha, and the Boys*, p. 264; spring, 1992, review of *Harry Gets an Uncle*, p. 60; fall, 1992, review of *Taxicab Tales*, p. 258; fall, 1993, review of *When Grandma Almost Fell off the Mountain and Other Stories* and *A Turkey Drive and Other Tales*, p. 290; spring, 1994, review of *Leave That Cricket Be, Alan Lee*, p. 69; fall, 1994, review of *Harry's Birthday*, p. 303; spring, 1995, review of *When Aunt Lucy Rode a Mule and Other Stories*, p. 69, review of *Something Terrible Happened*, p. 90; fall, 1995, review of *Chickens! Chickens!*, p. 279; fall, 1996, review of *Black Elephant with a Brown Ear (in Alabama)*, p. 296; fall, 1997, review of *Surprise! Surprise! It's Grandfather's Birthday*, p. 277; spring, 1998, review of *Tale of a Tadpole*, p. 43, review of *Harry's Pony*, p. 57; fall, 1998, review of *Hearsay*, p. 336; spring, 2001, review of *Ma Jiang and the Orange Ants*, p. 48.

Hungry Mind Review, summer, 1995, review of *Chickens! Chickens!*, p. 47.

Instructor, August, 1998, review of *Harry in Trouble*, p. 17.

Kirkus Reviews, February 1, 1983, review of *Harry's Visit*, p. 120; September 1, 1983, review of *Jesse's Ghost and Other Stories*, p. J164; May 1, 1984, review of *Harry's Dog*, p. J35; March 1, 1987, review of *I Only Made Up the Roses*, p. 379; January 1, 1989, review of *Harry in Trouble,* p. 53; April 1, 1989, review of *The Take-along Dog,* p. 552; August 1, 1989, review of *Ruthann and Her Pig,* p. 1165; February 1, 1993; April 1, 1993, p. 463; March 1, 1991, review of *Fat Fanny, Beanpole Bertha, and the Boys,* p. 320; July 1, 1991, review of *Harry Gets an Uncle,* p. 866; February 15 1992, review of *Taxicab Tales,* p. 259; April 1, 1993, review of *A Turkey Drive and Other Tales,* p. 463; July 15, 1993, review of *Leave That Cricket Be, Alan Lee,* p. 939; May 15, 1994, review of *Harry's Birthday,* p. 704; October 15, 1994, review of *Something Terrible Happened,* p. 1414; March 15, 1995, review of *Chickens! Chickens!,* p. 392; February 15, 1996, review of *Black Elephant with a Brown Ear (in Alabama),* p. 299; June 15, 1997, review of *Harry's Pony,* p. 956, review of *Tale of a Tadpole,* p. 1115; May 1, 1998, *Hearsay,* 664; September 15, 2001, review of *Beauty and the Serpent: Thirteen Tales of Unnatural Animals,* p. 1365.

Kliatt Young Adult Paperback Book Guide, January, 1997, review of *Something Terrible Happened,* p. 10.

Language Arts, October, 1989, review of *The Take-along Dog,* p. 678.

Learning, January, 1990, review of *Ruthann and Her Pig,* p. 33; January, 1998, review of *Tale of a Tadpole,* p. 43.

Library Talk, January, 1992, review of *Harry Gets an Uncle,* p. 47; November, 1993, review of *Leave That Cricket Be, Alan Lee,* p. 61; September, 1994, review of *When Grandma Almost Fell off the Mountain and Other Stories,* p. 13; November, 1994, review of *Harry's Birthday,* p. 39; March, 1995, review of *Leave That Cricket Be, Alan Lee,* p. 36.

Los Angeles Times Book Review, January 19, 1986, review of *Harry's Mom,* p. 10.

New York Times Book Review, May 21, 1995, review of *Chickens! Chickens!,* p. 22.

Parents, December, 1989, review of *Ruthann and Her Pig,* p. 227.

Publishers Weekly, September 16, 1983, review of *Jesse's Ghost and Other Stories,* p. 126; April 24, 1987, review of *I Only Made Up the Roses,* p. 72; February 10, 1989, review of *Harry in Trouble,* p. 71; July 28, 1989, review of *Ruthann and Her Pig,* p. 222; March 22, 1991, review of *Fat Fanny, Beanpole Bertha, and the Boys,* p. 80; February 17, 1992, review of *Taxicab Tales,* p. 63; March 8, 1993, review of *When Grandma Almost Fell off the Mountain and Other Stories,* p. 77; April 19, 1993, review of *A Turkey Drive and Other Tales,* p. 62; September 6, 1993, review of *Leave That Cricket Be, Alan Lee,* p. 97; August 1, 1994, p. 79; October 10, 1994, review of *Something Terrible Happened,* p. 70; January 2, 1995, review of *Chickens! Chickens!,* p. 76; September 1, 1997, review of *Tale of a Tadpole,* p. 103; May 18, 1998, review of *Hearsay,* p. 80; June 22, 1998, review of *He's Sorry, She's Sorry, They're Sorry Too: Stories.*

Reading Teacher, October, 1984, review of *Harry's Visit,* p. 69; May, 1990, review of *Harry in Trouble* and *The Take-along Dog,* p. 672; February, 1994, review of *Leave That Cricket Be, Alan Lee,* p. 564; April, 1994, review of *Leave That Cricket Be, Alan Lee,* p. 564;

School Library Journal, May, 1983, review of *Harry's Visit,* p. 88; November, 1983, review of *Jesse's Ghost and Other Stories,* p. 82; August, 1984, review of *Harry's Dog,* p. 64; April, 1985, Heide Piehler, review of *The Kidnapping of Aunt Elizabeth,* p. 91; December, 1985, review of *Harry's Mom,* p. 110; May, 1987, review of *I Only Made Up the Roses,* p. 117; March, 1989, review of *Harry in Trouble,* p. 168; June, 1989, Pamela Miller, review of *The Take-along Dog,* p. 91; October, 1989, Sally Margolis, review of *Ruthann and Her Pig,* p. 121; February, 1991, review of *Fat Fanny, Beanpole Bertha, and the Boys,* p. 82; September, 1991, review of *Harry Gets an Uncle,* p. 239; April, 1992, Heidi Piehler, review of *Taxicab Tales,* pp. 98-99; April, 1993, review of *When Grandma Almost Fell off the Mountain and Other Stories,* p. 102; May, 1993, review of *A Turkey Drive and Other Tales,* p. 90; October, 1993, Jody McCoy, review of *Leave That Cricket Be, Alan Lee,* p. 108; May, 1994, review of *Harry's Birthday,* p. 103; November, 1994, Nancy Menaldi-Scanlan, review of *When Aunt Lucy Rode a Mule and Other Stories,* p. 88; April, 1995, review of *Chickens! Chickens!,* p. 114; May, 1996, Pam Gosner, review of *Black Elephant with a Brown Ear (in Alabama),* p. 96; May, 1997, review of *Surprise! Surprise! It's Grandfather's Birthday,* p. 110; August, 1997, review of *Harry's Pony,* p. 138; September, 1997, review of *Tale of a Tadpole,* p. 190; June, 1998, review of *Hearsay,* p. 151; July, 2000, Linda Plevak, review of *If You Ever Get Lost: The Adventures of Julia and Evan,* p. 86; December, 2000, Linda Ludke, review of *Ma Jiang and the Orange Ants,* p. 123; November,

2001, Star LaTronica, review of *Beauty and the Serpent*, p. 183.

Science Books and Films, March, 1998, review of *Tale of a Tadpole,* p. 51.

Village Voice, May 9, 1989, review of *Harry in Trouble,* p. 42.

Voice of Youth Advocates, June, 1985, Margaret Porter, review of *The Kidnapping of Aunt Elizabeth,* p. 134; June, 1987, Myrna Feldman, review of *I Only Made Up the Roses,* p. 82; October, 1994, review of *Something Terrible Happened,* p. 215; October, 1995, review of *Something Terrible Happened,* p. 210.

Washington Post Book World, May 13, 2001.

Wilson Library Bulletin, April, 1995, review of Harry's Birthday, p. 112; June, 1995, review of *When Aunt Lucy Rode a Mule and Other Stories,* p. 117.

R

RAZZELL, Mary (Catherine) 1930-

PERSONAL: Born February 20, 1930, in Calgary, Alberta, Canada; daughter of Stephen Braerie (a mechanic, air force flight sergeant, and instructor) and Margaret Elizabeth (a domestic worker and homemaker; maiden name, McConnell) Slinn; married Bill Razzell (a microbiologist), September 22, 1951 (divorced); married Eric Nicol (a writer), February 11, 1986; children: (first marriage) Daniel, Robin, Jim. *Ethnicity:* "Irish-English." *Education:* St. Paul's School of Nursing, Vancouver, British Columbia, Canada, R.N., 1951; also attended University of British Columbia. *Religion:* Roman Catholic. *Hobbies and other interests:* Reading, working out with weights, bike riding, walking, swimming, camping, baking, oral history.

ADDRESSES: Home—3993 West 36th Ave., Vancouver, British Columbia V6N 2S7, Canada. *E-mail*—mcslinn@telus.net.

CAREER: Writer, 1979—. Worked as a registered nurse at hospitals in Illinois and Vancouver, British Columbia, Canada, retiring in 1993; also certified childbirth educator.

MEMBER: Canadian Society of Children's Authors, Illustrators and Performers, Children's Literature Roundtable, Children's Writers and Illustrators of British Columbia.

AWARDS, HONORS: Poetry Prize, Knowledge TV Network, 1991, for "Death of My Mother"; also finalist for other awards, including Canada Council Children's Literature Prize, Sheila A. Egoff Children's Literature Prize, West Coast Book Prize Society, and Geoffrey Bilson Award for Historical Fiction, Canadian Children's Book Centre.

WRITINGS:

FICTION

Snow Apples, Groundwood Books (Toronto, Ontario, Canada), 1984.
Salmonberry Wine, Groundwood Books (Toronto, Ontario, Canada), 1987.
Night Fires, Groundwood Books (Toronto, Ontario, Canada), 1990.
White Wave, Groundwood Books (Toronto, Ontario, Canada), 1994.
Smuggler's Moon, Groundwood Books (Toronto, Ontario, Canada), 1999.
Haida Quest, Harbour Publishing (Madeira Park, British Columbia, Canada), 2002.

Author of short story "The Job," included in the anthology *Takes: Stories for Young Adults,* edited by R. P. MacIntyre, Thistledown Press (Saskatoon, Saskatchewan, Canada), 1996. Contributor of short stories to periodicals.

OTHER

The Secret Code of DNA (nonfiction), illustrated by J. O. Pennanen, Penumbra Press (Manotick, Ontario, Canada), 1986.

St. Mary's Catholic Church: The First Fifty Years, Elphinstone Pioneer Museum (Gibsons, British Columbia, Canada), 2000.

Contributor of poetry and articles to periodicals in Canada and elsewhere.

WORK IN PROGRESS: Turkey Weed, adult fiction; a young adult novel set in British Columbia during a typhoid outbreak in 1968 and 1969.

SIDELIGHTS: Mary Razzell's novels are rooted in places she has visited, people she has known, emotions she has wrestled with, and experiences she has weathered. "When I write," she once commented, "I'm trying to work out something that's bothering me, trying to find out why things happened. When the stories or books are written, I feel a sense of ease." Writer and critic Michele Landsberg detected this personal motivation in *Snow Apples,* Razzell's first book. In *Michele Landsberg's Guide to Children's Books,* she wrote, "One feels the presence of a passionate, sometimes angry, adult sensibility, reliving the bitter injustices as well as the intense yearnings of young womanhood."

In an interview with Dave Jenkinson of *Emergency Librarian,* Razzell said, "In all those YA books, the starting point's been something that's been bothering me that I'm trying to work out. Trying to work out my mother in *Snow Apples* and also Nels, my first love. . . . In *Salmonberry Wine,* I was trying to figure out how you come to terms with your ideals in a working world. *Night Fires* was an attempt to understand why a marriage of two intelligent people with good will, who seemed to be in love, didn't work out. With *White Wave,* I wanted to write about fishing, and I wanted to write about my father."

Family life was a conundrum for the young Razzell. She felt loved and encouraged by a father who was rarely home. At the same time, she felt unloved, discouraged, and even disparaged, by a mother who was never away. Razzell's father was a mechanic by trade and, she told *Emergency Librarian,* "a philanderer" by nature. By choice as much as necessity, he was away from home and out of touch for a great deal of her childhood. Her Catholic mother, who had come to Regina, Saskatchewan, Canada, from Belfast, Ireland, in 1921, found herself on her own with five children to raise and little in the way of reliable financial support. Still, she managed to eke out enough of a living to support her family through the Depression and war years.

The effort took its toll, however. Bitterly resentful and disappointed in the turn her life had taken, she vented much of her anger and frustration at home. There, as the second oldest child and only daughter, Razzell became a sounding board for her mother's hurt and disillusionment, and a target for much of the pessimism, criticism, and suspicion this hurt and disillusionment bred.

A government program that sponsored domestic and farm workers had brought Razzell's mother to Canada. Though she had only a grade-four education, she possessed a very strong love of language and a great love of literature. She wrote poetry and short stories, and her work was published occasionally in community papers along the British Columbia coast. She was also interested in history and politics and served as secretary of the North Hill Social Credit Party when she lived in Calgary. "My mother was a *Stone Angel* type of woman, strong and capable of doing whatever she had to do," Razzell once noted. "During the Depression, she took in boarders and did housecleaning. Unfortunately, 'doing whatever she had to do' had a price. It was as if the strength to do it came at the cost of any tenderness there might have been."

If tenderness was in short supply, though, there was lots of enthusiasm for language and literature. "The biggest thrill of my childhood was to get my own library card. My eldest brother, Steve, used to bring me home picture books on his card, from the time I was four until I was six," Razzell told the Canadian Children's Book Centre. She also recalled writing her first story in grade five. She still has it and remembers "the pleasure it gave me to use words, create pictures."

By the time she was ten, moving had become a regular feature of Razzell's young life. When her parents could no longer meet the mortgage payments, they lost their house in Calgary. This blow, coupled with her father's recurring pneumonia, prompted a move to British Columbia, Canada, and, after this, the family moved every year or two. Razzell believes that all the moving contributed to her eventual decision to become a writer. She once commented, "I thought, What's the use of making friends? I became solitary. School work and reading were my focuses."

When it came time to think about a career, though, writing was not even a speck on the horizon of possibilities. Although Razzell recalls an early impression that she might enjoy being a home economist, the cost of a university education was beyond the family's means. What could be managed was the $100 tuition fee for a nursing program in Vancouver and, in 1951, after three years of training at St. Paul's Hospital, Razzell received her registered nursing diploma.

She also married in 1951. However, there was no settling down. The pattern of frequent moves she had experienced as a child persisted in her new life with her husband, Bill Razzell, who was pursuing his academic studies in the United States. Razzell nursed while her husband completed his doctorate in microbiology and until she had children. After raising two sons and a daughter, she returned to nursing where, over the years, she worked her way through the gamut of hospital nursing services. She especially enjoyed doing an oral history of nursing in British Columbia for the Registered Nurses Association of British Columbia. She was a certified childbirth educator when she retired in 1993.

When her children were in high school, Razzell's early interest in writing resurfaced. She registered in a night-school writing course one day when she realized just how soon her children might be leaving home. Taking this course was an important first step toward changing careers. Razzell liked the teacher and sold an article. The heady thrill of seeing her name in print encouraged her to continue writing. A year later, she enrolled part-time at the University of British Columbia, tackling courses in literature and creative writing. The writing courses gave her the opportunity to study under authors George McWhirter and Carol Shields.

Razzell's efforts paid off. She began to sell articles, as well as poems and short stories. At this stage, she was writing a lot of short stories. "All my novels, except *Night Fires,* began as short stories," she related. In 1979, "Two Septembers," a forerunner of *Snow Apples,* shared second prize in a University of British Columbia Alumni Short Story Prize contest.

The inspiration for her short stories, which frequently feature a young girl from British Columbia's Sunshine Coast, tended to come from her own experiences. When Shields, her creative writing instructor at the time, became intrigued by this young girl and encouraged Razzell to write about her in greater depth, she started work on an adult novel.

Razzell was well into work on this novel when she learned from her husband, who was out of the country, that their marriage was over. Fortunately, the writing project gave her a focus at a hurtful and difficult time. She finished the book but set it aside, feeling that it was too personal to publish while her mother was still alive. When she finally decided to seek a publisher, she sent it to her agent in London, England. Although she had experienced success selling a story which was a chapter in *Snow Apples* to the British Broadcasting Corporation, there were no takers for the book. The British market for first novels was flat.

Still, Eric Nicol, a writer Razzell met in 1979 when he served on the judging panel for the University of British Columbia Alumni Short Story Prize, provided encouragement on the home front. When he suggested that Douglas and McIntyre, a Vancouver publisher, might be interested in her book, Razzell followed his advice. The response was heartening. Although Douglas and McIntyre was not publishing fiction at the time, their representative offered to refer the book to Patsy Aldana, publisher of Groundwood Books in Toronto.

Aldana's interest sparked another metamorphosis in Razzell's work. Her adult novel, based on a short story, was destined to be rewritten for a young adult audience. "What was originally a memoir," Razzell once remarked, "was cut from 70,000 to 40,000 words. I also had to change the voice to a more immediate one." The publishing deadline was very tight but, with Aldana's help, Razzell met it, and *Snow Apples* was published in 1984. Looking back on the experience, Razzell said, "If I had a chance to do it again, I'd rewrite the sex scene. As it was, it was left as originally written."

Razzell's introduction to Groundwood Books was fortuitous; she found not only a good fit for her voice, but also a working relationship that was comfortable and supportive. "Groundwood treats you so well, you get spoiled," she stated. The collaboration has resulted in the publication of several more novels.

Reflecting on why she writes, Razzell once commented, "I think about what happens when you have young people who start out with high hopes and expectations. I'm trying to say, 'Look at things clearly, don't get caught up in what's not real.' When I was fifteen, the books I had access to told me I only had to look pretty and be nice. That disgusted me. I knew from experience it wasn't true."

Razzell writes in a small but comfortable study she inherited from Eric Nicol when they married in 1986. She tends to start with pen and paper. First drafts go into the computer for corrections. "If the writing is not going well, or if I have an emotional scene," she told the Canadian Children's Book Centre, "I go back to pencil and paper—the work flows more freely."

The personal nature of Razzell's work sometimes makes the editing process more difficult. For example, she wishes she had declined a request to change the setting of one of her books to the 1980s from the 1940s. "While I like contemporary young people, I can't pretend to know what's in their minds and what their experiences have been," she once explained. "What I can write about is my own truth. I have to be very careful that I don't allow my truth, which is real and will ring true to the reader, to be overcome by what someone else wants."

Razzell and her young adult novels about families, identity and strong young women have attracted critical attention. All the books except *Night Fires* have been contenders for literary awards and Razzell's gritty approach has been widely praised. In *The New Republic of Childhood: A Critical Guide to Canadian Children's Literature in English,* Sheila Egoff and Judith Saltman cited Razzell as one of the young adult novelists who has "created moving and realistic stories that offer authentic patterns of behavior and sharp insights about life." In *Quill & Quire,* Phyllis Simon noted, "Razzell does not shy away from controversial topics in her YA writing." And, in *Michele Landsberg's Guide to Children's Books,* Landsberg wrote that Razzell has achieved "what more clinical authors have failed to do: [she] forcefully conveys the driving urgency of teenage eroticism and the need for love."

Recently, a reader's question stopped Razzell in her tracks. "I was amazed," she said, "when I was asked, 'Why are your males so awful?' I answered, 'Are they? If they are, it's just what the males I knew were like.'" Still, the question caused her to think. "I think, perhaps, I've matured with my new book," she stated at the time. "I may have worked out my angst and, if so, I can go on to my imagination."

BIOGRAPHICAL AND CRITICAL SOURCES:

BOOKS

Egoff, Sheila, and Judith Saltman, *The New Republic of Childhood: A Critical Guide to Canadian Children's Literature in English,* Oxford University Press (New York, NY), 1990, p. 87.

Landsberg, Michele, *Michele Landsberg's Guide to Children's Books,* Penguin (New York, NY), 1985, p. 170, revised edition published as *Reading for the Love of It,* Prentice Hall Canada (Toronto, Ontario, Canada), 1987, p. 220.

Saltman, Judith, *Modern Canadian Children's Books,* Oxford University Press (New York, NY), 1987, pp. 71-72.

PERIODICALS

Books in Canada, August-September, 1987, pp. 34-36.
Canadian Book Review Annual, 1984, pp. 341-342; 1990, p. 325; 1994, pp. 497-498.
Canadian Children's Literature, Volume 49, 1988, pp. 49-51; Volume 66, 1992, pp. 74-75.
Children's Choices of Canadian Books, Volume 4, number 2, p. 68; Volume 6, number 2, May 1989, p. 71.
CM: Reviewing Journal of Canadian Materials for Young People, September, 1987, pp. 193-194; September, 1994, p. 139.
Emergency Librarian, March-April, 1995, interview by Dave Jenkinson, pp. 61-64.
Globe and Mail (Toronto, Ontario, Canada), November 17, 1984, p. B5; June 27, 1987, p. E20.
Quill & Quire, April, 1994, article by Phyllis Simon, p. 40.

OTHER

Canadian Children's Book Centre, unpublished notes, 1989.

* * *

REPLANSKY, Naomi 1918-

PERSONAL: Born May 23, 1918, in New York, NY; daughter of Sol and Fannie (Ginsberg) Replansky; companion of Eva Kollisch. *Education:* Attended Hunter College (now of the City University of New York), 1935-38; University of California—Los Angeles, B.A., 1956.

ADDRESSES: Home—711 Amsterdam Ave., No. 8E, New York, NY 10025.

CAREER: Poet. Worked at a variety of jobs, including office worker, factory worker, teacher, and computer programmer. Pitzer College, Claremont, CA, poet in residence, 1981; Henry Street Settlement and Educational Alliance, New York, NY, teacher of writing workshops, 1982-94.

MEMBER: PEN American Center, Poetry Society of America, Poets House, Phi Beta Kappa.

AWARDS, HONORS: National Book Award nomination, 1952, for *Ring Song.*

WRITINGS:

Ring Song (poetry), Scribner (New York, NY), 1952.
(Translator) Bertolt Brecht, *St. Joan of the Stockyards* (play), produced in New York, NY, 1978.
Twenty-one Poems, Old and New (chapbook), Gingko (New York, NY), 1988.
The Dangerous World: New and Selected Poems, 1934-1994, Another Chicago Press (Chicago, IL), 1994.

Work represented in numerous anthologies, including *No More Masks! An Anthology of Twentieth-Century American Woman Poets,* edited by Florence Howe, 1993; and *Inventions of Farewell: A Book of Elegies,* edited by Sandra M. Gilbert, W. W. Norton (New York, NY), 2001. Contributor of poetry and translations of the works of Hofmannsthal, Claudius, and Brecht to American and European magazines.

Collection of author's manuscripts is housed in the Berg Collection, New York Public Library, New York, NY.

SIDELIGHTS: Poet Naomi Replansky rose to prominence in the early 1950s when her first full-length collection of poems, *Ring Song,* was nominated for the National Book Award. However, such kudos were accompanied by blistering reviews by several critics. Replansky published only occasionally for four decades, finally emerging with *The Dangerous World: New and Selected Poems, 1934-1994.*

Written primarily during the poet's twenties and thirties, *Ring Song* reflects the creativity of a "self-taught, working-class woman who learned the craft of poetry while working in factories and stores," according to *Contemporary Women Poets* essayist Denise Wiloch. While several critics had praise for the collection—among them M. L. Rosenthal of the *New Republic,* who deemed Replansky's verses "alive and bright with color and feeling"—there were also criticisms, issuing mainly from the "patriarchal poetry establishment" of the mid-1950s, according to a reviewer in the *Bloomsbury Review.* Lawrence Ferlinghetti, reviewing *Ring Song* in the *San Francisco Chronicle,* maintained that the volume contained choppy writing and surmised that Replansky neglects the use of "her mind . . . when writing, as if merely to observe were enough." Unfortunately, Ferlinghetti, continued, such skills of observation were not yet mature.

After publication, Replansky maintained a literary silence for some years until the release of her 1994 offering, *The Dangerous World: New and Selected Poems, 1934-1994.* Elizabeth Gunderson in *Booklist* wrote of the poetry collection, "With timeless grace, she sets each poem simmering with powerful phrasing and universal experience . . . Replansky brings us ageless work in a collection that should not be missed."

BIOGRAPHICAL AND CRITICAL SOURCES:

BOOKS

Blair, Virginia, and others, editors, *Feminist Companion to Literature in English,* Yale University Press (New Haven, CT), 1990.
Contemporary Women Poets, St. James Press (Detroit, MI), 1997.
Gershgoren-Novak, Estelle, editor, *Poets of the Non-Existent City,* University of New Mexico Press (Albuquerque, NM), 2002.

PERIODICALS

Bloomsbury Review, January-February, 1995, review of *Ring Song,* p. 20.
Booklist, September 1, 1952, p. 49; October 15, 1994, Elizabeth Gunderson, review of *The Dangerous World: New and Selected Poems, 1934-1994,* p. 395.

Bridges: Journal for Jewish Feminists and Our Friends, Volume 9, number 2, 2002, interview, pp. 99-103.
Lamp in the Spine (St. Paul, MN), 1973-74.
Los Angeles Times Book Review, March 23, 2003, p. R3.
Nation, September 12, 1952.
New Republic, January 5, 1953, M. L. Rosenthal, review of *Ring Song,* p. 128.
New York Times, August 31, 1952, p. 11.
Publishers Weekly, September 26, 1994, p. 60.
San Francisco Chronicle, September 7, 1952, Lawrence Ferlinghetti, review of *Ring Song,* p. 21.
Saturday Review, September 6, 1952, A. M. Sullivan, review of *Ring Song.*
Voices: Journal of Poetry, January-April, 1953, H. W. Wells, review of *Ring Song,* pp. 55-56.
Women's Review of Books, December, 1995, pp. 11-12.

* * *

RUBIN, Hank 1916-

PERSONAL: Born May 21, 1916, in Portland, OR; son of Benjamin W. and Fannye Rubin; married, March, 1962; wife's name Lillian B. (a sociologist, psychotherapist, and writer); children: Marci. *Education:* University of California—Los Angeles, B.S., 1940; University of California—Berkeley, M.P.H., 1946.

ADDRESSES: *Home*—1333 Jones St., Apt. 808, San Francisco, CA 94109. *Agent*—Ed Knappman, New England Publishing Associates, P.O. Box 5, Chester, CT 06412.

CAREER: Teagarden Products, Oakland, CA, food technologist and jelly taster, 1954-58; *Vintage,* New York, NY, worked as managing editor; owner and executive chef of three restaurants (Pot Luck, Cruchons, and Black Sheep) in Berkeley, CA, between 1965 and 1974; co-proprietor of a small winery in Bordeaux, France. Wine Media, New York, NY, member, 1990—. Volunteer teacher at high schools in San Francisco, CA, 1992-2002. *Military service:* Army of the Republic of Spain, blood transfusionist, 1937-38. U.S. Army Air Forces, medical administrative officer during World War II; became first lieutenant.

WRITINGS:

Spain's Cause Was Mine: A Memoir of an American Medic in the Spanish Civil War, Southern Illinois University Press (Carbondale, IL), 1997.
The Kitchen Answer Book: 5,000 Answers to All of Your Kitchen and Cooking Questions, Capital Books (Dulles, VA), 2002.

Author of weekly wine column, *San Francisco Chronicle,* 1965-79; wine columnist, *Civilta del Bere.* Contributor to periodicals, including *San Jose Mercury, Wine Spectator,* and *Wine Enthuasiast.* Wine editor, *Bon Appetit,* 1968-83.

WORK IN PROGRESS: *Vino non Veritas* (tentative title), "a thousand misconceptions about wine in various countries"; research on substitutes and alternatives for food items.

S

SCHENKKAN, Robert (Frederic, Jr.) 1953-

PERSONAL: Surname is pronounced "Shank-in"; born March 19, 1953, in Chapel Hill, NC; son of Robert Frederic (a public television executive) and Jean (McKenzie) Schenkkan; married Mary Anne Dorward (an actress), December 1, 1984; children: Sara Victoria, Joshua McHenry. *Education:* University of Texas at Austin, B.A. (magna cum laude), 1975; Cornell University, M.F.A., 1977.

ADDRESSES: Home—Seattle, WA. *Agent*—Bill Craver, Writers & Artists, 19 West 44th St., No. 1000, New York, NY 10036.

CAREER: Playwright. Actor in theater, film, and television.

MEMBER: Screen Actors Guild, American Federation of Television and Radio Artists, Actors' Equity Association, New Dramatists, Dramatists Guild, Writers Guild, Ensemble Studio Theatre, Phi Beta Kappa.

AWARDS, HONORS: Best of the Fringe Award from Edinburgh Festival, 1984, for *The Survivalist;* Creative Artists Public Service Program (CAPS) grant from state of New York, 1985, for *Final Passages;* Playwrights Forum Award, 1988, for *Tall Tales;* Julie Harris Playwright Award from Beverly Hills Theatre Guild, 1989, for *Heaven on Earth;* grants from Arthur Foundation and Vogelstein Foundation, 1989, Pulitzer Prize for Drama, Columbia University, 1992, Penn Center West award, 1993, all for *The Kentucky Cycle;* grants from Fund for New American Plays, 1990, and California Arts Council, 1991; literary award, PEN Centre USA West, 1992; Antoinette Perry Award Nomination for best play, 1994, for *The Kentucky Cycle.*

WRITINGS:

PLAYS

Final Passages (first produced as *Derelict* in Buffalo, NY, 1982), published in *Plays in Process,* Theatre Communications Group, 1983, published by Dramatists Play Service, 1993.
Intermission (one-act; see also below), produced in Louisville, KY, 1982.
Lunchbreak (one-act; see also below), produced in Louisville, KY, 1982.
The Survivalist (one-act; see also below), produced Off Broadway, 1983.
Tachinoki, produced in Los Angeles, CA, at Ensemble Studio Theatre, 1987.
Tall Tales (one-act), produced in Colorado, 1988.
Heaven on Earth, produced Off Broadway, 1989, published by Dramatists Play Service, 1992.
The Kentucky Cycle (nine one-act plays), produced in Seattle, WA, 1991, published by Dramatists Play Service, 1995.
Conversations with the Spanish Lady (one-act; see also below), 1992, published as *Conversations with the Spanish Lady and Other One-Act Plays,* 1993.
Four One Act Plays: Conversations with the Spanish Lady, Lunch Break, Intermission, and the Survivalist, Dramatists Play Service, 1995.

The Dream Thief, 1998, published by Dramatic Publishing, 1999.

The Handler, 1999.

Plays included in collections, including *Burns & Mantle's Best Plays of 1993.*

SCREENPLAYS

Crazy Horse (made-for-TV movie), Turner Network Television (TNT), 1996.

Also author of scripts for *Magic* (Showtime), *The Long Ride Home* (Fox Family), *Our Fritz* (Warner Brothers), and *West of the Rising Son* (Interscope).

WORK IN PROGRESS: An adaptation of Graham Greene's novel *The Quiet American* as a film script for Paramount Pictures.

SIDELIGHTS: Robert Schenkkan's plays have been produced Off Broadway, in regional theaters across the United States, and in Canada and England. He is also an accomplished actor who has appeared in, among other things, *Star Trek: The Next Generation.* His festival appearances include the Humana Festival at the Actors Theatre of Louisville, the Edinburgh Festival, and the DuMaurier Festival. Schenkkan's work has been developed at the O'Neill Playwrights' Conference and the Sundance Playwright's Institute.

Schenkkan won national recognition for his 1991 play *The Kentucky Cycle.* When it first opened in Seattle, it broke records for ticket sales, and it went on to become the first play to win a Pulitzer Prize without having been performed in New York. Set on one plot of land in rural Appalachia, *The Kentucky Cycle* follows the suffering-filled lives of three families from the Revolutionary War until 1975. It takes six hours to tell the whole tale; actually nine separate one-act plays, *The Kentucky Cycle* is usually staged in two parts.

Several reviewers noted how dark *The Kentucky Cycle* is. "Firearms or knives are used in seven of the plays. The other two practice violence of the soul," depicting a man losing his freedom and another losing his beloved lush homestead, noted *Time* critic William A. Henry III. While *Denver Post* reviewer Dianne Zuckerman also noted the "greed, violence and generational retribution" in *The Kentucky Cycle,* she thought the tale as a whole was "a crackling good yarn." "While Schenkkan's insights [into the suffering of women, ethnic minorities, and the poor] aren't new, his dramatic skill gives fresh clout to the familiar struggle between the haves and the have-nots," she declared.

Schennkan's first play for children, *The Dream Thief,* premiered in 1998. Susan and Jamie are the children of a writer and an actress, both of whom are struggling at the moment. Their father's largest problem is that he has lost the biological ability to dream, which has affected his sleep in potentially life-threatening ways, as well as his ability to write. Through a series of imaginative encounters in the Land of Nod featuring the Sandman (who looks suspiciously like Susan and Jamie's father) and Twinkle, the little star (who looks like their mother), the children get their parents' dreams back, thus fulfilling the play's premise as described by *Shepherd Express* contributor Gordon Spencer: "Without dreams we cannot live either biologically or psychologically." Spencer praised the play in his review, calling it "imaginative, intelligent, funny, [and] contemporary."

Schenkkan is also the author of the play *The Handler,* about a Southern family which participates in a church which handles poisonous snakes as part of its worship. The play opens with the husband, Geordi, just being released from jail. He had been convicted of manslaughter for accidently running over his young daughter when he was driving drunk. One early scene features Geordi in church with his wife, Terri. Each is praying, Geordi for forgiveness for killing his child, Terri for God not to forgive him. The audience soon finds out that Terri's wish was the one which was granted: when Geordi decides to handle the snakes, for the first time in his life, he is bitten in the neck and killed. However, he rises from the dead in the middle of his funeral service, bringing a horde of reporters to their small town. Geordi flees into the mountains and descends into his own personal hell in preparation for his eventual reconciliation with his wife. According to Walter Bilderback, who reviewed the play for *American Theatre,* in *The Handler* Schenkkan "has created moments of hypnotic power and poetic ecstasy that far surpass his accomplishment in *The Kentucky Cycle.*"

BIOGRAPHICAL AND CRITICAL SOURCES:

BOOKS

Contemporary Theatre, Film, and Television, Volume 4, Gale (Detroit, MI), 1987.

PERIODICALS

American Theatre, April, 2000, Walter Bilderback, "Dangerous Salvation," p. 34.
Booklist, September 1, 1993, review of *The Kentucky Cycle,* p. 28.
Children's Book & Play Review, January, 2001, review of *The Dream Thief,* pp. 38+.
Christian Science Monitor, November 30, 1993, Frank Scheck, "Appalachia Stint Fuels Pulitzer-Winning Play."
Denver Post, August 25, 2000, Diane Zuckerman, "Hunger Artists Show Tells Saga of a Nation."
Los Angeles Times, April 8, 1992, Don Shirley, "Drama Pulitzer Breaks N.Y. Monopoly"; April 27, 1995, Don Shirley, "'Cycle' Retains Power in its Return to L.A."
New Yorker, November 20, 1989, Edith Oliver, review of *Heaven on Earth,* p. 110.
New York Times, November 12, 1989; July 5, 1996, John J. O'Connor, review of *Crazy Horse,* pp. B3, D9.
Rocky Mountain News, August 18, 2000, Lisa Bornstein, "An Epic Look at Cursed Lives"; August 25, 2000, Lisa Bornstein, "'Kentucky Cycle' Wobbles to Its End."
Shepherd Express, November 19, 1998, Gordon Spencer, "The Thief of Dreams."
Time, November 22, 1993, William A. Henry III, review of *The Kentucky Cycle,* p. 72.

OTHER

Bradley University, http://www.bradley.edu/ (June 19, 2002).
Kennedy Center Fund for New American Plays, http://www.kennedy-center.org/ (May 15, 2002).*

* * *

SCHNUR, Steven 1952-

PERSONAL: Born April 8, 1952. *Education:* Sarah Lawrence College, B.A., 1974; Hunter College of City University, M.A., 1980.

ADDRESSES: Home—19 Montrose Rd., Scarsdale, NY 10583.

CAREER: Bernard M. Baruch College of the City University of New York, New York, NY, instructor, 1977; Union of American Hebrew Congregations, New York, NY, editor, 1981-92; Sarah Lawrence College, Bronxville, NY, Writing Institute faculty, 1990—; *Reform Judaism* (magazine), literary editor, 1994-98; writer. Mercy College, adjunct professor, 1991-92.

MEMBER: Author's Guild.

AWARDS, HONORS: Washington Irving Book Award, Westchester Library Association (WLA), for *Daddy's Home! Reflections of a Family Man;* Sydney Taylor Book Award, Association of Jewish Libraries, 1994, Best Children's Book Award, Women's Zionist Organization, 1996, Premio Verghereto (Italy), 1999, and Washington Irving Children's Choice Award, WLA, all for *The Shadow Children;* Notable Children's Trade Book in the Field of Social Studies citation, National Council for the Social Studies/Children's Book Council, 1995, for *The Shadow Children,* and 1996, for *The Tie Man's Miracle: A Chanukah Tale;* Washington Irving Children's Choice Award, WLA, 1998, for *The Tie Man's Miracle;* Washington Irving Children's Choice Honor Book, WLA, 1998, and Best Books for Young Adults citation, American Library Association, both for *Beyond Providence;* Young Adult Choice selection, International Reading Association, 1999, for *The Koufax Dilemma.*

WRITINGS:

FOR CHILDREN

The Narrowest Bar Mitzvah, illustrated by Victor Lazarro, Union of American Hebrew Congregations (New York, NY), 1986.
The Return of Morris Schumsky, illustrated by Victor Lazarro, Union of American Hebrew Congregations (New York, NY), 1987.
Hannah and Cyclops, Bantam (New York, NY), 1990.
The Shadow Children, illustrated by Herbert Tauss, Morrow Junior Books (New York, NY), 1994.
The Tie Man's Miracle: A Chanukah Tale, illustrated by Stephen T. Johnson, Morrow Junior Books (New York, NY), 1995.

Beyond Providence, Harcourt Brace (San Diego, CA), 1996.

The Koufax Dilemma, Morrow Junior Books (New York, NY), 1997.

Autumn: An Alphabet Acrostic, illustrated by Leslie Evans, Clarion Books (New York, NY), 1997.

Spring: An Alphabet Acrostic, illustrated by Leslie Evans, Clarion Books (New York, NY), 1999.

Spring Thaw, illustrated by Stacey Schuett, Viking (New York, NY), 2000.

Night Lights, illustrated by Stacey Schuett, Frances Foster Books (New York, NY), 2000.

Summer: An Alphabet Acrostic, illustrated by Leslie Evans, Clarion Books (New York, NY), 2001.

Winter: An Alphabet Acrostic, illustrated by Leslie Evans, Clarion Books (New York, NY), 2002.

(Adapter) Henry David Thoreau, *Henry David's House,* illustrated by Peter M. Fiore, Charlesbridge (Watertown, MA), 2002.

OTHER

Daddy's Home!: Reflections of a Family Man, illustrated by Cheryl Gross, Crown (New York, NY), 1990, published as *Father's Day,* Avon Books (New York, NY), 1991.

This Thing Called Love: Thoughts of an Out-of-Step Romantic, Morrow (New York, NY), 1992.

9/11, Acorn Press (New York, NY), 2002.

Contributor to periodicals, including *New York Times, Reform Judaism, Christian Science Monitor, Woman's Day, New Woman, Moxie, First for Women, Twins, Denver Quarterly, Commentary,* and *Real People.*

SIDELIGHTS: Steven Schnur began his writing career with family stories for young readers featuring Jewish themes in books such as *The Narrowest Bar Mitzvah* and *The Return of Morris Schumsky,* which deal with family traditions and ceremonies, and *The Shadow Children* and *The Tie Man's Miracle: A Chanukah Tale,* which treat the Holocaust. Since then, Schnur has branched out to write more wide-ranging material for both beginning readers and older children as well as essays for adults. His later picture books, including a quartet of acrostics arranged around the seasons, often deal with nature or human interactions with the natural world.

Among his Jewish family works are his first book, *The Narrowest Bar Mitzvah,* and *The Return of Morris Schumsky.* The former tells of how Alex's bar mitzvah is almost ruined when a water main break the night before the event swamps the synagogue and ruins the refreshments. After some quick planning by Alex's family, the celebration is moved to Grandpa's six-foot-wide house. As noted by reviewer Ruth Shire in *School Library Journal,* Alex's grandparents have a "starring role and a very special relationship with their grandchildren" in this family story, which also features Grandfather's unusual house. In the second novel, Grandpa disappears on the morning of his granddaughter's wedding, only to reappear in the nick of time for the event with some friends from a local nursing home. The book was described as a "charming and evocative" story by a *Publishers Weekly* reviewer and praised by Ruth Shire in *School Library Journal* for its "strong characterizations" and "good portrayal of positive values."

More serious themes are dealt with in his 1994 offering, *The Shadow Children,* the story of eleven-year-old Etienne, who is spending the summer on his grandfather's farm in the French countryside after World War II. One day Etienne encounters the ghosts of Jewish children who had been sheltered on the farm during the war—until Etienne's grandfather and the other villagers, confronted by the Nazis and fearing for their own lives, let the children be taken away in cattle cars. In a review for *Horn Book,* Nancy Vasilakis singled out the book as a "thought-provoking novel." While noting that the book's theme of "unredeemed guilt" might prove difficult for middle graders, she affirmed that "there is no mistaking the book's importance" and its "power to grip the imagination and the conscience." Describing the author's narrative as "spare and beautiful," *Booklist*'s Hazel Rochman predicted that upon completion of *The Shadow Children,* "Readers will be moved to ask: what would I have done."

Schnur again undertakes the challenge presented by the topic of the Holocaust in *The Tie Man's Miracle,* a picture book for ages five and up. A Holocaust survivor who sells neckties door to door is invited to join young Seth's family for a Chanukah seder. Seth's baby sister Hannah reminds the old man of one of the five children he lost, along with his wife, in World War II. During the meal, Mr. Hoffman, the old man, describes a Chanukah belief in his village that if the nine candles on the menorah all burn out at the same instant, the smoke from them will carry a holiday prayer "straight to the ear of God." After Mr. Hoffman leaves, Seth silently prays that the old man will get his family back. At that moment smoke rises from all nine columns, and the boy sees a vision of light and hears laughter and voices calling, "Papa, Papa." The reader never learns what happens to the tie man, but every year Seth and Hannah make their prayers on the eighth night of Chanukah. Writing in *Horn Book,* reviewer Hanna B. Zeiger found *The Tie Man's Miracle* a "touching tale that links remembrance of the Holocaust with . . . Hanukkah in a sensitive and accessible way." While noting that Schnur has introduced a "delicate topic" carefully, a *Publishers Weekly* critic still found the Chanukah setting an "uncomfortable backdrop for a discussion of an ugly period in history." *School Library Journal* contributor Jane Marino, however, praised how the author "effectively weaves together the elements of miracle, mystery, and faith" in a story that explores the "mystery" of Chanukah.

In *Beyond Providence,* the setting features a rundown farm in upstate New York around the turn of the century. Nat Burns, the twelve-year-old narrator, and his older brother Eric, who wants to be an artist, both suffer at the hands of their embittered father, whose temper and bad leg just exacerbate the situation. The boys' mother has run away from the contentious household, only to die in a boating accident, and their father's thirty-year-old niece Kitty has come to help out around the house. Later they are joined by Nat's Uncle Zeke, who brings a badly needed sense of humor to the household. Kitty, who refuses to let the family become antisocial, falls in love with a much younger man from a neighboring farm. Eventually the family works out its problems, and when Nat turns sixteen, his father presents him with his piece of land and a summer cabin. *Booklist* reviewer Francis Bradburn found *Beyond Providence* "an exceptional book for that special group of readers that enjoys introspective, superbly crafted fiction." A *Kirkus Reviews* writer similarly noted the book's "lyrical prose" and concluded, "it's a novel that grows on readers with each turn of the page."

Like his hero Sandy Koufax, the Dodger pitcher who refused to pitch in a World Series game because it fell on Yom Kippur, fifth-grader Danny is also a pitcher who happens to be Jewish. In *The Koufax Dilemma,* Danny must decide whether baseball is more important than celebrating the first night of Passover with his mom, who is divorced from his dad, and her new boyfriend. Schnur has put several potential conflicts into play here, and in resolving them, according to *School Library Journal* reviewer Jack Forman, Danny relies "less on Koufax's model than on the unusually understanding adults in his life." Writing in the *Bulletin of the Center for Children's Books,* Amy E. Brandt stated that "the moral dilemma suggested by the title is reduced to adult lectures," but admitted that "readers may well relate to Danny's frustrations." Forman similarly observed that Danny is a "winning character . . . appealing, even in his childish obstinacy." As Stephanie Zvirin concluded in *Booklist:* "Danny's responses ring true: overdramatic and sometimes illogical, they are right on target."

In addition to his books dealing with Jewish themes, Schnur has also written other well-received works for youngsters. Between 1997 and 2002, Schnur and illustrator Leslie Evans published four picture books about the seasons. Beginning with *Autumn,* each book title carries the subtitle "an alphabet acrostic," that is, a poem in which the first letter of each line spells out a word when viewed vertically. After the first picture book made its debut, *Horn Book Guide* contributor Peter D. Sieruta favorably commented on Schnur's "evocative prose," which went on to be a hallmark of the quartet. *Booklist*'s Carolyn Phelan claimed the author's "best acrostics are fresh and imaginative," describing *Spring* overall as an "attractive" picture book with good classroom applications. *School Library Journal* critic Grace Oliff also dubbed *Spring* "innovative and lovely." Several reviewers appreciated *Summer,* including Steven Engelfried of *School Library Journal,* who praised the rhythm and "sheer inventiveness" of these poems that are composed within such a strict form, and Hazel Rochman of *Booklist,* who predicted that children and crossword puzzle enthusiasts would be "caught by the word game." A *Kirkus Reviews* critic also applauded *Summer,* dubbing it "another tour de force" for its technical virtuosity and evocative illustrations. With their final volume, *Winter,* the duo "produc[es] another visually and verbally entrancing title" to complete "a most satisfying quartet" concluded a *Kirkus Reviews* contributor.

The picture books *Spring Thaw, Night Lights,* and *Henry David's House* also deal with nature, particularly people's interactions with it. *Spring Thaw,* which *Booklist*'s Carolyn Phelan described as "more a lyrical mood piece than a story," shows the advent of spring through small events in the countryside. In *Night Lights,* Melinda "counts" the lights she can see as she prepares for bed, beginning with one nightlight on her wall and ending up with the million stars up above. While the literal-minded child might become frustrated as the numbers get larger, counting is not really the point after reaching fifty, Phelan noted in *Booklist*. Instead, this "beautiful" book in rhyming text would be a "satisfying choice" for readers and listeners needing a quiet bedtime book. Indeed, according to Marlene Gawron of *School Library Journal*, in "this lovely picture book," the theme of broadening one's perspective "is intriguing and well captured." And as the title suggests, *Henry David's House* is about Henry David Thoreau's life in the woods at Walden Pond. For this picture book adaptation of Thoreau's 1854 book, *Walden, or Life in the Woods,* Schnur selected highlights of Thoreau's book, which were then illustrated in pastel watercolor and oil paintings. According to Nancy Menaldi-Scanlan of *School Library Journal*, *Henry David's House* "will be particularly useful to teachers of art and science" as well as to English teachers wishing to introduce Thoreau's work.

BIOGRAPHICAL AND CRITICAL SOURCES:

BOOKS

Schnur, Steven, *The Tie Man's Miracle: A Chanukah Tale,* illustrated by Stephen T. Johnson, Morrow Junior Books (New York, NY), 1995.

PERIODICALS

Booklist, November 14, 1994, Hazel Rochman, review of *The Shadow Children,* p. 603; April 1, 1996, Frances Bradburn, review of *Beyond Providence,* pp. 1356-1357; March 15, 1997, Stephanie Zvirin, review of *The Koufax Dilemma;* April 1, 1999, Carolyn Phelan, review of *Spring: An Alphabet Acrostic,* p. 1418; March 1, 2000, Carolyn Phelan, review of *Spring Thaw,* p. 1252; May 1, 2000, Carolyn Phelan, review of *Night Lights,* p. 1680; July, 2000, Hazel Rochman, review of *The Tie Man's Miracle: A Chanukah Tale,* p. 2027; March 15, 2001, Hazel Rochman, review of *Summer: An Alphabet Acrostic,* p. 1393; April 1, 2002, John Peters, review of *Henry David's House,* p. 1340.
Bulletin of the Center for Children's Books, May, 1997, Amy E. Brandt, review of *The Koufax Dilemma.*
Horn Book, January-February, 1995, Nancy Vasilakis, review of *The Shadow Children,* p. 61; November-December, 1995, Hanna B. Zeiger, review of *The Tie Man's Miracle,* p. 730.
Horn Book Guide, spring, 1998, Peter D. Sieruta, review of *Autumn: An Alphabet Acrostic,* p. 151.
Kirkus Reviews, November 15, 1994, pp. 603, 1543; April 1, 1996, review of *Beyond Providence,* p. 536; December 15, 1999, review of *Spring Thaw,* p. 1963; February 1, 2001, review of *Summer,* p. 189; February 1, 2002, review of *Henry David's House,* p. 190; October 1, 2002, review of *Winter: An Alphabet Acrostic,* pp. 1479-1480.
Publishers Weekly, August 14, 1987, William Griffin, review of *The Return of Morris Schumsky,* p. 73; November 14, 1994, p. 69; September 18, 1995, review of *The Tie Man's Miracle,* p. 92; March 29, 1999, review of *Spring,* p. 106; October 7, 2002, "Encore Performances," review of *Winter,* p. 75.
School Library Journal, April, 1987, Ruth Shire, review of *The Narrowest Bar Mitzvah,* p. 104; May, 1988, Ruth Shire, review of *The Return of Morris Schumsky,* p. 101; October, 1995, Jane Marino, review of *The Tie Man's Miracle,* p. 41; April, 1996, p. 158; May, 1997, Jack Forman, review of *The Koufax Dilemma;* April, 1999, Grace Oliff, review of *Spring,* p. 124; February, 2000, Kathleen M. Kelly MacMillan, review of *Spring Thaw,* p. 103; July, 2000, Marlene Gawron, review of *Night Lights,* p. 86; April, 2001, Steven Engelfried, review of *Summer,* p. 135; May, 2002, Nancy Menaldi-Scanlan, review of *Henry David's House,* p. 178.
Voice of Youth Advocates, June, 1996, p. 101.

* * *

SHEPARD, Lucius 1947-

PERSONAL: Born August 21, 1947, in Lynchburg, VA; son of William (a writer) and Lucy (a teacher) Shepard; married; wife's name Joyce (an anthropologist), 1966; children: Gullivar. *Politics:* Radical. *Hobbies and other interests:* Rock music, world music.

ADDRESSES: Home—1010 Taylor Ave. N, No. 2, Seattle, WA 98109. *Agent*—Ralph Vicinanza, 111 Eighth Ave., New York, NY 10001.

CAREER: Self-employed as a musician during the 1970s and early 1980s; writer.

MEMBER: Science Fiction Writers of America.

AWARDS, HONORS: Campbell Award for best new writer, World Science Fiction Society, 1985, for *Green Eyes; Science Fiction Chronicle* Reader Award, 1986, for story "Salvador"; Nebula Award for best novella, Science Fiction Writers of America, 1987, for *R & R;* World Fantasy Award for best story collection, *Locus* magazine, 1988, and *New York Times* notable book citation, 1992, both for *The Jaguar Hunter;* World Fantasy Award for best story collection, 1992, for *The Ends of the Earth;* Hugo Award for Best Novella, World Science Fiction Society, 1993, for *Barnacle Bill the Spacer;* Hugo Award nomination for Best Novella, World Science Fiction Society, 2001, and the *Locus Award,* both for *Radiant Green Star.*

WRITINGS:

Cantata of Death, Weakmind & Generation (poems), Lillabulero Press (Chapel Hill, NC), 1967.
Sports and Music, M. V. Ziesing Books (Shingletown, CA), 1993.
Vermillion (comic book series), DC Comics (New York, NY), 1996-97.
Two Trains Running, Golden Gryphon Press (Urbana, IL), 2004.

NOVELS

Green Eyes, Ace Books (New York, NY), 1984.
Life during Wartime (novel), Bantam (New York, NY), 1987.
Kalimantan, Legend (London, England), 1990, St. Martin's Press (New York, NY), 1992.
The Golden, Bantam Books (New York, NY), 1993.
A Handbook of American Prayer, Mark V. Ziesing (Shingletown, CA), 1996.
Valentine: A Novel, Four Walls Eight Windows (New York, NY), 2002.
Louisiana Breakdown, Golden Gryphon Press (Urbana, IL), 2003.

NOVELLAS

The Scalehunter's Beautiful Daughter, Mark V. Ziesing (Willimantic, CT), 1988.

The Father of Stones, Washington Science Fiction (Baltimore, MD), 1989.
(With Robert Frazier) *Nantucket Slayrides: Three Short Novels,* Eel Grass Press (Nantucket, MA), 1989.
Colonel Rutherford's Colt (e-book), ElectricStory.com, 2002, Subterranean (Burton, MI), 2003.
Aztechs, Subterranean (Burton, MI), 2003.

SHORT STORY COLLECTIONS

The Jaguar Hunter, Arkham House (Sauk City, WI), 1987.
The Ends of the Earth, illustrated by Jeffrey K. Potter, Arkham House (Sauk City, WI), 1991.
Barnacle Bill the Spacer, and Other Stories, Millennium (London, England), 1998, also published as *Beast of the Heartland, and Other Stories,* Four Walls Eight Windows (New York, NY), 1999.

Author of award-winning novellas *R & R* and *Radiant Green Star.* Contributor of stories to science fiction magazines and anthologies, including *Universe 13, Universe 14, The Clarion Awards, Fantasy and Science Fiction, Playboy,* and *Isaac Asimov's Science Fiction Magazine.* Also author of screenplays.

ADAPTATIONS: Life during Wartime has been optioned for film.

WORK IN PROGRESS: Comic book series "The Bamboo Union," set in contemporary Vietnam.

SIDELIGHTS: Nebula Award-winning science fiction and fantasy writer Lucius Shepard garnered mainstream recognition and critical acclaim with his 1984 novel, *Green Eyes.* Since then Shepard has emerged as an important figure in what one critic called "terror fiction"—short stories and novels that transcend genre by incorporating elements of horror, science fiction, and psychological drama. To quote Paul di Filippo in the *St. James Guide to Horror, Ghost and Gothic Writers,* Shepard has produced "an astonishing array of demonstrably classic stories," all of which succeed on the "sheer quality of his writing." The critic continued: "Shepard is a consummate stylist, possessing a seemingly limitless ability to spin off sparkling original metaphors and concrete visualizations of the bizarre. With a rich vocabulary that enlists all of the reader's senses, he conjures mind-movies of surpassing vividness. Secondly, Shepard's imagination is as extensive as his experience. Able to spin endless variations on his basic plot scenario, Shepard always offers enough variety to keep readers intrigued."

Shepard left home at the age of fifteen and spent much of the next two decades traveling around the world. He also played in a rock band and experimented with drugs. Di Filippo wrote: "As years passed and Shepard tumbled around the globe, supporting himself both licitly and illicitly, he developed a fascination with those places best characterized as 'the ends of the earth,' a touchstone phrase for Shepard, and one he employs consistently. . . . Like Thoreau in the Maine woods, Shepard finds these locales—from Borneo to the Caribbean, but most vitally, Latin America—to be places where essentials of evil and good, duty and desire can be examined and confronted without the obscuring smoke of civilization."

Set in Louisiana in the near future, Shepard's first novel, *Green Eyes,* resurrects the time-honored zombie theme with a contemporary twist. Shepard brings the dead to life in a secret, government-funded lab by infecting genetically modified graveyard bacteria into the brains of the recently deceased. The zombies emerge with occult powers and an awesome capacity for good or evil, but their new lives are cut short by the fatally overbreeding bacteria, which make their eyes glow phosphorescent green.

From this premise, Shepard weaves a gothic adventure story laden with moral and social overtones. The zombie/poet protagonist, Donnell Harrison, escapes from the lab with his female therapist and hides out in decrepit, sinister New Orleans neighborhoods where he discovers his affinity for voodoo and becomes a faith healer. In reviews of *Green Eyes,* critics particularly praised Shepard's imaginative narrative and lyrical prose. "The fascinating premise of the story and the superior writing make *Green Eyes* a book you shouldn't miss," remarked Gene Deweese in *Science Fiction Review.*

The surreal also figures prominently in Shepard's second novel, *Life during Wartime.* The book is set in the jungles of Central America, where United States military forces are engaged in a protracted, Vietnam War-like conflict with shadowy guerrillas. As the story unfolds, the war has long since lost any sense of greater purpose and has assumed its own momentum as the occupying U.S. soldiers fight endlessly in a mindless haze of tropical heat, powerful drugs, and homicidal rapture. As in *Green Eyes,* political and moral themes underlie this war story. The exotic setting, critics observed, allows Shepard to display his gift for highly imaginative, surreal description. "In literary terms, *Life during Wartime* is a war between science fiction and magical realism, and Shepard uses both to superb effect," remarked *Times Literary Supplement* contributor Paul Kincaid. The reviewer added: "Shepard is a writer of startling power and originality, whose prose is as lush and fruitful as the jungles in which he sets his story." Di Filippo contended of the work: "As a portrait of corruption and redemption, as a phantasmagoric allegory, *Life during Wartime* has few parallels in modern genre literature."

Shepard also chose exotic locales for the stories in his collections *The Jaguar Hunter* and *The Ends of the Earth* and for his 1991 novel *Kalimantan. Kalimantan,* set in Borneo, details how two men attempt to control a miracle drug—developed by a witch doctor—that allows passage to another world. The typical heroes of the tales in *The Jaguar Hunter* are young Americans who had been disillusioned by the Vietnam War and who are living abroad in such places as Latin America, Katmandu, and the Caribbean. "The stories," commented Richard Gehr in the *Village Voice,* "are alternately tragic and redemptive, and never dull." *Times Literary Supplement* contributor Colin Greenland observed that in *The Jaguar Hunter* Shepard "deploys romance to enlarge and enrich his theme of alienation," and added that "his prose is full, even sumptuous, yet keen." In *Review of Contemporary Fiction,* Irving Malin deemed *The Jaguar Hunter* "a remarkable collection." Shepard's writing was also praised in reviews of *The Ends of the Earth,* with *Booklist* contributor Roland Green deeming him "one of the leading lights of literary science fiction."

At first glance, *The Golden* seems to be a standard gothic tale of vampires and their prey, but Shepard molds his tale of the bizarre goings-on at Castle Banat into a treatment of vampires as aliens seeking an especially nutritious kind of blood. "With its portrayal of power-mad immortals . . . engaged in feuds and schemes more bloody and recondite than those found in Roger Zelazny's 'Amber' books, and with its focus on the historical past, *The Golden* stakes out new territory for Shepard," Di Filippo observed. The critic concluded that Shepard "is an outsider at home nowhere and everywhere, one whose sad, wise gaze is turned not without compassion on every person he depicts—and on himself most unsparingly of all."

The 2002 romantic novel *Valentine* represents something of a departure for Shepard. In this story, two ex-lovers find themselves reunited under intense circumstances. Taking shelter together from a hurricane, Russell and Kay (who is now married), are afforded enough privacy to discover that there is much more to their connection than past and present lust. Critics deemed the book readable, but a bit flat in terms of substance. A *Kirkus Reviews* contributor concluded that the book is "heavily erotic, lightly plotted: a lover's confection, with a certain sweetness but little sustenance." Similarly, a critic for *Publishers Weekly* commented that although Shepard succeeds in creating exciting love scenes, "he fails to flesh out the plot with anything other than the constant coupling of his two lovers." Bonnie Johnston of *Booklist*, however, found the book to be a good balance of passion and "philosophical musings," declaring the novel "haunting and magical."

Shepard has stated that in most of his work the plot is driven by the characters. In an interview with *Event Horizon*, he said, "I guess that most of the people I write about are people who are trapped by circumstances that are partly of their own making. They are flawed people, and they think they see something better for themselves, but in the end their flaws overwhelm them, and so they are forced to make some kind of rational accommodation with their failure."

Shepard has continued to garner awards and gather a devoted following among science fiction fans, although he occasionally steps outside of the science fiction and fantasy genres. He discussed the evolution of his work in an *Omni* interview in which he commented, "I think I have to leave it to readers to define how the work has changed, but I feel that my characters in the new stuff are much more idiosyncratic, much more clearly articulated, and that the stories I'm telling are much more peculiar than the old ones, even if they aren't science fiction or fantasy. My appreciation of the world, it seems, has grown more perversely individual."

BIOGRAPHICAL AND CRITICAL SOURCES:

BOOKS

St. James Guide to Horror, Ghost and Gothic Writers, St. James Press (Detroit, MI), 1998, pp. 527-529.

PERIODICALS

Booklist, February 1, 1991, p. 1115; January 1, 2002, p. 814.
Bookwatch, August, 1999, p. 9.
Kirkus Reviews, February 1, 1991, p. 146; November 15, 1991; November 15, 2001, p. 1576.
Library Journal, May 1, 2002, p. 88.
Los Angeles Times Book Review, December 13, 1987, p. 13.
Magazine of Fantasy and Science Fiction, December 1999, p. 33.
New York Times Book Review, June 7, 1987.
Publishers Weekly, November 15, 1991, p. 66; January 9, 1995, p. 24; March 22, 1999, p. 75; November 12, 2001, p. 32.
Review of Contemporary Fiction, spring, 1990, p. 319-320.
Science Fiction Chronicle, July, 1998, p. 46.
Science Fiction Review, May, 1984, p. 23.
Times Literary Supplement, June 20, 1986, p. 683; October 21, 1988, p. 1180; March 31, 1989.
Village Voice, August 18, 1987, p. 52.
Washington Post, February 11, 1988.
Washington Post Book World, April 22, 1984, p. 11; May 24, 1987, p. 6; June 26, 1988; February 23, 1992, p. 10.

ONLINE

ElectricStory.com, www.electricstory.com/ (December 2, 2003).
Four Walls Eight Windows, www.fourwalleightwindows.com/ (December 2, 2003).*

* * *

SIDKY, H. 1956-

PERSONAL: Born November 22, 1956, in New York, NY. *Ethnicity:* "Caucasian." *Education:* Rocky Mountain College, B.A., 1978; University of Miami, Coral Gables, FL, M.A. (cum laude), 1985; Ohio State University, Ph.D. (cum laude), 1994.

ADDRESSES: *Home*—6 Jeffrey Dr., Oxford, OH 45056. *Office*—Department of Anthropology, Miami University, Oxford, OH 45056. *E-mail*—sidkyh@muohio.edu.

CAREER: Miami University, Oxford, OH, assistant professor, 1994-2000, associate professor of anthropology, 2000—. Conducted field research among the Islamic people of Afghanistan, 1979, among the Rapanui of Easter Island, 1989, among the Hunzakut people of Northern Pakistan, 1990-91 and 1998, and in Alice Springs, Northern Territory, Australia, 1998, 2001; conducted ethnographic field research in the Jiri Valley and Kathmandu Valley, Nepal, 1999 and 2000. Performed forensic facial reconstructions for the coroner's offices of Marion County and Franklin County, OH, 1988-89.

MEMBER: American Anthropological Association, Society for Anthropological Sciences, Sigma Xi, Phi Kappa Phi.

AWARDS, HONORS: Grants from Ohio State University, for research on Easter Island, 1989, and in the Hunza state (now in northwestern Pakistan), 1990-91; award from Philip and Elaina Hampton Fund for Faculty International Initiatives, Miami University, 1999.

WRITINGS:

Hunza: An Ethnographic Outline, Illustrated Book Publishers (Jaipur, India), 1995.
Irrigation and State Formation in Hunza: The Anthropology of a Hydraulic Kingdom, University Press of America (Lanham, MD), 1996.
Witchcraft, Lycanthropy, Drugs, and Disease: An Anthropological Study of the European Witch-Persecutions, Peter Lang (New York, NY), 1997.
The Greek Kingdom of Bactria: From Alexander to Eucratides the Great, University Press of America (Lanham, MD), 2000.
(With Janardan Subedi) *Bitan: Oracles and Healers in the Karakorams,* Illustrated Book Publishers (Jaipur, India), 2000.
(With Janardan Subedi and James Hamill) *Halfway to the Mountain: The Jirels of Eastern Nepal; An Ethnographic Description,* Tribhuvan University Press (Kathmandu, Nepal), 2002.

A Critique of Postmodern Anthropology: In Defense of Disciplinary Origins and Traditions, Edwin Mellen Press (Lewiston, NY), 2003.

Contributor of articles and reviews to academic journals, including *Anthropological Linguistics, Central Asiatic Journal, Asian Folklore Studies, Asian Affairs, Asian Culture Quarterly,* and *Eastern Anthropologist.* Editor, *MESA Folklore Bulletin,* 1992.

WORK IN PROGRESS: *Perspectives on Culture: An Introduction to Theory in Cultural Anthropology; Phombos and Jhankris: Spirit Masters and Healers,* with Janardan Subedi.

* * *

SILVER, Lee M(errill) 1952-

PERSONAL: Born April 27, 1952, in Philadelphia, PA; son of Joseph and Ethel (Goodman) Silver; married Susan Remis, August 25, 1985; children: Rebecca, Ari, Maxwell. *Education:* University of Pennsylvania, B.A., M.S., 1973; Harvard University, Ph.D., 1978. *Politics:* Democrat. *Religion:* Jewish.

ADDRESSES: *Office*—Princeton University, Princeton, NJ 08544. *Agent*—Theresa Park, Sanford J. Greenburger Associates, 55 Fifth Ave., New York, NY. *E-mail*—lsilver@princeton.edu.

CAREER: Cornell University, Medical School, New York, NY, assistant professor of genetics, 1979-80; Yeshiva University, Albert Einstein College of Medicine, Bronx, NY, visiting assistant professor of genetics, 1980; Cold Spring Harbor Laboratory, Cold Spring Harbor, NY, senior scientist, 1980-84; State University of New York—Stony Brook, Stony Brook, NY, assistant professor of genetics, 1981-84; Princeton University, Princeton, NJ, professor, 1984—.

MEMBER: International Mammalian Genome Society, Genetics Society of America, American Association for the Advancement of Science (fellow).

AWARDS, HONORS: Fellow, National Endowment for the Humanities, 1978-79; postdoctoral fellow, Sloan-Kettering Cancer Institute, 1977-80; Merit Award, National Institute for the Humanities, 1995.

WRITINGS:

(Editor, with Gail R. Martin and Sidney Strickland) *Teratocarcinoma Stem Cells,* Cold Spring Harbor Laboratory (Cold Spring Harbor, NY), 1983.
Mouse Genetics: Concepts and Applications, Oxford University Press (New York, NY), 1995.
Remaking Eden: Cloning and Beyond in a Brave New World, Avon (New York, NY), 1997.
(With Leland Hartwell, Leroy Hood, Michael L. Goldberg, and others) *Genetics: From Genes to Genomes with Genetics,* McGraw-Hill (New York, NY), 1999, 2nd edition, in press.

Editor in chief, *Mammalian Genome,* 1990-2001.

WORK IN PROGRESS: *The Last Taboo: Biotechnology and the Reconstruction of the Human Soul,* publication by Ecco Publishers (New York, NY) expected in 2004.

SIDELIGHTS: The study of mice in the laboratory has been important for the understanding of human genetics, biology, and disease for close to 100 years. Lee M. Silver's book, *Mouse Genetics: Concepts and Applications,* describes how mice came to be used by researchers as laboratory animals and includes chapters about the animals' reproduction and their genomes (chromosomes with the genes or inherited factors they contain), as well as gene mapping. Readers of this text can also learn about computer databases designed for mouse researchers and sources for obtaining laboratory mice. B. W. Auclair wrote in *Choice* that "students and researchers involved in mouse genetic research will find Silver's book a welcome addition to their shelves," and called the book a "well-written overview." Michael Potter and Beverly Mock assessed *Mouse Genetics* as "a unique synthesis of modern molecular genetics and the biology of the laboratory mouse" in *Science.* These reviewers also pointed out the growing need for familiarity with the biology of "this fascinating creature," and they labeled the book as understandable, practical, and unified, with a "pleasing and easy style." "Silver's insightful interest in the evolution of genomes surfaces over and over again in the text, making this book an exciting introduction to the comprehensive biology that is involved in the intriguing mysteries of the evolutionary process," Potter and Mock concluded.

Silver's next work, *Remaking Eden: Cloning and Beyond in a Brave New World,* examines the science and the moral and ethical concerns surrounding the latest technologies in human genetics and reproduction, including genetic screening and enhancement, cloning, and surrogate motherhood. The author "entertains even the wildest and most speculative notions because—as he argues persuasively—the future is already here," reported Paul Raeburn in the *New York Times Book Review.* "Many genetic and reproductive manipulations that seem to be science fiction are far closer to reality than we recognize," Raeburn continued.

In *Remaking Eden,* Silver argues that government will be unable to regulate or intervene in the use of genetic and reproductive technologies because parents will demand them in order to choose and shape their children's genetic characteristics, perhaps to create "designer" children from a computerized menu or to eliminate from a child the genes that carry a disease or enhance a gene in such a way as to prevent an illness. According to Raeburn, Silver "finds dizzying layers of contradiction in most religious and ethical arguments against one or another reproductive or genetic technology."

Silver also addresses the possible impacts of genetics technology on society and the entire human race (such as black-market cloning or the creation of a new species of humans) in *Remaking Eden,* and he joins the debate about when human life begins. Raeburn noted that Silver "argues that human reproduction does not belong at the center of the biological universe." Another reviewer for *Publishers Weekly* wrote that Silver presents his material clearly and called *Remaking Eden* "a scientifically astute guide to thorny territory."

A biologist, geneticist, and teacher of bioethics, Silver also coedited *Teratocarcinoma Stem Cells,* a collection of papers presented at a meeting of researchers at the Cold Spring Harbor Laboratory in September, 1982.

BIOGRAPHICAL AND CRITICAL SOURCES:

PERIODICALS

Choice, December, 1995, B. W. Auclair, review of *Mouse Genetics: Concepts and Applications,* p. 642.

New York Times Book Review, January 11, 1998, Paul Raeburn, review of *Remaking Eden: Cloning and Beyond in a Brave New World,* pp. 11-12.

Publishers Weekly, November 3, 1997, review of *Remaking Eden,* p. 75.

Science, December 8, 1995, Michael Potter and Beverly Mock, review of *Mouse Genetics,* pp. 1692-1693.

* * *

SNYDER, Don J. 1950-

PERSONAL: Born August 11, 1950, in Lansdale, PA; son of Richard (a pastor) and Peggy (Schwartz) Snyder; married Colleen McQuinn, December 14, 1985; children: Erin, Nell, Jack, Cara. *Education:* Colby College, B.A., 1972; University of Iowa, M.F.A., 1986. *Hobbies and other interests:* Sailing.

ADDRESSES: Home—Scarborough, ME. *Agent*—c/o Author Mail, Doubleday, 1745 Broadway, New York, NY 10019.

CAREER: Freelance writer, 1972—. Colby College, Waterville, ME, writer-in-residence, 1986; Colgate University, Hamilton, NY, writer-in-residence, 1989-1993; Columbia College, New York, NY, visiting writer, 2004.

AWARDS, HONORS: James A. Michener fellowship, Copernicus Society of America and James A. Michener, 1986; teaching writing fellowship in fiction, Iowa Writers Workshop, 1986.

WRITINGS:

FICTION

Veterans Park, F. Watts (New York, NY), 1987.
From the Point, F. Watts (New York, NY), 1988.
Night Crossing, Knopf (New York, NY), 2001.
Fallen Angel (also see below), Pocket Books (New York, NY), 2001.
Winter Dreams, Doubleday (New York, NY), 2003.
Fallen Angel (screenplay), Columbia Broadcasting System, 2003.

NONFICTION

A Soldier's Disgrace, Yankee Books, 1987.
The Cliff Walk: A Memoir of a Job Lost and a Life Found, Little, Brown (Boston, MA), 1997.
Of Time and Memory: A Mother's Story, Knopf (New York, NY), 1999.

Contributor of articles and stories to periodicals including, *Yankee, Boston Globe Sunday Magazine, Saturday Evening Post, NorthEast,* and *Reader's Digest.*

ADAPTATIONS: The Cliff Walk: A Memoir of a Job Lost and a Life Found, has been adapted to audiocassette.

SIDELIGHTS: Don J. Snyder's book *A Soldier's Disgrace* is the story of Ronald Alley, a U.S. Army major who was captured in Korea in 1950. Alley survived three years as a prisoner of war, then returned to the United States, only to face court martial and be convicted of collaboration with the enemy. He became the only American military officer to be imprisoned for such a crime in this century, even though hundreds of other military personnel conducted themselves as he did, trading bits of noncrucial intelligence information for the lives of other prisoners. According to Patrick Reardon in the *Chicago Tribune,* Alley approached journalist Don Snyder for help in clearing his name of the charges but died of a heart attack before any action could be taken. "Almost against his will," reported Reardon, "Snyder took up the search for truth that, for four years, became the obsession of his life." With the assistance of Alley's widow, Snyder tried to have the major's conviction overturned; *A Soldier's Disgrace* describes Alley's ordeal as well as Snyder's efforts on his behalf.

After losing his job at Colgate College to downsizing, Synder was confident he would find another quickly. Settling for a job as an unskilled construction worker to support his family, Synder sat down and wrote *The Cliff Walk: A Memoir of a Job Lost and a Life Found.* Carol Stern, writing in *Library Journal,* described the audiocassette tape version of the book "an articulate memoir." And Duanne Veidelis, writing in *Christian Science Monitor,* commented that "the subtleties of each phase of his awakening are just that—subtle. But this makes his tale convincing." *New York Times Book*

Review contributor Anne Matthews observed, "Over the last decade, millions of Americans pushed out of good jobs have largely left in stoic silence. But Mr. Snyder is a natural protester and contrarian. His testament of loss makes grim, instructive reading for upwardly mobile baby boomers, elected officials, academics on both sides of the tenure line and women tied to men whose employment is in jeopardy, or could be." "This honest, articulate memoir skillfully explores the psychological as well as the financial pain that comes with the loss of a statusy job and income," concluded a *Publishers Weekly* reviewer.

Another of Snyder's nonfiction works is *Of Time and Memory: A Mother's Story*. *Library Journal* critic Joyce Sparrow described the book as a "memoir, which reads like an intriguing love story, detail[ing] one man's attempt to find out the woman who dies sixteen days after giving birth to him and his twin brother in 1950." Through "exhaustive efforts" Snyder searches medical records, visits family friends, and locates personnel to discover what his mother had been like. GraceAnne A. DeCandido, writing in *Booklist*, observed, "in his search, [Snyder] re-creates the flesh-and-blood person who bore him and learns what it cost her." A reviewer for *Publishers Weekly* further stated that "Snyder's painstaking evocation of his emotional odyssey in search of a young woman with extraordinary courage will resonate with most readers."

Snyder once told *CA:* "My only aspiration as a writer is to drive a wedge against the world's greed and indifference. All of my novels and my nonfiction book[s] are about people who try to live decent lives, believe in good things, and then wake up one morning to discover that *nothing* is the way they thought it was. My only interests beyond my world of fiction are the Maine Charitable Foundation, my wife and daughters, and sailing. I want my books to provide me with a way to take care of people less fortunate than I."

BIOGRAPHICAL AND CRITICAL SOURCES:

PERIODICALS

Booklist, April 15, 1997, David Rouse, review of *The Cliff Walk: A Memoir of a Job Lost and a Life Found,* p. 1369; August, 1999, GraceAnne A. DeCandido, review of *Of Time and Memory: A Mother's Story,* p. 2013; April 15, 2001, Carie Bissey, review of *Night Crossing,* p. 1537.

Chicago Tribune, September 29, 1987.

Christian Science Monitor, September 8, 1997, Duanne Veidelis, "Finding Dignity in Pounding Nails," p. 13.

Library Journal, May 1, 1997, Bellinda Wise, review of *The Cliff Walk,* p. 116; August, 1999, Joyce Sparrow, review of *Of Time and Memory,* p. 106; September 15, 2000, Carol Stern, review of *The Cliff Walk,* p. 130; March 15, 2001, David W. Henderson, review of *Night Crossing,* p. 106.

Los Angeles Times Book Review, September 27, 1987.

New York Times Book Review, May 18, 1997, Anne Matthews, "Without a Parachute," p. 38.

People Weekly, October 6, 1997, Curtis Rist, "Handy Lesson: Sacked As a College Professor, Don Snyder Labored Manually to Learn Dignity," pp. 79-80.

Publishers Weekly, February 17, 1997, review of *The Cliff Walk,* p. 200; July 26, 1999, review of *Of Time and Memory,* p. 71; June 18, 2001, review of *Night Crossing,* p. 57; August 27, 2001, review of *Fallen Angel,* p. 47.

* * *

SOREL, Julia
See DREXLER, Rosalyn

* * *

SPIEGELMAN, Art 1948-
(Joe Cutrate, Al Flooglebuckle, Skeeter Grant)

PERSONAL: Born February 15, 1948, in Stockholm, Sweden; immigrated to United States; naturalized citizen; son of Vladek (in sales) and Anja (Zylberberg) Spiegelman; married Françoise Mouly (a publisher), July 12, 1977; children: Nadja Rachel, Dashiell Alan. *Education:* Attended Harpur College (now State University of New York at Binghamton), 1965-68.

ADDRESSES: Agent—Deborah Karl, 52 West Clinton Ave., Irvington, NY 10533; Steven Barclay Agency, 12 Western Avenue, Petaluma, CA 94952.

CAREER: Freelance artist and writer. Topps Chewing Gum, Inc., Brooklyn, NY, creative consultant, artist,

Art Spiegelman

designer, editor, and writer for novelty packaging and bubble gum cards and stickers, including Wacky Packages and Garbage Pail Kids, 1966-89; *New Yorker,* staff artist and writer, 1991-2003. Instructor in studio class on comics, San Francisco Academy of Art, 1974-75; instructor in history and aesthetics of comics at New York School of Visual Arts, 1979-87.

MEMBER: PEN.

AWARDS, HONORS: Playboy Editorial Award for best comic strip, and Yellow Kid Award (Italy) for best comic strip author, both 1982; Regional Design Award, *Print* magazine, 1983, 1984, and 1985; Joel M. Cavior Award for Jewish Writing, and National Book Critics Circle nomination, both 1986, both for *Maus: A Survivors Tale, My Father Bleeds History;* Inkpot Award, San Diego Comics Convention, and Stripschappenning Award (Netherlands) for best foreign comics album, both 1987; Special Pulitzer Prize, for both *Maus: A Survivors Tale, My Father Bleeds History* and *Maus: A Survivors Tale II, and Here My Troubles Began;* National Book Critics Circle Award, *Los Angeles Times* award, and American Book Award, Before Columbus Foundation Award, both 1992, both for *Maus: A Survivors Tale II, and Here My Troubles Began;* Guggenheim fellowship, 1990; National Book Critics Circle nomination, 1991; two nominations for Harvey Awards for *Jack Cole and Plastic Man: Forms Stretched to Their Limits.*

WRITINGS:

COMICS

The Complete Mr. Infinity, S. F. Book Co. (New York, NY), 1970.
The Viper Vicar of Vice, Villainy, and Vickedness, privately printed, 1972.
Zip-a-Tune and More Melodies, S. F. Book Co. (New York, NY), 1972.
(Compiling editor, with Bob Schneider) *Whole Grains: A Book of Quotations,* D. Links (New York, NY), 1972.
Ace Hole, Midget Detective, Apex Novelties (New York, NY), 1974.
Language of Comics, State University of New York at Binghamton, 1974.
Breakdowns: From Maus to Now: An Anthology of Strips, Belier Press (New York, NY), 1977.
Work and Turn, Raw Books (New York, NY), 1979.
Every Day Has Its Dog, Raw Books (New York, NY), 1979.
Two-fisted Painters Action Adventure, Raw Books (New York, NY), 1980.
(Contributor) Nicole Hollander, Skip Morrow, and Ron Wolin, editors, *Drawn Together: Relationships Lampooned, Harpooned, and Cartooned,* Crown (New York, NY), 1983.
Maus: A Survivors Tale, Pantheon (New York, NY), Volume I: *My Father Bleeds History,* 1986, Volume II: *And Here My Troubles Began,* 1991.
(Editor) Françoise Mouly, *Raw: The Graphic Aspirin for War Fever,* Raw Books & Graphics (New York, NY), 1986.
(Editor, with Françoise Mouly, and contributor) *Read Yourself Raw: Comix Anthology for Damned Intellectuals,* Pantheon (New York, NY), 1987.
(Editor, with Françoise Mouly, and contributor) Mark Beyer, *Agony,* Pantheon (New York, NY), 1987.
(Editor, with Françoise Mouly, and contributor), Gary Panter, *Jimbo: Adventures in Paradise,* Pantheon (New York, NY), 1988.

Raw: Open Wounds from the Cutting Edge of Commix, No. 1, Penguin (New York, NY), 1989.

Raw, No. 2, edited by Françoise Mouly, Penguin (New York, NY), 1990.

(Editor, with Françoise Mouly and R. Sikoryak) *Warts and All/Drew Friedman and Josh Alan Friedman,* Penguin (New York, NY), 1990.

Raw 3: High Culture for Lowbrows, Viking (New York, NY), 1991.

(Editor, with R. Sikoryak) Charles Burns, *Skin Deep: Tales of Doomed Romance,* Penguin (New York, NY), 1992.

The Complete Maus (CD-ROM), Voyager (New York, NY), 1994.

(Illustrator) Joseph Moncure March, *The Wild Party: The Lost Classic,* Pantheon (New York, NY), 1994.

(Editor, with R. Sikoryak) *The Narrative Corpse,* Raw Books & Gates of Heck (Richmond, VA), 1995.

I'm a Dog! (children's book), HarperCollins (New York, NY), 1997.

(Author of introduction) Bob Adelman, editor, *Tijuana Bibles: Art and Wit in America's Forbidden Funnies, 1930s-1950s,* Simon & Schuster (New York, NY), 1997.

(Editor, with Françoise Mouly) *Little Lit: Folklore and Fairy Tale Funnies,* HarperCollins (New York, NY), 2000.

(Editor, with Françoise Mouly) *Little Lit 2: Strange Stories for Strange Kids,* Joana Cotler Books/RAW (New York, NY), 2001.

(With Chip Kidd) *Jack Cole and Plastic Man: Forms Stretched to Their Limits,* Chronicle Books (San Francisco, CA), 2001.

(Editor, with Françoise Mouly) *It Was a Dark and Silly Night . . . ,* HarperCollins (New York, NY), 2003.

Contributor to books, including *The Apex Treasury of Underground Comics,* edited by Don Donahue and Susan Goodrich, D. Links (New York, NY), 1974; and *The Complete Color Polly and Her Pals,* Volume 1: *The Surrealist Period, 1926-1927,* Remco Worldservice (New York, NY), 1990. Also contributor to numerous underground comics. Editor of *Douglas Comix,* 1972, and (with Bill Griffith; and contributor) *Arcade, the Comics Revue,* 1975-76; founding coeditor and contributor, *Raw,* 1980—. Some works appear under the pseudonyms Joe Cutrate, Al Flooglebuckle, and Skeeter Grant.

WORK IN PROGRESS: *Drawn to Death: A Three-Panel Opera* with composer Phillip Johnston; the comic series *In the Shadow of No Towers.*

SIDELIGHTS: The two-volume graphic-novel saga *Maus: A Survivors Tale* has been cited as "among the remarkable achievements in comics" by Dale Luciano in the *Comics Journal.* The comic, an epic parable of the Holocaust that substitutes mice and cats for human Jews and Nazis, marks a zenith in the artistic career of writer and illustrator Art Spiegelman. Prior to the creation of *Maus* Spiegelman made a name for himself on the underground comics scene, and was a significant presence in graphic art beginning in his teen years when he wrote, printed, and distributed his own comics magazine. In the early 1980s Spiegelman and his wife, Françoise Mouly, produced the first issue of *Raw,* an underground comics—or as Spiegelman and Mouly refer to them, "comix"—anthology that grew into a highly respected alternative press by the middle of its first decade. It was not until the publication of the volume of *Maus* in 1986, however, that a wide range of readers became aware of Spiegelman's visionary talent and his considerable impact on the realm of comics. In an interview with Joey Cavalieri for *Comics Journal,* Spiegelman called *Maus* "the point where my work starts. . . . Up to that point, I feel like I'd been floundering. . . . All of a sudden, I found my own voice, my own needs, things that I wanted to do in comics."

The first volume of *Maus: A Survivor's Tale,* subtitled *My Father Bleeds History,* starts with Spiegelman, representing himself as a humanoid mouse, going to his father, Vladek, for information about the Holocaust. As Vladek's tale begins, he and his wife, Anja, are living in Poland with their young child, Richieu, at the outset of World War II. The Nazis, portrayed as cats, have overrun much of Eastern Europe, and their oppression is felt by everyone, especially the Jews/mice. The story recounts Vladek's service in the Polish army and subsequent incarceration in a German war prison. When he finally returns to Anja and his son, the Nazi "Final Solution"—to exterminate the entire Jewish race—is well underway. There is talk of Jews being rounded up and shipped off to camps where they are either put to strenuous work or put to death. Vladek and Anja's attempt to flee is thwarted and they are sent to Auschwitz, Poland, the site of one of the most notorious camps. As the first section of *Maus: A Survivor's Tale* concludes, Richieu has been taken from his parents by the Nazis—never to be seen again—and Vladek and Anja are separated and put in crowded train cars for shipment to Auschwitz.

As the second *Maus* volume, *And Here My Troubles Began,* opens, Art and his wife, Françoise, are visiting

Vladek at his summer home in the Catskills. During the visit Art and his father resume their discussion. Vladek recounts how he and Anja were put in separate camps, he in the Auschwitz facility, she in the neighboring Birkenau. The horrors and inhumanity of concentration-camp life are related in graphic detail. Vladek recalls the discomfort of cramming three or four men into a bunk that is only a few feet wide and the ignominy of scrounging for any scrap of food to sate his unending hunger. His existence at Auschwitz is marked by agonizing physical labor, severe abuse at the hands of the Nazis, and the ever-present fear that he—or Anja—may be among the next Jews sent to the gas chambers. Despite these overwhelming incentives to abandon hope, Vladek is bolstered by his clandestine meetings with Anja and the discovery of supportive allies among his fellow prisoners. In an encounter with a former priest, Vladek is told that the numerals in his serial identification, which the Nazis tattooed upon their victims, add up to eighteen, a number signifying life.

Vladek manages to hold on through several harrowing incidents, including a bout with typhus. As the war ends and the Allied troops make their way toward Auschwitz, Vladek and some fellow prisoners flee the camp and eventually make their way to safety. In the haste of his escape, however, Vladek loses contact with Anja and does not know if she is alive. Their reunion marks a happy point in Vladek's tale. As the book continues Vladek and Anja desperately search orphanages in Europe for Richieu, to no avail. They eventually immigrate to Sweden, where Art is born, and from there the family moves to America. However, the horrors of the war have scarred Anja permanently, and in 1968 she commits suicide. The book concludes with Art visiting Vladek just before Vladek's death in 1982.

Although *Maus* is essentially the story of Vladek and Anja's ordeal, Spiegelman has stated that *Maus* is also, in part, "a meditation on my own awareness of myself as a Jew." There are deeply personal passages depicting conversations between Art and his psychiatrist, Pavel, who, like Vladek, survived the Nazi's attempted purge. Their conversation ranges from Anja's suicide to the guilt Art feels for being successful in light of his father's tribulation. As much as *Maus* serves as a piece of edifying literature, it also provided its creator with an opportunity to confront his personal demons. As Spiegelman wrote in the *Village Voice*, *Maus* was motivated "by an impulse to look dead-on at the root cause of my own deepest fears and nightmares."

Not surprisingly, *Maus* sparked much critical discussion, much of it regarding Spiegelman's use of animals in the place of humans. When he began the book, Spiegelman made no mention of Jews or Nazis. The protagonists were mice, persecuted because they are "Maus." Likewise, the antagonists were cats, or "Die Katzen," and they chase mice, although "chasing" the mice means rounding them up in camps for work, torture, and extermination. The closest the strip came to an outright identification with the Holocaust was in naming the concentration camp "Mauschwitz." As Spiegelman began the expanded version of *Maus* however, he found it necessary to write in terms of "Jews" and "Nazis" when going into detail. He decided to maintain his characters as animals, however, citing a fear that using human characters would turn the work into a "corny" plea for sympathy. He explained to Joey Cavalieri in *Comics Journal,* "To use these ciphers, the cats and mice, is actually a way to allow you past the cipher at the people who are experiencing it. So it's really a much more direct way of dealing with the material."

Luciano agreed with Spiegelman's reasoning in his description of *Maus:* "By making the characters cats and mice, the result is that the characters 'human' qualities are highlighted all the more, to an inexplicably poignant effect." "By relating a story of hideous inhumanity in non-human terms," declared *Los Angeles Times Book Review* contributor James Colbert, "*Maus* and *Maus II* allow us as readers to go outside ourselves and to look objectively at ourselves and at otherwise unspeakable events." Luciano continued, "The situations recalled and acted-out in *Maus* place the characters in a variety of delicate situations: they express themselves with a simplicity and candor that is unsettling because it is so accurately *human.*" "And while the presentation is enormously effective (and while the events Mr. Spiegelman relates are factually accurate, in most ways a memoir)," Colbert concluded, "the fact is, too that these events did not take place among mice, cats and dogs. That is fiction—and it is fiction of the very highest order."

Full recognition of *Maus*'s influence came in 1992, when Spiegelman received a special Pulitzer Prize for the work. The event marked a change in his status as a writer—he joined the prestigious *New Yorker* magazine as a contributing editor and artist the same year—and launched another round of *Maus* commentary from critics. A special exhibition, "Art Spiegelman: The Road to Maus," featuring the artist's sketches and stories used in the composition of the work, opened at the Galerie St. Etienne late the same year. The exhibition—as well as the related CD-ROM that appeared in 1994—shows how the work evolved both out of the author's relationship with his father and his own need to understand himself. *Maus* goes "further than many Holocaust memoirs," wrote April Austin in the *Christian Science Monitor,* "because they portray the difficulties of *living with* a Holocaust survivor. Spiegelman achieves this by writing himself . . . into the stories, breaking into his mouse-father's narrative with descriptions of their present-day conversations."

Spiegelman's appointment as contributing artist at the *New Yorker* sparked a new wave of controversy, as many were taken aback by the graphic content of his interior and cover illustrations. The artist, working with newly appointed editor-in-chief Tina Brown, helped create a new style for the magazine as Brown worked to change the magazine's content and image. "In case you hadn't noticed or are one of the *New Yorker* traditionalists who refuse to pick up the magazine these days," declared Sean Mitchell in the *Los Angeles Times,* "it now contains comic strips by Spiegelman, Edward Sorel and other artists who once toiled mainly in the pages of the nation's 'underground' and alternative media. The truth is, they are—many of them, anyway—comic strips of a high order." Spiegelman kindled intense controversy for cover illustrations, one being a Valentine's Day cover showing a Hasidic Jewish man embracing a black woman. Mitchell noted of these covers that they are "meant not just to be plainly understood but also to reach up and tattoo your eyeballs with images once unimaginable in the magazine of old moneyed taste." Other covers included depictions of a naked press corps reviewing a fashion show model in spiked heels.

Spiegelman viewed his appointment not as an escape from the *New Yorker* tradition, but as a return to it. He told Mitchell that during the "Pre-Tina" era "it was a kind of live wire—like Peter Arno's cartoons were pretty hot for their moment. Charles Addams was considered rather morbid. It wasn't all those cartoons about businessmen in suits talking to each other over martinis." He continued to relish the creative freedom given him at the magazine until the events of September 11, 2001, changed the creative climate of the nation. Spiegelman resigned from the *New Yorker* in February of 2003. His reasons, as explained to an interviewer for the Italian *Corriere della Sera* and posted in translation on *Electronic Iraq:* "From the time that the Twin Towers fell, it seems as if I've been living in internal exile, or like a political dissident confined to an island. I no longer feel in harmony with American culture, especially now that the entire media has become conservative and tremendously timid. . . . On the contrary, I am more and more inclined to provocation."

In addition to his own cartoon work, beginning in 2000 Spiegelman has collaborated with his wife, Françoise Mouly, on the "Little Lit" comic book series, which collects pieces by noted cartoonists and illustrators of children's books such as Ian Falconer, Jules Feiffer, Walt Kelly, Barbara McClintock, and Maurice Sendak, as well as by Spiegelman. *Folklore and Fairy Tale Funnies,* the first book in the series, begins with Spiegelman's story of "Prince Rooster." Also included in this volume are renditions of "Princess and the Pea" and "Jack and the Beanstalk" along with a Japanese folktale called "The Fisherman and the Sea Princess." Artists Bruce McCall, Charles Burns, and Chris Ware contributed brainteasers, scratchboard hide-and-seek games, and a board game.

"Little Lit" raised the controversy characteristic of most Spiegelman enterprises. Appraising *Folklore and Fairy Tale Funnies,* a *Horn Book* review stated that "Many of the stories are illustrated with an affectionately retro flair." Claude Lalumiere wrote in *January Magazine* that the work is "a pretentious collection of misplaced nostalgia" that seems written more for adults than for children, even though it is advertised and recommended for the latter. "Spiegelman and Mouly's sophisticated collection . . . lingers at the crossroad between kids and adults, classics and parodies," commented a more appreciative *Publishers Weekly* critic. In a *Booksense* interview with Christopher Monte Smith, Spiegelman stated the reasons for focusing on fairy tales: "The tales are kinetic, filled with transformations. There's a lot to draw and see. Fairy tales and folklore . . . offer archetypal themes and memorable situations. We wanted to do a book for all ages, that could hold the interest of very young children and grown-ups."

Maurice Sendak and Jules Feiffer are among the cartoonists represented in the second "Little Lit" installment, *Strange Stories for Strange Kids*. One of the comics is based upon David Sedaris's story "Pretty Ugly." This volume also contains an original 1942 episode of the classic comic strip "Barnaby," produced by the late Crockett Johnson, as well as activity pages and jokes. The volume makes up "an exceptionally strong set of stories and games for kids that will also be appealing to teens and adults," noted a writer for *Rational Magic*. Grace Oliff of *School Library Journal* stated, "The stories all possess a sharp intelligence and unique imagination," while in a *Horn Book* review, Roger Sutton found the cartoons and stories "purposeful . . . even when absurd." *Booklist*'s Gillian Engberg felt that *Strange Stories for Strange Kids* "will excite readers of many ages," and Andrew D. Arnold in a *Time* review called the book "a delightful album of sophisticated, G-rated comix." Arnold concluded: "Thanks to the intelligence of editors Spiegelman and Mouly, you can't be too old to appreciate *Little Lit: Strange Stories for Strange Kids*."

Jack Cole and Plastic Man: Forms Stretched to Their Limits is a memorial by Spiegelman and Chip Kidd to an early cartoonist and his quirky superhero. Trained via a mail-order illustration course prior to beginning his career as a professional cartoonist in 1936, Jack Cole originally worked in the crime and horror comic-book genre until becoming a cartoonist for *Playboy*. His most notable creation was Plastic Man, a criminal who becomes a stretchable superhero as the result of a chemical accident. *Jack Cole and Plastic Man* includes a 1999 *New Yorker* essay about Cole's life which was written by Spiegelman. Kidd, a book designer, arranged to reprint Cole's cartoons in paper stocks that imitate the original work.

Jack Cole and Plastic Man "is an excellent memorial to an innovative American cartoonist," remarked a *Publishers Weekly* reviewer, while a writer for *DC Comics* online called the book "a fascinating back story [with] a colorful cast of characters." "Spiegelman and Kidd have assembled an attractive and innovative package," said Noel Murray in an *Onion A. V. Club* article, adding that because of its nostalgic feel, the work should "be held, smelled, and felt as much as read."

BIOGRAPHICAL AND CRITICAL SOURCES:

BOOKS

Contemporary Literary Criticism, Volume 76, Gale (Detroit, MI), 1993.

Witek, Joseph, *Comic Books As History: The Narrative Art of Jack Jackson, Art Spiegelman, and Harvey Pekar*, University Press of Mississippi (Jackson, MS), 1989.

PERIODICALS

Booklist, December 15, 2001, Gillian Engberg, review of *Little Lit: Strange Stories for Strange Kids*, p. 726.
Boston Globe, November 23, 1994, p. 25.
Bulletin of the Center for Children's Books, January, 2002, review of *Little Lit*, p. 185.
Christian Science Monitor, December 14, 1992, p. 14.
Comics Journal, August, 1981, Joey Cavalieri, "An Interview with Art Spiegelman and Françoise Mouly," pp. 98-125; December, 1986, pp. 43-45; April, 1989, pp. 110-1117.
Commonweal, December 5, 1997, p. 20; April 6, 2001, review of *Little Lit*, p. 22.
Entertainment Weekly, October 14, 2001, review of *Jack Cole and Plastic Man: Forms Stretched to Their Limit*, p. 12; November 2, 2001, review of *Little Lit*, p. 70.
Globe and Mail, December 15, 2001, review of *Little Lit*, p. D19.
Horn Book, September, 2000, Roger Sutton, review of *Little Lit*, p. 590; January-February, 2002, Roger Sutton, review of *Little Lit 2: Strange Stories for Strange Kids*, p. 73.
Library Journal, February 1, 2002, review of *Jack Cole and Plastic Man*, p. 57.
Los Angeles Times, December 18, 1994, p. 7.
Los Angeles Times Book Review, November 8, 1992, p. 2.
New Yorker, December 10, 2001, review of *Jack Cole and Plastic Man*, p. 107.
New York Times, February 11, 1994, p. D17.
New York Times Book Review, November 3, 1991, pp. 1, 35-36; January 20, 2002, review of *Little Lit 2*, p. 14.
Publishers Weekly, April 26, 1991; January 31, 1994, pp. 26-27; October 10, 1994, p. 61; September 4, 2000, review of *Little Lit*, p. 106; September 3, 2001, review of *Jack Cole and Plastic Man*, p. 67; November 19, 2001, review of *Little Lit 2*, p. 66.
Rolling Stone, November 20, 1986, pp. 103-106, 146-148.
School Library Journal, March, 2002, Grace Oliff, review of *Little Lit 2*, p. 221.

Times Educational Supplement, December 2, 1994, p. 7.

Village Voice, June 6, 1989, pp. 21-22.

Voice of Youth Advocates, October, 2001, review of *Little Lit,* p. 271.

ONLINE

Art and Culture Network, http://www.artandculture.com/ (June 2, 2003).

Booksense, http://www.booksense.com/ (June 2, 2003), Christopher Monte Smith, interview with Art Spiegelman.

DC Comics, http://dccomics.com/beyond_comics/ (January 2, 2004), review of *Jack Cole and Plastic Man.*

Electronic Iraq, http://www.electroniciraq.net (February 11, 2003), interview with Spiegelman from *Corriere della Sera.*

January Magazine, http://www.januarymagazine.com/ (June 2, 2003), Claude Lalumiere, review of *Little Lit: Folklore and Fairy Tale Funnies.*

Onion A. V. Club, http://www.theonionavclub.com/ (June 2, 2003), Noel Murray, review of *Jack Cole and Plastic Man.*

Rational Magic, http://www.rationalmagic.com/ (June 2, 2003), review of *Little Lit 2: Strange Stories for Strange Kids.*

Steven Barclay Agency Web site, http://www.barclayagency.com/ (November 16, 2003).*

* * *

STOWERS, Carlton 1942-

PERSONAL: Born April 14, 1942, in Brownwood, TX; son of Ira (in sales) and Fay (a secretary; maiden name, Stephenson) Stowers; married Betty Darby, October 7, 1962; married Lynne Livingston, November 30, 1975; married Pat Cruce, March 2, 1981; children: Anson, Ashley. *Education:* Attended University of Texas, 1961-63. *Religion:* Episcopalian.

ADDRESSES: Home—1015 Randy Rd., Cedar Hill, TX 75104. *E-mail*—cstowers@worldnet.att.net.

CAREER: Associated with *Amarillo Daily News,* Amarillo, TX, 1966-69, and *Lubbock Avalanche Journal,* Lubbock, TX, 1970-73; freelance writer, 1974-76; *Dal-*

Carlton Stowers

las Morning News, Dallas, TX, sportswriter and columnist, 1976-81; affiliated with *Dallas Cowboys Weekly,* 1981-89; writer for, and associate producer of, weekly television series "Countdown to 84," USA Cable network, 1984; staff writer for *Dallas Observer,* 2000—.

AWARDS, HONORS: Edgar Allan Poe Award for Best Fact Crime Book, Mystery Writers of America, 1986, for *Careless Whispers,* and 1999, for *To the Last Breath;* Oppie Award for Reporting, Southwestern Booksellers, 1986, for *Careless Whispers;* Violent Crown Book Award, nonfiction category, Writers' League of Texas, 2002, for *Within These Walls: Memoirs of a Death House Chaplain;* recipient of other national and state awards for magazine and newspaper journalism.

WRITINGS:

The Randy Matson Story, Tafnews (Los Altos, CA), 1971.

Spirit, Berkley, 1973.
(With Wilbur Evans) *Champions: University of Texas Track and Field,* Strode, 1978.
The Overcomers, Word Books (Waco, TX), 1978.
(With Trent Jones) *Where the Rainbows Wait,* Playboy Press, 1978.
(Editor) *Happy Trails to You* (autobiography of Roy Rogers and Dale Evans), Word Books (Waco, TX), 1979.
Journey to Triumph, Taylor Publishing, 1982.
The Unsinkable Titanic Thompson, Eakin Press, 1982.
Dallas Cowboys Bluebook III, Taylor Publishing, 1982.
Friday Night Heroes, Eakin Press, 1983.
Partners in Blue, Taylor Publishing, 1983.
Dallas Cowboys Bluebook IV, Taylor Publishing, 1983.
(With Billy Olson) *Reaching Higher,* Word Books (Waco, TX), 1984.
The Dallas Cowboys: The First 25 Years, with foreword by James Michener, Taylor Publishing, 1984.
The Cowboy Chronicles, Eakin Press, 1984.
Careless Whispers: The True Story of a Triple Murder and the Determined Lawman Who Wouldn't Give Up, Taylor Publishing, 1984.
The Cotton Bowl: The First 50 Years, Host Communications, 1986.
Real Winning: Faith in the Lives of Thirteen Great Athletes, Word Books (Waco, TX), 1986.
(With William C. Dear) *Please . . . Don't Kill Me* (nonfiction), Houghton, 1989.
(With Larry Wansley) *The FBI Undercover,* Pocket Books, 1989.
Innocence Lost, Pocket Books, 1990.
Open Secrets: A True Story of Love, Jealousy, and Murder, Pocket Books (New York, NY), 1994.
Sins of the Son, Hyperion (New York, NY), 1995.
(With Marcus Allen) *Marcus: The Autobiography of Marcus Allen,* St. Martin's Press (New York, NY), 1997.
To the Last Breath: Three Women Fight for the Truth behind a Child's Tragic Murder, St. Martin's Press (New York, NY), 1998.
(With Marcus Allen) *Strength of the Heart,* Andrews McMeel (Kansas City, MO), 2000.
(With Reverend Carroll Picket) *Within These Walls: Memoirs of a Death House Chaplain,* St. Martin's Press (New York, NY), 2002.
Scream at the Sky, St. Martin's Press (New York, NY), 2003.

Contributor to periodicals, including *Good Housekeeping, Sports Illustrated, TV Guide, Inside Sports,* and *People.*

Author's works has been translated into German, French, Japanese, Dutch, and Spanish.

ADAPTATIONS: Careless Whispers was the basis for *Sworn to Vengeance,* filmed for CBS and broadcast as the CBS movie of the week; *Open Secrets* was the basis for the ABC mini series *Telling Secrets.*

SIDELIGHTS: Carlton Stowers has written numerous books about true crime and about sports and athletes. Stowers, for example, worked with Marcus Allen on his self-titled autobiography. Allen attained brief notoriety in the wake of the O. J. Simpson murder trial when rumors arose that he had had an affair with Nicole Brown Simpson (O. J.'s wife, and one of the murder victims). In *Sporting News,* Steve Gietschier wrote that although the political commentary seems to be more Stowers's than Allen's, "the football passages tend to ring true." Other critics reached conflicting conclusions about the book's success in giving the reader a compelling portrait of its subject. While Terry Jo Madden of *Library Journal* found that the book provided "few insights into his personal life," a reviewer for *Publishers Weekly* found in the book's pages "a reflective man."

In 2002 he teamed up with Reverend Carroll Pickett for *Within These Walls: Memoirs of a Death House Chaplain.* Pickett served as the chaplain for the Huntsville, Texas, prison for fifteen years, speaking with death-row inmates in the days leading to their executions. The book, which won the 2002 Violet Crown Award for nonfiction, reveals his emotional and spiritual journey that led him to devote much of his retirement to opposing the death penalty. Frances Sandiford of *Library Journal* concluded, "This book, more than most others on the same subject, is likely to appeal to the general reader." A *Publishers Weekly* reviewer commented that "this thoughtful, gripping recollection offers a rare, firsthand perspective on the use of capital punishment." Similarly, John Green of *Booklist* commented that the book provides a "gripping look at America's prisons from a unique, and much needed, perspective." A critic for *Kirkus Reviews,* however, remarked that the book will fail to convince "eye-for-an-eye types" and may even make supporters question some of his perspectives. Ultimately, the critic concluded that the book would be ideal for anyone considering prison ministries.

Stowers once told *CA:* "The greatest enjoyment I receive from my work is the variety of projects I'm involved in. A newspaper background has provided me with the kind of work habits necessary to work swiftly and on more than one project at a time. In recent years I've dealt more attention to nonfiction books and have also found that television writing provides me a welcome respite from the long narrative of print journalism on occasion. I'm fortunate that a variety of subjects interests me; therefore I don't devote my efforts to a particular field even though I continue to do a considerable amount of sportswriting."

BIOGRAPHICAL AND CRITICAL SOURCES:

PERIODICALS

Armchair Detective, fall, 1995, review of *Sins of the Son,* p. 460.
Booklist, May 1, 2002, John Green, review of *Within These Walls: Memoirs of a Death House Chaplain,* p. 1490.
Kirkus Reviews, May 15, 1990, review of *Innocence Lost,* p. 716; April 15, 1994, review of *Open Secrets,* p. 541; May 15, 1995, review of *Sins of the Son,* p. 698; January 1, 1998, review of *To the Last Breath,* p. 44; March 15, 2002, review of *Within These Walls: Memoirs of a Death House Chaplain,* p. 39.
Library Journal, November 15, 1986, review of *Careless Whispers,* p. 108; July, 1990, review of *Innocence Lost,* p. 111-13; May 15, 1994, review of *Open Secrets,* p. 85; July, 1995, review of *Sins of the Son,* p. 101; September 1, 1997, Terry Jo Madden, review of *Marcus: The Autobiography of Marcus Allen,* p. 186-187; May 15, 2002, Frances Sandiford, review of *Within These Walls: Memoirs of a Death House Chaplain,* p. 112-113.
New York Times Book Review, October 15, 1989; December 10, 1995, review of *Sins of the Son,* p. 26.
Publishers Weekly, September 19, 1986, review of *Careless Whispers,* p. 128; August 9, 1991, review of *Innocence Lost,* p. 55; April 11, 1994, review of *Open Secrets,* p. 44; May 22, 1995, review of *Sins of the Son,* p. 41; August 28, 1995, review of *Open Secrets,* p. 111; July 21, 1997, review of *Marcus: The Autobiography of Marcus Allen,* p. 193; December 15, 1997, review of *To the Last Breath,* p. 42; April 29, 2002, review of *Within These Walls: Memoirs of a Death House Chaplain,* p. 53.
School Library Journal, November, 1990, review of *Innocence Lost,* p. 155.

Sporting News, October 27, 1997, Steve Gietschier, review of *Marcus: The Autobiography of Marcus Allen,* p. 7.

* * *

SUMMERLIN, Vernon

PERSONAL: Born in Grenada, MS; married Cathy McAllister (a writer), January 1, 1987.

ADDRESSES: Home—5550 Boy Scout Rd., Franklin, TN 37064.

CAREER: Writer and public speaker. *Tennessee Angler,* editor and publisher; WDCN-TV, Nashville, TN, field host for *Tennessee Outdoorsman; Outdoors with Vern and Doug,* cohost of weekly statewide radio program; *Tennessee Angler Radio,* producer and host of daily four-minute radio broadcast; *Gallivant: Whimsical Travel,* cofounder, 2003. Lecturer on fishing and writing at a community college.

MEMBER: Outdoor Writers Association of America, Southeastern Outdoor Press Association (past president), Tennessee Outdoor Writers Association (past president).

AWARDS, HONORS: Named Friend of Fisheries, Tennessee chapter, American Fisheries Society, 1998; more than thirty awards for writing, radio and television work, and photography.

WRITINGS:

Two Dozen Fishin' Holes: A Guide to Middle Tennessee, Rutledge Hill Press (Nashville, TN), 1992.
(With wife, Cathy Summerlin) *Traveling the Trace,* Rutledge Hill Press (Nashville, TN), 1995.
(With Cathy Summerlin) *Traveling the Southern Highlands,* Rutledge Hill Press (Nashville, TN), 1997.
(With Cathy Summerlin) *Traveling Tennessee,* Rutledge Hill Press (Nashville, TN), 1998.
(With Cathy Summerlin) *Highroad Guide to the Tennessee Mountains,* Longstreet Press (Marietta, GA), c. 1998.

(With Cathy Summerlin) *Traveling Tennessee: A Complete Tour Guide to the Volunteer State from the Highlands of the Smoky Mountains to the Banks of the Mississippi River,* Rutledge Hill Press (Nashville, TN), 1999.

(With Doug Markham) *The Compleat Tennessee Angler: Everything You Need to Know about Fishing in the Volunteer State,* Rutledge Hill Press (Nashville, TN), 1999.

(With Jimmy Holt) *The Great Outdoorsman Cookbook,* Rutledge Hill Press (Nashville, TN), 2001.

(With Cathy Summerlin) *Traveling Florida,* John F. Blair (Winston-Salem, NC), 2003.

Author of a weekly self-syndicated outdoor column appearing in Tennessee newspapers. Contributor of articles and photographs to magazines, including *Field and Stream, Outdoor Life, Bass Master, North American Fisherman, Tennessee Sportsman, Chevy Outdoors,* and *National Geographic Traveler.*

T

THOMAS, Frances 1943-

PERSONAL: Born October 21, 1943, in Aberdare, South Wales; daughter of David Elwyn (a teacher) and Agnes (a teacher; maiden name, Connor) Thomas; married Richard Rathbone (a university professor), 1965; children: Harriet, Lucy. *Education:* Queen Mary College, London University, B.A. (with honors), 1965. *Politics:* Labour Party.

ADDRESSES: Home—London, England. *Agent*—David Higham Associates, 5-8, Lower John St., London W1R 4HA, England. *E-mail*—frances.thomas@btinternet.com.

CAREER: Writer. Former school teacher.

AWARDS, HONORS: Tir na n-Og Prize, 1981, Welsh Books Council, for *The Blindfold Track,* 1986, for *The Region of the Summer Stars,* and 1992, for *Who Stole a Bloater?;* Whitbread First Novel runner-up award, 1986, and Welsh Arts Council Fiction Prize, 1991, both for *Seeing Things;* Scottish Arts Council Award, 1999, for *Supposing.*

WRITINGS:

FOR YOUNG PEOPLE

The Blindfold Track (first novel in *Taliesin* trilogy), Macmillan (London, England), 1980.

Secrets, illustrated by L. Acs, Hamish Hamilton (London, England), 1982.

A Knot of Spells (second novel in *Taliesin* trilogy), Barn Owl Press (Port Talbot, Wales), 1983.

Dear Comrade (for young adults), Bodley Head (London, England), 1983.

Zak (for young adults), Bodley Head (London, England), 1984.

The Region of the Summer Stars (third novel in *Taliesin* trilogy), Barn Owl Press (Port Talbot, Wales), 1985.

Cityscape (for young adults), Heinemann (London, England), 1988.

Jam for Tea, Collins Educational (Glasgow, Scotland), 1989.

The Prince and the Cave, Pont Books/WJEC Welsh History Project, 1991.

Who Stole a Bloater?, Seren Books (Bridgend, Wales), 1991.

The Bear and Mr. Bear, illustrated by Ruth Brown, Dutton's Children's Books (New York, NY), 1994, published in England as *Mr. Bear and the Bear,* Andersen Press (London, England), 1994.

Supposing, illustrated by Ross Collins, Bloomsbury Books (London, England), 1998, published as *What If?,* Hyperion Books for Children (New York, NY), 1998.

Polly's Running Away Book, illustrated by Sally Gardner, Bloomsbury Books (London, England), 2000, published as *Polly's Really Secret Diary,* Delacorte Press (New York, NY), 2002.

Maybe One Day, illustrated by Ross Collins, Bloomsbury Books (London, England), 2001, published as *One Day, Daddy,* Hyperion Books for Children (New York, NY), 2001.

Polly's Absolutely Worst Birthday Ever, illustrated by Sally Gardner, Delacorte Press (New York, NY), 2003.

I Found Your Diary, Anderson Press (London, England), 2004.

FOR ADULTS

Seeing Things (novel), Gollancz (London, England), 1986.

The Fall of Man (novel), Gollancz (London, England), 1989.

Christina Rossetti: A Biography, Self Publishing Association, 1992, Virago (London, England), 1994.

ADAPTATIONS: *Who Stole a Bloater?* was dramatized by Jackanory on BBC television in 1993.

SIDELIGHTS: Author Frances Thomas was born in Wales and grew up in London, England. She was educated in a convent school before attending London University. She began writing in 1980.

Thomas began her writing career, appropriately enough, with a historical fantasy set in her homeland. Referring to the Celtic epic, *The Mabinogion,* for inspiration, Thomas decided to write about the legend of Taliesin. *The Blindfold Track,* the first of Thomas's three books on the subject, follows the adventures of the boy Gwion, who is abandoned as a child, raised by a prince, and taught by Merlin the magician, eventually becoming the famed bard Taliesin. Margery Fisher of *Growing Point* wrote that in this retelling, Thomas depicts a "modern psychological view of a boy growing up" in a time now veiled in legend. Although *School Librarian* contributor Dennis Hamley felt that the dialogue was too "modern-sounding," *Junior Bookshelf* reviewer R. Baines called Thomas's first tale "a well-written, absorbing and enjoyable book." *The Blindfold Track* won the 1981 Tir na n-Og Prize, and Thomas followed this success three years later with a sequel, *A Knot of Spells,* which tells how Taliesin leaves his position as bard to the king of Powys in order to protect the twin children of a queen who is dying in another Welsh kingdom. "The book mingles high politics and archaeology, military exploits and romantic affections," according to Fisher of *Growing Point,* who added that this time the magical elements of Taliesin's story are "subordinated" in favor of concentrating on the characters' relationships. In this complex tale, noted *Junior Bookshelf* contributor D. A. Young, an "enthusiasm for all things Welsh on the part of a reader" is helpful in maintaining interest in the involved storyline.

Thomas, who has educated dyslexic children in her home, has also written other books for young readers that feature a present-day setting. *Dear Comrade* follows the written correspondences between Kate Bannister and Paul Miles as they slowly grow to love each other despite their completely opposing political views (he leans to the right, and she to the left). Kate and Paul argue about the law and other political matters, never coming to a consensus (though they do change their views a little), so that the reader must decide for himself who is in the right. Dennis Hamley, writing in *School Librarian,* found the two characters "convincing, funny and moving."

Thomas's next young adult novel is *Zak.* Told from the perspective of a teenager named Mark, *Zak* is about teens who are unhappy with who they are. Mark is bored silly by his life at school and at home, until a new kid named Zak comes to his school. Zak impresses everyone with his stories of living in Los Angeles with his father, whom he insists is a famous rock star. But when Mark visits Zak's home, he realizes the lies behind these stories. The book ends with Zak's disappearance and Mark going back to his original best friend and making amends. Young readers "will sympathise with the boredom and be entertained by Mark's contempt for adults," Margaret Campbell said in *School Librarian.*

In *Cityscape* Thomas demonstrates again her ability to write in different genres: in this case, science fiction/fantasy. Fifteen-year-old Debra Stober discovers on her route to school that an old Jacobean mansion has doors that lead to cities in other worlds. She "travels" to a world in the future ruled by the Guardians, who suppress their people by denying them the right to read books. Debra becomes attracted to Cal, a handsome man who is leading a democratic rebellion that needs Debra's help because she knows how to read and write. By teaching these people to read, Debra gains a new sense of purpose and inner pride that inspires her to accept the dangerous mission of going to the Poison Tower where the Guardians have secreted away all the books. The Guardians are overthrown, but Debra is disillusioned when she later returns to the city to discover that Cal is becoming just as corrupt as the Guardians were. Debra rejects the other world in favor of her home, to which she returns to begin a relationship with a new boyfriend. "Among the proliferation of metaphors for growing up," commented Fisher of *Growing Point,* "the image of alternative cityscapes provides valid insights into teenage personality and problems."

In addition to novels like these, Thomas has written picture books for young children, including *Secrets* and the more recent *The Bear and Mr. Bear. Secrets* is a simple story about "the social need for discretion and self-control," according to *Growing Point* reviewer Margery Fisher. It tells how two boys seek out their own secret when a friend refuses to tell them hers. *The Bear and Mr. Bear* is a sensitive tale about a man who takes pity on a dancing bear that is abused by its trainer. He buys the bear and sets him loose on the grounds of his home. The man, who is called Mr. Bear by the town's children because of his grumpy disposition, empathizes with the sad bear, and man and animal find solace and comfort in each other's company. *School Library Journal* contributor Tom S. Hurlburt called the book a "heartfelt, uplifting story."

In 2002, Thomas published *Polly's Really Secret Diary,* starring a young girl who writes, "This is my Running Away Diary." Polly is fed up with her life: her hamster has run off, her three-year-old sister is getting on her nerves, her best friend has dumped her for someone else, and her mother is pregnant and preoccupied. Polly keeps track of the money she is collecting to run away, and provides a running commentary on all the people who annoy her. A *School Library Journal* reviewer praised the book's British flavor, as well as Thomas's humor and energy.

Having written historical fantasy, realistic young adult novels, fantasy for teens, and picture books for small children, Thomas has proven her diversity as a writer. Thomas continued to demonstrate her versatility by also writing novels for adults, publishing her first biography for adults in 1992, *Christina Rossetti.*

Thomas once told *CA,* "I love writing for children—it's great fun, and I think they're the best and most inspired readers. I write because it's a process of finding out about things and also because I enjoy it enormously. I don't really have a special writing process—the only way to write is just to get down to it, even if you don't feel especially inspired."

BIOGRAPHICAL AND CRITICAL SOURCES:

PERIODICALS

Booklist, January 15, 1995, pp. 938, 940; July, 1999, John Peters, review of *What If?,* p. 1955; June 1, 2002, Kelly Milner Halls, review of *Polly's Really Secret Diary,* p. 1726.

Books, autumn, 1998, review of *Supposing,* p. 21; autumn, 2001, review of *Polly's Absolutely Worst Birthday Ever,* p. 18.

Books for Keeps, November, 1987; November, 2001, review of *Polly's Running Away Book,* p. 25.

Books for Your Children, spring, 1985, p. 18; summer, 1995, p. 21.

Center for Children's Books, September, 1999, review of *What If?,* p. 3; October, 2001, review of *One Day, Daddy,* p. 79.

Children's Book Review Service, August, 1999, *What If?,* p. 163.

Growing Point, September, 1980, p. 3767; January, 1983, pp. 4004-4005; May, 1984, p. 4263; January, 1989, pp. 5092-5093.

Junior Bookshelf, August, 1980, p. 201; February, 1983, p. 34; June, 1984, p. 146; February, 1985, pp. 49-50; December, 1988, pp. 297-98; February, 1995, p. 12.

Kirkus Reviews, June 1, 1999, review of *What If?,* p. 890.

Publishers Weekly, December 12, 1994, p. 62; June 18, 2001, review of *One Day, Daddy,* p. 80; June 3, 2002, review of *Polly's Really Secret Diary,* p. 88.

School Librarian, June, 1981, p. 157; June, 1983, p. 143; June, 1984, pp. 153-154; March, 1985, p. 63; winter, 2001, review of *Polly's Absolutely Worst Birthday Ever,* September, 2001, p. 207.

School Library Journal, March, 1995, p. 187; September, 2001, Carolyn Janssen, review of *One Day, Daddy,* p. 207.

Times Literary Supplement, November 25, 1983.

ONLINE

E-Zone, Midlothian Libraries On-Line for Kids, http://www.midlothian.gov.uk/Library/ezoneft.htm/ (August 21, 2002), author biography.

THOMAS, Marlo 1938-

PERSONAL: Born November 21, 1938, in Detroit, MI; daughter of Danny Thomas (a comedian and entertainer); married Phil Donahue (a talk-show host), May 21, 1980; stepchildren: five. *Education:* Attended University of Southern California.

ADDRESSES: Home—New York, NY. *Agent*—c/o Author Mail, McGraw Hill Ryerson Ltd., 300 Water St., Whitbey, Ontario L1N 9B6, Canada.

CAREER: Actress, producer, entertainer, and activist.

AWARDS, HONORS: Fame and *Photoplay,* Most Promising Newcomer Award for performance in TV series, *That Girl;* Emmy Awards for TV specials*Free to Be . . . You and Me,* 1974, *The Body Human: Facts for Girls,* 1981, *Free to Be . . . a Family,* 1989, and *Nobody's Child.*

WRITINGS:

(Editor, with Carole Hart and others) *Free to Be . . . You and Me,* McGraw Hill (New York, NY), 1974.
(Editor, with Christopher Cerf and others) *Free to Be . . . a Family,* Bantam (New York, NY), 1987.
(Creator and coauthor) *Free to Be . . . You and Me: Stories, Songs, and Poems,* Running Press Book Pub. (Philadelphia, PA), 1998.

ADAPTATIONS: TV adaptation and recording of *Free to Be . . . You and Me,* 1974.

SIDELIGHTS: Marlo Thomas, daughter of celebrity comedian Danny Thomas, has enjoyed a successful television and theater career as an actress and producer, with several Emmy Awards to her credit. She also produced two popular children's anthologies, which were released as books, records, and TV specials. Born in 1938 in Detroit, Michigan, Thomas grew up in Beverly Hills, California, and attended the University of Southern California. She began acting with minor television roles and in summer stock. After appearing in the TV series *The Joey Bishop Show,* she starred in her own hit sitcom, *That Girl,* for which she

Marlo Thomas

received the Most Promising Newcomer Awards from both *Fame* and *Photoplay.* This role made Thomas a celebrity in her own right.

An outspoken feminist, Thomas developed the children's book *Free to Be . . . You and Me,* also released as a recording and a TV special, in 1974. This was a compilation of nonsexist stories, songs, and poems gleaned from a wide variety of sources and aimed at promoting healthy attitudes toward identity in young children. Such notable authors as Judy Blume, Judith Viorst, and Shel Silverstein contributed to the project, which covered subjects such as divorce, sibling rivalry, friendship, and stereotypes. Critics appreciated the book's laudable intentions and found it visually attractive but were less enthusiastic about the textual sections. A *School Library Journal* reviewer was troubled by the book's confusing mix of reading levels, while a *Booklist* critic noted that some of the material "falls flat." Though reviewers' praise for the book remained moderate, it proved a popular success. The TV special, which Thomas produced, won an Emmy Award.

Thomas followed *Free to Be . . . You and Me* with several other TV projects related to feminist principles. The educational program *The Body Human: Facts for Girls,* in which she appeared, won an Emmy Award in 1981. She also appeared in and co-produced another educational special, *Love, Sex . . . and Marriage.* In 1987 Thomas produced a sequel to her first book, this time aimed at issues surrounding divorce, stepparents, single parents, and nontraditional family structures. Like its predecessor, the new volume, *Free to Be . . . a Family,* is an anthology of songs, poems, jokes, and stories from leading children's writers. The book, Thomas explains in the introduction, focuses on all "the different kinds of families you can imagine, all the different kinds of households we love in and live in." As with the first volume, critics found this effort a mixed bag. Thomas served as host and executive producer for the TV version of *Free to Be . . . a Family,* which won an Emmy Award in 1989.

In 1980 Thomas surprised her fans by marrying popular talk-show host Phil Donahue. Though several in the entertainment community doubted that the marriage would survive Thomas's feminist ideals, they were proven wrong. Despite the strains of maintaining two high-profile careers and raising four of Donahue's five teenagers from his previous marriage, the couple remained together. Thomas continued to take acting roles in television, appearing in *It Happened One Christmas, The Lost Honor of Kathryn Beck, Consenting Adult, Nobody's Child, Leap of Faith, Held Hostage: The Sis and Jerry Levin Story, Ultimate Betrayal,* and *Reunion.* Her theater credits include *Thieves, Social Security, The Shadow Box,* and *Six Degrees of Separation,* and she appeared in the films *Jenny, Thieves,* and *In the Spirit.* In addition to her Emmys for the two "Free to Be . . ." productions, Thomas won an Emmy Award for *Nobody's Child.* Thomas and her husband live and work in New York City and have a second home at the Connecticut shore.

BIOGRAPHICAL AND CRITICAL SOURCES:

PERIODICALS

Booklist, April 15, 1974, p. 944; December 15, 1987, p. 705.

Good Housekeeping, June, 1995, pp. 94.
Publishers Weekly, December 25, 1987, p. 74.
School Library Journal, May 1974, p. 1470.*

* * *

THOMPSON, M(ichael) W(elman) 1928-

PERSONAL: Born August 13, 1928, in London, England; son of Hartley (a merchant) and Lyla (Welman) Thompson; married Ann Elizabeth Crockatt (a musician), October 10, 1964; children: Elizabeth. *Ethnicity:* "Caucasian." *Education:* Pembroke College, Cambridge, M.A., 1952, Ph.D., 1953. *Politics:* "Variable, mainly conservative." *Religion:* Church of England.

ADDRESSES: Home—2 Offa Lea, Newton, Cambridge CB2 5PW, England. *E-mail*—michaelandann@offalea.fsnct.co.uk.

CAREER: Ministry of Works, Department of the Environment, Welsh Office, Cardiff, Wales, inspector of ancient monuments and head of ancient monuments branch in Wales, 1974-84; writer, 1984—. *Military service:* British Army, 1946-48; became sergeant.

MEMBER: Prehistoric Society (past vice-president), Society for Medieval Archaeology (president, 1991-95), Society of Antiquaries of London (fellow), Cambridge Antiquarian Society (president, 1990-92).

WRITINGS:

Farnham Castle, Surrey, H.M.S.O. (London, England), 1961.
Tattershall Castle, Lincolnshire, National Trust (London, England), 1974.
Kenilworth Castle, Warwickshire, H.M.S.O. (London, England), 1977.
General Pitt-Rivers, Moonraker Press (Bradford-on-Avon, Wiltshire, England), 1977.
Ruins: Their Preservation and Display, British Museum Publications (London, England), 1981.
(Editor) *The Journeys of Sir Richard Colt Hoare through Wales and England,* Alan Sutton (Stroud, Gloucestershire, England), 1983.

The Decline of the Castle, Cambridge University Press (Cambridge, England), 1988.

The Cambridge Antiquarian Society, 1890-1990, Cambridge Antiquarian Society (Cambridge, England), 1990.

The Rise of the Castle, Cambridge University Press (Cambridge, England), 1991.

The Medieval Hall: The Basis of Secular Domestic Life, 600-1600 A.D., Scolar Press (Aldershot, England), 1995.

Medieval Bishops' Houses in England and Wales, Ashgate Publishing (Aldershot, England), 1998.

Cloister, Abbot, and Precinct in Medieval Monasteries, Tempus (Stroud, Gloucestershire, England), 2001.

Author of guide books on English castles. Contributor to archaeology journals. Review editor, *Medieval Archaeology,* 1964-73.

TRANSLATOR

Aleksandr Mongait, *Archaeology in the U.S.S.R.,* Penguin (New York, NY), 1961.

S. A. Semenov, *Prehistoric Technology,* Barnes & Noble (New York, NY), 1964.

Sergei Rudenko, *Frozen Tombs of Siberia,* J. M. Dent (London, England), 1970.

A. V. Artsikhovsky and B. A. Kolchin, *Novgorod the Great,* Evelyn, Adams & Mackay (London, England), 1967.

SIDELIGHTS: M. W. Thompson once told *CA:* "After earning a doctorate at Cambridge, concerned with mesolithic cultures in Spain, I decided the more active life of government preservation work was more suited to my temperament. The nature of my work, preserving castles and abbeys, promoted an interest that led to my books. The Russian translations were the result of a publisher's invitation and my own interest in the subjects chosen. Colt Hoare's diaries, surviving at the Cardiff Public Library, prompted me to edit his travels.

"My writings have not followed a planned course, but have been responses to things I have encountered. I found the notebooks kept by Pitt-Rivers on his travels, and I found the travel journals of Sir Richard Colt Hoare. Such people, whose main achievements are outside their professions, arouse my interest.

"In the last few years I have returned to my professional interests in medieval buildings. Surprisingly, in certain subjects like the hall, people hold strong views, and I have found myself caught up in controversies that may have whetted my appetite! I have also developed a taste for monasteries and have written about them."

Recently Thompson added: "I have found that my writing has been helped by foreign travel, usually eastward as far as China. Recently trips to Latin America (Peru, Guatemala, Mexico) have allowed me to see exciting Inca, Maya, and Aztec remains."

* * *

THORNTON, Bruce S. 1953-

PERSONAL: Born August 2, 1953, in Fresno County, CA; son of Glen S. (a cattle rancher and barber) and Grace G. (a cattle rancher) Thornton; married Jacalyn Golston, 1977; children: Isaac, Cole. *Ethnicity:* "American." *Education:* University of California—Los Angeles, B.A. (magna cum laude), 1975, Ph.D., 1983. *Politics:* "Reluctant Democrat." *Religion:* Protestant. *Hobbies and other interests:* Basketball, chess.

ADDRESSES: *Home*—919 East Yale Ave., Fresno, CA 93704. *Office*—Department of Foreign Languages and Literatures, California State University—Fresno, 2320 East San Ramon Ave., Fresno, CA 93740-8030; fax: 559-278-7878. *E-mail*—bruce_thornton@csufresno.edu.

CAREER: California State University—Fresno, Fresno, CA, lecturer, 1977-78, 1982-89, assistant professor, 1989-91, associate professor, 1991-96, professor of classics and humanities, 1996—, chair, Department of Foreign Languages and Literatures, beginning 1996. Kings River Community College, lecturer, 1983-85.

MEMBER: National Association of Scholars, Phi Kappa Phi.

WRITINGS:

Eros the Killer: The Myth of Ancient Greek Sexuality, Westview Press (Boulder, CO), 1998.

Plagues of the Mind: The New Epidemic of False Knowledge, Praeger (New York, NY), 1998.

(Coauthor) *Bonfire of the Humanities: Rescuing the Classics in an Impoverished Age,* ISI Books (Wilmington, DE), 2000.

Greek Ways: How the Greeks Created Western Civilization, Encounter Books (San Francisco, CA), 2000.

Humanities Handbook, Prentice Hall (Tappan, NJ), 2000.

Searching for Joaquin: Myth, Murieta, and History in California, Encounter Books (San Francisco, CA), 2003.

A Student's Guide to the Classics, ISI Books (Wilmington, DE), 2003.

Contributor of articles and reviews to periodicals, including *Heterodoxy, Arion, Measure, Classical and Modern Literature, English Language Notes,* and *American Journal of Philology.*

SIDELIGHTS: Bruce S. Thornton once told *CA:* "Writing, for me, is primarily about pleasure: the pleasures of using language, playing with ideas, gathering knowledge, and speaking my piece. What Horace saw as the purpose of poetry, 'delight and instruction,' should be the purpose of all writing. To speak the truth as we know it, to explode error, to have sheer fun with words and ideas: very few activities are more rewarding or enjoyable. I write for the same reason I breathe: to keep the soul alive."

* * *

TOTEN, Teresa 1955-

PERSONAL: Born October 13, 1955, in Zagreb, Yugoslavia (now Croatia); immigrated to Canada, 1955; became Canadian citizen; daughter of Adam (a real estate agent) and Jan (a cook) Vukovic; married Ken Toten (a banker), September 22, 1979; children: Sasha, Nikki. *Ethnicity:* Croatian. *Education:* University of Toronto, B.A. (honors, political economy), 1978; M.A., 1979; attended writing workshops at George Brown College, Toronto, 1986-95. *Politics:* "Left of center." *Religion:* Roman Catholic. *Hobbies and other interests:* Working with children's groups to promote all aspects of children's literature and book production; travel; sports, especially tennis, basketball, walking.

Teresa Toten

ADDRESSES: *Home*—62 Lynwood Avenue, Toronto, Ontario M4V 1K4, Canada. *E-mail*—Teresatoten@aol.com.

CAREER: Writer, 1995—. Radio Canada, Montreal, Quebec, Canada, freelance writer and broadcaster, 1980; Royal Commission on Conditions of Foreign Service, Ottawa, Ontario, Canada, senior analyst, 1982; Canada Museum Construction Corporation, Ottawa, assistant to the chair, 1982-1984; Canadian Institute for International Peace and Security, Ottawa, corporate secretary, 1984-1985; freelance book reviewer, 1996— .

MEMBER: Canadian Society of Children's Authors, Illustrators and Performers (CANSCAIP), Canadian Children's Book Centre, Writers' Union of Canada, Artist with the Learning through the Arts Programme, International Board on Books for Young People, and the Ontario Arts Council Writers in the Schools Programme.

AWARDS, HONORS: Imperial Order of Daughters of the Empire (IODE) Book Award finalist, Municipal Chapter of Toronto IODE, 1995, Violet Downey Book

Award finalist, National Chapter of Canada IODE, 1995, Ruth Schwartz Children's Book Award finalist, Ontario Arts Council, 1995, Canadian Library Association Notable Book, 1996, and Our Choice selection, Canadian Children's Book Centre, 1996-97, all for *The Onlyhouse;* Governor-General's Literary Award nominee, Canada Council for the Arts, 2001, for *The Game;* Young Adult Canadian Book Award nominee, Canadian Library Association, Children's Book of the Year, Alberta Book Publishers' Association, White Raven Citation, *Voice of Youth Advocates* Best List, Book of the Year Award, Bronze, *ForeWord Magazine,* White Pine Award Finalist, and Best Book Award for Young Adults, all 2002, for *The Game;* American Library Association award, (best book for young adults category), 2003, for *The Game.*

WRITINGS:

The Onlyhouse (Northern Lights Young Novels), Red Deer College Press (Red Deer, Alberta, Canada), 1995.
The Game, Red Deer Press (Calgary, Alberta, Canada), 2001.

A chapter of *The Onlyhouse* appears in *Girl's Own: An Anthology of Canadian Fiction,* edited by Sarah Ellis, Penguin/Viking (New York, NY), 2001.

WORK IN PROGRESS: Me and the Blondes, a novel for young adults.

SIDELIGHTS: Canadian author Teresa Toten began to write books for children and young adults in the mid-1990s, acting upon a lifelong interest in writing. The positive critical response to Toten's first novel alone speaks volumes about her arrival on the Canadian children's literature scene. Selected for the short lists of several important literary awards and included on the "best books" lists of both the Canadian Children's Book Centre and the Canadian Library Association, *The Onlyhouse* is a story about roots, identity, and belonging. Presented from the perspective of eleven-year-old Lucy, it tells about an immigrant child's experiences in Toronto in the 1960s. Toten's second novel also received much critical praise. *The Game,* which tells the story of a troubled teen struggling to piece her life together in a rehabilitation clinic, was nominated for both the Governor-General's Literary Award and the Young Adult Canadian Book Award.

Quill & Quire reviewer Kenneth Oppel described Toten's narrative voice as "so authentic and compelling it draws us with instant enthusiasm into the story." Toten's work has been compared with the popular humor-tinged, realistic fiction Brian Doyle writes for pre-teens. "The laugh-alouds are a delight," said Sarah Ellis in a review of *The Onlyhouse* for *Resource Links.* "Even better are the rueful smiles with sadness at their edges."

Toten's parents married in Croatia. Her father, a Canadian citizen with Croatian roots, met Toten's mother on one of his visits "home." After their wedding, he returned to Canada to tackle the red tape that would allow his wife to leave Croatia and join him. By the time the immigration process untangled two years later, Toten had already been born. She was an infant in 1955 when her parents finally reunited in Toronto.

Shortly after the family's reunion, however, Toten's father died. Her mother was suddenly a single parent in a new country. Like Lucy's mother in *The Onlyhouse,* Toten's mother worked hard to achieve the immigrant dream of buying a home in a well-established, middle-class neighborhood. As a child, Toten called that Toronto home an "only house." There were two reasons for her description: the house was detached, and it was the first and therefore the only house she and her mother had ever lived in. The "only house" image was important to Toten as a child and its impact remained with her as an adult. When Red Deer College Press accepted her autobiographical novel for publication, Toten knew its title had to be *The Onlyhouse.*

Toten grew up and went to school in a neighborhood much like the one in her book. She completed high school and earned two academic degrees at the University of Toronto. In 1979, she married Ken Toten, moved to Montreal, and worked as a writer and broadcaster. A year later, the couple moved to Ottawa. During their five years in Canada's capital, Toten worked for a variety of government-affiliated organizations.

In 1985, the Totens returned to Toronto. After the birth of their first child in 1986, Toten began to pursue her lifelong interest in writing. She attended a series of writing workshops at George Brown College. An exercise in one of the workshops required her to write a scene about being ten years old. *The Onlyhouse,* based on Toten's own childhood, grew out of that assignment.

The Onlyhouse relives much of Toten's experience of moving from Toronto's lively, mixed Kensington Market district to the quiet, homogeneous Davisville neighborhood. As she wrote *The Onlyhouse,* she worked hard at portraying the diverse and distinctive communities that characterized Toronto in the 1960s and continue to characterize it today.

"Most of all, I wanted to tell the story of a child who feels quite different from the norm and wants very much to belong, to be part of the inside group," Toten once commented. "Lucy, the main character, and I have a lot in common and the other characters are a combination of real people I've known." Toten's Lucy impressed author Sarah Ellis. In a *Quill & Quire* article on great books for girls, Ellis included Lucy in a discussion of characters "who show passion, imagination, and humor in the face of oppression." She described Lucy specifically as "gregarious, optimistic, articulate and a bit of a goof."

The central character of Toten's second novel, *The Game,* faces a different set of challenges and obstacles. The reader meets Danielle Webster in Riverwood Youth Center, an institute for troubled teens; placed there by her mother after attempting suicide, Dani is struggling to make sense of her troubled past. Abused by her father and neglected by her mother, Dani slowly becomes friends with her roommate Scratch, a self-mutilator, and his friend Kevin, who also attempted suicide after his family refused to accept his homosexuality. Bev Greenberg, a contributor to *Herizons,* noted that Toten's "excellent use of dialogue lends credibility to the story by showing the slow development of a rapport between Danielle and the others at the Center." These budding friendships provide a supportive network for Dani as she tries to confront her problems.

Toten builds a sense of mystery surrounding Dani's past, revealing it in excerpts from her parents' letters and samples from Dani's sessions with her therapist. Most compelling, however, are the series of brief memories and flashbacks that punctuate the narrative. These memories revolve around the mysterious "game" that Dani had played with her younger sister Kelly. Although Dani originally tries to escape these painful memories, she later learns that she must confront them in order to find the truth.

Toten handles her difficult subject matter skillfully, using well-developed characters to bring humanity to the story. "*The Game* treats both its characters and its readers with great respect," Margaret Mackey commented in *Resource Links.* Toten crafts her characters "with consummate skill and a fine radar for current teen culture and language," noted *CM* reviewer Anne Letain.

Toten is a passionate reader and admires the work of Canadian authors for children such as Brian Doyle, Sarah Ellis, and Tim Wynne-Jones. During Canadian Children's Book Week in 1996, she had the opportunity to revisit the greater Toronto area as one of the Canadian Children's Book Centre's touring authors. She is an energetic advocate for children's literature and particularly enjoys working with groups of children; she also serves as Program Chair for the Canadian Society of Children's Authors, Illustrators, and Performers.

Toten lives in Toronto, where she teaches creative writing workshops and tutors English-as-a-Second-Language students as a volunteer. She once remarked, "I want to continue to write about the theme of belonging, what it is that motivates our need for this very human desire, and how we go about achieving it. I hope my writing will reach children who will feel less alone when they read it."

BIOGRAPHICAL AND CRITICAL SOURCES:

PERIODICALS

Booklist, February 15, 2002, Michael Cart, review of *The Game,* p. 1010.
Children's Book News, spring, 1996, pp. 13-14; winter, 1997, pp. 7-12.

Herizons, summer, 2002, Bev Greenberg, review of *The Game,* p. 32.

Quill & Quire, December, 1995, Kenneth Oppel, review of *The Onlyhouse,* p. 12; July, 1997, Sarah Ellis, "Great Canadian Books for Girls," p. 51; July, 2001, p. 48.

Resource Links, February, 1996, Sarah Ellis, review of *The Onlyhouse,* p. 118; October, 2001, Margaret Mackey, review of *The Game,* p. 43.

School Library Journal, July, 1996, pp. 86-87.

ONLINE

CANSCAIP, http://www.canscaip.org/ (February 18, 2003), biography of Teresa Toten.

CM: Canadian Review of Materials, http://www.umanitoba.ca/outreach/cm/ (November 16, 2001), Anne Letain, review of *The Game.*

Red Deer Press, http://www.reddeerpress.com/ (February 18, 2003), review of *The Game.*

V

VANDIVER, Frank E(verson) 1925-

PERSONAL: Born December 9, 1925, in Austin, TX; son of Harry Schultz (a mathematician) and Maude Folmsbee (Everson) Vandiver; married Carol Sue Smith (died, 1979); married Renee Aubry Carmody, 1980; children: (first marriage) Nita, Nancy, Frank Alexander. *Education:* University of Texas, M.A., 1949; Tulane University, Ph.D., 1951.

ADDRESSES: Office—The Mosher Institute of International Policy Studies, Texas A&M University, 2400 TAMU Blocker Bldg., College Station, TX 77843-2400. *Agent*—Paul R. Reynolds, Inc., 12 East 41st St., New York, NY 10017. *E-mail*—f-vandiver@tamu.edu.

CAREER: United States Civil Service, San Antonio, TX, historian, 1944-45; Air Force historian, Montgomery, AL, 1951-52; Washington University, St. Louis, MO, instructor, 1952-53, assistant professor of history, 1953-55; Rice University, Houston, TX, assistant professor, 1955-56, associate professor, 1956-58, professor of history, 1958-65, Harrison Masterson, Jr. Professor of History, 1965-79, chair of department of history and political science, 1962, chair of department of history, 1968-69, master of Margaret Root Brown College, 1964-66, acting president of University, 1969-70, provost, 1970-79, vice president, 1975-79; North Texas State University, Denton, president, 1979-81; Texas A & M University, College Station, president, 1981-88, president emeritus, 1988—; Mosher Institute for International Policy Studies, institute program director, 1988—; Harmsworth Professor of American History,

Frank E. Vandiver

Oxford University, 1963-64; visiting professor of military history, United States Military Academy, 1973-74; Fortenbaugh Lecturer, Gettysburg College, 1974. Member of advisory council, Office of the Chief of Military History, Department of the Army, 1969-74; executive director, American Revolution Bicentennial Commission of Texas, 1970-72; chairman of the board, 1992-98, acting interim president, 1997-98, The

American University in Cairo, Egypt; Member of board of trustees, United States Commission on Military History.

MEMBER: American Historical Association, Society of American Historians (fellow; councilor, 1966; member of board of directors, 1969—), Organization of American Historians, P.E.N., National Council of the Humanities (vice chair, 1976-78), White House Historical Society, Jefferson Davis Association (president, 1963—), Confederate Memorial Literary Society, Southern Historical Association (vice president, 1974-75; president, 1975-76), Texas State Historical Association (fellow), Texas Institute of Letters (president, 1960-62), Bicentennial Association of Texas (president, 1972-73), Philosophical Society of Texas (president, 1977-78), San Jacinto Museum of History Association (member of board of trustees, 1975—), Cosmos Club.

AWARDS, HONORS: Rockefeller fellow, 1946-48; Guggenheim fellow, 1955; Carr Collins Prize from Texas Institute of Letters, 1958, for *Mighty Stonewall*; American Philosophical Society research grants, 1954, 1955, and 1960; honorary degree from Oxford University, 1963; Harry S. Truman Award from Kansas City Civil War Round Table, 1966; Jefferson Davis Award from Confederate Memorial Literary Society, 1970, and Fletcher Pratt Award from New York Civil War Round Table, 1971, for *Their Tattered Flags: The Epic of the Confederacy;* Regent's Award from Lincoln Academy of Illinois, 1973; outstanding civilian service medal from Department of the Army, 1974; Americanism Award from Sons of the American Revolution, 1974; outstanding graduate alumnus award, Tulane University, 1974; George R. Brown Award from Rice University, 1975 and 1978; honorary doctorate from Austin College, 1977, Lincoln College, 1989; award from Grand Order of Filippo Mazzi, 1978; National Book Award nomination, 1978, for *Black Jack: The Life and Times of John J. Pershing;* Best Book Award from *Texas Books in Review,* 1978, for *Black Jack: The Life and Times of John J. Pershing;* Friends of the Dallas Public Library Award, Texas Institute of Letters, 1978, for *Black Jack: The Life and Times of John J. Pershing;* T. Harry Williams Memorial Award, 1985; Ima Hogg Award, 1992; President's Medal, The American University of Cairo, 1999.

WRITINGS:

Ploughshares into Swords: Josiah Gorgas and Confederate Ordnance, University of Texas Press (Arlington, TX), 1952, new edition, Texas A & M University Press (College Station, TX), 1994.

Rebel Brass: The Confederate Command System, Louisiana State University Press (Baton Rouge, LA), 1956.

Mighty Stonewall, McGraw-Hill (New York, NY), 1957.

Jubal's Raid: General Early's Famous Attack on Washington in 1864, McGraw-Hill (New York, NY) 1960.

(With W. H. Nelson) *Fields of Glory: A Pictorial Narrative of American Wars,* Dutton (New York, NY), 1960.

Basic History of the Confederacy, Van Nostrand (New York, NY), 1962.

The Making of a President: Jefferson Davis, 1861, Virginia Civil War Commission (Richmond, VA), 1962.

The First Public War, 1861-1865 (address before the conference of the Public Relations Society of America), Foundation for Public Relations Research and Education (New York, NY), 1962.

Jefferson Davis and the Confederate State, Clarendon Press (New York, NY), 1964.

(With others) *John J. Pershing,* Silver Burdett (New York, NY), 1967.

Their Tattered Flags: The Epic of the Confederacy, Harper's Magazine Press (New York, NY), 1970.

The Southwest: South or West? (from an address delivered to the annual meeting of the Southern Historical Association, Dallas, TX, 1974), drawings by Jo Alys Downs, Texas A&M University Press (College Station, TX), 1975.

Black Jack: The Life and Times of John J. Pershing, Texas A&M Press (College Station, TX), 1977.

The Long Loom of Lincoln (from a lecture delivered at the Foellinger-Freimann Botanical Conservatory in Fort Wayne, IN, 1986), Louis A. Warren Lincoln Library and Museum (Fort Wayne, IN), 1987.

(With J. C. Martin, W. T. Kendall, and James Kochan) *Texas Forever!! The Paintings,* Oak Creek Press (Sedona, AZ), 1990.

Blood Brothers: A Short History of the Civil War, Texas A&M University Press (College Station, TX), 1992.

(Author of foreword) *The Diaries of Josiah Gorgas, New Edition,* edited by Sarah Wiggins, University of Alabama Press (Tuscaloosa, AL), 1995.

Civil War Battlefields and Landmarks: A Guide to the National Park Sites (with official National Park Service maps), Random House (New York, NY), 1996.

Shadows of Vietnam: Lyndon Johnson's Wars, Texas A&M University Press (College Station, TX), 1997.

1001 Things Everyone Should Know about the Civil War, Doubleday (New York, NY), 1999.

(Author of foreword) Jill Edwards, editor, *Al-Alamein Revisited: The Battle of Al Alamein and its Historical Implications,* American University of Cairo (Cairo, Egypt), 2000.

(Author of foreword) James Hannah, editor, *The Great War Reader,* Texas A&M University Press (College Station, TX), 2000.

1001 Things Everyone Should Know about World War II, Broadway Books (New York, NY), 2002, paperback edition, 2003.

EDITOR

The Civil War Diary of General Josiah Gorgas, University of Alabama Press (Tuscaloosa, AL), 1947.

Confederate Blockade-Running through Bermuda, 1861-1865, University of Texas Press (Arlington, TX) 1947.

Joseph E. Johnston, *Narrative of Military Operations,* University of Indiana Press (Bloomington, IN), 1959.

Jubal A. Early, *War Memoirs,* University of Indiana Press (Bloomington, IN), 1960.

The Idea of the South, University of Chicago Press (Chicago, IL), 1964.

Contributor to books, including *The American Tragedy: The Civil War in Retrospect,* Hampden-Sydney College Press (Hampden-Sydney, VA), 1959; *Lincoln for the Ages,* edited by R. G. Newman, Doubleday (New York, NY), 1960; (with Martin Hardwick Hall and Homer L. Kerr) *Essays on the American Civil War,* edited by William F. Holmes and Harold M. Hollingsworth, introduction by E. C. Barksdale, University of Texas (Arlington, TX), 1968.

Contributor of articles about American and European military history to *American People's Encyclopedia,* 1952, *Encyclopedia Americana,* 1960, 1963, *World Book,* 1961, *Encyclopedia Britannica,* 1963, *Encyclopedia of World Biography,* 1972, *Dictionary of American Biography,* 1972, *New Book of Knowledge,* 1974, and *Encyclopedia of Southern History,* 1978. Also contributor of more than sixty additional articles to historical journals, and of more than one hundred book reviews to *New York Times, New York Herald Tribune, Saturday Review,* and historical journals. Associate editor, *Journal of Southern History,* 1959-62. Chief advisory editor, *The Papers of Jefferson Davis,* 1963—; member of editorial advisory board, *The Papers of U. S. Grant,* 1977—.

ADAPTATIONS: Some of the author's works have been adapted for audio cassette.

SIDELIGHTS: Frank E. Vandiver has long been a student of military and southern history, and his numerous books reflect this interest and fascination. Several of his books are biographies of great leaders and men of power. For example, Vandiver's book *Mighty Stonewall* is "a definitive biography of the great military genius," according to a reviewer for *Kirkus Reviews.* "This will stand out as a brilliant study of strategy and tactics in those campaigns in which the army of the Shenandoah bore the brunt. . . . Vandiver, a Texan, has done an exacting job of scholarship. . . . his will appeal primarily to that large market of avid armchair strategists who demand exact reportage of battles and campaigns and the men who fought them." H. T. Kane of the *Chicago Sunday Tribune* called the book "a major historical work, a brilliantly successful one. . . . The author is that comparative rarity, a professor who writes like a writer, with zest and deep capacity."

Vandiver is also frequently praised for his objectivity and fairness in reporting and interpreting facts. His book *Their Tattered Flags: The Epic of the Confederacy,* "which is intended to redress the slight, tries to atone for the literary syrup as well as the pedantry that has smothered the Confederates," E. M. Thomas commented in *Saturday Review.* "It attempts to compensate for the ahistorical ax-grinding that too often has glorified the inglorious, castigated the noble, and ignored the human qualities of the Confederate experience. And it succeeds. Vandiver has written a balanced, brilliant, literate history that Confederates themselves might recognize as their own. . . . The author weaved description and analysis together with a narrative that flows. Not only does [he] sketch his myriad characters masterfully, he allows them to develop with the course of events. . . . [This book] is a monumental achievement."

In 1978 Vandiver's *Black Jack: The Life and Times of John J. Pershing* was nominated for the National Book Award. *Black Jack* is a biography of General John J.

Pershing, the commander of the American Expeditionary Forces during World War I. Reviewers and readers alike were impressed with Vandiver's thoroughness, honesty, and accuracy, as well as with his ability to bring Pershing to life. A critic for *Publishers Weekly,* impressed with the research Vandiver prepared for *Black Jack,* observed that the book contains "more than 1,000 pages of text, a 22-page bibliography and hundreds of footnotes." "An eminent military historian," *Library Journal* reviewer Michel Ridgeway wrote, "Vandiver has written what may safely be described as a definitive biography of General Pershing. There is much to praise in this publication: the scholarship is extremely thorough, impeccably though not obstrusively, footnoted; the prose is lucid and readable; and the illustrations and maps are well-chosen. The portrait of Pershing that emerges is as honest and complete as could be done." Philip Terzian also appreciated Vandiver's biography of Pershing. He remarked in the *New Republic:* "This is one of the finest biographies that has been written of an American general, a masterful account of a military career that is both broad and deep. It is difficult to sew together the threads of character and events and to humanize the image of a totem like Pershing, but Vandiver has succeeded, and stylishly, too."

In *Shadows of Vietnam: Lyndon Johnson's Wars,* Vandiver "cultivates the challenging ground between scholarly and popular history," according to Richard Moser in the *Historian.* Vandiver drew on memoirs, oral history, archives, and secondary sources to reconstruct Lyndon Johnson's years in the White House and as commander in chief of the U.S. armed forces. In addition to providing a detailed portrait of Johnson, Vandiver also presents Johnson's advisors and military personnel. Vandiver portrays Johnson's dilemma: despite calls for a wider war in Vietnam, he was haunted by the danger of sparking a nuclear holocaust. In the end, as Moser commented, "despite political prowess and the possession of unprecedented public power, Johnson became another casualty of the war in Vietnam." Vandiver shows how this happened, giving readers insight into Johnson's character as well as into events of the time. In *Presidential Studies Quarterly,* Robert Previch wrote, "If you want to know precisely what went wrong in Vietnam, this is the book for you," and Previch noted, "What makes it so special is the author's ability to take the reader back to the events as they were happening."

Asked by Broadway Books to participate in the popular and acclaimed "1001 Things Everyone Ought to Know" series, Vandiver wrote *1001 Things Everyone Should Know about the Civil War* and *1001 Things Everyone Should Know about World War II.* The books are organized chronologically and form highly readable, entertaining works of reference for both the generalist and the enthusiast.

BIOGRAPHICAL AND CRITICAL SOURCES:

PERIODICALS

America, January 17, 1998, Wilson Miscamble, review of *Shadows of Vietnam: Lyndon Johnson's Wars,* p. 22.

Booklist, October 15, 1992, review of *Blood Brothers: A Short History of the Civil War,* p. 400; June 1, 1995, Joseph Keppler, review of *Voices of Valor: Words of the Civil War,* p. 1803; May 15, 1997, Margaret Flanagan review of *Shadows of Vietnam,* p. 1560.

Book Week, May 10, 1964.

Choice, October, 1968; October, 1997, review of *Shadows of Vietnam,* p. 359.

Civil War Book Review, summer, 1997, review of *1001 Things Everyone Should Know about the Civil War,* p. 15.

Civil War History, June, 1997, Ethan Rafuse, review of *Civil War Battlefields and Landmarks: A Guide to the National Park Sites,* p. 161.

Historian, spring, 1999, Richard Moser, review of *Shadows of Vietnam,* p. 691.

Journal of American History, March, 1994, review of *Blood Brothers,* p. 1475; October, 1993, p. 720.

Journal of Military History, October, 1993, review of *Blood Brothers,* p. 720; July, 1998, review of *Shadows of Vietnam,* p. 679.

Journal of Southern History, May, 1994, review of *Blood Brothers,* p. 401; May, 1997, review of *Civil War Battlefields and Landmarks,* p. 462.

Kirkus Reviews, April 1, 1957; March 1, 1997, review of *Shadows of Vietnam,* p. 369.

Library Journal, February 1, 1970; October 1, 1977; October 15, 1992, review of *Blood Brothers,* p. 400; May 1, 2002, Mel Lane, review of *1001 Things Everyone Should Know about World War II,* p. 92.

Marine Corps Gazette, October, 1997, review of *Shadows of Vietnam,* p. 70.

Military Review, May/June 1998, review of *Shadows of Vietnam,* p. 96.

New Republic, July 9, 1977.
New York Times Book Review, October 18, 1970.
Pacific Historical Review, February, 1999, Robert McMahon, review of *Shadows of Vietnam,* p. 131.
Presidential Studies Quarterly, fall, 1997, Robert Previdi, review of *Shadows of Vietnam,* p. 839.
Publishers Weekly, April 18, 1977; September 14, 1992, p. 118; April 7, 1997, review of *Shadows of Vietnam,* p. 84; September 14, 1992, review of *Blood Brothers,* p. 118.
Reference and Research Book News, February, 1995, review of *Rebel Brass: The Confederate Command System,* p. 12; March, 1995, review of *Ploughshares into Swords: Josiah Gorgas and Confederate Ordnance,* p. 13.
Saturday Review, March 28, 1970.
Social Science Quarterly, December, 1989, review of *Mighty Stonewall,* p. 1007.
Virginia Quarterly Review, spring, 1995, review of *Ploughshares into Swords,* p. 69.

ONLINE

Houston Chronicle Online, http://www.chron.com/ (August 21, 2002), Lynwood Abram, review of *Shadows of Vietnam: Lyndon Johnson's Wars.*

*   *   *

VAZSONYI, Nicholas 1963-

PERSONAL: Born May 31, 1963, in Traverse City, MI; son of Balint (a concert pianist) and Barbara (Whittington) Vazsonyi; married Agnes Mueller (a professor of German studies), March 1, 1996; children: Leah. *Education:* Indiana University—Bloomington, B.A. (summa cum laude), 1982; University of California—Los Angeles, M.A., 1988, Ph.D., 1993.

ADDRESSES: Home—2500 Blossom St., Columbia, SC 29205. *Office*—German Studies Program, University of South Carolina—Columbia, Columbia, SC 29208; fax: 803-777-0454. *E-mail*—vazsonyi@sc.edu.

CAREER: Telemusic, Inc., Bloomington, IN, artistic director, 1984-86, 1988-90; Vanderbilt University, Nashville, TN, assistant professor of German, 1994-97; University of South Carolina—Columbia, Columbia, SC, assistant professor, 1997-2001, associate professor of German, 2001—.

MEMBER: Goethe Society of North America, Modern Language Association of America, American Association of Teachers of German, German Studies Association, American Society for Eighteenth-Century Studies, Phi Beta Kappa.

AWARDS, HONORS: Grant from German Academic Exchange Service, 1997.

WRITINGS:

Lukacs Reads Goethe: From Aestheticism to Stalinism, Camden House (Columbia, SC), 1997.
(Editor) *Searching for Common Ground: Diskurse zur deutschen Identität, 1750-1871,* Böhlau Verlag (Cologne, Germany), 2000.
(Editor) *Wagner's "Meistersinger": Performance, History, Representation,* University of Rochester Press (Rochester, NY), 2003.

Documentary films for MPI Home Video include *Mozart, Beethoven, Schubert,* and *Brahms,* all 1989.

WORK IN PROGRESS: Research on the "Wagner industry."

W-Z

WARD, Margaret 1950-

PERSONAL: Born August 4, 1950, in Iserlohn, Germany; daughter of William (a British army officer) and Grace (a nurse; maiden name, O'Reilly) Ward; companion of Paddy Hillyard (a university lecturer); children: Fintan, Medbh. *Ethnicity:* "Irish." *Education:* Queen's University, Belfast, Northern Ireland, B.A., 1973. *Politics:* Northern Ireland Women's Coalition; "socialist-feminist."

ADDRESSES: *Office*—Democratic Dialogue, 23 University St., Belfast BT7 1FY, Northern Ireland; fax: 028-9022-0050. *E-mail*—mward45@hotmail.com.

CAREER: Queen's University, Belfast, Northern Ireland, junior research fellow at Institute of Irish Studies, 1979-81; Belfast City Council, Belfast, women's development officer in Department of Community Services, 1984-86; University of the West of England, Bristol, part-time lecturer, 1991-93; Bath Spa University College, Bath, England, research fellow in history, 1993-99; Democratic Dialogue, Belfast, assistant director, 2000—. Queen's University, member of advisory committee, Centre for the Advancement of Women in Politics.

MEMBER: British Association of Irish Studies (vice chair, 1996-99), Irish Women's Network.

WRITINGS:

Unmanageable Revolutionaries: Women and Irish Nationalism, Pluto Press (London, England), 1983, reprinted with new introduction, 1995.

Maud Gonne: A Life, Pandora Press (London, England), 1990.

(Editor) *In Their Own Voice: Women and Irish Nationalism,* Attic Press (Dublin, Ireland), 1995.

Hanna Sheehy-Skeffington: A Life, International Specialized Book Services (Portland, OR), 1997.

The Northern Ireland Assembly and Women: Assessing the Gender Deficit, Democratic Dialogue (Belfast, Northern Ireland), 2000.

(Editor, with Louise Ryan) *Soldiers, New Women, and Wicked Hags: Women and Irish Nationalism,* Irish Academic Press (Dublin, Ireland), 2003.

Contributor to books, including *Contesting Politics: Women in Ireland, North and South,* edited by Yvonne Galligan, Eilis Ward, and Rick Wilford, Westview Press (Boulder, CO), 1999; *Gendered Nations: Europe and Beyond,* edited by Ida Blom, Karen Hagemann, and Catherine Hall, Berg Publishers (New York, NY), 2000; *Female Activists: Irish Women and Change, 1900-1960,* edited by Mary Cullen and Maria Luddy, Woodfield Press (Dublin, Ireland), 2001; *The Irish Revolution, 1913-1923,* edited by Joost Augusteijn, Palgrave (Basingstoke, Hampshire, England), 2002; and *Motherhood in Ireland,* edited by Patricia Kennedy, Mercier Press (Dublin, Ireland), 2003. Contributor to journals, including *Women's History Review, Race and Class, Feminist Review, Journal of Gender Studies, Honest Ulsterman, Hecate,* and *History Ireland.* Member of editorial advisory board, *Irish Studies Review* and *Saothar.*

WORK IN PROGRESS: *Anna Parnell: A Biography,* publication by Cork University Press (Dublin, Ireland) expected in 2005.

SIDELIGHTS: Margaret Ward once told *CA:* "I grew up in Belfast, Northern Ireland, and from 1968 was active in the movement for civil rights. I later became a founding member of a number of feminist groups in Belfast and, as a graduate student in the department of political science at Queen's University, I became interested in researching the history of women's involvement in Irish political movements. One fundamental issue was understanding why articulate and politically active women were excluded from the public sphere when the Irish Free State was formed in 1922. My research helped the feminist groups to which I belonged develop a critique of contemporary Irish society. Due to political differences with my thesis supervisor, I did not submit my dissertation. It was published as *Unmanageable Revolutionaries: Women and Irish Nationalism,* a book that has been influential in many different circles.

"Since then I have focused upon suffrage and other feminist issues in further exploration of the relevance of feminism to modern Ireland. Biographical studies have provided an accessible means of putting this research into context. I have analyzed nationalist involvement in my biography of Maud Gonne, and my study of Hanna Sheehy-Skeffington, a suffragist and Sinn Feiner, examines the relationship between these political commitments."

Ward recently added: "I returned to Belfast in 1999. In my post as assistant director of the independent think-tank Democratic Dialogue, I have been engaged in research on the position of women in public life in Northern Ireland and, in particular, on the role played by women in the Northern Ireland Assembly. While I have continued my writing as a historian, the majority of my work is now on contemporary issues. One focus has been the difficulties of bringing up children in societies in conflict. How do mothers explain the origins of inter-communal strife to their children? How do they keep children safe? Are they responsible (unwittingly) for the transmission of sectarian attitudes?

"As an activist in the political party the Northern Ireland Women's Coalition, I have been responsible for coordinating party policy and writing our election manifesto for the Assembly elections of 2003."

WRIGHT, N. T(om) 1948-

PERSONAL: Born December 1, 1948, in Morpeth, Northumberland, England; son of N. I. (a company director) and F. (a homemaker; maiden name, Forman) Wright; married Margaret E. A. Fiske, August 14, 1971; children: Julian, Rosamund, Harriet, Oliver. *Ethnicity:* "British." *Education:* Exeter College, Oxford, B.A. (humanities; with first class honors), 1971, B.A. (theology; with first class honors), 1973, M.A., 1975; Merton College, Oxford, D.Phil., 1981, D.D., 2000. *Religion:* Church of England. *Hobbies and other interests:* Golf, cricket, hill walking, the classical world, music, poetry, travel.

ADDRESSES: Office—Auckland Castle, Bishop Auckland, County Durham DL14 7NR, England; fax: 01-388-605-204. *E-mail*—bishop.of.durham@durham.anglican.org.

CAREER: Ordained priest of Church of England, 1976; Cambridge University, Downing College, Cambridge, England, fellow and chaplain, 1978-81; McGill University, Montreal, Quebec, Canada, assistant professor of New Testament language and literature, 1981-86; Oxford University, Worcester College, Oxford, England, lecturer in New Testament studies, fellow, and chaplain, 1986-92; Church of England, canon theologian of Coventry Cathedral, 1992-99, dean of Lichfield, 1993—, canon of Westminster, 2000-03, bishop of Durham, 2003—. Institute for Christian Studies, Toronto, Ontario, Canada, fellow, 1991—. Montreal Diocesan Theological College, honorary professor, 1981-86; University of Otago, Burns Lecturer, 1996; Yale University, Shaffer Lecturer, 1996; Harvard University, visiting professor, 1999; Union Seminary, Richmond, VA, Sprunt Lecturer, 2000; University of Manchester, Manson Memorial Lecturer, 2000; St. Michael's Seminary, Baltimore, MD, visiting lecturer, 2000; Baylor University, Parchman Lecturer at George W. Truett Theological Seminary, 2001, visiting lecturer, 2002; Pontifical Gregorian University, Rome, Italy, McCarthy Visiting Professor, 2002; Cambridge University, Hulsean Lecturer, 2003; University of Sheffield, Stephenson Lecturer, 2003; also speaker at White House Bible Study Group and C. S. Lewis Institute, both Washington, DC. International Anglican Doctrinal and Theological Commission, member, 2001—. Affiliated with the videotapes *Jesus: The New*

Way (six-part series), Gateway Films, 1998; *Paul* and *Resurrection,* both Tabgha Films, 1999; and *Romans* and *The Gospels,* both Tabgha Films, 2000; presenter of televised religious services; guest on media programs in England and abroad, including productions of Public Broadcasting Service and National Public Radio in the United States; consultant for British television series *The Apostles* and *Son of God.*

MEMBER: Society for New Testament Studies, Society of Biblical Literature (chair of Historical Jesus Section, 1998-2001), Institute for Biblical Research, Tyndale Fellowship for Biblical Research, Anglican Association of Biblical Scholars.

AWARDS, HONORS: Research fellow, Society for the Promotion of Christian Knowledge, 2000-03; D.D., University of Aberdeen, 2001.

WRITINGS:

Small Faith, Great God, Fleming Revell (Old Tappan, NJ), 1978.
(Editor) *The Work of John Frith,* Sutton Courtenay Press (Appleford, England), 1983.
The Epistles of Paul to the Colossians and to Philemon, Eerdmans (Grand Rapids, MI), 1987.
(Editor, with L. D. Hurst) *The Glory of Christ in the New Testament: Studies in Christology in Memory of George Bradford Caird,* Oxford University Press (Oxford, England), 1987.
(With Stephen Neill) *The Interpretation of the New Testament, 1861-1986,* Oxford University Press (Oxford, England), 1988.
The Climax of the Covenant: Christ and the Law in Pauline Theology, T. & T. Clark (Edinburgh, Scotland), 1991, Fortress (Minneapolis, MN), 1992.
Bringing the Church to the World, Bethany House (Minneapolis, MN), 1992, published as *New Tasks for a Renewed Church,* Hodder & Stoughton, (London, England), 1992.
The Crown and the Fire, SPCK (London, England), 1992, Eerdmans (Grand Rapids, MI), 1995.
Christian Origins and the Question of God, Fortress (Minneapolis, MN), Volume I: *The New Testament and the People of God,* 1992, Volume II: *Jesus and the Victory of God,* 1996, Volume III: *The Resurrection of the Son of God,* 2003.

Who Was Jesus?, Eerdmans (Grand Rapids, MI), 1992.
Following Jesus: Biblical Reflections on Christian Discipleship, SPCK (London, England), 1994, Eerdmans (Grand Rapids, MI), 1995.
The Lord and His Prayer, Eerdmans (Grand Rapids, MI), 1996.
The Original Jesus, Eerdmans (Grand Rapids, MI), 1996.
For All God's Worth, Eerdmans (Grand Rapids, MI), 1997.
What St. Paul Really Said, Eerdmans (Grand Rapids, MI), 1997.
A Moment of Prayer, Eerdmans (Grand Rapids, MI), 1997.
A Moment of Quiet, Eerdmans (Grand Rapids, MI), 1997.
A Moment of Peace, Eerdmans (Grand Rapids, MI), 1997.
A Moment of Celebration, Eerdmans (Grand Rapids, MI), 1997.
Reflecting the Glory, Augsburg (Minneapolis, MN), 1997.
The Way of the Lord: Christian Pilgrimage in the Holy Land and Beyond, Eerdmans (Grand Rapids, MI), 1999.
The Millennium Myth, Westminster John Knox Press (Louisville, KY), 1999 (published in England as *The Myth of the Millennium,* SPCK, London, 1999).
The Challenge of Jesus: Rediscovering Who Jesus Was and Is, Inter-Varsity Press (Downers Grove, IL), 1999.
(With Marcus J. Borg) *The Meaning of Jesus: Two Visions,* HarperSanFrancisco (San Francisco, CA), 1999.
(Editor, with Sven K. Soderlund, and contributor) *Romans and the People of God: Essays in Honor of Gordon D. Fee on the Occasion of His 65th Birthday,* Eerdmans (Grand Rapids, MI), 1999.
Holy Communion for Amateurs, Hodder & Stoughton (London, England), 1999.
Twelve Months of Sundays: Reflections on Bible Readings, SPCK (London, England), *Year C,* 2000, *Year A,* 2001, *Year B,* 2002.
Mark for Everyone, SPCK (London, England), 2001.
Luke for Everyone, SPCK (London, England), 2001.
Paul for Everyone: Galatians and Thessalonians, SPCK (London, England), 2002.
Matthew for Everyone, two volumes, SPCK (London, England), 2002.

The Contemporary Quest for Jesus, Fortress (Minneapolis, MN), 2002.

Paul for Everyone: The Prison Letters, SPCK (London, England), 2002.

John for Everyone, two volumes, SPCK (London, England), 2002.

Paul for Everyone: 1 Corinthians, SPCK (London, England), 2003.

Paul for Everyone: 2 Corinthians, SPCK (London, England), 2003.

Contributor to books, including *Between Two Horizons: Spanning New Testament Studies and Systematic Theology,* edited by Joel B. Green and Max Turner, Eerdmans (Grand Rapids, MI), 2000; *Jesus Then and Now: Images of Jesus in History and Christology,* edited by Marvin Meyer and Charles Hughes, Trinity Press International (Harrisburg, PA), 2001; *Into God's Presence: Prayer in the New Testament,* edited by R. L. Longenecker, Eerdmans (Grand Rapids, MI), 2001; *The Incarnation,* edited by S. T. Davis, D. Kendall, and G. O'Collins, Oxford University Press (Oxford, England), 2002; and *New Interpreter's Bible,* Abingdon (Nashville, TN), 2002. Contributor to periodicals, including *Scottish Journal of Theology, Sewanee Theological Review, Ex Auditu, Journal of Biblical Literature, Theology, Journal of Theological Studies, Themelios, Studia Biblica, Tyndale Bulletin,* and *Gregorianum.* Assistant editor, *Journal for the Study of the New Testament,* 1991-96.

Wright's books have been published in Chinese, Dutch, Norwegian, Swedish, French, Finnish, and German.

WORK IN PROGRESS: Additional volumes of *Christian Origins and the Question of God,* for Fortress (Minneapolis, MN), Volume IV: *Paul and the Justice of God,* completion expected c. 2005, Volume V: *The Gospels and the Story of God,* c. 2007, and Volume VI: *The Early Christians and the Purpose of God,* c. 2009; *A Critical and Exegetical Commentary on the Epistle to the Philippians,* T. & T. Clark (Edinburgh, Scotland); additional volumes for the series *The New Testament for Everyone,* SPCK (London, England); *The Message of Malachi,* Inter-Varsity Press (Downers Grove, IL); *Romans in a Week,* Eerdmans (Grand Rapids, MI); *Galatians,* Eerdmans (Grand Rapids, MI); *Luke,* Black; *A Jesus Reader,* SPCK (London, England).

WYATT, Robert Lee III 1940-

PERSONAL: Born January 27, 1940, in Grandfield, OK; son of Robert Lee, Jr. (a farmer and rancher) and Melba Ruth (Green) Wyatt; married Louise Carole Bard, October 28, 1961; children: Melanie Dawn, Robert Lee IV. *Ethnicity:* "Caucasian." *Education:* University of Oklahoma, B.A., 1963, M.Ed., 1988, Ph.D., 1990. *Politics:* Democrat. *Religion:* Southern Baptist. *Hobbies and other interests:* Painting in watercolors, acting and directing in the theater, talking.

ADDRESSES: Home—2331 Stephanie Cir., Ada, OK 74820. *Office*—College of Education, East Central University, Box J-1, Ada, OK 74820. *E-mail*—bwyatt@wilnet1.com.

CAREER: High school English teacher in Las Cruces, NM, 1963-69; General Dynamics Corp., Fort Worth, TX, writer and director of airplane construction films, 1969-70; high school teacher of English, journalism, and drama, Grandfield, OK, 1970-87; East Central University, Ada, OK, professor of education, 1990—. *Big Pasture News,* owner and publisher, 1976-86.

MEMBER: National Council of Teachers of English, National Council for Social Studies, Association of Teacher Educators.

AWARDS, HONORS: Named Oklahoma State Teacher of the Year, 1985.

WRITINGS:

Devol: Gateway to the Big Pasture, Walsworth Publishing (Marceline, MO), 1974.

Grandfield: Hub of the Big Pasture, Walsworth Publishing (Marceline, MO), Volume I, 1975, Volume II, 1976.

The History of the Haverstock Tent Show, Southern Illinois University Press (Carbondale, IL), 1997.

(With Sandra Looper) *So You Have to Have a Portfolio: A Teacher's Guide to Preparation and Presentation,* Corwin (Thousand Oaks, CA), 1999.

(With Elaine White) *Making Your First Year a Success: The Secondary Teacher's Survival Guide,* Corwin (Thousand Oaks, CA), 2002.

WORK IN PROGRESS: Two young adult novels, *Queen Victoria's Jubilee* and *Last Drag down Main Street;* a third novel, *Seven Kids, A Model T Ford, and Shall We Gather at the River;* revising *So You Have to Have a Portfolio: A Teacher's Guide to Preparation and Presentation.*

SIDELIGHTS: Robert Lee Wyatt III once told *CA:* "I write for self-fulfillment. I love to tell stories, and writing preserves the stories. My primary influences are my family and my students' lives. I do occasionally pick up the shred of a story from a news article, which I file for future reference.

"I write on things I know about. I think that is the secret. I do research for accuracy, but I know my subject before I begin to write. Taking bare facts and then weaving around them is good writing. I like to read it, so that is how I like to write."

* * *

ZAILLIAN, Steven 1953-

PERSONAL: Born January 30, 1953, in CA. *Education:* San Francisco State University, B.A., 1975.

CAREER: Screenplay writer, director, and producer. Director of films, including *Searching for Bobby Fischer,* Paramount, 1993; producer and director of *A Civil Action,* Paramount, 1998.

MEMBER: Writer's Guild.

AWARDS, HONORS: Academy Award nomination for best screenplay adaptation, Academy of Motion Picture Arts and Sciences, 1990, and Writer's Guild Award nomination for best adapted screenplay, 1991, both for *Awakenings;* Academy Award for best screenplay adaptation, British Academy of Film and Theatre Arts (BAFTA) Award for best adapted screenplay, Chicago Film Critics Association Award, Golden Globe Award, Humanitas Prize, Friends of USC Libraries Scripter Award, and Writers Guild of America Award for best screenplay, all 1993, all for *Schindler's List;* MTV Movie award for best new filmmaker, and Tokyo International Film Festival special jury prize, both 1993, both for *Searching for Bobby Fischer;* ShoWest Con-

Steven Zaillian

vention Award for Screenwriter of the Year, 1994; Scripter Award, and Writers Guild of America nomination, both 1999, both for *A Civil Action;* Academy Award nomination for best writing, screenplay written directly for the screen (with Jay Cocks and Kenneth Lonergan), 2003, for *Gangs of New York.*

WRITINGS:

SCREENPLAYS

The Falcon and the Snowman (adapted from the book by Robert Lindsey), Orion Pictures, 1985.
Awakenings (adapted from the book by Oliver Sacks), Columbia, 1990.
Jack the Bear (adapted from the novel by Dan McCall), Twentieth Century-Fox, 1993.
Schindler's List (adapted from the book by Thomas Keneally), Universal, 1993.
(And director) *Searching for Bobby Fischer* (adapted from the book by Fred Waitzkin), Paramount, 1993.

(With Donald Stewart and John Milius) *Clear and Present Danger* (adapted from the novel by Tom Clancy), Paramount, 1994.

Mission: Impossible (based on the television series), Paramount, 1996.

A Civil Action (adapted from the book by Jonathan Harr), Paramount, 1998.

(With David Mamet) *Hannibal* (adapted from the book by Thomas Harris), Metro-Goldwyn-Mayer, 2001.

(With Jay Cocks and Kenneth Lonergan) *Gangs of New York*, Miramax, 2002.

Also uncredited author of rewrites for films, including *Crimson Tide, Primal Fear,* and *Amistad.*

SIDELIGHTS: Steven Zaillian is an accomplished screenwriter and filmmaker who has demonstrated his talents in adapting both novels and nonfiction for the screen. Zaillian began his screenwriting career in 1985 with *The Falcon and the Snowman,* a film he derived, with director John Schlesinger, from Robert Lindsey's nonfiction account of a Central Intelligence Agency (CIA) associate who provides secret information to Soviet agents, enlisting his drug-using friend as an intermediary. This scheme initially proves lucrative for the partners, but the hero eventually suffers guilt over his actions and determines to end his treasonous behavior even as his partner uses their profits to maintain his drug habit. The ensuing conflict between the pair leads, inevitably, to an encounter with American law enforcement.

Awakenings, Zaillian's 1990 screen credit, is an adaptation of neurologist Oliver Sacks's book about his experience with a group of victims of the encephalitis epidemic that took place between 1916 and 1927, whom he briefly revives with the chemical L-dopa in 1969, after they have suffered decades of virtual paralysis. In the film, which was directed by Penny Marshall, the fictional Dr. Malcolm Sayer is portrayed as an emotionally withdrawn physician who experiences difficulties interacting with others. Through his involvement with one revived patient, Leonard Lowe, Sayer attains a greater appreciation for human interaction. Lowe, meanwhile, declines from effusive exuberance to derangement and depression as the L-dopa begins to exert a profoundly negative effect, and the patient's decline culminates in an emotional climax.

Upon its release, *Awakenings* enjoyed popular success but was generally considered a sentimentalized adaptation of Sacks's book. *Chicago Tribune* contributor Dave Kehr was among the reviewers who deemed the film moving yet unnecessarily manipulative. *Awakenings,* he declared, "is a film that unquestionably succeeds on its own terms," but added that "those terms are deeply suspect." He concluded that the film "consistently swaps meaning for superficial effect." Similarly, *New York Times* reviewer Janet Maslin contended that *Awakenings* "both sentimentalizes its story and oversimplifies it beyond recognition." Desson Howe, in his *Washington Post* review, acknowledged that *Awakenings* "has all the appropriate poignant provocations." Among the supporters of the film was *Washington Post* reviewer Rita Kempley, who hailed the film as "literate and passionate" and "cause for rejoicing." And *Newsweek*'s David Ansen, who faulted the filmmakers for turning "Sacks's tragic but fiercely compassionate vision to banal movie conventions," conceded that "at its best [*Awakenings* has] real power."

Zaillian followed *Awakenings* with the 1993 film *Jack the Bear,* which he adapted from Dan McCall's novel about a father and his two young sons. In the film the family must contend with a host of problems, including the father's alcoholism and kidnapping of the younger son. In addition to these challenges, the family copes with living in an unstable neighborhood replete with a drug addict, a Nazi sympathizer, and attack dogs. *Time* reviewer Richard Schickel was among the reviewers who characterized *Jack the Bear* as unconvincing and uncompelling. Schickel was especially unimpressed with the kidnapping episode. "This crisis is purely arbitrary," he wrote. "So is its eventual resolution."

Zaillian found more resounding critical favor with his next film, *Searching for Bobby Fischer,* which also marked his debut as a director. The film is an adaptation of Fred Waitzkin's book about his son, a seven-year-old chess prodigy. In the film Waitzkin tries to nurture his son's impressive chess-playing abilities even while the son's mother works to maintain the child's integrity and innocence. The film also concerns the boy's relationship with his mentors, a chess hustler named Vinnie and a more sophisticated, driven, chess master named Bruce Pandolfini. *Newsweek* contributor David Ansen called the film "stirring," while *Wall Street Journal* reviewer Julie Salamon described it as "an entertaining excursion into a fascinating subculture."

Zaillian has also won acclaim as the screenwriter for director Steven Spielberg's epic film *Schindler's List,* a drama set during the Holocaust. The film, which is based on Thomas Keneally's book of the same title, concerns true-life figure Oskar Schindler, a flamboyant, charismatic businessman who managed to save hundreds of Jews by providing them with employment in his munitions factory during World War II. The film traces Schindler's schemes to keep making a profit even as the Nazis commit countless atrocities across Europe, but also concerns the fate of the Jews who manage to find employment in Schindler's factory, and those who were not so fortunate, and were left to face the horrors of the concentration camps.

After its 1993 release, Schindler's List was hailed by critics as a powerful and important work. New Yorker critic Terrence Rafferty proclaimed it "a great movie," and Commonweal contributor Richard Alleva was equally laudatory, dubbing Schindler's List "very good indeed" and "splendid." Schindler's List received further acclaim from the Academy of Motion Picture Arts and Sciences, whose members accorded the film's producers an Academy Award ("Oscar") for best film, Spielberg an Oscar for best director, and Zaillian an Academy award for best screenplay adaptation.

In 1994 Zaillian was listed with Donald Stewart and John Milius as screenwriters for the suspenseful Clear and Present Danger, an adaptation of Tom Clancy's popular novel about government agent Jack Ryan's battle against South American drug kingpins and nefarious American agents. While Ryan pursues matters through proper channels, a band of guerrilla fighters, acting under a U.S. agency's authority, launch an attack on the drug lord's stronghold. The drug lord reacts by bombing nearby American officials, including Ryan, who thereupon determines to personally handle the drug lord's demise. Terrence Rafferty, writing in the New Yorker, called the film "a sleek, classically proportioned suspense thriller," while David Denby, in his New York appraisal, noted the film's impressive "Hollywood craftsmanship" and added that Clear and Present Danger is a "swiftly moving tale of many layers."

A Civil Action, which appeared in 1998, is based upon Jonathan Harr's nonfiction account of a group of families living in Woburn, Massachusetts, who sued Beatrice Foods and W. R. Grace for contaminating the town's drinking water and thereby causing an inordinate number of cases of childhood leukemia—twenty-eight—resulting in sixteen deaths. The families engage Jan Schlichtmann, a high-profile personal-injury lawyer, to defend them in court, and the film depicts Schlichtmann's inward and outer battles and his subsequent transformation while working on the case. Zaillian remarked in an online Writers' Guild interview that his major challenge in adapting the book was actually the book's strength: its "relentless accumulation of detail . . . describing a legal case of epic scale." He found it challenging to preserve the book's integrity and scope within a two-hour time frame. "Writer/director Steven Zaillian has turned in another sharp, funny, and compelling film" wrote Kerry Douglas Dye for Leisure Suit Media. The critic added that, while "justice doesn't triumph in any satisfying way. . . . the movie is still a pleasure."

Zaillian's screenplay for Hannibal serves as a sequel to the movie The Silence of the Lambs; both works have their foundation in a trilogy of popular novels written by Thomas Harris. The chief protagonist in both films is the serial killer Hannibal Lecter, whose criminal trademark is his cannibalistic tendency. In Hannibal the killer is pitted against an old enemy, Mason Verger, a pedophile and former acquaintance of Lecter whom Lecter horribly mutilated on a previous occasion. The movie turns on Verger's efforts to avenge himself upon Hannibal for that deed. In an interview with Douglas Eby for TalentDeveloment, Zaillian said: "I was ambivalent [about Hannibal] because it was a sequel, and I'm generally not interested in sequels. But they [Dino DeLaurentiis and Ridley Scott] talked to me for about three weeks about the story. . . . It was a wonderful process of really talking about the story and what it should be."

The film Gangs of New York, released in 2002, was co-written by Zaillian, Jay Cocks, and Kenneth Lonergan, and directed by Martin Scorsese. Taking place in the later 1800s, the story focuses upon a group of men called the Native Americans who violently oppose immigrants, and especially, immigrants who follow the Catholic religion. William Cutting, commonly known as Bill the Butcher, leads the Native Americans in their deadly actions. A young Irish-American man named Amsterdam Vallon, who is the son of one of Cutting's victims, hides his identity in order to come nearer to the gang leader so that he can eventually avenge his father's murder. Lisa Schwarzbaum, in Entertainment Weekly online, remarked that although the film "groans and lumbers under too many ruts of narrative didacticism," it is also "vast and hugely ambitious."

BIOGRAPHICAL AND CRITICAL SOURCES:

PERIODICALS

Chicago Tribune, December 20, 1990.
Commonweal, February 11, 1994, pp. 16-18.
Nation, January 7, 1991, pp. 22-24.
New Republic, January 7, 1991, pp. 32-33; September 20, 1993, pp. 36-38; December 13, 1993, p. 30.
Newsweek, December 24, 1990, p. 62; August 30, 1993, pp. 52-53.
New York, August 15, 1994, pp. 54-55.
New Yorker, April 5, 1993, pp. 102-03; December 20, 1993, pp. 129-32; August 15, 1994, pp. 75-77.
New York Times, December 20, 1990.
Time, March 29, 1993.
Variety, August 1, 1994, pp. 44-45.
Wall Street Journal, August 26, 1993, p. A9.
Washington Post, January 11, 1991.

ONLINE

Entertainment Weekly Online, http://www.ew.com/ (September 25, 2003), Lisa Schwarzbaum, review of *Gangs of New York.*
LeisureSuit Media, http://www.leisuresuit.net/Webzine/ (June 3, 2003), Kerry Douglas Dye, review of *A Civil Action.*
TalentDevelopment, http://www.talentdevelop.com/ (June 3, 2003), Douglas Eby, interview with Zaillian.
Writers' Guild of America Web site, http://www.wga.org/ (June 3, 2003), Alan Waldman, interview with Zaillian.*